Life Examined

Life Examined

Foundational Themes in Ethical and Socio-Political Thought

Edited by Nick Garside,
Jonathan Lavery,
and Charles Wells

broadview press

BROADVIEW PRESS – www.broadviewpress.com
Peterborough, Ontario, Canada

Founded in 1985, Broadview Press remains a wholly independent publishing house. Broadview's focus is on academic publishing; our titles are accessible to university and college students as well as scholars and general readers. With over 600 titles in print, Broadview has become a leading international publisher in the humanities, with world-wide distribution. Broadview is committed to environmentally responsible publishing and fair business practices.

Library and Archives Canada Cataloguing in Publication

Title: Life examined : foundational themes in ethical and socio-political thought / edited by Nick Garside, Jonathan Lavery, and Charles Wells.
Other titles: Life examined (2019)
Names: Garside, Nick, 1972– editor. | Lavery, Jonathan, 1965– editor. | Wells, Charles, 1978– editor.
Description: Includes bibliographical references.
Identifiers: Canadiana 20190135905 | ISBN 9781554813841 (softcover)
Subjects: LCSH: Ethics—Textbooks. | LCSH: Political sociology—Textbooks. | LCGFT: Textbooks.
Classification: LCC BJ1012 .L54 2019 | DDC 170—dc23

Broadview Press handles its own distribution in North America:
PO Box 1243, Peterborough, Ontario K9J 7H5, Canada
555 Riverwalk Parkway, Tonawanda, NY 14150, USA
Tel: (705) 743-8990; Fax: (705) 743-8353
email: customerservice@broadviewpress.com

Distribution is handled by Eurospan Group in the UK, Europe, Central Asia, Middle East, Africa, India, Southeast Asia, Central America, South America, and the Caribbean. Distribution is handled by Footprint Books in Australia and New Zealand.

Canada Broadview Press acknowledges the financial support of the Government of Canada for our publishing activities.

Copy-edited by Michel Pharand
Book Design by Em Dash Design

PRINTED IN CANADA

The editors wish to dedicate work on *Life Examined* to the people whose love has made their own lives rich and meaningful:

Elizabeth Bender, Flora Garside, and Jack Garside;
Amelia Lavery, Julie Fields (d. 2014), Sadie Fields, and Tamsen Fields;
Kate Rossiter, Ruby Wells, and Barnaby Wells.

Contents

Acknowledgements

Work on this book has been ably assisted by several of our students who were supported by work-study programs funded by Wilfrid Laurier University. The editors are grateful for this financial support to the following student-assistants: Peter Aloussis, Jacob Makohin, Carla Lopez, Matthew Orrock, Sharon Kaur, Lucas Barbosa, and Erin McHarge.

We are also grateful to Broadview Press for taking on this project, in particular, to Stephen Latta for his patient and sage advice throughout the entire process of putting together the manuscript. We must also acknowledge the editorial guidance of Michel Pharand, Joe Davies, and Tara Lowes, who saved us from countless errors and missteps. Thanks also to Leslie Dema, who supported this work as it evolved and took shape.

The editors owe a special debt of gratitude to Dag Herbjørnsrud at the Centre for Global and Comparative Ideas in Norway, who provided the primary source materials for Zar'a Yaqob. As far as we are aware, *Life Examined* is the first general anthology to include this intriguing, seminal figure.

Lastly, we must acknowledge the suggestions and advice offered so generously by friends, colleagues, and former colleagues. The number of people on this list is, unfortunately, too long to fit comfortably here.

Introduction

> "Life is not a spectacle or a feast; it is a predicament."
>
> —GEORGE SANTAYANA

The Aims of *Life Examined*

Readings collected here are designed to spur the examination of life. Both the title and focus of this collection are inspired by Socrates's contention that an unexamined life is not worth living. In declaring this to jurors at his trial he was not simply striking a dramatic pose. He was forcing on them a provocative and sharply focused choice: either accept his way of life or kill him. The further suggestion from George Santayana that life is a *predicament* elucidates thorny implications in Socrates's provocation. A predicament—that is, a trying situation or plight without a clearly best solution—demands a special clarity of thought, for it tests our mettle as much as our intelligence. The predicament of life boils down to asking, "How ought we to live?" Any answer is bound to be complex and will inevitably release a swarm of further questions. Why choose one way of life rather than another? Why act in one way rather than others? What do we owe to other people and to ourselves? Answers to these and other difficult questions need to be carefully formulated, and they must be tested both by our faculties of critical reflection and by the life they entail. There are no guarantees that we can *solve* the predicament of life. But there appears to be no way a thoughtful person can avoid grappling with it, for it springs from enduring elements of the human condition and circumstances that perennially recur in communal living.

An *examination* of life should be distinguished from simply noting our immediate response to circumstances or difficulties. Throughout the course of life we mull over personal choices, embark on careers, enter into relationships, affiliate ourselves with social causes, and so forth. We usually act on values that are barely articulated. In the moment, so to speak, we typically lack the luxury of time to pause and formulate in words the active principles of right and wrong guiding us. But sometimes we are compelled to pause over these matters, especially when the best course is uncertain or when something spurs second guessing about decisions already made. In that pause we summon our first thoughts about what makes life fulfilling, often putting principles into words for the first time. In part, human life is a predicament because guiding principles—even our own, personal values—are not transparent to us, so articulating them requires insight. We must, therefore, distinguish between (1) the *active principles* that guide our conduct, and (2) the *articulated principles* by which we understand that conduct. In deliberating, we may say, for example, "people are inherently selfish," or "people are potentially altruistic," or "my first obligation is to myself," or "I have equal obligations to other people," and other such precepts. Articulating active principles in this way can, at times, immediately suggest an answer to the difficulty before us, even a momentous moral difficulty. But in the face of a genuine predicament—something morally and deeply problematic, perhaps not conclusively resolvable—our first articulated thoughts are often followed by further thoughts about whether these articulated principles stand on good conceptual grounds or whether there are compelling reasons to revise them. Ultimately, considerations of this sort lead to reflections upon our fundamental values, human nature, and the place of humanity in the cosmos. We must, therefore, further distinguish both our active and articulated principles from (3) *reflective principles*.

When we assemble the results of reflection into an interrelated body of thoughts, assessing their systematic cogency, we have embarked on a genuine examination. The *examination of life* therefore is an exercise in articulating our fundamental values and active principles, and critically re-evaluating these in light of their independent acceptability or logical implications. This kind of examination is both exhilarating and laborious. Exhilarating because it helps orient us more self-consciously in the world and among other people, in addition to all the practical benefits of providing sharper concepts for clear-headed ethical deliberation. But the process is also laborious because ethical concepts often elude precise formulation or a conclusive defence. Fortunately, we are not travelling in completely uncharted territory, for others have explored these regions ahead of us and have discovered several paths that we might seriously consider for ourselves. We must each find our own route, but we are not without resources. The readings collected in *Life Examined* are accordingly designed to help identify landmarks and constellations for navigation, not to prescribe a single route or to direct your way step-by-step.

Socrates did not merely utter a single provocative challenge to his fellow Athenians. He exemplified the life and activity that uncompromising self-examination demands. This kind of life was for him a mission, and in 399 BCE he was tried, convicted, sentenced to death, and executed because he refused to compromise.[1] The court concluded that he was a serious danger to the moral fabric of the city. What exactly was he doing that seemed so dangerous? According to all reports, talking to people, inquiring into the nature of justice, the essence of humanity, how one ought to live, etc. His interlocutors were implored to answer questions about these matters and prodded to develop their answers systematically. Then, most importantly, Socrates raised objections to problematic details in their answers. Many people feared that this kind of examination would undermine public confidence in morality. Moreover, his investigations were keenly followed by a devoted group of young men. They gravitated to Socrates and adopted his investigative procedures for themselves, so his influence was undeniable. Apparently, it was the influence of his example that prosecutors wanted to eradicate, and in the end the only way to accomplish that purpose was to eliminate him. At one point during the trial Socrates raises the possibility that he might be released on the condition that he give up his investigations (something that many jurors would have preferred to execution). He raises the suggestion only to reject it, however, adding the point mentioned earlier, that "the unexamined life is not worth living" (*Apology* 38a).[2] He lived this kind of life, he lived *for* it, and he died for it. To appreciate the significance of this stand, we must consider both the activity that animated Socrates's own life and its historical consequences.

---

1 BCE is an abbreviation for "Before the Common Era," and CE abbreviates "Common Era." Other abbreviations that are commonly found in scholarship and valuable to know are "e.g.," "i.e.," and "etc." "E.g." abbreviates the Latin "exempla grata," which means "for example" in English; "i.e.," abbreviates the Latin "id est," which means "that is"; "etc." abbreviates the Latin "etcetera," which means "and so on."

2 All references to the *Apology* (sometimes called *Socrates's Apology*) are to the dialogue written by Plato and found in Chapter 1 of this book. Alphanumerical citations of passages refer to the standard pagination that may be found in the margins of most editions. *Apology* translates the Greek word *apologia*, which means "defence," and has nothing to do with contrition.

The trial was a pivotal moment in history. Not merely Athenian history, but Western history in general, for it resonated well beyond the city and the circle of Socrates's close acquaintances. In this respect, efforts to discourage anyone from following his example failed spectacularly. The moral resolve Socrates demonstrated throughout his life and on trial spurred one young friend, Plato, to found a school, the Academy. Plato's Academy was in many respects a prototype of the modern university: a sub-community dedicated to leading-edge research and the training of novice scholars. One student of the Academy was Aristotle, who went on to found a school of his own in Athens (called the Lyceum). Shortly after Aristotle's death in 322 BCE additional schools were opened there by, among others, Epicurus and Zeno of Citium (whose followers were first called Zenonians, then eventually Stoics). As a result of these and other developments, Athens remained a hub for higher education throughout antiquity, until the Emperor Justinian closed all of its pagan institutions in 529 CE. In short, within a few generations Athens transformed from being the sort of city that executed Socrates for advocating self-examination among his personal acquaintances to being one of the major intellectual centres of antiquity. The reputation of ancient Athens as a centre for learning survives to this day, but it was not that sort of place in Socrates's lifetime.

In what does an examined life consist? An answer to this question is suggested in a line from Socrates's defence speech that falls immediately prior to the one quoted above. There Socrates declares to the jury that, "the greatest good for a man [is] to talk every day about virtue and other things you hear me converse about when I examine both myself and others ..." (38a). Accordingly, the life he advocates is not simply guided by virtue and other fundamental concepts. It is dedicated to the investigation of these things. Second, it is not a dispassionate investigation of claims that no one takes seriously or that we would never consult for guidance. The kind of activity Socrates envisions consists of examining values that he and others believe to be fundamental. These are not mere abstract concepts, but values that he and his interlocutors embodied and put into words—namely, what we call active and articulated principles above. Socrates's investigations always began with something sincerely believed by himself or his interlocutor. This kind of examination is not conducted in solitude. It is undertaken with others, and so a third feature of a Socratic examination is its social and interpersonal character.

A fourth feature of this life deserves more elaboration than the first three. It is this: its investigations must be critical, not dogmatic. Our initial articulated principles are the point of departure for a life examined, not a fortress to be defended at all costs. We must both expose ourselves to the critical examination of our companions and subject their opinions to our own critical examination. It takes faith and courage to risk exposure and confrontation in this way, for painful discoveries about the inadequacies of cherished ideals await anyone who does so. Moreover, if in this examination we expose flaws in long-held principles we may come to think that *nothing* is worthy of our commitment. Here Socrates's example is especially helpful, because he seems to have had more faith in his capacity to deal with such discoveries than he had in the principles being examined. Elsewhere in the *Apology* he claims for himself a special kind of superiority in wisdom: he is wiser than others to the extent that he did not think he knew anything important, while his interlocutors were unaware of their own comparable deficiencies (*Apology* 23b). This is an unusual way to characterize wisdom, i.e., as a combination of ignorance and self-awareness. But perhaps there is something to it. For this frame of mind did not prevent Socrates from acting decisively in battle, in daily life, or in his personal relationships (to judge by the biographical details in his defence speech). He had both the courage to abide by his principles when it was time to act and, it seems, the courage to challenge these very principles in moments of self-examination. It is a matter of debate whether this peculiar combination of ethically principled conduct and personal humility is ultimately coherent, but let us set that aside (that is, until Chapter 3). It is enough for the moment to note the distinction Socrates draws between wisdom as a kind of substantive knowledge (which apprehends something substantive, such as arithmetical equations, the colours of a rainbow, the rate of inflation, goodness, and so forth) and self-knowledge (which apprehends the limits of what one knows).

A fifth noteworthy feature of Socrates's example is the social-political function he claimed for his activities. This function is not mentioned in the two passages quoted above. Elsewhere in the speech he makes the audacious claim that he is on a divine mission from the god Apollo to save the city from its uncritical habits. He says:

> Indeed, men of Athens, I am making this defence hardly at all for my own sake, as one might suppose, but for yours, so you will not commit a wrong concerning the god's gift to you by condemning me. If you were to execute me you would not easily find another person like me, who is—although it is rather funny to say—attached to the city by the god just as though to a great and noble horse that's somewhat sluggish because of its size and needs to be provoked by a gadfly.[3] This is just the way, I think, the god attached me to the city, the sort of person who never ceases provoking you and persuading you and reproaching each one of you the whole day long everywhere I settle. (*Apology* 30d–31a)

As a gadfly, Socrates was both independent of the city and inseparable from it. He was independent insofar as he was detached from popular opinions. And he was inseparable from Athens insofar as he was devoted utterly to its welfare as he understood it—that is, as a community incapable of realizing its full potential without collective self-examination. His investigations must therefore be understood as embodying a divine mission, a civic duty, and a unique brand of patriotism.

The aims of *Life Examined* are Socratic in spirit rather than doctrine. Claims Socrates makes in the *Apology* must be read as contributions to a debate, not as awesome lore. As you will see, other figures collected here disagree with Socrates, some profoundly. The *Apology*, which opens Chapter 1 (1.2), thus, sets the tone for a complex and extended debate. This debate is then picked up by Immanuel Kant (1.3) and Naomi Klein (1.4), then carried into subsequent chapters.[4] Using Socrates's investigations as our point of reference, there are five features to note about this book:

i. Every chapter is oriented around fundamental values.
ii. The debates are of practical significance, even when the subject is highly theoretical.
iii. An examination of human life must be conducted with other people.
iv. An examination of human life must be critical.
v. This critical examination has both personal and social-political significance.

Reading, Learning, and Life

We can imagine how in a conversation it is possible for claims and counter-claims to be subjected to critical scrutiny by participants. A genuine conversation of this sort between two or more people seems both possible and desirable. Plato dramatizes many such conversations: one character asks a question; another

3 It is worth noting that the Greek word translated here as "gadfly" may also be translated as "spur." Indeed, "spur" may be preferable in light of the relationship conveyed by the analogy between the city and a horse.

4 Part of the scholarly apparatus for this book has been devised to facilitate efficient internal referencing. Citations for readings found elsewhere in the book will be provided in brackets and indicated by the chapter and reading number as designated in the Table of Contents. For example, here 1.3 refers to Chapter 1, reading number 3 (by Immanuel Kant) and 1.4 refers to Chapter 1, reading number 4 (by Naomi Klein); 1.2 refers to two readings by Plato, the *Apology* (which is more precisely indicated by 1.2.1–1.2.3) and the *Crito* (1.2.4).

responds with a claim; the claim is analyzed; the analysis unearths problems; the original claim is refined or another one is formulated in its stead; then the whole process begins again. Given the emphasis Socrates places on conversation and interpersonal relationships, it is natural to wonder whether there is any role for reading in an examination of life. Can reading replicate or foster anything comparable to the give-and-take dynamics of a Socratic investigation?

Add to these doubts further reservations about a connection between reading and the special quality of wisdom. It does not seem possible to sum up wisdom in a tidy package that can be conveyed as a doctrine, conceived either as a kind of substantive knowledge or as self-knowledge. Like recognizing whether or not a note is in tune, the ethical judgement required for wisdom seems to be a matter for experiential learning, not book learning. People with perfect pitch can catch an off-note, but such judgement cannot be transmitted to someone who is tone-deaf or tin-eared. Reading about music will not furnish it either. So why read, if our goal is wisdom or ethical insight into life? Neither wisdom nor insight seems to admit of simple formulation in words or transmission in print. Rather than respond to the question in general terms, let us consider the following stories.

Near the end of Robertson Davies's novel *The Lyre of Orpheus* a talented young composer, Hulda Schnakenburg, has been suffering the consequences of some reckless decisions.[5] She is intelligent but not well-read. As it happens, Hulda is working with several bookish colleagues to produce an opera. At one point, she is in the hospital and becomes overwhelmed by self-pity during a visit from one of these colleagues. The visitor teases Hulda, calling her "Mrs. Gummidge," after a Dickens character renowned for self-pity. She fails to recognize the allusion and asks who Mrs. Gummidge is. The visitor replies, "If you're a good girl and get well soon I'll lend you the book." Hulda has grown tired of book-talk by this point. She replies, "Oh, someone in a book. All you people ... seem to live out of books. As if everything was in books." The visitor then replies with some advice, "Well, ... if you'd read a few books you wouldn't have to meet everything as if it had never happened before, and take every blow on the chin. You'd see a few things coming...." The point is instructive: while reading is not a substitute for life and experience, it can prepare us for problems and difficulties that otherwise might hit us square on the chin. In a sense, reading about fictional characters or the lives of other people expand experience beyond the boundaries of one's personal life. We might see a few things coming, and we would be less bewildered in our encounters with the unfamiliar. We might even find fewer things unfamiliar. Reading can sharpen our perceptions and reduce the uncertainty that comes inevitably with new experiences or adversity.

While fiction can sharpen our perceptions and help us see a few things coming, theoretical, non-fiction can help refine the concepts and principles with which we deliberate. Life, after all, is not only perceived, it is conceived. Readings of the sort included in *Life Examined* can be helpful in deliberating over a difficult decision, especially when we must depend on ethical concepts such as duty, courage, right, wrong, and so forth. Inevitably, in such moments we rely on ethical concepts however we happen to conceive of them. Thoughtful reflection over the meaning, scope, applicability, and defensibility of these terms can, if we are diligent, refine our active and articulated principles. Such refinements will not solve problems for us, but we may be less overwhelmed by complications if we think clearly than if not. Not only might we see more things coming, we might understand them better when they arrive.

Our second story comes from Heda Kovály's memoir, *Under a Cruel Star*.[6] Kovály was a young woman living in the former Czechoslovakia under German occupation during World War II. In the fall of 1941 she was among thousands of Jews forcibly transported out of Prague. First, everyone was ordered to gather

5 Robertson Davies, *The Lyre of Orpheus*. Penguin Books Canada, 1988, 414.
6 Heda Magolis Kovály, *Under a Cruel Star: A Life in Prague, 1941–1968*. Translated by Frani Epstein and Helen Epstein, Plunkett Lake Press, 1986, 6–9.

in a single building before being taken by train to Poland. For two difficult days everyone was crammed together waiting to be transported. Conditions in the crowded, suffocating transport station were harrowing, with sick people dying, children crying incessantly, and everyone pushed to the psychological breaking point. Not only had these people lost virtually everything they owned, they were terrified about what the Nazis had planned for them (justifiably so, it turns out). Wandering through this scene, Kovály spotted one elderly man wearing a well-kept suit and sitting calmly on his black trunk. She writes: "In the middle of all that chaos, among all those people ... he looked as incongruous as if he were sitting there naked." After greeting her politely, this fellow explained that he had been a classicist in Vienna. When asked, he explains to Kovály that he did not dress more practically because he disliked changing his habits under the pressure of circumstances. "In any event ... he considered it most important to maintain equanimity [in arduous conditions]. Then he began talking about classical literature and ancient Rome." In the mad atmosphere of the transport station the two new friends occupied themselves with pleasant conversation of this sort for the next two days. Later, in Lodz, they were separated from each other. Kovály later worked in the Jewish ghetto there with a physician administering to the sick and dying. One day they were directed to the flat of a very sick man, who turned out to be her friend, the classicist. He had died shortly before they arrived. They found him lying on a dirty mattress with a book open on his chest, looking surprisingly peaceful. Apparently, he had been reading up to the moment of his death.

In both the chaos of the transport station and the destitution of the ghetto, Kovály's friend found refuge in his learning. He was by then too old to survive the deprivations of Nazi mistreatment, but he was not disturbed by the indignities imposed upon him. Books and learning helped preserve him in difficult circumstances and, Kovály suggests, comforted him until the final moments of his life. All the learning in the world would not suffice to help an old man escape death in the conditions forced upon ghetto dwellers under Nazi occupation. In fact, had he lived long enough to be transported to a death camp, he certainly would have been among the first designated for the gas chamber. No application of learning would have saved this man's life, but its possession helped preserve his equanimity. This is perhaps the greatest benefit of an education, and it cannot be measured in material or economic terms: like love or music, education can preserve us against the storms of life. So not only can book-learning help refine our concepts and sharpen our powers of deliberation, it provides its own unique form of fulfilment. This idea is summed up nicely by the ancient philosopher, Heraclitus. "Education," he declared, "is a second sun to the educated." Just as the sun illuminates the world and is the source of all life on Earth, so does education illuminate experience and sustain an educated mind.

In reading we encounter ideas, hypotheses, suggestions, stories, theories, precepts, and arguments. If we read critically, attend to the range of positions on offer, and explore these issues with other people (e.g., friends, classmates, professors, etc.), reading can help us live better—or at least help us deal better with the predicament of life. Authors and books cannot deliberate for us, but they can help us formulate our own questions more precisely and clarify the principles on which we act. Furthermore, as Kovály's classicist friend illustrates, learning is valuable in itself as a comfort and source of strength, over and above any utility it may serve. The readings collected here are presented with many purposes in mind: some offer direct guidance for practical problems; others draw our attention to ethical and political problems that we might otherwise not notice; others help refine the conceptual tools with which we deliberate individually and collectively; and, lastly, each one in its own way promises the satisfaction of understanding something for its own sake.

In addition to the anthologized readings that are the core of Chapters 1–8, you will find the following materials designed to frame these texts: (1) several aphoristic epigrams to prime the pump of reflection; (2) chapter introductions, outlining the conceptual issues at stake in each respective chapter and previewing the readings in relation to each other; (3) individual reading introductions to frame each contribution; (4) "Review Questions," which are designed to draw attention to interpretive problems in the readings and analytical problems important to the chapter; lastly, each chapter closes with (5) suggestions for "Further Reading."

UNIT I

Self-Examination, Individual and Collective

CHAPTER 1

Ethical Crises, Self-examination, and Citizenship

A thinker who cherishes the comforts of home isn't much of a thinker.

—CONFUCIUS

Socrates was the first who brought down philosophy from the heavens, placed it in cities, introduced it into families, and obliged it to examine into life and morals, and good and evil.

—CICERO

The more I read about [Socrates], the less I wonder that they poisoned him.

—THOMAS BABINGTON MACAULAY

People think the world needs a republic, and they think it needs a new social order, and a new religion, but it never occurs to anyone that what the world really needs, confused as it is by much learning, is a new Socrates.

—SØREN KIERKEGAARD

The one who wakes us wounds us.

—FRIEDRICH NIETZSCHE

A very popular error: having the courage of one's convictions; rather it is a matter of having the courage for an attack on one's convictions!!!

—FRIEDRICH NIETZSCHE

Practically, thinking means that each time you are confronted with some difficulty in life you must make up your mind anew.

—HANNAH ARENDT

The deeper my crisis, the clearer my choices.

—ANDREW BOYD

1.1 Introduction

Each reading in this chapter emerged out of a momentous ethical crisis. Plato's *Apology of Socrates* and *Crito* memorialize the politically charged series of events that ended with Socrates's execution in 399 BCE. Immanuel Kant's "What Is Enlightenment?" identifies a crisis in the moral condition of late eighteenth-century Europe, when he thought people were balking at a special kind of liberty that is implicit in a full commitment to reason. And our excerpts from Naomi Klein's *This Changes Everything* analyze irrational economic and ideological sources of climate-change denial. Each reading responds to a crisis that is distinctive of its historical moment, but all of the crises highlight distinctive features of human judgement that seem to endure from era to era, from antiquity to Enlightenment-era Europe to the present. Indeed, in all three cases our readings are embedded in a crisis, and each one offers an analysis of the structure of that particular crisis, a diagnosis of its causes, and prescriptions for its resolution. Instructively, these solutions are formulated as enduring general lessons, and not merely as a way out of the crisis at hand. Let us first identify some trends that help frame these crises before we turn to consider the readings themselves.

Our earliest crisis took place in ancient Athens, where Socrates was tried, convicted, and executed on charges of corrupting the youth and religious innovation (impiety). By his own admission, Socrates associated with any young man who took an interest in his investigations, either as interlocutors or as spectators while he interrogated others (*Apol* 23c–d). As well, he speaks openly about a divine spirit (*daimonion* in Greek) who intervenes to discourage him from wrongdoing. Socrates thus acknowledges the apparent grounds for both charges against him, but these are not the true source of his legal troubles. That source resides elsewhere. For many years, he had been a vocal critic of his fellow Athenians, including the city's most prominent citizens and leaders. His criticisms focused on superficial thinking that led people to value material comfort and social prestige over the health of their own souls. For most of Socrates's life, Athens had enjoyed great prosperity, much of it attained by imperial domination over other parts of Greece. At the same time, the city was riven by deep political factions, with reactionary conservatives on one side and radical democrats on the other. At issue were (a) economic questions about how to divide among themselves wealth accumulated from mining, trade, and tribute paid to Athens by client states in its empire, as well as (b) political questions about domestic and imperial policy. Nearly everyone, it seems, was driven by unhealthy competitive values: wealth, reputation, and honours were prized over wisdom (*Apol* 29d–e). He diagnoses the cause of these misguided values to be shallow, unreflective habits of thought and action. To correct these habits, Socrates prods jurors and spectators at his trial to embrace the kind of critical self-examination that his investigations embody.

More than 2000 years later, Kant expressed comparable concerns about his fellow Prussians. Like Socrates, he was frustrated by the moral and intellectual defects of his contemporaries. Mature, self-regulating liberty is, he thought, within everyone's grasp, if only people would shake off an uncritical dependence on institutional orthodoxies, a dependence that artificially constrains intellectual growth and moral development. Kant's concerns originate from what he regarded as a tension in eighteenth-century European life: Enlightenment science pulled in one direction by providing a model for people to appreciate the life-guiding potential of cultivated, critical intelligence, a potential that seemed to be appreciated by Prussia's reigning monarch; pulling in another direction were stale traditions and superstitions to which people clung in their practical lives. Kant diagnoses the cause of moral immaturity very directly as a failure of courage: in general, the Prussian laity, if not most Europeans, preferred to hand over responsibility for the most important decisions in their lives to ecclesiastical authorities and institutions. Kant proposes free public debate to counteract this sort of dependence. This single measure is advanced as a first step towards salutary reforms across all of society, which he thought must necessarily begin with a few individuals before spreading out to the masses.

Naomi Klein is primarily troubled about what she sees as our ineffectual response to climate change and impending environmental catastrophe. As it happens, two of her central concerns pick up on Kant's programmatic points: (1) a widespread failure of courage and (2) a degraded state of public debate. The failure of courage is, according to her analysis, more sharply focussed than Kant's complaints about his fellow Prussians. For Klein, a tendency for wishful thinking has prevented the majority of well-informed people from confronting the enormity of an environmental disaster currently unfolding as a result of climate change. Making matters worse, debate over anthropogenic climate change has been infected by misinformation and propaganda from people whose interests are vested in industries generating vast amounts of pollution. Klein diagnoses the cause of these problems to be a faulty political-economic ideology and a dangerous industrial model. The ideology is neoliberalism and the industrial model is extractivism.

Neoliberalism understands every social contribution entirely in terms of a capacity to participate in the economy. In a deregulated market, individual freedom is thereby exercised as consumer choice. Wealth is understood to be a sign of merit because deregulated markets are presumed to distribute it in a fair competition. Accordingly, greater freedom enjoyed by the wealthy few is considered to be properly earned, and moreover it may be rightfully expanded to take increasingly more control of political institutions and processes that govern everyone. As Klein portrays the current situation, the wealthiest members of society exercise this freedom by reducing their own tax burdens and further deregulating the markets as a way to further expand their own wealth. As a consequence of this disturbing pattern, small, powerful groups dominate political and economic life. What is most disturbing for Klein, natural resource industries have been extremely successful at taking control of political institutions and bending the international economy to their own advantage. Extractivism fits into this system as an economic dependence on natural resources extracted from the earth. Oil, natural gas, minerals, timber, and other natural resources are conceived of as private property, not as public property or as something beyond the reach of proprietorial claims. As such, these resources are commodified and sold for profit by private owners on the international market.

The consequence of neoliberal and extractivist ideological dominance is an unprecedented global threat of environmental catastrophe. Klein's prescription for this crisis is, in part, embodied in her own work: exposing the errors of neoliberalism and extractivism. More than anything else, we need a better model for industrial production, one that will help guide the regulation of industries that currently dominate the global economy. To this end, she implores readers to cultivate a new regard for the environment that does not consign all of its value to the private economic advantage of a few industries.

Two grand trends are observable in the movement from Plato to Kant to Klein: (1) the scale of "community," which expands at each successive crisis; and (2) a shifting conception of practical rationality, which in each case is put forth both as being essential for resolving its respective crisis and as an enduring source of guidance for life.

(1) In ancient Greece citizenship was a relation between an individual and a single city. This, in fact, is the germ of "politics," since *polis* is the Greek word for city. By modern times the scope of political life had expanded beyond the bounds of individual cities and had come to include entire nations. Kant, for instance, understands citizenship in terms of Prussian nationalism. Lastly, because the environmental crisis on which Klein focuses attention is global, she understands national citizenship in an international context. Consequently, from Socrates to Kant to Klein we see a transition from municipal to national to international conceptions of citizenship.

(2) Presuppositions about the practical function of rationality are less readily summarized than those

about citizenship; nevertheless, a clear pattern emerges when we consider how in each crisis the rationale for proposed solutions relates to religion and science. Over time, connections between practical rationality and religion become looser while connections between practical rationality and science become tighter. (This neat, linear pattern is not universally the case, by the way. Secular movements in antiquity and spiritual movements in the modern era will be explored in later chapters of *Life Examined*.)

Socrates presumes that practical guidance from religion will harmonize fundamentally with reason, even though the rational grounds for sacred precepts are ultimately inscrutable to human judgement. Rationality and divine judgement are expected to converge ultimately. This applies both to the directives Socrates receives from his personal spiritual guide and a declaration from Apollo that he is the wisest man. The spiritual guidance that discourages him from erring in speech or action is confirmed to be correct upon reflection (in the form of retrospective deliberation, 31d). Even when divine guidance initially *appears* to be wrong, it turns out unexpectedly to be rationally confirmed. The oracular revelation from Apollo's priestess in Delphi that Socrates is the wisest man clashes with the self-evident fact that he knows nothing (21b). Owing to the exalted source of this pronouncement, however, he makes a special effort to interpret what might be meant by it, for it is inconceivable to think that a god would lie (21b). In a subsequent inquiry, Socrates concludes that Apollo is correct: he is comparatively wiser than everyone else, but only because everyone else suffers from delusions of knowledge that they do not genuinely possess (21b–23b). So, rather than rejecting a divine judgement out of hand, Socrates finds a way to reinterpret it as something acceptable and consistent with his self-evident ignorance.

For Kant, however, religious institutions and orthodox beliefs are susceptible of critical assessment across the board, just as secular institutions and non-sacred beliefs are. We must, Kant thinks, demand that church institutions and orthodox beliefs satisfy abstract criteria for rational coherence (such as consistency, non-arbitrariness, non-circularity, etc.). Indeed, the demand that our beliefs be rationally coherent is practical insofar as tests for coherence (in terms of consistency, non-arbitrariness, non-circularity, and so on) root out indefensible beliefs, even those sanctioned by venerable religious authorities. For Kant, we have no obligations to make heroic interpretive efforts of the kind Socrates made in response to Apollo's judgement.

Klein's commitment to practical rationality as a guide for life turns out to be even stronger than Kant's. Additionally, her arguments presuppose that recent discoveries of environmental science are rationally authoritative, making it irrational for anyone to adhere to convictions that fly in the face of its evidence-based findings. This is why she focuses her critical attention on climate-change deniers. Klein is primarily worried about orthodoxies that derive primarily from ideology, not from religion. But differences between religion and ideology are almost negligible for her, since the grip these ideologies have on climate-change deniers is indistinguishable from religious conviction.

Let us now consider in more detail the three crises in light of the readings associated with each one.

* * *

Crisis is an especially suitable term to describe Socrates's situation. The English word *crisis* derives from the Greek word *krisis*, which was the ancient legal term for "trial." This etymology is revealing, for legal trials are very often turning points in which decisive change is immanent (i.e., a crisis in the ordinary sense of the word). This is almost inevitably the case for the defendant in a criminal trial, since a court's verdict has the effect of directing that person's life down one course or another. No matter how abstractly we conceive of justice or how impersonally legal procedures are conducted, the business of a trial is deeply personal and morally charged. For this reason, a court's proceedings are also trials in the non-legal sense: "That which puts one to the test; especially a painful test of one's endurance, patience, or faith"; for this reason, affliction, trouble, and misfortune are apt synonyms

(*OED*). A trial can indeed test the endurance, patience, and faith of a defendant as the court's machinery works inexorably towards its verdict.

For the moment, two historical facts are notable about Socrates's trial: (1) his immunity to the kinds of fears that haunt most defendants, and (2) the neat reversal of history which has cast the convicted defendant in a far more favourable light than the jury that convicted him. According to surviving accounts, Socrates was indifferent to the trial's outcome for himself personally. Most surprisingly, he seemed unconcerned that prosecutors were seeking the death penalty. Ignoring tactical advice from friends about how to counter the charges against him successfully, Socrates took a highly unconventional approach to his defence. He refused to pursue whatever means were necessary to win an acquittal. Against all expectation, he acknowledged having caused grave discomfort for numerous Athenians, admitted having done this intentionally, proclaimed himself to be doing all these things as an agent of the god Apollo, and used the occasion of his trial to explain the civic function of his unwelcomed investigations into the moral and intellectual limitations of his interlocutors. As he explains to the jury, "I am not making this defense on my own behalf.... It is on your behalf, that you may make no error about the god's gift to you by condemning me" (30d). He did not consider himself to be faced with a crisis in the ordinary, English sense of the word. A shift of focus away from his own fate to that of Athens proved to be prophetic, for Socrates's trial did ultimately turn out to be momentous for his city and for Western history.

At seventy years of age, and having surpassed by many years the life expectancy of an average Athenian, Socrates had good reason to believe that he was approaching the natural end of his life. Being charged with capital offenses compelled him to defend his conduct publically in court. The defence speech he delivered, however, made little attempt to extend his mortal life. Instead, he used the occasion as an opportunity to defend his *way of life*, which was oriented around obsessively exploring ethical questions. To carry out this inquiry he conscripted anyone who would talk to him. Some interlocutors found his aggressive questioning objectionable. As he makes clear, this was the principal reason he was hated (28a). The sharp belligerence of his trial cross-examination of Meletus is no doubt some indication of the pushy way he pursued these inquiries (24d–27e). Shortly after completing this cross-examination, Socrates vows that, if he is acquitted, he will resume critically examining each and every Athenian he meets (29c–30b). To some jurors this no doubt sounded like a threat. He later ridicules commonplace and undignified tactics typically used by other defendants trying desperately to get their lives spared, namely, begging for mercy and parading their families before the court for sympathy (34b–35b); this ridicule is a blunt provocation, since some of these former defendants were undoubtedly present to hear it. The trial was thus transformed into an opportunity for Socrates to expose the moral frailties of both Athenian institutions and his fellow Athenians. Thus, the verdict in his case became a crucial moral test for the jurors: either accept his way of life or eliminate him. By pressing this stark choice upon them so forcibly, Socrates revealed deep tensions in Athenian society and brought about a political crisis.

By 1784, when Immanuel Kant published "What Is Enlightenment?" a series of divisive religious wars across Europe had given way to an age of comparative tolerance. At the same time, the natural sciences had secured a central place in Western culture. Isaac Newton, for example, had constructed a powerful, systematic theory of physics that explained the cosmos better than all rival accounts. It is difficult to overestimate the influence of Newton's *Mathematical Principles of Natural Philosophy* (1687). Newton's success at deciphering motion out to the farthest reaches of the heavens seemed to throw open the limits to what human beings could imagine discovering. Optimism for science was virtually boundless in some influential circles, and a string of impressive advances in mechanics, chemistry, electricity, and so on seemed to confirm this optimism.

Throughout the eighteenth century, Newton's mechanical account of motion was taken to exemplify "knowledge" in its fullest development. Not only is it a spectacular piece of modern science, the systematic ordering and universal scope of Newtonian mechanics was regarded as a model of knowledge far beyond physics. The axiomatic structure of Newton's theory was emulated even in work on the regulation of society. Social and political thinkers wanted their theories to be as comprehensive in their domain as Newtonian mechanics in physics.

Animating "What Is Enlightenment?" is an incongruity Kant observed between the scientific progress pioneered by Newton and other scientists, on the one hand, and moral stagnation in conventional behaviour on the other. Because the physical sciences had advanced dramatically, the behaviour of material bodies was by then very well understood. However, these scientific achievements only served to highlight unachieved human potential in the moral sphere, where vice and wrongdoing remained commonplace (a perennial complaint by moralists, up to the present). Even worse, despite great funds of knowledge at their disposal from physical and social scientific research, devotees of popular religion seemed unwilling to accept full responsibility for themselves as independent agents. In short, many people looked outwardly to religious conventions to find their moral compass points rather than looking inwardly to their own faculties of judgement. How could development in the moral sphere lag so far behind the sciences? Kant thought that an uncritical regard for religious orthodoxies had made people timid. In his estimation, individuals simply deferred to exercise independent judgement, preferring instead the comforts of traditional conventional values. This is why Kant characterizes the immaturity of his contemporaries as "self-incurred." If, however, old habits of dependence could be shed, each person would be self-regulated and fully mature. As long as the vast majority of people resisted mature self-regulation, however, humanity would be in the grip of a moral crisis.

Kant's exhortation to self-determination is in important respects updated for the twenty-first century in Naomi Klein's contribution to this chapter. While the trajectory of scientific progress since 1800 follows lines that Kant might have anticipated, many of its features and implications could not have been predicted in his day. Large-scale industrial manufacturing and complex global trade relations could not have been foreseen by anyone living before the advent of steam-power, the electrical grid, nuclear energy, and the infrastructure that sustains contemporary life. As Klein portrays matters, both the dynamics of our present economy and the political structures that support them are incapable of reversing the environmental degradation currently threatening human survival. Indeed, these very political and economic conditions created that threat. Industries dedicated to resource extraction have been extremely proficient at transforming the natural world to suit their own purposes, and they have done so at the expense of other important things. Moreover, according to Klein, deregulated capitalism and a political tolerance for inequality have handed over a disproportionate share of the benefits from technological progress to a small class of people. In Klein's opinion, these political-economic conditions are insupportable in the face of a currently unfolding environmental catastrophe. To complicate matters, public debate has been narrowed in pathological ways that exclude effectual lines of inquiry into global-scale environmental reform. Tapping into the spirit of Socrates, she prods readers to critically examine the political and economic factors that are simultaneously spurring on an environmental catastrophe and actively sabotaging deliberation about solutions. If Klein and climate scientists are correct, at stake in this dispute is nothing less than the survival of humanity as a species. For this reason, Klein argues, our current political and economic system has brought on a global existential crisis.

1.2 Plato (427–347 BCE)

The enduring significance of Socrates's trial for Western history is due almost entirely to the first reading in this chapter. Plato's *Apology* records Socrates's stirring defence of the examined life. This is not the only historical record of Socrates's trial, but it is our only extant eye-witness account of the day. Another contemporary account from Xenophon is shorter and, by virtue of being second-hand, less influential than Plato's. For this reason Plato's *Apology* is the primary source for scholarship on both Socrates and his trial. Our text is not a word-for-word transcription of what Socrates and others said in court, however. It is a literary re-presentation of essential details, not court stenography.

Transcripts of trial speeches were not entered into an official record in ancient Athens. Plato wrote his account of Socrates's trial for a variety of purposes, among which three stand out: (1) to record an event that he regarded as significant but that might otherwise be forgotten; (2) to establish his friend's legacy, or at least to counter discreditable rumours about someone he admired; and (3) to promote the examined life. Most likely, Plato aimed to capture the spirit of Socrates's trial speeches and their essential messages rather than to record each and every word. This is historiography after the fashion of Socrates's near contemporary, Thucydides (widely regarded as the first serious historian). Thucydides was an Athenian general who wrote an authoritative history of the Peloponnesian War between Athens and Sparta (427–404 BCE). His *History* includes numerous long speeches, but he does not claim word-for-word accuracy for its reports. Thucydides writes: since "each speaker appeared to me to say roughly what was required about the particular circumstances in which he was involved ... this is how I set it down, sticking as closely as I could to the entire content of what was actually said" (*The History of the Peloponnesian War*, Book I, Section 22). Speeches reconstructed in this way are as much the product of informed historical imagination as they are of infallible memory, testimony, and documentation. Taken in a similar spirit, Plato's *Apology of Socrates* has as much authenticity as any such account may claim. In any case, Plato's text has acquired tremendous cultural significance, whether or not it is factually accurate in every detail, and that significance is enough to merit a central place on any university student's reading list.

The institutional framework of Athenian criminal justice is sufficiently different from ours as to require an explanation. First, criminal indictments were issued directly by private citizens, not by a public prosecutor or professional police force. Trials were instigated by citizen-prosecutors and conducted without the supervision of specially trained judges. Defendants were expected to represent themselves. All-male juries varied in size, some as large as 1,501 citizens. Socrates's jury of 501 was common. Large juries were used to frustrate attempts at bribery and corruption. Jurors were assigned on the day a trial was conducted and proceedings were completed in a single sitting (additional measures to prevent bribery and corruption).

Prosecutors addressed the jury first, making their case for conviction with a time-limited speech. The defendant was then given equal time to respond. Strictly speaking, the defendant's speech is the apology, *apologia* being the Greek term for "defence speech" (and which does not imply contrition). Upon completion of the prosecution and defence speeches, jurors voted in a secret ballot. The verdict fell in favour of whichever side secured 50 per cent of the votes plus one (i.e., 251 for a jury of 501). After an acquittal, the trial ended immediately. After a conviction, deliberations over the penalty took the form of two additional speeches. First the prosecution proposed what it considered to be an appropriate punishment, and then the defendant proposed another. A second secret ballot decided the outcome based on the majority's preference.

Some historical details of Socrates's trial are well understood. First, he faced three prosecutors, Meletus, Anytus, and Lycon, who indicted him for (i) corrupting the youth and (ii) impiety. These charges may strike us as imprecise, but the principal prosecutorial burden was to demonstrate that a defendant's actions constitute a danger to the city rather than being in strict violation of precisely formulated statutes. In this case, the prosecutors seemed to be relying on a general antipathy towards Socrates, not evidence of the sort that we might expect in court today (e.g., expert and eye-witness testimony, physical exhibits, documentation, etc.). Prosecutors counted on his unpopularity to make their task easier, as Socrates points out (28a). General antipathy is not surprising: Socrates's investigations often humiliated interlocutors by refuting them (23a); young men in his circle followed his example and conducted similar investigations of their own (23b–c); many people thought that he belonged to a controversial class of teachers known as sophists (20d); he claimed to be on a special divine mission (28a–34b) and guided by a divine guardian or voice (*daimonion*) that communicated only to him (31c–d); he pursued his investigations aggressively (29c–30a) and with a political—perhaps even revolutionary—purpose (30e). He was critical of conventional morality, democratic institutions, and official political authorities. Socrates was a genuinely controversial figure, whether or not he was a legitimate danger to society.

In addition to the jury, a crowd gathered to observe the trial, and it got raucous at times—as was common in an Athenian court. More than once, Socrates asks the audience not to make a disturbance (17d, 27b, 30c); presumably, spectators were responding audibly to one of his provocative points. We must not imagine everyone sitting respectfully in a hushed chamber, solemnly attending to Socrates's every word. Imagine, instead, a large, unruly, and fractious crowd at a political rally. Audience members may murmur among themselves, shout out objections, and stamp their feet while some among them attempt to hush objections and reduce any din that might drown out the podium speaker.

The complete text of Plato's *Apology of Socrates* consists of three separate speeches. They recount what Socrates said but nothing is reported directly from the prosecution speeches. We must glean some of the content of these unrecorded speeches indirectly from Socrates's response to particular points in them and from a brief exchange between Socrates and the chief prosecutor, Meletus (24c–25c). Since the first speech is complex we have inserted headings to demarcate 6 subsections (1.2.1; 17a–35d). In addition to the inserted subheadings, our texts of the *Apology* and *Crito* incorporate standard pagination used by scholars to precisely cite passages in Plato's dialogues; these are inserted directly into the text within square brackets as [17a–42a] for the *Apology*, and as [43a–54e] for *Crito*.

[1] The Defence Speech proper begins with a prologue (17a–18a) in which Socrates informs jurors that this is his first appearance before the court in any capacity and so he is unfamiliar with its conventional modes of address.

[2] Next (18a–19a), Socrates summarizes the charges against him and distinguishes two sets of accusers: the current accusers, Meletus, Lycon, and Anytus, are responsible for the two official charges; additionally, a large, amorphous group of earlier accusers had been for years misrepresenting him as a busybody and babbler (stock complaints about intellectuals of all stripes, including the sophists with whom Socrates was sometimes confused).

[3] Because the damage to Socrates's reputation from his earlier accusers is greater and more insidious than the official charges, he responds to them first (19b–24b). He claims to have been misrepresented in three ways: (1) that he teaches, (2) that he accepts money for teaching, and (3) that he possesses a special kind of knowledge that passes for wisdom. He denies allegation (1) on conceptual grounds: as someone who knows nothing, it is by definition impossible for him to teach (19e–20c). He denies allegation (2) on factual grounds: he has never accepted money for talking to people (19d–20a), a claim the prosecutors provide no witnesses to contradict (34a–b). Allegation (3), like allegation (1), is denied primarily on conceptual grounds, but accompanied by a complex explanation: Socrates is wiser than others only because he is aware of his own dearth of knowledge, whereas others do not possess such self-awareness about their ignorance (23a). His detailed response to allegation (3) diagnoses the deep source of animosity against him: it's not superiority in positive wisdom on his part that people resent; it's that he exposes in others the false pretense of wisdom (22e–23a).

[4] After addressing the slanders of his earlier accusers Socrates responds to the official charges against him, most of which is a cross-examination of Meletus (24c–27e). Here again, his defence is based partly on conceptual grounds, partly on factual grounds. Conceptually, he tries to show that the prosecutors do not understand the very terms their charges invoke. The official indictment seems formulated to trigger reputation-based hostility towards Socrates, not based on a clear understanding of how youths are benefitted or corrupted, nor is it based on evidence of impious conduct by Socrates. Furthermore, if Socrates happens to corrupt anyone, he does so unintentionally (which means that he ought to be corrected, not punished), and he publically observes conventional religious practices (which means he has done nothing wrong in that regard). Accordingly, he discounts the official charges as being without merit. Still, as he is aware, they never posed the real threat against him—that comes from the unofficial accusations.

Meletus's cross-examination instructively illustrates a pattern of Socratic questioning: first he elicits from his interlocutor an answer to a question; next he elicits elaboration of key terms in that answer; and lastly he explores the systematic implications of this elaboration and the original answer to his question. Poorly formulated claims tend to collapse after full elaboration and rigorous scrutiny of this sort. If Socrates's rough treatment of Meletus is typical of his manner towards other interlocutors, we can appreciate why Athenians had grown impatient with him.

[5] Arguably, the moral heart of the Defence Speech is the fifth subsection (28b–34b), for here Socrates explains the mission that gives purpose to all of his activities. In effect, it sums up the guiding principles of a novel and unique way of life. This life is founded on the conviction that he has been commissioned by Apollo to help Athenians examine their own lives. He sees himself as a gadfly, stinging the morally sluggish and powerful horse of Athens to examine itself critically (30d–e). Socrates accepts this mission as a civic duty, yet he fulfils this civic function in the capacity of a private citizen rather than seeking the kind of political influence available to someone in public office (31c–32). [6] Lastly, the Defence Speech closes with an epilogue (34b–35d) in which Socrates directs jurors to render their decision according to the impartial standard of justice alone and to reject the accusations against him.

Evidently, Socrates's *apologia* was not persuasive, for the jury voted to convict him. The prosecutors then advocated for capital punishment in speeches that are not recorded.

Socrates's Sentencing Speech (1.2.2; 35e–38b) is shorter than his Defence Speech and structured more simply. It begins in a way that is strictly consistent with his defence: being convinced that he is not guilty, he refuses to concede that any punishment would be appropriate for what he does. In this defiant spirit, Socrates initially floats a proposal based not on what the jurors are likely to accept, but on strict consideration of the value of his missionary services on their behalf. From this point of view, Socrates deserves an honour reserved for Olympic victors: free meals for life in the Council House (which is comparable to the House of Commons in Ottawa, the British Palace of Westminster in London, or the Capitol Building in Washington). This proposal is withdrawn shortly after being introduced, but some jurors no doubt resented his chutzpah for mentioning it at all. After ruling out other alternatives to capital punishment, Socrates ultimately proposes a fine that will be paid by some of his friends (Plato among them). Perhaps not surprisingly, more jurors voted for execution than conviction, which officially completes the trial.

In a final, Departing Speech (1.2.3; 38b–42a), Socrates addresses separately those who voted against him and those who supported him. His opponents are faulted for blundering tactically. Nature was preparing to rid them of a seventy-year-old nuisance without any effort on their part (38c). Now, however, they have stirred up others who will not forget Socrates and will predictably carry on his mission (38c–d). Socrates's friends are then comforted with an argument that death ought not to be feared (39d–41c).

The sequel to the *Apology*, Plato's *Crito*, is set in a jail cell three days before Socrates's execution (1.2.4). It begins with Crito arriving early in the morning to spirit Socrates away to safety in Thessaly, where presumably he would live out a natural life. Socrates's response to the plan is striking, for he pauses at the threshold to deliberate about the best course of action. In particular, Socrates refuses to flee until they have fully considered whether the plan is defensible. After setting aside as irrelevant some concerns voiced by Crito based on conventional opinion (44b–48a), they consider, in particular, whether Crito's plan is morally defensible (48b–49e). The position they reach anticipates by four centuries the more famous Christian injunction in Matthew 5:38–42 to turn the other cheek when someone strikes you; in other words, you must not harm a person who harms you. Two distinctive details in the *Crito* version of this prohibition deserve special note: (1) a premise asserting that justice is intrinsic to a good life, and (2) the conclusion that justice forbids us from acting to harm any other person. In short, the prohibition against harm admits of no exceptions, even when one has suffered wrong at the hands of another.

The no-harm principle that concludes this exchange applies in a wide range of circumstances, but it may fairly be asked whether Socrates's current situation is one of them. The principle forbids an agent from harming other people, but it is difficult to identify any *person* who would be harmed by Socrates's flight from Athens. Apparently, there are good grounds to believe that his guards will not suffer painful repercussions, that his prosecutors and opponents will be as satisfied by his self-imposed exile as by his execution, and that no other person could be harmed by his escape. If these reasonable assumptions are correct, then Socrates and Crito appear to have run into an argumentative dead-end. On reflection, the principle formulated at *Crito* 49e appears not to provide guidance in the situation at hand.

Deliberations between Socrates and Crito shift abruptly when in the next beat Socrates introduces an audacious and completely new set of considerations (50a). In short, he elevates the discussion, shifting the focus from a single *interpersonal* moral constraint imposed by the no-harm principle to a comprehensive set of abstract political principles (i.e., concerning the relationship between individual citizens and the state). Socrates maintains that his *political* obligations as a citizen of Athens are more compelling than his interpersonal obligations to all other individuals. To the city he owes his birth and education, and his debt in this regard is even greater than that which he owes to his parents (50c–51e). How exactly this is the case Socrates does not explain. In part, the argument seems to presuppose fifth-century citizenship laws that discouraged Athenian citizens from marrying non-Athenians. This prohibition gave his parents a strong incentive to eschew marrying Corinthians, Thebans, or any other non-Athenians. And in part, the argument seems to rest on the fact that children are socialized by an entire community and not simply by their parents. Other considerations may also factor in here, but the fundamental point is that a citizen incurs weighty debts to a society simply by virtue of being born and reared in it. In particular, citizens of a particular society who enjoy the protection of its laws must, as a direct consequence, obey those same laws.

According to the final pages of Plato's *Crito*, the law imposes formally binding obligations on a citizen, but these obligations are not absolute and are not imposed inflexibly (50a–54d). Legal and civic obligations are binding insofar as one cannot opt out of them by choice alone. Still, there is a protocol by which a citizen can alter the specific content of a civic obligation, a "persuade or obey" rule: obey the law as it stands, or persuade the city to formally withdraw that particular legal obligation (51b–c). Because Athens was a participatory democracy, citizens enjoyed the opportunity to address the Assembly directly and to advocate changing any law. When a petition of this sort was successful, the refurbished legal code bound everyone equally; if unsuccessful, then the dissident citizen remained obliged to obey the law, despite personal misgivings. Citizens are not tyrannically bound to an inflexible system of law as long as there is a mechanism to redefine those obligations. If, however, a citizen makes no effort to persuade the city to change its laws, then that person *implicitly* consents to obey its laws as they stand. Merely remaining in the city is a signal of implicit consent to any obligations specified in its legal code. As it happens, Socrates never voiced objections to Athenian laws, and he never emigrated, in which case he must accept the court's judgement about his mission.

Over and above all of the other political principles articulated in Plato's *Crito*, one stands out: the rule of law. The rule of law maintains that what ought to govern a society is not any person or group of people (e.g., a dictator, benevolent monarch, or democratically elected government). Rather, a just society is ruled by its laws, which simultaneously protect every citizen and oblige obedience from every citizen. Socrates introduces this fundamental principle by imagining the laws of Athens standing like a person in the doorway, chastising them as he is poised to flee (50a–54d). This thought experiment disguises the impasse that might have stymied any direct application of the no-harm principle as it was set out in the previous exchange (48b–49e). Just at the moment when a formidable argumentative obstacle appears, Socrates expands the scope of that which merits protection from the no-harm principle to include fundamental institutions of civil society—that is, in addition to individual persons, civil institutions can be harmed. (Rhetorically, this shift is disguised by Socrates's *personification* of Athenian law.) From this argument Socrates and Crito conclude that they are on the verge of committing an especially egregious sort of injustice, one that effectively undermines the legal foundation of society. After a lifetime spent enjoying the protection of Athenian law, Socrates cannot now escape his obligations to respect its authority. This special sort of injustice constitutes an existential threat to the legal system and the integrity of society, since laws depend for their authority on the obedience of citizens. On the basis of this conclusion, Socrates is convinced that he ought to remain in Athens and accept his legally sanctioned punishment (54d).

In order to assess Plato's arguments it is helpful to consider whether or not the mission described in the *Apology* was genuinely beneficial to Athens. Are Socrates's critical efforts healthy for a community or do they undermine civil order? Additionally, you might consider whether or not the purely critical posture Socrates adopts in his investigations is in any way instructive. Do we learn anything constructive in the wake of an argument that simply exposes someone's claim to be false or ill-conceived? Turning to Plato's *Crito*, you might consider whether the shift in focus from interpersonal ethics to political ethics in the final pages of the dialogue is warranted. Does the argument in the final pages of the *Crito* (50a–54d) simply and unproblematically extend the no-harm principle (49e), or does it stretch the scope of that principle's application beyond reasonable limits? You might also consider the tenability of Socrates's argument about the overriding obligations of a citizen to the state, as well as its implications about consent and the rule of law. And lastly, Socrates's defiance in Plato's *Apology* seems to have given way to obedience in *Crito*. Can these two portrayals be reconciled with each other?

1.2.1 Apology of Socrates, *Defense Speech (17a–35d)*

[1. Prologue (17a–18a)]

[17a] How you were affected, men of Athens,[1] by my accusers, I do not know. But I, even I myself almost forgot who I was because of them, so persuasively did they speak. And yet they have said practically nothing true. I was especially amazed by one of the many lies they told, the one in which they said that you should take care not to be deceived by me because I am a skilled speaker. [17b] Their lack of shame—since they will be exposed immediately by what I do, when I show myself not to be a clever speaker at all—this seems to me to be most disgraceful of them. Unless of course they mean to call "clever" someone who speaks the truth. Because if they mean this, then I would indeed admit—not in the way they do—that I am an orator.

So, as I say, these men have said little or nothing that is true, whereas from me you will hear the whole truth. [17c] Not, by Zeus, beautified speeches like theirs, men of Athens, and not ornamented with fine phrases and words, but you will hear me say the words that come to me spoken at random—for I believe what I say is just—and let none of you expect otherwise. After all, it would surely not be fitting, gentlemen, for someone of my age to come before you composing speeches, as it might be for a young man. And this most of all, men of Athens, I beg and request of you: if in these speeches you hear me defending myself in the language I also typically use in the marketplace by the tables, where many of you have heard me, as well as elsewhere, don't be surprised and don't make a disturbance because of it. [17d] Because this is exactly how it is: I have now come before the court for the first time, at seventy years of age.[2] So I am simply a stranger to the manner of speech here. And so, just as you would certainly have sympathy for me if I actually happened to be a stranger and spoke in the accent and manner in which I had been raised, I now particularly ask you for this just request, at least as it seems to me, to disregard my manner of speech—maybe it's better, maybe it's worse—and to consider only the following and pay attention to it: whether I say just things or not. [18a] For this is the virtue of a judge, while of an orator it is to speak the truth.

1 *men of Athens* The proper form of address is "judges" or "gentlemen of the jury," which Socrates uses later. (See 40a.)

2 *seventy* The year is 399 BCE, which puts Socrates's birth at 469 BCE. Other references to Socrates's age are made by him at 17c, 25d, 34e, 37d, *Crito* 43b, 49a, 52e.

[2. The Two Sets of Accusers, Earlier and Recent (18a–19a)]

It is right for me to defend myself, men of Athens, first against the earliest untrue accusations made against me and the earliest accusers, and then against the later accusations and the later accusers. [18b] For many of my accusers came to you many years ago now, saying nothing true, and I fear these more than Anytus and his friends,[3] though indeed they are dangerous too. But these men are more dangerous, gentlemen, the ones who, taking most of you aside from childhood, influenced you and made accusations against me that are not in fact true: that there is a certain Socrates, a clever man, a student of things in the sky who has investigated everything under the earth, and who makes the weaker speech the stronger. [18c] These people, men of Athens, having spread this allegation, are my fearsome accusers, for those who have heard them think that the people who study these things do not acknowledge the gods either. Moreover, these accusers are numerous and have been making accusations for a long time now. And what's more, they spoke to you at an age when you would be liable to believe them—some of you being children and youths—crudely making accusations against an absent person with no one else to make a rebuttal.

[18d] What is most unreasonable is that one can't know and name the names of these people, except if one happens to be a comic playwright.[4] These people who misled you with envy and slander—and others who, having themselves been persuaded, then persuade others—all of these are hardest to deal with. For it is not possible to summon them here to court or to cross-examine any of them, but it is necessary to defend myself just as if shadow-boxing, and conduct a cross-examination without anyone responding. So you too must accept that my accusers are twofold, as I said, those who accused me recently and those whom I mentioned from long ago, and believe that I must first defend myself against the latter. [18e] For you heard their accusations against me earlier and much more often than those of the later people.

Well then. I must make a defense, men of Athens, and in such a short time must try to banish this prejudice from you that you have held for a long time. [19a] I would like it to turn out this way—that I will succeed in defending myself—if that would be better for both you and me. But I think this is difficult, and just what it is I'm attempting doesn't escape me at all. Nevertheless, let the case proceed in whatever way the god favors; I must obey the law and make my defense.

[3. Defence against the Earlier Accusers (19b–24b)]

[19b] Let us consider, then, from the beginning, what the accusation is, from which the prejudice against me arose that Meletus believed when he brought this charge against me. Well then. What precisely did the accusers say when they accused me? Just as if they were charging me, it is necessary to read out their indictment: "Socrates is guilty of meddling, of inquiring into things under the earth and in the heavens, of making the weaker speech the stronger, and of teaching these very things"—something like this. [19c] For even you yourselves have seen these things in the comedy of Aristophanes, a certain Socrates being carried

3 *Anytus and his friends* His friends were Meletus and Lycon; the three of them were prosecuting. The leader of the prosecution was Meletus, a young man who probably held a grudge against Socrates; Anytus hated the sophists and probably regarded Socrates as one of them; Lycon was a rhetorician. Anytus is mentioned in particular because he was the most politically influential of these, having played an important part in the restoration of Athenian democracy.

4 *a comic playwright* In his play *Clouds* of 423, Aristophanes had portrayed a Socrates who was head of a "Thinkery" of students engaged in natural science and cosmological speculation, as well as in argumentation. Aristophanes is named in 19c. His caricature of Socrates seems to combine two types: the natural scientist and the sophist.

around up there,[5] insisting that he walks on air and spouting off a lot of other nonsense that I do not claim to know anything about, either great or small. I don't speak in order to dishonor such knowledge, if someone is wise about such things—I hope I am not somehow prosecuted by Meletus on such great charges—but in fact I have nothing to do with them, men of Athens, and I call on the majority of you as witnesses, and I expect you to teach and inform one another, those of you who have ever heard me in conversation—and this includes many of you. [19d] Tell one another if any of you heard me ever discussing such things, either a lot or a little. And from this you will realize that the same is true of the other things that the many say about me.

But in fact none of them is the case. And indeed, if you have heard from anyone that I endeavor to teach people and make money, this is not true. [19e] Though again, I think that it is a fine thing if an individual is able to teach people,[6] such as Gorgias of Leontini and Prodicus of Chios and Hippias of Elis. For each of these people, gentlemen, going into each of the cities, to the young—who could associate with whomever they want from their own citizens for free—they convince them to leave their company and join them, paying them money, and to feel grateful besides!

[20a] For that matter, there is currently another wise man, from Paros, whom I have discovered is in town because I happened to meet a man who has paid more money to sophists than all the others combined, Callias, son of Hipponicus. So I asked him—because he has two sons—"Callias," I said, "If colts or calves had been born to you as sons, we could find and hire a trainer who would make them well-bred with respect to the appropriate virtue; he would be some horse-trainer or farmer.[20b] But as it is, since they are humans, whom do you have in mind to hire as a trainer for them? Who is knowledgeable about such virtue, of the human being and of the citizen? Because I assume you have looked into it, since you have sons. Is there someone," I said, "or not?" "Certainly," said he. "Who?" I said, "And where from? And for how much does he teach?" "Evenus, Socrates," he said, "from Paros, for five mina."[7] [20c] And I considered Evenus blessed, if he really has this skill and teaches for such a sweet-sounding price. I at any rate would be proud of myself and be boastful, if I knew these things. But in fact I don't know them, men of Athens.

Perhaps some one of you might respond, "But Socrates, what is *your* profession? Where have these slanders against you come from? For surely it's not by busying yourself with the usual things that so much hearsay and talk has arisen, but by doing something different from most people. Then tell us what it is, so that we don't judge your case rashly." [20d] The person who says this seems to me to speak justly, and I will try to show you what it is, precisely, that won me this reputation and notoriety.

Listen, then. And while I will perhaps appear to some of you to be joking, rest assured that I will tell you the whole truth. For I, men of Athens, have acquired this reputation due to nothing other than a certain wisdom. What sort of wisdom is this? Quite likely it is human wisdom. There's a good chance that I actually have this kind of wisdom, while those men I was speaking of just now might perhaps be wise with a wisdom more than human—or I don't know how I should put it, for I certainly don't have it, and whoever says so is lying and is saying it to slander me. [20e] But don't interrupt me, men of Athens, not even if I strike you as talking big. The story I will tell you is not my own, but I will refer you to a trustworthy source for what I say, because regarding whether it is wisdom of a sort and of what sort it is I will present to you as my witness the god in Delphi.[8]

[21a] You know Chaerephon, I presume. He was a companion of mine from youth and a comrade of yours

---

5 *Socrates being carried around up there* In the play, the satire of Socrates's desire to inquire into higher things is given physical form through the depiction of Socrates in a hanging basket.

6 *able to teach people* The names given are all names of sophists (20a).

7 *five mina* (See also 38b for "a mina of silver.") A mina was 100 silver drachmas (see 26e, 36b), and a drachma was equivalent to 6 obols. Daily earnings ranged from 2–6 obols. Admission to the theatre was 2 obols. Pay for being a judge (jury duty) was 2 obols.

8 *the god in Delphi* At Delphi one could ask questions of the god Apollo via his oracle, a priestess known as the Pythia.

in the democracy and joined you in the recent exile[9] and returned with you. And you know how Chaerephon was, how zealous he was about whatever he pursued, and so for example when he went to Delphi he was so bold as to ask this—and, as I say, don't interrupt, gentlemen—he asked if there was anyone wiser than me. The Pythia then replied that no one was wiser. And his brother here will bear witness to you about these things, since he himself has died.

[21b] Think about why I am bringing this up: it's because I'm going to teach you where the prejudice against me came from. Because when I heard this I pondered in the following way: "Whatever does the god mean? And what riddle is he posing? For I am not aware of being wise in anything great or small. What in the world does he mean, then, when he says that I am wisest? For certainly he does not lie; he is not permitted to." And for a long time I puzzled over his meaning.

Then, very reluctantly, I embarked on a sort of trial of him. I went to one of the people who are thought to be wise, hoping to refute the oracle there if anywhere, and reply to its pronouncement: "This man here is wiser than me, though you said I was." [21c] So, scrutinizing this fellow—there's no need to refer to him by name; he was one of the politicians I had this sort of experience with when I examined him, men of Athens—in talking with him it seemed to me that while this man was considered to be wise both by many other people and especially by himself, he was not. And so I tried to show him that he took himself to be wise, but was not. [21d] As a result I became hated by this man and by many of those present.

And so, as I was going away, I was thinking to myself, "I am at least wiser than this man. It's likely that neither of us knows anything worthwhile, but whereas he thinks he knows something when he doesn't know it, I, when I don't know something, don't think I know it either. It's likely, then, that by this I am indeed wiser than him in some small way, that I don't think myself to know what I don't know." [21e] Next, I went to another one of the people thought to be wiser than him and things seemed the same to me, and so I made an enemy of that man as well as of many others.

So, after this, I now went to one after another, realizing with pain and fear that I was becoming hated. But nevertheless I thought it necessary to consider the god's oracle to be of the utmost importance, so I had to continue going to all of the people thought to know something, investigating the meaning of the oracle. [22a] And by the dog, men of Athens, because I must tell you the truth, my experience was really something like the following: in my divine search those held in highest esteem seemed to me to be lacking just about the most, while others thought to be poorer were better men as far as wisdom is concerned.

I have to represent my wanderings to you as though I were undertaking various labors[10] only to find that the oracle was quite irrefutable. After the politicians I went to the poets, including those of tragedies and those of dithyrambs[11] and others, so that there I would catch myself being more ignorant than them. [22b] Reading the works which I thought they had really labored over, I would ask them what they meant, so that at the same time I might also learn something from them. I am ashamed to tell you the truth, gentlemen, but nevertheless it must be told. Practically anybody present, so to speak, could have better explained what they had written. [22c] And so, as before, I quickly realized the following about the poets: that they do not write what they write because of their wisdom but because they have a certain nature and are possessed, like the seers and fortune-tellers, who also say many fine things but know nothing about what they're saying. It seemed clear to me that the poets had had a similar experience. And at once I understood that, because of their writing, they thought themselves to be the wisest of all men even about other things, but they weren't. And so I departed from them thinking

9 *in the democracy ... the recent exile* Athens was subject to violent political turmoil between rival factions who wanted to restrict the ruling positions to a small number (oligarchs) or broaden it to more (democrats).

10 *labors* Alluding to the labours of Heracles, a series of difficult tasks the mythological hero performed as penance.

11 *dithyrambs* Hymns to the god Dionysus, sung by a chorus.

that I was superior to them in the same way as I was to the politicians.

[22d] So finally I went to the crafters, because I was aware that while I knew practically nothing, I knew that I would find that they knew many fine things. And in this I was not mistaken—they knew things I didn't and in this they were wiser than me. But, men of Athens, the noble crafters seemed to me to have the same flaw that the poets also had. Because each of them performed his craft well, he considered himself to be most wise about the greatest things—and this sour note of theirs overshadowed their wisdom. [22e] And so I asked myself on behalf of the oracle whether I would prefer to be just as I am—neither being at all wise in the ways that they are wise nor ignorant in the ways they are ignorant—or to be both, as they are. And I answered myself and the oracle that it would be best for me to be as I am.

[23a] As a result of this quest, men of Athens, a lot of hatred developed against me, and of the most difficult and oppressive kind, such that from it many slanders arose, and I gained this reputation for being wise. For on each occasion the bystanders thought that I myself was wise about the subject on which I was examining the other person. But in fact it's likely, gentlemen, that in truth the god is wise, and by this pronouncement he means the following: that human wisdom is worth little or nothing. [23b] And he appears to be using me as an example, speaking of this man Socrates and even using my name, just as if he said, "Human beings, he among you is wisest who knows like Socrates that he is actually worthless with respect to wisdom." That's why, both then and now, I go around in accordance with the god, searching and making inquiries of anyone, citizen or stranger, whom I think to be wise. And if I then learn that he isn't, I assist the god and show him that he is not wise. And because of this busyness I lack the time to participate in any public affairs worth mentioning or any private business, but I am in great poverty because of my service to the god.

[23c] Furthermore, the young people follow me around of their own accord, those with the most leisure, the sons of the very wealthy. They delight in hearing me examine people and they often imitate me, having a go at examining others afterwards. And, I think, they discover a great number of people who think they know something but know little or nothing. [23d] As a result, the people who are examined by them then grow angry with me, but not themselves, and they say that Socrates is a most vile person and corrupts the young. And whenever anyone asks them, "By doing what and by teaching what?," they have nothing to say and do not know, but, so as to not appear at a loss, they say these things that are handy against all philosophers, about "the heavenly things and the things under the earth" and "not acknowledging the gods" and "making the weaker speech the stronger." I believe it's because they don't want to tell the truth, that they are obviously pretending to know something even though they know nothing. [23e] Since they are ambitious and impetuous, I think, and there are many of them and they speak about me ruthlessly and persuasively, they have filled up your ears, badmouthing me violently for a long time. On the strength of this, Meletus attacked me along with Anytus and Lycon, Meletus complaining on behalf of the writers, Anytus on behalf of the crafters and the politicians, and Lycon on behalf of the orators.

[24a] And so, as I said in the beginning, I would be amazed if I could rid you of this slander in such a short time, since it has become so powerful. This, I assure you, men of Athens, is the truth, and in speaking I conceal nothing, either big or small, nor hold anything back. Indeed I am quite aware that I am hated on account of these very things, which is an indication that I tell the truth, and that this is the slander against me and that these are the causes. And if you inquire into these things, either now or later, this is what you'll find.

[4. Defence against the Recent Accusers and the Official Charges (24b–28a)]

[24b] Concerning the charges of my initial accusers, let this defense before you be enough. Next I will try to defend myself against Meletus, the good and patriotic man, as he says, and the later accusers. And once more, as though they are different accusers, let's take up their indictment in turn. It goes something like this: he says Socrates is guilty of corrupting the young and not acknowledging the gods that the city does, but other strange spiritual things. [24c] The complaint is something along these lines. Let's examine this complaint point by point.

He says that I am guilty of corrupting the young. But I say, men of Athens, that Meletus is guilty, that he jokes in earnest, carelessly bringing a person to trial, pretending to be serious about and to trouble himself over various matters, none of which was ever an interest of his. This is how it is, as I will try to demonstrate.

[24d] Socrates: Here, Meletus, do tell me: don't you take making the young as good as possible to be your highest priority?

Meletus: I certainly do.

Socrates: Come now, tell these men, who makes them better? It's clear that you know. It's certainly a concern of yours, since upon discovering the one who corrupts them—me, as you claim—you bring me in front of these people here and accuse me. Come, state who is the one who makes them better and reveal to them who it is.... You see, Meletus, that you are silent and unable to speak? Doesn't it seem shameful to you, and sufficient proof of exactly what I'm claiming, that it meant nothing to you? So tell us, my good man, who makes them better?

Meletus: The laws.

[24e] Socrates: But that's not what I'm asking, best of men, but what man, whoever knows this very thing—the laws—in the first place?

Meletus: These men, Socrates, the judges.

Socrates: What do you mean, Meletus? These men can educate the young and make them better?

Meletus: Definitely.

Socrates: All of them, or some can and others can't?

Meletus: All of them.

Socrates: Well done, by Hera! And what a great number of benefactors you speak of. What next? Do these listeners[12] make them better or not?

[25a] Meletus: These too.

Socrates: Who else? The councilors?

Meletus: The councilors too.

Socrates: Well then, Meletus, surely those in the assembly, the assemblymen, they don't corrupt the young people? So do they all make them better, too?

Meletus: These too.

Socrates: Every Athenian, it seems, makes them fine and good except for me, and I alone corrupt them. Is this what you mean?

Meletus: That's exactly what I mean.

Socrates: You charge me with a great misfortune. [25b] But answer me: do you think it's like this with horses? That everyone makes them better, while one person is their corrupter? Or isn't it the complete opposite of this: one individual can make them better—or very few, the horse-trainers—while the many corrupt the horses if they deal with them and use them? Isn't this how it is, Meletus, concerning both horses and every other animal? ... It certainly is, whether you and Anytus agree or disagree. It would be a great blessing for the young if only a single person corrupted them, and all the others benefited them. [25c] But, Meletus, you have sufficiently demonstrated that you never before cared about the young, and you clearly reveal your indifference in that you have given no thought at all to the matters you indict me on.

Still, before Zeus, Meletus, tell us whether it is better to live among good citizens or wicked ones? ... Answer, my good man—I'm not asking anything difficult, you know. Don't the wicked always do something bad to those who are constantly closest to them, while the good do something good?

Meletus: Certainly.

12 *these listeners* Those attending Socrates's trial; ordinary Athenian citizens.

[25d] Socrates: But is there anyone who wishes to be harmed by those he associates with rather than to be helped? ... Keep answering, my good man, for the law also requires you to answer. Is there anyone who wants to be harmed?

Meletus: Of course not.

Socrates: Come then, do you bring me here on charges of intentionally or unintentionally corrupting the young and making them worse?

Meletus: Intentionally, I say.

[25e] Socrates: What then, Meletus? Are you so much wiser at your age than I am at mine that you know that the wicked always do something bad to those who are very close to them, and the good do good, while I, on the other hand, have fallen into such great ignorance that I don't also know this—that if I make one of my associates bad, I risk being harmed by him? And so I would do this great evil intentionally, as you claim?

I don't believe you, Meletus, and I think that no one else does. [26a] And either I do not corrupt, or if I do corrupt, I do so unintentionally, and so you are lying either way. If I corrupt unintentionally, the procedure is not to prosecute me here for such offenses, but to take me aside privately and teach and admonish me, since it is clear that if I learn, I will cease doing what I do unintentionally. You, however, fled from me and were unwilling to associate with me and teach me, but prosecuted me here, where the procedure is to prosecute those who need punishment rather than instruction.

[26b] And so, men of Athens, what I was saying is now clear, that Meletus never troubled himself about these matters in the slightest.

Nevertheless, tell us, Meletus, how do I corrupt the young, according to you? Or rather, isn't it clear from the indictment you wrote that I corrupt them by teaching them not to acknowledge the gods that the city recognizes, but other strange spiritual things? Don't you say that I corrupt them by teaching these things?

Meletus: That's absolutely what I'm saying.

[26c] Socrates: But by the gods, Meletus, the very gods that the discussion is currently about, speak even more clearly to me and these people here, because I can't tell whether you mean that I teach the young to believe that there are some gods—and so I believe there are gods and am not entirely godless nor guilty of this—not, however, the gods that the city believes in but others, and this is what you prosecute me for, that they are different, or, whether you mean that I do not acknowledge gods at all, and teach this to others?

Meletus: That's what I mean, that you don't acknowledge the gods at all.

[26d] Socrates: Incredible Meletus, why do you say that? I don't believe the sun, or even the moon, to be gods,[13] like other men do?

Meletus: No, by Zeus, judges, since he says that the sun is a stone and the moon is earth.

Socrates: Do you think you are prosecuting Anaxagoras, my dear Meletus? Do you have so much contempt for these men, and think them to be so unfamiliar with literature that they do not know that the books of Anaxagoras of Clazomenae are full of such claims? [26e] And what's more, do you think that the young learn these things from me, which they can buy sometimes for a drachma, at most, on the floor of the agora and can mock Socrates for, if he pretends they are his, especially when they are so distinctive? By Zeus, is this how I appear to you? Believing that there are no gods?

Meletus: You certainly don't, by Zeus; none whatsoever.

Socrates: You are unbelievable, Meletus, and are so even to yourself, I think. For the man seems to me, men of Athens, to be exceedingly arrogant and uncontrolled, and clumsily lodged this indictment out of hubris and lack of discipline and youthful zeal. [27a] He appears to be testing me, as though setting a riddle: "Will the wise Socrates realize that I am being facetious and contradicting myself, or will I deceive him and the other listeners?" For it looks to me as though he is saying contradictory things in his indictment, just as if he said "Socrates is guilty of not acknowledging the gods, and of acknowledging the gods." This is just like a riddler.

13 *I don't believe ... to be gods* Sun and moon worship were common in Greece.

Now join me in examining, gentlemen, in what way he seems to be saying these things. [27b] And you, Meletus, answer us. And as I begged of you all at the beginning, remember not to interrupt if I speak in my customary way.

Is there anyone, Meletus, who believes there are human matters, but does not believe in humans? ... Gentlemen, make him answer and not digress about other things. Is there anyone who does not believe there are horses, but believes there are equestrian matters? Or that there are not flute-players but there are flute-playing matters? ... There is not, best of men—since you are unwilling to answer I will answer on behalf of you and these others. [27c] But at least answer the next question: Is there anyone who believes there are spiritual matters but does not believe there are spirits?

Meletus: There is not.

Socrates: How delightful, that you answered reluctantly when compelled by these men. And so you say that I acknowledge and teach about spirits, and whether they be novel or old I at any rate believe in spiritual matters, according to your accusation, and you even swear this in the indictment. But if I believe in spiritual matters, surely it is unavoidably necessary that I believe in spirits too. Isn't that so? ... Of course it is. I take it that you agree, since you're not answering. [27d] Now, don't we think the spirits are either gods or the children of gods? Do you agree or not?

Meletus: Yes indeed.

Socrates: Well then, since I believe in spirits, as you say, then if, on the one hand, the spirits are gods of some sort, this would be what I am claiming you are riddling and being facetious about, saying that while I don't believe in gods, at the same time again I do believe in gods, since I indeed believe in spirits.

If, on the other hand, the spirits are certain illegitimate children of gods—either by nymphs or by some others that they're said to come from—who among men would think the children of gods exist, but not gods? [27e] Similarly, it would be strange if someone believed in the children of horses, or of asses too, namely mules, but did not believe in horses and asses.

And so, Meletus, it must be that you brought this indictment in order to test us about these things, or were at a loss as to what true crime you might charge me with. How you could persuade anyone with even a little intelligence that the same man does not believe in both spiritual and divine matters, or again, that this same man believes in neither spirits nor gods nor heroes—it's not possible!

[28a] And so, men of Athens, it seems to me that it doesn't take much of a defense to show I am not guilty of what Meletus charges me with, and even this is enough. What I said earlier, on the other hand—that I incurred a great hatred and from many people—you know well to be true. This is what convicts me, if indeed it convicts me, and not Meletus or Anytus, but the slander and malice of many people. And I know that these people have convicted, and will convict, many other good men; there is no fear that they will stop with me.

[5. Socrates's Divine Mission (28b–34b)]

[28b] Perhaps then someone might say, "Aren't you ashamed, Socrates, that you engaged in the kind of practice that now places you at risk of dying?" In reply to this I would justly say, "You do not speak well, Sir, if you think a man who is worth anything should take the risk of living or dying into account, rather than looking only to this: whether when he acts he acts justly or unjustly, and does the deeds of a good man or a bad one." [28c] For those demigods who met their ends in Troy would be fools according to you, especially the son of Thetis,[14] who thought so little of the risk in comparison with enduring some disgrace that, when his mother, a god, told him, when he was eager to kill Hector, something

14 *son of Thetis* The son of Thetis is Achilles. His reply to his mother's prophecy is from *Iliad* 18.98.

like this, as I recall: "Son, if you avenge the slaying of your comrade Patroclus[15] and kill Hector, you will be killed—because immediately after Hector," she said, "your fate is at hand," he, hearing this, belittled death and the danger and feared much more living as a coward and not avenging his friends. [28d] He said, "May I die at once, having served justice to the unjust, and not remain here, a laughing stock by the curved ships, a burden upon the earth." Do you think he cared about death or danger?

This is how it is, men of Athens, in reality. Wherever someone positions himself, thinking it to be for the best, or is positioned by his commander, he must, it seems to me, remain there and face the danger, and not put death or anything else ahead of disgrace. [28e] I would have done a terrible thing, men of Athens, if, when positioned by the officers, those whom you elected to command me at Potideia and Amphipolis and Delium,[16] I remained where these men stationed me and risked dying, just like anyone else, but when stationed by the god, as I believed and accepted—required to live my life seeking wisdom and examining both myself and others—I had abandoned my station for fear of death or anything else. [29a] That would be terrible, and truly under such circumstances someone could justly bring me to court for not believing that there are gods, defying the oracle and fearing death and thinking myself to be wise when I am not.

Indeed, to fear death, gentlemen, is nothing other than to regard oneself as wise when one is not; for it is to regard oneself as knowing what one does not know. No one knows whether death is not the greatest of all the goods for man, but they fear it as if they knew it to be the greatest of evils. [29b] And indeed, how could this ignorance not be reproachable, the ignorance of believing one knows what one does not know? But I, gentlemen, am perhaps superior to the majority of men to this extent and in this regard, and if indeed I seem to be wiser in any way than anyone, it would be in this, that I am not so certain about how things are in Hades and I do not think that I know.

But wrongdoing and defiance of one's superiors, whether god or man, *that* I know to be evil and shameful. So I will never fear nor flee things that for all I know could turn out to be good, rather than the evils that I know to be evil. [29c] So if you now acquitted me—rejecting Anytus, who said that either I should not have been brought here to trial in the first place, or, now that I have, executing me is unavoidable, and who tells you that if I were acquitted, your sons, practicing what Socrates teaches, will at once be thoroughly corrupted—if, referring to this, you said to me, "Socrates, we are not at present persuaded by Anytus and we acquit you but on the following condition, namely that you no longer spend your time on this quest and search for wisdom, and that if you are caught still doing this, you will die"—[29d] if, as I was saying, you were to acquit me on these conditions, I would say to you, "I cherish and love you, men of Athens, but I am more obedient to the god than to you, and so long as I have breath and am able I will not cease seeking wisdom and appealing and demonstrating to every one of you I come across, saying my customary things: Best of men, you are an Athenian, of the greatest and most renowned city in regard to wisdom and power. [29e] Are you not ashamed that you care about how you will acquire as much money as possible, and reputation and honor, while you do not care or worry about wisdom and truth and how your soul might be as good as possible?"

And if one of you disputes this and says that he does care, right away I will not let him go or leave him but will question and cross-examine and refute him, and if he does not appear to possess virtue, but he says he does, I will reproach him for considering the most valuable things to be of the least importance and the most worthless to be of the greatest importance. [30a] I will do this for anyone I meet, young and old,

15 *Hector ... Patroclus* In the *Iliad*, Hector is a prince of Troy who kills Achilles's comrade, Patroclus, in battle.

16 *Potideia and Amphipolis and Delium* Part of the Peloponnesian War (431–404 BCE) between the Athenian empire and a league led by Sparta, these were battles in which Socrates fought as a citizen-soldier.

stranger and citizen, though more for the citizens, insofar as they are closer to me in blood.

Rest assured that the god commands this, and I believe there has never been a greater good for the city than my service to the god. For I go around doing nothing other than persuading you, both young and old, not to care for your wealth and your bodies ahead of, or as intensely as, caring for how your soul might be as good as possible, saying that virtue does not come from wealth, but from virtue come wealth and all other human goods, both private and public. [30b] So if I corrupt the young by saying these things, they would be harmful; but if anyone claims that I say anything different from this, he is talking nonsense. "Men of Athens," I would say, "either be persuaded by Anytus or not, or acquit me or not, in light of the fact that I would not act differently, not even if I am destined to die again and again."

[30c] Do not create a disturbance, men of Athens, but keep to what I begged of you, not to make a disturbance at what I say and to listen, since I think by listening you might even be helped. For I am about to say a few other things to you at which you will perhaps cry out; but don't do this, no matter what. Rest assured that if you kill me for being the kind of person I describe, you will not harm me more than yourselves. Neither Meletus nor Anytus can do me any harm; it is not possible, since I think it is not permitted for a better man to be harmed by a worse one. [30d] Perhaps he will kill or exile or disenfranchise me, but while he and many others probably think that these are somehow great evils, I do not. It is a much greater evil to do what this man here is doing at this moment, attempting to put a man to death unjustly.

Indeed, men of Athens, I am making a defense hardly at all for my own sake, as one might suppose, but for yours, so you will not commit a wrong concerning the god's gift to you by condemning me. [30e] If you were to execute me you would not easily find another person like me, who is—although it is rather funny to say—attached to the city by the god just as though to a great and noble horse that's somewhat sluggish because of its size and needs to be provoked by a gadfly. This is just the way, I think, the god attached me to the city, the sort of person who never ceases provoking you and persuading you and reproaching each one of you the whole day long everywhere I settle. [31a] You won't easily get another person like this, gentlemen, and if you are persuaded by me, you will spare me. Or, being annoyed just like people roused from sleep, you might perhaps swat me, and persuaded by Anytus would put me to death without a second thought. And then you could live out your days in slumber, unless out of his concern for you the god sends you someone else.

[31b] You can tell from the following that I am the kind of person who is given by the god to the city: it is not human to disregard all my affairs and to endure the neglect of my household for so many years now but always be acting for your sake, going to each person privately just like a father or elder brother, urging you to pay attention to virtue. If I had gained something from these actions and received payment for inciting you in this way, they would make some sense. But you yourselves see now that my accusers, while so shameless in every other charge, lacked the audacity to present a witness to the effect that I ever charged anyone a fee or asked for one. [31c] For I believe I provide adequate witness that I am telling the truth: my poverty.

Perhaps it might be thought strange that I go around giving advice and getting myself involved privately, while I do not dare go to our assembly to advise the city publicly. [31d] The reason for this is something you have heard me say often and in many places: that something divine and spiritual comes to me, which Meletus jokingly included in the indictment. This has been coming to me as a kind of voice, beginning in childhood, and, whenever it comes, it always diverts me from what I am about to do but never toward anything. This is what prevented me from doing anything political, and I think it was entirely right to oppose me. Rest assured, men of Athens, if long ago I had tried my hand at political matters, long ago I would have perished and benefited neither you nor myself. [31e] And do not be offended by my telling the truth; there is no man who could save himself from you or any other populace while honestly opposing you and preventing many unjust and unlawful things from happening in the city. [32a] Rather, someone who genuinely fights for what is just, if he wishes to survive even for a short time, must act privately and not engage in public life.

I will provide you with ample evidence for this—not words, but what you admire, deeds. Listen to what happened to me, so that you may know that I did not yield to anyone, fearing death over justice, even though I might then have lost my life by not yielding. [32b] What I will relate is tiresome and lawyerly, but true. I, men of Athens, never held any office in the city apart from being on the council. And it so happened that our tribe, Antiochis, was presiding when you resolved to try as a group—contrary to law, as you all came to realize later—the ten generals[17] who did not rescue the people forsaken in the naval battle. At that time I alone of the committee members was opposed to you doing anything contrary to the laws and I voted against it. [32c] With the orators ready to indict and arrest me, and you inciting them and raising a ruckus, I thought it more important for me to risk everything with law and justice on my side than to side with you for fear of imprisonment or death, when you were contemplating unjust actions.

This was when the city was still a democracy. But again, when the oligarchy came to power, the Thirty summoned me and four others into the Rotunda and ordered us to bring Leon the Salaminian[18] from Salamis for execution; they made many such demands of a lot of other people, in order to tarnish as many as possible with their guilt. [32d] Then once again I demonstrated, not in speech but in action, that I couldn't care less about death, if it's not too crude to put it that way, but I care the world about this: that I avoid doing anything unjust or unholy. That regime did not intimidate me into doing something unjust, even though it was so powerful. And so when we exited the Rotunda, the other four left for Salamis and brought back Leon, but I left and headed home. And I might have been put to death for this, if the regime had not been overthrown soon after. [32e] There are many who will bear witness to these events before you.

Do you think I would have lasted for so many years if I had engaged in politics and, acting in the manner worthy of a good man, I came to the aid of the just decisions and rightly made them my utmost concern? Far from it, men of Athens, and neither would any other man. [33a] Throughout my whole life, I have shown myself to be the same sort of man in public—if I did anything at all—as in private, never joining anyone in anything illegal—neither those whom they say—slandering me—are my students, nor anyone else.

I have never been anyone's teacher, but if anybody desired to listen to me talking and fulfilling my mission, whether young or old, I never rejected anyone. [33b] Nor do I converse if I receive money but refuse to if I don't, but I allow rich and poor alike to question me, and likewise if anyone wishes to hear whatever I have to say in reply. And if any of them turn out to be good, or not good, I cannot justly be held responsible, since I never promised any instruction to any of them nor did I teach them. And if someone says that he learned anything from me or heard privately something all the others did not hear, rest assured that he is not speaking the truth.

[33c] But why then do people enjoy spending a lot of time with me? You have heard why, men of Athens—I told you the whole truth. It is because they enjoy hearing me expose those who think themselves wise but are not, for it is not unpleasant. I was commanded to do this, as I say, by the god, both in oracles and dreams and in every way that any divine fate at all ever ordered a man to do anything whatsoever. This is the truth, men of Athens, and easily tested. [33d] Because if I am indeed corrupting some of the young and have corrupted others, then surely if any of them realized when they were older that I recommended

---

17 *the ten generals* After the successful battle of Arginusae, the Athenian generals tasked with retrieving survivors at sea were unable to do so because of a violent storm. Many Athenians were outraged, and the generals were tried as a group and sentenced to death. Socrates opposed the decision on the grounds that Athenian law prohibited a group trial for those accused of a capital crime.

18 *Leon the Salaminian* Leon was an Athenian commander and war hero.

something evil at some point when they were young, they should have come forward just now to accuse me and avenge themselves. If they themselves were reluctant, someone from their family—a father or brother or some other relative—should call it to mind and take revenge, if they ever suffered any evil at my hands.

In any case, many of them are present here, whom I can see. [33e] First there is Crito here, who is my contemporary and from my district and the father of this man, Critoboulus. Next there is Lysanias of Sphettus, father of Aeschines here. Also, this here is Antiphon of Cephissos, father of Epigenes. These others have brothers who spent their time in this way: Nicostratus son of Theozotides, brother of Theodotus—Theodotus who died, which means that he could not have begged him not to testify—and Paralios here, son of Demodocus, whose brother was Theages. [34a] And here is Adeimantus, son of Ariston, the brother of Plato here, and Aeantodorus, brother of this man, Apollodorus. I have many others I could mention to you, some of whom Meletus certainly should have brought forth as a witness during his own presentation. If he forgot then, let him call them now—I yield my time—and let him speak if he has anyone of this kind.

Instead you will find the complete opposite of this, gentlemen; they are all ready to help me, the corruptor, the one who harms their kin, as Meletus and Anytus claim. [34b] Those who were corrupted perhaps would have a reason to help me. But the uncorrupted, who are already old men and who are their relatives, do they have any other reason for helping me except the right and just one, that they know just as well as Meletus does that he is lying, while I tell the truth?

[6. Epilogue (34b–35d)]

Well then, gentlemen. What *I* would say in my defense is this and maybe other similar points. [34c] One of you, perhaps, might then be angry when he is reminded of his own conduct—if, when contesting a lesser charge than this one, he begged and beseeched the judges with many tears, bringing forth his children so that they would pity him even more, with other members of his family and many friends, whereas I will do none of this, even though I run, I might suppose, the ultimate risk. Someone who brought this to mind might be more hard-hearted towards me and, feeling resentful, might cast his vote in anger. [34d] If this is really how any of you feel—I don't expect that it is, but if so—it seems reasonable for me to say to that person, "I, Sir, have a family, you know, and was not born 'from oak or from rock'—this is again an expression of Homer[19]—but from human beings, so that I have a family too, and indeed sons, men of Athens, three of them, one already a teenager and two who are children. But nonetheless I will not beg you to acquit me by bringing any of them here."

So why then won't I do any of these things? Not out of stubbornness, men of Athens, nor out of disrespect for you. [34e] Whether or not I am confident in the face of death is another story, but with respect to my good name, and yours and the whole city's, I don't think it's right for me to do any of these things at my age and with my reputation. [35a] Be it true or false, people have at any rate decided that Socrates is superior to most men in some respect, and if any of you who are reputed to be superior in wisdom or courage or any other virtue acted like that, it would be shameful. I have often seen people like this when they are on trial, men of some reputation but carrying on remarkably, as though they thought that something terrible will happen if they die, as if they would be immortal if you did not kill them.

[35b] I think these people bring shame upon the city, so that some stranger might think that the foremost of the Athenians in virtue, whom the Athenians nominate ahead of themselves for offices and other honors, they are no better than women. Those of you

19 *an expression of Homer* From *Odyssey* 19.163.

who are reputed to be something in any way whatsoever, men of Athens, should not do these things, and if we do them you should not permit it but be very clear about it, that you will more readily convict a person who puts on these miserable theatrics and makes a laughingstock of the city than one who holds his peace.

[35c] Apart from reputation, gentlemen, I do not think it is right to beg the judges nor to be acquitted by begging, but to teach and persuade instead. The judge does not sit for this reason—to hand out justice as a gift—but for the purpose of judging the case. He did not swear to do favors for whomever he feels like, but to judge according to the laws. We should not accustom you to breaking your oath and neither should you accustom yourselves; neither of us would then be acting piously. Do not, then, men of Athens, expect that I should act towards you in a way that I think is neither fine nor just nor holy, especially when, by Zeus, I am charged precisely with impiety by Meletus here. [35d] Clearly, if by begging I persuaded and convinced you who had sworn an oath, I would be teaching you to not believe that the gods exist, and in defending myself I would stupidly be accusing myself of not believing in the gods. But this is not at all how things are, since I do believe in them, men of Athens, unlike all of my accusers. And I trust you and the god to decide my case in whatever way you think is best both for me and for you.

[The judges vote and Socrates is found guilty by 281 votes to 220. The next stage of the trial involves each side proposing a penalty. The prosecution proposes the death penalty. Socrates must respond with a proposal of his own.]

1.2.2 Apology of Socrates, *Sentencing Speech (35e–38b)*

[35e] Many things contribute to my lack of anger, men of Athens, over what has just happened—that you found me guilty. [36a] And I am not surprised that what happened happened. Indeed, I am much more amazed at the final tally of each of the votes, since I, at least, did not think the difference would be so small, but larger. It now appears that if only thirty votes had changed sides, I would have been acquitted. I myself think that I was acquitted of Meletus's charges, and not just acquitted, as it is clear to everyone that if Anytus and Lycon had not joined him in accusing me, he would have owed a thousand drachmas for not receiving a fifth of the votes.[20]

[36b] The man proposes death as my penalty. Well then. Shall I make a counterproposal to you,[21] men of Athens? Or is it clear what I deserve? What, then? What do I deserve to suffer or pay, knowing that I have not gone about quietly throughout my life but, paying no attention to what the masses care about—money and estate and generalships and political power and other offices and clubs and political parties present in the city—[36c] and realizing that in reality I am too honorable a person to pursue these things and survive, I did not pursue the affairs that it would likely have helped neither you nor myself for me to get into, but I set out to accomplish the greatest good, as I declare, by going to each of you privately, trying to persuade each one of you not to put concern for any of his own affairs ahead of concern for how he himself might be as good and wise as possible, nor to put the affairs of the city ahead of the city itself, and to care for other things in the same way—what do I deserve for being such a person? [36d] Something good, men of Athens, if I must indeed make a proposal truly in accordance

20 *a fifth of the votes* Because it was considered a matter of public interest to punish impiety, Socrates's accusers would not have had to pay any court fees. To discourage frivolous suits, however, Athenian law levied a substantial fine against plaintiffs who failed to obtain at least one in five of the jury's votes.

21 *Shall I make a counterproposal to you* No penalty was specified by law for some crimes, including the crime of which Socrates has been convicted. Instead, the prosecution and defendant both proposed a penalty and the jurors had to decide which of the two recommended penalties to impose.

with merit. And more than that, some good which is fitting for me. What then is fitting for a poor man, a benefactor who needs to be at leisure to instruct you? There is nothing more fitting, men of Athens, than to feed such a man in the town hall, even more so than when one of you has won a race at Olympia on a single horse or in a two- or four-horse chariot. For while he makes you think that you are happy, I make you so, and while he does not need the nourishment, I do. [36e] So if I must propose a penalty according to justice based on merit, I propose this: dinners in the town hall.

[37a] Perhaps in saying this I seem to be speaking to you in much the same way as I spoke about pitying and imploring—out of arrogance. But it is not that, men of Athens, but rather because of the following sort of thing: I am convinced that I wrong no man willingly. But I cannot convince you of this, since we have been talking it over with each other for only a short time, whereas, I think, if your practice was the same as other people's, to deliberate about death penalty cases not just for one day but for many, you would be convinced. [37b] But, as it stands, it's not easy to demolish great prejudices in a short time.

Since I am convinced that I never do wrong, I certainly won't wrong myself and say against myself that I deserve something bad and proposing something of the sort for myself. Why should I? Because I'm afraid of something? So that I can avoid what Meletus proposes for me, when I claim not to know whether it is good or bad? Should I choose something that I am sure is something bad instead of this, and propose it as a penalty? What? Prison? [37c] And why must I live in the prison, enslaved to the Eleven[22] who are appointed to the office at the time? Then how about a fine, with imprisonment until I have paid? But in my case this is the same as what I just said, since I don't have any money to pay with.

Well then, shall I propose exile? You would probably accept this. But I would have an excessive love of life, men of Athens, if I were so stupid that I was unable to see that when you, my fellow citizens, could not bear my discussions and speeches, but they became so burdensome and so resented that you now seek to be free of them—would others willingly put up with them? [37d] Far from it, men of Athens. It would be a fine life for me, a man going into exile at my age, to spend my life being driven out and traipsing from one city to another. I'm quite sure that wherever I might go, the young will listen to me speak, just like here. [37e] And if I drive them away, they themselves will persuade their elders to drive me away; and if I don't drive them away, their fathers and relations will do so on their behalf.

Perhaps someone might say, "Can't you live quietly and peacefully in exile, Socrates, for our sake?" This is the hardest thing of all to make some of you believe. For if I say that this would be to disobey the god and so, because of this, I cannot live peacefully, you would think I was being ironic and not believe me. [38a] If instead I say that in fact this is the greatest good for a man, to talk every day about virtue and the other things you hear me converse about when I examine both myself and others, and that the unexamined life is not worth living for a man, you would believe this even less if I said it. As I say, this is how things are, gentlemen; but it is not easy to persuade you.

And besides, I am not accustomed to thinking of myself as worthy of anything bad. [38b] If I had money, I would have proposed as much money as I could pay, since it wouldn't have harmed me at all. But as it is I can't, unless you are willing to demand of me as much as I can pay. And perhaps I could somehow pay you a mina of silver. So I propose that amount....

Plato here, men of Athens, and Crito and Critoboulus and Apollodorus, they order me to propose thirty minas, and they guarantee it. So I propose that amount, and these men will be dependable guarantors of your silver. [The jury votes in favor of the death penalty, 361 to 140.]

---

22 *the Eleven* Elected officials in charge of prisons, executions, and confiscations. See [Aristotle's] *Athenian Constitution* 52.

1.2.3 Apology of Socrates, *Departing Speech (38c–42a)*

[38c] Men of Athens, among those who wish to criticize the city you will gain the reputation and take the blame for putting to death Socrates, a wise man—they will say I am wise, even if I am not, those people who wish to rebuke you—for the sake of a little time, because if you had waited a short while, this would have happened for you of its own accord, since you see that I am already advanced in years and that death is near.

[38d] I say this not to all of you, but to those who voted to execute me. And I say the following to those same people: perhaps you think, men of Athens, that I was condemned because I lacked the words that would convince you, as if I thought I must do and say everything possible to escape the charge. Far from it. I was condemned by a lack, certainly not of words, but of audacity and shamelessness and by my unwillingness to say to you what would be sweetest for you to hear—me lamenting and wailing and doing and saying many other things that, as I say, are unworthy of me, which you are used to hearing from other people. [38e] But I did not think at the time that I must do anything slavish on account of the danger.

Nor do I now regret how I defended myself—I would much rather choose to die having made this kind of defense than live having made the other kind. [39a] Neither on trial nor in war should I or anyone else contrive to avoid death by doing everything possible. Indeed, in battles it often becomes clear that a man could escape death by throwing aside his arms and begging his pursuers for mercy, and there are many other ways of fleeing death in each dangerous situation, provided one has the shamelessness to do and say anything.

It's not that it's not difficult to escape death, gentlemen, but it's much harder to escape wickedness, since it runs faster than death. [39b] And now, because I am a slow old man, I am being overtaken by the slower of the two, and my accusers, because they are clever and keen, by the swifter, by evil. And I am going away now, having been condemned to death by you, while they have been condemned by the truth to depravity and injustice. And both I and they will keep to our punishment. Perhaps this is how it had to be, and I suppose it's appropriate.

[39c] Next, I want to foretell the future to you my condemners, since I am now at the moment when men especially prophesy: whenever they are about to die. I declare that retribution will come to you swiftly after my death, you men who have killed me, and more troublesome, by Zeus, than the retribution you took when you sentenced me to die. [39d] You have done this just now by trying to avoid giving an account of your life, but I think the complete opposite will happen: you will have more prosecutors—whom I was holding back until now, though you did not notice—and as they are younger they will be more troublesome, and you will be more enraged. If you think that killing people will prevent anyone from rebuking you for not living properly, you are not thinking straight, since this escape is scarcely possible nor noble, whereas escape from the other is noblest and easiest: not by cutting down others but equipping oneself so that one can be as good as possible. With this prophecy to you who sentence me, I depart.

[39e] I would gladly converse with those who acquitted me, concerning what has come to pass, while the officials are busy and I am not yet on my way to the place where I must die when I arrive. Wait with me, gentlemen, for that long, since nothing prevents us from chatting together while we can. [40a] Since you are my friends, I want to show to you the meaning of what has just happened to me.

Something surprising happened to me, judges—and by calling you "judges" I would be using the word appropriately. Always in the past my usual divine prophetic sense was very strong and would even oppose me on detailed points if I was about to do something improper. And what happened to me just now, as you see yourselves, was what people might think, and do think, to be the worst of evils. [40b] And yet the sign of the god has not opposed me, not when I left home at dawn, nor when I arrived here in court, nor at any point during my speech when I was about to say something, whereas in many other speeches it has often stopped me, right as I was speaking. But now in this affair it has not been opposed to anything I have said or done.

So what do I take to be the cause of this? I will tell you. [40c] There's a good chance that what has happened to me is a good thing and that we understand death incorrectly, those of us who think death is something bad. I have strong evidence for this, since it is impossible that my customary sign would have failed to oppose me, unless I was about to do something good.

Let us also consider how there is great hope that it's a good thing in the following way: Now, death is one of two things, since it's either a kind of not being and the dead person has no perception of anything, or, according to what is said, it is a certain change and migration of the soul from its place here to another place.

[40d] And if it is the absence of perception and the kind of sleep when someone sleeps without having any dreams, death would be a wonderful gift—because I think if someone had to pick out the night when he slept so soundly that he did not have a dream and compared the other nights and days of his life with this night, and after considering them he had to say how many days and nights he had lived in his life that were better and more sweet than this night, I think that he—not only a private citizen but the great king—would find it easy to count them in comparison with other days and nights. [40e] If death is like this, I say it is a gift, since all of time would seem to be nothing more than a single night.

If, in turn, death is a kind of migration from here to another place, and what's said is true and perhaps all of the dead are there, what greater good could there be than this, judges? [41a] If someone who arrives in Hades, having moved on from these so-called judges here, finds those who were truly judges, who are said to act as judges there—Minos and Radamanthus and Aeacus and Triptolemus and as many other demigods who were judges in their own lifetimes—would it be unpleasant to depart? Or to spend time with Orpheus and Musaeus and Hesiod and Homer, how much would any of you give? [41b] I am willing to die many times if this is true, since I personally would find life there to be most amazing, if I could meet with Palamedes and Ajax son of Telamon, and anyone of the ancients who died as a result of an unjust decision, and measure my experience against theirs. I think it would not be unpleasant. And the greatest thing would be examining them and finding out which of them is wise and who thinks so but isn't, just like I do to people here.

[41c] How much would you give, judges, to quiz the leader of the great army against Troy, or Odysseus, or Sisyphus,[23] or many others one might mention, both men and women there whom it would be indescribably marvelous to debate and pass the time with and question? I should certainly hope that the people there would not put someone to death for that, since the people there are not just immortal for the rest of time but happier than those here in other respects, if what is said is true.

And so you too must be optimistic about death, judges, and hold this one thing to be true, that for a good man there is nothing evil in either living or dying. [41d] And neither do his deeds go unnoticed by the gods. My actions just now did not happen by themselves, but it is clear to me that it was to my advantage to die now and be released from my troubles. Because of this, my sign never deterred me. And I am not at all angry at those who voted against me and not much at my accusers—though they did not vote against me or accuse me with this in mind, but instead did so intending to harm me, and they deserve to be blamed for this.

23 *Minos ... Sisyphus* Most of the figures mentioned in this passage are mythological: Minos, Radamanthus, and Aeacus were mortal sons of Zeus, rewarded with the position of judges of the dead because they had established the first just laws on earth; Triptolemus was a demigod who brought agriculture to earth; Orpheus was a singer and a poet, and founder of the Orphic religious cult; Musaeus was a producer of sacred poetry and oracles; Palamedes was a clever inventor; Ajax was a king and Greek hero in the Trojan War; Odysseus was a cunning and eloquent Greek hero of the Trojan War, and protagonist of the *Odyssey*; Sisyphus was a king punished in the underworld by having perpetually to push a rock uphill. Possibly real figures were two revered Greek poets: Homer, author of the *Iliad* and the *Odyssey*, and Hesiod, whose only surviving works are *Works and Days* and the *Theogony*.

[41e] Nonetheless, I beg them for this much: revenge yourselves on my sons, when they have grown, gentlemen, by giving them the same trouble I gave you, if they seem to prioritize money or anything else ahead of virtue or if they think themselves to be something that they are not. Reproach them as I reproached you, for not caring about what they ought to and for thinking that they are something when they are worth nothing. [42a] If you would do this, I will have been served justice by you, and my sons, too.

But now it really is time to depart, I to die and you to go on living. But which of us goes to a better life is unclear to everyone except to the god.

1.2.4 Crito

[43a] Socrates: Why have you come at this hour, Crito? Or isn't it still early?

Crito: It certainly is.

Socrates: About what time is it?

Crito: Just before dawn.

Socrates: I'm surprised that the prison guard was willing to let you in.

Crito: He is used to me by now, Socrates, since I visit here so often. And besides, I have done him a good turn.

Socrates: Did you get here just now or a while ago?

Crito: Quite a while ago.

[43b] Socrates: So how come you didn't wake me up immediately, but sat by in silence?

Crito: By Zeus, no, Socrates. I wish I myself were not so sleepless and sorrowful, and so I have been marveling at you, when I see how peacefully you've been sleeping. I deliberately didn't wake you so that you would pass the time as peacefully as possible. And indeed, many times before I have thought you fortunate in your demeanor towards your entire life, and even more so in your present misfortune, so easily and calmly do you bear it.

Socrates: It's because it would be out of tune, Crito, to be angry, at my age, if I must finally die.

[43c] Crito: And yet others of your age, Socrates, have been caught up in such misfortunes, but their age does not prevent them from being angry at their fate.

Socrates: That's true. But why did you come so early?

Crito: Carrying troubling news, Socrates—though not for you, as it appears—but deeply troubling for me and all of your friends, and I, it seems, am among the most heavily burdened.

[43d] Socrates: What is it? Has the ship arrived from Delos, upon whose arrival I must die?

Crito: No, it hasn't arrived, but it looks like it will arrive today, based on the report of some people who have come from Sounion[24] and who left when it was there. It's clear from this that it will arrive today, and you will have to end your life tomorrow, Socrates.

Socrates: May it be for the best, Crito. If this pleases the gods, so be it. However, I don't think it will come today.

[44a] Crito: Where do you get your evidence for this?

24 *Sounion* The tip of Attica; a headland 200 feet above sea level, bearing a temple to Poseidon, where ships headed for Athens could be sighted early.

Socrates: I will tell you. I must be put to death sometime the day after the ship arrives?

Crito: That's what the authorities in these matters say, at least.

Socrates: In that case, I don't think it will arrive this coming day, but the next. My evidence is something I saw in a dream a little while ago during the night. It's likely that you chose a very good time not to wake me.

Crito: Well, what was the dream?

Socrates: A woman appeared, coming towards me, fine and good-looking, wearing white clothing. [44b] She called to me and said, "Socrates, you shall arrive in fertile Phthia on the third day."[25]

Crito: What a strange dream, Socrates.

Socrates: But obvious, at least as it appears to me, Crito.

Crito: Too obvious, perhaps. But, my supernatural Socrates, even now listen to me and be saved. If you die, for me it won't be just one misfortune: apart from being separated from the kind of friend the like of which I will never find again, many people, moreover, who do not know me and you well will think that I could have saved you if I were willing to spend the money, but that I didn't care to. [44c] And wouldn't this indeed be the most shameful reputation, that I would seem to value money above friends? For the many will not believe that it was you yourself who refused to leave here, even though we were urging you to.

Socrates: But why, blessed Crito, should we care so much about the opinion of the many? The best people, who are more deserving of our attention, will believe that the matter was handled in just the way it was.

[44d] Crito: But surely you see, Socrates, that we must pay attention to the opinion of the many, too. The present circumstances make it clear that the many can inflict not just the least of evils but practically the greatest, when one has been slandered amongst them.

Socrates: If they were of any use, Crito, the many would be able to do the greatest evils, and so they would also be able to do the greatest goods, and that would be fine. But as it is they can do neither, since they cannot make a man either wise or foolish, but they do just whatever occurs to them.

[44e] Crito: Well, let's leave that there. But tell me this, Socrates. You're not worried, are you, about me and your other friends, how, if you were to leave here, the informers would make trouble for us because we stole you away from here, and we would be compelled either to give up all our property or a good deal of money, or suffer some other punishment at their hands? [45a] If you have any such fear, let it go, because it is our obligation to run this risk in saving you and even greater ones if necessary. So trust me and do not refuse.

Socrates: I certainly am worried about these things, Crito, and lots of others too.

Crito: Well don't fear them. Indeed, some people only need to be given a little silver and they're willing to rescue you and get you out of here. And on top of that, don't you see how cheap those informers are and that we wouldn't need to spend a lot of money on them? [45b] My money is at your disposal, and is, I think, sufficient. Furthermore, even if, because of some concern for me, you think you shouldn't spend my money, there are these visitors here who are prepared to spend theirs. One of them has brought enough silver for this very purpose, Simmias of Thebes, and Cebes too is willing, and very many others. So, as I say, don't give up on saving yourself because you are uneasy about these things.

25 *fertile Phthia ... third day* In the *Iliad* 9.363, Achilles threatens to leave Troy and return home, saying "in three days shall I be in Phthia."

And don't let what you said in the court get to you, that you wouldn't know what to do with yourself as an exile. Wherever you go, there are places they will welcome you. [45c] And if you want to go to Thessaly, I have some friends there who will think highly of you and provide you with safety, so that no one in Thessaly will harass you.

What's more, Socrates, what you are doing doesn't seem right to me, giving yourself up when you could be saved, ready to have happen to you what your enemies would urge—and did urge—in their wish to destroy you.

[45d] I also think you are betraying your sons, whom you could raise and educate, by going away and abandoning them, and, as far as you are concerned, they can experience whatever happens to come their way, when it's likely that as orphans they'll get the usual orphans' treatment of orphans. One should either not have children or endure the hardship of raising and educating them. But it looks to me as though you are taking the laziest path, whereas you must choose the path a good and brave man would choose, especially when you keep saying that you care about virtue your whole life long.

[45e] So I am ashamed both on your behalf and on behalf of us, your friends, that this whole affair surrounding you will be thought to have happened due to some cowardice on our part: the hearing of the charge in court, that it came to trial when it need not have,[26] and the legal contest itself, how it was carried on, and, as the absurd part of the affair, that by some badness and cowardice on our part we will be thought to have let this final act get away from us, since we did not save you, nor you save yourself, when it was possible and we could have done so if we were of the slightest use. [46a] So see, Socrates, whether this is both evil and shameful, for you and for us as well. Think over—or rather, there's no longer time for thinking but only for deciding—this one consideration, because everything must be done this coming night; if we hang around any longer it will be impossible and we'll no longer be able to. So in every way, Socrates, believe me and do not refuse.

[46b] Socrates: My dear Crito, your eagerness would be worth a lot if it were in pursuit of something righteous, but the more it is not, the more difficult it is to deal with. We must therefore examine whether we should do this or not, because as always, and not just now for the first time, I am the sort of person who is persuaded in my soul by nothing other than the argument which seems best to me upon reflection. At present I am not able to abandon the arguments I previously made, now that this misfortune has befallen me, but they appear about the same to me, and I defer to and honor the ones I did before. [46c] If we have nothing better than them to offer under the present circumstances, rest assured that I will not agree with you, not if, even more so than at present, the power of the multitude were to spook us as though we were children, imposing chains and deaths and monetary fines upon us.

What's the most reasonable way we can examine this matter? By first resuming this argument that you give about reputations. [46d] Was it correct on each occasion when we said that one must pay attention to the opinions of some people and not to others'? Was this the correct thing to say before I had to die, whereas now it has become obvious that it was said only for the sake of argument and was actually just child's play and hot air?

I am determined to examine this together with you, Crito, whether it appears different when I consider it in this condition, or the same, and whether we should ignore it or be persuaded by it. [46e] It is always put like this, I think, by people who think there is something in it, the way I put it just now: that it is necessary to pay serious attention to some of the opinions that men hold and not to others. By the gods, Crito, doesn't this seem correct to you? [47a] Because you, as far as any human can tell, are in no danger of being executed tomorrow and the present misfortune should

26 *when it need not have* Socrates could have left the country and so avoided the trial.

not lead you astray. Have a look, then. Is it fair enough to say that one should not value every human opinion but only some and not others? And not the opinions of everyone but of some and not others? What do you say? Isn't this right?

Crito: Yes, that's right.

Socrates: Shouldn't we value the good opinions, and not the worthless ones?

Crito: Yes.

Socrates: Aren't the good ones the opinions of the wise, while the worthless ones come from the ignorant?

Crito: Of course.

[47b] Socrates: So then, what did we say, again, about cases such as this: should a man in training, who takes it seriously, pay any heed to the praise and blame and opinion of everyone, or only to one person, the one who is a doctor or a trainer?

Crito: Only to the one.

Socrates: So he should fear the criticisms and welcome the praises of that one person, and not those of the many?

Crito: Clearly.

Socrates: He must practice and exercise, and eat and drink, in the way that seems best to that one person, the trainer and expert, more than to all the others together.

Crito: That's right.

[47c] Socrates: Well then. If he disobeys this one man and dishonors his opinion and his praises and instead honors those of the many who know nothing, won't he suffer harm?

Crito: How could he not?

Socrates: What is this harm, and what does it tend to do, and in what part of the disobedient person?

Crito: It's clear that it's in the body, since this is what it destroys.

[47d] Socrates: Well said. Isn't it the same with the other things—not to go over them all, but in particular justice and injustice and shameful and fine things and good and bad, which are what our current discussion is about—whether we must follow the opinion of the many and fear it or instead the opinion of the one person, if there is someone who has knowledge, whom we must defer to and fear more than all the others together? If we do not heed his opinion we will corrupt and harm that part of us which becomes better with justice and is destroyed by injustice. Or don't you think so?

Crito: I do indeed, Socrates.

Socrates: Tell me, if we do not follow the opinion of the person who knows and so destroy that part of us which is improved by what is wholesome and corrupted by what sickens, is life worth living when that part is ruined? [47e] This is the body, I suppose, isn't it?

Crito: Yes.

Socrates: Then is life worth living with a wretched and corrupt body?

[48a] Crito: Not at all.

Socrates: And is life worth living after the part of us which injustice injures and justice benefits has been corrupted? Or do you think this is unimportant in comparison with the body, this part of us, whatever it is, that injustice and justice affect?

Crito: Not at all.

Socrates: But more valuable?

Crito: Much more.

Socrates: So, best of men, we must not pay much heed to what the many will say to us, but to what the one who knows about just and unjust things will say—to that one person, and to the truth itself. So you were wrong, at the beginning, to bring this up, that we must heed the opinion of the many concerning just things and noble things and good things and their opposites. "But in spite of that," someone might declare, "the many can put us to death."

[48b] Crito: That too is obvious. For someone might say so, Socrates. You're right.

Socrates: But, you wonderful fellow, it seems to me that the following statement, which we have been over before, remains just the same as before. So examine again whether or not it still holds true for you, that it's not living that should be our priority, but living well.

Crito: Why, of course it's still true.

Socrates: And that this is living well and finely and justly, does that remain true or not?

Crito: It remains true.

Socrates: Therefore, based on what you've agreed, we must consider the following: whether it is just or unjust for me to try to leave here, when I was not acquitted by the Athenians. [48c] And if it seems just let's try it, and if not, let's abandon it. As for the points you make about spending money and reputation and the upbringing of children, Crito, I suspect that these are really questions belonging to people who would casually put someone to death and resurrect him, if they could, without any thought—to the members of the multitude.

As for us, since the argument requires it, I suppose we should examine precisely what we just mentioned: whether we will act justly by giving money and thanks to those who will get me out of here—both you in the lead and me being led—or whether we will in fact act unjustly by doing all of this. [48d] If we think that we're acting unjustly by doing these things, I don't think we should take into consideration whether we will die if we hold our ground and keep our peace, or anything else we will suffer—only whether we're acting unjustly.

Crito: I think you put that well, Socrates. See what we should do, then.

Socrates: Let's look together, my good man, and if at any point you have an objection to what I am saying, make it and I will persuade you; if not, you blessed man, finally quit saying the same thing over and over, that I have to get out of here against the will of the Athenians. [48e] I think it is most important to act with your consent and not against your will. See, then, that the starting point of the inquiry is laid down to your satisfaction and try to answer the questions in the way you think best.

[49a] Crito: I shall certainly try.

Socrates: Do we say that we should never willingly act unjustly, or that we should in some instances and not in others? Or is acting unjustly never good or noble, as we often agreed on previous occasions? Or have all our previous agreements been overturned in these last few days, and did we fail to notice long ago, Crito, that when we have serious discussions with one another, we ourselves, at our age, are no different from children? [49b] Or more than anything isn't what we used to say still true? Whether the many agree or not, and whether we must also suffer harsher things than these or gentler, nevertheless acting unjustly is evil and shameful in every way for the person who does it. Do we say this or not?

Crito: We do.

Socrates: And so one must never act unjustly.

Crito: By no means.

Socrates: And so one should not repay an injustice with an injustice, as the many think, since one should never act unjustly.

[49c] Crito: It appears not.

Socrates: What next? Should one cause harm, Crito, or not?

Crito: Presumably not, Socrates.

Socrates: And then? Is returning a harm for a harm just, as the many say, or not just?

Crito: Not at all.

Socrates: Because harming a man in any way is no different from doing an injustice.

Crito: That's true.

Socrates: One must neither repay an injustice nor cause harm to any man, no matter what one suffers because of him. [49d] And see to it, Crito, that in agreeing with this you are not agreeing contrary to what you believe, because I know that few people believe it or will believe it. And so there is no common ground between those who hold this belief and those who don't; when they see each other's positions they are bound to despise one other. So think carefully about whether you yourself agree and believe, and let us begin thinking from here: that it is never right to act unjustly, or to return an injustice, or to retaliate when one has suffered some harm by repaying the harm. Do you reject or accept this starting principle? [49e] For it still seems good to me now, as it did long ago, but if it seemed some other way to you, speak up and educate me. If you're sticking to what we said before, listen to what comes next.

Crito: I do stick to it, and I accept it. Go ahead.

Socrates: Here in turn is the next point. Or rather, I'll ask you: when someone has made an agreement with someone else, and it is just, must he keep to it or betray it?

Crito: He must keep to it.

Socrates: Observe what follows from this. [50a] If we leave here without having persuaded the city, are we doing someone a harm—and those whom we should least of all harm—or not? And are we keeping to the just agreements we made, or not?

Crito: I'm unable to respond to what you're asking, Socrates; for I do not know.

Socrates: Well, look at it this way. If the laws and the community of the city came to us when we were about to sneak away from here—or whatever it should be called—and, standing over us, were to ask, "Tell me, Socrates, what are you intending to do? [50b] By attempting this deed, aren't you planning to do nothing other than destroy us, the laws, and the civic community, as much as you can? Or does it seem possible to you that any city where the verdicts reached have no force but are made powerless and corrupted by private citizens could continue to exist and not be in ruins?"

What will we say, Crito, to these questions and others like them? Because there's a lot more a person could say, especially an orator, on behalf of this law we're destroying, which makes sovereign the verdicts that have been decided. [50c] Or will we say to them, "The city treated us unjustly and did not decide the case properly"? Will we say this or something like it?

Crito: By Zeus, that's what we'll say, Socrates.

Socrates: What if the laws then said, "Socrates, did we agree on this, we and you, to honor the decisions that the city makes?" And if we were surprised to hear them say this, perhaps they would say, "Socrates, don't be surprised at what we're saying, but answer, since you are accustomed to using questions and answers. Come then, what reason can you give us and the city for trying to destroy us? [50d] Did we not, to begin with, give birth to you? And wasn't it through us that your father married your mother and conceived you? So show those of us, the laws concerning marriages, what fault you find that keeps them from being good?" "I find no fault with them," I would say.

"What about the laws concerning the upbringing and education of children, by which you too were raised? Or didn't those of us, the laws established on this matter, give good instructions when they directed your father to educate you in the arts and gymnastics?" [50e] "They did," I would say.

"Well, then. Since you have been born and brought up and educated, could you say that you were not our offspring and slave from the beginning, both you and your ancestors? And if this is so, do you suppose that justice between you and us is based on equality, and do you think that whatever we might try to do to you, it is just for you to do these things to us in return? Justice between you and your father, or your master if you happened to have one, was not based on equality, so that you could not do whatever you had suffered in return, neither speak back when crossed nor strike back when struck nor many other such things. [51a] Will you be allowed to do this to your homeland and the laws, so that, if we try to destroy you, thinking this to be just, you will in return try to destroy us the laws and your homeland with as much power as you have and claim that you're acting justly in doing so—the man who truly cares about virtue?

"Are you so wise that it has slipped your mind that the homeland deserves more honor and reverence and worship than your mother and father and all of your other ancestors? And that she is held in higher esteem both by the gods and by men of good sense? [51b] And that when she is angry you should show her more respect and compliance and obedience than your father, and either convince her or do what she commands, and suffer without complaining if she orders you to suffer something? And that whether it is to be beaten or imprisoned, or to be wounded or killed if she leads you into war, you must do it? And that this is just, and that you must not be daunted or withdraw or abandon your position, but at war and in the courts and everywhere you must do what the city and the homeland order, or convince her by appealing to what is naturally just? [51c] And that it is not holy to use force against one's mother or father, and it is so much worse to do so against one's homeland?" What will we say to this, Crito? That the laws speak the truth? Or not?

Crito: It looks so to me.

Socrates: "Consider, then, Socrates," the laws might say, "if what we say is true: that it is not just for you to try what you're now attempting to do to us. [51d] For we gave birth to you, brought you up, educated you, and gave you and all the other citizens every good thing we could, and yet even so we pronounce that any Athenian who wishes, once he has been admitted as an adult and sees the affairs of the city and us the laws, has the power, if he is not pleased with us, to take his possessions and leave for wherever he wants. And if any among you wants to live in a colony because we and the city do not satisfy him, or if he wants to go somewhere else and live as a foreigner, none of us laws stands in the way or forbids him from taking his possessions with him and leaving for wherever he wants.

[51e] "But whoever remains with us, having observed how we decide lawsuits and take care of other civic matters, we claim that this man by his action has now made an agreement with us to do what we command him to do, and we claim that anyone who does not obey is guilty three times over: he disobeys us who gave birth to him; and who raised him; and because, despite agreeing to be subject to us, he does not obey us or persuade us that we are doing something improper. [52a] And we give him an alternative and don't angrily press him to do what we order; and although we allow either of two possibilities—either to persuade us or to comply—he does neither of these.

"We say that you especially will be liable to these charges, Socrates, if indeed you carry out your plans, and you not least of the Athenians but most of all." If, then, I would say, "How do you mean?," perhaps they would scold me justly, saying that I most of all among the Athenians have made this agreement. [52b] They might say, "Socrates, we have great evidence for this, that we and the city satisfy you. For you would never have spent more of your life here than all of the other Athenians unless it seemed particularly good to you. You never left the city for a festival, except once to the Isthmus, but never went anywhere else except on military duty, nor did you ever make another trip like other Athenians do, nor did any urge seize you to get to know a different city or other laws, but we and our city were sufficient for you. [52c] So decidedly did you choose us and agree to be governed by us that, among other things, you had children in it, because the city was satisfactory to you.

"Moreover, at your trial you could have proposed exile, if you had wished, and what you're now trying to do to the city without her consent, you could have done then with her consent. At the time, you prided yourself on not being angry if you had to die, and you chose death, you said, in preference to exile. But now you neither feel shame in the face of those words nor have you any respect for us the laws. [52d] By trying to destroy us you are doing what the most despicable slave would do, trying to run away contrary to the contract and the agreement by which you agreed to be governed by us. So answer us first on this particular point: do we speak the truth when we say that you agreed to be governed by us in deed and not merely in words?" What can we say to this, Crito? Mustn't we agree?

Crito: We must, Socrates.

[52e] Socrates: "Aren't you," they might say, "going against your contracts and agreements with us, which you were not forced to agree to, nor deceived about, nor compelled to decide upon in a short time, but over seventy years, in which time you could have gone away if we did not satisfy you and these agreements did not appear just to you. [53a] You did not prefer Lacedaemon[27] or Crete, each of which you claim is well-governed, nor any of the other Hellenic cities or the foreign ones, but you left her less often than the lame and the blind and the other disabled people. Evidently the city and also we the laws were so much more pleasing to you than to other Athenians, for is a city pleasing to anyone without its laws? Now then, won't you keep to what you agreed? You will, if you are convinced by us, at any rate, Socrates; and at least you won't make yourself ridiculous by leaving the city.

"Just think about what good will it do you and your friends if you break them and do wrong in one of these ways. [53b] It's pretty clear that your friends will risk exile along with you and disenfranchisement from the city and confiscation of their property. And if you first go to one of the closest cities, to Thebes or to Megara—since both are well-governed—you will come as an enemy, Socrates, of those governments, and everyone who cares about their cities will regard you suspiciously, thinking that you are a destroyer of the laws.[28] [53c] And you will confirm the opinion of the judges, so that they will think they judged the case correctly, since whoever is a destroyer of the laws would certainly be considered in some way a destroyer of young and foolish men.

"Will you flee, then, from well-governed cities and from the most civilized people? Is it worth it to you to live like this? Will you associate with them, Socrates, and feel no shame when talking with them? What will you say, Socrates? What you said here, that virtue and justice are of the greatest value to humans, and along with lawfulness and the laws? And you don't think the conduct of such a Socrates will appear shameful? One should think so.

27 *Lacedaemon* Sparta.
28 *Thebes or to Megara ... destroyer of the laws* These were oligarchical states neighbouring Athens. Socrates would be seen as an enemy because he was a law-breaker.

[53d] "But will you leave these places and go to Crito's friends in Thessaly?[29] There is plenty of disorder and disobedience there and they might listen with pleasure to you, about how you amusingly ran away from prison wearing some costume or a peasant's vest or something else of the sort that runaways typically dress themselves in, altering your appearance. But still, will no one say that an old man, who probably only has a short time left in his life, was so greedy in his desire to live that he dared to violate the greatest laws? [53e] Perhaps not, if you do not annoy anyone. But if you do, Socrates, you will hear many dishonorable things about yourself. You will surely spend your life sucking up to everyone and living like a slave. What else will you do in Thessaly but feast, as though you had traveled to Thessaly for dinner? And those speeches, the ones about justice and the other virtues, where will they be?

[54a] "Is it for the sake of your children that you want to live, so that you can raise and educate them? What are you going do, in that case? You'll raise and educate them by bringing them to Thessaly and making them outsiders, so that they will enjoy that benefit too? Or if not that, will they grow up better if they are raised and educated with you away from them but alive, because your friends will take care of them? But is it that if you go to Thessaly, they'll look after them, whereas if you go to Hades, they won't? If those who claim to be your friends are any good, you must believe they will.

[54b] "So be convinced by us who brought you up, Socrates, and do not put children or life or anything else ahead of justice, so that when you go to Hades you will be able to provide all this as your defense to those who rule there. Since neither in this world, nor in the next when you arrive, will this action be thought better or more just or more pious for you and your friends to do. But as it is you leave us, if indeed you depart, having been done an injustice not by us, the laws, but by men. [54c] If you return the injustice, however, and repay the harm and flee in shame, having violated your agreement and contract with us and harmed those who least of all should be harmed—yourself, your friends, your homeland, and us—we will make life hard for you while you're alive, and then our brothers, the laws in Hades, will not receive you favorably, knowing that you tried to destroy us too, as far as you were able. So do not be persuaded by Crito to do what he says instead of what we say."

[54d] Rest assured, my dear friend Crito, that this is what I seem to hear, just as the Corybants[30] seem to hear the pipes, and the echo from these words resonates within me and makes me unable to hear anything else. So know that, based on my current beliefs, at least, if you speak against them you will speak in vain. Nevertheless, if you honestly think you can achieve anything more, speak.

Crito: No, Socrates. I am unable to speak.

[54e] Socrates: Then let it be, Crito, and let us act in this way, since this is where the god leads us.

29 *Thessaly* The Athenians associated this place with gluttony and debauchery.
30 *Corybants* Priests of the Asiatic goddess Cybele. The rites of the Corybants were accompanied by wild music and dancing.

1.3 Immanuel Kant (1724–1804)

Even those who disagree with controversial claims made in Socrates's Defence Speech (1.2.1) concede that it was courageous of him to voice such claims in a capital trial. Courage is thereby dramatized by Plato, even if its meaning or function are never explicitly elucidated in either his *Apology* or *Crito*. Kant goes a step further in "What Is Enlightenment?" by making courage thematic. Indeed, we should read Kant's essay as an exhortation to enlightenment, i.e., an attempt to encourage readers towards its pursuit (after all *en-courage* means literally "to instill the quality of courage in someone"). Enlightenment, like wisdom, is not something one simply receives; it must be earned. There is something ennobling about the mere aspiration for enlightenment for Kant, even if one's efforts are unsuccessful. This is because the independence of judgement required for its pursuit is nearly identified with maturity. To be mature one must think for oneself, often in defiance of institutional orthodoxies and conventional opinions. For these reasons, enlightenment and courage are twin themes in Kant's essay. Enlightenment is the psychological and political quality Kant champions, courage its precondition. His formulation of the Enlightenment's motto sums up this relationship: "Have courage to use your own understanding!"

Kant addresses two audiences, each with a distinctive purpose: his fellow Prussians are, by turns, coaxed and shamed into adopting the Enlightenment's motto; his monarch, Frederick II, is praised for endorsing Enlightenment values and implored to accept the dissemination of these same values throughout society. By identifying the pursuit of enlightenment with maturity, Kant makes it especially awkward for readers to decline the challenge he puts to them. How can any adult object to maturity? At the same time, he reassures the monarch that new-found independence among his subjects can be conjoined with obedience to his civil authority.

With respect to both audiences, Kant's analysis is in keeping with a general trend in modern times towards political liberalism. As its very name suggests, liberalism is a political theory that makes liberty or freedom its central principle. How liberty ought to be conceived, and how it relates to equality had been subjects of extensive debate for over a century by the time Kant published his essay. Schemes for promoting individual liberty date back to 1688 and John Locke's *Two Treatises of Government* (see 5.3). Subsequent liberal theorists refined and challenged important elements of Locke's account, but always with an eye to establishing the liberty rights of individual citizens. More importantly, in the Glorious Revolution in England (1688–89) the Catholic James II, who clashed with Parliament, was replaced on the throne by the Protestant William of Orange. Among many other things, this revolution established the supremacy of an elected Parliament over the monarchy. Significantly, in retaining its monarchy England declined to found itself as a republic. A century later, in 1789, revolutionaries ousted the French monarchy and founded the first Republic of France in the name of individual liberty and the universal franchise. Kant's 1784 essay was published while revolutionary ideas were fermenting in

France, Germany, and elsewhere, and it stakes a claim in several timely political debates. In particular, Kant takes a stand on the nature of individual liberty and on questions about whether that liberty is best promoted by a republican government or a constitutional monarchy.

Readers today may be surprised to see Kant defend hereditary monarchy as an instrument of individual liberty. But the violence of pre-eighteenth-century religious warfare in Europe made the stable, primarily secular monarchies of Kant's own day appear politically viable. The comparatively non-violent transition of England's Glorious Revolution was a model of civility when compared to the violent foundation France's first Republic in a revolution that culminated with the beheading of Louis XVI. As Kant presents it, a benevolent monarchy can both stabilize the foundation of society and promote individual liberty across it. This explains why "What Is Enlightenment?" must address two audiences as it does: a political commitment to individual liberty means something quite different to citizens who are encouraged to desire mature liberty than it does to the monarch who may feel threatened by his subjects' possession of it. It is therefore crucial that Kant sharply distinguish liberty as it operates independently of religious authority and liberty as it operates independently of a duly constituted political authority. Objections to religious authority on one side are thus balanced by an endorsement of political authority on the other.

The religious authorities that Kant most strenuously discourages people from heeding are the Roman Catholic Church and hierarchical, doctrinaire forms of Protestantism. He has no objections to religious faith that rests on the individual's direct engagement with sacred texts and precepts; self-examined faith of this sort is consistent with individual liberty. In taking this position, Kant thereby endorses some fundamental tenets of the Protestant Reformation that stand in sharp opposition to both Counter-Reformation tenets of the Catholic Church and formalistic strains of Protestantism. In Catholicism, for example, the Church had for centuries presented itself as an indispensable intermediary between the faithful and God, making the institutional hierarchy appear to be essential for individual salvation. According to central strands of the Reformation movement that began with Martin Luther in the early sixteenth century, individual salvation comes from each person's direct, personal relationship to God. In this regard, Kant's essay is not anti-religious *per se*; it simply takes a stand on one of the central religious disputes of the day. Eighteenth-century Prussia was less secular than twenty-first-century Canada, so we must be careful not to read Kant's position as irreligious, even when he criticizes particular religious attitudes or institutions.

Having declared the essential value of self-regulated or self-examined individual judgement, Kant turns to political freedom. Because individual judgement fulfils our moral and intellectual potential, freedom of thought is indispensable in the political sphere. Citizens ought to be free to enter into public debate and argue as their personal judgement dictates. Political constraints on free thought, speech, or independent judgement constitute an offence against the maturity that Kant encourages. Still, no matter how vigorously citizens argue with each other or how heated debate becomes, they must never resort to violence or illegality. For this reason, freedom of speech and unrestrained public debate must be combined with obligations in our conduct to obey the sovereign authority of the monarch. This is not the same as obedience to the rule of law as it is formulated in Plato's *Crito* (see 1.2, introduction) because it is not clear that Frederick's own conduct as a monarch-legislator is bound by Prussian law in the way that an Athenian citizen-legislator is bound by the laws of a democratic Athenian assembly. (This important theoretical issue is taken up in Chapter 4.) This is why, as a separate matter, Kant assures Frederick II that the free use of reason in public debate can co-exist with obedience. Hence, the king is implored to tell to his Prussian subjects, "Argue as much as you like and about whatever you like, but obey!" Naturally, this mantra serves as a directive to Kant's fellow Prussian citizens too: don't let debate lead to civil disorder or political subversion.

Both Kant's assurance to Frederick and his directive to all Prussians presuppose a programmatic distinction between the public use of reason and the private use of reason. How exactly Kant distinguishes between "public" and "private" here is not self-evident, since this is not how we ordinarily use the two terms. Ordinarily, "private" designates the domain of activity in which an individual person may reasonably expect to exercise a measure of unfettered control (e.g., in one's own home or with one's own family there), whereas "public" designates any place outside that sphere (e.g., the street outside one's home or with strangers there). As Kant uses the terms, they designate two different roles in which a person might operate: "public" means that the person speaks as a member of the general public, contributing to civic debate without special obligations beyond citizenship; "private" means speaking with a special obligation to represent whoever employs that person. The special obligations that constrain private reason cannot be overridden, but there are contexts in which a person who is employed as a minister, civic administer, office clerk, etc., can speak independently of their functionary role. In those contexts, they ought to be as free to reason publically as anyone else. A single person speaking on two occasions can switch roles if the two contexts allow it: when arguing as an independent citizen anything that person says or thinks ought to be uncensored by civil authorities; however, when serving a function within the state or when acting in a professional capacity (e.g., as a minister of a congregation, an administer of a school, as a clerk in an office, etc.) the same person is bound by special role-defined obligations. Accordingly, one can operate in what is ordinarily a public sphere, yet act in what Kant would designate a private capacity. It is therefore incumbent upon someone with special obligations to make it clear in which capacity they are speaking on any potentially ambiguous occasion; conversely, it is essential for official censors to ascertain in which capacity that person is speaking, i.e., publicly or privately.

In order to assess Kant's position it is helpful to consider whether all of his fine-grain distinctions are tenable. For example, is it theoretically coherent or practically possible to distinguish between public and private uses of reason? Also, is it categorically different to disregard a civil authority rather than a religious authority? Additionally, you might consider whether freedom of thought is compatible with total obedience to civil authorities. In particular, you might also consider whether genuine freedom for ordinary citizens can be satisfied by a monarchy, as Kant supposes.

"What Is Enlightenment?"

Enlightenment is man's emergence from his self-imposed nonage.[1] Nonage is the inability to use one's own understanding without another's guidance. This nonage is self-imposed if its cause lies not in lack of understanding but in indecision and lack of courage to use one's own mind without another's guidance. *Dare to know!* (*Sapere aude.*) "Have the courage to use your own understanding," is therefore the motto of the enlightenment.

Laziness and cowardice are the reasons why such a large part of mankind gladly remain minors all their lives, long after nature has freed them from external guidance. They are the reasons why it is so easy for others to set themselves up as guardians. It is so comfortable to be a minor. If I have a book that thinks for me, a pastor who acts as my conscience, a physician who prescribes my diet, and so on—then I have no need to exert myself. I have no need to think, if only I can pay; others will take care of that disagreeable business for me. Those guardians who have kindly taken supervision upon themselves see to it that the overwhelming majority of mankind—among them the entire fair sex—should consider the step to maturity, not only as hard, but as extremely dangerous. First, these guardians make their domestic cattle stupid and carefully prevent the docile creatures from taking a single step without the leading-strings to which they have fastened them. Then they show them the danger that would threaten them if they should try to walk by themselves. Now this danger is really not very great; after stumbling a few times they would, at last, learn to walk. However, examples of such failures intimidate and generally discourage all further attempts.

Thus it is very difficult for the individual to work himself out of the nonage which has become almost second nature to him. He has even grown to like it, and is at first really incapable of using his own understanding because he has never been permitted to try it. Dogmas and formulas, these mechanical tools designed for reasonable use—or rather abuse—of his natural gifts, are the fetters of an everlasting nonage. The man who casts them off would make an uncertain leap over the narrowest ditch, because he is not used to such free movement. That is why there are only a few men who walk firmly, and who have emerged from nonage by cultivating their own minds.

It is more nearly possible, however, for the public to enlighten itself; indeed, if it is only given freedom, enlightenment is almost inevitable. There will always be a few independent thinkers, even among the self-appointed guardians of the multitude. Once such men have thrown off the yoke of nonage, they will spread about them the spirit of a reasonable appreciation of man's value and of his duty to think for himself. It is especially to be noted that the public which was earlier brought under the yoke by these men afterwards forces these very guardians to remain in submission, if it is so incited by some of its guardians who are themselves incapable of any enlightenment. That shows how pernicious it is to implant prejudices: they will eventually revenge themselves upon their authors or their authors' descendants. Therefore, a public can

1 *nonage* Literally, this is "no age" or the age of legal minority.

achieve enlightenment only slowly. A revolution may bring about the end of a personal despotism or of avaricious tyrannical oppression, but never a true reform of modes of thought. New prejudices will serve, in place of the old, as guidelines for the unthinking multitude.

This enlightenment requires nothing but *freedom*—and the most innocent of all that may be called "freedom": freedom to make public use of one's reason in all matters. Now I hear the cry from all sides: "Do not argue!" The officer says: "Do not argue—drill!" The tax collector: "Do not argue—pay!" The pastor: "Do not argue—believe!" Only one ruler in the world says: "Argue as much as you please, but obey!" We find restrictions on freedom everywhere. But which restriction is harmful to enlightenment? Which restriction is innocent, and which advances enlightenment? I reply: the public use of one's reason must be free at all times, and this alone can bring enlightenment to mankind.

On the other hand, the private use of reason may frequently be narrowly restricted without especially hindering the progress of enlightenment. By "public use of one's reason" I mean that use which a man, as *scholar*, makes of it before the reading public. I call "private use" that use which a man makes of his reason in a civic post that has been entrusted to him. In some affairs affecting the interest of the community a certain [governmental] mechanism is necessary in which some members of the community remain passive. This creates an artificial unanimity which will serve the fulfillment of public objectives, or at least keep these objectives from being destroyed. Here arguing is not permitted: one must obey. Insofar as a part of this machine considers himself at the same time a member of a universal community—a world society of citizens—(let us say that he thinks of himself as a scholar rationally addressing his public through his writings) he may indeed argue, and the affairs with which he is associated in part as a passive member will not suffer. Thus it would be very unfortunate if an officer on duty and under orders from his superiors should want to criticize the appropriateness or utility of his orders. He must obey. But as a scholar he could not rightfully be prevented from taking notice of the mistakes in the military service and from submitting his views to his public for its judgement. The citizen cannot refuse to pay the taxes levied upon him; indeed, impertinent censure of such taxes could be punished as a scandal that might cause general disobedience. Nevertheless, this man does not violate the duties of a citizen if, as a scholar, he publicly expresses his objections to the impropriety or possible injustice of such levies. A pastor, too, is bound to preach to his congregation in accord with the doctrines of the church which he serves, for he was ordained on that condition. But as a scholar he has full freedom, indeed the obligation, to communicate to his public all his carefully examined and constructive thoughts concerning errors in that doctrine and his proposals concerning improvement of religious dogma and church institutions. This is nothing that could burden his conscience. For what he teaches in pursuance of his office as representative of the church, he represents as something which he is not free to teach as he sees it. He speaks as one who is employed to speak in the name and under the orders of another. He will say: "Our church teaches this or that; these are the proofs which it employs." Thus he will benefit his congregation as much as possible by presenting doctrines to which he may not subscribe with full conviction. He can commit himself to teach them because it is not completely impossible that they may contain hidden truth. In any event, he has found nothing in the doctrines that contradicts the heart of religion. For if he believed that such contradictions existed he would not be able to administer his office with a clear conscience. He would have to resign it. Therefore the use which a scholar makes of his reason before the congregation that employs him is only a private use, for no matter how sizable, this is only a domestic audience. In view of this he, as preacher, is not free and ought not to be free, since he is carrying out the orders of others. On the other hand, as the scholar who speaks to his own public (the world) through his writings, the minister in the public use of his reason enjoys unlimited freedom to use his own reason and to speak for himself. That the spiritual guardians of the people should themselves be treated as minors is an absurdity which would result in perpetuating absurdities.

But should a society of ministers, say a Church Council, ... have the right to commit itself by oath to a certain unalterable doctrine, in order to secure perpetual guardianship over all its members and through them over the people? I say that this is quite impossible. Such a contract, concluded to keep all further enlightenment from humanity, is simply null and void even if it should be confirmed by the sovereign power, by parliaments, and the most solemn treaties. An epoch cannot conclude a pact that will commit succeeding ages, prevent them from increasing their significant insights, purging themselves of errors, and generally progressing in enlightenment. That would be a crime against human nature whose proper destiny lies precisely in such progress. Therefore, succeeding ages are fully entitled to repudiate such decisions as unauthorized and outrageous. The touchstone of all those decisions that may be made into law for a people lies in this question: Could a people impose such a law upon itself? Now it might be possible to introduce a certain order for a definite short period of time in expectation of better order. But, while this provisional order continues, each citizen (above all, each pastor acting as a scholar) should be left free to publish his criticisms of the faults of existing institutions. This should continue until public understanding of these matters has gone so far that, by uniting the voices of many (although not necessarily all) scholars, reform proposals could be brought before the sovereign to protect those congregations which had decided according to their best lights upon an altered religious order, without, however, hindering those who want to remain true to the old institutions. But to agree to a perpetual religious constitution which is not publicly questioned by anyone would be, as it were, to annihilate a period of time in the progress of man's improvement. This must be absolutely forbidden.

A man may postpone his own enlightenment, but only for a limited period of time. And to give up enlightenment altogether, either for oneself or one's descendants, is to violate and to trample upon the sacred rights of man. What a people may not decide for itself may even less be decided for it by a monarch, for his reputation as a ruler consists precisely in the way in which he unites the will of the whole people within his own. If he only sees to it that all true or supposed [religious] improvement remains in step with the civic order, he can for the rest leave his subjects alone to do what they find necessary for the salvation of their souls. Salvation is none of his business; it *is* his business to prevent one man from forcibly keeping another from determining and promoting his salvation to the best of his ability. Indeed, it would be prejudicial to his majesty if he meddled in these matters and supervised the writings in which his subjects seek to bring their [religious] views into the open, even when he does this from his own highest insight, because then he exposes himself to the reproach: *Caesar non est supra grammaticos.*[2] It is worse when he debases his sovereign power so far as to support the spiritual despotism of a few tyrants in his state over the rest of his subjects.

When we ask, Are we now living in an enlightened age? the answer is, No, but we live in an age of enlightenment. As matters now stand it is still far from true that men are already capable of using their own reason in religious matters confidently and correctly without external guidance. Still, we have some obvious indications that the field of working towards the goal [of religious truth] is now opened. What is more, the hindrances against general enlightenment or the emergence from self-imposed nonage are gradually diminishing. In this respect this is the age of enlightenment and the century of Frederick [the Great].

A prince ought not to deem it beneath his dignity to state that he considers it his duty not to dictate anything to his subjects in religious matters, but to leave them complete freedom. If he repudiates the arrogant word "tolerant," he is himself enlightened; he deserves to be praised by a grateful world and posterity as that man who was the first to liberate mankind

2 Caesar is not above grammarians.

from dependence, at least on the government, and let everybody use his own reason in matters of conscience. Under his reign, honorable pastors, acting as scholars and regardless of the duties of their office, can freely and openly publish their ideas to the world for inspection, although they deviate here and there from accepted doctrine. This is even more true of every person not restrained by any oath of office. This spirit of freedom is spreading beyond the boundaries [of Prussia] even where it has to struggle against the external hindrances established by a government that fails to grasp its true interest. [Frederick's Prussia] is a shining example that freedom need not cause the least worry concerning public order or the unity of the community. When one does not deliberately attempt to keep men in barbarism, they will gradually work out of that condition by themselves.

I have emphasized the main point of the enlightenment—man's emergence from his self-imposed nonage—primarily in religious matters, because our rulers have no interest in playing the guardian to their subjects in the arts and sciences. Above all, nonage in religion is not only the most harmful but the most dishonorable. But the disposition of a sovereign ruler who favors freedom in the arts and sciences goes even further: he knows that there is no danger in permitting his subjects to make public use of their reason and to publish their ideas concerning a better constitution, as well as candid criticism of existing basic laws. We already have a striking example [of such freedom], and no monarch can match the one whom we venerate.

But only the man who is himself enlightened, who is not afraid of shadows, and who commands at the same time a well disciplined and numerous army as guarantor of public peace—only he can say what [the sovereign of] a free state cannot dare to say: "Argue as much as you like, and about what you like, but obey!" Thus we observe here as elsewhere in human affairs, in which almost everything is paradoxical, a surprising and unexpected course of events: a large degree of civic freedom appears to be of advantage to the intellectual freedom of the people, yet at the same time it establishes insurmountable barriers. A lesser degree of civic freedom, however, creates room to let that free spirit expand to the limits of its capacity. Nature, then, has carefully cultivated the seed within the hard core—namely the urge for and the vocation of free thought. And this free thought gradually reacts back on the modes of thought of the people, and men become more and more capable of acting in freedom. At last free thought acts even on the fundamentals of government and the state finds it agreeable to treat man, who is now more than a machine, in accord with his dignity.

1.4 Naomi Klein (1970–)

While both Socrates and Immanuel Kant work within a framework that acknowledges religious commitments, Naomi Klein draws upon environmental sciences that operate within an entirely secular framework. The crisis she has in view, climate-change, was discovered by environmental science, and environmental scientists have also proposed numerous measures to resolve it. Indeed, she criticizes climate-change deniers as dogmatically rejecting overwhelming scientific evidence of global warming. Her principal targets are extractivism and neoliberalism, as we note above (1.1). In some regards, these targets are more sharply defined than those criticized by Socrates and Kant.

Extractivism applies to an economy that is based on the trade of natural resources. The underlying assumption is that oil, natural gas, minerals, timber, and other natural resources may be conceived of as private property. As such, these resources are commodities to be sold for profit by private owners on the international market. The neoliberal political order that purports to sustain extractivist industrial practices advocates for minimal government intervention, including the reduction of wealth redistribution programs that tax one part of society (e.g., those with high incomes) to support another part (e.g., the ill, temporarily unemployed, indigent, or homeless). As Klein characterizes neoliberalism, the social value of any person or group is measured entirely by a capacity to participate in a deregulated market economy. Individual freedom is thus exercised entirely as consumer choice, and corporations furnish opportunities to exercise that freedom by providing marketable products and services. Wealth is a sign of merit because deregulated markets are presumed to distribute both money and political influence in a fair competition. Inequalities of wealth and political influence within society thus become inevitable, self-perpetuating, and greater over time. According to Klein, natural resources industries have been extremely successful at taking control of the political order and bending the international economic system to their own advantage, often by delimiting the range of opportunities available for collective political action to promote the common good. Political institutions, which were founded for the common good of all, have thus been co-opted for the private benefit of a small, influential group within society.

Klein invokes here a third variation of the public/private distinction that we noted earlier in connection with both Socrates and Kant. Socrates uses the distinction in passing without defining the terms (*Apol* 31c–33b). "Public" and "private" differentiate two potential contexts for his mission to morally reform Athens. He might have sought political office and conducted his work publically, i.e., in the democratic Assembly; instead, however, he spurned official politics and operated as a private citizen, talking to individual Athenians in private conversations. As we noted above (1.3, introduction) Kant uses the public/private distinction in a special, technical sense. In reasoning publically, a citizen speaks without any special obligations over and above membership in the community; in reasoning privately a person speaks as someone with special obligations, as someone performing a function for the state or an employer. For Kant, the public use of reason should be entirely free, whereas the private use of reason is bound by whatever obligations fall to a person because of their special functionary role. Klein applies the distinction to indicate what kind of material or financial interest is at stake in any particular situation: the material interest of an individual or a group of individuals who stand to benefit at the exclusion of others is "private," whereas the collective material interest of everyone is "public." She accuses climate-change deniers in the resource extraction industry of being disingenuous: they present economic policies that are designed to benefit themselves at the cost of others misleadingly as if they benefit everyone.

According to Klein, two kinds of "denial" are paralyzing environmental policy reform. Of course, first, there is the explicit denial of those who deny either that climate change is real or who doubt that human pollution causes it. In some ways, she is waging a battle of ideas with opponents who simply refuse to accept the evidence of environmental science. But for the most part, her criticisms of this position are as much psychological as they are conceptual or logical. Her diagnosis of problems in the ideological framework of climate-change denial is really a charge of motivated reasoning: such doubts are a function of resource industry self-interest, not any evidence against climate change itself. Self-interest and motivated reasoning are more difficult to refute than unsound reasoning or misinformation, which is why Klein often aims to disable deniers by undermining their credibility rather than refuting their arguments directly. The second kind of denial addressed by Klein takes the form of weak-willed acknowledgement that evidence of climate change is legitimate. To these people the problem either seems to require a miracle that will emerge without active political intervention or is simply unsolvable. Skepticism about environmental science is not the problem here, only the disengaged sense of agency felt by the vast majority of people who feel defeated or overwhelmed by the situation—Klein admits that she was formerly inclined this way herself. She attempts to activate this group in two ways simultaneously: (a) provoking their indignation at the motivated reasoning generating climate-change denial, and (b) fostering hope that environmental disaster can be averted with prompt action.

In order to assess Klein's position, it is helpful to consider whether her efforts to impugn the credibility of climate-change denial depend too heavily on psychological speculation about the motives of doubters and not enough on the evidence against their claims. Has she fairly and accurately characterized the substantive position of her opponents? Has she accurately diagnosed their motives? Do we have sufficient grounds to reject climate-change denial on the basis of her arguments? And do we have sufficient grounds to accept Klein's own activist claims? Over and above the position Klein adopts for herself and the climate-change denial she attacks, we might ask whether the hope she uses to spur prompt action among those who accept climate-change is realistic, given the evidence she herself advances about impending environmental disaster. She presents environmental problems in stark and dramatic terms. Does this evidence really provide grounds for hope of the sort she advocates?

~

from This Changes Everything

I denied climate change for longer than I care to admit. I knew it was happening, sure. Not like Donald Trump and the Tea Partiers going on about how the continued existence of winter proves it's all a hoax. But I stayed pretty hazy on the details and only skimmed most of the news stories, especially the really scary ones. I told myself the science was too complicated and that the environmentalists were dealing with it. And I continued to behave as if there was nothing wrong with the shiny card in my wallet attesting to my "elite" frequent flyer status.

A great many of us engage in this kind of climate change denial. We look for a split second and then we look away. Or we look but then turn it into a joke ("more signs of the Apocalypse!"). Which is another way of looking away.

Or we look but tell ourselves comforting stories about how humans are clever and will come up with a technological miracle that will safely suck the carbon out of the skies or magically turn down the heat of the sun. Which, I was to discover while researching this book, is yet another way of looking away.

Or we look but try to be hyper-rational about it ("dollar for dollar it's more efficient to focus on economic development than climate change, since wealth is the best protection from weather extremes")—as if having a few more dollars will make much difference when your city is underwater. Which is a way of looking away if you happen to be a policy wonk.

Or we look but tell ourselves we are too busy to care about something so distant and abstract—even though we saw the water in the subways in New York City, and the people on their rooftops in New Orleans, and know that no one is safe, the most vulnerable least of all. And though perfectly understandable, this too is a way of looking away.

Or we look but tell ourselves that all we can do is focus on ourselves. Meditate and shop at farmers' markets and stop driving—but forget trying to actually change the systems that are making the crisis inevitable because that's too much "bad energy" and it will never work. And at first it may appear as if we are looking, because many of these lifestyle changes are indeed part of the solution, but we still have one eye tightly shut.

Or maybe we do look—really look—but then, inevitably, we seem to forget. Remember and then forget again. Climate change is like that; it's hard to keep it in your head for very long. We engage in this odd form of on-again-off-again ecological amnesia for perfectly rational reasons. We deny because we fear that letting in the full reality of this crisis will change everything. And we are right.

We know that if we continue on our current path of allowing emissions to rise year after year, climate change will change everything about our world. Major cities will very likely drown, ancient cultures will be swallowed by the seas, and there is a very high chance that our children will spend a great deal of their lives fleeing and recovering from vicious storms and extreme droughts. And we don't have to do anything to bring about this future. All we have to do is nothing. Just continue to do what we are doing now, whether it's counting on a techno-fix or tending to our gardens or telling ourselves we're unfortunately too busy to deal with it.

All we have to do is *not* react as if this is a full-blown crisis. All we have to do is keep on denying how frightened we actually are. And then, bit by bit, we will have arrived at the place we most fear, the thing from which we have been averting our eyes. No additional effort required.

There are ways of preventing this grim future, or at least making it a lot less dire. But the catch is that these also involve changing everything. For us high consumers, it involves changing how we live, how our economies function, even the stories we tell about our place on earth. The good news is that many of these changes are distinctly un-catastrophic. Many are downright exciting. But I didn't discover this for a long while. I remember the precise moment when I stopped averting my eyes to the reality of climate change, or at least when I first allowed my eyes to rest there for a good while. It was in Geneva, in April 2009, and I was meeting with Bolivia's ambassador to the World Trade Organization (WTO), who was then a surprisingly young woman named Angélica Navarro Llanos....

She had recently given a speech at a United Nations climate conference in which she laid out the case for these kinds of wealth transfers, and she gave me a copy. "Millions of people," it read, "in small islands, least-developed countries, landlocked countries as well as vulnerable communities in Brazil, India and China, and all around the world—are suffering from the effects of a problem to which they did not contribute.... If we are to curb emissions in the next decade, we need a massive mobilization larger than any in history. We need a Marshall Plan for the Earth. This plan must mobilize financing and technology transfer on scales never seen before. It must get technology onto the ground in every country to ensure we reduce emissions while raising people's quality of life. We have only a decade."[1] ...

We had all just watched as trillions of dollars were marshaled in a moment when our elites decided to declare a crisis. If the banks were allowed to fail, we were told, the rest of the economy would collapse. It was a matter of collective survival, so the money had to be found. In the process, some rather large fictions at the heart of our economic system were exposed (Need more money? Print some!). A few years earlier, governments took a similar approach to public finances after the September 11 terrorist attacks. In many Western countries, when it came to constructing the security/surveillance state at home and waging war abroad, budgets never seemed to be an issue.

Climate change has never received the crisis treatment from our leaders, despite the fact that it carries the risk of destroying lives on a vastly greater scale than collapsed banks or collapsed buildings. The cuts to our greenhouse gas emissions that scientists tell us are necessary in order to greatly reduce the risk of catastrophe are treated as nothing more than gentle suggestions, actions that can be put off pretty much indefinitely. Clearly, what gets declared a crisis is an expression of power and priorities as much as hard facts. But we need not be spectators in all this: politicians aren't the only ones with the power to declare a crisis. Mass movements of regular people can declare one too.

Slavery wasn't a crisis for British and American elites until abolitionism turned it into one. Racial discrimination wasn't a crisis until the civil rights movement turned it into one. Sex discrimination wasn't a crisis until feminism turned it into one. Apartheid wasn't a crisis until the anti-apartheid movement turned it into one.

In the very same way, if enough of us stop looking away and decide that climate change is a crisis worthy of Marshall Plan levels of response, then it will become one, and the political class will have to respond, both by making resources available and by bending the free market rules that have proven so pliable when elite interests are in peril. We occasionally catch glimpses of this potential when a crisis puts climate change at the front of our minds for a while. "Money is no object in this relief effort. Whatever money is needed for it will be spent," declared British prime minister David Cameron—Mr. Austerity himself—when large parts of his country were underwater from historic flooding in February 2014 and the public was enraged that his government was not doing more to help.[2]

Listening to Navarro Llanos describe Bolivia's perspective, I began to understand how climate change—if treated as a true planetary emergency akin to those rising flood waters—could become a galvanizing force for humanity, leaving us all not just safer from extreme weather, but with societies that are safer and fairer in all kinds of other ways as well. The resources required to rapidly move away from fossil fuels and prepare for the coming heavy weather could pull huge swaths of humanity out of poverty, providing services now sorely lacking, from clean water to electricity. This is a vision of the future that goes beyond just surviving or enduring climate change, beyond "mitigating" and "adapting" to it in the grim language of the United Nations. It is a vision in which we collectively use the crisis to leap somewhere that seems, frankly, better than where we are right now....

... [C]limate change has become an existential crisis for the human species. The only historical precedent for a crisis of this depth and scale was the Cold War fear that we were heading toward nuclear holocaust, which would have made much of the planet uninhabitable....

So my mind keeps coming back to the question: what is wrong with us? What is really preventing us from putting out the fire that is threatening to burn down our collective house?

I think the answer is far more simple than many have led us to believe: we have not done the things

1 Angélica Navarro Llanos, "Climate Debt: The Basis of a Fair and Effective Solution to Climate Change," presentation to Technical Briefing on Historical Responsibility, Ad Hoc Working Group on Long-term Cooperative Action, United Nations Framework Convention on Climate Change, Bonn, Germany, June 4, 2009.

2 "British PM Warns of Worsening Floods Crisis," Agence France-Presse, February 11, 2014.

that are necessary to lower emissions because those things fundamentally conflict with deregulated capitalism, the reigning ideology for the entire period we have been struggling to find a way out of this crisis. We are stuck because the actions that would give us the best chance of averting catastrophe—and would benefit the vast majority—are extremely threatening to an elite minority that has a stranglehold over our economy, our political process, and most of our major media outlets. That problem might not have been insurmountable had it presented itself at another point in our history. But it is our great collective misfortune that the scientific community made its decisive diagnosis of the climate threat at the precise moment when those elites were enjoying more unfettered political, cultural, and intellectual power than at any point since the 1920s. Indeed, governments and scientists began talking seriously about radical cuts to greenhouse gas emissions in 1988—the exact year that marked the dawning of what came to be called "globalization," with the signing of the agreement representing the world's largest bilateral trade relationship between Canada and the United States, later to be expanded into the North American Free Trade Agreement (NAFTA) with the inclusion of Mexico.[3]

When historians look back on the past quarter century of international negotiations, two defining processes will stand out. There will be the climate process: struggling, sputtering, failing utterly to achieve its goals. And there will be the corporate globalization process, zooming from victory to victory: from that first free trade deal to the creation of the World Trade Organization to the mass privatization of the former Soviet economies to the transformation of large parts of Asia into sprawling free-trade zones to the "structural adjusting" of Africa....

The three policy pillars of this new era are familiar to us all: privatization of the public sphere, deregulation of the corporate sector, and lower corporate taxation, paid for with cuts to public spending. Much has been written about the real-world costs of these policies—the instability of financial markets, the excesses of the super-rich, and the desperation of the increasingly disposable poor, as well as the failing state of public infrastructure and services. Very little, however, has been written about how market fundamentalism has, from the very first moments, systematically sabotaged our collective response to climate change, a threat that came knocking just as this ideology was reaching its zenith.

The core problem was that the stranglehold that market logic secured over public life in this period made the most direct and obvious climate responses seem politically heretical. How, for instance, could societies invest massively in zero-carbon public services and infrastructure at a time when the public sphere was being systematically dismantled and auctioned off? How could governments heavily regulate, tax, and penalize fossil fuel companies when all such measures were being dismissed as relics of "command and control" communism? And how could the renewable energy sector receive the supports and protections it needed to replace fossil fuels when "protectionism" had been made a dirty word? ...

With hindsight, it's hard to see how it could have turned out otherwise. The twin signatures of this era have been the mass export of products across vast distances (relentlessly burning carbon all the way), and the import of a uniquely wasteful model of production, consumption, and agriculture to every corner of the world (also based on the profligate burning of fossil fuels). Put differently, the liberation of world markets, a process powered by the liberation of unprecedented amounts of fossil fuels from the earth, has dramatically sped up the same process that is liberating Arctic ice from existence.

As a result, we now find ourselves in a very difficult and slightly ironic position. Because of those decades of hardcore emitting exactly when we were supposed to be cutting back, the things we must do to avoid catastrophic warming are no longer just in conflict with

3 Spencer Weart, *The Discovery of Global Warming* (Cambridge, MA: Harvard University Press, 2008), 149.

the particular strain of deregulated capitalism that triumphed in the 1980s. They are now in conflict with the fundamental imperative at the heart of our economic model: grow or die....

I'll be delving deeper into those numbers in Chapter 2 [not included here], but the bottom line is what matters here: our economic system and our planetary system are now at war. Or, more accurately, our economy is at war with many forms of life on earth, including human life. What the climate needs to avoid collapse is a contraction in humanity's use of resources; what our economic model demands to avoid collapse is unfettered expansion. Only one of these sets of rules can be changed, and it's not the laws of nature.

Fortunately, it is eminently possible to transform our economy so that it is less resource-intensive, and to do it in ways that are equitable, with the most vulnerable protected and the most responsible bearing the bulk of the burden. Low-carbon sectors of our economies can be encouraged to expand and create jobs, while high-carbon sectors are encouraged to contract. The problem, however, is that this scale of economic planning and management is entirely outside the boundaries of our reigning ideology. The only kind of contraction our current system can manage is a brutal crash, in which the most vulnerable will suffer most of all.

So we are left with a stark choice: allow climate disruption to change everything about our world, or change pretty much everything about our economy to avoid that fate. But we need to be very clear: because of our decades of collective denial, no gradual, incremental options are now available to us....

That's tough for a lot of people in important positions to accept, since it challenges something that might be even more powerful than capitalism, and that is the fetish of centrism—of reasonableness, seriousness, splitting the difference, and generally not getting overly excited about anything. This is the habit of thought that truly rules our era, far more among the liberals who concern themselves with matters of climate policy than among conservatives, many of whom simply deny the existence of the crisis. Climate change presents a profound challenge to this cautious centrism because half measures won't cut it: "all of the above energy" programs, as U.S. President Barack Obama describes his approach, has about as much chance of success as an all of the above diet, and the firm deadlines imposed by science require that we get very worked up indeed....

The challenge, then, is not simply that we need to spend a lot of money and change a lot of policies; it's that we need to think differently, radically differently, for those changes to be remotely possible. Right now, the triumph of market logic, with its ethos of domination and fierce competition, is paralyzing almost all serious efforts to respond to climate change. Cutthroat competition between nations has deadlocked U.N. climate negotiations for decades: rich countries dig in their heels and declare that they won't cut emissions and risk losing their vaulted position in the global hierarchy; poorer countries declare that they won't give up their right to pollute as much as rich countries did on their way to wealth, even if that means deepening a disaster that hurts the poor most of all. For any of this to change, a worldview will need to rise to the fore that sees nature, other nations, and our own neighbors not as adversaries, but rather as partners in a grand project of mutual reinvention....

When public opinion on the big social and political issues changes, the trends tend to be relatively gradual. Abrupt shifts, when they come, are usually precipitated by dramatic events. Which is why pollsters were so surprised by what had happened to perceptions about climate change in just four years. A 2007 Harris poll found that 71 percent of Americans believed that the continued burning of fossil fuels would alter the climate. By 2009 the figure had dropped to 51 percent. In June 2011 the number was down to 44 percent—well under half the population. Similar trends have been tracked in the U.K. and Australia. Scott Keeter, director of survey research at the Pew Research Center for People & the Press, described the statistics in the United States as "among the largest shifts over a short period of time seen in recent public opinion history."[4]

The overall belief in climate change has rebounded somewhat since its 2010–11 low in the United States. (Some have hypothesized that experience with extreme weather events could be contributing, though "the evidence is at best very sketchy at this point," says Riley Dunlap, a sociologist at Oklahoma State University who specializes in the politics of climate change.) But what remains striking is that on the right-wing side of the political spectrum, the numbers are still way down.[5]

It seems hard to believe today, but as recently as 2008, tackling climate change still had a veneer of bipartisan support, even in the United States. That year, Republican stalwart Newt Gingrich did a TV spot with Democratic congresswoman Nancy Pelosi, then Speaker of the House, in which they pledged to join forces and fight climate change together. And in 2007, Rupert Murdoch—whose Fox News channel relentlessly amplifies the climate change denial movement—launched an incentive program at Fox to encourage employees to buy hybrid cars (Murdoch announced he had purchased one himself).

Those days of bipartisanship are decidedly over. Today, more than 75 percent of self-identified Democrats and liberals believe humans are changing the climate—a level that, despite yearly fluctuations, has risen only slightly since 2001. In sharp contrast, Republicans have overwhelmingly chosen to reject the scientific consensus. In some regions, only about 20 percent of self-identified Republicans accept the science. This political rift can also be found in Canada. According to an October 2013 poll conducted by Environics, only 41 percent of respondents who identify with the ruling Conservative Party believe that climate change is real and human-caused, while 76 percent of supporters of the left-leaning New Democratic Party and 69 percent of supporters of the centrist Liberal Party believe it is real. And the same phenomenon has once again been documented in Australia and the U.K., as well as Western Europe.[6]

Ever since this political divide opened up over climate change, a great deal of social science research has been devoted to pinpointing precisely how and why political beliefs are shaping attitudes toward global warming. According to Yale's Cultural Cognition Project, for example, one's "cultural worldview"—that would be political leanings or ideological outlook to the rest of us—explains "individuals' beliefs about global warming more powerfully than any other individual characteristic." More powerfully, that is, than age, ethnicity, education, or party affiliation.

The Yale researchers explain that people with strong "egalitarian" and "communitarian" worldviews (marked by an inclination toward collective action and social justice, concern about inequality, and suspicion of corporate power) overwhelmingly accept the scientific consensus on climate change. Conversely, those with strong "hierarchical" and "individualistic" worldviews (marked by opposition to government assistance for the poor and minorities, strong support

---

4 "Big Drop in Those Who Believe That Global Warming Is Coming," Harris Interactive, press release, December 2, 2009; "Most Americans Think Devastating Natural Disasters Are Increasing," Harris Interactive, press release, July 7, 2011; personal interview with Scott Keeter, September 12, 2011.

5 Lydia Saad, "A Steady 57% in U.S. Blame Humans for Global Warming," Gallup Politics, March 18, 2014; "October 2013 Political Survey: Final Topline," Pew Research Center for the People & the Press, October 9–13, 2013, p. 1; personal email communication with Riley Dunlap, March 29, 2014.

6 DEMOCRATS AND LIBERALS: Aaron M. McCright and Riley E. Dunlap, "The Politicization of Climate Change and Polarization in the American Public's Views of Global Warming 2001–2010," *The Sociological Quarterly* 52 (2011): 188, 193; Saad, "A Steady 57% in U.S. Blame Humans for Global Warming"; REPUBLICANS: Anthony Leiserowitz et al., "Politics and Global Warming: Democrats, Republicans, Independents, and the Tea Party," Yale Project on Climate Change Communication and George Mason University Center for Climate Change Communication, 2011, pp. 3–4; 20 PERCENT: Lawrence C. Hamilton, "Climate Change: Partisanship, Understanding, and Public Opinion," Carsey Institute, Spring 2011, p. 4; OCTOBER 2013 POLL: "Focus Canada 2013: Canadian Public Opinion About Climate Change," The Environics Institute, November 18, 2013, http://www.environicsinstitute.org; AUSTRALIA, U.K., AND WESTERN EUROPE: Bruce Tranter, "Political Divisions over Climate Change and Environmental Issues in Australia," Environmental Politics 20 (2011): 78–96; Ben Clements, "Exploring public opinion on the issue of climate change in Britain," *British Politics* 7 (2012): 183–202; Aaron M. McCright, Riley E. Dunlap, and Sandra T. Marquart-Pyatt, "Climate Change and Political Ideology in the European Union," Michigan State University, working paper, 2014.

for industry, and a belief that we all pretty much get what we deserve) overwhelmingly reject the scientific consensus.[7]

The evidence is striking. Among the segment of the U.S. population that displays the strongest "hierarchical" views, only 11 percent rate climate change as a "high risk," compared with 69 percent of the segment displaying the strongest "egalitarian" views.[8]

Yale law professor Dan Kahan, the lead author on this study, attributes the tight correlation between "worldview" and acceptance of climate science to "cultural cognition," the process by which all of us—regardless of political leanings—filter new information in ways that will protect our "preferred vision of the good society." If new information seems to confirm that vision, we welcome it and integrate it easily. If it poses a threat to our belief system, then our brain immediately gets to work producing intellectual antibodies designed to repel the unwelcome invasion.[9]

As Kahan explained in *Nature*, "People find it disconcerting to believe that behavior that they find noble is nevertheless detrimental to society, and behavior that they find base is beneficial to it. Because accepting such a claim could drive a wedge between them and their peers, they have a strong emotional predisposition to reject it." In other words, it is always easier to deny reality than to allow our worldview to be shattered, a fact that was as true of die-hard Stalinists at the height of the purges as it is of libertarian climate change deniers today. Furthermore, leftists are equally capable of denying inconvenient scientific evidence. If conservatives are inherent system justifiers, and therefore bridle before facts that call the dominant economic system into question, then most leftists are inherent system questioners, and therefore prone to skepticism about facts that come from corporations and government. This can lapse into the kind of fact resistance we see among those who are convinced that multinational drug companies have covered up the link between childhood vaccines and autism. No matter what evidence is marshaled to disprove their theories, it doesn't matter to these crusaders—it's just the system covering up for itself.

This kind of defensive reasoning helps explain the rise of emotional intensity that surrounds the climate issue today. As recently as 2007, climate change was something most everyone acknowledged was happening—they just didn't seem to care very much. (When Americans are asked to rank their political concerns in order of priority, climate change still consistently comes in last.)[10]

But today there is a significant cohort of voters in many countries who care passionately, even obsessively, about climate change. What they care about, however, is exposing it as a "hoax" being perpetrated by liberals to force them to change their light bulbs, live in Soviet-style tenements, and surrender their SUVs. For these right-wingers, opposition to climate change has become as central to their belief system as low taxes, gun ownership, and opposition to abortion. Which is why some climate scientists report receiving the kind of harassment that used to be reserved for doctors who perform abortions. In the Bay Area of California, local Tea Party activists have disrupted municipal meetings when minor sustainability strategies are being discussed, claiming they are part of a U.N.-sponsored plot to usher in world government. As Heather Gass of the East Bay Tea Party put it in an open letter after one such gathering: "One day (in 2035) you will wake up in subsidized government housing, eating government subsidized food, your kids will

7 Dan Kahan, "Cultural Cognition as a Conception of the Cultural Theory of Risk," in *Handbook of Risk Theory: Epistemology, Decision Theory, Ethics, and Social Implications of Risk*, ed. Sabine Roeser et al. (London: Springer, 2012), 731.

8 Kahan et al., "The Second National Risk and Culture Study," p. 4.

9 Dan Kahan, "Fixing the Communications Failure," *Nature* 463 (2010): 296; Dan Kahan et al., "Book Review—Fear of Democracy: A Cultural Evaluation of Sunstein on Risk," *Harvard Law Review* 119 (2006): 1083.

10 Rebecca Rifkin, "Climate Change Not a Top Worry in U.S.," Gallup, March 12, 2014; "Deficit Reduction Declines as Policy Priority," Pew Research Center for the People & the Press, January 27, 2014; "Thirteen Years of the Public's Top Priorities," Pew Research Center for the People & the Press, January 27, 2014, http://www.people-press.org.

be whisked off by government buses to indoctrination training centers while you are working at your government assigned job on the bottom floor of your urban transit center village because you have no car and who knows where your aging parents will be but by then it will be too late! WAKE UP!!!!"[11]

Clearly there is something about climate change that has some people feeling very threatened indeed.

Unthinkable Truths

... A 2013 study by Riley Dunlap and political scientist Peter Jacques found that a striking 72 percent of climate denial books, mostly published since the 1990s, were linked to right-wing think tanks, a figure that rises to 87 percent if self-published books (increasingly common) are excluded.

Many of these institutions were created in the late 1960s and early 1970s, when U.S. business elites feared that public opinion was turning dangerously against capitalism and toward, if not socialism, then an aggressive Keynesianism. In response, they launched a counterrevolution, a richly funded intellectual movement that argued that greed and the limitless pursuit of profit were nothing to apologize for and offered the greatest hope for human emancipation that the world had ever known. Under this liberationist banner, they fought for such policies as tax cuts, free trade deals, for the auctioning off of core state assets from phones to energy to water—the package known in most of the world as "neoliberalism."

At the end of the 1980s, after a decade of Margaret Thatcher at the helm in the U.K. and Ronald Reagan in the United States, and with communism collapsing, these ideological warriors were ready to declare victory: history was officially over and there was, in Thatcher's often repeated words, "no alternative" to their market fundamentalism. Filled with confidence, the next task was to systematically lock in the corporate liberation project in every country that had previously held out, which was usually best accomplished in the midst of political turmoil and large-scale economic crises, and further entrenched through free trade agreements and membership in the World Trade Organization.

It had all been going so well. The project had even managed to survive, more or less, the 2008 financial collapse directly caused by a banking sector that had been liberated of so much burdensome regulation and oversight. But to those gathered here at the Heartland conference, climate change is a threat of a different sort. It isn't about the political preferences of Republicans versus Democrats; it's about the physical boundaries of the atmosphere and ocean. If the dire projections coming out of the IPCC are left unchallenged, and business as usual is indeed driving us straight toward civilization-threatening tipping points, then the implications are obvious: the ideological crusade incubated in think tanks like Heartland, Cato, and Heritage will have to come to a screeching halt. Nor have the various attempts to soft-pedal climate action as compatible with market logic (carbon trading, carbon offsets, monetizing nature's "services") fooled these true believers one bit. They know very well that ours is a global economy created by, and fully reliant upon, the burning of fossil fuels and that a dependency that foundational cannot be changed with a few gentle market mechanisms. It requires heavy-duty interventions: sweeping bans on polluting activities, deep subsidies for green alternatives, pricey penalties for violations, new taxes, new public works programs, reversals of privatizations—the list of ideological outrages goes on and on. Everything, in short, that these think tanks—which have always been public proxies for far more powerful corporate interests—have been busily attacking for decades.

And there is also the matter of "global equity" that keeps coming up in the climate negotiations. The equity debate is based on the simple scientific

11 Heather Gass, "EBTP at the One Bay Area Agenda 21 Meeting," East Bay Tea Party, May 7, 2011, http://www.theeastbayteaparty.com.

fact that global warming is caused by the accumulation of greenhouse gases in the atmosphere over two centuries. That means that the countries that got a large head start on industrialization have done a great deal more emitting than most others. And yet many of the countries that have emitted least are getting hit by the impacts of climate change first and worst (the result of geographical bad luck as well as the particular vulnerabilities created by poverty). To address this structural inequity sufficiently to persuade fast-growing countries like China and India not to destabilize the global climate system, earlier emitters, like North America and Europe, will have to take a greater share of the burden at first. And there will obviously need to be substantial transfers of resources and technology to help battle poverty using low carbon tools. This is what Bolivia's climate negotiator Angélica Navarro Llanos meant when she called for a Marshall Plan for the Earth. And it is this sort of wealth redistribution that represents the direst of thought crimes at a place like the Heartland Institute.

Even climate action at home looks suspiciously like socialism to them; all the calls for high-density affordable housing and brand-new public transit are obviously just ways to give backdoor subsidies to the undeserving poor. Never mind what this war on carbon means to the very premise of global free trade, with its insistence that geographical distance is a mere fiction to be collapsed by Walmart's diesel trucks and Maersk's container ships.

More fundamentally than any of this, though, is their deep fear that if the free market system really has set in motion physical and chemical processes that, if allowed to continue unchecked, threaten large parts of humanity at an existential level, then their entire crusade to morally redeem capitalism has been for naught. With stakes like these, clearly greed is not so very good after all. And that is what is behind the abrupt rise in climate change denial among hardcore conservatives: they have come to understand that as soon as they admit that climate change is real, they will lose the central ideological battle of our time—whether we need to plan and manage our societies to reflect our goals and values, or whether that task can be left to the magic of the market....

And for many conservatives, particularly religious ones, the challenge goes deeper still, threatening not just faith in markets but core cultural narratives about what humans are doing here on earth. Are we masters, here to subdue and dominate, or are we one species among many, at the mercy of powers more complex and unpredictable than even our most powerful computers can model? As Robert Manne, a professor of politics at La Trobe University in Melbourne, puts it, climate science is for many conservatives "an affront to their deepest and most cherished basic faith: the capacity and indeed the right of 'mankind' to subdue the Earth and all its fruits and to establish a 'mastery' over Nature." For these conservatives, he notes, "such a thought is not merely mistaken. It is intolerable and deeply offensive. Those preaching this doctrine have to be resisted and indeed denounced."[12] ...

Which is why the ideological warriors gathered at the Marriott have concluded that there is really only one way to beat a threat this big: by claiming that thousands upon thousands of scientists are lying and that climate change is an elaborate hoax. That the storms aren't really getting bigger, it's just our imagination. And if they are, it's not because of anything humans are doing—or could stop doing. They deny reality, in other words, because the implications of that reality are, quite simply, unthinkable.

So here's my inconvenient truth: I think these hardcore ideologues understand the real significance of climate change better than most of the "warmists" in the political center, the ones who are still insisting that the response can be gradual and painless and that we don't need to go to war with anybody, including the fossil fuel companies. Before I go any further, let me be absolutely clear: as 97 percent of the world's climate scientists attest, the Heartlanders are completely wrong about the science. But when it

12 Robert Manne, "How Can Climate Change Denialism Be Explained?" *The Monthly*, December 8, 2011.

comes to the political and economic *consequences* of those scientific findings, specifically the kind of deep changes required not just to our energy consumption but to the underlying logic of our liberalized and profit-seeking economy, they have their eyes wide open. The deniers get plenty of the details wrong (no, it's not a communist plot; authoritarian state socialism, as we will see, was terrible for the environment and brutally extractivist), but when it comes to the scope and depth of change required to avert catastrophe, they are right on the money.

About That Money …

… According to one recent study, for instance, the denial-espousing think tanks and other advocacy groups making up what sociologist Robert Brulle calls the "climate change counter-movement" are collectively pulling in more than $900 million per year for their work on a variety of right-wing causes, most of it in the form of "dark money"—funds from conservative foundations that cannot be fully traced.[13]

This points to the limits of theories like cultural cognition that focus exclusively on individual psychology. The deniers are doing more than protecting their personal worldviews—they are protecting powerful political and economic interests that have gained tremendously from the way Heartland and others have clouded the climate debate. The ties between the deniers and those interests are well known and well documented. Heartland has received more than $1 million from ExxonMobil together with foundations linked to the Koch brothers and the late conservative funder Richard Mellon Scaife. Just how much money the think tank receives from companies, foundations, and individuals linked to the fossil fuel industry remains unclear because Heartland does not publish the names of its donors, claiming the information would distract from the "merits of our positions." Indeed, leaked internal documents revealed that one of Heartland's largest donors is anonymous—a shadowy individual who has given more than $8.6 million specifically to support the think tank's attacks on climate science.

Meanwhile, scientists who present at Heartland climate conferences are almost all so steeped in fossil fuel dollars that you can practically smell the fumes. To cite just two examples, the Cato Institute's Patrick Michaels, who gave the 2011 conference keynote, once told CNN that 40 percent of his consulting company's income comes from oil companies (Cato itself has received funding from ExxonMobil and Koch family foundations). A Greenpeace investigation into another conference speaker, astrophysicist Willie Soon, found that between 2002 and 2010, 100 percent of his new research grants had come from fossil fuel interests.[14] …

Plan B: Get Rich off a Warming World

One of the most interesting findings of the many recent studies on climate perceptions is the clear connection between a refusal to accept the science of climate change and social and economic privilege. Overwhelmingly, climate change deniers are not only conservative but also white and male, a group with higher than average incomes. And they are more likely than other adults to be highly confident in their views, no matter how demonstrably false. A much discussed paper on this topic by sociologists Aaron McCright and Riley Dunlap

13 Robert J. Brulle, "Institutionalizing Delay: Foundation Funding and the Creation of U.S. Climate Change Counter-Movement Organizations," *Climatic Change* 122 (2014): 681.

14 "Money Troubles: How to Kick-Start the Economy," *Fareed Zakaria* GPS, CNN, August 15, 2010; "Factsheet: Cato Institute," ExxonSecrets.org, Greenpeace USA, http://www.exxonsecrets.org; "Koch Industries Climate Denial Front Group: Cato Institute," Greenpeace USA, http://www.greenpeace.org; "Case Study: Dr. Willie Soon, a Career Fueled by Big Oil and Coal," Greenpeace USA, June 28, 2011, http://www.greenpeace.org.

(memorably titled "Cool Dudes") found that as a group, conservative white men who expressed strong confidence in their understanding of global warming were almost six times as likely to believe climate change "will never happen" as the rest of the adults surveyed. McCright and Dunlap offer a simple explanation for this discrepancy: "Conservative white males have disproportionately occupied positions of power within our economic system. Given the expansive challenge that climate change poses to the industrial capitalist economic system, it should not be surprising that conservative white males' strong system-justifying attitudes would be triggered to deny climate change."[15]

But deniers' relative economic and social privilege doesn't just give them more to lose from deep social and economic change; it gives them reason to be more sanguine about the risks of climate change should their contrarian views turn out to be false. This occurred to me as I listened to yet another speaker at the Heartland conference display what can only be described as an utter absence of empathy for the victims of climate change. Larry Bell (the space architect) drew plenty of laughs when he told the crowd that a little heat isn't so bad: "I moved to Houston intentionally!" (Houston was, at that time, in the midst of what would turn out to be Texas's worst single-year drought on record.) Australian geologist Bob Carter offered that "the world actually does better from our human perspective in warmer times." And Patrick Michaels said people worried about climate change should do what the French did after the devastating 2003 heat wave across Europe killed nearly fifteen thousand people in France alone: "they discovered Walmart and air-conditioning."[16]

I listened to these zingers as an estimated thirteen million people in the Horn of Africa faced starvation on parched land. What makes this callousness among deniers possible is their firm belief that if they're wrong about climate science, a few degrees of warming isn't something wealthy people in industrialized countries have to worry much about.[17] ("When it rains, we find shelter. When it's hot, we find shade," Texas congressman Joe Barton explained at an energy and environment subcommittee hearing.)[18]

As for everyone else, well, they should stop looking for handouts and get busy making money. (Never mind that the World Bank warned in a 2012 report that for poor countries, the increased cost of storms, droughts, and flooding is already so high that it "threatens to roll back decades of sustainable development.") ...

... Unless our culture goes through some sort of fundamental shift in its governing values, how do we honestly think we will "adapt" to the people made homeless and jobless by increasingly intense and frequent natural disasters? How will we treat the climate refugees who arrive on our shores in leaky boats? How will we cope as freshwater and food become ever more scarce?

We know the answers because the process is already under way. The corporate quest for natural resources will become more rapacious, more violent. Arable land in Africa will continue to be seized to provide food and fuel to wealthier nations, unleashing a new stage of neocolonial plunder layered on top of the most plundered places on earth (as journalist Christian Parenti documents so well in *Tropic of Chaos*). When heat stress and vicious storms wipe out small farms and fishing villages, the land will be handed over to

15 Personal email communication with Aaron McCright, September 30, 2011; Aaron McCright and Riley Dunlap, "Cool Dudes: The Denial of Climate Change among Conservative White Males in the United States," *Global Environmental Change* 21 (2011): 1167, 1171.

16 Session 5: Sharpening the Scientific Debate (video), The Heartland Institute; Chris Hooks, "State Climatologist: Drought Officially Worst on Record," *Texas Tribune*, April 4, 2011; Keynote Address (video), The Heartland Institute, July 1, 2011; "France Heat Wave Death Toll Set at 14,802," Associated Press, September 25, 2003; Keynote Address (video), The Heartland Institute, June 30, 2011.

17 Much of this confidence is based on fantasy. Though the ultra-rich may be able to buy a measure of protection for a while, even the wealthiest nation on the planet can fall apart in the face of a major shock (as Hurricane Katrina showed). And no society, no matter how well financed or managed, can truly adapt to massive natural disasters when one comes fast and furious on the heels of the last.

18 "World Bank Boosts Aid for Horn of Africa Famine," Agence France-Presse, September 24, 2011; "Mankind Always Adapts to Climate, Rep. Barton Says," Republicans on the House and Energy Commerce Committee, press release, March 25, 2009, http://republicans.energycommerce.house.gov.

large developers for mega-ports, luxury resorts, and industrial farms. Once self-sufficient rural residents will lose their lands and be urged to move into increasingly crowded urban slums—for their own protection, they will be told. Drought and famine will continue to be used as pretexts to push genetically modified seeds, driving farmers further into debt.[19]

In the wealthier nations, we will protect our major cities with costly sea-walls and storm barriers while leaving vast areas of coastline that are inhabited by poor and Indigenous people to the ravages of storms and rising seas. We may well do the same on the planetary scale, deploying techno-fixes, to lower global temperatures that will pose far greater risks to those living in the tropics than in the Global North (more on this later [not included here]). And rather than recognizing that we owe a debt to migrants forced to flee their lands as a result of our actions (and inactions), our governments will build ever more high-tech fortresses and adopt even more draconian anti-immigration laws. And, in the name of "national security," we will intervene in foreign conflicts over water, oil, and arable land, or start those conflicts ourselves. In short our culture will do what it is already doing, only with more brutality and barbarism, because that is what our system is built to do....

For a long time, environmentalists spoke of climate change as a great equalizer, the one issue that affected everyone, rich or poor. It was supposed to bring us together. Yet all signs are that it is doing precisely the opposite, stratifying us further into a society of haves and have-nots, divided between those whose wealth offers them a not insignificant measure of protection from ferocious weather, at least for now, and those left to the mercy of increasingly dysfunctional states.

The Meaner Side of Denial

As the effects of climate change become impossible to ignore, the crueler side of the denial project—now lurking as subtext—will become explicit. It has already begun. At the end of August 2011, with large parts of the world still suffering under record high temperatures, the conservative blogger Jim Geraghty published a piece in *The Philadelphia Inquirer* arguing that climate change "will help the U.S. economy in several ways and enhance, not diminish, the United States' geopolitical power." He explained that since climate change will be hardest on developing countries, "many potentially threatening states will find themselves in much more dire circumstances." And this, he stressed, was a good thing: "Rather than our doom, climate change could be the centerpiece of ensuring a second consecutive American Century." Got that? Since people who scare Americans are unlucky enough to live in poor, hot places, climate change will cook them, leaving the United States to rise like a phoenix from the flames of global warming.[20, 21]

Expect more of this monstrousness. As the world warms, the ideology so threatened by climate science—the one that tells us it's everyone for themselves, that victims deserve their fate, that we can master nature—will take us to a very cold place indeed. And it will only get colder, as theories of racial superiority, barely under

19 Christian Parenti, *Tropic of Chaos: Climate Change and the New Geography of Violence* (New York: Nation Books, 2011).

20 In early 2011, Joe Read, a newly elected representative to the Montana state legislature, made history by introducing the first bill to officially declare climate change a good thing. "Global warming is beneficial to the welfare and business climate of Montana," the bill stated. Read explained, "Even if it does get warmer, we're going to have a longer growing season; it could be very beneficial to the state of Montana. Why are we going to stop this progress?" The bill did not pass.

21 Jim Geraghty, "Climate Change Offers Us an Opportunity," *Philadelphia Inquirer*, August 28, 2011; FOOTNOTE: "House Bill No. 459," 2011 Montana Legislature, February 15, 2011; Brad Johnson, "Wonk Room Interviews Montana Legislator Who Introduced Bill to Declare Global Warming 'Natural'," ThinkProgress Green, February 17, 2011.

the surface in parts of the denial movement, make a raging comeback.[22, 23] In the grossly unequal world this ideology has done so much to intensify and lock in, these theories are not optional: they are necessary to justify the hardening of hearts to the largely blameless victims of climate change in the Global South and to the predominantly African American cities like New Orleans that are most vulnerable in the Global North....

The Polluter Pays

... [I]f we accept that governments are broke, and they're not likely to introduce "quantitative easing" (aka printing money) for the climate system as they have for the banks, where is the money supposed to come from? Since we have only a few short years to dramatically lower our emissions, the only rational way forward is to fully embrace the principle already well established in Western law: the polluter pays.

The fossil fuel companies have known for decades that their core product was warming the planet, and yet they have not only failed to adapt to that reality, they have actively blocked progress at every turn. Meanwhile, oil and gas companies remain some of the most profitable corporations in history, with the top five oil companies pulling in $900 billion in profits from 2001 to 2010. ExxonMobil still holds the record for the highest corporate profits ever reported in the United States, earning $41 billion in 2011 and $45 billion in 2012. These companies are rich, quite simply, because they have dumped the cost of cleaning up their mess onto regular people around the world. It is this situation that, most fundamentally, needs to change....

... [I]t's safe to assume that if fossil fuel companies are going to help pay for the shift to renewable energy, and for the broader costs of a climate destabilized by their pollution, it will be because they are forced to do so by law. Just as tobacco companies have been obliged to pay the costs of helping people to quit smoking, and BP has had to pay for much of the cleanup of its oil spill in the Gulf of Mexico, it is high time for the industry to at least split the bill for the climate crisis....

The question is: how do we stop fossil fuel profits from continuing to hemorrhage into executive paychecks and shareholder pockets—and how do we do it soon, before the companies are significantly less profitable or out of business because we have moved to a new energy system? ... A steep carbon tax would be a straightforward way to get a piece of the profits, as long as it contained a generous redistributive mechanism—a tax cut or income credit—that compensated poor and middle-class consumers for increased fuel and heating prices.... An even more direct route to getting a piece of those pollution profits would be for governments to negotiate much higher royalty rates on oil, gas, and coal extraction, with the revenues going to "heritage trust funds" that would be dedicated to building the post-fossil fuel future, as well as to helping communities and workers adapt to these new realities....

But the extractive industries shouldn't be the only targets of the "polluter pays" principle. The U.S. military is by some accounts the largest single consumer of petroleum in the world. In 2011, the Department of Defense released, at minimum, 56.6 million metric tons of CO_2 equivalent into the atmosphere, more

22 In a telling development, the American Freedom Alliance hosted its own conference challenging the reality of climate change in Los Angeles in June 2011. Part of the Alliance's stated mission is "to identify threats to Western civilization," and it is known for its fearmongering about "the Islamic penetration of Europe" and similar supposed designs in the U.S. Meanwhile, one of the books on sale at the Heartland conference was *Going Green* by Chris Skates, a fictional "thriller" in which climate activists plot with Islamic terrorists to destroy America's electricity grid.

23 "Mission Statement," American Freedom Alliance, http://www.americanfreedom alliance.org; Chris Skates, *Going Green: For Some It Has Nothing to Do with the Environment* (Alachua, FL: Bridge-Logos, 2011).

than the U.S. based operations of ExxonMobil and Shell combined.[24] So surely the arms companies should pay their share. The car companies have plenty to answer for too, as do the shipping industry and the airlines.

Moreover, there is a simple, direct correlation between wealth and emissions—more money generally means more flying, driving, boating, and powering of multiple homes. One case study of German consumers indicates that the travel habits of the most affluent class have an impact on climate 250 percent greater than that of their lowest-earning neighbors.[25]

That means any attempt to tax the extraordinary concentration of wealth at the very top of the economic pyramid, as documented so persuasively by Thomas Piketty among many others, would—if partially channeled into climate financing—effectively make the polluters pay. As journalist and climate and energy policy expert Gar Lipow puts it, "We should tax the rich more because it is the fair thing to do, and because it will provide a better life for most of us, and a more prosperous economy. However, providing money to save civilization and reduce the risk of human extinction is another good reason to bill the rich for their fair share of taxes." But it must be said that a "polluter pays" principle would have to reach beyond the super rich. According to Stephen Pacala, director of the Princeton Environmental Institute and codirector of Princeton's Carbon Mitigation Initiative, the roughly 500 million richest of us on the planet are responsible for about half of all global emissions. That would include the rich in every country in the world, notably in countries like China and India, as well significant parts of the middle classes in North America and Europe.[26, 27]

Taken together, there is no shortage of options for equitably coming up with the cash to prepare for the coming storms while radically lowering our emissions to prevent catastrophic warming.

Consider the following list, by no means complete:

- A "low-rate" financial transaction tax—which would hit trades of stocks, derivatives, and other financial instruments—could bring in nearly $650 billion at the global level each year, according to a 2011 resolution of the European Parliament (and it would have the added bonus of slowing down financial speculation).[28]
- Closing tax havens would yield another windfall. The U.K.-based Tax Justice Network estimates that in 2010, the private financial wealth of individuals stowed unreported in tax havens around the globe was somewhere between $21 trillion and $32 trillion. If that money were brought into the light and its earnings taxed at a 30 percent rate, it would yield at least $190 billion in income tax revenue each year.[29]
- A 1 percent "billionaire's tax," floated by the U.N., could raise $46 billion annually.[30]
- Slashing the military budgets of each of the top ten military spenders by 25 percent could free up another $325 billion, using 2012 numbers reported by the Stockholm International Peace Research

24 U.S. Department of Defense emissions were calculated using the federal Greenhouse Gas Inventory for fiscal year 2011 (total Scope 1 emissions, excluding biogenic). "Fiscal Year 2011 Greenhouse Gas Inventory," U.S. Department of Energy, Office of Energy Efficiency and Renewable Energy, June 14, 2013, http://energy.gov; "Greenhouse Gas 100 Polluters Index," Political Economy Research Institute, University of Massachusetts Amherst, June 2013, http://www.peri.umass.edu.

25 Bargar Aamaas, Jens Borken-Kleefeld, and Glen P. Peters, "The Climate Impact of Travel Behavior: A German Case Study with Illustrative Mitigation Options," *Environmental Science & Policy* 33 (2013): 273, 276.

26 This is why the persistent positing of population control as a solution to climate change is a distraction and moral dead end. As this research makes clear, the most significant cause of rising emissions is not the reproductive behavior of the poor but the consumer behaviors of the rich.

27 Thomas Piketty, *Capital in the Twenty-First Century*, trans. Arthur Goldhammer (Cambridge, MA: Harvard University Press, 2014); Gar Lipow, *Solving the Climate Crisis through Social Change: Public Investment in Social Prosperity to Cool a Fevered Planet* (Santa Barbara: Praeger, 2012), 56; Stephen W. Pacala, "Equitable Solutions to Greenhouse Warming: On the Distribution of Wealth, Emissions and Responsibility Within and Between Nations," presentation to International Institute for Applied Systems Analysis, November 2007, p. 3.

28 "Innovative Financing at a Global and European Level," European Parliament, resolution, March 8, 2011, http://www.europarl.europa.eu.

29 "Revealed: Global Super-Rich Has at Least $21 Trillion Hidden in Secret Tax Havens," Tax Justice Network, press release, July 22, 2012.

30 "World Economic and Social Survey 2012: In Search of New Development Finance," United Nations Department of Economic and Social Affairs, 2012, p. 44.

Institute. (Granted, probably the toughest sell of all, particularly in the U.S.)[31]

- A $50 tax per metric ton of CO_2 emitted in developed countries would raise an estimated $450 billion annually, while a more modest $25 carbon tax would still yield $250 billion per year, according to a 2011 report by the World Bank, the International Monetary Fund, and the Organisation for Economic Co-operation and Development (OECD), among others.[32]
- Phasing out fossil fuel subsidies globally would conservatively save governments a total $775 billion in a single year, according to a 2012 estimate by Oil Change International and the Natural Resources Defense Council.[33]

If these various measures were taken together, they would raise more than $2 trillion annually. Certainly enough for a very healthy start to finance a Great Transition (and avoid a Great Depression). And that doesn't count any royalty increases on fossil fuel extraction. Of course, for any of these tax crackdowns to work, key governments would have to coordinate their responses so that corporations had nowhere to hide—a difficult task, though far from impossible, and one frequently bandied about at G20 summits....

... This carelessness is at the core of an economic model some political scientists call "extractivism," a term originally used to describe economies based on removing ever more raw materials from the earth, usually for export to traditional colonial powers, where "value" was added. And it's a habit of thought that goes a long way toward explaining why an economic model based on endless growth ever seemed viable in the first place. Though developed under capitalism, governments across the ideological spectrum now embrace this resource-depleting model as a road to development, and it is this logic that climate change calls profoundly into question.

Extractivism is a nonreciprocal, dominance-based relationship with the earth, one purely of taking. It is the opposite of stewardship, which involves taking but also taking care that regeneration and future life continue. Extractivism is the mentality of the mountaintop remover and the old-growth clear-cutter. It is the reduction of life into objects for the use of others, giving them no integrity or value of their own—turning living complex ecosystems into "natural resources," mountains into "overburden" (as the mining industry terms the forests, rocks, and streams that get in the way of its bulldozers). It is also the reduction of human beings either into labor to be brutally extracted, pushed beyond limits, or, alternatively, into social burden, problems to be locked out at borders and locked away in prisons or reservations. In an extractivist economy, the interconnections among these various objectified components of life are ignored; the consequences of severing them are of no concern.

Extractivism is also directly connected to the notion of sacrifice zones—places that, to their extractors, somehow don't count and therefore can be poisoned, drained, or otherwise destroyed, for the supposed greater good of economic progress. This toxic idea has always been intimately tied to imperialism, with disposable peripheries being harnessed to feed a glittering center, and it is bound up too with notions of racial superiority, because in order to have sacrifice zones, you need to have people and cultures who count so little that they are considered deserving of sacrifice. Extractivism ran rampant under colonialism because relating to the world as a frontier of conquest—rather than as home—fosters this particular brand of irresponsibility. The colonial mind nurtures the belief that there is always somewhere else to go

31 Sam Perlo-Freeman, et al., "Trends in World Military Expenditure, 2012," Stockholm International Peace Research Institute, April 2013 http://sipri.org.

32 "Mobilizing Climate Finance: A Paper Prepared at the Request of G20 Finance Ministers," World Bank Group, October 6, 2011, p.15, http://www.imf.org.

33 "Governments Should Phase Out Fossil Fuel Subsidies or Risk Lower Economic Growth, Delayed Investment in Clean Energy and Unnecessary Climate Change Pollution," Oil Change International and Natural Resources Defense Council, June 2012, p. 2.

to and exploit once the current site of extraction has been exhausted.

These ideas predate industrial-scale extraction of fossil fuels. And yet the ability to harness the power of coal to power factories and ships is what, more than any single other factor, enabled these dangerous ideas to conquer the world....

The Ultimate Extractivist Relationship

If the modern-day extractive economy has a patron saint, the honor should probably go to Francis Bacon. The English philosopher, scientist, and statesman is credited with convincing Britain's elites to abandon, once and for all, pagan notions of the earth as a life-giving mother figure to whom we owe respect and reverence (and more than a little fear) and accept the role as her dungeon master. "For you have but to follow and as it were hound nature in her wanderings," Bacon wrote in *De Augmentis Scientiarum* in 1623, "and you will be able, when you like, to lead and drive her afterwards to the same place again.... Neither ought a man to make scruple of entering and penetrating into these holes and corners, when the inquisition of truth is his sole object."[34] (Not surprisingly, feminist scholars have tilled volumes analyzing the ex-Lord Chancellor's metaphor choices.)

These ideas of a completely knowable and controllable earth animated not only the Scientific Revolution but, critically, the colonial project as well, which sent ships crisscrossing the globe to poke and prod and bring the secrets, and wealth, back to their respective crowns. The mood of human invincibility that governed this epoch was neatly encapsulated in the words of clergyman and philosopher William Derham in his 1713 book *Physico-Theology*: "We can, if need be, ransack the whole globe, penetrate into the bowels of the earth, descend to the bottom of the deep, travel to the farthest regions of this world, to acquire wealth."[35]

And yet despite this bravado, throughout the 1700s, the twin projects of colonialism and industrialization were still constrained by nature on several key fronts. Ships carrying both slaves and the raw materials they harvested could sail only when winds were favorable, which could lead to long delays in the supply chain. The factories that turned those raw materials into finished products were powered by huge water wheels. They needed to be located next to waterfalls or rapids which made them dependent on the flow and levels of rivers....

Beginning in 1776, a Scottish engineer named James Watt perfected and manufactured a power source that offered solutions to all these vulnerabilities. Lawyer and historian Barbara Freese describes Watt's steam engine as "perhaps the most important invention in the creation of the modern world"—and with good reason.[36] ...

As Britain's urban population ballooned, two factors tipped the balance in favor of the steam engine. The first was the new machine's insulation from nature's fluctuations: unlike water wheels, steam engines worked at the same rate all the time, so long as there was coal to feed them and the machinery wasn't broken. The flow rates of rivers were of no concern. Steam engines also worked anywhere, regardless of the geography, which meant that factory owners could shift production from more remote areas to cities like London, Manchester, and Lancaster, where there were gluts of willing industrial workers, making it far easier to fire troublemakers and put down strikes....

Unlike the energy it replaced, power from fossil fuel always required sacrifice zones—whether in the black lungs of the coal miners or the poisoned waterways

---

34 Francis Bacon, *De Dignitate et Augmentis Scientiarum*, *Works*, ed. James Spedding, Robert Leslie Ellis, and Douglas Devon Heath, Vol. 4 (London: Longmans Green, 1870), 296.

35 William Derham, *Physico-Theology: or, A Demonstration of the Being and Attributes of God, from His Works of Creation* (London: Printed for Robinson and Roberts, 1768), 110.

36 Barbara Freese, *Coal: A Human History* (New York: Penguin; 2004), 44.

surrounding the mines. But these prices were seen as worth paying in exchange for coal's intoxicating promise of freedom from the physical world—a freedom that unleashed industrial capitalism's full force to dominate both workers and other cultures. With their portable energy creator, the industrialists and colonists of the 1800s could now go wherever labor was cheapest and most exploitable, and wherever resources were most plentiful and valuable....

Little wonder then that the introduction of Watt's steam engine coincided with explosive levels of growth in British manufacturing, such that in the eighty years between 1760 and 1840, the country went from importing 2.5 million pounds of raw cotton to importing 366 million pounds of raw cotton, a genuine revolution made possible by the potent and brutal combination of coal at home and slave labor abroad.[37] ...

Tipping the Balance

... [T]he most powerful lever for change in the Global South is the same as in the Global North: the emergence of positive, practical, and concrete alternatives to dirty development that do not ask people to choose between higher living standards and toxic extraction....

And there are alternatives—models of development that do not require massive wealth stratification, tragic cultural losses, or ecological devastation....

One proposal receiving increasing attention is for a "global feed-in tariff," which would create an internationally administered fund to support clean energy transitions throughout the developing world. The architects of this plan—economist Tariq Banuri and climate expert Niclas Hällström—estimate that a $100 billion annual investment for ten to fourteen years "could effectively help 1.5 billion people gain access to energy, while taking decisive steps toward a renewable energy future in time to prevent all our societies from suffering from climate catastrophe."[38]

Sunita Narain, director general of one of the most influential environmental organizations in India, the New Delhi-based Centre for Science and Environment, stresses that the solution is not for the wealthy world to contract its economies while allowing the developing world to pollute its way to prosperity (even if this were possible). It is for developing countries to "develop differently. We do not want to first pollute and then clean up. So we need money, we need technology, to be able to do things differently."[39] And that means the wealthy world must pay its climate debts....

Sunita Narain hears these objections often. "I'm always being told—especially by my friends in America—that ... issues of historical responsibility are something that we should not talk about. What my forefathers did is not my responsibility." But, she said in an interview, this overlooks the fact that those past actions have a direct bearing on why some countries are rich and others are poor. "Your wealth today has a relationship with the way society has drawn on nature, and overdrawn on nature. That has to be paid back. That's the historical responsibility issues that we need to confront."[40]

These debates are, of course, familiar from other reparations battles. In Latin America, progressive economists have long argued that Western powers owe an "ecological debt" for centuries of colonial land grabs and resource extraction, while Africa and Caribbean governments have, at various points (most notably the 2001 World Conference Against Racism in Durban, South Africa) called for reparations to be paid for transatlantic slavery. After receding for more than a decade after the Durban conference, these claims were back

---

37 Jackson J. Spielvogel, *Western Civilization: A Brief History, Volume II: Since 1500*, 8th ed. (Boston: Wadsworth, 2014), 445.
38 "Climate Change Leadership—Politics and Culture," CSD Uppsala, http://www.csduppsala.uu.se; Tariq Banuri and Niclas Hällström, "A Global Programme to Tackle Energy Access and Climate Change," *Development Dialogue* no. 61, September 2012, p. 275.
39 "'The Most Obdurate Bully in the Room': U.S. Widely Criticized for Role at Climate Talks," Democracy Now!, December 7, 2012.
40 Personal interview with Sunita Narain, director general, Centre for Science and Environment, May 6, 2013.

in the news in 2013 when fourteen Caribbean nations banded together to make a formal reparations claim to Britain, France, the Netherlands, and other European countries that participated in the slave trade. "Our constant search and struggle for development resources is linked directly to the historical inability of our nations to accumulate wealth from the efforts of our peoples during slavery and colonialism," said Baldwin Spencer, prime minister of Antigua and Barbuda, in July 2013. The goal of reparations, he argued, was to break the chains of dependency once and for all.[41]

The rich world, for the most part, pretty much ignores these calls, dismissing it all as ancient history, much as the U.S. government manages to disregard calls for slavery reparations from African Americans (though in the spring of 2014, the calls grew distinctly louder, thanks to breakthrough reporting by *The Atlantic*'s Ta-Nehisi Coates, which once again rekindled the debate).[42] But the case for climate debt is a little different. We can debate the legacy of colonialism, and we can argue about how much slavery shapes modern underdevelopment. But the science of climate change doesn't leave much room for that kind of disagreement. Carbon leaves an unmistakable trail, the evidence etched in coral and ice cores. We can accurately measure how much carbon we can collectively emit into the atmosphere and who has taken up what share of that budget over the past two hundred years or so.

On the other hand, all of these various suppressed and neglected debts are not separate from one another but are better understood as different chapters in the same, continuous story. It was planet-warming coal that powered the textile mills and sugar refineries in Manchester and London that needed to be fed with ever more raw cotton and sugarcane from the colonies, most of it harvested by slave labor. And Eric Williams, the late scholar and Trinidad's first prime minister, famously argued that profits from slavery directly subsidized the growth of industrialization in England, a process that we now know led inextricably to climate change....

The research project delved into the fact that when the British Parliament ruled to abolish slavery in its colonies in 1833, it pledged to compensate British slave owners for the loss of their human property—a backward form of reparations for the perpetrators of slavery, not its victims. This led to payouts adding up to £20 million—a figure that, according to *The Independent*, "represented a staggering 40 per cent of the Treasury's annual spending budget and, in today's terms, calculated as wage values, equates to around £16.5bn." Much of that money went directly into the coal-powered infrastructure of the now roaring Industrial Revolution—from factories to railways to steamships. These, in turn, were the tools that took colonialism to a markedly more rapacious stage, with the scars still felt to this day.[43]

Coal didn't create structural inequality—the boats that enabled the transatlantic slave trade and first colonial land grabs were powered by wind, and the early factories powered by water wheels. But the relentless and predictable power of coal certainly supercharged the process, allowing both human labor and natural resources to be extracted at rates previously unimaginable, laying down the bones of the modern global economy.

And now it turns out that the theft did not end when slavery was abolished, or when the colonial project faltered. In fact, it is still in progress, because the emissions from those early steamships and roaring factories were the beginning of the buildup of excess

41 Nicole Itano, "No Unity at Racism Conference," *Christian Science Monitor*, September 7, 2001; Declaration of the World Conference Against Racism, Racial Discrimination, Xenophobia and Related Intolerance, http://www.un.org; Ben Fox, "Caribbean Nations Seeking Compensation for Slavery," Associated Press, July 25, 2013; "Statement by the Honorable Baldwin Spencer, Prime Minister of Antigua and Barbuda to 34th Regular Meeting of the Conference of Heads of Government of the Caribbean Community, July 2013—On the Issue of Reparations for Native Genocide and Slavery," Caribbean Community Secretariat, press release, July 6, 2013.

42 Ta-Nehisi Coates, "The Case for Reparations," *The Atlantic*, May 21, 2014.

43 Sanchez Manning, "Britain's Colonial Shame: Slave-owners Given Huge Payouts After Abolition," *Independent*, February 24, 2013; "Legacies of British Slave-ownership," University College London.

atmospheric carbon. So another way of thinking about this history is that, starting two centuries ago, coal helped Western nations to deliberately appropriate other people's lives and lands; and as the emissions from that coal (and later oil and gas) continually built up in the atmosphere, it gave these same nations the means to inadvertently appropriate their descendants' sky as well, gobbling up most of our shared atmosphere's capacity to safely absorb carbon.

As a direct result of these centuries of serial thefts—of land, labor, and atmospheric space—developing countries today are squeezed between the impacts of global warming, made worse by persistent poverty, and by their need to alleviate that poverty, which, in the current economic system, can be done most cheaply and easily by burning a great deal more carbon, dramatically worsening the climate crisis. They cannot break this deadlock without help, and that help can only come from those countries and corporations that grew wealthy, in large part, as a result of those illegitimate appropriations.

The difference between this reparations claim and older ones is not that the case is stronger. It's that it does not rest on ethics and morality alone: wealthy countries do not just need to help the Global South move to a low-emissions economic path because it's the right thing to do. We need to do it because our collective survival depends on it.

At the same time, we need common agreement that having been wronged does not grant a country the right to repeat the same crime on an even grander scale. Just as having been raped does not bestow the right to rape, or having been robbed the right to steal, having been denied the opportunity to choke the atmosphere with pollution in the past does not grant anyone the right to choke it today. Especially because today's polluters know full well the catastrophic implications of that pollution in ways that early industrialists did not....

Without human interference, plants grow in different varieties next to one another and as perennials, reseeding themselves year after year, with their roots staying put and growing ever longer and deeper. This combination of diversity and perennialism keeps soil healthy, stable, and fertile: the roots hold the soil in place, the plants allow rain water to be more safely slowly absorbed, and different plants provide different fertility functions (some, like legumes and clover, are better at fixing nitrogen, critical to forming the building blocks of plant life), while diversity controls pests and invasive weeds.

It's a self-sustaining cycle, with decomposing plants serving as natural fertilizer for new plants and the life cycle being constantly renewed. Maintaining this cycle, according to the farmer and philosopher Wendell Berry, must be the centerpiece of humanity's relationship with nature. "The problem of sustainability is simple enough to state," he says. "It requires that the fertility cycle of birth, growth, maturity, death, and decay ... should turn continuously in place, so that the law of return is kept and nothing is wasted."[44] Simple enough: respect fertility, keep it going.

But when humans started planting single crops that needed to be replanted year after year, the problem of fertility loss began. The way industrial agriculture deals with this problem is well known: irrigate heavily to make up for the fact that annual plants do a poor job of retaining moisture (a growing problem as fresh water becomes more scarce), and lay on the chemicals, both to fertilize and ward off invasive pests and weeds.

This in turn creates a host of new environmental and health problems, including massive aquatic dead zones caused by agricultural runoff. In other words, rather than solving the fertility problem in the soil, we have simply moved it, transforming a land-based crisis into an ocean-based one....

Many traditional agricultural societies have developed methods to maintain soil fertility despite planting annual crops. The maize-growing cultures of Mesoamerica, for example, allowed fields to lie fallow so they could regenerate and incorporated nitrogen-fixing legumes such as beans into mixtures of crops grown side by side. These methods,

44 Wendell Berry, "It All Turns on Affection," Jefferson Lecture in the Humanities, Washington, D.C., April 23, 2012, http://www.neh.gov.

which mimic the way similar plants grow in the wild, have succeeded in keeping land fertile for thousands of years. Healthy soil also has the added bonus of sequestering carbon (helping to control emissions), and polycultures are less vulnerable to being wiped out by extreme weather.[45] ...

Coming Back to Life

In early 2013, I came across a speech by Mississauga Nishnaabeg writer and educator Leanne Simpson, in which she describes her people's teachings and governance structures like this: "Our systems are designed to promote more life."[46] The statement stopped me in my tracks. It struck me that this guiding purpose was the very antithesis of extractivism, which is based on the premise that life can be drained indefinitely, and which, far from promoting future life, specializes in turning living systems into garbage, whether it's the piles of "overburden" lining the roads in the Alberta tar sands, or the armies of discarded people roving the world looking for temporary work, or the particulates and gases that choke the atmosphere that were once healthy parts of ecosystems. Or, indeed, the cities and towns turned to rubble after being hit by storms made more powerful by the heat those gases are trapping.

After listening to the speech, I wrote to Simpson and asked whether she would be willing to tell me more about what lay behind that statement....

We ended up having a long, wide-ranging conversation about the difference between an extractivist mind-set (which Simpson describes bluntly as "stealing" and taking things "out of relationship") and a regenerative one. She described Anishinaabe systems as "a way of living designed to generate life, not just human life but the life of all living things." This is a concept of balance, or harmony, common to many Indigenous cultures and is often translated to mean "the good life." But Simpson told me that she preferred the translation "continuous rebirth," which she first heard from fellow Anishinaabe writer and activist Winona LaDuke.[47]

It's understandable that we associate these ideas today with an Indigenous worldview: it is primarily such cultures that have kept this alternate way of seeing the world alive in the face of the bulldozers of colonialism and corporate globalization. Like seed savers safeguarding the biodiversity of the global seed stock, other ways of relating to the natural world and one another have been safeguarded by many Indigenous cultures, based partly on a belief that a time will come when these intellectual seeds will be needed and the ground for them will become fertile once again.

One of the most important developments in the emergence of what I have been referring to as Blockadia is that, as this movement has taken shape, and as Indigenous people have taken on leadership roles within it, these long-protected ways of seeing are spreading in a way that has not occurred for centuries. What is emerging, in fact, is a new kind of reproductive rights movement, one fighting not only for the reproductive rights of women, but for the reproductive rights of the planet as a whole—for the decapitated mountains, the drowned valleys, the clear-cut forests, the fracked water tables, the strip-mined hillsides, the poisoned rivers, the "cancer villages." All of life has the right to renew, regenerate, and heal itself.

Based on this principle, countries like Bolivia and Ecuador—with large Indigenous populations—have enshrined the "rights of Mother Earth" into law, creating powerful new legal tools that assert the right of

45 Charles C. Mann, *1491: New Revelations of the Americas Before Columbus* (New York: Vintage, 2006), 226.
46 "Leanne Simpson Speaking at Beit Zatoun Jan 23rd 2012" (video), YouTube, Dreadedstar's Channel, January 25, 2012.
47 Personal interview with Leanne Simpson, February 22, 2013.

ecosystems not only to exist but to "regenerate."[48, 49] The gender essentialism of the term still makes some people uncomfortable. But it seems to me that the specifically female nature is not of central importance. Whether we choose to see the earth as a mother, a father, a parent, or an ungendered force of creation, what matters is that we are acknowledging that we are not in charge, that we are part of a vast living system on which we depend. The earth, wrote the great ecologist Stan Rowe, is not merely "resource" but "source."

These legal concepts are now being adopted and proposed in non-Indigenous contexts, including in North America and Europe, where increasingly, communities trying to protect themselves from the risks of extreme extraction are passing their own "rights of nature" ordinances. In 2010 the Pittsburgh City Council passed such a law, explicitly banning all natural gas extraction and stating that nature has "inalienable and fundamental rights to exist and flourish" in the city. A similar effort in Europe is attempting to make ecocide a crime under international law. The campaign defines ecocide as "the extensive damage to, destruction of or loss of ecosystem(s) of a given territory, whether by human agency or by other causes, to such an extent that peaceful enjoyment by the inhabitants of that territory has been or will be severely diminished."[50]

As Indigenous-inspired ideas have spread in these somewhat surprising contexts, something else is happening too: many people are remembering their own cultures' stewardship traditions, however deeply buried, and recognizing humanity's role as one of life promotion. The notion that we could separate ourselves from nature, that we did not need to be in perpetual partnership with the earth around us, is, after all, a relatively new concept, even in the West. Indeed it was only once humans came up with the lethal concept of the earth as an inert machine and man its engineer, that some began to forget the duty to protect and promote the natural cycles of regeneration on which we all depend....

---

48 When Ecuador adopted a new constitution in 2008, it became the first country to enshrine the rights of nature in law. Article 71 of the country's constitution states: "Nature or *Pachamama*, where the life is created and reproduced, has as a right that its existence is integrally respected as well as the right of the maintenance and regeneration of its vital cycles, structures, functions and evolutionary processes. Every person, community, people or nationality can demand from the public authority that these rights of nature are fulfilled." Similar principles were enshrined in the "Peoples Agreement" of the World People's Conference on Climate Change and the Rights of Mother Earth, which was adopted by 30,000 members of international civil society gathered in Cochabamba, Bolivia, in April 2010. Noting that, "the regenerative capacity of the planet has been already exceeded," the agreement asserts that the earth has "the right to regenerate its bio-capacity and to continue its vital cycles and processes free of human alteration."

49 John Vidal, "Bolivia Enshrines Natural World's Rights with Equal Status for Mother Earth," *Guardian*, April 10, 2011; Clare Kendall, "A New Law of Nature," *Guardian*, September 23, 2008; FOOTNOTE: Edgardo Lander, "Extractivism and Protest Against It in Latin America," presented at the Question of Power: Alternatives for the Energy Sector in Greece and Its European and Global Context, Athens, October 2013; República del Ecuador, Constitución de la República del Ecuador de 2008, Capítulo Séptima: Derechos de la Naturaleza, art. 71; "Peoples Agreement of Cochabamba," World People's Conference on Climate Change and the Rights of Mother Earth, April 24, 2010, http://pwccc.wordpress.com.

50 Fiona Harvey, "Vivienne Westwood Backs Ecocide Law," *Guardian*, January 16, 2014; "FAQ Ecocide," End Ecocide in Europe, April 16, 2013, https://www.endecocide.eu.

1.5 Review Questions

1. How would Kant and/or Klein interpret Socrates's claim to be on a divine mission? How would Kant and/or Klein assess the value of this mission?
2. In the expansion of political life from a municipal to a national to an international context, are there any qualitative changes in the nature of citizenship apart from the scale of one's community?
3. Do Klein's criticisms of climate-change denial apply to the sort of skepticism advocated by Socrates?
4. Could Socrates's doubts about what we can know compel him to reject Kant's optimism about science or Klein's endorsement of environmental science?
5. How would Socrates or Kant address climate-change denial differently than Klein does?
6. To what extent, if any, could either Socrates or Klein accept the political liberalism presupposed by Kant?
7. Are there any common themes in the critical approaches of Socrates, Kant, and Klein?
8. To what extent, if any, do Socrates, Kant, and Klein subscribe to comparable values?

1.6 Further Reading

Angus, Ian. *Facing the Anthropocene: Fossil Capitalism and the Crisis of the Earth System*. Monthly Review Press, 2016.

Aristophanes. *Clouds*. Translated by Peter Meineke, Hackett, 1993.

Brickhouse, Thomas, and Nicholas Smith. *The Trial and Execution of Socrates: Sources and Controversies*. Oxford University Press, 2002.

Cassirer, Ernst. *Kant's Life and Thought*. Translated by James Haden, Yale University Press, 1981.

Ferguson, John. *Socrates: A Sourcebook*. Macmillan for the Open University, 1990.

Foucault, Michel. "What Is Enlightenment?" In The *Foucault Reader*, by P. Rabinow, 32-50. Pantheon Books, 1984.

Kant, Immanual. *Perpetual Peace and Other Essays*. Translated by Ted Humphrey, Hackett, 1983.

Lang, Mabel. *Socrates in the Agora*. American School for Classical Studies, 1978.

McKibben, Bill. *Falter: Has the Human Game Begun to Play Itself Out?* Henry Holt and Co., 2019.

Moore, Jason W. (Ed.). *Anthropocene or Capitalocene? Nature, History and the Crisis of Capitalism*. PM Press, 2016.

Xenophon. "The Apology of Socrates." *Conversations of Socrates*, translated by Hugh Tredennick and Robin Waterfield, Penguin, 1990.

UNIT II

Rationality, Knowledge, and Normative Inquiry

CHAPTER 2

Critical Judgement, Scientific Reasoning, and Modes of Argumentation

Not straight away have Gods laid bare the order of things to mortal creatures,
But by searching, in time and incrementally such creatures discover for themselves.

—XENOPHANES, FRAGMENT 21B18

Eyes and ears are dissembling witnesses for people with barbarian souls.

—HERACLITUS, FRAGMENT 22B107

Nature is wont to hide.

—HERACLITUS, FRAGMENT 22B123

... no particular that exists exists apart, for each part partakes of all.

—ANAXAGORAS, FRAGMENT 59B6

Thought originates from two lines, one legitimate and the other illegitimate. Belonging to the illegitimate sort are sight, hearing, smell, taste, and touch. From these the legitimate sort is set apart.... For when finer discernment is needed and the illegitimate line of thought is not able to discern sharply by its sight, or by hearing, or smell, or taste, or touch, the legitimate one comes to the fore.

—DEMOCRITUS, FRAGMENT 68B11

Double is the genesis of transient things and double their passing.
Confluent bodies come together and dissolve with each generation,
For each successor emerges from the dissolution of its scattering predecessor.
Indeed, composites are ceaselessly, continually interchanging elements:
at one moment uniting together at the behest of Love,
the next flying apart at the instigation of antagonizing Strife.

—EMPEDOCLES, FRAGMENT 31B38

Geometry ... is the source—indeed the motherland—of all other knowledge.

—PHILOLAUS, FRAGMENT 44A7A

2.1 Introduction

What criteria must be satisfied for us to say that a person *knows* something? And according to what criteria may we declare someone's deliberations to be *rational*? In both cases, our position is similar to that of a musician striking a tuning fork to test whether C# is playing true on a piano. The pitch of the string must harmonize with the pitch of the fork. Since a tuning fork operates independently of both its user and the instrument, we can describe the pianist as consulting an independent standard to formulate a judgement about the string's tuning. Similarly, we must discover independent standards to consult about whether a particular claim is known, whether a particular deliberative process is rational, and so forth. Normative standards of this sort are more abstract and complex than the ring of a tuning fork, but their function is formally comparable. If someone's level of understanding meets the standard of knowledge, we have grounds to say that this person knows something. If someone's conduct or outwardly expressed thoughts exhibit the right kind of order, we have grounds to characterize them as rational.

We attribute "knowledge" or "rationality" when appropriate conditions have been satisfied. We are thus led to a crucial question: What are the precise conditions that must be satisfied in each case? We are here asking about two distinct sets of conditions: one set needs to differentiate knowledge from belief, subjective feelings of certainty, dogmatic adherence to a claim, and similar cognitive states; another set needs to differentiate rational deliberation from random selection on one side and from rationalization on the other. Drawing such distinctions in order to define normative standards precisely is even more abstract than formulating judgements themselves. Bearing in mind that the principal concerns of *Life Examined* are ethical, we must be careful not to dwell for long on questions remote from practical knowledge and rationality. But since our Chapter 1 readings push knowledge and rationality to the fore, we shall pause over these concepts for this chapter. To some extent, then, the present issues must be bracketed off from ethical issues in other chapters. Nevertheless, questions about what human beings can know and our capacities to be rational recur in virtually all ethical debates. It is therefore worthwhile to consider knowledge and rationality independently of ethics, as we do here.

Let us consider knowledge first. One crucial way to distinguish *knowledge* from other cognitive states is to note how it must be warranted in a special way by evidence. Evidence is not strictly required for someone to believe, feel subjectively certain about, or dogmatically adhere to a claim such as "Earth orbits the sun." When we maintain the same proposition as knowledge, however, we are expected to provide evidence to support the claim. For knowledge, it is not enough to have a strong attachment to what we claim; what we claim must be supported by independent evidence of the right sort and degree. The sincerity of one's beliefs, feelings, or adherence indicates something about the psychology of the person making a claim, but very little about evidence warranting that claim. Knowledge *requires* evidence in a way that other cognitive states do not.

The scientific texts in the present chapter throw into relief three important features of knowledge. (1) Scientific knowledge is articulate, which is to say that in a scientific context we expect claims to be intelligible and capable of being communicated. In some cases a claim may be expressed as a proposition stated in plain language and intelligible to nearly anyone (e.g., "Earth orbits the sun"). In other contexts it must be expressed in a technical formula that may be cryptic to most people but perfectly intelligible to specialists (e.g., $f = \frac{1}{2}mv^2$); even so, the technical formulation must be intelligible within a community, and not merely to the person claiming it. Scientific knowledge is therefore articulate rather than brute. (2) Any particular knowledge claim is systematically related to a large body of claims, which is why "Earth orbits the sun" is plausible only in relation to a large number of interconnected propositions about the solar system, galaxy, and other celestial phenomena. Knowledge claims are therefore systematic rather than isolated. Lastly (3), within a well-ordered body of knowledge, claims will be ranked according to their relative systematic importance, which means that some parts of the system are conceptually more central than other parts. Central to Newton's mechanical physics, for example, are universal laws of inertia, impelled forces, causal dynamics, gravity, and so on; all mechanical claims derived from this system are conceptually dependent on its axiomatic laws and basic definitions. A body of knowledge therefore consists of hierarchically ordered claims and concepts. Accordingly, in ethics, as in science, a claim cannot count as knowledge unless it is (1) articulate, (2) systematically related to other claims, and (3) that system is hierarchically ordered. Perhaps this is too much to expect in ethical contexts (many of our authors think not), but these three criteria will be useful points of reference for all of our investigations, and readings in Chapter 2 illustrate what to look for.

Rationality does not present neatly specifiable outward features of the sort we used to characterize knowledge. Indeed, rarely are the deliberations that constitute a person's thoughts or actions directly observable, nor are the specific qualities that make a deliberative process rational or irrational. For this reason, we often supply (rather than examine directly) the reasons that purport to guide a person's conduct or thinking. Deliberative processes are not merely *observed*, they must be *interpreted*. Ordinarily, we presuppose a degree of orderliness in the way the universe and people operate, and then diagnose something as irrational when evidence suggests otherwise. In law, rebuttable presumptions function this way (e.g., a trial defendant's innocence and an agent's intentionality (*mens reas*) are presumed by a court until refuted by evidence to the contrary). Normative standards of rationality may be explicated more realistically as expectations rather than as precise criteria. Here our critical faculties turn out to be indispensable.

Focal points for our critical expectations may be analyzed in terms of a process with (a) a starting point, (b) a purpose, and (c) operations that link its commencement and completion. First (a), we decline to characterize someone's actions or thoughts as being rational if they appear to be unsupported by evidence; in such cases, the starting point of an action or the rationale for their thinking seems unjustifiable or manifestly wrong. Second (b), we decline to characterize an action or series of thoughts as being rational if its discernible purpose seems unjustifiable or manifestly wrong; in such cases, the problem is a misguided aim or objective. Lastly (c), we decline to characterize actions or thoughts as being rational if the sequence of operations from commencement to completion is incoherent; in such cases, the problem lies at some point in the step-to-step sequence of the actions or thoughts. In the extreme case of insanity, we may conclude that a person's deliberative processes are simultaneously baseless, purposeless, and random. To appreciate how criticism filters out irrationality in these three ways, consider Galileo's critical assessment of the geocentric worldview (some details included in 2.5.2).

The geocentric worldview posits Earth as the centre of the universe, with all celestial bodies revolving around it as the moon does. A theoretical statement of geocentrism was put forth by Aristotle (384–322 BCE) and was later elaborated with geometrical models by Ptolemy (87–150 CE). It remained the predominant account of the cosmos until the Modern era. Geocentricism was initially appealing because it is consistent with ordinary observations of the sun, moon, and the "fixed" constellations, which Ptolemy's model seemed to explain in impressive detail. In the seventeenth century, however, Galileo (1564–1642) made astronomical observations that undermined evidentiary *support* for geocentrism (raising doubts about expectation (a) above). Using one of the earliest telescopes, he observed Venus waxing and waning, just as our moon does—a pattern which can be better explained by supposing Venus to be orbiting the sun rather than Earth. Also, he observed with his telescope four satellites orbiting Jupiter, not Earth. Even before Galileo, astronomers had already noticed that the planets seem to move in irregular patterns, when we try to plot them on paths orbiting Earth—as Ptolemy's model attempts to do. Half a century before Galileo, Copernicus (1473–1543) had proposed an alternative model in which all the planets (including Earth) orbit the Sun (i.e., heliocentrism). Galileo's observations seemed to him more consistent with Copernicus's heliocentric model than Ptolemy's geocentric one. In any case, because of evidence marshalled against geocentrism by Galileo, it was difficult to defend the theory as being rational.

Galileo also criticized purely theological arguments that purported to specify a moral and symbolic *purpose* for the geocentric worldview (as per expectation (b) above). According to one influential rationale, human beings have a central role in a divinely created order, so it is fitting that we should inhabit the centre of the cosmos. The geocentric account was therefore tightly bound with Church doctrine about God's providential concern for humanity. Allegedly, accounts of divine intervention in human affairs presupposed a geocentric cosmos. Joshua's successful military campaign against the Amorites was cited as one such account: at God's command the sun and moon stood still in order to facilitate victory for the Israelites (Joshua 10:12–13). Accepting for the sake of argument a literal reading of the passage, Galileo asks: which kind of fundamental motion is it more reasonable to suppose was altered in this episode, (i) a rotational motion of Earth within an otherwise undisturbed cosmic pattern or (ii) an orbital motion of the entire cosmos around a motionless Earth? Both possibilities are equally consistent with Joshua 10, but (i) is simpler (because only one thing needs to cease moving) and therefore more reasonable to accept. The geocentric position is unnecessarily complicated in this case. Moreover, sparse and unsystematic references to celestial phenomena in scripture suggest that these texts are agnostic about the *physical* cosmos. In short, divine providence does not require the physical cosmos to be geocentric. So, Galileo concluded, there is little purpose in maintaining the geocentric position, just as there is insufficient evidentiary support for it.

Lastly, there were additional problems with the way seventeenth-century Aristotelians disregarded Galileo's empirical evidence. In particular, unsatisfactory replies to telescopic observations of Venus and Jupiter violated expectation (c) above. Some of the most persistent adherents to the geocentric worldview refused to countenance any challenge to the ultimate authority of Aristotle. (Incidentally, Aristotle himself did not accept appeals to authority, and he had great respect for empirical research.) Reportedly, at least one opponent simply declined to look through a telescope at the moons of Jupiter. Not only was this an evasion rather than a response to Galileo's criticism, it confuses the rational functions of theory and observation: a geocentric universe was proposed originally by Aristotle as a theory to explain observations that were available at that time; Ptolemy refined the theory to accommodate these observations in a mathematically detailed geocentric model; ultimately, Galileo's seventeenth-century opponents refused to admit new observations of Venus and the moons of Jupiter into the total body of evidence because these observations clashed with their preferred theory. For both Aristotle and Ptolemy, observational evidence came first, but for their seventeenth-century defenders the theory came first. In the end, Galileo's opponents could not control what would be recognized as evidence by later astronomers, and the geocentric theory became obsolete despite their dogmatic adherence to it. It is, Galileo suggests, irrational to subscribe to a geocentric worldview in the face of reliable observations to the contrary: to understand the physical world, we must use physical evidence, not authorities and theories that conflict with our observations.

What lessons can we learn from the ultimate eclipse of a worldview that predominated for centuries?

First, distinct standards of knowledge and rationality relate differently to evidence. Knowledge is directly dependent upon the quality of available evidence, whereas rationality depends on our capacity to manage whatever evidence happens to be available. When the quality of available evidence is poor we cannot meet the standard of knowledge, however strongly we may believe something. By contrast, genuinely rational thought and action remain possible when evidence is slim, partial or unavailable. Poor evidence is managed rationally by operating within its limits. (This is how Socrates can justify his conduct as being rational while professing personal ignorance.) Consider for a moment Aristotle's original geocentric account of the cosmos: using unaided observations of the sun, moon, and stars, he formulated a theoretical hypothesis with some support. Using Aristotle's evidence and additional observations, Ptolemy improved the theory by systematically coordinating available data within an abstract geometrical model. At the same time, however, systematic organization of the data exposed an anomaly in the theory. In order to accommodate observations of Mercury, Venus, Mars, Jupiter, and Saturn, Ptolemy needed to incorporate in his model inelegant extra circles. In Ptolemy's model, the planetary orbits do not conform to the simple circular obits of the moon, sun, and "fixed" stars around Earth; in addition to a big orbital motion around Earth, each planet is supposed to move in an epicycle around the line of orbit. Using virtually the same set of observations as Ptolemy, Copernicus was able to formulate a more elegant hypothetical account that eliminated the need to add planetary epicycles. Galileo then provided further evidence about Venus and Jupiter that made Copernicus's heliocentric hypothesis more powerful. At what point in this chronology does "knowledge" enter the story? Arguably, never, given the quality of evidence available at each stage. Still, we can decline to call any of these hypotheses knowledge yet be impressed by the ways in which the evidence was managed. This is because in general knowledge is evidence-dependent (i.e., it is only possible when satisfactory evidence is available), whereas rationality has to do with a capacity to manage whatever evidence is at hand.

A second lesson also concerns the relationship between a theory and the evidence that is supposed to support it. As the eventual demise of geocentrism illustrates, when there is a discrepancy between evidence and theory, we have a stronger rational commitment to our evidence than to the theory. In empirical sciences a discrepancy of this sort is rectified by rejecting or revising the theory. Even observations which were not available when a theory was originally proposed must support it as they are admitted into the total body of evidence. A theory cannot be maintained on rational grounds by ruling out relevant evidence, as several of Galileo's contemporary opponents tried to do in discounting telescopic observations. Nor can empirical research be directed by a theory that is preferred independently of evidence; otherwise, the theory is being rationalized, not rationally supported. This lesson also applies to the heliocentric position that Galileo preferred, by the way. Eventually, astronomers restricted the scope of the heliocentric account, for it explains only our local solar system and not the rest of the universe; even Copernicus's model of our solar system had to be discarded when evidence against it was found.

The second lesson takes us to the centre of an enduring controversy about scientific argumentation and the fundamental way in which evidence supports a theory. In empirical science, observational evidence is either (i) the basis of theoretical speculation or (ii) used to test theoretical speculations. To appreciate the difference between these two possibilities consider the question, "How do we get the general and abstract claims that comprise a theory?" Do they come from (i) a process that first collects a body of empirical evidence, and then draws logical inferences to these abstract and general claims? This is called *induction*. If so, then scientific theories are *based* on evidence. Or (ii) do we construct abstract and general claims in purely theoretical operations and then investigate whether empirical evidence can be found that corresponds with these claims? This is called theoretical *modelling*. If this is the case, then general and abstract claims in science are not derived from observations and experiments inductively; rather, observations and experiments *test* the predictive power of theoretical models. To appreciate the difference between induction and modelling, consider Copernicus's heliocentric account. Did he gather observational data, and then draw logical inferences to describe circular paths for the fixed stars, planets, and Earth around the sun? Or did he construct a purely geometrical model of concentric circles, which proved to be superior to Ptolemy's geocentric model in application? Selections provided below include some authors who emphasize induction (esp. Bacon, 2.4) and others who emphasize modelling (esp. Popper, 2.10). The logical and technical details of this debate are beyond the scope of this book, but the essential controversy can be elaborated schematically if we clarify a few central concepts.

So far, we have been using the terms "evidence" and "theory" without analyzing them. Before turning to the readings, it will be helpful to specify roughly what they mean and to indicate two ways in which they relate to each other. In all cases, the analysis here is formulated in terms of argumentation rather than science, because in fact the ranges of these terms extend well beyond the limits of scientific reasoning. They are quite simply patterns of reasoning.

By "evidence" we mean any observation, physical item, set of data, or text that admits of formulation in any of the following kinds of proposition (this list is not exhaustive, nor are the items mutually exclusive):

1. *Particular claims*: propositions about particular entities, as opposed to those about the general classes in which particular entities are members (e.g., "The moon orbits Earth." [vs. "All satellites orbit a planet."])
2. *Concrete claims*: propositions about concrete objects, as opposed to claims about the qualities borne by these objects (e.g., "Snow is white." [vs. "White light is composed of red, orange, yellow, green, blue, indigo, and violet."])
3. *Observational claims*: propositions that report what is presented to our faculties of sight, hearing, touch, taste, or smell (e.g., "The male cardinal repeated a series of whistles and trills prior to mating with the female cardinal.")
4. *Experimental observation claims*: in an experimental setting, a propositional report about what is presented to our faculties of sight, hearing, touch, taste, or smell (e.g., "The litmus paper turned red after being submerged in vinegar; it turned blue when submerged in milk.")
5. *Data*: precisely and systematically encoded instances or details of a phenomenon, gathered either in an experimental setting or outside an experimental setting (e.g., "In a survey of adults between 21 and 30 years of age, 276 of 1,000 respondents reported feeling anxious about their long-term employment prospects.")
6. *Textual materials*: entire texts or passages of text, either quoted or paraphrased (e.g., "The first word of Homer's epic poem *Odyssey* is *andra*, 'man'.")

By "theory" we mean any claim formulated as a generalization, abstraction, definition, interpretation, or speculative hypothesis of the following sorts (again, the list is neither exhaustive nor are the items on it mutually exclusive):

A. *General claim*: propositions about classes of entities, as opposed to those about particular members of a class (e.g., "All satellites orbit a planet." [vs. "The moon orbits Earth."])
B. *Abstract claims*: propositions about a quality, as opposed to those about concrete bearers of qualities (e.g., "White light is composed of red, orange, yellow, green, blue, indigo, and violet." [vs. "Snow is white."])
C. *Speculative claims*: propositions that extrapolate from what is observed or whatever data has been collected to affirm something that is unobserved, such as a causal principle or future event (e.g., "The moon's orbit around Earth is caused by gravity.")
D. *Interpretive claims*: propositions about the meaning or significance of a text, passage, or artifact (e.g., "Hamlet's question 'to be or not to be?' begins a long soliloquy in which he moves from suicidal despair to vengeful scheming against his uncle.")
E. *Definitions*: propositions that specify the meaning of a term or phrase as it is used, stipulated,

or determined by its essential qualities (e.g., "According to Newton, atoms must be conceived of as 'solid, massy, hard, impenetrable, moveable particles' out of which all composite material things are composed.")

Evidentiary support for a theory is facilitated by the way items on list 1–6 correspond with items on list A–E. Some of the connections are obvious: particular claims (1) correspond to general claims (A); concrete claims (2) to abstract claims (B); observations (3), experimental observations (4), and data (5) to speculative claims (C); and textual materials (5) to interpretive claims (D). We should not always expect such straightforward correspondences, however, for textual materials are not the only things that require interpretation (D); for instance, archaeological artifacts (e.g., arrow heads, pottery shards, etc.) need to be interpreted, so a concrete claim (2) sometimes requires interpretive claims (D). Lastly, definitions (E) do not align with any particular item on list 1–6, because a word and phrase in any claim whatsoever may require defining (i.e., in 1–6 and A–D).

Reasoning as an operation of rational argumentation may be understood as the movement of thought. For example, a botanist's reasoning might move between observations of individual Ash trees to general claims about the Ash tree species, or a biblical scholar might move between a single motif in scripture to an interpretive claim about theology. We can convey this kind of movement with an arrow (→) to indicate where the motion begins and where it ends. The controversy about whether evidentiary support for a theory comes as an inductive inference or as model testing focuses on the direction of this movement. The movement of thought from evidentiary claims of 1–6 to the theoretical claims of A–E may be described as arguing up; conversely, the movement from theoretical claims (A–E) to evidentiary claims (1–6) may be described as arguing down.

These analytical tools can help clarify the controversy over induction and modelling. Each side in this dispute may be diagrammed schematically. The inductive position maintains that scientific reasoning begins with evidence to be found in observation, experiments, or data about particular or concrete things that lead up to theoretical claims. If our evidence is good and sufficient, it can serve as the basis of reliable theoretical claims. This is arguing up (because such reasoning begins with what is evident on the ground, so to speak, and moves to higher principles):

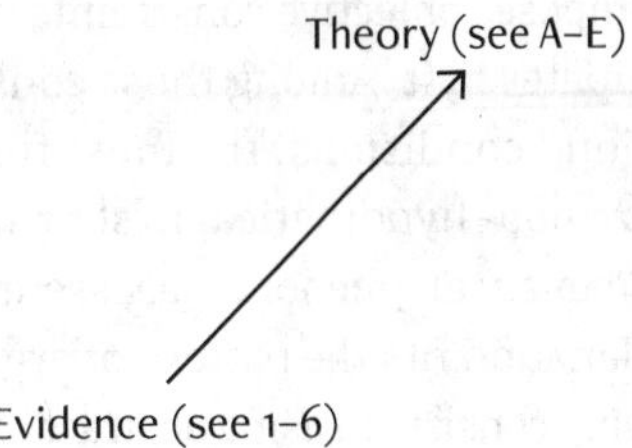

By contrast, the modelling position maintains that scientific argumentation begins with theoretical claims that predict observations, experimental results, or data about particular and concrete things. If our theoretical model is precise and accurate, it will survive such tests. This is arguing down (because the movement begins at higher principles):

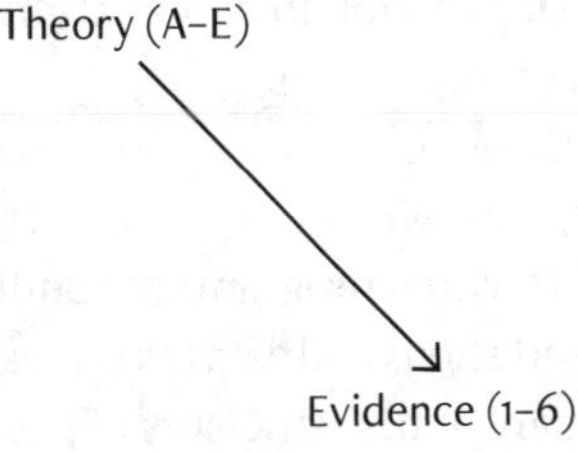

These diagrams will be useful for framing the readings selected for this chapter.

* * *

Our excerpt from Plato's *Meno* (2.2) illustrates hypothetical modelling. In trying to construct a square with a total area of 8 units, Socrates and an unnamed boy begin with a 2 x 2 square. They critically assess two hypotheses that are proven to be false before they find a satisfactory answer. As hypotheses, all of the proposed answers are accepted provisionally, even the final (and correct) one that turns out to be satisfactory. When they arrive at this satisfactory answer, the boy is challenged to thinking further about the problem and its result, investigating it in greater detail in order to ground their answer in a non-hypothetical principle (i.e., an answer that is firmly established, not provisionally accepted for the sake of argument). In 2.3 Aristotle presents science as a social enterprise that imposes objective constraints on everyone who participates in it. Among those constraints are "satisfaction" conditions, the most fundamental of which are non-hypothetical first principles that ultimately explain all phenomena. Essentially, a scientific explanation fits the pattern of arguing down: understanding consists in using abstract concepts and generalizations to explain how or why something is as it is. In 2.4, Francis Bacon objects to the model-theoretic approach that Aristotle advocates. Bacon argues that science in his day was not properly grounded in empirical research; to remedy this problem, he advocates for an ambitious inductive program that will provide a basis for subsequent theoretical work. Both Aristotle and Bacon want knowledge to be established on non-hypothetical first principles, Aristotle first asserting their function in explanations and Bacon suggesting a route to them.

The next three readings are seminal contributions to modern science. One of Galileo's contributions was a systematic research program that built speculative claims on observations and data (as is illustrated by our earlier summary of his criticisms of geocentricism). As we see in 2.5, he also made notable contributions to purely theoretical science. First, he considered mathematics to be indispensable, and it has remained integral to almost all subsequent scientific research since this time. Second, he helped resurrect the ancient atomistic theory of matter. Atomism was originally formulated in the fourth century BCE by Democritus, but it had been neglected for centuries. On the basis of atomism, Galileo argues the only real properties are those associated with imperceptibly small atoms (solidity, mass, position, speed). These qualities can be assigned well-defined scientific functions. Ordinary descriptors, such as colour, smoothness, cold, sweet, melodic, etc., cannot serve a scientific function because their very existence depends on our perceptual faculties. Following Galileo's atomistic and mathematical methodology, Newton developed a comprehensive, axiomatic, and geometrically ordered account of the physical universe. Newton considered the axiomatic laws of nature on which the theory was based (see 2.6) to have been properly grounded by the sort of empirical induction Bacon encouraged. Indeed, Newton insisted that his axioms were certain because they have been discovered by empirical research, and he objected to science that proceeded on the basis of hypotheses or pure supposition (2.6). Charles Darwin's theory of species evolution in biology is comparable in influence to Newtonian mechanics in physics. And in keeping with a wider trend to understand the physical world entirely in terms of physical causes, Darwin wanted to understand the emergence of natural species entirely in terms of natural causes (2.7). Species, according to his research, are mutable and not permanently set, which he explains in terms of an evolution from earlier life forms. Those species which exist today exist because they possess qualities that make them suitable for our present living conditions. In the long course of evolutionary history, some earlier species mutated into new species (e.g., small dinosaurs into birds), some survived unchanged for long periods (e.g., sharks), and some became extinct (e.g., dodo birds and passenger pigeons). Survivor species are selected naturally by the living conditions of their time, and when conditions change so will the array of species populating an area.

The next two selections introduce some contemporary science into this survey and illustrate two recent developments, one in biology and one in physics. An excerpt from a seminal article by Svante Arrhenius investigates a significant change in the living conditions on Earth (2.8). "On the Influence of Carbonic Acid in the Air upon the Temperature of the Ground" presents the earliest evidence we have of climate change due to atmospheric pollution. Here again, we see how thoroughly science has incorporated mathematical ideas and mathematically processed data, because Arrhenius's results are derived from data analysis. The second contemporary piece is an excerpt from Albert Einstein's popular summary of relativity theory (2.9). Relativity so thoroughly incorporates mathematics that Einstein needed to develop parts of tensor calculus to complete some of the physics. (Likewise, Newton had to develop infinitesimal calculus to elaborate his mechanical theories.) According to relativity theory, the speed of light (299,792,458 metres per second) is the absolute limit for all motion. Light has no mass, and anything with mass (even a single hydrogen atom) is unable to match or exceed that speed. Einstein's theory leads to some counter-intuitive consequences. For example, the theory entails that the shape of space is affected by the gravitational field of a massive object and, on that basis, it predicts that light will bend as it passes a massive object. As it happens, this very phenomenon was observed shortly after Einstein published his theory when Arthur Eddington undertook an expedition to observe an eclipse: a star that ought to have been behind the sun was visible in the darkened sky during the eclipse, because light from that star was bent towards us, as relativity entails.

Chapter 2 closes with two influential accounts of scientific rationality. First, Karl Popper (2.10) presents an account that makes theories the starting point of scientific reasoning. He doubts that induction can serve as the basis for establishing fundamental scientific principles. Indeed, for logical reasons he doubts that theories can be inductively based, as Bacon (2.4) had insisted. Rather, Popper argues, theories are proposed with the kind of provisional status of the hypotheses that we find in Plato's *Meno* (2.2). A theory must generate hypothetical claims that are wide in scope and precise in detail to qualify as scientific, according to Popper. Such theories generate predictions that are testable by empirical research. A theory that fails such testing has been falsified, in which case it needs to be rejected or refined. If, however, a prediction is found to be true, then the theory has not been falsified. Indeed, the most we can say in that case is that the theory remains provisionally acceptable; according to Popper, it is not possible to say that it has been verified, confirmed, or proven to be true. There remains always the possibility that it will fail a test in the future. Thomas Kuhn (2.11) expresses a comparable degree of skepticism about the degree of rational support available to a scientific theory. Whereas Popper accounts for scientific evolution from a logical point of view, Kuhn examines scientific practice from a historical point of view. According to Kuhn, science is organized around "paradigms." A paradigm consists of a methodology, vocabulary, and set of questions for research. People working with the same paradigm participate in a shared enterprise, whereas people working in different paradigms may not even be able to communicate with each other directly (e.g., Aristotle's physics vs. Einstein's relativistic physics). When the scientific community moves to a new paradigm (as physics did first in the seventeenth century, then again in the twentieth), it undergoes a revolution. Unlike Popper, Kuhn is not inclined to characterize such changes as an evolution or as progress. Rather, the community of scientists decide collectively that the novel problems set out by a new paradigm are more interesting than unsolved problems in an old one.

2.2 Plato (427–347 BCE)

We begin with Plato's *Meno*, which among other things illustrates how an inquiry into ethical knowledge and ethical rationality can lead to wider questions about the nature of knowledge and rationality irrespective of ethics. Preceding the excerpt below is an exchange in which a young man named Meno asks Socrates whether virtue can be taught.

After several false starts, Meno expresses frustration with the strict conditions Socrates imposes on a satisfactory answer. Socrates demands well-formulated definitions, logically coherent inferences, and theoretically sophisticated answers to his questions. To show by analogy how to meet these conditions, Socrates undertakes a geometrical exercise, which is included here.

Our passage comes from the second quarter of the *Meno*. Here Socrates introduces a doctrine about learning, namely, that we are born with unexplicated knowledge within us. Since knowledge is innate (rather than based inductively on experience), learning may be conceived metaphorically as "remembering." To illustrate his meaning, Socrates interviews a slave boy who has never studied geometry. By responding to a series of questions from Socrates, the boy arrives at a sophisticated insight about plane geometry: to double the area of a square, the diagonal of the original square must be used as the new base (see Figs. 1–5, below).

The interview between Socrates and the boy raises several points that are crucial for the history of science and argumentation: (1) the need for rigorous procedures in step-by-step reasoning or argumentation; (2) the use of hypotheses to develop an idea independently of evidence about its truth; (3) the need to test hypotheses for their internal coherence and implications; and (4) the impressive power of geometry as a tool of scientific reasoning.

(1) Procedures for step-by-step argumentation: Logicians have developed techniques for proving and disproving claims. Using a limited number of procedural rules that are both intuitive and corroborated by various technical means, abstract inferential reasoning can be subject to rigorous standards. A systematic set of inference rules had not yet been developed by 402 BCE, when this dialogue is set (Aristotle did this two generations later), but Socrates's questions are usually formulated to take his interlocutor from one claim to another by intuitive inferences. In the following passage, Socrates directs an investigation into how to double the area of a square. In three successive stages, Socrates elicits an answer to his question about how to construct such a square; he then explores logical implications to each answer. In our *Meno* passage, notice how Socrates and the boy add details to their diagrams one at a time in discrete steps.

(2) A hypothesis is a provisional answer to a question, which is accepted for the purpose of an investigation. By so characterizing an "answer," investigators signal that it is provisional rather than conclusive. In hypothetical reasoning, we leave aside direct considerations for the truth of a claim in order to explore the logical implications of a proposed answer. If the logical implications are unacceptable, then we can reject the hypothesis. If the logical implications are acceptable, we may continue to accept it provisionally. In our *Meno* passage, notice that the first two answers to the problem are rejected because each is shown to imply a patently wrong answer; Socrates no doubt knew these answers were wrong before following each line of argument. But by initially accepting the answers

hypothetically he and the boy are able to investigate each one for the sake of argument and rule it out rationally.

(3) Socrates and the boy ultimately reject the first two hypotheses; however, they accept the third when it yields the desired construction. This three-phase investigation illustrates how hypotheses are tested. There is a crucial difference between (i) accepting a claim as an article of faith and (ii) accepting it on the basis of a test. Articles of faith must be accepted independently of evidence (even, in some cases, in defiance of evidence). In a scientific or academic context, however, theoretical, general, and abstract claims are not accepted on faith. Either we have evidence to accept a claim or we take it as a hypothesis that must be tested: the result of the test will determine its acceptability. Notice in our *Meno* passage that Socrates proves *to the boy* that the first two hypotheses are wrong; the boy is testing each provisional answer by pursuing the logical implications until the results are clear to him.

(4) Geometry was one of the first sciences to elaborate sophisticated standards of rigour, and understandably, people remain impressed with its discoveries. For this reason, it retains a central place among the sciences. This regard for geometry and other branches of mathematics predates Socrates and Plato in Western history, and it is found in a wide range of cultures. As we shall see, Aristotle (2.3) sharply differentiates geometry and physics into separate domains, so that at most the systematic and hierarchical ordering of geometrical theorizing can function as an analogy for physical reasoning. Galileo (2.5) and Newton (2.6), on the other hand, incorporate geometry into the body of physical science. In this respect, Galileo and Newton resurrect the position of Plato by incorporating geometry and mathematics within physics.

~

from Meno *81e–86b*

Socrates: ... The soul, then, as being immortal, and having been born again many times, and having seen all things that exist, whether in this world or in the world below, has knowledge of them all; and it is no wonder that she should be able to call to remembrance all that she ever knew about virtue, and about everything; for as all nature is akin, and the soul has learned all things; there is no difficulty in her eliciting or as men say learning, out of a single recollection, all the rest, if a man is strenuous and does not faint; for all enquiry and all learning is but recollection. And therefore we ought not to listen to this sophistical argument about the impossibility of enquiry: for it will make us idle; and is sweet only to the sluggard; but the other saying will make us active and inquisitive. In that confiding, I will gladly enquire with you into the nature of virtue.

Meno: Yes, Socrates; but what do you mean by saying that we do not learn, and that what we call learning is only a process of recollection? Can you teach me how this is?

Socrates: I told you, Meno, just now that you were a rogue, and now you ask whether I can teach you, when I am saying that there is no teaching, but only recollection; and thus you imagine that you will involve me in a contradiction.

Meno: Indeed, Socrates, I protest that I had no such intention. I only asked the question from habit; but if you can prove to me that what you say is true, I wish that you would.

Socrates: It will be no easy matter, but I will try to please you to the utmost of my power. Suppose that you call one of your numerous attendants, that I may demonstrate on him.

Meno: Certainly. Come hither, boy.

Socrates: He is Greek, and speaks Greek, does he not?

Meno: Yes, indeed; he was born in the house.

Socrates: Attend now to the questions which I ask him, and observe whether he learns of me or only remembers.

Meno: I will.

Socrates: Tell me, boy, do you know that a figure like this is a square?

Boy: I do.

Socrates: And you know that a square figure has these four lines equal?

Boy: Certainly.

Socrates: And these lines which I have drawn through the middle of the square are also equal?

Boy: Yes.

Socrates: A square may be of any size?

Boy: Certainly.

Socrates: And if one side of the figure be of two feet, and the other side be of two feet, how much will the whole be? Let me explain: if in one direction the space was of two feet, and in other direction of one foot, the whole would be of two feet taken once? [see Fig. 1]

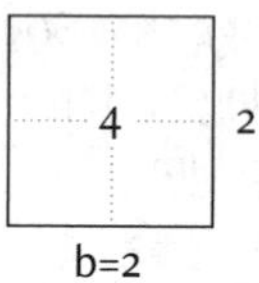

[Fig. 1:] Socrates asks the boy to construct a square with an area that is double that of a square constructed on a base of 2 units. The original square is thus $2 \times 2 = 4$ units.

Boy: Yes.

Socrates: But since this side is also of two feet, there are twice two feet?

Boy: There are.

Socrates: Then the square is of twice two feet?

Boy: Yes.

Socrates: And how many are twice two feet? Count and tell me.

Boy: Four, Socrates.

Socrates: And might there not be another square twice as large as this, and having like this the lines equal?

Boy: Yes.

Socrates: And of how many feet will that be?

Boy: Of eight feet. [see Fig. 2]

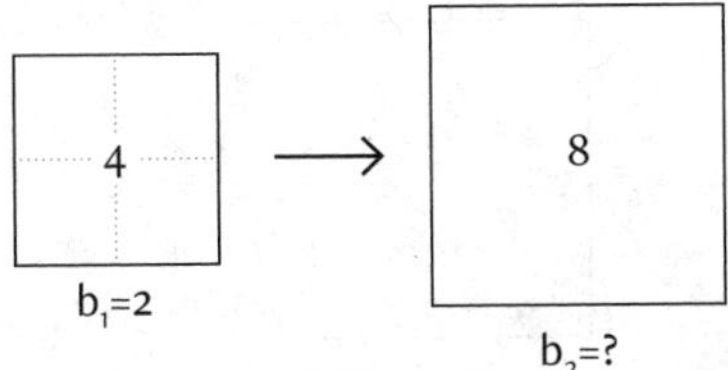

[Fig. 2:] The goal is to construct a second square that is 8 units from the original 4-unit square. The problem is to find the base of this 8-unit² figure.

Socrates: And now try and tell me the length of the line which forms the side of that double square: this is two feet—what will that be?

Boy: Clearly, Socrates, it will be double. [see Fig. 3]

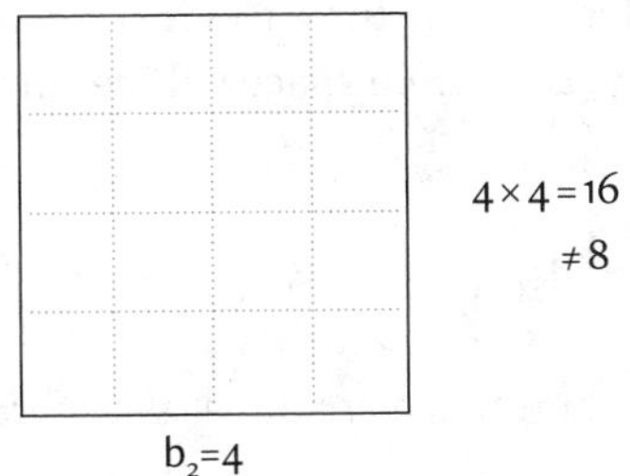

[Fig. 3:] As a first hypothesis, the boy suggests doubling the 2-unit base of the original square.

Socrates: Do you observe, Meno, that I am not teaching the boy anything, but only asking him questions; and now he fancies that he knows how long a line is necessary in order to produce a figure of eight square feet; does he not?

Meno: Yes.

Socrates: And does he really know?

Meno: Certainly not.

Socrates: He only guesses that because the square is double, the line is double.

Meno: True.

Socrates: Observe him while he recalls the steps in regular order. (To the Boy.) Tell me, boy, do you assert that a double space comes from a double line? Remember that I am not speaking of an oblong, but of a figure equal every way, and twice the size of this—that is to say of eight feet; and I want to know whether you still say that a double square comes from a double line?

Boy: Yes.

Socrates: But does not this line become doubled if we add another such line here?

Boy: Certainly.

Socrates: And four such lines will make a space containing eight feet?

Boy: Yes.

Socrates: Let us describe such a figure: Would you not say that this is the figure of eight feet?

Boy: Yes.

Socrates: And are there not these four divisions in the figure, each of which is equal to the figure of four feet?

Boy: True.

Socrates: And is not that four times four?

Boy: Certainly.

Socrates: And four times is not double?

Boy: No, indeed.

Socrates: But how much?

Boy: Four times as much.

Socrates: Therefore the double line, boy, has given a space, not twice, but four times as much.

Boy: True.

Socrates: Four times four are sixteen—are they not?

Boy: Yes.

Socrates: What line would give you a space of eight feet, as this gives one of sixteen feet;—do you see?

Boy: Yes.

Socrates: And the space of four feet is made from this half line?

Boy: Yes.

Socrates: Good; and is not a space of eight feet twice the size of this, and half the size of the other?

Boy: Certainly.

Socrates: Such a space, then, will be made out of a line greater than this one, and less than that one?

Boy: Yes; I think so.

Socrates: Very good; I like to hear you say what you think. And now tell me, is not this a line of two feet and that of four?

Boy: Yes.

Socrates: Then the line which forms the side of eight feet ought to be more than this line of two feet, and less than the other of four feet?

Boy: It ought.

Socrates: Try and see if you can tell me how much it will be.

Boy: Three feet. [see Fig. 4]

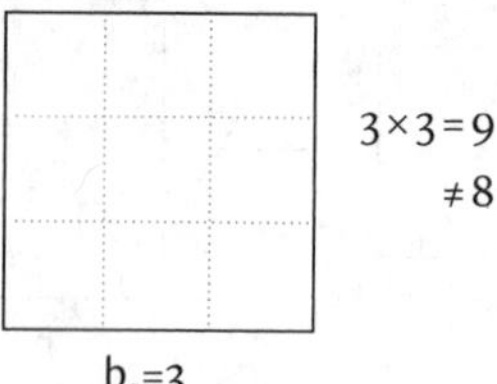

[Fig. 4:] As a second hypothesis, the boy suggests adding one unit to the base of the original square.

Socrates: Then if we add a half to this line of two, that will be the line of three. Here are two and there is one; and on the other side, here are two also and there is one: and that makes the figure of which you speak?

Boy: Yes.

Socrates: But if there are three feet this way and three feet that way, the whole space will be three times three feet?

Boy: That is evident.

Socrates: And how much are three times three feet?

Boy: Nine.

Socrates: And how much is the double of four?

Boy: Eight.

Socrates: Then the figure of eight is not made out of three?

Boy: No.

Socrates: But from what line?—tell me exactly; and if you would rather not reckon, try and show me the line.

Boy: Indeed, Socrates, I do not know.

Socrates: Do you see, Meno, what advances he has made in his power of recollection? He did not know at first, and he does not know now, what is the side of a figure of eight feet: but then he thought that he knew, and answered confidently as if he knew, and had no difficulty; now he has a difficulty, and neither knows nor fancies that he knows.

Meno: True.

Socrates: Is he not better off in knowing his ignorance?

Meno: I think that he is.

Socrates: If we have made him doubt, and given him the "torpedo's shock," have we done him any harm?[1]

Meno: I think not.

Socrates: We have certainly, as would seem, assisted him in some degree to the discovery of the truth; and now he will wish to remedy his ignorance, but then he would have been ready to tell all the world again and again that the double space should have a double side.

Meno: True.

Socrates: But do you suppose that he would ever have enquired into or learned what he fancied that he knew, though he was really ignorant of it, until he had fallen into perplexity under the idea that he did not know, and had desired to know?

Meno: I think not, Socrates.

Socrates: Then he was the better for the torpedo's touch?

Meno: I think so.

Socrates: Mark now the farther development. I shall only ask him, and not teach him, and he shall share the enquiry with me: and do you watch and see if you find me telling or explaining anything to him, instead of eliciting his opinion. Tell me, boy, is not this a square of four feet which I have drawn?

Boy: Yes.

Socrates: And now I add another square equal to the former one?

Boy: Yes.

Socrates: And a third, which is equal to either of them?

Boy: Yes.

Socrates: Suppose that we fill up the vacant corner?

Boy: Very good.

Socrates: Here, then, there are four equal spaces?

Boy: Yes.

Socrates: And how many times larger is this space than this other?

Boy: Four times.

Socrates: But it ought to have been twice only, as you will remember.

Boy: True.

Socrates: And does not this line, reaching from corner to corner, bisect each of these spaces?

1 In a passage not excerpted here (80a–b), Meno complains to Socrates that their investigation into virtue has left him confused and utterly unable to speak, as if he'd been stung by a torpedo fish (often called a stingray). Now that Socrates has induced the same state in the boy, he is pointing out the value of this state to Meno.

Boy: Yes.

Socrates: And are there not here four equal lines which contain this space?

Boy: There are.

Socrates: Look and see how much this space is.

Boy: I do not understand.

Socrates: Has not each interior line cut off half of the four spaces?

Boy: Yes.

Socrates: And how many spaces are there in this section?

Boy: Four.

Socrates: And how many in this?

Boy: Two.

Socrates: And four is how many times two?

Boy: Twice.

Socrates: And this space is of how many feet?

Boy: Of eight feet.

Socrates: And from what line do you get this figure?

Boy: From this.

Socrates: That is, from the line which extends from corner to corner of the figure of four feet? [see Fig. 5:]

Boy: Yes.

Socrates: And that is the line which the learned call the diagonal. And if this is the proper name, then you, Meno's slave, are prepared to affirm that the double space is the square of the diagonal?

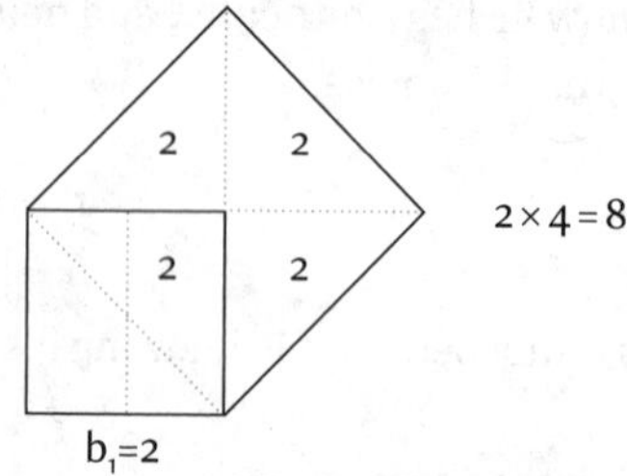

[Fig. 5:] As a third hypothesis, Socrates suggests using the diagonal of the original square, which allows them to construct a square according to the original specifications (i.e., to find a square exactly 8 units^2 from a square of 4 units^2).

Boy: Certainly, Socrates.

Socrates: What do you say of him, Meno? Were not all these answers given out of his own head?

Meno: Yes, they were all his own.

Socrates: And yet, as we were just now saying, he did not know?

Meno: True.

Socrates: But still he had in him those notions of his—had he not?

Meno: Yes.

Socrates: Then he who does not know may still have true notions of that which he does not know?

Meno: He has.

Socrates: And at present these notions have just been stirred up in him, as in a dream; but if he were frequently asked the same questions, in different forms, he would know as well as any one at last?

Meno: I dare say.

Socrates: Without any one teaching him he will recover his knowledge for himself, if he is only asked questions?

Meno: Yes.

Socrates: And this spontaneous recovery of knowledge in him is recollection?

Meno: True.

Socrates: And this knowledge which he now has must he not either have acquired or always possessed?

Meno: Yes.

Socrates: But if he always possessed this knowledge he would always have known; or if he has acquired the knowledge he could not have acquired it in this life, unless he has been taught geometry; for he may be made to do the same with all geometry and every other branch of knowledge. Now, has any one ever taught him all this? You must know about him, if, as you say, he was born and bred in your house.

Meno: And I am certain that no one ever did teach him.

Socrates: And yet he has the knowledge?

Meno: The fact, Socrates, is undeniable.

Socrates: But if he did not acquire the knowledge in this life, then he must have had and learned it at some other time?

Meno: Clearly he must.

Socrates: Which must have been the time when he was not a man?

Meno: Yes.

Socrates: And if there have been always true thoughts in him, both at the time when he was and was not a man, which only need to be awakened into knowledge by putting questions to him, his soul must have always possessed this knowledge, for he always either was or was not a man?

Meno: Obviously.

Socrates: And if the truth of all things always existed in the soul, then the soul is immortal. Wherefore be of good cheer, and try to recollect what you do not know, or rather what you do not remember.

Meno: I feel, somehow, that I like what you are saying.

Socrates: And I, Meno, like what I am saying. Some things I have said of which I am not altogether confident. But that we shall be better and braver and less helpless if we think that we ought to enquire, than we should have been if we indulged in the idle fancy that there was no knowing and no use in seeking to know what we do not know;—that is a theme upon which I am ready to fight, in word and deed, to the utmost of my power.

Meno: There again, Socrates, your words seem to me excellent.

2.3 Aristotle (384–322 BCE)

Aristotle was both a working empirical scientist and a theorist who speculated about the purposes and procedures of science. Within science, he contributed to logic, psychology, mechanical physics, astronomy, and biology, among other things. Much of his empirical work is obsolete, but his theoretical account of scientific reasoning has endured. He conceived of science (called "natural philosophy" until recently) as a social enterprise that helps fulfill a psychological impulse to understand the world as it appears to us.

Selections below from his *Metaphysics* elaborate the social dynamics and the psychological impulse behind scientific curiosity, which he says begins in wonder (2.3.1). Most significantly, in investigating the world as part of this enterprise, we ourselves are transformed: we fulfill a social impulse to coordinate our activities, satisfy the wonder and curiosity that drives this impulse in each of us individually, and we apprehend the world from a different perspective.

Selections from Aristotle's *Physics* elaborate the basic causal mechanisms that satisfy these impulses (2.3.2). The word "physis" (i.e., nature) designates change that comes about by virtue of an internal source (e.g., the DNA that guides the maturation of acorns into oak trees, and tadpoles into frogs). This is differentiated from "technē" (i.e., art), which designates changes that originate from an external source (e.g., a carpenter's art changes raw wood into a table, or a potter's art that turns a mound of clay into a bowl). A key term for Aristotle's account of causation is "form," which in a biological context, for example, is the species (i.e., all pine trees of the same species share the same form, which helps differentiate them from oaks, maples, etc.). Geometrical objects of the same type also share a form, so form in natural science and form in geometry must be differentiated in one crucial respect: according to Aristotle, natural forms regulate changes in the material world, whereas geometrical forms are immaterial and changeless. We see here how Aristotle locates geometry and natural sciences in separate domains. As we shall see, Galileo and Newton make geometry and mathematics central to the study of nature, so they do not accept this sharp distinction.

Lastly, selections from Aristotle's *Posterior Analytics* describe a structural framework within which scientific knowledge explains natural phenomena (2.3.3), whereas Plato maintains in our *Meno* passage that knowledge is innate or inborn (see 2.2), Aristotle, has us learning from our predecessors (albeit with a critical eye); that is, new knowledge must be integrated with inherited knowledge (the past is part our "foundation," so to speak, see also 2.3.1).

The theoretical basis of science is an apparatus of general and abstract claims that identify the causal principles of what appears to us (e.g., a universal principle of gravity explains why a 10 kg object weighs 22 pounds on earth and only 5.8 pounds on the moon). (1) From a scientific point of view, universal principles are "first" (i.e., first in importance). (2) In coming to learn such general and abstract principles, however, one first encounters particular phenomena (e.g., heavy objects under the influence of gravity). So for Aristotle there are two senses of "first knowledge": (1) explanatory priority, in which general and abstract principles are first conceptually, and (2) empirical priority, in which particular, material objects are first experientially. We begin with (2) but the aim of science is (1).

2.3.1 *from* Metaphysics *I, 1–2; II, 1 (Trans. W.D. Ross)*

Book I

PART 1

All men by nature desire to know. An indication of this is the delight we take in our senses; for even apart from their usefulness they are loved for themselves; and above all others the sense of sight. For not only with a view to action, but even when we are not going to do anything, we prefer seeing (one might say) to everything else. The reason is that this, most of all the senses, makes us know and brings to light many differences between things.

By nature animals are born with the faculty of sensation, and from sensation memory is produced in some of them, though not in others. And therefore the former are more intelligent and apt at learning than those which cannot remember; those which are incapable of hearing sounds are intelligent though they cannot be taught, e.g., the bee, and any other race of animals that may be like it; and those which besides memory have this sense of hearing can be taught.

The animals other than man live by appearances and memories, and have but little of connected experience; but the human race lives also by art and reasonings. Now from memory experience is produced in men; for the several memories of the same thing produce finally the capacity for a single experience. And experience seems pretty much like science and art, but really science and art come to men through experience; for 'experience made art', as Polus says, 'but inexperience luck.' Now art arises when from many notions gained by experience one universal judgement about a class of objects is produced. For to have a judgement that when Callias was ill of this disease this did him good, and similarly in the case of Socrates and in many individual cases, is a matter of experience; but to judge that it has done good to all persons of a certain constitution, marked off in one class, when they were ill of this disease, e.g., to phlegmatic or bilious people when burning with fevers—this is a matter of art.

With a view to action experience seems in no respect inferior to art, and men of experience succeed even better than those who have theory without experience. (The reason is that experience is knowledge of individuals, art of universals, and actions and productions are all concerned with the individual; for the physician does not cure man, except in an incidental way, but Callias or Socrates or some other called by some such individual name, who happens to be a man. If, then, a man has the theory without the experience, and recognizes the universal but does not know the individual included in this, he will often fail to cure; for it is the individual that is to be cured.) But yet we think that knowledge and understanding belong to art rather than to experience, and we suppose artists to be wiser than men of experience (which implies that Wisdom depends in all cases rather on knowledge); and this because the former know the cause, but the latter do not. For men of experience know that the thing is so, but do not know why, while the others know the 'why' and the cause. Hence we think also that the masterworkers in each craft are more honourable and know in a truer sense and are wiser than the manual workers, because they know the causes of the things that are done (we think the manual workers are like certain lifeless things which act indeed, but act without knowing what they do, as fire burns,—but while the lifeless things perform each of their functions by a natural tendency, the labourers perform them through habit); thus we view them as being wiser not in virtue of being able to act, but of having the theory for themselves and knowing the causes. And in general it is a sign of the man who knows and of the man who does not know, that the former can teach, and therefore we think art more truly knowledge than experience is; for artists can teach, and men of mere experience cannot.

Again, we do not regard any of the senses as Wisdom; yet surely these give the most authoritative knowledge of particulars. But they do not tell us the 'why' of anything—e.g., why fire is hot; they only say that it is hot.

At first he who invented any art whatever that went beyond the common perceptions of man was naturally admired by men, not only because there was something useful in the inventions, but because he was thought wise and superior to the rest. But as more arts were invented, and some were directed to the necessities of life, others to recreation, the inventors of the latter were naturally always regarded as wiser than the inventors of the former, because their branches of knowledge did not aim at utility. Hence when all such inventions were already established, the sciences which do not aim at giving pleasure or at the necessities of life were discovered, and first in the places where men first began to have leisure. This is why the mathematical arts were founded in Egypt; for there the priestly caste was allowed to be at leisure.

We have said in the *Ethics* what the difference is between art and science and the other kindred faculties; but the point of our present discussion is this, that all men suppose what is called Wisdom to deal with the first causes and the principles of things; so that, as has been said before, the man of experience is thought to be wiser than the possessors of any sense-perception whatever, the artist wiser than the men of experience, the masterworker than the mechanic, and the theoretical kinds of knowledge to be more of the nature of Wisdom than the productive. Clearly then Wisdom is knowledge about certain principles and causes.

PART 2

... That [knowledge of fundamental principles and causes] is not a science of production is clear even from the history of the earliest philosophers. For it is owing to their wonder that men both now begin and at first began to philosophize; they wondered originally at the obvious difficulties, then advanced little by little and stated difficulties about the greater matters, e.g., about the phenomena of the moon and those of the sun and of the stars, and about the genesis of the universe. And a man who is puzzled and wonders thinks himself ignorant (whence even the lover of myth is in a sense a lover of Wisdom, for the myth is composed of wonders); therefore since they philosophized in order to escape from ignorance, evidently they were pursuing science in order to know, and not for any utilitarian end. And this is confirmed by the facts; for it was when almost all the necessities of life and the things that make for comfort and recreation had been secured, that such knowledge began to be sought. Evidently then we do not seek it for the sake of any other advantage; but as the man is free, we say, who exists for his own sake and not for another's, so we pursue this as the only free science, for it alone exists for its own sake....

Book II

PART 1

The investigation of the truth is in one way hard, in another easy. An indication of this is found in the fact that no one is able to attain the truth adequately, while, on the other hand, we do not collectively fail, but every one says something true about the nature of things, and while individually we contribute little or nothing to the truth, by the union of all a considerable amount is amassed. Therefore, since the truth seems to be like the proverbial door, which no one can fail to hit, in this respect it must be easy, but the fact that we can have a whole truth and not the particular part we aim at shows the difficulty of it.

Perhaps, too, as difficulties are of two kinds, the cause of the present difficulty is not in the facts but in us. For as the eyes of bats are to the blaze of day, so is the reason in our soul to the things which are by nature most evident of all.

It is just that we should be grateful, not only to those with whose views we may agree, but also to those who have expressed more superficial views; for these also contributed something, by developing before us the powers of thought. It is true that if there had been no Timotheus we should have been without much of our lyric poetry; but if there had been no Phrynis there would have been no Timotheus. The same holds good of those who have expressed views about the truth; for from some thinkers we have inherited certain opinions, while the others have been responsible for the appearance of the former.

It is right also that philosophy should be called knowledge of the truth. For the end of theoretical knowledge is truth, while that of practical knowledge is action (for even if they consider how things are, practical men do not study the eternal, but what is relative and in the present). Now we do not know a truth without its cause; and a thing has a quality in a higher degree than other things if in virtue of it the similar quality belongs to the other things as well (e.g., fire is the hottest of things; for it is the cause of the heat of all other things); so that that causes derivative truths to be true is most true. Hence the principles of eternal things must be always most true (for they are not merely sometimes true, nor is there any cause of their being, but they themselves are the cause of the being of other things), so that as each thing is in respect of being, so is it in respect of truth.

2.3.2 *from* Physics II, 1–2 *(Trans. R.P. Hardie and R.K. Gaye)*

Book II

PART 1

Of things that exist, some exist by nature, some from other causes. By 'nature' the animals and their parts exist, and the plants and the simple bodies (earth, fire, air, water)—for we say that these and the like exist 'by nature'.

All the things mentioned present a feature in which they differ from things which are not constituted by nature. Each of them has within itself a principle of motion and of stationariness (in respect of place, or of growth and decrease, or by way of alteration). On the other hand, a bed and a coat and anything else of that sort, qua receiving these designations, i.e., in so far as they are products of art—have no innate impulse to change. But in so far as they happen to be composed of stone or of earth or of a mixture of the two, they do have such an impulse, and just to that extent which seems to indicate that nature is a source or cause of being moved and of being at rest in that to which it belongs primarily, in virtue of itself and not in virtue of a concomitant attribute.

I say 'not in virtue of a concomitant attribute', because (for instance) a man who is a doctor might cure himself. Nevertheless it is not in so far as he is a patient that he possesses the art of medicine: it merely has happened that the same man is doctor and patient—and that is why these attributes are not always found together. So it is with all other artificial products. None of them has in itself the source of its own production. But while in some cases (for instance houses and the other products of manual labour) that principle is in something else external to the thing, in others those which may cause a change in themselves in virtue of a concomitant attribute—it lies in the things themselves (but not in virtue of what they are).

'Nature' then is what has been stated. Things 'have a nature' which have a principle of this kind. Each of them is a substance; for it is a subject, and nature always implies a subject in which it inheres.

The term 'according to nature' is applied to all these things and also to the attributes which belong to them in virtue of what they are, for instance the property of fire to be carried upwards—which is not a 'nature' nor 'has a nature' but is 'by nature' or 'according to nature'.

What nature is, then, and the meaning of the terms 'by nature' and 'according to nature', has been stated. That nature exists, it would be absurd to try to prove; for it is obvious that there are many things of this kind, and to prove what is obvious by what is not is the mark of a man who is unable to distinguish what is self-evident from what is not. (This state of mind is clearly possible. A man blind from birth might reason about colours. Presumably therefore such persons must be talking about words without any thought to correspond.) ...

PART 2

We have distinguished, then, the different ways in which the term 'nature' is used [omitted from Part 1].

The next point to consider is how the mathematician differs from the physicist [i.e., naturalist or natural scientist]. Obviously physical bodies contain surfaces and volumes, lines and points, and these are the subject-matter of mathematics.

Further, is astronomy different from physics or a department of it? It seems absurd that the physicist should be supposed to know the nature of sun or moon, but not to know any of their essential attributes, particularly as the writers on physics obviously do discuss their shape also and whether the earth and the world are spherical or not.

Now the mathematician, though he too treats of these things, nevertheless does not treat of them as the limits of a physical body; nor does he consider the attributes indicated as the attributes of such bodies. That is why he separates them; for in thought they are separable from motion, and it makes no difference, nor does any falsity result, if they are separated. The holders of the theory of Forms do the same, though they are not aware of it; for they separate the objects of physics, which are less separable than those of mathematics. This becomes plain if one tries to state in each of the two cases the definitions of the things and of their attributes. 'Odd' and 'even', 'straight' and 'curved', and likewise 'number', 'line', and 'figure', do not involve motion; not so 'flesh' and 'bone' and 'man'—these are defined like 'snub nose', not like 'curved'.

Similar evidence is supplied by the more physical of the branches of mathematics, such as optics, harmonics, and astronomy. These are in a way the converse of geometry. While geometry investigates physical lines but not qua physical, optics investigates mathematical lines, but qua physical, not qua mathematical....

2.3.3 *from* Posterior Analytics *I, 1–2 (Trans. G.R.G. Mure)*

Book I

PART 1

All instruction given or received by way of argument proceeds from pre-existent knowledge. This becomes evident upon a survey of all the species of such instruction. The mathematical sciences and all other speculative disciplines are acquired in this way, and so are the two forms of dialectical reasoning, syllogistic and inductive; for each of these latter make use of old knowledge to impart new, the syllogism assuming an audience that accepts its premisses, induction exhibiting the universal as implicit in the clearly known particular. Again, the persuasion exerted by rhetorical arguments is in principle the same, since they use either example, a kind of induction, or enthymeme, a form of syllogism.

The pre-existent knowledge required is of two kinds. In some cases admission of the fact must be assumed, in others comprehension of the meaning of the term used, and sometimes both assumptions are essential. Thus, we assume that every predicate can be either truly affirmed or truly denied of any subject, and that 'triangle' means so and so; as regards 'unit' we have to make the double assumption of the meaning of the word and the existence of the thing. The reason is that these several objects are not equally obvious to us. Recognition of a truth may in some cases contain as factors both previous knowledge and also knowledge acquired simultaneously with that recognition—knowledge, this latter, of the particulars actually falling under the universal and therein already virtually known. For example, the student knew beforehand that the angles of every triangle are equal to two right angles; but it was only at the actual moment at which he was being led on to recognize this as true in the instance before him that he came to know 'this figure inscribed in the semicircle' to be a triangle. For some things (viz. the singulars finally reached which are not predicable of anything else as subject) are only learnt in this way, i.e., there is here no recognition through a middle of a minor term as subject to a major. Before he was led on to recognition or before he actually drew a conclusion, we should perhaps say that in a manner he knew, in a manner not.

If he did not in an unqualified sense of the term know the existence of this triangle, how could he know without qualification that its angles were equal to two right angles? No: clearly he knows not without qualification but only in the sense that he knows universally. If this distinction is not drawn, we are faced with the dilemma in the *Meno* [80d-e] either a man will learn nothing or what he already knows; for we cannot accept the solution which some people offer. A man is asked, 'Do you, or do you not, know that every pair is even?' He says he does know it. The questioner then produces a particular pair, of the existence, and so a fortiori of the evenness, of which he was unaware. The solution which some people offer is to assert that they do not know that every pair is even, but only that everything which they know to be a pair is even: yet what they know to be even is that of which they have demonstrated evenness, i.e., what they made the subject of their premiss, viz. not merely every triangle or number which they know to be such, but any and every number or triangle without reservation. For no premiss is ever couched in the form 'every number which you know to be such', or 'every rectilinear figure which you know to be such': the predicate is always construed as applicable to any and every instance of the thing. On the other hand, I imagine there is nothing to prevent a man in one sense knowing what he is learning, in another not knowing it. The strange thing would be, not if in some sense he knew what he was learning, but if he were to know it in that precise sense and manner in which he was learning it.

PART 2

We suppose ourselves to possess unqualified scientific knowledge of a thing, as opposed to knowing it in the accidental way in which the sophist knows, when we think that we know the cause on which the fact depends, as the cause of that fact and of no other, and, further, that the fact could not be other than it is. Now that scientific knowing is something of this sort is evident—witness both those who falsely claim it and those who actually possess it, since the former merely imagine themselves to be, while the latter are also actually, in the condition described. Consequently, the proper object of unqualified scientific knowledge is something which cannot be other than it is....

2.4 Francis Bacon (1561–1626)

In late medieval times, most research in natural philosophy (i.e., science) operated within the framework set out in Aristotle's Organon, a six-book set outlining normative principles for sound reasoning (and which includes *Posterior Analytics*, 2.3.3). Francis Bacon was among several modern authors who found this framework unsatisfactory. In addition, he had revolutionary ideas about both the social enterprise of science and scientific reasoning. In both respects, he wanted modern science to find an entirely new footing at the beginning of the Enlightenment.

Bacon wanted his contemporaries to work independently of traditional knowledge (see CXXII, below). The tradition his contemporaries had inherited heavily emphasized theoretical work, book-centred research, and respect for authority (and was accordingly "dogmatical" in his opinion, see XCVI). To overcome the limits of this tradition, he advocates for a thoroughgoing empirical research program that derives theoretical speculative claims from inductive reasoning.

In his opinion, speculative natural philosophy ought to be based on properly conducted research in natural history, which for him consisted of methodically recorded observations of natural phenomena and experimental results (see CI). From this base, low-level axioms must be derived inductively (axioms being general and abstract claims). Claims of greater generality and abstraction can be derived from these as research progresses. Sound research therefore begins on the ground and works upwards: we gather empirical evidence about as many and various falling objects as we can observe, for example; then and only then do we inductively draw general and abstract inferences about what regulates these phenomena (see CIII–CXII). Further coordinated research will then use these results to generate higher abstractions and more general claims. For example, observations of a few falling apples should lead to experiments with free falling objects of various weights, to interpretive claims based on these observations, to speculative claims about what causes free fall on Earth, and finally to very abstract and universal claims about gravitation. As we shall see, this is how Newton understood his own research (2.6).

Whereas Socrates reasons from mere hypotheses in doubling the size of a square (with no direct regard for truth at first), the program of inquiry Bacon advocates begins with empirical claims that can be assessed directly. (The results of a hypothetical argument indicate only that the conclusion is consistent or inconsistent with a prior claim, not whether the conclusion is true or false in itself. Our other commitments thus come into play when we critically assess a hypothetical claim; we assess the hypothesis *indirectly*, not directly.) According to Bacon, only *after* we gather reliable observations, experimental results, and data can we draw inferences to general and abstract claims.

And whereas Aristotle's account of scientific explanation has us arguing down from the causal principles in a theory to the particular phenomena that need explanation, Bacon's account of induction has us arguing up from particular phenomena to causal principles. In this respect, Bacon's account is incompatible with Plato's *Meno* (2.2), but it may complement the account in Aristotle's *Posterior Analytics* (2.3.3).

from Novum Organum (The New Organon)

XCV. Those who have treated of the sciences have been either empirics or dogmatical. The former like ants only heap up and use their store, the latter like spiders spin out their own webs. The bee, a mean between both, extracts matter from the flowers of the garden and the field, but works and fashions it by its own efforts. The true labor of philosophy resembles hers, for it neither relies entirely or principally on the powers of the mind, nor yet lays up in the memory the matter afforded by the experiments of natural history and mechanics in its raw state, but changes and works it in the understanding. We have good reason, therefore, to derive hope from a closer and purer alliance of these faculties (the experimental and rational) than has yet been attempted.

XCVI. Natural philosophy is not yet to be found unadulterated, but is impure and corrupted—by logic in the school of Aristotle, by natural theology in that of Plato, by mathematics in the second school of Plato (that of Proclus and others) which ought rather to terminate natural philosophy than to generate or create it. We may, therefore, hope for better results from pure and unmixed natural philosophy.

XCVII. No one has yet been found possessed of sufficient firmness and severity to resolve upon and undertake the task of entirely abolishing common theories and notions, and applying the mind afresh, when thus cleared and levelled, to particular researches; hence our human reasoning is a mere farrago and crude mass made up of a great deal of credulity and accident, and the puerile notions it originally contracted.

But if a man of mature age, unprejudiced senses, and clear mind, would betake himself anew to experience and particulars, we might hope much more from such a one; in which respect we promise ourselves the fortune of Alexander the Great....

XCVIII. The foundations of experience (our sole resource) have hitherto failed completely or have been very weak; nor has a store and collection of particular facts, capable of informing the mind or in any way satisfactory, been either sought after or amassed. On the contrary, learned, but idle and indolent, men have received some mere reports of experience, traditions as it were of dreams, as establishing or confirming their philosophy, and have not hesitated to allow them the weight of legitimate evidence. So that a system has been pursued in philosophy with regard to experience resembling that of a kingdom or state which would direct its councils and affairs according to the gossip of city and street politicians, instead of the letters and reports of ambassadors and messengers worthy of credit. Nothing is rightly inquired into, or verified, noted, weighed, or measured, in natural history; indefinite and vague observation produces fallacious and uncertain information. If this appear strange, or our complaint somewhat too unjust (because Aristotle himself, so distinguished a man and supported by the wealth of so great a king, has completed an accurate history of animals, to which others with greater diligence but less noise have made considerable additions, and others again have composed copious histories and notices of plants, metals, and fossils), it will arise from a want of sufficiently attending to and comprehending our present observations; for a natural history compiled on its own account, and one collected for the mind's information as a foundation for philosophy, are two different things. They differ in several respects, but principally in this—the former contains only the varieties of natural species without the experiments of mechanical arts; for as in ordinary life every person's disposition, and the concealed feelings of the mind and passions are most drawn out when they are disturbed—so the secrets of nature betray themselves more readily when tormented by art than when left to their own course. We must begin, therefore, to entertain hopes of natural philosophy then only, when we have a better compilation of natural history, its real basis and support.

XCIX. Again, even in the abundance of mechanical experiments, there is a very great scarcity of those which best inform and assist the understanding. For the mechanic, little solicitous about the investigation of truth, neither directs his attention, nor applies his hand to anything that is not of service to his business. But our hope of further progress in the sciences will then only be well founded, when numerous experiments shall be received and collected into natural history, which, though of no use in themselves, assist materially in the discovery of causes and axioms; which experiments we have termed enlightening, to distinguish them from those which are profitable. They possess this wonderful property and nature, that they never deceive or fail you; for being used only to discover the natural cause of some object, whatever be the result, they equally satisfy your aim by deciding the question.

C. We must not only search for, and procure a greater number of experiments, but also introduce a completely different method, order, and progress of continuing and promoting experience. For vague and arbitrary experience is (as we have observed), mere groping in the dark, and rather astonishes than instructs. But when experience shall proceed regularly and uninterruptedly by a determined rule, we may entertain better hopes of the sciences.

CI. But after having collected and prepared an abundance and store of natural history, and of the experience required for the operations of the understanding or philosophy, still the understanding is as incapable of acting on such materials of itself, with the aid of memory alone, as any person would be of retaining and achieving, by memory, the computation of an almanac. Yet meditation has hitherto done more for discovery than writing, and no experiments have been committed to paper. We cannot, however, approve of any mode of discovery without writing, and when that comes into more general use, we may have further hopes.

CII. Besides this, there is such a multitude and host, as it were, of particular objects, and lying so widely dispersed, as to distract and confuse the understanding; and we can, therefore, hope for no advantage from its skirmishing, and quick movements and incursions, unless we put its forces in due order and array, by means of proper and well arranged, and, as it were, living tables of discovery of these matters, which are the subject of investigation, and the mind then apply itself to the ready prepared and digested aid which such tables afford.

CIII. When we have thus properly and regularly placed before the eyes a collection of particulars, we must not immediately proceed to the investigation and discovery of new particulars or effects, or, at least, if we do so, must not rest satisfied therewith. For, though we do not deny that by transferring the experiments from one art to another (when all the experiments of each have been collected and arranged, and have been acquired by the knowledge, and subjected to the judgment of a single individual), many new experiments may be discovered tending to benefit society and mankind, by what we term literate experience; yet comparatively insignificant results are to be expected thence, while the more important are to be derived from the new light of axioms, deduced by certain method and rule from the above particulars, and pointing out and defining new particulars in their turn. Our road is not a long plain, but rises and falls, ascending to axioms, and descending to effects.

CIV. Nor can we suffer the understanding to jump and fly from particulars to remote and most general axioms (such as are termed the principles of arts and things), and thus prove and make out their intermediate axioms according to the supposed unshaken truth of the former. This, however, has always been done to the present time from the natural bent of the understanding, educated too, and accustomed to this very method, by the syllogistic mode of demonstration. But we can then only augur well for the sciences, when the assent shall proceed by a true scale and successive steps, without interruption or breach, from particulars to the lesser axioms, thence to the intermediate (rising one above the other), and lastly, to the most general. For the lowest axioms differ but little from bare experiment; the highest and most general (as they are esteemed at present), are notional, abstract, and of no real weight. The intermediate are true, solid, full of life, and upon them depend the business and fortune of mankind; beyond these are the really general, but not abstract, axioms, which are truly limited by the intermediate.

We must not then add wings, but rather lead and ballast to the understanding, to prevent its jumping or flying, which has not yet been done; but whenever this takes place, we may entertain greater hopes of the sciences.

CV. In forming axioms, we must invent a different form of induction from that hitherto in use; not only for the proof and discovery of principles (as they are called), but also of minor, intermediate, and, in short, every kind of axioms. The induction which proceeds by simple enumeration is puerile, leads to uncertain conclusions, and is exposed to danger from one contradictory instance, deciding generally from too small a number of facts, and those only the most obvious. But a really useful induction for the discovery and demonstration of the arts and sciences, should separate nature by proper rejections and exclusions, and then conclude for the affirmative, after collecting a sufficient number of negatives. Now this has not been done, nor even attempted, except perhaps by Plato, who certainly uses this form of induction in some measure, to sift definitions and ideas. But much of what has never yet entered the thoughts of man must necessarily be employed, in order to exhibit a good and legitimate mode of induction or demonstration, so as even to render it essential for us to bestow more pains upon it than have hitherto been bestowed on [purely deductive and theoretical] syllogisms. The assistance of induction is to serve us not only in the discovery of axioms, but also in defining our notions. Much indeed is to be hoped from such an induction as has been described.

CVI. In forming our axioms from induction, we must examine and try whether the axiom we derive be only fitted and calculated for the particular instances from which it is deduced, or whether it be more extensive and general. If it be the latter, we must observe, whether it confirm its own extent and generality by giving surety, as it were, in pointing out new particulars, so that we may neither stop at actual discoveries, nor with a careless grasp catch at shadows and abstract forms, instead of substances of a determinate nature: and as soon as we act thus, well authorized hope may with reason be said to beam upon us.

CVII. Here, too, we may again repeat what we have said above, concerning the extending of natural philosophy and reducing particular sciences to that one, so as to prevent any schism or dismembering of the sciences; without which we cannot hope to advance.

CXII. In the meantime let no one be alarmed at the multitude of particulars, but rather inclined to hope on that very account. For the particular phenomena of the arts and nature are in reality but as a handful, when compared with the fictions of the imagination removed and separated from the evidence of facts. The termination of our method is clear, and I had almost said near at hand; the other admits of no termination, but only of infinite confusion. For men have hitherto dwelt but little, or rather only slightly touched upon experience, while they have wasted much time on theories and the fictions of the imagination. If we had but any one who could actually answer our interrogations of nature, the invention of all causes and sciences would be the labor of but a few years.

CXXII. Again, it may be objected to us as being singular and harsh, that we should with one stroke and assault, as it were, banish all authorities and sciences, and that too by our own efforts, without requiring the assistance and support of any of the ancients.

Now we are aware, that had we been ready to act otherwise than sincerely, it was not difficult to refer our present method to remote ages, prior to those of the Greeks (since the sciences in all probability flourished more in their natural state, though silently, than when they were paraded with the fifes and trumpets of the Greeks); or even (in parts, at least) to some of the Greeks themselves, and to derive authority and honor from thence; as men of no family labor to raise and form nobility for themselves in some ancient line, by the help of genealogies. Trusting, however, to the evidence of facts, we reject every kind of fiction and imposture; and think it of no more consequence to our subject, whether future discoveries were known to the ancients, and set or rose according to the vicissitudes of events and lapse of ages, than it would be of importance to mankind to know whether the new world be the island of Atlantis, and known to the ancients, or be now discovered for the first time.

With regard to the universal censure we have bestowed, it is quite clear, to any one who properly considers the matter, that it is both more probable and more modest than any partial one could have been. For if the errors had not been rooted in the primary notions, some well conducted discoveries must have corrected others that were deficient. But since the errors were fundamental, and of such a nature, that men may be said rather to have neglected or passed over things, than to have formed a wrong or false judgment of them, it is little to be wondered at, that they did not obtain what they never aimed at, nor arrive at a goal which they had not determined, nor perform a course which they had neither entered upon nor adhered to.

With regard to our presumption, we allow that if we were to assume a power of drawing a more perfect straight line or circle than any one else, by superior steadiness of hand or acuteness of eye, it would lead to a comparison of talent; but if one merely assert that he can draw a more perfect line or circle with a ruler or compasses, than another can by his unassisted hand or eye, he surely cannot be said to boast of much. Now this applies not only to our first original attempt, but also to those who shall hereafter apply themselves to the pursuit. For our method of discovering the sciences merely levels men's wits, and leaves but little to their superiority, since it achieves everything by the most certain rules and demonstrations. Whence (as we have often observed), our attempt is to be attributed to fortune rather than talent, and is the offspring of time rather than of wit. For a certain sort of chance has no less effect upon our thoughts than on our acts and deeds.

CXXV. Others may object that we are only doing that which has already been done, and that the ancients followed the same course as ourselves. They may imagine, therefore, that, after all this stir and exertion, we shall at last arrive at some of those systems that prevailed among the ancients: for that they, too, when commencing their meditations, laid up a great store of instances and particulars, and digested them under topics and titles in their commonplace books, and so worked out their systems and arts, and then decided upon what they discovered, and related now and then some examples to confirm and throw light upon their doctrine; but thought it superfluous and troublesome to publish their notes, minutes, and commonplaces, and therefore followed the example of builders who remove the scaffolding and ladders when the building is finished. Nor can we indeed believe the case to have been otherwise. But to any one, not entirely forgetful of our previous observations, it will be easy to answer this objection or rather scruple; for we allow that the ancients had a particular form of investigation and discovery, and their writings show it. But it was of such a nature, that they immediately flew from a few instances and particulars (after adding some common notions, and a few generally received opinions most in vogue) to the most general conclusions or the principles of the sciences, and then by their intermediate propositions deduced their inferior conclusions, and tried them by the test of the immovable and settled truth of the first, and so constructed their art. Lastly, if some new particulars and instances were brought forward, which contradicted their dogmas, they either with great subtilty reduced them to one system, by distinctions or explanations of their own rules, or got rid of them clumsily as exceptions, laboring most pertinaciously in the meantime to accommodate the causes of such as were not contradictory to their own principles. Their natural history and their experience were both far from being what they ought to have been, and their flying off to generalities ruined everything.

CXXX. But it is time for us to lay down the art of interpreting nature, to which we attribute no absolute necessity (as if nothing could be done without it) nor perfection, although we think that our precepts are most useful and correct. For we are of opinion, that if men had at their command a proper history of nature and experience, and would apply themselves steadily to it, and could bind themselves to two things: 1, to lay aside received opinions and notions; 2, to restrain themselves, till the proper season, from generalization, they might, by the proper and genuine exertion of their minds, fall into our way of interpretation without the aid of any art. For interpretation is the true and natural act of the mind, when all obstacles are removed: certainly, however, everything will be more ready and better fixed by our precepts.

Yet do we not affirm that no addition can be made to them; on the contrary, considering the mind in its connection with things, and not merely relatively to its own powers, we ought to be persuaded that the art of invention can be made to grow with the inventions themselves.

2.5 Galileo Galilei (1564–1642)

While Francis Bacon outlined a general program and methodology for Enlightenment-era research, Galileo Galilei exemplified the spirit of the age in an active research program. In keeping with Bacon's exhortations, Galileo made observational studies of particular phenomena (e.g., the moons of Jupiter, and the phases of Venus), and he collected experimental data (on falling objects, among other things). He also reflected carefully on both his own patterns of reasoning and on general principles of reasoning that ought to guide any scientific program.

Like Bacon, Galileo wants to set aside authorities (for which he criticizes a contemporary who wrote under the pen name of Sarsi). Instead, one must learn to interpret nature by understanding natural processes directly, in their own terms (see 2.5.1). The language of the universe is, Galileo declares, mathematics; one must therefore learn mathematics in order to read the book of nature. Mathematics is not merely something after which scientific knowledge should pattern itself in this case. Nor is the study of nature entirely separable from mathematics because the two fields study entirely separate objects ("changing" phenomena in physics vs. "unchanging" figures and number in mathematics), as Aristotle maintains (2.3.2). Mathematics is, in Galileo's opinion, an indispensable part of natural philosophy (2.5.1).

Galileo also summarizes an approach to complex phenomena that conceptually organizes everything with a few simple principles. This strategy is called *reductionism*, and it both predates Galileo and remains commonplace today. Any time we conceive of complex phenomena in terms of simple elements and principles, we proceed reductively. In his case, the material world is *reduced to* (i.e., conceived of entirely in terms of) atoms and composites of atoms, the behaviour of which conform to mathematical patterns. Atoms exhibit a small number of simple "primary" qualities such as solidity, speed, and position, and these qualities admit of description in terms of mathematical formulae (2.5.1). The qualities we ordinarily attribute to phenomena by our senses (colours by sight, flavours by taste, textures by touch, etc.) are "secondary" and have no scientific function; secondary qualities are confined to the theatre of our sensory experience, and they are not objectively present *in* phenomena (2.5.1). When a feather passes over the surface of our skin, contact with nerve endings registers the primary qualities, and only when we process it internally are sensations *interpreted* as ticklish. The reductionist approach to scientific inquiry sets aside secondary qualities, describing only primary qualities that derive from the solidity, direction, etc., of material objects.

Like both Aristotle (2.3.2) and Bacon (2.4), Galileo implores us to understand the natural world by discovering natural causes; therefore our explanations must invoke natural principles. For Galileo natural causes admit of mathematical description (a significant departure from Aristotle, 2.3.2). This approach excludes supernatural causes, as we see in our excerpt from Galileo's letter to the Grand Duchess Christina (2.5.2).

2.5.1 *from* The Assayer

... In Sarsi I seem to discern the firm belief that in philosophizing one must support oneself upon the opinion of some celebrated author, as if our minds ought to remain completely sterile and barren unless wedded to the reasoning of some other person. Possibly he thinks that philosophy is a book of fiction by some writer, like the *Iliad* or *Orlando Furioso*, productions in which the least important thing is whether what is written there is true. Well, Sarsi, that is not how matters stand. Philosophy is written in this grand book, the universe, which stands continually open to our gaze. But the book cannot be understood unless one first learns to comprehend the language and read the letters in which it is composed. It is written in the language of mathematics, and its characters are triangles, circles, and other geometric figures without which it is humanly impossible to understand a single word of it; without these, one wanders about in a dark labyrinth.

Sarsi seems to think that our intellect should be enslaved to that of some other man.... But even on that assumption I do not see why he selects Tycho.... Tycho could not extricate himself from his own explanation of diversity in the apparent motion of his comet; but now Sarsi expects my mind to be satisfied and set at rest by a little poetic flower that is not followed by any fruit at all. It is this that Guiducci rejected when he quite rightly said that nature takes no delight in poetry. That is a very true statement, even though Sarsi appears to disbelieve it and acts as if acquainted with neither nature nor poetry. He seems not to know that fables and fictions are in a way essential to poetry, which could not exist without them, while any sort of falsehood is so abhorrent to nature that it is as absent there as darkness is in light....

Perhaps Sarsi believes that all the host of good philosophers may be enclosed within four walls. I believe that they fly, and that they fly alone, like eagles, and not in flocks like starlings. It is true that because eagles are rare birds they are little seen and less heard, while birds that fly like starlings fill the sky with shrieks and cries, and wherever they settle befoul the earth beneath them. Yet if true philosophers are like eagles they are not [unique] like the phoenix. The crowd of fools who know nothing, Sarsi, is infinite. Those who know very little of philosophy are numerous. Few indeed are they who really know some part of it, and only One knows all.

To put aside hints and speak plainly, and dealing with science as a method of demonstration and reasoning capable of human pursuit, I hold that the more this partakes of perfection the smaller the number of propositions it will promise to teach, and fewer yet will it conclusively prove. Consequently the more perfect it is the less attractive it will be, and the fewer its followers. On the other hand magnificent titles and many grandiose promises attract the natural curiosity of men and hold them forever involved in fallacies and chimeras, without ever offering them one single sample of that sharpness of true proof by which the taste may be awakened to know how insipid is the ordinary fare of philosophy. Such things will keep an infinite number of men occupied, and that man will indeed be fortunate who, led by some unusual inner light, can turn from dark and confused labyrinths in which he might have gone perpetually winding with the crowd and becoming ever more entangled.

Hence I consider it not very sound to judge a man's philosophical opinions by the number of his followers. Yet though I believe the number of disciples of the best philosophy may be quite small. I do not conclude conversely that those opinions and doctrines are necessarily perfect which have few followers, for I know well enough that some men hold opinions so erroneous as to be rejected by everyone else. But from which of those sources the two authors mentioned by Sarsi derive the scarcity of their followers I do not know, for I have not studied their works sufficiently to judge....

Long experience has taught me this about the status of mankind with regard to matters requiring thought: the less people know and understand about them, the more positively they attempt to argue concerning them, while on the other hand to know and understand a multitude of things renders men cautious in passing judgment upon anything new.

Once upon a time, in a very lonely place, there lived a man endowed by nature with extraordinary curiosity and a very penetrating mind. For a pastime he raised birds, whose songs he much enjoyed; and he observed with great admiration the happy contrivance by which they could transform at will the very air they breathed into a variety of sweet songs.

One night this man chanced to hear a delicate song close to his house, and being unable to connect it with anything but some small bird he set out to capture it. When he arrived at a road he found a shepherd boy who was blowing into a kind of hollow stick while moving his fingers about on the wood, thus drawing from it a variety of notes similar to those of a bird, though by quite a different method. Puzzled, but impelled by his natural curiosity, he gave the boy a calf in exchange for this flute and returned to solitude. But realizing that if he had not chanced to meet the boy he would never have learned of the existence of a new method of forming musical notes and the sweetest songs, he decided to travel to distant places in the hope of meeting with some new adventure.

The very next day he happened to pass by a small hut within which he heard similar tones; and in order to see whether this was a flute or a bird he went inside. There he found a small boy who was holding a bow in his right hand and sawing upon some fibers stretched over a hollowed piece of wood. The left hand supported the instrument, and the fingers of the boy were moving so that he drew from this a variety of notes, and most melodious ones too, without any blowing. Now you who participate in this man's thoughts and share his curiosity may judge of his astonishment. Yet finding himself now to have two unanticipated ways of producing notes and melodies, he began to perceive that still others might exist.

His amusement was increased when upon entering a temple he heard a sound, and upon looking behind the gates discovered that this had come from the hinges and fastenings as he opened it. Another time, led by curiosity, he entered an inn expecting to see someone lightly bowing the strings of a violin, and instead he saw a man rubbing his fingertip around the rim of a goblet and drawing forth a pleasant tone from that. Then he observed that wasps, mosquitoes, and flies do not form single notes by breathing, as did the birds, but produce their steady sounds by swift beating of their wings. And as his wonder grew, his conviction proportionately diminished that he knew how sounds were produced; nor would all his previous experiences have sufficed to teach him or even allow him to believe that crickets derive their sweet and sonorous shrilling by scraping their wings together, particularly as they cannot fly at all.

Well, after this man had come to believe that no more ways of forming tones could possibly exist—after having observed, in addition to all the things already mentioned, a variety of organs, trumpets, fifes, stringed instruments, and even that little tongue of iron which is placed between the teeth and which makes strange use of the oral cavity for sounding box and of the breath for vehicle of sound—when, I say, this man believed he had seen everything, he suddenly found himself once more plunged deeper into ignorance and bafflement than ever. For having captured in his hands a cicada, he failed to diminish its strident noise either by closing its mouth or stopping its wings, yet he could not see it move the scales that covered its body, or any other thing. At last he lifted up the armor of its chest and there he saw some thin hard ligaments beneath; thinking the sound might come from their vibration, he decided to break them in order to silence it. But nothing happened until his needle drove too deep, and transfixing the creature he took away its life with its voice, so that he was still unable to determine whether the song had originated in those ligaments. And by this experience his knowledge was reduced to diffidence, so that when asked how sounds were created he used to answer tolerantly that although he knew a few ways, he was sure that many more existed which were not only unknown but unimaginable.

I could illustrate with many more examples Nature's bounty in producing her effects, as she employs means we could never think of without our senses and our experiences to teach them to us—and sometimes even these are insufficient to remedy our lack of understanding. So I should not be condemned for being unable to determine precisely the way in which comets are produced, especially in view of the fact that I have never boasted that I could do this, knowing that they may originate in some manner that is far beyond our power of imagination. The difficulty of comprehending how the cicada forms its song even when we have it singing to us right in our hands ought to be more than enough to excuse us for not knowing how comets are formed at such immense distances. Let us therefore go no further than our original intention, which was to set forth the questions that appeared to upset the old theories, and to propose a few new ideas....

I cannot but be astonished that Sarsi should persist in trying to prove by means of witnesses something that I may see for myself at any time by means of experiment. Witnesses are examined in doubtful matters which are past and transient, not in those which are actual and present. A judge must seek by means of witnesses to determine whether Peter injured John last night, but not whether John was injured, since the judge can see that for himself. But even in conclusions which can be known only by reasoning, I say that the testimony of many has little more value than that of few, since the number of people who reason well in complicated matters is much smaller than that of those who reason badly. If reasoning were like hauling I should agree that several reasoners would be worth more than one, just as several horses can haul more sacks of grain than one can. But reasoning is like racing and not like hauling, and a single Arabian steed can outrun a hundred plowhorses. So when Sarsi brings in this multitude of authors it appears to me that instead of strengthening his conclusion he merely ennobles our case by showing that we have outreasoned many men of great reputation.

If Sarsi wants me to believe with Suidas that the Babylonians cooked their eggs by whirling them in slings, I shall do so; but I must say that the cause of this effect was very different from what he suggests. To discover the true cause I reason as follows: "If we do not achieve an effect which others formerly achieved, then it must be that in our operations we lack something that produced their success. And if there is just one single thing we lack, then that alone can be the true cause. Now we do not lack eggs, nor slings, nor sturdy fellows to whirl them; yet our eggs do not cook, but merely cool down faster if they happen to be hot. And since nothing is lacking to us except being Babylonians, then being Babylonians is the cause of the hardening of eggs, and not friction of the air." And this is what I wished to discover. Is it possible that Sarsi has never observed the coolness produced on his face by the continual change of air when he is riding post? If he has, then how can he prefer to believe things related by other men as having happened two thousand years ago in Babylon rather than present events which he himself experiences? ...

Sarsi says he does not wish to be numbered among those who affront the sages by disbelieving and contradicting them. I say I do not wish to be counted as an ignoramus and an ingrate toward Nature and toward God; for if they have given me my senses and my reason, why should I defer such great gifts to the errors of some man? Why should I believe blindly and stupidly what I wish to believe, and subject the freedom of my intellect to someone else who is just as liable to error as I am? ...

It now remains for me to tell Your Excellency, as I promised, some thoughts of mine about the proposition "motion is the cause of heat," and to show in what sense this may be true. But first I must consider what it is that we call heat, as I suspect that people in general have a concept of this which is very remote from the truth. For they believe that heat is a real phenomenon, or property, or quality, which actually resides in the material by which we feel ourselves warmed.[1] Now I say that whenever I conceive any material or corporeal substance, I immediately feel the need to think of it as bounded, and as having this or that shape; as being large or small in relation to other things, and in some specific place at any given time; as being in motion or at rest; as touching or not touching some other body; and as being one in number, or few, or many. From these conditions I cannot separate such a substance by any stretch of my imagination. But that it must be white or red, bitter or sweet, noisy or silent, and of sweet or foul odor, my mind does not feel compelled to bring in as necessary accompaniments. Without the senses as our guides, reason or imagination unaided would probably never arrive at qualities like these. Hence I think that tastes, odors, colors, and so on are no more than mere names so far as the object in which we place them is concerned, and that they reside only in the consciousness. Hence if the living creature were removed, all these qualities would be wiped away and annihilated. But since we have imposed upon them special names, distinct from those of the other and real qualities mentioned previously, we wish to believe that they really exist as actually different from those.

I may be able to make my notion clearer by means of some examples. I move my hand first over a marble statue and then over a living man. As to the effect flowing from my hand, this is the same with regard to both objects and my hand; it consists of the primary phenomena of motion and touch, for which we have no

1 The ensuing passages are generally considered to entitle Galileo to credit for anticipating the fundamental concepts of the empiricist philosophy developed chiefly by John Locke at the close of the seventeenth century. The basic tenets are of course much older, belonging to the atomism of Democritus (b. 460 BCE), a doctrine which was particularly repugnant to Aristotle. While this exposition is of no little philosophical and scientific interest (inasmuch as empiricism, rightly or wrongly, has been closely associated with the development of modern science), Galileo was no philosophical empiricist. He attached no less importance to reason than to experiment, and he had no doubt about the independent truth of mathematical propositions, the denial of which has always involved empiricist philosophers in serious difficulty with the best logicians.

further names. But the live body which receives these operations feels different sensations according to the various places touched. When touched upon the soles of the feet, for example, or under the knee or armpit, it feels in addition to the common sensation of touch a sensation on which we have imposed a special name, "tickling." This sensation belongs to us and not to the hand. Anyone would make a serious error if he said that the hand, in addition to the properties of moving and touching, possessed another faculty of "tickling," as if tickling were a phenomenon that resided in the hand that tickled. A piece of paper or a feather drawn lightly over any part of our bodies performs intrinsically the same operations of moving and touching, but by touching the eye, the nose, or the upper lip it excites in us an almost intolerable titillation, even though elsewhere it is scarcely felt. This titillation belongs entirely to us and not to the feather; if the live and sensitive body were removed it would remain no more than a mere word. I believe that no more solid an existence belongs to many qualities which we have come to attribute to physical bodies—tastes, odors, colors, and many more.

A body which is solid and, so to speak, quite material, when moved in contact with any part of my person produces in me the sensation we call touch. This, though it exists over my entire body, seems to reside principally in the palms of the hands and in the finger tips, by whose means we sense the most minute differences in texture that are not easily distinguished by other parts of our bodies. Some of these sensations are more pleasant to us than others.... The sense of touch is more material than the other senses; and, as it arises from the solidity of matter, it seems to be related to the earthly element.

Perhaps the origin of two other senses lies in the fact that there are bodies which constantly dissolve into minute particles, some of which are heavier than air and descend, while others are lighter and rise up. The former may strike upon a certain part of our bodies that is much more sensitive than the skin, which does not feel the invasion of such subtle matter. This is the upper surface of the tongue; here the tiny particles are received, and mixing with and penetrating its moisture, they give rise to tastes, which are sweet or unsavory according to the various shapes, numbers, and speeds of the particles. And those minute particles which rise up may enter by our nostrils and strike upon some small protuberances which are the instrument of smelling; here likewise their touch and passage is received to our like or dislike according as they have this or that shape, are fast or slow, and are numerous or few. The tongue and nasal passages are providently arranged for these things, as the one extends from below to receive descending particles, and the other is adapted to those which ascend. Perhaps the excitation of tastes may be given a certain analogy to fluids, which descend through air, and odors to fires, which ascend.

Then there remains the air itself, an element available for sounds, which come to us indifferently from below, above, and all sides—for we reside in the air and its movements displace it equally in all directions. The location of the ear is most fittingly accommodated to all positions in space. Sounds are made and heard by us when the air—without any special property of "sonority" or "transonority"—is ruffled by a rapid tremor into very minute waves and moves certain cartilages of a tympanum in our ear. External means capable of thus ruffling the air are very numerous, but for the most part they may be reduced to the trembling of some body which pushes the air and disturbs it. Waves are propagated very rapidly in this way, and high tones are produced by frequent waves and low tones by sparse ones.

To excite in us tastes, odors, and sounds I believe that nothing is required in external bodies except shapes, numbers, and slow or rapid movements. I think that if ears, tongues, and noses were removed, shapes and numbers and motions would remain, but not odors or tastes or sounds. The latter, I believe, are nothing more than names when separated from living beings, just as tickling and titillation are nothing but names in the absence of such things as noses and armpits. And as these four senses are related to the four elements, so I believe that vision, the sense eminent above all others in the proportion of the finite to the infinite, the temporal to the instantaneous, the quantitative to the indivisible, the illuminated to the obscure—that vision, I say, is related to light itself. But of this sensation and the things pertaining to it I pretend to understand but little; and since even a long time would not suffice to explain that trifle, or even to hint at an explanation, I pass this over in silence.

Having shown that many sensations which are supposed to be qualities residing in external objects have no real existence save in us, and outside ourselves are mere names, I now say that I am inclined to believe heat to be of this character. Those materials which produce heat in us and make us feel warmth, which are known by the general name of "fire," would then be a multitude of minute particles having certain shapes and moving with certain velocities. Meeting with our bodies, they penetrate by means of their extreme subtlety, and their touch as felt by us when they pass through our substance is the sensation we call "heat." This is pleasant or unpleasant according to the greater or smaller speed of these particles as they go pricking and penetrating; pleasant when this assists our necessary transpiration, and obnoxious when it causes too great a separation and dissolution of our substance. The operation of fire by means of its particles is merely that in moving it penetrates all bodies, causing their speedy or slow dissolution in proportion to the number and velocity of the fire-corpuscles and the density or tenuity of the bodies. Many materials are such that in their decomposition the greater part of them passes over into additional tiny corpuscles, and this dissolution continues so long as these continue to meet with further matter capable of being so resolved. I do not believe that in addition to shape, number, motion, penetration and touch there is any other quality in fire corresponding to "heat"; this belongs so intimately to us that when the live body is taken away, heat becomes no more than a simple name....

2.5.2 *from "Letter to the Grand Duchess Christina"*

Galileo Galilei
To
The Most Serene
Grand Duchess Mother:

Some years ago, as Your Serene Highness well knows, I discovered in the heavens many things that had not been seen before our own age. The novelty of these things, as well as some consequences which followed from them in contradiction to the physical notions commonly held among academic philosophers, stirred up against me no small number of professors—as if I had placed these things in the sky with my own hands in order to upset nature and overturn the sciences. They seemed to forget that the increase of known truths stimulates the investigation, establishment, and growth of the arts; not their diminution or destruction.

Showing a greater fondness for their own opinions than for truth, they sought to deny and disprove the new things which, if they had cared to look for themselves, their own senses would have demonstrated to them. To this end they hurled various charges and published numerous writings filled with vain arguments, and they made the grave mistake of sprinkling these with passages taken from places in the Bible which they had failed to understand properly, and which were ill suited to their purposes.

These men would perhaps not have fallen into such error had they but paid attention to a most useful doctrine of St. Augustine's, relative to our making positive statements about things which are obscure and hard to understand by means of reason alone. Speaking of a certain physical conclusion about the heavenly bodies, he wrote: "Now keeping always our respect for moderation in grave piety, we ought not to believe anything inadvisedly on a dubious point, lest in favor to our error we conceive a prejudice against something that truth hereafter may reveal to be not contrary in any way to the sacred books of either the Old or the New Testament."[2]

Well, the passage of time has revealed to everyone the truths that I previously set forth; and, together with the truth of the facts, there has come to light the great difference in attitude between those who simply and dispassionately refused to admit the discoveries to be true, and those who combined with their incredulity some reckless passion of their own. Men who were well grounded in astronomical and physical science were persuaded as soon as they received my first message. There were others who denied them or remained in doubt only because of their novel and unexpected character, and because they had not yet had the opportunity to see for themselves. These men have by degrees come to be satisfied. But some, besides allegiance to their original error, possess I know not what fanciful interest in remaining hostile not so much toward the things in question as toward their discoverer. No longer being able to deny them, these men now take refuge in obstinate silence, but being more than ever exasperated by that which has pacified and quieted other men, they divert their thoughts to other fancies and seek new ways to damage me.

I should pay no more attention to them than to those who previously contradicted me—at whom I always laugh, being assured of the eventual outcome—were it not that in their new calumnies and persecutions I perceive that they do not stop at proving themselves more learned than I am (a claim which I scarcely contest), but go so far as to cast against me imputations of crimes which must be, and are, more abhorrent to me than death itself. I cannot remain satisfied merely to know that the injustice of this is recognized by those who are acquainted with these men and with me, as perhaps it is not known to others.

Persisting in their original resolve to destroy me and everything mine by any means they can think of, these men are aware of my views in astronomy and philosophy. They know that as to the arrangement of the parts of the universe, I hold the sun to be situated motionless in the center of the revolution of the celestial orbs while the earth rotates on its axis and revolves about the sun. They know also that I support this position not only by refuting the arguments of Ptolemy and Aristotle, but by producing many counterarguments; in particular, some which relate to physical effects whose causes can perhaps be assigned in no other way. In addition there are astronomical arguments derived from many things in my new celestial discoveries that plainly confute the Ptolemaic system while admirably agreeing with and confirming the contrary hypothesis. Possibly because they are disturbed by the known truth of other propositions of mine which differ from those commonly held, and therefore mistrusting their defense so long as they confine themselves to the field of philosophy, these men have resolved to fabricate a shield for their fallacies out of the mantle of pretended religion and the authority of the Bible. These they apply, with little judgment, to the refutation of arguments that they do not understand and have not even listened to.

First they have endeavored to spread the opinion that such propositions in general are contrary to the Bible and are consequently damnable and heretical. They know that it is human nature to take up causes whereby a man may oppress his neighbor, no matter how unjustly, rather than those from which a man may receive some just encouragement. Hence they have had no trouble in finding men who would preach the damnability and heresy of the new doctrine from their very pulpits with unwonted confidence, thus doing impious and inconsiderate injury not only to that doctrine and its followers but to all mathematics and mathematicians in general. Next, becoming bolder, and hoping (though vainly) that this seed which first took root in their hypocritical minds would send out branches and ascend to heaven, they began scattering rumors

2 *De Genesi ad literam*, end of bk. ii (citations of theological works are taken from Galileo's marginal notes, without verification).

among the people that before long this doctrine would be condemned by the supreme authority. They know, too, that official condemnation would not only suppress the two propositions which I have mentioned, but would render damnable all other astronomical and physical statements and observations that have any necessary relation or connection with these.

In order to facilitate their designs, they seek so far as possible (at least among the common people) to make this opinion seem new and to belong to me alone. They pretend not to know that its author, or rather its restorer and confirmer, was Nicholas Copernicus; and that he was not only a Catholic, but a priest and a canon. He was in fact so esteemed by the church that when the Lateran Council under Leo X took up the correction of the church calendar, Copernicus was called to Rome from the most remote parts of Germany to undertake its reform. At that time the calendar was defective because the true measures of the year and the lunar month were not exactly known. The Bishop of Fossombrone, then in charge of this matter, assigned Copernicus to seek more light and greater certainty concerning the celestial motions by means of constant study and labor. With Herculean toil he set his admirable mind to this task, and he made such great progress in this science and brought our knowledge of the heavenly motions to such precision that he became celebrated as an astronomer. Since that time not only has the calendar been regulated by his teachings, but tables of all the motions of the planets have been calculated as well.

Having reduced his system into six books, he published these at the instance of the Cardinal of Capua[3] and the Bishop of Culm.[4] And since he had assumed his laborious enterprise by order of the supreme pontiff, he dedicated this book *On the celestial revolutions* to Pope Paul III. When printed, the book was accepted by the holy Church, and it has been read and studied by everyone without the faintest hint of any objection ever being conceived against its doctrines. Yet now that manifest experiences and necessary proofs have shown them to be well grounded, persons exist who would strip the author of his reward without so much as looking at his book, and add the shame of having him pronounced a heretic. All this they would do merely to satisfy their personal displeasure conceived without any cause against another man, who has no interest in Copernicus beyond approving his teachings.

Now as to the false aspersions which they so unjustly seek to cast upon me, I have thought it necessary to justify myself in the eyes of all men, whose judgment in matters of religion and of reputation I must hold in great esteem. I shall therefore discourse of the particulars which these men produce to make this opinion detested and to have it condemned not merely as false but as heretical. To this end they make a shield of their hypocritical zeal for religion. They go about invoking the Bible, which they would have minister to their deceitful purposes. Contrary to the sense of the Bible and the intention of the holy Fathers, if I am not mistaken, they would extend such authorities until even in purely physical matters—where faith is not involved—they would have us altogether abandon reason and the evidence of our senses in favor of some biblical passage, though under the surface meaning of its words this passage may contain a different sense.

I hope to show that I proceed with much greater piety than they do, when I argue not against condemning this book, but against condemning it in the way they suggest—that is, without understanding it, weighing it, or so much as reading it. For Copernicus never discusses matters of religion or faith, nor does he use arguments that depend in any way upon the authority of sacred writings which he might have interpreted erroneously. He stands always upon physical conclusions pertaining to the celestial motions, and deals with them by astronomical and geometrical demonstrations, founded primarily upon sense experiences and very exact observations. He did not ignore the Bible, but he knew very well that if his doctrine were

3 Nicholas Schoenberg, spoken of by Copernicus as "celebrated in all fields of scholarship."

4 Tiedmann Giese, to whom Copernicus referred in his preface as "that scholar, my good friend."

proved, then it could not contradict the Scriptures when they were rightly understood. And thus at the end of his letter of dedication, addressing the pope, he said:

"If there should chance to be any exegetes ignorant of mathematics who pretend to skill in that discipline, and dare to condemn and censure this hypothesis of mine upon the authority of some scriptural passage twisted to their purpose, I value them not, but disdain their unconsidered judgment. For it is known that Lactantius—a poor mathematician though in other respects a worthy author—writes very childishly about the shape of the earth when he scoffs at those who affirm it to be a globe. Hence it should not seem strange to the ingenious if people of that sort should in turn deride me. But mathematics is written for mathematicians, by whom, if I am not deceived, these labors of mine will be recognized as contributing something to their domain, as also to that of the Church over which Your Holiness now reigns."[5]

Such are the people who labor to persuade us that an author like Copernicus may be condemned without being read, and who produce various authorities from the Bible, from theologians, and from Church Councils to make us believe that this is not only lawful but commendable. Since I hold these to be of supreme authority, I consider it rank temerity for anyone to contradict them—when employed according to the usage of the holy Church. Yet I do not believe it is wrong to speak out when there is reason to suspect that other men wish, for some personal motive, to produce and employ such authorities for purposes quite different from the sacred intention of the holy Church.

Therefore I declare (and my sincerity will make itself manifest) not only that I mean to submit myself freely and renounce any errors into which I may fall in this discourse through ignorance of matters pertaining to religion, but that I do not desire in these matters to engage in disputes with anyone, even on points that are disputable. My goal is this alone; that if, among errors that may abound in these considerations of a subject remote from my profession, there is anything that may be serviceable to the holy Church in making a decision concerning the Copernican system, it may be taken and utilized as seems best to the superiors. And if not, let my book be torn and burnt, as I neither intend nor pretend to gain from it any fruit that is not pious and Catholic. And though many of the things I shall reprove have been heard by my own ears, I shall freely grant to those who have spoken them that they never said them, if that is what they wish, and I shall confess myself to have been mistaken. Hence let whatever I reply be addressed not to them, but to whoever may have held such opinions.

The reason produced for condemning the opinion that the earth moves and the sun stands still is that in many places in the Bible one may read that the sun moves and the earth stands still. Since the Bible cannot err, it follows as a necessary consequence that anyone takes an erroneous and heretical position who maintains that the sun is inherently motionless and the earth movable.

With regard to this argument, I think in the first place that it is very pious to say and prudent to affirm that the holy Bible can never speak untruth—whenever its true meaning is understood. But I believe nobody will deny that it is often very abstruse, and may say things which are quite different from what its bare words signify. Hence in expounding the Bible if one were always to confine oneself to the unadorned grammatical meaning, one might fall into error. Not only contradictions and propositions far from true might thus be made to appear in the Bible, but even grave heresies and follies. Thus it would be necessary to assign to God feet, hands, and eyes, as well as corporeal and human affections, such as anger, repentance, hatred, and sometimes even the forgetting of things past and ignorance of those to come. These propositions uttered by the Holy Ghost were set down in that manner by the sacred scribes in order to accommodate them to the capacities of the common people, who are rude and unlearned. For the sake of those who deserve to be separated from the herd, it

5 *De Revolutionibus* (Nuremberg, 1543), f. iiii.

is necessary that wise expositors should produce the true senses of such passages, together with the special reasons for which they were set down in these words. This doctrine is so widespread and so definite with all theologians that it would be superfluous to adduce evidence for it.

Hence I think that I may reasonably conclude that whenever the Bible has occasion to speak of any physical conclusion (especially those which are very abstruse and hard to understand), the rule has been observed of avoiding confusion in the minds of the common people which would render them contumacious toward the higher mysteries. Now the Bible, merely to condescend to popular capacity, has not hesitated to obscure some very important pronouncements, attributing to God himself some qualities extremely remote from (and even contrary to) His essence. Who, then, would positively declare that this principle has been set aside, and the Bible has confined itself rigorously to the bare and restricted sense of its words, when speaking but casually of the earth, of water, of the sun, or of any other created thing? Especially in view of the fact that these things in no way concern the primary purpose of the sacred writings, which is the service of God and the salvation of souls—matters infinitely beyond the comprehension of the common people.

This being granted, I think that in discussions of physical problems we ought to begin not from the authority of scriptural passages, but from sense-experiences and necessary demonstrations; for the holy Bible and the phenomena of nature proceed alike from the divine Word, the former as the dictate of the Holy Ghost and the latter as the observant executrix of God's commands. It is necessary for the Bible, in order to be accommodated to the understanding of every man, to speak many things which appear to differ from the absolute truth so far as the bare meaning of the words is concerned. But Nature, on the other hand, is inexorable and immutable; she never transgresses the laws imposed upon her, or cares a whit whether her abstruse reasons and methods of operation are understandable to men. For that reason it appears that nothing physical which sense-experience sets before our eyes, or which necessary demonstrations prove to us, ought to be called in question (much less condemned) upon the testimony of biblical passages which may have some different meaning beneath their words. For the Bible is not chained in every expression to conditions as strict as those which govern all physical effects; nor is God any less excellently revealed in Nature's actions than in the sacred statements of the Bible. Perhaps this is what Tertullian meant by these words:

"We conclude that God is known first through Nature, and then again, more particularly, by doctrine; by Nature in His works, and by doctrine in His revealed word."

From this I do not mean to infer that we need not have an extraordinary esteem for the passages of holy Scripture. On the contrary, having arrived at any certainties in physics, we ought to utilize these as the most appropriate aids in the true exposition of the Bible and in the investigation of those meanings which are necessarily contained therein, for these must be concordant with demonstrated truths. I should judge that the authority of the Bible was designed to persuade men of those articles and propositions which, surpassing all human reasoning, could not be made credible by science, or by any other means than through the very mouth of the Holy Spirit.

Yet even in those propositions which are not matters of faith, this authority ought to be preferred over that of all human writings which are supported only by bare assertions or probable arguments, and not set forth in a demonstrative way. This I hold to be necessary and proper to the same extent that divine wisdom surpasses all human judgment and conjecture.

2.6 Isaac Newton (1643–1727)

Only Charles Darwin and Albert Einstein rival Isaac Newton's influence in Western science. Newton's *Opticks* (1704; not included here) presents a sophisticated account of light based on innovative research techniques (e.g., prism experiments that reveal the composite quality of white light), among other things. More importantly, the Classical Mechanics of *Mathematical Principles of Natural Philosophy* (1687) exemplify Aristotle's vision of a systematic explanatory theory that can causally explain particular phenomena (2.3.1). Newton had grand ambitions for his scientific theory: results must be based not on mere hypotheses requiring us to set aside questions about the truth of our fundamental principles (see "Rules of Reasoning," Rule IV); in his estimation, everything in his theory is based on non-hypothetical first principles, that is, axioms. Subsequent developments in physics raise doubts about this characterization of these axioms (see in particular Einstein, 2.9), but the success of Newton's comprehensive theory compels us to take this characterization seriously. He was convinced, additionally, that the axioms were based on methodical experimental research (i.e., derived inductively, as Bacon recommends in 2.4).

Like Galileo, Newton adopted both a reductionist approach to physical explanations and an atomism account of matter. To this end, he summarizes a crude theory of the atom that was current at the time: the material world is composed of hard, solid, impenetrable, and indestructible particles (see "Rules of Reasoning in Philosophy," Rule III). Nineteenth-century chemists and twentieth-century particle physicists developed sophisticated techniques to expose the variety and structure of sub-microscopic phenomena; out of this research emerged our periodic table of elements and devices for splitting the atom. Nevertheless, Newton's crude atomism was sufficient for his own purposes, which was to explain how material objects behave according to a few simple laws.

Even before stating its axioms, *Mathematical Principles of Natural Philosophy* (2.6) begins with definitions of basic concepts (e.g., mass, force, inertia, etc.). Next, the three principal axioms articulate fundamental laws of nature (e.g., of inertia, of transmitted energy, and of reciprocal action). From these laws he proves a series of propositions in a geometrical procedure that is comparable to that which is illustrated in Plato's *Meno* (2.2). (Unlike the *Meno* proofs, however, the point of departure is not a provisionally accepted hypothesis, but foundational axioms.) In geometrical fashion, Newton moves systematically from abstract laws to conclusions about increasingly detailed phenomena. At one point, he proves how derived forces work (see "Corollary I"), and at another that large spherical bodies such as Earth, the moon, or the sun can be treated as centred on geometrical points (see "Proposition LXXVI"). Ultimately, he is able to explain the behaviour of falling objects, projectiles, ocean tides, the orbit of the moon around Earth, the orbit of planets around the sun, comets, and so forth (see "Appearances or Phaenomena" and "System of the World"). Such explanatory detail is what makes Newton's Classical Mechanics a central achievement of Western science.

Among the most controversial and influential contributions in Newton's theory is the principle of gravity. Gravity acts as a force of attraction, explaining why falling objects accelerate towards the centre of our planet, why the moon and planetary objects tend to be spherical, why the moon orbits Earth, why Earth and other planets orbit the sun, why comets return regularly, and so on. Newton, however, could not explain how gravitational forces can act at a distance (e.g., Earth drawing an apple towards its centre or holding the moon in orbit). Other forces in his system act by contact (e.g., a cue ball communicating its momentum to another billiard ball). While Newton was convinced that nature admits of no "occult" causes, such as "action at a distance," he accepted gravity on the basis of overwhelming empirical evidence. Despite gravity being inexplicable in some respects and at odds with the material, atomistic framework of the rest of Classical Mechanics, it is presented as a natural cause of natural phenomena.

from Philosophiae Naturalis Principia Mathematica (Mathematical Principles of Natural Philosophy)

Book I

DEFINITIONS

DEFINITION I: *The quantity of matter is the measure of the same, arising from its density and bulk conjunctly.*
Thus air of a double density, in a double space, is quadruple in quantity; in a triple space, sextuple in quantity. The same thing is to be understood of snow, and fine dust or powders, that are condensed by compression or liquefaction; and of all bodies that are by any causes whatever differently condensed. I have no regard in this place to a medium, if any such there is, that freely pervades the interstices between the parts of bodies. It is this quantity that I mean hereafter everywhere under the name of body or mass. And the same is known by the weight of each body; for it is proportional to the weight, as I have found by experiments on pendulums, very accurately made, which shall be shewn hereafter.

DEFINITION II: *The quantity of motion is the measure of the same, arising from the velocity and quantity of matter conjunctly.*
The motion of the whole is the sum of the motions of all the parts; and therefore in a body double in quantity, with equal velocity, the motion is double; with twice the velocity, it is quadruple.

DEFINITION III: The vis insita,[1] *or innate force of matter, is a power of resisting, by which every body, as much as in it lies, endeavours to persevere in its present state, whether it be of rest, or of moving uniformly forward in a right line.*
This force is ever proportional to the body whose force it is; and differs nothing from the inactivity of the mass, but in our manner of conceiving it. A body, from the inactivity of matter, is not without difficulty put out of its state of rest or motion. Upon which account, this vis insita, may, by a most significant name, be called *vis inertiæ*, or force of inactivity.

1 I.e., "force in place," which is to say the innate force in a quantity of matter. Since this force constitutes a resistance to an impelled force, Newton also uses the name "vis inertiæ," which is Latin for force of inactivity.

But a body exerts this force only when another force, impressed upon it, endeavours to change its condition; and the exercise of this force may be considered both as resistance and impulse; it is resistance, in so far as the body, for maintaining its present state, withstands the force impressed; it is impulse, in so far as the body, by not easily giving way to the impressed force of another, endeavours to change the state of that other. Resistance is usually ascribed to bodies at rest, and impulse to those in motion; but motion and rest, as commonly conceived, are only relatively distinguished; nor are those bodies always truly at rest, which commonly are taken to be so.

DEFINITION IV: *An impressed force is an action exerted upon a body, in order to change its state, either of rest, or of moving uniformly forward in a right line.*
This force consists in the action only; and remains no longer in the body, when the action is over. For a body maintains every new state it acquires, by its *vis inertiæ* only. Impressed forces are of different origins as from percussion, from pressure, from centripetal force. ...

AXIOMS, OR LAWS OF MOTION

LAW I: *Every body perseveres in its state of rest, or of uniform motion in a right line, unless it is compelled to change that state by forces impressed thereon.*
Projectiles persevere in their motions, so far as they are not retarded by the resistance of the air, or impelled downwards by the force of gravity. A top, whose parts by their cohesion are perpetually drawn aside from rectilinear motions, does not cease its rotation, otherwise than as it is retarded by the air. The greater bodies of the planets and comets, meeting with less resistance in more free spaces, preserve their motions both progressive and circular for a much longer time.

LAW II: *The alteration of motion is ever proportional to the motive force impressed; and is made in the direction of the right line in which that force is impressed.*
If any force generates a motion, a double force will generate double the motion, a triple force triple the motion, whether that force be impressed altogether and at once, or gradually and successively. And this motion (being always directed the same way with the generating force), if the body moved before, is added to or subducted from the former motion, according as they directly conspire with or are directly contrary to each other; or obliquely joined, when they are oblique, so as to produce a new motion compounded from the determination of both.

LAW III: *To every action there is always opposed an equal reaction: or the mutual actions of two bodies upon each other are always equal, and directed to contrary parts.*
Whatever draws or presses another is as much drawn or pressed by that other. If you press a stone with your finger, the finger is also pressed by the stone. If a horse draws a stone tied to a rope, the horse (if I may so say) will be equally drawn back towards the stone: for the distended rope, by the same endeavour to relax or unbend itself, will draw the horse as much towards the stone, as it does the stone towards the horse, and will obstruct the progress of the one as much as it advances that of the other. If a body impinge upon another, and by its force change the motion of the other, that body also (because of the equality of the mutual pressure) will undergo an equal change, in its own motion, towards the contrary part. The changes made by these actions are equal, not in the velocities but in the motions of bodies; that is to say, if the bodies are not hindered by any other impediments. For, because the motions are equally changed, the changes of the velocities made towards contrary parts are reciprocally proportional to the bodies. This law takes place also in attractions, as will be proved in the next scholium.

COROLLARY I: *A body by two forces conjoined will describe the diagonal of a parallelogram, in the same time that it would describe the sides, by those forces apart.*

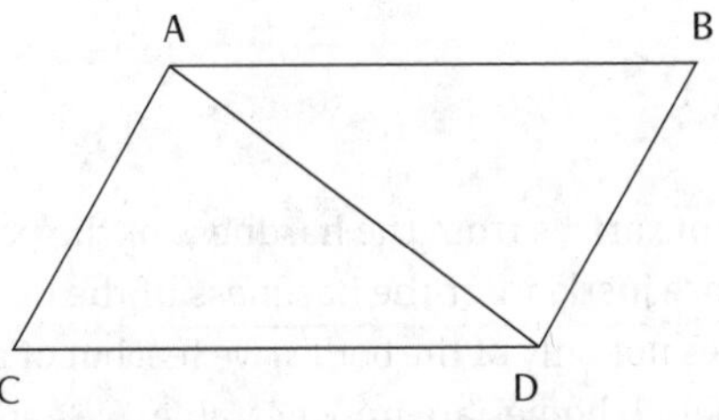

If a body in a given time, by the force M impressed apart in the place A, should with an uniform motion be carried from A to B; and by the force N impressed apart in the same place, should be carried from A to C; complete the parallelogram ABCD, and, by both forces acting together, it will in the same time be carried in the diagonal from A to D. For since the force N acts in the direction of the line AC, parallel to BD, this force (by the second law) will not at all alter the velocity generated by the other force M, by which the body is carried towards the line BD. The body therefore will arrive at the line BD in the same time, whether the force N be impressed or not; and therefore at the end of that time it will be found somewhere in the line BD. By the same argument, at the end of the same time it will be found somewhere in the line CD. Therefore it will be found in the point D, where both lines meet. But it will move in a right line from A to D, by Law I.

...

PROPOSITION LXXVI. THEOREM XXXVI.

If spheres be however dissimilar (as to density of matter and attractive force) in the same ratio onward from the centre to the circumference; but every where similar, at every given distance from the centre, on all sides round about; and the attractive force of every point decreases in the duplicate ratio of the distance of the body attracted; I say, that the whole force with which one of these spheres attracts the other will be reciprocally proportional to the square of the distance of the centres.

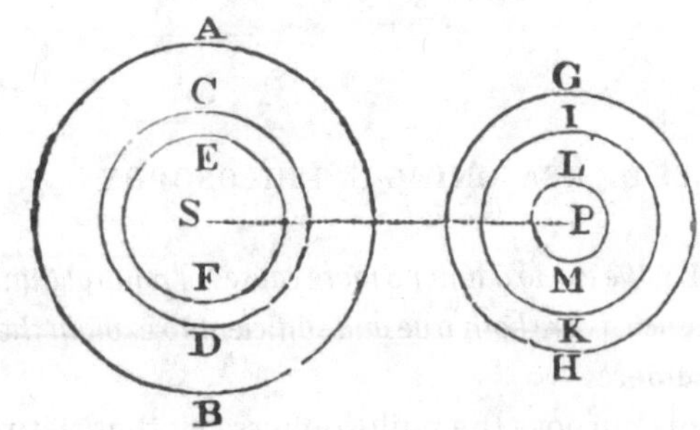

Imagine several concentric similar spheres, AB, CD, EF, &c., the innermost of which added to the outermost may compose a matter more dense towards the centre, or subducted from them may leave the same more lax and rare. Then, by Prop. LXXV, these spheres will attract other similar concentric spheres GH, IK, LM, &c., each the other, with forces reciprocally proportional to the square of the distance SP. And, by composition or division, the sum of all those forces, or the excess of any of them above the others; that is, the entire force with which the whole sphere AB (composed of any concentric spheres or of their differences) will attract the whole sphere GH (composed of any concentric spheres or their differences) in the same ratio. Let the number of the concentric spheres be increased *in infinitum*, so that the density of the matter together with the attractive force may, in the progress from the circumference to the centre, increase or decrease according to any given law; and by the addition of matter not attractive, let the deficient density be supplied, that so the spheres may acquire any form desired; and the force with which one of these attracts the other will be still, by the former reasoning, in the same ratio of the square of the distance inversely. Q.E.D.[2]

2 I.e., "quod erat demonstrandum," which is Latin for "as has been demonstrated" and indicates that the proposition has now been proven.

Cor. 1. Hence if many spheres of this kind, similar in all respects, attract each other mutually, the accelerative attractions of each to each, at any equal distances of the centres, will be as the attracting spheres.

Cor. 2. And at any unequal distances, as the attracting spheres applied to the squares of the distances between the centres....

Book III

RULES OF REASONING IN PHILOSOPHY

RULE I: *We are to admit no more causes of natural things than such as are both true and sufficient to explain their appearances.*
To this purpose the philosophers say that Nature does nothing in vain, and more is in vain when less will serve; for Nature is pleased with simplicity, and affects not the pomp of superfluous causes.

RULE II: *Therefore to the same natural effects we must, as far as possible, assign the same causes.*
As to respiration in a man and in a beast; the descent of stones in Europe and in America; the light of our culinary fire and of the sun; the reflection of light in the earth, and in the planets.

RULE III: *The qualities of bodies, which admit neither intension nor remission of degrees, and which are found to belong to all bodies within the reach of our experiments, are to be esteemed the universal qualities of all bodies whatsoever.*
For since the qualities of bodies are only known to us by experiments, we are to hold for universal all such as universally agree with experiments; and such as are not liable to diminution can never be quite taken away. We are certainly not to relinquish the evidence of experiments for the sake of dreams and vain fictions of our own devising; nor are we to recede from the analogy of Nature, which uses to be simple, and always consonant to itself. We no other way know the extension of bodies than by our senses, nor do these reach it in all bodies; but because we perceive extension in all that are sensible, therefore we ascribe it universally to all others also. That abundance of bodies are hard, we learn by experience; and because the hardness of the whole arises from the hardness of the parts, we therefore justly infer the hardness of the undivided particles not only of the bodies we feel but of all others. That all bodies are impenetrable, we gather not from reason, but from sensation. The bodies which we handle we find impenetrable, and thence conclude impenetrability to be an universal property of all bodies whatsoever. That all bodies are moveable, and endowed with certain powers (which we call the *vires inertiae*) of persevering in their motion, or in their rest, we only infer from the like properties observed in the bodies which we have seen. The extension, hardness, impenetrability, mobility, and *vis inertiae* of the whole, result from the extension, hardness, impenetrability, mobility, and *vires inertiae* of the parts; and thence we conclude the least particles of all bodies to be also all extended, and hard and impenetrable, and moveable, and endowed with their proper *vires inertia*. And this is the foundation of all philosophy. Moreover, that the divided but contiguous particles of bodies may be separated from one another, is matter of observation; and, in the particles that remain undivided, our minds are able to distinguish yet lesser parts, as is mathematically demonstrated. But whether the parts so distinguished, and not yet divided, may, by the powers of Nature, be actually divided and separated from one another, we cannot certainly determine. Yet, had we the proof of but one experiment that any undivided particle, in breaking a hard and solid body, suffered a division, we might by virtue of this rule conclude that the undivided as well as the divided particles may be divided and actually separated to infinity.

Lastly, if it universally appears, by experiments and astronomical observations, that all bodies about the earth gravitate towards the earth, and that in proportion to the quantity of matter which they severally contain; that the moon likewise, according to the quantity of its matter, gravitates towards the earth; that, on the other hand, our sea gravitates towards the moon; and all the planets mutually one towards another; and the comets in like manner towards the sun; we must, in consequence of this rule, universally allow that all bodies whatsoever are endowed with a principle of mutual gravitation. For the argument from the appearances concludes with more force for the universal gravitation of all bodies than for their impenetrability; of which, among those in the celestial regions, we have no experiments, nor any manner of observation. Not that I affirm gravity to be essential to bodies: by their *vis insita* I mean nothing but their *vis inertiae*. This is immutable. Their gravity is diminished as they recede from the earth.

RULE IV: *In experimental philosophy we are to look upon propositions collected by general induction from phaenomena as accurately or very nearly true, notwithstanding any contrary hypotheses that may be imagined, till such time as other phaenomena occur, by which they may either be made more accurate, or liable to exceptions.* This rule we must follow, that the argument of induction may not be evaded by hypotheses.

APPEARANCES OR PHAENOMENA[3]

PHAENOMENON III: *That the five primary planets, Mercury, Venus, Mars, Jupiter, and Saturn, with their several orbits, encompass the sun.*

That Mercury and Venus revolve about the sun, is evident from their moon-like appearances. When they shine out with a full face, they are, in respect of us, beyond or above the sun; when they appear half full, they are about the same height on one side or other of the sun; when horned, they are below or between us and the sun; and they are sometimes, when directly under, seen like spots traversing the sun's disk. That Mars surrounds the sun, is as plain from its full face when near its conjunction with the sun, and from the gibbous figure which it shews in its quadratures.[4] And the same thing is demonstrable of Jupiter and Saturn, from their appearing full in all situations; for the shadows of their satellites that appear sometimes upon their disks make it plain that the light they shine with is not their own, but borrowed from the sun.

...

PROPOSITIONS ...

PROPOSITION II. THEOREM II.

That the forces by which the primary planets are continually drawn off from rectilinear motions, and retained in their proper orbits, tend to the sun; and are reciprocally as the squares of the distances of the places of those planets from the sun's centre.

The former part of the Proposition is manifest from Phaen. V, and Prop. II, Book I; the latter from Phaen. IV, and Cor. 6, Prop. IV, of the same Book. But this part of the Proposition is, with great accuracy, demonstrable from the quiescence of the aphelion points;[5] for a very small aberration from the *reciprocal* duplicate proportion would (by Cor. 1, Prop. XLV, Book I) produce a motion of the apsides[6] sensible enough in every single revolution, and in many of them enormously great.

PROPOSITION III. THEOREM III.

That the force by which the moon is retained in its orbit tends to the earth; and is reciprocally as the square of the distance of its place from the earth's centre.

The former part of the Proposition is evident from Phaen. VI, and Prop. II or III, Book I; the latter from the very slow motion of the moon's apogee; which in every single revolution amounting but to 3° 3′ *in consequentia*, may be neglected....

3 The term "phaenomena" is the Greek plural for appearances. The singular is "phaenomenon" and is abbreviated as "phaen" elsewhere in Newton's text.

4 I.e., the position of Mars (or the Moon or any outer planet) when a straight line from it to Earth is at right angles to the straight line from the sun to Earth.

5 The aphelion point is that part of a planet's orbit that is farthest from the sun.

6 I.e., the two points in an astronomical orbit lying closest to and farthest from the centre of attraction.

PROPOSITION IV ...

That the moon gravitates towards the earth, and by the force of gravity is continually drawn off from a rectilinear motion, and retained in its orbit.

...

PROPOSITION V. THEOREM V.

That the circumjovial planets[7] *gravitate towards Jupiter; the circumsaturnal towards Saturn; the circumsolar towards the sun; and by the forces of their gravity are drawn off from rectilinear motions, and retained in curvilinear orbits.*

For the revolutions of the circumjovial planets about Jupiter, of the circumsaturnal about Saturn, and of Mercury and Venus, and the other circumsolar planets,[8] about the sun, are appearances of the same sort with the revolution of the moon about the earth; and therefore, by Rule II, must be owing to the same sort of causes; especially since it has been demonstrated, that the forces upon which those revolutions depend tend to the centres of Jupiter, of Saturn, and of the sun; and that those forces, in receding from Jupiter, from Saturn, and from the sun, decrease in the same proportion, and according to the same law, as the force of gravity does in receding from the earth.

Cor. 1. There is, therefore, a power of gravity tending to all the planets; for, doubtless, Venus, Mercury, and the rest, are bodies of the same sort with Jupiter and Saturn. And since all attraction (by Law III) is mutual, Jupiter will therefore gravitate towards all his[9] own satellites, Saturn towards his, the earth towards the moon, and the sun towards all the primary planets.

Cor. 2. The force of gravity which tends to any one planet is reciprocally as the square of the distance of places from that planet's centre.

Cor. 3. All the planets do mutually gravitate towards one another, by Cor. 1 and 2. And hence it is that Jupiter and Saturn, when near their conjunction; by their mutual attractions sensibly disturb each other's motions. So the sun disturbs the motions of the moon; and both sun and moon disturb our sea, as we shall hereafter explain.

SCHOLIUM.[10]

The force which retains the celestial bodies in their orbits has been hitherto called centripetal force;[11] but it being now made plain that it can be no other than a gravitating force, we shall hereafter call it gravity. For the cause of that centripetal force which retains the moon in its orbit will extend itself to all the planets, by Rule I, II, and IV.

PROPOSITION VI. THEOREM VI.

That all bodies gravitate towards every planet; and that the weights of bodies towards any one planet, at equal distances from the centre of the planet, are proportional to the quantities of matter which they severally contain.

It has been, now of a long time, observed by others, that all sorts of heavy bodies (allowance being made for the inequality of retardation which they suffer from a small power of resistance in the air) descend to the earth *from equal heights* in equal times; and that equality of times we may distinguish to a great accuracy, by the help of pendulums. I tried the thing in gold, silver, lead, glass, sand, common salt, wood, water, and wheat. I provided two wooden boxes, round and equal: I filled the one with wood, and suspended an equal weight of gold (as exactly as I could) in the centre of oscillation of the other. The boxes hanging by equal threads of 11 feet made a couple of pendulums perfectly equal in weight and figure, and equally receiving the resistance of the air. And, placing the one by the other, I observed them to play together forward

---

7 I.e., satellites of Jupiter. Similarly, circumsaturnal planets are satellites of Saturn.

8 I.e., planets that orbit the sun, which includes those named here and will eventually include Uranus, Neptune, and Pluto (which had not yet been discovered in Newton's time).

9 In using personal pronouns here Newton is being poetic, reminding us that the names of the planets were originally the same as Roman gods.

10 I.e., a note added to illustrate or further develop a point established in the central argument.

11 I.e., a force that draws the revolving body towards the centre of its orbital circle.

and backward, for a long time, with equal vibrations. And therefore the quantity of matter in the gold (by Cor. 1 and 6, Prop. XXIV, Book II) was to the quantity of matter in the wood as the action of the motive force (or *vis motrix*) upon all the gold to the action of the same upon all the wood: that is, as the weight of the one to the weight of the other: and the like happened in the other bodies. By these experiments, in bodies of the same weight, I could manifestly have discovered a difference of matter less than the thousandth part of the whole, had any such been. But, without all doubt, the nature of gravity towards the planets is the same as towards the earth. For, should we imagine our terrestrial bodies removed to the orb of the moon, and there, together with the moon, deprived of all motion, to be let go, so as to fall together towards the earth, it is certain, from what we have demonstrated before, that, in equal times, they would describe equal spaces with the moon, and of consequence are to the moon, in quantity of matter, as their weights to its weight....

But further; the weights of all the parts of every planet towards any other planet are one to another as the matter in the several parts; for if some parts did gravitate more, others less, than for the quantity of their matter, then the whole planet, according to the sort of parts with which it most abounds, would gravitate more or less than in proportion to the quantity of matter in the whole. Nor is it of any moment whether these parts are external or internal; for if, for example, we should imagine the terrestrial bodies with us to be raised up to the orb of the moon, to be there compared with its body: if the weights of such bodies were to the weights of the external parts of the moon as the quantities of matter in the one and in the other respectively; but to the weights of the internal parts in a greater or less proportion, then likewise the weights of those bodies would be to the weight of the whole moon in a greater or less proportion; against what we have shewed above.

Cor. 1. Hence the weights of bodies do not depend upon their forms and textures; for if the weights could be altered with the forms, they would be greater or less, according to the variety of forms, in equal matter; altogether against experience.

Cor. 2. Universally, all bodies about the earth gravitate towards the earth; and the weights of all, at equal distances from the earth's centre, are as the quantities of matter which they severally contain. This is the quality of all bodies within the reach of our experiments; and therefore (by Rule III) to be affirmed of all bodies whatsoever.

PROPOSITION VII. THEOREM VII.
That there is a power of gravity tending to all bodies, proportional to the several quantities of matter which they contain.

That all the planets mutually gravitate one towards another, we have proved before; as well as that the force of gravity towards every one of them, considered apart, is reciprocally as the square of the distance of places from the centre of the planet. And thence (by Prop. LXIX, Book I, and its Corollaries) it follows, that the gravity tending towards all the planets is proportional to the matter which they contain.

Moreover, since all the parts of any planet A gravitate towards any other planet B; and the gravity of every part is to the gravity of the whole as the matter of the part to the matter of the whole; and (by Law III) to every action corresponds an equal re-action; therefore the planet B will, on the other hand, gravitate towards all the parts of the planet A; and its gravity towards any one part will be to the gravity towards the whole as the matter of the part to the matter of the whole. Q.E.D.

Cor. 1. Therefore the force of gravity towards any whole planet arises from, and is compounded of, the forces of gravity towards all its parts. Magnetic and electric attractions afford us examples of this; for all attraction towards the whole arises from the attractions towards the several parts. The thing may be easily understood in gravity, if we consider a greater planet, as formed of a number of lesser planets, meeting together in one globe; for *hence it would appear that* the force of the whole must arise from the forces of the component parts. If it is objected, that, according to this law, all bodies with us must mutually gravitate one towards another, whereas no such gravitation any where appears, I answer, that since the gravitation towards these bodies is to the gravitation towards the whole earth as these bodies are to the whole earth, the gravitation towards them must be far less than to fall under the observation of our senses.

Cor. 2. The force of gravity towards the several equal particles of any body is reciprocally as the square of the distance of places from the particles; as appears from Cor. 3, Prop. LXXIV, Book I.

...

PROPOSITION IX. THEOREM IX.

That the force of gravity, considered downward from the surface of the planets, decreases nearly in the proportion of the distances from their centres.

If the matter of the planet were of an uniform density, this Proposition would be accurately true (by Prop. LXXIII. Book I). The error, therefore, can be no greater than what may arise from the inequality of the density.

...

THE SYSTEM OF THE WORLD.

It was the ancient opinion of not a few, in the earliest ages of philosophy, that the fixed stars stood immoveable in the highest parts of the world; that under the fixed stars the planets were carried about the sun; that the earth, as one of the planets, described an annual course about the sun, while by a diurnal motion[12] it was in the mean time revolved about its own axis; and that the sun, as the common fire which served to warm the whole, was fixed in the centre of the universe.

...

But our purpose is only to trace out the quantity and properties of this force from the phaenomena (...), and to apply what we discover in some simple cases as principles, by which, in a mathematical way, we may estimate the effects thereof in more involved cases; for it would be endless and impossible to bring every particular to direct and immediate observation.

We said, *in a mathematical way*, to avoid all questions about the nature or quality of this force, which we would not be understood to determine by any hypothesis; and therefore call it by the general name of a centripetal force, as it is a force which is directed towards some centre; and as it regards more particularly a body in that centre, we call it circum-solar,[13] circum-terrestrial,[14] circum-jovial;[15] and in like manner in respect of other central bodies.

That by means of centripetal forces the planets may be retained in certain orbits, we may easily understand, if we consider the motions of projectiles...; for a stone projected is by the pressure of its own weight forced out of the rectilinear path, which by the projection alone it should have pursued, and made to describe a curve line in the air; and through that crooked way is at last brought down to the ground; and the greater the velocity is with which it is projected, the farther it goes before it falls to the earth. We may therefore suppose the velocity to be so increased, that it would describe an arc of 1, 2, 5, 10, 100, 1000 miles before it arrived at the earth, till at last, exceeding the limits of the earth, it should pass quite by without touching it.

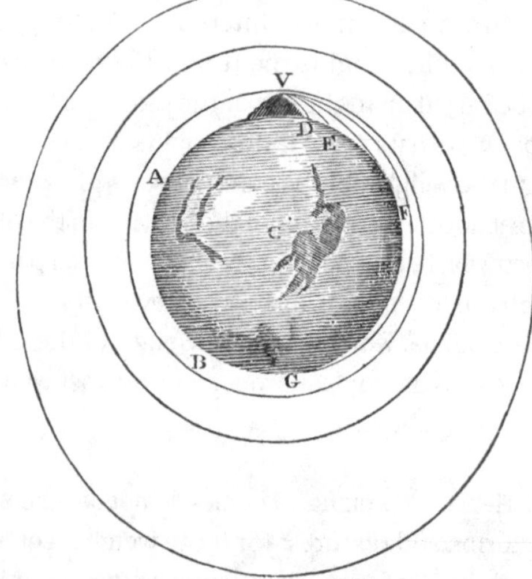

12 I.e., motion that is completed in a day.
13 I.e., revolving around the sun.
14 I.e., revolving around Earth.
15 I.e., revolving around Jupiter.

Let AFB represent the surface of the earth, C its centre, VD, VE, VF, the curve lines which a body would describe, if projected in an horizontal direction from the top of an high mountain successively with more and more velocity (...); and, because the celestial motions are scarcely retarded by the little or no resistance of the spaces in which they are performed, to keep up the parity of cases, let us suppose either that there is no air about the earth, or at least that it is endowed with little or no power of resisting; and for the same reason that the body projected with a less velocity describes the lesser arc VD, and with a greater velocity the greater arc VE, and, augmenting the velocity, it goes farther and farther to F and G, if the velocity was still more and more augmented, it would reach at last quite beyond the circumference of the earth, and return to the mountain from which it was projected.

And since the areas which by this motion it describes by a radius drawn to the centre of the earth are (by Prop. 1, Book 1, *Princip. Math.*) proportional to the times in which they are described, its velocity, when it returns to the mountain, will be no less than it was at first; and, retaining the velocity, it will describe the same curve over and over, by the same law.

But if we now imagine bodies to be projected in the directions of lines parallel to the horizon from greater heights, as of 5, 10, 100, 1000, or more miles, or rather as many semi-diameters of the earth, those bodies, according to their different velocity, and the different force of gravity in different heights, will describe arcs either concentric with the earth, or variously eccentric, and go on revolving through the heavens in those trajectories, just as the planets do in their orbs.

As when a stone is projected obliquely, that is, any way but in the perpendicular direction, the perpetual deflection thereof towards the earth from the right line in which it was projected is a proof of its gravitation to the earth, no less certain than its direct descent when only suffered to fall freely from rest; so the deviation of bodies moving in free spaces from rectilinear paths, and perpetual deflection therefrom towards any place, is a sure indication of the existence of some force which from all quarters impels those bodies towards that place.

And as, from the supposed existence of gravity, it necessarily follows that all bodies about the earth must press downwards, and therefore must either descend directly to the earth, if they are let fall from rest, or at least perpetually deviate from right lines towards the earth, if they are projected obliquely; so from the supposed existence of a force directed to any centre, it will follow, by the like necessity, that all bodies upon which this force acts must either descend directly to that centre, or at least deviate perpetually towards it from right lines, if otherwise they should have moved obliquely in these right lines.

And how from the motions given we may infer the forces, or from the forces given we may determine the motions, is shewn in the two first Books of our *Principles of Philosophy*.

...

That there are centripetal forces actually directed to the bodies of the sun, of the earth, and other planets, I thus infer.

The moon revolves about our earth, and by radii drawn to its centre (...) describes areas nearly proportional to the times in which they are described, as is evident from its velocity compared with its apparent diameter; for its motion is slower when its diameter is less (and therefore its distance greater), and its motion is swifter when its diameter is greater.

The revolutions of the satellites of Jupiter about that planet are more regular (...); for they describe circles concentric with Jupiter by equable motions, as exactly as our senses can distinguish.

And so the satellites of Saturn are revolved about this planet with motions nearly (...) circular and equable, scarcely disturbed by any eccentricity hitherto observed.

That Venus and Mercury are revolved about the sun, is demonstrable from their moon-like appearances (...); when they shine with a full face, they are in those parts of their orbs which in respect of the earth lie beyond the sun; when they appear half full, they are in those parts which lie over against the sun; when horned, in those parts which lie between the earth and the sun; and sometimes they pass over the sun's disk, when directly interposed between the earth and the sun.

And Venus, with a motion almost uniform, describes an orb nearly circular and concentric with the sun.

But Mercury, with a more eccentric motion, makes remarkable approaches to the sun, and goes off again by turns; but it is always swifter as it is near to the sun, and therefore by a radius drawn to the sun still describes areas proportional to the times.

Lastly, that the earth describes about the sun, or the sun about the earth, by a radius from the one to the other, areas exactly proportional to the times, is demonstrable from the apparent diameter of the sun compared with its apparent motion.

These are astronomical experiments; from which it follows, by Prop. I, II, III, in the first Book of our *Principles*, and their Corollaries..., that there are centripetal forces actually directed (either accurately or without considerable error) to the centres of the earth, of Jupiter, of Saturn, and of the sun. In Mercury, Venus, Mars, and the lesser planets, where experiments are wanting, the arguments from analogy must be allowed in their place.

That those forces ... decrease in the duplicate proportion of the distances from the centre of every planet, appears by Cor. VI, Prop. IV, Book I; for the periodic times of the satellites of Jupiter are one to another ... in the sesquiplicate[16] proportion of their distances from the centre of this planet.

2.7 Charles Darwin (1809–1882)

Charles Darwin's *The Origin of Species* (1859) introduced evolution as a bold new idea for biology. Before evolution theory, natural species were presumed to have existed always in their present forms. His fundamental insight (which was co-discovered by Alfred Russel Wallace) is that the origin of each species is both historical and natural (i.e., not supernatural, as in creation). Evolution is the process by which life first emerged from simple forms, then gradually evolved to complex and variegated ones.

Just as breeders "artificially" select individuals with the most desirable traits to breed from their livestock paddock, kennel, or coop (e.g., for milk production, herding, egg production, etc.), so do natural conditions in the environment "select" some individuals for survival and reproduction among all the wildlife on Earth. Variations among species "fit" some birds for cracking open nuts, some for extracting insects from tree bark, some for drawing nectar from flowering plants, and so forth. Each variation affects the probability that individual members will reproduce to leave offspring with similar traits. Variations within a local species population (e.g., longer or shorter beaks) will "fit" individual members to local conditions, and these members will pass their own particular traits to their offspring. This is survival of the fittest. Species with members who can successfully pass along their traits will survive while other species struggle with the same living conditions. Both intra-species and inter-species competition for resources (food, habitation, mates, etc.) determine the constitution of future life. In a process that Darwin

16 I.e., the orbital times for the different satellites relate to each other in a geometrical ratio of 3:2.

calls natural selection a relation between natural conditions and inherited traits determine which individuals and species survive.

The economist Thomas Malthus (1766–1834) first identified the dynamic forces that govern competition for resources among individuals and populations: the rate of reproduction always tends to increase the size of a population, but available land cannot furnish a corresponding increase of resources. Extending this principle to biological species, Darwin notes that, in the struggle for existence, only some members of each generation can survive, and the survivors are those individuals who out-compete others for these limited resources. Survivors reproduce, sometimes leaving offspring that replicate a parent's traits almost perfectly, sometimes not. Over the long course of natural history, trait changes in the species get introduced by offspring who differ from their parents. Whether these changes are incremental (e.g., with each generation being slightly larger than its predecessors) or sudden (e.g., a mutation), such changes can result in a new species. In this way, evolution over an extremely long time explains the variety and variability of life on Earth.

from The Origin of Species

Introduction

... In considering the origin of species, it is quite conceivable that a naturalist, reflecting on the mutual affinities of organic beings, on their embryological relations, their geographical distribution, geological succession, and other such facts, might come to the conclusion that species had not been independently created, but had descended, like varieties, from other species. Nevertheless, such a conclusion, even if well founded, would be unsatisfactory, until it could be shown how the innumerable species, inhabiting this world have been modified, so as to acquire that perfection of structure and coadaptation which justly excites our admiration. Naturalists continually refer to external conditions, such as climate, food, etc., as the only possible cause of variation. In one limited sense, as we shall hereafter see, this may be true; but it is preposterous to attribute to mere external conditions, the structure, for instance, of the woodpecker, with its feet, tail, beak, and tongue, so admirably adapted to catch insects under the bark of trees. In the case of the mistletoe, which draws its nourishment from certain trees, which has seeds that must be transported by certain birds, and which has flowers with separate sexes absolutely requiring the agency of certain insects to bring pollen from one flower to the other, it is equally preposterous to account for the structure of this parasite, with its relations to several distinct organic beings, by the effects of external conditions, or of habit, or of the volition of the plant itself.

It is, therefore, of the highest importance to gain a clear insight into the means of modification and coadaptation. At the commencement of my observations it seemed to me probable that a careful study of domesticated animals and of cultivated plants would offer the best chance of making out this obscure problem. Nor have I been disappointed; in this and in all other perplexing cases I have invariably found that our knowledge, imperfect though it be, of variation under domestication, afforded the best and safest clue....

Chapter I. Variation under Domestication

... CAUSES OF VARIABILITY

When we look to the individuals of the same variety or sub-variety of our older cultivated plants and animals, one of the first points which strikes us, is, that they generally differ much more from each other, than do the individuals of any one species or variety in a state of nature. When we reflect on the vast diversity of the plants and animals which have been cultivated, and which have varied during all ages under the most different climates and treatment, I think we are driven to conclude that this greater variability is simply due to our domestic productions having been raised under conditions of life not so uniform as, and somewhat different from, those to which the parent-species have been exposed under nature....

... Any variation which is not inherited is unimportant for us. But the number and diversity of inheritable deviations of structure, both those of slight and those of considerable physiological importance, are endless. Dr. Prosper Lucas' treatise, in two large volumes, is the fullest and the best on this subject. No breeder doubts how strong is the tendency to inheritance; that like produces like is his fundamental belief: doubts have been thrown on this principle only by theoretical writers. When any deviation of structure often appears, and we see it in the father and child, we cannot tell whether it may not be due to the same cause having acted on both; but when among individuals, apparently exposed to the same conditions, any very rare deviation, due to some extraordinary combination of circumstances, appears in the parent—say, once among several million individuals—and it reappears in the child, the mere doctrine of chances almost compels us to attribute its reappearance to inheritance....

The laws governing inheritance are for the most part unknown; no one can say why the same peculiarity in different individuals of the same species, or in different species, is sometimes inherited and sometimes not so; why the child often reverts in certain characteristics to its grandfather or grandmother or more remote ancestor; why a peculiarity is often transmitted from one sex to both sexes, or to one sex alone, more commonly but not exclusively to the like sex....

... When we look to the hereditary varieties or races of our domestic animals and plants, and compare them with closely allied species, we generally perceive in each domestic race, as already remarked, less uniformity of character than in true species. Domestic races often have a somewhat monstrous character; by which I mean, that, although differing from each other and from other species of the same genus, in several trifling respects, they often differ in an extreme degree in some one part, both when compared one with another, and more especially when compared with the species under nature to which they are nearest allied....

PRINCIPLES OF SELECTION ANCIENTLY FOLLOWED, AND THEIR EFFECTS

Let us now briefly consider the steps by which domestic races have been produced, either from one or from several allied species. Some effect may be attributed to the direct and definite action of the external conditions of life, and some to habit; but he would be a bold man who would account by such agencies for the differences between a dray and race-horse, a greyhound and bloodhound, a carrier and tumbler pigeon. One of the most remarkable features in our domesticated races is that we see in them adaptation, not indeed to the animal's or plant's own good, but to man's use or fancy.... When we compare the dray-horse and race-horse, the dromedary and camel, the various breeds of sheep fitted either for cultivated land or mountain pasture, with the wool of one breed good for one purpose, and that of another breed for another purpose; when we compare the many breeds of dogs, each good for man in different ways; when we compare the game-cock, so pertinacious in battle, with other breeds so little quarrelsome, with "everlasting layers" which never desire to sit, and with the bantam so small and elegant; when we compare the host of agricultural, culinary, orchard, and flower-garden races of plants, most useful to man at different seasons and for different purposes, or so beautiful in his eyes, we must, I think, look further than to mere variability. We cannot suppose that all the breeds were suddenly produced as perfect and as useful as we now see them; indeed, in many cases, we know that this has not been their history. The key is man's power of accumulative selection: nature gives successive variations; man adds them up in certain directions useful to him. In this sense he may be said to have made for himself useful breeds.

The great power of this principle of selection is not hypothetical. It is certain that several of our eminent breeders have, even within a single lifetime, modified to a large extent their breeds of cattle and sheep....

... UNCONSCIOUS SELECTION

At the present time, eminent breeders try by methodical selection, with a distinct object in view, to make a new strain or sub-breed, superior to anything of the kind in the country. But, for our purpose, a form of selection, which may be called unconscious, and which results from every one trying to possess and breed from the best individual animals, is more important. Thus, a man who intends keeping pointers naturally tries to get as good dogs as he can, and afterwards breeds from his own best dogs, but he has no wish or expectation of permanently altering the breed. Nevertheless we may infer that this process, continued during centuries, would improve and modify any breed, in the same way as Bakewell, Collins, &c., by this very same process, only carried on more methodically, did greatly modify, even during their lifetimes, the forms and qualities of their cattle....

... By a similar process of selection, and by careful training, English racehorses have come to surpass in fleetness and size the parent Arabs, so that the latter, by the regulations for the Goodwood Races, are favoured in the weights which they carry. Lord Spencer and others have shown how the cattle of England have increased in weight and in early maturity, compared with the stock formerly kept in this country. By comparing the accounts given in various old treatises of the former and present state of carrier and tumbler pigeons in Britain, India, and Persia, we can trace the stages through which they have insensibly passed, and come to differ so greatly from the rock-pigeon.

THE TERM, STRUGGLE FOR EXISTENCE, USED IN A WIDE SENSE

... A struggle for existence inevitably follows from the high rate at which all organic beings tend to increase. Every being, which during its natural lifetime produces several eggs or seeds, must suffer destruction during some period of its life, and during some season or occasional year, otherwise, on the principle of geometrical increase, its numbers would quickly become so inordinately great that no country could support the product. Hence, as more individuals are produced than can possibly survive, there must in every case be a struggle for existence, either one individual with another of the same species, or with the individuals of distinct species, or with the physical conditions of life. It is the doctrine of Malthus applied with manifold force to the whole animal and vegetable kingdoms; for in this case there can be no artificial increase of food, and no prudential restraint from marriage. Although some species may be now increasing, more or less rapidly, in numbers, all cannot do so, for the world would not hold them.

There is no exception to the rule that every organic being naturally increases at so high a rate, that, if not destroyed, the earth would soon be covered by the progeny of a single pair. Even slow-breeding man has doubled in twenty-five years, and at this rate, in less than a thousand years, there would literally not be standing room for his progeny....

... In looking at Nature, it is most necessary to keep the foregoing considerations always in mind—never to forget that every single organic being may be said to be striving to the utmost to increase in numbers; that each lives by a struggle at some period of its life; that heavy destruction inevitably falls either on the young or old during each generation or at recurrent intervals. Lighten any check, mitigate the destruction ever so little, and the number of the species will almost instantaneously increase to any amount.

NATURE OF THE CHECKS TO INCREASE

The causes which check the natural tendency of each species to increase are most obscure....

The amount of food for each species, of course, gives the extreme limit to which each can increase; but very frequently it is not the obtaining food, but the serving as prey to other animals, which determines the average number of a species....

When a species, owing to highly favourable circumstances, increases inordinately in numbers in a small tract, epidemics—at least, this seems generally to occur with our game animals—often ensue; and here we have a limiting check independent of the struggle for life....

On the other hand, in many cases, a large stock of individuals of the same species, relatively to the numbers of its enemies, is absolutely necessary for its preservation....

... STRUGGLE FOR LIFE MOST SEVERE BETWEEN INDIVIDUALS AND VARIETIES OF THE SAME SPECIES

As the species of the same genus usually have, though by no means invariably, much similarity in habits and constitution, and always in structure, the struggle will generally be more severe between them, if they come into competition with each other, than between the species of distinct genera. We see this in the recent extension over parts of the United States of one species of swallow having caused the decrease of another species. The recent increase of the missel-thrush in parts of Scotland has caused the decrease of the song-thrush. How frequently we hear of one species of rat taking the place of another species under the most different climates! ...

A corollary of the highest importance may be deduced from the foregoing remarks, namely, that the structure of every organic being is related, in the most essential yet often hidden manner, to that of all other organic beings, with which it comes into competition for food or residence, or from which it has to escape, or on which it preys. This is obvious in the structure of the teeth and talons of the tiger; and in that of the legs and claws of the parasite which clings to the hair on the tiger's body....

Chapter IV. Natural Selection; or the Survival of the Fittest

... How will the struggle for existence, briefly discussed in the last chapter, act in regard to variation? Can the principle of selection, which we have seen is so potent in the hands of man, apply under nature? I think we shall see that it can act most efficiently. Let the endless number of slight variations and individual differences occurring in our domestic productions, and, in a lesser degree, in those under nature, be borne in mind; as well as the strength of the hereditary tendency. Under domestication, it may truly be said that the whole organisation becomes in some degree plastic. But the variability, which we almost universally meet with in our domestic productions is not directly produced, as Hooker and Asa Gray have well remarked, by man; he can neither originate varieties nor prevent their occurrence; he can only preserve and accumulate such as do occur. Unintentionally he exposes organic beings to new and changing conditions of life, and variability ensues; but similar changes of conditions might and do occur under nature. Let it also be borne in mind how infinitely complex and close-fitting are the mutual relations of all organic beings to each other and to their physical conditions of life; and consequently what infinitely varied diversities of structure might be of use to each being under changing conditions of life. Can it then be thought improbable, seeing that variations useful to man have undoubtedly occurred, that other variations useful in some way to each being in the great and complex battle of life, should occur in the course of many successive generations? If such do occur, can we doubt (remembering that many more individuals are born than can possibly survive) that individuals having any advantage, however slight, over others, would have the best chance of surviving and procreating their kind? On the other hand, we may feel sure that any variation in the least degree injurious would be rigidly destroyed. This preservation of favourable individual differences and variations, and the destruction of those which are injurious, I have called Natural Selection, or the Survival of the Fittest. Variations neither useful nor injurious would not be affected by natural selection, and would be left either a fluctuating element, as perhaps we see in certain polymorphic species, or would ultimately become fixed, owing to the nature of the organism and the nature of the conditions.

Several writers have misapprehended or objected to the term Natural Selection. Some have even imagined that natural selection induces variability, whereas it implies only the preservation of such variations as arise and are beneficial to the being under its conditions of life.... Others have objected that the term selection implies conscious choice in the animals which become modified; and it has even been urged that, as plants have no volition, natural selection is not applicable to them! In the literal sense of the word, no doubt, natural selection is a false term.... It has been said that I speak of natural selection as an active power or Deity.... Every one knows what is meant and is implied by such metaphorical expressions; and they are almost necessary for brevity. So again it is difficult to avoid personifying the word Nature; but I mean by nature, only the aggregate action and product of many natural laws, and by laws the sequence of events as ascertained by us. With a little familiarity such superficial objections will be forgotten.

... As man can produce, and certainly has produced, a great result by his methodical and unconscious means of selection, what may not natural selection effect? Man can act only on external and visible characters: Nature, if I may be allowed to personify the natural preservation or survival of the fittest, cares nothing for appearances, except in so far as they are useful to any being. She can act on every internal organ, on every shade of constitutional difference, on the whole machinery of life. Man selects only for his own good; Nature only for that of the being which she tends. Every selected character is fully exercised by her, as is implied by the fact of their selection.... How fleeting are the wishes and efforts of man! How short his time, and consequently how poor will be his results, compared with those accumulated by Nature during whole geological periods! Can we wonder, then, that Nature's productions should be far "truer" in character than man's productions; that they should be infinitely better adapted to the most complex conditions of life, and should plainly bear the stamp of far higher workmanship?

It may metaphorically be said that natural selection is daily and hourly scrutinising, throughout the world, the slightest variations; rejecting those that are bad, preserving and adding up all that are good; silently and insensibly working, whenever and wherever opportunity offers, at the improvement of each organic being in relation to its organic and inorganic conditions of life. We see nothing of these slow changes in progress, until the hand of time has marked the long lapse of ages, and then so imperfect is our view into long-past geological ages that we see only that the forms of life are now different from what they formerly were. ...

SEXUAL SELECTION

... This leads me to say a few words on what I have called sexual selection. This form of selection depends, not on a struggle for existence in relation to other organic beings or to external conditions, but on a struggle between the individuals of one sex, generally the males, for the possession of the other sex. The result is not death to the unsuccessful competitor, but few or no offspring. Sexual selection is, therefore, less rigorous than natural selection. Generally, the most vigorous males, those which are best fitted for their places in nature, will leave most progeny. But in many cases victory depends not so much on general vigour, but on having special weapons, confined to the male sex. A hornless stag or spurless cock would have a poor chance of leaving numerous offspring....

Among birds, the contest is often of a more peaceful character.

All those who have attended to the subject, believe that there is the severest rivalry between the males of many species to attract, by singing, the females. The rock-thrush of Guiana, birds of paradise, and some others, congregate, and successive males display with the most elaborate care, and show off in the best manner, their gorgeous plumage; they likewise perform strange antics before the females, which, standing by as spectators, at last choose the most attractive partner....

... Isolation, also, is an important element in the modification of species through natural selection. In a confined or isolated area, if not very large, the organic and inorganic conditions of life will generally be almost uniform; so that natural selection will tend to modify all the varying individuals of the same species in the same manner. Intercrossing with the inhabitants of the surrounding districts, will also be thus prevented....

... Although isolation is of great importance in the production of new species, on the whole I am inclined to believe that largeness of area is still more important, especially for the production of species which shall prove capable of enduring for a long period, and of spreading widely. Throughout a great and open area, not only will there be a better chance of favourable variations, arising from the large number of individuals of the same species there supported, but the conditions of life are much more complex from the large number of already existing species; and if some of these many species become modified and improved, others will have to be improved in a corresponding degree, or they will be exterminated.... Finally, I conclude that, although small isolated areas have been in some respects highly favourable for the production of new species, yet that the course of modification will generally have been more rapid on large areas; and what is more important, that the new forms produced on large areas, which already have been victorious over many competitors, will be those that will spread most widely, and will give rise to the greatest number of new varieties and species....

...

EXTINCTION CAUSED BY NATURAL SELECTION

... Natural selection acts solely through the preservation of variations in some way advantageous, which consequently endure. Owing to the high geometrical rate of increase of all organic beings, each area is already fully stocked with inhabitants, and it follows from this, that as the favoured forms increase in number, so, generally, will the less favoured decrease and become rare. Rarity, as geology tells us, is the precursor to extinction. We can see that any form which is represented by few individuals will run a good chance of utter extinction, during great fluctuations in the nature or the seasons, or from a temporary increase in the number of its enemies. But we may go further than this; for as new forms are produced, unless we admit that specific forms can go on indefinitely increasing in number, many old forms must become extinct....

We have seen that the species which are most numerous in individuals have the best chance of producing favourable variations within any given period. We have evidence of this, in the facts stated in the second chapter, showing that it is the common and diffused or dominant species which offer the greatest number of recorded varieties. Hence, rare species will be less quickly modified or improved within any given period; they will consequently be beaten in the race for life by the modified and improved descendants of the commoner species.

...

DIVERGENCE OF CHARACTER

... How, then, does the lesser difference between varieties become augmented into the greater difference between species? ...

... In practice, a fancier is, for instance, struck by a pigeon having a slightly shorter beak; another fancier is struck by a pigeon having a rather longer beak; and on the acknowledged principle that "fanciers do not and will not admire a medium standard, but like extremes," they both go on (as has actually occurred with the sub-breeds of the tumbler-pigeon) choosing and breeding from birds with longer and longer beaks, or with shorter and shorter beaks. Again, we may suppose that at an early period of history, the men of one nation or district required swifter horses, while those of another required stronger and bulkier horses. The early differences would be very slight; but, in the course of time, from the continued selection of swifter horses in the one case, and of stronger ones in the other, the differences would become greater, and would be noted as forming two sub-breeds. Ultimately after the lapse of centuries, these sub-breeds would become converted into two well-established and distinct breeds. As the differences became greater, the inferior animals with intermediate characters, being neither very swift nor very strong, would not have been used for breeding, and will thus have tended to disappear. Here, then, we see in man's productions the action of what may be called the principle of divergence, causing differences, at first barely appreciable, steadily to increase, and the breeds to diverge in character, both from each other and from their common parent.

But how, it may be asked, can any analogous principle apply in nature? I believe it can and does apply most efficiently (though it was a long time before I saw how), from the simple circumstance that the more diversified the descendants from any one species become in structure, constitution, and habits, by so much will they be better enabled to seize on many and widely diversified places in the polity of nature, and so be enabled to increase in numbers....

... The truth of the principle that the greatest amount of life can be supported by great diversification of structure, is seen under many natural circumstances. In an extremely small area, especially if freely open to immigration, and where the contest between individual and individual must be very severe, we always find great diversity in its inhabitants.... The advantage of diversification of structure in the inhabitants of the same region is, in fact, the same as that of the physiological division of labour in the organs of the same individual body—a subject so well elucidated by Milne Edwards. No physiologist doubts that a stomach by being adapted to digest vegetable matter alone, or flesh alone, draws most nutriment from these substances. So in the general economy of any land, the more widely and perfectly the animals and plants are diversified for different habits of life, so will a greater number of individuals be capable of there supporting themselves. A set of animals, with their organisation but little diversified, could hardly compete with a set more perfectly diversified in structure....

SUMMARY OF CHAPTER IV

If under changing conditions of life organic beings present individual differences in almost every part of their structure, and this cannot be disputed; if there be, owing to their geometrical rate of increase, a severe struggle for life at some age, season or year, and this certainly cannot be disputed; then, considering the infinite complexity of the relations of all organic beings to each other and to their conditions of life, causing an infinite diversity in structure, constitution, and habits, to be advantageous to them, it would be a most extraordinary fact if no variations had ever occurred useful to each being's own welfare, in the same manner as so many variations have occurred useful to man. But if variations useful to any organic being ever do occur, assuredly individuals thus characterised will have the best chance of being preserved in the struggle for life; and from the strong principle of inheritance, these will tend to produce offspring similarly characterised. This principle of preservation, or the survival of the fittest, I have called natural selection. It leads to the improvement of each creature in relation to its organic and inorganic conditions of life; and consequently, in most cases, to what must be regarded as an advance in organisation. Nevertheless, low and simple forms will long endure if well fitted for their simple conditions of life.

Natural selection, on the principle of qualities being inherited at corresponding ages, can modify the egg, seed, or young as easily as the adult. Among many animals sexual selection will have given its aid to ordinary selection by assuring to the most vigorous and best adapted males the greatest number of offspring. Sexual selection will also give characters useful to the males alone in their struggles or rivalry with other males; and these characters will be transmitted to one sex or to both sexes, according to the form of inheritance which prevails.

Whether natural selection has really thus acted in adapting the various forms of life to their several conditions and stations, must be judged by the general tenour and balance of evidence given in the following chapters. But we have already seen how it entails extinction; and how largely extinction has acted in the world's history, geology plainly declares. Natural selection, also, leads to divergence of character; for the more organic beings diverge in structure, habits and constitution, by so much the more can a large number be supported on the area,—of which we see proof by looking to the inhabitants of any small spot, and to the productions naturalised in foreign lands. Therefore, during the modification of the descendants of any one species, and during the incessant struggle of all species to increase in numbers, the more diversified the descendants become, the better will be their chance of success in the battle for life. Thus the small differences distinguishing varieties of the same species, steadily tend to increase, till they equal the greater differences between species of the same genus, or even of distinct genera.

We have seen that it is the common, the widely diffused, and widely ranging species, belonging to the larger genera within each class, which vary most; and these tend to transmit to their modified offspring that superiority which now makes them dominant in their own countries. Natural selection, as has just been remarked, leads to divergence of character and to much extinction of the less improved and intermediate forms of life. On these principles, the nature of the affinities, and the generally well defined distinctions between the innumerable organic beings in each class throughout the world, may be explained. It is a truly wonderful fact—the wonder of which we are apt to overlook from familiarity—that all animals and all plants throughout all time and space should be related to each other in groups, subordinate to groups, in the manner which we everywhere behold—namely, varieties of the same species most closely related, species of the same genus less closely and unequally related, forming sections and sub-genera, species of distinct genera much less closely related, and genera related in different degrees, forming sub-families, families, orders, sub-classes, and classes. The several subordinate groups in any class cannot be ranked in a single file, but seem clustered round points, and these round other points, and so on in almost endless cycles. If species had been independently created, no explanation would have been possible of this kind of classification; but it is explained through inheritance and the complex action of natural selection, entailing extinction and divergence of character, as we have seen illustrated in the diagram.

The affinities of all the beings of the same class have sometimes been represented by a great tree. I believe this simile largely speaks the truth. The green and budding twigs may represent existing species; and those produced during former years may represent the long succession of extinct species. At each period of growth all the growing twigs have tried to branch out on all sides, and to overtop and kill the surrounding twigs and branches, in the same manner as species and groups of species have at all times overmastered other species in the great battle for life. The limbs divided into great branches, and these into lesser and lesser branches, were themselves once, when the tree was young, budding twigs; and this connexion of the former and present buds by ramifying branches may well represent the classification of all extinct and living species in groups subordinate to groups. Of the many twigs which flourished when the tree was a mere bush, only two or three, now grown into great branches, yet survive and bear the other branches; so with the species which lived during long-past geological periods, very few have left living and modified descendants. From the first growth of the tree, many a limb and branch has decayed and dropped off; and these fallen branches of various sizes may represent those whole orders, families, and genera which have now no living representatives, and which are known to us only in a fossil state. As we here and there see a thin, straggling branch springing from a fork low down in a tree, and which by some chance has been favoured and is still alive on its summit, so we occasionally see an animal like the Ornithorhynchus or Lepidosiren, which in some small degree connects by its affinities two large branches of life, and which has apparently been saved from fatal competition by having inhabited a protected station. As buds give rise by growth to fresh buds, and these, if vigorous, branch out and overtop on all sides many a feebler branch, so by generation I believe it has been with the great Tree of Life, which fills with its dead and broken branches the crust of the earth, and covers the surface with its ever-branching and beautiful ramifications.

2.8 Svante Arrhenius (1859–1927)

Habitat is one of the things for which organisms compete in the struggle for existence, along with food, mates, and so on (see 2.7). Ordinarily, we think of habitat in terms of a localized space somewhere within the biosphere enclosed between Earth's crust and its upper atmosphere. Environmental sciences, however, have helped us understand habitat as a function of large-scale conditions set by climate and global patterns of warming and cooling. Studies of glacial ice and tree rings, for example, have revealed strong correlations between temperature, atmospheric conditions and the availability of food sources in the past. Atmospheric boundaries are more fluid than geographical boundaries, so environmental sciences help us understand habitability as a global condition.

Quite simply, if the planet gets colder (e.g., the ice age of 12,000 years ago) or warmer (e.g., global warming today), then changing living conditions will make it so difficult for some species to survive that they go extinct. Large dinosaur species could not survive sudden, catastrophic environmental changes 65 million years ago, for example.

The following excerpt from Swedish scientist Svante Arrhenius is a seminal contribution to environmental science. Here Arrhenius presents the first evidence that carbon dioxide (CO_2, "carbonic acid") in Earth's atmosphere affects global temperature. In short, Arrhenius is the first to notice current trends in global warming. Not only does he identify a correlation between increasing levels of atmospheric CO_2 and temperature, he explains the chemical process that regulates this relationship. Chemists already understood the process by which gaseous CO_2 absorbs heat in experimental conditions. In the article from which our passage is excerpted, Arrhenius establishes a statistically significant correlation in the environmental data, and he explains that correlation as a function of this well-established chemistry: light from the sun is absorbed by atmospheric CO_2 particles in such a way as to heat the surface of the planet.

~

from "On the Influence of Carbonic Acid in the Air upon the Temperature of the Ground"

The London, Edinburgh, and Dublin Philosophical Magazine and Journal of Science [Fifth Series][1]

April 1896

1. Introduction: Observations of Langley on Atmospherical Absorption

A great deal has been written on the influence of the absorption of the atmosphere upon the climate. Tyndall[2] in particular has pointed out the enormous importance of this question. To him it was chiefly the diurnal and annual variations of the temperature that were lessened by this circumstance. Another side of the question, that has long attracted the attention of physicists, is this: Is the mean temperature of the ground in any way influenced by the presence of heat-absorbing gases in the atmosphere? Fournier[3] maintained that the atmosphere acts like the glass of a hot-house, because it lets through the light rays of the sun but retains the dark rays from the ground. This idea was elaborated by Pouillet;[4] and Langley was by some of his researches led to the view, that "the temperature of the earth under direct sunshine, even though our atmosphere were present as now, would probably fall to -200° C., if that atmosphere did not possess the quality of selective absorption."[5] This view, which was founded on too wide a use of Newton's law of cooling, must be abandoned, as Langley himself in a later memoir showed that the full moon, which certainly does not possess any sensible heat-absorbing atmosphere, has a "mean effective temperature" of about 45° C.[6]

The air retains heat (light or dark) in two different ways. On the one hand, the heat suffers a selective diffusion on its passage through the air; on the other hand, some of the atmospheric gases absorb considerable quantities of heat. These two actions are very different. The selective diffusion is extraordinarily great for the ultra-violet rays, and diminishes continuously with increasing wave-length of the light, so that it is insensible for the rays that form the chief

1 Extract from a paper presented to the Royal Swedish Academy of Sciences, 11th December 1895. Communicated by the Author.
2 'Heat a Mode of Motion,' 2nd ed. p. 405 (Lond., 1865).
3 *Mem. De l'Ac. R. d. Sci. de l'Inst. de France*, t. vii. 1827.
4 *Comptes rendus*, t. vii. P. 41 (1838).
5 Langley, 'Professional Papers of the Signal Service,' No. 15. "Researches on Solar Heat," p. 123 (Washington, 1884).
6 Langley, 'The Temperature of the Moon.' Mem. Of the National Academy of Sciences, vol. iv. 9th mem. p. 193 (1890).

part of the radiation from a body of the mean temperature of the earth.[7]

The selective absorption of the atmosphere is, according to the researches of Tyndall, Lecher and Pernter, Röntgen, Heine, Langley, Ångström, Paschen, and others,[8] of a wholly different kind. It is not exerted by the chief mass of the air, but in a high degree by aqueous vapour and carbonic acid, which are present in the air in small quantities. Further, this absorption is not continuous over the whole spectrum, but nearly insensible in the light part of it, and chiefly limited to the long-waved part, where it manifests itself in very well-defined absorption-bands, which fall off rapidly on both sides.[9] The influence of this absorption is comparatively small on the heat from the sun, but must be of great importance in the transmission of rays from the earth. Tyndall held the opinion that the water-vapour has the greatest influence, whilst other authors, for instance Lecher and Pernter, are inclined to think that the carbonic acid plays the more important part. The researches of Paschen show that these gases are both very effective, so that probably sometimes the one, sometimes the other, may have the greater effect according to the circumstances.

7 Langley, 'Prof Papers,' No. 15, p. 151. I have tried to calculate a formula for the value of the absorption due to the selective reflexion, as determined by Langley. Among the different formulae examined, the following agrees best with the experimental results:—

$$\log a = b\,(1/\lambda) + c\,(1/\lambda)^3.$$

I have determined the coefficients of this formula by aid of the method of least squares, and have found

$$b = -0.0463, \qquad c = 0.008204.$$

a represents the strength of a ray of the wave-length λ (expressed in μ) after it has entered with the strength 1 and passed through the air-mass 1. The close agreement with experiment will be seen from the following table:—

λ	$a^{1/7.6}$ (*obs*).	$a^{1/7.6}$ (*calc*.).	Prob. error.
0.358 μ	0.904	0.911	
0.383	0.920	0.923	0.0047
0.416	0.935	0.934	
0.440	0.942	0.941	
0.468	0.950	0.947	0.0028
0.550	0.960	0.960	
0.615	0.968	0.967	
0.781	0.978	0.977	
0.870	0.982	0.980	0.0017
1.01	0.985	0.984	
1.20	0.987	0.987	
1.50	0.989	0.990	0.0011
2.59	0.990	0.993	0.0018

For ultraviolet rays the absorption becomes extremely great in accordance with facts.

As one may see from the probable errors which I have placed alongside for the least concordant values and also for the one value (1.50 μ), where the probable error is extremely small, the differences are just of the magnitude that one might expect in an exactly fitting formula. The curves for the formula and for the experimental values cut each other at four points (1/λ = 2.43, 1.83, 1.28, and 0.82 respectively). From the formula we may estimate the value of the selective reflection for those parts of the spectrum that prevail in the heat from the moon and the earth (angle of deviation = 38 -36°, λ= 10.4-24.4μ). We find that the absorption from this cause varies between 0.5 and 1 p.c. for air-mass 1. This insensible action, which is wholly covered by the experimental errors, I have neglected in the ... calculations.

8 Vide Winkelmann, *Handbuch der Physik.*

9 Cf., e.g., Trabert, *Meteorologische Zeitschrift*, Bd. ii. p. 238 (1894).

2.9 Albert Einstein (1879–1955)

Albert Einstein's Relativity Theory returns to some of the fundamental claims in Isaac Newton's work on light and gravity (2.6). Relativity was developed in two stages and presents a new approach to mechanics (i.e., the behaviour of physical objects in space and time). First, Einstein's *Special Theory of Relativity* (published in 1905) posits new laws to explain motion in "inertial systems," that is, when an object is not accelerating or decelerating with respect to its framework (it is called the "special theory" because it covers only one species of motion). Second, the *General Theory* (1916) expands the scope of relativity to explain motion in both inertial and non-inertial systems ("non-inertial motion" is acceleration or deceleration with respect to a framework). Most importantly for our purposes, the *General Theory* introduces a novel account of gravity, which seems to overcome a problem that Newton could not solve.

Newton's first law is the principle of inertia: all objects at rest will remain at rest until a force is imposed on them, and all objects in motion will remain in motion (in a straight line) until they meet external resistance (2.6). Accelerated motion enters the picture with Newton's second law for impelled forces: the momentum transmitted to a motionless object accelerates that object in the direction of the impelled force; similarly, a moving object decelerates upon meeting resistance (2.6). Recall also that Newton posited gravity as a universal phenomenon that is intrinsically associated with mass (2.6). The effects of gravity can be described in terms of geometrical proportions: it is simultaneously directly proportional to the masses of the objects (m_1 and m_2), and inversely proportional to the distance between them; hence, the formula $g = m_1m_2 /d^2$. Still, Newton was uncomfortable with the idea that gravitational forces act at a distance. Because every other force in his system required contact in order to produce an effect, gravity seems exceptional. This problem is compounded by Newton's explicit rejection of "occult forces" (i.e., non-natural forces, 2.6). Einstein's general theory of relativity redefines several key concepts to resolve these tensions in Classical Mechanics, in particular those related to gravitation.

We see the final stage of Einstein's solution to these problems in the opening pages of the following passage. First, in our excerpt from Ch. XX of *The Meaning of Relativity* he notes that there is no fundamental difference between (a) the effect of accelerated motion and (b) the effect of gravity. Both accelerated motion and gravity manifest as a continuously exerted force impelling objects in a particular direction. What Classical Mechanics treats as two distinct principles (acceleration and gravity) Relativity treats together. Second, Einstein has the benefit of twentieth-century chemistry and atom theory, which no longer conceived of atoms as tiny, solid particles; rather, atoms have a complex structure and do not "fill" their space as continuously solid matter, so at the sub-microscopic level contact is not essential to causal relations, as Newton had supposed. Third, Newton conceived of space as an empty and neutral backdrop to the dynamic interactions of discrete objects. According to General Relativity, however, massive objects are analyzed as "fields" that change the shape of space around them; mass and space interact dynamically, and the law of gravity describes the diminishing extent of a field, not a force that reaches out into inert, empty space.

With regard to argumentation, Einstein disagrees with Newton and Bacon about the value of induction. According to the final pages of the following selection, observations *test* theoretical models and equations, and are not the basis of them. In our excerpt from Ch. XXI, Einstein expresses dissatisfaction with a key presupposition of Classical Mechanics: why should we use as our primary frame of reference inertial systems (K) rather than non-inertial ones (K′)? Newton presents a set of equations that describe mechanical causes within an inertial frame of reference (i.e., linear motion or rest is the fundamental state of things as Law I indicates), whereas the equations derived from General Relativity theory do not accept this assumption (the equations are not included here). How then can we choose between one set of equations and another (or, what is the same thing, one theory and another)? In the history of science, the question was decided in favour of General Relativity when it was able to explain and predict things that Classical Mechanics could not. In an appendix to *The Meaning of Relativity* Einstein summarizes three experimental observations that can be explained by General Relativity and not by Newton's Classical Mechanics. Our excerpt from the appendix includes one of these cases, that of Arthur Eddington's expedition to test one unique implication of Einstein's equations: light bending in the curved space around a massive object; in 1919, Eddington observed this phenomenon when light from a star that was physically *behind* the sun was visible during an eclipse. Einstein interprets this result and others as 'confirming' General Relativity.

~

from The Meaning of Relativity

Chapter XIX
The Gravitational Field

"If we pick up a stone and then let it go, why does it fall to the ground?" The usual answer to this question is: "Because it is attracted by the earth." Modern physics formulates the answer rather differently for the following reason. As a result of the more careful study of electromagnetic phenomena, we have come to regard action at a distance as a process impossible without the intervention of some intermediary medium. If, for instance, a magnet attracts a piece of iron, we cannot be content to regard this as meaning that the magnet acts directly on the iron through the intermediate empty space, but we are constrained to imagine—after the manner of Faraday—that the magnet always calls into being something physically real in the space around it, that something being what we call a "magnetic field." In its turn this magnetic field operates on the piece of iron, so that the latter strives to move towards the magnet. We shall not discuss here the justification for this incidental conception, which is indeed a somewhat arbitrary one. We shall only mention that with its aid electromagnetic phenomena can be theoretically represented much more satisfactorily than without it, and this applies particularly to the transmission of electromagnetic waves. The effects of gravitation also are regarded in an analogous manner.

The action of the earth on the stone takes place indirectly. The earth produces in its surroundings a gravitational field, which acts on the stone and produces its motion of fall. As we know from experience, the intensity of the action on a body diminishes according to a quite definite law, as we proceed farther and farther away from the earth. From our point of view this means: The law governing the properties of the gravitational field in space must be a perfectly definite one, in order correctly to represent the diminution of gravitational action with the distance from operative bodies. It is something like this: The body (*e.g.*, the earth) produces a field in its immediate neighbourhood directly: the intensity and direction of the field at points farther removed from the body are thence determined by the law which governs the properties in space of the gravitational fields themselves.

In contrast to electric and magnetic fields, the gravitational field exhibits a most remarkable property, which is of fundamental importance for what follows. Bodies which are moving under the sole influence of a gravitational field receive an acceleration, *which does not in the least depend either on the material or on the physical state of the body.* For instance, a piece of lead and a piece of wood fall in exactly the same manner in a gravitational field (*in vacuo*), when they start off from rest or with the same initial velocity. This law, which holds most accurately, can be expressed in a different form in the light of the following consideration.

According to Newton's law of motion, we have

(Force) = (inertial mass) × (acceleration),

where the "inertial mass" is a characteristic constant of the accelerated body. If now gravitation is the cause of the acceleration, we then have

(Force) = (gravitational mass) × (intensity of the gravitational field),

where the "gravitational mass" is likewise a characteristic constant for the body. From these two relations follows:

$$(\text{acceleration}) = \frac{(\text{gravitational mass})}{(\text{inertial mass})} \times (\text{intensity of the gravitational field}).$$

If now, as we find from experience, the acceleration is to be independent of the nature and the condition of the body and always the same for a given gravitational field, then the ratio of the gravitational to the inertial mass must likewise be the same for all bodies. By a suitable choice of units we can thus make this ratio equal to unity. We then have the following law: The *gravitational* mass of a body is equal to its *inertial* mass.

It is true that this important law had hitherto been recorded in mechanics, but it had not been *interpreted.* A satisfactory interpretation can be obtained only if we recognise the following fact: *The same* quality of a body manifests itself according to circumstances as "inertia" or as "weight" (lit. "heaviness"). In the following section we shall show to what extent this is actually the case, and how this question is connected with the general postulate of relativity....

Chapter XX
The Equality of Inertial and Gravitational Mass as an Argument for the General Postulate of Relativity

We imagine a large portion of empty space, so far removed from stars and other appreciable masses, that we have before us approximately the conditions required by the fundamental law of Galilei. It is then possible to choose a Galileian reference-body for this part of space (world), relative to which points at rest remain at rest and points in motion continue permanently in uniform rectilinear motion. As reference-body let us imagine a spacious chest resembling a room with an observer inside who is equipped with apparatus. Gravitation naturally does not exist for this observer. He must fasten himself with strings to the floor, otherwise the slightest impact against the floor will cause him to rise slowly towards the ceiling of the room.

To the middle of the lid of the chest is fixed externally a hook with rope attached, and now a "being" (what kind of a being is immaterial to us) begins pulling at this with a constant force. The chest together with the observer then begin to move "upwards" with a uniformly accelerated motion. In course of time their velocity will reach unheard-of values—provided that we are viewing all this from another reference-body which is not being pulled with a rope.

But how does the man in the chest regard the process? The acceleration of the chest will be transmitted to him by the reaction of the floor of the chest. He must therefore take up this pressure by means of his legs if he does not wish to be laid out full length on the floor. He is then standing in the chest in exactly the same way as anyone stands in a room of a house on our earth. If he release a body which he previously had in his hand, the acceleration of the chest will no longer be transmitted to this body, and for this reason the body will approach the floor of the chest with an accelerated relative motion. The observer will further convince himself *that the acceleration of the body towards the floor of the chest is always of the same magnitude, whatever kind of body he may happen to use for the experiment.*

Relying on his knowledge of the gravitational field (as it was discussed in the preceding section [not included here]), the man in the chest will thus come to the conclusion that he and the chest are in a gravitational field which is constant with regard to time. Of course he will be puzzled for a moment as to why the chest does not fall in this gravitational field. Just then, however, he discovers the hook in the middle of the lid of the chest and the rope which is attached to it, and he consequently comes to the conclusion that the chest is suspended at rest in the gravitational field.

Ought we to smile at the man and say that he errs in his conclusion? I do not believe we ought to if we wish to remain consistent; we must rather admit that his mode of grasping the situation violates neither reason nor known mechanical laws. Even though it is being accelerated with respect to the "Galileian space" first considered, we can nevertheless regard the chest as being at rest. We have thus good grounds for extending the principle of relativity to include bodies of reference which are accelerated with respect to each other, and as a result we have gained a powerful argument for a generalised postulate of relativity.

We must note carefully that the possibility of this mode of interpretation rests on the fundamental property of the gravitational field of giving all bodies the same acceleration, or, what comes to the same thing, on the law of the equality of inertial and gravitational mass. If this natural law did not exist, the man in the accelerated chest would not be able to interpret the behaviour of the bodies around him on the supposition of a gravitational field, and he would not be justified on the grounds of experience in supposing his reference-body to be "at rest."

Suppose that the man in the chest fixes a rope to the inner side of the lid, and that he attaches a body to the free end of the rope. The result of this will be to stretch the rope so that it will hang "vertically" downwards. If we ask for an opinion of the cause of tension in the rope, the man in the chest will say: "The suspended body experiences a downward force in the gravitational field, and this is neutralised by the tension of the rope; what determines the magnitude of the tension of the rope is the *gravitational mass* of the suspended body." On the other hand, an observer who is poised freely in space will interpret the condition of things thus: "The rope must perforce take part in the accelerated motion of the chest, and it transmits this motion to the body attached to it. The tension of the rope is just large enough to effect the acceleration of the body. That which determines the magnitude of the tension of the rope is the *inertial mass* of the body." Guided by this example, we see that our extension of the principle of relativity implies the *necessity* of the law of the equality of inertial and gravitational mass. Thus we have obtained a physical interpretation of this law.

From our consideration of the accelerated chest we see that a general theory of relativity must yield important results on the laws of gravitation. In point of fact, the systematic pursuit of the general idea of relativity has supplied the laws satisfied by the gravitational field. Before proceeding farther, however, I must warn the reader against a misconception suggested by these considerations. A gravitational field exists for the man in the chest, despite the fact that there was no such field for the co-ordinate system first chosen. Now we might easily suppose that the existence of a gravitational field is always only an *apparent* one. We might also think that, regardless of the kind of gravitational field which may be present, we could always choose another reference-body such that *no* gravitational field exists with reference to it. This is by no means true for all gravitational fields, but only for those of quite special form. It is, for instance, impossible to choose a body of reference such that, as judged from it, the gravitational field of the earth (in its entirety) vanishes....

Chapter XXI
In What Respects Are the Foundations of Classical Mechanics and of the Special Theory of Relativity Unsatisfactory?

We have already stated several times that classical mechanics starts out from the following law: Material particles sufficiently far removed from other material particles continue to move uniformly in a straight line or continue in a state of rest. We have also repeatedly emphasised that this fundamental law can only be valid for bodies of reference *K*[1] which possess certain unique states of motion, and which are in uniform translational motion relative to each other. Relative to other reference-bodies *K* the law is not valid. Both in classical mechanics and in the special theory of relativity we therefore differentiate between reference-bodies *K* relative to which the recognised "laws of nature" can be said to hold, and reference-bodies *K* relative to which these laws do not hold.

But no person whose mode of thought is logical can rest satisfied with this condition of things. He asks: "How does it come that certain reference-bodies (or their states of motion) are given priority over other reference-bodies (or their states of motion)? *What is the reason for this preference?* In order to show clearly what I mean by this question, I shall make use of a comparison.

I am standing in front of a gas range. Standing alongside of each other on the range are two pans so much alike that one may be mistaken for the other. Both are half full of water. I notice that steam is being emitted continuously from the one pan, but not from the other. I am surprised at this, even if I have never seen either a gas range or a pan before. But if I now notice a luminous something of bluish colour under the first pan but not under the other, I cease to be astonished, even if I have never before seen a gas flame. For I can only say that this bluish something will cause the emission of the steam, or at least *possibly* it may do so. If, however, I notice the bluish something in neither case, and if I observe that the one continuously emits steam whilst the other does not, then I shall remain astonished and dissatisfied until I have discovered some circumstance to which I can attribute the different behaviour of the two pans.

Analogously, I seek in vain for a real something in classical mechanics (or in the special theory of

1 Editor's note: *K* here indicates a frame of reference that is inertial, a presupposition of Newton's laws of Classical Mechanics. *K′*, however, indicates a frame of reference that is non-inertial (or accelerating).

relativity) to which I can attribute the different behaviour of bodies considered with respect to the referencesystems K and K'.[2] Newton saw this objection and attempted to invalidate it, but without success. But E. Mach recognised it most clearly of all, and because of this objection he claimed that mechanics must be placed on a new basis. It can only be got rid of by means of a physics which is conformable to the general principle of relativity, since the equations of such a theory hold for every body of reference, whatever may be its state of motion.[3] ...

Appendix III
The Experimental Confirmation of the General Theory of Relativity

From a systematic theoretical point of view, we may imagine the process of evolution of an empirical science to be a continuous process of induction. Theories are evolved and are expressed in short compass as statements of a large number of individual observations in the form of empirical laws, from which the general laws can be ascertained by comparison. Regarded in this way, the development of a science bears some resemblance to the compilation of a classified catalogue. It is, as it were, a purely empirical enterprise.

But this point of view by no means embraces the whole of the actual process; for it slurs over the important part played by intuition and deductive thought in the development of an exact science. As soon as a science has emerged from its initial stages, theoretical advances are no longer achieved merely by a process of arrangement. Guided by empirical data, the investigator rather develops a system of thought which, in general, is built up logically from a small number of fundamental assumptions, the so-called axioms. We call such a system of thought a *theory*. The theory finds the justification for its existence in the fact that it correlates a large number of single observations, and it is just here that the "truth" of the theory lies.

Corresponding to the same complex of empirical data, there may be several theories, which differ from one another to a considerable extent. But as regards the deductions from the theories which are capable of being tested, the agreement between the theories may be so complete that it becomes difficult to find any deductions in which the two theories differ from each other. As an example, a case of general interest is available in the province of biology, in the Darwinian theory of the development of species by selection in the struggle for existence, and in the theory of development which is based on the hypothesis of the hereditary transmission of acquired characters.

We have another instance of far-reaching agreement between the deductions from two theories in Newtonian mechanics on the one hand, and the general theory of relativity on the other. This agreement goes so far, that up to the present we have been able to find only a few deductions from the general theory of relativity which are capable of investigation, and to which the physics of pre-relativity days does not also lead, and this despite the profound difference in the fundamental assumptions of the two theories. In what follows, we shall again consider these important deductions, and we shall also discuss the empirical evidence appertaining to them which has hitherto been obtained....

(B) DEFLECTION OF LIGHT BY A GRAVITATIONAL FIELD

In Section XXII [not included here] it has been already mentioned that according to the general theory of relativity, a ray of light will experience a curvature of its path when passing through a gravitational field, this

2 The objection is of importance more especially when the state of motion of the reference-body is of such a nature that it does not require any external agency for its maintenance, *e.g.*, in the case when the reference-body is rotating uniformly.

3 Editor's note: For practical reasons we have not included these equations here. They are technical in form and quite opaque to non-specialists. They are still used by physicists today.

curvature being similar to that experienced by the path of a body which is projected through a gravitational field. As a result of this theory, we should expect that a ray of light which is passing close to a heavenly body would be deviated towards the latter. For a ray of light which passes the sun at a distance of Δ sun-radii from its centre, the angle of deflection (a) should amount to

$$a = \frac{1.7 \text{ seconds of arc}}{\Delta}$$

It may be added that, according to the theory, half of this deflection is produced by the Newtonian field of attraction of the sun, and the other half by the geometrical modification ("curvature") of space caused by the sun.

This result admits of an experimental test by means of the photographic registration of stars during a total eclipse of the sun. The only reason why we must wait for a total eclipse is because at every other time the atmosphere is so strongly illuminated by the light from the sun that the stars situated near the sun's disc are invisible. The predicted effect can be seen clearly from the accompanying diagram. If the sun (S) were not present, a star which is practically infinitely distant would be seen in the direction D_1, as observed from the earth. But as a consequence of the deflection of light from the star by the sun, the star will be seen in the direction D_2, i.e., at a somewhat greater distance from the centre of the sun than corresponds to its real position.

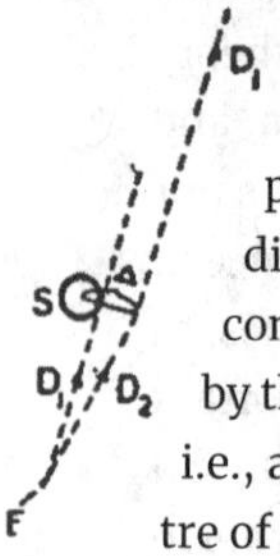

In practice, the question is tested in the following way. The stars in the neighbourhood of the sun are photographed during a solar eclipse. In addition, a second photograph of the same stars is taken when the sun is situated at another position in the sky, *i.e.*, a few months earlier or later. As compared with the standard photograph, the positions of the stars on the eclipse photograph ought to appear displaced radially outwards (away from the centre of the sun) by an amount corresponding to the angle a.

We are indebted to the Royal Society and to the Royal Astronomical Society for the investigation of this important deduction. Undaunted by the war and by difficulties of both a material and a psychological nature aroused by the war, these societies equipped two expeditions—to Sobral (Brazil), and to the island of Principe (West Africa)—and sent several of Britain's most celebrated astronomers (Eddington, Cottingham, Crommelin, Davidson), in order to obtain photographs of the solar eclipse of 29th May, 1919. The relative discrepancies to be expected between the stellar photographs obtained during the eclipse and the comparison photographs amounted to a few hundredths of a millimetre only. Thus great accuracy was necessary in making the adjustments required for the taking of the photographs, and in their subsequent measurement.

The results of the measurements confirmed the theory in a thoroughly satisfactory manner. The rectangular components of the observed and of the calculated deviations of the stars (in seconds of arc) are set forth in the following table of results:

Number of the Star	First Co-ordinate		Second Co-ordinate	
	Observed	Calculated	Observed	Calculated
11	- 0.19	- 0.22	+0.16	+0.02
5	+0.29	+0.31	- 0.46	- 0.43
4	+0.11	+0.10	+0.83	+0.74
3	+0.20	+0.12	+ 1.00	+0.87
6	+0.10	+0.04	+0.57	+0.40
10	- 0.08	+0.09	+0.35	+0.32
2	+0.95	+0.85	- 0.27	- 0.09

2.10 Karl Popper (1904–1994)

Like Aristotle, Karl Popper traces the source of our impulse to conduct scientific research to "amazement" (an alternative translation of "wonder" in Aristotle's *Metaphysics*, 2.3.1). Popper focuses on scientific argumentation rather than the content of science, and his analysis aims to demarcate scientific reasoning from other kinds of reasoning (in particular, commonsense). On all but one essential point, Popper's account of scientific argumentation agrees with Einstein. That one point of difference is crucial, however: unlike Einstein, he does not think that a scientific theory can be "confirmed" by a successful prediction.

First, Popper thinks that there is no infallible *base* on which scientific knowledge sits and which thereby warrants all other claims as certain. Induction, in particular, is logically inadequate to serve such a purpose. No matter how many white swans we observe, there is never sufficient inductive evidence to assert with certainty that "All swans are white." Indeed, for Europeans this general claim was falsified (to use Popper's term) when explorers first sighted black swans in Australia. More importantly, no matter how many objects we observe behaving under the influence of gravity, we can never rule out the possibility of future exceptions. Because unobserved exceptions are always possible, induction can never certify a general claim. Logicians call this the problem of induction. In the long, complex debate over this problem, Popper and Einstein stand diametrically opposed to Bacon (2.4) and Newton (2.6).

According to Popper, working scientists avoid the problem of induction by reversing the relationship between evidence and theory posited by Bacon. In science, as in commonsense, we rely on our natural impulse to formulate abstract and general claims. This impulse is fallible, however, so all such theoretical claims must be accepted provisionally rather than conclusively. Whenever this impulse is activated we generate several hypotheses, and then we search for the most acceptable one in a process of elimination. In both commonsense and science, provisionally accepted claims that survive testing remain acceptable, and those that do not are cast aside.

Central to both scientific and commonsense reasoning are problems that we want to solve. The core structure of commonsense reasoning is a three-stage process: identification of a problem (finding food for one's next meal); the tentative proposal of solutions (look in places x, y, and z); elimination by trial and error of unsuccessful proposed solutions (not x or y). In science, the problems and solutions are entirely theoretical, and the elimination proceeds by empirical testing. Scientific reasoning is therefore objective and more rigorous than commonsense, but its basic operation is not intrinsically more complex than commonsense. Four stages mark scientific reasoning: (1) an existing problem captures someone's attention; (2) tentative theories are formulated to solve the problem; (3) attempts are made to eliminate theories that do not work; (4) new problems are generated from the critical discussion of the surviving theories. Since critical discussion identifies new problems, the cycle from (1)–(4) is continuous and has no set starting point.

Throughout the history of science this process of theory-generation, testing, and revision has eliminated innumerable false solutions to problems. Popper calls the operation of theory-elimination *falsification* because a theory that generates an inaccurate prediction must be false. The remaining theories, which have not been falsified, have been subjected to intense critical scrutiny. In this way, science makes progress, even if it never arrives at certain conclusions. A criterion for accepting and rejecting theories thereby justifies characterizing the history of science in terms of evolutionary progress.

from "The Logic and Evolution of Scientific Theory"

A *problem* arises for the animal if an expectation proves to have been wrong. This then leads to testing movements, to attempts to replace the wrong expectation with a new one.

If a higher organism is too often disappointed in its expectations, it caves in. It cannot solve the problem; it perishes.

I would like to present what I have said so far about learning through trial and error in a three-stage model. The model has the following three stages:

1 *the problem;*
2 *the attempted solutions;*
3 *the elimination.*

So, the first stage in our model is *the problem*. The problem arises when some kind of disturbance takes place—a disturbance either of innate expectations or of expectations that have been discovered or learnt through trial and error.

The second stage in our model consists of *attempted solutions*—that is, attempts *to solve the problem*.

The third stage in our model is the *elimination* of unsuccessful solutions.

Pluralism is essential to this three-stage model. The first stage, the problem itself, may appear in the singular; but not the second stage, which I have called 'attempted solutions' in the plural. Already in the case of animals we speak of testing movements, in the plural. There would be little sense in calling one particular movement a testing movement.

Stage 2, the attempted solutions, are [sic] thus testing movements and therefore in the plural; they are subject to the process *of elimination* in the third stage of our model.

Stage 3, the *elimination*, is *negative*. The elimination is fundamentally the elimination of *mistakes*. If an unsuccessful or misguided solution is eliminated, the problem remains unsolved and gives rise to new attempted solutions.

But what happens if an attempted solution is eventually successful? Two things happen. First, the successful solution is *learnt*. Among animals this usually means that, when a similar problem appears again, the earlier testing movements, including unsuccessful ones, are briefly and sketchily repeated in their original order; they are run through until the successful solution is reached.

Learning means that unsuccessful or discarded solutions drop more and more to the level of passing references, so that eventually the successful attempt at a solution appears to be almost the only one left. This is the elimination procedure, which depends upon a pluralism of attempted solutions.

The organism may be said to have thus learnt a new *expectation*. We may describe its behaviour by saying that it expects the problem to be solved through testing movements and, in the end, through the final testing movement that is not eliminated.

As we shall soon see, the development of this expectation by the organism has its scientific counterpart in the formation of hypotheses or theories. But before I turn to the formation of scientific theories, I should like to point out another biological application of my three-stage model. My *three-stage model*,

1 *the problem;*
2 *the attempted solutions;*
3 *the elimination,*

may also be understood as the schema of Darwin's theory of evolution. It is applicable not only to the evolution of the individual organism but also to *the evolution of species*. In the language of our three-stage model, a change in either the environmental conditions or the inner structure of the organism produces a *problem*. It is *a problem of species adaptation*: that is, the species can survive only if it solves the problem through a change in its genetic structure. How does this happen in the Darwinian view of things? Our genetic apparatus is such that changes or mutations occur again and again in the genetic structure. Darwinism assumes that, in the terms of our model, these mutations function as Stage 2 *attempted solutions*. Most mutations are fatal: they are deadly for the bearer of the mutation, for the organism in which they occur. But in this way they are *eliminated*, in accordance with Stage 3 of our model. In our three-stage model, then, we must again stress the essential pluralism of the second stage of *attempted solutions*. If there were not *very many* mutations, they would not be worth considering as attempted solutions. We must assume that sufficient *mutability* is essential to the functioning of our genetic apparatus.

Now I can finally turn to my main theme, the theory or logic of science.

My first thesis here is that science is a biological phenomenon. Science has arisen out of prescientific knowledge; it is a quite remarkable continuation of commonsense knowledge, which may in turn be seen as a continuation of animal knowledge.

My second hypothesis is that our three-stage model is also *applicable to science*.

I mentioned at the outset that, as the Greek philosophers already saw, science starts with *problems*, from *amazement* about something that may be quite ordinary in itself but becomes a problem or a source of amazement for scientific thinkers. My thesis is that each new development in science can be understood only in this way, that its starting point is a *problem* or *problem situation* (which means the appearance of a problem in a certain state of our accumulated knowledge).

This point is extremely important. The old theory of science taught, and still teaches, that the starting point for science is our sense perception or sensory observation. This sounds at first thoroughly reasonable and persuasive, but it is fundamentally wrong. One can easily show this by stating the thesis: *without a problem, no observation*. If I asked you: 'Please, observe!', then linguistic usage would require you to answer by asking me: 'Yes, but what? *What* am I supposed to observe?' In other words, you ask me to set a *problem* that can be solved through your observation; and if I do not give you a *problem* but only an *object*, that is already something but it is by no means enough. For instance, if I say to you: 'Please look at your watch', you will still not know what I actually want to have observed. But things are different once I set you the most trivial *problem*. Perhaps you will not be interested in the problem, but at least you will know what you are supposed to find out through your perception or observation....

What is distinctive about science? What is the key difference between an amoeba and a great scientist such as ... Einstein?

The answer to this question is that the distinctive feature of science is conscious application of the *critical method*; in Stage 3 of our model, the stage of error elimination, we act in a consciously critical manner.

The critical method alone explains the extraordinarily rapid growth of the scientific form of knowledge, the extraordinary progress of science.

All prescientific knowledge, whether animal or human, is *dogmatic*; and science begins with the invention of the non-dogmatic critical method.

At any event, the invention of the critical method presupposes a descriptive human *language* in which critical *arguments* can take shape. Possibly it presupposes even writing. For the essence of the critical method is that our attempted solutions, our theories, and our hypotheses, can be formulated and objectively *presented* in language, so that they become *objects of consciously critical investigation*....

My thesis is that the step from my unspoken thought: 'It will rain today' to the same spoken proposition 'It will rain today' is a hugely important step, a step over an abyss, so to speak. At first this step, the expression of a thought, does not seem so great at all. But to formulate something in speech means that what used to be part of my personality, my expectations and perhaps fears, is now objectively to hand and therefore available for general critical discussion. The difference is also huge for me personally. The proposition—the prediction, for example—detaches itself from me when it is formulated in speech. It becomes independent of my moods, hopes, and fears. It is *objectified*. It can be *experimentally* endorsed by others as well as by myself, but it can also be *experimentally* disputed. The pros and cons can be weighed and discussed. People can take sides for and against the prediction....

I should now like to recall my three-stage model:

1 *problem;*
2 *attempted solutions;*
3 *elimination,*

and my remark that this schema of how new knowledge is acquired is applicable all the way from the amoeba to Einstein.

What is the difference? This question is decisive for the theory of science.

The crucial difference appears in Stage 3, in the *elimination* of attempted solutions.

In the prescientific development of knowledge, *elimination* is something that happens to us: the environment eliminates our attempted solutions; we are not active in the elimination but only passively involved; we *suffer* the elimination, and if it too often destroys our attempted solutions, or if it destroys an attempted solution that was previously successful, it thereby destroys not only the attempted solution but also ourselves as its bearers. This is clear in the case of Darwinian selection.

The crucial novelty of the scientific method and approach is simply that we are actively interested and involved in elimination. The attempted solutions are objectified; we are no longer personally identified with our attempted solutions. However much we may or may not be aware of the three-stage model, the novelty in the scientific approach is that we actively seek to eliminate our attempted solutions. We subject them to criticism, and this criticism operates with every means that we have at our disposal and are able to produce. For example, instead of waiting until our environment refutes a theory or an attempted solution, we try to modify the environment in such a way that it is *as unfavourable as possible* to our attempted solutions. We thus put our theories to the test—indeed, we try to eliminate our theories, for we ourselves should like to discover those theories that are *false*.

The question of how the amoeba differs crucially from Einstein may thus be answered as follows.

The amoeba shuns falsification: its expectation is part of itself, and prescientific bearers of an expectation or a hypothesis are often destroyed by refutation of the expectation or the hypothesis. Einstein, however, made his hypothesis objective. The hypothesis is something outside him, and the scientist can destroy the hypothesis through criticism without perishing along with it. In science we get our hypotheses to die for us.

I have now reached my own hypothesis.... My main thesis is that what distinguishes the scientific approach from the prescientific approach is the method of *attempted falsification*. Every attempted solution, every theory, is tested as rigourously as it is possible for us to test it. But a rigourous examination is always an attempt to discover *weakness* in what is being examined. Our testing of theories is also an attempt to detect their weaknesses. The testing of a theory is thus an attempt to refute or *falsify* the theory.

... Although the taking of sides undoubtedly has a function in scientific method, it is in my view important that the individual researcher should be aware of the underlying significance of attempts at falsification and of sometimes successful falsification. For the scientific method is not *cumulative*...; it is fundamentally *revolutionary*. Scientific progress essentially consists in the replacement of earlier theories by later theories. These new theories must be capable of solving the problems that the old theories solved, and of solving them at least as well. Thus Einstein's theory solves the problems of planetary motion and macro-mechanics in general, at least as well as, and *perhaps better than*, Newton's theory does. But the revolutionary theory starts from new assumptions, and in its conclusions it goes beyond and directly contradicts the old theory. This contradiction allows it to devise experiments that can distinguish the old from the new theory, but only in the sense that they can falsify at least one of the two theories. In fact, the experiments may prove the superiority of the surviving theory, but not its truth; and the surviving theory may soon be overtaken in its turn.

Once a scientist grasps that this is how things stand, he will himself adopt a critical attitude towards his own pet theory. He will prefer to test it himself and even to falsify it, rather than leave this to his critics.

... We are always learning a whole host of things through falsification. We learn not only *that* a theory is wrong; we learn *why* it is wrong. Above all else, we gain a *new and more sharply focused problem*; and a new problem, as we already know, is the real starting point for a new development in science.

You will perhaps have been surprised that I have so often mentioned my three-stage model. I have done this partly to prepare you for a very similar four-stage model, which is typical of science and the dynamics of scientific development. The four-stage model may be derived from our three-stage model (problem, attempted solutions, elimination), because what we do is call the first stage 'the old problem' and the fourth stage 'the new problems'. If we further replace 'attempted solutions' with 'tentative theories', and 'elimination' with 'attempted elimination through discussion', we arrive at the four-stage model characteristic of scientific theory.

So it looks like this:

1 *the old problem;*
2 *formation of tentative theories;*
3 *attempts at elimination through critical discussion, including experimental testing;*
4 *the new problems that arise from the critical discussion of our theories....*

An important conclusion from my main thesis refers to the question of how empirical scientific theories differ from other theories....

An empirical scientific theory differs from other theories because it may be undone by possible experimental results: that is to say, possible experimental results can be described that would falsify the theory if we were actually to obtain them....

The falsifiability criterion may be illustrated by many theories. For example, the theory that vaccination protects against smallpox is falsifiable: if someone who has really been vaccinated still gets smallpox, the theory is falsified.

This example may also be used to show that the falsifiability criterion has problems of its own. If one out of a million vaccinated people get smallpox, we will hardly consider our theory to be falsified. Rather, we will assume that something was wrong with the vaccination or with the vaccine material. And in principle such an escape route is always possible. When we are faced with a falsification, we can always talk our way out somehow or other; we can introduce an auxiliary hypothesis and reject the falsification. We can '*immunize*' our theories against all possible falsification (to use an expression of Professor Hans Albert's).

It is not always simple, then, to apply the falsifiability criterion. Yet the falsifiability criterion does have its value. It is applicable to the theory of smallpox vaccination even if the application is not always quite so simple. If the proportion of vaccinated people who get smallpox is roughly the same as (or perhaps even greater than) the proportion of unvaccinated people who get smallpox, then all scientists will give up the theory of vaccine protection....

The idea of approximation to the truth—like the idea of truth as a regulative principle—presupposes a *realistic view of the world*. It does *not* presuppose that reality is as our scientific theories describe it; but it does presuppose that there is a reality and that we and our theories—which are ideas we have ourselves created and are therefore always idealizations—can draw closer and closer to an adequate description of reality, if we employ the four-stage method of trial and error....

2.11 Thomas Kuhn (1922–1996)

Thomas Kuhn, like Karl Popper, considers science to be a problem-solving enterprise. Whereas Popper approaches science from a logical point of view and characterizes its Western history in terms of evolutionary progress, Thomas Kuhn analyzes that history in sociological terms that do not admit of progress. Unlike Popper, Kuhn does not discern a special reasoning process or pattern of logic distinguishing science from other human activities. Science is that which scientists do. What passes for science in a scientific community simply is science. What unifies members of a particular scientific community is not a pattern of reasoning, but a paradigm. Kuhn defines "paradigm" loosely, but it functions comparably with "theory" in Popper's account: a *paradigm* is a set of basic concepts, research methods, and shared assumptions that help coordinate work by members of the same scientific community.

According to Kuhn, scientific research proceeds in one of two ways: (1) *normal science* is directed towards solving established problems; (2) *revolutionary science* abandons historically established problems for new ones. Kuhn sometimes characterizes normal science in terms of puzzle-solving, because its problems are treated like puzzles that can be solved by the resources at hand. Basic concepts, research methods, and fundamental assumptions are so deeply ingrained that scientists expect their results to support the paradigm. Occasionally, a scientific community comes to an impasse and concludes that the paradigm does not have sufficient resources for the problems they are working on. When scientists lose confidence in a paradigm, the community faces a crisis. In this period of crisis, a rival paradigm can attract the allegiance of working scientists. A community-wide shift of allegiance from one paradigm to another is a scientific revolution. Just as in a political revolution, the fundamental structure of a community changes dramatically in a scientific revolution: novel problems set out by a new paradigm become the focus of research and the problems from the old paradigm are simply left unsolved.

According to Popper, transitions such as that from Aristotelian physics to Newton's Classical Mechanics to Einstein's Relativity Theory are guided by an independent criterion: falsifiability; i.e., a theory that has been falsified guides the community to eliminate it from the list of possibilities. Kuhn, however, thinks that in a revolutionary crisis there is no higher standard to guide this choice than the consensus of a scientific community. If Kuhn is correct, then no objective criterion justifies a community's preference for one paradigm over another. The history of science cannot therefore be characterized in terms of progress or evolution in Kuhn's account.

from The Structure of Scientific Revolutions

... Normal science, the activity in which most scientists inevitably spend almost all their time, is predicated on the assumption that the scientific community knows what the world is like. Much of the success of the enterprise derives from the community's willingness to defend that assumption, if necessary at considerable cost. Normal science, for example, often suppresses fundamental novelties because they are necessarily subversive of its basic commitments. Nevertheless, so long as those commitments retain an element of the arbitrary, the very nature of normal research ensures that novelty shall not be suppressed for very long. Sometimes a normal problem, one that ought to be solvable by known rules and procedures, resists the reiterated onslaught of the ablest members of the group within whose competence it falls. On other occasions a piece of equipment designed and constructed for the purpose of normal research fails to perform in the anticipated manner, revealing an anomaly that cannot, despite repeated effort, be aligned with professional expectation. In these and other ways besides, normal science repeatedly goes astray. And when it does—when, that is, the profession can no longer evade anomalies that subvert the existing tradition of scientific practice—then begin the extraordinary investigations that lead the profession at last to a new set of commitments, a new basis for the practice of science. The extraordinary episodes in which that shift of professional commitments occurs are the ones known in this essay as scientific revolutions. They are the tradition-shattering complements to the tradition-bound activity of normal science....

But if the aim of normal science is not major substantive novelties—if failure to come near the anticipated result is usually failure as a scientist—then why are these problems undertaken at all? ... Though its outcome can be anticipated, often in detail so great that what remains to be known is itself uninteresting, the way to achieve that outcome remains very much in doubt. Bringing a normal research problem to a conclusion is achieving the anticipated in a new way, and it requires the solution of all sorts of complex instrumental, conceptual, and mathematical puzzles. The man who succeeds proves himself an expert puzzle-solver, and the challenge of the puzzle is an important part of what usually drives him on.

The terms 'puzzle' and 'puzzle-solver' highlight several of the themes that have become increasingly prominent in the preceding pages. Puzzles are, in the entirely standard meaning here employed, that special category of problems that can serve to test ingenuity or skill in solution. Dictionary illustrations are 'jigsaw puzzle' and 'crossword puzzle,' and it is the characteristics that these share with the problems of normal science that we now need to isolate. One of them has just been mentioned. It is no criterion of goodness in a puzzle that its outcome be intrinsically interesting or important. On the contrary, the really pressing problems, e.g., a cure for cancer or the design of a lasting peace, are often not puzzles at all, largely because they may not have any solution. Consider the jigsaw puzzle whose pieces are selected at random from each of two different puzzle boxes. Since that problem is likely to defy (though it might not) even the most ingenious of men, it cannot serve as a test of skill in solution. In any usual sense it is not a puzzle at all. Though intrinsic value is no criterion for a puzzle, the assured existence of a solution is.

We have already seen, however, that one of the things a scientific community acquires with a paradigm is a criterion for choosing problems that, while the paradigm is taken for granted, can be assumed to have solutions. To a great extent these are the only problems that the community will admit as scientific or encourage its members to undertake. Other problems, including many that had previously been standard, are rejected as metaphysical, as the concern of another discipline, or sometimes as just too problematic to be worth the time....

Normal science, the puzzle-solving activity we have just examined, is a highly cumulative enterprise, eminently successful in its aim, the steady extension of the scope and precision of scientific knowledge. In all these respects it fits with great precision the most usual image of scientific work. Yet one standard product of the scientific enterprise is missing. Normal science does not aim at novelties of fact or theory and, when successful, finds none. New and unsuspected phenomena are, however, repeatedly uncovered by scientific research, and radical new theories have again and again been invented by scientists. History even suggests that the scientific enterprise has developed a uniquely powerful technique for producing surprises of this sort. If this characteristic of science is to be reconciled with what has already been said, then research under a paradigm must be a particularly effective way of inducing paradigm change. That is what fundamental novelties of fact and theory do. Produced inadvertently by a game played under one set of rules, their assimilation requires the elaboration of another set. After they have become parts of science, the enterprise, at least of those specialists in whose particular field the novelties lie, is never quite the same again....

... Discovery commences with the awareness of anomaly, i.e., with the recognition that nature has somehow violated the paradigm-induced expectations that govern normal science. It then continues with a more or less extended exploration of the area of anomaly. And it closes only when the paradigm theory has been adjusted so that the anomalous has become the expected. Assimilating a new sort of fact demands a more than additive adjustment of theory, and until that adjustment is completed—until the scientist has learned to see nature in a different way—the new fact is not quite a scientific fact at all....

... So long as the tools a paradigm supplies continue to prove capable of solving the problems it defines, science moves fastest and penetrates most deeply through confident employment of those tools. The reason is clear. As in manufacture so in science—retooling is an extravagance to be reserved for the occasion that demands it. The significance of crises is the indication they provide that an occasion for retooling has arrived.

Let us then assume that crises are a necessary precondition for the emergence of novel theories and ask next how scientists respond to their existence. Part of the answer, as obvious as it is important, can be discovered by noting first what scientists never do when confronted by even severe and prolonged anomalies. Though they may begin to lose faith and then to consider alternatives, they do not renounce the paradigm that has led them into crisis. They do not, that is, treat anomalies as counterinstances, though in the vocabulary of philosophy of science that is what they are. In part this generalization is simply a statement from historic fact, based upon examples like those given above and, more extensively, below. These hint what our later examination of paradigm rejection will disclose more fully: once it has achieved the status of paradigm, a scientific theory is declared invalid only if an alternate candidate is available to take its place. No process yet disclosed by the historical study of scientific development at all resembles the methodological stereotype of falsification by direct comparison with nature. That remark does not mean that scientists do not reject scientific theories, or that experience and experiment are not essential to the process in which they do so. But it does mean—what will ultimately be a central point—that the act of judgment that leads scientists to reject a previously accepted theory is always based upon more than a comparison of that theory with the world. The decision to reject one paradigm is always simultaneously the decision to accept another, and the judgment leading to that decision involves the comparison of both paradigms with nature *and* with each other....

... [T]here is no such thing as research without counterinstances. For what is it that differentiates normal science from science in a crisis state? Not, surely, that the former confronts, no counterinstances. On the contrary, what we previously called the puzzles that constitute normal science exist only because no paradigm that provides a basis for scientific research ever completely resolves all its problems. The very few that have ever seemed to do so (e.g., geometric optics) have shortly ceased to yield research problems at all and have instead become tools for engineering. Excepting those that are exclusively instrumental, every problem that normal science sees as a puzzle can be seen, from another viewpoint, as a counterinstance and thus as a source of crisis.... Furthermore, even the existence of crisis does not by itself transform a puzzle into a counterinstance. There is no such sharp dividing line. Instead, by proliferating versions of the paradigm, crisis loosens the rules of normal puzzle-solving in ways that ultimately permit a new paradigm to emerge. There are, I think, only two alternatives: either no scientific theory ever confronts a counterinstance, or all such theories confront counterinstances at all times.

... Normal science does and must continually strive to bring theory and fact into closer agreement, and that activity can easily be seen as testing or as a search for confirmation or falsification. Instead, its object is to solve a puzzle for whose very existence the validity of the paradigm must be assumed. Failure to achieve a solution discredits only the scientist and not the theory. Here, even more than above, the proverb applies: "It is a poor carpenter who blames his tools." ...

The transition from a paradigm in crisis to a new one from which a new tradition of normal science can emerge is far from a cumulative process, one achieved by an articulation or extension of the old paradigm. Rather it is a reconstruction of the field from new fundamentals, a reconstruction that changes some of the field's most elementary theoretical generalizations as well as many of its paradigm methods and applications.... One perceptive historian, viewing a classic case of a science's reorientation by paradigm change, recently described it as "picking up the other end of the stick," a process that involves "handling the same bundle of data as before, but placing them in a new system of relations with one another by giving them a different framework."[1] Others who have noted this aspect of scientific advance have emphasized its similarity to a change in visual gestalt: the marks on paper that were first seen as a bird are now seen as an antelope, or vice versa.[2] ...

... Almost always the men who achieve these fundamental inventions of a new paradigm have been either very young or very new to the field whose paradigm they change.[3] And perhaps that point need not have been made explicit, for obviously these are the men who, being little committed by prior practice to the traditional rules of normal science, are particularly likely to see that those rules no longer define a

1 Herbert Butterfield, *The Origins of Modern Science, 1300–1800* (London, 1949), pp. 1–7.

2 Hanson, *op. cit.*, chap. i.

3 This generalization about the role of youth in fundamental scientific research is so common as to be a cliché. Furthermore, a glance at almost any list of fundamental contributions to scientific theory will provide impressionistic confirmation. Nevertheless, the generalization badly needs systematic investigation. Harvey C. Lehman (*Age and Achievement* [Princeton, 1953]) provides many useful data; but his studies make no attempt to single out contributions that involve fundamental reconceptualization. Nor do they inquire about the special circumstances, if any, that may accompany relatively late productivity in the sciences.

playable game and to conceive another set that can replace them.

The resulting transition to a new paradigm is scientific revolution....

... Why should a change of paradigm be called a revolution? In the face of the vast and essential differences between political and scientific development, what parallelism can justify the metaphor that finds revolutions in both?

One aspect of the parallelism must already be apparent. Political revolutions are inaugurated by a growing sense, often restricted to a segment of the political community, that existing institutions have ceased adequately to meet the problems posed by an environment that they have in part created. In much the same way, scientific revolutions are inaugurated by a growing sense, again often restricted to a narrow subdivision of the scientific community, that an existing paradigm has ceased to function adequately in the exploration of an aspect of nature to which that paradigm itself had previously led the way. In both political and scientific development the sense of malfunction that can lead to crisis is prerequisite to revolution....

This genetic aspect of the parallel between political and scientific development should no longer be open to doubt. The parallel has, however, a second and more profound aspect upon which the significance of the first depends. Political revolutions aim to change political institutions in ways that those institutions themselves prohibit. Their success therefore necessitates the partial relinquishment of one set of institutions in favor of another, and in the interim, society is not fully governed by institutions at all. Initially it is crisis alone that attenuates the role of political institutions as we have already seen it attenuate the role of paradigms. In increasing numbers individuals become increasingly estranged from political life and behave more and more eccentrically within it. Then, as the crisis deepens, many of these individuals commit themselves to some concrete proposal for the reconstruction of society in a new institutional framework. At that point the society is divided into competing camps or parties, one seeking to defend the old institutional constellation, the others seeking to institute some new one. And, once that polarization has occurred, *political recourse fails*. Because they differ about the institutional matrix within which political change is to be achieved and evaluated, because they acknowledge no supra-institutional framework for the adjudication of revolutionary difference, the parties to a revolutionary conflict must finally resort to the techniques of mass persuasion, often including force. Though revolutions have had a vital role in the evolution of political institutions, that role depends upon their being partially extrapolitical or extrainstitutional events.

... Like the choice between competing political institutions, that between competing paradigms proves to be a choice between incompatible modes of community life. Because it has that character, the choice is not and cannot be determined merely by the evaluative procedures characteristic of normal science, for these depend in part upon a particular paradigm, and that paradigm is at issue. When paradigms enter, as they must, into a debate about paradigm choice, their role is necessarily circular. Each group uses its own paradigm to argue in that paradigm's defense.

The resulting circularity does not, of course, make the arguments wrong or even ineffectual. The man who premises a paradigm when arguing in its defense can nonetheless provide a clear exhibit of what scientific practice will be like for those who adopt the new view of nature. That exhibit can be immensely persuasive, often compellingly so. Yet, whatever its force, the status of the circular argument is only that of persuasion. It cannot be made logically or even probabilistically compelling for those who refuse to step into the circle. The premises and values shared by the two parties to a debate over paradigms are not sufficiently extensive for that. As in political revolutions, so in paradigm choice—there is no standard higher than the assent of the relevant community. To discover how scientific revolutions are effected, we shall therefore have to examine not only the impact of nature and of logic, but also the techniques of persuasive argumentation effective within the quite special groups that constitute the community of scientists....

... To the extent, as significant as it is incomplete, that two scientific schools disagree about what is a problem and what a solution, they will inevitably talk through each other when debating the relative merits of their respective paradigms. In the partially circular arguments that regularly result, each paradigm will be shown to satisfy more or less the criteria that it dictates for itself and to fall short of a few of those dictated by its opponent.... Which problems is it more significant to have solved? Like the issue of competing standards, that question of values can be answered only in terms of criteria that lie outside of normal science altogether, and it is that recourse to external criteria that most obviously makes paradigm debates revolutionary....

... Given a paradigm, interpretation of data is central to the enterprise that explores it.

But that interpretive enterprise—and this was the burden of the paragraph before last—can only articulate a paradigm, not correct it. Paradigms are not corrigible by normal science at all. Instead, as we have already seen, normal science ultimately leads only to the recognition of anomalies and to crises. And these are terminated, not by deliberation and interpretation, but by a relatively sudden and unstructured event like the gestalt switch. Scientists then often speak of the "scales falling from the eyes" or of the "lightning flash" that "inundates" a previously obscure puzzle, enabling its components to be seen in a new way that for the first time permits its solution. On other occasions the relevant illumination comes in sleep.[4] No ordinary sense of the term 'interpretation' fits these flashes of intuition through which a new paradigm is born....

... I suggest that there are excellent reasons why revolutions have proved to be so nearly invisible. Both scientists and laymen take much of their image of creative scientific activity from an authoritative source that systematically disguises—partly for important functional reasons—the existence and significance of scientific revolutions....

As the source of authority, I have in mind principally textbooks of science together with both the popularizations and the philosophical works modeled on them. All three of these categories—until recently no other significant sources of information about science have been available except through the practice of research—have one thing in common. They address themselves to an already articulated body of problems, data, and theory, most often to the particular set of paradigms to which the scientific community is committed at the time they are written....

... Textbooks ... being pedagogic vehicles for the perpetuation of normal science, have to be rewritten in whole or in part whenever the language, problem-structure, or standards of normal science change. In short, they have to be rewritten in the aftermath of each scientific revolution, and, once rewritten, they inevitably disguise not only the role but the very existence of the revolutions that produced them. Unless he has personally experienced a revolution in his own lifetime, the historical sense either of the working scientist or of the lay reader of textbook literature extends only to the outcome of the most recent revolutions in the field.

Textbooks thus begin by truncating the scientist's sense of his discipline's history and then proceed to supply a substitute for what they have eliminated. Characteristically, textbooks of science contain just a bit of history, either in an introductory chapter or, more often, in scattered references to the great heroes of an earlier age. From such references both students and professionals come to feel like participants in a long-standing historical tradition. Yet the textbook-derived tradition in which scientists come to sense their participation is one that, in fact, never existed. For reasons that are both obvious and highly functional, science textbooks (and too many of the older histories of science) refer only to that part of the work of past scientists that can easily be viewed as contributions to the statement and solution of the texts' paradigm

4 [Jacques] Hadamard, *Subconscient, intuition, et logique dans la recherche scientifique* (*Conférence faite au Palais de la Découverte le 8 Décembre 1945* [Alençon, n.d.]), pp. 7–8. A much fuller account, though one exclusively restricted to mathematical innovations, is the same author's *The Psychology of Invention in the Mathematical Field* (Princeton, 1949).

problems. Partly by selection and partly by distortion, the scientists of earlier ages are implicitly represented as having worked upon the same set of fixed problems and in accordance with the same set of fixed canons that the most recent revolution in scientific theory and method has made seem scientific. No wonder that textbooks and the historical tradition they imply have to be rewritten after each scientific revolution. And no wonder that, as they are rewritten, science once again comes to seem largely cumulative....

... Many of the puzzles of contemporary normal science did not exist until after the most recent scientific revolution. Very few of them can be traced back to the historic beginning of the science within which they now occur. Earlier generations pursued their own problems with their own instruments and their own canons of solution....

... [T]heories, of course, do "fit the facts," but only by transforming previously accessible information into facts that, for the preceding paradigm, had not existed at all. And that means that theories too do not evolve piecemeal to fit facts that were there all the time. Rather, they emerge together with the facts they fit from a revolutionary reformulation of the preceding scientific tradition, a tradition within which the knowledge-mediated relationship between the scientist and nature was not quite the same....

... Any new interpretation of nature, whether a discovery or a theory, emerges first in the mind of one or a few individuals. It is they who first learn to see science and the world differently, and their ability to make the transition is facilitated by two circumstances that are not common to most other members of their profession. Invariably their attention has been intensely concentrated upon the crisis-provoking problems; usually, in addition, they are men so young or so new to the crisis-ridden field that practice has committed them less deeply than most of their contemporaries to the world view and rules determined by the old paradigm. How are they able, what must they do, to convert the entire profession or the relevant professional subgroup to their way of seeing science and the world? What causes the group to abandon one tradition of normal research in favor of another? ...

... In the sciences the testing situation never consists, as puzzle-solving does, simply in the comparison of a single paradigm with nature. Instead, testing occurs as part of the competition between two rival paradigms for the allegiance of the scientific community.

Closely examined, this formulation displays unexpected and probably significant parallels to two of the most popular contemporary philosophical theories about verification....

A very different approach to this whole network of problems has been developed by Karl R. Popper who denies the existence of any verification procedures at all.[5] Instead, he emphasizes the importance of falsification, i.e., of the test that, because its outcome is negative, necessitates the rejection of an established theory. Clearly, the role thus attributed to falsification is much like the one this essay assigns to anomalous experiences, i.e., to experiences that, by evoking crisis, prepare the way for a new theory. Nevertheless, anomalous experiences may not be identified with falsifying ones. Indeed, I doubt that the latter exist. As has repeatedly been emphasized before, no theory ever solves all the puzzles with which it is confronted at a given time; nor are the solutions already achieved often perfect. On the contrary, it is just the incompleteness and imperfection of the existing data-theory fit that, at any time, define many of the puzzles that characterize normal science. If any and every failure to fit were ground for theory rejection, all theories ought to be rejected at all times. On the other hand, if only severe failure to fit justifies theory rejection, then the Popperians will require some criterion of "improbability" or of "degree of falsification." In developing one they will almost certainly encounter the same network of difficulties that has haunted the advocates of the various probabilistic verification theories.

Many of the preceding difficulties can be avoided by recognizing that both of these prevalent and

5 K.R. Popper, *The Logic of Scientific Discovery* (New York, 1959), esp. chaps. i–iv.

opposed views about the underlying logic of scientific inquiry have tried to compress two largely separate processes into one. Popper's anomalous experience is important to science because it evokes competitors for an existing paradigm. But falsification, though it surely occurs, does not happen with, or simply because of, the emergence of an anomaly or falsifying instance. Instead, it is a subsequent and separate process that might equally well be called verification since it consists in the triumph of a new paradigm over the old one.... To the historian, at least, it makes little sense to suggest that verification is establishing the agreement of fact with theory. All historically significant theories have agreed with the facts, but only more or less. There is no more precise answer to the question whether or how well an individual theory fits the facts. But questions much like that can be asked when theories are taken collectively or even in pairs. It makes a great deal of sense to ask which of two actual and competing theories fits the facts *better*....

This formulation, however, makes the task of choosing between paradigms look both easier and more familiar than it is. If there were but one set of scientific problems, one world within which to work on them, and one set of standards for their solution, paradigm competition might be settled more or less routinely by some process like counting the number of problems solved by each. But, in fact, these conditions are never met completely. The proponents of competing paradigms are always at least slightly at cross-purposes. Neither side will grant all the non-empirical assumptions that the other needs in order to make its case.... Though each may hope to convert the other to his way of seeing his science and its problems, neither may hope to prove his case. The competition between paradigms is not the sort of battle that can be resolved by proofs.

... [T]he proponents of competing paradigms will often disagree about the list of problems that any candidate for paradigm must resolve. Their standards or their definitions of science are not the same....

... In a sense that I am unable to explicate further, the proponents of competing paradigms practice their trades in different worlds.... Just because it is a transition between incommensurables, the transition between competing paradigms cannot be made a step at a time, forced by logic and neutral experience. Like the gestalt switch, it must occur all at once (though not necessarily in an instant) or not at all.

How, then, are scientists brought to make this transposition? Part of the answer is that they are very often not.... Darwin, in a particularly perceptive passage at the end of his *Origin of Species*, wrote: "Although I am fully convinced of the truth of the views given in this volume..., I by no means expect to convince experienced naturalists whose minds are stocked with a multitude of facts all viewed, during a long course of years, from a point of view directly opposite to mine.... [B]ut I look with confidence to the future,—to young and rising naturalists, who will be able to view both sides of the question with impartiality."[6] And Max Planck, surveying his own career in his *Scientific Autobiography*, sadly remarked that "a new scientific truth does not triumph by convincing its opponents and making them see the light, but rather because its opponents eventually die, and a new generation grows up that is familiar with it."[7]

... [I]n these matters neither proof nor error is at issue. The transfer of allegiance from paradigm to paradigm is a conversion experience that cannot be forced. Lifelong resistance, particularly from those whose productive careers have committed them to an older tradition of normal science, is not a violation of scientific standards but an index to the nature of scientific research itself. The source of resistance is the assurance that the older paradigm will ultimately solve all its problems, that nature can be shoved into the box the paradigm provides. Inevitably, at times of revolution, that assurance seems stubborn and pigheaded as

6 Charles Darwin, *On the Origin of Species* ... (authorized edition from 6th English ed.; New York, 1889), II, pp. 295–96.
7 Max Planck, *Scientific Autobiography and Other Papers*, trans. F. Gaynor (New York, 1949), pp. 33–34.

indeed it sometimes becomes. But it is also something more. That same assurance is what makes normal or puzzle-solving science possible. And it is only through normal science that the professional community of scientists succeeds, first, in exploiting the potential scope and precision of the older paradigm and, then, in isolating the difficulty through the study of which a new paradigm may emerge.

Still, to say that resistance is inevitable and legitimate, that paradigm change cannot be justified by proof, is not to say that no arguments are relevant or that scientists cannot be persuaded to change their minds....

Probably the single most prevalent claim advanced by the proponents of a new paradigm is that they can solve the problems that have led the old one to a crisis. When it can legitimately be made, this claim is often the most effective one possible....

Claims of this sort are particularly likely to succeed if the new paradigm displays a quantitative precision strikingly better than its older competitor....

The claim to have solved the crisis-provoking problems is, however, rarely sufficient by itself. Nor can it always legitimately be made....

... [T]here is also another sort of consideration that can lead scientists to reject an old paradigm in favor of a new. These are the arguments, rarely made entirely explicit, that appeal to the individual's sense of the appropriate or the aesthetic—the new theory is said to be "neater," "more suitable," or "simpler" than the old....

To see the reason for the importance of these more subjective and aesthetic considerations, remember what a paradigm debate is about. When a new candidate for paradigm is first proposed, it has seldom solved more than a few of the problems that confront it, and most of those solutions are still far from perfect....

... Usually the opponents of a new paradigm can legitimately claim that even in the area of crisis it is little superior to its traditional rival. Of course, it handles some problems better, has disclosed some new regularities. But the older paradigm can presumably be articulated to meet these challenges as it has met others before.... Even in the area of crisis, the balance of argument and counterargument can sometimes be very close indeed. And outside that area the balance will often decisively favor the tradition.... In short, if a new candidate for paradigm had to be judged from the start by hardheaded people who examined only relative problem-solving ability, the sciences would experience very few major revolutions. Add the counterarguments generated by what we previously called the incommensurability of paradigms, and the sciences might experience no revolutions at all.

But paradigm debates are not really about relative problem-solving ability, though for good reasons they are usually couched in those terms. Instead, the issue is which paradigm should in the future guide research on problems many of which neither competitor can yet claim to resolve completely. A decision between alternate ways of practicing science is called for, and in the circumstances that decision must be based less on past achievement than on future promise. The man who embraces a new paradigm at an early stage must often do so in defiance of the evidence provided by problem-solving. He must, that is, have faith that the new paradigm will succeed with the many large problems that confront it, knowing only that the older paradigm has failed with a few. A decision of that kind can only be made on faith....

... Why should the enterprise sketched above move steadily ahead in ways that, say, art, political theory, or philosophy does not? Why is progress a perquisite reserved almost exclusively for the activities we call science? ...

... In music, the graphic arts, and literature, the practitioner gains his education by exposure to the works of other artists, principally earlier artists. Textbooks, except compendia of or handbooks to original creations, have only a secondary role. In history, philosophy, and the social sciences, textbook literature has a greater significance. But even in these fields the elementary college course employs parallel readings in original sources, some of them the "classics" of the field, others the contemporary research reports that practitioners write for each other. As a result, the student in any one of these disciplines is constantly made aware of the immense variety of problems that the members of his future group have, in the course of time, attempted to solve. Even more important, he has constantly before him a number of competing and incommensurable solutions to these problems, solutions that he must ultimately evaluate for himself.

Contrast this situation with that in at least the contemporary natural sciences. In these fields the student relies mainly on textbooks until, in his third or fourth year of graduate work, he begins his own research....

... [F]or normal-scientific work, for puzzle-solving within the tradition that the textbooks define, the scientist is almost perfectly equipped. Furthermore, he is well equipped for another task, as well—the generation through normal science of significant crises. When they arise, the scientist is not, of course, equally well prepared. Even though prolonged crises are probably reflected in less rigid educational practice, scientific training is not well designed to produce the man who will easily discover a fresh approach. But so long as somebody appears with a new candidate for paradigm—usually a young man or one new to the field—the loss due to rigidity accrues only to the individual. Given a generation in which to effect the change, individual rigidity is compatible with a community that can switch from paradigm to paradigm when the occasion demands. Particularly, it is compatible when that very rigidity provides the community with a sensitive indicator that something has gone wrong.

... Revolutions close with a total victory for one of the two opposing camps. Will that group ever say that the result of its victory has been something less than progress? That would be rather like admitting that they had been wrong and their opponents right. To them, at least, the outcome of revolution must be progress, and they are in an excellent position to make certain that future members of their community will see past history in the same way....

... The developmental process described in this essay has been a process of evolution *from* primitive beginnings—a process whose successive stages are characterized by an increasingly detailed and refined understanding of nature. But nothing that has been or will be said makes it a process of evolution *toward* anything. Inevitably that lacuna will have disturbed many readers. We are all deeply accustomed to seeing science as the one enterprise that draws constantly nearer to some goal set by nature in advance.

But need there be any such goal? Can we not account for both science's existence and its success in terms of evolution from the community's state of knowledge at any given time? Does it really help to imagine that there is some one full, objective, true account of nature and that the proper measure of scientific achievement is the extent to which it brings us closer to that ultimate goal? If we can learn to substitute evolution-from-what-we-do-know for evolution-toward-what-we-wish-to-know, a number of vexing problems may vanish in the process....

... When Darwin first published his theory of evolution by natural selection in 1859, what most bothered many professionals was neither the notion of species change nor the possible descent of man from apes. The evidence pointing to evolution, including the evolution of man, had been accumulating for decades, and the idea of evolution had been suggested and widely disseminated before. Though evolution, as such, did encounter resistance, particularly from some religious groups, it was by no means the greatest of the difficulties the Darwinians faced. That difficulty stemmed from an idea that was more nearly Darwin's own. All the well-known pre-Darwinian evolutionary theories—those of Lamarck, Chambers, Spencer, and the German *Naturphilosophen*—had taken evolution to be a goal-directed process. The "idea" of man and of the contemporary flora and fauna was thought to have been present from the first creation of life, perhaps in the mind of God. That idea or plan had provided the direction and the guiding force to the entire evolutionary process. Each new stage of evolutionary development was a more perfect realization of a plan that had been present from the start.[8]

8 Loren Eiseley, *Darwin's Century: Evolution and the Men Who Discovered It* (New York, 1958), chaps. ii, iv–v.

For many men the abolition of that teleological kind of evolution was the most significant and least palatable of Darwin's suggestions.[9] The *Origin of Species* recognized no goal set either by God or nature. Instead, natural selection, operating in the given environment and with the actual organisms presently at hand, was responsible for the gradual but steady emergence of more elaborate, further articulated, and vastly more specialized organisms. Even such marvelously adapted organs as the eye and hand of man—organs whose design had previously provided powerful arguments for the existence of a supreme artificer and an advance plan—were products of a process that moved steadily *from* primitive beginnings but *toward* no goal. The belief that natural selection, resulting from mere competition between organisms for survival, could have produced man together with the higher animals and plants was the most difficult and disturbing aspect of Darwin's theory. What could 'evolution,' 'development,' and 'progress' mean in the absence of a specified goal? ...

2.12 Review Questions

1. How do the separate accounts of mathematics and geometry from Plato and Aristotle complement or conflict with each other?

2. How do Aristotle's ideas about the separateness of mathematics and geometry from physics factor in transition to modern, Enlightenment science?

3. How do Aristotle's ideas about the social enterprise of science compare with Bacon's? Or with those of Popper or Kuhn?

4. How does Newton's Classical Mechanics fulfill the purposes of science articulated by either Aristotle or Galileo?

5. How do Popper's ideas about evolution and progress in science cohere with Darwin's ideas about evolution in biology?

6. What is the best way to characterize the results of Eddington's observations of the 1919 eclipse? As a confirmation of Relativity Theory, or as evidence that Relativity Theory is superior to Classical Mechanics?

7. Einstein thinks that observational research confirmed General Relativity, and Popper thinks that no theory is ever confirmed. Rather, Popper says, we ought to say that it has passed all tests that might falsify it. How might a conversation go on this question between these two figures?

---

9 For a particularly acute account of one prominent Darwinian's struggle with this problem, see A. Hunter Dupree, *Asa Gray, 1810–1888* (Cambridge, Mass., 1959), pp. 295–306, 355–83.

8. One way to consider the debate between Popper and Kuhn is to imagine a conversation between figures from different eras. For example: Is it possible for Aristotle to recognize whether the ideas of Galileo or Newton or Darwin or Einstein are superior to his own? Einstein thinks that General Relativity solves a problem that Newton tried to address. Are he and Popper correct to think that, in principle, Newton could agree with this assessment? Is Kuhn correct to say that scientists operating within different paradigms do not really communicate with each other?

2.13 Further Reading

Darwin, Charles. *On the Origin of Species*. Edited by Joseph Carroll, Broadview Press, 2003.

Einstein, Albert. *Relativity: The Special and General Theory*. Translated by Robert W. Lawson, Methuen & Co., 1920.

Galilei, Galileo. *The Essential Galileo*. Edited and Translated by Maurice A. Finocchiaro, Hackett, 2008.

Giere, Ronald, et al. *Understanding Scientific Reasoning*. 5th ed., Thomson Wadsworth, 2006.

Martin, Robert M. *Scientific Thinking*. Broadview Press, 2000.

Popper, Karl. "Back to the Presocratics." *Conjectures and Refutations: The Growth of Scientific Knowledge*. Basic Books, 1963, 136–53.

CHAPTER 3

Wisdom, Enlightenment, and the Uncertainty of Human Life

Alas, how terrifying is wisdom that profits not the one possessing it.

—SOPHOCLES

To a fool, wise counsel is unintelligible.

—EURIPIDES

Respect for a sage is a credit to the admirer.

—EPICURUS

Intellect is a magnitude of intensity, not a magnitude of extension: which is why in this respect one sage can confidently take on ten thousand, and a thousand fools do not make a sage.

—ARTHUR SCHOPENHAUER

It is quite true what philosophy says; that life must be understood backwards. But then one forgets the other principle: that it must be lived forwards.

—SØREN KIERKEGAARD

3.1 Introduction

Of the many concepts weaving their way through Socrates's trial speeches, three are thematically central: human nature, goodness, and wisdom. All three converge in his critical remark that Athenians care more for wealth, reputation, and honours than for the state of their own souls (*Apology* 29d–30c). In keeping with Socrates's theoretical inclinations, the charge presupposes a package of normative principles. First, each of us is endowed with a special potential by *nature*, i.e., an inner principle which is realized as a condition of the soul; accordingly, every person has an ethical responsibility to fulfill this psychological potential.[1] Next, to fulfill a special potential is to realize something good: *goodness* is a fundamental

1 The Greek noun for soul, *psyché*, is the root of "psychology" (*psyché-logos*, literally soul-structure).

normative principle; in other dialogues Plato goes even further, positing goodness as a principle regulating the entire cosmos, including the human soul and its distinctive capacities. Lastly, the psychological condition that fulfills our special potential is wisdom. Together these form a neat conceptual triad: the highest expression of human nature is wisdom, which we may understand provisionally to be an apprehension of goodness. Essentially, Socrates is here accusing his fellow citizens of squandering their lives on trivialities when only wisdom could possibly fulfill their deepest impulses. And because the accusation presupposes a rich set of normative principles, it has the force of a general lesson for anyone.

Turning to wisdom specifically, Socrates makes some surprising claims about both its nature and his own reputation for it. When the question of his reputation is first raised, wisdom is presumed to be a special kind of knowledge with its own substantive subject matter. It seemed to Socrates initially implausible that the Oracle in Delphi would single him out as the wisest man. How could he, not "being wise in anything great or small," be wisest? Surely, he thinks, someone else knows more than he about the subject of such knowledge. By the time he finishes interviewing politicians, poets, and crafters, his conception of wisdom evolves and bifurcates into two species: (i) wisdom as a form of substantive knowledge, which is the province of a god, in this case Apollo; (ii) wisdom as self-knowledge, which is the most that Socrates can claim for himself and which consists primarily in self-awareness about the limits of his substantive knowledge. His superiority over other people with respect to wisdom is not, therefore, on any subject of substantive knowledge. Indeed, in saying that the god alone is wise, he seems to suggest that substantive wisdom lies beyond the potential of human nature (23a).

As with almost everything else Socrates says, his account of wisdom is contestable. Indeed, there are many rival accounts of wisdom as the pinnacle of human potential. There are also rival accounts of human potential positing something other than wisdom as its highest expression, in particular, enlightenment. Lastly, there are accounts objecting to both ideals. The present chapter includes a range of alternatives to Socrates's account, each falling into one of the following three categories: (1) accounts of wisdom, (2) accounts of enlightenment, and (3) critical responses objecting to the necessity and desirability of either wisdom or enlightenment. Let us begin with category (1), which is represented by the largest number of contributions in the present chapter.

Two generic theoretical strategies may be discerned among the rival accounts of wisdom included here, one (i) focusing on the polarity between wisdom and its opposite (either ignorance or folly), the other (ii) focusing on fine-grain distinctions between wisdom and related concepts (such as foresight, cleverness, and insight). These strategies constitute distinctive exercises in conceptual geography. (i) Because the first strategy differentiates polar opposites, we may call it an Antipodal[2] approach: like the north and south poles, wisdom and its polar opposite are separated by great distances; accordingly, theoretical contrasts drawn between them can leave unanalyzed vast regions lying between the poles. By contrast, a Regional approach differentiates neighbouring concepts from each other, providing precise analysis of wisdom and some closely related concepts; this approach can leave the opposite poles unanalyzed. The two approaches are different, but they are not mutually exclusive and are potentially complementary. Indeed, in the present chapter Thomas Aquinas adopts both approaches (3.9).

One point needs to be clarified before we review positions taking the Antipodal approach, for wisdom seems to have two antonyms: ignorance and folly. *Ignorance* is a generic deprivation of knowledge or an incorrect apprehension of some state of affairs. It is thus not contrasted with wisdom specifically, but with all knowledge. When invoked as a contrast to

2 "Antipodes" is Greek for "having the opposite (anti) feet (podes)," which we can imagine as two people lying head-to-head with their feet as far apart from each other as that relative positioning allows. The extreme opposition here is of two diametrically separated parts within the same large, complex whole.

wisdom, ignorance signifies uninformed judgement about what is the right thing to do or about what normative principles ought to regulate one's judgements and actions. The politicians Socrates exposes in the *Apology* as exhibiting only counterfeit wisdom illustrate a deprivation of substantive knowledge because they cannot answer Socrates's questions satisfactorily (21a–c). They fail to meet the specific standard of wisdom because they fail to meet the generic standard of knowledge. *Folly* is more specific than ignorance and signifies something additional to simple, uninformed judgement. It has ethical implications built into its essence, for it is ignorance compounded by a disregard for appropriate values or normative constraints. Socrates implies this about Meletus, who he accuses of "carelessly bringing a person to trial, pretending to be serious about and to trouble himself over various matters, none of which was ever an interest of his" (24c). It is an additional element of indifference to independent standards that separates the fool from someone who suffers from simple ignorance. In this respect, folly may be more sharply contrasted with wisdom than ignorance, since it is an opposite with respect both to all knowledge and to knowledge with an inherent moral dimension. This is why ignorance is commonly not perceived as inherently vicious, while folly is.

Several accounts included in the present chapter draw a programmatic contrast between wisdom and folly as polar opposites. While these accounts of wisdom fit the same formal template, materially they differ because, in each case, wisdom is constituted by a special combination of elements. Siddhartha Gautama, the founder of Buddhism, characterizes the paradigmatic sage as someone who stands outside the fray of conventional social dynamics and is indifferent to the temptations of material pleasure; the fool, by contrast, is dedicated to material things and social standing under the misapprehension that they are intrinsically valuable (3.2.3, 3.2.4). Similarities with Socrates's account are notable here, but we must not overemphasize them. The Buddhist sage finds a degree of tranquility that is unlike anything Socrates seems to have enjoyed, and Socrates's emphasis on self-knowledge is less plausible in light of Buddhist skepticism about the existence of a "self" or "ego" as the focus of such knowledge. A second way to contrast wisdom and folly is put forth by Solomon in his *Proverbs* (3.4). Here folly is virtually identified as a combination of sin and irrationality, which is exemplified by the fool's refusal to accept sound counsel; wisdom, by contrast, involves both a desire for substantial moral knowledge and an understanding of righteous divine guidance. Similarly, in his *Summa Theologiae* Thomas Aquinas portrays wisdom as a virtue of the intellect that is a reliable source of moral guidance, whereas folly is a stupefaction of the heart and intellect that results in sin (3.9.1). Lastly, Cleanthes contrasts wisdom and folly in terms of one's rational conformity with divine and impersonal laws that govern the universe: exhibiting an austere and self-effacing obedience to divine law, a stoic lives in harmony with it and thereby finds peace of mind, whereas the fool puts up futile resistance (3.6). Each of these four accounts thus formulates a distinctive version of the wisdom/folly contrast by relating the two in terms of morality, intelligence, knowledge, and rationality.

The Regional approach elucidates wisdom without programmatic reference to its polar opposite, although none preclude the contrast. In relating wisdom to near synonyms, these accounts focus on concepts related to other forms of practical intelligence, which may coordinate with wisdom or overlap with it but must nevertheless be theoretically differentiated from it. Here the purpose is to develop a systematic taxonomy, situating wisdom in relation to a cluster of concepts (rather than a diametrical opposite) as well as defining the concept itself. Numerous terms reside in the same neighbourhood as wisdom. Of these, foresight, cleverness, and insight stand out, and a brief survey of these three concepts will help clarify our expectations about wisdom. Each of these other forms of practical intelligence is valuable in its own way, but none in the way that satisfies some basic expectations for an account of wisdom: a distinctive capacity that functions normatively to help us assess what purposes are worth pursuing and how to accomplish these purposes ethically, along with a discursive understanding of these things.

First, *Foresight* signifies the anticipation of future difficulties or opportunities, a capacity often associated with wisdom; however, while wisdom can manifest as foresight, the two are not identical because foresight does not entail judgement about what to do with such knowledge. We can foresee that people will suffer health complications from smoking cigarettes, for example, but in itself this sort of knowledge does not help us assess social policies to curtail it. *Cleverness* signifies an intellectual capacity that operates independently of ethical principles or constraints, whereas wisdom has no such independence. An incorrigible scoundrel can be clever, but it would be counter-intuitive to conceive of "wisdom" in a way that includes villains such as Iago or Voldemort. Socrates draws attention to this distinction when commenting on the purported wisdom of crafters (in Greek "those who possess *techné*," i.e., technical know-how; *Apology* 22d–e). Someone with technical know-*how* can accomplish a particular purpose expediently, but in itself such knowledge does not guide them as to when, whether, or why that purpose is worth pursuing. *Insight* signifies a capacity to appreciate the meaning or ethical significance of a situation. Insight, however, need not be accompanied by a discursive understanding; someone with insight may directly apprehend the ethical significance of a situation but not be able to explain themselves. Without using the term "insight," Socrates distinguishes this concept from wisdom when he observes that inspired poets cannot explain their own profound compositions (*Apology* 22a–c).

The Regional approach to wisdom is represented in the present chapter by Confucius, Aristotle, Epicurus, and again Thomas Aquinas. Sayings and anecdotes associated with Confucius reveal a teacher who was ever alert to the misguided plans and purposes of those susceptible to his influence (3.3). Confucius exhibits an impressive degree of self-knowledge, but additionally his confidently asserted opinions and eloquent counsel suggest the possession of substantive wisdom. Part of Confucius's eloquence consists in judging when to speak and when to recognize the limits of speech. Sometimes that limit is determined by the subject matter, sometimes by the circumstances, and sometimes by the capacities of his pupils. In any case, because his sagacity is channeled into teaching, whatever theoretical content he draws upon is secondary to its practical expression in word or deed. Aristotle's account, by contrast, is theoretical and systematic, even if his subject is practical wisdom (3.5). He differentiates practical wisdom from technical knowledge on one side, and both speculative wisdom and theoretical wisdom on the other. Like technical knowledge, practical wisdom is exhibited in action. And like speculative and theoretical wisdom, practical wisdom apprehends substantive causal principles. Unlike all of these other forms of knowledge, however, practical wisdom guides deliberation for action, the ultimate purpose of which is "happiness" (and by which Aristotle means a good life that includes speculative wisdom about the cosmos and theoretical wisdom about conceptual matters). Epicurus, like Aristotle, puts wisdom in service to a good life, although his conception of a good life is defined more narrowly in terms of pleasure (3.7). By pleasure, Epicurus means "freedom from pain," which includes both physical and psychological pain. In particular, the materialist worldview and simple lifestyle of an Epicurean sage is designed to promote equanimity by releasing the sage from the complications of insatiable desires and the fear of death. Lastly, in *Summa Contra Gentiles*, Thomas Aquinas draws theoretical distinctions along the lines similar to those traced by Aristotle, but within a framework of Christian faith (3.9.2). The framework makes a significant difference in this case because the role of faith in wisdom is wider than that which Aristotle ascribes to substantive knowledge. Indeed, because the revelations of scripture are for him more authoritative than the discoveries of the intellect, faith grounds practical wisdom.

As we note elsewhere (1.1), the Western tradition that was for centuries oriented culturally, intellectually, and spiritually around *wisdom* shifted its focus to *enlightenment* in the modern era (roughly, 1500–1870). Even before the advent of the eighteenth-century movement known as The Enlightenment, however, two of its distinctive values had become commonplace: (i) the independence of mature judgement from tradition, and (ii) a commitment to the authority of reason over tradition. Like the debate over wisdom, debate in this chapter over the content of enlightenment as a state of mind or the meaning of the term is highly theoretical. Our point of departure for this debate is the synoptic encapsulation of it as a modern, European ideal in Immanuel Kant's "What Is Enlightenment?" (1.3). As Kant understands it, institutional religion has a civic function which it can fulfill well or poorly. Insofar as a religion supports the moral development of citizens, fostering their maturation, it fulfills that function well. If, however, otherwise mature adults become dependent on its institutions in the exercise of their judgement, then a religious institution fails. Kant's commitments to reason disqualify him from assessing religion on theological grounds, which is consigned to matters of faith. In his opinion, theological claims can be neither rationally grounded nor rationally refuted. From the point of view of reason, then, enlightenment must function independently of religious doctrine.

Three figures take up the theme of enlightenment as a distinct concept, namely, Gautama Buddha, Zar'a Yaqob, and Edmund Burke. Our earliest contribution, from Siddhartha Gautama, is a special case since it provides our only Eastern account of enlightenment (3.2). But, also, while the Buddha's ideas were originally disseminated independently of existing religious institutions, eventually Buddhism evolved into a religion with its own institutions and denominational factions. And lastly, Buddhism is a special case because some of the selections included here also contribute directly to our debate over wisdom. To the extent that *enlightenment* is conceptually distinct from wisdom, it is described as a desirable state of consciousness rather than as a normative capacity.[3] Enlightenment seems to be episodic in the life of a sage (3.2.3), so wisdom and enlightenment cannot be identical concepts. Moreover, rituals and practices (such as meditation) that are tightly associated with enlightenment are associated less tightly with wisdom *per se*. The sage functions in a social capacity, reproaching and counselling others. The Buddhist state of enlightenment, by contrast, seems to require a complete release from social relations. Conceptually, non-attachment requires a release from everything (material possessions, erotic desires, even the ego), and a sage's social relations seem to be among the last to go. Perhaps the persistence of social relations explains why Gautama is called the compassionate Buddha.

As the only African figure represented here, the seventeen-century Ethiopian, Zar'a Yaqob, is also a special case (3.10). Nevertheless, his account of enlightenment is conceptually more in keeping with the European tradition than Gautama Buddha's. In some ways Zar'a Yaqob's ideas about enlightenment anticipate Kant, even though there were no known contacts between himself and anyone connected to the European Enlightenment. In particular, he refers deliberative judgements to rationality in operations that must be performed independently of institutional authorities. Still, there are distinctive elements in Zar'a Yaqob's account of enlightenment, some in the presentation of his ideas and some in their content. Zar'a Yaqob's remarks about enlightenment are conveyed autobiographically, not defended in an argumentative essay. In content, Zar'a Yaqob's religious independence was exercised less as a critical response to institutional authority and more as an ecumenical attitude towards all religions. He wants to learn from every religion without being bound exclusively by any particular doctrine. Whereas Kant displays an even-handed detachment from all theological views, Zar'a Yaqob seems equally friendly to all of them. This, unfortunately, created difficulty for

3 Sometimes the terminology is not common from author to author, and in some cases an author will use the terms "wisdom" or "enlightenment," but qualified in some way. Our Buddhist contribution is unique in this chapter for invoking both terms, each with its own content.

him when nothing less than partisan allegiance was tolerable to local authorities.

Lastly, the present chapter presents conservative objections to enlightenment values by Kant's English contemporary Edmund Burke (3.12). Whereas Enlightenment authors encouraged people to think and act independently of traditional beliefs and values, Burke argues that sound judgement depends on them. Prejudices, which are antithetical to enlightenment values, are in his opinion indispensable for individual and collective agency: prejudices are the outward expression of time-tested knowledge. It is not always possible for an individual to fathom the implicit wisdom of the institutions and habits that govern our collective lives because these things became deeply enmeshed in the fabric of society incrementally and over vast stretches of time. If we reflect on the fundamental elements of our shared civic life Burke is confident that we shall see how subtle and ingeniously they work for our benefit. Still, we will inevitably encounter novel situations that our institutions were not prepared for specifically. In situations of this sort, we ought to change as little as possible. For this reason he advocates on behalf of reform, in contrast to Enlightenment authors who, in the name of abstract principles, looked more favourably upon the prospect of a political revolution. Here we see Burke reacting against the dominant intellectual trends of his day, preferring a less abstract brand of rationality and encouraging respect for historically important institutions.

In the second half of the nineteenth century—two generations after Kant and Burke—all sources of authority came under critical scrutiny. Beginning with Friedrich Nietzsche, suspicious regard for authority expanded beyond Enlightenment-era reservations about traditional beliefs and values to include reason, knowledge, and any institution thought to command unconditional respect. We cannot be saved from uncertainty by civil institutions, knowledge, reason, wisdom, or grace, Nietzsche insists. At best, we can learn to disregard the illusory authority of these things and live without any objective or external, normative guidance. Accordingly, a fundamental issue to consider in the present chapter concerns whether or not we can eliminate uncertainty at all—either with wisdom or enlightenment. This possibility necessitates the inclusion of (a) historically significant voices of skepticism and (b) post-Enlightenment voices objecting to both enlightenment and wisdom. Representing skepticism are Sextus Empiricus (3.8) and David Hume (3.11), and representing the post-Enlightenment period are Friedrich Nietzsche (3.13) and Albert Camus (3.14).

Of these voices, the skeptics are historically earlier, Sextus Empiricus being an ancient author and Hume predating Kant. In general, skeptics doubt the possibility of knowledge, thereby automatically ruling out both wisdom and enlightenment. Instead, skeptics refer judgements and choices to fallible customs, traditions, appearances, or sentiments. (Edmund Burke, incidentally, voices comparable doubts about enlightenment, but he prefers to present customs and traditions *as* wisdom (3.12).) In particular, Sextus doubts the Hellenistic era project to devise principles for the Art of Life as it was pursued by stoics and epicureans. He argues that any rational criterion for truth or goodness specified as part of this art is bound to be problematic for one of many reasons. As a consequence of this problem, doubts can never be eliminated. By default, we fall back on the sort of practical criteria that have nothing to do with art or any kind of "knowledge" at all, namely, customs, traditions, and appearances. David Hume objects more directly to eighteenth-century Enlightenment enthusiasm for rationality. Many of his contemporaries attempted to ground morality on fundamental rational bases or on a systematic set of principles. Hume argues that this project is entirely wrong-headed, since rationality is not normative: neither moral principles nor human moral motivation is ever guided by our rational faculties. Sentiments, not reasons, govern morality, and rationality serves our non-rational faculties by identifying ways to accomplish the dictates of our sentiments.

Post-Enlightenment thinkers (sometimes called "post-modernists") tend to challenge all purported sources of authoritative guidance, including customs, traditions, and anything purporting to be objectively normative. Even the idea of truth itself is challenged by Friedrich Nietzsche (3.13). In *The Birth of Tragedy* (not included here), he asserts provocatively that "knowledge kills action." If so, for genuine human agency, inspiration of the sort that Socrates attributes to poets (Apology 22b–c), is better than knowledge: independence comes from being inspired by one's own self-generated values, not from being guided by knowledge conceived of as a set of substantive normative principles. Anyone who is not inspired by a creative, self-generated conception of their own life or values is, according to Nietzsche, necessarily led by externally imposed values. Albert Camus takes this impulse one step further: our healthiest attitude consists in rebelling against the prevailing order of the cosmos (3.14). In doing this we confer value on something by investing in it, thereby giving meaning to life. Not all post-Enlightenment figures rebel strenuously against authority as Nietzsche and Camus do, but such doubts about institutional and moral authority are typical of the era. Accordingly, recent work in ethical theory tends to focus narrowly on clarifying our ethical concepts or critically investigating the institutions of authority that govern our collective lives. Religion, traditional morality, moral theory, science, technology, legal institutions, and popular media have been subject to special scrutiny by post-Enlightenment authors. This is not to say that we are encouraged to discard all institutions of civil society, only that presuppositions about authority, including the authority of knowledge, can no longer be taken for granted.

3.2 Siddhartha Gautama (563–483 BCE, Buddhism)

The sermons and weighty proclamations of Siddhartha Gautama, the Buddha, seem more in keeping with the ordinary expectations of a sage than Socrates's modest self-awareness. Whereas Socrates is known as a gadfly critic of his fellow Athenians, Gautama is known as the Compassionate Buddha. Certainly, Gautama Buddha's sermons have an air of profundity. The Four Noble Truths are stated in his first sermon at Benares ("First Sermon," 3.2.1): (1) life is painful; (2) ignorant desire leads us astray; attachments and delusions cause suffering; (3) we can be released from pain and suffering by overcoming ego-centricity; (4) the way to salvation is embodied in the Noble Eightfold Path, a list of eight requirements for spiritual success. The precepts put forth by the Buddha are formulated as self-evident postulates rather than argued conclusions. The items listed as part of the Noble Eightfold Path, for example, are formulaically posited as "Right ... [views/intentions/speech/etc.]." Apart from brief elaboration in "The Synopsis of Truth" (3.2.2) and "The Path" (3.2.5), these precepts are not sufficiently directive to be doctrinaire. Evidently, this lack of specificity has a purpose: spiritual fulfillment is an internal condition that cannot be generated by adopting doctrines or following a rule-governed procedure. Fundamental to such fulfillment is non-attachment, a state of release from all striving and desire, even—paradoxically—the ego-centric desire for spiritual fulfillment. The culmination of this release is a state of consciousness that Buddhists call "enlightenment."

Two of the readings included here are character sketches, one of "The Fool" (3.2.3) and one of "The Wise Man" (i.e., "the sage" in gender-neutral terms, 3.2.4). The Sanskrit word for wisdom or insight is *pranjā*. The fool is characterized as being oblivious to wisdom due to ego-centric attachments; even instruction and association with a sage cannot convey *pranjā* to anyone with such attachments. The sage, however, may rightfully instruct and admonish others, as Gautama did; this is how wisdom is expressed as compassion. The sage is characterized in terms of non-attachment, purity, and simplicity, so this instruction must be undertaken non-dogmatically.

3.2.1 "First Sermon at Benares"[1]

These two extremes, O monks, are not to be practised by one who has gone forth from the world. What are the two? That conjoined with the passions, low, vulgar, common, ignoble, and useless, and that conjoined with self-torture, painful, ignoble, and useless. Avoiding these two extremes the Tathāgata[2] has gained the knowledge of the Middle Way, which gives sight and knowledge, and tends to calm, to insight, enlightenment, *nirvāṇa*.

What, O monks, is the Middle Way, which gives sight...? It is the noble Eightfold Path, namely, right views, right intention, right speech, right action, right livelihood, right effort, right mindfulness, right concentration. This, O monks, is the Middle Way....

(1) Now this, O monks, is the noble truth of pain: birth is painful, old age is painful, sickness is painful, death is painful, sorrow, lamentation, dejection, and despair are painful. Contact with unpleasant things is painful, not getting what one wishes is painful. In short the five *khandhas* of grasping are painful.[3]

(2) Now this, O monks, is the noble truth of the cause of pain: that craving which leads to rebirth, combined with pleasure and lust, finding pleasure here and there, namely, the craving for passion, the craving for existence, the craving for non-existence.

(3) Now this, O monks, is the noble truth of the cessation of pain: the cessation without a remainder of that craving, abandonment, forsaking, release, non-attachment.

(4) Now this, O monks, is the noble truth of the way that leads to the cessation of pain: this is the noble Eightfold Path, namely, right views, right intention, right speech, right action, right livelihood, right effort, right mindfulness, right concentration....

As long as in these noble truths my threefold knowledge and insight duly with its twelve divisions was not well purified, even so long, O monks, in the world with its gods, Māra,[4] Brahmā,[5] with ascetics, *brāhmins*, gods, and men, I had not attained the highest complete enlightenment. Thus I knew.

But when in these noble truths my threefold knowledge and insight duly with its twelve divisions was well purified, then, O monks, in the world ... I had attained the highest complete enlightenment. Thus I knew. Knowledge arose in me; insight arose that the release of my mind is unshakable; this is my last existence; now there is no rebirth.

1 *Saṁyutta-nikāya* v. 420; in Edward J. Thomas, *The Life of Buddha as Legend and History* (New York: Alfred A. Knopf, 1927), pp. 87–88.
2 "Tathāgata" is a name for the Buddha. Literally it means one who has "thus come."
3 The five *khandhas* (groups or aggregates) are form, feeling (or sensation), perception (volitional disposition), predispositions (or impressions), and consciousness.
4 The goddess of temptation.
5 God in the role of creator.

3.2.2 *"The Synopsis of Truth"*[6]

Thus have I heard. Once when the Lord was staying at Benares in the Isipatana deerpark, he addressed the almsmen as follows: It was here in this very deerpark at Benares that the Truth-finder, *Arahat* [*arhat*] all-enlightened, set a-rolling the supreme Wheel of the Doctrine—which shall not be turned back from its onward course by recluse or *brāhmin*, god or Māra or Brahmā or by anyone in the universe,—the announcement of the Four Noble Truths, the teaching, declaration, and establishment of those Four Truths, with their unfolding, exposition, and manifestation.

What are these four?—The announcement, teaching ... and manifestation of the Noble Truth of suffering[7]—of the origin of suffering—of the cessation of suffering—of the path that leads to the cessation of suffering.

Follow, almsmen, Sāriputta and Moggallāna and be guided by them; they are wise helpers unto their fellows in the higher life.... Sāriputta is able to announce, teach ... and manifest the Four Noble Truths in all their details.

Having thus spoken, the Blessed One arose and went into his own cell.

The Lord had not been gone long when the reverent Sāriputta proceeded to the exposition of the Truth-finder's Four Noble Truths, as follows:

What, reverend sirs, is the Noble Truth of suffering?—Birth is a suffering; decay is a suffering; death is a suffering; grief and lamentation, pain, misery and tribulation are sufferings; it is a suffering not to get what is desired;—in brief all the factors of the five-fold grip on existence are suffering.

Birth is, for living creatures of each several class, the being born or produced, the issue, the arising or the re-arising, the appearance of the impressions,[8] the growth of faculties.

Decay, for living creatures of each several class, is the decay and decaying, loss of teeth, grey hair, wrinkles, a dwindling term of life, sere faculties.

Death, for living creatures of each several class, is the passage and passing hence, the dissolution, disappearance, dying, death, decease, the dissolution of the impressions, the discarding of the dead body.

Grief is the grief, grieving, and grievousness, the inward grief and inward anguish of anyone who suffers under some misfortune or is in the grip of some type of suffering.

Lamentation is the lament and lamentation, the wailing and the lamenting of anyone who suffers under some misfortune or is in the grip of some type of suffering.

Pain is any bodily suffering or bodily evil, and suffering bred of bodily contact, any evil feeling.

Misery is mental suffering and evil, any evil feeling of the mind.

Tribulation is the tribulation of heart and mind, the state to which tribulation brings them, in anyone who suffers under some misfortune or is in the grip of some type of suffering.

There remains not to get what is desired. In creatures subject to birth—or decay—or death—or grief and lamentation, pain, misery, and tribulation—the desire arises not to be subject thereto but to escape them. But escape is not to be won merely by desiring it; and failure to win it is another suffering.

What are in brief all the factors of the fivefold grip on existence which are sufferings?—They are: the factors of form, feeling, perception, impressions, and consciousness.

The foregoing, sirs, constitutes the Noble Truth of suffering.

What now is the Noble Truth of the origin of suffering? It is any craving that makes for re-birth and is

6 *Majjhima-nikāya*, iii. 248–52: in *Further Dialogues of the Buddha*, II, translated by Lord Chalmers, Sacred Books of the Buddhists, VI (London: Oxford University Press, 1927), pp. 296–99.

7 "Suffering" has been substituted for the translator's "ill" in this selection. Other frequent translations are "misery" and "pain."

8 "Impressions," "dispositions," or "predispositions" would appear to be a better translation of *saṁskāras* than the translator's "plastic forces."

tied up with passion's delights and culls satisfaction now here now there—such as the craving for sensual pleasure, the craving for continuing existence, and the craving for annihilation.

Next, what is the Noble Truth of the cessation of suffering?—It is the utter and passionless cessation of this same craving,—the abandonment and rejection of craving, deliverance from craving, and aversion from craving.

Lastly, what is the Noble Truth of the Path that leads to the cessation of suffering?—It is just the Noble Eightfold Path, consisting of right outlook, right resolves, right speech, right acts, right livelihood, right endeavour, right mindfulness and right rapture of concentration.

Right outlook is to know suffering, the origin of suffering, the cessation of suffering, and the path that leads to the cessation of suffering.

Right resolves are the resolve to renounce the world and to do no hurt or harm.

Right speech is to abstain from lies and slander, from reviling, and from tattle.

Right acts are to abstain from taking life, from stealing, and from lechery.

Right livelihood is that by which the disciple of the Noble One supports himself, to the exclusion of wrong modes of livelihood.

Right endeavour is when an almsman brings his will to bear, puts forth endeavour and energy, struggles and strives with all his heart, to stop bad and wrong qualities which have not yet arisen from ever arising, to renounce those which have already arisen, to foster good qualities which have not yet arisen, and, finally, to establish, clarify, multiply, enlarge, develop, and perfect those good qualities which are there already.

Right mindfulness is when realizing what the body is—what feelings are—what the heart is—and what the mental states are—an almsman dwells ardent, alert, and mindful, in freedom from the wants and discontents attendant on any of these things.

Right rapture of concentration is when, divested of lusts and divested of wrong dispositions, an almsman develops, and dwells in, the first ecstasy with all its zest and satisfaction, a state bred of aloofness and not divorced from observation and reflection. By laying to rest observation and reflection, he develops and dwells in inward serenity, in [the] focussing of heart, in the zest and satisfaction of the second ecstasy, which is divorced from observation and reflection and is bred of concentration—passing thence to the third and fourth ecstasies.

This, sirs, constitutes the Noble Truth of the Path that leads to the cessation of suffering....

3.2.3 "The Fool"

1. Long is the night to him who is awake, long is the *yojana* (a space of nine or twelve miles) to him who is weary; long is the chain of existence to the foolish who do not know the true law. (60)

2. If on a journey (a traveller) does not meet his better or equal let him firmly pursue his journey by himself; there is no companionship with a fool. (61)

3. The fool is tormented thinking "these sons belong to me," "this wealth belongs to me." He himself does not belong to himself. How, then, can sons be his? How can wealth be his? (62)

4. The fool who knows his foolishness is wise at least to that extent; but a fool who thinks himself wise is called a fool indeed. (63)

5. If a fool be associated with a wise man even all his life, he does not perceive the truth even as a spoon (does not perceive) the taste of soup. (64)

6. But if a thoughtful man be associated with a wise man even for a minute, he will soon perceive the truth even as the tongue (perceives) the taste of soup. (65)

7. Fools of little understanding, being enemies to themselves, wander about doing evil deeds which bear bitter fruits. (66)

8. That deed is not well done, which, having been done, brings remorse, whose reward one receives weeping and with a tearful countenance. (67)

9. But that deed is well done, which, having been done, does not bring remorse, whose reward one receives delighted and happy. (68)

10. So long as an evil deed does not bear fruit, the fool thinks that it is like honey; but when it bear fruit, then the fool suffers grief. (69)

11. Let a fool month after month eat his food with the tip (of a blade) of *kuśa* grass; nevertheless he is not worth the sixteenth part of those who have well understood the law. (70)

12. An evil deed, like newly drawn milk, does not turn (at once); smouldering, like fire covered by ashes, it follows the fool. (71)

13. The knowledge that a fool acquires, far from being to his advantage, destroys his bright share of merit and cleaves his head. (72)

14. Let the fool wish for false reputation, for precedence among the mendicants, for lordship in convents, and worship among other groups. (73)

15. "Let both the householders and the monks think that this is done by me. Let them follow my pleasure in what should be done and what should not be done." Such is the wish of the fool and so his desire and pride increase. (74)

16. One is the road that leads to gain; another is the road that leads to *nirvāṇa*. Let the mendicant, the disciple of the Buddha, having learnt this, not seek the respect of men but strive after wisdom. (75)

3.2.4 *"The Wise Man"*

1. If a person sees a wise man who reproaches him (for his faults), who shows what is to be avoided, he should follow such a wise man as he would a revealer of hidden treasures. It fares well and not ill with one who follows such a man. (76)

2. Let him admonish, let him instruct, let him restrain from the impure. He becomes beloved of the good and hated by the evil. (77)

3. One should not associate with friends who are evil-doers nor with persons who are despicable; associate with friends who are virtuous, associate with the best of men. (78)

4. He who drinks in the law lives happily with a serene mind. The wise man ever rejoices in the law made known by the elect (or the Āryas). (79)

5. Engineers (who build canals and aqueducts) lead the water (wherever they like), fletchers make the arrow straight, carpenters carve the wood; wise people fashion (discipline) themselves. (80)

6. As a solid rock is not shaken by the wind, so wise men are not moved amidst blame and praise. (81)

7. Even as a deep lake is clear and calm, so also wise men become tranquil after they have listened to the laws. (82)

8. Good people walk on whatever happens to them. Good people do not prattle, yearning for pleasures. The wise do not show variation (elation or depression), whether touched by happiness or else by sorrow. (83)

9. He who, for his own sake or for the sake of another, does not wish for a son or wealth or a kingdom, if he does not wish for his own prosperity by unfair means he certainly is virtuous, wise, and religious. (84)

10. Few amongst men are those who reach the farther shore: the other people here run along (this) shore. (85)

11. But those who, when the law has been well preached to them, follow the law, will pass to the other shore, [beyond] the dominion of death which is difficult to overcome. (86)

12. Let the wise man leave the way of darkness and follow the way of light. After going from his home to a homeless state, that retirement so hard to love. (87)

13. Let him there look for enjoyment. Putting away all pleasures, calling nothing his own, let the wise man cleanse himself from all the impurities of the heart. (88)

14. Those whose minds are well grounded in the (seven) elements of enlightenment, who without clinging to anything rejoice in freedom from attachment, whose appetites have been conquered, who are full of light, attain *nirvāṇa* in this world. (89)

3.2.5 "The Path"

1. Of paths the eightfold is the best; of truths the (best are) four sayings (truths); of virtues freedom from attachment is the best; of men (literally two-footed beings) he who is possessed of sight. (273)

2. This is the path; there is none other that leads to the purifying of insight. You follow this (path). This will be to confuse (escape from) Māra (Death, sin). (274)

3. Going on this path, you will end your suffering. This path was preached by me when I became aware of the removal of the thorns (in the flesh). (275)

4. You yourself must strive. The Blessed Ones are (only) preachers. Those who enter the path and practise meditation are released from the bondage of Māra (Death, sin). (276)

5. "All created things are impermanent (transitory)." When one by wisdom realizes (this), he heeds not (is superior to) (this world of) sorrow; this is the path to purity. (277)

6. "All created things are sorrowful." When one by wisdom realizes (this) he heeds not (is superior to) (this world of) sorrow; this is the path to purity. (278)

7. "All the elements of being are non-self." When one by wisdom realizes (this), he heeds not (is superior to) (this world of) sorrow; this is the path to purity. (279)

8. He who does not get up when it is time to get up, who, though young and strong, is full of sloth, who is weak in resolution and thought, that lazy and idle man will not find the way to wisdom. (280)

9. Guarding his speech, restraining well his mind, let a man not commit anything wrong with his body. He who keeps these three roads of action clear will achieve the way taught by the wise. (281)

10. From meditation springs wisdom; from lack of meditation there is loss of wisdom. Knowing this twofold path of progress and decline, a man should place himself in such a way that his wisdom increases. (282)

11. Cut down the (whole) forest, not the tree (only); danger comes out of the forest. Having cut down both the forest and desire, O mendicants, do you attain freedom. (283)

12. As long indeed as the desire, however small, of a man for women is not destroyed, so long is his mind attached (to existence) as a sucking calf is to its mother. (284)

13. Cut out the love of self as you would an autumn lily with the hand. Cherish the path to peace, to *nirvāṇa* pointed out by the Buddha. (285)

14. "Here I shall dwell in the rain, here in winter and summer" thus the fool thinks; he does not think of the obstacle (of life). (286)

15. As a great flood carries off a sleeping village, death takes off and goes with that man who is giddy (with the possession of) children and cattle, whose mind is distracted (with the desire for worldly goods). (287)

16. Sons are no protection, nor father, nor relations; for one who is seized by death, there is no safety in kinsmen. (288)

17. Realizing the significance of this, the wise and righteous man should even quickly clear the path leading to release. (289)

3.3 Confucius (551–478 BCE)

The Analects collects sayings and anecdotes from the life of Confucius (more accurately rendered as Master Cong). Like Socrates and Siddhartha Gautama, Confucius did not write, but the exemplary way he lived his life and the things he said about that life inspired others to record these things. Passages of two sorts are included here: (1) some passages sketch a picture of Confucius as a sage providing counsel; (2) others help fill out the network of concepts that inform the Confucian tradition's account of wisdom and noble-mindedness. Most comprehensive editions of *The Analects* intersperse passages that depict the master's character and passages that convey his ideas, and we have followed that precedent here. Concentrating on Confucius's conceptual remarks, we can see that wisdom or noble-mindedness requires study, the proper observance of ritual, attention to duty, modesty, and reverence.

The character of Confucius that emerges from *The Analects* is of someone dedicated to virtue, ritual, tradition, family and community, and learning. While many sayings in *The Analects* are directive and straight-forward, many remarks are suggestive rather than explicit. There is an underlying integrity to this combination of principles, but Confucius never developed a "system" to relate them explicitly. For this reason Confucianism must be understood as a tradition rather than a system of ideas. Confucius's personal charisma and his spiritual influence were so great, however, that later figures were inspired to construct abstract and general theories systematizing the tradition.

~

from The Analects

Book 1. CHAP. IV. The philosopher Tsang said, 'I daily examine myself on three points:—whether, in transacting business for others, I may have been not faithful;—whether, in intercourse with friends, I may have been not sincere;—whether I may have not mastered and practised the instructions of my teacher.'

Book 2. CHAP. IV. The Master said, 'At fifteen, I had my mind bent on learning. At thirty, I stood firm. At forty, I had no doubts. At fifty, I knew the decrees of Heaven. At sixty, my ear was an obedient organ for the reception of truth. At seventy, I could follow what my heart desired, without transgressing what was right.'

Book 2. CHAP. XI. The Master said, 'If a man keeps cherishing his old knowledge, so as continually to be acquiring new, he may be a teacher of others.'

Book 2. CHAP. XII. The Master said, 'The accomplished scholar is not a utensil.'

Book 3. CHAP. XXIV. The border warden at Yi requested to be introduced to the Master, saying, 'When men of superior virtue have come to this, I have never been denied the privilege of seeing them.' The followers of the sage introduced him, and when he came out from the interview, he said, 'My friends, why are you distressed by your master's loss of office? The kingdom has long been without the principles of truth and right;

Heaven is going to use your master as a bell with its wooden tongue.'

Book 6. CHAP. XXI. The Master said, 'The wise find pleasure in water; the virtuous find pleasure in hills. The wise are active; the virtuous are tranquil. The wise are joyful; the virtuous are long-lived.'

Book 6. CHAP. XXVII. The Master said, 'Perfect is the virtue which is according to the Constant Mean! Rare for a long time has been its practise among the people.'

Book 6. CHAP. XXVIII. Tsze-kung said, 'Suppose the case of a man extensively conferring benefits on the people, and able to assist all, what would you say of him? Might he be called perfectly virtuous?'

The Master said, 'Why speak only of virtue in connexion with him? Must he not have the qualities of a sage? Even Yao and Shun were still solicitous about this. Now the man of perfect virtue, wishing to be established himself, seeks also to establish others; wishing to be enlarged himself, he seeks also to enlarge others. To be able to judge of others by what is nigh in ourselves;—this may be called the art of virtue.'

Book 7. CHAP. VI. 1. The Master said, 'Let the will be set on the path of duty. Let every attainment in what is good be firmly grasped. Let perfect virtue be accorded with. Let relaxation and enjoyment be found in the polite arts.'

Book 7. CHAP. VIII. The Master said, 'I do not open up the truth to one who is not eager to get knowledge, nor help out any one who is not anxious to explain himself. When I have presented one corner of a subject to any one, and he cannot from it learn the other three, I do not repeat my lesson.'

Book 7. CHAP. XI. The Master said, 'If the search for riches is sure to be successful, though I should become a groom with whip in hand to get them, I will do so. As the search may not be successful, I will follow after that which I love.'

Book 7. CHAP. XIX. The Master said, 'I am not one who was born in the possession of knowledge; I am one who is fond of antiquity, and earnest in seeking it there.'

Book 7. CHAP. XXVII. The Master said, 'There may be those who act without knowing why. I do not do so. Hearing much and selecting what is good and following it; seeing much and keeping it in memory:—this is the second style of knowledge.'

Book 7. CHAP. XXXIII. The Master said, 'The sage and the man of perfect virtue;—how dare I rank myself with them? It may simply be said of me, that I strive to become such without satiety, and teach others without weariness.'

Kung-hsi Hwa said, 'This is just what we, the disciples, cannot imitate you in.'

Book 8. CHAP. VII. The philosopher Tsang said, 'The officer may not be without breadth of mind and vigorous endurance. His burden is heavy and his course is long.

'Perfect virtue is the burden which he considers it is his to sustain;—is it not heavy? Only with death does his course stop;—is it not long?'

Book 12. CHAP. I. 1. Yen Yuan asked about perfect virtue. The Master said, 'To subdue one's self and return to propriety, is perfect virtue. If a man can for one day subdue himself and return to propriety, all under heaven will ascribe perfect virtue to him. Is the practice of perfect virtue from a man himself, or is it from others?'

Yen Yuan said, 'I beg to ask the steps of that process.'

The Master replied, 'Look not at what is contrary to propriety; listen not to what is contrary to propriety; speak not what is contrary to propriety; make no movement which is contrary to propriety.'

Yen Yuan then said, 'Though I am deficient in intelligence and vigour, I will make it my business to practise this lesson.'

Book 14. CHAP. XIII. Tsze-lu asked what constituted a COMPLETE man. The Master said, 'Suppose a man with the knowledge of Tsang Wu-chung, the freedom from covetousness of Kung-ch'o, the bravery of Chwang of Pien, and the varied talents of Zan Ch'iu; add to these the accomplishments of the rules of propriety and music:—such a one might be reckoned a COMPLETE man.' He then added, 'But what is the necessity for a complete man of the present day to have all these things? The man, who in the view of gain, thinks of righteousness; who in the view of danger is prepared to give up his life; and who does not forget an old agreement however far back it extends:—such a man may be reckoned a COMPLETE man.'

Book 15. CHAP. XVIII. The Master said, 'The superior man is distressed by his want of ability. He is not distressed by men's not knowing him.'

Book 15. CHAP. XX. The Master said, 'What the superior man seeks is in himself. What the mean man seeks is in others.'

Book 15. CHAP. XXX. The Master said, 'I have been the whole day without eating, and the whole night without sleeping:—occupied with thinking. It was of no use. The better plan is to learn.'

Book 16. CHAP. VIII. Confucius said, 'There are three things of which the superior man stands in awe. He stands in awe of the ordinances of Heaven. He stands in awe of great men. He stands in awe of the words of sages. The mean man does not know the ordinances of Heaven, and consequently does not stand in awe of them. He is disrespectful to great men. He makes sport of the words of sages.'

Book 17. CHAP. VIII. The Master said, 'Yu, have you heard the six words to which are attached six beclouding s?'

Yu replied, 'I have not.'

'Sit down, and I will tell them to you. There is the love of being benevolent without the love of learning;—the beclouding here leads to a foolish simplicity. There is the love of knowing without the love of learning;—the beclouding here leads to dissipation of mind. There is the love of being sincere without the love of learning;—the beclouding here leads to an injurious disregard of consequences. There is the love of straightforwardness without the love of learning;—the beclouding here leads to rudeness. There is the love of boldness without the love of learning;—the beclouding here leads to insubordination. There is the love of firmness without the love of learning;—the beclouding here leads to extravagant conduct.'

Book 17. CHAP. XIX. The Master said, 'I would prefer not speaking.'

Tsze-kung said, 'If you, Master, do not speak, what shall we, your disciples, have to record?'

The Master said, 'Does Heaven speak? The four seasons pursue their courses, and all things are continually being produced, but does Heaven say anything?'

3.4 Solomon (tenth century BCE)

Proverbs contains sage advice, prophetic warnings, and gnomic utterances attributed to the ancient Israelite king, Solomon. Solomon's renowned wisdom comes not only from what he said, but also from his character, and the insightful judgements he made as leader of his people. This reputation was based primarily on his conduct, and it is preserved in the accounts that ultimately became *Proverbs, Ecclesiastes*, and *The Song of Solomon*, central books of the Hebrew Old Testament. A profound respect for knowledge and compassion for his subjects is evident both in the words preserved in those sacred texts and his legendary good judgement as it is depicted there. Solomon's wisdom combines the desire to learn, the ability to learn, the application of learning to life, submission to divine judgement, and recognition of the limits of learning.

from Proverbs

Chapter 1

1. The parables of Solomon, the son of David, king of Israel,
2. To know wisdom, and instruction:
3. To understand the words of prudence: and to receive the instruction of doctrine, justice, and judgement, and equity:
4. To give subtilty to little ones, to the young man knowledge and understanding.
5. A wise man shall hear, and shall be wiser: and he that understandeth shall possess governments.
6. He shall understand a parable and the interpretation, the words of the wise, and their mysterious sayings.
7. The fear of the Lord is the beginning of wisdom. Fools despise wisdom and instruction.
8. My son, hear the instruction of thy father, and forsake not the law of thy mother:
9. That grace may be added to thy head, and a chain of gold to thy neck.
10. My son, if sinners shall entice thee, consent not to them.
11. If they shall say: Come with us, let us lie in wait for blood, let us hide snares for the innocent without cause:
12. Let us swallow him up alive like hell, and whole as one that goeth down into the pit.
13. We shall find all precious substance, we shall fill our houses with spoils.
14. Cast in thy lot with us, let us all have one purse.
15. My son, walk not thou with them, restrain thy foot from their paths.
16. For their feet run to evil, and make haste to shed blood.
17. But a net is spread in vain before the eyes of them that have wings.
18. And they themselves lie in wait for their own blood, and practise deceits against their own souls.
19. So the ways of every covetous man destroy the souls of the possessors.
20. Wisdom preacheth abroad, she uttereth her voice in the streets:
21. At the head of multitudes she crieth out, in the entrance of the gates of the city she uttereth her words, saying:
22. O children, how long will you love childishness, and fools covet those things which are hurtful to themselves, and the unwise hate knowledge?

23. Turn ye at my reproof: behold I will utter my spirit to you, and will shew you my words.
24. Because I called, and you refused: I stretched out my hand, and there was none that regarded.
25. You have despised all my counsel, and have neglected my reprehensions.
26. I also will laugh in your destruction, and will mock when that shall come to you which you feared.
27. When sudden calamity shall fall on you, and destruction, as a tempest, shall be at hand: when tribulation and distress shall come upon you:
28. Then shall they call upon me, and I will not hear: they shall rise in the morning, and shall not find me:
29. Because they have hated instruction, and received not the fear of the Lord,
30. Nor consented to my counsel, but despised all my reproof.
31. Therefore they shall eat the fruit of their own way, and shall be filled with their own devices.
32. The turning away of little ones shall kill them, and the prosperity of fools shall destroy them.
33. But he that shall hear me, shall rest without terror, and shall enjoy abundance, without fear of evils.

Chapter 2

1. My son, if thou wilt receive my words, and wilt hide my commandments with thee,
2. That thy ear may hearken to wisdom: incline thy heart to know prudence.
3. For if thou shalt call for wisdom, and incline thy heart to prudence:
4. If thou shalt seek her as money, and shalt dig for her as for a treasure:
5. Then shalt thou understand the fear of the Lord, and shalt find the knowledge of God:
6. Because the Lord giveth wisdom: and out of his mouth cometh prudence and knowledge.
7. He wilt keep the salvation of the righteous, and protect them that walk in simplicity,
8. Keeping the paths of justice, and guarding the ways of saints.
9. Then shalt thou understand justice, and judgement, and equity, and every good path.
10. If wisdom shall enter into thy heart, and knowledge please thy soul:
11. Counsel shall keep thee, and prudence shall preserve thee,
12. That thou mayst be delivered from the evil way, and from the man that speaketh perverse things....

Chapter 3

...

13. Blessed is the man that findeth wisdom, and is rich in prudence:
14. The purchasing thereof is better than the merchandise of silver, and her fruit than the chief and purest gold:
15. She is more precious than all riches: and all the things that are desired, are not to be compared to her.
16. Length of days is in her right hand, and in her left hand riches and glory.
17. Her ways are beautiful ways, and all her paths are peaceable.
18. She is a tree of life to them that lay hold on her: and he that shall retain her is blessed....

Chapter 8

1. Doth not wisdom cry aloud, and prudence put forth her voice?
2. Standing in the top of the highest places by the way, in the midst of the paths,

3. Beside the gates of the city, in the very doors she speaketh, saying:
4. O ye men, to you I call, and my voice is to the sons of men.
5. O little ones understand subtlety, and ye unwise, take notice.
6. Hear, for I will speak of great things: and my lips shall be opened to preach right things.
7. My mouth shall meditate truth, and my lips shall hate wickedness.
8. All my words are just, there is nothing wicked, nor perverse in them.
9. They are right to them that understand, and just to them that find knowledge.
10. Receive my instruction, and not money: choose knowledge rather than gold.
11. For wisdom is better than all the most precious things: and whatsoever may be desired cannot be compared to it.
12. I, wisdom, dwell in counsel, and am present in learned thoughts.
13. The fear of the Lord hateth evil; I hate arrogance, and pride, and every wicked way, and a mouth with a double tongue.
14. Counsel and equity is mine, prudence is mine, strength is mine.
15. By me kings reign, and lawgivers decree just things.
16. By me princes rule, and the mighty decree justice.
17. I love them that love me: and they that in the morning early watch for me, shall find me.
18. With me are riches and glory, glorious riches and justice.
19. For my fruit is better than gold and the precious stone, and my blossoms than choice silver.
20. I walk in the way of justice, in the midst of the paths of judgement,
21. That I may enrich them that love me, and may fill their treasures....

3.5 Aristotle (384–322 BCE)

Book VI of the *Nicomachean Ethics* outlines Aristotle's account of practical wisdom. Here Aristotle distinguishes practical wisdom from wisdom in the arts (technical knowledge, *techné*) and scientific knowledge (*episteme*). Essentially, practical wisdom is desirable as a guide to deliberation. Technical knowledge is too specialized to count as wisdom and deals with matters over which we do not deliberate. An application of technical knowledge presupposes that we have already identified our purpose, whereas deliberation has to do with finding a purpose. A car mechanic, for example, can diagnose and change a damaged engine, but this does not help us decide whether these repairs are worthwhile. Scientific knowledge, however, differs from practical wisdom in not being confined to human matters and, again, does not concern matters over which we deliberate. Whatever intricate details scientists discover about the chemistry of biological life will not help us decide how to conduct our own life. Additionally, Aristotle explores what is involved in deliberation and judgement and what differentiates wisdom from cleverness.

Aristotle's inquiry into practical wisdom in Book VI is framed by the larger subject of his *Nicomachean Ethics*, that is, the good life. This frame is established in Book I, where he adopts a teleological approach to ethics and analyzes human life in terms of a broadly conceived single purpose, happiness (*eudaimonia*). By happiness he means not a mood or passing state of mind. The Greek word here is instructive: *Eudaimonia* translates literally as "good" (eu) "spirit" (daimon), which metaphorically conveys the impression of a semi-divine figure overseeing one's welfare. For happiness, i.e., a "good life," one must develop one's rational faculties. Practical wisdom, therefore, is not merely an instrumental good that secures for us other good things (such as wealth, honours, pleasure, etc.); it is an intrinsic good, something that fulfills our special potential.

from Nicomachean Ethics, *Books I and VI*

Book I

CHAPTER I

Every art, and every science reduced to a teachable form, and in like manner every action and moral choice, aims, it is thought, at some good: for which reason a common and by no means a bad description of the Chief Good is, "that which all things aim at."

Now there plainly is a difference in the Ends proposed: for in some cases they are acts of working, and in others certain works or tangible results beyond and beside the acts of working: and where there are certain Ends beyond and beside the actions, the works are in their nature better than the acts of working. Again, since actions and arts and sciences are many, the Ends likewise come to be many: of the healing art, for instance, health; of the ship-building art, a vessel; of the military art, victory; and of domestic management, wealth; are respectively the Ends.

And whatever of such actions, arts, or sciences range under some one faculty (as under that of horsemanship the art of making bridles, and all that are connected with the manufacture of horse-furniture in general; this itself again, and every action connected with war, under the military art; and in the same way others under others), in all such, the Ends of the master-arts are more choice-worthy than those ranging under them, because it is with a view to the former that the latter are pursued.

(And in this comparison it makes no difference whether the acts of working are themselves the Ends of the actions, or something further beside them, as is the case in the arts and sciences we have been just speaking of.)

CHAPTER II

Since then of all things which may be done there is some one End which we desire for its own sake, and with a view to which we desire everything else; and since we do not choose in all instances with a further End in view (for then men would go on without limit, and so the desire would be unsatisfied and fruitless), this plainly must be the Chief Good, i.e., the best thing of all.

Surely then, even with reference to actual life and conduct, the knowledge of it must have great weight; and like archers, with a mark in view, we shall be more likely to hit upon what is right: and if so, we ought to try to describe, in outline at least, what it is and of which of the sciences and faculties it is the End.

Now one would naturally suppose it to be the End of that which is most commanding and most inclusive: and to this description, *politikae* [politics] plainly answers: for this it is that determines which of the sciences should be in the communities, and which kind individuals are to learn, and what degree of proficiency is to be required. Again; we see also ranging under this the most highly esteemed faculties, such as the art military, and that of domestic management, and Rhetoric. Well then, since this uses all the other practical sciences, and moreover lays down rules as to what men are to do, and from what to abstain, the

End of this must include the Ends of the rest, and so must be The Good of Man. And grant that this is the same to the individual and to the community, yet surely that of the latter is plainly greater and more perfect to discover and preserve: for to do this even for a single individual were a matter for contentment; but to do it for a whole nation, and for communities generally, were more noble and godlike.

CHAPTER III

Such then are the objects proposed by our treatise, which is of the nature of *politikae* [politics]: and I conceive I shall have spoken on them satisfactorily, if they be made as distinctly clear as the nature of the subject-matter will admit: for exactness must not be looked for in all discussions alike, any more than in all works of handicraft. Now the notions of nobleness and justice, with the examination of which *politikea* [politics] is concerned, admit of variation and error to such a degree, that they are supposed by some to exist conventionally only, and not in the nature of things: but then, again, the things which are allowed to be goods admit of a similar error, because harm comes to many from them: for before now some have perished through wealth, and others through valour.

We must be content then, in speaking of such things and from such data, to set forth the truth roughly and in outline; in other words, since we are speaking of general matter and from general data, to draw also conclusions merely general. And in the same spirit should each person receive what we say: for the man of education will seek exactness so far in each subject as the nature of the thing admits, it being plainly much the same absurdity to put up with a mathematician who tries to persuade instead of proving, and to demand strict demonstrative reasoning of a Rhetorician.

Now each man judges well what he knows, and of these things he is a good judge: on each particular matter then he is a good judge who has been instructed in *it*, and in a general way the man of general mental cultivation.

Hence the young man is not a fit student of Moral Philosophy, for he has no experience in the actions of life, while all that is said presupposes and is concerned with these: and in the next place, since he is apt to follow the impulses of his passions, he will hear as though he heard not, and to no profit, the end in view being practice and not mere knowledge.

And I draw no distinction between young in years, and youthful in temper and disposition: the defect to which I allude being no direct result of the time, but of living at the beck and call of passion, and following each object as it rises. For to them that are such the knowledge comes to be unprofitable, as to those of imperfect self-control: but, to those who form their desires and act in accordance with reason, to have knowledge on these points must be very profitable.

Book VI

CHAPTER V

As for Practical Wisdom, we shall ascertain its nature by examining to what kind of persons we in common language ascribe it.

It is thought then to be the property of the Practically Wise man to be able to deliberate well respecting what is good and expedient for himself, not in any definite line, as what is conducive to health or strength, but what to living well. A proof of this is that we call men Wise in this or that, when they calculate well with a view to some good end in a case where there is no definite rule. And so, in a general way of speaking, the man who is good at deliberation will be Practically Wise. Now no man deliberates respecting things which cannot be otherwise than they are, nor such as lie not within the range of his own action: and so, since Knowledge requires strict demonstrative reasoning, of which Contingent matter does not admit (I say Contingent matter, because all matters of deliberation must be Contingent and deliberation cannot take place with respect to things which are Necessarily), Practical Wisdom cannot be Knowledge nor Art; nor the former, because what falls under the province of Doing must be Contingent; not the latter, because Doing and Making are different in kind.

It remains then that it must be "a state of mind true, conjoined with Reason, and apt to Do, having for its object those things which are good or bad for Man:" because of Making something beyond itself is always the object, but cannot be of Doing because the very well-doing is in itself an End.

For this reason we think Pericles and men of that stamp to be Practically Wise, because they can see what is good for themselves and for men in general, and we also think those to be such who are skilled in domestic management or civil government. In fact, this is the reason why we call the habit of perfected self-mastery by the name which in Greek it bears, etymologically signifying "that which preserves the Practical Wisdom": for what it does preserve is the Notion I have mentioned, i.e., one's own true interest. For it is not every kind of Notion which the pleasant and the painful corrupt and pervert, as, for instance, that "the three angles of every rectilineal triangle are equal to two right angles," but only those bearing on moral action.

For the Principles of the matters of moral action are the final cause of them: now to the man who has been corrupted by reason of pleasure or pain the Principle immediately becomes obscured, nor does he see that it is his duty to choose and act in each instance with a view to this final cause and by reason of it: for viciousness has a tendency to destroy the moral Principle: and so Practical Wisdom must be "a state conjoined with reason, true, having human good for its object, and apt to do."

Then again Art admits of degrees of excellence, but Practical Wisdom does not: and in Art he who goes wrong purposely is preferable to him who does so unwittingly, but not so in respect of Practical Wisdom or the other Virtues. It plainly is then an Excellence of a certain kind, and not an Art.

Now as there are two parts of the Soul which have Reason, it must be the Excellence of the Opinionative [which we called before calculative or deliberative], because both Opinion and Practical Wisdom are exercised upon Contingent matter. And further, it is not simply a state conjoined with Reason, as is proved by the fact that such a state may be forgotten and so lost while Practical Wisdom cannot....

CHAPTER VII

Science is a term we use principally in two meanings: in the first place, in the Arts we ascribe it to those who carry their arts to the highest accuracy; Phidias, for instance, we call a Scientific or cunning sculptor; Polycleitus a Scientific or cunning statuary; meaning, in this instance, nothing else by Science than an excellence of art: in the other sense, we think some to be Scientific in a general way, not in any particular line or in any particular thing, just as Homer says of a man in his Margites; "Him the Gods made neither a digger of the ground, nor ploughman, nor in any other way Scientific."

So it is plain that Science must mean the most accurate of all Knowledge; but if so, then the Scientific man must not merely know the deductions from the First Principles but be in possession of truth respecting the First Principles. So that Science must be equivalent to Intuition and Knowledge; it is, so to speak, Knowledge of the most precious object.

I say of the most precious things, because it is absurd to suppose *politikae* [politics], or Practical Wisdom, to be the highest, unless it can be shown that Man is the most excellent of all that exists in the Universe. Now if "healthy" and "good" are relative terms, differing when applied to men or to fish, but "white" and "straight" are the same always, men must allow that the Scientific is the same always, but the Practically Wise varies: for whatever provides all things well for itself, to this they would apply the term Practically Wise, and commit these matters to it; which is the reason, by the way, that they call some brutes Practically Wise, such that is as plainly have a faculty of forethought respecting their own subsistence.

And it is quite plain that Science and *politikae* [politics] cannot be identical: because if men give the name of Science to that faculty which is employed upon what is expedient for themselves, there will be many instead of one, because there is not one and the same faculty employed on the good of all animals collectively, unless in the same sense as you may say there is one art of healing with respect to all living beings.

If it is urged that man is superior to all other animals, that makes no difference: for there are many other things more Godlike in their nature than Man, as, most obviously, the elements of which the Universe is composed.

It is plain then that Science is the union of Knowledge and Intuition, and has for its objects those things which are most precious in their nature. Accordingly, Anaxagoras, Thales, and men of that stamp, people call Scientific, but not Practically Wise because they see them ignorant of what concerns themselves; and they say that what they know is quite out of the common run certainly, and wonderful, and hard, and very fine no doubt, but still useless because they do not seek after what is good for them as men.

But Practical Wisdom is employed upon human matters, and such as are objects of deliberation (for we say, that to deliberate well is most peculiarly the work of the man who possesses this Wisdom), and no man deliberates about things which cannot be otherwise than they are, nor about any save those that have some definite End and this End good resulting from Moral Action; and the man to whom we should give the name of Good in Counsel, simply and without modification, is he who in the way of calculation has a capacity for attaining that of practical goods which is the best for Man.

3.6 Cleanthes (331–232 BCE, Stoicism)

Alexander the Great's empire extended from Macedonia to Egypt to India. The Hellenistic era is dated from the year of his death, 323 BCE (a year before his teacher, Aristotle, in 322 BCE). In the wake of this military campaign Greek ideas disseminated to the outer boundaries of his conquest, and the reciprocal flow of non-Greek ideas making their way back to Greece, introduced a cosmopolitanism that had been unimaginable in previous times. (Before this era Greeks referred to non-Greeks as "barbarians" because the unintelligible speech of other languages sounded to them like "bar bar bar bar.") The unified empire collapsed into four different regional empires after his death, but a cultural shift was irreversible by this point. A great deal of cultural intermingling had exported Greek ideas to previously unknown realms, and non-Greek ideas were already drifting back to Greece. In this context three schools of thought emerged that reflect in their own ways the new international scope of ethics, Stoicism, Epicureanism, and Skepticism.

Ultimately, stoicism came to dominate the Roman Empire. One emperor, Marcus Aurelius (121–180 CE), was an avowed stoic, and his *Mediations* survive to this day as a popular source of insight. And Epictetus (55–135) was a freed slave who became an influential stoic teacher. Their dedication to duty, willingness to set aside personal inclinations to fulfill a social role, and commitment to reason made stoics dutiful functionaries for the empire. Cleanthes, who lived in the Roman Republic and before the Empire was founded by Augustus in 27 BCE, was among the earliest figures in the school, and his poem "Hymn to Zeus" summarizes several stoic themes: providence, the priority of reason over everything else, cosmic governance by divine law, wisdom as obedience to objective regulative principles, and folly as ego-centric resistance to the same principle, among others.

~

"Hymn to Zeus"

Most glorious of Immortals, mighty God,
Invoked by many a name, O sovran King
Of universal Nature, piloting
This world in harmony with Law,—all hail!

Thee it is meet that mortals should invoke,
For we Thine offspring are, and sole of all
Created things that live and move on earth
Receive from Thee the image of the One.

Therefore I praise Thee, and shall hymn Thy power
Unceasingly. Thee the wide world obeys,
As onward ever in its course it rolls
Where'er Thou guidest, and rejoices still
Beneath Thy sway: so strong a minister
Is held by Thine unconquerable hands,—
That two-edged thunderbolt of living fire
That never fails.

    Under its dreadful blow
All Nature reels; therewith Thou dost direct
The Universal Reason which, commixt
With all the greater and the lesser lights,
Moves thro' the Universe.

    How great Thou art,
The Lord supreme for ever and for aye!
No work is wrought apart from Thee, O God,
Or in the world, or in the heaven above,
Or on the deep, save only what is done
By sinners in their folly.

    Nay, Thou canst
Make the rough smooth, bring wondrous order forth
From chaos; in Thy sight unloveliness

Seems beautiful; for so Thou hast fitted things
Together, good and evil, that there reigns
One everlasting Reason in them all.

The wicked heed not this, but suffer it
To slip, to their undoing; these are they
Who, yearning ever to secure the good,
Mark not nor hear the law of God, by wise
Obedience unto which they might attain
A nobler life, with Reason harmonized.

But now, unbid, they pass on divers paths
Each his own way, yet knowing not the truth,—
Some in unlovely striving for renown,
Some bent on lawless gains, on pleasure some,
Working their own undoing, self-deceived.

O Thou most bounteous God that sittest throned
In clouds, the Lord of lightning, save mankind
From grievous ignorance!

Oh, scatter it
Far from their souls, and grant them to achieve
True knowledge, on whose might Thou dost rely
To govern all the world in righteousness;

That so, being honoured, we may Thee requite
With honour, chanting without pause Thy deeds,
As all men should: since greater guerdon ne'er
Befalls or man or god than evermore
Duly to praise the Universal Law.

3.7 Epicurus (341–271 BCE)

Epicurus's "Letter to Menoeceus" summarizes Epicurean ethics, which are based on pleasure (*hedon*, hence hedonism). By pleasure, Epicurus means simply "absence of pain." In this letter he identifies prudently sought pleasure of this sort as the central feature in the life of a sage. Unlike the stoics, Epicureans were pure materialists. They disavowed abstract principles and abstract impersonal duties. They also denied the influence of supernatural forces in human life: if gods exist, they have nothing to do with us, so we cannot depend on providence. An epicurean sage, therefore, eliminates external dependence as much as possible: simple living, simple food, and withdrawal from political life. Dependence on anything outside one's direct control comes with the risk of pain. So pleasure does not involve voluptuous sensuous experiences for a traditional epicurean. For this reason, Epicurus and his followers retreated to his garden in Athens and refrained from participating in public life.

Epicurus's letter, therefore, summarizes the art of life as he understood it. Since material comfort (i.e., a painless life) was essential to the good life, neither systematic completeness nor theoretical precision was important to Epicurus. "Rationality" is identified with prudential self-regulation. The soul is material and the function of reason is tactical and entirely instrumental: it must help us avoid pain. In its speculative functions, reason helps us understand that death is final and that, without the prospect of a punitive afterlife, it is not to be feared. On this single question about the fear of death, they agree with Socrates (*Apology* 40b–41d). Otherwise, they objected to most of his claims and presuppositions: the immateriality of the soul, the intrinsic value of reason, the possibility of an afterlife, and so on.

"Letter to Menoeceus"

Greeting.

Let no one be slow to seek wisdom when he is young nor weary in the search thereof when he is grown old. For no age is too early or too late for the health of the soul. And to say that the season for studying philosophy has not yet come, or that it is past and gone, is like saying that the season for happiness is not yet or that it is now no more. Therefore, both old and young ought to seek wisdom, the former in order that, as age comes over him, he may be young in good things because of the grace of what has been, and the latter in order that, while he is young, he may at the same time be old, because he has no fear of the things which are to come. So we must exercise ourselves in the things which bring happiness, since, if that be present, we have everything, and, if that be absent, all our actions are directed toward attaining it.

Those things which without ceasing I have declared to you, those do, and exercise yourself in those, holding them to be the elements of right life. First believe that God is a living being immortal and happy, according to the notion of a god indicated by the common sense of humankind.... For truly there are gods, and knowledge of them is evident; but they are not such as the multitude believe, seeing that people do not steadfastly maintain the notions they form respecting them. Not the person who denies the gods worshipped by the multitude, but he who affirms of the gods what the multitude believes about them is truly impious. For the utterances of the multitude about the gods are not true preconceptions but false assumptions; hence it is that the greatest evils happen to the wicked and the greatest blessings happen to the good from the hand of the gods, seeing that they are always favorable to their own good qualities and take pleasure in people like to themselves, but reject as alien whatever is not of their kind.

Accustom yourself to believe that death is nothing to us, for good and evil imply awareness, and death is the privation of all awareness; therefore a right understanding that death is nothing to us makes the mortality of life enjoyable, not by adding to life an unlimited time, but by taking away the yearning after immortality. For life has no terror; for those who thoroughly apprehend that there are no terrors for them in ceasing to live. Foolish, therefore, is the person who says that he fears death, not because it will pain when it comes, but because it pains in the prospect. Whatever causes no annoyance when it is present, causes only a groundless pain in the expectation. Death, therefore, the most awful of evils, is nothing to us, seeing that, when we are, death is not come, and, when death is come, we are not. It is nothing, then, either to the living or to the dead, for with the living it is not and the dead exist no longer. But in the world, at one time people shun death as the greatest of all evils, and at another time choose it as a respite from the evils in life. The wise person does not deprecate life nor does he fear the cessation of life. The thought of life is no offense to him, nor is the cessation of life regarded as an evil. And even as people choose of food not merely and simply the larger portion, but the more pleasant, so the wise seek to enjoy the time which is most pleasant and not merely that which is longest. And he who admonishes the young to live well and the old to make a good end speaks foolishly, not merely because of the desirability of life, but because the same exercise at once teaches to live well and to die well. Much worse is he who says that it were good not to be born, but when once one is born to pass with all speed through the gates of Hades. For if he truly believes this, why does he not depart from life? It were easy for him to do so, if once he were firmly convinced. If he speaks only in mockery, his words are foolishness, for those who hear believe him not.

We must remember that the future is neither wholly ours nor wholly not ours, so that neither must we count upon it as quite certain to come nor despair of it as quite certain not to come.

We must also reflect that of desires some are natural, others are groundless; and that of the natural some are necessary as well as natural, and some natural only. And of the necessary desires some are necessary if we are to be happy, some if the body is to be rid of uneasiness, some if we are even to live. He who has a clear and certain understanding of these things will direct every preference and aversion toward securing health of body and tranquillity of mind, seeing that this is the sum and end of a happy life. For the end of all our actions is to be free from pain and fear, and, when once we have attained all this, the tempest of the soul is laid; seeing that the living creature has no need to go in search of something that is lacking, nor to look to anything else by which the good of the soul and of the body will be fulfilled. When we are pained, then, and then only, do we feel the need of pleasure. For this reason we call pleasure the alpha and omega of a happy life. Pleasure is our first and kindred good. It is the starting-point of every choice and of every aversion, and to it we come back, inasmuch as we make feeling the rule by which to judge of every good thing. And since pleasure is our first and native good, for that reason we do not choose every pleasure whatever, but often pass over many pleasures when a greater annoyance ensues from them. And often we consider pains superior to pleasures when submission to the pains for a long time brings us as a consequence a greater pleasure. While therefore all pleasure because it is naturally akin to us is good, not all pleasure is worthy of choice, just as all pain is an evil and yet not all pain is to be shunned. It is, however, by measuring one against another, and by looking at the conveniences and inconveniences, that all these matters must be judged. Sometimes we treat the good as an evil, and the evil, on the contrary, as a good. Again, we regard independence of outward things as a great good, not so as in all cases to use little, but so as to be contented with little if we have not much, being honestly persuaded that they have the sweetest enjoyment of luxury who stand least in need of it, and that whatever is natural is easily procured and only the vain and worthless hard to win. Plain fare gives as much pleasure as a costly diet, when once the pain of want has been removed, while bread and water confer the highest possible pleasure when they are brought to hungry lips. To habituate one's self, therefore, to simple and inexpensive diet supplies all that is needful for health, and enables a person to meet the necessary requirements of life without shrinking and it places us in a better condition when we approach at intervals a costly fare and renders us fearless of fortune.

When we say, then, that pleasure is the end and aim, we do not mean the pleasures of the prodigal or the pleasures of sensuality, as we are understood to do by some through ignorance, prejudice, or willful misrepresentation. By pleasure we mean the absence of pain in the body and of trouble in the soul. It is not an unbroken succession of drinking-bouts and of merrymaking, not sexual love, not the enjoyment of the fish and other delicacies of a luxurious table, which produce a pleasant life; it is sober reasoning, searching out the grounds of every choice and avoidance, and banishing those beliefs through which the greatest disturbances take possession of the soul. Of all this the end is prudence. For this reason prudence is a more precious thing even than the other virtues, for as a life of pleasure which is not also a life of prudence, honor, and justice; nor lead a life of prudence, honor, and justice, which is not also a life of pleasure. For the virtues have grown into one with a pleasant life, and a pleasant life is inseparable from them.

Who, then, is superior in your judgment to such a person? He holds a holy belief concerning the gods, and is altogether free from the fear of death. He has diligently considered the end fixed by nature, and understands how easily the limit of good things can be reached and attained, and how either the duration or the intensity of evils is but slight. Destiny which some introduce as sovereign over all things, he laughs to scorn, affirming rather that some things happen of necessity, others by chance, others through our own agency. For he sees that necessity destroys responsibility and that chance or fortune is inconstant; whereas our own actions are free, and it is to them that praise and blame naturally attach. It were better, indeed, to accept the legends of the gods than to bow beneath destiny which the natural philosophers have imposed. The one holds out some faint hope that we may escape if we honor the gods, while the necessity of the naturalists is deaf to all entreaties. Nor does he hold chance to be a god, as the world in general does, for in the acts of a god there is no disorder; nor to be a cause, though an uncertain one, for he believes that no good or evil is dispensed by chance to people so as to make life happy, though it supplies the starting-point of great good and great evil. He believes that the misfortune of the wise is better than the prosperity of the fool. It is better, in short, that what is well judged in action should not owe its successful issue to the aid of chance.

Exercise yourself in these and kindred precepts day and night, both by yourself and with him who is like to you; then never, either in waking or in dream, will you be disturbed, but will live as a god among people. For people lose all appearance of mortality by living in the midst of immortal blessings.

3.8 Sextus Empiricus (160–210, Skepticism)

Pyrrhonism is a branch of ancient skepticism that objected to abstract theorizing. Our representative skeptic here is Sextus Empiricus, a medical doctor who collected skeptical arguments and presented the most comprehensive defence of the school's position on a range of questions. In one chapter of *Against the Ethicists*, "Does there exist any art of life?" Sextus formulates objections to a project undertaken by most of the other Hellenistic schools, in particular the stoics, the epicureans, and the peripatetics (i.e., the followers of Aristotle). These schools maintained that there is an "art of living" (in Latin, *ars vivendi*), and each school articulated what it took to be the fundamental principles of this art. Sextus raises doubts about the possibility and desirability of such an art. Indeed, because skeptics doubt that human beings can know anything, an *art* of living or any other source of wisdom is ruled out. One of the arguments from this chapter, along with a previous chapter, is included below. Essentially, Sextus argues that the goal of this purported "art," imperturbability of mind (*ataraxia*), is frustrated by dogmatic commitments. Peace of mind, or imperturbability, is better satisfied by suspending judgement (*epoché*).

In particular, skeptics had doubts about the prospect of being guided by abstract theoretical principles. To refer our judgements about right and wrong or to decide a course of action on the basis of a general or abstract principle seemed dogmatic to skeptics. Basing one's judgement or decision on such a principle may pass for being rational among others who accept the principle, but it's not possible to ground the principle on an independent criterion (see 4.4.1). A central problem for Hellenistic schools was finding a criterion (i.e., a standard of judgement). For epicureans, pleasure (defined as absence of pain) was the criterion; for stoics and peripatetics reason, properly defined. Skeptics disavowed these as dogmatic, adhering instead to appearances and custom (4.4.1). All this is in keeping with the name "skeptic," which is derived from the Greek *skeptomai* (i.e., to search, to look carefully, to examine).

from Against the Ethicists

Chapter V.—Is He Who Suspends Judgement Regarding the Nature of Things Good and Evil in All Respects Happy?

He, then, is happy who lives to the end without perturbation and, as Timon said, existing in a state of quietness and calm—

> For on all sides calm was prevailing,

And—

> Him when thus I descried in a calm
> with no winds to disquiet.

And of the goods and evils which are said to exist some are introduced by belief, others by necessity. Thus by [rational] belief are introduced all those which men pursue or avoid of their own judgement,—as, for example, amongst things external, wealth and fame and noble birth and friendship, and everything of the kind, are called desirable and good; and, amongst qualities of the body, beauty and strength and sound condition; and, amongst qualities of the soul, courage and justice and wisdom and virtue in general; and the opposites of these are regarded as things to be avoided. But by necessity are brought about all such things as befall us because of an irrational affection of sense, and all that some natural necessity brings about, "but no one would willingly choose them," or avoid them,—such as pain and pleasure. Hence, since there exists such a difference as this in these things, the fact that it is only the man who suspends judgement about all things who lives to the end an unperturbed life in respect of the goods and evils due to belief we have already established, both in our previous discussion of the Sceptic "end," and also on the present occasion when we showed that it is not possible to be happy if one assumes the existence of anything good and evil by nature. For he who does this is tossed about with endless perturbations, through avoiding these things and pursuing those, and drawing upon himself many evils because of the goods, and being afflicted by many times more evils because of his belief about evils....

Chapter VI.—Does There Exist any Art of Life?

We have proved sufficiently that it is possible to live a satisfactory life by adopting suspension of judgement about all things....

Also, if the science of life,—that is, wisdom,—is cognisant of things good and evil and neither, either it is other than the goods whereof it is said to be the science, or it is itself the good, even as some of them assert in their definition—"Good is virtue or what partakes of virtue." And if it is other than the goods whereof it is said to be the science, it will not be a science at all; for every science is the knowledge of certain existing things, but we have previously shown that goods and evils are non-existent, so that neither will there exist any science of goods and evils. But if it is itself the good and claims to be the science of the goods, it will be the science of itself; and this again is absurd. For the things which form the object of a science are conceived before the science. Thus medicine is said to be the science of things healthy and morbid and neither; but the healthy and morbid things are in existence before medicine and precede it. And again: Music is the science of things in tune and out of tune, rhythmical and unrhythmical; but previous to these Music does not exist.... If, then, wisdom is the science of itself, it must have existed before itself; but nothing can have existed before itself; so that neither in this way can it be asserted that any art of life exists.

3.9 St. Thomas Aquinas (1225–1274)

Thomas Aquinas was a leading figure of medieval Catholic theology and philosophy. He drew upon both Christian doctrine and Aristotle's ideas to articulate positions on an extraordinary range of issues. His priority in this regard lay with Christianity, but Aristotelian philosophy was central to his efforts to systematize Catholic doctrine. In particular, he sought a way to reconcile a life of faith with a commitment to reason in its speculative and practical functions.

Our passages from *Summa Theologiae* elaborate on the nature of practical wisdom, in particular how it relates to both spiritual grace and the intellectual capacities of reason. Wisdom manifests as rectitude of judgement directed towards higher things. For Aquinas, the highest object of contemplation is God. Both love (i.e., charity) and intelligence or reason participate in wisdom. Accordingly, folly is a deficiency of the heart and the intellect.

Our passages from *Summa Contra Gentiles* address directly the relationship between faith and reason. As it turns out, for him revelations of faith and discoveries of reason do not conflict. The compatibility of faith and reason is evident on both substantive and moral matters, and both have roles to play in scientific knowledge and moral agency. Some important questions reason cannot answer (on God's eternality, the universe's creation, and salvation of the soul after death, to name only three). While both the grace of revealed religion and the discoveries of our rational faculties provide normative guidance for human life, religious doctrine is broader in scope than reason. On some questions only revelation, and not reason, provides guidance for the faithful. Reason is a natural endowment that allows human beings to occupy a special place within the created universe. We alone can participate actively in the rational order of things.

One final note about the unusual organization of *Summa Theologiae*: this highly formalized text is less forbidding if a few things are borne in mind. All the major questions are addressed systematically in a series of "Articles." Each article is oriented around a subsidiary question, expressed in the interrogative mood. Within each article, views opposing that of Aquinas are presented first as numbered "Objections." These objections are followed by an authoritative answer to the question from a church father, passage of scripture, or a revered author such as Aristotle. The voice of authority is brought in to correct errors that have been already stated as objections, so it is introduced formulaically with "On the contrary,..." Aquinas then answers the question in his own voice, opening with "I answer that ..." Lastly, each objection is given a direct reply as a "Reply to objection 1 (or 2 or 3 ...)." In some cases in this and the next chapter we have selected only essential parts of an article, namely, the question, the voice of authority, and Aquinas's answer. Question 45, Second Article that begins 3.9.1 is a complete example of this format, however.

~

3.9.1 *from* Summa Theologiae

Book II; Part II

QUESTION 45: OF THE GIFT OF WISDOM

We must now consider the gift of wisdom which corresponds to charity; and firstly, wisdom itself, secondly, the opposite vice....

SECOND ARTICLE [II–II, Q. 45, ART. 2]

Whether Wisdom Is in the Intellect As Its Subject?

Objection 1: It would seem that wisdom is not in the intellect as its subject. For Augustine says (*Ep.* cxx) that "wisdom is the charity of God." Now charity is in the will as its subject, and not in the intellect, as stated [elsewhere]. Therefore wisdom is not in the intellect as its subject.

Obj. 2: Further, it is written (*Ecclus.* 6:23): "The wisdom of doctrine is according to her name," for wisdom (*sapientia*) may be described as "sweet-tasting science (*sapida scientia*)," and this would seem to regard the appetite to which it belongs to taste spiritual pleasure or sweetness. Therefore wisdom is in the appetite rather than in the intellect.

Obj. 3: Further, the intellective power is sufficiently perfected by the gift of understanding. Now it is superfluous to require two things where one suffices for the purpose. Therefore wisdom is not in the intellect.

On the contrary, Gregory says (*Moral.* ii, 49) that "wisdom is contrary to folly." But folly is in the intellect. Therefore wisdom is also.

I answer that, ... wisdom denotes a certain rectitude of judgment according to the Eternal Law. Now rectitude of judgment is twofold: first, on account of perfect use of reason, secondly, on account of a certain connaturality with the matter about which one has to judge. Thus, about matters of chastity, a man after inquiring with his reason forms a right judgment, if he has learnt the science of morals, while he who has the habit of chastity judges of such matters by a kind of connaturality.

Accordingly it belongs to the wisdom that is an intellectual virtue to pronounce right judgment about Divine things after reason has made its inquiry, but it belongs to wisdom as a gift of the Holy Ghost to judge aright about them on account of connaturality with them: thus Dionysius says (*Div. Nom.* ii) that "Hierotheus is perfect in Divine things, for he not only learns, but is patient of, Divine things."

Now this sympathy or connaturality for Divine things is the result of charity, which unites us to God, according to *1 Cor.* 6:17: "He who is joined to the Lord, is one spirit." Consequently wisdom which is a gift, has its cause in the will, which cause is charity, but it has its essence in the intellect, whose act is to judge aright....

Reply Obj. 1: Augustine is speaking of wisdom as to its cause, whence also wisdom (*sapientia*) takes its name, in so far as it denotes a certain sweetness (*saporem*). Hence the *Reply to the Second Objection* is evident, that is if this be the true meaning of the text quoted. For, apparently this is not the case, because such an exposition of the text would only fit the Latin word for wisdom, whereas it does not apply to the Greek and perhaps not in other languages. Hence it would seem that in the text quoted wisdom stands for the renown of doctrine, for which it is praised by all.

Reply Obj. 3: The intellect exercises a twofold act, perception and judgment. The gift of understanding regards the former; the gift of wisdom regards the latter according to the Divine ideas, the gift of knowledge, according to human ideas.

THIRD ARTICLE [II–II, Q. 45, ART. 3]
Whether Wisdom Is Merely Speculative, or Practical Also?

Objection 1: It would seem that wisdom is not practical but merely speculative. For the gift of wisdom is more excellent than the wisdom which is an intellectual virtue. But wisdom, as an intellectual virtue, is merely speculative. Much more therefore is wisdom, as a gift, speculative and not practical.

Obj. 2: Further, the practical intellect is about matters of operation which are contingent. But wisdom is about Divine things which are eternal and necessary. Therefore wisdom cannot be practical.

Obj. 3: Further, Gregory says (*Moral.* vi, 37) that "in contemplation we seek the Beginning which is God, but in action we labor under a mighty bundle of wants." Now wisdom regards the vision of Divine things, in which there is no toiling under a load, since according to *Wis.* 8:16, "her conversation hath no bitterness, nor her company any tediousness." Therefore wisdom is merely contemplative, and not practical or active.

On the contrary, It is written (*Col.* 4:5): "Walk with wisdom towards them that are without." Now this pertains to action. Therefore wisdom is not merely speculative, but also practical.

I answer that, As Augustine says (*De Trin.* xii, 14), the higher part of the reason is the province of wisdom, while the lower part is the domain of knowledge. Now the higher reason according to the same authority (*De Trin.* xii, 7) "is intent on the consideration and consultation of the heavenly," i.e., Divine...; it considers them, in so far as it contemplates Divine things in themselves, and it consults them, in so far as it judges of human acts by Divine things, and directs human acts according to Divine rules.

Accordingly wisdom as a gift, is not merely speculative but also practical.

Reply Obj. 1: The higher a virtue is, the greater the number of things to which it extends, as stated in *De Causis*, prop. x, xvii. Wherefore from the very fact that wisdom as a gift is more excellent than wisdom as an intellectual virtue, since it attains to God more intimately by a kind of union of the soul with Him, it is able to direct us not only in contemplation but also in action.

Reply Obj. 2: Divine things are indeed necessary and eternal in themselves, yet they are the rules of the contingent things which are the subject-matter of human actions.

Reply Obj. 3: A thing is considered in itself before being compared with something else. Wherefore to wisdom belongs first of all contemplation which is the vision of the Beginning, and afterwards the direction of human acts according to the Divine rules. Nor from the direction of wisdom does there result any bitterness or toil in human acts; on the contrary the result of wisdom is to make the bitter sweet, and labor a rest.

FOURTH ARTICLE [II–II, Q. 45, ART. 4]
Whether Wisdom Can Be Without Grace, and with Mortal Sin? ...

On the contrary, It is written (*Wis.* 1:4): "Wisdom will not enter into a malicious soul, nor dwell in a body subject to sins."

I answer that, The wisdom which is a gift of the Holy Ghost, as stated above (A. 1), enables us to judge aright of Divine things, or of other things according to Divine rules, by reason of a certain connaturalness or union with Divine things, which is the effect of charity, as stated [elsewhere]. Hence the wisdom of which we are speaking presupposes charity. Now charity is incompatible with mortal sin, as shown [elsewhere]. Therefore it follows that the wisdom of which we are speaking cannot be together with mortal sin....

FIFTH ARTICLE [II–II, Q. 45, ART. 5]
Whether Wisdom Is in All Who Have Grace?...

On the contrary, Whoever is without mortal sin, is beloved of God; since he has charity, whereby he loves God, and God loves them that love Him (*Prov.* 8:17). Now it is written (*Wis.* 7:28) that "God loveth none but him that dwelleth with wisdom." Therefore wisdom is in all those who have charity and are without mortal sin.

I answer that, The wisdom of which we are speaking, as stated above (A. 4), denotes a certain rectitude of judgment in the contemplation and consultation of Divine things, and as to both of these men obtain various degrees of wisdom through union with Divine things. For the measure of right judgment attained by some, whether in the contemplation of Divine things or in directing human affairs according to Divine rules, is no more than suffices for their salvation. This measure is wanting to none who is without mortal sin through having sanctifying grace, since if nature does not fail in necessaries, much less does grace fail: wherefore it is written (*1 John* 2:27): "(His) unction teacheth you of all things."

Some, however, receive a higher degree of the gift of wisdom, both as to the contemplation of Divine things (by both knowing more exalted mysteries and being able to impart this knowledge to others) and as to the direction of human affairs according to Divine rules (by being able to direct not only themselves but also others according to those rules). This degree of wisdom is not common to all that have sanctifying grace, but belongs rather to the gratuitous graces, which the Holy Ghost dispenses as He will, according to *1 Cor.* 12:8: "To one indeed by the Spirit is given the word of wisdom," etc....

QUESTION 46: OF FOLLY WHICH IS OPPOSED TO WISDOM ...

FIRST ARTICLE [II–II, Q. 46, ART. 1]
Whether Folly Is Contrary to Wisdom?...

On the contrary, Gregory says (*Moral.* ii, 26) that "the gift of wisdom is given as a remedy against folly."

I answer that, *Stultitia* (Folly) seems to take its name from *stupor*; wherefore Isidore says (loc. cit.): "A fool is one who through dullness (*stuporem*) remains unmoved." And folly differs from fatuity, according to the same authority (*Etym.* x), in that folly implies apathy in the heart and dullness in the senses, while fatuity denotes entire privation of the spiritual sense. Therefore folly is fittingly opposed to wisdom.

For "sapiens" (*wise*) as Isidore says (*Etym.* x) "is so named from *sapor* (savor), because just as the taste is quick to distinguish between savors of meats, so is a wise man in discerning things and causes." Wherefore it is manifest that *folly* is opposed to *wisdom* as its contrary, while *fatuity* is opposed to it as a pure negation: since the fatuous man lacks the sense of judgment, while the fool has the sense, though dulled, whereas the wise man has the sense acute and penetrating.

SECOND ARTICLE [II–II, Q. 46, ART. 2]
Whether Folly Is a Sin?

Objection 1: It would seem that folly is not a sin. For no sin arises in us from nature. But some are fools naturally. Therefore folly is not a sin.

Obj. 2: Further, "Every sin is voluntary," according to Augustine (*De Vera Relig.* xiv). But folly is not voluntary. Therefore it is not a sin.

Obj. 3: Further, every sin is contrary to a Divine precept. But folly is not contrary to any precept. Therefore folly is not a sin.

On the contrary, It is written (*Prov.* 1:32): "The prosperity of fools shall destroy them." But no man is destroyed save for sin. Therefore folly is a sin.

I answer that, Folly, as stated above (A. 1), denotes dullness of sense in judging, and chiefly as regards the highest cause, which is the last end and the sovereign good. Now a man may in this respect contract dullness in judgment in two ways. First, from a natural indisposition, as in the case of idiots, and such like folly is no sin. Secondly, by plunging his sense into earthly things, whereby his sense is rendered incapable of perceiving Divine things, according to *1 Cor.* 2:14, "The sensual man perceiveth not these things that are of the Spirit of God," even as sweet things have no savor for a man whose taste is infected with an evil humor: and such like folly is a sin.

This suffices for the *Reply to the First Objection*.

Reply Obj. 2: Though no man wishes to be a fool, yet he wishes those things of which folly is a consequence, viz. to withdraw his sense from spiritual things and to plunge it into earthly things. The same thing happens in regard to other sins; for the lustful man desires pleasure, without which there is no sin, although he does not desire sin simply, for he would wish to enjoy the pleasure without sin.

Reply Obj. 3: Folly is opposed to the precepts about the contemplation of truth, of which we have spoken above (Q. 16) when we were treating of knowledge and understanding.

3.9.2 *from* Summa Contra Gentiles

Book I

CHAPTER 7: THAT THE TRUTH OF REASON IS NOT OPPOSED TO THE TRUTH OF THE CHRISTIAN FAITH

[1] Now, although the truth of the Christian faith which we have discussed surpasses the capacity of the reason, nevertheless that truth that the human reason is naturally endowed to know cannot be opposed to the truth of the Christian faith. For that with which the human reason is naturally endowed is clearly most true; so much so, that it is impossible for us to think of such truths as false. Nor is it permissible to believe as false that which we hold by faith, since this is confirmed in a way that is so clearly divine. Since, therefore, only the false is opposed to the true, as is clearly evident from an examination of their definitions, it is impossible that the truth of faith should be opposed to those principles that the human reason knows naturally.

[2] Furthermore, that which is introduced into the soul of the student by the teacher is contained in the knowledge of the teacher—unless his teaching is fictitious, which it is improper to say of God. Now, the knowledge of the principles that are known to us naturally has been implanted in us by God; for God is the Author of our nature. These principles, therefore, are also contained by the divine Wisdom. Hence, whatever is opposed to them is opposed to the divine Wisdom, and, therefore, cannot come from God. That which we hold by faith as divinely revealed, therefore, cannot be contrary to our natural knowledge....

[7] From this we evidently gather the following conclusion: whatever arguments are brought forward against the doctrines of faith are conclusions incorrectly derived from the first and self-evident principles imbedded in nature. Such conclusions do not have the force of demonstration; they are arguments that are either probable or sophistical. And so, there exists the possibility to answer them.

CHAPTER 8: HOW THE HUMAN REASON IS RELATED TO THE TRUTH OF FAITH

[1] There is also a further consideration. Sensible things, from which the human reason takes the origin of its knowledge, retain within themselves some sort of trace of a likeness to God. This is so imperfect, however, that it is absolutely inadequate to manifest the substance of God. For effects bear within themselves, in their own way, the likeness of their causes, since an agent produces its like; yet an effect does not always reach to the full likeness of its cause. Now, the human reason is related to the knowledge of the truth of faith (a truth which can be most evident only to those who see the divine substance) in such a way that it can gather certain likenesses of it, which are yet not sufficient so that the truth of faith may be comprehended as being understood demonstratively or through itself. Yet it is useful for the human reason to exercise itself in such arguments, however weak they may be, provided only that there be present no presumption to comprehend or to demonstrate. For to be able to see something of the loftiest realities, however thin and weak the sight may be, is, as our previous remarks indicate, a cause of the greatest joy....

Book III

CHAPTER 2: HOW EVERY AGENT ACTS FOR AN END

[1] The first thing that we must show, then, is that in acting every agent intends an end.

[2] In the case of things which obviously act for an end we call that toward which the inclination of the agent tends the end. For, if it attains this, it is said to attain its end; but if it fails in regard to this, it fails in

regard to the end intended, as is evident in the case of the physician working for the sake of health, and of the man who is running toward a set objective. As far as this point is concerned, it makes no difference whether the being tending to an end is a knowing being or not. For, just as the target is the end for the archer, so is it the end for the motion of the arrow. Now every inclination of an agent tends toward something definite. A given action does not stem from merely any power but heating comes from heat, cooling from cold. Thus it is that, actions are specifically distinguished by virtue of diversity of active powers. In fact, an action may sometimes terminate in something which is made, as building does in a house, and as healing does in health. Sometimes, however, it does not, as in the cases of understanding and sensing. Now, if an action does in fact terminate in some thing that is made, the inclination of the agent tends through the action toward the thing that is produced. But if it does not terminate in a product, then the inclination of the agent tends toward the action itself. So, it must be that every agent in acting intends an end, sometimes the action itself, sometimes a thing produced by the action.

[3] Again, with reference to all things that act for an end, we say that the ultimate end is that beyond which the agent seeks nothing else; thus, the action of a physician goes as far as health, but when it is attained there is no desire for anything further. Now, in the action of all agents, one may find something beyond which the agent seeks nothing further. Otherwise, actions would tend to infinity, which is impossible. Since "it is impossible to proceed to infinity," the agent could not begin to act, because nothing is moved toward what cannot be reached. Therefore, every agent acts for an end....

CHAPTER 3: THAT EVERY AGENT ACTS FOR A GOOD

[1] Next after this we must show that every agent acts for a good.

[2] That every agent acts for an end has been made clear from the fact that every agent tends toward something definite. Now, that toward which an agent tends in a definite way must be appropriate to it, because the agent would not be inclined to it except by virtue of some agreement with it. But, what is appropriate to something is good for it. So, every agent acts for a good.

[3] Again, the end is that in which the appetitive inclination of an agent or mover, and of the thing moved, finds its rest. Now, the essential meaning of the good is that it provides a terminus for appetite, since "the good is that which all desire." Therefore, every action and motion are for the sake of a good.

[4] Besides, every action and movement are seen to be ordered in some way toward being, either that it may be preserved in the species or in the individual, or that it may be newly acquired. Now, the very fact of being is a good, and so all things desire to be. Therefore, every action and movement are for the sake of a good.

[5] Moreover, every action and movement are for the sake of some perfection. Even if the action itself be the end, it is clear that it is a secondary perfection of the agent. But, if the action be a changing of external matter, it is obvious that the mover intends to bring about some perfection in the thing that is moved. Even the thing that is moved also tends toward this, if it be a case of natural movement. Now, we call what is perfect a good. So, every action and movement are for the sake of a good.

[6] Furthermore, every agent acts in so far as it is in act, and in acting it tends to produce something like itself. So, it tends toward some act. But every act has something of good in its essential character, for there is no evil thing that is not in a condition of potency falling short of its act. Therefore, every action is for the sake of a good....

CHAPTER 25: THAT TO UNDERSTAND GOD IS THE END OF EVERY INTELLECTUAL SUBSTANCE

[1] Since all creatures, even those devoid of understanding, are ordered to God as to an ultimate end, all achieve this end to the extent that they participate somewhat in His likeness. Intellectual creatures attain it in a more special way, that is, through their

proper operation of understanding Him. Hence, this must be the end of the intellectual creature, namely, to understand God.

[2] The ultimate end of each thing is God, as we have shown. So, each thing intends, as its ultimate end, to be united with God as closely as is possible for it. Now, a thing is more closely united with God by the fact that it attains to His very substance in some manner, and this is accomplished when one knows something of the divine substance, rather than when one acquires some likeness of Him. Therefore, an intellectual substance tends to divine knowledge as an ultimate end.

[3] Again, the proper operation of a thing is an end for it, for this is its secondary perfection. That is why whatever is fittingly related to its proper operation is said to be virtuous and good. But the act of understanding is the proper operation of an intellectual substance. Therefore, this act is its end. And that which is most perfect in this operation is the ultimate end, particularly in the case of operations that are not ordered to any products, such as the acts of understanding and sensing. Now, since operations of this type are specified by their objects, through which they are known also, any one of these operations must be more perfect when its object is more perfect. And so, to understand the most perfect intelligible object, which is God, is the most perfect thing in the genus of this operation of understanding. Therefore, to know God by an act of understanding is the ultimate end of every intellectual substance....

[15] And so, it is said in Matthew (5:8): "Blessed are the clean of heart, for they shall see God"; and in John (17:3): "This is eternal life, that they may know Thee, the only true God." ...

CHAPTER 111: THAT RATIONAL CREATURES ARE SUBJECT TO DIVINE PROVIDENCE IN A SPECIAL WAY

[1] From the points which have been determined above, it is manifest that divine providence extends to all things. Yet we must note that there is a special meaning for providence in reference to intellectual and rational creatures, over and above its meaning for other creatures. For they do stand out above other creatures, both in natural perfection and in the dignity of their end. In the order of natural perfection, only the rational creature holds dominion over his acts, moving himself freely in order to perform his actions. Other creatures, in fact, are moved to their proper workings rather than being the active agents of these operations, as is clear from what has been said. And in the dignity of their end, for only the intellectual creature reaches the very ultimate end of the whole of things through his own operation, which is the knowing and loving of God; whereas other creatures cannot attain the ultimate end except by a participation in its likeness. Now, the formal character of every work differs according to the diversity of the end and of the things which are subject to the operation; thus, the method of working in art differs according to the diversity of the end and of the subject matter. For instance, a physician works in one way to get rid of illness and in another way to maintain health, and he uses different methods for bodies differently constituted. Likewise, in the government of a state, a different plan of ordering must be followed, depending on the varying conditions of the persons subject to this government and on the different purposes to which they are directed. For soldiers are controlled in one way, so that they may be ready to fight; while artisans will be managed in another way, so that they may successfully carry out their activities. So, also, there is one orderly plan in accord with which rational creatures are subjected to divine providence, and another by means of which the rest of creatures are ordered.

3.10 Zar'a Yaqob (1599–1692)

Zar'a Yaqob, of Ethiopia, was encouraged to record his experiences and thoughts by a student, Walda Heywat. The *Treatise of Zar'a Yaqob*, which narrates events of his life and articulates his principal insights, presents several Enlightenment ideas independently of contemporaneous developments in France, England, Germany, and other countries ordinarily associated with the historical movement known as The Enlightenment. In one respect, he represents a tradition separate from the European West, as do Siddhartha Gautama (3.2) and Confucius (3.3). In another respect, he might have contributed directly to debates going on in Europe in his own lifetime—if only channels of communication between London and Paris had extended as far as Addis Ababa.

Like Kant, Zar'a encourages everyone to formulate scientific and moral judgements by their own lights and according to the standard truth. Also like Kant, he had serious concerns about the malignant influence of institutional religion on independent judgement. Unlike Kant, however, his frustrations in this regard grew out of difficult personal adversity. Evidently, Zar'a Yaqob and Walda Heywat belonged to a dissenting school in which students were encouraged to think independently rather than to accept any particular doctrines. At some points in his life, this independence of opinion created problems for Zar'a Yaqob, and he was persecuted for religious heresy. Because Zar'a was willing to consider without judgement the claims of any religion, he was often perceived as a heretic by those affiliated with institutional religious sects. His own spiritual beliefs seem to be ecumenical rather than irreligious, but it was not possible for him to safely and openly express these ideas. In the 1630s he withdrew to a cave for two years, until a serious threat to his life passed. The following passage presents part of the story of his life and some of the insights that substantiate his designation as an Enlightenment thinker—if not, strictly speaking, a figure from the historical European Enlightenment.

~

from Treatise of Zar'a Yaqob

[His Banishment, his Enemy *Wâldä Yohannəs* and King *Susənyos*]

While I was teaching in my district, many of my friends came to dislike me. During this period there was no real friendship and as a result men became jealous of one another. I surpassed the others in knowledge and in love of one's neighbour and I was on good terms with all, even with the *Franğ* and the Copts. And while I was teaching and interpreting the Books, I used to say: "The *Franğ* say this and this" or "The Copts say that and that," and I did not say "This is good, that is bad," but I said: "All these things are good if we ourselves are good." Hence I was disliked by all: the Copts took me for a *Franğ*, the *Franğ* for a Copt. They brought a charge against me many times to the king; but God saved me. At that time, a certain enemy of mine, *Wâldä Yohannəs*, a priest from Aksum and a friend of the king, went [to bring a charge against me:] since the love of kings could be won by a perfidious tongue.

This betrayer went to the king and said this about me: "Truly this man misleads the people and tells them we should rise for the sake of our faith, kill the king and expel the *Franğ*." He also said many other similar words against me. But being aware of all this and frightened by it, I took three measures of gold which I possessed and the Psalms of David, with which I prayed, and fled at night. I did not tell anyone where I was going. I reached a place close to the *Täkkäd* River, and the next day, as I felt hungry I went out in fear to beg the farmers for some bread. I ate what they gave me and ran away. I lived in this manner for many days. On my way to Shoa, I found an uninhabited location. There was a beautiful cave at the foot of a deep valley, and I said [to myself:] I shall live here unnoticed. I lived there for two years until [King] *Susənyos* died. At times I would leave [the cave] and go to the market or to the country of the Ahmara as they took me for a hermit who goes about begging and gave me enough to appease my hunger. People however, did not know where I dwelt. Alone in my cave, I felt I was living in heaven. Knowing the boundless badness of men, I disliked contact with them. I built a fence of stone and thorny bush so that wild animals would not endanger my life at night, and I made an exit through which I could escape if ever people searched for me; there I lived peacefully praying with all my heart on the Psalms of David and trusting God was hearing me....

I thought, saying to myself: "What will men tell me other than what is in their heart?" Indeed each one says: "My faith is right, and those who believe in another faith believe in falsehood, and are the enemies of God." These days the *Franğ* tell us: "Our faith is right, yours is false." We on the other hand tell them: "It is not so; your faith is wrong, ours is right." If we also ask the Mohammedans and the Jews, they will claim the same thing, and who would be the judge for such a kind of argument? No single human being [can judge:] for all men are plaintiffs and defendants between themselves. Once I asked a *Franğ* scholar many things concerning our faith; he interpreted a well-known Ethiopian scholar and he also interpreted all things according to his own faith. If I had asked the Mohammedans and the Jews, they also would have interpreted according to their own faith; then, where could I obtain a judge that tells the truth? As my faith appears true to me, so does another one find his own faith true; but truth is one. While thinking over this matter, I said: "O my creator, wise among the wise and just among the just, who created me with an intelligence, help me to understand, for men lack wisdom and truthfulness; as David said, no man can be relied upon."

I thought further and said: "Why do men lie over problems of such great importance, even to the point of destroying themselves?" and they seemed to do so because although they pretend to know all, they know nothing. Convinced they know all, they do not attempt to investigate the truth. As David said: "Their hearts are curdled like milk" [Psalm CXIX: 70]. Their heart is curdled because they assume what they have is heard from their predecessors and they do not inquire whether it is true or false.... I said to myself: "Why is it that all men did not adhere to truth, instead of [believing] falsehood?" [The cause] seemed to be the nature of man which is weak and sluggish. Men aspire to know truth and hidden things of nature, but this endeavour is difficult and can only be attained with great labour and patience, as Solomon said: "With the help of wisdom I have been at pains to study all that is done under heaven; oh, what a weary task God has given mankind to labour at!" [*Ecclesiastes* 1: 13]. Hence people hastily accept what they have heard from their fathers and shy away from any [critical] examination.... I have learnt more while living alone in a cave than when I was living with scholars....

I hated to go back to my previous profession, for I did not wish to teach falsehood, [knowing] that if I thought the truth, people would not listen to me, but would hate me, accuse me and persecute me. But I preferred to feed on the fruit of my work, ignored by men and secluded with the wisdom God had taught me, rather than to live richly in the house of sinners.

But my enemy the hyprocritical *Wâldä Yohannəs*, who brought accusation against me to King *Susənyos*, came back to the faith of the Copts; [to say the truth] he had no particular faith except that which afforded him material advantages at any given time. He was perfidious enough to become the friend of King *Fasilädäs* once he had presented himself to the king; kings love the hypocrite and the treacherous. Having heard that I was living peacefully in ənfəraz, *Wâldä Yohannəs* once more began accusing me, saying: "He is a *Franğ* master and teaches in secret the doctrine of the *Franğ*"; the same he said to the chief of ənfəraz. His betrayal grieved me sadly; at first he has said I was the enemy of the *Franğ* and now he was saying I was their friend. With a heavy heart I said: "May God snatch away perfidious lips!" For many days I prayed the words of Psalm XXXIV ("Accuse") and of Psalm CVIII ("Lord, break your silence"). And God heard my voice; for this man later became the head of several regions in *Dämbəya*; the people hated him so much that they killed him. His corpse was found in his house, but the murderer was not found; another man took his post and his wealth.

People took me for a Christian when I was dealing with them; but in my heart I did not believe in anything except in God who created all and conserves all, as he had taught me. I thought and said: "Will it be a sin in the eyes of God if I pretend to be what I am not and deceive men?" But I said [to myself]: "Men want to be deceived; if I tell them the truth, instead of listening to me they will curse me and persecute me; it is useless to open my thoughts to them; it will harm me greatly. And therefore I shall be with men as one of theirs; but with God I shall be as he taught me." In order that those who will come after me will know me, I have written down those things I hide within me until my death. I entreat any wise and inquisitive man who may come after I am dead to add his thoughts to mine. Behold, I have begun an inquiry such as has not been attempted before. You can complete what I have begun so that the people of our country will become wise with the help of God and arrive at the science of truth, lest they believe in falsehood, trust in depravity, go from vanity to vanity, that they know the truth and love their brother, lest they quarrel about their empty faith as they have been doing till now. If there is an intelligent [man] who understands these things and even higher ones, and who teaches and writes them, let God give him all he wishes in his heart and bring to completion all he longs for and satisfy him with all the things of the world as he satisfied me; as he made me joyous and happy in this world, let him also make this man joyous and happy. As to the one who will criticize [me] on account of this book and who will not understand it so that he may benefit therefrom, let God pay him according to his merit. Amen.

... O my brother, you who read this my book, know that I have written it in a great fear of God who absolutely guards me from telling lies; I do not fear men, nor am I frightened by their faces, nor have I anything to do with those who write and teach falsehood and vanity. If anyone asks me: "Is it only you who know the truth; the others besides you, do they not know it also?"

I answer: "No, not I alone, but many have known and loved the truth as I do, but they did not dare teach it openly because they feared the curse of blind men and expulsion from their congregation. But the rest of the people did not know, because they have made no research, no inquiry in order to distinguish truth from falsehood, but they accepted and believed what they heard from their fathers without inquiry. Hence the children of Christians are Christians, the children of Mohammedans are Mohammedans, the children of Jews are Jews; there is no reason for their faith other than this. They have heard from childhood that the faith of their parents is true, and they have believed in it without examination or [proper] knowledge. All fight for their faith affirming it is the true one. But it is not possible that all faiths of men be true, because they disagree between themselves. It is possible, however, that all be false because falsehood is many, but truth is one."

O my brother, lift up your mind to that perfect essence that created you with intelligence, and look at it with the eye of your intelligence, and recognize the light of science which your creator has shown you. Do not listen to the voice of those who speak ill of you and call you a denier of the creator if you reject the doctrine that they teach you; they do not know their creator; and there is no wisdom among them. Do not believe what men teach you before you have examined all they teach you and have distinguished the true from the false, because men can lie and you do not know whether they teach you the truth or falsehood.

Similarly do not believe what is written in books until you have examined it and found it to be right. For books are written by men who are likely to write false things.

3.11 David Hume (1711–1776)

David Hume was a leading figure in the Scottish Enlightenment who resurrected ancient skeptical arguments to check the ambitions many of his contemporaries had for reason and knowledge. Like ancient skeptics, he doubted that speculative reason could furnish reliable normative principles. Against attempts to ground morality on rational principles or to discover indubitable moral principles, he argued that moral knowledge is not available to us and that reason has a sharply delimited function. Our prospects for wisdom or enlightenment are low, in Hume's estimation. Unlike Socrates, however, there is for Hume no normative function for rationality in the absence of substantive knowledge. In one provocative passage, he maintains that "It is not contrary to reason to prefer the destruction of the whole world to the scratching of my finger." For Hume irrationality and immorality are not nearly synonymous, as they are for Socrates, Aristotle, and the stoics, in particular. All of our preferences, including our moral choices, come from another source, namely, subjective emotions, sentiments, and passions.

Moral deliberation requires a person to determine (a) what to do and (b) how to accomplish this. The crucial question for Hume concerns (a) what to do. In every case, he observes, the answer comes from our emotional or sentimental faculties, sometimes called our "passions." Passions move or direct us, not our rational faculties. Indeed, early in our selection he writes: "Reason is, and ought only to be the slave of the passions, and can never pretend to any other office than to serve and obey." In many respects, Hume's position that morality does not admit of rational direction is commonplace, but in the eighteenth century it was highly controversial.

from A Treatise of Human Nature

Book II

SECT. III OF THE INFLUENCING MOTIVES OF THE WILL

Nothing is more usual in philosophy, and even in common life, than to talk of the combat of passion and reason, to give the preference to reason, and assert that men are only so far virtuous as they conform themselves to its dictates. Every rational creature, it is said, is obliged to regulate his actions by reason; and if any other motive or principle challenge the direction of his conduct, he ought to oppose it, till it be entirely subdued, or at least brought to a conformity with that superior principle. On this method of thinking the greatest part of moral philosophy, antient and modern, seems to be founded; nor is there an ampler field, as well for metaphysical arguments, as popular declamations, than this supposed pre-eminence of reason above passion. The eternity, invariableness, and divine origin of the former have been displayed to the best advantage: The blindness, unconstancy, and deceitfulness of the latter have been as strongly insisted on. In order to shew the fallacy of all this philosophy, I shall endeavour to prove first, that reason alone can never be a motive to any action of the will; and secondly, that it can never oppose passion in the direction of the will.

The understanding exerts itself after two different ways, as it judges from demonstration or probability; as it regards the abstract relations of our ideas, or those relations of objects, of which experience only gives us information. I believe it scarce will be asserted, that the first species of reasoning alone is ever the cause of any action. As its proper province is the world of ideas, and as the will always places us in that of realities, demonstration and volition seem, upon that account, to be totally removed from each other. Mathematics, indeed, are useful in all mechanical operations, and arithmetic in almost every art and profession: But it is not of themselves they have any influence: Mechanics are the art of regulating the motions of bodies to some designed end or purpose; and the reason why we employ arithmetic in fixing the proportions of numbers, is only that we may discover the proportions of their influence and operation. A merchant is desirous of knowing the sum total of his accounts with any person: Why? but that he may learn what sum will have the same effects in paying his debt, and going to market, as all the particular articles taken together. Abstract or demonstrative reasoning, therefore, never influences any of our actions, but only as it directs our judgment concerning causes and effects; which leads us to the second operation of the understanding.

It is obvious, that when we have the prospect of pain or pleasure from any object, we feel a consequent emotion of aversion or propensity, and are carryed to avoid or embrace what will give us this uneasiness or satisfaction. It is also obvious, that this emotion rests not here, but making us cast our view on every side, comprehends whatever objects are connected with its original one by the relation of cause and effect. Here then reasoning takes place to discover this relation; and according as our reasoning varies, our actions receive a subsequent variation. But it is evident in this case that the impulse arises not from reason, but is only directed by it. It is from the prospect of pain or pleasure that the aversion or propensity arises towards any object: And these emotions extend themselves to the causes and effects of that object, as they are pointed out to us by reason and experience. It can never in the least concern us to know, that such objects are causes, and such others effects, if both the causes and effects be indifferent to us. Where the objects themselves do not affect us, their connexion can never give them any influence; and it is plain, that as reason is nothing but the discovery of this connexion, it cannot be by its means that the objects are able to affect us.

Since reason alone can never produce any action, or give rise to volition, I infer, that the same faculty is as incapable of preventing volition, or of disputing the preference with any passion or emotion. This consequence is necessary. It is impossible reason could have the latter effect of preventing volition, but by giving an impulse in a contrary direction to our passion; and that impulse, had it operated alone, would have been able to produce volition. Nothing can oppose or retard the impulse of passion, but a contrary impulse; and if this contrary impulse ever arises from reason, that latter faculty must have an original influence on the will, and must be able to cause, as well as hinder any act of volition. But if reason has no original influence, it is impossible it can withstand any principle, which has such an efficacy, or ever keep the mind in suspence [sic] a moment. Thus it appears, that the principle, which opposes our passion, cannot be the same with reason, and is only called so in an improper sense. We speak not strictly and philosophically when we talk of the combat of passion and of reason. Reason is, and ought only to be the slave of the passions, and can never pretend to any other office than to serve and obey them. As this opinion may appear somewhat extraordinary, it may not be improper to confirm it by some other considerations.

A passion is an original existence, or, if you will, modification of existence, and contains not any representative quality, which renders it a copy of any other existence or modification. When I am angry, I am actually possest with the passion, and in that emotion have no more a reference to any other object, than when I am thirsty, or sick, or more than five foot high. It is impossible, therefore, that this passion can be opposed by, or be contradictory to truth and reason; since this contradiction consists in the disagreement of ideas, considered as copies, with those objects, which they represent.

What may at first occur on this head, is, that as nothing can be contrary to truth or reason, except what has a reference to it, and as the judgments of our understanding only have this reference, it must follow, that passions can be contrary to reason only so far as they are accompanyed with some judgment or opinion. According to this principle, which is so obvious and natural, it is only in two senses, that any affection can be called unreasonable. First, When a passion, such as hope or fear, grief or joy, despair or security, is founded on the supposition or the existence of objects, which really do not exist. Secondly, When in exerting any passion in action, we chuse means insufficient for the designed end, and deceive ourselves in our judgment of causes and effects. Where a passion is neither founded on false suppositions, nor chuses means insufficient for the end, the understanding can neither justify nor condemn it. It is not contrary to reason to prefer the destruction of the whole world to the scratching of my finger. It is not contrary to reason for me to chuse my total ruin, to prevent the least uneasiness of an Indian or person wholly unknown to me. It is as little contrary to reason to prefer even my own acknowledged lesser good to my greater, and have a more ardent affection for the former than the latter. A trivial good may, from certain circumstances, produce a desire superior to what arises from the greatest and most valuable enjoyment; nor is there any thing more extraordinary in this, than in mechanics to see a one pound weight raise up a hundred by the advantage of its situation. In short, a passion must be accompanyed with some false judgment in order to its being unreasonable; and even then, it is not the passion, properly speaking, which is unreasonable, but the judgment.

The consequences are evident. Since a passion can never, in any sense, be called unreasonable, but when founded on a false supposition or when it chuses means insufficient for the designed end, it is impossible, that reason and passion can ever oppose each other, or dispute for the government of the will and actions. The moment we perceive the falsehood of any supposition, or the insufficiency of any means, our passions yield to our reason without any opposition. I may desire any fruit as of an excellent relish; but whenever you convince me of my mistake, my longing ceases. I may will the performance of certain actions as means of obtaining any desired good; but as my willing of these actions is only secondary, and founded on the supposition, that they are causes of the proposed effect; as soon as I discover the falshood [sic] of that supposition, they must become indifferent to me.

It is natural for one, that does not examine objects with a strict philosophic eye, to imagine, that those actions of the mind are entirely the same, which produce not a different sensation, and are not immediately distinguishable to the feeling and perception. Reason, for instance, exerts itself without producing any sensible emotion; and except in the more sublime disquisitions of philosophy, or in the frivolous subtilties of the school, scarce ever conveys any pleasure or uneasiness. Hence it proceeds, that every action of the mind, which operates with the same calmness and tranquillity, is confounded with reason by all those, who judge of things from the first view and appearance. Now it is certain, there are certain calm desires and tendencies, which, though they be real passions, produce little emotion in the mind, and are more known by their effects than by the immediate feeling or sensation. These desires are of two kinds; either certain instincts originally implanted in our natures, such as benevolence and resentment, the love of life, and kindness to children; or the general appetite to good, and aversion to evil, considered merely as such. When any of these passions are calm, and cause no disorder in the soul, they are very readily taken for the determinations of reason, and are supposed to proceed from the same faculty, with that, which judges of truth and falshood. Their nature and principles have been supposed the same, because their sensations are not evidently different.

Beside these calm passions, which often determine the will, there are certain violent emotions of the same kind, which have likewise a great influence on that faculty. When I receive any injury from another, I often feel a violent passion of resentment, which makes me desire his evil and punishment, independent of all considerations of pleasure and advantage to myself. When I am immediately threatened with any grievous ill, my fears, apprehensions, and aversions rise to a great height, and produce a sensible emotion.

The common error of metaphysicians has lain in ascribing the direction of the will entirely to one of these principles, and supposing the other to have no influence. Men often act knowingly against their interest: For which reason the view of the greatest possible good does not always influence them. Men often counter-act a violent passion in prosecution of their interests and designs: It is not therefore the present uneasiness alone, which determines them. In general we may observe, that both these principles operate on the will; and where they are contrary, that either of them prevails, according to the general character or present disposition of the person. What we call strength of mind, implies the prevalence of the calm passions above the violent; though we may easily observe, there is no man so constantly possessed of this virtue, as never on any occasion to yield to the sollicitations of passion and desire. From these variations of temper proceeds the great difficulty of deciding concerning the actions and resolutions of men, where there is any contrariety of motives and passions.

Book III Of Morals

Part I Of Virtue and Vice in General

SECT. I MORAL DISTINCTIONS NOT DERIVED FROM REASON

... It has been observed, that nothing is ever present to the mind but its perceptions; and that all the actions of seeing, hearing, judging, loving, hating, and thinking, fall under this denomination. The mind can never exert itself in any action, which we may not comprehend under the term of perception; and consequently that term is no less applicable to those judgments, by which we distinguish moral good and evil, than to every other operation of the mind. To approve of one character, to condemn another, are only so many different perceptions.

Now as perceptions resolve themselves into two kinds, viz. impressions and ideas, this distinction gives rise to a question, with which we shall open up our present enquiry concerning morals. WHETHER IT IS BY MEANS OF OUR IDEAS OR IMPRESSIONS WE DISTINGUISH BETWIXT VICE AND VIRTUE, AND PRONOUNCE AN ACTION BLAMEABLE OR PRAISEWORTHY? This will immediately cut off all loose discourses and declamations, and reduce us to something precise and exact on the present subject.

Those who affirm that virtue is nothing but a conformity to reason; that there are eternal fitnesses and unfitnesses of things, which are the same to every rational being that considers them; that the immutable measures of right and wrong impose an obligation, not only on human creatures, but also on the Deity himself: All these systems concur in the opinion, that morality, like truth, is discerned merely by ideas, and by their juxta-position and comparison. In order, therefore, to judge of these systems, we need only consider, whether it be possible, from reason alone, to distinguish betwixt moral good and evil, or whether there must concur some other principles to enable us to make that distinction.

If morality had naturally no influence on human passions and actions, it were in vain to take such pains to inculcate it; and nothing would be more fruitless than that multitude of rules and precepts, with which all moralists abound. Philosophy is commonly divided into speculative and practical; and as morality is always comprehended under the latter division, it is supposed to influence our passions and actions, and to go beyond the calm and indolent judgments of the understanding. And this is confirmed by common experience, which informs us, that men are often governed by their duties, and are deterred from some actions by the opinion of injustice, and impelled to others by that of obligation.

Since morals, therefore, have an influence on the actions and affections, it follows, that they cannot be derived from reason; and that because reason alone, as we have already proved, can never have any such influence. Morals excite passions, and produce or prevent actions. Reason of itself is utterly impotent in this particular. The rules of morality therefore, are not conclusions of our reason.

No one, I believe, will deny the justness of this inference; nor is there any other means of evading it, than by denying that principle, on which it is founded. As long as it is allowed, that reason has no influence on our passions and action, it is in vain to pretend, that morality is discovered only by a deduction of reason. An active principle can never be founded on an inactive; and if reason be inactive in itself, it must remain so in all its shapes and appearances, whether it exerts itself in natural or moral subjects, whether it considers the powers of external bodies, or the actions of rational beings.

SECT. II MORAL DISTINCTIONS DERIVED FROM A MORAL SENSE

Thus the course of the argument leads us to conclude, that since vice and virtue are not discoverable merely by reason, or the comparison of ideas, it must be by means of some impression or sentiment they occasion, that we are able to mark the difference betwixt them. Our decisions concerning moral rectitude and depravity are evidently perceptions; and as all perceptions are either impressions or ideas, the exclusion of the one is a convincing argument for the other. Morality, therefore, is more properly felt than judged of; though this feeling or sentiment is commonly so soft and gentle, that we are apt to confound it with an idea, according to our common custom of taking all things for the same, which have any near resemblance to each other.

The next question is, Of what nature are these impressions, and after what manner do they operate upon us? Here we cannot remain long in suspense, but must pronounce the impression arising from virtue, to be agreeable, and that proceeding from vice to be uneasy. Every moment's experience must convince us of this. There is no spectacle so fair and beautiful as a noble and generous action; nor any which gives us more abhorrence than one that is cruel and treacherous. No enjoyment equals the satisfaction we receive from the company of those we love and esteem; as the greatest of all punishments is to be obliged to pass our lives with those we hate or contemn. A very play or romance may afford us instances of this pleasure, which virtue conveys to us; and pain, which arises from vice.

Now since the distinguishing impressions, by which moral good or evil is known, are nothing but particular pains or pleasures; it follows, that in all enquiries concerning these moral distinctions, it will be sufficient to shew the principles, which make us feel a satisfaction or uneasiness from the survey of any character, in order to satisfy us why the character is laudable or blameable. An action, or sentiment, or character is virtuous or vicious; why? because its view causes a pleasure or uneasiness of a particular kind. In giving a reason, therefore, for the pleasure or uneasiness, we sufficiently explain the vice or virtue. To have the sense of virtue, is nothing but to feel a satisfaction of a particular kind from the contemplation of a character.

The very feeling constitutes our praise or admiration. We go no farther; nor do we enquire into the cause of the satisfaction. We do not infer a character to be virtuous, because it pleases: But in feeling that it pleases after such a particular manner, we in effect feel that it is virtuous. The case is the same as in our judgments concerning all kinds of beauty, and tastes, and sensations. Our approbation is implyed in the immediate pleasure they convey to us....

3.12 Edmund Burke (1729–1797)

Edmund Burke was a British member of parliament, writer, and influential conservative thinker. He was horrified by the 1789 French Revolution that overthrew a monarchy to found a secular republic. *Reflections on the Revolution in France* (1791) is an extended exploration of his concerns. These derived partly from the French Revolution in particular and partly from general features of revolution in any well-established community. Our interests here focus on general problems he notes about political revolutions.

Like Hume, Burke doubts ambitious theoretical schemes. Abstractions and general claims are prone to imprecision, if not likely to be false. It is simply too much to expect success from any revolution that severs the present from the past in order to build something from the ground up. Traditional knowledge is a more reliable normative guide, in Burke's opinion, than theoretical knowledge. Collectively, communities have accumulated a vast body of implicit knowledge that has proven to be useful innumerable times. Even prejudices are valuable as outward manifestations of assimilated traditional beliefs and values. In Burke's opinion, they are not—as champions of the Enlightenment often maintained—uncritical reflexes. Wisdom, in Burke's view, is possessed by the historically extended community and passed from generation to generation. Social change must never be revolutionary because the post-revolutionary age will not have traditional beliefs and values for guidance. Burke's position on social questions is, therefore, conservative because each generation must conserve what it inherits. Still, circumstances change all the time and those who live today cannot simply replicate the past. For this reason, Burke advocates on behalf of reform over revolution. Had the French reformed its political institutions from an absolute monarchy to a constitutional monarchy, they might have retained valuable links to their own past and avoided the kind of violence associated with the Reign of Terror and other aspects of the French Revolution.

from Reflections on the Revolution in France

Dear Sir,—You are pleased to call again, and with some earnestness, for my thoughts on the late proceedings in France. I will not give you reason to imagine that I think my sentiments of such value as to wish myself to be solicited about them. They are of too little consequence to be very anxiously either communicated or withheld. My errors, if any, are my own. My reputation alone is to answer for them.

You see, Sir, by the long letter I have transmitted to you, that, though I do most heartily wish that France may be animated by a spirit of rational liberty, and that I think you bound, in all honest policy, to provide a permanent body in which that spirit may reside, and an effectual organ by which it may act, it is my misfortune to entertain great doubts concerning several material points in your late transactions....

I flatter myself that I love a manly, moral, regulated liberty as well as any gentleman of that society, be he who he will; and perhaps I have given as good proofs of my attachment to that cause, in the whole course of my public conduct. I think I envy liberty as little as they do to any other nation. But I cannot stand forward, and give praise or blame to anything which relates to human actions and human concerns on a simple view of the object, as it stands stripped of every relation, in all the nakedness and solitude of metaphysical abstraction. Circumstances (which with some gentlemen pass for nothing) give in reality to every political principle its distinguishing color and discriminating effect. The circumstances are what render every civil and political scheme beneficial or noxious to mankind. Abstractedly speaking, government, as well as liberty, is good; yet could I, in common sense, ten years ago, have felicitated France on her enjoyment of a government, (for she then had a government,) without inquiry what the nature of that government was, or how it was administered? Can I now congratulate the same nation upon its freedom? Is it because liberty in the abstract may be classed amongst the blessings of mankind, that I am seriously to felicitate a madman who has escaped from the protecting restraint and wholesome darkness of his cell on his restoration to the enjoyment of light and liberty? Am I to congratulate a highwayman and murderer who has broke prison upon the recovery of his natural rights? This would be to act over again the scene of the criminals condemned to the galleys, and their heroic deliverer, the metaphysic Knight of the Sorrowful Countenance.[1]

When I see the spirit of liberty in action, I see a strong principle at work; and this, for a while, is all I can possibly know of it. The wild gas, the fixed air, is plainly broke loose: but we ought to suspend our judgment until the first effervescence is a little subsided, till the liquor is cleared, and until we see something deeper than the agitation of a troubled and frothy surface. I must be tolerably sure, before I venture publicly to congratulate men upon a blessing, that they have really received one. Flattery corrupts both the receiver and the giver; and adulation is not of more service to the people than to kings. I should therefore suspend my congratulations on the new liberty of France, until I was informed how it had been combined with government, with public force, with the discipline and obedience of armies, with the collection of an effective and well-distributed revenue, with morality and religion, with solidity and property, with peace and order, with civil and social manners. All these (in their way) are good things, too; and without them, liberty is not a benefit whilst it lasts, and is not likely to continue long. The effect of liberty to individuals is, that they may do what they please: we ought to see what it will please them to do, before we risk congratulations, which may be soon turned into complaints. Prudence would dictate this in the case of separate, insulated, private men. But liberty, when men act in bodies, is power. Considerate people, before they declare themselves, will observe the use which is made of power,—and particularly of so trying a thing as new power in new persons, of whose principles, tempers, and dispositions they have little or no experience, and in situations where those who appear the most stirring in the scene may possibly not be the real movers....

On the forenoon of the fourth of November last, Doctor Richard Price, a Non-Conforming minister[2] of eminence, preached at the Dissenting meeting-house of the Old Jewry, to his club or society, a very extraordinary miscellaneous sermon,[3] in which there are some good moral and religious sentiments, and not ill expressed, mixed up with a sort of porridge of various political opinions and reflections: but the Revolution in France is the grand ingredient in the caldron.... For my part, I looked on that sermon as the public declaration of a man much connected with literary caballers and intriguing philosophers, with political theologians and theological politicians, both at home and abroad. I know they set

1 The reference here is to an episode in Miguel de Cervantes's *Don Quixote*, Part I, Ch. 22. In this episode Don Quixote, who calls himself the Knight of the Sorrowful Countenance, releases a chain gang of condemned criminals under the delusion that they have been unjustly imprisoned. The prisoners repay his benefaction by abusing him and embarking on a rampage.

2 That is, a minister in a denomination other than the Anglican Church, the official (i.e., conforming) religion of England.

3 Richard Price's sermon, "A Discourse on the Love of Our Country," aims to (a) defend the revolution in France that deposed Louis XVI as the overthrow of a tyrannical regime and (b) maintain the legitimacy of the English monarchy on grounds of popular support. Burke, by contrast, aims to defend monarchy in general as a sound, time-tested form of aristocracy (i.e., literally the "rule of the best").

him up as a sort of oracle; because, with the best intentions in the world, he naturally philippizes,[4] and chants his prophetic song in exact unison with their designs....

If the noble Seekers [a seventeenth-century sect] should find nothing to satisfy their pious fancies in the old staple of the national [i.e., Anglican] Church, or in all the rich variety to be found in the well-assorted warehouses of the Dissenting congregations, Dr. Price advises them to improve upon Non-Conformity, and to set up, each of them, a separate meeting-house upon his own particular principles. It is somewhat remarkable that this reverend divine should be so earnest for setting up new churches, and so perfectly indifferent concerning the doctrine which may be taught in them. His zeal is of a curious character. It is not for the propagation of his own opinions, but of any opinions. It is not for the diffusion of truth, but for the spreading of contradiction. Let the noble teachers but dissent, it is no matter from whom or from what. This great point once secured, it is taken for granted their religion will be rational and manly. I doubt whether religion would reap all the benefits which the calculating divine computes from this "great company of great preachers." It would certainly be a valuable addition of nondescripts to the ample collection of known classes, genera, and species, which at present beautify the *hortus siccus* of Dissent.... I should only stipulate that these ... coronets should keep some sort of bounds in the democratic and levelling principles which are expected from their titled pulpits. The new evangelists will, I dare say, disappoint the hopes that are conceived of them. They will not become, literally as well as figuratively, polemic divines,—nor be disposed so to drill their congregations, that they may, as in former blessed times, preach their doctrines to regiments of dragoons and corps of infantry and artillery. Such arrangements, however favorable to the cause of compulsory freedom, civil and religious, may not be equally conducive to the national tranquillity. These few restrictions I hope are no great stretches of intolerance, no very violent exertions of despotism....

You will observe, that, from Magna Charta to the Declaration of Right, it has been the uniform policy of our Constitution to claim and assert our liberties as an entailed inheritance derived to us from our forefathers, and to be transmitted to our posterity,—as an estate specially belonging to the people of this kingdom, without any reference whatever to any other more general or prior right. By this means our Constitution preserves a unity in so great a diversity of its parts. We have an inheritable crown, an inheritable peerage, and a House of Commons and a people inheriting privileges, franchises, and liberties from a long line of ancestors.

This policy appears to me to be the result of profound reflection,—or rather the happy effect of following Nature, which is wisdom without reflection, and above it. A spirit of innovation is generally the result of a selfish temper and confined views. People will not look forward to posterity, who never look backward to their ancestors. Besides, the people of England well know that the idea of inheritance furnishes a sure principle of conservation, and a sure principle of transmission, without at all excluding a principle of improvement. It leaves acquisition free; but it secures what it acquires. Whatever advantages are obtained by a state proceeding on these maxims are locked fast as in a sort of family settlement, grasped as in a kind of mortmain forever. By a constitutional policy working after the pattern of Nature, we receive, we hold, we transmit our government and our privileges, in the same manner in which we enjoy and transmit our property and our lives. The institutions of policy, the goods of fortune, the gifts of Providence, are handed down to us, and from us, in the same course and order. Our political system is placed in a just correspondence and symmetry with the order of the world, and with the mode of existence decreed to a permanent body composed of transitory parts,—wherein, by the disposition of a stupendous wisdom, moulding together the great mysterious incorporation of the human race, the whole, at one time, is never old or middle-aged or young, but, in a condition of unchangeable constancy, moves on through

4 "Philippizing" is invective oratory characteristic of speeches (philippics) denouncing Philip of Macedon by the Athenian politician Demosthenes.

the varied tenor of perpetual decay, fall, renovation, and progression. Thus, by preserving the method of Nature in the conduct of the state, in what we improve we are never wholly new, in what we retain we are never wholly obsolete. By adhering in this manner and on those principles to our forefathers, we are guided, not by the superstition of antiquarians, but by the spirit of philosophic analogy. In this choice of inheritance we have given to our frame of polity the image of a relation in blood: binding up the Constitution of our country with our dearest domestic ties; adopting our fundamental laws into the bosom of our family affections; keeping inseparable, and cherishing with the warmth of all their combined and mutually reflected charities, our state, our hearths, our sepulchres, and our altars.

Through the same plan of a conformity to Nature in our artificial institutions, and by calling in the aid of her unerring and powerful instincts to fortify the fallible and feeble contrivances of our reason, we have derived several other, and those no small benefits, from considering our liberties in the light of an inheritance. Always acting as if in the presence of canonized forefathers, the spirit of freedom, leading in itself to misrule and excess, is tempered with an awful gravity. This idea of a liberal descent inspires us with a sense of habitual native dignity, which prevents that upstart insolence almost inevitably adhering to and disgracing those who are the first acquirers of any distinction. By this means our liberty becomes a noble freedom. It carries an imposing and majestic aspect. It has a pedigree and illustrating ancestors. It has its bearings and its ensigns armorial. It has its gallery of portraits, its monumental inscriptions, its records, evidences, and titles. We procure reverence to our civil institutions on the principle upon which Nature teaches us to revere individual men: on account of their age, and on account of those from whom they are descended. All your sophisters cannot produce anything better adapted to preserve a rational and manly freedom than the course that we have pursued, who have chosen our nature rather than our speculations, our breasts rather than our inventions, for the great conservatories and magazines of our rights and privileges....

Government is not made in virtue of natural rights, which may and do exist in total independence of it,—and exist in much greater clearness, and in a much greater degree of abstract perfection: but their abstract perfection is their practical defect. By having a right to everything they want everything. Government is a contrivance of human wisdom to provide for human wants. Men have a right that these wants should be provided for by this wisdom. Among these wants is to be reckoned the want, out of civil society, of a sufficient restraint upon their passions. Society requires not only that the passions of individuals should be subjected, but that even in the mass and body, as well as in the individuals, the inclinations of men should frequently be thwarted, their will controlled, and their passions brought into subjection. This can only be done by a power out of themselves, and not, in the exercise of its function, subject to that will and to those passions which it is its office to bridle and subdue. In this sense the restraints on men, as well as their liberties, are to be reckoned among their rights. But as the liberties and the restrictions vary with times and circumstances, and admit of infinite modifications, they cannot be settled upon any abstract rule; and nothing is so foolish as to discuss them upon that principle.

The moment you abate anything from the full rights of men each to govern himself, and suffer any artificial, positive limitation upon those rights, from that moment the whole organization of government becomes a consideration of convenience. This it is which makes the constitution of a state, and the due distribution of its powers, a matter of the most delicate and complicated skill. It requires a deep knowledge of human nature and human necessities, and of the things which facilitate or obstruct the various ends which are to be pursued by the mechanism of civil institutions. The state is to have recruits to its strength and remedies to its distempers. What is the use of discussing a man's abstract right to food or medicine? The question is upon the method of procuring and administering them. In that deliberation I shall always advise to call in the aid of the farmer and the physician, rather than the professor of metaphysics.

The science of constructing a commonwealth, or renovating it, or reforming it, is, like every other experimental science, not to be taught *a priori*.[5] Nor is it a short experience that can instruct us in that practical science; because the real effects of moral causes are not always immediate, but that which in the first instance is prejudicial may be excellent in its remoter operation, and its excellence may arise even from the ill effects it produces in the beginning. The reverse also happens; and very plausible schemes, with very pleasing commencements, have often shameful and lamentable conclusions. In states there are often some obscure and almost latent causes, things which appear at first view of little moment, on which a very great part of its prosperity or adversity may most essentially depend. The science of government being, therefore, so practical in itself, and intended for such practical purposes, a matter which requires experience, and even more experience than any person can gain in his whole life, however sagacious and observing he may be, it is with infinite caution that any man ought to venture upon pulling down an edifice which has answered in any tolerable degree for ages the common purposes of society, or on building it up again without having models and patterns of approved utility before his eyes.

When ancient opinions and rules of life are taken away, the loss cannot possibly be estimated. From that moment we have no compass to govern us, nor can we know distinctly to what port we steer. Europe, undoubtedly, taken in a mass, was in a flourishing condition the day on which your Revolution was completed. How much of that prosperous state was owing to the spirit of our old manners and opinions is not easy to say; but as such causes cannot be indifferent in their operation, we must presume, that, on the whole, their operation was beneficial.

We are but too apt to consider things in the state in which we find them, without sufficiently adverting to the causes by which they have been produced, and possibly may be upheld. Nothing is more certain than that our manners, our civilization, and all the good things which are connected with manners and with civilization, have, in this European world of ours, depended for ages upon two principles, and were, indeed, the result of both combined: I mean the spirit of a gentleman, and the spirit of religion. The nobility and the clergy, the one by profession, and the other by patronage, kept learning in existence, even in the midst of arms and confusions, and whilst governments were rather in their causes than formed. Learning paid back what it received to nobility and to priesthood, and paid it with usury, by enlarging their ideas, and by furnishing their minds. Happy, if they had all continued to know their indissoluble union, and their proper place! Happy, if learning, not debauched by ambition, had been satisfied to continue the instructor, and not aspired to be the master! Along with its natural protectors and guardians, learning will be cast into the mire and trodden down under the hoofs of a swinish multitude.

If, as I suspect, modern letters owe more than they are always willing to own to ancient manners, so do other interests which we value full as much as they are worth. Even commerce, and trade, and manufacture, the gods of our economical politicians, are themselves perhaps but creatures, are themselves but effects, which, as first causes, we choose to worship. They certainly grew under the same shade in which learning flourished. They, too, may decay with their natural protecting principles. With you, for the present at least, they all threaten to disappear together. Where trade and manufactures are wanting to a people, and the spirit of nobility and religion remains, sentiment supplies, and not always ill supplies, their place; but if commerce and the arts should be lost in an experiment to try how well a state may stand without these old fundamental principles, what sort of a thing must be a nation of gross, stupid, ferocious, and at the same time poor and sordid barbarians, destitute of religion, honor, or manly pride, possessing nothing at present, and hoping for nothing hereafter? ...

You see, Sir, that in this enlightened age I am bold enough to confess that we are generally men of untaught

5 That is, science derived independently (*a priori*) of experience, or by rationality alone—as, for example, geometry.

feelings: that, instead of casting away all our old prejudices, we cherish them to a very considerable degree; and, to take more shame to ourselves, we cherish them because they are prejudices; and the longer they have lasted, and the more generally they have prevailed, the more we cherish them. We are afraid to put men to live and trade each on his own private stock of reason; because we suspect that the stock in each man is small, and that the individuals would do better to avail themselves of the general bank and capital of nations and of ages. Many of our men of speculation, instead of exploding general prejudices, employ their sagacity to discover the latent wisdom which prevails in them. If they find what they seek, (and they seldom fail,) they think it more wise to continue the prejudice, with the reason involved, than to cast away the coat of prejudice, and to leave nothing but the naked reason; because prejudice, with its reason, has a motive to give action to that reason, and an affection which will give it permanence. Prejudice is of ready application in the emergency; it previously engages the mind in a steady course of wisdom and virtue, and does not leave the man hesitating in the moment of decision, skeptical, puzzled, and unresolved. Prejudice renders a man's virtue his habit, and not a series of unconnected acts. Through just prejudice, his duty becomes a part of his nature.

Your literary men, and your politicians, and so do the whole clan of the enlightened among us, essentially differ in these points. They have no respect for the wisdom of others; but they pay it off by a very full measure of confidence in their own. With them it is a sufficient motive to destroy an old scheme of things, because it is an old one. As to the new, they are in no sort of fear with regard to the duration of a building run up in haste; because duration is no object to those who think little or nothing has been done before their time, and who place all their hopes in discovery. They conceive, very systematically, that all things which give perpetuity are mischievous, and therefore they are at inexpiable war with all establishments. They think that government may vary like modes of dress, and with as little ill effect; that there needs no principle of attachment, except a sense of present conveniency, to any constitution of the state. They always speak as if they were of opinion that there is a singular species of compact between them and their magistrates, which binds the magistrate, but which has nothing reciprocal in it, but that the majesty of the people has a right to dissolve it without any reason but its will. Their attachment to their country itself is only so far as it agrees with some of their fleeting projects: it begins and ends with that scheme of polity which falls in with their momentary opinion.

These doctrines, or rather sentiments, seem prevalent with your new statesmen. But they are wholly different from those on which we have always acted in this country....

3.13 Friedrich Nietzsche (1844–1900)

Friedrich Nietzsche was an accomplished classicist who drew upon this learning and a talent for colourful writing to skewer moral and scientific authorities. One of his books, *Twilight of the Idols*, is subtitled "How One Philosophizes with a Hammer," and another bears the provocative title *The Antichrist*. Evidently, his personality was less polemical than his authorial persona. Nevertheless, his avowed ambition to re-value all values signals a profound dissatisfaction with traditional conceptions of morality and conventional ethics.

The passages in the present chapter come from Nietzsche's *Joyful Wisdom*. Here he explores the historical contingency of what passes for knowledge in Western culture. Science, for example, is presented as a series of discoveries about the substantive order of things. A grand presumption has been posited to portray science and moral theory as authoritative: there is an independently existing world of ordered facts lurking behind the appearances that present themselves to us; science endeavours to expose nature, including human nature. If we release ourselves from this illusory presumption, we will experience an exhilarating freedom. In the most famous and provocative passage below, Nietzsche tells the story of a mad man who informs everyone that God is dead (sect. 125). In light of this freedom and without divine providence, the principal task of a human being is to shape one's life according to one's personal tastes (sect. 290).

from Joyful Wisdom

37

Owing to Three Errors.—Science has been furthered during recent centuries, partly because it was hoped that God's goodness and wisdom would be best understood therewith and thereby—the principal motive in the soul of great Englishmen (like Newton); partly because the absolute utility of knowledge was believed in, and especially the most intimate connection of morality, knowledge, and happiness—the principal motive in the soul of great Frenchmen (like Voltaire); and partly because it was thought that in science there was something unselfish, harmless, self-sufficing, lovable, and truly innocent to be had, in which the evil human impulses did not at all participate—the principal motive in the soul of Spinoza, who felt himself divine, as a knowing being:—it is consequently owing to three errors that science has been furthered.

39

Altered Taste.—The alteration of the general taste is more important than the alteration of opinions; opinions, with all their proving, refuting, and intellectual masquerade, are merely symptoms of altered taste, and are certainly *not* what they are still so often claimed to be, the causes of the altered taste. How does the general taste alter? By the fact of individuals, the powerful and influential persons, expressing and tyrannically enforcing without any feeling of shame, *their hoc est ridiculum, hoc est absurdum*; the decisions, therefore, of their taste and their disrelish:—they thereby lay a constraint upon many people, out of which there gradually grows a habituation for still more, and finally a *necessity for all.* The fact, however, that these individuals feel and "taste" differently, has usually its origin in a peculiarity of their mode of life, nourishment, or digestion, perhaps in a surplus or deficiency of the inorganic salts in their blood and brain, in short in their *physis*; they have, however, the courage to avow their physical constitution, and to lend an ear even to the most delicate tones of its requirements: their aesthetic and moral judgments are those "most delicate tones" of their *physis*.[6]

6 "Physis" is "nature."

110

Origin of Knowledge.—Throughout immense stretches of time the intellect produced nothing but errors; some of them proved to be useful and preservative of the species: he who fell in with them, or inherited them, waged the battle for himself and his offspring with better success. Those erroneous articles of faith which were successively transmitted by inheritance, and have finally become almost the property and stock of the human species, are, for example, the following:—that there are enduring things, that there are equal things, that there are things, substances, and bodies, that a thing is what it appears, that our will is free, that what is good for me is also good absolutely. It was only very late that the deniers and doubters of such propositions came forward,—it was only very late that truth made its appearance as the most impotent form of knowledge. It seemed as if it were impossible to get along with truth, our organism was adapted for the opposite; all its higher functions, the perceptions of the senses, and in general every kind of sensation co-operated with those primevally embodied, fundamental errors. Moreover, those propositions became the very standards of knowledge according to which the "true" and the "false" were determined—throughout the whole domain of pure logic. The *strength* of conceptions does not, therefore, depend on their degree of truth, but on their antiquity, their embodiment, their character as conditions of life. Where life and knowledge seemed to conflict, there has never been serious contention; denial and doubt have there been regarded as madness. The exceptional thinkers like the Eleatics, who, in spite of this, advanced and maintained the antitheses of the natural errors, believed that it was possible also *to live* these counterparts: it was they who devised the sage as the man of immutability, impersonality and universality of intuition, as one and all at the same time, with a special faculty for that reverse kind of knowledge; they were of the belief that their knowledge was at the same time the principle of *life*. To be able to affirm all this, however, they had to *deceive* themselves concerning their own condition: they had to attribute to themselves impersonality and unchanging permanence, they had to mistake the nature of the philosophic individual, deny the force of the impulses in cognition, and conceive of reason generally as an entirely free and self-originating activity; they kept their eyes shut to the fact that they also had reached their doctrines in contradiction to valid methods, or through their longing for repose or for exclusive possession or for domination. The subtler development of sincerity and of scepticism finally made these men impossible; their life also, and their judgments, turned out to be dependent on the primeval impulses and fundamental errors of all sentient being.—The subtler sincerity and scepticism arose wherever two antithetical maxims appeared to be *applicable* to life, because both of them were compatible with the fundamental errors; where, therefore, there could be contention concerning a higher or lower degree of *utility* for life; and likewise where new maxims proved to be, not necessarily useful, but at least not injurious, as expressions of an intellectual impulse to play a game that was like all games innocent and happy. The human brain was gradually filled with such judgments and convictions; and in this tangled skein there arose ferment, strife and lust for power. Not only utility and delight, but every kind of impulse took part in the struggle for "truths": the intellectual struggle became a business, an attraction, a calling, a duty, an honour—: cognizing and striving for the true finally arranged themselves as needs among other needs. From that moment, not only belief and conviction, but also examination, denial, distrust and contradiction became *forces*; all "evil" instincts were subordinated to knowledge, were placed in its service, and acquired the prestige of the permitted, the honoured, the useful, and finally the appearance and innocence of the *good*. Knowledge, thus became a portion of life itself, and as life it became a continually growing power: until finally the cognitions and those primeval, fundamental errors clashed with each other, both as life, both as power, both in the same man. The thinker is now the being in whom the impulse to truth and those life preserving errors wage their first conflict, now that the impulse to truth has also *proved* itself to be a life-preserving power. In comparison with the importance of this conflict everything else is indifferent; the final question concerning the conditions of life is here raised, and the first attempt is here made to answer it by experiment. How far is truth susceptible of embodiment?—that is the question, that is the experiment.

111

Origin of the Logical.—Where has logic originated in men's heads? Undoubtedly out of the illogical, the domain of which must originally have been immense. But numberless beings who reasoned otherwise than we do at present, perished; albeit that they may have come nearer to truth than we! ... In itself every high degree of circumspection in conclusions, every sceptical inclination, is a great danger to life. No living being might have been preserved unless the contrary inclination—to affirm rather than suspend judgment, to mistake and fabricate rather than wait, to assent rather than deny, to decide rather than be in the right—had been cultivated with extraordinary assiduity.—The course of logical thought and reasoning in our modern brain corresponds to a process and struggle of impulses, which singly and in themselves are all very illogical and unjust; we experience usually only the result of the struggle, so rapidly and secretly does this primitive mechanism now operate in us.

115

The Four Errors.—Man has been reared by his errors: firstly, he saw himself always imperfect; secondly, he attributed to himself imaginary qualities; thirdly, he felt himself in a false position in relation to the animals and nature; fourthly, he always devised new tables of values, and accepted them for a time as eternal and unconditioned, so that at one time this, and at another time that human impulse or state stood first, and was ennobled in consequence. When one has deducted the effect of these four errors, one has also deducted humanity, humaneness, and "human dignity."

124

In the Horizon of the Infinite.—We have left the land and have gone aboard ship! We have broken down the bridge behind us,—nay, more, the land behind us! Well, little ship! look out! Beside thee is the ocean; it is true it does not always roar, and sometimes it spreads out like silk and gold and a gentle reverie. But times will come when thou wilt feel that it is infinite, and that there is nothing more frightful than infinity. Oh, the poor bird that felt itself free, and now strikes against the walls of this cage! Alas, if homesickness for the land should attack thee, as if there had been more *freedom* there,—and there is no "land" any longer!

125

The Madman.—Have you ever heard of the madman who on a bright morning lighted a lantern and ran to the market-place calling out unceasingly: "I seek God! I seek God!"—As there were many people standing about who did not believe in God, he caused a great deal of amusement. Why! is he lost? said one. Has he strayed away like a child? said another. Or does he keep himself hidden? Is he afraid of us? Has he taken a sea-voyage? Has he emigrated?—the people cried out laughingly, all in a hubbub. The insane man jumped into their midst and transfixed them with his glances. "Where is God gone?" he called out. "I mean to tell you! *We have killed him*,—you and I! We are all his murderers! But how have we done it? How were we able to drink up the sea? Who gave us the sponge to wipe away the whole horizon? What did we do when we loosened this earth from its sun? Whither does it now move? Whither do we move? Away from all suns? Do we not dash on unceasingly? Backwards, sideways, forewards, in all directions? Is there still an above and below? Do we not stray, as through infinite nothingness? Does not empty space breathe upon us? Has it not become colder? Does not night come on continually, darker and darker? Shall we not have to light lanterns in the morning? Do we not hear the noise of the grave-diggers who are burying God? Do we not smell the divine putrefaction?—for even Gods putrefy! God is dead! God remains dead! And, we have killed him! How shall we console ourselves, the most murderous of all murderers? The holiest and the mightiest that the world has hitherto possessed, has bled to death under our knife,—who will wipe the blood from us? With what water could we cleanse ourselves? What lustrums, what sacred games shall we have to devise? Is not the magnitude of this deed too great for us? Shall we not ourselves have to become Gods, merely to seem worthy of it? There never was a greater event,—and on account of it, all who are born after us belong to a higher history than any history hitherto!"—Here the madman was silent and looked again at his hearers; they also were silent and looked at him in surprise. At last he threw his lantern on the ground, so that it broke in pieces and was extinguished. "I come too early," he then said, "I am not yet at the right time. This prodigious event is still on its way, and is travelling,—it has not yet reached men's ears. Lightning and thunder need time, the light of the stars needs time, deeds need time, even after they are done, to be seen and heard. This deed is as yet further from them than the furthest star,—*and yet they have done it!*"—It is further stated that the madman made his way into different churches on the same day, and there intoned his *Requiem aeternam deo*. When led out and called to account, he always gave the reply: "What are these churches now, if they are not the tombs and monuments of God?"—

290

One Thing Is Needful.—To "give style" to one's character—that is a grand and a rare art! He who surveys all that his nature presents in its strength and in its weakness, and then fashions it into an ingenious plan, until everything appears artistic and rational, and even the weaknesses enchant the eye—exercises that admirable art. Here there has been a great amount of second nature added, there a portion of first nature has been taken away:—in both cases with long exercise and daily labour at the task. Here the ugly, which does not permit of being taken away, has been concealed, there it has been re-interpreted into the sublime. Much of the vague, which refuses to take form, has been reserved and utilised for the perspectives:—it is meant to give a hint of the remote and immeasurable. In the end, when the work has been completed, it is revealed how it was the constraint of the same taste that organised and fashioned it in whole and in part: whether the taste was good or bad is of less importance than one thinks,—it is sufficient that it was *a taste!*—It will be the strong imperious natures which experience their most refined joy in such constraint, in such confinement and perfection under their own law; the passion of their violent volition lessens at the sight of all disciplined nature, all conquered and ministering nature: even when they have palaces to build and gardens to lay out, it is not to their taste to allow nature to be free.—It is the reverse with weak characters who have not power over themselves, and *hate* the restriction of style: they feel that if this repugnant constraint were laid upon them, they would necessarily become *vulgarised* under it: they become slaves as soon as they serve, they hate service. Such intellects—they may be intellects of the first rank—are always concerned with fashioning and interpreting themselves and their surroundings as *free* nature—wild, arbitrary, fantastic, confused and surprising: and it is well for them to do so, because only in this manner can they please themselves! For one thing is needful: namely, that man should *attain to* satisfaction with himself—be it but through this or that fable and artifice: it is only then that man's aspect is at all endurable! He who is dissatisfied with himself is ever ready to avenge himself on that account: we others will be his victims, if only in having always to endure his ugly aspect. For the aspect of the ugly makes one mean and sad.

3.14 Albert Camus (1913–1960)

During World War II, Albert Camus worked underground on behalf of the resistance movement in Nazi-occupied France. Otherwise, he was very much a public intellectual, writing novels, essays, and journalism—for which he won the Nobel Prize for literature in 1957. His fiction and non-fictional works explore human alienation in a universe that is benignly indifferent to our purposes.

His book *The Myth of Sisyphus* is an extended essay on the absurdity of our human condition. In living and acting we make choices based on preferences. We are simultaneously aware of the values implicit in these choices and of the fact that they cannot be grounded in objective principles. Nevertheless, we act as a kind of revolt against the potential hopelessness of our situation. Agency thus constitutes an investment in something, a task that gives one's life value. The ancient story of Sisyphus raises questions about the meaning of life, and Camus retells it to explore some of his own ideas. According to the ancient myth, Sisyphus was punished by the gods to roll a huge, heavy rock up a hill. Every time he reaches the top, the rock rolls back down, whereupon he must begin the task anew. Endless, futile labour seems, on the face of it, to be a cruel fate, but Camus imagines that Sisyphus must be happy. Sisyphus has a task that is all his own, and his existence thereby has a purpose that both fulfills him and gives meaning to everything. In understanding his own situation clearly, Sisyphus achieves a state of *lucidity*. In place of wisdom or enlightenment, Camus posits "lucid consciousness" as the condition that constitutes human fulfillment.

~

from The Myth of Sisyphus

What then is that incalculable feeling that deprives the mind of the sleep necessary to life? A world that can be explained even with bad reasons is a familiar world. But, on the other hand, in a universe suddenly divested of illusions and lights, man feels an alien, a stranger. His exile is without remedy since he is deprived of the memory of a lost home or the hope of a promised land. This divorce between man and his life, the actor and his setting, is properly the feeling of absurdity. All healthy men having thought of their own suicide, it can be seen, without further explanation, that there is a direct connection between this feeling and the longing for death.

The subject of this essay is precisely this relationship between the absurd and suicide, the exact degree to which suicide is a solution to the absurd. The principle can be established that for a man who does not cheat what he believes to be true must determine his action. Belief in the absurdity of existence must then dictate his conduct. It is legitimate to wonder, clearly and without false pathos, whether a conclusion of this importance requires forsaking as rapidly as possible an incomprehensible condition. I am speaking, of course, of men inclined to be in harmony with themselves.

Stated clearly, this problem may seem both simple and insoluble. But it is wrongly assumed that simple questions involve answers that are no less simple and that evidence implies evidence. *A priori* and reversing the terms of the problem, just as one does or does not kill oneself, it seems that there are but two philosophical solutions, either yes or no. This would be too easy. But allowance must be made for those who, without concluding, continue questioning. Here I am only slightly indulging in irony: this is the majority. I notice also that those who answer 'no' act as if they thought 'yes'. As a matter of fact, if I accept the Nietzschean criterion, they think yes in one way or another. On the other hand, it often happens that those who commit suicide were assured of the meaning of life. These contradictions are constant. It may even be said that they have never been so keen as on this point where, on the contrary, logic seems so desirable....

Absurd Walls

Like great works, deep feelings always mean more than they are conscious of saying. The regularity of an impulse or a repulsion in a soul is encountered again in habits of doing or thinking, is reproduced in consequences of which the soul itself knows nothing. Great feelings take with them their own universe, splendid or abject. They light up with their passion an exclusive world in which they recognize their climate. There is a universe of jealousy, of ambition, of selfishness or of generosity. A universe—in other words a metaphysic and an attitude of mind. What is true of already specialized feelings will be even more so of emotions basically as indeterminate, simultaneously as vague and as 'definite', as remote and as 'present' as those furnished us by beauty or aroused by absurdity.

At any street corner the feeling of absurdity can strike any man in the face. As it is, in its distressing nudity, in its light without effulgence, it is elusive. But that very difficulty deserves reflection. It is probably true that a man remains for ever unknown to us and that there is in him something irreducible that escapes us. But *practically* I know men and recognize them by their behaviour, by the totality of their deeds, by the consequences caused in life by their presence. Likewise, all those irrational feelings which offer no purchase to analysis. I can define them *practically*, appreciate them *practically*, by gathering together the sum of their consequences in the domain of the intelligence, by seizing and noting all their aspects, by outlining their universe. It is certain that apparently, though I have seen the same actor a hundred times, I shall not for that reason know him any better personally. Yet if I add up the heroes he has personified and if I say that I know him a little better at the hundredth character counted off, this will be felt to contain an element of truth. For this apparent paradox is also an apologue. There is a moral to it. It teaches that a man defines himself by his make-believe as well as by his sincere impulses. There is thus a lower key of feelings, inaccessible in the heart but partially disclosed by the acts they imply and the attitudes of mind they assume. It is clear that in this way I am defining a method. But it is also evident that that method is one of analysis and not of knowledge. For methods imply metaphysics; unconsciously they disclose conclusions that they often claim not to know yet. Similarly the last pages of a book are already contained in the first pages. Such a link is inevitable. The method defined here acknowledges the feeling that all true knowledge is impossible. Solely appearances can be enumerated and the climate make itself felt.

Perhaps we shall be able to overtake that elusive feeling of absurdity in the different but closely related worlds of intelligence, of the art of living, or of art itself. The climate of absurdity is in the beginning. The end is the absurd universe and that attitude of mind which lights the world with its true colours to bring out the privileged and implacable visage which that attitude has discerned in it.

*

All great deeds and all great thoughts have a ridiculous beginning. Great works are often born on a street-corner or in a restaurant's revolving door. So it is with absurdity. The absurd world more than others derives its nobility from that abject birth. In certain situations, replying 'nothing' when asked what one is thinking about may be pretence in a man. Those who are loved are well aware of this. But if that reply is sincere, if it symbolizes that odd state of soul in which the void becomes eloquent, in which the chain of daily gestures is broken, in which the heart vainly seeks the link that will connect it again, then it is as it were the first sign of absurdity.

It happens that the stage-sets collapse. Rising, tram, four hours in the office or factory, meal, tram, four hours of work, meal, sleep and Monday, Tuesday, Wednesday, Thursday, Friday and Saturday, according to the same rhythm—this path is easily followed most of the time. But one day the 'why' arises and everything begins in that weariness tinged with amazement. 'Begins'—this is important. Weariness comes at the end of the acts of a mechanical life, but at the same time it inaugurates the impulse of consciousness. It awakens consciousness and provokes what follows. What follows is the gradual return into the chain or it is the definitive awakening. At the end of the awakening comes, in time, the consequence: suicide or recovery. In itself weariness has something sickening about it. Here, I must conclude that it is good. For everything begins with consciousness and nothing is worth anything except through it. There is nothing original about these remarks. But they are obvious; that is enough for a while, during a sketchy reconnaissance in the origins of the absurd. Mere 'anxiety', as Heidegger says, is at the source of everything.

Likewise and during every day of an unillustrious life, time carries us. But a moment always comes when we have to carry it. We live on the future: 'tomorrow', later on', 'when you have made your way', 'you will understand when you are old enough'. Such irrelevancies are wonderful, for, after all, it's a matter of dying. Yet a time comes when a man notices or says that he is thirty. Thus he asserts his youth. But simultaneously he situates himself in relation to time. He takes his place in it. He admits that he stands at a certain point on a curve that he acknowledges having to travel to its end. He belongs to time and, by the horror that seizes him, he recognizes his worst enemy. Tomorrow, he was longing for tomorrow, whereas everything in him ought to reject it. The revolt of the flesh is the absurd.[1]

A step lower and strangeness creeps in: perceiving that the world is 'dense', sensing to what degree a stone is foreign and irreducible to us, with what intensity nature or a landscape can negate us. At the heart of all beauty lies something inhuman, and these hills, the softness of the sky, the outline of these trees at this very minute lose the illusory meaning with which we had clothed them, henceforth more remote than a lost paradise. The primitive hostility of the world rises up to face us across millennia. For a second we cease to understand it because for centuries we have understood in it solely the images and designs that we had attributed to it beforehand, because henceforth we lack the power to make use of that artifice. The world evades us because it becomes itself again. That stage-scenery masked by habit becomes again what it is. It withdraws at a distance from us. Just as there are days when, under the familiar face of a woman, we see as a stranger her we had loved months or years ago, perhaps we shall come even to desire what suddenly leaves us so alone. But

1 But not in the proper sense. This is not a definition, but rather an *enumeration* of the feelings that may admit of the absurd. Still, the enumeration finished, the absurd has nevertheless not been exhausted.

the time has not yet come. Just one thing: that denseness and that strangeness of the world is the absurd.

Men, too, secrete the inhuman. At certain moments of lucidity, the mechanical aspect of their gestures, their meaningless pantomime make silly everything that surrounds them. A man is talking on the telephone behind a glass partition; you cannot hear him but you see his incomprehensible dumb-show: you wonder why he is alive. The discomfort in the face of man's own inhumanity, this incalculable tumble before the image of what we are, this 'nausea', as a writer of today calls it, is also the absurd. Likewise the stranger who at certain seconds comes to meet us in a mirror, the familiar and yet alarming brother we encounter in our own photographs is also the absurd.

I come at last to death and to the attitude we have towards it. On this point everything has been said and it is only proper to avoid pathos. Yet one will never be sufficiently surprised that everyone lives as if no one 'knew'. This is because in reality there is no experience of death. Properly speaking, nothing has been experienced but what has been lived and made conscious. Here, it is barely possible to speak of the experience of others' deaths. It is a substitute, an illusion, and it never quite convinces us. That melancholy convention cannot be persuasive. The horror comes in reality from the mathematical aspect of the event. If time frightens us, this is because it works out the problem and the solution comes afterwards. All the pretty speeches about the soul will have their contrary convincingly proved, at least for a time. From this inert body on which a slap makes no mark the soul has disappeared. This elementary and definitive aspect of the adventure constitutes the absurd feeling. Under the fatal lighting of that destiny, its uselessness becomes evident. No code of ethics and no effort are justifiable *a priori* in the face of the cruel mathematics that command our condition.

Let me repeat: all this has been said over and over. I am limiting myself here to making a rapid classification and to pointing out these obvious themes. They run through all literatures and all philosophies. Everyday conversation feeds on them. There is no question of re-inventing them. But it is essential to be sure of these facts in order to be able to question oneself subsequently on the primordial question. I am interested—let me repeat again—not so much in absurd discoveries as in their consequences. If one is assured of these facts, what is one to conclude, how far is one to go to elude nothing? Is one to die voluntarily or to hope in spite of everything? Beforehand, it is necessary to take the same rapid inventory on the plane of the intelligence....

The Myth of Sisyphus

The gods had condemned Sisyphus to ceaselessly rolling a rock to the top of a mountain, whence the stone would fall back of its own weight. They had thought with some reason that there is no more dreadful punishment than futile and hopeless labour.

If one believes Homer, Sisyphus was the wisest and most prudent of mortals. According to another tradition, however, he was disposed to practise the profession of highwayman. I see no contradiction in this. Opinions differ as to the reasons why he became the futile labourer of the underworld. To begin with, he is accused of a certain levity in regard to the gods. He stole their secrets. Aegina, the daughter of Aesopus, was carried off by Jupiter. The father was shocked by that disappearance and complained to Sisyphus. He, who knew of the abduction, offered to tell about it on condition that Aesopus would give water to the citadel of Corinth. To the celestial thunderbolts he preferred the benediction of water. He was punished for this in the underworld. Homer tells us also that Sisyphus had put Death in chains. Pluto could not endure the sight of his deserted, silent empire. He dispatched the god of war who liberated Death from the hands of her conqueror.

It is said also that Sisyphus, being near to death, rashly wanted to test his wife's love. He ordered her to cast his unburied body into the middle of the public square. Sisyphus woke up in the underworld. And there, annoyed by an obedience so contrary to human love, he obtained from Pluto permission to return to earth in order to chastise his wife. But when he had seen again the face of this world, enjoyed water and sun, warm stones and the sea, he no longer wanted to go back to the infernal darkness. Recalls, signs of anger, warnings were of no avail. Many years more, he lived facing the curve of the gulf, the sparkling sea, and the smiles of earth. A decree of the gods was necessary. Mercury came and seized the impudent man by the collar and, snatching him from his joys, led him forcibly back to the underworld where his rock was ready for him.

You have already grasped that Sisyphus is the absurd hero. He *is*, as much through his passions as through his torture. His scorn of the gods, his hatred of death, and his passion for life won him that unspeakable penalty in which the whole being is exerted towards accomplishing nothing. This is the price that must be paid for the passions of this earth. Nothing is told us about Sisyphus in the underworld. Myths are made for the imagination to breathe life into them. As for this myth, one sees merely the whole effort of a body straining to raise the huge stone, to roll it and push it up a slope a hundred times over; one sees the face screwed up, the cheek tight against the stone, the shoulder bracing the clay-covered mass, the foot wedging it, the fresh start with arms outstretched, the wholly human security of two earth-clotted hands. At the very end of his long effort measured by skyless space and time without depth, the purpose is achieved. Then Sisyphus watches the stone rush down in a few moments towards that lower world whence he will have to push it up again towards the summit. He goes back down to the plain.

It is during that return, that pause, that Sisyphus interests me. A face that toils so close to stones is already stone itself! I see that man going back down with a heavy yet measured step towards the torment of which he will never know the end. That hour, like a breathing-space which returns as surely as his suffering, that is the hour of consciousness. At each of those moments when he leaves the heights and gradually sinks towards the lairs of the gods, he is superior to his fate. He is stronger than his rock.

If this myth is tragic, that is because its hero is conscious. Where would his torture be, indeed, if at every step the hope of succeeding upheld him? The workman of today works every day in his life at the same tasks and this fate is no less absurd. But it is tragic only at the rare moments when it becomes conscious. Sisyphus, proletarian of the gods, powerless and rebellious, knows the whole extent of his wretched condition; it is what he thinks of during his descent. The lucidity that was to constitute his torture at the same time crowns his victory. There is no fate that cannot be surmounted by scorn.

*

If the descent is thus sometimes performed in sorrow, it can also take place in joy. The word is not too much. Again I fancy Sisyphus returning towards his rock, and the sorrow was in the beginning. When the images of earth cling too tightly to memory, when the call of happiness becomes too insistent, it happens that melancholy rises in man's heart: this is the rock's victory, this is the rock itself. The boundless grief is too heavy to bear. These are our nights of Gethsemane. But crushing truths perish from being acknowledged. Thus Oedipus at the outset obeys fate without knowing it. But from the moment he knows, his tragedy begins. Yet at the same moment, blind and desperate, he realizes that the only bond linking him to the world is the cool hand of a girl. Then a tremendous remark rings out: 'Despite so many ordeals, my advanced age and the nobility of my soul make me conclude that all is well.' Sophocles' Oedipus, like Dostoievsky's Kirilov, thus gives the recipe for the absurd victory. Ancient wisdom confirms modern heroism.

One does not discover the absurd without being tempted to write a manual of happiness. 'What! by such narrow ways ...' There is but one world, however. Happiness and the absurd are two sons of the same earth. They are inseparable. It would be a mistake to say that happiness necessarily springs from the absurd discovery. It happens as well that the feeling of the absurd springs from happiness. 'I conclude that all is well,' says Oedipus, and that remark is sacred. It echoes in the wild and limited universe of man. It teaches that all is not, has not been, exhausted. It drives out of this world a god who had come into it with dissatisfaction and a preference for futile sufferings. It makes of fate a human matter, which must be settled among men.

All Sisyphus' silent joy is contained therein. His fate belongs to him. His rock is his thing. Likewise, the absurd man, when he contemplates his torment, silences all the idols. In the universe suddenly restored to its silence, the myriad wondering little voices of the earth rise up. Unconscious, secret calls, invitations from all the faces, they are the necessary reverse and price of victory. There is no sun without shadow, and it is essential to know the night. The absurd man says yes and his effort will henceforth be unceasing. If there is a personal fate, there is no higher destiny or at least there is but one which he concludes is inevitable and despicable. For the rest, he knows himself to be the master of his days. At that subtle moment when man glances backward over his life, Sisyphus returning towards his rock, in that slight pivoting, he contemplates that series of unrelated actions which becomes his fate, created by him, combined under his memory's eye and soon sealed by his death. Thus, convinced of the wholly human origin of all that is human, a blind man eager to see who knows that the night has no end, he is still on the go. The rock is still rolling.

I leave Sisyphus at the foot of the mountain! One always finds one's burden again. But Sisyphus teaches the higher fidelity that negates the gods and raises rocks. He, too, concludes that all is well. This universe henceforth without a master seems to him neither sterile nor futile. Each atom of that stone, each mineral flake of that night-filled mountain, in itself forms a world. The struggle itself towards the heights is enough to fill a man's heart. One must imagine Sisyphus happy.

3.15 Review Questions

1. To what extent, if any, are the doubts about wisdom from the skeptics (Sextus Empiricus, Hume, Camus) a product of exceedingly high demands on what wisdom must provide?

2. Does Nietzsche's attack on wisdom as a form of knowledge also undermine the other sources of guidance suggested by Sextus Empiricus and Hume?

3. How does the account of wisdom from one of our Eastern authors (Siddhartha Gautama, Confucius) compare with one of our Western authors?

4. To what extent, if any, is Socrates's distinction between human and divine wisdom in line with the skeptical doubts of Sextus Empiricus and Hume?

5. For Thomas Aquinas and Edmund Burke, wisdom and a good life necessarily involve some degree of conformity. Are these accounts consistent with the idea that a wise person is self-sufficient or thinks independently?

6. What is the relationship between the Epicurean account of a good life based on pleasure (or freedom from pain) and Hume's account based on the passions?

7. How does Hume's attack on the naturalistic fallacy relate to Nietzsche's attack on moral goodness as a corruption of what is "natural"?

8. To what extent does the ancient skeptical attack on wisdom correspond with doubts about moral authority voiced by Nietzsche and Camus?

3.16 Further Reading

Boethius. *The Consolation of Philosophy*. Translated by V.E. Watts, Penguin, 1969.
Kekes, John. *Moral Wisdom and Good Lives*. Cornell University Press, 1995.
Spinoza, Baruch. *The Ethics*. Translated by Samuel Shirley, Hackett Publishing Company, 1982.
Williams, Bernard. *Ethics and the Limits of Philosophy*. Harvard University Press, 1985.
Wolf, Susan. *Meaning in Life and Why It Matters*. Princeton University Press, 2010.

CHAPTER 4

Laws, Rules, and Duties

Citizens ought to fight for their law as for their city wall.

—HERACLITUS

All the laws of humanity are nourished by a single divine law, which rules according to its own bidding and is superabundant for all.

—HERACLITUS

A law that is unjust is to be considered no law at all.

—ST. AUGUSTINE OF HIPPO

It is superstitious to put one's faith in convention; but it is arrogant to be unwilling to submit to it.

—BLAISE PASCAL

There is no crueler tyranny than that which is perpetuated under the shield of law and in the name of justice.

—BARON DE MONTESQUIEU

Custom reconciles us to everything.

—EDMUND BURKE

... the law is a ass—a idiot. If that's the eye of the law, the law is a bachelor; and the worst I wish the law is that his eye may be opened by experience—by experience."

—CHARLES DICKENS, MR. BUMBLE, FROM *OLIVER TWIST*

When men are pure, laws are useless; when men are corrupt, laws are broken.

—BENJAMIN DISRAELI

The difference between a slave and a citizen is that the slave is subject to a master and the citizens to the laws. It may happen that the master is very gentle and the laws very harsh. Everything lies in the difference between caprice and rule.

—SIMONE WEIL

Tradition is the most sublime form of necrophilia.

—HANS KUDSZUS

4.1 Introduction

Socrates performs his gadfly function in two ways, one personal and one political. First, he makes a personal accusation against individual Athenians for neglecting the state of their souls in favour of wealth, reputation, and honours (*Apology* 29d–30c). Wisdom, not these other pursuits, ought to be every person's life-guiding ambition. Wisdom is thus affirmed to be a standard of *personal goodness*, and accordingly Chapter 3 surveys alternative conceptions of individual wisdom and enlightenment. At the same time, Socrates's characterization of Athens as "a great and noble horse that's somewhat sluggish because of its size" is a separate accusation against the city collectively (30e). Clearly, by his lights, Athens does not measure up to a *political standard* of goodness. In what, then, does this standard consist?

One central task of political theory is to answer this question by identifying the essential qualities of a well-functioning community. To this end, we turn now from personal ethics and individual self-examination to political ethics and collective self-examination. Readings in Chapter 4 focus on rules regulating social relations, and those in Chapter 5 focus on the political implications of economic relations. Rules at the centre of Chapter 4 constitute the basic formal conditions of communal life, whereas economic relations at the centre of Chapter 5 constitute its basic material conditions.

Our point of departure in the present chapter is Plato's *Crito*, where Socrates argues that law is absolutely indispensable for communal life (see 1.2.4 for details). The conversation between Socrates and his friend Crito takes place between the end of the trial and the execution of its sentence. Ordinarily, capital punishment in Athens was carried out within days of a trial. Socrates's execution, however, was delayed due to an annual one-month moratorium of the practice. Evidently, friends seized the opportunity to plot his escape. During this period of incarceration Socrates was allowed to receive visitors, and on this occasion Crito informs him that arrangements have been made for his immediate departure (by bribing guards, etc.). Typically, Socrates refuses to do anything without first deliberating over the rational and moral defensibility of Crito's plan, so they pause over the question of his escape.

Eventually Socrates convinces Crito that their final decision must be made in accordance with justice (48b–49b). When they turn to consider a citizen's political obligations to this standard, Socrates adopts the point of view of Athenian law (50a–54d). What he says on its behalf is a sharp rebuke of Crito's plan: escape would effectively usurp the entire Athenian legal system. Because Crito's plan constitutes a threat to the very existence of that system, acting on it would be a grievous violation of political justice. Socrates insists further that no individual citizen can justifiably disobey the law. The principle Socrates articulates here is central to political theory: the rule of law, according to which society ought to be ruled by its legal institutions and not any person or group, including a duly elected government. Law is therefore sovereign.[1] For a citizen, political justice requires a kind of submission. For the city, it requires operating according to properly constituted legal principles. A properly constituted legal system is thus authorized to govern the lives of its citizens, and justice prevails when both a state and its citizens are coordinated by this formal relationship.[2]

While some political theorists do not follow Socrates and make the rule of law an absolute condition of justice, almost all acknowledge that law has some kind

---

1 Note that in the expression "rule of law" the term "rule" is a synonym for sovereign, not maxim. Accordingly, we might equally call this principle "sovereignty of the law." Apart from the phrase "rule of law," in this introduction "rule" should be read as being short for "rule for action" and synonymous with "maxim."

2 It remains important to ask how Athens has failed to satisfy justice by being "sluggish," as Socrates characterizes it in his trial (*Apology* 30e). We shall pause over the point, but it must be noted.

of authority. Two issues emerge from acknowledging law's authority: (1) an ambiguity as to how we are to understand "law" and (2) the need to specify the precise source of its authority. (1) First, a three-part ambiguity. The term "law" might be taken to mean any one of the following: (a) written statutes of *positive law* which explicitly and officially regulate human conduct within a particular jurisdiction; (b) *conventions*, *customs*, or *norms* which informally regulate a social group; or (c) independently existing abstract *moral principles* from which written, positive laws are supposed to be derived. In all three cases, "law" functions as a rule for action by prescribing or proscribing specific forms of conduct. But what kind of rule is most fundamental—a statute, a convention, or a moral principle? The question is practical as well as theoretical, for no one wants to submit to rules of the wrong sort. Each of the three interpretive strategies has defenders, and every particular interpretation offered by our theorists identifies the source of law's authority. On what basis can we say that the law is authoritative and thereby obliges the obedience of individual citizens? Theoretical selections in the present chapter attempt to disambiguate key terms in order to answer this question.

We might initially suppose that in the *Crito* the rule of law refers to the written laws of Athens. This may indeed be correct, but it may also be historically anachronistic to attribute it to Socrates in 399 BCE. Codified written law was a recent innovation at that point in Athenian history, for not until 410–399 BCE did Athens undertake to systematize and inscribe all of its laws in a single, public location (in this case, in stone on the walls of a building). This initiative was highly controversial, for some people complained that laws were not merely rendered internally consistent but altered in the process. It is not impossible, but it seems unlikely that Socrates would maintain without argument that citizens owed submission to something so controversial.

Nevertheless, even if Socrates himself does not mean "written statutes" in the *Crito*, other theorists have defended the authority of written law. This theoretical position is called *legal positivism* because it maintains that positive, written laws are authoritative, that there is no other standard of justice, and that we must submit to them if we are to live together in a civil society. This is an influential standpoint for both the interpretation of law and its place in human life, and it is defended here by Thomas Hobbes and Baron de Montesquieu. For both Hobbes and Montesquieu, law gets its authority entirely by virtue of the political authority of the legislative body instituting it, and in both cases law serves its purpose by stabilizing social relations. According to Hobbes, citizens submit to the authority of the state and are thereby compelled to obey its laws in return for the legal protection of their lives and property. According to Montesquieu, the variability of temperament of different populations requires different legal regimes, which in some jurisdictions will be republican, in others monarchal, and in others still despotic. These are examined anthropologically with an eye to their distinctive features, not measured against a common, independent standard by Montesquieu. Because positivism identifies justice as whatever is encoded in law, it is crucial among positivists that that state be duly constituted. Once that is established, however, individuals must submit to the law as a fundamental condition of citizenship.

What can the alternative, "*unwritten* law," mean? And how can it operate as an authoritative standard of justice? The two alternatives to legal positivism presuppose distinctive and incompatible conceptions of "unwritten law." The first alternative maintains that it refers to socially embodied conventions, customs, or norms, and that these rules are authoritative. This position is called conventionalism. The second alternative maintains that natural laws of morality are objective analogously to natural laws of mechanics (such as Newton's laws of gravity, inertia, reaction, etc., 2.6) and because of their alleged priority in nature moral laws are more authoritative than positive laws. Purportedly they provide an independent and superior standpoint from which to formulate and assess positive, written statutes. This theoretical strategy is called natural law theory. Both conventionalism and natural law theory encounter one special conceptual problem in addition to the question of authority noted above, namely "How do we determine the content of an unwritten law?" Positive laws expressly convey their content as the text of documents (a constitution, criminal code, contract law, etc.), but neither of our two non-positivist strategies can point directly to anything as tangible as this for guidance. Let us consider the conventionalist approach first.

Differences between unwritten social conventions, customs, and norms on the one hand and written statutes on the other are substantial. A written text can be parsed, glossed, and analyzed, because rival interpretations of a written legal rule always have a common point of reference: the text of the law, which usually includes a set of definitions restricting interpretation to within a limited range of possibilities. An unwritten convention, by contrast, is a pattern of practice which may admit of interpretation in terms of a rule. Still, something that admits of a rule-based interpretation is not the same as what we find in positive law, namely, explicit rules in concrete statutes. A written text focuses debate, even when interpretations of the text vary. Without a comparable common point of reference, however, conventions are difficult to specify precisely.

Even when a convention is formulated in an adage or maxim, problems arise. Consider, for example, the convention of respecting our elders. For the sake of illustration, consider the maxim, "Respect your elders." Does "respect" here require us simply to listen to what an elder has to say, or does it require us to obey every command? Does "your elders" include everyone who is older than you, or only senior citizens? Both "respect" and "elder" admit of more than one interpretation, and conventional practices provide little guidance to choose between alternatives. Even if these terms are clarified and everyone endorses the rule as formulated, there will be a great deal of disagreement as to what constitutes conformity to or violation of the rule. People claiming allegiance to the same conventionally formulated rule may yet behave differently. In such cases there seems to be no straightforward way to adjudicate rival interpretations of the key terms or to fix the scope of the convention-rule.

Where we happen to find a discernable consensus about the meaning and application of a particular convention or custom, it usually rests on tradition. In such cases, custom has a more restricted scope than convention. "Custom" is narrowed by the implication of being a convention with a historical origin. Characterizing a custom as traditional suggests that it extends back to a distant and indefinite time. Over the history of a community, the interpretation of its customs can be clarified and disambiguated in practical ways, and these developments may address some of the problems identified in the previous paragraph. Let us imagine for the moment a distinct group in which there is a clear consensus about what is meant by "respect your elders." This common understanding must take shape as specific patterns of behaviour that get passed down from generation to generation. In such cases, tradition is not only a potential resource to sharpen the meaning of a custom, it is invoked as its source of authority.

Long-standing patterns of conduct, and any adages associated with them, are thought to be authoritative because they have endured and withstood the test of time. In this chapter, Confucius is the best representative of this position (4.2). His legendary wisdom owes its conceptual foundation to ritual forms of conduct, ceremonies, and traditions that he submitted to personally. Much of his advice is in the spirit of the poet Pindar, who is quoted approvingly by another conventionalist, Herodotus: "Custom is king of all" (4.3). For both Confucius and Herodotus traditional rules in a particular community are sovereign because they owe their origins to insightful predecessors from the distant past. A third version of this position comes from ancient skeptics, who submit to customs despite acknowledging that they are manifestly fallible (4.4). According to skeptics, we simply have nothing better to go by. Incidentally, Edmund Burke endorses the value of traditional customs in contrast to abstract Enlightenment ideals (4.9; see also 3.12). For Burke, long-standing social institutions, such as the English courts, Parliament, and the monarchy, stabilize customs by translating them into positive laws. Legislation thus constitutes an official consensus about their meaning.

Natural law theory, the last theoretical strategy in the present chapter, is defended by Thomas Aquinas, Immanuel Kant, and Martin Luther King, Jr. According to natural law theory, a positive statute is authoritative if and only if it conforms to a higher law. These higher laws are thought to be part of the natural fabric of the universe or to derive from human nature, hence the name "*natural* law theory." A moral agent is obliged to submit to a properly constituted positive law by virtue of the law's conformity to a higher moral principle. Conversely, any positive law that is not so derived does not oblige our submission. The higher principle is our measuring stick to determine whether or not we are bound by a positive law.

Martin Luther King, Jr. goes a step further in applying this measure: when a positive law offends a natural moral principle (e.g., the equality of persons), every citizen has an obligation to actively do something to change that law (4.13). In particular, King advocates for "civil disobedience," according to which people flagrantly violate unjust positive laws in hope that compelling enforcement will expose their objectionable qualities. On this basis he argues that moral principles justify his own openly illegal campaign to protest Alabama's racial segregation laws. In his opinion these positive laws were morally unjust, even though they technically satisfied the legal conditions for justice. In this situation, civil disobedience is advocated as a way for citizens to submit to the moral law without being complicit in the injustices of a morally objectionable positive law. A similar rationale is put forth by Nelson Mandela about his activist efforts to challenge racial segregation in the notorious Apartheid legal code of twentieth-century South Africa (see 8.11).

If, like socially embedded conventions, higher laws are unwritten, then it is fair to ask again, "How do we specify the content of such unwritten laws?" In order to arrive at some consensus about what a natural moral law enjoins, we must first settle disagreements about its interpretation. According to Thomas Aquinas, our capacity for reason solves this problem (4.5). By virtue of this capacity, we discover moral laws, which (if they are indeed discovered) are necessarily objective. Because (i) everyone has the same capacity and (ii) the discoveries of rational deliberation purport to be objective, it is theoretically possible for a society to arrive at a well-grounded consensus about positive laws. In the framework of a rationally constituted legal system, legislators formulate positive laws that accord with natural law, judges apply these laws, and citizens obey them. In short, legal justice is measured by, and ought to be informed by, moral standards. Rationally constituted positive laws thereby compel the submission of citizens because of their rationality, not their traditional (as conventionalism maintains) or legislative source (as legal positivism maintains).

Additionally, we often deliberate over questions of moral right and wrong in the absence of any legal framework whatsoever. A conscientious person gets no guidance from the legal system when contemplating whether to tell a white lie, whether or not to honour a promise, or whether they have a duty to develop a special talent, to name only three examples. In the present chapter Immanuel Kant's version of natural law theory aims for the sort of generality that can provide guidance in all such situations (4.8). According to Kant, every rational being has direct insight into an axiomatic law-like principle that grounds morality: the Categorical Imperative. This imperative tests every possible course of action to determine whether it conforms to duty. In particular, it directs us to act on a maxim that we could conceivably institute as a universal law. In one respect, we act with complete freedom since the laws we obey are those we institute ourselves. In another respect, we submit to a rational procedure that identifies morally compelling duties. Kant thus characterizes human deliberation over right and wrong as our voluntary submission to law-like rules. This account is, incidentally, not included here as a contribution to legal theory *per se*. Laws discovered by applying the Categorical Imperative are operational results of a deliberative procedure, not enacted legislation.

In sum, theoretical readings in the present chapter urge us to adopt a particular perspective with respect to the rules we live by collectively. Legal positivism asks us to think like jurists, conventionalism asks us to think like social scientists or historians, and natural law theory asks us to think like moral legislators.

Our last author, Friedrich Nietzsche, discourages us from adopting any of these perspectives. His contribution here is entirely critical, attacking the idea that our deliberations over right and wrong can be grounded in rationality, humane conventions, or defensible laws (4.10). Indeed, not only does natural law theory strike him as implausible, he thinks submission to reason pathologically suppresses our most primitive natural instinct, something he calls the "will to power." This natural, ego-centric instinct is also more powerful and more admirable than submission to either conventional morality or any legal code. Here we find a position that seems to invert Socrates's submission to Athenian law in Plato's *Crito*, for Nietzsche regards submission of any sort as "slave morality."

Also included in this chapter are two documents that throw into sharper relief issues central to the theoretical questions in our other readings. First, the *Nuremberg Laws* (1935) instituted by the Nazis excluded Jews from German society by suspending basic political rights (4.11). This was one of a series of legislative manoeuvres that led to the Holocaust, the Nazi campaign to systematically murder millions of Jews, homosexuals, gypsies, communists, and members of other "undesirable" groups. It is worthwhile to ask whether and how legal reforms embodied in the *Nuremberg Laws* can be assessed from each of the theoretical perspectives explored in this chapter. Our second document is the *United Nations Declaration of Human Rights* (1948), which was drafted in the wake of World War II to prevent genocide and state-sponsored murder of the sort perpetrated by the Nazis (4.12). Here again, we can ask how each of the different theoretical positions would assess this attempt to institute a legal system that aspires to operate on an international scale.

4.2 Confucius (551–478 BCE)

General introductory remarks about Confucius and *The Analects* are found in 3.3.

For the most part, what Confucius says about law subscribes to a version of Conventionism, and in particular the branch that recognizes as sovereign traditional customs. Rectitude of names, speech, and conduct is exemplified by careful attention to ritual ceremonies and propriety. Ceremony is a pattern of conduct in which all players act according to shared, prescribed rules. Because shared rules prescribe what can and cannot be done, each person can expect certain things from other people. In the hierarchical civilization presupposed by these remarks, respect for ritual at the highest level promotes order throughout society. Also, in interpersonal situations, reciprocity (*shu*) is asserted as a universal moral principle. If everything operates according to the conventions of propriety, then there ought to be no need for litigation between individual citizens or the use of force by the state.

from The Analects

Book 2. CHAP. III. The Master said, 'If the people be led by laws, and uniformity sought to be given them by punishments, they will try to avoid the punishment, but have no sense of shame. If they be led by virtue, and uniformity sought to be given them by the rules of propriety, they will have the sense of shame, and moreover will become good.'

Book 3. CHAP. XVII. Tsze-kung wished to do away with the offering of a sheep connected with the inauguration of the first day of each month. The Master said, 'Ts'ze, you love the sheep; I love the ceremony.'

Book 8. CHAP. II. 1. The Master said, 'Respectfulness, without the rules of propriety, becomes laborious bustle; carefulness, without the rules of propriety, becomes timidity; boldness, without the rules of propriety, becomes insubordination; straightforwardness, without the rules of propriety, becomes rudeness.

'When those who are in high stations perform well all their duties to their relations, the people are aroused to virtue. When old friends are not neglected by them, the people are preserved from meanness.'

Book 8. CHAP. IX. The Master said, 'The people may be made to follow a path of action, but they may not be made to understand it.'

Book 12. CHAP. XIII. The Master said, 'In hearing litigations, I am like any other body. What is necessary, however, is to cause the people to have no litigations.'

Book 13. The Duke of Sheh informed Confucius, saying, 'Among us here there are those who may be styled upright in their conduct. If their father have stolen a sheep, they will bear witness to the fact.'

Confucius said, 'Among us, in our part of the country, those who are upright are different from this. The father conceals the misconduct of the son, and the son conceals the misconduct of the father. Uprightness is to be found in this.'

Book 15. CHAP. XXIII. Tsze-kung asked, saying, 'Is there one word which may serve as a rule of practice for all one's life?'

The Master said, 'Is not RECIPROCITY [*shu*] such a word? What you do not want done to yourself, do not do to others.'

4.3 Herodotus (490–425 BCE)

Herodotus is the first recognizable historian in the Western tradition. In Greek, the title of his book is simply *History*, which translates literally as "inquiries." It is, accordingly, much more variegated than a simple account of the past. For in addition to being a narrative history of events in Greece and neighbouring regions, it contains a rich amalgam of anthropology, geography, architectural criticism, mythography, and gossip.

Usually Herodotus's conventionalism is implicit rather than explicit in his long account of ancient history. But in the following passage he declares a theoretical position at the end by quoting a line from the poet Pindar. The line, "Custom is king of all," declares our collective habitual practices to be authoritative about what is right and wrong. The example of the Persian King Cambyses (reigned 530–522 BCE), who disregards custom, illustrates the injustices that result in violating long-standing community values. Not only was his successor, Darius (521–486 BCE), more sensible, he explored the value-guiding function of custom in interviews with Greeks and Callatians (from India) about funereal practices.

from The History of Herodotus, *Book 3.38*

Thus it appears certain to me, by a great variety of proofs, that Cambyses was raving mad; he would not else have set himself to make a mock of holy rites and long-established usages. For if one were to offer men to choose out of all the customs in the world such as seemed to them the best, they would examine the whole number, and end by preferring their own; so convinced are they that their own usages far surpass those of all others. Unless, therefore, a man was mad, it is not likely that he would make sport of such matters. That people have this feeling about their laws may be seen by very many proofs: among others, by the following. Darius, after he had got the kingdom, called into his presence certain Greeks who were at hand, and asked, "What he should pay them to eat the bodies of their fathers when they died?" To which they answered, that there was no sum that would tempt them to do such a thing. He then sent for certain Indians, of the race called Callatians, men who eat their fathers, and asked them, while the Greeks stood by, and knew by the help of an interpreter all that was said, "What he should give them to burn the bodies of their fathers at their decease?" The Indians exclaimed aloud, and bade him forbear such language. Such is men's wont herein; and Pindar was right, in my judgment, when he said, "Custom is the king o'er all."

4.4 Skepticism

Because ancient skeptics were doubtful about theoretical knowledge, they could not accept natural law, which requires an apprehension of abstract principles. But skeptics can accept conventions and positive law. They can endorse any or all positive laws, current conventions, and traditional customs, providing the guidance is not taken dogmatically. By "non-dogmatic" acceptance they mean that a law, convention, or custom is consulted without being taken for the authoritative truth. For this reason, skeptical endorsement of positive law is not an endorsement of legal positivism, since legal positivism is based on several theoretical claims about human nature. Truth or objective truth is, according to Sextus Empiricus, not available to human judgement, because we have access only to appearances (4.4.1). Without a criterion of truth, no rule can be authoritative, because even here they formulaically suspend judgement about the truth of all matters; however, if we bear in mind the fallibility of conventions and laws, they have practical value. As ground for doubt about a criterion of truth, skeptics observe the disparity of customs from culture to culture. Both Pyrrho of Elis (365–270 BCE), one of the earliest skeptics, and Philo Judaeus (30 BCE–45CE) invoke the fact that different cultures have different customs and laws as evidence that there is no universal criterion of truth.

4.4.1 Sextus Empiricus (160–210 CE), from Outlines of Pyrrhonism

Chapter XI
The Criterion of Scepticism

That we pay attention to appearances is clear from what we say about the criterion of the Sceptic discipline. Now, the word "criterion" is used in two senses. First, it is the standard one takes for belief in reality or non reality. This we shall discuss in our refutation. Second, it is the standard of action the observance of which regulates our actions in life. It is this latter about which we now speak. Now, we say that the criterion of the Sceptic discipline is the appearance, and it is virtually the sense-presentation to which we give this name, for this is dependent on feeling and involuntary affection and hence is not subject to question. Therefore no one, probably, will dispute that an object has this or that appearance; the question is whether it is in reality as it appears to be. Now, we cannot be entirely inactive when it comes to the observances of everyday life. Therefore, while living undogmatically, we pay due regard to appearances. This observance of the requirements of daily life seems to be fourfold, with the following particular heads: the guidance of nature, the compulsion of the feelings, the tradition of laws and customs, and the instruction of the arts. It is by the guidance of nature that we are naturally capable of sensation and thought. It is by the compulsion of the feelings that hunger leads us to food and thirst leads us to drink. It is by virtue of the tradition of laws and customs that in everyday life we accept piety as good and impiety as evil. And it is by virtue of the instruction of the arts that we are not inactive in those arts which we employ. All these statements, however, we make without prejudice.

Chapter XII
The End of Scepticism

The next point to go through would be the end of Scepticism. An end is "that at which all actions or thoughts are directed, and which is itself directed at nothing, in other words, the ultimate of desirable things." Our assertion up to now is that the Sceptic's end, where matters of opinion are concerned, is mental tranquillity; in the realm of things unavoidable, moderation of feeling is the end. His initial purpose in philosophizing was to pronounce judgement on appearances. He wished to find out which are true and which false, so as to attain mental tranquillity. In doing so, he met with contradicting alternatives of equal force. Since he could not decide between them, he withheld judgement. Upon his suspension of judgement there followed, by chance, mental tranquillity in matters of opinion. For the person who entertains the opinion that anything is by nature good or bad is continually disturbed. When he lacks those things which seem to him to be good, he believes he is being pursued, as if by the Furies, by those things which are by nature bad, and pursues what he believes to be the good things. But when he has acquired them, he encounters further perturbations. This is because his elation at the acquisition is unreasonable and immoderate, and also because in his fear of a reversal all his exertions go to prevent the loss of the things which to him seem good. On the other side there is the man who leaves undetermined the question what things are good and bad by nature. He does not exert himself to avoid anything or to seek after anything, and hence he is in a tranquil state.

The Sceptic, in fact, had the same experience as that related in the story about Apelles the artist.[1] They say that when Apelles was painting a horse, he wished to represent the horse's foam in the painting. His attempt was so unsuccessful that he gave it up and at the same time flung at the picture his sponge, with which he had wiped the paints off his brush. As it struck the picture, the sponge produced an image of horse's foam. So it was with the Sceptics. They were in hopes of attaining mental tranquillity, thinking that they could do this by arriving at some rational judgement which would dispel the inconsistencies involved in both appearances and thoughts. When they found this impossible, they withheld judgement. While they were in this state, they made a chance discovery. They found that they were attended by mental tranquillity as surely as a body by its shadow.

Nevertheless, we do not suppose the Sceptic to be altogether free from disturbance; rather, we say that when he is disturbed, it is by things which are unavoidable. Certainly we concede that he is sometimes cold and thirsty, and that he suffers in other such ways. But even here there is a difference. Two circumstances combine to the detriment of the ordinary man: he is hindered both by the feelings themselves and not less by the fact that he believes these conditions to be evil by nature. The Sceptic, on the other hand, rejects this additional notion that each of these things is evil by nature, and thus he gets off more easily. These, then, are our reasons for saying that the Sceptic's end is mental tranquillity where matters of opinion are concerned, and moderate feeling in the realm of things unavoidable. Some notable Sceptics have, however, added to these a third: suspension of judgement in investigations.

Chapter XIV

…

The Tenth Mode

There is a tenth mode, this one concerned chiefly with ethics. This is the argument from disciplines, customs, laws, mythical beliefs, and dogmatic notions. Now, a "discipline" is a choice of a way of life or of some objective, made by one person or by many. A case in point would be Diogenes, or the Laconians. A law is a written covenant among men who live in organized states, the transgressor of which is punished. A custom or habit (there is no difference) is a common acceptance by many men of a certain thing. Here the transgressor is not punished at all. Examples: It is a law not to commit adultery, but a custom not to have intercourse with a woman publicly. Mythical belief is an acceptance of unhistorical and fictitious events, such as—among others—the tales told of Kronos (for there are many who are led to believe these tales). A dogmatic notion is acceptance of a thing in so far as the acceptance seems to be confirmed by a line of reasoning or by some proof, for example, that atoms[2] are the elements of existing things, or homoeomeries, or minimal bodies, or something else.

Each of these we oppose sometimes to itself, sometimes to each of the others. We oppose custom to custom, for instance, in this way. Some of the Ethiopians tattoo their babies, while we do not. And Persians think that the use of bright-coloured, dragging garments is seemly, while we think it is unbecoming. And the Indians have intercourse with their women in public, whereas most other peoples hold this to be shameful. We oppose law to law in the following manner. With the Romans, he who relinquishes claim to the property inherited from his father is not obliged

1 Apelles was a contemporary of Alexander the Great and also of Pyrrho, the Skeptic, in the fourth century BCE. He was famous not only for his portrait of Alexander holding a thunderbolt and another picture of Venus rising from the sea, but also for his unceasing efforts at self-improvement in his art. The proverb *Nulla dies sine linea* is not only ascribed to him but could be broadly applied to the researches of the Skeptics from Pyrrho to Sextus's medical Skeptics.

2 Democritus, Epicurus, and Lucretius the Epicurean held the first view, Anaxagoras believed in the homoeomeries, and Diodorus Cronos, whose school was absorbed into the Stoics, believed in the minimal bodies.

to pay his father's debts, but with the Rhodians one must pay them in any event. And among the Tauri of Scythia there was a law that strangers should be sacrificed to Artemis, while with us the ritual killing of humans is forbidden. We oppose discipline to discipline when we set the discipline of Diogenes in opposition to that of Aristippus, or that of the Laconians to that of the Italians. We oppose mythical belief to mythical belief when we say that in one version Zeus is spoken of as the father of gods and men, while in another version it is Oceanus. To quote:

> Ocean, sire of the gods, and Tethys their
> mother.[3]

And we set dogmatic notions against one other when we say that some declare that there is only one element, while others assume that they are infinite in number. We do so also when we say that some believe the soul to be mortal, others immortal; and that some declare that human affairs are directed by divine providence, while others claim providence has no hand in them.

We oppose custom to the other things, as for example to a law, when we say that with Persian men it is a custom to indulge in homosexual practices, while with the Romans this practice is prohibited by law. This is also the case when we say that with us adultery is forbidden, while with the Massagetae the custom is traditionally an indifferent matter, as Eudoxus of Cnidos records in the first book of his *Voyage*. And whereas intercourse with our daughters is prohibited by our laws, with the Persians it is a custom to marry thus if one possibly can. Among the Egyptians men marry their sisters, a practice which with us is prohibited by law. The opposition of custom to discipline is seen in the fact that whereas most men have intercourse with their wives in private, Crates did so with Hipparchia in public.[4] And Diogenes went about with only a one-sleeved tunic, while we dress as is customary. Custom is opposed to mythical belief when the stories have it that Kronos devoured his own children, since it is our custom to provide for our children. And while it is habitual practice with us to venerate the gods as being good and unaffected by evils, the poets represent them as getting wounded and being envious of one another. And custom is opposed to dogmatic notion when Epicurus says, in opposition to our custom of begging favours of the gods, that the Divinity does not pay any attention to us; and when Aristippus thinks that dressing in women's clothes is a matter of indifference, whereas we consider this a shameful thing.

We have discipline opposed to law when in the face of a law which forbids the striking of a freeman or a well-born man, pancratiasts strike each other because of the discipline of the life they follow; and when gladiators, for the same reason, kill each other even though homicide is forbidden. We oppose mythical belief to discipline when we say that the myths tell of Heracles that he carded wool and endured the lot of a slave,[5] and that he did things that no one, exercising even a moderate choice, would have done, whereas Heracles' discipline of life was a noble one. Discipline is opposed to dogmatic notion when athletes pursue glory as something good, and for its sake take upon themselves a laborious discipline of life, while many philosophers have the dogmatic notion that glory is a trivial thing. We oppose law to mythical belief when the poets portray the gods as committing adultery and practising paederasty, whereas with us these practices are forbidden by law. And we oppose law to dogmatic notion when Chrysippus says that having intercourse with mothers or sisters is a matter of indifference, while the law forbids this. And we oppose mythical belief to dogmatic notion when the poets tell of Zeus coming down and having intercourse with mortal women, while with the dogmatists it is believed that this is impossible. And the Poet says that Zeus, in his

3 Homer, *Iliad* XIV 201. (—Tr.)

4 While this seems to us the very opposite of what we call "discipline," the point is that Crates's "discipline," or way of life, permitted this. (—Tr.)

5 Homer, *Odyssey* XXII 423 (the passage in Homer does not refer to Heracles). (—Tr.)

grief over Sarpedon, "poured down showers of blood to the earth,"[6] yet it is a dogma of philosophers that the Deity is impassive; and philosophers confute the story of the horse-centaurs, and offer us the horse-centaur as an example of non-reality.

Now, it would be possible to take up many other examples for each of the antitheses mentioned above, but for a brief account these will be sufficient. However, since this mode too points out how great the discrepancy in things is, we shall not be able to say what quality an object possesses according to nature, but only what quality it appears to possess with reference to a particular discipline, a particular law, a particular custom, and so on with each of the others. This mode also, then, compels us to suspend judgement regarding the nature of external objects. And so in this manner, through the ten modes, we end with suspension of judgement.

4.4.2 Diogenes Laertius (3rd century CE), from "Life of Pyrrho" in **Lives and Opinions of the Eminent Philosophers,** *Book IX*

The difficulties which they suggest, relating to the agreement subsisting between what appears to the senses, and what is comprehended by the intellect, divide themselves into ten modes of argument, according to which the subject and object of our knowledge is incessantly changing. And these ten modes Pyrrho lays down in the following manner....

The fifth mode is conversant with laws, and established customs, and belief in mythical traditions, and the conventions of art, and dogmatical opinions. This mode embraces all that relates to vice, and to honesty; to the true, and to the false; to the good, and to the bad; to the Gods, and to the production, and destruction of all visible objects. Accordingly, the same action is just in the case of some people, and unjust in that of others. And good in the case of some, and bad in that of others. On this principle we see that the Persians do not think it unnatural for a man to marry his daughter; but among the Greeks it is unlawful. Again, the Massagetæ, as Eudoxus tells us in the first book of his Travels over the World, have their women in common; but the Greeks do not. And the Cilicians delight in piracy, but the Greeks avoid it. So again, different nations worship different Gods; and some believe in the providence of God, and others do not. The Egyptians embalm their dead, and then bury them; the Romans burn them; the Pæonians throw them into the lakes. All these considerations show that we ought to suspend our judgment....

4.4.3 Philo Judaeus (30 BCE–45 CE), from **On Drunkenness**

... XLVII. (192) Since, then, this is the state of affairs with respect to these matters, it is worthwhile to appreciate correctly the simplicity, or rashness, or impudence of those who pretend to be able with ease to form an opinion, so as to assent to or deny what is stated with respect to anything whatever. For if the simple faculties are wanting, but the mingled powers and those which are formed by contributions from many sources are within sight, and if it is impossible for those which are invisible to be seen, and if we are unable to comprehend separately the character of all the component parts which are united to make up each faculty, then what remains except that we must think it necessary to suspend our judgment? (193) And then, too, do not those facts which are diffused over nearly the whole world, and which have caused both to Greeks and barbarians such erroneous judgments, exhort us not to be too ready in giving our credence

6 Homer, Iliad XVI 459. (—Tr.)

to what is not seen? And what are these facts? Surely they are the instructions which we have received from our childhood, and our national customs and ancient laws, of which it is admitted that there is not a single one which is of equal force among all people; but it is notorious that they vary according to the different countries, and nations, and cities, aye, and even still more, in every village and private house, and even with respect to men, and women, and infant children, in almost every point. (194) At all events, what are accounted disgraceful actions among us, are by others looked upon as honourable; what we think becoming, others call unseemly; what we pronounce just, others renounce as iniquitous; others think our holy actions impious, our lawful deeds lawless: and further, what we think praiseworthy, they find fault with; what we think worthy of all honour, is, in the eyes of others, deserving of punishment; and, in fact, they think most things to be of a contrary character to what we think. (195) And why need I be prolix and dwell further on this subject, when I am called off by other more important points? If then, any one, leaving out of the question all other more remarkable subjects of speculation, were to choose to devote his time to an investigation of the subject here proposed, namely, to examine the education, and customs, and laws of every different nation, and country, and place, and city; of all subjects and rulers; of all men, whether renowned or inglorious, whether free or slaves, whether ignorant or endowed with knowledge, he would spend not one day or two, nor a month, nor even a year, but his whole life, even though he were to reach a great age, in the investigation; and he would nevertheless still leave a vast number of subjects unexamined, uninvestigated, and unmentioned, without perceiving it. (196) Therefore, since there are some persons and things removed from other persons and things, not by a short distance only, but since they are utterly different, it then follows of necessity that the perceptions which occur to men of different things must also differ, and that their opinions must be at variance with one another.

XLVIII. (197) And since this is the case, who is so foolish and ridiculous as to affirm positively that such and such a thing is just, or wise, or honourable, or expedient? For whatever this man defines as such, someone else, who from his childhood, has learnt a contrary lesson, will be sure to deny. (198) But I am not surprised if a confused and mixed multitude, being the inglorious slave of customs and laws, however introduced and established, accustomed from its very cradle to obey them as if they were masters and tyrants, having their souls beaten and buffeted, as it were, and utterly unable to conceive any lofty or magnanimous thoughts, believes at once every tradition which is represented to it, and leaving its mind without any proper training, assents to and denies propositions without examination and without deliberation....

4.5 St. Thomas Aquinas (1225–1274)

General introductory remarks about Thomas Aquinas and the unusual format of a Thomistic article are found in 3.9.

Thomas Aquinas provides a systematic and comprehensive account of Natural Law theory. According to his account, three levels of law govern the cosmos. First, God's creative and providential agency operates according to Eternal Law. The Eternal Law is rational, but not apprehensible by human reason. Natural Law, which is one level below Eternal Law, is available to us. Natural Law includes the rule-governed conduct of the material universe, such as gravity and laws of mechanics. More importantly, it also includes moral rules that govern human agency by virtue of our mature, rational faculties. Below Natural Laws are Human Laws, which are the positive, written statutes, etc. that are formulated by worldly administrators. From this point of view, Aquinas characterizes human laws as mutable in light of natural law, and as being more morally compelling than custom. Lastly, he addresses Socrates's situation in Plato's *Crito* from general considerations of the obligations of a citizen to natural law. As it turns out, the justly condemned are not justified in evading punishment whereas the unjustly condemned are.

~

from Summa Theologiae

Question 90: Of the Essence of Law

We have now to consider the extrinsic principles of acts. Now the extrinsic principle inclining to evil is the devil, of whose temptations we have spoken in the First Part (Q. 114). But the extrinsic principle moving to good is God, Who both instructs us by means of His Law, and assists us by His Grace: wherefore in the first place we must speak of law; in the second place, of grace.

Concerning law, we must consider: (1) Law itself in general; (2) its parts....

FIRST ARTICLE [I–II, Q. 90, ART. 1]: WHETHER LAW IS SOMETHING PERTAINING TO REASON?

Obj. 1: It would seem that law is not something pertaining to reason. For the Apostle says (*Rom.* 7:23): "I see another law in my members," etc. But nothing pertaining to reason is in the members; since the reason does not make use of a bodily organ. Therefore law is not something pertaining to reason.

Obj. 2: Further, in the reason there is nothing else but power, habit, and act. But law is not the power itself of reason. In like manner, neither is it a habit of reason: because the habits of reason are the intellectual virtues of which we have spoken above (Q. 57). Nor again is it an act of reason: because then law would cease, when the act of reason ceases, for instance, while we are asleep. Therefore law is nothing pertaining to reason.

Obj. 3: Further, the law moves those who are subject to it to act aright. But it belongs properly to the will to move to act, as is evident from what has been said above (Q. 9, A. 1). Therefore law pertains, not to the reason, but to the will; according to the words of the Jurist (*Lib.* i, ff., *De Const. Prin. leg.* i): "Whatsoever pleaseth the sovereign, has force of law."

On the contrary, It belongs to the law to command and to forbid. But it belongs to reason to command, as stated above (Q. 17, A. 1). Therefore law is something pertaining to reason.

I answer that, Law is a rule and measure of acts, whereby man is induced to act or is restrained from acting: for *lex* (law) is derived from *ligare* (to bind), because it binds one to act. Now the rule and measure of human acts is the reason, which is the first principle of human acts, as is evident from what has been stated above (Q. 1, A. 1, ad 3); since it belongs to the reason to direct to the end, which is the first principle in all matters of action, according to the Philosopher (*Phys.* ii). Now that which is the principle in any genus, is the rule and measure of that genus: for instance, unity in the genus of numbers, and the first movement in the genus of movements. Consequently it follows that law is something pertaining to reason.

Reply Obj. 1: Since law is a kind of rule and measure, it may be in something in two ways. First, as in that which measures and rules: and since this is proper to reason, it follows that, in this way, law is in the reason alone. Secondly, as in that which is measured and ruled. In this way, law is in all those things that are inclined to something by reason of some law: so that any inclination arising from a law, may be called a law, not essentially but by participation as it were. And thus the inclination of the members to concupiscence is called "the law of the members."

Reply Obj. 2: Just as, in external action, we may consider the work and the work done, for instance the work of building and the house built; so in the acts of reason, we may consider the act itself of reason, i.e. to understand and to reason, and something produced by this act. With regard to the speculative reason, this is first of all the definition; secondly, the proposition; thirdly, the syllogism or argument. And since also the practical reason makes use of a syllogism in respect of the work to be done, as stated above (Q. 13, A. 3; Q. 76, A. 1) and since as the Philosopher teaches (*Ethic.* vii, 3); hence we find in the practical reason something that holds the same position in regard to operations, as, in the speculative intellect, the proposition holds in regard to conclusions. Such like universal propositions of the practical intellect that are directed to actions have the nature of law. And these propositions are sometimes under our actual consideration, while sometimes they are retained in the reason by means of a habit.

Reply Obj. 3: Reason has its power of moving from the will, as stated above (Q. 17, A. 1): for it is due to the fact that one wills the end, that the reason issues its commands as regards things ordained to the end. But in order that the volition of what is commanded may have the nature of law, it needs to be in accord with some rule of reason. And in this sense, is to be understood the saying that the will of the sovereign has the force of law; otherwise the sovereign's will would savor of lawlessness rather than of law.

Question 91: Of the Various Kinds of Law

We must now consider the various kinds of law: under which head there are six points of inquiry:

(1) Whether there is an eternal law?
(2) Whether there is a natural law?
(3) Whether there is a human law? ...

FIRST ARTICLE [I-II, Q. 91, ART. 1]: WHETHER THERE IS AN ETERNAL LAW? ...

On the contrary ... Augustine says (*De Lib. Arb.* i, 6): "That Law which is the Supreme Reason cannot be understood to be otherwise than unchangeable and eternal."

I answer that, As stated above (Q. 90, A. 1, ad 2; AA. 3, 4), a law is nothing else but a dictate of practical reason emanating from the ruler who governs a perfect community. Now it is evident, granted that the world is ruled by Divine Providence, as was stated in the First Part (Q. 22, AA. 1, 2), that the whole community of the universe is governed by Divine Reason. Wherefore the very Idea of the government of things in God the Ruler of the universe, has the nature of a law. And since the Divine Reason's conception of things is not subject to time but is eternal, according to Prov. 8:23, therefore it is that this kind of law must be called eternal....

SECOND ARTICLE [I-II, Q. 91, ART. 2]: WHETHER THERE IS IN US A NATURAL LAW?

Objection 1: It would seem that there is no natural law in us. Because man is governed sufficiently by the eternal law: for Augustine says (*De Lib. Arb.* i) that "the eternal law is that by which it is right that all things should be most orderly." But nature does not abound in superfluities as neither does she fail in necessaries. Therefore no law is natural to man.

Obj. 2: Further, by the law man is directed, in his acts, to the end, as stated above (Q. 90, A. 2). But the directing of human acts to their end is not a function of nature, as is the case in irrational creatures, which act for an end solely by their natural appetite; whereas man acts for an end by his reason and will. Therefore no law is natural to man.

Obj. 3: Further, the more a man is free, the less is he under the law. But man is freer than all the animals, on account of his free-will, with which he is endowed above all other animals. Since therefore other animals are not subject to a natural law, neither is man subject to a natural law.

On the contrary, A gloss on *Rom.* 2:14: "When the Gentiles, who have not the law, do by nature those things that are of the law," comments as follows: "Although they have no written law, yet they have the natural law, whereby each one knows, and is conscious of, what is good and what is evil."

I answer that, As stated above (Q. 90, A. 1, ad 1), law, being a rule and measure, can be in a person in two ways: in one way, as in him that rules and measures; in another way, as in that which is ruled and measured, since a thing is ruled and measured, in so far as it partakes of the rule or measure. Wherefore, since all things subject to Divine providence are ruled and measured by the eternal law, as was stated above (A. 1); it is evident that all things partake somewhat of the eternal law, in so far as, namely, from its being imprinted on them, they derive their respective inclinations to their proper acts and ends. Now among all others, the rational creature is subject to Divine providence in the most excellent way, in so far as it partakes of a share of providence, by being provident both for itself and for others. Wherefore it has a share of the Eternal Reason, whereby it has a natural inclination to its proper act and end: and this participation of the eternal law in the rational creature is called the natural law. Hence the Psalmist after saying (*Ps.* 4:6): "Offer up the sacrifice of justice," as though someone asked what the works of justice are, adds: "Many say, Who showeth us good things?" in answer to which question he says: "The light of Thy countenance, O Lord, is signed upon us": thus implying that the light of natural reason, whereby we discern what is good and what is evil, which is the function of the natural law, is nothing else than an imprint on us of the Divine light. It is therefore evident that the natural law is nothing else than the rational creature's participation of the eternal law.

Reply Obj. 1: This argument would hold, if the natural law were something different from the eternal law: whereas it is nothing but a participation thereof, as stated above.

Reply Obj. 2: Every act of reason and will in us is based on that which is according to nature, as stated above (Q. 10, A. 1): for every act of reasoning is based on principles that are known naturally, and every act of appetite in respect of the means is derived from the natural appetite in respect of the last end. Accordingly the first direction of our acts to their end must needs be in virtue of the natural law.

Reply Obj. 3: Even irrational animals partake in their own way of the Eternal Reason, just as the rational creature does. But because the rational creature partakes thereof in an intellectual and rational manner, therefore the participation of the eternal law in the rational creature is properly called a law, since a law is something pertaining to reason, as stated above (Q. 90, A. 1). Irrational creatures, however, do not partake thereof in a rational manner, wherefore there is no participation of the eternal law in them, except by way of similitude.

THIRD ARTICLE [I–II, Q. 91, ART. 3]: WHETHER THERE IS A HUMAN LAW?

Obj. 1: It would seem that there is not a human law. For the natural law is a participation of the eternal law, as stated above (A. 2). Now through the eternal law "all things are most orderly," as Augustine states (*De Lib. Arb.* i, 6). Therefore the natural law suffices for the ordering of all human affairs. Consequently there is no need for a human law.

Obj. 2: Further, a law bears the character of a measure, as stated above (Q. 90, A. 1). But human reason is not a measure of things, but vice versa, as stated in *Metaph.* x, text. 5. Therefore no law can emanate from human reason.

Obj. 3: Further, a measure should be most certain, as stated in *Metaph.* x, text. 3. But the dictates of human reason in matters of conduct are uncertain, according to *Wis.* 9:14: "The thoughts of mortal men are fearful, and our counsels uncertain." Therefore no law can emanate from human reason.

On the contrary, Augustine (*De Lib. Arb.* i, 6) distinguishes two kinds of law, the one eternal, the other temporal, which he calls human.

I answer that, As stated above (Q. 90, A. 1, ad 2), a law is a dictate of the practical reason. Now it is to be observed that the same procedure takes place in the practical and in the speculative reason: for each proceeds from principles to conclusions, as stated above (ibid.). Accordingly we conclude that just as, in the speculative reason, from naturally known indemonstrable principles, we draw the conclusions of the various sciences, the knowledge of which is not imparted to us by nature, but acquired by the efforts of reason, so too it is from the precepts of the natural law, as from general and indemonstrable principles, that the human reason needs to proceed to the more particular determination of certain matters. These particular determinations, devised by human reason, are called human laws, provided the other essential conditions of law be observed, as stated above (Q. 90, AA. 2, 3, 4). Wherefore Tully says in his *Rhetoric* (*De Invent. Rhet.* ii) that "justice has its source in nature; thence certain things came into custom by reason of their utility; afterwards these things which emanated from nature and were approved by custom, were sanctioned by fear and reverence for the law."

Reply Obj. 1: The human reason cannot have a full participation of the dictate of the Divine Reason, but according to its own mode, and imperfectly. Consequently, as on the part of the speculative reason, by a natural participation of Divine Wisdom, there is in us the knowledge of certain general principles, but not proper knowledge of each single truth, such as that contained in the Divine Wisdom; so too, on the part of the practical reason, man has a natural participation of the eternal law, according to certain general principles, but not as regards the particular determinations of individual cases, which are, however, contained in the eternal law. Hence the need for human reason to proceed further to sanction them by law.

Reply Obj. 2: Human reason is not, of itself, the rule of things: but the principles impressed on it by nature, are general rules and measures of all things relating to human conduct, whereof the natural reason is the rule and measure, although it is not the measure of things that are from nature.

Reply Obj. 3: The practical reason is concerned with practical matters, which are singular and contingent: but not with necessary things, with which the speculative reason is concerned. Wherefore human laws cannot have that inerrancy that belongs to the demonstrated conclusions of sciences. Nor is it necessary for every measure to be altogether unerring and certain, but according as it is possible in its own particular genus....

Question 93: Of the Eternal Law

SIXTH ARTICLE [I–II, Q. 93, ART. 6]: WHETHER ALL HUMAN AFFAIRS ARE SUBJECT TO THE ETERNAL LAW? ...

I answer that, There are two ways in which a thing is subject to the eternal law, as explained above (A. 5): first, by partaking of the eternal law by way of knowledge; secondly, by way of action and passion, i.e., by partaking of the eternal law by way of an inward motive principle: and in this second way, irrational creatures are subject to the eternal law, as stated above (A. 5). But since the rational nature, together with that which it has in common with all creatures, has something proper to itself inasmuch as it is rational, consequently it is subject to the eternal law in both ways; because while each rational creature has some knowledge of the eternal law, as stated above (A. 2), it also has a natural inclination to that which is in harmony with the eternal law; for "we are naturally adapted to the recipients of virtue" (*Ethic.* ii, 1).

Both ways, however, are imperfect, and to a certain extent destroyed, in the wicked; because in them the natural inclination to virtue is corrupted by vicious habits, and, moreover, the natural knowledge of good is darkened by passions and habits of sin. But in the good both ways are found more perfect: because in them, besides the natural knowledge of good, there is the added knowledge of faith and wisdom; and again, besides the natural inclination to good, there is the added motive of grace and virtue.

Accordingly, the good are perfectly subject to the eternal law, as always acting according to it: whereas the wicked are subject to the eternal law, imperfectly as to their actions, indeed, since both their knowledge of good, and their inclination thereto, are imperfect; but this imperfection on the part of action is supplied on the part of passion, in so far as they suffer what the eternal law decrees concerning them, according as they fail to act in harmony with that law. Hence Augustine says (*De Lib. Arb.* i, 15): "I esteem that the righteous act according to the eternal law; and (*De Catech. Rud.* xviii): Out of the just misery of the souls which deserted Him, God knew how to furnish the inferior parts of His creation with most suitable laws." ...

Question 94: Of the Natural Law

FOURTH ARTICLE [I–II, Q. 94, ART. 4]: WHETHER THE NATURAL LAW IS THE SAME IN ALL MEN? ...

I answer that, As stated above (AA. 2, 3), to the natural law belong those things to which a man is inclined naturally: and among these it is proper to man to be inclined to act according to reason. Now the process of reason is from the common to the proper, as stated in *Phys.* i. The speculative reason, however, is differently situated in this matter, from the practical reason. For, since the speculative reason is busied chiefly with necessary things, which cannot be otherwise than they are, its proper conclusions, like the universal principles, contain the truth without fail. The practical reason, on the other hand, is busied with contingent matters, about which human actions are concerned: and consequently, although there is necessity in the general principles, the more we descend to matters of detail, the more frequently we encounter defects. Accordingly then in speculative matters truth is the same in all men, both as to principles and as to conclusions: although the truth is not known to all as regards the conclusions, but only as regards the principles which are called common notions. But in matters of action, truth or practical rectitude is not the same for all, as to matters of detail, but only as to the general principles: and where there is the same rectitude in matters of detail, it is not equally known to all.

It is therefore evident that, as regards the general principles whether of speculative or of practical reason, truth or rectitude is the same for all, and is equally known by all. As to the proper conclusions of the speculative reason, the truth is the same for all, but is not equally known to all: thus it is true for all that the three angles of a triangle are together equal to two right angles, although it is not known to all. But as to the proper conclusions of the practical reason, neither is the truth or rectitude the same for all, nor, where it is the same, is it equally known by all. Thus it is right and true for all to act according to reason: and from this principle it follows as a proper conclusion, that goods entrusted to another should be restored to their owner. Now this is true for the majority of cases: but it may happen in a particular case that it would be injurious, and therefore unreasonable, to restore goods held in trust; for instance, if they are claimed for the purpose of fighting against one's country. And this principle will be found to fail the more, according as we descend further into detail, e.g., if one were to say that goods held in trust should be restored with such and such a guarantee, or in such and such a way; because the greater the number of conditions added, the greater the number of ways in which the principle may fail, so that it be not right to restore or not to restore.

Consequently we must say that the natural law, as to general principles, is the same for all, both as to rectitude and as to knowledge. But as to certain matters of detail, which are conclusions, as it were, of those general principles, it is the same for all in the majority of cases, both as to rectitude and as to knowledge; and yet in some few cases it may fail, both as to rectitude, by reason of certain obstacles (just as natures subject to generation and corruption fail in some few cases on account of some obstacle), and as to knowledge, since in some the reason is perverted by passion, or evil habit, or an evil disposition of nature; thus formerly, theft, although it is expressly contrary to the natural law, was not considered wrong among the Germans, as Julius Caesar relates (*De Bello Gall.* vi)....

Question 95: Of Human Law

We must now consider human law; and (1) this law considered in itself; (2) its power; (3) its mutability....

(1) Its utility.
(2) Its origin....

FIRST ARTICLE [I–II, Q. 95, ART. 1]: WHETHER IT WAS USEFUL FOR LAWS TO BE FRAMED BY MEN? ...

I answer that, As stated above (Q. 63, A. 1; Q. 94, A. 3), man has a natural aptitude for virtue; but the perfection of virtue must be acquired by man by means of some kind of training. Thus we observe that man is helped by industry in his necessities, for instance, in food and clothing. Certain beginnings of these he has from nature, viz. his reason and his hands; but he has not the full complement, as other animals have, to whom nature has given sufficiency of clothing and food. Now it is difficult to see how man could suffice for himself in the matter of this training: since the perfection of virtue consists chiefly in withdrawing man from undue pleasures, to which above all man is inclined, and especially the young, who are more capable of being trained. Consequently a man needs to receive this training from another, whereby to arrive at the perfection of virtue. And as to those young people who are inclined to acts of virtue, by their good natural disposition, or by custom, or rather by the gift of God, paternal training suffices, which is by admonitions. But since some are found to be depraved, and prone to vice, and not easily amenable to words, it was necessary for such to be restrained from evil by force and fear, in order that, at least, they might desist from evil-doing, and leave others in peace, and that they themselves, by being habituated in this way, might be brought to do willingly what hitherto they did from fear, and thus become virtuous. Now this kind of training, which compels through fear of punishment, is the discipline of laws. Therefore in order that man might have peace and virtue, it was necessary for laws to be framed: for, as the Philosopher says (*Polit.* i, 2), "as man is the most noble of animals if he be perfect in virtue, so is he the lowest of all, if he be severed from law and righteousness"; because man can use his reason to devise means of satisfying his lusts and evil passions, which other animals are unable to do....

SECOND ARTICLE [I–II, Q. 95, ART. 2]: WHETHER EVERY HUMAN LAW IS DERIVED FROM THE NATURAL LAW? ...

I answer that, As Augustine says (*De Lib. Arb.* i, 5) "that which is not just seems to be no law at all": wherefore the force of a law depends on the extent of its justice. Now in human affairs a thing is said to be just, from being right, according to the rule of reason. But the first rule of reason is the law of nature, as is clear from what has been stated above (Q. 91, A. 2, ad 2). Consequently every human law has just so much of the nature of law, as it is derived from the law of nature. But if in any point it deflects from the law of nature, it is no longer a law but a perversion of law.

But it must be noted that something may be derived from the natural law in two ways: first, as a conclusion from premises, secondly, by way of determination of certain generalities. The first way is like to that by which, in sciences, demonstrated conclusions are drawn from the principles: while the second mode is likened to that whereby, in the arts, general forms are particularized as to details: thus the craftsman needs to determine the general form of a house to some particular shape. Some things are therefore derived from the general principles of the natural law, by way of conclusions; e.g., that "one must not kill" may be derived as a conclusion from the principle that "one should do harm to no man": while some are derived therefrom by way of determination; e.g., the law of nature has it that the evil-doer should be punished; but that he be punished in this or that way, is a determination of the law of nature.

Accordingly both modes of derivation are found in the human law. But those things which are derived in the first way, are contained in human law not as emanating therefrom exclusively, but have some force from the natural law also. But those things which are derived in the second way, have no other force than that of human law....

Question 96: Of the Power of Human Law

We must now consider the power of human law....

FOURTH ARTICLE [I–II, Q. 96, ART. 4]: WHETHER HUMAN LAW BINDS A MAN IN CONSCIENCE? ...

I answer that, Laws framed by man are either just or unjust. If they be just, they have the power of binding in conscience, from the eternal law whence they are derived, according to *Prov.* 8:15: "By Me kings reign, and lawgivers decree just things." Now laws are said to be just, both from the end, when, to wit, they are ordained to the common good—and from their author, that is to say, when the law that is made does not exceed the power of the lawgiver—and from their form, when, to wit, burdens are laid on the subjects, according to an equality of proportion and with a view to the common good. For, since one man is a part of the community, each man in all that he is and has, belongs to the community; just as a part, in all that it is, belongs to the whole; wherefore nature inflicts a loss on the part, in order to save the whole: so that on this account, such laws as these, which impose proportionate burdens, are just and binding in conscience, and are legal laws.

On the other hand laws may be unjust in two ways: first, by being contrary to human good, through being opposed to the things mentioned above—either in respect of the end, as when an authority imposes on his subjects burdensome laws, conducive, not to the common good, but rather to his own cupidity or vainglory—or in respect of the author, as when a man makes a law that goes beyond the power committed to him—or in respect of the form, as when burdens are imposed unequally on the community, although with a view to the common good. The like are acts of violence rather than laws; because, as Augustine says (*De Lib. Arb.* i, 5), "a law that is not just, seems to be no law at all." Wherefore such laws do not bind in conscience, except perhaps in order to avoid scandal or disturbance, for which cause a man should even yield his right, according to *Matt.* 5:40, 41: "If a man . . . take away thy coat, let go thy cloak also unto him; and whosoever will force thee one mile, go with him another two."

Secondly, laws may be unjust through being opposed to the Divine good: such are the laws of tyrants inducing to idolatry, or to anything else contrary to the Divine law: and laws of this kind must nowise be observed, because, as stated in *Acts* 5:29, "we ought to obey God rather than man." ...

FIFTH ARTICLE [I–II, Q. 96, ART. 5]: WHETHER ALL ARE SUBJECT TO THE LAW?

Objection 1: It would seem that not all are subject to the law. For those alone are subject to a law for whom a law is made. But the Apostle says (*1 Tim.* 1:9): "The law is not made for the just man." Therefore the just are not subject to the law.

Obj. 2: Further, Pope Urban says [*Decretals. caus.* xix, qu. 2]: "He that is guided by a private law need not for any reason be bound by the public law." Now all spiritual men are led by the private law of the Holy Ghost, for they are the sons of God, of whom it is said (*Rom.* 8:14): "Whosoever are led by the Spirit of God, they are the sons of God." Therefore not all men are subject to human law.

Obj. 3: Further, the jurist says [*Pandect. Justin.* i, ff., tit. 3, *De Leg. et Senat.*] that "the sovereign is exempt from the laws." But he that is exempt from the law is not bound thereby. Therefore not all are subject to the law.

On the contrary, The Apostle says (*Rom.* 13:1): "Let every soul be subject to the higher powers." But subjection to a power seems to imply subjection to the laws framed by that power. Therefore all men should be subject to human law.

I answer that, As stated above (Q. 90, AA. 1, 2; A. 3, ad 2), the notion of law contains two things: first, that it is a rule of human acts; secondly, that it has coercive power. Wherefore a man may be subject to law in two ways. First, as the regulated is subject to the regulator: and, in this way, whoever is subject to a power, is subject to the law framed by that power. But it may happen in two ways that one is not subject to a power. In one way, by being altogether free from its authority: hence the subjects of one city or kingdom are not bound by the laws of the sovereign of another city or kingdom, since they are not subject to his authority. In another way, by being under a yet higher law; thus the subject of a proconsul should be ruled by his command, but not in those matters in which the subject receives his orders from the emperor: for in these matters, he is not bound by the mandate of the lower authority, since he is directed by that of a higher. In this way, one who is simply subject to a law, may not be subject thereto in certain matters, in respect of which he is ruled by a higher law.

Secondly, a man is said to be subject to a law as the coerced is subject to the coercer. In this way the virtuous and righteous are not subject to the law, but only the wicked. Because coercion and violence are contrary to the will: but the will of the good is in harmony with the law, whereas the will of the wicked is discordant from it. Wherefore in this sense the good are not subject to the law, but only the wicked.

Reply Obj. 1: This argument is true of subjection by way of coercion: for, in this way, "the law is not made for the just men": because "they are a law to themselves," since they "show the work of the law written in their hearts," as the Apostle says (*Rom.* 2:14, 15). Consequently the law does not enforce itself upon them as it does on the wicked.

Reply Obj. 2: The law of the Holy Ghost is above all law framed by man: and therefore spiritual men, in so far as they are led by the law of the Holy Ghost, are not subject to the law in those matters that are inconsistent with the guidance of the Holy Ghost. Nevertheless the very fact that spiritual men are subject to law, is due to the leading of the Holy Ghost, according to *1 Pet.* 2:13: "Be ye subject ... to every human creature for God's sake."

Reply Obj. 3: The sovereign is said to be "exempt from the law," as to its coercive power; since, properly speaking, no man is coerced by himself, and law has no coercive power save from the authority of the sovereign. Thus then is the sovereign said to be exempt from the law, because none is competent to pass sentence on him, if he acts against the law. Wherefore on *Ps.* 50:6: "To Thee only have I sinned," a gloss says that "there is no man who can judge the deeds of a king." But as to the directive force of law, the sovereign is subject to the law by his own will, according to the statement (*Extra, De Constit. cap. Cum omnes*) that "whatever law a man makes for another, he should keep himself. And a wise authority [Dionysius Cato, *Dist. de Moribus*] says: 'Obey the law that thou makest thyself.'" Moreover the Lord reproaches those who "say and do not"; and who "bind heavy burdens and lay them on men's shoulders, but with a finger of their own they will not move them" (*Matt.* 23:3, 4). Hence, in the judgment of God, the sovereign is not exempt from the law, as to its directive force; but he should fulfil it to his own free-will and not of constraint. Again the sovereign is above the law, in so far as, when it is expedient, he can change the law, and dispense in it according to time and place....

Question 97: Of Change in Laws

We must now consider change in laws....

(1) Whether human law is changeable? ...
(2) Whether it is abolished by custom, and whether custom obtains the force of law? ...

FIRST ARTICLE [I–II, Q. 97, ART. 1]: WHETHER HUMAN LAW SHOULD BE CHANGED IN ANY WAY? ...

On the contrary ... Augustine says (*De Lib. Arb.* i, 6): "A temporal law, however just, may be justly changed in course of time."

I answer that, As stated above (Q. 91, A. 3), human law is a dictate of reason, whereby human acts are directed. Thus there may be two causes for the just change of human law: one on the part of reason; the other on the part of man whose acts are regulated by law. The cause on the part of reason is that it seems natural to human reason to advance gradually from the imperfect to the perfect. Hence, in speculative sciences, we see that the teaching of the early philosophers was imperfect, and that it was afterwards perfected by those who succeeded them. So also in practical matters: for those who first endeavored to discover something useful for the human community, not being able by themselves to take everything into consideration, set up certain institutions which were deficient in many ways; and these were changed by subsequent lawgivers who made institutions that might prove less frequently deficient in respect of the common weal.

On the part of man, whose acts are regulated by law, the law can be rightly changed on account of the changed condition of man, to whom different things are expedient according to the difference of his condition. An example is proposed by Augustine (*De Lib. Arb.* i, 6): "If the people have a sense of moderation and responsibility, and are most careful guardians of the common weal, it is right to enact a law allowing such a people to choose their own magistrates for the government of the commonwealth. But if, as time goes on, the same people become so corrupt as to sell their votes, and entrust the government to scoundrels and criminals; then the right of appointing their public officials is rightly forfeit to such a people, and the choice devolves to a few good men." ...

THIRD ARTICLE [I–II, Q. 97, ART. 3]: WHETHER CUSTOM CAN OBTAIN FORCE OF LAW? ...

I answer that, All law proceeds from the reason and will of the lawgiver; the Divine and natural laws from the reasonable will of God; the human law from the will of man, regulated by reason. Now just as human reason and will, in practical matters, may be made manifest by speech, so may they be made known by deeds: since seemingly a man chooses as good that which he carries into execution. But it is evident that by human speech, law can be both changed and expounded, in so far as it manifests the interior movement and thought of human reason. Wherefore by actions also, especially if they be repeated, so as to make a custom, law can be changed and expounded; and also something can be established which obtains force of law, in so far as by repeated external actions, the inward movement of the will, and concepts of reason are most effectually declared; for when a thing is done again and again, it seems to proceed from a deliberate judgment of reason. Accordingly, custom has the force of a law, abolishes law, and is the interpreter of law....

Question 69: Of Sins Committed against Injustice by the Defendant

[II–II, Q. 69, ART. 4] WHETHER A MAN WHO IS CONDEMNED TO DEATH MAY LAWFULLY DEFEND HIMSELF IF HE CAN?

Objection 1: It would seem that a man who is condemned to death may lawfully defend himself if he can. For it is always lawful to do that to which nature inclines us, as being of natural right, so to speak. Now, to resist corruption is an inclination of nature not only in men and animals but also in things devoid of sense. Therefore if he can do so, the accused, after condemnation, may lawfully resist being put to death.

Obj. 2: Further, just as a man, by resistance, escapes the death to which he has been condemned, so does he by flight. Now it is lawful seemingly to escape death by flight, according to *Ecclus.* 9:18, "Keep thee far from the man that hath power to kill [and not to quicken]" [*The words in the brackets are not in the Vulgate]. Therefore it is also lawful for the accused to resist.

Obj. 3: Further, it is written (*Prov.* 24:11): "Deliver them that are led to death: and those that are drawn to death forbear not to deliver." Now a man is under greater obligation to himself than to another. Therefore it is lawful for a condemned man to defend himself from being put to death.

On the contrary, The Apostle says (*Rom.* 13:2): "He that resisteth the power, resisteth the ordinance of God: and they that resist, purchase to themselves damnation." Now a condemned man, by defending himself, resists the power in the point of its being ordained by God "for the punishment of evil-doers, and for the praise of the good" [*1 Pet.* 2:14]. Therefore he sins in defending himself.

I answer that, A man may be condemned to death in two ways. First justly, and then it is not lawful for the condemned to defend himself, because it is lawful for the judge to combat his resistance by force, so that on his part the fight is unjust, and consequently without any doubt he sins.

Secondly a man is condemned unjustly: and such a sentence is like the violence of robbers, according to *Ezech.* 22:21, "Her princes in the midst of her are like wolves ravening the prey to shed blood." Wherefore even as it is lawful to resist robbers, so is it lawful, in a like case, to resist wicked princes; except perhaps in order to avoid scandal, whence some grave disturbance might be feared to arise.

Reply Obj. 1: Reason was given to man that he might ensue those things to which his nature inclines, not in all cases, but in accordance with the order of reason. Hence not all self-defense is lawful, but only such as is accomplished with due moderation.

Reply Obj. 2: When a man is condemned to death, he has not to kill himself, but to suffer death: wherefore he is not bound to do anything from which death would result, such as to stay in the place whence he would be led to execution. But he may not resist those who lead him to death, in order that he may not suffer what is just for him to suffer. Even so, if a man were condemned to die of hunger, he does not sin if he partakes of food brought to him secretly, because to refrain from taking it would be to kill himself.

Reply Obj. 3: This saying of the wise man does not direct that one should deliver a man from death in opposition to the order of justice: wherefore neither should a man deliver himself from death by resisting against justice.

4.6 Thomas Hobbes (1588–1679)

In *Leviathan* Thomas Hobbes develops a systematic statement of positivism. His argument begins with an account of the state of nature, in which human beings are characterized as essentially selfish and in a condition of war with each other. Under the constant spectre of violent death, we agree to enter into a social contract with each other. In the civil society that is founded on this contract we all live under the aegis of an authoritarian state (either a single ruler or a small number of them). People surrender their natural liberty for the security and protection of the state. The state regulates society by means of laws, which institute for the first time a common conception of justice. Because laws are authorized as the positive act of the state, this position is called *legal positivism*. On this issue, Hobbes's position is opposed to that of Thomas Aquinas and Martin Luther King, Jr.

Once the laws are legislated and promulgated by the state, they are authoritative and not subject to critical assessment from the citizens who must obey them. A consequence of this position is that individual citizens are free only to the extent that they may do anything that is not forbidden explicitly by law. The only exception is someone who has been sentenced to die by capital punishment. Each citizen gives up natural liberty for the purpose of self-preservation. If that function disappears, as in the case of a condemned criminal, that person is no longer bound by the law. Of course, the state locks up condemned prisoners until a death sentence can be executed, so escape is usually not possible. But, according to Hobbes, someone in Socrates's position would be justified in fleeing (notice the argument on pp. 256–57 about the invalidity of a covenant not to defend oneself). On the question of ones's obligations to accept capital punishment, Hobbes's answer is opposed to that of Socrates and Thomas Aquinas.

~

from Leviathan

Chapter XIV, Of the First and Second Naturall Lawes, and of Contracts

The RIGHT OF NATURE, which Writers commonly call Jus Naturale, is the Liberty each man hath, to use his own power, as he will himselfe, for the preservation of his own Nature; that is to say, of his own Life; and consequently, of doing any thing, which in his own Judgement, and Reason, hee shall conceive to be the aptest means thereunto.

By LIBERTY, is understood, according to the proper signification of the word, the absence of externall Impediments: which Impediments, may oft take away part of a mans power to do what hee would; but cannot hinder him from using the power left him, according as his judgement, and reason shall dictate to him.

A LAW OF NATURE, (Lex Naturalis,) is a Precept, or generall Rule, found out by Reason, by which a man is forbidden to do, that, which is destructive of his life, or taketh away the means of preserving the same; and to omit, that, by which he thinketh it may be best preserved. For though they that speak of this subject, use to confound Jus, and Lex, Right and Law; yet they ought to be distinguished; because RIGHT, consisteth in liberty to do, or to forbeare; Whereas LAW, determineth, and bindeth to one of them: so that Law, and Right, differ as much, as Obligation, and Liberty; which in one and the same matter are inconsistent.

And because the condition of Man, (as hath been declared in the precedent Chapter) is a condition of Warre of every one against every one; in which case every one is governed by his own Reason; and there is nothing he can make use of, that may not be a help unto him, in preserving his life against his enemyes; It followeth, that in such a condition, every man has a Right to every thing; even to one anothers body. And therefore, as long as this naturall Right of every man to every thing endureth, there can be no security to any man, (how strong or wise soever he be,) of living out the time, which Nature ordinarily alloweth men to live.

And consequently it is a precept, or generall rule of Reason, "That every man, ought to endeavour Peace, as farre as he has hope of obtaining it; and when he cannot obtain it, that he may seek, and use, all helps, and advantages of Warre." The first branch, of which Rule, containeth the first, and Fundamentall Law of Nature; which is, "To seek Peace, and follow it." The Second, the summe of the Right of Nature; which is, "By all means we can, to defend our selves."

From this Fundamentall Law of Nature, by which men are commanded to endeavour Peace, is derived this second Law; "That a man be willing, when others are so too, as farre-forth, as for Peace, and defence of himselfe he shall think it necessary, to lay down this right to all things; and be contented with so much liberty against other men, as he would allow other men against himselfe." For as long as every man holdeth this Right, of doing any thing he liketh; so long are all men in the condition of Warre. But if other men will not lay down their Right, as well as he; then there is no Reason for any one, to devest himselfe of his: For that were to expose himselfe to Prey, (which no man is bound to) rather than to dispose himselfe to Peace. This is that Law of the Gospell; "Whatsoever you require that others should do to you, that do ye to them." And that Law of all men, "Quod tibi feiri non vis, alteri ne feceris."

To Lay Downe a mans Right to any thing, is to Devest himselfe of the Liberty, of hindring another of the benefit of his own Right to the same. For he that renounceth, or passeth away his Right, giveth not to any other man a Right which he had not before; because there is nothing to which every man had not Right by Nature: but onely standeth out of his way, that he may enjoy his own originall Right, without hindrance from him; not without hindrance from another. So that the effect which redoundeth to one man, by another mans defect of Right, is but so much diminution of impediments to the use of his own Right originall.

Right is layd aside, either by simply Renouncing it; or by Transferring it to another. By Simply RENOUNCING; when he cares not to whom the benefit thereof redoundeth. By TRANSFERRING; when he intendeth the benefit thereof to some certain person, or persons. And when a man hath in either manner abandoned, or granted away his Right; then is he said to be OBLIGED, or BOUND, not to hinder those, to whom such Right is granted, or abandoned, from the benefit of it: and that he Ought, and it his DUTY, not to make voyd that voluntary act of his own: and that such hindrance is INJUSTICE, and INJURY, as being Sine Jure; the Right being before renounced, or transferred. So that Injury, or Injustice, in the controversies of the world, is somewhat like to that, which in the disputations of Scholers is called Absurdity. For as it is there called an Absurdity, to contradict what one maintained in the Beginning: so in the world, it is called Injustice, and Injury, voluntarily to undo that, which from the beginning he had voluntarily done. The way by which a man either simply Renounceth, or Transferreth his Right, is a Declaration, or Signification, by some voluntary and sufficient signe, or signes, that he doth so Renounce, or Transferre; or hath so Renounced, or Transferred the same, to him that accepteth it. And these Signes are either Words onely, or Actions onely; or (as it happeneth most often) both Words and Actions. And the same are the BONDS, by which men are bound, and obliged: Bonds, that have their strength, not from their own Nature, (for nothing is more easily broken then a mans word,) but from Feare of some evill consequence upon the rupture.

Whensoever a man Transferreth his Right, or Renounceth it; it is either in consideration of some Right reciprocally transferred to himselfe; or for some other good he hopeth for thereby. For it is a voluntary act: and of the voluntary acts of every man, the object is some Good To Himselfe. And therefore there be some Rights, which no man can be understood by any words, or other signes, to have abandoned, or transferred. As first a man cannot lay down the right of resisting them, that assault him by force, to take away his life; because he cannot be understood to ayme thereby, at any Good to himselfe. The same may be sayd of Wounds, and Chayns, and Imprisonment; both because there is no benefit consequent to such patience; as there is to the patience of suffering another to be wounded, or imprisoned: as also because a man cannot tell, when he seeth men proceed against him by violence, whether they intend his death or not. And lastly the motive, and end for which this renouncing, and transferring or Right is introduced, is nothing else but the security of a mans person, in his life, and in the means of so preserving life, as not to be weary of it. And therefore if a man by words, or other signes, seem to despoyle himselfe of the End, for which those signes were intended; he is not to be understood as if he meant it, or that it was his will; but that he was ignorant of how such words and actions were to be interpreted.

The mutuall transferring of Right, is that which men call CONTRACT.

There is difference, between transferring of Right to the Thing; and transferring, or tradition, that is, delivery of the Thing it selfe. For the Thing may be delivered together with the Translation of the Right; as in buying and selling with ready mony; or exchange of goods, or lands: and it may be delivered some time after.

Again, one of the Contractors, may deliver the Thing contracted for on his part, and leave the other to perform his part at some determinate time after, and in the mean time be trusted; and then the Contract on his part, is called PACT, or COVENANT: Or both parts may contract now, to performe hereafter: in which cases, he that is to performe in time to come, being trusted, his performance is called Keeping Of Promise, or Faith; and the fayling of performance (if it be voluntary) Violation Of Faith.

When the transferring of Right, is not mutuall; but one of the parties transferreth, in hope to gain thereby friendship, or service from another, or from his friends; or in hope to gain the reputation of Charity, or Magnanimity; or to deliver his mind from the pain of compassion; or in hope of reward in heaven; This is not Contract, but GIFT, FREE GIFT, GRACE: which words signifie one and the same thing.

Signes of Contract, are either Expresse, or By Inference. Expresse, are words spoken with understanding of what they signifie; And such words are either of the time Present, or Past; as, I Give, I Grant, I Have Given, I Have Granted, I Will That This Be Yours: Or of the future; as, I Will Give, I Will Grant; which words of the future, are called Promise.

Signes by Inference, are sometimes the consequence of Words; sometimes the consequence of Silence; sometimes the consequence of Actions; sometimes the consequence of Forbearing an Action: and generally a signe by Inference, of any Contract, is whatsoever sufficiently argues the will of the Contractor.

Words alone, if they be of the time to come, and contain a bare promise, are an insufficient signe of a Free-gift and therefore not obligatory. For if they be of the time to Come, as, To Morrow I Will Give, they are a signe I have not given yet, and consequently that my right is not transferred, but remaineth till I transferre it by some other Act. But if the words be of the time Present, or Past, as, "I have given, or do give to be delivered to morrow," then is my to morrows Right given away to day; and that by the vertue of the words, though there were no other argument of my will. And there is a great difference in the signification of these words, Volos Hoc Tuum Esse Cras, and Cros Dabo; that is between "I will that this be thine to morrow," and, "I will give it to thee to morrow:" For the word I Will, in the former manner of speech, signifies an act of the will Present; but in the later, it signifies a promise of an act of the will to Come: and therefore the former words, being of the Present, transferre a future right; the later, that be of the Future, transferre nothing. But if there be other signes of the Will to transferre a Right, besides Words; then, though the gift be Free, yet may the Right be understood to passe by words of the future: as if a man propound a Prize to him that comes first to the end of a race, The gift is Free; and though the words be of the Future, yet the Right passeth: for if he would not have his words so be understood, he should not have let them runne.

Signes Of Contract Are Words Both Of The Past, Present, and Future In Contracts, the right passeth, not onely where the words are of the time Present, or Past; but also where they are of the Future; because all Contract is mutuall translation, or change of Right; and therefore he that promiseth onely, because he hath already received the benefit for which he promiseth, is to be understood as if he intended the Right should passe: for unlesse he had been content to have his words so understood, the other would not have performed his part first. And for that cause, in buying, and selling, and other acts of Contract, A Promise is equivalent to a Covenant; and therefore obligatory.

He that performeth first in the case of a Contract, is said to MERIT that which he is to receive by the performance of the other; and he hath it as Due. Also when a Prize is propounded to many, which is to be given to him onely that winneth; or mony is thrown amongst many, to be enjoyed by them that catch it; though this be a Free Gift; yet so to Win, or so to Catch, is to Merit, and to have it as DUE. For the Right is transferred in the Propounding of the Prize, and in throwing down the mony; though it be not determined to whom, but by the Event of the contention. But there is between these two sorts of Merit, this difference, that In Contract, I Merit by vertue of my own power, and the Contractors need; but in this case of Free Gift, I am enabled to Merit onely by the benignity of the Giver; In Contract, I merit at The Contractors hand that hee should depart with his right; In this case of gift, I Merit not that the giver should part with his right; but that when he has parted with it, it should be mine, rather than anothers. And this I think to be the meaning of that distinction of the Schooles, between Meritum Congrui, and Meritum Condigni. For God Almighty, having promised Paradise to those men (hoodwinkt with carnall desires,) that can walk through this world according to the Precepts, and Limits prescribed by him; they say, he that shall so walk, shall Merit Paradise Ex Congruo. But because no man can demand a right to it, by his own Righteousnesse, or any other power in himselfe, but by the Free Grace of God onely; they say, no man can Merit Paradise Ex Condigno. This I say, I think is the meaning of that distinction; but because Disputers do not agree upon the signification of their own termes of Art, longer than it serves their turn; I will not affirme any thing of their meaning: onely this I say; when a gift is given indefinitely, as a prize to be contended for, he that winneth Meriteth, and may claime the Prize as Due.

If a Covenant be made, wherein neither of the parties performe presently, but trust one another; in the condition of meer Nature, (which is a condition of Warre of every man against every man,) upon any reasonable suspition, it is Voyd; But if there be a common Power set over them bothe, with right and force sufficient to compell performance; it is not Voyd. For he that performeth first, has no assurance the other will performe after; because the bonds of words are too weak to bridle mens ambition, avarice, anger, and other Passions, without the feare of some coerceive Power; which in the condition of meer Nature, where all men are equall, and judges of the justnesse of their own fears cannot possibly be supposed. And therefore he which performeth first, does but betray himselfe to his enemy; contrary to the Right (he can never abandon) of defending his life, and means of living.

But in a civill estate, where there is a Power set up to constrain those that would otherwise violate their faith, that feare is no more reasonable; and for that cause, he which by the Covenant is to perform first, is obliged so to do.

The cause of Feare, which maketh such a Covenant invalid, must be alwayes something arising after the Covenant made; as some new fact, or other signe of the Will not to performe; else it cannot make the

Covenant Voyd. For that which could not hinder a man from promising, ought not to be admitted as a hindrance of performing.

He that transferreth any Right, transferreth the Means of enjoying it, as farre as lyeth in his power. As he that selleth Land, is understood to transferre the Herbage, and whatsoever growes upon it; Nor can he that sells a Mill turn away the Stream that drives it. And they that give to a man The Right of government in Soveraignty, are understood to give him the right of levying mony to maintain Souldiers; and of appointing Magistrates for the administration of Justice.

To make Covenant with bruit Beasts, is impossible; because not understanding our speech, they understand not, nor accept of any translation of Right; nor can translate any Right to another; and without mutuall acceptation, there is no Covenant.

To make Covenant with God, is impossible, but by Mediation of such as God speaketh to, either by Revelation supernaturall, or by his Lieutenants that govern under him, and in his Name; For otherwise we know not whether our Covenants be accepted, or not. And therefore they that Vow any thing contrary to any law of Nature, Vow in vain; as being a thing unjust to pay such Vow. And if it be a thing commanded by the Law of Nature, it is not the Vow, but the Law that binds them.

The matter, or subject of a Covenant, is alwayes something that falleth under deliberation; (For to Covenant, is an act of the Will; that is to say an act, and the last act, of deliberation;) and is therefore alwayes understood to be something to come; and which is judged Possible for him that Covenanteth, to performe.

And therefore, to promise that which is known to be Impossible, is no Covenant. But if that prove impossible afterwards, which before was thought possible, the Covenant is valid, and bindeth, (though not to the thing it selfe,) yet to the value; or, if that also be impossible, to the unfeigned endeavour of performing as much as is possible; for to more no man can be obliged.

Men are freed of their Covenants two wayes; by Performing; or by being Forgiven. For Performance, is the naturall end of obligation; and Forgivenesse, the restitution of liberty; as being a retransferring of that Right, in which the obligation consisted.

Covenants entred into by fear, in the condition of meer Nature, are obligatory. For example, if I Covenant to pay a ransome, or service for my life, to an enemy; I am bound by it. For it is a Contract, wherein one receiveth the benefit of life; the other is to receive mony, or service for it; and consequently, where no other Law (as in the condition, of meer Nature) forbiddeth the performance, the Covenant is valid. Therefore Prisoners of warre, if trusted with the payment of their Ransome, are obliged to pay it; And if a weaker Prince, make a disadvantageous peace with a stronger, for feare; he is bound to keep it; unlesse (as hath been sayd before) there ariseth some new, and just cause of feare, to renew the war. And even in Commonwealths, if I be forced to redeem my selfe from a Theefe by promising him mony, I am bound to pay it, till the Civill Law discharge me. For whatsoever I may lawfully do without Obligation, the same I may lawfully Covenant to do through feare: and what I lawfully Covenant, I cannot lawfully break.

A former Covenant, makes voyd a later. For a man that hath passed away his Right to one man to day, hath it not to passe to morrow to another: and therefore the later promise passeth no Right, but is null.

A Covenant not to defend my selfe from force, by force, is alwayes voyd. For (as I have shewed before) no man can transferre, or lay down his Right to save himselfe from Death, Wounds, and Imprisonment, (the avoyding whereof is the onely End of laying down any Right,) and therefore the promise of not resisting force, in no Covenant transferreth any right; nor is obliging. For though a man may Covenant thus, "Unlesse I do so, or so, kill me;" he cannot Covenant thus "Unless I do so, or so, I will not resist you, when you come to kill me." For man by nature chooseth the lesser evill, which is danger of death in resisting; rather than the greater, which is certain and present death in not resisting. And this is granted to be true by all men, in that they lead Criminals to Execution, and Prison, with armed men, notwithstanding that such Criminals have consented to the Law, by which they are condemned.

A Covenant to accuse ones Selfe, without assurance of pardon, is likewise invalide. For in the condition of Nature, where every man is Judge, there is no place for Accusation: and in the Civill State, the Accusation is followed with Punishment; which being Force, a man is not obliged not to resist. The same is also true, of the Accusation of those, by whose Condemnation a man falls into misery; as of a Father, Wife, or Benefactor. For the Testimony of such an Accuser, if it be not willingly given, is praesumed to be corrupted by Nature; and therefore not to be received: and where a mans Testimony is not to be credited, his not bound to give it. Also Accusations upon Torture, are not to be reputed as Testimonies. For Torture is to be used but as means of conjecture, and light, in the further examination, and search of truth; and what is in that case confessed, tendeth to the ease of him that is Tortured; not to the informing of the Torturers: and therefore ought not to have the credit of a sufficient Testimony: for whether he deliver himselfe by true, or false Accusation, he does it by the Right of preserving his own life.

The force of Words, being (as I have formerly noted) too weak to hold men to the performance of their Covenants; there are in mans nature, but two imaginable helps to strengthen it. And those are either a Feare of the consequence of breaking their word; or a Glory, or Pride in appearing not to need to breake it. This later is a Generosity too rarely found to be presumed on, especially in the pursuers of Wealth, Command, or sensuall Pleasure; which are the greatest part of Mankind. The Passion to be reckoned upon, is Fear; whereof there be two very generall Objects: one, the Power of Spirits Invisible; the other, the Power of those men they shall therein Offend. Of these two, though the former be the greater Power, yet the feare of the later is commonly the greater Feare. The Feare of the former is in every man, his own Religion: which hath place in the nature of man before Civill Society. The later hath not so; at least not place enough, to keep men to their promises; because in the condition of meer Nature, the inequality of Power is not discerned, but by the event of Battell. So that before the time of Civill Society, or in the interruption thereof by Warre, there is nothing can strengthen a Covenant of Peace agreed on, against the temptations of Avarice, Ambition, Lust, or other strong desire, but the feare of that Invisible Power, which they every one Worship as God; and Feare as a Revenger of their perfidy. All therefore that can be done between two men not subject to Civill Power, is to put one another to swear by the God he feareth: Which Swearing or OATH, is a Forme Of Speech, Added To A Promise; By Which He That Promiseth, Signifieth, That Unlesse He Performe, He Renounceth The Mercy Of His God, Or Calleth To Him For Vengeance On Himselfe. Such was the Heathen Forme, "Let Jupiter kill me else, as I kill this Beast." So is our Forme, "I shall do thus, and thus, so help me God." And this, with the Rites and Ceremonies, which every one useth in his own Religion, that the feare of breaking faith might be the greater.

By this it appears, that an Oath taken according to any other Forme, or Rite, then his, that sweareth, is in vain; and no Oath: And there is no Swearing by any thing which the Swearer thinks not God. For though men have sometimes used to swear by their Kings, for feare, or flattery; yet they would have it thereby understood, they attributed to them Divine honour. And that Swearing unnecessarily by God, is but prophaning of his name: and Swearing by other things, as men do in common discourse, is not Swearing, but an impious Custome, gotten by too much vehemence of talking.

It appears also, that the Oath addes nothing to the Obligation. For a Covenant, if lawfull, binds in the sight of God, without the Oath, as much as with it; if unlawfull, bindeth not at all; though it be confirmed with an Oath.

Chapter XV, Other Laws of Nature

From that law of Nature, by which we are obliged to transferre to another, such Rights, as being retained, hinder the peace of Mankind, there followeth a Third; which is this, That Men Performe Their Covenants Made: without which, Covenants are in vain, and but Empty words; and the Right of all men to all things remaining, wee are still in the condition of Warre.

And in this law of Nature, consisteth the Fountain and Originall of JUSTICE. For where no Covenant hath preceded, there hath no Right been transferred, and every man has right to every thing; and consequently, no action can be Unjust. But when a Covenant is made, then to break it is Unjust: And the definition of INJUSTICE, is no other than The Not Performance Of Covenant. And whatsoever is not Unjust, is Just.

But because Covenants of mutuall trust, where there is a feare of not performance on either part, (as hath been said in the former Chapter,) are invalid; though the Originall of Justice be the making of Covenants; yet Injustice actually there can be none, till the cause of such feare be taken away; which while men are in the naturall condition of Warre, cannot be done. Therefore before the names of Just, and Unjust can have place, there must be some coercive Power, to compell men equally to the performance of their Covenants, by the terrour of some punishment, greater than the benefit they expect by the breach of their Covenant; and to make good that Propriety, which by mutuall Contract men acquire, in recompence of the universall Right they abandon: and such power there is none before the erection of a Common-wealth. And this is also to be gathered out of the ordinary definition of Justice in the Schooles: For they say, that "Justice is the constant Will of giving to every man his own." And therefore where there is no Own, that is, no Propriety, there is no Injustice; and where there is no coerceive Power erected, that is, where there is no Common-wealth, there is no Propriety; all men having Right to all things: Therefore where there is no Common-wealth, there nothing is Unjust. So that the nature of Justice, consisteth in keeping of valid Covenants: but the Validity of Covenants begins not but with the Constitution of a Civill Power, sufficient to compell men to keep them: And then it is also that Propriety begins....

On this law, dependeth another, "That at the entrance into conditions of Peace, no man require to reserve to himselfe any Right, which he is not content should be reserved to every one of the rest." As it is necessary for all men that seek peace, to lay down certaine Rights of Nature; that is to say, not to have libertie to do all they list: so is it necessarie for mans life, to retaine some; as right to governe their owne bodies; enjoy aire, water, motion, waies to go from place to place; and all things else without which a man cannot live, or not live well. If in this case, at the making of Peace, men require for themselves, that which they would not have to be granted to others, they do contrary to the precedent law, that commandeth the acknowledgement of naturall equalitie, and therefore also against the law of Nature. The observers of this law, are those we call Modest, and the breakers Arrogant Men. The Greeks call the violation of this law pleonexia; that is, a desire of more than their share.

Also "If a man be trusted to judge between man and man," it is a precept of the Law of Nature, "that he deale Equally between them." For without that, the Controversies of men cannot be determined but by Warre. He therefore that is partiall in judgment, doth what in him lies, to deterre men from the use of Judges, and Arbitrators; and consequently, (against the fundamentall Lawe of Nature) is the cause of Warre....

And seeing every man is presumed to do all things in order to his own benefit, no man is a fit Arbitrator in his own cause: and if he were never so fit; yet Equity allowing to each party equall benefit, if one be admitted to be Judge, the other is to be admitted also; & so the controversie, that is, the cause of War, remains, against the Law of Nature.

For the same reason no man in any Cause ought to be received for Arbitrator, to whom greater profit, or honour, or pleasure apparently ariseth out of the victory of one party, than of the other: for he hath taken (though an unavoydable bribe, yet) a bribe; and no man can be obliged to trust him. And thus also the controversie, and the condition of War remaineth, contrary to the Law of Nature....

The Lawes of Nature are Immutable and Eternall, For Injustice, Ingratitude, Arrogance, Pride, Iniquity, Acception of persons, and the rest, can never be made lawfull. For it can never be that Warre shall preserve life, and Peace destroy it.

The same Lawes, because they oblige onely to a desire, and endeavour, I mean an unfeigned and constant endeavour, are easie to be observed. For in that they require nothing but endeavour; he that endeavoureth their performance, fulfilleth them; and he that fulfilleth the Law, is Just.

And the Science of them, is the true and onely Moral Philosophy. For Morall Philosophy is nothing else but the Science of what is Good, and Evill, in the conversation, and Society of mankind. Good, and Evill, are names that signifie our Appetites, and Aversions; which in different tempers, customes, and doctrines of men, are different: And divers men, differ not onely in their Judgement, on the senses of what is pleasant, and unpleasant to the tast, smell, hearing, touch, and sight; but also of what is conformable, or disagreeable to Reason, in the actions of common life. Nay, the same man, in divers times, differs from himselfe; and one time praiseth, that is, calleth Good, what another time he dispraiseth, and calleth Evil: From whence arise Disputes, Controversies, and at last War. And therefore so long as man is in the condition of meer Nature, (which is a condition of War,) as private Appetite is the measure of Good, and Evill: and consequently all men agree on this, that Peace is Good, and therefore also the way, or means of Peace, which (as I have shewed before) are Justice, Gratitude, Modesty, Equity, Mercy, & the rest of the Laws of Nature, are good; that is to say, Morall Vertues; and their contrarie Vices, Evill. Now the science of Vertue and Vice, is Morall Philosophie; and therfore the true Doctrine of the Lawes of Nature, is the true Morall Philosophie. But the Writers of Morall Philosophie, though they acknowledge the same Vertues and Vices; Yet not seeing wherein consisted their Goodnesse; nor that they come to be praised, as the meanes of peaceable, sociable, and comfortable living; place them in a mediocrity of passions: as if not the Cause, but the Degree of daring, made Fortitude; or not the Cause, but the Quantity of a gift, made Liberality.

These dictates of Reason, men use to call by the name of Lawes; but improperly: for they are but Conclusions, or Theoremes concerning what conduceth to the conservation and defence of themselves; whereas Law, properly is the word of him, that by right hath command over others. But yet if we consider the same Theoremes, as delivered in the word of God, that by right commandeth all things; then are they properly called Lawes.

Ch. XVII, Of the Causes, Generation, and Definition of a Common-wealth

The finall Cause, End, or Designe of men, (who naturally love Liberty, and Dominion over others,) in the introduction of that restraint upon themselves, (in which wee see them live in Common-wealths,) is the foresight of their own preservation, and of a more contented life thereby; that is to say, of getting themselves out from that miserable condition of Warre, which is necessarily consequent (as hath been shewn) to the naturall Passions of men, when there is no visible Power to keep them in awe, and tye them by feare of punishment to the performance of their Covenants, and observation of these Lawes of Nature set down [above]....

It is true, that certain living creatures, as Bees, and Ants, live sociably one with another, (which are therefore by Aristotle numbred amongst Politicall creatures;) and yet have no other direction, than their particular judgements and appetites; nor speech, whereby one of them can signifie to another, what he thinks expedient for the common benefit: and therefore some man may perhaps desire to know, why Man-kind cannot do the same. To which I answer,

First, that men are continually in competition for Honour and Dignity, which these creatures are not; and consequently amongst men there ariseth on that ground, Envy and Hatred, and finally Warre; but amongst these not so.

Secondly, that amongst these creatures, the Common good differeth not from the Private; and being by nature enclined to their private, they procure thereby the common benefit. But man, whose Joy consisteth in comparing himselfe with other men, can relish nothing but what is eminent.

Thirdly, that these creatures, having not (as man) the use of reason, do not see, nor think they see any fault, in the administration of their common businesse: whereas amongst men, there are very many, that thinke themselves wiser, and abler to govern the Publique, better than the rest; and these strive to reforme and innovate, one this way, another that way; and thereby bring it into Distraction and Civill warre.

Fourthly, that these creatures, though they have some use of voice, in making knowne to one another their desires, and other affections; yet they want that art of words, by which some men can represent to others, that which is Good, in the likenesse of Evill; and Evill, in the likenesse of Good; and augment, or diminish the apparent greatnesse of Good and Evill; discontenting men, and troubling their Peace at their pleasure.

Fifthly, irrationall creatures cannot distinguish betweene Injury, and Dammage; and therefore as long as they be at ease, they are not offended with their fellowes: whereas Man is then most troublesome, when he is most at ease: for then it is that he loves to shew his Wisdome, and controule the Actions of them that governe the Common-wealth.

Lastly, the agreement of these creatures is Naturall; that of men, is by Covenant only, which is Artificiall: and therefore it is no wonder if there be somewhat else required (besides Covenant) to make their Agreement constant and lasting; which is a Common Power, to keep them in awe, and to direct their actions to the Common Benefit.

The only way to erect such a Common Power, as may be able to defend them from the invasion of Forraigners, and the injuries of one another, and thereby to secure them in such sort, as that by their owne industrie, and by the fruites of the Earth, they may nourish themselves and live contentedly; is, to conferre all their power and strength upon one Man, or upon one Assembly of men, that may reduce all their Wills, by plurality of voices, unto one Will: which is as much as to say, to appoint one man, or Assembly of men, to beare their Person; and every one to owne, and acknowledge himselfe to be Author of whatsoever he that so beareth their Person, shall Act, or cause to be Acted, in those things which concerne the Common Peace and Safetie; and therein to submit their Wills, every one to his Will, and their Judgements, to his Judgment. This is more than Consent, or Concord; it is a reall Unitie of them all, in one and the same Person, made by Covenant of every man with every man, in such manner, as if every man should say to every man, "I Authorise and give up my Right of Governing my selfe, to this Man, or to this Assembly of men, on this condition, that thou give up thy Right to him, and Authorise all his Actions in like manner." This done, the Multitude so united in one Person, is called a COMMON-WEALTH, in latine CIVITAS. This is the Generation of that great LEVIATHAN, or rather (to speake more reverently) of that Mortall God, to which wee owe under the Immortall God, our peace and defence. For by this Authoritie, given him by every particular man in the Common-Wealth, he hath the use of so much Power and Strength conferred on him, that by terror thereof, he is inabled to forme the wills of them all, to Peace at home, and mutuall ayd against their enemies abroad.

And in him consisteth the Essence of the Commonwealth; which (to define it,) is "One Person, of whose Acts a great Multitude, by mutuall Covenants one with another, have made themselves every one the Author, to the end he may use the strength and means of them all, as he shall think expedient, for their Peace and Common Defence."

And he that carryeth this Person, as called SOVERAIGNE, and said to have Soveraigne Power; and every one besides, his SUBJECT.

The attaining to this Soveraigne Power, is by two wayes. One, by Naturall force; as when a man maketh his children, to submit themselves, and their children to his government, as being able to destroy them if they refuse, or by Warre subdueth his enemies to his will, giving them their lives on that condition. The other, is when men agree amongst themselves, to submit to some Man, or Assembly of men, voluntarily, on confidence to be protected by him against all others. This later, may be called a Politicall Common-wealth, or Common-wealth by Institution; and the former, a Common-wealth by Acquisition. And first, I shall speak of a Common-wealth by Institution.

Chapter XXVI, Of Civill Lawes

By CIVILL LAWES, I understand the Lawes, that men are therefore bound to observe, because they are Members, not of this, or that Common-wealth in particular, but of a Common-wealth. For the knowledge of particular Lawes belongeth to them, that professe the study of the Lawes of their severall Countries; but the knowledge of Civill Law in generall, to any man. The antient Law of Rome was called their Civil Law, from the word Civitas, which signifies a Common-wealth; And those Countries, which having been under the Roman Empire, and governed by that Law, retaine still such part thereof as they think fit, call that part the Civill Law, to distinguish it from the rest of their own Civill Lawes. But that is not it I intend to speak of here; my designe being not to shew what is Law here, and there; but what is Law; as Plato, Aristotle, Cicero, and divers others have done, without taking upon them the profession of the study of the Law.

And first it is manifest, that Law in generall, is not Counsell, but Command; nor a Command of any man to any man; but only of him, whose Command is addressed to one formerly obliged to obey him. And as for Civill Law, it addeth only the name of the person Commanding, which is Persona Civitatis, the Person of the Common-wealth.

Which considered, I define Civill Law in this Manner. "CIVILL LAW, Is to every Subject, those Rules, which the Common-wealth hath Commanded him, by Word, Writing, or other sufficient Sign of the Will, to make use of, for the Distinction of Right, and Wrong; that is to say, of what is contrary, and what is not contrary to the Rule." ...

4.7 Charles-Louis de Secondat, Baron de La Brède et de Montesquieu (1689–1755)

Montesquieu (the name by which this author is usually known) presents a comprehensive theoretical account of human laws, along with an institutional account of the creation, preservation, and application of human law. To this end he differentiates among positive law, divine law, and physical law. Theoretically, positive laws are analogous to divine laws and physical laws, except that positive laws are subject to errors of formulation and implementation. Due to human ignorance, error is inevitable, but errors in positive law may be corrected and avoided with a sound understanding of the framework Montesquieu aims to provide.

Institutionally, Book II, Chapter 1 of *The Spirit of the Laws* distinguishes three forms of government: republics, monarchies, and despotisms. Each of these has its own distinctive relationship to positive law, and any particular state is functional or dysfunctional to the extent that its legal system is appropriately suited to its specific form of government. Strictly speaking, this framework is called Legalism. Both republicanism and monarchy—insofar as each operates according to its own distinctive virtue—are capable of functioning well; at the same time, each is susceptible of its own distinctive type of corruption. Good laws in a republic must promote virtue, and in a monarchy they promote honour; bad laws corrupt by undermining these specific aims. Despotism, however, is inherently corrupt and is sustained only by accidental, contingent conditions (of climate or religion, for example).

~

from The Spirit of the Laws

Book I. Of Laws in General

CHAP. I. OF THE RELATION OF LAWS TO DIFFERENT BEINGS

Laws, in their most general signification, are the necessary relations arising from the nature of things. In this sense, all beings have their laws; the Deity his laws, the material world its laws, the intelligence superior to man their laws, the beasts their laws, man his laws.

They who assert, that a blind fatality produced the various effects we behold in this world, talk very absurdly; for can any thing be more unreasonable than to pretend that a blind fatality could be productive of intelligent beings?

There is then a primitive reason; and laws are the relations subsisting between it and different beings, and the relations of these to one another.

God is related to the universe as creator and preserver: the laws by which he created all things are those by which he preserves them. He acts according to these rules, because he knows them; he knows them, because he made them; and he made them, because they are relative to his wisdom and power.

Since we observe that the world, though formed by the motion of matter, and void of understanding, subsists through so long a succession of ages, its motions must certainly be directed by invariable laws: and, could we imagine another world, it must also have constant rules, or it would inevitably perish.

Thus the creation, which seems an arbitrary act, supposeth laws as invariable as those of the fatality of the atheists. It would be absurd to say, that the Creator might govern the world without those rules, since without them it could not subsist.

These rules are a fixed and invariable relation. In bodies moved, the motion is received, increased, diminished, lost, according to the relations of the quantity of matter and velocity: each diversity is uniformity; each change is constancy.

Particular intelligent beings may have laws of their own making; but they have some likewise which they never made. Before there were intelligent beings, they were possible; they had therefore possible relations, and consequently possible laws. Before laws were made, there were relations of possible justice. To say that there is nothing just or unjust, but what is commanded or forbidden by positive laws, is the same as saying that, before the describing of a circle, all the radii were not equal.

We must therefore acknowledge relations of justice antecedent to the positive law by which they are established: as for instance, that, if human societies existed, it would be right to conform to their laws; if there were intelligent beings that had received a benefit of another being, they ought to shew their gratitude; if one intelligent being had created another intelligent being, the latter ought to continue in its original state of dependence; if one intelligent being injures another, it deserves a retaliation; and so on.

But the intelligent world is far from being so well governed as the physical: for, though the former has also its laws, which of their own nature are invariable, it does not conform to them so exactly as the physical world. This is because, on the one hand, particular intelligent beings are of a finite nature, and consequently liable to error; and, on the other, their nature requires them to be free agents. Hence they do not steadily conform to their primitive laws; and even those of their own instituting they frequently infringe.

Whether brutes be governed by the general laws of motion, or by a particular movement, we cannot determine. Be that as it may, they have not a more intimate relation to God than the rest of the material world; and sensation is of no other use to them, than in the relation they have either to other particular beings, or to themselves.

By the allurement of pleasure they preserve the individual, and by the same allurement they preserve their species. They have natural laws, because they are united by sensation; positive laws they have none, because they are not connected by knowledge: and yet they do not invariably conform to their natural laws: these are better observed by vegetables, that have neither understanding nor sense.

Brutes are deprived of the high advantages which we have; but they have some which we have not. They have not our hopes; but they are without our fears: they are subject, like us, to death, but without knowing it: even most of them are more attentive than we to self-preservation, and do not make so bad a use of their passions.

Man, as a physical being, is, like other bodies, governed by invariable laws. As an intelligent being, he incessantly transgresses the laws established by God, and changes those of his own instituting. He is left to his private direction, though a limited being, and subject, like all finite intelligences, to ignorance and error: even his imperfect knowledge he loseth; and, as a sensible creature, he is hurried away by a thousand impetuous passions. Such a being might every instant forget his Creator; God has therefore reminded him of his duty by the laws of religion. Such a being is liable every moment to forget himself; philosophy has provided against this by the laws of morality. Formed to live in society, he might forget his fellow-creatures; legislators have, therefore, by political and civil laws, confined him to his duty.

CHAP. II. OF THE LAWS OF NATURE

Antecedent to the above-mentioned laws are those of nature; so called because they derive their force entirely from our frame and existence. In order to have a perfect knowledge of these laws, we must consider man before the establishment of society; the laws received in such a state would be those of nature.

The law, which, impressing on our minds the idea of a Creator, inclines us toward him, is the first in importance, though not in order, of natural laws. Man, in a state of nature, would have the faculty of knowing before he had acquired any knowledge. Plain it is that his first ideas would not be of a speculative nature: he would think of the preservation of his being before he would investigate its original. Such a man would feel nothing in himself, at first, but impotency and weakness: his fears and apprehensions would be excessive; as appears from instances (were there any necessity of proving it) of savages found in forests trembling at the motion of a leaf, and flying from every shadow.

In this state, every man, instead of being sensible of his equality, would fancy himself inferior: there would, therefore, be no danger of their attacking one another; peace would be the first law of nature.

The natural impulse, or desire, which Hobbes attributes to mankind, of subduing one another, is far from being well founded. The idea of empire and dominion is so complex, and depends on so many other notions, that it could never be the first which occurred to the human understanding.

Hobbes enquires, "For what reason men go armed, and have locks and keys to fasten their doors, if they be not naturally in a state of war?" But is it not obvious, that he attributes to mankind, before the establishment of society, what can happen but in consequence of this establishment, which furnishes them with motives for hostile attacks and self-defence?

Next to a sense of his weakness, man would soon find that of his wants. Hence, another law of nature would prompt him to seek for nourishment.

Fear, I have observed, would induce men to shun one another; but the marks of this fear, being reciprocal, would soon engage them to associate. Besides, this association would quickly follow from the very pleasure one animal feels at the approach of another of the same species. Again, the attraction arising from the difference of sexes would enhance this pleasure, and the natural inclination they have for each other would form a third law.

Besides the sense or instinct which man possesses in common with brutes, he has the advantage of acquired knowledge; and thence arises a second tie, which brutes have not. Mankind have therefore a new motive of uniting, and a fourth law of nature results from the desire of living in society.

CHAP. III. OF POSITIVE LAWS

As soon as mankind enter into a state of society, they lose the sense of their weakness; equality ceases, and then commences the state of war.

Each particular society begins to feel its strength; whence arises a state of war betwixt different nations. The individuals likewise of each society become sensible of their force: hence the principal advantages of this society they endeavour to convert to their own emolument; which constitutes a state of war betwixt individuals.

These two different kinds of states give rise to human laws. Considered as inhabitants of so great a planet, which necessarily contains a variety of nations, they have laws relative to their mutual intercourse, which is what we call the law of nations. As members of a society that must be properly supported, they have laws relative to the governors and the governed; and this we distinguish by the name of politic law. They have also another sort of laws, as they stand in relation to each other; by which is understood the civil law.

The law of nations is naturally founded on this principle, that different nations ought in time of peace to do one another all the good they can, and in time of war as little injury as possible, without prejudicing their real interests.

The object of war is victory; that of victory is conquest; and that of conquest, preservation. From this and the preceding principle all those rules are derived which constitute the law of nations....

Besides the law of nations relating to all societies, there is a polity, or civil constitution, for each, particularly considered. No society can subsist without a form of government. "The united strength of individuals," as Gravina well observes, "constitutes what we call the body politic."

The general strength may be in the hands of a single person, or of many. Some think that, nature having established paternal authority, the most natural government was that of a single person. But the example of paternal authority proves nothing: for, if the power of a father be relative to a single government, that of brothers after the death of a father, and that of cousin-germans after the decease of brothers, refer to a government of many. The political power necessarily comprehends the union of several families.

Better is it to say, that the government most conformable to nature is that which best agrees with the humour and disposition of the people in whose favour it is established.

The strength of individuals cannot be united without a conjunction of all their wills. "The conjunction of those wills," as Gravina again very justly observes, "is what we call the civil state."

Law in general is human reason, inasmuch as it governs all the inhabitants of the earth; the political and civil laws of each nation ought to be only the particular cases in which human reason is applied.

They should be adapted in such a manner to the people for whom they are framed, that it is a great chance if those of one nation suit another.

They should be relative to the nature and principle of each government; whether they form it, as may be said of political laws; or whether they support it, as in the case of civil institutions.

They should be relative to the climate of each country, to the quality of its soil, to its situation and extent, to the principal occupation of the natives, whether husbandmen, huntsmen, or shepherds: they should have a relation to the degree of liberty which the constitution will bear, to the religion of the inhabitants, to their inclinations, riches, numbers, commerce, manners, and customs. In fine, they have relations to each other, as also to their origin, to the intent of the legislator, and to the order of things on which they are established; in all which different lights they ought to be considered.

This is what I have undertaken to perform in the following work. These relations I shall examine, since all these together constitute what I call the Spirit of Laws.

I have not separated the political from the civil institutions; for, as I do not pretend to treat of laws, but of their spirit, and as this spirit consists in the various relations which the laws may have to different objects, it is not so much my business to follow the natural order of laws, as that of these relations and objects....

Book II. Of Laws Directly Derived from the Nature of Government

CHAP. I. OF THE NATURE OF THREE DIFFERENT GOVERNMENTS

There are three species of government; republican, monarchical, and despotic. In order to discover their nature, it is sufficient to recollect the common notion, which supposes three definitions, or rather three facts: "That a republican government is that in which the body or only a part of the people is possessed of the supreme power: monarchy, that in which a single person governs by fixed and established laws: a despotic government, that in which a single person directs every thing by his own will and caprice."

This is what I call the nature of each government: we must now inquire into those laws which directly conform to this nature, and consequently are the fundamental institutions.

CHAP. II. OF THE REPUBLICAN GOVERNMENT, AND THE LAWS RELATIVE TO DEMOCRACY

When the body of the people is possessed of the supreme power, this is called a democracy. When the supreme power is lodged in the hands of a part of the people, it is then an aristocracy.

In a democracy the people are in some respects the sovereign, and in others the subject.

There can be no exercise of sovereignty but by their suffrages, which are their own will: now, the sovereign's will is the sovereign himself. The laws, therefore, which establish the right of suffrage, are fundamental to this government. And indeed it is as important to regulate, in a republic, in what manner, by whom, to whom, and concerning what, suffrages are to be given, as it is, in a monarchy, to know who is the prince, and after what manner he ought to govern.

Libanius says, that at "Athens a stranger who intermeddled in the assemblies of the people was punished with death." This is because such a man usurped the rights of sovereignty....

The people, in whom the supreme power resides, ought to have the management of every thing within their reach: what exceeds their abilities must be conducted by their ministers....

The people are extremely well qualified for choosing those whom they are to intrust with part of their authority. They have only to be determined by things to which they cannot be strangers, and by facts that are obvious to sense. They can tell when a person has fought many battles, and been crowned with success; they are therefore very capable of electing a general. They can tell when a judge is assiduous in his office, gives general satisfaction, and has never been charged with bribery: this is sufficient for choosing a prætor. They are struck with the magnificence or riches of a fellow-citizen: no more is requisite for electing an ædile. These are facts of which they can have better information in a public forum than a monarch in his palace. But are they capable of conducting an intricate affair, of seizing and improving the opportunity and critical moment of action? No; this surpasses their abilities....

As most citizens have sufficient abilities to choose, though unqualified to be chosen, so the people, though capable of calling others to an account for their administration, are incapable of conducting the administration themselves.

The public business must be carried on, with a certain motion, neither too quick nor too slow. But the motion of the people is always either too remiss or too violent. Sometimes, with a hundred thousand arms, they overturn all before them; and sometimes, with a hundred thousand feet, they creep like insects....

The suffrage by lot is natural to democracy, as that by choice is to aristocracy.

The suffrage by lot is a method of electing that offends no one; but animates each citizen with the pleasing hope of serving his country.

Yet, as this method is in itself defective, it has been the endeavour of the most eminent legislators to regulate and amend it....

It is likewise a fundamental law, in democracies, that the people should have the sole power to enact laws. And yet there are a thousand occasions on which it is necessary the senate should have a power of decreeing: nay, it is frequently proper to make some trial of a law before it is established. The constitutions of Rome and Athens were excellent. The decrees of the senate had the force of laws for the space of a year, but did not become perpetual till they were ratified by the consent of the people.

CHAP. IV. OF THE RELATION OF LAWS TO THE NATURE OF MONARCHICAL GOVERNMENT

The intermediate, subordinate, and dependent powers constitute the nature of monarchical government; I mean of that in which a single person governs by fundamental laws. I said, the intermediate, subordinate, and dependent powers: and indeed, in monarchies, the prince is the source of all power, political and civil. These fundamental laws necessarily suppose the intermediate channels through which the power flows; for, if there be only the momentary and capricious will of a single person to govern the state, nothing can be fixed, and of course there is no fundamental law.

The most natural intermediate and subordinate power is that of the nobility. This, in some measure, seems to be essential to a monarchy, whose fundamental maxim is, No monarch, no nobility; no nobility, no monarch: but there may be a despotic prince....

Far am I from being prejudiced in favour of the privileges of the clergy; however, I should be glad their jurisdiction were once fixed. The question is not, whether their jurisdiction was justly established; but, whether it be really established; whether it constitutes a part of the laws of the country, and is in every respect relative to those laws; whether, between two powers acknowledged independent, the conditions ought not to be reciprocal; and whether it be not equally the duty of a good subject to defend the prerogative of the prince, and to maintain the limits which from time immemorial he has prescribed to his authority.

Though the ecclesiastic power be so dangerous in a republic, yet it is extremely proper in a monarchy, especially of the absolute kind. What would become of Spain and Portugal, since the subversion of their laws, were it not for this only barrier against the incursions of arbitrary power? a barrier ever useful when there is no other: for, since a despotic government is productive of the most dreadful calamities to human nature, the very evil that restrains it is beneficial to the subject.

In the same manner as the ocean, threatening to overflow the whole earth, is stopped by weeds and pebbles, that lie scattered along the shore; so monarchs, whose power seems unbounded, are restrained by the smallest obstacles, and suffer their natural pride to be subdued by supplication and prayer.

The English, to favour their liberty, have abolished all the intermediate powers of which their monarchy was composed. They have a great deal of reason to be jealous of this liberty: were they ever to be so unhappy as to lose it, they would be one of the most servile nations upon earth....

It is not enough to have intermediate powers in a monarchy; there must be also a depositary of the laws. This depositary can only be the judges of the supreme courts of justice, who promulgatee the new laws, and revive the obsolete. The natural ignorance of the nobility, their indolence, and contempt of civil government, require there should be a body invested with a power of reviving and executing the laws, which would be otherwise buried in oblivion. The prince's council are not a proper depositary: they are naturally the depositary of the momentary will of the prince, and not of the fundamental laws. Besides, the prince's council is continually changing; it is neither permanent nor numerous; neither has it a sufficient share of the confidence of the people; consequently it is incapable to set them right in difficult conjunctures, or to reduce them to proper obedience.

Despotic governments, where there are no fundamental laws, have no such kind of depositary. Hence it is that religion has generally so much influence in those countries, because it forms a kind of permanent depositary; and, if this cannot be said of religion, it may of the customs that are respected instead of laws.

CHAP. V. OF THE LAWS RELATIVE TO THE NATURE OF A DESPOTIC GOVERNMENT

From the nature of despotic power it follows, that the single person, invested with this power, commits the execution of it also to a single person. A man, whom his senses continually inform that he himself is every thing, and his subjects nothing, is naturally lazy, voluptuous, and ignorant. In consequence of this, he neglects the management of public affairs. But, were he to commit the administration to many, there would be continual disputes among them; each would form intrigues to be his first slave, and he would be obliged to take the reins into his own hands. It is, therefore, more natural for him to resign it to a vizir, and to invest him with the same power as himself. The creation of a vizir is a fundamental law of this government....

The more extensive the empire, the larger the seraglio; and consequently the more voluptuous the prince. Hence the more nations such a sovereign has to rule, the less he attends to the cares of government; the more important his affairs, the less he makes them the subject of his deliberations....

Book V. That the Laws, Given by the Legislator, Ought to Be Relative to the Principle of Government

CHAP. XIII. AN IDEA OF DESPOTIC POWER

When the savages of Louisiana are desirous of fruit, they cut the tree to the root, and gather the fruit. This is an emblem of despotic government.

CHAP. XIV. IN WHAT MANNER THE LAWS ARE RELATIVE TO THE PRINCIPLES OF DESPOTIC GOVERNMENT

The principle of despotic government is fear: but a timid, ignorant, and faint-spirited people have no occasion for a great number of laws.

Every thing ought to depend here on two or three ideas: hence there is no necessity that any new notions should be added. When we want to break a horse, we take care not to let him change his master, his lesson, or his pace. Thus an impression is made on his brain by two or three motions, and no more....

Such a state is happiest when it can look upon itself as the only one in the world, when it is environed with deserts, and separated from those people whom they call barbarians. Since it cannot depend on the militia, it is proper it should destroy a part of itself.

As fear is the principle of despotic government, its end is tranquillity: but this tranquillity cannot be called a peace; no, it is only the silence of those towns which the enemy is ready to invade.

Since the strength does not lie in the state, but in the army that founded it; in order to defend the state, the army must be preserved, how formidable soever to the prince. How, then, can we reconcile the security of the government to that of the prince's person? ...

Book VI. Consequences of the Principles of Different Governments with Respect to the Simplicity of Civil and Criminal Laws, the Form of Judgements, and the Inflicting of Punishments

CHAP. I. OF THE SIMPLICITY OF CIVIL LAWS IN DIFFERENT GOVERNMENTS

Monarchies do not permit of so great a simplicity of laws as despotic governments: for, in monarchies, there must be courts of judicature: these must give their decisions: the decisions must be preserved and learnt, that we may judge in the same manner to-day as yesterday, and that the lives and property of the citizens may be as certain and fixt as the very constitution of the state.

In monarchies, the administration of justice, which decides not only in whatever belongs to life and property, but likewise to honour, demands very scrupulous enquiries. The delicacy of the judge increases in proportion to the increase of his trust, and of the importance of the interests on which he determines.

We must not therefore be surprised to find so many rules, restrictions, and extensions, in the laws of those countries; rules that multiply the particular cases, and seem to make of reason itself an art.

The difference of rank, birth, and condition, established in monarchical governments, is frequently attended with distinctions in the nature of property; and the laws relative to the constitution of this government may augment the number of these distinctions. Hence, among us, goods are divided into real estates, purchases, dowries, paraphernalia, paternal and maternal inheritances; moveables of different kinds; estates held in fee-simple or in tail; acquired by descent or conveyance; allodial, or held by soccage; ground-rents, or annuities. Each sort of goods is subject to particular rules, which must be complied with in the disposal of them. These things must needs diminish the simplicity of the laws....

The monarch, who knows each of his provinces, may establish different laws, or tolerate different customs. But, as the despotic prince knows nothing, and can attend to nothing, he must take general measures, and govern by a rigid and inflexible will, which, throughout his whole dominions, produces the same effect: in short, every thing bends under his feet.

In proportion as the decisions of the courts of judicature are multiplied in monarchies, the law is loaded with decrees that sometimes contradict one another; either because succeeding judges are of a different way of thinking, or because the same causes are sometimes well, and at other times ill, defended; or, in fine, by reason of an infinite number of abuses, to which all human regulations are liable. This is a necessary evil, which the legislator redresses from time to time, as contrary even to the spirit of moderate governments: for, when people are obliged to have recourse to courts of judicature, this should come from the nature of the constitution, and not from the contradiction or uncertainty of the law....

One of the privileges least burthensome to society, and especially to him who confers it, is that of pleading in one court preferably to another. Here new difficulties arise, when it becomes a question before which court we shall plead.

Far different is the case of the people under despotic governments. In those countries I can see nothing that the legislator is able to decree, or the magistrate to judge. As the lands belong to the prince, it follows that there are scarce any civil laws in regard to landed property. From the right the sovereign has to successions it follows likewise that there are none relating to inheritances. The monopolies, established by the prince for himself in some countries, render all sorts of commercial laws quite useless....

I forgot to observe, that, as what we call honour is a thing hardly known in those countries, the several difficulties relating to this article, though of such importance with us, are with them quite out of the question. Despotic power is self-sufficient: round it there is an absolute vacuum. Hence it is, that, when travellers favour us with the description of countries where arbitrary sway prevails, they seldom make mention of civil laws.

All occasions, therefore, of wrangling and lawsuits are here removed. And to this, in part, it is owing that litigious people, in those countries, are so roughly handled: as the injustice of their demand is neither screened, palliated, nor protected, by an infinite number of laws, of course it is immediately discovered.

...

CHAP. IX. OF THE SEVERITY OF PUNISHMENTS IN DIFFERENT GOVERNMENTS

The severity of punishments is fitter for despotic governments, whose principle is terror, than for a monarchy or a republic, whose spring is honour and virtue.

In moderate governments, the love of one's country, shame, and the fear of blame, are restraining motives, capable of preventing a multitude of crimes. Here the greatest punishment of a bad action is conviction. The civil laws have, therefore, a softer way of correcting, and do not require so much force and severity.

In those states, a good legislator is less bent upon punishing, than preventing, crimes; he is more attentive to inspire good morals than to inflict penalties.

It is a constant remark of the Chinese authors, that, the more the penal laws were increased in their empire, the nearer they drew towards a revolution. This is because punishments were augmented in proportion as the public morals were corrupted.

It would be an easy matter to prove, that, in all, or almost all, the governments of Europe, penalties have increased or diminished in proportion as those governments favoured or discouraged liberty.

In despotic governments, people are so unhappy as to have a greater dread of death than regret for the loss of life; consequently, their punishments ought to be more severe. In moderate states, they are more afraid of losing their lives than apprehensive of the pain of dying; those punishments, therefore, which deprive them simply of life, are sufficient.

Men, in excess of happiness or misery, are equally inclinable to severity; witness conquerors and monks. It is mediocrity alone, and a mixture of prosperous and adverse fortune, that inspire us with lenity and pity.

What we see practised by individuals is equally observable in regard to nations. In countries inhabited by savages, who lead a very hard life, and in despotic governments, where there is only one person on whom fortune lavishes her favours, while the miserable subjects lie exposed to her insults, people are equally cruel. Lenity reigns in moderate governments.

When, in reading history, we observe the cruelty of the sultans in the administration of justice, we shudder at the very thought of the miseries of human nature.

In moderate governments, a good legislator may make use of every thing by way of punishment. Is it not very extraordinary, that one of the chief penalties, at Sparta, was to deprive a person of the power of lending out his wife, or of receiving the wife of another man, and to oblige him to have no company at home but virgins? In short, whatever the law calls a punishment, is such effectively.

4.8 Immanuel Kant (1724–1804)

The theory Kant sets out represents a general approach to morality labelled *deontology*, which literally translates from its Greek origins as "necessary rules." According to Kant, morality is a system of duties that derive from a single moral principle, that is, a single necessary rule. Because this rule identifies what is necessary for a person to do to conform to morality it operates as an imperative. And because it identifies what to do irrespective of that person's personal preferences, interests, desires, or circumstances, it applies categorically, that is, unconditionally. For these reasons, he calls this the Categorical Imperative. The Categorical Imperative is to be distinguished first from Hypothetical Imperatives that specify what to do to satisfy specifiable conditions: *if* you want to run a complete marathon, you must train daily; *if* you want to become a physician, you must study medicine; *if* you desire to see the Taj Mahal at sunrise, you must go to India, and so on. The imperatives specified here by "you must ..." are compelling on the hypothesis or condition that precedes it. By contrast, the rules of morality apply unconditionally, or in Kant's terms categorically. The Categorical Imperative functions as a test to assess whether a proposed course of action conforms to our duties; a proposed course of action that fails the test violates a moral duty.

According to Kant, the only thing that is good without qualification is a good will. In the following passage he explains the conditions that must be satisfied for a good will. The Categorical Imperative is central to this account. Two versions of the Categorical Imperative are formulated here and applied in four representative instances. The first formulation he considers to be a purely formal principle, and it consists of a four-step testing procedure: (1) identify a prospective course of action (let's use X as a variable here); (2) use that action to formulate a maxim (i.e., a rule, "I ought to do X"); (3) restate the maxim as a universal rule that everyone ought to obey (i.e., "everyone ought to do X"); and (4) consider whether you could will that the universal rule be imposed as a law. The second formulation, which he calls the practical imperative, is supposed to select exactly the same duties as the first formulation, except that the moral agent focuses on the moral value of the patient of the action: does the proposed course of action honour the intrinsic worth of anyone's humanity? If not, then it violates a moral duty; if it does, then it is permissible.

The four examples included in this passage represent four types of duty: respectively, (1) a perfect duty to oneself, (2) a perfect duty to others, (3) an imperfect (meritorious) duty to oneself, and (4) an imperfect (meritorious) duty to others. Perfect duties admit of no further deliberation, whereas imperfect duties grant that an agent can decide when to apply it even if it is not possible to be released from it entirely. So, for example, Kant maintains that a person has an imperfect duty to charity: an agent who is *never* charitable thereby violates the duty, but no single opportunity for charity is perfectly compelling.

~

from Fundamental Principles of the Metaphysics of Morals

Section One

... The second proposition [of morality] is: That an action done from duty derives its moral worth, not from the purpose which is to be attained by it, but from the maxim by which it is determined, and therefore does not depend on the realization of the object of the action, but merely on the principle of volition by which the action has taken place, without regard to any object of desire. It is clear from what precedes that the purposes which we may have in view in our actions, or their effects regarded as ends and springs of the will, cannot give to actions any unconditional or moral worth. In what, then, can their worth lie, if it is not to consist in the will and in reference to its expected effect? It cannot lie anywhere but in the principle of the will without regard to the ends which can be attained by the action. For the will stands between its a priori principle, which is formal, and its a posteriori spring, which is material, as between two roads, and as it must be determined by something, it follows that it must be determined by the formal principle of volition when an action is done from duty, in which case every material principle has been withdrawn from it.

The third proposition, which is a consequence of the two preceding, I would express thus: Duty is the necessity of acting from respect for the law. I may have inclination for an object as the effect of my proposed action, but I cannot have respect for it, just for this reason, that it is an effect and not an energy of will. Similarly I cannot have respect for inclination, whether my own or another's; I can at most, if my own, approve it; if another's, sometimes even love it; i.e., look on it as favourable to my own interest. It is only what is connected with my will as a principle, by no means as an effect—what does not subserve my inclination, but overpowers it, or at least in case of choice excludes it from its calculation—in other words, simply the law of itself, which can be an object of respect, and hence a command. Now an action done from duty must wholly exclude the influence of inclination and with it every object of the will, so that nothing remains which can determine the will except objectively the law, and subjectively pure respect for this practical law, and consequently the maxim that I should follow this law even to the thwarting of all my inclinations.

Thus the moral worth of an action does not lie in the effect expected from it, nor in any principle of action which requires to borrow its motive from this expected effect. For all these effects—agreeableness of one's condition and even the promotion of the happiness of others—could have been also brought about by other causes, so that for this there would have been no need of the will of a rational being; whereas it is in this alone that the supreme and unconditional good can be found. The pre-eminent good which we call moral can therefore consist in nothing else than the conception of law in itself, which certainly is only possible in a rational being, in so far as this conception, and not the expected effect, determines the will. This is a good which is already present in the person who acts accordingly, and we have not to wait for it to appear first in the result.

But what sort of law can that be, the conception of which must determine the will, even without paying any regard to the effect expected from it, in order that this will may be called good absolutely and without qualification? As I have deprived the will of every impulse which could arise to it from obedience to any law, there remains nothing but the universal conformity of its actions to law in general, which alone is to serve the will as a principle, i.e., I am never to act otherwise than so that I could also will that my maxim should become a universal law. Here, now, it is the simple conformity to law in general, without assuming any particular law applicable to certain actions, that serves the will as its principle and must so serve it, if duty is not to be a vain delusion and a chimerical notion. The common reason of men in its practical judgements perfectly coincides with this and always has in view the principle here suggested. Let the question be, for example: May I when in distress make a promise with the intention not to keep it? I readily distinguish here between the two significations which the question may have: Whether it is prudent, or whether it is right, to make a false promise? The former may undoubtedly often be the case. I see clearly indeed that it is not enough to extricate myself from a present difficulty by means of this subterfuge, but it must be well considered whether there may not hereafter spring from this lie much greater inconvenience than that from which I now free myself, and as, with all my supposed cunning, the consequences cannot be so easily foreseen but that credit once lost may be much more injurious to me than any mischief which I seek to avoid at present, it should be considered whether it would not be more prudent to act herein according to a universal maxim and to make it a habit to promise nothing except with the intention of keeping it. But it is soon clear to me that such a maxim will still only be based on the fear of consequences. Now it is a wholly different thing to be truthful from duty and to be so from apprehension of injurious consequences. In the first case, the very notion of the action already implies a law for me; in the second case, I must first look about elsewhere to see what results may be combined with it which would affect myself. For to deviate from the principle of duty is beyond all doubt wicked; but to be unfaithful to my maxim of prudence may often be very advantageous to me, although to abide by it is certainly safer. The shortest way, however, and an unerring one, to discover the answer to this question whether a lying promise is consistent with duty, is to ask myself, "Should I be content that my maxim (to extricate myself from difficulty by a false promise) should hold good as a universal law, for myself as well as for others?" and should I be able to say to myself, "Every one may make a deceitful promise when he finds himself in a difficulty from which he cannot otherwise extricate himself?" Then I presently become aware that while I can will the lie, I can by no means will that lying should be a universal law. For with such a law there would be no promises at all, since it would be in vain to allege my intention in regard to my future actions to those who would not believe this allegation, or if they over hastily did so would pay me back in my own coin. Hence my maxim, as soon as it should be made a universal law, would necessarily destroy itself.

I do not, therefore, need any far-reaching penetration to discern what I have to do in order that my will may be morally good. Inexperienced in the course of the world, incapable of being prepared for all its contingencies, I only ask myself: Canst thou also will that thy maxim should be a universal law? If not, then it must be rejected, and that not because of a disadvantage accruing from it to myself or even to others, but because it cannot enter as a principle into a possible universal legislation, and reason extorts from me immediate respect for such legislation. I do not indeed as yet discern on what this respect is based (this the philosopher may inquire), but at least I understand this, that it is an estimation of the worth which far outweighs all worth of what is recommended by inclination, and that the necessity of acting from pure respect for the practical law is what constitutes duty, to which every other motive must give place, because it is the condition of a will being good in itself, and the worth of such a will is above everything....

Second Section

...

Everything in nature works according to laws. Rational beings alone have the faculty of acting according to the conception of laws, that is according to principles, i.e., have a will. Since the deduction of actions from principles requires reason, the will is nothing but practical reason. If reason infallibly determines the will, then the actions of such a being which are recognised as objectively necessary are subjectively necessary also, i.e., the will is a faculty to choose that only which reason independent of inclination recognises as practically necessary, i.e., as good. But if reason of itself does not sufficiently determine the will, if the latter is subject also to subjective conditions (particular impulses) which do not always coincide with the objective conditions; in a word, if the will does not in itself completely accord with reason (which is actually the case with men), then the actions which objectively are recognised as necessary are subjectively contingent, and the determination of such a will according to objective laws is obligation, that is to say, the relation of the objective laws to a will that is not thoroughly good is conceived as the determination of the will of a rational being by principles of reason, but which the will from its nature does not of necessity follow.

The conception of an objective principle, in so far as it is obligatory for a will, is called a command (of reason), and the formula of the command is called an imperative.

All imperatives are expressed by the word ought [or shall], and thereby indicate the relation of an objective law of reason to a will, which from its subjective constitution is not necessarily determined by it (an obligation). They say that something would be good to do or to forbear, but they say it to a will which does not always do a thing because it is conceived to be good to do it. That is practically good, however, which determines the will by means of the conceptions of reason, and consequently not from subjective causes, but objectively, that is on principles which are valid for every rational being as such. It is distinguished from the pleasant, as that which influences the will only by means of sensation from merely subjective causes, valid only for the sense of this or that one, and not as a principle of reason, which holds for everyone.

A perfectly good will would therefore be equally subject to objective laws (viz., laws of good), but could not be conceived as obliged thereby to act lawfully, because of itself from its subjective constitution it can only be determined by the conception of good. Therefore no imperatives hold for the Divine will, or in general for a holy will; ought is here out of place, because the volition is already of itself necessarily in unison with the law. Therefore imperatives are only formulae to express the relation of objective laws of all volition to the subjective imperfection of the will of this or that rational being, e.g., the human will.

Now all imperatives command either hypothetically or categorically. The former represent the practical necessity of a possible action as means to something else that is willed (or at least which one might possibly will). The categorical imperative would be that which represented an action as necessary of itself without reference to another end, i.e., as objectively necessary.

Since every practical law represents a possible action as good and, on this account, for a subject who is practically determinable by reason, necessary, all imperatives are formulae determining an action which is necessary according to the principle of a will good in some respects. If now the action is good only as a means to something else, then the imperative is hypothetical; if it is conceived as good in itself and consequently as being necessarily the principle of a will which of itself conforms to reason, then it is categorical.

Thus the imperative declares what action possible by me would be good and presents the practical rule in relation to a will which does not forthwith perform an action simply because it is good, whether because the subject does not always know that it is good, or because, even if it know this, yet its maxims might be opposed to the objective principles of practical reason.

Accordingly the hypothetical imperative only says that the action is good for some purpose, possible or actual. In the first case it is a problematical, in the second an assertorial practical principle. The categorical imperative which declares an action to be objectively necessary in itself without reference to any purpose, i.e., without any other end, is valid as an apodeictic (practical) principle.

Whatever is possible only by the power of some rational being may also be conceived as a possible purpose of some will; and therefore the principles of action as regards the means necessary to attain some possible purpose are in fact infinitely numerous. All sciences have a practical part, consisting of problems expressing that some end is possible for us and of imperatives directing how it may be attained. These may, therefore, be called in general imperatives of skill. Here there is no question whether the end is rational and good, but only what one must do in order to attain it. The precepts for the physician to make his patient thoroughly healthy, and for a poisoner to ensure certain death, are of equal value in this respect, that each serves to effect its purpose perfectly. Since in early youth it cannot be known what ends are likely to occur to us in the course of life, parents seek to have their children taught a great many things, and provide for their skill in the use of means for all sorts of arbitrary ends, of none of which can they determine whether it may not perhaps hereafter be an object to their pupil, but which it is at all events possible that he might aim at; and this anxiety is so great that they commonly neglect to form and correct their judgement on the value of the things which may be chosen as ends.

There is one end, however, which may be assumed to be actually such to all rational beings (so far as imperatives apply to them, viz., as dependent beings), and, therefore, one purpose which they not merely may have, but which we may with certainty assume that they all actually have by a natural necessity, and this is happiness. The hypothetical imperative which expresses the practical necessity of an action as means to the advancement of happiness is assertorial. We are not to present it as necessary for an uncertain and merely possible purpose, but for a purpose which we may presuppose with certainty and a priori in every man, because it belongs to his being. Now skill in the choice of means to his own greatest well-being may be called prudence, in the narrowest sense. And thus the imperative which refers to the choice of means to one's own happiness, i.e., the precept of prudence, is still always hypothetical; the action is not commanded absolutely, but only as means to another purpose.

Finally, there is an imperative which commands a certain conduct immediately, without having as its condition any other purpose to be attained by it. This imperative is categorical. It concerns not the matter of the action, or its intended result, but its form and the principle of which it is itself a result; and what is essentially good in it consists in the mental disposition, let the consequence be what it may. This imperative may be called that of morality.

There is a marked distinction also between the volitions on these three sorts of principles in the dissimilarity of the obligation of the will. In order to mark this difference more clearly, I think they would be most suitably named in their order if we said they are either rules of skill, or counsels of prudence, or commands (laws) of morality. For it is law only that involves the conception of an unconditional and objective necessity, which is consequently universally valid; and commands are laws which must be obeyed, that is, must be followed, even in opposition to inclination. Counsels, indeed, involve necessity, but one which can only hold under a contingent subjective condition, viz., they depend on whether this or that man reckons this or that as part of his happiness; the categorical imperative, on the contrary, is not limited by any condition, and as being absolutely, although practically, necessary, may be quite properly called a command....

When I conceive a hypothetical imperative, in general I do not know beforehand what it will contain until I am given the condition. But when I conceive a categorical imperative, I know at once what it contains. For as the imperative contains besides the law only the necessity that the maxims shall conform to this law, while the law contains no conditions restricting it, there remains nothing but the general statement that the maxim of the action should conform to a universal law, and it is this conformity alone that the imperative properly represents as necessary.

There is therefore but one categorical imperative, namely, this: Act only on that maxim whereby thou canst at the same time will that it should become a universal law.

Now if all imperatives of duty can be deduced from this one imperative as from their principle, then, although it should remain undecided what is called duty is not merely a vain notion, yet at least we shall be able to show what we understand by it and what this notion means.

Since the universality of the law according to which effects are produced constitutes what is properly called nature in the most general sense (as to form), that is the existence of things so far as it is determined by general laws, the imperative of duty may be expressed thus: Act as if the maxim of thy action were to become by thy will a universal law of nature.

We will now enumerate a few duties, adopting the usual division of them into duties to ourselves and to others, and into perfect and imperfect duties.

1. A man reduced to despair by a series of misfortunes feels wearied of life, but is still so far in possession of his reason that he can ask himself whether it would not be contrary to his duty to himself to take his own life. Now he inquires whether the maxim of his action could become a universal law of nature. His maxim is: "From self-love I adopt it as a principle to shorten my life when its longer duration is likely to bring more evil than satisfaction." It is asked then simply whether this principle founded on self-love can become a universal law of nature. Now we see at once that a system of nature of which it should be a law to destroy life by means of the very feeling whose special nature it is to impel to the improvement of life would contradict itself and, therefore, could not exist as a system of nature; hence that maxim cannot possibly exist as a universal law of nature and, consequently, would be wholly inconsistent with the supreme principle of all duty.

2. Another finds himself forced by necessity to borrow money. He knows that he will not be able to repay it, but sees also that nothing will be lent to him unless he promises stoutly to repay it in a definite time. He desires to make this promise, but he has still so much conscience as to ask himself: "Is it not unlawful and inconsistent with duty to get out of a difficulty in this way?" Suppose however that he resolves to do so: then the maxim of his action would be expressed thus: "When I think myself in want of money, I will borrow money and promise to repay it, although I know that I never can do so." Now this principle of self-love or of one's own advantage may perhaps be consistent with my whole future welfare; but the question now is, "Is it right?" I change then the suggestion of self-love into a universal law, and state the question thus: "How would it be if my maxim were a universal law?" Then I see at once that it could never hold as a universal law of nature, but would necessarily contradict itself. For supposing it to be a universal law that everyone when he thinks himself in a difficulty should be able to promise whatever he pleases, with the purpose of not keeping his promise, the promise itself would become impossible, as well as the end that one might have in view in it, since no one would consider that anything was promised to him, but would ridicule all such statements as vain pretences.

3. A third finds in himself a talent which with the help of some culture might make him a useful man in many respects. But he finds himself in comfortable circumstances and prefers to indulge in pleasure rather than to take pains in enlarging and improving his happy natural capacities. He asks, however, whether his maxim of neglect of his natural gifts, besides agreeing with his inclination to indulgence, agrees also with what is called duty. He sees then that a system of nature could indeed subsist with such a universal law although men (like the South Sea islanders) should let their talents rest and resolve to devote their lives merely to idleness, amusement, and propagation of their species—in a word, to enjoyment; but he cannot possibly will that this should be a universal law of nature, or be implanted in us as such by a natural instinct. For, as a rational being, he necessarily wills that his faculties be developed, since they serve him and have been given him, for all sorts of possible purposes.

4. A fourth, who is in prosperity, while he sees that others have to contend with great wretchedness and that he could help them, thinks: "What concern is it of mine? Let everyone be as happy as Heaven pleases, or as he can make himself; I will take nothing from him nor even envy him, only I do not wish to contribute anything to his welfare or to his assistance in distress!" Now no doubt if such a mode of thinking were a universal law, the human race might very well subsist and doubtless even better than in a state in which everyone talks of sympathy and good-will, or even takes

care occasionally to put it into practice, but, on the other side, also cheats when he can, betrays the rights of men, or otherwise violates them. But although it is possible that a universal law of nature might exist in accordance with that maxim, it is impossible to will that such a principle should have the universal validity of a law of nature. For a will which resolved this would contradict itself, inasmuch as many cases might occur in which one would have need of the love and sympathy of others, and in which, by such a law of nature, sprung from his own will, he would deprive himself of all hope of the aid he desires.

These are a few of the many actual duties, or at least what we regard as such, which obviously fall into two classes on the one principle that we have laid down. We must be able to will that a maxim of our action should be a universal law. This is the canon of the moral appreciation of the action generally. Some actions are of such a character that their maxim cannot without contradiction be even conceived as a universal law of nature, far from it being possible that we should will that it should be so. In others this intrinsic impossibility is not found, but still it is impossible to will that their maxim should be raised to the universality of a law of nature, since such a will would contradict itself. It is easily seen that the former violate strict or rigorous (inflexible [i.e., perfect]) duty; the latter only laxer (meritorious [i.e., imperfect]) duty. Thus it has been completely shown how all duties depend as regards the nature of the obligation (not the object of the action) on the same principle.

If now we attend to ourselves on occasion of any transgression of duty, we shall find that we in fact do not will that our maxim should be a universal law, for that is impossible for us; on the contrary, we will that the opposite should remain a universal law, only we assume the liberty of making an exception in our own favour or (just for this time only) in favour of our inclination. Consequently if we considered all cases from one and the same point of view, namely, that of reason, we should find a contradiction in our own will, namely, that a certain principle should be objectively necessary as a universal law, and yet subjectively should not be universal, but admit of exceptions. As however we at one moment regard our action from the point of view of a will wholly conformed to reason, and then again look at the same action from the point of view of a will affected by inclination, there is not really any contradiction, but an antagonism of inclination to the precept of reason, whereby the universality of the principle is changed into a mere generality, so that the practical principle of reason shall meet the maxim half way. Now, although this cannot be justified in our own impartial judgement, yet it proves that we do really recognise the validity of the categorical imperative and (with all respect for it) only allow ourselves a few exceptions, which we think unimportant and forced from us.

We have thus established at least this much, that if duty is a conception which is to have any import and real legislative authority for our actions, it can only be expressed in categorical and not at all in hypothetical imperatives. We have also, which is of great importance, exhibited clearly and definitely for every practical application the content of the categorical imperative, which must contain the principle of all duty if there is such a thing at all. We have not yet, however, advanced so far as to prove a priori that there actually is such an imperative, that there is a practical law which commands absolutely of itself and without any other impulse, and that the following of this law is duty.

With the view of attaining to this, it is of extreme importance to remember that we must not allow ourselves to think of deducing the reality of this principle from the particular attributes of human nature. For duty is to be a practical, unconditional necessity of action; it must therefore hold for all rational beings (to whom an imperative can apply at all), and for this reason only be also a law for all human wills. On the contrary, whatever is deduced from the particular natural characteristics of humanity, from certain feelings and propensions, nay, even, if possible, from any particular tendency proper to human reason, and which need not necessarily hold for the will of every rational being; this may indeed supply us with a maxim, but not with a law; with a subjective principle on which we may have a propension and inclination to act, but not with an objective principle on which we should be enjoined to act, even though all our propensions, inclinations, and natural dispositions were opposed to it. In fact, the sublimity and intrinsic dignity of the command in duty are so much the more evident, the less the subjective impulses favour it and the more they oppose it, without being able in the slightest degree to weaken the obligation of the law or to diminish its validity....

Supposing, however, that there were something whose existence has in itself an absolute worth, something which, being an end in itself, could be a source of definite laws; then in this and this alone would lie the source of a possible categorical imperative, i.e., a practical law.

Now I say: man and generally any rational being exists as an end in himself, not merely as a means to be arbitrarily used by this or that will, but in all his actions, whether they concern himself or other rational beings, must be always regarded at the same time as an end. All objects of the inclinations have only a conditional worth, for if the inclinations and the wants founded on them did not exist, then their object would be without value. But the inclinations, themselves being sources of want, are so far from having an absolute worth for which they should be desired that on the contrary it must be the universal wish of every rational being to be wholly free from them. Thus the worth of any object which is to be acquired by our action is always conditional. Beings whose existence depends not on our will but on nature's, have nevertheless, if they are irrational beings, only a relative value as means, and are therefore called things; rational beings, on the contrary, are called persons, because their very nature points them out as ends in themselves, that is as something which must not be used merely as means, and so far therefore restricts freedom of action (and is an object of respect). These, therefore, are not merely subjective ends whose existence has a worth for us as an effect of our action, but objective ends, that is, things whose existence is an end in itself; an end moreover for which no other can be substituted, which they should subserve merely as means, for otherwise nothing whatever would possess absolute worth; but if all worth were conditioned and therefore contingent, then there would be no supreme practical principle of reason whatever.

If then there is a supreme practical principle or, in respect of the human will, a categorical imperative, it must be one which, being drawn from the conception of that which is necessarily an end for everyone because it is an end in itself, constitutes an objective principle of will, and can therefore serve as a universal practical law. The foundation of this principle is: rational nature exists as an end in itself. Man necessarily conceives his own existence as being so; so far then this is a subjective principle of human actions. But every other rational being regards its existence similarly, just on the same rational principle that holds for me: so that it is at the same time an objective principle, from which as a supreme practical law all laws of the will must be capable of being deduced. Accordingly the practical imperative will be as follows: So act as to treat humanity, whether in thine own person or in that of any other, in every case as an end withal, never as means only. We will now inquire whether this can be practically carried out.

4.9 Edmund Burke (1729–1797)

General introductory remarks for Edmund Burke are found in 3.12.

from Reflections on the Revolution in France

[Richard Price's] doctrines affect our Constitution in its vital parts. He tells the Revolution Society, in this political sermon, that his Majesty "is almost the only lawful king in the world, because the only one who owes his crown to the choice of his people." As to the kings of the world, all of whom (except one) this arch-pontiff of the rights of men, with all the plenitude and with more than the boldness of the Papal deposing power in its meridian fervor of the twelfth century, puts into one sweeping clause of ban and anathema, and proclaims usurpers by circles of longitude and latitude over the whole globe, it behooves them to consider how they admit into their territories these apostolic missionaries, who are to tell their subjects they are not lawful kings. That is their concern. It is ours, as a domestic interest of some moment, seriously to consider the solidity of the only principle upon which these gentlemen acknowledge a king of Great Britain to be entitled to their allegiance.

This doctrine, as applied to the prince now on the British throne, either is nonsense, and therefore neither true nor false, or it affirms a most unfounded, dangerous, illegal, and unconstitutional position. According to this spiritual doctor of politics, if his Majesty does not owe his crown to the choice of his people, he is no lawful king. Now nothing can be more untrue than that the crown of this kingdom is so held by his Majesty. Therefore, if you follow their rule, the king of Great Britain, who most certainly does not owe his high office to any form of popular election, is in no respect better than the rest of the gang of usurpers, who reign, or rather rob, all over the face of this our miserable world, without any sort of right or title to the allegiance of their people. The policy of this general doctrine, so qualified, is evident enough. The propagators of this political gospel are in hopes their abstract principle (their principle that a popular choice is necessary to the legal existence of the sovereign magistracy) would be overlooked, whilst the king of Great Britain was not affected by it. In the mean time the ears of their congregations would be gradually habituated to it, as if it were a first principle admitted without dispute. For the present it would only operate as a theory, pickled in the preserving juices of pulpit eloquence, and laid by for future use. *Condo et compono quæ mox depromere passim.* By this policy, whilst our government is soothed with a reservation in its favor, to which it has no claim, the security which it has in common with all governments, so far as opinion is security, is taken away.

Thus these politicians proceed, whilst little notice is taken of their doctrines; but when they come to be examined upon the plain meaning of their words and the direct tendency of their doctrines, then equivocations and slippery constructions come into play. When they say the king owes his crown to the choice of his people, and is therefore the only lawful sovereign in the world, they will perhaps tell us they mean to say no more than that some of the king's predecessors have been called to the throne by some sort of choice, and therefore he owes his crown to the choice of his people. Thus, by a miserable subterfuge, they hope to render their proposition safe by rendering it nugatory. They are welcome to the asylum they seek for their offence, since they take refuge in their folly. For, if you admit this interpretation, how does their idea of election differ from our idea of inheritance? And how does the settlement of the crown in the Brunswick line, derived from James the First, come to legalize our monarchy rather than that of any of the neighboring countries? At some time or other, to be sure, all the beginners of dynasties were chosen by those who called them to govern. There is ground enough for the opinion that all the kingdoms of Europe were at a remote period elective, with more or fewer limitations in the objects of choice. But whatever kings might have been here or elsewhere a thousand years ago, or in whatever manner the ruling dynasties of England or France may have begun, the king of Great Britain is at this day king by a fixed rule of succession, according to the laws of his country; and whilst the legal conditions of the compact of sovereignty are performed by him, (as they are performed,) he holds his crown in contempt of the choice of the Revolution Society, who have not a single vote for a king amongst them, either individually or collectively: though I make no doubt they would soon erect themselves into an electoral college, if things were ripe to give effect to their claim.

His Majesty's heirs and successors, each in his time and order, will come to the crown with the same contempt of their choice with which his Majesty has succeeded to that he wears.

...

The ceremony of cashiering kings, of which these gentlemen talk so much at their ease, can rarely, if ever, be performed without force. It then becomes a case of war, and not of constitution. Laws are commanded to hold their tongues amongst arms; and tribunals fall to the ground with the peace they are no longer able to uphold. The Revolution of 1688 was obtained by a just war, in the only case in which any war, and much more a civil war, can be just. "*Justa bella quibus NECESSARIA.*" The question of dethroning, or, if these gentlemen, like the phrase better, "cashiering kings," will always be, as it has always been, an extraordinary question of state, and wholly out of the law: a question (like all other questions of state) of dispositions, and of means, and of probable consequences, rather than of positive rights. As it was not made for common abuses, so it is not to be agitated by common minds. The speculative line of demarcation, where obedience ought to end and resistance must begin, is faint, obscure, and not easily definable. It is not a single act or a single event which determines it. Governments must be abused and deranged indeed, before it can be thought of; and the prospect of the future must be as bad as the experience of the past. When things are in that lamentable condition, the nature of the disease is to indicate the remedy to those whom Nature has qualified to administer in extremities this critical, ambiguous, bitter potion to a distempered state. Times and occasions and provocations will teach their own lessons. The wise will determine from the gravity of the case; the irritable, from sensibility to oppression; the high-minded, from disdain and indignation at abusive power in unworthy hands; the brave and bold, from the love of honorable danger in a generous cause: but, with or without right, a revolution will be the very last resource of the thinking and the good.

The third head of right asserted by the pulpit of the Old Jewry, namely, the "right to form a government for ourselves," has, at least, as little countenance from anything done at the Revolution, either in precedent or principle, as the two first of their claims. The Revolution was made to preserve our ancient indisputable laws and liberties, and that ancient constitution of government which is our only security for law and liberty. If you are desirous of knowing the spirit of our Constitution, and the policy which predominated in that great period which has secured it to this hour, pray look for both in our histories, in our records, in our acts of Parliament and journals of Parliament, and not in the sermons of the Old Jewry, and the after-dinner toasts of the Revolution Society. In the former you will find other ideas and another language. Such a claim is as ill-suited to our temper and wishes as it is unsupported by any appearance of authority. The very idea of the fabrication of a new government is enough to fill us with disgust and horror. We wished at the period of the Revolution, and do now wish, to derive all we possess as an inheritance from our forefathers. Upon that body and stock of inheritance we have taken care not to inoculate any scion alien to the nature of the original plant. All the reformations we have hitherto made have proceeded upon the principle of reference to antiquity; and I hope, nay, I am persuaded, that all those which possibly may be made hereafter will be carefully formed upon analogical precedent, authority, and example.

...

In the famous law of the 3rd of Charles the First, called the Petition of Right, the Parliament says to the king, "Your subjects have inherited this freedom": claiming their franchises, not on abstract principles, "as the rights of men," but as the rights of Englishmen, and as a patrimony derived from their forefathers. Selden, and the other profoundly learned men who drew this Petition of Right, were as well acquainted, at least, with all the general theories concerning the "rights of men" as any of the discoursers in our pulpits or on your tribune: full as well as Dr. Price, or as the Abbé Sièyes. But, for reasons worthy of that practical wisdom which superseded their theoretic science, they preferred this positive, recorded, hereditary title to all which can be dear to the man and the citizen to that vague, speculative right which exposed their sure inheritance to be scrambled for and torn to pieces by every wild, litigious spirit.

The same policy pervades all the laws which have since been made for the preservation of our liberties. In the 1st of William and Mary, in the famous statute called the Declaration of Right, the two Houses utter not a syllable of "a right to frame a government for themselves." You will see that their whole care was to secure the religion, laws, and liberties that had been long possessed, and had been lately endangered. "Taking into their most serious consideration the best means for making such an establishment that their religion, laws, and liberties might not be in danger of being again subverted," they auspicate all their proceedings by stating as some of those best means, "in the first place," to do "as their ancestors in like cases have usually done for vindicating their ancient rights and liberties, to declare";—and then they pray the king and queen "that it may be declared and enacted that all and singular the rights and liberties asserted and declared are the true ancient and indubitable rights and liberties of the people of this kingdom."

You will observe, that, from Magna Charta to the Declaration of Right, it has been the uniform policy of our Constitution to claim and assert our liberties as an entailed inheritance derived to us from our forefathers, and to be transmitted to our posterity,—as an estate specially belonging to the people of this kingdom, without any reference whatever to any other more general or prior right. By this means our Constitution preserves an unity in so great a diversity of its parts. We have an inheritable crown, an inheritable peerage, and a House of Commons and a people inheriting privileges, franchises, and liberties from a long line of ancestors.

This policy appears to me to be the result of profound reflection,—or rather the happy effect of following Nature, which is wisdom without reflection, and above it. A spirit of innovation is generally the result of a selfish temper and confined views. People will not look forward to posterity, who never look backward to their ancestors. Besides, the people of England well know that the idea of inheritance furnishes a sure principle of conservation, and a sure principle of transmission, without at all excluding a principle of improvement. It leaves acquisition free; but it secures what it acquires. Whatever advantages are obtained by a state proceeding on these maxims are locked fast as in a sort of family settlement, grasped as in a kind of mortmain forever. By a constitutional policy working after the pattern of Nature, we receive, we hold, we transmit our government and our privileges, in the same manner in which we enjoy and transmit our property and our lives. The institutions of policy, the goods of fortune, the gifts of Providence, are handed down to us, and from us, in the same course and order. Our political system is placed in a just correspondence and symmetry with the order of the world, and with the mode of existence decreed to a permanent body composed of transitory parts,—wherein, by the disposition of a stupendous wisdom, moulding together the great mysterious incorporation of the human race, the whole, at one time, is never old or middle-aged or young, but, in a condition of unchangeable constancy, moves on through the varied tenor of perpetual decay, fall, renovation, and progression. Thus, by preserving the method of

Nature in the conduct of the state, in what we improve we are never wholly new, in what we retain we are never wholly obsolete. By adhering in this manner and on those principles to our forefathers, we are guided, not by the superstition of antiquarians, but by the spirit of philosophic analogy. In this choice of inheritance we have given to our frame of polity the image of a relation in blood: binding up the Constitution of our country with our dearest domestic ties; adopting our fundamental laws into the bosom of our family affections; keeping inseparable, and cherishing with the warmth of all their combined and mutually reflected charities, our state, our hearths, our sepulchres, and our altars.

Through the same plan of a conformity to Nature in our artificial institutions, and by calling in the aid of her unerring and powerful instincts to fortify the fallible and feeble contrivances of our reason, we have derived several other, and those no small benefits, from considering our liberties in the light of an inheritance. Always acting as if in the presence of canonized forefathers, the spirit of freedom, leading in itself to misrule and excess, is tempered with an awful gravity. This idea of a liberal descent inspires us with a sense of habitual native dignity, which prevents that upstart insolence almost inevitably adhering to and disgracing those who are the first acquirers of any distinction. By this means our liberty becomes a noble freedom. It carries an imposing and majestic aspect. It has a pedigree and illustrating ancestors. It has its bearings and its ensigns armorial. It has its gallery of portraits, its monumental inscriptions, its records, evidences, and titles. We procure reverence to our civil institutions on the principle upon which Nature teaches us to revere individual men: on account of their age, and on account of those from whom they are descended. All your sophisters cannot produce anything better adapted to preserve a rational and manly freedom than the course that we have pursued, who have chosen our nature rather than our speculations, our breasts rather than our inventions, for the great conservatories and magazines of our rights and privileges.

You might, if you pleased, have profited of our example, and have given to your recovered freedom a correspondent dignity. Your privileges, though discontinued, were not lost to memory. Your Constitution, it is true, whilst you were out of possession, suffered waste and dilapidation; but you possessed in some parts the walls, and in all the foundations, of a noble and venerable castle. You might have repaired those walls; you might have built on those old foundations. Your Constitution was suspended before it was perfected; but you had the elements of a Constitution very nearly as good as could be wished. In your old states you possessed that variety of parts corresponding with the various descriptions of which your community was happily composed; you had all that combination and all that opposition of interests, you had that action and counteraction, which, in the natural and in the political world, from the reciprocal struggle of discordant powers draws out the harmony of the universe. These opposed and conflicting interests, which you considered as so great a blemish in your old and in our present Constitution, interpose a salutary check to all precipitate resolutions. They render deliberation a matter, not of choice, but of necessity; they make all change a subject of compromise, which naturally begets moderation; they produce temperaments, preventing the sore evil of harsh, crude, unqualified reformations, and rendering all the headlong exertions of arbitrary power, in the few or in the many, forever impracticable. Through that diversity of members and interests, general liberty had as many securities as there were separate views in the several orders; whilst by pressing down the whole by the weight of a real monarchy, the separate parts would have been prevented from warping and starting from their allotted places.

You had all these advantages in your ancient states; but you chose to act as if you had never been moulded into civil society, and had everything to begin anew. You began ill, because you began by despising everything that belonged to you. You set up your trade without a capital. If the last generations of your country appeared without much lustre in your eyes, you might have passed them by, and derived your claims from a more early race of ancestors. Under a pious predilection for those ancestors, your imaginations would have realized in them a standard of virtue and wisdom beyond the vulgar practice of the hour; and you would have risen with the example to whose imitation you aspired. Respecting your forefathers, you would have been taught to respect yourselves. You would not have chosen to consider the French as a people of yesterday, as a nation of low-born, servile wretches until the emancipating year of 1789. In order to furnish, at the expense of your honor, an excuse to your apologists here for several enormities of yours, you would not have been content to be represented as a gang of Maroon slaves, suddenly broke loose from the house of bondage, and therefore to be pardoned for your abuse of the liberty to which you were not accustomed, and were ill fitted. Would it not, my worthy friend, have been wiser to have you thought, what I for one always thought you, a generous and gallant nation, long misled to your disadvantage by your high and romantic sentiments of fidelity, honor, and loyalty; that events had been unfavorable to you, but that you were not enslaved through any illiberal or servile disposition; that, in your most devoted submission, you were actuated by a principle of public spirit; and that it was your country you worshipped, in the person of your king? Had you made it to be understood, that, in the delusion of this amiable error, you had gone further than your wise ancestors,—that you were resolved to resume your ancient privileges, whilst you preserved the spirit of your ancient and your recent loyalty and honor; or if, diffident of yourselves, and not clearly discerning the almost obliterated Constitution of your ancestors, you had looked to your neighbors in this land, who had kept alive the ancient principles and models of the old common law of Europe, meliorated and adapted to its present state,—by following wise examples you would have given new examples of wisdom to the world. You would have rendered the cause of liberty venerable in the eyes of every worthy mind in every nation. You would have shamed despotism from the earth, by showing that freedom was not only reconcilable, but, as, when well disciplined, it is, auxiliary to law. You would have had an unoppressive, but a productive revenue. You would have had a flourishing commerce to feed it. You would have had a free Constitution, a potent monarchy, a disciplined army, a reformed and venerated clergy,—a mitigated, but spirited nobility, to lead your virtue, not to overlay it; you would have had a liberal order of commons, to emulate and to recruit that nobility; you would have had a protected, satisfied, laborious, and obedient people, taught to seek and to recognize the happiness that is to be found by virtue in all conditions,—in which consists the true moral equality of mankind, and not in that monstrous fiction which, by inspiring false ideas and vain expectations into men destined to travel in the obscure walk of laborious life, serves only to aggravate and embitter that real inequality which it never can remove, and which the order of civil life establishes as much for the benefit of those whom it must leave in an humble state as those whom it is able to exalt to a condition more splendid, but not more happy. You had a smooth and easy career of felicity and glory laid open to you, beyond anything recorded in the history of the world; but you have shown that difficulty is good for man.

Compute your gains; see what is got by those extravagant and presumptuous speculations which have taught your leaders to despise all their predecessors, and all their contemporaries, and even to despise themselves, until the moment in which they became truly despicable. By following those false lights, France has bought undisguised calamities at a higher price than any nation has purchased the most unequivocal blessings. France has bought poverty by crime. France has not sacrificed her virtue to her interest; but she has abandoned her interest, that she might prostitute her virtue. All other nations have begun the fabric of a new government, or the reformation of an old, by establishing originally, or by enforcing with greater exactness, some rites or other of religion. All other people have laid the foundations of civil freedom in severer manners, and a system of a more austere and masculine morality. France, when she let loose the reins of regal authority, doubled the license of a ferocious dissoluteness in manners, and of an insolent irreligion in opinions and practices,—and has extended through all ranks of life, as if she were communicating some privilege, or laying open some secluded benefit, all the unhappy corruptions that usually were the disease of wealth and power. This is one of the new principles of equality in France.

France, by the perfidy of her leaders, has utterly disgraced the tone of lenient council in the cabinets of princes, and disarmed it of its most potent topics. She has sanctified the dark, suspicious maxims of tyrannous distrust, and taught kings to tremble at (what will hereafter be called) the delusive plausibilities of moral politicians. Sovereigns will consider those who advise them to place an unlimited confidence in their people as subverters of their thrones,—as traitors who aim at their destruction, by leading their easy good-nature, under specious pretences, to admit combinations of bold and faithless men into a participation of their power. This alone (if there were nothing else) is an irreparable calamity to you and to mankind. Remember that your Parliament of Paris told your king, that, in calling the states together, he had nothing to fear but the prodigal excess of their zeal in providing for the support of the throne. It is right that these men should hide their heads. It is right that they should bear their part in the ruin which their counsel has brought on their sovereign and their country. Such sanguine declarations tend to lull authority asleep,—to encourage it rashly to engage in perilous adventures of untried policy,—to neglect those provisions, preparations, and precautions which distinguish benevolence from imbecility, and without which no man can answer for the salutary effect of any abstract plan of government or of freedom. For want of these, they have seen the medicine of the state corrupted into its poison. They have seen the French rebel against a mild and lawful monarch, with more fury, outrage, and insult than ever any people has been known to rise against the most illegal usurper or the most sanguinary tyrant. Their resistance was made to concession; their revolt was from protection; their blow was aimed at a hand holding out graces, favors, and immunities.

This was unnatural. The rest is in order. They have found their punishment in their success. Laws overturned; tribunals subverted; industry without vigor; commerce expiring; the revenue unpaid, yet the people impoverished; a church pillaged, and a state not relieved; civil and military anarchy made the constitution of the kingdom; everything human and divine sacrificed to the idol of public credit, and national bankruptcy the consequence; and, to crown all, the paper securities of new, precarious, tottering power, the discredited paper securities of impoverished fraud and beggared rapine, held out as a currency for the support of an empire, in lieu of the two great recognized species that represent the lasting, conventional credit of mankind, which disappeared and hid themselves in the earth from whence they came, when the principle of property, whose creatures and representatives they are, was systematically subverted.

Were all these dreadful things necessary? Were they the inevitable results of the desperate struggle of determined patriots, compelled to wade through blood and tumult to the quiet shore of a tranquil and prosperous liberty? No! nothing like it. The fresh ruins of France, which shock our feelings wherever we can turn our eyes, are not the devastation of civil war: they are the sad, but instructive monuments of rash and ignorant counsel in time of profound peace. They are the display of inconsiderate and presumptuous, because unresisted and irresistible, authority. The persons who have thus squandered away the precious treasure of their crimes, the persons who have made this prodigal and wild waste of public evils, (the last stake reserved for the ultimate ransom of the state,) have met in their progress with little, or rather with no opposition at all. Their whole march was more like a triumphal procession than the progress of a war. Their pioneers have gone before them, and demolished and laid everything level at their feet. Not one drop of their blood have they shed in the cause of the country they have ruined. They have made no sacrifices to their projects of greater consequence than their shoe-buckles, whilst they were imprisoning their king, murdering their fellow-citizens, and bathing in tears and plunging in poverty and distress thousands of worthy men and worthy families. Their cruelty has not even been the base result of fear. It has been the effect of their sense of perfect safety, in authorizing treasons, robberies, rapes, assassinations, slaughters, and burnings, throughout their harassed land. But the cause of all was plain from the beginning.

This unforced choice, this fond election of evil, would appear perfectly unaccountable, if we did not consider the composition of the National Assembly: I do not mean its formal constitution, which, as it now stands, is exceptionable enough, but the materials of which in a great measure it is composed, which is of ten thousand times greater consequence than all the formalities in the world. If we were to know nothing of this assembly but by its title and function, no colors could paint to the imagination anything more venerable. In that light, the mind of an inquirer, subdued by such an awful image as that of the virtue and wisdom of a whole people collected into one focus, would pause and hesitate in condemning things even of the very worst aspect. Instead of blamable, they would appear only mysterious. But no name, no power, no function, no artificial institution whatsoever, can make the men, of whom any system of authority is composed, any other than God, and Nature, and education, and their habits of life have made them. Capacities beyond these the people have not to give. Virtue and wisdom may be the objects of their choice; but their choice confers neither the one nor the other on those upon whom they lay their ordaining hands. They have not the engagement of Nature, they have not the promise of Revelation for any such powers.

After I had read over the list of the persons and descriptions elected into the Tiers État, nothing which they afterwards did could appear astonishing. Among them, indeed, I saw some of known rank, some of shining talents; but of any practical experience in the state not one man was to be found. The best were only men of theory. But whatever the distinguished few may have been, it is the substance and mass of the body which constitutes its character, and must finally determine its direction. In all bodies, those who will lead must also, in a considerable degree, follow. They must conform their propositions to the taste, talent, and disposition of those whom they wish to conduct: therefore, if an assembly is viciously or feebly composed in a very great part of it, nothing but such a supreme degree of virtue as very rarely appears in the world, and for that reason cannot enter into calculation, will prevent the men of talents disseminated through it from becoming only the expert instruments of absurd projects. If, what is the more likely event, instead of that unusual degree of virtue, they should be actuated by sinister ambition and a lust of meretricious glory, then the feeble part of the assembly, to whom at first they conform, becomes, in its turn, the dupe and instrument of their designs. In this political traffic, the leaders will be obliged to bow to the ignorance of their followers, and the followers to become subservient to the worst designs of their leaders.

To secure any degree of sobriety in the propositions made by the leaders in any public assembly, they ought to respect, in some degree perhaps to fear, those whom they conduct. To be led any otherwise than blindly, the followers must be qualified, if not for actors, at least for judges; they must also be judges of natural weight and authority. Nothing can secure a steady and moderate conduct in such assemblies, but that the body of them should be respectably composed, in point of condition in life, of permanent property, of education, and of such habits as enlarge and liberalize the understanding.

In the calling of the States-General of France, the first thing that struck me was a great departure from the ancient course. I found the representation for the third estate composed of six hundred persons. They were equal in number to the representatives of both the other orders. If the orders were to act separately, the number would not, beyond the consideration of the expense, be of much moment. But when it became apparent that the three orders were to be melted down into one, the policy and necessary effect of this numerous representation became obvious. A very small desertion from either of the other two orders must throw the power of both into the hands of the third. In fact, the whole power of the state was soon resolved into that body. Its due composition became, therefore, of infinitely the greater importance.

Judge, Sir, of my surprise, when I found that a very great proportion of the Assembly (a majority, I believe, of the members who attended) was composed of practitioners in the law. It was composed, not of distinguished magistrates, who had given pledges to their country of their science, prudence, and integrity,—not of leading advocates, the glory of the bar,—not of renowned professors in universities,—but for the far greater part, as it must in such a number, of the inferior, unlearned, mechanical, merely instrumental members of the profession. There were distinguished exceptions; but the general composition was of obscure provincial advocates, of stewards of petty local jurisdictions, country attorneys, notaries, and the whole train of the ministers of municipal litigation, the fomenters and conductors of the petty war of village vexation. From the moment I read the list, I saw distinctly, and very nearly as it has happened, all that was to follow.

The degree of estimation in which any profession is held becomes the standard of the estimation in which the professors hold themselves. Whatever the personal merits of many individual lawyers might have been, (and in many it was undoubtedly very considerable,) in that military kingdom no part of the profession had been much regarded, except the highest of all, who often united to their professional offices great family splendor, and were invested with great power and authority. These certainly were highly respected, and even with no small degree of awe. The next rank was not much esteemed; the mechanical part was in a very low degree of repute.

Whenever the supreme authority is vested in a body so composed, it must evidently produce the consequences of supreme authority placed in the hands of men not taught habitually to respect themselves,—who had no previous fortune in character at stake,—who could not be expected to bear with moderation or to conduct with discretion a power which they themselves, more than any others, must be surprised to find in their hands. Who could flatter himself that these men, suddenly, and as it were by enchantment, snatched from the humblest rank of subordination, would not be intoxicated with their unprepared greatness? Who could conceive that men who are habitually meddling, daring, subtle, active, of litigious dispositions and unquiet minds, would easily fall back into their old condition of obscure contention, and laborious, low, and unprofitable chicane? Who could doubt but that, at any expense to the state, of which they understood nothing, they must pursue their private interests, which they understood but too well? It was not an event depending on chance or contingency. It was inevitable; it was necessary; it was planted in the nature of things. They must join (if their capacity did not permit them to lead) in any project which could procure to them a litigious constitution,—which could lay open to them those innumerable lucrative jobs which follow in the train of all great convulsions and revolutions in the state, and particularly in all great and violent permutations of property. Was it to be expected that they would attend to the stability of property, whose existence had always depended upon whatever rendered property questionable, ambiguous, and insecure? Their objects would be enlarged with their elevation; but their disposition, and habits, and mode of accomplishing their designs must remain the same.

Well! but these men were to be tempered and restrained by other descriptions, of more sober minds and more enlarged understandings. Were they, then, to be awed by the supereminent authority and awful dignity of a handful of country clowns, who have seats in that assembly, some of whom are said not to be able to read and write,—and by not a greater number of traders, who, though somewhat more instructed, and more conspicuous in the order of society, had never known anything beyond their counting-house? No! both these descriptions were more formed to be overborne and swayed by the intrigues and artifices of lawyers than to become their counterpoise. With such a dangerous disproportion, the whole must needs be governed by them.

...

We know that the British House of Commons, without shutting its doors to any merit in any class, is, by the sure operation of adequate causes, filled with everything illustrious in rank, in descent, in hereditary and in acquired opulence, in cultivated talents, in military, civil, naval, and politic distinction, that the country can afford. But supposing, what hardly can be supposed as a case, that the House of Commons should be composed in the same manner with the *Tiers État* in France,—would this dominion of chicane be borne with patience, or even conceived without horror? God forbid I should insinuate anything derogatory to that profession which is another priesthood, administering the rights of sacred justice! But whilst I revere men in the functions which belong to them, and would do as much as one man can do to prevent their exclusion from any, I cannot, to flatter them, give the lie to Nature. They are good and useful in the composition; they must be mischievous, if they preponderate so as virtually to become the whole. Their very excellence in their peculiar functions may be far from a qualification for others. It cannot escape observation, that, when men are too much confined to professional and faculty habits, and, as it were, inveterate in the recurrent employment of that narrow circle, they are rather disabled than qualified for whatever depends on the knowledge of mankind, on experience in mixed affairs, on a comprehensive, connected view of the various, complicated, external, and internal interests which go to the formation of that multifarious thing called a State.

After all, if the House of Commons were to have an wholly professional and faculty composition, what is the power of the House of Commons, circumscribed and shut in by the immovable barriers of laws, usages, positive rules of doctrine and practice, counterpoised by the House of Lords, and every moment of its existence at the discretion of the crown to continue, prorogue, or dissolve us? The power of the House of Commons, direct or indirect, is, indeed, great: and long may it be able to preserve its greatness, and the spirit belonging to true greatness, at the full!—and it will do so, as long as it can keep the breakers of law in India from becoming the makers of law for England. The power, however, of the House of Commons, when least diminished, is as a drop of water in the ocean, compared to that residing in a settled majority of your National Assembly. That assembly, since the destruction of the orders, has no fundamental law, no strict convention, no respected usage to restrain it. Instead of finding themselves obliged to conform to a fixed constitution, they have a power to make a constitution which shall conform to their designs. Nothing in heaven or upon earth can serve as a control on them. What ought to be the heads, the hearts, the dispositions, that are qualified, or that dare, not only to make laws under a fixed constitution, but at one heat to strike out a totally new constitution for a great kingdom, and in every part of it, from the monarch on the throne to the vestry of a parish? But "Fools rush in where angels fear to tread."

In such a state of unbounded power, for undefined and undefinable purposes, the evil of a moral and almost physical inaptitude of the man to the function must be the greatest we can conceive to happen in the management of human affairs.

Having considered the composition of the third estate, as it stood in its original frame, I took a view of the representatives of the clergy. There, too, it appeared that full as little regard was had to the general security of property, or to the aptitude of the deputies for their public purposes, in the principles of their election. That election was so contrived as to send a very large proportion of mere country curates to the great and arduous work of new-modelling a state: men who never had seen the state so much as in a picture; men who knew nothing of the world beyond the bounds of an obscure village; who, immersed in hopeless poverty, could regard all property, whether secular or ecclesiastical, with no other eye than that of envy; among whom must be many who, for the smallest hope of the meanest dividend in plunder, would readily join in any attempts upon a body of wealth in which they could hardly look to have any share, except in a general scramble. Instead of balancing the power of the active chicaners in the other assembly, these curates must necessarily become the active coadjutors, or at best the passive instruments, of those by whom they had been habitually guided in their petty village concerns. They, too, could hardly be the most conscientious of their kind, who, presuming upon their incompetent understanding, could intrigue for a trust which led them from their natural relation to their flocks, and their natural spheres of action, to undertake the regeneration of kingdoms. This preponderating weight, being added to the force of the body of chicane in the *Tiers État*, completed that momentum of ignorance, rashness, presumption, and lust of plunder, which nothing has been able to resist.

4.10 Friedrich Nietzsche (1844–1900)

Whether they are understood as abstract principles, statutes or customs, "rules of society" constrain individual agents, and obeying these rules constitutes a kind of submission (4.10.1). Taking guidance from a statute or custom, by contrast, is submission to an external fact, and taking it from an abstract principle is submission to a fiction. For Nietzsche, submission to any external constraint is born of weakness or powerlessness. He therefore characterizes the kind of widespread submission that marks modern life as "slave morality," which is contrasted with a kind of creative, daring noble individual who acts independently of statutes, customs, and conventions (4.10.3). The label "slave morality" is derived from an analogy: a moral agent who obeys any rule is like a slave who obeys a master. Independent action makes noble agency a law unto itself. "Slave morality" is sustained by timorous, gossipy propaganda that devalues bold independence. What he calls a "Master morality" is marked by an attitude of *désintéressement* [disinterestedness] towards these common values (4.10.3). In *On the Genealogy of Morals* he diagnoses the sustaining motivation of slave morality as *ressentiment* [resentment] (see 7.4). Slave morality differentiates "good" from "evil," whereas the noble agent differentiates "good" from "bad." Not only do they define goodness differently, but slave morality identifies as "evil" the creative and daring noble agent. Thus, the noble agent is the very thing that slave morality resents and that Nietzsche celebrates.

Our longest selection here comes from *Beyond Good and Evil* (4.10.3). The attack on stoicism in this passage applies not merely to the ideas of historical stoics, such as Cleanthes (see 3.6). Stoic submission to impersonal forces such as law and reason are emblematic of a general tendency among ethical and moral theorists to conceive moral goodness in terms of obedience to abstract principles. Against this, he celebrates an ego-centric natural impulse that he calls the "will to power" (4.10.2). The fullest expression of this instinct is, by Nietzsche's account, noble. His celebration of nobility here is very romantic in the way it sets a lone, heroic figure against popular, conventional, and abstract notions of good citizenship. Elsewhere in his work, he portrays the common run of humanity as being no better than cud-chewing cattle, that is, creatures content with domestic ease and too servile to think or act independently. Nietzsche scholars often debate the extent to which his account is meant seriously, and how much of it is intended to provoke and shock us into resisting the temptations of domestic ease. These exegetical concerns are not merely academic, for at least one circle of readers took him seriously and literally: Nazis, who venerated their own self-image as the blond beast that Nietzsche celebrates in *The Genealogy of Morals* (see 7.4). For this reason, in assessing the following passages we should (a) consider the possibility that his remarks may be hyperbolic rather than propagandistic, and (b) whether in his ideas we can find the seeds of Himmler's remarks in 7.6.

Lastly, it is helpful to consider the thought experiment in the present excerpt from *Joyful Wisdom* in light of Kant's Categorical Imperative (4.10.4). Nietzsche asks how we would respond to hearing that all of history, including every moment of our own lives will be repeated endlessly in eternally recurring cycles. Would we relish the prospect or dread it? Whereas the Categorical Imperative asks whether we can accept the idea that a maxim of a particular action be made into a universal law, "eternal recurrence" asks whether we can accept our current way of life.

4.10.1 *from* Human, All Too Human

96.

CUSTOM AND MORALITY.—To be moral, correct, and virtuous is to be obedient to an old-established law and custom. Whether we submit with difficulty or willingly is immaterial, enough that we do so. He is called "good" who, as if naturally, after long precedent, easily and willingly, therefore, does what is right, according to whatever this may be (as, for instance, taking revenge, if to take revenge be considered as right, as amongst the ancient Greeks). He is called good because he is good "for something"; but as goodwill, pity, consideration, moderation, and such like, have come, with the change in manners, to be looked upon as "good for something," as useful, the good-natured and helpful have, later on, come to be distinguished specially as "good." (In the beginning other and more important kinds of usefulness stood in the foreground.) To be evil is to be "not moral" (immoral), to be immoral is to be in opposition to tradition, however sensible or stupid it may be; injury to the community (the "neighbour" being understood thereby) has, however, been looked upon by the social laws of all different ages as being eminently the actual "immorality," so that now at the word "evil" we immediately think of voluntary injury to one's neighbour. The fundamental antithesis which has taught man the distinction between moral and immoral, between good and evil, is not the "egoistic" and "un-egoistic," but the being bound to the tradition, law, and solution thereof. How the tradition has *arisen* is immaterial, at all events without regard to good and evil or any immanent categorical imperative, but above all for the purpose of preserving a *community*, a generation, an association, a people; every superstitious custom that has arisen on account of some falsely explained accident, creates a tradition, which it is moral to follow; to separate one's self from it is dangerous, but more dangerous for the *community* than for the individual (because the Godhead punishes the community for every outrage and every violation of its rights, and the individual only in proportion). Now every tradition grows continually more venerable, the farther off lies its origin, the more this is lost sight of; the veneration paid it accumulates from generation to generation, the tradition at last becomes holy and excites awe; and thus in any case the morality of piety is a much older morality than that which requires un-egoistic actions.

4.10.2 *from* The Antichrist

2

What is good? All that enhances the feeling of power, the Will to Power, and power itself in man. What is bad?—All that proceeds from weakness. What is happiness?—The feeling that power is *increasing*,—that resistance has been overcome.

Not contentment, but more power; not peace at any price, but war; not virtue, but efficiency (virtue in the Renaissance sense, *virtù*, free from all moralic acid). The weak and the botched shall perish: first principle of our humanity. And they ought even to be helped to perish.

What is more harmful than any vice?—Practical sympathy with all the botched and the weak—Christianity.

4.10.3 *from* Beyond Good and Evil *(from Ch. 9: What Is Noble?)*

Section 9

Do you want to *live* "according to nature"? O you noble Stoics,[1] what a verbal swindle! Imagine a being like nature—extravagant without limit, indifferent without limit, without purposes and consideration, without pity and justice, simultaneously fruitful, desolate, and unknown—imagine indifference itself as a power—how *could* you live in accordance with this indifference? Living—isn't that precisely a will to be something different from what this nature is? Isn't living appraising, preferring, being unjust, being limited, wanting to be different? And if your imperative "live according to nature" basically means what amounts to "live according to life"—how could you *not* do that? Why make a principle out of what you yourselves are and must be? The truth of the matter is quite different: while you pretend to be in raptures as you read the canon of your law out of nature, you want something which is the reverse of this, you weird actors and self-deceivers! Your pride wants to prescribe to and incorporate into nature, this very nature, your morality, your ideal. You demand that nature be "in accordance with the Stoa," and you'd like to make all existence merely living in accordance with your own image—as a huge and eternal glorification and universalizing of Stoicism! With all your love of truth, you force yourselves for such a long time and with such persistence and hypnotic rigidity to look at nature *falsely*, that is, stoically, until you are no longer capable of seeing nature as anything else—and some abysmal arrogance finally inspires you with the lunatic hope that, *because* you know how to tyrannize over yourselves—Stoicism is self-tyranny—nature also allows herself to be tyrannized. Is the Stoic then not a *part* of nature? ... But this is an ancient, eternal story: what happened then with the Stoics is still happening today, as soon as a philosophy begins to believe in itself. It always creates a world in its own image. It cannot do anything different. Philosophy is this tyrannical drive itself, the most spiritual will to power, to a "creation of the world," to the *causa prima* [first cause].

...

1 The Stoics: A Greek philosophical school (founded in 306 BCE) teaching patient endurance and repression of the emotions.

Section 260

As the result of a stroll though the many more sophisticated and cruder moral systems which up to this point have ruled or still rule on earth, I found certain characteristics routinely return with each other, bound up together, until finally two basic types revealed themselves to me and a fundamental difference sprang up. There is *master morality*, and there is *slave morality*—to this I immediately add that in all higher and more mixed cultures attempts at a mediation between both moralities make an appearance as well, even more often, a confusion and mutual misunderstanding between the two, in fact, sometimes their close juxtaposition—even in the same person, within a single soul. Distinctions in moral value have arisen either among a ruling group which was happily conscious of its difference with respect to the ruled—or among the ruled, the slaves and dependent people of every degree. In the first case, when it's the masters who establish the idea of the "good," the elevated and proud conditions of the soul emotionally register as the distinguishing and defining order of rank. The noble man separates his own nature from that of people in whom the opposite of such exalted and proud states expresses itself. He despises them. We should notice at once that in this first kind of morality the opposites "good" and "bad" mean no more than "noble" and "despicable"—the opposition between "good" and "evil" has another origin. The despised one is the coward, the anxious, the small, the man who thinks about narrow utility, also the suspicious man with his inhibited look, the self-abasing man, the species of human dogs who allow themselves to be mistreated, the begging flatterer, and, above all, the liar:—it is a basic belief of all aristocrats that the common folk are liars. "We tellers of the truth"—that's what the nobility called itself in ancient Greece. It's evident that distinctions of moral worth everywhere were first applied to *men* and then later, by extension, were established for *actions*; hence, it is a serious mistake when historians of morality take as a starting point questions like "Why was the compassionate action praised?" The noble kind of man experiences *himself* as a person who determines value and who does not need other people's approval. He makes the judgment "What is harmful to me is harmful in itself." He understands himself as something which in general first confers honour on things, as something which *creates values*. Whatever he recognizes in himself he honours. Such a morality is self-glorification. In the foreground stands the feeling of fullness, the power which wants to overflow, the happiness of high tension, the consciousness of riches which wants to give presents and provide:—the noble man also helps the unfortunate, however not, or hardly ever, from pity, but more in response to an impulse which the excess of power produces. The noble person honours the powerful man in himself and also the man who has power over himself, who understands how to speak and how to keep silent, who takes delight in dealing with himself severely and toughly, and who respects, above all, severity and toughness. "Wotan set a hard heart in my breast," it says in an old Scandinavian saga: that's poetry emerging from the soul of a proud Viking—and justifiably so. A man of this sort is simply proud of the fact that he has *not* been made for pity. That's why the hero of the saga adds a warning, "In a man whose heart is not hard when he is still young it will never become hard." Noble and brave men who think this way are furthest removed from that morality which sees the badge of morality specifically in pity or in actions for others or in *désintéressement* [disinterestedness]. The belief in oneself, pride in oneself, a fundamental hostility and irony against "selflessness" belong to noble morality, just as much as an easy contempt and caution before feelings of pity and the "warm heart." Powerful men are the ones who *understand* how to honour; that is their art, their realm of invention. The profound reverence for age and for ancestral tradition—all justice stands on this double reverence—the belief and the prejudice favouring forefathers and working against newcomers are typical in the morality of the powerful, and when, by contrast, the men of "modern ideas" believe almost instinctively in "progress" and the "future" and increasingly lack any respect for age, then in that attitude the ignoble origin of these "ideas" already reveals itself well enough. However, a morality of the rulers is most alien and embarrassing to present taste because of the severity of its basic principle that man has duties only with respect to those like him, that man should act towards those beings of lower rank, towards everything foreign, at his own discretion, or "as his heart dictates," and, in any case, "beyond good and evil." Here pity and things like that may belong. The capacity for and obligation to a long gratitude and a long revenge—both only within the circle of one's peers—the sophistication in paying back again, the refined idea in friendship, a certain necessity to have enemies (as, so to speak, drainage ditches for the feelings of envy, quarrelsomeness, and high spirits—basically in order to be capable of being a good *friend*): all those are typical characteristics of a noble morality, which, as indicated, is not the morality of "modern ideas" and which is thus nowadays difficult to sympathize with, as well as difficult to dig up and expose. Things are different with the second type of moral system, *slave morality*. Suppose the oppressed, depressed, suffering, and unfree people, those ignorant of themselves and tired out, suppose they moralize: what will be the common feature of their moral estimates of value? Probably a pessimistic suspicion directed at the entire human situation will express itself, perhaps a condemnation of man, along with his situation. The gaze of a slave is not well disposed towards the virtues of the powerful; he possesses scepticism and mistrust; he has a *subtlety* of mistrust of everything "good" that is honoured in those virtues—he would like to persuade himself that even happiness is not genuine there. By contrast, those characteristics will be pulled forward and flooded with light which serve to mitigate existence for those who suffer: here respect is given to pity, to the obliging hand ready to help, to the warm heart, to patience, diligence, humility, and friendliness—for these are here the most useful characteristics and almost the only means to endure the pressure of existence. Slave morality is essentially a morality of utility. Here is the focus for the origin of that famous opposition of "good" and "*evil*":—people sense power and danger within evil, a certain terror, subtlety, and strength that does not permit contempt to spring up. According to slave morality, the "evil" man thus inspires fear; according to master morality, it is precisely the "good" man who inspires and desires to inspire fear, while the "bad" man is felt as despicable. This opposition reaches its peak when, in accordance with the consequences of slave morality, finally a trace of disregard is also attached to the "good" of this morality—it may be light and benevolent—because within the way of thinking of the slave the good person must definitely be the *harmless* person: he is good natured, easy to deceive, perhaps a bit stupid, *un bonhomme* [a good fellow]. Wherever slave morality gains predominance the language reveals a tendency to bring the words "good" and "stupid" into closer proximity. A final basic difference: the longing *for freedom*, the instinct for happiness, and the refinements of the feeling for freedom belong just as necessarily to slave morality and morals as art and enthusiasm in reverence and in devotion are the regular symptoms of an aristocratic way of thinking and valuing. From this we can without further ado understand why love as *passion*—which is our European specialty—must clearly have a noble origin: as is well known, its invention belongs to the Provencal knightly poets, those splendidly inventive men of the "*gay saber*" [gay science] to whom Europe owes so much—almost its very self.

Section 261

Vanity is among the things that are perhaps hardest for a noble man to understand: he will be tempted even to deny its existence where another kind of man thinks he has grasped it with both hands. For him the problem is imagining to himself beings who seek to elicit a good opinion of themselves which they themselves do not possess—and which, as a result, they also have not "earned"—people who, nonetheless, themselves later *believe* in this good opinion. Half of this seems to the noble man so tasteless and disrespectful of oneself and the other half so unreasonably baroque, that he would be happy to understand vanity as an exception and has doubts about it in most cases when people talk of it. For example, he'll say: "I can make a mistake about my own value and yet on the other hand still demand that my value, precisely as I determine it, is recognized by others—that, however, is not vanity (but arrogance or, in the more frequent cases, something called "humility" and "modesty"). Or again, "For many reasons I can take pleasure in the good opinion of others, perhaps because I honour and love them and enjoy all of their pleasures, perhaps also because their good opinion underscores and strengthens the faith I have in my own good opinion of myself, or perhaps because the good opinion of others, even in cases where I do not share it, is still useful to me or promises to be useful—but all that is not vanity." The noble man must first compel himself, particularly with the help of history, to see that since time immemorial, in all the levels of people dependent in some way or other, the common man *was* only what people *thought of him*:—not being at all accustomed to set values himself, he measured even himself by no value other than by how his masters assessed him (that is the essential *right of masters*, to create values). We should understand that, as the consequence of an immense atavism, the common man even today still always *waits* first for an opinion about himself and then instinctively submits himself to it: however, that is by no means merely to a "good" opinion, but also to a bad and unreasonable one (think, for example, of the greatest part of the self-assessment and self-devaluing which devout women learn from their father confessors and the devout Christian in general learns from his church). Now, in accordance with the slow arrival of the democratic order of things (and its cause, the blood mixing between masters and slaves), the originally noble and rare impulse to ascribe to oneself a value on one's own and "to think well" of oneself will really become more and more encouraged and widespread. But in every moment, it has working against it an older, more extensive, and more deeply incorporated tendency—and where the phenomenon of "vanity" is concerned, this older tendency becomes master over the more recent one. The vain person takes pleasure in *every* good opinion which he hears about himself (quite apart from all considerations of its utility and equally apart from its truth or falsity), just as he suffers from every bad opinion. For he submits to both; he *feels* himself subjected to them on the basis of that oldest of instincts for submission which breaks out in him. It is "the slave" in the blood of the vain man, a trace of the slave's roguishness—and how much of the "slave" still remains nowadays in woman, for example!—that tries to *tempt* him into good opinions of himself; in the same way it's the slave who later prostrates himself immediately in front of these opinions, as if he had not summoned them up.—To state the matter once again: vanity is an atavism.

Section 262

A *species* arises, a type becomes established and strong, under the long struggle with essentially unchanging, *unfavourable* conditions. By contrast, we know from the experience of breeders that species which receive an ultra-abundant nourishment and, in general, an increase in protection and care immediately tend towards variety in the type in the strongest manner and are rich in wonders and monstrosities (as well as monstrous vices). Now, let's look at an aristocratic commonwealth—for example, an ancient Greek *polis* [city state] or Venice—as an organization, whether voluntary or involuntary, for the purpose of *breeding*. There are men there living together who rely upon one another and who want their species to succeed mainly because it *has to* succeed or run the fearful risk of being annihilated. Here there is a lack of that advantage, that excess, that protection under which variations are encouraged. The species senses the need for itself as a species, as something which, particularly thanks to its hardness, uniformity, and simplicity of form, can generally succeed and enable itself to keep going in the constant struggles with neighbours or with the rebellious oppressed people or with those who threaten rebellion. The most varied experience teaches them which characteristics they have to thank, above all, for the fact that they are still there, in spite of all the gods and men, that they have always been victorious up to this point. These characteristics they call virtues, and they cultivate only these virtues to any great extent. They do that with severity—in fact, they desire severity. Every aristocratic morality is intolerant in its education of the young, its provisions for women, its marriage customs, its relationships between young and old, and its penal laws (which fix their eyes only on those who are deviants)—it reckons intolerance itself among the virtues, under the name "justice." A type with few but very strong characteristics, a species of strict, warlike, shrewdly laconic people, close-knit and reserved (and, as such, having the most sophisticated feelings for the charm and nuances of society) in this way establishes itself over and above the changes in the generations. The constant struggle with unvarying, *unfavourable* conditions is, as mentioned, the factor that makes a type fixed and hard. Finally, however, at some point a fortunate time arises, which lets the immense tension ease. Perhaps there are no more enemies among the neighbours, and the means for living, even for enjoying life, are there in abundance. With one blow the bond and the compulsion of the old discipline are torn apart: that discipline no longer registers as necessary, as a condition of existence—if it wished to remain in existence, it could do so only as a form of *luxury*, as an archaic *taste*. Variation, whether as something abnormal (something higher, finer, and rarer) or as degeneration and monstrosity, suddenly bursts onto the scene in the greatest abundance and splendour; the individual dares to be individual and stand apart. At these historical turning points there appear alongside each other and often involved and mixed up together marvellous, multifaceted, jungle-like growths, an upward soaring, a kind of *tropical* tempo in competitiveness for growing and an immense annihilation and self-destruction, thanks to the wild egoisms turned against each other and, as it were, exploding, which wrestle with one another "for sun and light" and no longer know how to derive any limit, any restraint, or any consideration from the morality they have had up to that point. This very morality was the one which built up such immense power, which bent the bow in such a threatening manner—now, at this moment, it is and is becoming "outdated." The dangerous and disturbing point is reached where the greater, more multifaceted, and more comprehensive life *lives beyond* the old morality; the "individual" stands there, forced to give himself his own laws, his own arts and tricks for self-preservation, self-raising, and self-redemption. Nothing but new *what-for*'s, nothing but new *how-to*'s, no common formulas any more, misunderstanding and contempt bound up together, decay, spoilage, and the highest desires tied together in a ghastly way, the genius of the race brimming over from all the horns of plenty with good and bad, an ominous simultaneous presence of spring and autumn, full of new charms and veils, characteristic of young, still unexhausted, still unwearied depravity. Once again there's danger there, the mother of morality, great danger, this time transferred into the individual, into one's neighbour and friend, into the alleyways, into one's own child, into one's own heart, into all the narrowest and most secret parts of one's wishes and desires. What will the moral philosophers who emerge at such a time now have to preach? They discover, these keen observers and street loafers, that things are quickly coming to an end, that everything around them is going rotten and spreading corruption, that nothing lasts until the day after tomorrow, except for one kind of person, the incurably *mediocre*. Only the mediocre have the prospect of succeeding, of reproducing themselves—they are the people of the future, the only survivors, "Be like them! Become mediocre!"—from now on that's the only morality that still makes sense, that people still hear.—But it is difficult to preach, this morality of mediocrity!—it may never admit what it is and what it wants! It must speak about restraint and worth and duty and love of one's neighbour—it will have difficulty *concealing its irony*!

...

Section 264

One cannot erase from a human being's soul those actions which his ancestors loved most and carried out most steadfastly: whether they were, for example, industrious savers attached to a writing table and money box, modest and bourgeois in their desires, as well as modest in their virtues, or whether they were accustomed to live giving orders from morning until night, fond of harsh entertainment and, along with that, perhaps of even harsher duties and responsibilities; or whether, finally, they had at some time or other once sacrificed the old privileges of their birth and possessions in order to live entirely for their faith—for their "god"—as men of an unrelenting and delicate conscience, which blushes when confronted with any compromise. It is in no way possible that a man does *not* possess in his body the characteristics and preferences of his parents and forefathers, no matter what appearance might say to the contrary. This is the problem of race. If we know something about the parents, then we may draw a conclusion about the child: some unpleasant excess or other, some lurking envy, a crude habit of self-justification—these three together have at all times made up the essential type of the rabble—something like that must be passed onto the child as surely as corrupt blood, and with the help of the best education and culture people will succeed only in *deceiving* others about such heredity. And nowadays what else do education and culture want! In our age, one very much of the people—I mean to say our uncouth age—"education" and "culture" *must* basically be the art of deception—to mislead about the origin of the inherited rabble in one's body and soul. Today an educator who preached truthfulness above everything else and constantly shouted at his students "Be true! Be natural! Act as you really are!"—even such a virtuous and true-hearted jackass would after some time learn to take hold of that *furca* [pitchfork] of Horace,[2] in order to *naturam expellere* [drive out nature]. With what success? "Rabble" *usque recurret* [will always return].

Section 265

At the risk of annoying innocent ears, I propose the following: egoism belongs to the nature of the noble soul; I mean that unshakeable faith that to a being such as "we are" other beings must be subordinate by nature and have to sacrifice themselves. The noble soul takes this fact of its egoism without any question mark and without the feeling that there is anything harsh, compelled, or arbitrary in it, much more as something that may be established in the fundamental law of things. If he sought out a name for this, he would say "It is justice itself." In some circumstances which make him hesitate at first, he admits that there are those with rights equal to his own. As soon as he has cleared up this question of rank, he moves among these equals who have the same rights as his with the same confident modesty and sophisticated reverence which he has in his dealings with himself—in accordance with an inborn heavenly mechanism which all the stars understand. It is one *more* part of his egoism, this sophistication and self-restraint in his relations with his equals—every star is such an egoist—: his soul honours *itself* in them and in the rights which it

2 Quintus Horatius Flaccus (65–8 BCE), an important poet in classical Rome.

concedes to them. It has no doubt that the exchange of respect and rights, as the *essential quality* of all interactions, also belongs to the natural condition of things. The noble soul gives as it takes, out of the passionate and sensitive instinct for repayment, which lies deep within it. The idea "favour" has no sense and agreeable fragrance *inter pares* [among equals]; there may be a sublime manner of allowing presents from above to wash over one, as it were, and of drinking them up thirstily like water drops, but for these arts and gestures the noble soul has no skill. Here its egoism hinders it: in general, it is not happy to look "up above"—instead it looks either directly *forward*, horizontally and slowly, or down—*it knows that it is on a height.*

4.10.4 *from* Joyful Wisdom

341

The Heaviest Burden.—What if a demon crept after thee into thy loneliest loneliness some day or night, and said to thee: "This life, as thou livest it at present, and hast lived it, thou must live it once more, and also innumerable times; and there will be nothing new in it, but every pain and every joy and every thought and every sigh, and all the unspeakably small and great in thy life must come to thee again, and all in the same series and sequence—and similarly this spider and this moonlight among the trees, and similarly this moment, and I myself. The eternal sandglass of existence will ever be turned once more, and thou with it, thou speck of dust!"—Wouldst thou not throw thyself down and gnash thy teeth, and curse the demon that so spake? Or hast thou once experienced a tremendous moment in which thou wouldst answer him: "Thou art a God, and never did I hear anything so divine!" If that thought acquired power over thee as thou art, it would transform thee, and perhaps crush thee; the question with regard to all and everything: "Dost thou want this once more, and also for innumerable times?" would lie as the heaviest burden upon thy activity! Or, how wouldst thou have to become favourably inclined to thyself and to life, so as *to long for nothing more ardently* than for this last eternal sanctioning and sealing?

4.11 From *Nuremberg Laws* (1935, German Legislation)

Since the end of World War II, jurists and scholars have debated whether the Nazi regime that murdered millions of unarmed civilians possessed a properly constituted "legal system." Not all of its heinous activities were carried out in the theatre of war. In many cases, its victims were processed through courts of law that were overseen by qualified judges and in accordance with long-established practices. But there is much debate over whether the institutions and agents of the court were fulfilling an independent function that legitimized some Nazi atrocities ("legitimize" literally means "to make law"), or whether it functioned as a legal system only in appearance, that is, as a mere extension of a violent political regime. This controversy goes far beyond the scope of this text, but it is worth considering in light of the present chapter. In particular, it is worth considering in light of the theorists included elsewhere in this chapter.

The passage here is historically significant, as being one of the first steps towards the Holocaust in which millions of unarmed civilians were systematically murdered. The *Nuremberg Laws* effectively denaturalized anyone of Jewish descent, thereby depriving them of protection from the law as German citizens. From the perspective of Natural Law theory, not every act of legislation is genuine law. How might Natural law theory assess the Nuremberg laws? From the perspective of Legal Positivism, any legislation that originates from a constituted state is properly authorized. Can this theory formulate any objections to the *Nuremberg Laws*? Some of the practical consequences of the legislation presented here are considered in a chilling speech by Heinrich Himmler that encourages members of the squadrons who carried out the Holocaust (see 7.6), and Hannah Arendt speculates on the bureaucratic mindset that facilitated the atrocity (see 7.7).

Reich Citizenship Law of September 15, 1935 (Translated from *Reichsgesetzblatt* I, 1935, p. 1146)

The Reichstag has unanimously enacted the following law, which is promulgated herewith:

Article 1

1. A subject of the state is a person who enjoys the protection of the German Reich and who in consequence has specific obligations toward it.
2. The status of subject of the state is acquired in accordance with the provisions of the Reich and the Reich Citizenship Law.

Article 2

1. A Reich citizen is a subject of the state who is of German or related blood, and proves by his conduct that he is willing and fit to faithfully serve the German people and Reich.
2. Reich citizenship is acquired through the granting of a Reich citizenship certificate.
3. The Reich citizen is the sole bearer of full political rights in accordance with the law.

Article 3

The Reich Minister of the Interior, in coordination with the Deputy of the Führer, will issue the legal and administrative orders required to implement and complete this law.

Nuremberg, September 15, 1935
At the Reich Party Congress of Freedom

The Führer and Reich Chancellor
[signed] Adolf Hitler

The Reich Minister of the Interior
[signed] Frick

Law for the Protection of German Blood and German Honor of September 15, 1935 (Translated from *Reichsgesetzblatt* I, 1935, pp. 1146–47)

Moved by the understanding that purity of German blood is the essential condition for the continued existence of the German people, and inspired by the inflexible determination to ensure the existence of the German nation for all time, the Reichstag has unanimously adopted the following law, which is promulgated herewith:

Article 1

1. Marriages between Jews and subjects of the state of German or related blood are forbidden. Marriages nevertheless concluded are invalid, even if concluded abroad to circumvent this law.
2. Annulment proceedings can be initiated only by the state prosecutor.

Article 2

Extramarital relations between Jews and subjects of the state of German or related blood are forbidden.

Article 3

Jews may not employ in their households female subjects of the state of German or related blood who are under 45 years old.

Article 4

1. Jews are forbidden to fly the Reich or national flag or display Reich colors.
2. They are, on the other hand, permitted to display the Jewish colors. The exercise of this right is protected by the state.

Article 5

1. Any person who violates the prohibition under Article 1 will be punished with a prison sentence.
2. A male who violates the prohibition under Article 2 will be punished with a jail term or a prison sentence.
3. Any person violating the provisions under Articles 3 or 4 will be punished with a jail term of up to one year and a fine, or with one or the other of these penalties.

Article 6

The Reich Minister of the Interior, in coordination with the Deputy of the Führer and the Reich Minister of Justice, will issue the legal and administrative regulations required to implement and complete this law.

Article 7

The law takes effect on the day following promulgation, except for Article 3, which goes into force on January 1, 1936.

Nuremberg, September 15, 1935
At the Reich Party Congress of Freedom

The Führer and Reich Chancellor
[signed] Adolf Hitler

The Reich Minster of the Interior
[signed] Frick

The Reich Minister of Justice
[signed] Dr. Gürtner

The Deputy of the Führer
[signed] R. Hess

4.12 From *UN Declaration of Human Rights* (1948, United Nations Proclamation)

The United Nations was formed in the aftermath of World War II. One of its functions is to set international rules for the conduct of states. Ordinarily authority and enforcement of a law is the function of a sovereign state; sovereignty of the state empowers it to enforce laws. The United Nations does not have any kind of sovereignty over nations, but member nations bind themselves to some basic principles. One of the signature documents of the United Nations is the *Declaration of Human Rights*, most of which is included here.

~

Preamble

Whereas recognition of the inherent dignity and of the equal and inalienable rights of all members of the human family is the foundation of freedom, justice and peace in the world,

Whereas disregard and contempt for human rights have resulted in barbarous acts which have outraged the conscience of mankind, and the advent of a world in which human beings shall enjoy freedom of speech and belief and freedom from fear and want has been proclaimed as the highest aspiration of the common people,

Whereas it is essential, if man is not to be compelled to have recourse, as a last resort, to rebellion against tyranny and oppression, that human rights should be protected by the rule of law,

Whereas it is essential to promote the development of friendly relations between nations,

Whereas the peoples of the United Nations have in the Charter reaffirmed their faith in fundamental human rights, in the dignity and worth of the human person and in the equal rights of men and women and have determined to promote social progress and better standards of life in larger freedom,

Whereas Member States have pledged themselves to achieve, in co-operation with the United Nations, the promotion of universal respect for and observance of human rights and fundamental freedoms,

Whereas a common understanding of these rights and freedoms is of the greatest importance for the full realization of this pledge,

Now, Therefore THE GENERAL ASSEMBLY proclaims THIS UNIVERSAL DECLARATION OF HUMAN RIGHTS as a common standard of achievement for all peoples and all nations, to the end that every individual and every organ of society, keeping this Declaration constantly in mind, shall strive by teaching and education to promote respect for these rights and freedoms and by progressive measures, national and international, to secure their universal and effective recognition and observance, both among the peoples of Member States themselves and among the peoples of territories under their jurisdiction.

Article 1

All human beings are born free and equal in dignity and rights. They are endowed with reason and conscience and should act towards one another in a spirit of brotherhood.

Article 2

Everyone is entitled to all the rights and freedoms set forth in this Declaration, without distinction of any kind, such as race, colour, sex, language, religion, political or other opinion, national or social origin, property, birth or other status. Furthermore, no distinction shall be made on the basis of the political, jurisdictional or international status of the country or territory to which a person belongs, whether it be independent, trust, non-self-governing or under any other limitation of sovereignty.

Article 3

Everyone has the right to life, liberty and security of person.

Article 4

No one shall be held in slavery or servitude; slavery and the slave trade shall be prohibited in all their forms.

Article 5

No one shall be subjected to torture or to cruel, inhuman or degrading treatment or punishment.

Article 6

Everyone has the right to recognition everywhere as a person before the law.

Article 7

All are equal before the law and are entitled without any discrimination to equal protection of the law. All are entitled to equal protection against any discrimination in violation of this Declaration and against any incitement to such discrimination.

Article 8

Everyone has the right to an effective remedy by the competent national tribunals for acts violating the fundamental rights granted him by the constitution or by law.

Article 9

No one shall be subjected to arbitrary arrest, detention or exile.

Article 10

Everyone is entitled in full equality to a fair and public hearing by an independent and impartial tribunal, in the determination of his rights and obligations and of any criminal charge against him.

Article 11

(1) Everyone charged with a penal offence has the right to be presumed innocent until proved guilty according to law in a public trial at which he has had all the guarantees necessary for his defence.

(2) No one shall be held guilty of any penal offence on account of any act or omission which did not constitute a penal offence, under national or international law, at the time when it was committed. Nor shall a heavier penalty be imposed than the one that was applicable at the time the penal offence was committed.

Article 12

No one shall be subjected to arbitrary interference with his privacy, family, home or correspondence, nor to attacks upon his honour and reputation. Everyone has the right to the protection of the law against such interference or attacks.

Article 13

(1) Everyone has the right to freedom of movement and residence within the borders of each state.

(2) Everyone has the right to leave any country, including his own, and to return to his country.

Article 14

(1) Everyone has the right to seek and to enjoy in other countries asylum from persecution.

(2) This right may not be invoked in the case of prosecutions genuinely arising from non-political crimes or from acts contrary to the purposes and principles of the United Nations.

Article 15

(1) Everyone has the right to a nationality.

(2) No one shall be arbitrarily deprived of his nationality nor denied the right to change his nationality.

Article 16

(1) Men and women of full age, without any limitation due to race, nationality or religion, have the right to marry and to found a family. They are entitled to equal rights as to marriage, during marriage and at its dissolution.

(2) Marriage shall be entered into only with the free and full consent of the intending spouses.

(3) The family is the natural and fundamental group unit of society and is entitled to protection by society and the State.

Article 17

(1) Everyone has the right to own property alone as well as in association with others.

(2) No one shall be arbitrarily deprived of his property.

Article 18

Everyone has the right to freedom of thought, conscience and religion; this right includes freedom to change his religion or belief, and freedom, either alone or in community with others and in public or private, to manifest his religion or belief in teaching, practice, worship and observance.

Article 19

Everyone has the right to freedom of opinion and expression; this right includes freedom to hold opinions without interference and to seek, receive and impart information and ideas through any media and regardless of frontiers.

Article 20

(1) Everyone has the right to freedom of peaceful assembly and association.

(2) No one may be compelled to belong to an association.

Article 21

(1) Everyone has the right to take part in the government of his country, directly or through freely chosen representatives.

(2) Everyone has the right of equal access to public service in his country.

(3) The will of the people shall be the basis of the authority of government; this will shall be expressed in periodic and genuine elections which shall be by universal and equal suffrage and shall be held by secret vote or by equivalent free voting procedures.

Article 22

Everyone, as a member of society, has the right to social security and is entitled to realization, through national effort and international co-operation and in accordance with the organization and resources of each State, of the economic, social and cultural rights indispensable for his dignity and the free development of his personality.

Article 23

(1) Everyone has the right to work, to free choice of employment, to just and favourable conditions of work and to protection against unemployment.

(2) Everyone, without any discrimination, has the right to equal pay for equal work.

(3) Everyone who works has the right to just and favourable remuneration ensuring for himself and his family an existence worthy of human dignity, and supplemented, if necessary, by other means of social protection.

(4) Everyone has the right to form and to join trade unions for the protection of his interests.

Article 24

Everyone has the right to rest and leisure, including reasonable limitation of working hours and periodic holidays with pay.

Article 25

(1) Everyone has the right to a standard of living adequate for the health and well-being of himself and of his family, including food, clothing, housing and medical care and necessary social services, and the right to security in the event of unemployment, sickness, disability, widowhood, old age or other lack of livelihood in circumstances beyond his control.

(2) Motherhood and childhood are entitled to special care and assistance. All children, whether born in or out of wedlock, shall enjoy the same social protection.

Article 26

(1) Everyone has the right to education. Education shall be free, at least in the elementary and fundamental stages. Elementary education shall be compulsory. Technical and professional education shall be made generally available and higher education shall be equally accessible to all on the basis of merit.

(2) Education shall be directed to the full development of the human personality and to the strengthening of respect for human rights and fundamental freedoms. It shall promote understanding, tolerance and friendship among all nations, racial or religious groups, and shall further the activities of the United Nations for the maintenance of peace.

(3) Parents have a prior right to choose the kind of education that shall be given to their children.

Article 27

(1) Everyone has the right freely to participate in the cultural life of the community, to enjoy the arts and to share in scientific advancement and its benefits.

(2) Everyone has the right to the protection of the moral and material interests resulting from any scientific, literary or artistic production of which he is the author.

Article 28

Everyone is entitled to a social and international order in which the rights and freedoms set forth in this Declaration can be fully realized.

Article 29

(1) Everyone has duties to the community in which alone the free and full development of his personality is possible.

(2) In the exercise of his rights and freedoms, everyone shall be subject only to such limitations as are determined by law solely for the purpose of securing due recognition and respect for the rights and freedoms of others and of meeting the just requirements of morality, public order and the general welfare in a democratic society.

(3) These rights and freedoms may in no case be exercised contrary to the purposes and principles of the United Nations.

Article 30

Nothing in this Declaration may be interpreted as implying for any State, group or person any right to engage in any activity or to perform any act aimed at the destruction of any of the rights and freedoms set forth herein.

4.13 Martin Luther King Jr. (1929–1968)

"Civil disobedience" was one tactic used by anti-segregationists in the American civil rights movement of the 1960s, the movement with which Dr. King is associated. His open letter from a Birmingham, Alabama jail cell to other participants in this movement attempts to justify his own controversial use of civil disobedience. The tactic itself is simple: a citizen who objects to a particular law openly violates it in order to compel its enforcement. No attempt is made to evade detection or capture; quite the contrary, getting arrested and charged is essential for its purpose, so these are atypical examples of illegality. Theoretically, a law is violated in this case, but not the rule of law because the person accepts the legal consequences without resistance.

The expression "civil disobedience" was coined by Henry David Thoreau in an essay with that title in 1849. Traditionally, disobeying a law has been be characterized as "uncivilized" or "uncivil" because the legal system and the rules associated with it are considered to have a civilizing influence upon society. *Civil* disobedience is, therefore, almost an oxymoron, since those who use the tactic claim as their purpose the improvement of civility, not a disregard for it. The underlying rationale for civil disobedience derives from the Natural Law principle that positive laws do not necessarily bind a person's conscience. Conceivably, a person may justifiably not feel bound to obey a law if it violates a principle of moral conscience. Moreover, as King argues, by means of civil disobedience a citizen can expose to view a particular unjust law in what is otherwise considered to be a just system of law. Once exposed, the law can no longer serve as an invisible force of compulsion among the citizens. After being so exposed, legislators and legal officials must address the alleged wrongness of the law and its enforcement.

from "Letter from the Birmingham City Jail"

AUGUST 1963

Letter from Birmingham Jail

While confined here in the Birmingham city jail, I came across your recent statement calling our present activities "unwise and untimely." Seldom, if ever, do I pause to answer criticism of my work and ideas. If I sought to answer all of the criticisms that cross my desk, my secretaries would be engaged in little else in the course of the day, and I would have no time for constructive work. But since I feel that you are men of genuine good will and your criticisms are sincerely set forth, I would like to answer your statement in what I hope will be patient and reasonable terms.

I think I should give the reason for my being in Birmingham, since you have been influenced by the argument of "outsiders coming in." I have the honor of serving as president of the Southern Christian Leadership Conference, an organization operating in every Southern state, with headquarters in Atlanta, Georgia. We have some eighty-five affiliate organizations all across the South, one being the Alabama Christian Movement for Human Rights. Whenever necessary and possible, we share staff, educational and financial resources with our affiliates. Several months ago our local affiliate here in Birmingham invited us to be on call to engage in a nonviolent direct-action program if such were deemed necessary. We readily consented, and when the hour came we lived up to our promises. So I am here, along with several members of my staff, because we were invited here. I am here because I have basic organizational ties here.

Beyond this, I am in Birmingham because injustice is here. Just as the eighth-century prophets left their little villages and carried their "thus saith the Lord" far beyond the boundaries of their hometowns; and just as the Apostle Paul left his little village of Tarsus and carried the gospel of Jesus Christ to practically every hamlet and city of the Greco-Roman world, I too am compelled to carry the gospel of freedom beyond my particular hometown. Like Paul, I must constantly respond to the Macedonian call for aid.

Moreover, I am cognizant of the interrelatedness of all communities and states. I cannot sit idly by in Atlanta and not be concerned about what happens in Birmingham. Injustice anywhere is a threat to justice everywhere. We are caught in an inescapable network of mutuality, tied in a single garment of destiny. Whatever affects one directly affects all indirectly. Never again can we afford to live with the narrow, provincial "outside agitator" idea. Anyone who lives inside the United States can never be considered an outsider.

You deplore the demonstrations that are presently taking place in Birmingham. But I am sorry that your statement did not express a similar concern for the conditions that brought the demonstrations into being. I am sure that each of you would want to go beyond the superficial social analyst who looks merely at effects and does not grapple with underlying causes. I would not hesitate to say that it is unfortunate that so-called demonstrations are taking place in Birmingham at this time, but I would say in more emphatic terms that it is even more unfortunate that the white power structure of this city left the Negro community with no other alternative.

In any nonviolent campaign there are four basic steps: collection of the facts to determine whether injustices are alive, negotiation, self-purification, and direct action. We have gone through all of these steps in Birmingham. There can be no gainsaying of the fact that racial injustice engulfs this community. Birmingham is probably the most thoroughly segregated city in the United States. Its ugly record of police brutality is known in every section of this country. Its unjust treatment of Negroes in the courts is a notorious reality. There have been more unsolved bombings of Negro homes and churches in Birmingham than in any other city in this nation. These are the hard, brutal, and unbelievable facts. On the basis of them, Negro leaders sought to negotiate with the city fathers. But the political leaders consistently refused to engage in good-faith negotiation.

Then came the opportunity last September to talk with some of the leaders of the economic community. In these negotiating sessions certain promises were made by the merchants, such as the promise to remove the humiliating racial signs from the stores. On the basis of these promises, Reverend Shuttlesworth and the leaders of the Alabama Christian Movement for Human Rights agreed to call a moratorium on any type of demonstration. As the weeks and months unfolded, we realized that we were the victims of a broken promise. The signs remained. As in so many experiences of the past, we were confronted with blasted hopes, and the dark shadow of a deep disappointment settled upon us. So we had no alternative except that of preparing for direct action, whereby we would present our very bodies as a means of laying our case before the conscience of the local and national community. We were not unmindful of the difficulties involved. So we decided to go through a process of self-purification. We started having workshops on nonviolence and repeatedly asked ourselves the questions, "Are you able to accept blows without retaliating?" and "Are you able to endure the ordeals of jail?" We decided to set our direct-action program around the Easter season, realizing that, with exception of Christmas, this was the largest shopping period of the year. Knowing that a strong economic withdrawal program would be the by-product of direct action, we felt that this was the best time to bring pressure on the merchants for the needed changes. Then it occurred to us that the March election was ahead, and so we speedily decided to postpone action until after election day. When we discovered that Mr. Conner was in the runoff, we decided again to postpone action so that the demonstration could not be used to cloud the issues. At this time we agreed to begin our nonviolent witness the day after the runoff.

This reveals that we did not move irresponsibly into direct action. We, too, wanted to see Mr. Conner defeated, so we went through postponement after postponement to aid in this community need. After this we felt that direct action could be delayed no longer.

You may well ask, "Why direct action, why sit-ins, marches, and so forth? Isn't negotiation a better path?" You are exactly right in your call for negotiation. Indeed, this is the purpose of direct action. Nonviolent direct action seeks to create such a crisis and establish such creative tension that a community that has consistently refused to negotiate is forced to confront the issue. It seeks so to dramatize the issue that it can no longer be ignored. I just referred to the creation of tension as a part of the work of the nonviolent resister. This may sound rather shocking. But I must confess that I am not afraid of the word "tension." I have earnestly worked and preached against violent tension, but there is a type of constructive nonviolent tension that is necessary for growth. Just as Socrates felt that it was necessary to create a tension in the mind so that individuals could rise from the bondage of myths and half-truths to the unfettered realm of creative analysis and objective appraisal, we must see the need of having nonviolent gadflies to create the kind of tension in society that will help men to rise from the dark depths of prejudice and racism to the majestic heights of understanding and brotherhood. So, the purpose of direct action is to create a situation so crisis-packed that it will inevitably open the door to negotiation. We therefore concur with you in your call for negotiation. Too long has our beloved Southland been bogged down in the tragic attempt to live in monologue rather than dialogue.

One of the basic points in your statement is that our acts are untimely. Some have asked, "Why didn't you give the new administration time to act?" The only answer that I can give to this inquiry is that the new administration must be prodded about as much as the outgoing one before it acts. We will be sadly mistaken if we feel that the election of Mr. Boutwell will bring the millennium to Birmingham. While Mr. Boutwell is much more articulate and gentle than Mr. Conner, they are both segregationists, dedicated to the task of maintaining the status quo. The hope I see in Mr. Boutwell is that he will be reasonable enough to see the futility of massive resistance to desegregation. But he will not see this without pressure from the devotees of civil rights. My friends, I must say to you that we have not made a single gain in civil rights without determined legal and nonviolent pressure. History is the long and tragic story of the fact that privileged groups seldom give up their privileges voluntarily. Individuals may see the moral light and voluntarily give up their unjust posture; but, as Reinhold Niebuhr has reminded us, groups are more immoral than individuals.

We know through painful experience that freedom is never voluntarily given by the oppressor; it must be demanded by the oppressed. Frankly, I have never yet engaged in a direct-action movement that was "well timed" according to the timetable of those who have not suffered unduly from the disease of segregation. For years now I have heard the word "wait." It rings in the ear of every Negro with a piercing familiarity. This "wait" has almost always meant "never." It has been a tranquilizing thalidomide, relieving the emotional stress for a moment, only to give birth to an ill-formed infant of frustration. We must come to see with the distinguished jurist of yesterday that "justice too long delayed is justice denied." We have waited for more than three hundred and forty years for our God-given and constitutional rights. The nations of Asia and Africa are moving with jetlike speed toward the goal of political independence, and we still creep at horse-and-buggy pace toward the gaining of a cup of coffee at a lunch counter. I guess it is easy for those who have never felt the stinging darts of segregation to say "wait." But when you have seen vicious mobs lynch your mothers and fathers at will and drown your sisters and brothers at whim; when you have seen hate-filled policemen curse, kick, brutalize, and even kill your black brothers and sisters with impunity; when you see the vast majority of your twenty million Negro brothers smothering in an airtight cage of poverty in the midst of an affluent society; when you suddenly find your tongue twisted and your speech stammering as you seek to explain to your six-year-old daughter why she cannot go to the public amusement park that has just been advertised on television, and see tears welling up in her little eyes when she is told that Funtown is closed to colored children, and see the depressing clouds of inferiority begin to form in her little mental sky, and see her begin to distort her little personality by unconsciously developing a bitterness toward white people; when you have to concoct an answer for a five-year-old son asking in agonizing pathos, "Daddy, why do white people treat colored people so mean?"; when you take a cross-country drive and find it necessary to sleep night after night in the uncomfortable corners of your automobile because no motel will accept you; when you are humiliated day in and day out by nagging signs reading "white" and "colored"; when your first name becomes "nigger" and your middle name becomes "boy" (however old you are) and your last name becomes "John," and when your wife and mother are never given the respected title "Mrs."; when you are harried by day and haunted by night by the fact that you are a Negro, living constantly at tiptoe stance, never knowing what to expect next, and plagued with inner fears and outer resentments; when you are forever fighting a degenerating sense of "nobodyness"—then you will understand why we find it difficult to wait. There comes a time when the cup of endurance runs over and men are no longer willing to be plunged into an abyss of injustice where they experience the bleakness of corroding despair. I hope, sirs, you can understand our legitimate and unavoidable impatience.

You express a great deal of anxiety over our willingness to break laws. This is certainly a legitimate concern. Since we so diligently urge people to obey the Supreme Court's decision of 1954 outlawing segregation in the public schools, it is rather strange and paradoxical to find us consciously breaking laws. One may well ask, "How can you advocate breaking some laws and obeying others?" The answer is found in the fact that there are two types of laws: there are just laws, and there are unjust laws. I would agree with St. Augustine that "An unjust law is no law at all."

Now, what is the difference between the two? How does one determine when a law is just or unjust? A just law is a man-made code that squares with the moral law, or the law of God. An unjust law is a code that is out of harmony with the moral law. To put it in the terms of St. Thomas Aquinas, an unjust law is a human law that is not rooted in eternal and natural law. Any law that uplifts human personality is just. Any law that degrades human personality is unjust. All segregation statutes are unjust because segregation distorts the soul and damages the personality. It gives the segregator a false sense of superiority and the segregated a false sense of inferiority. To use the words of Martin Buber, the great Jewish philosopher, segregation substitutes an "I–it" relationship for the "I–thou" relationship and ends up relegating persons to the status of things. So segregation is not only politically, economically, and sociologically unsound, but it is morally wrong and sinful. Paul Tillich has said that sin is separation. Isn't segregation an existential expression of man's tragic separation, an expression of his awful estrangement, his terrible sinfulness? So I can urge men to obey the 1954 decision of the Supreme Court because it is morally right, and I can urge them to disobey segregation ordinances because they are morally wrong.

Let us turn to a more concrete example of just and unjust laws. An unjust law is a code that a majority inflicts on a minority that is not binding on itself. This is difference made legal. On the other hand, a just law is a code that a majority compels a minority to follow, and that it is willing to follow itself. This is sameness made legal.

Let me give another explanation. An unjust law is a code inflicted upon a minority which that minority had no part in enacting or creating because it did not have the unhampered right to vote. Who can say that the legislature of Alabama which set up the segregation laws was democratically elected? Throughout the state of Alabama all types of conniving methods are used to prevent Negroes from becoming registered voters, and there are some counties without a single Negro registered to vote, despite the fact that the Negroes constitute a majority of the population. Can any law set up in such a state be considered democratically structured?

These are just a few examples of unjust and just laws. There are some instances when a law is just on its face and unjust in its application. For instance, I was arrested Friday on a charge of parading without a permit. Now, there is nothing wrong with an ordinance which requires a permit for a parade, but when the ordinance is used to preserve segregation and to deny citizens the First Amendment privilege of peaceful assembly and peaceful protest, then it becomes unjust.

Of course, there is nothing new about this kind of civil disobedience. It was seen sublimely in the refusal of Shadrach, Meshach, and Abednego to obey the laws of Nebuchadnezzar because a higher moral law was involved. It was practiced superbly by the early Christians, who were willing to face hungry lions and the excruciating pain of chopping blocks before submitting to certain unjust laws of the Roman Empire. To a degree, academic freedom is a reality today because Socrates practiced civil disobedience.

We can never forget that everything Hitler did in Germany was "legal" and everything the Hungarian freedom fighters did in Hungary was "illegal." It was "illegal" to aid and comfort a Jew in Hitler's Germany.

But I am sure that if I had lived in Germany during that time, I would have aided and comforted my Jewish brothers even though it was illegal. If I lived in a Communist country today where certain principles dear to the Christian faith are suppressed, I believe I would openly advocate disobeying these anti-religious laws.

I must make two honest confessions to you, my Christian and Jewish brothers. First, I must confess that over the last few years I have been gravely disappointed with the white moderate. I have almost reached the regrettable conclusion that the Negro's great stumbling block in the stride toward freedom is not the White Citizens Councillor or the Ku Klux Klanner but the white moderate who is more devoted to order than to justice; who prefers a negative peace which is the absence of tension to a positive peace which is the presence of justice; who constantly says, "I agree with you in the goal you seek, but I can't agree with your methods of direct action"; who paternalistically feels that he can set the timetable for another man's freedom; who lives by the myth of time; and who constantly advises the Negro to wait until a "more convenient season." Shallow understanding from people of good will is more frustrating than absolute misunderstanding from people of ill will. Lukewarm acceptance is much more bewildering than outright rejection.

In your statement you asserted that our actions, even though peaceful, must be condemned because they precipitate violence. But can this assertion be logically made? Isn't this like condemning the robbed man because his possession of money precipitated the evil act of robbery? Isn't this like condemning Socrates because his unswerving commitment to truth and his philosophical delvings precipitated the misguided popular mind to make him drink the hemlock? Isn't this like condemning Jesus because His unique God-consciousness and never-ceasing devotion to His will precipitated the evil act of crucifixion? We must come to see, as federal courts have consistently affirmed, that it is immoral to urge an individual to withdraw his efforts to gain his basic constitutional rights because the quest precipitates violence. Society must protect the robbed and punish the robber.

I had also hoped that the white moderate would reject the myth of time. I received a letter this morning from a white brother in Texas which said, "All Christians know that the colored people will receive equal rights eventually, but is it possible that you are in too great of a religious hurry? It has taken Christianity almost 2000 years to accomplish what it has. The teachings of Christ take time to come to earth." All that is said here grows out of a tragic misconception of time. It is the strangely irrational notion that there is something in the very flow of time that will inevitably cure all ills. Actually, time is neutral. It can be used either destructively or constructively. I am coming to feel that the people of ill will have used time much more effectively than the people of good will. We will have to repent in this generation not merely for the vitriolic words and actions of the bad people but for the appalling silence of the good people. We must come to see that human progress never rolls in on wheels of inevitability. It comes through the tireless efforts and persistent work of men willing to be coworkers with God, and without this hard work time itself becomes an ally of the forces of social stagnation.

You spoke of our activity in Birmingham as extreme. At first I was rather disappointed that fellow clergymen would see my nonviolent efforts as those of an extremist. I started thinking about the fact that I stand in the middle of two opposing forces in the Negro community. One is a force of complacency made up of Negroes who, as a result of long years of oppression, have been so completely drained of self-respect and a sense of "somebodyness" that they have adjusted to segregation, and, on the other hand, of a few Negroes in the middle class who, because of a degree of academic and economic security and because at points they profit by segregation, have unconsciously become insensitive to the problems of the masses. The other force is one of bitterness and hatred and comes perilously close to advocating violence. It is expressed in the various black nationalist groups that are springing up over the nation, the largest and best known being Elijah Muhammad's Muslim movement. This movement is nourished by the contemporary frustration over the continued existence of racial discrimination. It is made up of people who have lost faith in America, who have absolutely repudiated Christianity, and who have concluded that the white man is an incurable devil. I have tried to stand between these two forces, saying that we need not follow the do-nothingism of the complacent or the hatred and despair of the black nationalist. There is a more excellent way, of love and nonviolent protest. I'm grateful to God that, through the Negro church, the dimension of nonviolence entered our struggle. If this philosophy had not emerged, I am convinced that by now many streets of the South would be flowing with floods of blood. And I am further convinced that if our white brothers dismiss as "rabble-rousers" and "outside agitators" those of us who are working through the channels of nonviolent direct action and refuse to support our nonviolent efforts, millions of Negroes, out of frustration and despair, will seek solace and security in black nationalist ideologies, a development that will lead inevitably to a frightening racial nightmare.

Oppressed people cannot remain oppressed forever. The urge for freedom will eventually come. This is what has happened to the American Negro. Something within has reminded him of his birthright of freedom; something without has reminded him that he can gain it. Consciously and unconsciously, he has been swept in by what the Germans call the *Zeitgeist*, and with his black brothers of Africa and his brown and yellow brothers of Asia, South America, and the Caribbean, he is moving with a sense of cosmic urgency toward the promised land of racial justice. Recognizing this vital urge that has engulfed the Negro community, one should readily understand public demonstrations. The Negro has many pent-up resentments and latent frustrations. He has to get them out. So let him march sometime; let him have his prayer pilgrimages to the city hall; understand why he must have sit-ins and freedom rides. If his repressed emotions do not come out in these nonviolent ways, they will come out in ominous expressions of violence. This is not a threat; it is a fact of history. So I have not said to my people, "Get rid of your discontent." But I have tried to say that this normal and healthy discontent can be channeled through the creative outlet of nonviolent direct action. Now this approach is being dismissed as extremist. I must admit that I was initially disappointed in being so categorized.

But as I continued to think about the matter, I gradually gained a bit of satisfaction from being considered an extremist. Was not Jesus an extremist in love?—"Love your enemies, bless them that curse you, pray for them that despitefully use you." Was not Amos an extremist for justice?—"Let justice roll down like waters and righteousness like a mighty stream." Was not Paul an extremist for the gospel of Jesus Christ?—"I bear in my body the marks of the Lord Jesus." Was not Martin Luther an extremist?—"Here I stand; I can do no other so help me God." Was not John Bunyan an extremist?—"I will stay in jail to the end of my days before I make a mockery of my conscience." Was not Abraham Lincoln an extremist?—"This nation cannot survive half slave and half free." Was not Thomas Jefferson an extremist?—"We hold these truths to be self-evident, that all men are created equal." So the question is not whether we will be extremist, but what kind of extremists we will be. Will we be extremists for hate, or will we be extremists for love? Will we be extremists for the preservation of injustice, or will we be extremists for the cause of justice?

I had hoped that the white moderate would see this. Maybe I was too optimistic. Maybe I expected too much. I guess I should have realized that few members of a race that has oppressed another race can understand or appreciate the deep groans and passionate yearnings of those that have been oppressed, and still fewer have the vision to see that injustice must be rooted out by strong, persistent, and determined action. I am thankful, however, that some of our white brothers have grasped the meaning of this social revolution and committed themselves to it. They are still all too small in quantity, but they are big in quality. Some, like Ralph McGill, Lillian Smith, Harry Golden, and James Dabbs, have written about our struggle in eloquent, prophetic, and understanding terms. Others have marched with us down nameless streets of the South. They sat in with us at lunch counters and rode in with us on the freedom rides. They have languished in filthy roach-infested jails, suffering the abuse and brutality of angry policemen who see them as "dirty nigger lovers." They, unlike many of their moderate brothers, have recognized the urgency of the moment and sensed the need for powerful "action" antidotes to combat the disease of segregation.

Let me rush on to mention my other disappointment. I have been disappointed with the white church and its leadership. Of course, there are some notable exceptions. I am not unmindful of the fact that each of you has taken some significant stands on this issue. I commend you, Reverend Stallings, for your Christian stand this past Sunday in welcoming Negroes to your Baptist Church worship service on a nonsegregated basis. I commend the Catholic leaders of this state for integrating Springhill College several years ago.

But despite these notable exceptions, I must honestly reiterate that I have been disappointed with the church. I do not say that as one of those negative critics who can always find something wrong with the church. I say it as a minister of the gospel who loves the church, who was nurtured in its bosom, who has been sustained by its Spiritual blessings, and who will remain true to it as long as the cord of life shall lengthen.

I had the strange feeling when I was suddenly catapulted into the leadership of the bus protest in Montgomery several years ago that we would have the support of the white church. I felt that the white ministers, priests, and rabbis of the South would be some of our strongest allies. Instead, some few have been outright opponents, refusing to understand the freedom movement and misrepresenting its leaders; all too many others have been more cautious than courageous and have remained silent behind the anesthetizing security of stained-glass windows.

In spite of my shattered dreams of the past, I came to Birmingham with the hope that the white religious leadership of this community would see the justice of our cause and with deep moral concern serve as the channel through which our just grievances could get to the power structure. I had hoped that each of you would understand. But again I have been disappointed.

I have heard numerous religious leaders of the South call upon their worshipers to comply with a desegregation decision because it is the law, but I have longed to hear white ministers say, follow this decree because integration is morally right and the Negro is your brother. In the midst of blatant injustices inflicted upon the Negro, I have watched white churches stand on the sidelines and merely mouth pious irrelevancies and sanctimonious trivialities. In the midst of a mighty struggle to rid our nation of racial and economic injustice, I have heard so many ministers say, "Those are social issues which the gospel has nothing to do with," and I have watched so many churches commit themselves to a completely otherworldly religion which made a strange distinction between bodies and souls, the sacred and the secular.

There was a time when the church was very powerful. It was during that period that the early Christians rejoiced when they were deemed worthy to suffer for what they believed. In those days the church was not merely a thermometer that recorded the ideas and principles of popular opinion; it was the thermostat that transformed the mores of society. Wherever the early Christians entered a town the power structure got disturbed and immediately sought to convict them for being "disturbers of the peace" and "outside agitators." But they went on with the conviction that they were "a colony of heaven" and had to obey God rather than man. They were small in number but big in commitment. They were too God-intoxicated to be "astronomically intimidated." They brought an end to such ancient evils as infanticide and gladiatorial contest.

Things are different now. The contemporary church is so often a weak, ineffectual voice with an uncertain sound. It is so often the arch supporter of the status quo. Far from being disturbed by the presence of the church, the power structure of the average community is consoled by the church's often vocal sanction of things as they are.

But the judgment of God is upon the church as never before. If the church of today does not recapture the sacrificial spirit of the early church, it will lose its authentic ring, forfeit the loyalty of millions, and be dismissed as an irrelevant social club with no meaning for the twentieth century. I meet young people every day whose disappointment with the church has risen to outright disgust.

I hope the church as a whole will meet the challenge of this decisive hour. But even if the church does not come to the aid of justice, I have no despair about the future. I have no fear about the outcome of our struggle in Birmingham, even if our motives are presently misunderstood. We will reach the goal of freedom in Birmingham and all over the nation, because the goal of America is freedom. Abused and scorned though we may be, our destiny is tied up with the destiny of America. Before the Pilgrims landed at Plymouth, we were here. Before the pen of Jefferson scratched across the pages of history the majestic words of the Declaration of Independence, we were here. For more than two centuries our foreparents labored here without wages; they made cotton king; and they built the homes of their masters in the midst of brutal injustice and shameful humiliation—and yet out of a bottomless vitality our people continue to thrive and develop. If the inexpressible cruelties of slavery could not stop us, the opposition we now face will surely fail. We will win our freedom because the sacred heritage of our nation and the eternal will of God are embodied in our echoing demands.

I must close now. But before closing I am impelled to mention one other point in your statement that troubled me profoundly. You warmly commended the Birmingham police force for keeping "order" and "preventing violence." I don't believe you would have so warmly commended the police force if you had seen its angry violent dogs literally biting six unarmed, nonviolent Negroes. I don't believe you would so quickly commend the policemen if you would observe their ugly and inhuman treatment of Negroes here in the city jail; if you would watch them push and curse old Negro women and young Negro girls; if you would see them slap and kick old Negro men and young boys, if you would observe them, as they did on two occasions, refusing to give us food because we wanted to sing our grace together. I'm sorry that I can't join you in your praise for the police department.

It is true that they have been rather disciplined in their public handling of the demonstrators. In this sense they have been publicly "nonviolent." But for what purpose? To preserve the evil system of segregation. Over the last few years I have consistently preached that nonviolence demands that the means we use must be as pure as the ends we seek. So I have tried to make it clear that it is wrong to use immoral means to attain moral ends. But now I must affirm that it is just as wrong, or even more, to use moral means to preserve immoral ends.

I wish you had commended the Negro demonstrators of Birmingham for their sublime courage, their willingness to suffer, and their amazing discipline in the midst of the most inhuman provocation. One day the South will recognize its real heroes. They will be the James Merediths, courageously and with a majestic sense of purpose facing jeering and hostile mobs and the agonizing loneliness that characterizes the life of the pioneer. They will be old, oppressed, battered Negro women, symbolized in a seventy-two-year-old woman of Montgomery, Alabama, who rose up with a sense of dignity and with her people decided not to ride the segregated buses, and responded to one who inquired about her tiredness with ungrammatical profundity, "My feets is tired, but my soul is rested." They will be young high school and college students, young ministers of the gospel and a host of their elders courageously and nonviolently sitting in at lunch counters and willingly going to jail for conscience's sake. One day the South will know that when these disinherited children of God sat down at lunch counters they were in reality standing up for the best in the American dream and the most sacred values in our Judeo-Christian heritage.

Never before have I written a letter this long—or should I say a book? I'm afraid that it is much too long to take your precious time. I can assure you that it would have been much shorter if I had been writing from a comfortable desk, but what else is there to do when you are alone for days in the dull monotony of a narrow jail cell other than write long letters, think strange thoughts, and pray long prayers?

If I have said anything in this letter that is an understatement of the truth and is indicative of an unreasonable impatience, I beg you to forgive me. If I have said anything in this letter that is an overstatement of the truth and is indicative of my having a patience that makes me patient with anything less than brotherhood, I beg God to forgive me.

Yours for the cause of Peace and Brotherhood,

MARTIN LUTHER KING, JR.

4.14 Review Questions

1. Assess Socrates's argument about his duty to obey Athenian law in light of the theoretical arguments formulated by Aquinas (Natural Law), Hobbes (Positivism), or Montesquieu (Legalism).

2. In light of what Thomas Aquinas and Thomas Hobbes say about the obligations of someone condemned to capital punishment, how would they respond to Socrates's arguments in the *Crito* (1.2.4) about his own position?

3. Which strategy provides the best approach to defining "law"? Is it best conceived of as positive law, as convention (or custom or social norm), or as an application of moral principle?

4. How might each of the three theoretical perspectives assess the *Nuremberg Laws*?

5. How might each of the three theoretical perspectives assess the *UN Declaration of Human Rights*?

6. How might legal positivism or conventionalism respond to Martin Luther King, Jr.'s defence of civil disobedience?

7. How might different authors from each of the perspectives formulate distinctive responses to the previous two questions?

8. How can we identify a bad law?

9. Are individual citizens obliged to obey a law that they believe is a bad law?

10. Does an individual citizen have an obligation to resist or disobey a bad law?

4.15 Further Reading

Aeschylus. *Oresteia Trilogy*. Translated by Peter Meineck, Hackett Publishing, 1998.
Benedict, Ruth. *Patterns of Culture*. Houghton Mifflin, 1934 [1989].
Canada Act and Canadian Charter of Rights and Freedoms. 1982.
Constitution of the United States. 1789.
Devlin, Patrick. *The Enforcement of Morals*. Oxford University Press, 1965.
Dworkin, Ronald. *Law's Empire*. Harvard University Press, 1986.
Hart, H.L.A. *The Concept of Law*. Oxford University Press, 1961.
Melville, Herman. *Billy Budd*. Broadview Press, 2016.
Rawls, John. *A Theory of Justice*. Harvard University Press, 1971.
Sophocles. *Antigone*. Translated by Paul Woodruff, Hackett Publishing, 2001.
Thoreau, Henry David. *Civil Disobedience*. Broadview Press, 2016.

CHAPTER 5

Property, Equality, and Economics

Republics end through luxury, monarchies through poverty.

—BARON DE MONTESQUIEU

If we command our wealth, we shall be rich and free. If our wealth commands us, we are poor indeed.

—EDMUND BURKE

The palace is not safe when the cottage is not happy.

—BENJAMIN DISRAELI

What is property? ... theft.

—PIERRE-JOSEPH PROUDHON

We slowly grow tired of the old, of what we safely possess, and we stretch our hands again; even the most beautiful landscape is no longer sure of our love after we have lived in it for three months, and some more distant coast excites our greed: possession usually diminishes the possession.

—FRIEDRICH NIETZSCHE

An "unemployed" existence is a worse negation than death itself.

—JOSÉ ORTEGA Y GASSET

In its majestic equality, the law forbids rich and poor alike to sleep under bridges, beg in the streets and steal loaves of bread.

—ANATOLE FRANCE

5.1 Introduction

Equality has been an elusive ideal since the Golden Age of democratic Athens in the fifth century BCE. Socrates, a poor stonemason, had as much right as the wealthiest Athenian to address the democratic assembly, to protect his personal interests in a court of law, or to prosecute a crime. Athenians took pride in the equal access individual citizens had to their legal and political institutions. At the same time, however,

Athenian women were entirely disenfranchised, wealth was highly concentrated among a small number of land-owners, and the city housed tens of thousands of slaves. Equality in some respects and exclusively among male citizens stood side by side with inequality in these other respects. Comparable combinations of equality and inequality were taken for granted in Enlightenment-era Europe. Kant, for example, maintained that every person is endowed with the same inherent dignity as everyone else while happily accepting hereditary monarchal rule (1.3). More recently, Naomi Klein describes the current global economy as being dominated by a resource-extraction industry that channels economic benefits to a relatively small number of people while the consequences of climate change are being borne by everyone (1.4).

Strict equality in every respect seems to be an implausible theoretical ideal, and it may well be undesirable to strive for it in practice. For this reason, debate usually turns on how to coordinate equality with other values, such as liberty, dignity, prosperity, civility, and so on. These other values help determine in which respects equality is desirable and in which inequality is tolerated. Equality and liberty may be at odds with each other, for example, whereas equality and civility may be perfectly compatible.

One domain in which equality operates as a paramount guiding ideal is the law. Laws are formulated in general terms that apply to everyone equally. We are all equally protected from physical violence by legal proscriptions against assault, just as we are all equally bound to obey these same laws. In principle, it is both irrational and unjust for one citizen to receive either more or less protection from the law than other citizens. It would be unacceptable if a law against assault protected me from being assaulted by you but not you from being assaulted by me. From a legal perspective, each person has the same status as every other person. Equality of status establishes a condition known as *formal equality*, which means that like cases must be treated alike. A notable symbol of formal equality is prominently displayed outside many courthouses: statues depicting Justice as a female figure wearing a blindfold and holding a balance-scale. Her blindfold signals an impartiality that ignores differences between people, and her balance-scale signals the measure of fairness with which legal judgements must be administered. Impartial, legal justice is a basic expectation in countries with an independent legal system (i.e., a legal system that is not simply a tool for despotic authority). In Chapter 5 we turn from frameworks of formal equality in the law (in Chapter 4) to accounts of economic conditions that produce *material equality* and *inequality*.

Underlying economic concepts in the present chapter is the brute fact that the planet has limited material resources to support life. Furthermore, some vital resources, such as food and water, are occasionally scarce (e.g., fruit during cold winters, potable water during droughts, etc.). There are roughly 2.25 acres of land on Earth for each person alive today (15.8 billion acres divided by approximately 7 billion people). Forty years ago, there were 7.9 acres per person. Crop yields are necessarily limited by the amount of arable land available for crop cultivation and livestock. Additionally, some land is undesirable or impractically located for farming, and some of it must be left as wilderness. Available land, and whatever living can be eked out of it, must service a large and rapidly expanding human population. Additionally, whatever food and other resources that are extracted from the Earth must be processed and distributed, and all waste products must be disposed of in some way. None of this is going to be done well if these challenges are addressed haphazardly. Indeed, such daunting challenges must be met systematically, if there is going to be hope of success on a vast, global scale. The two most viable economic systems devised to meet these challenges are *socialism* and *capitalism*. Most other systems, such as mediaeval feudalism and slave-labour, are simply not living options.

Variations of socialism and capitalism make both systems difficult to encapsulate in a simple formula. Still, they can be differentiated with reference to the ownership of natural resources and how these resources ought to be converted into material products. *Socialism* refers to either (i) an economic system based on collective ownership of resources and shared control of the means of production, distribution, and exchange of manufactured items, or (ii) a system marked by active state regulation and intervention in the private market for resources and manufactured items. Capitalism, by contrast, refers to a system based on private ownership of resources and control of the means of production, distribution, and exchange, all of which take place unimpeded by state regulation or intervention.

Consider, further, how each system relates politics and economics. Theoretically, economics and politics are intimately interrelated in a socialist system: the state plays an active role in producing and distributing material items for its citizens, directing these resources either by centralized state control of the economy (e.g., a communist state) or by using taxation to redistribute wealth from the rich to the poor (i.e., a welfare state). In a fully realized capitalist system, on the other hand, the economy functions independently of politics: an unregulated market for resources operates according to its own principles with the state playing no role in its day-to-day operations. Where market forces reign without state intervention formal equality is the only realistic kind of equality we can expect; where state intervention is active, the rationale for intervention is typically formulated in terms of material equality.

Even though the theoretical bases of the two systems are incompatible, for much of the last century strands of both socialism and capitalism have been interwoven in countries across the globe. In practice, tendencies towards both socialism and capitalism vie for influence. As a result, we see features of both systems in our own society, and partisan voices advocate constantly for one over the other. Some encourage more state regulation and intervention, and others insist that the market must be left alone. Where we find both a developed economy and a stable, established state, market transactions tend to be regulated to some extent, with active state intervention being limited to times of turmoil. It is for this reason difficult to find an example of a purely socialist system or of a purely capitalist system. Even China, which is ruled by an avowedly socialist Communist party, has fostered an enormous number of profitable capitalist ventures. And the United States of America, which is resolutely capitalist, has extensive social services. When combined, the two "systems" operate as ideological rivals engaged in a tense, ongoing debate. Usually this debate focuses on questions about how much wealth redistribution is fair to those who pay taxes, or how much market deregulation is beneficial for everyone. Objections to wealth redistribution can be framed as a violation of formal equality since the tax burden is inequitably distributed. And objections to market deregulation can be framed as a violation of material equality because it entrenches a division between rich and poor.

* * *

Most readings in the present chapter are drawn from Enlightenment- or post-Enlightenment-era sources. Primarily, this focus is due to the historical fact that economic systems from earlier eras are anachronistic now. Feudalism, for example, is simply no longer viable, whereas socialism and capitalism are. It was not until the seventeenth century that the conceptual elements of modern capitalism and socialism emerged. The lone exception to this historical restriction is a selection from Aristotle's *Politics* (5.2), which serves as our present point of departure for three purposes: (1) to illustrate relations of scale between macro- and micro-level economic forces; (2) to illustrate how politics and economics relate to each other independently of questions about state regulation or intervention; (3) to contrast a modern emphasis on freedom with ancient attitudes towards slavery. Aristotle's *Politics* thus illustrates both the roots of economic thinking—(1) and (2)—and a set of assumptions rejected entirely by modern economic thought (3).

Consider first the roots of economic thought. Aristotle's analysis illustrates the idea that large-scale economic dynamics are rooted in small-scale communal relations. This idea is implicit in the word *economics*, which is derived from the Greek terms "oikos" (home or house) and "nomos" (rules). In its original sense, economics referred to rules for managing a household. Today this is considered part of micro-economics. Small-scale economic principles for managing a household, an individual company, or a single corporate entity are generally contrasted with aggregated macro-economic descriptions of large populations (e.g., a country). Different principles apply for micro- and macro-economics, for the two scales are qualitatively as well as quantitatively different. Nevertheless, micro- and macro-economics are tightly bound together, because large-scale conditions provide the framework for small-scale decisions and innumerable small-scale decisions produce large-scale patterns. At the level of macro-economics, Aristotle makes plain a point indicated above: economic activity must be understood in relation to political life. As we note above, the precise nature of this relationship can be momentous. Aristotle's analytical division of society into different classes, including slaves, illustrates this very point. In one respect, slaves are purely economic resources, but the institution would never survive without a special political framework.

Aristotle's casual regard for slavery stands in sharp counterpoint to contemporary concerns about individual liberty, independence, and equality. While slavery is no longer a viable institution, it haunts modern political-economic thought as a spectre, something so repellant that no institution can be proposed that hints of it. Jean-Jacques Rousseau invokes it in his objections to private property (5.4), and Karl Marx and Friedrich Engels diagnose flaws in capitalism by tracing its problems back to ancient master-slave institutions (5.7.1). More directly, in a move that illustrates its repugnance, Locke repudiates slavery and warfare together (5.3). In sharp contrast to Aristotle, no other author in the present chapter takes slavery seriously. Enlightenment and post-Enlightenment values preclude it. Locke and Adam Smith favour individual liberty, independence of thought, voluntary associations. From a socialist perspective, Rousseau, Marx, Engels, and David Harvey (5.8) worry that capitalist economics replicate some of the unacceptable inequalities characteristic of slavery. Lastly, French author Alexis de Tocqueville (5.6) explores some of the paradoxical dynamics in nineteenth-century American society, parts of which still depended heavily on chattel slavery when he studied it during an 1831 tour of the country.

John Locke and Adam Smith would have called themselves liberals, not capitalists. Indeed, Locke never invokes the term "capital" as an economic concept. As Locke, Smith, and John Stuart Mill (6.6) defend classical liberalism, individual freedom is its guiding principle. In keeping with the Latin *liberalis* (for "independent" or "unconstrained"), classical liberalism is a comprehensive social theory that aims to reduce constraints upon individual agents as much as possible. Laws in a liberal society are designed to protect individuals from impediments to their natural and civil liberty. Only behaviour in the public sphere that affects other people is subject to legal sanction by the state, according to liberalism. The private sphere, on the other hand, is protected by "rights of non-interference."

In keeping with a fundamental commitment not to intervene in private affairs, a liberal state does not intervene in ordinary commerce. One exception is consumer protection, in particular, laws protecting individual citizens from being dominated economically by monopolies (i.e., when one person or group controls the market for a service or material item). Smith warns about the economic costs of a market monopoly, but in general, legal measures to prevent monopolies are designed to protect the liberty of individual citizens. The United States of America, for example, has a network of Anti-trust laws to prevent monopolies from taking advantage of customers who would otherwise have no other place to obtain a service or item. To protect consumers from gouging, the American government used these laws to dismantle Standard Oil in the early twentieth century and AT&T in the 1980s. Without competition, companies with a monopoly have the luxury of fixing prices to the disadvantage of their customers. Similar laws forbid collusion (in which "competitors" conspire to artificially inflate prices to their mutual benefit and the disadvantage of customers). Here we see the state acting to preserve a level of equality between buyers and sellers so that transactions are mutually beneficial rather than one-sided in favour of sellers.

John Locke's *Second Treatise on Government* is the origin of classical liberal theory (5.3). Here he confines the state's function to that of protecting individuals from threats against their lives, security, and *private property*. The selection here focuses on Locke's influential rationale for private property. According to his account, each individual person is naturally endowed with capacities to act in service to his or her own best interests, and the entire natural world is shared as *common property* by everyone. By labouring on natural resources, an individual appropriates a portion of that common property as private property. Even something as simple as collecting fallen apples from under a wild tree makes these apples the private property of a collector. Private property is thereby an extension of the person. State functions protecting the life and security of its citizens automatically include protecting private property. By protecting private property, the state indirectly protects trade. In its simplest form, a transaction might consist in one person bartering an extra bushel of apples to get a bushel of pears or a sack of potatoes. If private property were to consist entirely in perishable things such as apples and pears, and if all transactions were bartered, then economic activity would be unstable and transient. *Money*, which is tacitly agreed to serve as a common reference point for value, gets around this problem: coins, in particular, are more durable than fruit, vegetables, and other perishable items, so money earned at harvest time is available for use many months later when the apple farmer wants root vegetables but has no apples left to barter with.

Adam Smith clarifies the function of money, distinguishes it from capital, elaborates on the economic advantages of collective labour, and explains some fundamental principles of liberal macro-economics (5.5). First, our economic institutions differentiate *use-value* and *exchange-value*. While money may have no practical value in use, it has economic value in exchange. Second, *capital* includes both the money and property at someone's disposal in economic transactions. Someone need not have enough cash to finance a business venture, for example, if they have sufficient property (e.g., land) to use as collateral for a loan. Third, dividing labour in the production process improves the efficiency of industrial manufacturing, reduces the cost of production, and increases the number of material items available across society. In both production and trade, a great deal of cooperation is required, but, according to Smith, the fundamental motive behind these relations is self-interest. Workers participate to earn wages, factory owners to make profits, consumers to acquire the material items and services they want, and so on. These relations do not require political regulation or intervention by the state, according to Smith. Macro-economic trends and benefits are built upon the micro-level decisions of independent agents participating in a free market. At the macro-level, orderly patterns in the economy are spontaneously generated as if by the "invisible hand" of the market itself, not by centralized management. There are therefore two fundamental liberal objections to state economic management, one practical and one principled: the practical objection is that political management will be less efficient than the self-interest of individual decision-makers in a free market; the principled objection, which is elaborated elsewhere by John Stuart Mill, is that "paternalism" violates a liberal commitment to leave private decisions in the hands of individual agents (6.6).

Socialist voices are less audible than liberal ones in recent debates. In part, this is because some of the worst humanitarian travesties of the twentieth century were the result of socialist experiments in China, Russia, and Eastern Europe. The death and oppression of millions of people in Russia and China, in particular, make theorists wary of centralized economic planning and has muted voices in favour of full-scale socialism. Less ambitious socialist experiments in Scandinavia, North America, and Western Europe have been comparatively successful, but it is unclear to what extent these comparative successes are due to their socialist elements, liberal elements, or a combination of liberal and socialist elements. In any case, socialist themes in Jean-Jacques Rousseau's *Discourse upon the Origin and the Foundation of the Inequality among Mankind* (5.4) and the socialist agenda of Karl Marx and Friedrich Engels (5.7) are built upon criticism of classical liberal theory. More precisely, Rousseau's criticisms target Locke's defence of private property, whereas Marx and Engels target the sort of liberal-capitalism articulated by Smith. In the case of David Harvey (5.8), this critical tendency is repeated, but directed towards an updated version of liberalism that has been branded neoliberalism.

Rousseau diagnoses private property itself as the root of economic inequality and unhealthy social divisions. Relations between people of equal status are not only preferable, in his opinion, but are natural. Conversely, inequality is necessarily based on a corruption of natural relations. Not every form of inequality is intrinsically economic, but in civil society economic disparity between rich and poor is especially divisive. When inequalities become part of the fabric of society, they crystalize into divisions of class. Only oppressive institutions, deception, and violence can sustain these divisions, and so the political institutions of modern society are, in his opinion, fundamentally unjust. In light of these complaints, it should come as little surprise to learn that Rousseau's ideas were fuel for French revolutionaries in 1789.

Marx and Engels were also revolutionaries, and *The Communist Manifesto* was written with the expressed purpose to fuel revolutions across Europe in 1848. Like Rousseau, Marx and Engels identify class divisions as the source of widespread social injustice. Unlike Rousseau, they trace the origins of nineteenth-century class divisions to historically earlier times. In keeping with Aristotle, the earliest division is that between master and slave classes: control of resources in ancient Greece resided in the hands of the masters who were at liberty to exploit slave labour for their own benefit. As institutions of slavery diminished in European history, the division between master and slave evolved into that between feudal lord and peasant: control in the middle ages resided in the hands of land-owning lords who had the power to extract tribute taxes from peasants. In modern times, the power of land-ownership evolved into the power of factory owners, industrialists, financiers, and others who possess capital over those whose only marketable commodity is a capacity for labour: control now resides in the hands of a capitalist Bourgeoisie class over a wage-labouring Proletariat class.[1] Class divisions in this final stage are, like those of its ancient and mediaeval predecessors, only a passing phase to the next stage.

What Adam Smith described as an invisible hand generating spontaneous order in an unregulated market is for Marx and Engels the latest manifestation of historical laws. Class divisions are central to their analysis. Each political-economic system is associated with a specific kind of division and a particular set of historical conditions. Furthermore, each system has a natural lifespan, from its first emergence out of its predecessor's dissolution to a final transformation into its successor: ancient master-slave relations transformed into medieval lord-peasant-relations, which in turn transformed into modern capitalist-labourer relations. Each transformation is brought about by a crisis in its predecessor. In this way, one system prepares the way for the next, with underlying political and economic forces regulating the processes. If the crisis conditions of capitalism are favourable, then its class divisions will dissolve and everyone will belong to a single class. At this point, material inequalities will be eliminated and a global communist state will be established.

This prediction of a global communist revolution has yet to materialize, and it seems unlikely to occur in the near future. Nevertheless, Marxism has remained vital as a source of critical insight into contemporary liberal-capitalism. Marx, for example, diagnoses problems

1 For the sake of clarity, in this introduction we label these two groups capitalist and labour classes rather than the Bourgeoisie and Proletariat.

using the foundational tenets of capitalism (5.7.2). In particular, he identifies productive and financial practices that have divorced economic activity from beneficial and meaningful social functions. Workers labouring in industrial conditions are alienated and dehumanized. And financial arrangements are set up to promote the ever-expanding accumulation of capital among the capitalist class rather than generating socially functional products. These criticisms have been updated recently by David Harvey (5.8). According to Harvey, the sort of classical liberal-capitalism that Marx and Engels criticized has evolved into something new, neoliberalism. Harvey traces the source of neoliberalism to widespread deregulation in the United Kingdom and the United States in the final decades of the twentieth century. Classical liberalism contained within it a rationale for the state to protect individual citizens from being dominated by monopolies and colluding corporations. As Harvey describes it, political trends favouring deregulation and non-intervention by the state signal the emergence of a new economic system, hence the label neoliberalism. According to his analysis, without state regulation or intervention material inequalities that emerged in formerly liberal societies have been exacerbated and perpetuated by neoliberal economics.

It is worth noting before we close this introduction that material-economic equality and inequality cannot be isolated from other kinds of equality and inequality. Inequalities based on gender or racial differences, for example, have implications for unequal economic opportunities and legal status. These and other issues will be addressed in Unit III.

5.2 Aristotle (384–322 BCE)

Aristotle begins *Politics* by declaring that social life serves a purpose, i.e., we participate in society with a view to achieving something good. He asserts this as a *natural law*. No individual is self-sufficient, but human beings are able to survive because we have an innate social instinct. Speech and a capacity for collaborative work are indications of this instinct. Each individual contributes something to the group, and all of the separate contributions ensure both individual and collective survival. The inter-relation of these contributions is, in essence, an economy. It also happens to be an economy built upon a profound inequality.

The fundamental social unit is a family, which is naturally hierarchical according to Aristotle. Next in size and complexity is the village, which consists of several families. The city, a collection of villages, is the most complex of all and gives politics its name (*polis* is the Greek word for city). All of these social arrangements are expressions of our social nature.

Aristotle also considers the source and character of divisions within society. According to his analysis, in any complex system the natural arrangement is for the superior part to rule the inferior. It is, accordingly, natural for the soul to rule the body and for human beings to rule non-human animals. Aristotle then asks (1) whether there is a natural ruling principle in a household or city, and (2) whether anyone is naturally ruled as a slave. He answers (1) in terms of intelligence: since intelligence is the special virtue of a human being, intelligence ought to be the ruling principle in a community. To answer (2) he differentiates someone who is reduced to slavery by war or custom from someone who is so deficient in intelligence as to require guidance. People who fit the second description are natural slaves. In essence, a slave is a tool with some intelligence—more than a kitchen utensil or plough-ox, but not enough to think independently. In this respect, a slave can belong to someone as property. There are people who are intended by nature to be slaves.

from Politics I

Book I

PART I

Every state is a community of some kind, and every community is established with a view to some good; for mankind always act in order to obtain that which they think good. But, if all communities aim at some good, the state or political community, which is the highest of all, and which embraces all the rest, aims at good in a greater degree than any other, and at the highest good.

Some people think that the qualifications of a statesman, king, householder, and master are the same, and that they differ, not in kind, but only in the number of their subjects. For example, the ruler over a few is called a master; over more, the manager of a household; over a still larger number, a statesman or king, as if there were no difference between a great household and a small state. The distinction which is made between the king and the statesman is as follows: When the government is personal, the ruler is a king; when, according to the rules of the political science, the citizens rule and are ruled in turn, then he is called a statesman.

But all this is a mistake; for governments differ in kind, as will be evident to any one who considers the matter according to the method which has hitherto guided us. As in other departments of science, so in politics, the compound should always be resolved into the simple elements or least parts of the whole. We must therefore look at the elements of which the state is composed, in order that we may see in what the different kinds of rule differ from one another, and whether any scientific result can be attained about each one of them.

PART II

He who thus considers things in their first growth and origin, whether a state or anything else, will obtain the clearest view of them. In the first place there must be a union of those who cannot exist without each other; namely, of male and female, that the race may continue (and this is a union which is formed, not of deliberate purpose, but because, in common with other animals and with plants, mankind have a natural desire to leave behind them an image of themselves), and of natural ruler and subject, that both may be preserved. For that which can foresee by the exercise of mind is by nature intended to be lord and master, and that which can with its body give effect to such foresight is a subject, and by nature a slave; hence master and slave have the same interest. Now nature has distinguished between the female and the slave. For she is not niggardly, like the smith who fashions the Delphian knife for many uses; she makes each thing for a single use, and every instrument is best made when intended for one and not for many uses.... Out of these two relationships between man and woman, master and slave, the first thing to arise is the family, and Hesiod is right when he says, "First house and wife and an ox for the plough," for the ox is the poor man's slave. The family is the association established by nature for the supply of men's everyday wants, and the members of it are called by Charondas 'companions of the cupboard,' and by Epimenides the Cretan, 'companions of the manger.' But when several families are united, and the association aims at something more than the supply of daily needs, the first society to be formed is the village. And the most natural form of the village appears to be that of a colony from the family, composed of the children and grandchildren, who are said to be suckled 'with the same milk.' And this is the reason why Hellenic states were originally governed by kings; because the Hellenes were under royal rule before they came together, as [others] still are....

When several villages are united in a single complete community, large enough to be nearly or quite self-sufficing, the state comes into existence, originating in the bare needs of life, and continuing in existence for the sake of a good life. And therefore, if the earlier forms of society are natural, so is the state, for it is the end of them, and the nature of a thing is its end. For what each thing is when fully developed, we call its nature, whether we are speaking of a man, a horse, or a family. Besides, the final cause and end of a thing is the best, and to be self-sufficing is the end and the best.

Hence it is evident that the state is a creation of nature, and that man is by nature a political animal. And he who by nature and not by mere accident is without a state, is either a bad man or above humanity; he is like the "Tribeless, lawless, hearthless one," whom Homer denounces—the natural outcast is forthwith a lover of war; he may be compared to an isolated piece at draughts.

Now, that man is more of a political animal than bees or any other gregarious animals is evident. Nature, as we often say, makes nothing in vain, and man is the only animal whom she has endowed with the gift of speech. And whereas mere voice is but an indication of pleasure or pain, and is therefore found in other animals (for their nature attains to the perception of pleasure and pain and the intimation of them to one another, and no further), the power of speech is intended to set forth the expedient and inexpedient, and therefore likewise the just and the unjust. And it is a characteristic of man that he alone has any sense of good and evil, of just and unjust, and the like, and the association of living beings who have this sense makes a family and a state.

Further, the state is by nature clearly prior to the family and to the individual, since the whole is of necessity prior to the part; for example, if the whole body be destroyed, there will be no foot or hand, except in an equivocal sense, as we might speak of a stone hand; for when destroyed the hand will be no better than that. But things are defined by their working and power; and we ought not to say that they are the same when they no longer have their proper quality, but only that they have the same name. The proof that the state is a creation of nature and prior to the individual is that the individual, when isolated, is not self-sufficing; and therefore he is like a part in relation to the whole. But he who is unable to live in society, or who has no need because he is sufficient for himself, must be either a beast or a god: he is no part of a state. A social instinct is implanted in all men by nature, and yet he who first founded the state was the greatest of benefactors. For man, when perfected, is the best of animals, but, when separated from law and justice, he is the worst of all; since armed injustice is the more dangerous, and he is equipped at birth with arms, meant to be used by intelligence and virtue, which he may use for the worst ends. Wherefore, if he have not virtue, he is the most unholy and the most savage of animals, and the most full of lust and gluttony. But justice is the bond of men in states, for the administration of justice, which is the determination of what is just, is the principle of order in political society.

PART III

Seeing then that the state is made up of households, before speaking of the state we must speak of the management of the household. The parts of household management correspond to the persons who compose the household, and a complete household consists of slaves and freemen. Now we should begin by examining everything in its fewest possible elements; and the first and fewest possible parts of a family are master and slave, husband and wife, father and children. We have therefore to consider what each of these three relations is and ought to be: I mean the relation of master and servant, the marriage relation (the conjunction of man and wife has no name of its own), and thirdly, the procreative relation (this also has no proper name). And there is another element of a household, the so-called art of getting wealth, which, according to some, is identical with household management, according to others, a principal part of it; the nature of this art will also have to be considered by us.

Let us first speak of master and slave, looking to the needs of practical life and also seeking to attain some better theory of their relation than exists at present. For some are of opinion that the rule of a master is a science, and that the management of a household, and the mastership of slaves, and the political and royal rule, as I was saying at the outset, are all the same. Others affirm that the rule of a master over slaves is contrary to nature, and that the distinction between slave and freeman exists by law only, and not by nature; and being an interference with nature is therefore unjust.

PART IV

Property is a part of the household, and the art of acquiring property is a part of the art of managing the household; for no man can live well, or indeed live at all, unless he be provided with necessaries. And as in the arts which have a definite sphere the workers must have their own proper instruments for the accomplishment of their work, so it is in the management of a household. Now instruments are of various sorts; some are living, others lifeless; in the rudder, the pilot of a ship has a lifeless, in the look-out man, a living instrument; for in the arts the servant is a kind of instrument. Thus, too, a possession is an instrument for maintaining life. And so, in the arrangement of the family, a slave is a living possession, and property a number of such instruments; and the servant is himself an instrument which takes precedence of all other instruments. For if every instrument could accomplish its own work, obeying or anticipating the will of others, like the statues of Daedalus, or the tripods of Hephaestus, which, says the poet, "of their own accord entered the assembly of the Gods"; if, in like manner, the shuttle would weave and the plectrum touch the lyre without a hand to guide them, chief workmen would not want servants, nor masters slaves. Here, however, another distinction must be drawn; the instruments commonly so called are instruments of production, whilst a possession is an instrument of action. The shuttle, for example, is not only of use; but something else is made by it, whereas of a garment or of a bed there is only the use. Further, as production and action are different in kind, and both require instruments, the instruments which they employ must likewise differ in kind. But life is action and not production, and therefore the slave is the minister of action. Again, a possession is spoken of as a part is spoken of; for the part is not only a part of something else, but wholly belongs to it; and this is also true of a possession. The master is only the master of the slave; he does not belong to him, whereas the slave is not only the slave of his master, but wholly belongs to him. Hence we see what is the nature and office of a slave; he who is by nature not his own but another's man, is by nature a slave; and he may be said to be another's man who, being a human being, is also a possession. And a possession may be defined as an instrument of action, separable from the possessor.

PART V

But is there any one thus intended by nature to be a slave, and for whom such a condition is expedient and right, or rather is not all slavery a violation of nature?

There is no difficulty in answering this question, on grounds both of reason and of fact. For that some should rule and others be ruled is a thing not only necessary, but expedient; from the hour of their birth, some are marked out for subjection, others for rule.

And there are many kinds both of rulers and subjects (and that rule is the better which is exercised over better subjects—for example, to rule over men is better than to rule over wild beasts; for the work is better which is executed by better workmen, and where one man rules and another is ruled, they may be said to have a work); for in all things which form a composite whole and which are made up of parts, whether continuous or discrete, a distinction between the ruling and the subject element comes to light. Such a duality exists in living creatures, but not in them only; it originates in the constitution of the universe; even in things which have no life there is a ruling principle, as in a musical mode. But we are wandering from the subject. We will therefore restrict ourselves to the living creature, which, in the first place, consists of soul and body: and of these two, the one is by nature the ruler, and the other the subject. But then we must look for the intentions of nature in things which retain their nature, and not in things which are corrupted. And therefore we must study the man who is in the most perfect state both of body and soul, for in him we shall see the true relation of the two; although in bad or corrupted natures the body will often appear to rule over the soul, because they are in an evil and unnatural condition. At all events we may firstly observe in living creatures both a despotical and a constitutional rule; for the soul rules the body with a despotical rule, whereas the intellect rules the appetites with a constitutional and royal rule. And it is clear that the rule of the soul over the body, and of the mind and the rational element over the passionate, is natural and expedient; whereas the equality of the two or the rule of the inferior is always hurtful. The same holds good of animals in relation to men; for tame animals have a better nature than wild, and all tame animals are better off when they are ruled by man; for then they are preserved. Again, the male is by nature superior, and the female inferior; and the one rules, and the other is ruled; this principle, of necessity, extends to all mankind.

Where then there is such a difference as that between soul and body, or between men and animals (as in the case of those whose business is to use their body, and who can do nothing better), the lower sort are by nature slaves, and it is better for them as for all inferiors that they should be under the rule of a master. For he who can be, and therefore is, another's and he who participates in rational principle enough to apprehend, but not to have, such a principle, is a slave by nature. Whereas the lower animals cannot even apprehend a principle; they obey their instincts. And indeed the use made of slaves and of tame animals is not very different; for both with their bodies minister to the needs of life. Nature would like to distinguish between the bodies of freemen and slaves, making the one strong for servile labor, the other upright, and although useless for such services, useful for political life in the arts both of war and peace. But the opposite often happens—that some have the souls and others have the bodies of freemen. And doubtless if men differed from one another in the mere forms of their bodies as much as the statues of the Gods do from men, all would acknowledge that the inferior class should be slaves of the superior. And if this is true of the body, how much more just that a similar distinction should exist in the soul? but the beauty of the body is seen, whereas the beauty of the soul is not seen. It is clear, then, that some men are by nature free, and others slaves, and that for these latter slavery is both expedient and right.

PART VI

But that those who take the opposite view have in a certain way right on their side, may be easily seen. For the words slavery and slave are used in two senses. There is a slave or slavery by law as well as by nature. The law of which I speak is a sort of convention—the law by which whatever is taken in war is supposed to belong to the victors. But this right many jurists impeach, as they would an orator who brought forward an unconstitutional measure: they detest the notion that, because one man has the power of doing violence and is superior in brute strength, another shall be his slave and subject. Even among philosophers there is a difference of opinion. The origin of the dispute, and what makes the views invade each other's territory, is as follows: in some sense virtue, when furnished with means, has actually the greatest power of exercising force; and as superior power is only found where there is superior excellence of some kind, power seems to imply virtue, and the dispute to be simply one about justice (for it is due to one party identifying justice with goodwill while the other identifies it with the mere rule of the stronger). If these views are thus set out separately, the other views have no force or plausibility against the view that the superior in virtue ought to rule, or be master. Others, clinging, as they think, simply to a principle of justice (for law and custom are a sort of justice), assume that slavery in accordance with the custom of war is justified by law, but at the same moment they deny this. For what if the cause of the war be unjust? And again, no one would ever say he is a slave who is unworthy to be a slave. Were this the case, men of the highest rank would be slaves and the children of slaves if they or their parents chance to have been taken captive and sold. Wherefore Hellenes do not like to call Hellenes slaves, but confine the term to barbarians. Yet, in using this language, they really mean the natural slave of whom we spoke at first; for it must be admitted that some are slaves everywhere, others nowhere. The same principle applies to nobility. Hellenes regard themselves as noble everywhere, and not only in their own country, but they deem the barbarians noble only when at home, thereby implying that there are two sorts of nobility and freedom, the one absolute, the other relative. The Helen of Theodectes says: "Who would presume to call me servant who am on both sides sprung from the stem of the Gods?" What does this mean but that they distinguish freedom and slavery, noble and humble birth, by the two principles of good and evil? They think that as men and animals beget men and animals, so from good men a good man springs. But this is what nature, though she may intend it, cannot always accomplish.

We see then that there is some foundation for this difference of opinion, and that all are not either slaves by nature or freemen by nature, and also that there is in some cases a marked distinction between the two classes, rendering it expedient and right for the one to be slaves and the others to be masters: the one practicing obedience, the others exercising the authority and lordship which nature intended them to have. The abuse of this authority is injurious to both; for the interests of part and whole, of body and soul, are the same, and the slave is a part of the master, a living but separated part of his bodily frame. Hence, where the relation of master and slave between them is natural they are friends and have a common interest, but where it rests merely on law and force the reverse is true.

5.3 John Locke (1632–1704)

Like his English predecessor Thomas Hobbes (4.6), John Locke imagines what life for human beings would be like without the institutions of civil society. In this way, both authors theoretically separate those elements of social life which originate in our deepest nature from those which are the product of artificial socialization. Everything begins with an account of human beings in a "state of nature." In contrast to Hobbes, Locke portrays human relations in this state as being fundamentally peaceful (Hobbes imagines it as a state of war). According to Locke, violence and exploitation are contrary to our nature, and we accordingly have natural rights to life, liberty, and security. As an extension of these fundamental rights, every person has a property right over his or her own body, and this extends even further to the things acquired through physical labour.

In a state of nature *private property* is initially acquired from *common property*, which includes anything in the natural world over which no one has yet established a claim. To claim something as private property, we need only mix our labour with part of the stock of common property. Locke's example is someone who acquires acorns for food: in gathering loose acorns from the ground the person has improved the condition of these items by making them useful for human consumption. The only natural restriction to this mode of acquisition is a "spoils limitation," which forbids a person from acquiring so much of a perishable good that it spoils before it can be used; spoiled goods waste something that ought to have been left available for someone else to acquire. Once someone has a private property right over something, no one else may possess it without the consent of its owner. The owner, however, may use it, give it away, or exchange it for someone else's property. A property owner's right to transfer his or her property to another person is the origin of all our economic relations, for that means it can be bartered or sold at the owner's pleasure. And because property ownership is a natural right, it exists prior to when the laws and institutions of civil society were founded.

We found civil society and submit to the laws of a properly constituted state in order to formally empower a third party to protect individual rights. We do this to avoid the predictable consequence of passionate over-reaction from individuals seeking retribution for themselves in response to a violation of their rights. Victims of theft or assault, for example, are susceptible of being violent with perpetrators if they must prosecute their own cases. When one person has violated the natural right of another, the intervention of an independent police force and court system can better restore order. Still, this is the extent to which state intervention is justifiable, according to Locke. State intervention beyond this will impede the individual liberty of citizens. Because the paramount value in Locke's theory is individual liberty, he is properly classified as a liberal. Indeed, his work is the origin of modern liberal theory. The emphasis on individual liberty and natural rights in Locke's theory automatically rules out slavery, which is why he repudiates it near the beginning of the selection here.

~

from Second Treatise on Government

Chapter III. Of the State of War

Sect. 16. The state of war is a state of enmity and destruction: and therefore declaring by word or action, not a passionate and hasty, but a sedate settled design upon another man's life, puts him in a state of war with him against whom he has declared such an intention, and so has exposed his life to the other's power to be taken away by him, or any one that joins with him in his defence, and espouses his quarrel; it being reasonable and just, I should have a right to destroy that which threatens me with destruction: for, by the fundamental law of nature, man being to be preserved as much as possible, when all cannot be preserved, the safety of the innocent is to be preferred: and one may destroy a man who makes war upon him, or has discovered an enmity to his being, for the same reason that he may kill a wolf or a lion; because such men are not under the ties of the common law of reason, have no other rule, but that of force and violence, and so may be treated as beasts of prey, those dangerous and noxious creatures, that will be sure to destroy him whenever he falls into their power.

Sect. 17. And hence it is, that he who attempts to get another man into his absolute power, does thereby put himself into a state of war with him; it being to be understood as a declaration of a design upon his life: for I have reason to conclude, that he who would get me into his power without my consent, would use me as he pleased when he had got me there, and destroy me too when he had a fancy to it; for no body can desire to have me in his absolute power, unless it be to compel me by force to that which is against the right of my freedom, i.e., make me a slave. To be free from such force is the only security of my preservation; and reason bids me look on him, as an enemy to my preservation, who would take away that freedom which is the fence to it; so that he who makes an attempt to enslave me, thereby puts himself into a state of war with me. He that, in the state of nature, would take away the freedom that belongs to any one in that state, must necessarily be supposed to have a design to take away every thing else, that freedom being the foundation of all the rest; as he that, in the state of society, would take away the freedom belonging to those of that society or commonwealth, must be supposed to design to take away from them every thing else, and so be looked on as in a state of war.

Sect. 18. This makes it lawful for a man to kill a thief, who has not in the least hurt him, nor declared any design upon his life, any farther than, by the use of force, so to get him in his power, as to take away his money, or what he pleases, from him; because using force, where he has no right, to get me into his power, let his pretence be what it will, I have no reason to suppose, that he, who would take away my liberty, would not, when he had me in his power, take away every thing else. And therefore it is lawful for me to treat him as one who has put himself into a state of war with me, i.e., kill him if I can; for to that hazard does he justly expose himself, whoever introduces a state of war, and is aggressor in it....

Chapter IV. Of Slavery

Sect. 22. The natural liberty of man is to be free from any superior power on earth, and not to be under the will or legislative authority of man, but to have only the law of nature for his rule. The liberty of man, in society, is to be under no other legislative power, but that established, by consent, in the commonwealth; nor under the dominion of any will, or restraint of any law, but what that legislative shall enact, according to the trust put in it....

Sect. 23. This freedom from absolute, arbitrary power, is so necessary to, and closely joined with a man's preservation, that he cannot part with it, but by what forfeits his preservation and life together: for a man, not having the power of his own life, cannot, by compact, or his own consent, enslave himself to any one, nor put himself under the absolute, arbitrary power of another, to take away his life, when he pleases. No body can give more power than he has himself; and he that cannot take away his own life, cannot give another power over it. Indeed, having by his fault forfeited his own life, by some act that deserves death; he, to whom he has forfeited it, may (when he has him in his power) delay to take it, and make use of him to his own service, and he does him no injury by it: for, whenever he finds the hardship of his slavery outweigh the value of his life, it is in his power, by resisting the will of his master, to draw on himself the death he desires.

Sect. 24. This is the perfect condition of slavery, which is nothing else, but the state of war continued, between a lawful conqueror and a captive: for, if once compact enter between them, and make an agreement for a limited power on the one side, and obedience on the other, the state of war and slavery ceases, as long as the compact endures: for, as has been said, no man can, by agreement, pass over to another that which he hath not in himself, a power over his own life....

Chapter V. Of Property

Sect. 25. ... It seems to some a very great difficulty, how any one should ever come to have a property in any thing ... upon a supposition that God gave the world to Adam, and his posterity in common.... But I shall endeavour to shew, how men might come to have a property in several parts of that which God gave to mankind in common, and that without any express compact of all the commoners.

Sect. 26. ... The earth, and all that is therein, is given to men for the support and comfort of their being. And tho' all the fruits it naturally produces, and beasts it feeds, belong to mankind in common, as they are produced by the spontaneous hand of nature; and no body has originally a private dominion, exclusive of the rest of mankind, in any of them, as they are thus in their natural state: yet being given for the use of men, there must of necessity be a means to appropriate them some way or other, before they can be of any use, or at all beneficial to any particular man. The fruit, or venison, which nourishes the wild Indian, who knows no enclosure, and is still a tenant in common, must be his, and so his, i.e., a part of him, that another can no longer have any right to it, before it can do him any good for the support of his life.

Sect. 27. ... Every man has a property in his own person: this no body has any right to but himself. The labour of his body, and the work of his hands, we may say, are properly his. Whatsoever then he removes out of the state that nature hath provided, and left it in, he hath mixed his labour with, and joined to it something that is his own, and thereby makes it his property. It being by him removed from the common state nature hath placed it in, it hath by this labour something annexed to it, that excludes the common right of other men: for this labour being the unquestionable property of the labourer, no man but he can have a right to what that is once joined to, at least where there is enough, and as good, left in common for others.

Sect. 28. He that is nourished by the acorns he picked up under an oak, or the apples he gathered from the trees in the wood, has certainly appropriated them to himself. No body can deny but the nourishment is his. I ask then, when did they begin to be his? when he digested? or when he eat? or when he boiled? or when he brought them home? or when he picked them up? and it is plain, if the first gathering made them not his, nothing else could. That labour put a distinction between them and common: that added something to them more than nature, the common mother of all, had done; and so they became his private right. And will any one say, he had no right to those acorns or apples, he thus appropriated, because he had not the consent of all mankind to make them his? Was it a robbery thus to assume to himself what belonged to all in common? If such a consent as that was necessary, man had starved, notwithstanding the plenty God had given him. We see in commons, which remain so by compact, that it is the taking any part of what is common, and removing it out of the state nature leaves it in, which begins the property; without which the common is of no use. And the taking of this or that part, does not depend on the express consent of all the commoners....

Sect. 31. It will perhaps be objected to this, that if gathering the acorns, or other fruits of the earth, &c. makes a right to them, then any one may ingross as much as he will. To which I answer, Not so. The same law of nature, that does by this means give us property, does also bound that property too. God has given us all things richly.... But how far has he given it us? To enjoy. As much as any one can make use of to any advantage of life before it spoils, so much he may by his labour fix a property in: whatever is beyond this, is more than his share, and belongs to others. Nothing was made by God for man to spoil or destroy. And thus, considering the plenty of natural provisions there was a long time in the world, and the few spenders; and to how small a part of that provision the industry of one man could extend itself, and ingross it to the prejudice of others; especially keeping within the bounds, set by reason, of what might serve for his use; there could be then little room for quarrels or contentions about property so established.

Sect. 32. But the chief matter of property being now not the fruits of the earth, and the beasts that subsist on it, but the earth itself; as that which takes in and carries with it all the rest; I think it is plain, that property in that too is acquired as the former. As much land as a man tills, plants, improves, cultivates, and can use the product of, so much is his property. He by his labour does, as it were, inclose it from the common. Nor will it invalidate his right, to say every body else has an equal title to it; and therefore he cannot appropriate, he cannot inclose, without the consent of all his fellow-commoners, all mankind. God, when he gave the world in common to all mankind, commanded man also to labour, and the penury of his condition required it of him. God and his reason commanded him to subdue the earth, i.e., improve it for the benefit of life, and therein lay out something upon it that was his own, his labour. He that in obedience to this command of God, subdued, tilled and sowed any part of it, thereby annexed to it something that was his property, which another had no title to, nor could without injury take from him.

Sect. 33. Nor was this appropriation of any parcel of land, by improving it, any prejudice to any other man, since there was still enough, and as good left; and more than the yet unprovided could use. So that, in effect, there was never the less left for others because of his enclosure for himself: for he that leaves as much as another can make use of, does as good as take nothing at all. No body could think himself injured by the drinking of another man, though he took a good draught, who had a whole river of the same water left him to quench his thirst: and the case of land and water, where there is enough of both, is perfectly the same. ...

Sect. 35. It is true, in land that is common in England, or any other country, where there is plenty of people under government, who have money and commerce, no one can inclose or appropriate any part, without the consent of all his fellow-commoners; because this is left common by compact, i.e., by the law of the land, which is not to be violated. And though it be common, in respect of some men, it is not so to all mankind; but is the joint property of this country, or this parish.... The law man was under, was rather for appropriating.... So that God, by commanding to subdue, gave authority so far to appropriate: and the condition of human life, which requires labour and materials to work on, necessarily introduces private possessions.

Sect. 36. The measure of property nature has well set by the extent of men's labour and the conveniencies of life: no man's labour could subdue, or appropriate all; nor could his enjoyment consume more than a small part; so that it was impossible for any man, this way, to intrench upon the right of another, or acquire to himself a property, to the prejudice of his neighbour, who would still have room for as good, and as large a possession (after the other had taken out his) as before it was appropriated. This measure did confine every man's possession to a very moderate proportion, and such as he might appropriate to himself, without injury to any body, in the first ages of the world.... And the same measure may be allowed still without prejudice to any body, as full as the world seems: for supposing a man ... let him plant in some inland, vacant places of America, we shall find that the possessions he could make himself, upon the measures we have given, would not be very large, nor, even to this day, prejudice the rest of mankind, or give them reason to complain, or think themselves injured by this man's incroachment, though the race of men have now spread themselves to all the corners of the world, and do infinitely exceed the small number was at the beginning ... this I dare boldly affirm, that the same rule of propriety, (viz.) that every man should have as much as he could make use of, would hold still in the world ... since there is land enough in the world to suffice double the inhabitants, had not the invention of money, and the tacit agreement of men to put a value on it, introduced (by consent) larger possessions, and a right to them; which, how it has done, I shall by and by shew more at large.

Sect. 37. ... He who appropriates land to himself by his labour, does not lessen, but increase the common stock of mankind: for the provisions serving to the support of human life, produced by one acre of inclosed and cultivated land, are (to speak much within compass) ten times more than those which are yielded by an acre of land of an equal richness lying waste in common. And therefore he that incloses land, and has a greater plenty of the conveniencies of life from ten acres, than he could have from an hundred left to nature, may truly be said to give ninety acres to mankind: for his labour now supplies him with provisions out of ten acres, which were but the product of an hundred lying in common. I have here rated the improved land very low, in making its product but as ten to one, when it is much nearer an hundred to one: for I ask, whether in the wild woods and uncultivated waste of America, left to nature, without any improvement, tillage or husbandry, a thousand acres yield the needy and wretched inhabitants as many conveniencies of life, as ten acres of equally fertile land do in Devonshire, where they are well cultivated? Before the appropriation of land, he who gathered as much of the wild fruit, killed, caught, or tamed, as many of the beasts, as he could ... did thereby acquire a propriety in them: but if they perished, in his possession, without their due use; if the fruits rotted, or the venison putrified, before he could spend it, he offended against the common law of nature, and was liable to be punished; he invaded his neighbour's share, for he had no right, farther than his use called for any of them, and they might serve to afford him conveniencies of life.

Sect. 38. The same measures governed the possession of land too: whatsoever he tilled and reaped, laid up and made use of, before it spoiled, that was his peculiar right; whatsoever he enclosed, and could feed, and make use of, the cattle and product was also his. But if either the grass of his enclosure rotted on the ground, or the fruit of his planting perished without gathering, and laying up, this part of the earth, notwithstanding his enclosure, was still to be looked on as waste, and might be the possession of any other.... But as families increased, and industry inlarged their stocks, their possessions inlarged with the need of them; but yet it was commonly without any fixed property in the ground they made use of, till they incorporated, settled themselves together, and built cities; and then, by consent, they came in time, to set out the bounds of their distinct territories, and agree on limits between them and their neighbours; and by laws within themselves, settled the properties of those of the same society....

Sect. 40. Nor is it so strange, as perhaps before consideration it may appear, that the property of labour should be able to over-balance the community of land: for it is labour indeed that puts the difference of value on every thing; and let any one consider what the difference is between an acre of land planted with tobacco or sugar, sown with wheat or barley, and an acre of the same land lying in common, without any husbandry upon it, and he will find, that the improvement of labour makes the far greater part of the value. I think it will be but a very modest computation to say, that of the products of the earth useful to the life of man nine tenths are the effects of labour: nay, if we will rightly estimate things as they come to our use, and cast up the several expences about them, what in them is purely owing to nature, and what to labour, we shall find, that in most of them ninety-nine hundredths are wholly to be put on the account of labour.

...

Sect. 42. To make this a little clearer, let us but trace some of the ordinary provisions of life, through their several progresses, before they come to our use, and see how much they receive of their value from human industry. Bread, wine and cloth, are things of daily use, and great plenty; yet notwithstanding, acorns, water and leaves, or skins, must be our bread, drink and cloathing, did not labour furnish us with these more useful commodities: for whatever bread is more worth than acorns, wine than water, and cloth or silk, than leaves, skins or moss, that is wholly owing to labour and industry; the one of these being the food and raiment which unassisted nature furnishes us with; the other, provisions which our industry and pains prepare for us, which how much they exceed the other in value, when any one hath computed, he will then see how much labour makes the far greatest part of the value of things we enjoy in this world: and the ground which produces the materials, is scarce to be reckoned in, as any, or at most, but a very small part of it; so little, that even amongst us, land that is left wholly to nature, that hath no improvement of pasturage, tillage, or planting, is called, as indeed it is, waste; and we shall find the benefit of it amount to little more than nothing.

... It is not barely the plough-man's pains, the reaper's and thresher's toil, and the baker's sweat, is to be counted into the bread we eat; the labour of those who broke the oxen, who digged and wrought the iron and stones, who felled and framed the timber employed about the plough, mill, oven, or any other utensils, which are a vast number, requisite to this corn, from its being feed to be sown to its being made bread, must all be charged on the account of labour, and received as an effect of that: nature and the earth furnished only the almost worthless materials, as in themselves. It would be a strange catalogue of things, that industry provided and made use of, about every loaf of bread, before it came to our use, if we could trace them; iron, wood, leather, bark, timber, stone, bricks, coals, lime, cloth, dying drugs, pitch, tar, masts, ropes, and all the materials made use of in the ship, that brought any of the commodities made use of by any of the workmen, to any part of the work; all which it would be almost impossible, at least too long, to reckon up.

...

Sect. 46. The greatest part of things really useful to the life of man, and such as the necessity of subsisting made the first commoners of the world look after, as it doth the Americans now, are generally things of short duration; such as, if they are not consumed by use, will decay and perish of themselves: gold, silver and diamonds, are things that fancy or agreement hath put the value on, more than real use, and the necessary support of life. Now of those good things which nature hath provided in common, every one had a right (as hath been said) to as much as he could use.... He that gathered a hundred bushels of acorns or apples, had thereby a property in them.... He was only to look, that he used them before they spoiled, else he took more than his share, and robbed others. And indeed it was a foolish thing, as well as dishonest, to hoard up more than he could make use of. If he gave away a part to any body else, so that it perished not uselesly in his possession, these he also made use of. And if he also bartered away plums, that would have rotted in a week, for nuts that would last good for his eating a whole year, he did no injury; he wasted not the common stock; destroyed no part of the portion of goods that belonged to others, so long as nothing perished uselesly in his hands. Again, if he would give his nuts for a piece of metal, pleased with its colour; or exchange his sheep for shells, or wool for a sparkling pebble or a diamond, and keep those by him all his life he invaded not the right of others, he might heap up as much of these durable things as he pleased; the exceeding of the bounds of his just property not lying in the largeness of his possession, but the perishing of any thing uselesly in it.

Sect. 47. And thus came in the use of money, some lasting thing that men might keep without spoiling, and that by mutual consent men would take in exchange for the truly useful, but perishable supports of life.

Sect. 48. And as different degrees of industry were apt to give men possessions in different proportions, so this invention of money gave them the opportunity to continue and enlarge them: for supposing an island, separate from all possible commerce with the rest of the world, wherein there were but an hundred families, but there were sheep, horses and cows, with other useful animals, wholsome fruits, and land enough for corn for a hundred thousand times as many, but nothing in the island, either because of its commonness, or perishableness, fit to supply the place of money; what reason could any one have there to enlarge his possessions beyond the use of his family, and a plentiful supply to its consumption, either in what their own industry produced, or they could barter for like perishable, useful commodities, with others? Where there is not some thing, both lasting and scarce, and so valuable to be hoarded up, there men will not be apt to enlarge their possessions of land, were it never so rich, never so free for them to take: for I ask, what would a man value ten thousand, or an hundred thousand acres of excellent land, ready cultivated, and well stocked too with cattle, in the middle of the inland parts of America, where he had no hopes of commerce with other parts of the world, to draw money to him by the sale of the product? It would not be worth the enclosing, and we should see him give up again to the wild common of nature, whatever was more than would supply the conveniencies of life to be had there for him and his family.

...

Sect. 50. But since gold and silver, being little useful to the life of man in proportion to food, raiment, and carriage, has its value only from the consent of men, whereof labour yet makes, in great part, the measure, it is plain, that men have agreed to a disproportionate and unequal possession of the earth, they having, by a tacit and voluntary consent, found out, a way how a man may fairly possess more land than he himself can use the product of, by receiving in exchange for the overplus gold and silver, which may be hoarded up without injury to any one; these metals not spoiling or decaying in the hands of the possessor. This partage [sharing] of things in an inequality of private possessions, men have made practicable out of the bounds of society, and without compact, only by putting a value on gold and silver, and tacitly agreeing in the use of money: for in governments, the laws regulate the right of property, and the possession of land is determined by positive constitutions.

Sect. 51. And thus, I think, it is very easy to conceive, without any difficulty, how labour could at first begin a title of property in the common things of nature, and how the spending it upon our uses bounded it. So that there could then be no reason of quarrelling about title, nor any doubt about the largeness of possession it gave. Right and conveniency went together; for as a man had a right to all he could employ his labour upon, so he had no temptation to labour for more than he could make use of. This left no room for controversy about the title, nor for encroachment on the right of others; what portion a man carved to himself, was easily seen; and it was useless, as well as dishonest, to carve himself too much, or take more than he needed.

5.4 Jean-Jacques Rousseau (1712–1778)

Like Thomas Hobbes and John Locke, the Swiss-born Jean-Jacques Rousseau begins by speculating about human relationships in a state of nature. Whereas Hobbes posits a condition of natural insecurity and Locke posits natural liberty, Rousseau speculates that people must have existed in a natural state of independence. The natural relation in this state would be equality. Accordingly, any inequality in our present relations must be artificial, and anything that upsets this condition of equality is thereby naturally unjust. Since inequality was evident in virtually every society known to Rousseau and remains evident today, it is crucial to diagnose the cause of this injustice. According to him, the problem is private property.

According to Rousseau, human beings have simple natural needs. The simplicity of these natural needs means that we do not require social relations (as Aristotle thought). Still, human beings in the original state of nature bear no resentment towards each other and had no reason to fear each other (as Hobbes thought). As well, social relations in the state of nature would be transient, not formal and permanent. A natural love of independence would make ongoing associations or the founding of a state unattractive to people in this condition. What ruined this idyllic situation is private property. Fencing off a plot of land or laying claim to a natural resource excludes other people and thereby compels the claimant to defend the claim with violence or the threat of violence. Prior to the institution of private property, people had enough natural sympathy for each other to form temporary associations and to cooperate for specific purposes. After the institution of private property, however, associations were motivated by calculating self-interest and other people were regarded as potential threats to oneself.

Private property is thus the root of class divisions, the most fundamental of which is between rich and poor. Moreover, this division can only be maintained artificially by a state that is controlled by the rich in order to protect their property. Each person has as much natural right to liberty as every other person. However, if one person is rich and the other poor they can never be equal, and the rich person is in a position to extract services from the poor one. Moreover, because all land and resources in the modern world have been claimed by someone, those without property are left without any opportunity to fulfill their natural love of independence and liberty.

~

from A Discourse upon the Origin and the Foundation of the Inequality among Mankind

...

The philosophers, who have examined the foundations of society, have, every one of them, perceived the necessity of tracing it back to a state of nature, but not one of them has ever arrived there. Some of them have not scrupled to attribute to man in that state the ideas of justice and injustice, without troubling their heads to prove, that he really must have had such ideas, or even that such ideas were useful to him: others have spoken of the natural right of every man to keep what belongs to him, without letting us know what they meant by the word belong; others, without further ceremony ascribing to the strongest an authority over the weakest, have immediately struck out government, without thinking of the time requisite for men to form any notion of the things signified by the words authority and government. All of them, in fine, constantly harping on wants, avidity, oppression, desires and pride, have transferred to the state of nature ideas picked up in the bosom of society. In speaking of savages they described citizens....

Discourse First Part

... It is impossible to conceive, why, in this primitive state, one man should have more occasion for the assistance of another, than one monkey, or one wolf for that of another animal of the same species; or supposing that he had, what motive could induce another to assist him; or even, in this last case, how he, who wanted assistance, and he from whom it was wanted, could agree among themselves upon the conditions. Authors, I know, are continually telling us, that in this state man would have been a most miserable creature ... but, if I thoroughly understand this term miserable, it ... signifies nothing, but a privation attended with pain, and a suffering state of body or soul; now I would fain know what kind of misery can be that of a free being, whose heart enjoys perfect peace, and body perfect health? And which is aptest to become insupportable to those who enjoy it, a civil or a natural life? In civil life we can scarcely meet a single person who does not complain of his existence; many even throw away as much of it as they can.... Was ever any free savage known to have been so much as tempted to complain of life, and lay violent hands on himself? Let us therefore judge with less pride on which side real misery is to be placed.... Savage man ... had in his instinct alone everything requisite to live in a state of nature; in his cultivated reason he has barely what is necessary to live in a state of society.

It appears at first sight that, as there was no kind of moral relations between men in this state, nor any known duties, they could not be either good or bad, and had neither vices nor virtues.... But without deviating from the usual meaning of these terms, it is proper to suspend the judgment ... till ... we have examined whether there are more virtues or vices among civilized men; or whether the improvement of their understanding is sufficient to compensate the damage which they mutually do to each other, in proportion as they become better informed of the services which they ought to do; or whether, upon the whole, they would not be much happier in a condition, where they had nothing to fear or to hope from each other, than in that where they had submitted to an universal subserviency, and have obliged themselves to depend for everything upon the good will of those, who do not think themselves obliged to give anything in return.

But above all things let us beware concluding with Hobbes, that man, as having no idea of goodness, must be naturally bad; that he is vicious because he does not know what virtue is; that he always refuses to do any service to those of his own species, because he believes that none is due to them; that, in virtue of that right which he justly claims to everything he wants, he foolishly looks upon himself as proprietor of the whole universe.... This author, to argue from his own principles, should say that the state of nature, being that where the care of our own preservation interferes least with the preservation of others, was of course the most favourable to peace, and most suitable to mankind.... Hobbes did not consider that the same cause, which hinders savages from making use of their reason ... hinders them at the same time from making an ill use of their faculties ... so that we may say that savages are not bad, precisely because they don't know what it is to be good; for it is neither the development of the understanding, nor the curb of the law, but the calmness of their passions and their ignorance of vice that hinders them from doing ill: *tantus plus in illis proficit vitiorum ignorantia, quam in his cognito virtutis*. There is besides another principle that has escaped Hobbes, and which, having been given to man to moderate ... the blind and impetuous sallies of self-love, or the desire of self-preservation ... allays the ardour, with which he naturally pursues his private welfare, by an innate abhorrence to see beings suffer that resemble him. I shall not surely be contradicted, in granting to man the only natural virtue, which the most passionate detractor of human virtues could not deny him, I mean that of pity, a disposition suitable to creatures weak as we are, and liable to so many evils; a virtue so much the more universal, and withal useful to man, as it takes place in him of all manner of reflection; and so natural, that the beasts themselves sometimes give evident signs of it....

Such is the pure motion of nature, anterior to all manner of reflection; such is the force of natural pity, which the most dissolute manners have as yet found it so difficult to extinguish, since we every day see, in our theatrical representation, those men sympathize with the unfortunate and weep at their sufferings, who, if in the tyrant's place, would aggravate the torments of their enemies.... What is generosity, what clemency, what humanity, but pity applied to the weak, to the guilty, or to the human species in general? Even benevolence and friendship, if we judge right, will appear the effects of a constant pity, fixed upon a particular object: for to wish that a person may not suffer, what is it but to wish that he may be happy? ... Now it is evident that this identification must have been infinitely more perfect in the state of nature than in the state of reason. It is reason that engenders self-love, and reflection that strengthens it; it is reason that makes man shrink into himself; it is reason that makes him keep aloof from everything that can trouble or afflict him: it is philosophy that destroys his connections with other men; it is in consequence of her dictates that he mutters to himself at the sight of another in distress, You may perish for aught I care, nothing can hurt me. Nothing less than those evils, which threaten the whole species, can disturb the calm sleep of the philosopher, and force him from his bed. One man may with impunity murder another under his windows; he has nothing to do but clap his hands to his ears, argue a little with himself to hinder nature, that startles within him, from identifying him with the unhappy sufferer. Savage man wants this admirable talent; and for want of wisdom and reason, is always ready foolishly to obey the first whispers of humanity. In riots and street-brawls the populace flock together, the prudent man sneaks off. They are the dregs of the people, the poor basket and barrow-women, that part the combatants, and hinder gentle folks from cutting one another's throats.

It is therefore certain that pity is a natural sentiment, which, by moderating in every individual the activity of self-love, contributes to the mutual preservation of the whole species. It is this pity which hurries us without reflection to the assistance of those we see in distress; it is this pity which, in a state of nature, stands for laws, for manners, for virtue, with this advantage, that no one is tempted to disobey her sweet and gentle voice: it is this pity which will always hinder a robust savage from plundering a feeble child, or infirm old man, of the subsistence they have acquired with pain and difficulty, if he has but the least prospect of providing for himself by any other means: it is this pity which, instead of that sublime maxim of argumentative justice, Do to others as you would have others do to you, inspires all men with that other maxim of natural goodness a great deal less perfect, but perhaps more useful, Consult your own happiness with as little prejudice as you can to that of others. It is in a word, in this natural sentiment, rather than in fine-spun arguments, that we must look for the cause of that reluctance which every man would experience to do evil, even independently of the maxims of education....The human species would long ago have ceased to exist, had it depended entirely for its preservation on the reasonings of the individuals that compose it.

With passions so tame, and so salutary a curb, men, rather wild than wicked, and more attentive to guard against mischief than to do any to other animals, were not exposed to any dangerous dissensions: As they kept up no manner of correspondence with each other, and were of course strangers to vanity, to respect, to esteem, to contempt; as they had no notion of what we call Meum and Tuum, nor any true idea of justice; as they considered any violence they were liable to, as an evil that could be easily repaired, and not as an injury that deserved punishment; and as they never so much as dreamed of revenge, unless perhaps mechanically and unpremeditatedly, as a dog who bites the stone that has been thrown at him; their disputes could seldom be attended with bloodshed....

Let us conclude that savage man, wandering about in the forests, without industry, without speech, without any fixed residence, an equal stranger to war and every social connection, without standing in any shape in need of his fellows, as well as without any desire of hurting them, and perhaps even without ever distinguishing them individually one from the other, subject to few passions, and finding in himself all he wants, let us, I say, conclude that savage man thus circumstanced had no knowledge or sentiment but such as are proper to that condition, that he was alone sensible of his real necessities, took notice of nothing but what it was his interest to see, and that his understanding made as little progress as his vanity. If he happened to make any discovery, he could the less communicate it as he did not even know his children....

If I have enlarged so much upon the supposition of this primitive condition, it is because I thought it my duty, considering what ancient errors and inveterate prejudices I have to extirpate, to dig to the very roots, and show in a true picture of the state of nature, how much even natural inequality falls short in this state of that reality and influence which our writers ascribe to it.

In fact, we may easily perceive that among the differences, which distinguish men, several pass for natural, which are merely the work of habit and the different kinds of life adopted by men living in a social way. Thus a robust or delicate constitution, and the strength and weakness which depend on it, are oftener produced by the hardy or effeminate manner in which a man has been brought up, than by the primitive constitution of his body. It is the same thus in regard to the forces of the mind; and education not only produces a difference between those minds which are cultivated and those which are not, but even increases that which is found among the first in proportion to their culture.... If we compare the prodigious variety in the education and manner of living of the different orders of men in a civil state, with the simplicity and uniformity that prevails in the animal and savage life, where all the individuals make use of the same aliments, live in the same manner, and do exactly the same things, we shall easily conceive how much the difference between man and man in the state of nature must be less than in the state of society, and how much every inequality of institution must increase the natural inequalities of the human species.

But though nature in the distribution of her gifts should really affect all the preferences that are ascribed to her, what advantage could the most favoured derive from her partiality, to the prejudice of others, in a state of things, which scarce admitted any kind of relation between her pupils? Of what service can beauty be, where there is no love? What will wit avail people who don't speak, or craft those who have no affairs to transact? Authors are constantly crying out, that the strongest would oppress the weakest; but let them explain what they mean by the word oppression. One man will rule with violence, another will groan under a constant subjection to all his caprices: this is indeed precisely what I observe among us, but I don't see how it can be said of savage men.... One man might, indeed, seize on the fruits which another had gathered, on the game which another had killed, on the cavern which another had occupied for shelter; but how is it possible he should ever exact obedience from him, and what chains of dependence can there be among men who possess nothing? If I am driven from one tree, I have nothing to do but look out for another; if one place is made uneasy to me, what can hinder me from taking up my quarters elsewhere? But suppose I should meet a man so much superior to me in strength, and withal so wicked, so lazy and so barbarous as to oblige me to provide for his subsistence while he remains idle; he must resolve not to take his eyes from me a single moment, to bind me fast before he can take the least nap, lest I should kill him or give him the slip during his sleep: that is to say, he must expose himself voluntarily to much greater troubles than what he seeks to avoid, than any he gives me. And after all, let him abate ever so little of his vigilance; let him at some sudden noise but turn his head another way; I am already buried in the forest, my fetters are broke, and he never sees me again.

But without insisting any longer upon these details, every one must see that, as the bonds of servitude are formed merely by the mutual dependence of men one upon another and the reciprocal necessities which unite them, it is impossible for one man to enslave another, without having first reduced him to a condition in which he can not live without the enslaver's assistance; a condition which, as it does not exist in a state of nature, must leave every man his own master, and render the law of the strongest altogether vain and useless.

...

Second Part

The first man, who, after enclosing a piece of ground, took it into his head to say, "This is mine," and found people simple enough to believe him, was the true founder of civil society. How many crimes, how many wars, how many murders, how many misfortunes and horrors, would that man have saved the human species, who pulling up the stakes or filling up the ditches should have cried to his fellows: Be sure not to listen to this imposter; you are lost, if you forget that the fruits of the earth belong equally to us all, and the earth itself to nobody! ...

As long as men remained satisfied with their rustic cabins; as long as they confined themselves to the use of clothes made of the skins of other animals, and the use of thorns and fish-bones, in putting these skins together; as long as they continued to consider feathers and shells as sufficient ornaments, and to paint their bodies of different colours, to improve or ornament their bows and arrows, to form and scoop out with sharp-edged stones some little fishing boats, or clumsy instruments of music; in a word, as long as they undertook such works only as a single person could finish, and stuck to such arts as did not require the joint endeavours of several hands, they lived free, healthy, honest and happy, as much as their nature would admit, and continued to enjoy with each other all the pleasures of an independent intercourse; but from the moment one man began to stand in need of another's assistance; from the moment it appeared an advantage for one man to possess the quantity of provisions requisite for two, all equality vanished; property started up; labour became necessary; and boundless forests became smiling fields, which it was found necessary to water with human sweat, and in which slavery and misery were soon seen to sprout out and grow with the fruits of the earth.

...

To the tilling of the earth the distribution of it necessarily succeeded, and to property once acknowledged, the first rules of justice: for to secure every man his own, every man must have something. Moreover, as men began to extend their views to futurity, and all found themselves in possession of more or less goods capable of being lost, every one in particular had reason to fear, lest reprisals should be made on him for any injury he might do to others. This origin is so much the more natural, as it is impossible to conceive how property can flow from any other source but industry; for what can a man add but his labour to things which he has not made, in order to acquire a property in them? 'Tis the labour of the hands alone, which giving the husbandman a title to the produce of the land he has tilled gives him a title to the land itself, at least till he has gathered in the fruits of it, and so on from year to year; and this enjoyment forming a continued possession is easily transformed into a property....

Things thus circumstanced might have remained equal, if men's talents had been equal, and if, for instance, the use of iron, and the consumption of commodities had always held an exact proportion to each other; but as this proportion had no support, it was soon broken. The man that had most strength performed most labour; the most dexterous turned his labour to best account; the most ingenious found out methods of lessening his labour; the husbandman required more iron, or the smith more corn, and while both worked equally, one earned a great deal by his labour, while the other could scarce live by his. It is thus that natural inequality insensibly unfolds itself with that arising from a variety of combinations, and that the difference among men, developed by the difference of their circumstances, becomes more sensible, more permanent in its effects, and begins to influence in the same proportion the condition of private persons.

...

Behold then all our faculties developed; our memory and imagination at work, self-love interested; reason rendered active; and the mind almost arrived at the utmost bounds of that perfection it is capable of. Behold all our natural qualities put in motion; the rank and condition of every man established, not only as to the quantum of property and the power of serving or hurting others, but likewise as to genius, beauty, strength or address, merit or talents; and as these were the only qualities which could command respect, it was found necessary to have or at least to affect them. It was requisite for men to be thought what they really were not. To be and to appear became two very different things, and from this distinction sprang pomp and knavery, and all the vices which form their train. On the other hand, man, heretofore free and independent, was now in consequence of a multitude of new wants brought under subjection, as it were, to all nature, and especially to his fellows, whose slave in some sense he became even by becoming their master; if rich, he stood in need of their services, if poor, of their assistance; even mediocrity itself could not enable him to do without them. He must therefore have been continually at work to interest them in his happiness, and make them, if not really, at least apparently find their advantage in labouring for his: this rendered him sly and artful in his dealings with some, imperious and cruel in his dealings with others, and laid him under the necessity of using ill all those whom he stood in need of, as often as he could not awe them into a compliance with his will, and did not find it his interest to purchase it at the expense of real services. In fine, an insatiable ambition, the rage of raising their relative fortunes, not so much through real necessity, as to over-top others, inspire all men with a wicked inclination to injure each other, and with a secret jealousy so much the more dangerous, as to carry its point with the greater security, it often puts on the face of benevolence. In a word, sometimes nothing was to be seen but a contention of endeavours on the one hand, and an opposition of interests on the other, while a secret desire of thriving at the expense of others constantly prevailed. Such were the first effects of property, and the inseparable attendants of infant inequality.

Riches, before the invention of signs to represent them, could scarce consist in anything but lands and cattle, the only real goods which men can possess. But when estates increased so much in number and in extent as to take in whole countries and touch each other, it became impossible for one man to aggrandise himself but at the expense of some other; and the supernumerary inhabitants, who were too weak or too indolent to make such acquisitions in their turn, impoverished without losing anything, because while everything about them changed they alone remained the same, were obliged to receive or force their subsistence from the hands of the rich. And hence began to flow, according to the different characters of each, domination and slavery, or violence and rapine. The rich on their side scarce began to taste the pleasure of commanding, when they preferred it to every other; and making use of their old slaves to acquire new ones, they no longer thought of anything but subduing and enslaving their neighbours; like those ravenous wolves, who having once tasted human flesh, despise every other food, and devour nothing but men for the future.

... Equality once broken was followed by the most shocking disorders. It is thus that the usurpations of the rich, the pillagings of the poor, and the unbridled passions of all, by stifling the cries of natural compassion, and the as yet feeble voice of justice, rendered man avaricious, wicked and ambitious. There arose between the title of the strongest, and that of the first occupier a perpetual conflict, which always ended in battery and bloodshed. Infant society became a scene of the most horrible warfare: Mankind thus debased and harassed, and no longer able to retreat, or renounce the unhappy acquisitions it had made; labouring, in short merely to its confusion by the abuse of those faculties, which in themselves do it so much honour, brought itself to the very brink of ruin and destruction. ...

But it is impossible that men should not sooner or later have made reflections on so wretched a situation, and upon the calamities with which they were overwhelmed. The rich in particular must have soon perceived how much they suffered by a perpetual war, of which they alone supported all the expense, and in which, though all risked life, they alone risked any substance. Besides, whatever colour they might pretend to give their usurpations, they sufficiently saw that these usurpations were in the main founded upon false and precarious titles, and that what they had acquired by mere force, others could again by mere force wrest out of their hands, without leaving them the least room to complain of such a proceeding. Even those, who owed all their riches to their own industry, could scarce ground their acquisitions upon a better title. It availed them nothing to say, 'Twas I built this wall; I acquired this spot by my labour. Who traced it out for you, another might object, and what right have you to expect payment at our expense for doing that we did not oblige you to do? Don't you know that numbers of your brethren perish, or suffer grievously for want of what you possess more than suffices nature, and that you should have had the express and unanimous consent of mankind to appropriate to yourself of their common, more than was requisite for your private subsistence? Destitute of solid reasons to justify, and sufficient force to defend himself; crushing individuals with ease, but with equal ease crushed by numbers; one against all, and unable, on account of mutual jealousies, to unite with his equals against banditti united by the common hopes of pillage; the rich man, thus pressed by necessity, at last conceived the deepest project that ever entered the human mind: this was to employ in his favour the very forces that attacked him, to make allies of his enemies, to inspire them with other maxims, and make them adopt other institutions as favourable to his pretensions, as the law of nature was unfavourable to them.

With this view, after laying before his neighbours all the horrors of a situation, which armed them all one against another, which rendered their possessions as burdensome as their wants were intolerable, and in which no one could expect any safety either in poverty or riches, he easily invented specious arguments to bring them over to his purpose. "Let us unite," said he, "to secure the weak from oppression, restrain the ambitious, and secure to every man the possession of what belongs to him: Let us form rules of justice and peace, to which all may be obliged to conform, which shall not except persons, but may in some sort make amends for the caprice of fortune, by submitting alike the powerful and the weak to the observance of mutual duties. In a word, instead of turning our forces against ourselves, let us collect them into a sovereign power, which may govern us by wise laws, may protect and defend all the members of the association, repel common enemies, and maintain a perpetual concord and harmony among us."

Much fewer words of this kind were sufficient to draw in a parcel of rustics, whom it was an easy matter to impose upon, who had besides too many quarrels among themselves to live without arbiters, and too much avarice and ambition to live long without masters. All offered their necks to the yoke in hopes of securing their liberty; for though they had sense enough to perceive the advantages of a political constitution, they had not experience enough to see beforehand the dangers of it; those among them, who were best qualified to foresee abuses, were precisely those who expected to benefit by them; even the soberest judged it requisite to sacrifice one part of their liberty to ensure the other, as a man, dangerously wounded in any of his limbs, readily parts with it to save the rest of his body.

Such was, or must have been ... the origin of society and of the laws, which increased the fetters of the weak, and the strength of the rich; irretrievably destroyed natural liberty, fixed for ever the laws of property and inequality; changed an artful usurpation into an irrevocable title; and for the benefit of a few ambitious individuals subjected the rest of mankind to perpetual labour, servitude, and misery. We may easily conceive how the establishment of a single society rendered that of all the rest absolutely necessary, and how, to make head against united forces, it became necessary for the rest of mankind to unite in their turn. Societies once formed in this manner, soon multiplied or spread to such a degree, as to cover the face of the earth; and not to leave a corner in the whole universe, where a man could throw off the yoke, and withdraw his head from under the often ill-conducted sword which he saw perpetually hanging over it. The civil law being thus become the common rule of citizens, the law of nature no longer obtained but among the different societies, in which, under the name of the law of nations, it was qualified by some tacit conventions to render commerce possible, and supply the place of natural compassion, which, losing by degrees all that influence over societies which it originally had over individuals, no longer exists but in some great souls, who consider themselves as citizens of the world, and ... make the whole human race the object of their benevolence.

Political bodies, thus remaining in a state of nature among themselves, soon experienced the inconveniences which had obliged individuals to quit it; and this state became much more fatal to these great bodies, than it had been before to the individuals which now composed them. Hence those national wars, those battles, those murders, those reprisals, which make nature shudder and shock reason; hence all those horrible prejudices, which make it a virtue and an honour to shed human blood. The worthiest men learned to consider the cutting the throats of their fellows as a duty; at length men began to butcher each other by thousands without knowing for what; and more murders were committed in a single action, and more horrible disorders at the taking of a single town, than had been committed in the state of nature during ages together upon the whole face of the earth. Such are the first effects we may conceive to have arisen from the division of mankind into different societies. Let us return to their institution.

... Society at first consisted merely of some general conventions which all the members bound themselves to observe, and for the performance of which the whole body became security to every individual. Experience was necessary to show the great weakness of such a constitution, and how easy it was for those, who infringed it, to escape the conviction or chastisement of faults, of which the public alone was to be both the witness and the judge; the laws could not fail of being eluded a thousand ways; inconveniences and disorders could not but multiply continually, till it was at last found necessary to think of committing to private persons the dangerous trust of public authority, and to magistrates the care of enforcing obedience to the people: for to say that chiefs were elected before confederacies were formed, and that the ministers of the laws existed before the laws themselves, is a supposition too ridiculous to deserve I should seriously refute it.

It would be equally unreasonable to imagine that men at first threw themselves into the arms of an absolute master, without any conditions or consideration on his side; and that the first means contrived by jealous and unconquered men for their common safety was to run hand over head into slavery. In fact, why did they give themselves superiors, if it was not to be defended by them against oppression, and protected in their lives, liberties, and properties, which are in a manner the constitutional elements of their being? Now in the relations between man and man, the worst that can happen to one man being to see himself at the discretion of another, would it not have been contrary to the dictates of good sense to begin by making over to a chief the only things for the preservation of which they stood in need of his assistance? What equivalent could he have offered them for so fine a privilege? And had he presumed to exact it on pretense of defending them, would he not have immediately received the answer in the apologue? What worse treatment can we expect from an enemy? It is therefore past dispute, and indeed a fundamental maxim of political law, that people gave themselves chiefs to defend their liberty and not be enslaved by them. If we have a prince, said Pliny to Trajan, it is in order that he may keep us from having a master.

Political writers argue in regard to the love of liberty with the same philosophy that philosophers do in regard to the state of nature; by the things they see they judge of things very different which they have never seen, and they attribute to men a natural inclination to slavery, on account of the patience with which the slaves within their notice carry the yoke; not reflecting that it is with liberty as with innocence and virtue, the value of which is not known but by those who possess them, though the relish for them is lost with the things themselves....

As an unbroken courser erects his mane, paws the ground, and rages at the bare sight of the bit, while a trained horse patiently suffers both whip and spur, just so the barbarian will never reach his neck to the yoke which civilized man carries without murmuring but prefers the most stormy liberty to a calm subjection. It is not therefore by the servile disposition of enslaved nations that we must judge of the natural dispositions of man for or against slavery, but by the prodigies done by every free people to secure themselves from oppression. I know that the first are constantly crying up that peace and tranquillity they enjoy in their irons, and that *miserrimam servitutem pacem appellant*: but when I see the others sacrifice pleasures, peace, riches, power, and even life itself to the preservation of that single jewel so much slighted by those who have lost it; when I see free-born animals through a natural abhorrence of captivity dash their brains out against the bars of their prison; when I see multitudes of naked savages despise European pleasures, and brave hunger, fire and sword, and death itself to preserve their independency; I feel that it belongs not to slaves to argue concerning liberty.

As to paternal authority, from which several have derived absolute government and every other mode of society, it is sufficient, without having recourse to Locke and Sidney, to observe that nothing in the world differs more from the cruel spirit of despotism than the gentleness of that authority, which looks more to the advantage of him who obeys than to the utility of him who commands; that by the law of nature the father continues master of his child no longer than the child stands in need of his assistance; that after that term they become equal, and that then the son, entirely independent of the father, owes him no obedience, but only respect. Gratitude is indeed a duty which we are bound to pay, but which benefactors can not exact. Instead of saying that civil society is derived from paternal authority, we should rather say that it is to the former that the latter owes its principal force: No one individual was acknowledged as the father of several other individuals, till they settled about him. The father's goods, which he can indeed dispose of as he pleases, are the ties which hold his children to their dependence upon him, and he may divide his substance among them in proportion as they shall have deserved his attention by a continual deference to his commands. Now the subjects of a despotic chief, far from having any such favour to expect from him, as both themselves and all they have are his property, or at least are considered by him as such, are obliged to receive as a favour what he relinquishes to them of their own property. He does them justice when he strips them; he treats them with mercy when he suffers them to live. By continuing in this manner to compare facts with right, we should discover as little solidity as truth in the voluntary establishment of tyranny; and it would be a hard matter to prove the validity of a contract which was binding only on one side, in which one of the parties should stake everything and the other nothing, and which could turn out to the prejudice of him alone who had bound himself. ...

It therefore appears to me incontestably true, that not only governments did not begin by arbitrary power, which is but the corruption and extreme term of government, and at length brings it back to the law of the strongest, against which governments were at first the remedy, but even that, allowing they had commenced in this manner, such power being illegal in itself could never have served as a foundation to the rights of society, nor of course to the inequality of institution....

If there was no superior power capable of guaranteeing the fidelity of the contracting parties and of obliging them to fulfil their mutual engagements, they would remain sole judges in their own cause, and each of them would always have a right to renounce the contract, as soon as he discovered that the other had broke the conditions of it, or that these conditions ceased to suit his private convenience. Upon this principle, the right of abdication may probably be founded. Now, to consider as we do nothing but what is human in this institution, if the magistrate, who has all the power in his own hands, and who appropriates to himself all the advantages of the contract, has notwithstanding a right to divest himself of his authority; how much a better right must the people, who pay for all the faults of its chief, have to renounce their dependence upon him. But the shocking dissensions and disorders without number, which would be the necessary consequence of so dangerous a privilege, show more than anything else how much human governments stood in need of a more solid basis than that of mere reason, and how necessary it was for the public tranquillity, that the will of the Almighty should interpose to give to sovereign authority, a sacred and inviolable character, which should deprive subjects of the mischievous right to dispose of it to whom they pleased. If mankind had received no other advantages from religion, this alone would be sufficient to make them adopt and cherish it, since it is the means of saving more blood than fanaticism has been the cause of spilling. But to resume the thread of our hypothesis.

The various forms of government owe their origin to the various degrees of inequality between the members, at the time they first coalesced into a political body. Where a man happened to be eminent for power, for virtue, for riches, or for credit, he became sole magistrate, and the state assumed a monarchical form; if many of pretty equal eminence out-topped all the rest, they were jointly elected, and this election produced an aristocracy; those, between whose fortune or talents there happened to be no such disproportion, and who had deviated less from the state of nature, retained in common the supreme administration, and formed a democracy. Time demonstrated which of these forms suited mankind best. Some remained altogether subject to the laws; others soon bowed their necks to masters. The former laboured to preserve their liberty; the latter thought of nothing but invading that of their neighbours, jealous at seeing others enjoy a blessing which themselves had lost. In a word, riches and conquest fell to the share of the one, and virtue and happiness to that of the other....

By pursuing the progress of inequality in these different revolutions, we shall discover that the establishment of laws and of the right of property was the first term of it; the institution of magistrates the second; and the third and last the changing of legal into arbitrary power; so that the different states of rich and poor were authorized by the first epoch; those of powerful and weak by the second; and by the third those of master and slave, which formed the last degree of inequality, and the term in which all the rest at last end, till new revolutions entirely dissolve the government, or bring it back nearer to its legal constitution....

Political distinctions are necessarily attended with civil distinctions. The inequality between the people and the chiefs increase so fast as to be soon felt by the private members, and appears among them in a thousand shapes according to their passions, their talents, and the circumstances of affairs. The magistrate can not usurp any illegal power without making himself creatures, with whom he must divide it. Besides, the citizens of a free state suffer themselves to be oppressed merely in proportion as, hurried on by a blind ambition, and looking rather below than above them, they come to love authority more than independence. When they submit to fetters, 'tis only to be the better able to fetter others in their turn. It is no easy matter to make him obey, who does not wish to command; and the most refined policy would find it impossible to subdue those men, who only desire to be independent; but inequality easily gains ground among base and ambitious souls, ever ready to run the risks of fortune, and almost indifferent whether they command or obey, as she proves either favourable or adverse to them....

... Inequalities ... are of several kinds; but riches, nobility or rank, power and personal merit, being in general the principal distinctions, by which men in society measure each other ... riches is that in which they ultimately terminate, because, being the most immediately useful to the prosperity of individuals, and the most easy to communicate, they are made use of to purchase every other distinction. By this observation we are enabled to judge with tolerable exactness, how much any people has deviated from its primitive institution, and what steps it has still to make to the extreme term of corruption. I could show how much this universal desire of reputation, of honours, of preference, with which we are all devoured, exercises and compares our talents and our forces: how much it excites and multiplies our passions; and, by creating an universal competition, rivalship, or rather enmity among men, how many disappointments, successes, and catastrophes of every kind it daily causes among the innumerable pretenders whom it engages in the same career. I could show that it is to this itch of being spoken of, to this fury of distinguishing ourselves which seldom or never gives us a moment's respite, that we owe both the best and the worst things among us, our virtues and our vices, our sciences and our errors, our conquerors and our philosophers; that is to say, a great many bad things to a very few good ones. I could prove, in short, that if we behold a handful of rich and powerful men seated on the pinnacle of fortune and greatness, while the crowd grovel in obscurity and want, it is merely because the first prize what they enjoy but in the same degree that others want it, and that, without changing their condition, they would cease to be happy the minute the people ceased to be miserable.

... We should see the chiefs foment everything that tends to weaken men formed into societies by dividing them; everything that, while it gives society an air of apparent harmony, sows in it the seeds of real division; everything that can inspire the different orders with mutual distrust and hatred by an opposition of their rights and interest, and of course strengthen that power which contains them all.

'Tis from the bosom of this disorder and these revolutions, that despotism gradually rearing up her hideous crest, and devouring in every part of the state all that still remained sound and untainted, would at last issue to trample upon the laws and the people, and establish herself upon the ruins of the republic. The times immediately preceding this last alteration would be times of calamity and trouble: but at last everything would be swallowed up by the monster; and the people would no longer have chiefs or laws, but only tyrants. At this fatal period all regard to virtue and manners would likewise disappear; for despotism, *cui ex honesto nulla est spes*, tolerates no other master, wherever it reigns; the moment it speaks, probity and duty lose all their influence, and the blindest obedience is the only virtue the miserable slaves have left them to practise.

This is the last term of inequality, the extreme point which closes the circle and meets that from which we set out. 'Tis here that all private men return to their primitive equality, because they are no longer of any account; and that, the subjects having no longer any law but that of their master, nor the master any other law but his passions, all notions of good and principles of justice again disappear. 'Tis here that everything returns to the sole law of the strongest, and of course to a new state of nature different from that with which we began, in as much as the first was the state of nature in its purity, and the last the consequence of excessive corruption. There is, in other respects, so little difference between these two states, and the contract of government is so much dissolved by despotism, that the despot is no longer master than he continues the strongest, and that, as soon as his slaves can expel him, they may do it without his having the least right to complain of their using him ill. The insurrection, which ends in the death or despotism of a sultan, is as juridical an act as any by which the day before he disposed of the lives and fortunes of his subjects. Force alone upheld him, force alone overturns him.

Thus all things take place and succeed in their natural order; and whatever may be the upshot of these hasty and frequent revolutions, no one man has reason to complain of another's injustice, but only of his own indiscretion or bad fortune....

... In the long run our wants and our pleasures change objects.... Original man vanishing by degrees, society no longer offers to our inspection but an assemblage of artificial men and factitious passions, which are the work of all these new relations, and have no foundation in nature.... Savage man and civilised man differ so much at bottom in point of inclinations and passions, that what constitutes the supreme happiness of the one would reduce the other to despair. The first sighs for nothing but repose and liberty; he desires only to live, and to be exempt from labour.... On the contrary, the citizen always in motion, is perpetually sweating and toiling, and racking his brains to find out occupations still more laborious: He continues a drudge to his last minute; nay, he courts death to be able to live, or renounces life to acquire immortality. He cringes to men in power whom he hates, and to rich men whom he despises; he sticks at nothing to have the honour of serving them; he is not ashamed to value himself on his own weakness and the protection they afford him; and proud of his chains, he speaks with disdain of those who have not the honour of being the partner of his bondage.... The savage lives within himself, whereas the citizen, constantly beside himself, knows only how to live in the opinion of others; insomuch that it is, if I may say so, merely from their judgment that he derives the consciousness of his own existence. It is foreign to my subject to show how this disposition engenders so much indifference for good and evil, notwithstanding so many and such fine discourses of morality; how everything, being reduced to appearances, becomes mere art and mummery; honour, friendship, virtue, and often vice itself, which we at last learn the secret to boast of; how, in short, ever inquiring of others what we are, and never daring to question ourselves on so delicate a point, in the midst of so much philosophy, humanity, and politeness, and so many sublime maxims, we have nothing to show for ourselves but a deceitful and frivolous exterior, honour without virtue, reason without wisdom, and pleasure without happiness. It is sufficient that I have proved that this is not the original condition of man, and that it is merely the spirit of society, and the inequality which society engenders, that thus change and transform all our natural inclinations.

5.5 Adam Smith (1723–1790)

One of the most surprising details of John Locke's liberalism is the suggestion that money is a natural feature of human society. A century later, Adam Smith developed an economic theory that dispenses with speculative thought experiments to determine which elements of social life are natural and which artificial. Instead he focuses on patterns and operations distinctive to a complex national economy as he studied it in eighteenth-century Britain. *The Wealth of Nations*, in particular, explores the macro-economic dynamics of a modern liberal society.

A complex liberal economy requires efficient means of production, coordinated labour, large-scale manufacturing, and a free market. Smith begins with an account of manufacturing in which divided labour increases the rate of production significantly. By assigning each stage of production to one worker who can repeat an operation skillfully many times in a work-day, each operation can be completed very quickly. If each worker completes this one simple operation then passes the unfinished product to another for the next stage of production, then production of each item can be completed in a fraction of the time it would take a solo crafter. Here we encounter a conceptual limit to Locke's labour theory of value. No single worker can own the final product that comes from a production line of this sort. Each one of them makes a small contribution, with no single labourer having a decisive claim on it. Ultimately, whoever owns the shop owns the final product, which is then sold to a customer while the workers receive a wage for their contributions.

According to Smith, everyone who participates in the economy acts entirely for their own self-interest. Cooperation among workers, cooperation between workers and shop-owners, cooperation between shop-owners and customers, and so on, requires no benevolence whatsoever. Each person enters into transactions in order to get something that they believe is useful for themselves or money for themselves. The efficiency that Smith identifies in his account of production by divided labour extends all the way up to the macro-level of a national economy: by looking after their own interests everyone participating in an economy ensures efficiency at every step. This degree of efficiency may appear to be well-orchestrated, but, Smith insists, it is generated spontaneously. The economy functions "as if" there were an invisible hand regulating it, but there is no such agent. Indeed, if the state attempts to regulate the market, the spontaneous order will be upset and it will become less efficient.

~

from The Wealth of Nations

Book I. Of the Causes of Improvement in the Productive Powers of Labour, and of the Order According to Which Its Produce Is Naturally Distributed among the Different Ranks of the People

CHAPTER I. OF THE DIVISION OF LABOUR

The greatest improvements in the productive powers of labour, and the greater part of the skill, dexterity, and judgment, with which it is anywhere directed, or applied, seem to have been the effects of the division of labour....

To take an example, therefore, from a very trifling manufacture, but one in which the division of labour has been very often taken notice of, the trade of a pin-maker: a workman not educated to this business (which the division of labour has rendered a distinct trade), nor acquainted with the use of the machinery employed in it (to the invention of which the same division of labour has probably given occasion), could scarce, perhaps, with his utmost industry, make one pin in a day, and certainly could not make twenty. But in the way in which this business is now carried on, not only the whole work is a peculiar trade, but it is divided into a number of branches, of which the greater part are likewise peculiar trades. One man draws out the wire; another straights it; a third cuts it; a fourth points it; a fifth grinds it at the top for receiving the head; to make the head requires two or three distinct operations; to put it on is a peculiar business; to whiten the pins is another; it is even a trade by itself to put them into the paper; and the important business of making a pin is, in this manner, divided into about eighteen distinct operations, which, in some manufactories, are all performed by distinct hands, though in others the same man will sometimes perform two or three of them. I have seen a small manufactory of this kind, where ten men only were employed, and where some of them consequently performed two or three distinct operations. But though they were very poor, and therefore but indifferently accommodated with the necessary machinery, they could, when they exerted themselves, make among them about twelve pounds of pins in a day. There are in a pound upwards of four thousand pins of a middling size. Those ten persons, therefore, could make among them upwards of forty-eight thousand pins in a day. Each person, therefore, making a tenth part of forty-eight thousand pins, might be considered as making four thousand eight hundred pins in a day. But if they had all wrought separately and independently, and without any of them having been educated to this peculiar business, they certainly could not each of them have made twenty, perhaps not one pin in a day; that is, certainly, not the two hundred and fortieth, perhaps not the four thousand eight hundredth, part of what they are at present capable of performing, in consequence of a proper division and combination of their different operations.

... The division of labour, however, so far as it can be introduced, occasions, in every art, a proportionable increase of the productive powers of labour. The separation of different trades and employments from one another, seems to have taken place in consequence of this advantage. This separation, too, is generally carried furthest in those countries which enjoy the highest degree of industry and improvement; what is the work of one man, in a rude state of society, being generally that of several in an improved one....

This great increase in the quantity of work, which, in consequence of the division of labour, the same number of people are capable of performing, is owing to three different circumstances; first, to the increase of dexterity in every particular workman; secondly, to the saving of the time which is commonly lost in passing from one species of work to another; and, lastly, to the invention of a great number of machines which facilitate and abridge labour, and enable one man to do the work of many.

First, the improvement of the dexterity of the workmen, necessarily increases the quantity of the work he can perform; and the division of labour, by reducing every man's business to some one simple operation, and by making this operation the sole employment of his life, necessarily increases very much the dexterity of the workman. A common smith, who, though accustomed to handle the hammer, has never been used to make nails, if, upon some particular occasion, he is obliged to attempt it, will scarce, I am assured, be able to make above two or three hundred nails in a day, and those, too, very bad ones. A smith who has been accustomed to make nails, but whose sole or principal business has not been that of a nailer, can seldom, with his utmost diligence, make more than eight hundred or a thousand nails in a day. I have seen several boys, under twenty years of age, who had never exercised any other trade but that of making nails, and who, when they exerted themselves, could make, each of them, upwards of two thousand three hundred nails in a day....

Secondly, the advantage which is gained by saving the time commonly lost in passing from one sort of work to another, is much greater than we should at first view be apt to imagine it. It is impossible to pass very quickly from one kind of work to another, that is carried on in a different place, and with quite different tools. A country weaver, who cultivates a small farm, must lose a good deal of time in passing from his loom to the field, and from the field to his loom. When the two trades can be carried on in the same workhouse, the loss of time is, no doubt, much less. It is, even in this case, however, very considerable. A man commonly saunters a little in turning his hand from one sort of employment to another. When he first begins the new work, he is seldom very keen and hearty; his mind, as they say, does not go to it, and for some time he rather trifles than applies to good purpose. The habit of sauntering, and of indolent careless application, which is naturally, or rather necessarily, acquired by every country workman who is obliged to change his work and his tools every half hour, and to apply his hand in twenty different ways almost every day of his life, renders him almost always slothful and lazy, and incapable of any vigorous application, even on the most pressing occasions. Independent, therefore, of his deficiency in point of dexterity, this cause alone must always reduce considerably the quantity of work which he is capable of performing.

Thirdly, and lastly, everybody must be sensible how much labour is facilitated and abridged by the application of proper machinery. It is unnecessary to give any example. I shall only observe, therefore, that the invention of all those machines by which labour is so much facilitated and abridged, seems to have been originally owing to the division of labour. Men are much more likely to discover easier and readier methods of attaining any object, when the whole attention of their minds is directed towards that single object, than when it is dissipated among a great variety of things. But, in consequence of the division of labour, the whole of every man's attention comes naturally to be directed towards some one very simple object. It is naturally to be expected, therefore, that some one or other of those who are employed in each particular branch of labour should soon find out easier and readier methods of performing their own particular work, whenever the nature of it admits of such improvement. A great part of the machines made use of in those manufactures in which labour is most subdivided, were originally the invention of common workmen, who, being each of them employed in some very simple operation, naturally turned their thoughts towards finding out easier and readier methods of performing it....

It is the great multiplication of the productions of all the different arts, in consequence of the division of labour, which occasions, in a well-governed society, that universal opulence which extends itself to the lowest ranks of the people. Every workman has a great quantity of his own work to dispose of beyond what he himself has occasion for; and every other workman being exactly in the same situation, he is enabled to exchange a great quantity of his own goods for a great quantity or, what comes to the same thing, for the price of a great quantity of theirs. He supplies them abundantly with what they have occasion for, and they accommodate him as amply with what he has occasion for, and a general plenty diffuses itself through all the different ranks of the society.

...

CHAPTER II. OF THE PRINCIPLE WHICH GIVES OCCASION TO THE DIVISION OF LABOUR

This division of labour, from which so many advantages are derived, is not originally the effect of any human wisdom, which foresees and intends that general opulence to which it gives occasion. It is the necessary, though very slow and gradual, consequence of a certain propensity in human nature, which has in view no such extensive utility; the propensity to truck, barter, and exchange one thing for another.

... Man sometimes uses the same arts with his brethren, and when he has no other means of engaging them to act according to his inclinations, endeavours by every servile and fawning attention to obtain their good will. He has not time, however, to do this upon every occasion. In civilized society he stands at all times in need of the co-operation and assistance of great multitudes, while his whole life is scarce sufficient to gain the friendship of a few persons. In almost every other race of animals, each individual, when it is grown up to maturity, is entirely independent, and in its natural state has occasion for the assistance of no other living creature. But man has almost constant occasion for the help of his brethren, and it is in vain for him to expect it from their benevolence only. He will be more likely to prevail if he can interest their self-love in his favour, and shew them that it is for their own advantage to do for him what he requires of them. Whoever offers to another a bargain of any kind, proposes to do this. Give me that which I want, and you shall have this which you want, is the meaning of every such offer; and it is in this manner that we obtain from one another the far greater part of those good offices which we stand in need of. It is not from the benevolence of the butcher, the brewer, or the baker that we expect our dinner, but from their regard to their own interest. We address ourselves, not to their humanity, but to their self-love, and never talk to them of our own necessities, but of their advantages. Nobody but a beggar chooses to depend chiefly upon the benevolence of his fellow-citizens....

As it is by treaty, by barter, and by purchase, that we obtain from one another the greater part of those mutual good offices which we stand in need of, so it is this same trucking disposition which originally gives occasion to the division of labour.... The certainty of being able to exchange all that surplus part of the produce of his own labour, which is over and above his own consumption, for such parts of the produce of other men's labour as he may have occasion for, encourages every man to apply himself to a particular occupation, and to cultivate and bring to perfection whatever talent of genius he may possess for that particular species of business.

The difference of natural talents in different men, is, in reality, much less than we are aware of; and the very different genius which appears to distinguish men of different professions, when grown up to maturity, is not upon many occasions so much the cause, as the effect of the division of labour. The difference between the most dissimilar characters, between a philosopher and a common street porter, for example, seems to arise not so much from nature, as from habit, custom, and education....

CHAPTER III. THAT THE DIVISION OF LABOUR IS LIMITED BY THE EXTENT OF THE MARKET

As it is the power of exchanging that gives occasion to the division of labour, so the extent of this division must always be limited by the extent of that power, or, in other words, by the extent of the market. When the market is very small, no person can have any encouragement to dedicate himself entirely to one employment, for want of the power to exchange all that surplus part of the produce of his own labour, which is over and above his own consumption, for such parts of the produce of other men's labour as he has occasion for.

There are some sorts of industry, even of the lowest kind, which can be carried on nowhere but in a great town. A porter, for example, can find employment and subsistence in no other place.... A country carpenter deals in every sort of work that is made of wood; a country smith in every sort of work that is made of iron. The former is not only a carpenter, but a joiner, a cabinet-maker, and even a carver in wood, as well as a wheel-wright, a plough-wright, a cart and waggon-maker....

CHAPTER IV. OF THE ORIGIN AND USE OF MONEY

When the division of labour has been once thoroughly established, it is but a very small part of a man's wants which the produce of his own labour can supply. He supplies the far greater part of them by exchanging that surplus part of the produce of his own labour, which is over and above his own consumption, for such parts of the produce of other men's labour as he has occasion for. Every man thus lives by exchanging, or becomes, in some measure, a merchant, and the society itself grows to be what is properly a commercial society.

... Every prudent man in every period of society, after the first establishment of the division of labour, must naturally have endeavoured to manage his affairs in such a manner, as to have at all times by him, besides the peculiar produce of his own industry, a certain quantity of some one commodity or other, such as he imagined few people would be likely to refuse in exchange for the produce of their industry. Many different commodities, it is probable, were successively both thought of and employed for this purpose....

Different metals have been made use of by different nations for this purpose. Iron was the common instrument of commerce among the ancient Spartans, copper among the ancient Romans, and gold and silver among all rich and commercial nations.

... Before the institution of coined money, however, unless they went through this tedious and difficult operation, people must always have been liable to the grossest frauds and impositions; and instead of a pound weight of pure silver, or pure copper, might receive, in exchange for their goods, an adulterated composition of the coarsest and cheapest materials, which had, however, in their outward appearance, been made to resemble those metals. To prevent such abuses, to facilitate exchanges, and thereby to encourage all sorts of industry and commerce, it has been found necessary, in all countries that have made any considerable advances towards improvement, to affix a public stamp upon certain quantities of such particular metals, as were in those countries commonly made use of to purchase goods. Hence the origin of coined money, and of those public offices called mints; institutions exactly of the same nature with those of the aulnagers and stamp-masters of woollen and linen cloth. All of them are equally meant to ascertain, by means of a public stamp, the quantity and uniform goodness of those different commodities when brought to market.

...

The inconveniency and difficulty of weighing those metals with exactness, gave occasion to the institution of coins, of which the stamp, covering entirely both sides of the piece, and sometimes the edges too, was supposed to ascertain not only the fineness, but the weight of the metal. Such coins, therefore, were received by tale, as at present, without the trouble of weighing.

...

It is in this manner that money has become, in all civilized nations, the universal instrument of commerce, by the intervention of which goods of all kinds are bought and sold, or exchanged for one another.

What are the rules which men naturally observe, in exchanging them either for money, or for one another, I shall now proceed to examine. These rules determine what may be called the relative or exchangeable value of goods.

The word VALUE, it is to be observed, has two different meanings, and sometimes expresses the utility of some particular object, and sometimes the power of purchasing other goods which the possession of that object conveys. The one may be called 'value in use;' the other, 'value in exchange.' The things which have the greatest value in use have frequently little or no value in exchange; and, on the contrary, those which have the greatest value in exchange have frequently little or no value in use. Nothing is more useful than water; but it will purchase scarce any thing; scarce any thing can be had in exchange for it. A diamond, on the contrary, has scarce any value in use; but a very great quantity of other goods may frequently be had in exchange for it.

In order to investigate the principles which regulate the exchangeable value of commodities, I shall endeavour to shew,

First, what is the real measure of this exchangeable value; or wherein consists the real price of all commodities.

Secondly, what are the different parts of which this real price is composed or made up.

And, lastly, what are the different circumstances which sometimes raise some or all of these different parts of price above, and sometimes sink them below, their natural or ordinary rate; or, what are the causes which sometimes hinder the market price, that is, the actual price of commodities, from coinciding exactly with what may be called their natural price....

Book IV. Of Systems of Political Economy

Political economy, considered as a branch of the science of a statesman or legislator, proposes two distinct objects; first, to provide a plentiful revenue or subsistence for the people, or, more properly, to enable them to provide such a revenue or subsistence for themselves; and, secondly, to supply the state or commonwealth with a revenue sufficient for the public services. It proposes to enrich both the people and the sovereign.

...

CHAPTER II. OF RESTRAINTS UPON IMPORTATION FROM FOREIGN COUNTRIES OF SUCH GOODS AS CAN BE PRODUCED AT HOME

...

Every individual is continually exerting himself to find out the most advantageous employment for whatever capital he can command. It is his own advantage, indeed, and not that of the society, which he has in view. But the study of his own advantage naturally, or rather necessarily, leads him to prefer that employment which is most advantageous to the society.

First, every individual endeavours to employ his capital as near home as he can, and consequently as much as he can in the support of domestic industry, provided always that he can thereby obtain the ordinary, or not a great deal less than the ordinary profits of stock.

Thus, upon equal, or nearly equal profits, every wholesale merchant naturally prefers the home trade to the foreign trade of consumption, and the foreign trade of consumption to the carrying trade. In the home trade, his capital is never so long out of his sight as it frequently is in the foreign trade of consumption. He can know better the character and situation of the persons whom he trusts; and if he should happen to be deceived, he knows better the laws of the country from which he must seek redress. In the carrying trade, the capital of the merchant is, as it were, divided between two foreign countries, and no part of it is ever necessarily brought home, or placed under his own immediate view and command.... A capital employed in the home trade, it has already been shown, necessarily puts into motion a greater quantity of domestic industry, and gives revenue and employment to a greater number of the inhabitants of the country, than an equal capital employed in the foreign trade of consumption; and one employed in the foreign trade of consumption has the same advantage over an equal capital employed in the carrying trade. Upon equal, or only nearly equal profits, therefore, every individual naturally inclines to employ his capital in the manner in which it is likely to afford the greatest support to domestic industry, and to give revenue and employment to the greatest number of people of his own country.

Secondly, every individual who employs his capital in the support of domestic industry, necessarily endeavours so to direct that industry, that its produce may be of the greatest possible value.

The produce of industry is what it adds to the subject or materials upon which it is employed. In proportion as the value of this produce is great or small, so will likewise be the profits of the employer. But it is only for the sake of profit that any man employs a capital in the support of industry; and he will always, therefore, endeavour to employ it in the support of that industry of which the produce is likely to be of the greatest value, or to exchange for the greatest quantity either of money or of other goods.

But the annual revenue of every society is always precisely equal to the exchangeable value of the whole annual produce of its industry, or rather is precisely the same thing with that exchangeable value. As every individual, therefore, endeavours as much as he can, both to employ his capital in the support of domestic industry, and so to direct that industry that its produce may be of the greatest value; every individual necessarily labours to render the annual revenue of the society as great as he can. He generally, indeed, neither intends to promote the public interest, nor knows how much he is promoting it. By preferring the support of domestic to that of foreign industry, he intends only his own security; and by directing that industry in such a manner as its produce may be of the greatest value, he intends only his own gain; and he is in this, as in many other cases, led by an invisible hand to promote an end which was no part of his intention. Nor is it always the worse for the society that it was no part of it. By pursuing his own interest, he frequently promotes that of the society more effectually than when he really intends to promote it. I have never known much good done by those who affected to trade for the public good. It is an affectation, indeed, not very common among merchants, and very few words need be employed in dissuading them from it.

What is the species of domestic industry which his capital can employ, and of which the produce is likely to be of the greatest value, every individual, it is evident, can in his local situation judge much better than any statesman or lawgiver can do for him. The statesman, who should attempt to direct private people in what manner they ought to employ their capitals, would not only load himself with a most unnecessary attention, but assume an authority which could safely be trusted, not only to no single person, but to no council or senate whatever, and which would nowhere be so dangerous as in the hands of a man who had folly and presumption enough to fancy himself fit to exercise it.

To give the monopoly of the home market to the produce of domestic industry, in any particular art or manufacture, is in some measure to direct private people in what manner they ought to employ their capitals, and must in almost all cases be either a useless or a hurtful regulation. If the produce of domestic can be brought there as cheap as that of foreign industry, the regulation is evidently useless. If it cannot, it must generally be hurtful. It is the maxim of every prudent master of a family, never to attempt to make at home what it will cost him more to make than to buy....

What is prudence in the conduct of every private family, can scarce be folly in that of a great kingdom. If a foreign country can supply us with a commodity cheaper than we ourselves can make it, better buy it of them with some part of the produce of our own industry, employed in a way in which we have some advantage. The general industry of the country being always in proportion to the capital which employs it, will not thereby be diminished, no more than that of the above-mentioned artificers; but only left to find out the way in which it can be employed with the greatest advantage.

5.6 Alexis de Tocqueville (1805–1859)

Democracy in America presents an outsider's sociological impressions of the unique political experiment undertaken by the United States of America. When Alexis de Tocqueville arrived in the United States of America in 1831, no other country had attempted to institute democracy without first having overthrown an aristocracy. In France, Tocqueville's own country, democracy followed a violent revolution, which left the revolutionaries with a problem: what to do about the aristocrats? Long-established, class-based animosities persisted, destabilizing social relations and preventing both democracy and political equality from firmly taking hold. America never had an aristocratic class, so social relations did not have a history of class antagonisms to overcome. America did, of course, have some citizens with considerably more wealth than others. Unlike old-world aristocrats, however, those who prospered in the new world "constantly keep on easy terms with the lower classes." Habitual good relations prevent the infiltration of class resentments in American society, which preserves conditions for political equality. According to Tocqueville's analysis, citizens of a democracy love equality more than liberty. People will tolerate restrictions to their liberty, providing the restrictions are borne equally by everyone.

The equality that Tocqueville identifies in America is not economic: it is political. It is founded on "individualism," which he differentiates from "egoism." Individualism is a mature and calm love of self. Egoism, by contrast, is passionate and exaggerated self-love. Whereas egoism drives someone to put their own interest above all else and isolates that person from the community, individualism encourages people to think that their destiny lies in their own hands and does not discourage participation in social relations. In America, Tocqueville observed popular movements among citizens for informal and transient associations of all sorts—temperance leagues, for example. Such informal associations are preferred over official government involvement in social relations. Government administration of social life generates confusion because citizens then need to discriminate its *commands* in the form of laws and its *advice* in the administration of social life. For similar reasons, it is believed that industry and commerce ought to be left entirely in private hands and not consigned to the power in government.

As with any experiment, the results of American democracy are not guaranteed. Tocqueville ventures to identify some potential problems it may face. For one, it is vulnerable to a new and distinctive form of despotism. Traditional aristocracies and monarchies had given birth to violent tyrannical regimes. American democracy, however, is subject to a mild form of despotism that threatens to degrade and enfeeble its citizens rather than terrorize them. Tendencies to moderation and individualism will simply be turned against them. If elected leaders take on the role of guardians, the citizens will be reduced to a state of perpetual childhood, enslaving them "in the minor details of life."

from Democracy in America

Section 2: Influence of Democracy on the Feelings of Americans

CHAPTER I: WHY DEMOCRATIC NATIONS SHOW A MORE ARDENT AND ENDURING LOVE OF EQUALITY THAN OF LIBERTY

The first and most intense passion which is engendered by the equality of conditions is, I need hardly say, the love of that same equality. My readers will therefore not be surprised that I speak of it before all others. Everybody has remarked that in our time, and especially in France, this passion for equality is every day gaining ground in the human heart. It has been said a hundred times that our contemporaries are far more ardently and tenaciously attached to equality than to freedom; but as I do not find that the causes of the fact have been sufficiently analyzed, I shall endeavor to point them out.

It is possible to imagine an extreme point at which freedom and equality would meet and be confounded together. Let us suppose that all the members of the community take a part in the government, and that each of them has an equal right to take a part in it. As none is different from his fellows, none can exercise a tyrannical power: men will be perfectly free, because they will all be entirely equal; and they will all be perfectly equal, because they will be entirely free. To this ideal state democratic nations tend. Such is the completest form that equality can assume upon earth; but there are a thousand others which, without being equally perfect, are not less cherished by those nations.

The principle of equality may be established in civil society, without prevailing in the political world. Equal rights may exist of indulging in the same pleasures, of entering the same professions, of frequenting the same places—in a word, of living in the same manner and seeking wealth by the same means, although all men do not take an equal share in the government. A kind of equality may even be established in the political world, though there should be no political freedom there. A man may be the equal of all his countrymen save one, who is the master of all without distinction, and who selects equally from among them all the agents of his power. Several other combinations might be easily imagined, by which very great equality would be united to institutions more or less free, or even to institutions wholly without freedom. Although men cannot become absolutely equal unless they be entirely free, and consequently equality, pushed to its furthest extent, may be confounded with freedom, yet there is good reason for distinguishing the one from the other. The taste which men have for liberty, and that which they feel for equality, are, in fact, two different things; and I am not afraid to add that, amongst democratic nations, they are two unequal things.

Upon close inspection, it will be seen that there is in every age some peculiar and preponderating fact with which all others are connected; this fact almost always gives birth to some pregnant idea or some ruling passion, which attracts to itself, and bears away in its course, all the feelings and opinions of the time: it is like a great stream, towards which each of the surrounding rivulets seems to flow. Freedom has appeared in the world at different times and under various forms; it has not been exclusively bound to any social condition, and it is not confined to democracies. Freedom cannot, therefore, form the distinguishing characteristic of democratic ages. The peculiar and preponderating fact which marks those ages as its own is the equality of conditions; the ruling passion of men in those periods is the love of this equality. Ask not what singular charm the men of democratic ages find in being equal, or what special reasons they may have for clinging so tenaciously to equality rather than to the other advantages which society holds out to them: equality is the distinguishing characteristic of the age they live in; that, of itself, is enough to explain that they prefer it to all the rest.

But independently of this reason there are several others, which will at all times habitually lead men to prefer equality to freedom. If a people could ever succeed in destroying, or even in diminishing, the equality which prevails in its own body, this could only be accomplished by long and laborious efforts. Its social condition must be modified, its laws abolished, its opinions superseded, its habits changed, its manners corrupted. But political liberty is more easily lost; to neglect to hold it fast is to allow it to escape. Men therefore not only cling to equality because it is dear to them; they also adhere to it because they think it will last forever.

That political freedom may compromise in its excesses the tranquillity, the property, the lives of individuals, is obvious to the narrowest and most unthinking minds. But, on the contrary, none but attentive and clear-sighted men perceive the perils with which equality threatens us, and they commonly avoid pointing them out. They know that the calamities they apprehend are remote, and flatter themselves that they will only fall upon future generations, for which the present generation takes but little thought. The evils which freedom sometimes brings with it are immediate; they are apparent to all, and all are more or less affected by them. The evils which extreme equality may produce are slowly disclosed; they creep gradually into the social frame; they are only seen at intervals, and at the moment at which they become most violent habit already causes them to be no longer felt. The advantages which freedom brings are only shown by length of time; and it is always easy to mistake the cause in which they originate. The advantages of equality are instantaneous, and they may constantly be traced from their source. Political liberty bestows exalted pleasures, from time to time, upon a certain number of citizens. Equality every day confers a number of small enjoyments on every man. The charms of equality are every instant felt, and are within the reach of all; the noblest hearts are not insensible to them, and the most vulgar souls exult in them. The passion which equality engenders must therefore be at once strong and general. Men cannot enjoy political liberty unpurchased by some sacrifices, and they never obtain it without great exertions. But the pleasures of equality are self-proffered: each of the petty incidents of life seems to occasion them, and in order to taste them nothing is required but to live.

Democratic nations are at all times fond of equality, but there are certain epochs at which the passion they entertain for it swells to the height of fury. This occurs at the moment when the old social system, long menaced, completes its own destruction after a last intestine struggle, and when the barriers of rank are at length thrown down. At such times men pounce upon equality as their booty, and they cling to it as to some precious treasure which they fear to lose. The passion for equality penetrates on every side into men's hearts, expands there, and fills them entirely. Tell them not that by this blind surrender of themselves to an exclusive passion they risk their dearest interests: they are deaf. Show them not freedom escaping from their grasp, whilst they are looking another way: they are blind—or rather, they can discern but one sole object to be desired in the universe.

What I have said is applicable to all democratic nations: what I am about to say concerns the French alone. Amongst most modern nations, and especially amongst all those of the Continent of Europe, the taste and the idea of freedom only began to exist and to extend themselves at the time when social conditions were tending to equality, and as a consequence of that very equality. Absolute kings were the most efficient levellers of ranks amongst their subjects. Amongst these nations equality preceded freedom: equality was therefore a fact of some standing when freedom was still a novelty: the one had already created customs, opinions, and laws belonging to it, when the other, alone and for the first time, came into actual existence. Thus the latter was still only an affair of opinion and of taste, whilst the former had already crept into the habits of the people, possessed itself of their manners, and given a particular turn to the smallest actions of their lives. Can it be wondered that the men of our own time prefer the one to the other?

I think that democratic communities have a natural taste for freedom: left to themselves, they will seek it, cherish it, and view any privation of it with regret. But for equality, their passion is ardent, insatiable, incessant, invincible: they call for equality in freedom; and if they cannot obtain that, they still call for equality in slavery. They will endure poverty, servitude, barbarism—but they will not endure aristocracy. This is true at all times, and especially true in our own. All men and all powers seeking to cope with this irresistible passion, will be overthrown and destroyed by it. In our age, freedom cannot be established without it, and despotism itself cannot reign without its support.

CHAPTER II: OF INDIVIDUALISM IN DEMOCRATIC COUNTRIES

...

Amongst aristocratic nations, as families remain for centuries in the same condition, often on the same spot, all generations become as it were contemporaneous. A man almost always knows his forefathers, and respects them: he thinks he already sees his remote descendants, and he loves them. He willingly imposes duties on himself towards the former and the latter; and he will frequently sacrifice his personal gratifications to those who went before and to those who will come after him. Aristocratic institutions have, moreover, the effect of closely binding every man to several of his fellow-citizens. As the classes of an aristocratic people are strongly marked and permanent, each of them is regarded by its own members as a sort of lesser country, more tangible and more cherished than the country at large. As in aristocratic communities all the citizens occupy fixed positions, one above the other, the result is that each of them always sees a man above himself whose patronage is necessary to him, and below himself another man whose co-operation he may claim. Men living in aristocratic ages are therefore almost always closely attached to something placed out of their own sphere, and they are often disposed to forget themselves. It is true that in those ages the notion of human fellowship is faint, and that men seldom think of sacrificing themselves for mankind; but they often sacrifice themselves for other men. In democratic ages, on the contrary, when the duties of each individual to the race are much more clear, devoted service to any one man becomes more rare; the bond of human affection is extended, but it is relaxed.

Amongst democratic nations new families are constantly springing up, others are constantly falling away, and all that remain change their condition; the woof of time is every instant broken, and the track of generations effaced. Those who went before are soon forgotten; of those who will come after no one has any idea: the interest of man is confined to those in close propinquity to himself. As each class approximates to other classes, and intermingles with them, its members become indifferent and as strangers to one another. Aristocracy had made a chain of all the members of the community, from the peasant to the king: democracy breaks that chain, and severs every link of it. As social conditions become more equal, the number of persons increases who, although they are neither rich enough nor powerful enough to exercise any great influence over their fellow-creatures, have nevertheless acquired or retained sufficient education and fortune to satisfy their own wants. They owe nothing to any man, they expect nothing from any man; they acquire the habit of always considering themselves as standing alone, and they are apt to imagine that their whole destiny is in their own hands. Thus not only does democracy make every man forget his ancestors, but it hides his descendants, and separates his contemporaries from him; it throws him back forever upon himself alone, and threatens in the end to confine him entirely within the solitude of his own heart.

...

CHAPTER IV: THAT THE AMERICANS COMBAT THE EFFECTS OF INDIVIDUALISM BY FREE INSTITUTIONS

Despotism, which is of a very timorous nature, is never more secure of continuance than when it can keep men asunder; and all its influence is commonly exerted for that purpose. No vice of the human heart is so acceptable to it as egotism: a despot easily forgives his subjects for not loving him, provided they do not love each other. He does not ask them to assist him in governing the State; it is enough that they do not aspire to govern it themselves. He stigmatizes as turbulent and unruly spirits those who would combine their exertions to promote the prosperity of the community, and, perverting the natural meaning of words, he applauds as good citizens those who have no sympathy for any but themselves. Thus the vices which despotism engenders are precisely those which equality fosters. These two things mutually and perniciously complete and assist each other. Equality places men side by side, unconnected by any common tie; despotism raises barriers to keep them asunder; the former predisposes them not to consider their fellow-creatures, the latter makes general indifference a sort of public virtue.

Despotism then, which is at all times dangerous, is more particularly to be feared in democratic ages. It is easy to see that in those same ages men stand most in need of freedom. When the members of a community are forced to attend to public affairs, they are necessarily drawn from the circle of their own interests, and snatched at times from self-observation. As soon as a man begins to treat of public affairs in public, he begins to perceive that he is not so independent of his fellow-men as he had at first imagined, and that, in order to obtain their support, he must often lend them his co-operation.

...

I may here be met by an objection derived from electioneering intrigues, the meannesses of candidates, and the calumnies of their opponents. These are opportunities for animosity which occur the oftener the more frequent elections become. Such evils are doubtless great, but they are transient; whereas the benefits which attend them remain. The desire of being elected may lead some men for a time to violent hostility; but this same desire leads all men in the long run mutually to support each other; and if it happens that an election accidentally severs two friends, the electoral system brings a multitude of citizens permanently together, who would always have remained unknown to each other. Freedom engenders private animosities, but despotism gives birth to general indifference.

The Americans have combated by free institutions the tendency of equality to keep men asunder, and they have subdued it. The legislators of America did not suppose that a general representation of the whole nation would suffice to ward off a disorder at once so natural to the frame of democratic society, and so fatal: they also thought that it would be well to infuse political life into each portion of the territory, in order to multiply to an infinite extent opportunities of acting in concert for all the members of the community, and to make them constantly feel their mutual dependence on each other. The plan was a wise one. The general affairs of a country only engage the attention of leading politicians, who assemble from time to time in the same places; and as they often lose sight of each other afterwards, no lasting ties are established between them. But if the object be to have the local affairs of a district conducted by the men who reside there, the same persons are always in contact, and they are, in a manner, forced to be acquainted, and to adapt themselves to one another.

It is difficult to draw a man out of his own circle to interest him in the destiny of the State, because he does not clearly understand what influence the destiny of the State can have upon his own lot. But if it be proposed to make a road cross the end of his estate, he will see at a glance that there is a connection between this small public affair and his greatest private affairs; and he will discover, without its being shown to him, the close tie which unites private to general interest. Thus, far more may be done by intrusting to the citizens the administration of minor affairs than by surrendering to them the control of important ones, towards interesting them in the public welfare, and convincing them that they constantly stand in need one of the other in order to provide for it. A brilliant achievement may win for you the favor of a people at one stroke; but to earn the love and respect of the population which surrounds you, a long succession of little services rendered and of obscure good deeds—a constant habit of kindness, and an established reputation for disinterestedness—will be required. Local freedom, then, which leads a great number of citizens to value the affection of their neighbors and of their kindred, perpetually brings men together, and forces them to help one another, in spite of the propensities which sever them.

...

Many people in France consider equality of conditions as one evil, and political freedom as a second. When they are obliged to yield to the former, they strive at least to escape from the latter. But I contend that in order to combat the evils which equality may produce, there is only one effectual remedy—namely, political freedom.

CHAPTER V: OF THE USE WHICH THE AMERICANS MAKE OF PUBLIC ASSOCIATIONS IN CIVIL LIFE

I do not propose to speak of those political associations—by the aid of which men endeavor to defend themselves against the despotic influence of a majority—or against the aggressions of regal power. That subject I have already treated. If each citizen did not learn, in proportion as he individually becomes more feeble, and consequently more incapable of preserving his freedom single-handed, to combine with his fellow-citizens for the purpose of defending it, it is clear that tyranny would unavoidably increase together with equality.

Those associations only which are formed in civil life, without reference to political objects, are here adverted to. The political associations which exist in the United States are only a single feature in the midst of the immense assemblage of associations in that country. Americans of all ages, all conditions, and all dispositions, constantly form associations. They have not only commercial and manufacturing companies, in which all take part, but associations of a thousand other kinds—religious, moral, serious, futile, extensive, or restricted, enormous or diminutive. The Americans make associations to give entertainments, to found establishments for education, to build inns, to construct churches, to diffuse books, to send missionaries to the antipodes; and in this manner they found hospitals, prisons, and schools. If it be proposed to advance some truth, or to foster some feeling by the encouragement of a great example, they form a society. Wherever, at the head of some new undertaking, you see the government in France, or a man of rank in England, in the United States you will be sure to find an association. I met with several kinds of associations in America, of which I confess I had no previous notion; and I have often admired the extreme skill with which the inhabitants of the United States succeed in proposing a common object to the exertions of a great many men, and in getting them voluntarily to pursue it. I have since travelled over England, whence the Americans have taken some of their laws and many of their customs; and it seemed to me that the principle of association was by no means so constantly or so adroitly used in that country. The English often perform great things singly; whereas the Americans form associations for the smallest undertakings. It is evident that the former people consider association as a powerful means of action, but the latter seem to regard it as the only means they have of acting.

Thus the most democratic country on the face of the earth is that in which men have in our time carried to the highest perfection the art of pursuing in common the object of their common desires, and have applied this new science to the greatest number of purposes. Is this the result of accident? or is there in reality any necessary connection between the principle of association and that of equality? Aristocratic communities always contain, amongst a multitude of persons who by themselves are powerless, a small number of powerful and wealthy citizens, each of whom can achieve great undertakings single-handed. In aristocratic societies men do not need to combine in order to act, because they are strongly held together. Every wealthy and powerful citizen constitutes the head of a permanent and compulsory association, composed of all those who are dependent upon him, or whom he makes subservient to the execution of his designs. Amongst democratic nations, on the contrary, all the citizens are independent and feeble; they can do hardly anything by themselves, and none of them can oblige his fellow-men to lend him their assistance. They all, therefore, fall into a state of incapacity, if they do not learn voluntarily to help each other. If men living in democratic countries had no right and no inclination to associate for political purposes, their independence would be in great jeopardy; but they might long preserve their wealth and their cultivation: whereas if they never acquired the habit of forming associations in ordinary life, civilization itself would be endangered. A people amongst which individuals should lose the power of achieving great things single-handed, without acquiring the means of producing them by united exertions, would soon relapse into barbarism.

...

Feelings and opinions are recruited, the heart is enlarged, and the human mind is developed by no other means than by the reciprocal influence of men upon each other. I have shown that these influences are almost null in democratic countries; they must therefore be artificially created, and this can only be accomplished by associations.

...

Nothing, in my opinion, is more deserving of our attention than the intellectual and moral associations of America. The political and industrial associations of that country strike us forcibly; but the others elude our observation, or if we discover them, we understand them imperfectly, because we have hardly ever seen anything of the kind. It must, however, be acknowledged that they are as necessary to the American people as the former, and perhaps more so. In democratic countries the science of association is the mother of science; the progress of all the rest depends upon the progress it has made. Amongst the laws which rule human societies there is one which seems to be more precise and clear than all others. If men are to remain civilized, or to become so, the art of associating together must grow and improve in the same ratio in which the equality of conditions is increased.

Book Four: Influence of Democratic Opinions on Political Society

CHAPTER VI: WHAT SORT OF DESPOTISM DEMOCRATIC NATIONS HAVE TO FEAR

I had remarked during my stay in the United States, that a democratic state of society, similar to that of the Americans, might offer singular facilities for the establishment of despotism; and I perceived, upon my return to Europe, how much use had already been made by most of our rulers, of the notions, the sentiments, and the wants engendered by this same social condition, for the purpose of extending the circle of their power. This led me to think that the nations of Christendom would perhaps eventually undergo some sort of oppression like that which hung over several of the nations of the ancient world. A more accurate examination of the subject, and five years of further meditations, have not diminished my apprehensions, but they have changed the object of them. No sovereign ever lived in former ages so absolute or so powerful as to undertake to administer by his own agency, and without the assistance of intermediate powers, all the parts of a great empire: none ever attempted to subject all his subjects indiscriminately to strict uniformity of regulation, and personally to tutor and direct every member of the community. The notion of such an undertaking never occurred to the human mind; and if any man had conceived it, the want of information, the imperfection of the administrative system, and above all, the natural obstacles caused by the inequality of conditions, would speedily have checked the execution of so vast a design. When the Roman emperors were at the height of their power, the different nations of the empire still preserved manners and customs of great diversity; although they were subject to the same monarch, most of the provinces were separately administered; they abounded in powerful and active municipalities; and although the whole government of the empire was centred in the hands of the emperor alone, and he always remained, upon occasions, the supreme arbiter in all matters, yet the details of social life and private occupations lay for the most part beyond his control. The emperors possessed, it is true, an immense and unchecked power, which allowed them to gratify all their whimsical tastes, and to employ for that purpose the whole strength of the State. They frequently abused that power arbitrarily to deprive their subjects of property or of life: their tyranny was extremely onerous to the few, but it did not reach the greater number; it was fixed to some few main objects, and neglected the rest; it was violent, but its range was limited.

But it would seem that if despotism were to be established amongst the democratic nations of our days, it might assume a different character; it would be more extensive and more mild; it would degrade men without tormenting them. I do not question, that in an age of instruction and equality like our own, sovereigns might more easily succeed in collecting all political power into their own hands, and might interfere more habitually and decidedly within the circle of private interests, than any sovereign of antiquity could ever do. But this same principle of equality which facilitates despotism, tempers its rigor. We have seen how the manners of society become more humane and gentle in proportion as men become more equal and alike. When no member of the community has much power or much wealth, tyranny is, as it were, without opportunities and a field of action. As all fortunes are scanty, the passions of men are naturally circumscribed—their imagination limited, their pleasures simple. This universal moderation moderates the sovereign himself, and checks within certain limits the inordinate extent of his desires.

Independently of these reasons drawn from the nature of the state of society itself, I might add many others arising from causes beyond my subject; but I shall keep within the limits I have laid down to myself. Democratic governments may become violent and even cruel at certain periods of extreme effervescence or of great danger: but these crises will be rare and brief. When I consider the petty passions of our contemporaries, the mildness of their manners, the extent of their education, the purity of their religion, the gentleness of their morality, their regular and industrious habits, and the restraint which they almost all observe in their vices no less than in their virtues, I have no fear that they will meet with tyrants in their rulers, but rather guardians. I think then that the species of oppression by which democratic nations are menaced is unlike anything which ever before existed in the world: our contemporaries will find no prototype of it in their memories. I am trying myself to choose an expression which will accurately convey the whole of the idea I have formed of it, but in vain; the old words "despotism" and "tyranny" are inappropriate: the thing itself is new; and since I cannot name it, I must attempt to define it.

I seek to trace the novel features under which despotism may appear in the world. The first thing that strikes the observation is an innumerable multitude of men all equal and alike, incessantly endeavoring to procure the petty and paltry pleasures with which they glut their lives. Each of them, living apart, is as a stranger to the fate of all the rest—his children and his private friends constitute to him the whole of mankind; as for the rest of his fellow-citizens, he is close to them, but he sees them not—he touches them, but he feels them not; he exists but in himself and for himself alone; and if his kindred still remain to him, he may be said at any rate to have lost his country. Above this race of men stands an immense and tutelary power, which takes upon itself alone to secure their gratifications, and to watch over their fate. That power is absolute, minute, regular, provident, and mild. It would be like the authority of a parent, if, like that authority, its object was to prepare men for manhood; but it seeks on the contrary to keep them in perpetual childhood: it is well content that the people should rejoice, provided they think of nothing but rejoicing. For their happiness such a government willingly labors, but it chooses to be the sole agent and the only arbiter of that happiness: it provides for their security, foresees and supplies their necessities, facilitates their pleasures, manages their principal concerns, directs their industry, regulates the descent of property, and subdivides their inheritances—what remains, but to spare them all the care of thinking and all the trouble of living? Thus it every day renders the exercise of the free agency of man less useful and less frequent; it circumscribes the will within a narrower range, and gradually robs a man of all the uses of himself. The principle of equality has prepared men for these things: it has predisposed men to endure them, and oftentimes to look on them as benefits.

After having thus successively taken each member of the community in its powerful grasp, and fashioned them at will, the supreme power then extends its arm over the whole community. It covers the surface of society with a network of small complicated rules, minute and uniform, through which the most original minds and the most energetic characters cannot penetrate, to rise above the crowd. The will of man is not shattered, but softened, bent, and guided: men are seldom forced by it to act, but they are constantly restrained from acting: such a power does not destroy, but it prevents existence; it does not tyrannize, but it compresses, enervates, extinguishes, and stupefies a people, till each nation is reduced to be nothing better than a flock of timid and industrious animals, of which the government is the shepherd. I have always thought that servitude of the regular, quiet, and gentle kind which I have just described, might be combined more easily than is commonly believed with some of the outward forms of freedom; and that it might even establish itself under the wing of the sovereignty of the people. Our contemporaries are constantly excited by two conflicting passions; they want to be led, and they wish to remain free: as they cannot destroy either one or the other of these contrary propensities, they strive to satisfy them both at once. They devise a sole, tutelary, and all-powerful form of government, but elected by the people. They combine the principle of centralization and that of popular sovereignty; this gives them a respite; they console themselves for being in tutelage by the reflection that they have chosen their own guardians. Every man allows himself to be put in leading-strings, because he sees that it is not a person or a class of persons, but the people at large that holds the end of his chain. By this system the people shake off their state of dependence just long enough to select their master, and then relapse into it again. A great many persons at the present day are quite contented with this sort of compromise between administrative despotism and the sovereignty of the people; and they think they have done enough for the protection of individual freedom when they have surrendered it to the power of the nation at large. This does not satisfy me: the nature of him I am to obey signifies less to me than the fact of extorted obedience.

I do not however deny that a constitution of this kind appears to me to be infinitely preferable to one, which, after having concentrated all the powers of government, should vest them in the hands of an irresponsible person or body of persons. Of all the forms which democratic despotism could assume, the latter would assuredly be the worst. When the sovereign is elective, or narrowly watched by a legislature which is really elective and independent, the oppression which he exercises over individuals is sometimes greater, but it is always less degrading; because every man, when he is oppressed and disarmed, may still imagine, that whilst he yields obedience it is to himself he yields it, and that it is to one of his own inclinations that all the rest give way. In like manner I can understand that when the sovereign represents the nation, and is dependent upon the people, the rights and the power of which every citizen is deprived, not only serve the head of the State, but the State itself; and that private persons derive some return from the sacrifice of their independence which they have made to the public. To create a representation of the people in every centralized country, is therefore, to diminish the evil which extreme centralization may produce, but not to get rid of it. I admit that by this means room is left for the intervention of individuals in the more important affairs; but it is not the less suppressed in the smaller and more private ones. It must not be forgotten that it is especially dangerous to enslave men in the minor details of life. For my own part, I should be inclined to think freedom less necessary in great things than in little ones, if it were possible to be secure of the one without possessing the other. Subjection in minor affairs breaks out every day, and is felt by the whole community indiscriminately. It does not drive men to resistance, but it crosses them at every turn, till they are led to surrender the exercise of their will. Thus their spirit is gradually broken and their character enervated; whereas that obedience, which is exacted on a few important but rare occasions, only exhibits servitude at certain intervals, and throws the burden of it upon a small number of men. It is in vain to summon a people, which has been rendered so dependent on the central power, to choose from time to time the representatives of that power; this rare and brief exercise of their free choice, however important it may be, will not prevent them from gradually losing the faculties of thinking, feeling, and acting for themselves, and thus gradually falling below the level of humanity. I add that they will soon become incapable of exercising the great and only privilege which remains to them. The democratic nations which have introduced freedom into their political constitution, at the very time when they were augmenting the despotism of their administrative constitution, have been led into strange paradoxes. To manage those minor affairs in which good sense is all that is wanted—the people are held to be unequal to the task, but when the government of the country is at stake, the people are invested with immense powers; they are alternately made the playthings of their ruler, and his masters—more than kings, and less than men. After having exhausted all the different modes of election, without finding one to suit their purpose, they are still amazed, and still bent on seeking further; as if the evil they remark did not originate in the constitution of the country far more than in that of the electoral body. It is, indeed, difficult to conceive how men who have entirely given up the habit of self-government should succeed in making a proper choice of those by whom they are to be governed; and no one will ever believe that a liberal, wise, and energetic government can spring from the suffrages of a subservient people. A constitution, which should be republican in its head and ultra-monarchical in all its other parts, has ever appeared to me to be a short-lived monster. The vices of rulers and the ineptitude of the people would speedily bring about its ruin; and the nation, weary of its representatives and of itself, would create freer institutions, or soon return to stretch itself at the feet of a single master.

5.7 Karl Marx (1818–1883) and Friedrich Engels (1820–1893)

From a socialist perspective, the division of labour described in such detail by Adam Smith at the beginning of *The Wealth of Nations* (5.5) is not a marvel of efficient production. Rather, it is a dehumanizing process for workers. Production-line labour is not, according to Marx and Engels, an ingenious expansion of Locke's labour theory of value (5.3). Rather, on the basis of that theory, production-line work is corruptive. According to Locke, individuals acquire private property by mixing their labour with raw materials. Because labour improves the materials, it becomes the rightful property of the labourer. In production-line work, the opposite happens: a little bit of the labourer's humanity is lost forever in the final product. Marx and Engels call this process alienating labour. The labourer does not get to possess the product, only a wage. Moreover, whatever skills or dexterity are improved by means of this labour do not improve the labourer's distinctively *human* capacities.

Marx and Engels wrote *The Communist Manifesto* in 1848, during a year of political unrest across Europe. The *Manifesto* was intended to galvanize disgruntled workers and inspire a revolution. Ultimately, the moment passed, and there was no continent-wide revolution. It was almost 70 years before the Russian revolution responded to this call.

According to Marxism, history unfolds in epochs that are defined by distinctive material conditions. The most important of these conditions are class divisions. Each age is marked by distinctive class relations: masters and slaves in antiquity; land-owners and peasants in the Middle Ages; and, lastly, bourgeois capitalists and proletarian wage-labourers in modern times. In each case, one class dominates the other. As it happens, the conditions responsible for the dominance of capitalists over wage-labourers are the very conditions that make revolution possible: dispersed, wage-labourers cannot organize into a revolutionary class; collected together in cities and working at factories, however, the labouring class is in a position to apprehend its numerical superiority. The *Manifesto* was written to embolden workers to seize the moment and institute a communist state.

In *Kapital* Marx provides a comprehensive and critical account of capitalist economics. Here the broad sweep of history that makes the *Manifesto* stirring is supplemented with analytical detail. First, Marx observes an incongruity between the market as a source of commodities for use by consumers and the market as a source of income for the producers. Market speculation by capitalists turns the production and purchase of commodities into a means to accumulate more capital for those who already possess it, not a means to provide for the material needs of society. Money thereby becomes another commodity. Additionally, the production process turns labour into a commodity. Not only that, but the supply of labour is plentiful, and each individual labourer is replaceable. So labour is a cheap commodity. Whoever owns the shop or factory owns the means of production. After purchasing labour for the lowest price possible, that person owns the products of that labour. As the economy cycles through this process repeatedly, the capitalist class accumulates more capital at the expense of the labour class.

5.7.1 *Karl Marx and Friedrich Engels,* The Communist Manifesto

A spectre is haunting Europe—the spectre of Communism. All the Powers of old Europe have entered into a holy alliance to exorcise this spectre: Pope and Czar, Metternich and Guizot, French Radicals and German police-spies.

Where is the party in opposition that has not been decried as Communistic by its opponents in power? Where is the Opposition that has not hurled back the branding reproach of Communism, against the more advanced opposition parties, as well as against its reactionary adversaries?

Two things result from this fact.

I. Communism is already acknowledged by all European Powers to be itself a Power.
II. It is high time that Communists should openly, in the face of the whole world, publish their views, their aims, their tendencies, and meet this nursery tale of the Spectre of Communism with a Manifesto of the party itself.

To this end, Communists of various nationalities have assembled in London, and sketched the following Manifesto, to be published in the English, French, German, Italian, Flemish and Danish languages.

I. Bourgeois and Proletarians

The history of all hitherto existing societies is the history of class struggles.

Freeman and slave, patrician and plebeian, lord and serf, guild-master and journeyman, in a word, oppressor and oppressed, stood in constant opposition to one another, carried on an uninterrupted, now hidden, now open fight, a fight that each time ended, either in a revolutionary re-constitution of society at large, or in the common ruin of the contending classes.

In the earlier epochs of history, we find almost everywhere a complicated arrangement of society into various orders, a manifold gradation of social rank. In ancient Rome we have patricians, knights, plebeians, slaves; in the Middle Ages, feudal lords, vassals, guild-masters, journeymen, apprentices, serfs; in almost all of these classes, again, subordinate gradations.

The modern bourgeois society that has sprouted from the ruins of feudal society has not done away with class antagonisms. It has but established new classes, new conditions of oppression, new forms of struggle in place of the old ones. Our epoch, the epoch of the bourgeoisie, possesses, however, this distinctive feature: it has simplified the class antagonisms. Society as a whole is more and more splitting up into two great hostile camps, into two great classes, directly facing each other: Bourgeoisie and Proletariat.

From the serfs of the Middle Ages sprang the chartered burghers of the earliest towns. From these burgesses the first elements of the bourgeoisie were developed.

The discovery of America, the rounding of the Cape, opened up fresh ground for the rising bourgeoisie. The East-Indian and Chinese markets, the colonisation of America, trade with the colonies, the increase in the means of exchange and in commodities generally, gave to commerce, to navigation, to industry, an impulse never before known, and thereby, to the revolutionary element in the tottering feudal society, a rapid development.

The feudal system of industry, under which industrial production was monopolised by closed guilds, now no longer sufficed for the growing wants of the new markets. The manufacturing system took its place. The guild-masters were pushed on one side by the manufacturing middle class; division of labour between the different corporate guilds vanished in the face of division of labour in each single workshop.

Meantime the markets kept ever growing, the demand ever rising. Even manufacture no longer sufficed. Thereupon, steam and machinery revolutionised industrial production. The place of manufacture was taken by the giant, Modern Industry, the place of the industrial middle class, by industrial millionaires, the leaders of whole industrial armies, the modern bourgeois.

Modern industry has established the world-market, for which the discovery of America paved the way. This market has given an immense development to commerce, to navigation, to communication by land. This development has, in its time, reacted on the extension of industry; and in proportion as industry, commerce, navigation, railways extended, in the same proportion the bourgeoisie developed, increased its capital, and pushed into the background every class handed down from the Middle Ages.

We see, therefore, how the modern bourgeoisie is itself the product of a long course of development, of a series of revolutions in the modes of production and of exchange.

Each step in the development of the bourgeoisie was accompanied by a corresponding political advance of that class. An oppressed class under the sway of the feudal nobility, an armed and self-governing association in the mediaeval commune; here independent urban republic (as in Italy and Germany), there taxable "third estate" of the monarchy (as in France), afterwards, in the period of manufacture proper, serving either the semi-feudal or the absolute monarchy as a counterpoise against the nobility, and, in fact, corner-stone of the great monarchies in general, the bourgeoisie has at last, since the establishment of Modern Industry and of the world-market, conquered for itself, in the modern representative State, exclusive political sway. The executive of the modern State is but a committee for managing the common affairs of the whole bourgeoisie.

The bourgeoisie, historically, has played a most revolutionary part.

The bourgeoisie, wherever it has got the upper hand, has put an end to all feudal, patriarchal, idyllic relations. It has pitilessly torn asunder the motley feudal ties that bound man to his "natural superiors," and has left remaining no other nexus between man and man than naked self-interest, than callous "cash payment." It has drowned the most heavenly ecstasies of religious fervour, of chivalrous enthusiasm, of philistine sentimentalism, in the icy water of egotistical calculation. It has resolved personal worth into exchange value, and in place of the numberless and indefeasible chartered freedoms, has set up that single, unconscionable freedom—Free Trade. In one word, for exploitation, veiled by religious and political illusions, naked, shameless, direct, brutal exploitation.

The bourgeoisie has stripped of its halo every occupation hitherto honoured and looked up to with reverent awe. It has converted the physician, the lawyer, the priest, the poet, the man of science, into its paid wage labourers.

The bourgeoisie has torn away from the family its sentimental veil, and has reduced the family relation to a mere money relation.

The bourgeoisie has disclosed how it came to pass that the brutal display of vigour in the Middle Ages, which Reactionists so much admire, found its fitting complement in the most slothful indolence. It has been the first to show what man's activity can bring about. It has accomplished wonders far surpassing Egyptian pyramids, Roman aqueducts, and Gothic cathedrals; it has conducted expeditions that put in the shade all former Exoduses of nations and crusades.

The bourgeoisie cannot exist without constantly revolutionising the instruments of production, and thereby the relations of production, and with them the whole relations of society. Conservation of the old modes of production in unaltered form, was, on the contrary, the first condition of existence for all earlier industrial classes. Constant revolutionising of production, uninterrupted disturbance of all social conditions, everlasting uncertainty and agitation distinguish the bourgeois epoch from all earlier ones. All fixed, fast-frozen relations, with their train of ancient and venerable prejudices and opinions, are swept away, all new-formed ones become antiquated before they can ossify. All that is solid melts into air, all that is holy is profaned, and man is at last compelled to face with sober senses, his real conditions of life, and his relations with his kind.

The need of a constantly expanding market for its products chases the bourgeoisie over the whole surface of the globe. It must nestle everywhere, settle everywhere, establish connexions everywhere.

The bourgeoisie has through its exploitation of the world-market given a cosmopolitan character to production and consumption in every country. To the great chagrin of Reactionists, it has drawn from under the feet of industry the national ground on which it stood. All old-established national industries have been destroyed or are daily being destroyed. They are dislodged by new industries, whose introduction becomes a life and death question for all civilised nations, by industries that no longer work up indigenous raw material, but raw material drawn from the remotest zones; industries whose products are consumed, not only at home, but in every quarter of the globe. In place of the old wants, satisfied by the productions of the country, we find new wants, requiring for their satisfaction the products of distant lands and climes. In place of the old local and national seclusion and self-sufficiency, we have intercourse in every direction, universal inter-dependence of nations. And as in material, so also in intellectual production. The intellectual creations of individual nations become common property. National one-sidedness and narrow-mindedness become more and more impossible, and from the numerous national and local literatures, there arises a world literature.

The bourgeoisie, by the rapid improvement of all instruments of production, by the immensely facilitated means of communication, draws all, even the most barbarian, nations into civilisation. The cheap prices of its commodities are the heavy artillery with which it batters down all Chinese walls, with which it forces the barbarians' intensely obstinate hatred of foreigners to capitulate. It compels all nations, on pain of extinction, to adopt the bourgeois mode of production; it compels them to introduce what it calls civilisation into their midst, i.e., to become bourgeois themselves. In one word, it creates a world after its own image.

The bourgeoisie has subjected the country to the rule of the towns. It has created enormous cities, has greatly increased the urban population as compared with the rural, and has thus rescued a considerable part of the population from the idiocy of rural life. Just as it has made the country dependent on the towns, so it has made barbarian and semi-barbarian countries dependent on the civilised ones, nations of peasants on nations of bourgeois, the East on the West.

The bourgeoisie keeps more and more doing away with the scattered state of the population, of the means of production, and of property. It has agglomerated production, and has concentrated property in a few hands. The necessary consequence of this was political centralisation. Independent, or but loosely connected provinces, with separate interests, laws, governments and systems of taxation, became lumped together into one nation, with one government, one code of laws, one national class-interest, one frontier and one customs-tariff. The bourgeoisie, during its rule of scarce one hundred years, has created more massive and more colossal productive forces than have all preceding generations together. Subjection of Nature's forces to man, machinery, application of chemistry to industry and agriculture, steam-navigation, railways, electric telegraphs, clearing of whole continents for cultivation, canalisation of rivers, whole populations conjured out of the ground—what earlier century had even a presentiment that such productive forces slumbered in the lap of social labour?

We see then: the means of production and of exchange, on whose foundation the bourgeoisie built itself up, were generated in feudal society. At a certain stage in the development of these means of production and of exchange, the conditions under which feudal society produced and exchanged, the feudal organisation of agriculture and manufacturing industry, in one word, the feudal relations of property became no longer compatible with the already developed productive forces; they became so many fetters. They had to be burst asunder; they were burst asunder.

Into their place stepped free competition, accompanied by a social and political constitution adapted to it, and by the economical and political sway of the bourgeois class.

A similar movement is going on before our own eyes. Modern bourgeois society with its relations of production, of exchange and of property, a society that has conjured up such gigantic means of production and of exchange, is like the sorcerer, who is no longer able to control the powers of the nether world whom he has called up by his spells. For many a decade past the history of industry and commerce is but the history of the revolt of modern productive forces against modern conditions of production, against the property relations that are the conditions for the existence of the bourgeoisie and of its rule. It is enough to mention the commercial crises that by their periodical return put on its trial, each time more threateningly, the existence of the entire bourgeois society. In these crises a great part not only of the existing products, but also of the previously created productive forces, are periodically destroyed. In these crises there breaks out an epidemic that, in all earlier epochs, would have seemed an absurdity—the epidemic of over-production. Society suddenly finds itself put back into a state of momentary barbarism; it appears as if a famine, a universal war of devastation had cut off the supply of every means of subsistence; industry and commerce seem to be destroyed; and why? Because there is too much civilisation, too much means of subsistence, too much industry, too much commerce. The productive forces at the disposal of society no longer tend to further the development of the conditions of bourgeois property; on the contrary, they have become too powerful for these conditions, by which they are fettered, and so soon as they overcome these fetters, they bring disorder into the whole of bourgeois society, endanger the existence of bourgeois property. The conditions of bourgeois society are too narrow to comprise the wealth created by them. And how does the bourgeoisie get over these crises? On the one hand inforced destruction of a mass of productive forces; on the other, by the conquest of new markets, and by the more thorough exploitation of the old ones. That is to say, by paving the way for more extensive and more destructive crises, and by diminishing the means whereby crises are prevented.

The weapons with which the bourgeoisie felled feudalism to the ground are now turned against the bourgeoisie itself.

But not only has the bourgeoisie forged the weapons that bring death to itself; it has also called into existence the men who are to wield those weapons—the modern working class—the proletarians.

In proportion as the bourgeoisie, i.e., capital, is developed, in the same proportion is the proletariat, the modern working class, developed—a class of labourers, who live only so long as they find work, and who find work only so long as their labour increases capital. These labourers, who must sell themselves piece-meal, are a commodity, like every other article of commerce, and are consequently exposed to all the vicissitudes of competition, to all the fluctuations of the market.

Owing to the extensive use of machinery and to division of labour, the work of the proletarians has lost all individual character, and consequently, all charm for the workman. He becomes an appendage of the machine, and it is only the most simple, most monotonous, and most easily acquired knack, that is required of him. Hence, the cost of production of a workman is restricted, almost entirely, to the means of subsistence that he requires for his maintenance, and for the propagation of his race. But the price of a commodity, and therefore also of labour, is equal to its cost of production. In proportion therefore, as the repulsiveness of the work increases, the wage decreases. Nay more, in proportion as the use of machinery and division of labour increases, in the same proportion the burden of toil also increases, whether by prolongation of the working hours, by increase of the work exacted in a given time or by increased speed of the machinery, etc.

Modern industry has converted the little workshop of the patriarchal master into the great factory of the industrial capitalist. Masses of labourers, crowded into the factory, are organised like soldiers. As privates of the industrial army they are placed under the command of a perfect hierarchy of officers and sergeants. Not only are they slaves of the bourgeois class, and of the bourgeois State; they are daily and hourly enslaved by the machine, by the over-looker, and, above all, by the individual bourgeois manufacturer himself. The more openly this despotism proclaims gain to be its end and aim, the more petty, the more hateful and the more embittering it is.

The less the skill and exertion of strength implied in manual labour, in other words, the more modern industry becomes developed, the more is the labour of men superseded by that of women. Differences of age and sex have no longer any distinctive social validity for the working class. All are instruments of labour, more or less expensive to use, according to their age and sex.

No sooner is the exploitation of the labourer by the manufacturer, so far at an end, that he receives his wages in cash, than he is set upon by the other portions of the bourgeoisie, the landlord, the shopkeeper, the pawnbroker, etc.

The lower strata of the middle class—the small tradespeople, shopkeepers, retired tradesmen generally, the handicraftsmen and peasants—all these sink gradually into the proletariat, partly because their diminutive capital does not suffice for the scale on which Modern Industry is carried on, and is swamped in the competition with the large capitalists, partly because their specialized skill is rendered worthless by the new methods of production. Thus the proletariat is recruited from all classes of the population.

The proletariat goes through various stages of development. With its birth begins its struggle with the bourgeoisie. At first the contest is carried on by individual labourers, then by the workpeople of a factory, then by the operatives of one trade, in one locality, against the individual bourgeois who directly exploits them. They direct their attacks not against the bourgeois conditions of production, but against the instruments of production themselves; they destroy imported wares that compete with their labour, they smash to pieces machinery, they set factories ablaze, they seek to restore by force the vanished status of the workman of the Middle Ages.

At this stage the labourers still form an incoherent mass scattered over the whole country, and broken up by their mutual competition. If anywhere they unite to form more compact bodies, this is not yet the consequence of their own active union, but of the union of the bourgeoisie, which class, in order to attain its own political ends, is compelled to set the whole proletariat in motion, and is moreover yet, for a time, able to do so. At this stage, therefore, the proletarians do not fight their enemies, but the enemies of their enemies, the remnants of absolute monarchy, the landowners, the non-industrial bourgeois, the petty bourgeoisie. Thus the whole historical movement is concentrated in the hands of the bourgeoisie; every victory so obtained is a victory for the bourgeoisie.

But with the development of industry the proletariat not only increases in number; it becomes concentrated in greater masses, its strength grows, and it feels that strength more. The various interests and conditions of life within the ranks of the proletariat are more and more equalised, in proportion as machinery obliterates all distinctions of labour, and nearly everywhere reduces wages to the same low level. The growing competition among the bourgeois, and the resulting commercial crises, make the wages of the workers ever more fluctuating. The unceasing improvement of machinery, ever more rapidly developing, makes their livelihood more and more precarious;

the collisions between individual workmen and individual bourgeois take more and more the character of collisions between two classes. Thereupon the workers begin to form combinations (Trades Unions) against the bourgeois; they club together in order to keep up the rate of wages; they found permanent associations in order to make provision beforehand for these occasional revolts. Here and there the contest breaks out into riots.

Now and then the workers are victorious, but only for a time. The real fruit of their battles lies, not in the immediate result, but in the ever-expanding union of the workers. This union is helped on by the improved means of communication that are created by modern industry and that place the workers of different localities in contact with one another. It was just this contact that was needed to centralise the numerous local struggles, all of the same character, into one national struggle between classes. But every class struggle is a political struggle. And that union, to attain which the burghers of the Middle Ages, with their miserable highways, required centuries, the modern proletarians, thanks to railways, achieve in a few years.

This organisation of the proletarians into a class, and consequently into a political party, is continually being upset again by the competition between the workers themselves. But it ever rises up again, stronger, firmer, mightier. It compels legislative recognition of particular interests of the workers, by taking advantage of the divisions among the bourgeoisie itself. Thus the ten-hours' bill in England was carried.

Altogether collisions between the classes of the old society further, in many ways, the course of development of the proletariat. The bourgeoisie finds itself involved in a constant battle. At first with the aristocracy; later on, with those portions of the bourgeoisie itself, whose interests have become antagonistic to the progress of industry; at all times, with the bourgeoisie of foreign countries. In all these battles it sees itself compelled to appeal to the proletariat, to ask for its help, and thus, to drag it into the political arena. The bourgeoisie itself, therefore, supplies the proletariat with its own instruments of political and general education, in other words, it furnishes the proletariat with weapons for fighting the bourgeoisie.

Further, as we have already seen, entire sections of the ruling classes are, by the advance of industry, precipitated into the proletariat, or are at least threatened in their conditions of existence. These also supply the proletariat with fresh elements of enlightenment and progress.

Finally, in times when the class struggle nears the decisive hour, the process of dissolution going on within the ruling class, in fact within the whole range of society, assumes such a violent, glaring character, that a small section of the ruling class cuts itself adrift, and joins the revolutionary class, the class that holds the future in its hands. Just as, therefore, at an earlier period, a section of the nobility went over to the bourgeoisie, so now a portion of the bourgeoisie goes over to the proletariat, and in particular, a portion of the bourgeois ideologists, who have raised themselves to the level of comprehending theoretically the historical movement as a whole.

Of all the classes that stand face to face with the bourgeoisie today, the proletariat alone is a really revolutionary class. The other classes decay and finally disappear in the face of Modern Industry; the proletariat is its special and essential product. The lower middle class, the small manufacturer, the shopkeeper, the artisan, the peasant, all these fight against the bourgeoisie, to save from extinction their existence as fractions of the middle class. They are therefore not revolutionary, but conservative. Nay more, they are reactionary, for they try to roll back the wheel of history. If by chance they are revolutionary, they are so only in view of their impending transfer into the proletariat, they thus defend not their present, but their future interests, they desert their own standpoint to place themselves at that of the proletariat.

The "dangerous class," the social scum, that passively rotting mass thrown off by the lowest layers of old society, may, here and there, be swept into the movement by a proletarian revolution; its conditions of life, however, prepare it far more for the part of a bribed tool of reactionary intrigue.

In the conditions of the proletariat, those of old society at large are already virtually swamped. The proletarian is without property; his relation to his wife and children has no longer anything in common with the bourgeois family-relations; modern industrial labour, modern subjection to capital, the same in England as in France, in America as in Germany, has stripped him of every trace of national character. Law, morality, religion, are to him so many bourgeois prejudices, behind which lurk in ambush just as many bourgeois interests.

All the preceding classes that got the upper hand, sought to fortify their already acquired status by subjecting society at large to their conditions of appropriation. The proletarians cannot become masters of the productive forces of society, except by abolishing their own previous mode of appropriation, and thereby also every other previous mode of appropriation. They have nothing of their own to secure and to fortify; their mission is to destroy all previous securities for, and insurances of, individual property.

All previous historical movements were movements of minorities, or in the interests of minorities. The proletarian movement is the self-conscious, independent movement of the immense majority, in the interests of the immense majority. The proletariat, the lowest stratum of our present society, cannot stir, cannot raise itself up, without the whole superincumbent strata of official society being sprung into the air.

Though not in substance, yet in form, the struggle of the proletariat with the bourgeoisie is at first a national struggle. The proletariat of each country must, of course, first of all settle matters with its own bourgeoisie.

In depicting the most general phases of the development of the proletariat, we traced the more or less veiled civil war, raging within existing society, up to the point where that war breaks out into open revolution, and where the violent overthrow of the bourgeoisie lays the foundation for the sway of the proletariat.

Hitherto, every form of society has been based, as we have already seen, on the antagonism of oppressing and oppressed classes. But in order to oppress a class, certain conditions must be assured to it under which it can, at least, continue its slavish existence. The serf, in the period of serfdom, raised himself to membership in the commune, just as the petty bourgeois, under the yoke of feudal absolutism, managed to develop into a bourgeois. The modern laborer, on the contrary, instead of rising with the progress of industry, sinks deeper and deeper below the conditions of existence of his own class. He becomes a pauper, and pauperism develops more rapidly than population and wealth. And here it becomes evident, that the bourgeoisie is unfit any longer to be the ruling class in society, and to impose its conditions of existence upon society as an over-riding law. It is unfit to rule because it is incompetent to assure an existence to its slave within his slavery, because it cannot help letting him sink into such a state, that it has to feed him, instead of being fed by him. Society can no longer live under this bourgeoisie, in other words, its existence is no longer compatible with society.

The essential condition for the existence, and for the sway of the bourgeois class, is the formation and augmentation of capital; the condition for capital is wage-labour. Wage-labour rests exclusively on competition between the laborers. The advance of industry, whose involuntary promoter is the bourgeoisie, replaces the isolation of the labourers, due to competition, by their revolutionary combination, due to association. The development of Modern Industry, therefore, cuts from under its feet the very foundation on which the bourgeoisie produces and appropriates products. What the bourgeoisie, therefore, produces, above all, is its own grave-diggers. Its fall and the victory of the proletariat are equally inevitable.

II. Proletarians and Communists

In what relation do the Communists stand to the proletarians as a whole?

The Communists do not form a separate party opposed to other working-class parties.

They have no interests separate and apart from those of the proletariat as a whole.

They do not set up any sectarian principles of their own, by which to shape and mould the proletarian movement.

The Communists are distinguished from the other working-class parties by this only: (1) In the national struggles of the proletarians of the different countries, they point out and bring to the front the common interests of the entire proletariat, independently of all nationality. (2) In the various stages of development which the struggle of the working class against the bourgeoisie has to pass through, they always and everywhere represent the interests of the movement as a whole.

The Communists, therefore, are on the one hand, practically, the most advanced and resolute section of the working-class parties of every country, that section which pushes forward all others; on the other hand, theoretically, they have over the great mass of the proletariat the advantage of clearly understanding the line of march, the conditions, and the ultimate general results of the proletarian movement.

The immediate aim of the Communist is the same as that of all the other proletarian parties: formation of the proletariat into a class, overthrow of the bourgeois supremacy, conquest of political power by the proletariat.

The theoretical conclusions of the Communists are in no way based on ideas or principles that have been invented, or discovered, by this or that would-be universal reformer. They merely express, in general terms, actual relations springing from an existing class struggle, from a historical movement going on under our very eyes. The abolition of existing property relations is not at all a distinctive feature of Communism.

All property relations in the past have continually been subject to historical change consequent upon the change in historical conditions.

The French Revolution, for example, abolished feudal property in favour of bourgeois property.

The distinguishing feature of Communism is not the abolition of property generally, but the abolition of bourgeois property. But modern bourgeois private property is the final and most complete expression of the system of producing and appropriating products, that is based on class antagonisms, on the exploitation of the many by the few.

In this sense, the theory of the Communists may be summed up in the single sentence: Abolition of private property.

We Communists have been reproached with the desire of abolishing the right of personally acquiring property as the fruit of a man's own labour, which property is alleged to be the groundwork of all personal freedom, activity and independence.

Hard-won, self-acquired, self-earned property! Do you mean the property of the petty artisan and of the small peasant, a form of property that preceded the bourgeois form? There is no need to abolish that; the development of industry has to a great extent already destroyed it, and is still destroying it daily.

Or do you mean modern bourgeois private property?

But does wage-labour create any property for the labourer? Not a bit. It creates capital, i.e., that kind of property which exploits wage-labour, and which cannot increase except upon condition of begetting a new supply of wage-labour for fresh exploitation. Property, in its present form, is based on the antagonism of capital and wage-labour. Let us examine both sides of this antagonism.

To be a capitalist, is to have not only a purely personal, but a social status in production. Capital is a collective product, and only by the united action of many members, nay, in the last resort, only by the united action of all members of society, can it be set in motion.

Capital is, therefore, not a personal, it is a social power.

When, therefore, capital is converted into common property, into the property of all members of society, personal property is not thereby transformed into social property. It is only the social character of the property that is changed. It loses its class-character.

Let us now take wage-labour.

The average price of wage-labour is the minimum wage, i.e., that quantum of the means of subsistence, which is absolutely requisite in bare existence as a labourer. What, therefore, the wage-labourer appropriates by means of his labour, merely suffices to prolong and reproduce a bare existence. We by no means intend to abolish this personal appropriation of the products of labour, an appropriation that is made for the maintenance and reproduction of human life, and that leaves no surplus wherewith to command the labour of others. All that we want to do away with, is the miserable character of this appropriation, under which the labourer lives merely to increase capital, and is allowed to live only in so far as the interest of the ruling class requires it.

In bourgeois society, living labour is but a means to increase accumulated labour. In Communist society, accumulated labour is but a means to widen, to enrich, to promote the existence of the labourer.

In bourgeois society, therefore, the past dominates the present; in Communist society, the present dominates the past. In bourgeois society capital is independent and has individuality, while the living person is dependent and has no individuality.

And the abolition of this state of things is called by the bourgeois, abolition of individuality and freedom! And rightly so. The abolition of bourgeois individuality, bourgeois independence, and bourgeois freedom is undoubtedly aimed at.

By freedom is meant, under the present bourgeois conditions of production, free trade, free selling and buying.

But if selling and buying disappears, free selling and buying disappears also. This talk about free selling and buying, and all the other "brave words" of our bourgeoisie about freedom in general, have a meaning, if any, only in contrast with restricted selling and buying, with the fettered traders of the Middle Ages, but have no meaning when opposed to the Communistic abolition of buying and selling, of the bourgeois conditions of production, and of the bourgeoisie itself.

You are horrified at our intending to do away with private property. But in your existing society, private property is already done away with for nine-tenths of the population; its existence for the few is solely due to its non-existence in the hands of those nine-tenths. You reproach us, therefore, with intending to do away with a form of property, the necessary condition for whose existence is the non-existence of any property for the immense majority of society.

In one word, you reproach us with intending to do away with your property. Precisely so; that is just what we intend.

From the moment when labour can no longer be converted into capital, money, or rent, into a social power capable of being monopolised, i.e., from the moment when individual property can no longer be transformed into bourgeois property, into capital, from that moment, you say individuality vanishes.

You must, therefore, confess that by "individual" you mean no other person than the bourgeois, than the middle-class owner of property. This person must, indeed, be swept out of the way, and made impossible.

Communism deprives no man of the power to appropriate the products of society; all that it does is to deprive him of the power to subjugate the labour of others by means of such appropriation.

It has been objected that upon the abolition of private property all work will cease, and universal laziness will overtake us.

According to this, bourgeois society ought long ago to have gone to the dogs through sheer idleness; for those of its members who work, acquire nothing, and those who acquire anything, do not work. The whole of this objection is but another expression of the tautology: that there can no longer be any wage-labour when there is no longer any capital.

All objections urged against the Communistic mode of producing and appropriating material products, have, in the same way, been urged against the Communistic modes of producing and appropriating intellectual products. Just as, to the bourgeois, the disappearance of class property is the disappearance of production itself, so the disappearance of class culture is to him identical with the disappearance of all culture.

That culture, the loss of which he laments, is, for the enormous majority, a mere training to act as a machine.

But don't wrangle with us so long as you apply, to our intended abolition of bourgeois property, the standard of your bourgeois notions of freedom, culture, law, etc. Your very ideas are but the outgrowth of the conditions of your bourgeois production and bourgeois property, just as your jurisprudence is but the will of your class made into a law for all, a will, whose essential character and direction are determined by the economical conditions of existence of your class.

The selfish misconception that induces you to transform into eternal laws of nature and of reason, the social forms springing from your present mode of production and form of property—historical relations that rise and disappear in the progress of production—this misconception you share with every ruling class that has preceded you. What you see clearly in the case of ancient property, what you admit in the case of feudal property, you are of course forbidden to admit in the case of your own bourgeois form of property.

Abolition of the family! Even the most radical flare up at this infamous proposal of the Communists.

On what foundation is the present family, the bourgeois family, based? On capital, on private gain. In its completely developed form this family exists only among the bourgeoisie. But this state of things finds its complement in the practical absence of the family among the proletarians, and in public prostitution.

The bourgeois family will vanish as a matter of course when its complement vanishes, and both will vanish with the vanishing of capital.

Do you charge us with wanting to stop the exploitation of children by their parents? To this crime we plead guilty.

But, you will say, we destroy the most hallowed of relations, when we replace home education by social.

And your education! Is not that also social, and determined by the social conditions under which you educate, by the intervention, direct or indirect, of society, by means of schools, etc.? The Communists have not invented the intervention of society in education; they do but seek to alter the character of that intervention, and to rescue education from the influence of the ruling class.

The bourgeois clap-trap about the family and education, about the hallowed co-relation of parent and child, becomes all the more disgusting, the more, by the action of Modern Industry, all family ties among the proletarians are torn asunder, and their children transformed into simple articles of commerce and instruments of labour.

But you Communists would introduce community of women, screams the whole bourgeoisie in chorus.

The bourgeois sees in his wife a mere instrument of production. He hears that the instruments of production are to be exploited in common, and, naturally, can come to no other conclusion than that the lot of being common to all will likewise fall to the women.

He has not even a suspicion that the real point is to do away with the status of women as mere instruments of production.

For the rest, nothing is more ridiculous than the virtuous indignation of our bourgeois at the community of women which, they pretend, is to be openly and officially established by the Communists. The Communists have no need to introduce community of women; it has existed almost from time immemorial.

Our bourgeois, not content with having the wives and daughters of their proletarians at their disposal, not to speak of common prostitutes, take the greatest pleasure in seducing each other's wives.

Bourgeois marriage is in reality a system of wives in common and thus, at the most, what the Communists might possibly be reproached with, is that they desire to introduce, in substitution for a hypocritically concealed, an openly legalised community of women. For the rest, it is self-evident that the abolition of the present system of production must bring with it the abolition of the community of women springing from that system, i.e., of prostitution both public and private.

The Communists are further reproached with desiring to abolish countries and nationality.

The working men have no country. We cannot take from them what they have not got. Since the proletariat must first of all acquire political supremacy, must rise to be the leading class of the nation, must constitute itself the nation, it is, so far, itself national, though not in the bourgeois sense of the word.

National differences and antagonisms between peoples are daily more and more vanishing, owing to the development of the bourgeoisie, to freedom of commerce, to the world-market, to uniformity in the mode of production and in the conditions of life corresponding thereto.

The supremacy of the proletariat will cause them to vanish still faster. United action, of the leading civilised countries at least, is one of the first conditions for the emancipation of the proletariat.

In proportion as the exploitation of one individual by another is put an end to, the exploitation of one nation by another will also be put an end to. In proportion as the antagonism between classes within the nation vanishes, the hostility of one nation to another will come to an end.

The charges against Communism made from a religious, a philosophical, and, generally, from an ideological standpoint, are not deserving of serious examination.

Does it require deep intuition to comprehend that man's ideas, views and conceptions, in one word, man's consciousness, changes with every change in the conditions of his material existence, in his social relations and in his social life?

What else does the history of ideas prove, than that intellectual production changes its character in proportion as material production is changed? The ruling ideas of each age have ever been the ideas of its ruling class.

When people speak of ideas that revolutionise society, they do but express the fact, that within the old society, the elements of a new one have been created, and that the dissolution of the old ideas keeps even pace with the dissolution of the old conditions of existence.

When the ancient world was in its last throes, the ancient religions were overcome by Christianity. When Christian ideas succumbed in the 18th century to rationalist ideas, feudal society fought its death battle with the then revolutionary bourgeoisie. The ideas of religious liberty and freedom of conscience merely gave expression to the sway of free competition within the domain of knowledge.

"Undoubtedly," it will be said, "religious, moral, philosophical and juridical ideas have been modified in the course of historical development. But religion, morality, philosophy, political science, and law, constantly survived this change."

"There are, besides, eternal truths, such as Freedom, Justice, etc. that are common to all states of society. But Communism abolishes eternal truths, it abolishes all religion, and all morality, instead of constituting them on a new basis; it therefore acts in contradiction to all past historical experience."

What does this accusation reduce itself to? The history of all past society has consisted in the development of class antagonisms, antagonisms that assumed different forms at different epochs.

But whatever form they may have taken, one fact is common to all past ages, viz., the exploitation of one part of society by the other. No wonder, then, that the social consciousness of past ages, despite all the multiplicity and variety it displays, moves within certain common forms, or general ideas, which cannot completely vanish except with the total disappearance of class antagonisms.

The Communist revolution is the most radical rupture with traditional property relations; no wonder that its development involves the most radical rupture with traditional ideas.

But let us have done with the bourgeois objections to Communism.

We have seen above, that the first step in the revolution by the working class, is to raise the proletariat to the position of ruling as to win the battle of democracy.

The proletariat will use its political supremacy to wrest, by degrees, all capital from the bourgeoisie, to centralise all instruments of production in the hands of the State, i.e., of the proletariat organised as the ruling class; and to increase the total of productive forces as rapidly as possible.

Of course, in the beginning, this cannot be effected except by means of despotic inroads on the rights of property, and on the conditions of bourgeois production; by means of measures, therefore, which appear economically insufficient and untenable, but which, in the course of the movement, outstrip themselves, necessitate further inroads upon the old social order, and are unavoidable as a means of entirely revolutionising the mode of production.

These measures will of course be different in different countries.

Nevertheless in the most advanced countries, the following will be pretty generally applicable.

1. Abolition of property in land and application of all rents of land to public purposes.
2. A heavy progressive or graduated income tax.
3. Abolition of all right of inheritance.
4. Confiscation of the property of all emigrants and rebels.
5. Centralisation of credit in the hands of the State, by means of a national bank with State capital and an exclusive monopoly.
6. Centralisation of the means of communication and transport in the hands of the State.
7. Extension of factories and instruments of production owned by the State; the bringing into cultivation of waste-lands, and the improvement of the soil generally in accordance with a common plan.
8. Equal liability of all to labour. Establishment of industrial armies, especially for agriculture.
9. Combination of agriculture with manufacturing industries; gradual abolition of the distinction between town and country, by a more equable distribution of the population over the country.
10. Free education for all children in public schools. Abolition of children's factory labour in its present form. Combination of education with industrial production, &c., &c.

When, in the course of development, class distinctions have disappeared, and all production has been concentrated in the hands of a vast association of the whole nation, the public power will lose its political character. Political power, properly so called, is merely the organised power of one class for oppressing another. If the proletariat during its contest with the bourgeoisie is compelled, by the force of circumstances, to organise itself as a class, if, by means of a revolution, it makes itself the ruling class, and, as such, sweeps away by force the old conditions of production, then it will, along with these conditions, have swept away the conditions for the existence of class antagonisms and of classes generally, and will thereby have abolished its own supremacy as a class.

In place of the old bourgeois society, with its classes and class antagonisms, we shall have an association, in which the free development of each is the condition for the free development of all.

5.7.2 *Karl Marx,* Kapital: A Critique of Political Economy

Volume I

Part 2: Transformation of Money into Capital

CHAPTER 4: THE GENERAL FORMULA FOR CAPITAL

...

The first distinction we notice between money that is money only, and money that is capital, is nothing more than a difference in their form of circulation.

The simplest form of the circulation of commodities is C-M-C, the transformation of commodities into money, and the change of the money back again into commodities; or selling in order to buy. But alongside of this form we find another specifically different form: M-C-M, the transformation of money into commodities, and the change of commodities back again into money; or buying in order to sell....

The circuit C-M-C starts with one commodity, and finishes with another, which falls out of circulation and into consumption. Consumption, the satisfaction of wants, in one word, use-value, is its end and aim. The circuit M-C-M, on the contrary, commences with money and ends with money. Its leading motive, and the goal that attracts it, is therefore mere exchange-value.

In the simple circulation of commodities, the two extremes of the circuit have the same economic form. They are both commodities, and commodities of equal value. But they are also use-values differing in their qualities, as, for example, corn and clothes. The exchange of products, of the different materials in which the labour of society is embodied, forms here the basis of the movement. It is otherwise in the circulation M-C-M, which at first sight appears purposeless, because tautological. Both extremes have the same economic form. They are both money, and therefore are not qualitatively different use-values; for money is but the converted form of commodities, in which their particular use-values vanish. To exchange £100 for cotton, and then this same cotton again for £100, is merely a roundabout way of exchanging money for money, the same for the same, and appears to be an operation just as purposeless as it is absurd. One sum of money is distinguishable from another only by its amount. The character and tendency of the process M-C-M, is therefore not due to any qualitative difference between its extremes, both being money, but solely to their quantitative difference. More money is withdrawn from circulation at the finish than was thrown into it at the start. The cotton that was bought for £100 is perhaps resold for £100 + £10 or £110. The exact form of this process is therefore M-C-M′, where M′ = M + D M = the original sum advanced, plus an increment. This increment or excess over the original value I call "surplus-value." The value originally advanced, therefore, not only remains intact while in circulation, but adds to itself a surplus-value or expands itself. It is this movement that converts it into capital....

If, then, the expansion of value is once aimed at, there is just the same inducement to augment the value of the £110 as that of the £100; for both are but limited expressions for exchange-value, and therefore both have the same vocation to approach, by quantitative increase, as near as possible to absolute wealth....

Therefore, the final result of every separate circuit, in which a purchase and consequent sale are completed, forms of itself the starting-point of a new circuit. The simple circulation of commodities—selling in order to buy—is a means of carrying out a purpose unconnected with circulation, namely, the appropriation of use-values, the satisfaction of wants. The circulation of money as capital is, on the contrary, an end in itself, for the expansion of value takes place only within this constantly renewed movement. The circulation of capital has therefore no limits.

As the conscious representative of this movement, the possessor of money becomes a capitalist. His person, or rather his pocket, is the point from which the money starts and to which it returns. The expansion of value, which is the objective basis or main-spring of the circulation M-C-M, becomes his subjective aim, and it is only in so far as the appropriation of ever more and more wealth in the abstract becomes the sole motive of his operations, that he functions as a capitalist, that is, as capital personified and endowed with consciousness and a will. Use-values must therefore never be looked upon as the real aim of the capitalist; neither must the profit on any single transaction. The restless never-ending process of profit-making alone is what he aims at. This boundless greed after riches, this passionate chase after exchange-value, is common to the capitalist and the miser; but while the miser is merely a capitalist gone mad, the capitalist is a rational miser....

Buying in order to sell, or, more accurately, buying in order to sell dearer, M-C-M′, appears certainly to be a form peculiar to one kind of capital alone, namely, merchants' capital. But industrial capital too is money, that is changed into commodities, and by the sale of these commodities, is re-converted into more money. The events that take place outside the sphere of circulation, in the interval between the buying and selling, do not affect the form of this movement....

CHAPTER 6: THE BUYING AND SELLING OF LABOUR-POWER

...

In order that our owner of money may be able to find labour-power offered for sale as a commodity, various conditions must first be fulfilled. The exchange of commodities of itself implies no other relations of dependence than those which result from its own nature. On this assumption, labour-power can appear upon the market as a commodity, only if, and so far as, its possessor, the individual whose labour-power it is, offers it for sale, or sells it, as a commodity. In order that he may be able to do this, he must have it at his disposal, must be the untrammelled owner of his capacity for labour, i.e., of his person. He and the owner of money meet in the market, and deal with each other as on the basis of equal rights, with this difference alone, that one is buyer, the other seller; both, therefore, equal in the eyes of the law. The continuance of this relation demands that the owner of the labour-power should sell it only for a definite period, for if he were to sell it rump and stump, once for all, he would be selling himself, converting himself from a free man into a slave, from an owner of a commodity into a commodity. He must constantly look upon his labour-power as his own property, his own commodity, and this he can only do by placing it at the disposal of the buyer temporarily, for a definite period of time. By this means alone can he avoid renouncing his rights of ownership over it.

The second essential condition to the owner of money finding labour-power in the market as a commodity is this—that the labourer instead of being in the position to sell commodities in which his labour is incorporated, must be obliged to offer for sale as a commodity that very labour-power, which exists only in his living self.

In order that a man may be able to sell commodities other than labour-power, he must of course have the means of production, as raw material, implements, &c. No boots can be made without leather. He requires also the means of subsistence....

For the conversion of his money into capital, therefore, the owner of money must meet in the market with the free labourer, free in the double sense, that as a free man he can dispose of his labour-power as his own commodity, and that on the other hand he has no other commodity for sale, is short of everything necessary for the realisation of his labour-power....

CHAPTER 7: THE LABOUR-PROCESS AND THE PROCESS OF PRODUCING SURPLUS-VALUE

Section 1: The Labour-Process or the Production of Use-Values

...

The labour-process, turned into the process by which the capitalist consumes labour-power, exhibits two characteristic phenomena. First, the labourer works under the control of the capitalist to whom his labour belongs; the capitalist taking good care that the work is done in a proper manner, and that the means of production are used with intelligence, so that there is no unnecessary waste of raw material, and no wear and tear of the implements beyond what is necessarily caused by the work.

Secondly, the product is the property of the capitalist and not that of the labourer, its immediate producer. Suppose that a capitalist pays for a day's labour-power at its value; then the right to use that power for a day belongs to him, just as much as the right to use any other commodity, such as a horse that he has hired for the day. To the purchaser of a commodity belongs its use, and the seller of labour-power, by giving his labour, does no more, in reality, than part with the use-value that he has sold. From the instant he steps into the workshop, the use-value of his labour-power, and therefore also its use, which is labour, belongs to the capitalist.

By the purchase of labour-power, the capitalist incorporates labour, as a living ferment, with the lifeless constituents of the product. From his point of view, the labour-process is nothing more than the consumption of the commodity purchased, i.e., of labour-power; but this consumption cannot be effected except by supplying the labour-power with the means of production. The labour-process is a process between things that the capitalist has purchased, things that have become his property. The product of this process belongs, therefore, to him, just as much as does the wine which is the product of a process of fermentation completed in his cellar.

Section 2: The Production of Surplus-Value ...

Our capitalist has two objects in view: in the first place, he wants to produce a use-value that has a value in exchange, that is to say, an article destined to be sold, a commodity; and secondly, he desires to produce a commodity whose value shall be greater than the sum of the values of the commodities used in its production, that is, of the means of production and the labour-power, that he purchased with his good money in the open market. His aim is to produce not only a use-value, but a commodity also; not only use-value, but value; not only value, but at the same time surplus-value....

Let us examine the matter more closely. The value of a day's labour-power amounts to 3 shillings, because on our assumption half a day's labour is embodied in that quantity of labour-power, i.e., because the means of subsistence that are daily required for the production of labour-power, cost half a day's labour. But the past labour that is embodied in the labour-power, and the living labour that it can call into action; the daily cost of maintaining it, and its daily expenditure in work, are two totally different things. The former determines the exchange-value of the labour-power, the latter is its use-value. The fact that half a day's labour is necessary to keep the labourer alive during 24 hours, does not in any way prevent him from working a whole day. Therefore, the value of labour-power, and the value which that labour-power creates in the labour-process, are two entirely different magnitudes; and this difference of the two values was what the capitalist had in view, when he was purchasing the labour-power....

What really influenced him was the specific use-value which this commodity possesses of being a source not only of value, but of more value than it has itself. This is the special service that the capitalist expects from labour-power....

The labourer therefore finds, in the workshop, the means of production necessary for working, not only during six, but during twelve hours....

CHAPTER 25: THE GENERAL LAW OF CAPITALIST ACCUMULATION

Section 2: Relative Diminution of the Variable Part of Capital Simultaneously with the Progress of Accumulation and of the Concentration That Accompanies It

...

The laws of this centralisation of capitals, or of the attraction of capital by capital, cannot be developed here. A brief hint at a few facts must suffice. The battle of competition is fought by cheapening of commodities. The cheapness of commodities demands, *caeteris paribus*, on the productiveness of labour, and this again on the scale of production. Therefore, the larger capitals beat the smaller. It will further be remembered that, with the development of the capitalist mode of production, there is an increase in the minimum amount of individual capital necessary to carry on a business under its normal conditions. The smaller capitals, therefore, crowd into spheres of production which Modern Industry has only sporadically or incompletely got hold of. Here competition rages in direct proportion to the number, and in inverse proportion to the magnitudes, of the antagonistic capitals. It always ends in the ruin of many small capitalists, whose capitals partly pass into the hands of their conquerors, partly vanish....

Centralisation completes the work of accumulation by enabling industrial capitalists to extend the scale of their operations. Whether this latter result is the consequence of accumulation or centralisation, whether centralisation is accomplished by the violent method of annexation—when certain capitals become such preponderant centres of attraction for others that they shatter the individual cohesion of the latter and then draw the separate fragments to themselves—or whether the fusion of a number of capitals already formed or in process of formation takes place by the smoother process of organising joint-stock companies—the economic effect remains the same. Everywhere the increased scale of industrial establishments is the starting point for a more comprehensive organisation of the collective work of many, for a wider development of their material motive forces—in other words, for the progressive transformation of isolated processes of production, carried on by customary methods, into processes of production socially combined and scientifically arranged....

In time the old capital also reaches the moment of renewal from top to toe, when it sheds its skin and is reborn like the others in a perfected technical form, in which a smaller quantity of labour will suffice to set in motion a larger quantity of machinery and raw materials....

On the one hand, therefore, the additional capital formed in the course of accumulation attracts fewer and fewer labourers in proportion to its magnitude. On the other hand, the old capital periodically reproduced with change of composition, repels more and more of the labourers formerly employed by it.

Section 3: Progressive Production of a Relative Surplus Population or Industrial Reserve Army

...

In fact, it is capitalistic accumulation itself that constantly produces, and produces in the direct ratio of its own energy and extent, a relatively redundant population of labourers, i.e., a population of greater extent than suffices for the average needs of the self-expansion of capital, and therefore a surplus population....

But if a surplus labouring population is a necessary product of accumulation or of the development of wealth on a capitalist basis, this surplus population becomes, conversely, the lever of capitalistic accumulation, nay, a condition of existence of the capitalist mode of production. It forms a disposable industrial reserve army, that belongs to capital quite as absolutely as if the latter had bred it at its own cost. Independently of the limits of the actual increase of population, it creates, for the changing needs of the self-expansion of capital, a mass of human material always ready for exploitation....

The course characteristic of modern industry, viz., a decennial cycle (interrupted by smaller oscillations), of periods of average activity, production at high pressure, crisis and stagnation, depends on the constant formation, the greater or less absorption, and the re-formation of the industrial reserve army or surplus population. In their turn, the varying phases of the industrial cycle recruit the surplus population, and become one of the most energetic agents of its reproduction....

Up to this point it has been assumed that the increase or diminution of the variable capital corresponds rigidly with the increase or diminution of the number of labourers employed.

The number of labourers commanded by capital may remain the same, or even fall, while the variable capital increases. This is the case if the individual labourer yields more labour, and therefore his wages increase, and this although the price of labour remains the same or even falls, only more slowly than the mass of labour rises. Increase of variable capital, in this case, becomes an index of more labour, but not of more labourers employed. It is the absolute interest of every capitalist to press a given quantity of labour out of a smaller, rather than a greater number of labourers, if the cost is about the same. In the latter case, the outlay of constant capital increases in proportion to the mass of labour set in action; in the former that increase is much smaller. The more extended the scale of production, the stronger this motive. Its force increases with the accumulation of capital.

We have seen that the development of the capitalist mode of production and of the productive power of labour—at once the cause and effect of accumulation—enables the capitalist, with the same outlay of variable capital, to set in action more labour by greater exploitation (extensive or intensive) of each individual labour power. We have further seen that the capitalist buys with the same capital a greater mass of labour power, as he progressively replaces skilled labourers by less skilled, mature labour power by immature, male by female, that of adults by that of young persons or children....

The overwork of the employed part of the working class swells the ranks of the reserve, whilst conversely the greater pressure that the latter by its competition exerts on the former, forces these to submit to overwork and to subjugation under the dictates of capital. The condemnation of one part of the working class to enforced idleness by the overwork of the other part, and the converse, becomes a means of enriching the individual capitalists, and accelerates at the same time the production of the industrial reserve army on a scale corresponding with the advance of social accumulation.... Taking them as a whole, the general movements of wages are exclusively regulated by the expansion and contraction of the industrial reserve army, and these again correspond to the periodic changes of the industrial cycle. They are, therefore, not determined by the variations of the absolute number of the working population, but by the varying proportions in which the working class is divided into active and reserve army, by the increase or diminution in the relative amount of the surplus population, by the extent to which it is now absorbed, now set free....

Capital works on both sides at the same time. If its accumulation, on the one hand, increases the demand for labour, it increases on the other the supply of labourers by the "setting free" of them, whilst at the same time the pressure of the unemployed compels those that are employed to furnish more labour, and therefore makes the supply of labour, to a certain extent, independent of the supply of labourers. The action of the law of supply and demand of labour on this basis completes the despotism of capital. As soon, therefore, as the labourers learn the secret, how it comes to pass that in the same measure as they work more, as they produce more wealth for others, and as the productive power of their labour increases, so in the same measure even their function as a means of the self-expansion of capital becomes more and more precarious for them; as soon as they discover that the degree of intensity of the competition among themselves depends wholly on the pressure of the relative surplus population; as soon as, by Trades Unions, &c., they try to organise a regular co-operation between employed and unemployed in order to destroy or to weaken the ruinous effects of this natural law of capitalistic production on their class, so soon capital and its sycophant, Political Economy, cry out at the infringement of the "eternal" and so to say "sacred" law of supply and demand. Every combination of employed and unemployed disturbs the "harmonious" action of this law. But, on the other hand, as soon as (in the colonies, e.g.) adverse circumstances prevent the creation of an industrial reserve army and, with it, the absolute dependence of the working class upon the capitalist class, capital, along with its commonplace Sancho Panza, rebels against the "sacred" law of supply and demand, and tries to check its inconvenient action by forcible means and State interference.

5.8 David Harvey (1935–)

The British-born and American-based sociologist David Harvey identifies a novel political-economic system that emerged simultaneously in the United Kingdom, the United States of America, and China in the late 1970s. It was known as Thatcherism for a while, after the British prime minister, Margaret Thatcher, who advocated on behalf of free markets, international trade, private property rights, and reducing the welfare state. This new arrangement was recognizably liberal, but differed qualitatively from classical liberalism. No longer was the state an economic guardian protecting citizens from corporate dominance or a sponsor of welfare services. Instead, the state's principal function is to expand markets as far as possible, giving free reign to entrepreneurial impulses. It introduced a new social-political-economic ethic with deregulated markets and the transfer of formerly public assets into private hands. Because this new ethic differs in important respects from classical liberalism, Harvey designates the system "neoliberalism."

According to Harvey, the theory supporting neoliberalism is problematic and, in fact, many of its defenders instituted practices that did not cohere well with the theory. Despite "free market fundamentalism" and enthusiasm for economic competition, states have been activist with respect to creating a good environment for business and improving the capacity of consolidated multinational corporations to eliminate small competitors. In addition, without declaring this purpose, democratically elected governmental power has been curtailed. Elites and experts who are more responsive to lobbyists from industry than to citizens direct the neoliberal state managerially. Not only is this situation politically objectionable, according to Harvey, it exacerbates economic inequalities. The climate for good business at the centre of neoliberalism produces economic benefits, but they flow to the top at the expense of workers and ordinary citizens. As a result, neoliberalism has resurrected old class divisions along economic lines.

Emerging class divisions, economic crises in capitalism (e.g., the global financial collapse in 2008), political crises in democracy, and deteriorating working conditions for the vast majority of people, have generated a great deal of cynicism. As Harvey describes it, neoliberalism is unstable due to its internal contradictions, which has made it impossible to implement consistently. The result is widespread moral frustration. For this reason, in 2005, when his book was released, he anticipated the rise of nationalism and a backlash against progressive social programs such as affirmative action, environmentalism, and so forth.

~

from A Brief History of Neoliberalism

Introduction

... Neoliberalism is in the first instance a theory of political economic practices that proposes that human well-being can best be advanced by liberating individual entrepreneurial freedoms and skills within an institutional framework characterized by strong private property rights, free markets, and free trade. The role of the state is to create and preserve an institutional framework appropriate to such practices. The state has to guarantee, for example, the quality and integrity of money. It must also set up those military, defence, police, and legal structures and functions required to secure private property rights and to guarantee, by force if need be, the proper functioning of markets. Furthermore, if markets do not exist (in areas such as land, water, education, health care, social security, or environmental pollution) then they must be created, by state action if necessary. But beyond these tasks the state should not venture. State interventions in markets (once created) must be kept to a bare minimum because, according to the theory, the state cannot possibly possess enough information to second-guess market signals (prices) and because powerful interest groups will inevitably distort and bias state interventions (particularly in democracies) for their own benefit.

There has everywhere been an emphatic turn towards neoliberalism in political-economic practices and thinking since the 1970s. Deregulation, privatization, and withdrawal of the state from many areas of social provision have been all too common. Almost all states, from those newly minted after the collapse of the Soviet Union to old-style social democracies and welfare states such as New Zealand and Sweden, have embraced, sometimes voluntarily and in other instances in response to coercive pressures, some version of neoliberal theory and adjusted at least some policies and practices accordingly. Post-apartheid South Africa quickly embraced neoliberalism, and even contemporary China, as we shall see, appears to be headed in this direction. Furthermore, the advocates of the neoliberal way now occupy positions of considerable influence in education (the universities and many 'think tanks'), in the media, in corporate boardrooms and financial institutions, in key state institutions (treasury departments, the central banks), and also in those international institutions such as the International Monetary Fund (IMF), the World Bank, and the World Trade Organization (WTO) that regulate global finance and trade. Neoliberalism has, in short, become hegemonic as a mode of discourse. It has pervasive effects on ways of thought to the point where it has become incorporated into the common-sense way many of us interpret, live in, and understand the world.

The process of neoliberalization has, however, entailed much 'creative destruction', not only of prior institutional frameworks and powers (even challenging traditional forms of state sovereignty) but also of divisions of labour, social relations, welfare provisions, technological mixes, ways of life and thought, reproductive activities, attachments to the land and habits of the heart. In so far as neoliberalism values market exchange as 'an ethic in itself, capable of acting as a guide to all human action, and substituting for all previously held ethical beliefs', it emphasizes the significance of contractual relations in the marketplace.[1] It holds that the social good will be maximized by maximizing the reach and frequency of market transactions, and it seeks to bring all human action into the domain of the market. This requires technologies of information creation and capacities to accumulate, store, transfer, analyse, and use massive databases to guide decisions in the global marketplace. Hence neoliberalism's intense interest in and pursuit of information technologies (leading some to proclaim

1 P. Treanor, 'Neoliberalism: Origins, Theory, Definition', http://web.inter.nl.net/users/Paul.Treanor/neoliberalism.html.

the emergence of a new kind of 'information society'). These technologies have compressed the rising density of market transactions in both space and time. They have produced a particularly intensive burst of what I have elsewhere called 'time-space compression'. The greater the geographical range (hence the emphasis on 'globalization') and the shorter the term of market contracts the better.

1

Freedom's Just Another Word …

For any way of thought to become dominant, a conceptual apparatus has to be advanced that appeals to our intuitions and instincts, to our values and our desires, as well as to the possibilities inherent in the social world we inhabit. If successful, this conceptual apparatus becomes so embedded in common sense as to be taken for granted and not open to question. The founding figures of neoliberal thought took political ideals of human dignity and individual freedom as fundamental, as 'the central values of civilization'. In so doing they chose wisely, for these are indeed compelling and seductive ideals. These values, they held, were threatened not only by fascism, dictatorships, and communism, but by all forms of state intervention that substituted collective judgements for those of individuals free to choose.

Concepts of dignity and individual freedom are powerful and appealing in their own right. Such ideals empowered the dissident movements in eastern Europe and the Soviet Union before the end of the Cold War as well as the students in Tiananmen Square. The student movements that swept the world in 1968—from Paris and Chicago to Bangkok and Mexico City—were in part animated by the quest for greater freedoms of speech and of personal choice. More generally, these ideals appeal to anyone who values the ability to make decisions for themselves.

The idea of freedom, long embedded in the US tradition, has played a conspicuous role in the US in recent years. '9/11' was immediately interpreted by many as an attack on it. 'A peaceful world of growing freedom', wrote President Bush on the first anniversary of that awful day, 'serves American long-term interests, reflects enduring American ideals and unites America's allies.' 'Humanity', he concluded, 'holds in its hands the opportunity to offer freedom's triumph over all its age-old foes', and 'the United States welcomes its responsibilities to lead in this great mission'. This language was incorporated into the US National Defense Strategy document issued shortly thereafter. 'Freedom is the Almighty's gift to every man and woman in this world', he later said, adding that 'as the greatest power on earth we have an obligation to help the spread of freedom'.[2] …

The assumption that individual freedoms are guaranteed by freedom of the market and of trade is a cardinal feature of neoliberal thinking, and it has long dominated the US stance towards the rest of the world.[3] What the US evidently sought to impose by main force on Iraq was a state apparatus whose fundamental mission was to facilitate conditions for profitable capital accumulation on the part of both domestic and foreign capital. I call this kind of state apparatus a *neoliberal state*. The freedoms it embodies reflect the interests of private property owners, businesses, multinational corporations, and financial capital. Bremer invited the Iraqis, in short, to ride their horse of freedom straight into the neoliberal corral….

There is, however, one element within this transition that deserves specific attention. The crisis of

2 G.W. Bush, 'President Addresses the Nation in Prime Time Press Conference', 13 Apr. 2004; http://www.whitehouse.gov/news/releases/2004/0420040413-20.html.

3 G.W. Bush, 'Securing Freedom's Triumph', *New York Times*, 11 Sept. 2002, A33. *The National Security Strategy of the United State of America* can be found on the website: www.whitehouse.gov/nsc/nss.

capital accumulation in the 1970s affected everyone through the combination of rising unemployment and accelerating inflation.... Discontent was widespread and the conjoining of labour and urban social movements throughout much of the advanced capitalist world appeared to point towards the emergence of a socialist alternative to the social compromise between capital and labour that had grounded capital accumulation so successfully in the post-war period. Communist and socialist parties were gaining ground, if not taking power, across much of Europe and even in the United States popular forces were agitating for widespread reforms and state interventions. There was, in this, a clear *political* threat to economic elites and ruling classes everywhere, both in the advanced capitalist countries (such as Italy, France, Spain, and Portugal) and in many developing countries (such as Chile, Mexico, and Argentina). In Sweden, for example, what was known as the Rehn–Meidner plan literally offered to gradually buy out the owners' share in their own businesses and turn the country into a worker/share-owner democracy. But, beyond this, the *economic* threat to the position of ruling elites and classes was now becoming palpable. One condition of the post-war settlement in almost all countries was that the economic power of the upper classes be restrained and that labour be accorded a much larger share of the economic pie. In the US, for example, the share of the national income taken by the top 1 per cent of income earners fell from a pre-war high of 16 per cent to less than 8 per cent by the end of the Second World War, and stayed close to that level for nearly three decades. While growth was strong this restraint seemed not to matter. To have a stable share of an increasing pie is one thing. But when growth collapsed in the 1970s, when real interest rates went negative and paltry dividends and profits were the norm, then upper classes everywhere felt threatened. In the US the control of wealth (as opposed to income) by the top 1 per cent of the population had remained fairly stable throughout the twentieth century. But in the 1970s it plunged precipitously... as asset values (stocks, property, savings) collapsed. The upper classes had to move decisively if they were to protect themselves from political and economic annihilation.

The coup in Chile and the military takeover in Argentina, promoted internally by the upper classes with US support, provided one kind of solution. The subsequent Chilean experiment with neoliberalism demonstrated 'that the benefits of revived capital accumulation were highly skewed under forced privatization. The country and its ruling elites, along with foreign investors, did extremely well in the early stages. Redistributive effects and increasing social inequality have in fact been such a persistent feature of neoliberalization as to be regarded as structural to the whole project. Gerard Dumenil and Dominique Lévy, after careful reconstruction of the data, have concluded that neoliberalization was from the very beginning a project to achieve the restoration of class power. After the implementation of neoliberal policies in the late 1970s, the share of national income of the top 1 per cent of income earners in the US soared, to reach 15 per cent (very close to its pre-Second World War share) by the end of the century. The top 0.1 per cent of income earners in the US increased their share of the national income from 2 per cent in 1978 to over 6 per cent by 1999, while the ratio of the median compensation of workers to the salaries of CEOs increased from just over 30 to 1 in 1970 to nearly 500 to 1 by 2000.... Almost certainly, with the Bush administration's tax reforms now taking effect, the concentration of income and wealth in the upper echelons of society is continuing apace because the estate tax (a tax on wealth) is being phased out and taxation on income from investments and capital gains is being diminished, while taxation on wages and salaries is maintained.[4]

4 G. Dumenil and D. Levy, 'Neoliberal Dynamics: Towards A New Phase?', in K. van der Pijl, L. Assassi, and D. Wigan (eds.), *Global Regulation: Managing Crises after the Imperial Turn* (New York: Palgrave Macmillan, 2004), 41–63. See also Task Force on Inequality and American Democracy, *American Democracy in an Age of Rising Inequality* (American Political Science Association, 2004); T. Piketty and E. Saez, 'Income Inequality in the United States, 1913–1998', *Quarterly Journal of Economics* 118 (2003), 1–39.

The US is not alone in this: the top 1 per cent of income earners in Britain have doubled their share of the national income from 6.5 per cent to 13 per cent since 1982. And when we look further afield we see extraordinary concentrations of wealth and power emerging all over the place.... While there are exceptions to this trend (several East and South-East Asian countries have so far contained income inequalities within reasonable bounds, as has France ...), the evidence strongly suggests that the neoliberal turn is in some way and to some degree associated with the restoration or reconstruction of the power of economic elites.

We can, therefore, interpret neoliberalization either as a *utopian* project to realize a theoretical design for the reorganization of international capitalism or as a *political* project to re-establish the conditions for capital accumulation and to restore the power of economic elites. In what follows I shall argue that the second of these objectives has in practice dominated. Neoliberalization has not been very effective in revitalizing global capital accumulation, but it has succeeded remarkably well in restoring, or in some instances (as in Russia and China) creating, the power of an economic elite. The theoretical utopianism of neoliberal argument has, I conclude, primarily worked as a system of justification and legitimation for whatever needed to be done to achieve this goal. The evidence suggests, moreover, that when neoliberal principles clash with the need to restore or sustain elite power, then the principles are either abandoned or become so twisted as to be unrecognizable. This in no way denies the power of ideas to act as a force for historical-geographical change. But it does point to a creative tension between the power of neoliberal ideas and the actual practices of neoliberalization that have transformed how global capitalism has been working over the last three decades.

3

The Neoliberal State

The role of the state in neoliberal theory is reasonably easy to define. The practice of neoliberalization has, however, evolved in such a way as to depart significantly from the template that theory provides. The somewhat chaotic evolution and uneven geographical development of state institutions, powers, and functions over the last thirty years suggests, furthermore, that the neoliberal state may be an unstable and contradictory political form.

THE NEOLIBERAL STATE IN THEORY

According to theory, the neoliberal state should favour strong individual private property rights, the rule of law, and the institutions of freely functioning markets and free trade.[5] These are the institutional arrangements considered essential to guarantee individual freedoms. The legal framework is that of freely negotiated contractual obligations between juridical individuals in the marketplace. The sanctity of contracts and the individual right to freedom of action, expression, and choice must be protected. The state must therefore use its monopoly of the means of violence to preserve these freedoms at all costs. By extension, the freedom of businesses and corporations (legally regarded as individuals) to operate within this institutional framework of free markets and free trade is regarded as a fundamental good. Private enterprise and entrepreneurial initiative are seen as the keys to

5 H.-J. Chang, *Globalisation, Economic Development and the Role of the State* (London: Zed Books, 2003); B. Jessop, 'Liberalism, Neoliberalism, and Urban Governance: A State-Theoretical Perspective', *Antipode*, 3413 (2002), 452–72; N. Poulantzas, *State Power Socialism*, trans. P. Camiller (London: Verso, 1978); S. Clarke (ed.), *The State Debate* (London: Macmillan, 1991); S. Haggard and R. Kaufman (eds.), *The Politics of Economic Adjustment: International Constraints, Distributive Conflicts and the State* (Princeton: Princeton University Press, 1992); R. Nozick, *Anarchy, State and Utopia* (New York: Basic Books, 1977).

innovation and wealth creation. Intellectual property rights are protected (for example through patents) so as to encourage technological changes. Continuous increases in productivity should then deliver higher living standards to everyone. Under the assumption that 'a rising tide lifts all boats', or of 'trickle down', neoliberal theory holds that the elimination of poverty (both domestically and worldwide) can best be secured through free markets and free trade.

Neoliberals are particularly assiduous in seeking the privatization of assets. The absence of clear private property rights—as in many developing countries—is seen as one of the greatest of all institutional barriers to economic development and the improvement of human welfare. Enclosure and the assignment of private property rights is considered the best way to protect against the so-called 'tragedy of the commons' (the tendency for individuals to irresponsibly super-exploit common property resources such as land and water). Sectors formerly run or regulated by the state must be turned over to the private sphere and be deregulated (freed from any state interference). Competition—between individuals, between firms, between territorial entities (cities, regions, nations, regional groupings)—is held to be a primary virtue. The ground-rules for market competition must be properly observed, of course. In situations where such rules are not clearly laid out or where property rights are hard to define, the state must use its power to impose or invent market systems (such as trading in pollution rights). Privatization and deregulation combined with competition, it is claimed, eliminate bureaucratic red tape, increase efficiency and productivity, improve quality, and reduce costs, both directly to the consumer through cheaper commodities and services and indirectly through reduction of the tax burden. The neoliberal state should persistently seek out internal reorganizations and new institutional arrangements that improve its competitive position as an entity vis-à-vis other states in the global market.

While personal and individual freedom in the marketplace is guaranteed, each individual is held responsible and accountable for his or her own actions and well-being. This principle extends into the realms of welfare, education, health care, and even pensions (social security has been privatized in Chile and Slovakia, and proposals exist to do the same in the US). Individual success or failure are interpreted in terms of entrepreneurial virtues or personal failings (such as not investing significantly enough in one's own human capital through education) rather than being attributed to any systemic property (such as the class exclusions usually attributed to capitalism).

The free mobility of capital between sectors, regions, and countries is regarded as crucial. All barriers to that free movement (such as tariffs, punitive taxation arrangements, planning and environmental controls, or other locational impediments) have to be removed, except in those areas crucial to 'the national interest', however that is defined. State sovereignty over commodity and capital movements is willingly surrendered to the global market. International competition is seen as healthy since it improves efficiency and productivity, lowers prices, and thereby controls inflationary tendencies. States should therefore collectively seek and negotiate the reduction of barriers to movement of capital across borders and the opening of markets (for both commodities and capital) to global exchange. Whether or not this applies to labour as a commodity is, however, controversial. To the degree that all states must collaborate to reduce barriers to exchange, so co-ordinating structures such as the group of advanced capitalist nations (the US, Britain, France, Germany, Italy, Canada, and Japan) known as the G7 (now the G8 with the addition of Russia) must arise. International agreements between states guaranteeing the rule of law and freedoms of trade, such as those now incorporated in the World Trade Organization agreements, are critical to the advancement of the neoliberal project on the global stage.

Neoliberal theorists are, however, profoundly suspicious of democracy. Governance by majority rule is seen as a potential threat to individual rights and constitutional liberties. Democracy is viewed as a luxury, only possible under conditions of relative affluence coupled with a strong middle-class presence to guarantee political stability. Neoliberals therefore tend to favour governance by experts and elites. A strong preference exists for government by executive order and by judicial decision rather than democratic and parliamentary decision-making. Neoliberals prefer to insulate key institutions, such as the central bank, from democratic pressures. Given that neoliberal theory centres on the rule of law and a strict interpretation of constitutionality, it follows that conflict and opposition must be mediated through the courts. Solutions and remedies to any problems have to be sought by individuals through the legal system.

TENSIONS AND CONTRADICTIONS

There are some shadowy areas as well as points of conflict within the general theory of the neoliberal state. First, there is the problem of how to interpret monopoly power. Competition often results in monopoly or oligopoly, as stronger firms drive out weaker. Most neoliberal theorists consider this unproblematic (it should, they say, maximize efficiency) provided there are no substantial barriers to the entry of competitors (a condition often hard to realize and which the state may therefore have to nurture). The case of so-called 'natural monopolies' is more difficult. It makes no sense to have multiple competing electrical power grids, gas pipelines, water and sewage systems, or rail links between Washington and Boston. State regulation of provision, access, and pricing seems unavoidable in such domains. While partial deregulation may be possible (permitting competing producers to feed electricity into the same grid or run trains on the same tracks, for example) the possibilities for profiteering and abuse, as the California power crisis of 2002 abundantly showed, or for deadly muddle and confusion, as the British rail situation has proven, are very real.

The second major arena of controversy concerns market failure. This arises when individuals and firms avoid paying the full costs attributable to them by shedding their liabilities outside the market (the liabilities are, in technical parlance, 'externalized'). The classic case is that of pollution, where individuals and firms avoid costs by dumping noxious wastes free of charge in the environment. Productive ecosystems may be degraded or destroyed as a result. Exposure to dangerous substances or physical dangers in the workplace may affect human health and even deplete the pool of healthy labourers in the workforce. While neoliberals admit the problem and some concede the case for limited state intervention, others argue for inaction because the cure will almost certainly be worse than the disease. Most would agree, however, that if there are to be interventions these should work through market mechanisms (via tax impositions or incentives, trading rights of pollutants, and the like). Competitive failures are approached in a similar fashion. Rising transaction costs can be incurred as contractual and subcontractual relations proliferate. The vast apparatus of currency speculation, to take just one example, appears more and more costly at the same time as it becomes more and more fundamental to capturing speculative profits. Other problems arise when, say, all competing hospitals in a region buy the same sophisticated equipment that remains underutilized, thus driving up aggregate costs. The case here for cost containment through state planning, regulation, and forced co-ordination is strong, but again neoliberals are deeply suspicious of such interventions.

All agents acting in the market are generally presumed to have access to the same information. There are presumed to be no asymmetries of power or of information that interfere with the capacity of individuals to make rational economic decisions in their own interests. This condition is rarely, if ever, approximated in practice, and there are significant consequences.[6] Better informed and more powerful players have an advantage that can all too easily be parlayed into procuring even better information and greater relative power. The establishment of intellectual property rights

6 J. Stiglitz, *The Roaring Nineties* (New York: Norton, 2003), won his Nobel Prize for his studies on how asymmetries of information affected market behaviours and outcomes.

(patents), furthermore, encourages 'rent seeking'. Those who hold the patent rights use their monopoly power to set monopoly prices and to prevent technology transfers except at a very high cost. Asymmetric power relations tend, therefore, to increase rather than diminish over time unless the state steps in to counteract them. The neoliberal presumption of perfect information and a level playing field for competition appears as either innocently utopian or a deliberate obfuscation of processes that will lead to the concentration of wealth and, therefore, the restoration of class power.

The neoliberal theory of technological change relies upon the coercive powers of competition to drive the search for new products, new production methods, and new organizational forms. This drive becomes so deeply embedded in entrepreneurial common sense, however, that it becomes a fetish belief: that there is a technological fix for each and every problem. To the degree that this takes hold not only within corporations but also within the state apparatus (in the military in particular), it produces powerful independent trends of technological change that can become destabilizing, if not counterproductive. Technological developments can run amok as sectors dedicated solely to technological innovation create new products and new ways of doing things that as yet have no market (new pharmaceutical products are produced, for which new illnesses are then invented). Talented interlopers can, furthermore, mobilize technological innovations to undermine dominant social relations and institutions; they can, through their activities, even reshape common sense to their own pecuniary advantage. There is an inner connection, therefore, between technological dynamism, instability, dissolution of social solidarities, environmental degradation, deindustrialization, rapid shifts in time-space relations, speculative bubbles, and the general tendency towards crisis formation within capitalism.[7]

There are, finally, some fundamental political problems within neoliberalism that need to be addressed. A contradiction arises between a seductive but alienating possessive individualism on the one hand and the desire for a meaningful collective life on the other. While individuals are supposedly free to choose, they are not supposed to choose to construct strong collective institutions (such as trade unions) as opposed to weak voluntary associations (like charitable organizations). They most certainly should not choose to associate to create political parties with the aim of forcing the state to intervene in or eliminate the market. To guard against their greatest fears—fascism, communism, socialism, authoritarian populism, and even majority rule—the neoliberals have to put strong limits on democratic governance, relying instead upon undemocratic and unaccountable institutions (such as the Federal Reserve or the IMF) to make key decisions. This creates the paradox of intense state interventions and government by elites and 'experts' in a world where the state is supposed not to be interventionist. One is reminded of Francis Bacon's utopian tale *New Atlantis* (first published in 1626) where a Council of Wise Elders mandates all key decisions. Faced with social movements that seek collective interventions, therefore, the neoliberal state is itself forced to intervene, sometimes repressively, thus denying the very freedoms it is supposed to uphold. In this situation, however, it can marshal one secret weapon: international competition and globalization can be used to discipline movements opposed to the neoliberal agenda within individual states. If that fails, then the state must resort to persuasion, propaganda or, when necessary, raw force and police power to suppress opposition to neoliberalism. This was precisely Polanyi's fear: that the liberal (and by extension the neoliberal) utopian project could only ultimately be sustained by resort to authoritarianism. The freedom of the masses would be restricted in favour of the freedoms of the few....

This brings us, finally, to the problematic issue of the neoliberal state's approach to labour markets. Internally, the neoliberal state is necessarily hostile to

7 See D. Harvey, *Condition of Postmodernity* (Oxford: Basil Blackwell, 1989); Harvey, *The Limits to Capital* (Oxford: Basil Blackwell, 1982).

all forms of social solidarity that put restraints on capital accumulation. Independent trade unions or other social movements (such as the municipal socialism of the Greater London Council type), which acquired considerable power under embedded liberalism, have therefore to be disciplined, if not destroyed, and this in the name of the supposedly sacrosanct individual liberty of the isolated labourer.

... The general outcome is lower wages, increasing job insecurity, and in many instances loss of benefits and of job protections. Such trends are readily discernible in all states that have taken the neoliberal road. Given the violent assault on all forms of labour organization and labour rights and heavy reliance upon massive but largely disorganized labour reserves in countries such as China, Indonesia, India, Mexico, and Bangladesh, it would seem that labour control and maintenance of a high rate of labour exploitation have been central to neoliberalization all along. The restoration or formation of class power occurs, as always, at the expense of labour.

It is precisely in such a context of diminished personal resources derived from the job market that the neoliberal determination to transfer all responsibility for well-being back to the individual has doubly deleterious effects. As the state withdraws from welfare provision and diminishes its role in arenas such as health care, public education, and social services, which were once so fundamental to embedded liberalism, it leaves larger and larger segments of the population exposed to impoverishment.[8] The social safety net is reduced to a bare minimum in favour of a system that emphasizes personal responsibility. Personal failure is generally attributed to personal failings, and the victim is all too often blamed.

Behind these major shifts in social policy lie important structural changes in the nature of governance. Given the neoliberal suspicion of democracy, a way has to be found to integrate state decision-making into the dynamics of capital accumulation and the networks of class power that are in the process of restoration, or, as in China and Russia, in formation. Neoliberalization has entailed, for example, increasing reliance on public-private partnerships (this was one of the strong ideas pushed by Margaret Thatcher as she set up 'quasi-governmental institutions' such as urban development corporations to pursue economic development). Businesses and corporations not only collaborate intimately with state actors but even acquire a strong role in writing legislation, determining public policies, and setting regulatory frameworks (which are mainly advantageous to themselves). Patterns of negotiation arise that incorporate business and sometimes professional interests into governance through close and sometimes secretive consultation. The most blatant example of this was the persistent refusal of Vice-President Cheney to release the names of the consultative group that formulated the Bush administration's energy policy document of 2002; it almost certainly included Kenneth Lay, the head of Enron—a company accused of profiteering by deliberately fostering an energy crisis in California and which then collapsed in the midst of a huge accounting scandal. The shift from government (state power on its own) to governance (a broader configuration of state and key elements in civil society) has therefore been marked under neoliberalism.[9] In this respect the practices of the neoliberal and developmental state broadly converge.

The state typically produces legislation and regulatory frameworks that advantage corporations, and in some instances specific interests such as energy, pharmaceuticals, agribusiness, etc. In many of the instances of public–private partnerships, particularly at the municipal level, the state assumes much of the risk while the private sector takes most of the profits. If necessary, furthermore, the neoliberal state will resort to coercive legislation and policing tactics (anti-picketing rules, for example) to disperse or repress collective forms of opposition to corporate power. Forms of surveillance and policing multiply:

8 V. Navarro (ed.), *The Political Economy of Social Inequalities: Consequences for Health and the Quality of Life* (Amityville, NY: Haywood, 2002).

9 P. McCarney and R. Stren, *Governance on the Ground: Innovations and Discontinuities in the Cities of the Developing World* (Princeton: Woodrow Wilson Center Press, 2003); A. Dixit, *Lawlessness and Economics: Alternative Modes of Governance* (Princeton: Princeton University Press, 2004).

in the US, incarceration became a key state strategy to deal with problems arising among discarded workers and marginalized populations. The coercive arm of the state is augmented to protect corporate interests and, if necessary, to repress dissent. None of this seems consistent with neoliberal theory. The neoliberal fear that special-interest groups would pervert and subvert the state is nowhere better realized than in Washington, where armies of corporate lobbyists (many of whom have taken advantage of the 'revolving door' between state employment and far more lucrative employment by the corporations) effectively dictate legislation to match their special interests. While some states continue to respect the traditional independence of the Civil Service, this condition has everywhere been under threat in the course of neoliberalization. The boundary between the state and corporate power has become more and more porous. What remains of representative democracy is overwhelmed, if not totally though legally corrupted by money power....

From this account we can clearly see that neoliberalism does not make the state or particular institutions of the state (such as the courts and police functions) irrelevant, as some commentators on both the right and the left have argued.[10] There has, however, been a radical reconfiguration of state institutions and practices (particularly with respect to the balance between coercion and consent, between the powers of capital and of popular movements, and between executive and judicial power, on the one hand, and powers of representative democracy on the other).

But all is not well with the neoliberal state, and it is for this reason that it appears to be either a transitional or an unstable political form. At the heart of the problem lies a burgeoning disparity between the declared public aims of neoliberalism—the well-being of all—and its actual consequences—the restoration of class power. But beyond this there lies a whole series of more specific contradictions that need to be highlighted.

1. On the one hand the neoliberal state is expected to take a back seat and simply set the stage for market functions, but on the other it is supposed to be activist in creating a good business climate and to behave as a competitive entity in global politics. In its latter role it has to work as a collective corporation, and this poses the problem of how to ensure citizen loyalty. Nationalism is an obvious answer, but this is profoundly antagonistic to the neoliberal agenda. This was Margaret Thatcher's dilemma, for it was only through playing the nationalism card in the Falklands/Malvinas war and, even more significantly, in the campaign against economic integration with Europe, that she could win re-election and promote further neoliberal reforms internally. Again and again, be it within the European Union, in Mercosur (where Brazilian and Argentine nationalisms inhibit integration), in NAFTA, or in ASEAN, the nationalism required for the state to function effectively as a corporate and competitive entity in the world market gets in the way of market freedoms more generally.
2. Authoritarianism in market enforcement sits uneasily with ideals of individual freedoms. The more neoliberalism veers towards the former, the harder it becomes to maintain its legitimacy with respect to the latter and the more it has to reveal its anti-democratic colours. This contradiction is paralleled by a growing lack of symmetry in the power relation between corporations and individuals such as you and me. If 'corporate power steals your personal freedom' then the promise of neoliberalism comes to nothing.[11] This applies to individuals in the workplace as well as in the living space. It is one thing to maintain, for

10 K. Ohmae, *The End of the Nation State: The Rise of the Regional Economies* (New York: Touchstone Press, 1996).

11 J. Court, *Corporateering: How Corporate Power Steals Your Personal Freedom* (New York: J.P. Tarcher/Putnam, 2003).

example, that my health-care status is my personal choice and responsibility, but quite another when the only way I can satisfy my needs in the market is through paying exorbitant premiums to inefficient, gargantuan, highly bureaucratized but also highly profitable insurance companies. When these companies even have the power to define new categories of illness to match new drugs coming on the market, then something is clearly wrong.[12] Under such circumstances, maintaining legitimacy and consent, as we saw in Chapter 2 [not included here], becomes an even more difficult balancing act that can easily topple over when things start to go wrong.

3. While it may be crucial to preserve the integrity of the financial system, the irresponsible and self-aggrandizing individualism of operators within it produces speculative volatility, financial scandals, and chronic instability. The Wall Street and accounting scandals of recent years have undermined confidence and posed regulatory authorities with serious problems of how and when to intervene, internationally as well as nationally. International free trade requires some global rules of the game, and that calls forth the need for some kind of global governance (for example by the WTO). Deregulation of the financial system facilitates behaviours that call for re-regulation if crisis is to be avoided.[13]
4. While the virtues of competition are placed up front, the reality is the increasing consolidation of oligopolistic, monopoly, and transnational power within a few centralized multinational corporations: the world of soft-drinks competition is reduced to Coca Cola versus Pepsi, the energy industry is reduced to five huge transnational corporations, and a few media magnates control most of the flow of news, much of which then becomes pure propaganda.
5. At the popular level, the drive towards market freedoms and the commodification of everything can all too easily run amok and produce social incoherence. The destruction of forms of social solidarity and even, as Thatcher suggested, of the very idea of society itself, leaves a gaping hole in the social order. It then becomes peculiarly difficult to combat anomie and control the resultant anti-social behaviours such as criminality, pornography, or the virtual enslavement of others. The reduction of 'freedom' to 'freedom of enterprise' unleashes all those 'negative freedoms' that Polanyi saw as inextricably tied in with the positive freedoms. The inevitable response is to reconstruct social solidarities, albeit along different lines—hence the revival of interest in religion and morality, in new forms of associationism (around questions of rights and citizenship, for example) and even the revival of older political forms (fascism, nationalism, localism, and the like). Neoliberalism in its pure form has always threatened to conjure up its own nemesis in varieties of authoritarian populism and nationalism. As Schwab and Smadja, organizers of the once purely celebratory neoliberal annual jamboree at Davos, warned as early as 1996:
   - Economic globalization has entered a new phase. A mounting backlash against its effects, especially in the industrial democracies, is threatening a disruptive impact on economic activity and social stability in many countries. The mood in these democracies is one of helplessness and anxiety, which helps explain the rise of a new brand of populist politicians. This can easily turn into revolt.[14]

THE NEOCONSERVATIVE ANSWER

If the neoliberal state is inherently unstable, then what might replace it? In the US there are signs of a

12 D. Healy, *Let Them Eat Prozac: The Unhealthy Relationship between the Pharmaceutical Industry and Depression* (New York: New York University Press, 2004).

13 W. Bello, N. Bullard, and K. Malhotra (eds.), *Global Finance: New Thinking on Regulating Speculative Markets* (London: Zed Books, 2000).

14 K. Schwab and C. Smadja, cited in D. Harvey, *Spaces of Hope* (Edinburgh: Edinburgh University Press, 2000), 70.

distinctively neoconservative answer to this question. Reflecting on the recent history of China, Wang also suggests that, theoretically,

> such discursive narratives as 'neo-Authoritarianism', 'neoconservatism', 'classical liberalism', market extremism, national modernization ... all had close relationships of one sort or another with the constitution of neoliberalism. The successive displacement of these terms for one another (or even the contradictions among them) demonstrate the shifts in the structure of power in both contemporary China and the contemporary world at large.[15]

Whether or not this portends a more general reconfiguration of governance structures worldwide remains to be seen. It is, however, interesting to note how neoliberalization in authoritarian states such as China and Singapore seems to be converging with the increasing authoritarianism evident in neoliberal states such as the US and Britain. Consider, then, how the neoconservative answer to the inherent instability of the neoliberal state has evolved in the US.

Like the neoliberals that preceded them, the 'neocons' had long been nurturing their particular views on the social order, in universities (Leo Strauss at the University of Chicago being particularly influential) and well-funded think-tanks, and through influential publications (such as *Commentary*).[16] US neoconservatives favour corporate power, private enterprise, and the restoration of class power. Neoconservatism is therefore entirely consistent with the neoliberal agenda of elite governance, mistrust of democracy, and the maintenance of market freedoms. But it veers away from the principles of pure neoliberalism and has reshaped neoliberal practices in two fundamental respects: first, in its concern for order as an answer to the chaos of individual interests, and second, in its concern for an overweening morality as the necessary social glue to keep the body politic secure in the face of external and internal dangers.

In its concern for order, neoconservatism appears as a mere stripping away of the veil of authoritarianism in which neoliberalism sought to envelop itself. But it also proposes distinctive answers to one of the central contradictions of neoliberalism. If 'there is no such thing as society but only individuals' as Thatcher initially put it, then the chaos of individual interests can easily end up prevailing over order. The anarchy of the market, of competition, and of unbridled individualism (individual hopes, desires, anxieties, and fears; choices of lifestyle and of sexual habits and orientation; modes of self-expression and behaviours towards others) generates a situation that becomes increasingly ungovernable. It may even lead to a breakdown of all bonds of solidarity and a condition verging on social anarchy and nihilism.

In the face of this, some degree of coercion appears necessary to restore order. The neoconservatives therefore emphasize militarization as an antidote to the chaos of individual interests. For this reason, they are far more likely to highlight threats, real or imagined, both at home and abroad, to the integrity and stability of the nation. In the US this entails triggering what Hofstadter refers to as 'the paranoid style of American politics' in which the nation is depicted as besieged and threatened by enemies from within and without.[17] This style of politics has had a long history in the US. Neoconservatism is not new, and since the Second World War it has found a particular home in a powerful military-industrial complex that has a vested interest in permanent militarization. But the end of the Cold War posed the question of where the threat to US security was coming from. Radical Islam and China emerged as the top two candidates externally, and dissident internal movements (the Branch

15 H. Wang, *China's New Order: Society, Politics and Economy in Transition* (Cambridge, Mass.: Harvard University Press, 2003), 44.
16 J. Mann, *The Rise of the Vulcans: The History of Bush's War Cabinet* (New York: Viking Books, 2004); S. Drury, *Leo Strauss and the American Right* (New York: Palgrave Macmillan, 1999).
17 R. Hofstadter, *The Paranoid Style in American Politics and Other Essays* (Cambridge, Mass.: Harvard University Press, 1996).

Dravidians incinerated at Waco, militia movements that gave succour to the Oklahoma bombing, the riots that followed the beating of Rodney King in Los Angeles, and finally the disorders that broke out in Seattle in 1999) had to be targeted internally by stronger surveillance and policing. The very real emergence of the threat from radical Islam during the 1990s that culminated in the events of 9/11 finally came to the fore as the central focus for the declaration of a permanent 'war on terror' that demanded militarization both at home and abroad to guarantee the security of the nation. While, plainly, some sort of police/military response to the threat revealed by the two attacks on the World Trade Center in New York was called for, the arrival in power of neoconservatives guaranteed an overarching, and in the judgement of many an overreaching, response in the turn to extensive militarization at home and abroad.[18]

Neoconservatism has long hovered in the wings as a movement against the moral permissiveness that individualism typically promotes. It therefore seeks to restore a sense of moral purpose, some higher-order values that will form the stable centre of the body politic. This possibility is in a way presaged within the framework of neoliberal theories which, 'by questioning the very political foundation of interventionist models of economic management ... have brought issues of morality, justice and power—although in their own peculiar ways—back into economics'.[19] What the neoconservatives do is to change the 'peculiar ways' in which such questions enter into debate. Their aim is to counteract the dissolving effect of the chaos of individual interests that neoliberalism typically produces. They in no way depart from the neoliberal agenda of a construction or restoration of a dominant class power. But they seek legitimacy for that power, as well as social control through construction of a climate of consent around a coherent set of moral values. This immediately poses the question of which moral values should prevail. It would, for example, be entirely feasible to appeal to the liberal system of human rights since, after all, the aim of human rights activism, as Mary Kaldor argues, 'is not merely intervention to protect human rights but the creation of a moral community'.[20] In the US, doctrines of 'exceptionalism' and the long history of civil rights activism have certainly generated moral movements around issues such as civil rights, global hunger, and philanthropic engagement, as well as missionary zeal.

But the moral values that have now become central to the neoconservatives can best be understood as products of the particular coalition that was built in the 1970s, between elite class and business interests intent on restoring their class power, on the one hand, and an electoral base among the 'moral majority' of the disaffected white working class on the other. The moral values centred on cultural nationalism, moral righteousness, Christianity (of a certain evangelical sort), family values, and right-to-life issues, and on antagonism to the new social movements such as feminism, gay rights, affirmative action, and environmentalism. While this alliance was mainly tactical under Reagan, the domestic disorder of the Clinton years forced the moral values argument to the top of the agenda in the Republicanism of Bush the younger. It now forms the core of the moral agenda of the neoconservative movement.[21]

But it would be wrong to see this neoconservative turn as exceptional or peculiar to the US, even though there are special elements at work there that may not be present elsewhere. Within the US this assertion of moral values relies heavily on appeals to ideals of nation, religion, history, cultural tradition, and the like, and these ideals are by no means confined to the US. This brings one of the more troubling aspects of neoliberalization more sharply back into focus: the curious relationship between state and nation. In principle, neoliberal theory does not look with favour on

18 D. Harvey, *The New Imperialism* (Oxford: Oxford University Press, 2003), ch. 4.
19 Chang, *Globalisation*, 31.
20 M. Kaldor, *New and Old Wars: Organized Violence in a Global Era* (Cambridge: Polity, 1999), 130.
21 T. Frank, *What's the Matter with Kansas: How Conservatives Won the Hearts of America* (New York: Metropolitan Books, 2004).

the *nation* even as it supports the idea of a strong state. The umbilical cord that tied together state and nation under embedded liberalism had to be cut if neoliberalism was to flourish....

But, as we have seen, the neoliberal state needs nationalism of a certain sort to survive. Forced to operate as a competitive agent in the world market and seeking to establish the best possible business climate, it mobilizes nationalism in its effort to succeed. Competition produces ephemeral winners and losers in the global struggle for position, and this in itself can be a source of national pride or of national soul-searching. Nationalism around sports competitions between nations is a sign of this. In China, the appeal to nationalist sentiment in the struggle to procure the state's position (if not hegemony) in the global economy is overt (as is the intensity of its training programme for athletes for the Beijing Olympics). Nationalist sentiment is equally rife in South Korea and Japan, and in both instances this can be seen as an antidote to the dissolution of former bonds of social solidarity under the impact of neoliberalism. Strong currents of cultural nationalism are stirring within the old nation-states (such as France) that now constitute the European Union. Religion and cultural nationalism provided the moral heft behind the Hindu Nationalist Party's success in enhancing neoliberal practices in India in recent times. The invocation of moral values in the Iranian revolution and the subsequent turn to authoritarianism has not led to total abandonment of market-based practices there, even though the revolution was aimed at the decadence of unbridled market individualism....

Clearly, while there are dangers in the neoliberal dalliance with nationalism of a certain sort, the fierce neoconservative embrace of a national moral purpose is far more threatening. The picture of many states, each prepared to resort to draconian coercive practices while each espousing its own distinctive and supposedly superior moral values, competing on the world stage is not reassuring. What seems like an answer to the contradictions of neoliberalism can all too easily turn into a problem. The spread of neoconservative, if not outright authoritarian, power (of the sort Vladimir Putin exercises in Russia and the Communist Party exercises in China), albeit grounded very differently in different social formations, highlights the dangers of descent into competing and perhaps even warring nationalisms. If there is an inevitability at work, then it arises more out of the neoconservative turn than out of eternal truths attaching to supposed national differences. To avoid catastrophic outcomes therefore requires rejection of the neoconservative solution to the contradictions of neoliberalism.

5.9 Review Questions

1. According to Tocqueville, what is the difference between political liberty and equality of conditions, and why do we tend to fight for one and forget the other in "democratic ages"?

2. How does Tocqueville describe the new kind of despotism he warns might emerge out of democracy, and how is it different from traditional despotism?

3. What justification does Locke give for arguing that private property is a right that exists even in the state of nature?

4. Why does Locke believe the invention of money is necessary and useful to human civilization?

5. How does Smith describe the "division of labour" and why does it make productive processes more efficient?

6. What is Smith's "invisible hand of the market" and what does it do?

7. For Rousseau, why does the ownership of land lead people to treat each other increasingly badly?

8. What is the new "state of nature" that Rousseau warns the development of civilization is leading towards and how does it differ from his notion of the original state of nature?

9. According to Marx, what is the difference between money and capital, and why does one try to grow while the other only changes forms?

10. According to Marx, why does capitalism produce unemployment?

11. According to Harvey, what kind of freedom does neoliberalism pursue, and what does it actually produce?

12. How does Harvey define neoconservatism in relation to neoliberalism?

5.10 Further Reading

Brown, Wendy. "Neoliberalism and the End of Liberal Democracy." *Theory & Event*, vol. 7, no. 1, 2003.

Durkheim, Emile. *The Division of Labour in Society*. Translated by W.D. Halls, Macmillan Press, 1984.

Friedman, Milton. *Capitalism and Freedom*. University of Chicago Press, 2002.

Hayek, Friedrich. *The Constitution of Liberty*. University of Chicago Press, 1960.

Heilbroner, Robert. *The Worldly Philosophers: The Lives, Times, and Ideas of the Great Economic Thinkers*. 7th ed., Simon & Schuster, 1999.

Macpherson, C.B. *The Political Theory of Possessive Individualism*. Oxford University Press, 1962.

Marcuse, Herbert. *One Dimensional Man*. 2nd ed., Beacon Press, 1991.

Weber, Max. *The Protestant Ethic and the Spirit of Capitalism*. 4th ed., translated by Stephen Kahlberg, Oxford University Press, 2009.

Wilde, Oscar. *The Soul of Man under Socialism*. A.L. Humphreys, 1907.

UNIT III

Power, Violence, and Political Ethics

CHAPTER 6
Propaganda and Power

Power ought to serve as a check to power.

—MONTESQUIEU

All power comes from the people and never returns there.

—GABRIEL LAUB

The whole aim of practical politics is to keep the populace alarmed (and hence clamourous to be led to safety) by menacing it with an endless series of hobgoblins, all of them imaginary.

—H.L. MENKEN

Nearly all men can stand adversity, but if you want to test a man's character, give him power. 

—ABRAHAM LINCOLN

One is never unwillingly ordered around. When one is ordered around, it is always willingly.

—CHARLES PÉGUY

Force is as pitiless to the man who possesses it, or thinks he does, as it is to its victims; the second it crushes, the first it intoxicates. The truth is, nobody really possesses it.

—SIMONE WEIL

6.1 Introduction

Social and political power can be defined in a number of ways. It may be something inherent to an individual or group, or it may be a relationship that exists only between individuals and groups. It may be something transferred from one individual or group to another, or something that one individual or group imposes on another. It may be directional—from one individual or group to another—or structural—a relationship that all parties find themselves inside. It may be something that limits the freedom of an individual or group, or it may be the very basis on which an individual or group experiences itself as free. Readings in this chapter explore the relationship between power and ethics.

A good starting point from which to approach this chapter is to adopt a working definition of power as the ability of one individual or group to influence or determine what others believe or do. It is the ability to cause the will of another to conform to one's own, the ability to control, guide, and structure human activity and relations. Vital to note straightaway about this definition is that it presupposes the existence of freely deciding human subjects. Here, power is the ability of one freely deciding subject to control the decision-making of another, the ability to override what would otherwise have been his or her freedom. Although there are a host of external objects that we might desire to control on a daily basis, we reserve the term "power" for our control over other human subjects—that is, other freely deciding subjects who might deliberately resist efforts to control them. And although there is a host of external forces that might influence our beliefs and behaviours, we reserve the term "power" for the influence of other human subjects—subjects who have decided to try to influence us. When we use the term power, we therefore refer explicitly to a situation in which one individual or group's freedom to decide is replaced by the freedom of another individual or group to decide for them.

Focusing on the freely deciding human subject situates our working definition of power securely within the realm of ethics—especially those parts that originate from Enlightenment principles of rationality, universality, and critical reasoning. If, as Kant supposes (1.3), Enlightenment is premised on the notion that everyone has the ability and right to think rationally for themselves, then power is inherently problematic. Insofar as power is essentially the ability to interfere with or take away another subject's ability and right to think independently, it is possible to argue that power is inevitably immoral.

An antagonism between power and ethics is staged from the outset of *Life Examined* in Plato's *Apology*. Socrates argues that the court before which he stands accused is not being used as a tool of inquiry to judge whether he has violated the law, but as a tool of power, a weapon for his accusers to punish him. And what does Socrates believe he is being punished for? Arguably for pursuing ethical inquiry in a way that endangers his accusers' social and political power. Socratic inquiry is a threat to power, and power defends itself by repressing it ruthlessly.

But this is not the whole story. Many Enlightenment thinkers argue that the rational capacity and right to think independently is neither natural nor innate in human beings. It is, instead, cultivated and sustained by power itself. Locke and Burke, to name two examples, argue that the only way to regulate external influences, i.e., to create a space within which we are free to think and decide for ourselves, is for power to constrain and prevent undue interference from others. Another version of this same argument holds that power is essentially the only game in town: If one wishes to be free from power, the only tool one has at one's disposal to limit or restrain it is precisely some other source or form of power.

Kant stages this tension very nicely in his "What Is Enlightenment?" On the one hand, Kant's Enlightenment ideal envisions the independence of every mature adult. To this end, he asks power—in this case embodied in King Frederick of Prussia—to limit itself and provide a space of freedom within which freely deciding citizens can exercise their independence. On the other hand, Kant is also clear that this does not mean power should disappear. Kant argues that, while absolute freedom for all might succeed in challenging existing prejudices, it will only give rise to new prejudices in its turn, rather than leading to Enlightenment. To counter this tendency he argues for what he calls "artificial unanimity"—the ability of power to organize groups of subjects who might otherwise be at cross-purposes with each other into a cohesive unit pursuing a common goal.

In the present chapter, John Stuart Mill (6.6) conceives of liberty in a way that fits this Enlightenment understanding of power. For Mill, liberty is precisely the ability of a populace to protect itself from abuses of authorities with official power, the extent to which power can be made to restrain or check itself. What's more, Mill brings this question into relation with modern democracy, which can be understood as an attempt to resolve precisely this tension: In modern democracy, power is supposed to be possessed by the very people over whom it is exercised. And while this may help ensure that power limits itself, Mill argues that pure majority rule has its own tyrannical tendencies.

How, then, does power function? How is it possible for one individual or group to determine the beliefs and behaviours of others? While there are many answers to this question, some of which are enumerated by authors in this chapter, power relations between freely deciding human subjects can take two basic forms: first, there are what we might call coercive forms of power, techniques that change the environment around the subject in order to induce him or her to decide differently. The threat of physical violence is perhaps the most visible example here. Whereas someone might have made a particular decision had he or she been free to do so, the threat of physical violence can change the grounds for that decision.

In an earlier chapter Hobbes argues that coercive power is necessary for maintaining social cohesion (4.6). Excerpts from Niccolò Machiavelli's *The Prince* in this chapter enumerate various coercive techniques, including violence (which he calls "cruelty") and the threat of violence (which induces what he calls "fear"), the effectiveness of which he praises above other, more positive forms of coercion such as bribery or the promise of glory (6.5). In "Panopticism," Michel Foucault describes what he calls sovereign or exclusionary forms of power, which attach rewards and punishments to certain acts through a legal code (6.7). This system, in which one can freely decide to transgress the law in the face of painful consequences, has very much the structure of coercive power.

Second, and distinct from coercive power, there are what we might call deceptive forms of power. Rather than only manipulating a person's environment, deceptive power manipulates a person's decision-making process itself. While this may sound confusing or abstract, it boils down to manipulating individuals into thinking that they have made a free decision, when in fact they are obeying power. These techniques are especially important and problematic for two reasons: first, they can be much more difficult to resist than coercion. While one might accept physical violence as the cost of a particular decision—or even make that decision precisely in order to assert one's freedom in the face of coercive power—deceptive power heads off particular decisions in advance. One may not even realize that one is being subjected to it.

The reach of deceptive power is great and difficult to assess directly, primarily because appearances mask its fundamental operations. Machiavelli, who makes no bones about the expedience of coercion, argues that deception is one of the most important tools for gaining and retaining power. Even a powerful prince must appear to be morally upstanding in the course of violating moral standards. Noam Chomsky and Edward Herman argue that our contemporary mainstream news media functions as propaganda, a form of deceptive power that does not directly demand overt obedience. By providing the public with seemingly neutral, factual information, it counts on us to arrive at beliefs and values friendly to corporate and government interests. Michel Foucault contrasts traditional sovereign power, which tends to be coercive, with a new, deceptive form of power that he calls discipline. Here the success of discipline is its silent operation on the way we think. Rather than imposing power as an external force, discipline works by training individuals to impose power on themselves from within, thereby encouraging conformity and obedience unconsciously.

Deceptive power is also important to both *Life Examined* and human life because it operates primarily through discourse—in interpersonal transactions with words and images—which is also the medium for higher-order thinking about ethics and morality. To put it simply, on the face of it, the text you are reading right now might be as earnest as a Socratic inquiry, as deceptive as the mask of a Machiavellian prince, as sly as mass media propaganda, or as insidious as Foucauldian discipline. How would you know? On their own, words on the page do not reveal what kind of power relationship we are engaged in. The best we can do is think carefully and critically at every stage. Debate in this chapter over the relationship between discourse, power, and ethics begins with excerpts from three ancient sources: Confucius's *Analects*, Plato's *Gorgias*, and Aristotle's *The Art of Rhetoric*. Confucius makes the point that words are directive, that admonishment, advice, and other verbal operations are intrinsically ethical. We must speak carefully because we must deliberate carefully, and we must deliberate carefully because deliberation is the basis of action. In *Gorgias*, Plato launches a moral challenge to empirical rhetoric—that is, the skill of persuading people with language as it was taught by Gorgias, arguing that it is not a true art, like legislation. Here he repeats a distinction from the *Apology*: true arts, like philosophy and legislation, pursue truth, while counterfeit arts, like rhetoric and flattery, persuade people to believe things whether they are true or not. Persuasive speech need not be false to be worth condemning; it is enough that success in rhetoric be understood independently of the truth or falsity of someone's message. In this sense, Plato accuses rhetoric of putting itself at the disposal of deceptive power. Still, when a message is true, useful, illuminating, or insightful, some means must be found to communicate it. In *The Art of Rhetoric*, Aristotle argues that rhetoric can function as a true art, and it is also a necessary tool for disseminating the truth.

6.2 Confucius (551–478 BCE)

The following excerpts from *The Analects* consider two normative functions for words and speech: (1) moral guidance and (2) cognitive ordering. These are not the only functions language serves, but these two seem to be related insofar as they are ethically significant.

(1) Moral guidance, as distinct from physical coercion, leaves open the possibility that any advice, admonition, etc. offered will be declined by its recipient; as well, even when it is accepted, it may not be understood or translated into action. Truly persuasive speech issues in action, not mere assent or pleasure, and the true value of guidance over coercion lies in the autonomy of any resulting action (see *Analects* 9; XXV). Functioning in this capacity, words have a kind of social power that can be directed to benevolent purposes. No doubt, Confucius understood his own volition as a teacher in this light.

(2) Additionally, words and terms function in a cognitive capacity to shape how someone thinks independently of any direct guidance they may receive from others (see *Analects* 17; VIII). In this capacity, they have a psychological power, and this power is manifested in the deliberations that guide a person's action. It is only with great and careful effort that we can order our thoughts, but the task is necessary: both our humanity and our agency depend upon doing that well (13; III).

~

from The Analects

Book 9, Chap. XXV

The Master [Confucius] said, 'Can men refuse to assent to the words of strict admonition? But it is reforming the conduct because of them which is valuable. Can men refuse to be pleased with words of gentle advice? But it is unfolding their aim which is valuable. If a man be pleased with these words, but does not unfold their aim, and assents to those, but does not reform his conduct, I can really do nothing with him.'

Book 13, Chap. III

Tsze-lu said, 'The ruler of Wei has been waiting for you, in order with you to administer the government. What will you consider the first thing to be done?'

The Master replied, 'What is necessary is to rectify names.'

'So, indeed!' said Tsze-lu. 'You are wide of the mark! Why must there be such rectification?'

The Master said, 'How uncultivated you are, Yu! A superior man, in regard to what he does not know, shows a cautious reserve. If names be not correct, language is not in accordance with the truth of things. If language be not in accordance with the truth of things, affairs cannot be carried on to success. When affairs cannot be carried on to success, proprieties and music will not flourish. When proprieties and music do not flourish, punishments will not be properly awarded. When punishments are not properly awarded, the people do not know how to move hand or foot. Therefore a superior man considers it necessary that the names he uses may be spoken appropriately, and also that what he speaks may be carried out appropriately. What the superior man requires, is just that in his words there may be nothing incorrect.'

Book 17, Chap. VIII

The Master said, 'Yu, have you heard the six words to which are attached six becloudings?'

Yu replied, 'I have not.'

'Sit down, and I will tell them to you. There is the love of being benevolent without the love of learning;—the beclouding here leads to a foolish simplicity. There is the love of knowing without the love of learning;—the beclouding here leads to dissipation of mind. There is the love of being sincere without the love of learning;—the beclouding here leads to an injurious disregard of consequences. There is the love of straightforwardness without the love of learning;—the beclouding here leads to rudeness. There is the love of boldness without the love of learning;—the beclouding here leads to insubordination. There is the love of firmness without the love of learning;—the beclouding here leads to extravagant conduct.'

Book 20, Chap. III

The Master said, 'Without recognising the ordinances of Heaven, it is impossible to be a superior man. Without an acquaintance with the rules of Propriety, it is impossible for the character to be established. Without knowing the force of words, it is impossible to know men.'

6.3 Plato (427–347 BCE)

In this excerpt from *Gorgias*, Plato provides a critique of rhetoric: the skill of using language to persuade. Like the other dialogues, this one features Plato's teacher, Socrates, engaged in a kind of debate. Here, Socrates is speaking with Gorgias, a well-known and successful sophist, about whether rhetoric ought to be considered an art or only a kind of skill or talent without general principles. Plato argues that while justice is a true art that belongs to the category of politics, rhetoric is a counterfeit or false version of it.

The distinction that Plato sets up is subtle and can be difficult to understand. Plato's complaint that rhetoric does not have general principles, such as a set of categories describing what sorts of people there are in the world and what different techniques are available for convincing them, seems unfounded from our contemporary perspective. As early as Aristotle's *The Art of Rhetoric*, we see a rebuttal of Plato which provides precisely such a set of principles. And this is to say nothing of more contemporary developments such as the fields of propaganda, public relations, and marketing.

However, there are other ways to make sense of Plato's distinction. First, Plato makes clear that one of the things that bothers him about rhetoric is that it acts through seduction, appealing to irrationality and sensation rather than rationality and truth. While the practice of justice involves trying to arrive at the true difference between right and wrong, rhetoric tries to seduce the listener into believing that something is right or wrong without it necessarily being so. At this level, Plato sees rhetoric as essentially deceitful. Second, Gorgias himself admits that the aim of rhetoric is to transform everyone else in the world into one's slaves. Rhetoric's purpose is to produce an unequal power relationship through which one can control others, making it incompatible with Plato's understanding of the true arts, which always endeavour to discover universal truths that are in principle good for everyone. In *Phaedrus*, Socrates imagines rhetoric rehabilitated this way.

~

6.3.1 *from* Gorgias

Gorgias, 450b–453a

... GORGIAS: ... Socrates, the knowledge of the other arts has only to do with some sort of external action, as of the hand; but there is no such action of the hand in rhetoric which works and takes effect only through the medium of discourse. And therefore I am justified in saying that rhetoric treats of discourse.

SOCRATES: I am not sure whether I entirely understand you, but I dare say I shall soon know better; please to answer me a question:—you would allow that there are arts?

GORGIAS: Yes.

SOCRATES: As to the arts generally, they are for the most part concerned with doing, and require little or no speaking; in painting, and statuary, and many other arts, the work may proceed in silence; and of such arts I suppose you would say that they do not come within the province of rhetoric.

GORGIAS: You perfectly conceive my meaning, Socrates.

SOCRATES: But there are other arts which work wholly through the medium of language, and require either no action or very little, as, for example, the arts of arithmetic, of calculation, of geometry, and of playing draughts; in some of these speech is pretty nearly co-extensive with action, but in most of them the verbal element is greater—they depend wholly on words for their efficacy and power: and I take your meaning to be that rhetoric is an art of this latter sort?

GORGIAS: Exactly.

SOCRATES: And yet I do not believe that you really mean to call any of these arts rhetoric; although the precise expression which you used was, that rhetoric is an art which works and takes effect only through the medium of discourse; and an adversary who wished to be captious might say, 'And so, Gorgias, you call arithmetic rhetoric.' But I do not think that you really call arithmetic rhetoric any more than geometry would be so called by you.

GORGIAS: You are quite right, Socrates, in your apprehension of my meaning.

SOCRATES: Well, then, let me now have the rest of my answer:—seeing that rhetoric is one of those arts which works mainly by the use of words, and there are other arts which also use words, tell me what is that quality in words with which rhetoric is concerned:—Suppose that a person asks me about some of the arts which I was mentioning just now; he might say, 'Socrates, what is arithmetic?' and I should reply to him, as you replied to me, that arithmetic is one of those arts which take effect through words. And then he would proceed to ask: 'Words about what?' and I should reply, Words about odd and even numbers, and how many there are of each. And if he asked again: 'What is the art of calculation?' I should say, That also is one of the arts which is concerned wholly with words. And if he further said, 'Concerned with what?' I should say, like the clerks in the assembly, 'as aforesaid' of arithmetic, but with a difference, the difference being that the art of calculation considers not only the quantities of odd and even numbers, but also their numerical relations to themselves and to one another. And suppose, again, I were to say that astronomy is only words—he would ask, 'Words about what, Socrates?' and I should answer, that astronomy tells us about the motions of the stars and sun and moon, and their relative swiftness.

GORGIAS: You would be quite right, Socrates.

SOCRATES: And now let us have from you, Gorgias, the truth about rhetoric: which you would admit (would you not?) to be one of those arts which act always and fulfil all their ends through the medium of words?

GORGIAS: True.

SOCRATES: Words which do what? I should ask. To what class of things do the words which rhetoric uses relate?

GORGIAS: To the greatest, Socrates, and the best of human things.

SOCRATES: That again, Gorgias is ambiguous; I am still in the dark: for which are the greatest and best of human things? I dare say that you have heard men singing at feasts the old drinking song, in which the singers enumerate the goods of life, first health, beauty next, thirdly, as the writer of the song says, wealth honestly obtained.

GORGIAS: Yes, I know the song; but what is your drift?

SOCRATES: I mean to say, that the producers of those things which the author of the song praises, that is to say, the physician, the trainer, the money-maker, will at once come to you, and first the physician will say: 'O Socrates, Gorgias is deceiving you, for my art is concerned with the greatest good of men and not his.' And when I ask, Who are you? he will reply, 'I am a physician.' What do you mean? I shall say. Do you mean that your art produces the greatest good? 'Certainly,' he will answer, 'for is not health the greatest good? What greater good can men have, Socrates?' And after him the trainer will come and say, 'I too, Socrates, shall be greatly surprised if Gorgias can show more good of his art than I can show of mine.' To him again I shall say, Who are you, honest friend, and what is your business? 'I am a trainer,' he will reply, 'and my business is to make men beautiful and strong in body.' When I have done with the trainer, there arrives the money-maker, and he, as I expect, will utterly despise them all. 'Consider Socrates,' he will say, 'whether Gorgias or any one else can produce any greater good than wealth.' Well, you and I say to him, and are you a creator of wealth? 'Yes,' he replies. And who are you? 'A money-maker.' And do you consider wealth to be the greatest good of man? 'Of course,' will be his reply. And we shall rejoin: Yes; but our friend Gorgias contends that his art produces a greater good than yours. And then he will be sure to go on and ask, 'What good? Let Gorgias answer.' Now I want you, Gorgias, to imagine that this question is asked of you by them and by me; What is that which, as you say, is the greatest good of man, and of which you are the creator? Answer us.

GORGIAS: That good, Socrates, which is truly the greatest, being that which gives to men freedom in their own persons, and to individuals the power of ruling over others in their several states.

SOCRATES: And what would you consider this to be?

GORGIAS: What is there greater than the word which persuades the judges in the courts, or the senators in the council, or the citizens in the assembly, or at any other political meeting?—if you have the power of uttering this word, you will have the physician your slave, and the trainer your slave, and the money-maker of whom you talk will be found to gather treasures, not for himself, but for you who are able to speak and to persuade the multitude.

SOCRATES: Now I think, Gorgias, that you have very accurately explained what you conceive to be the art of rhetoric; and you mean to say, if I am not mistaken, that rhetoric is the artificer of persuasion, having this and no other business, and that this is her crown and end. Do you know any other effect of rhetoric over and above that of producing persuasion?

GORGIAS: No: the definition seems to me very fair, Socrates; for persuasion is the chief end of rhetoric.

Gorgias, 462b–466a

... POLUS: I will ask; and do you answer me, Socrates, the same question which Gorgias, as you suppose, is unable to answer: What is rhetoric?

SOCRATES: Do you mean what sort of an art?

POLUS: Yes.

SOCRATES: To say the truth, Polus, it is not an art at all, in my opinion.

POLUS: Then what, in your opinion, is rhetoric?

SOCRATES: A thing which, as I was lately reading in a book of yours, you say that you have made an art.

POLUS: What thing?

SOCRATES: I should say a sort of experience.[1]

POLUS: Does rhetoric seem to you to be an experience?

SOCRATES: That is my view, but you may be of another mind.

POLUS: An experience in what?

SOCRATES: An experience in producing a sort of delight and gratification.

POLUS: And if able to gratify others, must not rhetoric be a fine thing?

SOCRATES: What are you saying, Polus? Why do you ask me whether rhetoric is a fine thing or not, when I have not as yet told you what rhetoric is?

POLUS: Did I not hear you say that rhetoric was a sort of experience?

SOCRATES: Will you, who are so desirous to gratify others, afford a slight gratification to me?

POLUS: I will.

SOCRATES: Will you ask me, what sort of an art is cookery?

POLUS: What sort of an art is cookery?

SOCRATES: Not an art at all, Polus.

POLUS: What then?

SOCRATES: I should say an experience.

POLUS: In what? I wish that you would explain to me.

SOCRATES: An experience in producing a sort of delight and gratification, Polus.

POLUS: Then are cookery and rhetoric the same?

SOCRATES: No, they are only different parts of the same profession.

POLUS: Of what profession?

SOCRATES: I am afraid that the truth may seem discourteous; and I hesitate to answer, lest Gorgias should imagine that I am making fun of his own profession. For whether or no this is that art of rhetoric which Gorgias practises I really cannot tell:—from what he was just now saying, nothing appeared of what he thought of his art, but the rhetoric which I mean is a part of a not very creditable whole.

GORGIAS: A part of what, Socrates? Say what you mean, and never mind me.

SOCRATES: In my opinion then, Gorgias, the whole of which rhetoric is a part is not an art at all, but the habit of a bold and ready wit, which knows how to manage mankind: this habit I sum up under the word 'flattery'; and it appears to me to have many other parts, one of which is cookery, which may seem to be an art, but, as I maintain, is only an experience or routine and not an art:—another part is rhetoric, and the art of attiring and sophistry are two others: thus there are four branches, and four different things answering to them. And Polus may ask, if he likes, for he has not as yet been informed, what part of flattery is rhetoric: he did not see that I had not yet answered him when he proceeded to ask a further question: Whether I do not think rhetoric a fine thing? But I shall not tell him whether rhetoric is a fine thing or not, until I have first answered, 'What is rhetoric?' For that would not be

1 "Empeiria" may be translated also as "knack." In brief, Socrates thinks that the current state of rhetoric is unsystematic and incapable of being formulated in general principles. A knack can be refined with practice, but not formulated in a set of theoretical principles or transmitted in instruction.

right, Polus; but I shall be happy to answer, if you will ask me, What part of flattery is rhetoric?

POLUS: I will ask and do you answer? What part of flattery is rhetoric?

SOCRATES: Will you understand my answer? Rhetoric, according to my view, is the ghost or counterfeit of a part of politics.

POLUS: And noble or ignoble?

SOCRATES: Ignoble, I should say, if I am compelled to answer, for I call what is bad ignoble: though I doubt whether you understand what I was saying before.

GORGIAS: Indeed, Socrates, I cannot say that I understand myself.

SOCRATES: I do not wonder, Gorgias; for I have not as yet explained myself, and our friend Polus, colt by name and colt by nature, is apt to run away.

GORGIAS: Never mind him, but explain to me what you mean by saying that rhetoric is the counterfeit of a part of politics.

SOCRATES: I will try, then, to explain my notion of rhetoric, and if I am mistaken, my friend Polus shall refute me. We may assume the existence of bodies and of souls?

GORGIAS: Of course.

SOCRATES: You would further admit that there is a good condition of either of them?

GORGIAS: Yes.

SOCRATES: Which condition may not be really good, but good only in appearance? I mean to say, that there are many persons who appear to be in good health, and whom only a physician or trainer will discern at first sight not to be in good health.

GORGIAS: True.

SOCRATES: And this applies not only to the body, but also to the soul: in either there may be that which gives the appearance of health and not the reality?

GORGIAS: Yes, certainly.

SOCRATES: And now I will endeavour to explain to you more clearly what I mean: The soul and body being two, have two arts corresponding to them: there is the art of politics attending on the soul; and another art attending on the body, of which I know no single name, but which may be described as having two divisions, one of them gymnastic, and the other medicine. And in politics there is a legislative part, which answers to gymnastic, as justice does to medicine; and the two parts run into one another, justice having to do with the same subject as legislation, and medicine with the same subject as gymnastic, but with a difference. Now, seeing that there are these four arts, two attending on the body and two on the soul for their highest good; flattery knowing, or rather guessing their natures, has distributed herself into four shams or simulations of them; she puts on the likeness of some one or other of them, and pretends to be that which she simulates, and having no regard for men's highest interests, is ever making pleasure the bait of the unwary, and deceiving them into the belief that she is of the highest value to them. Cookery simulates the disguise of medicine, and pretends to know what food is the best for the body; and if the physician and the cook had to enter into a competition in which children were the judges, or men who had no more sense than children, as to which of them best understands the goodness or badness of food, the physician would be starved to death. A flattery I deem this to be and of an ignoble sort, Polus, for to you I am now addressing myself, because it aims at pleasure without any thought of the best. An art I do not call it, but only an experience, because it is unable to explain or to give a reason of the nature of its own applications. And I do not call any irrational thing an art; but if you dispute my words, I am prepared to argue in defence of them.

Cookery, then, I maintain to be a flattery which takes the form of medicine; and tiring,[2] in like manner, is a flattery which takes the form of gymnastic, and is knavish, false, ignoble, illiberal, working deceitfully by the help of lines, and colours, and enamels, and garments, and making men affect a spurious beauty to the neglect of the true beauty which is given by gymnastic.

I would rather not be tedious, and therefore I will only say, after the manner of the geometricians (for I think that by this time you will be able to follow)

as tiring: gymnastic:: cookery: medicine;

or rather,

as tiring: gymnastic:: sophistry: legislation;

and

as cookery: medicine:: rhetoric: justice.

And this, I say, is the natural difference between the rhetorician and the sophist, but by reason of their near connection, they are apt to be jumbled up together; neither do they know what to make of themselves, nor do other men know what to make of them. For if the body presided over itself, and were not under the guidance of the soul, and the soul did not discern and discriminate between cookery and medicine, but the body was made the judge of them, and the rule of judgment was the bodily delight which was given by them, then the word of Anaxagoras, that word with which you, friend Polus, are so well acquainted, would prevail far and wide: 'Chaos' would come again, and cookery, health, and medicine would mingle in an indiscriminate mass. And now I have told you my notion of rhetoric, which is, in relation to the soul, what cookery is to the body.... And now you may do what you please with my answer.

POLUS: What do you mean? Do you think that rhetoric is flattery?

SOCRATES: Nay, I said a part of flattery; if at your age, Polus, you cannot remember, what will you do by-and-by, when you get older?

6.3.2 *from* Phaedrus

Phaedrus, 270b–272a

SOCRATES: The method which proceeds without analysis is like the groping of a blind man. Yet, surely, he who is an artist ought not to admit of a comparison with the blind, or deaf. The rhetorician, who teaches his pupil to speak scientifically, will particularly set forth the nature of that being to which he addresses his speeches; and this, I conceive, to be the soul.

PHAEDRUS: Certainly.

SOCRATES: His whole effort is directed to the soul; for in that he seeks to produce conviction.

PHAEDRUS: Yes.

SOCRATES: Then clearly, ... any one ... who teaches rhetoric in earnest will give an exact description of the nature of the soul; which will enable us to see whether she be single and same, or, like the body,

2 Here "tiring" is a synonym for dress or adorn. It picks up "attire," which is used earlier.

multiform. That is what we should call showing the nature of the soul.

PHAEDRUS: Exactly.

SOCRATES: He will explain, secondly, the mode in which she acts or is acted upon.

PHAEDRUS: True.

SOCRATES: Thirdly, having classified men and speeches, and their kinds and affections, and adapted them to one another, he will tell the reasons of his arrangement, and show why one soul is persuaded by a particular form of argument, and another not.

PHAEDRUS: You have hit upon a very good way.

SOCRATES: Yes, that is the true and only way in which any subject can be set forth or treated by rules of art, whether in speaking or writing. But the writers of the present day, at whose feet you have sat, craftily conceal the nature of the soul which they know quite well. Nor, until they adopt our method of reading and writing, can we admit that they write by rules of art?

PHAEDRUS: What is our method?

SOCRATES: I cannot give you the exact details; but I should like to tell you generally, as far as is in my power, how a man ought to proceed according to rules of art.

PHAEDRUS: Let me hear.

SOCRATES: Oratory is the art of enchanting the soul, and therefore he who would be an orator has to learn the differences of human souls—they are so many and of such a nature, and from them come the differences between man and man. Having proceeded thus far in his analysis, he will next divide speeches into their different classes:—'Such and such persons,' he will say, 'are affected by this or that kind of speech in this or that way,' and he will tell you why. The pupil must have a good theoretical notion of them first, and then he must have experience of them in actual life, and be able to follow them with all his senses about him, or he will never get beyond the precepts of his masters. But when he understands what persons are persuaded by what arguments, and sees the person about whom he was speaking in the abstract actually before him, and knows that it is he, and can say to himself, 'This is the man or this is the character who ought to have a certain argument applied to him in order to convince him of a certain opinion';—he who knows all this, and knows also when he should speak and when he should refrain, and when he should use pithy sayings, pathetic appeals, sensational effects, and all the other modes of speech which he has learned;—when, I say, he knows the times and seasons of all these things, then, and not till then, he is a perfect master of his art; but if he fail in any of these points, whether in speaking or teaching or writing them, and yet declares that he speaks by rules of art, he who says 'I don't believe you' has the better of him. Well, the teacher will say, is this, Phaedrus and Socrates, your account of the so-called art of rhetoric, or am I to look for another?

PHAEDRUS: He must take this, Socrates, for there is no possibility of another, and yet the creation of such an art is not easy.

6.4 Aristotle (384–322 BCE)

In *The Art of Rhetoric*, Aristotle develops a set of general principles for rhetoric—the skill of using language to persuade—as well as a defence of its ethical legitimacy. In this sense, Aristotle is responding directly to Plato's *Gorgias*, in which Plato critiqued rhetoric for lacking general principles and for being essentially deceitful. Aristotle begins by enumerating and explaining three basic ways in which arguments can persuade: *logos*, the logical consistency of the argument; *ethos*, the authority or perceived legitimacy of the person making the argument; and *pathos*, the emotional receptivity of the audience.

Aristotle then develops two arguments for why rhetoric should not be condemned as essentially deceitful. First, he argues that there are some people who cannot be led to understand the truth of certain subjects. For these people, rhetoric is necessary to sway their opinions on those subjects. While this may sound like a prejudiced dismissal of certain people as too stupid to understand, it speaks to the need—already present in ancient Greece—for experts. In our contemporary world, subjects such as quantum physics, neurochemistry, and global finance are beyond most of us. As such, we rely on experts to tell us what we should think about them, which for Aristotle will fall into the category of rhetoric.

Second, Aristotle argues that truth has a natural persuasive power over falsehood. That is to say, it is naturally easier for us to believe things that are true and harder to convince people of things that are false. Therefore, argues Aristotle, if rhetoric is used on both sides of an argument the truth will tend to win out. While it may be tempting to try to produce counterexamples, the least one can say is that this resembles very closely our modern adversarial judicial system: the fairness of our trials is based on a process of producing rhetorical arguments for both sides and calling on an impartial third party to judge between them.

from Rhetoric

Book I

PART 1

Rhetoric is the counterpart of Dialectic.[1] Both alike are concerned with such things as come, more or less, within the general ken of all men and belong to no definite science. Accordingly all men make use, more or less, of both; for to a certain extent all men attempt to discuss statements and to maintain them, to defend themselves and to attack others. Ordinary people do this either at random or through practice and from acquired habit. Both ways being possible,

1 The Greek word "dialectic" refers to "reasoning in a step-by-step manner with at least two people."

the subject can plainly be handled systematically, for it is possible to inquire the reason why some speakers succeed through practice and others spontaneously; and every one will at once agree that such an inquiry is the function of an art....

It is clear, then, that rhetorical study, in its strict sense, is concerned with the modes of persuasion. Persuasion is clearly a sort of demonstration,[2] since we are most fully persuaded when we consider a thing to have been demonstrated....

Rhetoric is useful (1) because things that are true and things that are just have a natural tendency to prevail over their opposites, so that if the decisions of judges are not what they ought to be, the defeat must be due to the speakers themselves, and they must be blamed accordingly. Moreover, (2) before some audiences not even the possession of the exactest knowledge will make it easy for what we say to produce conviction. For argument based on knowledge implies instruction, and there are people whom one cannot instruct. Here, then, we must use, as our modes of persuasion and argument, notions possessed by everybody, as we observed in the *Topics*[3] when dealing with the way to handle a popular audience. Further, (3) we must be able to employ persuasion, just as strict reasoning can be employed, on opposite sides of a question, not in order that we may in practice employ it in both ways (for we must not make people believe what is wrong), but in order that we may see clearly what the facts are, and that, if another man argues unfairly, we on our part may be able to confute him. No other of the arts draws opposite conclusions: dialectic and rhetoric alone do this. Both these arts draw opposite conclusions impartially. Nevertheless, the underlying facts do not lend themselves equally well to the contrary views. No; things that are true and things that are better are, by their nature, practically always easier to prove and easier to believe in. Again, (4) it is absurd to hold that a man ought to be ashamed of being unable to defend himself with his limbs, but not of being unable to defend himself with speech and reason, when the use of rational speech is more distinctive of a human being than the use of his limbs. And if it be objected that one who uses such power of speech unjustly might do great harm, that is a charge which may be made in common against all good things except virtue, and above all against the things that are most useful, as strength, health, wealth, generalship. A man can confer the greatest of benefits by a right use of these, and inflict the greatest of injuries by using them wrongly.

It is clear, then, that rhetoric is not bound up with a single definite class of subjects, but is as universal as dialectic; it is clear, also, that it is useful. It is clear, further, that its function is not simply to succeed in persuading, but rather to discover the means of coming as near such success as the circumstances of each particular case allow. In this it resembles all other arts. For example, it is not the function of medicine simply to make a man quite healthy, but to put him as far as may be on the road to health; it is possible to give excellent treatment even to those who can never enjoy sound health. Furthermore, it is plain that it is the function of one and the same art to discern the real and the apparent means of persuasion, just as it is the function of dialectic to discern the real and the apparent syllogism.[4] ...

PART 2

Rhetoric may be defined as the faculty of observing in any given case the available means of persuasion. This is not a function of any other art. Every other art can instruct or persuade about its own particular subject-matter; for instance, medicine about what is healthy and unhealthy, geometry about the properties of magnitudes, arithmetic about numbers, and the same is true of the other arts and sciences. But rhetoric we look upon as the power of observing the means of persuasion on almost any subject presented to us; and that is why we say that, in its technical character,

2 By "demonstration" Aristotle means proving a claim by means of an argument based on accepted premises.
3 The title of a work by Aristotle.
4 A deductive argument. Unlike a demonstration argument, which rests on accepted premises, a syllogism may or may not have accepted premises.

it is not concerned with any special or definite class of subjects.

Of the modes of persuasion some belong strictly to the art of rhetoric and some do not. By the latter I mean such things as are not supplied by the speaker but are there at the outset-witnesses, evidence given under torture, written contracts, and so on. By the former I mean such as we can ourselves construct by means of the principles of rhetoric. The one kind has merely to be used, the other has to be invented.

Of the modes of persuasion furnished by the spoken word there are three kinds. The first kind depends on the personal character of the speaker [i.e., *ethos*]; the second on putting the audience into a certain frame of mind [i.e., *pathos*]; the third on the proof, or apparent proof, provided by the words of the speech itself [i.e., *logos*].

Persuasion is achieved, [first,] by the speaker's personal character when the speech is so spoken as to make us think him credible. We believe good men more fully and more readily than others: this is true generally whatever the question is, and absolutely true where exact certainty is impossible and opinions are divided. This kind of persuasion, like the others, should be achieved by what the speaker says, not by what people think of his character before he begins to speak. It is not true, as some writers assume in their treatises on rhetoric, that the personal goodness revealed by the speaker contributes nothing to his power of persuasion; on the contrary, his character may almost be called the most effective means of persuasion he possesses.

Secondly, persuasion may come through the hearers, when the speech stirs their emotions. Our judgements when we are pleased and friendly are not the same as when we are pained and hostile. It is towards producing these effects, as we maintain, that present-day writers on rhetoric direct the whole of their efforts. This subject shall be treated in detail when we come to speak of the emotions.

Thirdly, persuasion is effected through the speech itself when we have proved a truth or an apparent truth by means of the persuasive arguments suitable to the case in question.

There are, then, these three means of effecting persuasion. The man who is to be in command of them must, it is clear, be able (1) to reason logically, (2) to understand human character and goodness in their various forms, and (3) to understand the emotions—that is, to name them and describe them, to know their causes and the way in which they are excited. It thus appears that rhetoric is an offshoot of dialectic and also of ethical studies. Ethical studies may fairly be called political; and for this reason rhetoric masquerades as political science, and the professors of it as political experts—sometimes from want of education, sometimes from ostentation, sometimes owing to other human failings. As a matter of fact, it is a branch of dialectic and similar to it, as we said at the outset. Neither rhetoric nor dialectic is the scientific study of any one separate subject: both are faculties for providing arguments. This is perhaps a sufficient account of their scope and of how they are related to each other....

A statement is persuasive and credible either because it is directly self-evident or because it appears to be proved from other statements that are so. In either case it is persuasive because there is somebody whom it persuades. But none of the arts theorize about individual cases. Medicine, for instance, does not theorize about what will help to cure Socrates or Callias, but only about what will help to cure any or all of a given class of patients: this alone is business: individual cases are so infinitely various that no systematic knowledge of them is possible. In the same way the theory of rhetoric is concerned not with what seems probable to a given individual like Socrates or Hippias, but with what seems probable to men of a given type; and this is true of dialectic also. Dialectic does not construct its syllogisms out of any haphazard materials, such as the fancies of crazy people, but out of materials that call for discussion; and rhetoric, too, draws upon the regular subjects of debate. The duty of rhetoric is to deal with such matters as we deliberate upon without arts or systems to guide us, in the hearing of persons who cannot take in at a glance a complicated argument, or follow a long chain of reasoning. The subjects of our deliberation are such as seem to present us with alternative possibilities: about things that could not have been, and cannot now or in the future be, other than they are, nobody who takes them to be of this nature wastes his time in deliberation....

PART 5

It may be said that every individual man and all men in common aim at a certain end which determines what they choose and what they avoid. This end, to sum it up briefly, is happiness and its constituents. Let us, then, by way of illustration only, ascertain what is in general the nature of happiness,[5] and what are the elements of its constituent parts. For all advice to do things or not to do them is concerned with happiness and with the things that make for or against it; whatever creates or increases happiness or some part of happiness, we ought to do; whatever destroys or hampers happiness, or gives rise to its opposite, we ought not to do.

We may define happiness as prosperity combined with virtue; or as independence of life; or as the secure enjoyment of the maximum of pleasure; or as a good condition of property and body, together with the power of guarding one's property and body and making use of them. That happiness is one or more of these things, pretty well everybody agrees.

From this definition of happiness it follows that its constituent parts are: good birth, plenty of friends, good friends, wealth, good children, plenty of children, a happy old age, also such bodily excellences as health, beauty, strength, large stature, athletic powers, together with fame, honour, good luck, and virtue. A man cannot fail to be completely independent if he possesses these internal and these external goods; for besides these there are no others to have. (Goods of the soul and of the body are internal. Good birth, friends, money, and honour are external.) Further, we think that he should possess resources and luck, in order to make his life really secure. As we have already ascertained what happiness in general is, so now let us try to ascertain what of these parts of it is....

PART 8

The most important and effective qualification for success in persuading audiences and speaking well on public affairs is to understand all the forms of government and to discriminate their respective customs, institutions, and interests. For all men are persuaded by considerations of their interest, and their interest lies in the maintenance of the established order. Further, it rests with the supreme authority to give authoritative decisions, and this varies with each form of government; there are as many different supreme authorities as there are different forms of government. The forms of government are four—democracy, oligarchy, aristocracy, monarchy. The supreme right to judge and decide always rests, therefore, with either a part or the whole of one or other of these governing powers.

A democracy is a form of government under which the citizens distribute the offices of state among themselves by lot, whereas under oligarchy there is a property qualification, under aristocracy one of education. By education I mean that education which is laid down by the law; for it is those who have been loyal to the national institutions that hold office under an aristocracy. These are bound to be looked upon as 'the best men', and it is from this fact that this form of government has derived its name ('the rule of the best'). Monarchy, as the word implies, is the constitution in which one man has authority over all. There are two forms of monarchy: kingship, which is limited by prescribed conditions, and 'tyranny', which is not limited by anything.

We must also notice the ends which the various forms of government pursue, since people choose in practice such actions as will lead to the realization of their ends. The end of democracy is freedom; of oligarchy, wealth; of aristocracy, the maintenance of education and national institutions; of tyranny, the

5 The Greek word here, *eudaimonia*, refers not merely to a mood, as the English word suggests. Rather, it encompasses all that is included in Book I, Part 5, and refers to a well-lived and fully satisfying life—within the bounds of what is humanly possible.

protection of the tyrant. It is clear, then, that we must distinguish those particular customs, institutions, and interests which tend to realize the ideal of each constitution, since men choose their means with reference to their ends. But rhetorical persuasion is effected not only by demonstrative but by ethical argument; it helps a speaker to convince us, if we believe that he has certain qualities himself, namely, goodness, or goodwill towards us, or both together. Similarly, we should know the moral qualities characteristic of each form of government, for the special moral character of each is bound to provide us with our most effective means of persuasion in dealing with it. We shall learn the qualities of governments in the same way as we learn the qualities of individuals, since they are revealed in their deliberate acts of choice; and these are determined by the end that inspires them....

6.5 Niccolò Machiavelli (1469–1527)

Niccolò Machiavelli was an Italian philosopher, politician, and diplomat. Although he wrote during the Renaissance, many of his ideas anticipate modern Enlightenment thought, especially insofar as he celebrates rationality and critical thinking. *The Prince* presents itself as a kind of self-help book for the powerful and those who aspire to political power. In it, Machiavelli draws lessons from a series of historical examples, producing a set of recommendations about how to be (or become) an effective "Prince." The portrait he draws is of a ruthless leader who gains and secures political power by whatever means are useful.

One key feature of *The Prince* is that, in adopting the acquisition and maintenance of political power as its only aim, it dispenses explicitly with moral considerations. Machiavelli is constantly at pains to remind his reader that, if gaining and retaining power are one's only ends, then immorality should not discourage a prince from using the most effective means to achieve them. This policy goes beyond the notion that "the ends justify the means"—that if one's goals are good, accomplishing them immorally is excusable. Indeed, Machiavelli's message is arguably even more shocking: in essence, he encourages his reader to dispense with moral constraints altogether.

Another key feature of *The Prince* is that a great many of the tactics and strategies it recommends are based on deception. Wielding power over other human beings, Machiavelli argues, inevitably necessitates concealing various truths from them, especially one's own immorality. From Machiavelli's point of view, a Prince still needs to keep one eye on moral standards for his own political self-interest: he must trick others into believing that he has complied with them. It is for this reason that Machiavelli's name has become associated with underhanded and devious forms of manipulation, giving us the adjective "Machiavellian." It is also for this reason that *The Prince* was widely condemned, to the point of being banned by the Catholic Church.

from The Prince

Dedication: To the Magnificent Lorenzo Di Piero De' Medici:

Those who strive to obtain the good graces of a prince are accustomed to come before him with such things as they hold most precious, or in which they see him take most delight; whence one often sees horses, arms, cloth of gold, precious stones, and similar ornaments presented to princes, worthy of their greatness. Desiring therefore to present myself to your Magnificence with some testimony of my devotion towards you, I have not found among my possessions anything which I hold more dear than, or value so much as, the knowledge of the actions of great men, acquired by long experience in contemporary affairs, and a continual study of antiquity; which, having reflected upon it with great and prolonged diligence, I now send, digested into a little volume, to your Magnificence.

And although I may consider this work unworthy of your countenance, nevertheless I trust much to your benignity that it may be acceptable, seeing that it is not possible for me to make a better gift than to offer you the opportunity of understanding in the shortest time all that I have learnt in so many years, and with so many troubles and dangers; which work I have not embellished with swelling or magnificent words, nor stuffed with rounded periods, nor with any extrinsic allurements or adornments whatever, with which so many are accustomed to embellish their works; for I have wished either that no honour should be given it, or else that the truth of the matter and the weightiness of the theme shall make it acceptable.

Nor do I hold with those who regard it as a presumption if a man of low and humble condition dare to discuss and settle the concerns of princes; because, just as those who draw landscapes place themselves below in the plain to contemplate the nature of the mountains and of lofty places, and in order to contemplate the plains place themselves upon high mountains, even so to understand the nature of the people it needs to be a prince, and to understand that of princes it needs to be of the people.

Take then, your Magnificence, this little gift in the spirit in which I send it; wherein, if it be diligently read and considered by you, you will learn my extreme desire that you should attain that greatness which fortune and your other attributes promise. And if your Magnificence from the summit of your greatness will sometimes turn your eyes to these lower regions, you will see how unmeritedly I suffer a great and continued malignity of fortune.

Chapter VII. Concerning New Principalities Which Are Acquired Either by the Arms of Others or by Good Fortune

Those who solely by good fortune become princes from being private citizens have little trouble in rising, but much in keeping atop; they have not any difficulties on the way up, because they fly, but they have many when they reach the summit. Such are those to whom some state is given either for money or by the favour of him who bestows it....

States that rise unexpectedly, then, like all other things in nature which are born and grow rapidly, cannot leave their foundations and correspondencies fixed in such a way that the first storm will not overthrow them; unless, as is said, those who unexpectedly become princes are men of so much ability that they know they have to be prepared at once to hold that which fortune has thrown into their laps, and that those foundations, which others have laid BEFORE they became princes, they must lay AFTERWARDS....

Concerning these two methods of rising to be a prince by ability or fortune, I wish to adduce two examples within our own recollection, and these are Francesco Sforza and Cesare Borgia. Francesco, by proper means and with great ability, from being a private person rose to be Duke of Milan, and that which he had acquired with a thousand anxieties he kept with little trouble. On the other hand, Cesare Borgia, called by the people Duke Valentino, acquired his state during the ascendancy of his father, and on its decline he lost it, notwithstanding that he had taken every measure and done all that ought to be done by a wise and able man to fix firmly his roots in the states which the arms and fortunes of others had bestowed on him....

Alexander the Sixth, in wishing to aggrandize the duke, his son, had many immediate and prospective difficulties.... The duke, therefore, having acquired the Romagna and beaten the Colonnesi, while wishing to hold that and to advance further, was hindered by two things: the one, his forces did not appear loyal to him, the other, the goodwill of France: that is to say, he feared that the forces of the Orsini, which he was using, would not stand to him, that not only might they hinder him from winning more, but might themselves seize what he had won, and that the king might also do the same. Of the Orsini he had a warning when, after taking Faenza and attacking Bologna, he saw them go very unwillingly to that attack. And as to the king, he learned his mind when he himself, after taking the Duchy of Urbino, attacked Tuscany, and the king made him desist from that undertaking; hence the duke decided to depend no more upon the arms and the luck of others.

For the first thing he weakened the Orsini and Colonnesi parties in Rome, by gaining to himself all their adherents who were gentlemen, making them his gentlemen, giving them good pay, and, according to their rank, honouring them with office and command in such a way that in a few months all attachment to the factions was destroyed and turned entirely to the duke.... Having exterminated the leaders, and turned their partisans into his friends, the duke laid sufficiently good foundations to his power, having all the Romagna and the Duchy of Urbino; and the people now beginning to appreciate their prosperity, he gained them all over to himself. And as this point is worthy of notice, and to be imitated by others, I am not willing to leave it out....

When the duke occupied the Romagna he found it under the rule of weak masters, who rather plundered their subjects than ruled them, and gave them more cause for disunion than for union, so that the country was full of robbery, quarrels, and every kind of violence; and so, wishing to bring back peace and obedience to authority, he considered it necessary to give it a good governor. Thereupon he promoted Messer Ramiro d'Orco, a swift and cruel man, to whom he gave the fullest power. This man in a short time restored peace and unity with the greatest success. Afterwards the duke considered that it was not advisable to confer such excessive authority, for he had no doubt but that he would become odious, so he set up a court of judgment in the country, under a most excellent president, wherein all cities had their advocates. And because he knew that the past severity had caused some hatred against himself, so, to clear himself in the minds of the people, and gain them entirely to himself, he desired to show that, if any cruelty had been practised, it had not originated with him, but in the natural sternness of the minister. Under this pretence he took Ramiro, and one morning caused him to be executed and left on the piazza at Cesena with the block and a bloody knife at his side. The barbarity of this spectacle caused the people to be at once satisfied and dismayed....

The duke, finding himself now sufficiently powerful and partly secured from immediate dangers by having armed himself in his own way, and having in a great measure crushed those forces in his vicinity that could injure him if he wished to proceed with his conquest, had next to consider France....

But as to the future he had to fear, in the first place, that a new successor to the Church might not be friendly to him and might seek to take from him that which Alexander had given him, so he decided to act in four ways. Firstly, by exterminating the families of those lords whom he had despoiled.... Secondly, by winning to himself all the gentlemen of Rome.... Thirdly, by converting the college more to himself. Fourthly, by acquiring so much power before the Pope should die that he could by his own measures resist the first shock. Of these four things, at the death of Alexander, he had accomplished three. For he had killed as many of the dispossessed lords as he could lay hands on, and few had escaped; he had won over the Roman gentlemen, and he had the most numerous party in the college....

But Alexander died five years after he had first drawn the sword. He left the duke with the state of Romagna alone consolidated, with the rest in the air, between two most powerful hostile armies, and sick unto death. Yet there were in the duke such boldness and ability, and he knew so well how men are to be won or lost, and so firm were the foundations which in so short a time he had laid, that if he had not had those armies on his back, or if he had been in good health, he would have overcome all difficulties....

When all the actions of the duke are recalled, I do not know how to blame him, but rather it appears to be, as I have said, that I ought to offer him for imitation to all those who, by the fortune or the arms of others, are raised to government. Because he, having a lofty spirit and far-reaching aims, could not have regulated his conduct otherwise, and only the shortness of the life of Alexander and his own sickness frustrated his designs. Therefore, he who considers it necessary to secure himself in his new principality, to win friends, to overcome either by force or fraud, to make himself beloved and feared by the people, to be followed and revered by the soldiers, to exterminate those who have power or reason to hurt him, to change the old order of things for new, to be severe and gracious, magnanimous and liberal, to destroy a disloyal soldiery and to create new, to maintain friendship with kings and princes in such a way that they must help him with zeal and offend with caution, cannot find a more lively example than the actions of this man....

Chapter VIII. Concerning Those Who Have Obtained a Principality by Wickedness

Although a prince may rise from a private station in two ways, neither of which can be entirely attributed to fortune or genius, yet it is manifest to me that I must not be silent on them, although one could be more copiously treated when I discuss republics. These methods are when, either by some wicked or nefarious ways, one ascends to the principality, or when by the favour of his fellow-citizens a private person becomes the prince of his country. And speaking of the first method, it will be illustrated by two examples—one ancient, the other modern—and without entering further into the subject, I consider these two examples will suffice those who may be compelled to follow them.

Agathocles, the Sicilian, became King of Syracuse not only from a private but from a low and abject position. This man, the son of a potter, through all the changes in his fortunes always led an infamous life. Nevertheless, he accompanied his infamies with so much ability of mind and body that, having devoted himself to the military profession, he rose through its ranks to be Praetor of Syracuse. Being established in that position, and having deliberately resolved to make himself prince and to seize by violence, without obligation to others, that which had been conceded to him by assent, he came to an understanding for this purpose with Amilcar, the Carthaginian, who, with his army, was fighting in Sicily. One morning he assembled the people and the senate of Syracuse, as if he had to discuss with them things relating to the Republic, and at a given signal the soldiers killed all the senators and the richest of the people; these dead, he seized and held the princedom of that city without any civil commotion. And although he was twice routed by the Carthaginians, and ultimately besieged, yet not only was he able to defend his city, but leaving part of his men for its defence, with the others he attacked Africa, and in a short time raised the siege of Syracuse. The Carthaginians, reduced to extreme necessity, were compelled to come to terms with Agathocles, and, leaving Sicily to him, had to be content with the possession of Africa....

Therefore, he who considers the actions and the genius of this man will see nothing, or little, which can be attributed to fortune, inasmuch as he attained pre-eminence, as is shown above, not by the favour of any one, but step by step in the military profession, which steps were gained with a thousand troubles and perils, and were afterwards boldly held by him with many hazardous dangers. Yet it cannot be called talent to slay fellow-citizens, to deceive friends, to be without faith, without mercy, without religion; such methods may gain empire, but not glory. Still, if the courage of Agathocles in entering into and extricating himself from dangers be considered, together with his greatness of mind in enduring and overcoming hardships, it cannot be seen why he should be esteemed less than the most notable captain. Nevertheless, his barbarous cruelty and inhumanity with infinite wickedness do not permit him to be celebrated among the most excellent men. What he achieved cannot be attributed either to fortune or genius....

Oliverotto gave a solemn banquet to which he invited Giovanni Fogliani and the chiefs of Fermo. When the viands and all the other entertainments that are usual in such banquets were finished, Oliverotto artfully began certain grave discourses, speaking of the greatness of Pope Alexander and his son Cesare, and of their enterprises, to which discourse Giovanni and others answered; but he rose at once, saying that such matters ought to be discussed in a more private place, and he betook himself to a chamber, whither Giovanni and the rest of the citizens went in after him. No sooner were they seated than soldiers issued from secret places and slaughtered Giovanni and the rest. After these murders Oliverotto, mounted on horseback, rode up and down the town and besieged the chief magistrate in the palace, so that in fear the people were forced to obey him, and to form a government, of which he made himself the prince. He killed all the malcontents who were able to injure him, and strengthened himself with new civil and military ordinances, in such a way that, in the year during which he held the principality, not only was he secure in the city of Fermo, but he had become formidable to all his neighbours. And his destruction would have been as difficult as that of Agathocles if he had not allowed himself to be overreached by Cesare Borgia, who took him with the Orsini and Vitelli at Sinigalia, as was stated above. Thus one year after he had committed this parricide, he was strangled, together with Vitellozzo, whom he had made his leader in valour and wickedness.

Some may wonder how it can happen that Agathocles, and his like, after infinite treacheries and cruelties, should live for long secure in his country, and defend himself from external enemies, and never be conspired against by his own citizens; seeing that many others, by means of cruelty, have never been able even in peaceful times to hold the state, still less in the doubtful times of war. I believe that this follows from severities being badly or properly used. Those may be called properly used, if of evil it is possible to speak well, that are applied at one blow and are necessary to one's security, and that are not persisted in afterwards unless they can be turned to the advantage of the subjects. The badly employed are those which, notwithstanding they may be few in the commencement, multiply with time rather than decrease. Those who practise the first system are able, by aid of God or man, to mitigate in some degree their rule, as Agathocles did. It is impossible for those who follow the other to maintain themselves....

Hence it is to be remarked that, in seizing a state, the usurper ought to examine closely into all those injuries which it is necessary for him to inflict, and to do them all at one stroke so as not to have to repeat them daily; and thus by not unsettling men he will be able to reassure them, and win them to himself by benefits. He who does otherwise, either from timidity or evil advice, is always compelled to keep the knife in his hand; neither can he rely on his subjects, nor can they attach themselves to him, owing to their continued and repeated wrongs. For injuries ought to be done all at one time, so that, being tasted less, they offend less; benefits ought to be given little by little, so that the flavour of them may last longer.

And above all things, a prince ought to live amongst his people in such a way that no unexpected circumstances, whether of good or evil, shall make him change; because if the necessity for this comes in troubled times, you are too late for harsh measures; and mild ones will not help you, for they will be considered as forced from you, and no one will be under any obligation to you for them.

Chapter XII. How Many Kinds of Soldiery There Are, and Concerning Mercenaries

…

We have seen above how necessary it is for a prince to have his foundations well laid, otherwise it follows of necessity he will go to ruin. The chief foundations of all states, new as well as old or composite, are good laws and good arms; and as there cannot be good laws where the state is not well armed, it follows that where they are well armed they have good laws. I shall leave the laws out of the discussion and shall speak of the arms.

I say, therefore, that the arms with which a prince defends his state are either his own, or they are mercenaries, auxiliaries, or mixed. Mercenaries and auxiliaries are useless and dangerous; and if one holds his state based on these arms, he will stand neither firm nor safe; for they are disunited, ambitious, and without discipline, unfaithful, valiant before friends, cowardly before enemies; they have neither the fear of God nor fidelity to men, and destruction is deferred only so long as the attack is; for in peace one is robbed by them, and in war by the enemy. The fact is, they have no other attraction or reason for keeping the field than a trifle of stipend, which is not sufficient to make them willing to die for you. They are ready enough to be your soldiers whilst you do not make war, but if war comes they take themselves off or run from the foe; which I should have little trouble to prove, for the ruin of Italy has been caused by nothing else than by resting all her hopes for many years on mercenaries, and although they formerly made some display and appeared valiant amongst themselves, yet when the foreigners came they showed what they were. Thus it was that Charles, King of France, was allowed to seize Italy with chalk in hand; and he who told us that our sins were the cause of it told the truth, but they were not the sins he imagined, but those which I have related. And as they were the sins of princes, it is the princes who have also suffered the penalty....

I wish to demonstrate further the infelicity of these arms. The mercenary captains are either capable men or they are not; if they are, you cannot trust them, because they always aspire to their own greatness, either by oppressing you, who are their master, or others contrary to your intentions; but if the captain is not skilful, you are ruined in the usual way.

And if it be urged that whoever is armed will act in the same way, whether mercenary or not, I reply that when arms have to be resorted to, either by a prince or a republic, then the prince ought to go in person and perform the duty of a captain; the republic has to send its citizens, and when one is sent who does not turn out satisfactorily, it ought to recall him, and when one is worthy, to hold him by the laws so that he does not leave the command. And experience has shown princes and republics, single-handed, making the greatest progress, and mercenaries doing nothing except damage; and it is more difficult to bring a republic, armed with its own arms, under the sway of one of its citizens than it is to bring one armed with foreign arms. Rome and Sparta stood for many ages armed and free. The Switzers are completely armed and quite free....

Chapter XIII. Concerning Auxiliaries, Mixed Soldiery, and One's Own

Auxiliaries, which are the other useless arm, are employed when a prince is called in with his forces to aid and defend, as was done by Pope Julius in the most recent times; for he, having, in the enterprise against Ferrara, had poor proof of his mercenaries, turned to auxiliaries, and stipulated with Ferdinand, King of Spain, for his assistance with men and arms. These arms may be useful and good in themselves, but for him who calls them in they are always disadvantageous; for losing, one is undone, and winning, one is their captive....

Therefore, let him who has no desire to conquer make use of these arms, for they are much more hazardous than mercenaries, because with them the ruin is ready made; they are all united, all yield obedience to others; but with mercenaries, when they have conquered, more time and better opportunities are needed to injure you; they are not all of one community, they are found and paid by you, and a third party, which you have made their head, is not able all at once to assume enough authority to injure you. In conclusion, in mercenaries dastardy is most dangerous; in auxiliaries, valour. The wise prince, therefore, has always avoided these arms and turned to his own; and has been willing rather to lose with them than to conquer with the others, not deeming that a real victory which is gained with the arms of others.

I shall never hesitate to cite Cesare Borgia and his actions. This duke entered the Romagna with auxiliaries, taking there only French soldiers, and with them he captured Imola and Forli; but afterwards, such forces not appearing to him reliable, he turned to mercenaries, discerning less danger in them, and enlisted the Orsini and Vitelli; whom presently, on handling and finding them doubtful, unfaithful, and dangerous, he destroyed and turned to his own men. And the difference between one and the other of these forces can easily be seen when one considers the difference there was in the reputation of the duke, when he had the French, when he had the Orsini and Vitelli, and when he relied on his own soldiers, on whose fidelity he could always count and found it ever increasing; he was never esteemed more highly than when every one saw that he was complete master of his own forces....

Chapter XIV. That Which Concerns a Prince on the Subject of the Art of War

A prince ought to have no other aim or thought, nor select anything else for his study, than war and its rules and discipline; for this is the sole art that belongs to him who rules, and it is of such force that it not only upholds those who are born princes, but it often enables men to rise from a private station to that rank. And, on the contrary, it is seen that when princes have thought more of ease than of arms they have lost their states. And the first cause of your losing it is to neglect this art; and what enables you to acquire a state is to be master of the art. Francesco Sforza, through being martial, from a private person became Duke of Milan; and the sons, through avoiding the hardships and troubles of arms, from dukes became private persons. For among other evils which being unarmed brings you, it causes you to be despised, and this is one of those ignominies against which a prince ought to guard himself, as is shown later on. Because there is nothing proportionate between the armed and the unarmed; and it is not reasonable that he who is armed should yield obedience willingly to him who is unarmed, or that the unarmed man should be secure among armed servants. Because, there being in the one disdain and in the other suspicion, it is not possible for them to work well together. And therefore a prince who does not understand the art of war, over and above the other misfortunes already mentioned, cannot be respected by his soldiers, nor can he rely on them. He ought never, therefore, to have out of his thoughts this subject of war, and in peace he should addict himself more to its exercise than in war; this he can do in two ways, the one by action, the other by study.

As regards action, he ought above all things to keep his men well organized and drilled, to follow incessantly the chase, by which he accustoms his body to hardships, and learns something of the nature of localities, and gets to find out how the mountains rise, how the valleys open out, how the plains lie, and to understand the nature of rivers and marshes, and in all this to take the greatest care. Which knowledge is useful in two ways. Firstly, he learns to know his country, and is better able to undertake its defence; afterwards, by means of the knowledge and observation of that locality, he understands with ease any other which it may be necessary for him to study hereafter; because the hills, valleys, and plains, and rivers and marshes that are, for instance, in Tuscany, have a certain resemblance to those of other countries, so that with a knowledge of the aspect of one country one can easily arrive at a knowledge of others. And the prince that lacks this skill lacks the essential which it is desirable that a captain should possess, for it teaches him to surprise his enemy, to select quarters, to lead armies, to array the battle, to besiege towns to advantage....

Chapter XV. Concerning Things for Which Men, and Especially Princes, Are Praised or Blamed

It remains now to see what ought to be the rules of conduct for a prince towards subject and friends. And as I know that many have written on this point, I expect I shall be considered presumptuous in mentioning it again, especially as in discussing it I shall depart from the methods of other people. But, it being my intention to write a thing which shall be useful to him who apprehends it, it appears to me more appropriate to follow up the real truth of the matter than the imagination of it; for many have pictured republics and principalities which in fact have never been known or seen, because how one lives is so far distant from how one ought to live, that he who neglects what is done for what ought to be done, sooner effects his ruin than his preservation; for a man who wishes to act entirely up to his professions of virtue soon meets with what destroys him among so much that is evil.

Hence it is necessary for a prince wishing to hold his own to know how to do wrong, and to make use of it or not according to necessity. Therefore, putting on one side imaginary things concerning a prince, and discussing those which are real, I say that all men when they are spoken of, and chiefly princes for being more highly placed, are remarkable for some of those qualities which bring them either blame or praise; and thus it is that one is reputed liberal, another miserly, using a Tuscan term (because an avaricious person in our language is still he who desires to possess by robbery, whilst we call one miserly who deprives himself too much of the use of his own); one is reputed generous, one rapacious; one cruel, one compassionate; one faithless, another faithful; one effeminate and cowardly, another bold and brave; one affable, another haughty; one lascivious, another chaste; one sincere, another cunning; one hard, another easy; one grave, another frivolous; one religious, another unbelieving, and the like. And I know that every one will confess that it would be most praiseworthy in a prince to exhibit all the above qualities that are considered good; but because they can neither be entirely possessed nor observed, for human conditions do not permit it, it is necessary for him to be sufficiently prudent that he may know how to avoid the reproach of those vices which would lose him his state; and also to keep himself, if it be possible, from those which would not lose him it; but this not being possible, he may with less hesitation abandon himself to them. And again, he need not make himself uneasy at incurring a reproach for those vices without which the state can only be saved with difficulty, for if everything is considered carefully, it will be found that something which looks like virtue, if followed, would be his ruin; whilst something else, which looks like vice, yet followed brings him security and prosperity.

Chapter XVI. Concerning Liberality and Meanness

Commencing then with the first of the above-named characteristics, I say that it would be well to be reputed liberal. Nevertheless, liberality exercised in a way that does not bring you the reputation for it, injures you; for if one exercises it honestly and as it should be exercised, it may not become known, and you will not avoid the reproach of its opposite. Therefore, any one wishing to maintain among men the name of liberal is obliged to avoid no attribute of magnificence; so that a prince thus inclined will consume in such acts all his property, and will be compelled in the end, if he wish to maintain the name of liberal, to unduly weigh down his people, and tax them, and do everything he can to get money. This will soon make him odious to his subjects, and becoming poor he will be little valued by any one; thus, with his liberality, having offended many and rewarded few, he is affected by the very first trouble and imperilled by whatever may be the first danger; recognizing this himself, and wishing to draw back from it, he runs at once into the reproach of being miserly.

Therefore, a prince, not being able to exercise this virtue of liberality in such a way that it is recognized, except to his cost, if he is wise he ought not to fear the reputation of being mean, for in time he will come to be more considered than if liberal, seeing that with his economy his revenues are enough, that he can defend himself against all attacks, and is able to engage in enterprises without burdening his people; thus it comes to pass that he exercises liberality towards all from whom he does not take, who are numberless, and meanness towards those to whom he does not give, who are few.

We have not seen great things done in our time except by those who have been considered mean; the rest have failed. Pope Julius the Second was assisted in reaching the papacy by a reputation for liberality, yet he did not strive afterwards to keep it up, when he made war on the King of France; and he made many wars without imposing any extraordinary tax on his subjects, for he supplied his additional expenses out of his long thriftiness. The present King of Spain would not have undertaken or conquered in so many enterprises if he had been reputed liberal. A prince, therefore, provided that he has not to rob his subjects, that he can defend himself, that he does not become poor and abject, that he is not forced to become rapacious, ought to hold of little account a reputation for being mean, for it is one of those vices which will enable him to govern.

And if any one should say: Caesar obtained empire by liberality, and many others have reached the highest positions by having been liberal, and by being considered so, I answer: Either you are a prince in fact, or in a way to become one. In the first case this liberality is dangerous, in the second it is very necessary to be considered liberal; and Caesar was one of those who wished to become pre-eminent in Rome; but if he had survived after becoming so, and had not moderated his expenses, he would have destroyed his government. And if any one should reply: Many have been princes, and have done great things with armies, who have been considered very liberal, I reply: Either a prince spends that which is his own or his subjects' or else that of others. In the first case he ought to be sparing, in the second he ought not to neglect any opportunity for liberality. And to the prince who goes forth with his army, supporting it by pillage, sack, and extortion, handling that which belongs to others, this liberality is necessary, otherwise he would not be followed by soldiers. And of that which is neither yours nor your subjects' you can be a ready giver, as were Cyrus, Caesar, and Alexander; because it does not take away your reputation if you squander that of others, but adds to it; it is only squandering your own that injures you.

And there is nothing wastes so rapidly as liberality, for even whilst you exercise it you lose the power to do so, and so become either poor or despised, or else, in avoiding poverty, rapacious and hated. And a prince should guard himself, above all things, against being despised and hated; and liberality leads you to both. Therefore it is wiser to have a reputation for meanness which brings reproach without hatred, than to be compelled through seeking a reputation for liberality to incur a name for rapacity which begets reproach with hatred.

Chapter XVII. Concerning Cruelty and Clemency, and Whether It Is Better to Be Loved Than Feared

Coming now to the other qualities mentioned above, I say that every prince ought to desire to be considered clement and not cruel. Nevertheless he ought to take care not to misuse this clemency. Cesare Borgia was considered cruel; notwithstanding, his cruelty reconciled the Romagna, unified it, and restored it to peace and loyalty. And if this be rightly considered, he will be seen to have been much more merciful than the Florentine people, who, to avoid a reputation for cruelty, permitted Pistoia to be destroyed. Therefore a prince, so long as he keeps his subjects united and loyal, ought not to mind the reproach of cruelty; because with a few examples he will be more merciful than those who, through too much mercy, allow disorders to arise, from which follow murders or robberies; for these are wont to injure the whole people, whilst those executions which originate with a prince offend the individual only....

And of all princes, it is impossible for the new prince to avoid the imputation of cruelty, owing to new states being full of dangers....

Upon this a question arises: whether it be better to be loved than feared or feared than loved? It may be answered that one should wish to be both, but, because it is difficult to unite them in one person, it is much safer to be feared than loved, when, of the two, either must be dispensed with. Because this is to be asserted in general of men, that they are ungrateful, fickle, false, cowardly, covetous, and as long as you succeed they are yours entirely; they will offer you their blood, property, life, and children, as is said above, when the need is far distant; but when it approaches they turn against you. And that prince who, relying entirely on their promises, has neglected other precautions, is ruined; because friendships that are obtained by payments, and not by greatness or nobility of mind, may indeed be earned, but they are not secured, and in time of need cannot be relied upon; and men have less scruple in offending one who is beloved than one who is feared, for love is preserved by the link of obligation which, owing to the baseness of men, is broken at every opportunity for their advantage; but fear preserves you by a dread of punishment which never fails.

Nevertheless a prince ought to inspire fear in such a way that, if he does not win love, he avoids hatred; because he can endure very well being feared whilst he is not hated, which will always be as long as he abstains from the property of his citizens and subjects and from their women. But when it is necessary for him to proceed against the life of someone, he must do it on proper justification and for manifest cause, but above all things he must keep his hands off the property of others, because men more quickly forget the death of their father than the loss of their patrimony. Besides, pretexts for taking away the property are never wanting; for he who has once begun to live by robbery will always find pretexts for seizing what belongs to others; but reasons for taking life, on the contrary, are more difficult to find and sooner lapse. But when a prince is with his army, and has under control a multitude of soldiers, then it is quite necessary for him to disregard the reputation of cruelty, for without it he would never hold his army united or disposed to its duties.

Among the wonderful deeds of Hannibal this one is enumerated: that having led an enormous army, composed of many various races of men, to fight in foreign lands, no dissensions arose either among them or against the prince, whether in his bad or in his good fortune. This arose from nothing else than his inhuman cruelty, which, with his boundless valour, made him revered and terrible in the sight of his soldiers, but without that cruelty, his other virtues were not sufficient to produce this effect. And short-sighted writers admire his deeds from one point of view and from another condemn the principal cause of them. That it is true his other virtues would not have been sufficient for him may be proved by the case of Scipio, that most excellent man, not only of his own times but within the memory of man, against whom, nevertheless, his army rebelled in Spain; this arose from nothing but his too great forbearance, which gave his soldiers more license than is consistent with military discipline. For this he was upbraided in the Senate by Fabius Maximus, and called the corrupter of the Roman soldiery. The Locrians were laid waste by a legate of Scipio, yet they were not avenged by him, nor was the insolence of the legate punished, owing entirely to his easy nature. Insomuch that someone in the Senate, wishing to excuse him, said there were many men who knew much better how not to err than to correct the errors of others. This disposition, if he had been continued in the command, would have destroyed in time the fame and glory of Scipio; but, he being under the control of the Senate, this injurious characteristic not only concealed itself, but contributed to his glory.

Returning to the question of being feared or loved, I come to the conclusion that, men loving according to their own will and fearing according to that of the prince, a wise prince should establish himself on that which is in his own control and not in that of others; he must endeavour only to avoid hatred, as is noted.

Chapter XVIII. Concerning the Way in Which Princes Should Keep Faith

...

Every one admits how praiseworthy it is in a prince to keep faith, and to live with integrity and not with craft. Nevertheless our experience has been that those princes who have done great things have held good faith of little account, and have known how to circumvent the intellect of men by craft, and in the end have overcome those who have relied on their word. You must know there are two ways of contesting, the one by the law, the other by force; the first method is proper to men, the second to beasts; but because the first is frequently not sufficient, it is necessary to have recourse to the second. Therefore it is necessary for a prince to understand how to avail himself of the beast and the man. This has been figuratively taught to princes by ancient writers, who describe how Achilles and many other princes of old were given to the Centaur Chiron to nurse, who brought them up in his discipline; which means solely that, as they had for a teacher one who was half beast and half man, so it is necessary for a prince to know how to make use of both natures, and that one without the other is not durable. A prince, therefore, being compelled knowingly to adopt the beast, ought to choose the fox and the lion; because the lion cannot defend himself against snares and the fox cannot defend himself against wolves. Therefore, it is necessary to be a fox to discover the snares and a lion to terrify the wolves. Those who rely simply on the lion do not understand what they are about. Therefore a wise lord cannot, nor ought he to, keep faith when such observance may be turned against him, and when the reasons that caused him to pledge it exist no longer. If men were entirely good this precept would not hold, but because they are bad, and will not keep faith with you, you too are not bound to observe it with them. Nor will there ever be wanting to a prince legitimate reasons to excuse this non-observance. Of this endless modern examples could be given, showing how many treaties and engagements have been made void and of no effect through the faithlessness of princes; and he who has known best how to employ the fox has succeeded best....

But it is necessary to know well how to disguise this characteristic, and to be a great pretender and dissembler; and men are so simple, and so subject to present necessities, that he who seeks to deceive will always find someone who will allow himself to be deceived. One recent example I cannot pass over in silence. Alexander the Sixth did nothing else but deceive men, nor ever thought of doing otherwise, and he always found victims; for there never was a man who had greater power in asserting, or who with greater oaths would affirm a thing, yet would observe it less; nevertheless his deceits always succeeded according to his wishes, because he well understood this side of mankind....

Therefore it is unnecessary for a prince to have all the good qualities I have enumerated, but it is very necessary to appear to have them. And I shall dare to say this also, that to have them and always to observe them is injurious, and that to appear to have them is useful; to appear merciful, faithful, humane, religious, upright, and to be so, but with a mind so framed that should you require not to be so, you may be able and know how to change to the opposite.

And you have to understand this, that a prince, especially a new one, cannot observe all those things for which men are esteemed, being often forced, in order to maintain the state, to act contrary to fidelity, friendship, humanity, and religion. Therefore it is necessary for him to have a mind ready to turn itself accordingly as the winds and variations of fortune force it, yet, as I have said above, not to diverge from the good if he can avoid doing so, but, if compelled, then to know how to set about it....

For this reason a prince ought to take care that he never lets anything slip from his lips that is not replete with the above-named five qualities, that he may appear to him who sees and hears him altogether merciful, faithful, humane, upright, and religious. There is nothing more necessary to appear to have than this last quality, inasmuch as men judge generally more by the eye than by the hand, because it belongs to everybody to see you, to few to come in touch with you. Every one sees what you appear to be, few really know what you are, and those few dare not oppose themselves to the opinion of the many, who have the majesty of the state to defend them; and in the actions of all men, and especially of princes, which it is not prudent to challenge, one judges by the result.

For that reason, let a prince have the credit of conquering and holding his state, the means will always be considered honest, and he will be praised by everybody; because the vulgar are always taken by what a thing seems to be and by what comes of it; and in the world there are only the vulgar, for the few find a place there only when the many have no ground to rest on.

One prince of the present time, whom it is not well to name, never preaches anything else but peace and good faith, and to both he is most hostile, and either, if he had kept it, would have deprived him of reputation and kingdom many a time....

6.6 John Stuart Mill (1806–1873)

John Stuart Mill was a British philosopher and member of Parliament. In political theory, Mill was a foundational figure in modern Liberalism, and he advocated many ideas we continue to associate with that movement today, including the abolition of slavery, women's suffrage, and freedom of speech. He favoured democracy over other forms of government and objected to paternalism in theory and domestic politics. But at the same time he worked for the East India Company overseeing the British colonial occupation of India, and openly subscribed to the notion that Europeans were superior to Asians and thereby had the right (perhaps even a duty) to imperial rule. In this respect, his work embodies some of the same Enlightenment tensions as Kant's.

On Liberty is a key modern text about the relationship between modern democracy and political power in which Mill draws on and updates Enlightenment concepts for Victorian times. In it, he defines liberty as the ability of citizens to protect themselves from being abused by their own leaders. For Mill, people are "free" only insofar as those who have power over them are held in check. The central dynamic is a struggle between the individual liberty of a citizen and the official authority of those in public office. In *On Liberty*, Mill explores this distinctive polarity of modern democracy, a political system in which the citizens, in principle, have power over themselves. While it would be tempting to assert that there is no need for special protections for liberty in such a system, Mill argues that there is: in a democracy the majority holds the reins of power, and it is every bit as likely to be abusive towards individuals and minorities as any individual despot. Democracies therefore very much need measures to protect liberty.

In morality, Mill is a utilitarian. Utilitarianism has three core tenets: (1) the moral rightness or wrongness of an action or policy derives from its consequences; (2) the chief consequence to aim at is minimizing unhappiness and maximizing happiness; and (3) the happiness of any single person counts equally to that of other people. This theory is sometimes summed up as aiming to secure the greatest happiness for the greatest number of people. Since freedom contributes to happiness, Mill's political commitment to freedom is based on his utilitarian moral commitment to happiness. And since the mere threat of harm from other citizens and officials can undermine individual happiness, he makes protection against harm central to *On Liberty*. To this end, he accepts a single liberty-limiting principle: As long as you aren't hurting anybody else, you should be free to do whatever you want. While this political principle and the moral tenets of Mill's position are common and popular in contemporary Liberal democracies, they were radical when he first introduced them.

from On Liberty

Chapter I. Introductory

The subject of this Essay is ... Civil, or Social Liberty: the nature and limits of the power which can be legitimately exercised by society over the individual. A question seldom stated, and hardly ever discussed, in general terms, but which profoundly influences the practical controversies of the age by its latent presence, and is likely soon to make itself recognised as the vital question of the future. It is so far from being new, that in a certain sense, it has divided mankind, almost from the remotest ages; but in the stage of progress into which the more civilised portions of the species have now entered, it presents itself under new conditions, and requires a different and more fundamental treatment.

The struggle between Liberty and Authority is the most conspicuous feature in the portions of history with which we are earliest familiar.... But in old times this contest was between subjects, or some classes of subjects, and the government. By liberty, was meant protection against the tyranny of the political rulers. The rulers were conceived (except in some of the popular governments of Greece) as in a necessarily antagonistic position to the people whom they ruled. They consisted of a governing One, or a governing tribe or caste, who derived their authority from inheritance or conquest, who, at all events, did not hold it at the pleasure of the governed, and whose supremacy men did not venture, perhaps did not desire, to contest, whatever precautions might be taken against its oppressive exercise. Their power was regarded as necessary, but also as highly dangerous; as a weapon which they would attempt to use against their subjects, no less than against external enemies. To prevent the weaker members of the community from being preyed upon by innumerable vultures, it was needful that there should be an animal of prey stronger than the rest, commissioned to keep them down. But as the king of the vultures would be no less bent upon preying on the flock than any of the minor harpies, it was indispensable to be in a perpetual attitude of defence against his beak and claws. The aim, therefore, of patriots, was to set limits to the power which the ruler should be suffered to exercise over the community; and this limitation was what they meant by liberty. It was attempted in two ways. First, by obtaining a recognition of certain immunities, called political liberties or rights, which it was to be regarded as a breach of duty in the ruler to infringe, and which if he did infringe, specific resistance, or general rebellion, was held to be justifiable. A second, and generally a later expedient, was the establishment of constitutional checks; by which the consent of the community, or of a body of some sort, supposed to represent its interests, was made a necessary condition to some of the more important acts of the governing power.... And so long as mankind were content to combat one enemy by another, and to be ruled by a master, on condition of being guaranteed more or less efficaciously against his tyranny, they did not carry their aspirations beyond this point.

A time, however, came, in the progress of human affairs, when men ceased to think it a necessity of nature that their governors should be an independent power, opposed in interest to themselves. It appeared to them much better that the various magistrates of the State should be their tenants or delegates, revocable at their pleasure. In that way alone, it seemed, could they have complete security that the powers of government would never be abused to their disadvantage. By degrees, this new demand for elective and temporary rulers became the prominent object of the exertions of the popular party, wherever any such party existed; and superseded, to a considerable extent, the previous efforts to limit the power of rulers. As the struggle proceeded for making the ruling power emanate from the periodical choice of the ruled, some persons began to think that too much importance had been attached to the limitation of the power itself. *That* (it might seem) was a resource against rulers whose interests were habitually opposed to those of the people. What was now wanted was, that the rulers should be identified with the people; that their interest and will should be the interest and will of the nation. The nation did not need to be protected against its own will. There was no fear of its tyrannising over itself. Let the rulers be effectually responsible to it, promptly removable by it, and it could afford to trust them with power of which it could itself dictate the use to be made. Their power was but the nation's own power, concentrated, and in a form convenient for exercise....

But, in political and philosophical theories, as well as in persons, success discloses faults and infirmities which failure might have concealed from observation. The notion, that the people have no need to limit their power over themselves, might seem axiomatic, when popular government was a thing only dreamed about, or read of as having existed at some distant period of the past.... In time, however, a democratic republic came to occupy a large portion of the earth's surface, and made itself felt as one of the most powerful members of the community of nations; and elective and responsible government became subject to the observations and criticisms which wait upon a great existing fact. It was now perceived that such phrases as "self-government," and "the power of the people over themselves," do not express the true state of the case. The "people" who exercise the power are not always the same people with those over whom it is exercised; and the "self-government" spoken of is not the government of each by himself, but of each by all the rest. The will of the people, moreover, practically means, the will of the most numerous or the most active *part* of the people; the majority, or those who succeed in making themselves accepted as the majority: the people, consequently, *may* desire to oppress a part of their number; and precautions are as much needed against this, as against any other abuse of power. The limitation, therefore, of the power of government over individuals, loses none of its importance when the holders of power are regularly accountable to the community, that is, to the strongest party therein. This view of things, recommending itself equally to the intelligence of thinkers and to the inclination of those important classes in European society to whose real or supposed interests democracy is adverse, has had no difficulty in establishing itself; and in political speculations "the tyranny of the majority" is now generally included among the evils against which society requires to be on its guard.

Like other tyrannies, the tyranny of the majority was at first, and is still vulgarly, held in dread, chiefly as operating through the acts of the public authorities. But reflecting persons perceived that when society is itself the tyrant—society collectively, over the separate individuals who compose it—its means of tyrannising are not restricted to the acts which it may do by the hands of its political functionaries. Society can and does execute its own mandates: and if it issues wrong mandates instead of right, or any mandates at all in things with which it ought not to meddle, it practises a social tyranny more formidable than many kinds of political oppression, since, though not usually upheld by such extreme penalties, it leaves fewer means of escape, penetrating much more deeply into the details of life, and enslaving the soul itself. Protection, therefore, against the tyranny of the magistrate is not enough: there needs protection also against the tyranny of the prevailing opinion and feeling; against the tendency of society to impose, by other means than civil penalties, its own ideas and practices as rules of conduct on those who dissent from them; to fetter the development, and, if possible, prevent the formation, of any individuality not in harmony with its ways, and compel all characters to fashion themselves upon the model of its own. There is a limit to the legitimate interference of collective opinion with individual independence: and to find that limit, and maintain it against encroachment, is as indispensable to a good condition of human affairs, as protection against political despotism.

But though this proposition is not likely to be contested in general terms, the practical question, where to place the limit—how to make the fitting adjustment between individual independence and social control—is a subject on which nearly everything remains to be done. All that makes existence valuable to any one, depends on the enforcement of restraints upon the actions of other people. Some rules of conduct, therefore, must be imposed, by law in the first place, and by opinion on many things which are not fit subjects for the operation of law. What these rules should be, is the principal question in human affairs; but if we except a few of the most obvious cases, it is one of those which least progress has been made in resolving. No two ages, and scarcely any two countries, have decided it alike; and the decision of one age or country is a wonder to another. Yet the people of any given age and country no more suspect any difficulty in it, than if it were a subject on which mankind had always been agreed. The rules which obtain among themselves appear to them self-evident and self-justifying. This all but universal illusion is one of the examples of the magical influence of custom, which is not only, as the proverb says, a second nature, but is continually mistaken for the first. The effect of custom, in preventing any misgiving respecting the rules of conduct which mankind impose on one another, is all the more complete because the subject is one on which it is not generally considered necessary that reasons should be given, either by one person to others, or by each to himself. People are accustomed to believe, and have been encouraged in the belief by some who aspire to the character of philosophers, that their feelings, on subjects of this nature, are better than reasons, and render reasons unnecessary. The practical principle which guides them to their opinions on the regulation of human conduct, is the feeling in each person's mind that everybody should be required to act as he, and those with whom he sympathises, would like them to act. No one, indeed, acknowledges to himself that his standard of judgment is his own liking; but an opinion on a point of conduct, not supported by reasons, can only count as one person's preference; and if the reasons, when given, are a mere appeal to a similar preference felt by other people, it is still only many people's liking instead of one. To an ordinary man, however, his own preference, thus supported, is not only a perfectly satisfactory reason, but the only one he generally has for any of his notions of morality, taste, or propriety, which are not expressly written in his religious creed; and his chief guide in the interpretation even of that. Men's opinions, accordingly, on what is laudable or blamable, are affected by all the multifarious causes which influence their wishes in regard to the conduct of others, and which are as numerous as those which determine their wishes on any other subject. Sometimes their reason—at other times their prejudices or superstitions: often their social affections, not seldom their anti-social ones, their envy or jealousy, their arrogance or contemptuousness: but most commonly, their desires or fears for themselves—their legitimate or illegitimate self-interest. Wherever there is an ascendant class, a large portion of the morality of the country emanates from its class interests, and its feelings of class superiority. The morality between Spartans and Helots, between planters and negroes, between princes and subjects, between nobles and roturiers, between men and women, has been for the most part the creation of these class interests and feelings: and the sentiments thus generated, react in turn upon the moral feelings of the members of the ascendant class, in their relations among themselves. Where, on the other hand, a class, formerly ascendant, has lost its ascendancy, or where its ascendancy is unpopular, the prevailing moral sentiments frequently bear the impress of an impatient dislike of superiority. Another grand determining principle of the rules of conduct, both in act and forbearance, which have been enforced by law or opinion, has been the servility of mankind towards the supposed preferences or aversions of their temporal masters, or of their gods. This servility, though essentially selfish, is not hypocrisy; it gives rise to perfectly genuine sentiments of abhorrence; it made men burn magicians and heretics. Among so many baser influences, the general and obvious interests of society have of course had a share, and a large one, in the direction of the moral sentiments: less, however, as a matter of reason, and on their own account, than as a consequence of the sympathies and antipathies which grew out of them: and sympathies and antipathies which had little or nothing to do with the interests of society, have made themselves felt in the establishment of moralities with quite as great force.

The likings and dislikings of society, or of some powerful portion of it, are thus the main thing which has practically determined the rules laid down for general observance, under the penalties of law or opinion. And in general, those who have been in advance of society in thought and feeling have left this condition of things unassailed in principle, however they may have come into conflict with it in some of its details. They have occupied themselves rather in inquiring what things society ought to like or dislike, than in questioning whether its likings or dislikings should be a law to individuals. They preferred endeavouring to alter the feelings of mankind on the particular points on which they were themselves heretical, rather than make common cause in defence of freedom, with heretics generally. The only case in which the higher ground has been taken on principle and maintained with consistency, by any but an individual here and there, is that of religious belief: a case instructive in many ways, and not least so as forming a most striking instance of the fallibility of what is called the moral sense: for the *odium theologicum*, in a sincere bigot, is one of the most unequivocal cases of moral feeling. Those who first broke the yoke of what called itself the Universal Church, were in general as little willing to permit difference of religious opinion as that church itself. But when the heat of the conflict was over, without giving a complete victory to any party, and each church or sect was reduced to limit its hopes to retaining possession of the ground it already occupied; minorities, seeing that they had no chance of becoming majorities, were under the necessity of pleading to those whom they could not convert, for permission to differ. It is accordingly on this battle-field, almost solely, that the rights of the individual against society have been asserted on broad grounds of principle, and the claim of society to exercise authority over dissentients, openly controverted. The great writers to whom the world owes what religious liberty it possesses, have mostly asserted freedom of conscience as an indefeasible right, and denied absolutely that a human being is accountable to others for his religious belief. Yet so natural to mankind is intolerance in whatever they really care about, that religious freedom has hardly anywhere been practically realised, except where religious indifference, which dislikes to have its peace disturbed by theological quarrels, has added its weight to the scale. In the minds of almost all religious persons, even in the most tolerant countries, the duty of toleration is admitted with tacit reserves. One person will bear with dissent in matters of church government, but not of dogma; another can tolerate everybody, short of a Papist or a Unitarian; another, every one who believes in revealed religion; a few extend their charity a little further, but stop at the belief in a God and in a future state. Wherever the sentiment of the majority is still genuine and intense, it is found to have abated little of its claim to be obeyed. ...

The object of this Essay is to assert one very simple principle, as entitled to govern absolutely the dealings of society with the individual in the way of compulsion and control, whether the means used be physical force in the form of legal penalties, or the moral coercion of public opinion. That principle is, that the sole end for which mankind are warranted, individually or collectively, in interfering with the liberty of action of any of their number, is self-protection. That the only purpose for which power can be rightfully exercised over any member of a civilised community, against his will, is to prevent harm to others. His own good, either physical or moral, is not a sufficient warrant. He cannot rightfully be compelled to do or forbear because it will be better for him to do so, because it will make him happier, because, in the opinions of others, to do so would be wise, or even right. These are good reasons for remonstrating with him, or reasoning with him, or persuading him, or entreating him, but not for compelling him, or visiting him with any evil in case he do otherwise. To justify that, the conduct from which it is desired to deter him must be calculated to produce evil to some one else. The only part of the conduct of any one, for which he is amenable to society, is that which concerns others. In the part which merely concerns himself, his independence is, of right, absolute. Over himself, over his own body and mind, the individual is sovereign.

It is, perhaps, hardly necessary to say that this doctrine is meant to apply only to human beings in the maturity of their faculties. We are not speaking of children, or of young persons below the age which the law may fix as that of manhood or womanhood. Those who are still in a state to require being taken care of by others, must be protected against their own actions as well as against external injury. For the same reason, we may leave out of consideration those backward states of society in which the race itself may be considered as in its nonage. The early difficulties in the way of spontaneous progress are so great, that there is seldom any choice of means for overcoming them; and a ruler full of the spirit of improvement is warranted in the use of any expedients that will attain an end, perhaps otherwise unattainable. Despotism is a legitimate mode of government in dealing with barbarians, provided the end be their improvement, and the means justified by actually effecting that end. Liberty, as a principle, has no application to any state of things anterior to the time when mankind have become capable of being improved by free and equal discussion. Until then, there is nothing for them but implicit obedience to an Akbar or a Charlemagne, if they are so fortunate as to find one. But as soon as mankind have attained the capacity of being guided to their own improvement by conviction or persuasion (a period long since reached in all nations with whom we need here concern ourselves), compulsion, either in the direct form or in that of pains and penalties for non-compliance, is no longer admissible as a means to their own good, and justifiable only for the security of others.

It is proper to state that I forego any advantage which could be derived to my argument from the idea of abstract right, as a thing independent of utility. I regard utility as the ultimate appeal on all ethical questions; but it must be utility in the largest sense, grounded on the permanent interests of man as a progressive being. Those interests, I contend, authorise the subjection of individual spontaneity to external control, only in respect to those actions of each, which concern the interest of other people. If any one does an act hurtful to others, there is a *primâ facie* case for punishing him, by law, or, where legal penalties are not safely applicable, by general disapprobation. There are also many positive acts for the benefit of others, which he may rightfully be compelled to perform; such as, to give evidence in a court of justice; to bear his fair share in the common defence, or in any other joint work necessary to the interest of the society of which he enjoys the protection; and to perform certain acts of individual beneficence, such as saving a fellow-creature's life, or interposing to protect the defenceless against ill-usage, things which whenever it is obviously a man's duty to do, he may rightfully be made responsible to society for not doing. A person may cause evil to others not only by his actions but by his inaction, and in either case he is justly accountable to them for the injury. The latter case, it is true, requires a much more cautious exercise of compulsion than the former. To make any one answerable for doing evil to others, is the rule; to make him answerable for not preventing evil, is, comparatively speaking, the exception. Yet there are many cases clear enough and grave enough to justify that exception. In all things which regard the external relations of the individual, he is *de jure* amenable to those whose interests are concerned, and if need be, to society as their protector. There are often good reasons for not holding him to the responsibility; but these reasons must arise from the special expediencies of the case: either because it is a kind of case in which he is on the whole likely to act better, when left to his own discretion, than when controlled in any way in which society have it in their power to control him; or because the attempt to exercise control would produce other evils, greater than those which it would prevent. When such reasons as these preclude the enforcement of responsibility, the conscience of the agent himself should step into the vacant judgment seat, and protect those interests of others which have no external protection; judging himself all the more rigidly, because the case does not admit of his being made accountable to the judgment of his fellow-creatures.

But there is a sphere of action in which society, as distinguished from the individual, has, if any, only an indirect interest; comprehending all that portion of a person's life and conduct which affects only himself, or if it also affects others, only with their free, voluntary, and undeceived consent and participation. When I say only himself, I mean directly, and in the first instance: for whatever affects himself, may affect others *through* himself; and the objection which may be grounded on this contingency, will receive consideration in the sequel. This, then, is the appropriate region of human liberty. It comprises, first, the inward domain of consciousness; demanding liberty of conscience, in the most comprehensive sense; liberty of thought and feeling; absolute freedom of opinion and sentiment on all subjects, practical or speculative, scientific, moral, or theological. The liberty of expressing and publishing opinions may seem to fall under a different principle, since it belongs to that part of the conduct of an individual which concerns other people; but, being almost of as much importance as the liberty of thought itself, and resting in great part on the same reasons, is practically inseparable from it. Secondly, the principle requires liberty of tastes and pursuits; of framing the plan of our life to suit our own character; of doing as we like, subject to such consequences as may follow: without impediment from our fellow-creatures, so long as what we do does not harm them, even though they should think our conduct foolish, perverse, or wrong. Thirdly, from this liberty of each individual, follows the liberty, within the same limits, of combination among individuals; freedom to unite, for any purpose not involving harm to others: the persons combining being supposed to be of full age, and not forced or deceived.

No society in which these liberties are not, on the whole, respected, is free, whatever may be its form of government; and none is completely free in which they do not exist absolute and unqualified. The only freedom which deserves the name, is that of pursuing our own good in our own way, so long as we do not attempt to deprive others of theirs, or impede their efforts to obtain it. Each is the proper guardian of his own health, whether bodily, or mental and spiritual. Mankind are greater gainers by suffering each other to live as seems good to themselves, than by compelling each to live as seems good to the rest.

Though this doctrine is anything but new, and, to some persons, may have the air of a truism, there is no doctrine which stands more directly opposed to the general tendency of existing opinion and practice. Society has expended fully as much effort in the attempt (according to its lights) to compel people to conform to its notions of personal, as of social excellence....

Apart from the peculiar tenets of individual thinkers, there is also in the world at large an increasing inclination to stretch unduly the powers of society over the individual, both
even by that of legislati
the changes taking pla
society, and diminis
this encroachment i
spontaneously to di
grow more and mo
mankind, whether as
impose their own opinions and
of conduct on others, is so energetically sup
by some of the best and by some of the worst feelings incident to human nature, that it is hardly ever kept under restraint by anything but want of power; and as the power is not declining, but growing, unless a strong barrier of moral conviction can be raised against the mischief, we must expect, in the present circumstances of the world, to see it increase....

6.7 Michel Foucault (1926–1984)

Michel Foucault was a French philosopher whose work concentrated on the genealogy of ideas, borrowing that term from Friedrich Nietzsche. In practice, it usually begins by explicating a particular word or concept that we take for granted today (such as sex, madness, or discipline) by tracing the history of its transformation and development over time. In this way, we can uncover meanings, stories, and implications of that concept that we ordinarily overlook or forget. In *Discipline and Punish* Foucault explores the development of various legal, judicial, punitive, and correctional practices that emerged in the modern era to deal with criminality. Foucault argues that discipline should be understood as a distinct form of power comprising a series of techniques and practices that work to transform the behaviour of individuals. Ultimately, Foucault argues that discipline proved so effective at transforming criminality that it has expanded beyond its original scope, being now used to "correct" the sick, the mad, and the young. In short, contemporary forms of discipline "improve" the behaviour of ordinary citizens in their everyday lives. Hence discipline is at work everywhere in our contemporary society.

"Panopticism," a central and influential chapter from *Discipline and Punish*, shows how the principles of discipline were put to work by the British philosopher Jeremy Bentham in his proposal for a new architectural model for prisons: the panopticon. In this building, surveillance replaces violence as the principle means of control, a body of scientific knowledge is developed about the prisoners, and the prisoners are encouraged to internalize power and exercise it over themselves. This exploration produces an invaluable

...ght into the stealthy ways of power: even when no one else is actively wielding power ...ver us, we may be caught in its grip as a result of having been disciplined into wielding power over ourselves.

from Discipline and Punish

Panopticism

This enclosed, segmented space, observed at every point, in which the Individuals are inserted in a fixed place, in which the slightest movements are supervised, in which all events are recorded, in which an uninterrupted work of writing links the centre and periphery, in which power is exercised without division, according to a continuous hierarchical figure, in which each individual is constantly located, examined and distributed among the living beings, the sick and the dead—all this constitutes a compact model of the disciplinary mechanism. The plague is met by order; its function is to sort out every possible confusion: that of the disease, which is transmitted when bodies are mixed together; that of the evil, which is increased when fear and death overcome prohibitions. It lays down for each individual his place, his body, his disease and his death, his well-being, by means of an omnipresent and omniscient power that subdivides itself in a regular, uninterrupted way even to the ultimate determination of the individual, of what characterizes him, of what belongs to him, of what happens to him. Against the plague, which is a mixture, discipline brings into play its power, which is one of analysis. A whole literary fiction of the festival grew up around the plague: suspended laws, lifted prohibitions, the frenzy of passing time, bodies mingling together without respect, individuals unmasked, abandoning their statutory identity and the figure under which they had been recognized, allowing a quite different truth to appear. But there was also a political dream of the plague, which was exactly its reverse: not the collective festival, but strict divisions; not laws transgressed, but the penetration of regulation into even the smallest details of everyday life through the mediation of the complete hierarchy that assured the capillary functioning of power; not masks that were put on and taken off, but the assignment to each individual of his 'true' name, his 'true' place, his 'true' body, his 'true' disease. The plague as a form, at once real and imaginary, of disorder had as its medical and political correlative discipline. Behind the disciplinary mechanisms can be read the haunting memory of 'contagions', of the plague, of rebellions, crimes, vagabondage, desertions, people who appear and disappear, live and die in disorder.

If it is true that the leper gave rise to rituals of exclusion, which to a certain extent provided the model for and general form of the great Confinement, then the plague gave rise to disciplinary projects. Rather than the massive, binary division between one set of people and another, it called for multiple separations, individualizing distributions, an organization in depth of surveillance and control, an intensification and a ramification of power. The leper was caught up in a practice of rejection, of exile-enclosure; he was left to his doom in a mass among which it was useless to differentiate; those sick of the plague were caught up in a meticulous tactical partitioning in which individual differentiations were the constricting effects of a power that multiplied, articulated and subdivided itself; the great confinement on the one hand; the correct training on the other. The leper and his separation; the plague and its segmentations. The first is marked; the second analysed and distributed. The exile of the leper and the arrest of the plague do not bring with them the same political dream. The first is that of a pure community, the second that of a disciplined society. Two ways of exercising power over men, of controlling their relations, of separating out their dangerous mixtures. The plague-stricken town, traversed throughout with hierarchy, surveillance, observation, writing; the town immobilized by the functioning of an extensive power that bears in a distinct way over all individual bodies—this is the utopia of the perfectly governed city. The plague (envisaged as a possibility at least) is the trial in the course of which one may define ideally the exercise of disciplinary power. In order to make rights and laws function according to pure theory, the jurists place themselves in imagination in the state of nature; in order to see perfect disciplines functioning, rulers dreamt of the state of plague. Underlying disciplinary projects the image of the plague stands for all forms of confusion and disorder; just as the image of the leper, cut off from all human contact, underlies projects of exclusion.

They are different projects, then, but not incompatible ones. We see them coming slowly together, and it is the peculiarity of the nineteenth century that it applied to the space of exclusion of which the leper was the symbolic inhabitant (beggars, vagabonds, madmen and the disorderly formed the real population), the technique of power proper to disciplinary partitioning. Treat 'lepers' as 'plague victims', project the subtle segmentations of discipline onto the confused space of internment, combine it with the methods of analytical distribution proper to power, individualize the excluded, but use procedures of individualization to mark exclusion—this is what was operated regularly by disciplinary power from the beginning of the nineteenth century in the psychiatric asylum, the penitentiary, the reformatory, the approved school and, to some extent, the hospital. Generally speaking, all the authorities exercising individual control function according to a double mode; that of binary division and branding (mad/sane; dangerous/harmless; normal/abnormal); and that of coercive assignment, of differential distribution (who he is; where he must be; how he is to be characterized; how he is to be recognized; how a constant surveillance is to be exercised over him in an individual way, etc.). On the one hand, the lepers are treated as plague victims; the tactics of individualizing disciplines are imposed on the excluded; and, on the other hand, the universality of disciplinary controls makes it possible to brand the 'leper' and to bring into play against him the dualistic mechanisms of exclusion. The constant division between the normal and the abnormal, to which every individual is subjected, brings us back to our own time, by applying the binary branding and exile of the leper to quite different objects; the existence of a whole set of techniques and institutions for measuring, supervising and correcting the abnormal brings into play the disciplinary mechanisms to which the fear of the plague gave rise. All the mechanisms of power which, even today, are disposed around the abnormal individual, to brand him and to alter him, are composed of those two forms from which they distantly derive.

Bentham's *Panopticon* is the architectural figure of this composition. We know the principle on which it was based: at the periphery, an annular building; at the centre, a tower; this tower is pierced with wide windows that open onto the inner side of the ring; the peripheric building is divided into cells, each of which extends the whole width of the building; they have two windows, one on the inside, corresponding to the windows of the tower; the other, on the outside, allows the light to cross the cell from one end to the other. All that is needed, then, is to place a supervisor in a central tower and to shut up in each cell a madman, a patient, a condemned man, a worker or a schoolboy. By the effect of backlighting, one can observe from the tower, standing out precisely against the light, the small captive shadows in the cells of the periphery. They are like so many cages, so many small theatres, in which each actor is alone, perfectly individualized and constantly visible. The panoptic mechanism arranges spatial unities that make it possible to see constantly and to recognize immediately. In short, it reverses the principle of the dungeon; or rather of its three functions—to enclose, to deprive of light and to hide—it preserves only the first and eliminates the other two. Full lighting and the eye of a supervisor capture better than darkness, which ultimately protected. Visibility is a trap.

To begin with, this made it possible—as a negative effect—to avoid those compact, swarming, howling masses that were to be found in places of confinement, those painted by Goya or described by Howard. Each individual, in his place, is securely confined to a cell from which he is seen from the front by the supervisor; but the side walls prevent him from coming into contact with his companions. He is seen, but he does not see; is the object of information, never a subject in communication. The arrangement of his room, opposite the central tower, imposes on him an axial visibility; but the divisions of the ring, those separated cells, imply a lateral invisibility. And this invisibility is a guarantee of order. If the inmates are convicts, there is no danger of a plot, an attempt at collective escape, the planning of new crimes for the future, bad reciprocal influences; if they are patients, there is no danger of contagion; if they are madmen there is no risk of their committing violence upon one another; if they are schoolchildren, there is no copying, no noise, no chatter, no waste of time; if they are workers, there are no disorders, no theft, no coalitions, none of those distractions that slow down the rate of work, make it less perfect or cause accidents. The crowd, a compact mass, a locus of multiple exchanges, individualities merging together, a collective effect, is abolished and replaced by a collection of separated individualities. From the point of view of the guardian, it is replaced by a multiplicity that can be numbered and supervised; from the point of view of the inmates, by a sequestered and observed solitude (Bentham, 60–64).

Hence the major effect of the Panopticon: to induce in the inmate a state of conscious and permanent visibility that assures the automatic functioning of power. So to arrange things that the surveillance is permanent in its effects, even if it is discontinuous in its action; that the perfection of power should tend to render its actual exercise unnecessary; that this architectural apparatus should be a machine for creating and sustaining a power relation independent of the person who exercises it; in short, that the inmates should be caught up in a power situation of which they are themselves the bearers. To achieve this, it is at once too much and too little that the prisoner should be constantly observed by an inspector: too little, for what matters is that he knows himself to be observed; too much, because he has no need in fact of being so. In view of this, Bentham laid down the principle that power should be visible and unverifiable. Visible: the inmate will constantly have before his eyes the tall outline of the central tower from which he is spied upon. Unverifiable: the inmate must never know whether he is being looked at at any one moment; but he must be sure that he may always be so. In order to make the presence or absence of the inspector unverifiable, so that the prisoners, in their cells, cannot even see a shadow, Bentham envisaged not only venetian blinds on the windows of the central observation hall, but, on the inside, partitions that intersected the hall at right angles and, in order to pass from one quarter to the other, not doors but zig-zag openings; for the slightest noise, a gleam of light, a brightness in a half-opened door would betray the presence of the guardian.[1] The Panopticon is a machine for dissociating the see/being seen dyad: in the peripheric ring, one is totally seen, without ever seeing; in the central tower, one sees everything without ever being seen.[2]

It is an important mechanism, for it automatizes and disindividualizes power. Power has its principle not so much in a person as in a certain concerted distribution of bodies, surfaces, lights, gazes; in an

1 In the Postscript to the Panopticon, 1791, Bentham adds dark inspection galleries painted in black around the inspector's lodge, each making it possible to observe two storeys of cells.

2 In his first version of the Panopticon, Bentham had also imagined an acoustic surveillance, operated by means of pipes leading from the cells to the central tower. In the Postscript he abandoned the idea, perhaps because he could not introduce into it the principle of dissymmetry and prevent the prisoners from hearing the inspector as well as the inspector hearing them. Julius tried to develop a system of dissymmetrical listening (Julius, 18).

arrangement whose internal mechanisms produce the relation in which individuals are caught up. The ceremonies, the rituals, the marks by which the sovereign's surplus power was manifested are useless. There is a machinery that assures dissymmetry, disequilibrium, difference. Consequently, it does not matter who exercises power. Any individual, taken almost at random, can operate the machine: in the absence of the director, his family, his friends, his visitors, even his servants (Bentham, 45). Similarly, it does not matter what motive animates him: the curiosity of the indiscreet, the malice of a child, the thirst for knowledge of a philosopher who wishes to visit this museum of human nature, or the perversity of those who take pleasure in spying and punishing. The more numerous those anonymous and temporary observers are, the greater the risk for the inmate of being surprised and the greater his anxious awareness of being observed. The Panopticon is a marvellous machine which, whatever use one may wish to put it to, produces homogeneous effects of power.

A real subjection is born mechanically from a fictitious relation. So it is not necessary to use force to constrain the convict to good behaviour, the madman to calm, the worker to work, the schoolboy to application, the patient to the observation of the regulations. Bentham was surprised that panoptic institutions could be so light: there were no more bars, no more chains, no more heavy locks; all that was needed was that the separations should be clear and the openings well arranged. The heaviness of the old 'houses of security', with their fortress-like architecture, could be replaced by the simple, economic geometry of a 'house of certainty'. The efficiency of power, its constraining force have, in a sense, passed over to the other side—to the side or its surface of application. He who is subjected to a field of visibility, and who knows it, assumes responsibility for the constraints of power; he makes them play spontaneously upon himself; he inscribes in himself the power relation in which he simultaneously plays both roles; he becomes the principle of his own subjection. By this very fact, the external power may throw off its physical weight; it tends to the non-corporal; and, the more it approaches this limit, the more constant, profound and permanent are its effects: it is a perpetual victory that avoids any physical confrontation and which is always decided in advance.

... [T]he Panopticon also does the work of a naturalist. It makes it possible to draw up differences: among patients, to observe the symptoms of each individual, without the proximity of beds, the circulation of miasmas, the effects of contagion confusing the clinical tables; among schoolchildren, it makes it possible to observe performances (without there being any imitation or copying), to map aptitudes, to assess characters, to draw up rigorous classifications and, in relation to normal development, to distinguish 'laziness and stubbornness' from 'incurable imbecility'; among workers, it makes it possible to note the aptitudes of each worker, compare the time he takes to perform a task, and if they are paid by the day, to calculate their wages (Bentham, 60–64).

So much for the question of observation. But the Panopticon was also a laboratory; it could be used as a machine to carry out experiments, to alter behaviour, to train or correct individuals. To experiment with medicines and monitor their effects. To try out different punishments on prisoners, according to their crimes and character, and to seek the most effective ones. To reach different techniques simultaneously to the workers, to decide which is the best. To try out pedagogical experiments ... the Panopticon is a privileged place for experiments on men, and for analysing with complete certainty the transformations that may be obtained from them. The Panopticon may even provide an apparatus for supervising its own mechanisms. In this central tower, the director may spy on all the employees that he has under his orders: nurses, doctors, foremen, teachers, warders; he will be able to judge them continuously, alter their behaviour, impose upon them the methods he thinks best; and it will even be possible to observe the director himself. An inspector arriving unexpectedly at the centre of the Panopticon will be able to judge at a glance, without anything being concealed from him, how the entire establishment is functioning. And, in any case, enclosed as he is in the middle of this architectural mechanism, is not the director's own fate entirely bound up with it? The incompetent physician who has allowed contagion to spread, the incompetent prison governor or workshop manager will be the first victims of an epidemic or a revolt. '"By every tie I could devise", said the master of the Panopticon, "my own fate had been bound up by me with theirs"' (Bentham, 177). The Panopticon functions as a kind of laboratory of power. Thanks to its mechanisms of observation, it gains in efficiency and in the ability to penetrate into men's behaviour; knowledge follows the advances of power, discovering new objects of knowledge over all the surfaces on which power is exercised....

It is polyvalent in its applications; it serves to reform prisoners, but also to treat patients, to instruct schoolchildren, to confine the insane, to supervise workers, to put beggars and idlers to work. It is a type of location of bodies in space, of distribution of individuals in relation to one another, of hierarchical organization, of disposition of centres and channels of power, of definition of the instruments and modes of intervention of power, which can be implemented in hospitals, workshops, schools, prisons. Whenever one is dealing with a multiplicity of individuals on whom a task or a particular form of behaviour must be imposed, the panoptic schema may be used. It is—necessary modifications apart—applicable 'to all establishments whatsoever, in which, within a space not too large to be covered or commanded by buildings, a number of persons are meant to be kept under inspection' (Bentham, 40; although Bentham takes the penitentiary house as his prime example, it is because it has many different functions to fulfil—safe custody, confinement, solitude, forced labour and instruction).

In each of its applications, it makes it possible to perfect the exercise of power. It does this in several ways: because it can reduce the number of those who exercise it, while increasing the number of those on whom it is exercised. Because it is possible to intervene at any moment and because the constant pressure acts even before the offences, mistakes or crimes have been committed. Because, in these conditions, its strength is that it never intervenes, it is exercised spontaneously and without noise, it constitutes a mechanism whose effects follow from one another. Because, without any physical instrument other than architecture and geometry, it acts directly on individuals; it gives 'power of mind over mind'. The panoptic schema makes any apparatus of power more intense: it assures its economy (in material, in personnel, in time); it assures its efficacity by its preventative character, its continuous functioning and its automatic mechanisms. It is a way of obtaining from power 'in hitherto unexampled quantity', 'a great and new instrument of government ...; its great excellence consists in the great strength it is capable of giving to *any* institution it may be thought proper to apply it to (Bentham, 66)....

The panoptic schema, without disappearing as such or losing any of its properties, was destined to spread throughout the social body; its vocation was to become a generalized function....

The celebrated, transparent, circular cage, with its high tower, powerful and knowing, may have been for Bentham a project of a perfect disciplinary institution; but he also set out to show how one may 'unlock' the disciplines and get them to function in a diffused, multiple, polyvalent way throughout the whole social body. These disciplines, which the classical age had elaborated in specific, relatively enclosed places—barracks, schools, workshops—and whose total implementation had been imagined only at the limited and temporary scale of a plague-stricken town, Bentham dreamt of transforming into a network of mechanisms that would be everywhere and always alert, running through society without interruption in space or in time. The panoptic arrangement provides the formula for this generalization. It programmes, at the level of an elementary and easily transferable mechanism, the basic functioning of a society penetrated through and through with disciplinary mechanisms.

There are two images, then, of discipline. At one extreme, the discipline-blockade, the enclosed institution established on the edges of society, turned inwards towards negative functions: arresting evil, breaking communications, suspending time. At the other extreme, with panopticism, is the discipline-mechanism: a functional mechanism that must improve the exercise of power by making it lighter, more rapid, more effective, a design of subtle coercion for a society to come. The movement from one project to the other, from a schema of exceptional discipline to one of a generalized surveillance, rests on a historical transformation: the gradual extension of the mechanisms of discipline throughout the seventeenth and eighteenth centuries, their spread throughout the whole social body, the formation of what might be called in general the disciplinary society.

A whole disciplinary generalization—the Benthamite physics of power represents an acknowledgement of this—had operated throughout the classical age. The spread of disciplinary institutions, whose network was beginning to cover an ever larger surface and occupying above all a less and less marginal position, testifies to this: what was an islet, a privileged place, a circumstantial measure, or a singular model, became a general formula....

1. *The functional inversion of the disciplines*. At first, they were expected to neutralize dangers, to fix useless or disturbed populations, to avoid the inconveniences of over-large assemblies; now they were being asked to play a positive role, for they were becoming able to do so, to increase the possible utility of individuals. Military discipline is no longer a mere means of preventing looting, desertion or failure to obey orders among the troops; it has become a basic technique to enable the army to exist, not as an assembled crowd, but as a unity that derives from this very unity an increase in its forces; discipline increases the skill of each individual, coordinates these skills, accelerates movements, increases fire power, broadens the fronts of attack without reducing their vigour, increases the capacity for resistance, etc. The discipline of the workshop, while remaining a way of enforcing respect for the regulations and authorities, of preventing thefts or losses, tends to increase aptitudes, speeds, output and therefore profits; it still exerts a moral influence over behaviour, but more and more it treats actions in terms of their results, introduces bodies into a machinery, forces into an economy. When, in the seventeenth century, the provincial schools or the Christian elementary schools were founded, the justifications given for them were above all negative: those poor who were unable to bring up their children left them 'in ignorance of their obligations: given the difficulties they have in earning a living, and themselves having been badly brought up, they are unable to communicate a sound upbringing that they themselves never had'; this involves three major inconveniences: ignorance of God, idleness (with its consequent drunkenness, impurity, larceny, brigandage); and the formation of those gangs of beggars, always ready to stir up public disorder and 'virtually to exhaust the funds of the Hôtel-Dieu' (Demia, 60–61). Now, at the beginning of the Revolution, the end laid down for primary education was to be, among other things, to 'fortify', to 'develop the body', to prepare the child 'for a future in some mechanical work', to give him 'an observant eye, a sure hand and prompt habits' (Talleyrand's Report to the Constituent Assembly, 10 September 1791, quoted by Léon, 106). The disciplines function increasingly as techniques for making useful individuals. Hence their emergence from a marginal position on the confines of society, and detachment from the forms of exclusion or expiation, confinement or retreat. Hence the slow loosening of their kinship with religious regularities and enclosures. Hence also their rooting in the most important, most central and most productive sectors of society. They become attached to some of the great essential functions: factory production, the transmission of knowledge, the diffusion of aptitudes and skills, the war-machine. Hence, too, the double tendency one sees developing throughout the eighteenth century to increase the number of disciplinary institutions and to discipline the existing apparatuses....

With the police, one is in the indefinite world of a supervision that seeks ideally to reach the most elementary particle, the most passing phenomenon of the social body....

And, in order to be exercised, this power had to be given the instrument of permanent, exhaustive, omnipresent surveillance, capable of making all visible, as long as it could itself remain invisible. It had to be like a faceless gaze that transformed the whole social body into a field of perception: thousands of eyes posted everywhere, mobile attentions ever on the alert, a long, hierarchized network which, according to Le Maire, comprised for Paris the forty-eight *commissaires*, the twenty *inspecteurs*, then the 'observers', who were paid regularly, the '*basses mouches*', or secret agents, who were paid by the day, then the informers, paid according to the job done, and finally the prostitutes. And this unceasing observation had to be accumulated in a series of reports and registers; throughout the eighteenth century, an immense police text increasingly covered society by means of a complex documentary organization (on the police registers in the eighteenth century, cf. Chassaigne). And, unlike the methods of judicial or administrative writing, what was registered in this way were forms of behaviour, attitudes, possibilities, suspicions—a permanent account of individuals' behaviour....

'Discipline' may be identified neither with an institution nor with an apparatus; it is a type of power, a modality for its exercise, comprising a whole set of instruments, techniques, procedures, levels of application, targets; it is a 'physics' or an 'anatomy' of power, a technology. And it may be taken over either by 'specialized" institutions (the penitentiaries or 'houses of correction' of the nineteenth century), or by institutions that use it as an essential instrument for a particular end (schools, hospitals), or by pre-existing authorities that find in it a means of reinforcing or reorganizing their internal mechanisms of power (one day we should show how intra-familial relations, essentially in the parents-children cell, have become 'disciplined', absorbing since the classical age external schemata, first educational and military, then medical, psychiatric, psychological, which have made the family the privileged locus of emergence for the disciplinary question of the normal and the abnormal); or by apparatuses that have made discipline their principle of internal functioning (the disciplinarization of the administrative apparatus from the Napoleonic period), or finally by state apparatuses whose major, if not exclusive, function is to assure that discipline reigns over society as a whole (the police).

On the whole, therefore, one can speak of the formation of a disciplinary society in this movement that stretches from the enclosed disciplines, a sort of social 'quarantine', to an indefinitely generalizable mechanism of 'panopticism'. Nor because the disciplinary modality of power has replaced all the others; but because it has infiltrated the others, sometimes undermining them, but serving as an intermediary between them, linking them together, extending them and above all making it possible to bring the effects of power to the most minute and distant elements. It assures an infinitesimal distribution of the power relations.

A few years after Bentham, Julius gave this society its birth certificate (Julius, 384–6). Speaking of the panoptic principle, he said that there was much more there than architectural ingenuity: it was an event in the 'history of the human mind'. In appearance, it is merely the solution of a technical problem; but, through it, a whole type of society emerges. Antiquity had been a civilization of spectacle. 'To render accessible to a multitude of men the inspection of a small number of objects': this was the problem to which the architecture of temples, theatres and circuses responded. With spectacle, there was a predominance of public life, the intensity of festivals, sensual proximity. In these rituals in which blood flowed, society found new vigour and formed for a moment a single great body. The modern age poses the opposite problem: 'To procure for a small number, or even for a single individual, the instantaneous view of a great multitude.' In a society in which the principal elements are no longer the community and public life, but, on the one hand, private individuals and, on the other, the state, relations can be regulated only in a form that is the exact reverse of the spectacle: 'It was to the modern age, to the ever-growing influence of the state, to its ever more profound intervention in all the details and all the relations of social life, that was reserved the task of increasing and perfecting its guarantees, by using and directing towards that great aim the building and distribution of buildings intended to observe a great multitude of men at the same time.'

Julius saw as a fulfilled historical process that which Bentham had described as a technical programme. Our society is one not of spectacle, but of surveillance; under the surface of images, one invests bodies in depth; behind the great abstraction of exchange, there continues the meticulous, concrete training of useful forces; the circuits of communication are the supports of an accumulation and a centralization of knowledge; the play of signs defines the anchorages of power; it is not that the beautiful totality of the individual is amputated, repressed, altered by our social order, it is rather that the individual is carefully fabricated in it, according to a whole technique of forces and bodies....

... Historically, the process by which the bourgeoisie became in the course of the eighteenth century the politically dominant class was masked by the establishment of an explicit, coded and formally egalitarian juridical framework, made possible by the organization of a parliamentary, representative régime. But the development and generalization of disciplinary mechanisms constituted the other, dark side of these processes. The general juridical form that guaranteed a system of rights that were egalitarian in principle was supported by these tiny, everyday, physical mechanisms, by all those systems of micro-power that are essentially non-egalitarian and asymmetrical that we call the disciplines. And although, in a formal way, the representative régime makes it possible, directly or indirectly, with or without relays, for the will of all to form the fundamental authority of sovereignty, the disciplines provide, at the base, a guarantee of the submission of forces and bodies. The real, corporal disciplines constituted the foundation of the formal, juridical liberties. The contract may have been regarded as the ideal foundation of law and political power; panopticism constituted the technique, universally widespread, of coercion. It continued to work in depth on the juridical structures of society, in order to make the effective mechanisms of power function in opposition to the formal framework that it had acquired. The 'Enlightenment', which discovered the liberties, also invented the disciplines.

In appearance, the disciplines constitute nothing more than an infra-law. They seem to extend the general forms defined by law to the infinitesimal level of individual lives; or they appear as methods of training that enable individuals to become integrated into these general demands. They seem to constitute the same type of law on a different scale, thereby making it more meticulous and more indulgent. The disciplines should be regarded as a sort of counter-law. They have the precise role of introducing insuperable asymmetries and excluding reciprocities. First, because discipline creates between individuals a 'private' link, which is a relation of constraints entirely different from contractual obligation; the acceptance of a discipline may be underwritten by contract; the way in which it is imposed, the mechanisms it brings into play, the non-reversible subordination of one group of people by another, the 'surplus' power that is always fixed on the same side, the inequality of position of the different 'partners' in relation to the common regulation, all these distinguish the disciplinary link from the contractual link, and make it possible to distort the contractual link systematically from the moment it has as its content a mechanism of discipline. We know, for example, how many real procedures undermine the legal fiction of the work contract: workshop discipline is not the least important. Moreover, whereas the juridical systems define juridical subjects according to universal norms, the disciplines characterize, classify, specialize; they distribute along a scale, around a norm, hierarchize individuals in relation to one another and, if necessary, disqualify and invalidate. In any case, in the space and during the time in which they exercise their control and bring into play the asymmetries of their power, they effect a suspension of the law that is never total, but is never annulled either. Regular and institutional as it may be, the discipline, in its mechanism, is a 'counter-law'. And, although the universal juridicism of modern society seems to fix limits on the exercise of power, its universally widespread panopticism enables it to operate, on the underside of the law, a machinery that is both immense and minute, which supports, reinforces, multiplies the asymmetry of power and undermines the limits that are traced around the law....

What is now imposed on penal justice as its point of application, its 'useful' object, will no longer be the body of the guilty man set up against the body of the king; nor will it be the juridical subject of an ideal contract; it will be the disciplinary individual. The extreme point of penal justice under the Ancien Régime was the infinite segmentation of the body of the regicide: a manifestation of the strongest power over the body of the greatest criminal, whose total destruction made the crime explode into its truth. The ideal point of penality today would be an indefinite discipline: an interrogation without end, an investigation that would be extended without limit to a meticulous and ever more analytical observation, a judgement that would at the same time be the constitution of a file that was never closed, the calculated leniency of a penalty that would be interlaced with the ruthless curiosity of an examination, a procedure that would be at the same time the permanent measure of a gap in relation to an inaccessible norm and the asymptotic movement that strives to meet in infinity. The public execution was the logical culmination of a procedure governed by the Inquisition. The practice of placing individuals under 'observation' is a natural extension of a justice imbued with disciplinary methods and examination procedures. Is it surprising that the cellular prison, with its regular chronologies, forced labour, its authorities of surveillance and registration, its experts in normality, who continue and multiply the functions of the judge, should have become the modern instrument of penality? Is it surprising that prisons resemble factories, schools, barracks, hospitals, which all resemble prisons?

6.8 Edward S. Herman (1925–2017) and Noam Chomsky (1928–)

Noam Chomsky, a journalist, philosopher, and activist, is among the most influential intellectuals in the world. Since the 1960s Chomsky has been critical of American imperialism, militarism, and abusive forms of political and corporate power. He frequently criticizes the United States and its allies for their role in perpetuating poverty, violence, dictatorial forms of power, and environmental degradation worldwide, but he also works to expose various other oppressive and abusive actors on the global scene.

Manufacturing Consent was authored in the 1980s with his colleague Edward Herman, whose research concentrated on economics, politics, and mass media. It makes the argument that mainstream corporately-owned, profit-oriented journalism constitutes propaganda. Chomsky and Herman argue that, even when it is not consciously intended, market and political forces acting on news producers push them into only publishing stories that reflect positively on their owners, the prevailing capitalist, global economic system, and the nation-states within which these are situated. Much of Chomsky's work involves bringing to light various facts that he argues the mainstream press has conveniently forgotten.

Manufacturing Consent examines critically the institutional forces of the media industry in a democratic society. Unlike a totalitarian regime, democracies do not control the activities and behaviour of individual agents directly. Because consent of the people is essential in a democracy, the state and large corporations in Western democratic countries must convince people that these institutions serve everyone's best interests. Rather than allowing people to make their own spontaneous judgements on state and corporate interests, the media instead manufactures popular consent. It does this by means of propaganda that controls the terms and bounds of debate, and thereby regulates the very limits of thinkable thought.

from Manufacturing Consent

1
A Propaganda Model

The mass media serve as a system for communicating messages and symbols to the general populace. It is their function to amuse, entertain, and inform, and to inculcate individuals with the values, beliefs, and codes of behavior that will integrate them into the institutional structures of the larger society. In a world of concentrated wealth and major conflicts of class interest, to fulfil this role requires systematic propaganda.[1]

In countries where the levers of power are in the hands of a state bureaucracy, the monopolistic control over the media, often supplemented by official censorship, makes it clear that the media serve the ends of a dominant elite. It is much more difficult to see a propaganda system at work where the media are private and formal censorship is absent. This is especially true where the media actively compete, periodically attack and expose corporate and governmental malfeasance, and aggressively portray themselves as spokesmen for free speech and the general community interest. What is not evident (and remains undiscussed in the media) is the limited nature of such critiques, as well as the huge inequality in command of resources, and its effect both on access to a private media system and on its behavior and performance.

A propaganda model focuses on this inequality of wealth and power and its multilevel effects on mass-media interests and choices. It traces the routes by which money and power are able to filter out the news fit to print, marginalize dissent, and allow the government and dominant private interests to get their messages across to the public. The essential ingredients of our propaganda model, or set of news "filters," fall under the following headings: (1) the size, concentrated ownership, owner wealth, and profit orientation of the dominant mass-media firms; (2) advertising as the primary income source of the mass media; (3) the reliance of the media on information provided by government, business, and "experts" funded and approved by these primary sources and agents of power; (4) "flak" as a means of disciplining the media; and (5) "anticommunism" as a national religion and control mechanism. These elements interact with and reinforce one another. The raw material of news must pass through successive filters, leaving only the cleansed residue fit to print.

1 See note 4 of the preface [to *Manufacturing Consent*].

They fix the premises of discourse and interpretation, and the definition of what is newsworthy in the first place, and they explain the basis and operations of what amount to propaganda campaigns.

The elite domination of the media and marginalization of dissidents that results from the operation of these filters occurs so naturally that media news people, frequently operating with complete integrity and goodwill, are able to convince themselves that they choose and interpret the news "objectively" and on the basis of professional news values. Within the limits of the filter constraints they often are objective; the constraints are so powerful, and are built into the system in such a fundamental way, that alternative bases of news choices are hardly imaginable. In assessing the newsworthiness of the U.S. government's urgent claims of a shipment of MIGs to Nicaragua on November 5, 1984, the media do not stop to ponder the bias that is inherent in the priority assigned to government-supplied raw material, or the possibility that the government might be manipulating the news,[2] imposing its own agenda, and deliberately diverting attention from other material.[3] It requires a macro, alongside a micro- (story-by-story), view of media operations, to see the pattern of manipulation and systematic bias.

Let us turn now to a more detailed examination of the main constituents of the propaganda model, which will be applied and tested in the chapters that follow.

1.1. SIZE, OWNERSHIP, AND PROFIT ORIENTATION OF THE MASS MEDIA: THE FIRST FILTER

In their analysis of the evolution of the media in Great Britain, James Curran and Jean Seaton describe how, in the first half of the nineteenth century, a radical press emerged that reached a national working-class audience. This alternative press was effective in reinforcing class consciousness: it unified the workers because it fostered an alternative value system and framework for looking at the world, and because it "promoted a greater collective confidence by repeatedly emphasizing the potential power of working people to effect social change through the force of 'combination' and organized action."[4] This was deemed a major threat by the ruling elites. One MP asserted that the working-class newspapers "inflame passions and awaken their selfishness, contrasting their current condition with what they contend to be their future condition—a condition incompatible with human nature and those immutable laws which Providence has established for the regulation of civil society."[5] The result was an attempt to squelch the working-class media by libel laws and prosecutions, by requiring an expensive security bond as a condition for publication, and by imposing various taxes designed to drive out radical media by raising their costs. These coercive efforts were not effective, and by mid-century they had been abandoned in favor of the liberal view that the market would enforce responsibility.

---

2 Media representatives claim that what the government says is "newsworthy" in its own right. If, however, the government's assertions are transmitted without context or evaluation, and without regard to the government's possible manipulative intent, the media have set themselves up to be "managed." Their objectivity is "nominal," not substantive....

In early October 1986, memos were leaked to the press indicating that the Reagan administration had carried out a deliberate campaign of disinformation to influence events in Libya. The mass media, which had passed along this material without question, expressed a great deal of righteous indignation that they had been misled. To compound the absurdity, five years earlier the press had reported a CIA-run "disinformation program designed to embarrass Qaddafi and his government," along with terrorist operations to overthrow Qaddafi and perhaps assassinate him (*Newsweek*, Aug. 3, 1981; P. Edward Haley, *Qaddafi and the United States since 1969* [New York: Praeger, 1984], p. 272). But no lessons were learned. In fact, the mass media are gulled on an almost daily basis, but rarely have to suffer the indignity of government *documents* revealing their gullibility. With regard to Libya, the media have fallen into line for each propaganda ploy, from the 1981 "hit squads" through the Berlin discotheque bombing, swallowing each implausible claim, failing to admit error in retrospect, and apparently unable to learn from successive entrapment—which suggests willing error. See Noam Chomsky, *Pirates & Emperors* (New York: Claremont, 1986), chapter 3. As we show throughout the present book, a series of lies by the government, successively exposed, never seems to arouse skepticism in the media regarding the next government claim.

3 For a description of the government's strategy of deflecting attention away from the Nicaraguan election by the fabricated MIG story, and the media's service in this government program, see chapter 3 [of *Manufacturing Consent*] under "The MIG Crisis Staged during the Nicaraguan Election Week."

4 James Curran and Jean Seaton, *Power Without Responsibility: The Press and Broadcasting in Britain*, 2d ed. (London: Methuen, 1985), p. 24.

5 Quoted in ibid., p. 23.

Curran and Seaton show that the market *did* successfully accomplish what state intervention failed to do. Following the repeal of the punitive taxes on newspapers between 1853 and 1869, a new daily local press came into existence, but not one new local working-class daily was established through the rest of the nineteenth century. Curran and Seaton note that

> Indeed, the eclipse of the national radical press was so total that when the Labour Party developed out of the working-class movement in the first decade of the twentieth century, it did not obtain the exclusive backing of a single national daily or Sunday paper.[6]

One important reason for this was the rise in scale of newspaper enterprise and the associated increase in capital costs from the mid-nineteenth century onward, which was based on technological improvements along with the owners' increased stress on reaching large audiences. The expansion of the free market was accompanied by an "industrialization of the press." The total cost of establishing a national weekly on a profitable basis in 1837 was under a thousand pounds, with a break-even circulation of 6,200 copies. By 1867, the estimated start-up cost of a new London daily was 50,000 pounds. The *Sunday Express*, launched in 1918, spent over two million pounds before it broke even with a circulation of over 250,000.[7]

Similar processes were at work in the United States, where the start-up cost of a new paper in New York City in 1851 was $69,000; the public sale of the *St. Louis Democrat* in 1872 yielded $456,000; and city newspapers were selling at from $6 to $18 million in the 1920s.[8] The cost of machinery alone, of even very small newspapers, has for many decades run into the hundreds of thousands of dollars; in 1945 it could be said that "Even small-newspaper publishing is big business ... [and] is no longer a trade one takes up lightly even if he has substantial cash—or takes up at all if he doesn't."[9]

Thus the first filter—the limitation on ownership of media with any substantial outreach by the requisite large size of investment—was applicable a century or more ago, and it has become increasingly effective over time.[10] In 1986 there were some 1,500 daily newspapers, 11,000 magazines, 9,000 radio and 1,500 TV stations, 2,400 book publishers, and seven movie studios in the United States—over 25,000 media entities in all. But a large proportion of those among this set who were news dispensers were very small and local, dependent on the large national companies and wire services for all but local news. Many more were subject to common ownership, sometimes extending through virtually the entire set of media variants.[11] ...

Actually, while suggesting a media autonomy from corporate and government power that we believe to be incompatible with structural facts (as we describe below), Bagdikian[12] also may be understating the degree of effective concentration in news manufacture. It has long been noted that the media are tiered, with the top tier—as measured by prestige, resources, and outreach—comprising somewhere between ten and twenty-four systems.[13] It is this top tier, along with

6 Ibid., p. 34.

7 Ibid., pp. 38–39.

8 Alfred McClung Lee, *The Daily Newspaper in America* (New York: Macmillan, 1937), pp. 166, 173.

9 Earl Vance, "Freedom of the Press for Whom," *Virginia* (Summer 1945), quoted in *Survival of a Free, Competition Press: The Small Newspaper: Democracy's Grass Roots.* Report of the Chairman, Senate Small Business Committee, 80th Cong., 1st session, 1947, p. 54.

10 Note that we are speaking of media with substantial outreach—mass media. It has always been possible to start small-circulation journals and to produce mimeographed or photocopied news letters sent around to a tiny audience. But even small journals in the United States today typically survive only by virtue of contributions from wealthy financial angels.

11 In 1987, the Times-Mirror Company, for example, owned newspapers in Los Angeles, Baltimore, Denver, and Hartford, Connecticut, had book publishing and magazine subsidiaries, and owned cable systems and seven television stations.

12 Ben Bagdikian examines the conglomeration of private news media producers in Ben Bakdikian, *The Media Monopoly*, 2nd ed. (Boston: Beacon Press, 1987).

13 David L. Paletz and Robert M. Entman, *Media Power Politics* (New York: Free Press, 1981), p. 7; Stephen Hess, *The Government/Press Connection: Press Officers and Their Offices* (Washington: Brookings, 1984), pp. 99–100.

the government and wire services, that defines the news agenda and supplies much of the national and international news to the lower tiers of the media, and thus for the general public.[14] Centralization within the top tier was substantially increased by the post-World War II rise of television and the national networking of this important medium. Pre-television news markets were local, even if heavily dependent on the higher tiers and a narrow set of sources for national and international news; the networks provide national and international news from three national sources, and television is now the principal source of news for the public.[15] The maturing of cable, however, has resulted in a fragmentation of television audiences and a slow erosion of the market share and power of the networks....

Many of the large media companies are fully integrated into the market, and for the others, too, the pressures of stockholders, directors, and bankers to focus on the bottom line are powerful. These pressures have intensified in recent years as media stocks have become market favorites, and actual or prospective owners of newspapers and television properties have found it possible to capitalize increased audience size and advertising revenues into multiplied values of the media franchises—and great wealth.[16] This has encouraged the entry of speculators and increased the pressure and temptation to focus more intensively on profitability. Family owners have been increasingly divided between those wanting to take advantage of the new opportunities and those desiring a continuation of family control, and their splits have often precipitated crises leading finally to the sale of the family interest.[17]

This trend toward greater integration of the media into the market system has been accelerated by the loosening of rules limiting media concentration, cross-ownership, and control by non-media companies.[18] There has also

14 The four major Western wire services—Associated Press, United Press International, Reuters, and Agence-France-Presse—account for some 80 percent of the international news circulating in the world today. AP is owned by member newspapers; UPI is privately owned; Reuters was owned mainly by the British media until it went public in 1984, but control was retained by the original owners by giving lesser voting rights to the new stockholders; Agence-France-Presse is heavily subsidized by the French government. As is pointed out by Jonathan Fenby, the wire services "exist to serve markets," and their prime concern, accordingly, "is with the rich media markets of the United States, Western Europe, and Japan, and increasingly with the business community." They compete fiercely, but AP and UPI "are really U.S. enterprises that operate on an international scale.... Without their domestic base, the AP and UPI could not operate as international agencies. With it, they must be American organizations, subject to American pressures and requirements" (*The International News Services* [New York: Schocken, 1986], pp. 7, 9, 73–74). See also Anthony Smith, *The Geopolitics of Information: How Western Culture Dominates the World* (New York: Oxford University Press, 1980), chapter 3.

15 The fourteenth annual Roper survey, "Public Attitudes toward Television and Other Media in a Time of Change" (May 1985), indicates that in 1984, 64 percent of the sample mentioned television as the place "where you usually get most of your news about what's going on in the world today ..." (p. 3). It has often been noted that the television networks themselves depend heavily on the prestige newspapers, wire services, and government for their choices of news. Their autonomy as newsmakers can be easily exaggerated.

16 John Kluge, having taken the Metromedia system private in a leveraged buyout in 1984 worth $1.1 billion, sold off various parts of this system in 1985–86 for $5.5 billion, at a personal profit of some $3 billion (Gary Hector, "Are Shareholders Cheated by LBOs?" *Fortune*, Jan. 17, 1987, p. 100). Station KDLA-T.V. in Los Angeles, which had been bought by a management-outsider group in a leveraged buyout in 1983 for $245 million, was sold to the Tribune Company for $510 million two years later (Richard Stevenson, "Tribune in TV Deal for $510 Million," *New York Times*, May 7, 1985). See also "The Media Magnates: Why Huge Fortunes Roll Off the Presses," *Fortune*, October 12, 1987.

17 A split among the heirs of James E. Scripps eventually resulted in the sale of the *Detroit Evening News*. According to one news article, "Daniel Marentette, a Scripps family member and a self-described 'angry shareholder,' says family members want a better return on their money. 'We get better yields investing in a New York checking account,' says Mr. Marentette, who sells race horses" (Damon Darlin, "Takeover Rumors Hit Detroit News Parent' *Wall Street Journal*, July 18, 1985). The Bingham family division on these matters led to the sale of the *Louisville Courier-Journal*; the New Haven papers of the Jackson family were sold after years of squabbling, and "the sale price [of the New Haven papers], $185 million, has only served to publicize the potential value of family holdings of family newspapers elsewhere" (Geraldine Fabrikant, "Newspaper Properties, Hotter Than Ever," *New York Times*, Aug, 17, 1986).

18 The Reagan administration strengthened the control of existing holders of television-station licenses by increasing their term from three to five years, and its FCC made renewals essentially automatic. The FCC also greatly facilitated speculation and trading in television properties by a rule change reducing the required holding period before sale of a newly acquired property from three years to one year. The Reagan era FCC and Department of Justice also refused to challenge mergers and takeover bids that would significantly increase the concentration of power (GE-RCA) or media concentration (Capital Cities–ABC). Furthermore, beginning April 2, 1985, media owners could own as many as twelve television stations, as long as their total audience didn't exceed 25 percent of the nation's television households; and they could also hold twelve AM and twelve FM stations, as the 1953 "7-7-7 rule" was replaced with a "12-12-12 rule." See Herbert H. Howard, "Group and Cross-Media Ownership of Television Stations: 1985" (Washington: National Association of Broadcasters, 1985).

been an abandonment of restrictions—previously quite feeble anyway—on radio-TV commercials, entertainment-mayhem programming, and "fairness doctrine" threats, opening the door to the unrestrained commercial use of the airwaves.[19]

The greater profitability of the media in a deregulated environment has also led to an increase in takeovers and takeover threats, with even giants like CBS and Time, Inc., directly attacked or threatened. This has forced the managements of the media giants to incur greater debt and to focus ever more aggressively and unequivocally on profitability, in order to placate owners and reduce the attractiveness of their properties to outsiders.[20] They have lost some of their limited autonomy to bankers, institutional investors, and large individual investors whom they have had to solicit as potential "white knights."[21] ...

The control groups of the media are also brought into close relationships with the mainstream of the corporate community through boards of directors and social links. In the cases of NBC and the Group W television and cable systems, their respective parents, GE and Westinghouse, are themselves mainstream corporate giants, with boards of directors that are dominated by corporate and banking executives. Many of the other large media firms have boards made up predominantly of insiders, a general characteristic of relatively small and owner-dominated companies. The larger the firm and the more widely distributed the stock, the larger the number and proportion of outside directors. The composition of the outside directors of the media giants is very similar to that of large non-media corporations....

Another structural relationship of importance is the media companies' dependence on and ties with government. The radio-TV companies and networks all require government licenses and franchises and are thus potentially subject to government control or harassment. This technical legal dependency has been used as a club to discipline the media, and media policies that stray too often from an establishment orientation could activate this threat.[22] The media protect themselves from this contingency by lobbying and other political expenditures, the cultivation of political relationships, and care in policy. The political ties of the media have been impressive.... [F]ifteen of ninety-five outside directors of ten of the media giants are former government officials, and Peter Dreier gives a similar proportion in his study of large newspapers.[23] In television, the revolving-door flow of personnel between regulators and the regulated

19 This was justified by Reagan-era FCC chairman Mark Fowler on the grounds that market options are opening up and that the public should be free to choose. Criticized by Fred Friendly for doing away with the law's public interest standard, Fowler replied that Friendly "distrusts the ability of the viewing public to make decisions on its own through the marketplace mechanism, I do not." (Jeanne Saddler, "Clear Channel: Broadcast Takeovers Meet Less FCC Static, and Critics Are Upset," *Wall Street Journal*, June 11, 1985). Among other problems, Fowler ignores the fact that true freedom of choice involves the ability to select options that may not be offered by an oligopoly selling audiences to advertisers.

20 CBS increased its debt by about $1 billion in 1985 to finance the purchase of 21 percent of its own stock, in order to fend off a takeover attempt by Ted Turner. The *Wall Street Journal* noted that "With debt now standing at 60% of capital, it needs to keep advertising revenue up to repay borrowings and interest" (Peter Barnes, "CBS Profit Hinges on Better TV Ratings," June 6, 1986). With the slowed-up growth of advertising revenues; CBS embarked on an employment cutback of as many as six hundred broadcast division employees, the most extensive for CBS since the loss of cigarette advertising in 1971 (Peter Barnes, "CBS Will Cut up to 600 Posts in Broadcasting," *Wall Street Journal*, July 1,1986). In June 1986, Time, Inc., embarked on program to buy back as much as 10 million shares, or 16 percent of its common stock, at an expected cost of some $900 million, again to reduce the threat of a hostile takeover (Laura Landro, "Time Will Buy as Much as 16% of Its Common," *Wall Street Journal*, June 20, 1986).

21 In response to the Jesse Helms and Turner threats to CBS, Laurence Tisch, of Loews Corporation, was encouraged to increase his holdings in CBS stock, already at 11.7 percent. In August 1986, the Loews interest was raised to 24.9 percent, and Tisch obtained a position of virtual control. In combination with William Paley, who owned 8.1 percent of the shares, the chief executive officer of CBS was removed and Tisch took over that role himself, on a temporary basis (Peter Barnes, "Loews Increases Its Stake in CBS to Almost 25%," *Wall Street Journal*, Aug 12, 1986).

22 On the Nixon-Agnew campaign to bully the media by publicity attacks and threats, see Marilyn Lashner, *The Chilling Effect in TV News* (New York: Praeger, 1984). Lashner concluded that the Nixon White House's attempt to quiet the media "succeeded handily, at least as far as television is concerned ..." (p. 167). See also Fred Powledge, The *Engineering of Restraint: The Nixon 'Administration and the Press* (Washington: Public Affairs Press; 1971), and William E. Porter, *Assault on the Media: The Nixon Years* (Ann Arbor: University of Michigan Press, 1976).

23 Of the 290 directors in his sample of large newspapers, 36 had high-level positions—past or present—in the federal government (Dreier, "The Position of the Press," p. 303).

firms was massive during the years when the oligopolistic structure of the media and networks was being established.[24]

The great media also depend on the government for more general policy support. All business firms are interested in business taxes, interest rates, labor policies, and enforcement and nonenforcement of the antitrust laws. GE and Westinghouse depend on the government to subsidize their nuclear power and military research and development, and to create a favorable climate for their overseas sales. The *Reader's Digest*, *Time*, *Newsweek*, and movie- and television-syndication sellers also depend on diplomatic support for their rights to penetrate foreign cultures with U.S. commercial and value messages and interpretations of current affairs. The media giants, advertising agencies, and great multinational corporations have a joint and close interest in a favorable climate of investment in the Third World, and their interconnections and relationships with the government in these policies are symbiotic.[25]

In sum, the dominant media firms are quite large businesses; they are controlled by very wealthy people or by managers who are subject to sharp constraints by owners and other market-profit–oriented forces;[26] and they are closely interlocked, and have important common interests, with other major corporations, banks, and government. This is the first powerful filter that will affect news choices.

1.2. THE ADVERTISING LICENSE TO DO BUSINESS: THE SECOND FILTER

In arguing for the benefits of the free market as a means of controlling dissident opinion in the mid-nineteenth century, the Liberal chancellor of the British exchequer, Sir George Lewis, noted that the market would promote those papers "enjoying the preference of the advertising public."[27] Advertising did, in fact, serve as a powerful mechanism weakening the working-class press. Curran and Seaton give the growth of advertising a status comparable with the increase in capital costs as a factor allowing the market to accomplish what state taxes and harassment failed to do, noting that these "advertisers thus acquired a de facto licensing authority since, without their support, newspapers ceased to be economically viable."[28]

Before advertising became prominent, the price of a newspaper had to cover the costs of doing business. With the growth of advertising, papers that attracted ads could afford a copy price well below production costs. This put papers lacking in advertising at a serious disadvantage: their prices would tend to be higher, curtailing sales, and they would have less surplus to invest in improving the salability of the paper (features, attractive format, promotion, etc.). For this reason, an advertising-based system will tend to drive out of existence or into marginality the media companies and types that depend on revenue from sales alone. With advertising, the free market does not yield a neutral system in which final buyer choice decides. The *advertisers'* choices influence media

24 One study showed that of sixty-five FCC commissioners and high-level staff personnel who left the FCC between 1945 and 1970, twelve had come out of the private-communications sector before their FCC service, and thirty-four went into private-firm service after leaving the commission (Roger Noll et al., *Economic Aspects of Television Regulation* [Washington: Brookings, 1973], p. 23).

25 "The symbiotic growth of American television and global enterprise has made them so interrelated that they cannot be thought of as separate. They are essentially the same phenomenon: Preceded far and wide by military advisers, lobbyists, equipment salesmen, advertising specialists, merchandising experts, and telefilm salesmen as advance agents, the enterprise penetrates much of the non-socialist world. Television is simply its most visible portion" (Erik Barnouw, *The Sponsor* [New York: Oxford University Press, 1978], p: 158). For a broader picture, see Herbert I. Schiller, *Communication and Cultural Domination* (White Plains, N.Y.: International Arts and Sciences Press, 1976), especially chapters 3–4.

26 Is it not possible that if the populace "demands" program content greatly disliked by the owners, competition and the quest for profits will cause them to offer such programming? There is some truth in this, and it, along with the limited autonomy of media personnel, may help explain the "surprises" that crop up occasionally in the mass media. One limit to the force of public demand, however, is that the millions of customers have no means of registering their demand for products that are not offered to them. A further problem is that the owners' class interests are reinforced by a variety of other filters that we discuss below.

27 Quoted in Curran and Seaton, *Power Without Responsibility*, p. 31.

28 Ibid., p. 41.

prosperity and survival.[29] The ad-based media receive an advertising subsidy that gives them a price-marketing-quality edge, which allows them to encroach on and further weaken their ad-free (or ad-disadvantaged) rivals.[30] Even if ad-based media cater to an affluent ("upscale") audience, they easily pick-up a large part of the "down-scale" audience, and their rivals lose market share and are eventually driven out or marginalized.

In fact, advertising has played a potent role in increasing concentration even among rivals that focus with equal energy on seeking advertising revenue. A market share and advertising edge on the part of one paper or television station will give it additional revenue to compete more effectively—promote more aggressively, buy more salable features and programs—and the disadvantaged rival must add expenses it cannot afford to try to stem the cumulative process of dwindling market (and revenue) share. The crunch is often fatal, and it helps explain the death of many large-circulation papers and magazines and the attrition in the number of newspapers.[31]

From the time of the introduction of press advertising, therefore, working-class and radical papers have been at a serious disadvantage. Their readers have tended to be of modest means, a factor that has always affected advertiser interest. One advertising executive stated in 1856 that some journals are poor vehicles because "their readers are not purchasers, and any money thrown upon them is so much thrown away."[32] The same force took a heavy toll of the post–World War II social-democratic press in Great Britain, with the *Daily Herald*, *News Chronicle*, and *Sunday Citizen* failing or absorbed into establishment systems between 1960 and 1967, despite a collective average daily readership of 9.3 million. As James Curran points out, with 4.7 million readers in its last year, "the *Daily Herald* actually had almost double the readership of *The Times*, the *Financial Times* and the *Guardian* combined." What is more, surveys showed that its readers "thought more highly of their paper than the regular readers of any other popular newspaper," and "they also read more in their paper than the readers of other popular papers despite being overwhelmingly working class...."[33] The death of the *Herald*, as well as of the *News Chronicle* and *Sunday Citizen*, was in large measure a result of progressive strangulation by lack of advertising support. The *Herald*, with 8.1 percent of national daily circulation, got 3.5 percent of net advertising revenue; the *Sunday Citizen* got one-tenth of the net advertising revenue of the *Sunday Times* and one-seventh that of the *Observer* (on a per-thousand-copies basis). Curran argues persuasively that the loss of these three papers was an important contribution to the declining fortunes of the Labour party, in the case of the *Herald* specifically removing a mass-circulation institution that provided "an alternative framework of analysis and understanding that contested the dominant systems of representation in both broadcasting and the mainstream press."[34] A mass movement without any major media support, and subject to a great deal of active press hostility, suffers a serious disability, and struggles against grave odds.

The successful media today are fully attuned to the crucial importance of audience "quality": CBS proudly tells its shareholders that while it "continuously seeks

29 "... producers presenting patrons [advertisers] with the greatest opportunities to make a profit through their publics will receive support while those that cannot compete on this score will not survive" (Joseph Turow, *Media Industries: The Production of News and Entertainment* [New York: Longman, 1984], p. 52).

30 Noncommercial television is also at a huge disadvantage for the same reason, and will require a public subsidy to be able to compete. Because public television does not have the built-in-constraints of ownership by the wealthy, and the need to appease advertisers, it poses a threat to a narrow elite control of mass communications. This is why conservatives struggle to keep public television on a short leash, with annual funding decisions, and funding at a low level (see Barnouw, *The Sponsor*, pp. 179–82). Another option pursued in the Carter-Reagan era has been to force it into the commercial nexus by sharp defunding,

31 Bagdikian, *Media Monopoly*, pp. 118–26. "'The dominant paper ultimately thrives,' Gannett Chairman Allen H. Neuharth says. 'The weaker paper ultimately dies'" (Joseph B. White, "Knight-Ridder's No-Lose Plan Backfires," *Wall Street Journal*, Jan. 4, 1988).

32 Quoted in Curran and Seaton, *Power Without Responsibility*, p. 43.

33 "Advertising and the Press," in James Curran, ed., *The British Press: A Manifesto* (London: Macmillan, 1978), pp. 252–55.

34 Ibid., p. 254.

to maximize audience delivery," it has developed a new "sales tool" with which it approaches advertisers: "Client Audience Profile, or CAP, will help advertisers optimize the effectiveness of their network television schedules by evaluating audience segments in proportion to usage levels of advertisers' products and services."[35] In short, the mass media are interested in attracting audiences with buying power, not audiences per se; it is affluent audiences that spark advertiser interest today, as in the nineteenth century. The idea that the drive for large audiences makes the mass media "democratic" thus suffers from the initial weakness that its political analogue is a voting system weighted by income!

The power of advertisers over television programming stems from the simple fact that they buy and pay for the programs—they are the "patrons" who provide the media subsidy. As such, the media compete for their patronage, developing specialized staff to solicit advertisers and necessarily having to explain how their programs serve advertisers' needs. The choices of these patrons greatly affect the welfare of the media, and the patrons become what William Evan calls "normative reference organizations,"[36] whose requirements and demands the media must accommodate if they are to succeed.[37]

For a television network, an audience gain or loss of one percentage point in the Nielsen ratings translates into a change in advertising revenue of from $80 to $100 million a year, with some variation depending on measures of audience "quality." The stakes in audience size and affluence are thus extremely large, and in a market system there is a strong tendency for such considerations to affect policy profoundly. This is partly a matter of institutional pressures to focus on the bottom line, partly a matter of the continuous interaction of the media organization with patrons who supply the revenue dollars. As Grant Tinker, then head of NBC-TV, observed, television "is an advertising-supported medium, and to the extent that support falls out, programming will change."[38]

Working-class and radical media also suffer from the political discrimination of advertisers. Political discrimination is structured into advertising allocations by the stress on people with money to buy. But many firms will always refuse to patronize ideological enemies and those whom they perceive as damaging their interests, and cases of overt discrimination add to the force of the voting system weighted by income. Public-television station WNET lost its corporate funding from Gulf + Western in 1985 after the station showed the documentary "Hungry for Profit," which contains material critical of multinational corporate activities in the Third World. Even before the program was shown, in anticipation of negative corporate reaction, station officials "did all we could to get the program sanitized" (according to one station source).[39] The chief executive of Gulf + Western complained to the station that the program was "virulently anti-business if not anti-American," and that the station's carrying the program was not the behavior "of a friend" of the corporation. The London *Economist* says that "Most people believe that WNET would not make the same mistake again."[40]

In addition to discrimination against unfriendly media institutions, advertisers also choose selectively

35 *1984 CBS Annual Report*, p. 13.This is a further refinement in the measurement of "efficiency" in "delivering an audience." In the magazine business, the standard measure is CPM, or "costs per thousand," to an advertiser to reach buyers through a full-page, black-and-white ad. Recent developments, like CBS's CAP, have been in the direction of identifying the special characteristics of the audience delivered. In selling itself to advertisers, the *Soap Opera Digest* says: "But you probably want to know about our first milestone: today *Soap Opera Digest* delivers more women in the 18–49 category at the lowest CPM than any other women's magazine" (quoted in Turow, *Media Industries*, p. 55).

36 William Evan, *Organization Theory* (New York: Wiley, 1976), p. 123.

37 Turow asserts that "The continual interaction of producers and primary patrons plays a dominant part in setting the general boundary conditions for day-to-day production activity" (*Media Industries*, p. 51).

38 Quoted in Todd Gitlin, *Inside Prime Time* (New York: Pantheon, 1983), p. 253.

39 Pat Aufderheide, "What Makes Public TV Public?" *The Progressive* (January 1988).

40 "Castor oil or Camelot?" December 5, 1987. For further materials on such interventions, see Harry Hammitt, "Advertising Pressures on Media," Freedom of Information Center Report no. 367 (School of Journalism, University of Missouri at Columbia, February 1977). See also James Aronson, *Deadline for the Media* (New York: Bobbs-Merrill, 1972), pp. 261–63.

among programs on the basis of their own principles. With rare exceptions these are culturally and politically conservative.[41] Large corporate advertisers on television will rarely sponsor programs that engage in serious criticisms of corporate activities, such as the problem of environmental degradation, the workings of the military-industrial complex, or corporate support of and benefits from Third World tyrannies. Erik Barnouw recounts the history of a proposed documentary series on environmental problems by NBC at a time of great interest in these issues. Barnouw notes that although at that time a great many large companies were spending money on commercials and other publicity regarding environmental problems, the documentary series failed for want of sponsors. The problem was one of excessive objectivity in the series, which included suggestions of corporate or systemic failure, whereas the corporate message "was one of reassurance."[42]

Television networks learn over time that such programs will not sell and would have to be carried at a financial sacrifice, and that, in addition, they may offend powerful advertisers.[43] With the rise in the price of advertising spots, the forgone revenue increases; and with increasing market pressure for financial performance and the diminishing constraints from regulation, an advertising-based media system will gradually increase advertising time and marginalize or eliminate altogether programming that has significant public-affairs content.[44]

Advertisers will want, more generally, to avoid programs with serious complexities and disturbing controversies that interfere with the "buying mood." They seek programs that will lightly entertain and thus fit in with the spirit of the primary purpose of program purchases—the dissemination of a selling message. Thus over time, instead of programs like "The Selling of the Pentagon" it is a natural evolution of a market seeking sponsor dollars to offer programs such as "A Bird's-Eye View of Scotland," "Barry Goldwater's Arizona," "An Essay on Hotels," and "Mr. Rooney Goes to Dinner,"—a CBS program on "how Americans eat when they dine out, where they go and why."[45] There are exceptional cases of companies willing to sponsor serious programs, sometimes a result of recent embarrassments that call for a public-relations offset.[46] But even in these cases the companies will usually not want to sponsor close examination of sensitive and divisive issues—they prefer programs on Greek antiquities, the ballet, and items of cultural and national history and nostalgia. Barnouw points out an interesting contrast: commercial-television drama "deals almost wholly with the here and now, as processed via advertising budgets," but on public television, culture "has come to

41 According to Procter & Gamble's instructions to their ad agency, "There will be no material on any of our programs which could in any way further the concept of business as cold, ruthless, and lacking in all sentiment or spiritual motivation." The manager of corporate communications for General Electric has said: "We insist on a program environment that reinforces our corporate messages" (quoted in Bagdikian, *Media Monopoly*, p. 160). We may recall that GE now owns NBC-TV.

42 Barnouw, *The Sponsor*, p. 135.

43 Advertisers may also be offended by attacks on themselves or their products. On the tendency of the media to avoid criticism of advertised products even when very important to consumer welfare [e.g., the effects of smoking], see Bagdikian, *Media Monopoly*, pp. 168–73.

44 This is hard to prove statistically, given the poor data made available by the FCC over the years. The long-term trend in advertising time/programming time is dramatically revealed by the fact that in 1929 the National Association of Broadcasting adopted as a standard of commercial practice on radio following: "Commercial announcements shall not be broadcast between 7 and 11 P.M." William Paley testified before the Senate Commerce Committee in 1930 that only 22 percent of CBS's time was allocated to commercially sponsored programs, with the other 78 percent sustaining; and he noted that advertising took up only "seven-tenths of 1 percent of all our time" (quoted in *Public Service Responsibility of Broadcast Licensees*, FCC [Washington: GPO, Mar. 7, 1946], p. 42). Frank Wolf states in reference to public-affairs programming: "That such programs were even shown at all on commercial television may have been the result of FCC regulation" (*Television Programming for News and Public Affairs* [New York: Praeger, 1972], p. 138; see also pp. 99–139).

45 Barnouw, *The Sponsor*, p. 134.

46 For Alcoa's post-antitrust-suit sponsorship of Edward R. Murrow, and ITT's post-early-70s-scandals sponsorship of "The Big Blue Marble," see Barnouw, *The Sponsor*, ibid., pp. 51–52, 84–86. Barnouw shows that network news coverage of ITT was sharply constrained during the period of ITT program sponsorship.

mean 'other cultures.' ... American civilization, here and now, is excluded from consideration."[47]

Television stations and networks are also concerned to maintain audience "flow" levels, i.e., to keep people watching from program to program, in order to sustain advertising ratings and revenue. Airing program interludes of documentary-cultural matter that cause station switching is costly, and over time a "free," (i.e., ad-based) commercial system will tend to excise it. Such documentary-cultural-critical materials will be driven out of secondary media vehicles as well, as these companies strive to qualify for advertiser interest, although there will always be some cultural-political programming trying to come into being or surviving on the periphery of the mainstream media.

1.3. SOURCING MASS-MEDIA NEWS: THE THIRD FILTER

The mass media are drawn into a symbiotic relationship with powerful sources of information by economic necessity and reciprocity of interest. The media need a steady, reliable flow of the raw material of news. They have daily news demands and imperative news schedules that they must meet. They cannot afford to have reporters and cameras at all places where important stories may break. Economics dictates that they concentrate their resources where significant news often occurs, where important rumors and leaks abound, and where regular press conferences are held. The White House, the Pentagon, and the State Department, in Washington, D.C., are central nodes of such news activity. On a local basis, city hall and the police department are the subject of regular news "beats" for reporters. Business corporations and trade groups are also regular and credible purveyors of stories deemed newsworthy. These bureaucracies turn out a large volume of material that meets the demands of news organizations for reliable, scheduled flows. Mark Fishman calls this "the principle of bureaucratic affinity: only other bureaucracies can satisfy the input needs of a news bureaucracy."[48]

Government and corporate sources also have the great merit of being recognizable and credible by their status and prestige. This is important to the mass media. As Fishman notes,

> Newsworkers are predisposed to treat bureaucratic accounts as factual because news personnel participate in upholding a normative order of authorized knowers in the society. Reporters operate with the attitude that officials ought to know what it is their job to know.... In particular, a newsworker will recognize an official's claim to knowledge not merely as a claim, but as a credible, competent piece of knowledge. This amounts to a moral division of labor: officials have and give the facts; reporters merely get them.[49]

Another reason for the heavy weight given to official sources is that the mass media claim to be "objective" dispensers of the news. Partly to maintain the image of objectivity, but also to protect themselves from criticisms of bias and the threat of libel suits, they need material that can be portrayed as presumptively accurate.[50] This is also partly a matter of cost: taking information from sources that may be presumed credible reduces investigative expense, whereas material from sources that are not prima facie credible, or that will elicit criticism and threats, requires careful checking and costly research.

The magnitude of the public-information operations of large government and corporate bureaucracies that constitute the primary news sources is vast and ensures special access to the media. The Pentagon, for example, has a public-information service that involves

47 Barnouw, *The Sponsor*, p. 150.

48 Mark Fishman, *Manufacturing the News* (Austin: University of Texas Press, 1980), p. 143.

49 Ibid., pp. 144–45.

50 Gaye Tuchman, "Objectivity as Strategic Ritual: An Examination of Newsmen's Notions of Objectivity," *American Journal of Sociology* 77, no. 2 (1972), pp. 662–64.

many thousands of employees, spending hundreds of millions of dollars every year and dwarfing not only the public-information resources of any dissenting individual or group but the *aggregate* of such groups....

Only the corporate sector has the resources to produce public information and propaganda on the scale of the Pentagon and other government bodies. The AFSC and NCC cannot duplicate the Mobil Oil company's multimillion-dollar purchase of newspaper space and other corporate investments to get its viewpoint across.[51] The number of individual corporations with budgets for public information and lobbying in excess of those of the AFSC and NCC runs into the hundreds, perhaps even the thousands. A corporate *collective* like the U.S. Chamber of Commerce had a 1983 budget for research, communications, and political activities of $65 million.[52] By 1980, the chamber was publishing a business magazine (*Nation's Business*) with a circulation of 1.3 million and a weekly newspaper with 740,000 subscribers, and it was producing a weekly panel show distributed to 400 radio stations, as well as its own weekly panel-discussion programs carried by 128 commercial television stations.[53]

Besides the U.S. Chamber, there are thousands of state and local chambers of commerce and trade associations also engaged in public-relations and lobbying activities. The corporate and trade-association lobbying network community is "a network of well over 150,000 professionals,"[54] and its resources are related to corporate income, profits, and the protective value of public-relations and lobbying outlays. Corporate profits before taxes in 1985 were $295.5 billion. When the corporate community gets agitated about the political environment, as it did in the 1970s, it obviously has the wherewithal to meet the perceived threat. Corporate and trade-association image and issues advertising increased from $305 million in 1975 to $650 million in 1980.[55] So did direct-mail campaigns through dividend and other mail stuffers, the distribution of educational films, booklets and pamphlets, and outlays on initiatives and referendums, lobbying, and political and think-tank contributions. Aggregate corporate and trade-association political advertising and grass-roots outlays were estimated to have reached the billion-dollar-a-year level by 1978, and to have grown to $1.6 billion by 1984.[56]

To consolidate their preeminent position as sources, government and business-news promoters go to great pains to make things easy for news organizations. They provide the media organizations with facilities in which to gather; they give journalists advance copies of speeches and forthcoming reports; they schedule press conferences at hours well-geared to news deadlines;[57] they write press releases in usable language; and they carefully organize their press conferences and "photo opportunity" sessions.[58] It is the job of news officers "to meet the journalist's scheduled needs with material that their beat agency has generated at its own pace."[59]

In effect, the large bureaucracies of the powerful *subsidize* the mass media, and gain special access by their contribution to reducing the media's costs of

51 In 1980, Mobil Oil had a public-relations budget of $21 million and public-relations staff of seventy-three. Between 1976 and 1981 it produced at least a dozen televised special reports on such issues as gasoline prices, with a hired television journalist interviewing Mobil executives and other experts, that are shown frequently on television, often without indication of Mobil sponsorship. See A. Kent MacDougall, *Ninety Seconds to Tell It All* (Homewood, Ill.: Dow Jones-Irwin, 1981), pp. 117–20.

52 John S. Saloma III, *Ominous Politics: The New Conservative Labyrinth* (New York: Hill & Wang, 1984), p. 79.

53 MacDougall, *Ninety Seconds*, pp. 116–17.

54 Thomas B. Edsall, *The New Politics of Inequality* (New York: Norton, 1984), p. 110.

55 Peggy Dardenne, "Corporate Advertising," *Public Relations Journal* (November 1982), p. 36.

56 S. Prakash Sethi, *Handbook of Advocacy Advertising: Strategies and Applications* (Cambridge, Mass.: Ballinger, 1987), p. 22. See also Edsall, *New Politics*, chapter 3, "The Politicization of the Business Community"; and Saloma, *Ominous Politics*, chapter 6, "The Corporations: Making Our Voices Heard."

57 The April 14, 1986, U.S. bombing of Libya was the first military action timed to preempt attention on 7 P.M. prime-time television news. See Chomsky, *Pirates & Emperors*, p. 147.

58 For the masterful way the Reagan administration used these to manipulate the press, see "Standups," *The New Yorker*, December 2, 1985, pp. 81ff.

59 Fishman, *Manufacturing the News*, p. 153.

acquiring the raw materials of, and producing, news. The large entities that provide this subsidy become "routine" news sources and have privileged access to the gates. Non-routine sources must struggle for access, and may be ignored by the arbitrary decision of the gatekeepers. It should also be noted that in the case of the largesse of the Pentagon and the State Department's Office of Public Diplomacy, the subsidy is at the taxpayers' expense, so that, in effect, the citizenry pays to be propagandized in the interest of powerful groups such as military contractors and other sponsors of state terrorism.

Because of their services, continuous contact on the beat, and mutual dependency, the powerful can use personal relationships, threats, and rewards to further influence and coerce the media. The media may feel obligated to carry extremely dubious stories and mute criticism in order not to offend their sources and disturb a close relationship.[60] It is very difficult to call authorities on whom one depends for daily news liars, even if they tell whoppers. Critical sources may be avoided not only because of their lesser availability and higher cost of establishing credibility, but also because the primary sources may be offended and may even threaten the media using them.

Powerful sources may also use their prestige and importance to the media as a lever to deny critics access to the media: the Defense Department, for example, refused to participate in National Public Radio discussions of defense issues if experts from the Center for Defense Information were on the program; Elliott Abrams refused to appear on a program on human rights in Central America at the Kennedy School of Government, at Harvard University, unless the former ambassador, Robert White, was excluded as a participant;[61] Claire Sterling refused to participate in television-network shows on the Bulgarian Connection where her critics would appear.[62] In the last two of these cases, the authorities and brand-name experts were successful in monopolizing access by coercive threats.

Perhaps more important, powerful sources regularly take advantage of media routines and dependency to "manage" the media to manipulate them into following a special agenda and framework (as we will show in detail in the chapters that follow [not included here]).[63] Part of this management process consists of inundating the media with stories, which serve sometimes to foist a particular line and frame on the media (e.g., Nicaragua as illicitly supplying arms to the Salvadoran rebels), and at other times to help chase unwanted stories off the front page or out of the media altogether (the alleged delivery of MIGs to Nicaragua during the week of the 1984 Nicaraguan election). This strategy can be traced back at least as far as the Committee on Public Information, established to coordinate propaganda during World War I, which "discovered in 1917–18 that one of the best means of controlling news was flooding news channels with 'facts,' or what amounted to official information."[64]

The relation between power and sourcing extends beyond official and corporate provision of day-to-day news to shaping the supply of "experts." The dominance of official sources is weakened by the existence

60 On January 16, 1986, the American Friends Service Committee issued a news release, based on extended Freedom of Information Act inquiries, which showed that there had been 381 navy nuclear-weapons accidents and "incidents" in the period 1965–77, a figure far higher than that previously claimed. The mass media did not cover this hot story directly but through the filter of the navy's reply, which downplayed the significance of the new findings and eliminated or relegated to the background the AFSC's full range of facts and interpretation of the meaning of what they had uncovered. A typical heading: "Navy Lists Nuclear Mishaps: None of 630 Imperilled Public, Service Says," *Washington Post*, January 16, 1986.

61 The Harvard professor in charge of the program, Harvey Mansfield, stated that the invitation to White had been a mistake anyway, as he "is a representative of the far left," whereas the forum was intended to involve a debate "between liberals and conservatives" (*Harvard Crimson*, May 14, 1986).

62 See Edward S. Herman and Frank Brodhead, *The Rise and Fall of the Bulgarian Connection* (New York: Sheridan Square Publications; 1986), pp. 123–24.

63 Mark Hertsgaard, "How Reagan Seduced Us: Inside the President's Propaganda Factory," *Village Voice*, September 18, 1984; see also "Standups," cited in [note 18] above.

64 Stephen L. Vaughn, *Holding Fast the Inner Lines* (Chapel Hill: University of North Carolina Press, 1980), p. 194.

of highly respectable unofficial sources that give dissident views with great authority. This problem is alleviated by "co-opting the experts"[65]—i.e., putting them on the payroll as consultants, funding their research, and organizing think tanks that will hire them directly and help disseminate their messages. In this way bias may be structured, and the supply of experts may be skewed in the direction desired by the government and "the market."[66] As Henry Kissinger has pointed out, in this "age of the expert," the "constituency" of the expert is "those who have a vested interest in commonly held opinions; elaborating and defining its consensus at a high level has, after all, made him an expert."[67] It is therefore appropriate that this restructuring has taken place to allow the commonly held opinions (meaning those that are functional for elite interests) to continue to prevail.

This process of creating the needed body of experts has been carried out on a deliberate basis and a massive scale. Back in 1971, Judge Lewis Powell (later elevated to the Supreme Court) wrote a memo to the U.S. Chamber of Commerce urging business "to buy the top academic reputations in the country to add credibility to corporate studies and give business a stronger voice on the campuses."[68] One buys them, and assures that—in the words of Dr. Edwin Feulner, of the Heritage Foundation—the public-policy area "is awash with in-depth academic studies" that have the proper conclusions. Using the analogy of Procter & Gamble selling toothpaste, Feulner explained that "They sell it and resell it every day by keeping the product fresh in the consumer's mind." By the sales effort, including the dissemination of the correct ideas to "thousands of newspapers," it is possible to keep debate "within its proper perspective."[69]

In accordance with this formula, during the 1970s and early 1980s a string of institutions was created and old ones were activated to the end of propagandizing the corporate viewpoint. Many hundreds of intellectuals were brought to these institutions, where their work was funded and their outputs were disseminated to the media by a sophisticated propaganda effort.[70] The corporate funding and clear ideological purpose in the overall effort had no discernible effect on the credibility of the intellectuals so mobilized; on the contrary, the funding and pushing of their ideas catapulted them into the press....

1.4. FLAK AND THE ENFORCERS: THE FOURTH FILTER

"Flak" refers to negative responses to a media statement or program. It may take the form of letters, telegrams, phone calls, petitions, lawsuits, speeches and bills before Congress, and other modes of complaint, threat, and punitive action. It may be organized centrally or locally, or it may consist of the entirely independent actions of individuals.

If flak is produced on a large scale, or by individuals or groups with substantial resources, it can be both uncomfortable and costly to the media. Positions have to be defended within the organization and without, sometimes before legislatures and possibly even in courts. Advertisers may withdraw patronage. Television advertising is mainly of consumer goods that are readily subject to organized boycott. During the McCarthy years, many advertisers and radio and television stations were effectively coerced into quiescence and blacklisting of employees by the threats of determined Red hunters to boycott products. Advertisers are still concerned to avoid offending constituencies that might produce flak, and their demand for

65 Bruce Owen and Ronald Braeutigam, *The Regulation Game: Strategic Use of the Administrative Process* (Cambridge; Mass.: Ballinger, 1978), p. 7.
66 See Edward S. Herman, "The-Institutionalization of Bias in Economics," *Media, Culture and Society* (July 1982), pp. 275–91.
67 Henry Kissinger, *American Foreign Policy* (New York: Norton, 1969), p. 28.
68 Quoted in Alex Carey, "Managing Public Opinion: The Corporate Offensive" (University of New South Wales, 1986, mimeographed), p. 32.
69 Ibid., pp. 46–47, quoting Feulner papers given in 1978 and 1985.
70 For a good discussion of many of these organizations and their purposes, funding, networking, and outreach programs, see Saloma, *Ominous Politics*, chapters 4, 6, and 9.

suitable programming is a continuing feature of the media environment.[71] If certain kinds of fact, position, or program are thought likely to elicit flak, this prospect can be a deterrent.

The ability to produce flak, and especially flak that is costly and threatening, is related to power. Serious flak has increased in close parallel with business's growing resentment of media criticism and the corporate offensive of the 1970s and 1980s. Flak from the powerful can be either direct or indirect. The direct would include letters or phone calls from the White House to Dan Rather or William Paley, or from the FCC to the television networks asking for documents used in putting together a program, or from irate officials of ad agencies or corporate sponsors to media officials asking for reply time or threatening retaliation.[72] The powerful can also work on the media indirectly by complaining to their own constituencies (stockholders, employees) about the media, by generating institutional advertising that does the same, and by funding right-wing monitoring or think-tank operations designed to attack the media. They may also fund political campaigns and help put into power conservative politicians who will more directly serve the interests of private power in curbing any deviationism in the media.

Along with its other political investments of the 1970s and 1980s, the corporate community sponsored the growth of institutions such as the American Legal Foundation, the Capital Legal Foundation, the Media Institute, the Center for Media and Public Affairs, and Accuracy in Media (AIM). These may be regarded as institutions organized for the specific purpose of producing flak. Another and older flak-producing machine with a broader design is Freedom House. The American Legal Foundation, organized in 1980, has specialized in Fairness Doctrine complaints and libel suits to aid "media victims." The Capital Legal Foundation, incorporated in 1977, was the Scaife vehicle for Westmoreland's $120-million libel suit against CBS.[73]

The Media Institute, organized in 1972 and funded by corporate-wealthy patrons, sponsors monitoring projects, conferences, and studies of the media. It has focused less heavily on media failings in foreign policy, concentrating more on media portrayals of economic issues and the business community, but its range of interests is broad. The main theme of its sponsored studies and conferences has been the failure of the media to portray business accurately and to give adequate weight to the business point of view.[74] ...

The Center for Media and Public Affairs, run by Linda and Robert Lichter, came into existence in the mid-1980s as a "non-profit, non-partisan" research institute, with warm accolades from Patrick Buchanan, Faith Whittlesey, and Ronald Reagan himself, who recognized the need for an objective and fair press. Their *Media Monitor* and research studies continue their earlier efforts to demonstrate the liberal bias and anti-business propensities of the mass media.[75]

AIM was formed in 1969, and it grew spectacularly in the 1970s. Its annual income rose from $5,000 in 1971 to $1.5 million in the early 1980s, with funding mainly from large corporations and the wealthy heirs and foundations of the corporate system. At least eight separate oil companies were contributors to AIM in the early 1980s, but the wide representation in sponsors from the corporate community is impressive.[76] The function of AIM is to harass the media and put pressure on them to follow the corporate agenda and a hard-line,

71 See above [note re: Procter & Gamble and General Electric].

72 See "The Business Campaign Against 'Trial by TV,'" *Business Week*, June 22, 1980, pp. 77–79; William H. Miller, "Fighting TV Hatchet Jobs," *Industry Week*, January 12, 1981, pp. 61–64.

73 See Walter Schneir and Miriam Schneir, "Beyond Westmoreland: The Right's Attack on the Press," *The Nation*, March 30, 1985.

74 An ad widely distributed by United Technologies Corporation, titled "Crooks and Clowns on TV," is based on the Media Institute's study entitled *Crooks, Conmen and Clowns: Businessmen in TV Entertainment*, which contends that businessmen are treated badly in television entertainment programs.

75 See S. Robert Lichter, Stanley Rothman, and Linda Lichter, *The Media Elite* (Bethesda, Md.: Adler & Adler, 1986). For a good discussion of the Lichters' new center, see Alexander Cockburn, "Ashes and Diamonds," *In These Times*, July 8–21, 1987.

76 Louis Wolf, "Accuracy in Media Rewrites News and History," *Covert Action Information Bulletin* (Spring 1984), pp. 26–29.

right-wing foreign policy. It presses the media to join more enthusiastically in Red-scare bandwagons, and attacks them for alleged deficiencies whenever they fail to toe the line on foreign policy. It conditions the media to expect trouble (and cost increases) for violating right-wing standards of bias.[77]

Freedom House, which dates back to the early 1940s, has had interlocks with AIM, the World Anticommunist League, Resistance International, and U.S. government bodies such as Radio Free Europe and the CIA, and has long served as a virtual propaganda arm of the government and international right wing....

Although the flak machines steadily attack the mass media, the media treat them well. They receive respectful attention, and their propagandistic role and links to a larger corporate program are rarely mentioned or analyzed. AIM head, Reed Irvine's diatribes, are frequently published, and right-wing network flacks who regularly assail the "liberal media," such as Michael Ledeen,[78] are given Op-Ed column space, sympathetic reviewers, and a regular place on talk shows as experts. This reflects the power of the sponsors, including the well-entrenched position of the right wing in the mass media themselves.[79]

The producers of flak add to one another's strength and reinforce the command of political authority in its news-management activities. The government is a major producer of flak, regularly assailing, threatening, and "correcting" the media, trying to contain any deviations from the established line. News management itself is designed to produce flak. In the Reagan years, Mr. Reagan was put on television to exude charm to millions, many of whom berated the media when they dared to criticize the "Great Communicator."[80]

1.5. ANTICOMMUNISM AS A CONTROL MECHANISM

A final filter is the ideology of anticommunism. Communism as the ultimate evil has always been the specter haunting property owners, as it threatens the very root of their class position and superior status. The Soviet, Chinese, and Cuban revolutions were traumas to Western elites, and the ongoing conflicts and the well-publicized abuses of Communist states have contributed to elevating opposition to communism to a first principle of Western ideology and politics. This ideology helps mobilize the populace against an enemy, and because the concept is fuzzy it can be used against anybody advocating policies that threaten property interests or support accommodation with Communist states and radicalism. It therefore helps fragment the left and labor movements and serves as a political-control mechanism. If the triumph of communism is the worst imaginable result, the support of fascism abroad is justified as a lesser evil. Opposition to social democrats who are too soft on Communists and "play into their hands" is rationalized in similar terms.

Liberals at home, often accused of being pro-Communist or insufficiently anti-Communist, are kept continuously on the defensive in a cultural milieu in which anticommunism is the dominant religion. If they allow communism, or something that can be labeled communism, to triumph in the provinces while

77 AIM's impact is hard to gauge, but it must be recognized as only a part of a larger corporate-right-wing campaign of attack. It has common funding sources with such components of the conservative labyrinth as AEI, Hoover, the Institute for Contemporary Studies, and others (see Saloma, *Ominous Politics*, esp. chapters 2, 3, and 6), and has its own special role to play. AIM's head, Reed Irvine, is a frequent participant in television talk shows, and his letters to the editor and commentary are regularly published in the mass media. The media feel obligated to provide careful responses to his detailed attacks on their news and documentaries and the Corporation for Public Broadcasting even helped fund his group's reply to the PBS series on Vietnam. His ability to get the publisher of the *New York Times* to meet with him personally once a year—a first objective of any lobbyist—is impressive testimony to influence. On his contribution to the departure of Raymond Bonner from the *Times*, see Wolf, "Accuracy in Media Rewrites News and History," pp. 32–33.

78 For a discussion of Ledeen's views on the media, see Herman and Brodhead, *Bulgarian Connection*, pp. 166–70.

79 Among the contributors to AIM have been the Reader's Digest Association and the DeWitt Wallace Fund, Walter Annenberg, Sir James Goldsmith (owner of the French *L'Express*), and E.W. Scripps II, board chairman of a newspaper-television-radio system.

80 George Skelton, White House correspondent for the *Los Angeles Times*, noted that in reference to Reagan's errors of fact, "You write the stories once, twice, and you get a lot of mail saying, 'You're picking on the guy, you guys in the press make mistakes too.' And editors respond to that, so after a while the stories don't run anymore. We're intimidated" (quoted in Hertsgaard, "How Reagan Seduced Us").

they are in office, the political costs are heavy. Most of them have fully internalized the religion anyway, but they are all under great pressure to demonstrate their anti-Communist credentials. This causes them to behave very much like reactionaries. Their occasional support of social democrats often breaks down where the latter are insufficiently harsh on their own indigenous radicals or on popular groups that are organizing among generally marginalized sectors....

It should be noted that when anti-Communist fervor is aroused, the demand for serious evidence in support of claims of "communist" abuses is suspended, and charlatans can thrive as evidential sources. Defectors, informers, and assorted other opportunists move to center stage as "experts," and they remain there even after exposure as highly unreliable, if not downright liars.[81] Pascal Delwit and Jean-Michel Dewaele point out that in France, too, the ideologues of anticommunism "can do and say anything."[82] Analyzing the new status of Annie Kriegel and Pierre Daix, two former passionate Stalinists now possessed of a large and uncritical audience in France,[83] Delwit and Dewaele note:

> If we analyse their writings, we find all the classic reactions of people who have been disappointed in love. But no one dreams of criticising them for their past, even though it has marked them forever. They may well have been converted, but they have not changed.... no one notices the constants, even though they are glaringly obvious. Their best sellers prove, thanks to the support of the most indulgent and slothful critics anyone could hope for, that the public can be fooled. No one denounces or even notices the arrogance of both yesterday's eulogies and today's diatribes; no one cares that there is never any proof and that invective is used in place of analysis. Their inverted hyper-Stalinism—which takes the usual form of total Manichaeism—is whitewashed simply because it is directed against Communism. The hysteria has not changed, but it gets a better welcome in its present guise.[84]

The anti-Communist control mechanism reaches through the system to exercise a profound influence on the mass media. In normal times as well as in periods of Red scares, issues tend to be framed in terms of a dichotomized world of Communist and anti-Communist powers, with gains and losses allocated to contesting sides, and rooting for "our side" considered an entirely legitimate news practice. It is the mass media that identify, create, and push into the limelight a Joe McCarthy, Arkady Shevchenko, and Claire Sterling and Robert Leiken, or an Annie Kriegel and Pierre Daix. The ideology and religion of anticommunism is a potent filter.

1.6. DICHOTOMIZATION AND PROPAGANDA CAMPAIGNS

The five filters narrow the range of news that passes through the gates, and even more sharply limit what can become "big news," subject to sustained news campaigns. By definition, news from primary establishment sources meets one major filter requirement and is readily accommodated by the mass media. Messages from and about dissidents and weak, unorganized individuals and groups, domestic and foreign, are at an initial disadvantage in sourcing costs and credibility, and they often do not comport with the ideology or

81 See above, pp. 24–25; below, pp. 157–161 [in *Manufacturing Consent*].

82 "The Stalinists of Anti-Communism," in Ralph Miliband, John Saville, and Marcel Liebman, *Socialist Register, 1984: The Uses of Anticommunism* (London: Merlin Press, 1984), p. 337.

83 Daix, in 1949, referred to the Stalin concentration camps as "one of the Soviet Union's most glorious achievements," displaying "the complete suppression of man's exploitation of man" (quoted in Miliband et al., *Socialist Register*, p. 337). Kriegel, formerly a hardline Communist party functionary, was the author of a 1982 book explaining that the KGB organized the Sabra-Shatila massacres, employing German terrorists associated with the PLO and with the tacit cooperation of the CIA, in order to defame Israel as part of the Soviet program of international terrorism. For more on this profound study, and its influence, see Noam Chomsky, *Fateful Triangle* (Boston: South End Press, 1983), pp. 291–92, 374–75.

84 *Socialist Register*, p. 345.

interests of the gatekeepers and other powerful parties that influence the filtering process.[85]

Thus, for example, the torture of political prisoners and the attack on trade unions in Turkey will be pressed on the media only by human-rights activists and groups that have little political leverage. The U.S. government supported the Turkish martial-law government from its inception in 1980, and the U.S. business community has been warm toward regimes that profess fervent anticommunism, encourage foreign investment, repress unions, and loyally support U.S. foreign policy (a set of virtues that are frequently closely linked). Media that chose to feature Turkish violence against their own citizenry would have had to go to extra expense to find and check out information sources; they would elicit flak from government, business, and organized right-wing flak machines, and they might be looked upon with disfavor by the corporate community (including advertisers) for indulging in such a quixotic interest and crusade. They would tend to stand alone in focusing on victims that from the standpoint of dominant American interests were *unworthy*.[86]

In marked contrast, protest over political prisoners and the violation of the rights of trade unions in Poland was seen by the Reagan administration and business elites in 1981 as a noble cause, and, not coincidentally, as an opportunity to score political points. Many media leaders and syndicated columnists felt the same way. Thus information and strong opinions on human-rights violations in Poland could be obtained from official sources in Washington, and reliance on Polish dissidents would not elicit flak from the U.S. government or the flak machines. These victims would be generally acknowledged by the managers of the filters to be *worthy*. The mass media never explain *why* Andrei Sakharov is worthy and José Luis Massera, in Uruguay, is unworthy—the attention and general dichotomization occur "naturally" as a result of the working of the filters, but the result is the same as if a commissar had instructed the media: "Concentrate on the victims of enemy powers and forget about the victims of friends."[87]

Reports of the abuses of worthy victims not only pass through the filters; they may also become the basis of sustained propaganda campaigns. If the government or corporate community and the media feel that a story is useful as well as dramatic, they focus on it intensively and use it to enlighten the public....

Propaganda campaigns in general have been closely attuned to elite interests....

Conversely, propaganda campaigns will *not* be mobilized where victimization, even though massive,

---

85 Where dissidents are prepared to denounce official enemies, of course, they can pass through the mass-media filtering system, in the manner of the ex-Communist experts described in "Anticommunism as a Control Mechanism" (p. 29 [of *Manufacturing Consent*]).

86 See chapter 2 [of *Manufacturing Consent*], "Worthy and Unworthy Victims." Of interest in the Turkish case is the Western press's refusal to publicize the Turkish government's attacks on the press, including the U.S. press's own reporters in that country. UPI's reporter Ismet Imset, beaten up by the Turkish police and imprisoned under trumped-up charges, was warned by UPI not to publicize the charges against him, and UPI eventually fired him for criticizing their badly compromised handling of his case. See Chris Christiansen, "Keeping In With The Generals," *New Statesman*, January 4, 1985.

87 We believe that the same dichotomization applies in the domestic sphere. For example, both British and American analysts have noted the periodic intense focus on—and indignation over—"welfare chiselers" by the mass media, and the parallel de-emphasis of and benign attitudes toward the far more important fraud and tax abuses of business and the affluent. There is also a deep-seated reluctance on the part of the mass media to examine the structural causes of inequality and poverty. Peter Golding and Sue Middleton, after an extensive discussion of the long-standing "criminalization of poverty" and incessant attacks on welfare scroungers in Britain, point out that tax evasion, by contrast, is "acceptable, even laudable," in the press, that the tax evader "is not merely a victim but a hero." They note, also, that "The supreme achievement of welfare capitalism" has been to render the causes and condition of poverty almost invisible (*Images of Welfare: Press and Public Attitudes to Poverty* [Oxford: Martin Robertson, 1982], pp. 66–67, 98–100, 186, 193).

In a chapter entitled "The Deserving Rich," A.J. Liebling pointed out that in the United States as well, "The crusade against the destitute is the favorite crusade of the newspaper publisher," and that "There is no concept more generally cherished by publishers than that of the Undeserving Poor" (*The Press* [New York: Ballantine, 1964], pp. 78–79). Liebling went into great detail on various efforts of the media to keep welfare expenses and taxes down "by saying that they [the poor] have concealed assets; or bad character, or both" (pp. 78–79). These strategies not only divert, they also help split the employed working class from the unemployed and marginalized, and make these all exceedingly uncomfortable about participating in a degraded system of scrounging. See Peter Golding and Sue Middleton, "Attitudes to Claimants: A Culture of Contempt," in *Images of Welfare*, pp. 169ff. President Reagan's fabricated anecdotes about welfare chiselers, and his complete silence on the large-scale chiseling of his corporate sponsors, have fitted into a long tradition of cynical and heartless greed.

sustained, and dramatic, fails to meet the test of utility to elite interests....

Using a propaganda model, we would not only anticipate definitions of worth based on utility, and dichotomous attention based on the same criterion, we would also expect the news stories about worthy and unworthy victims (or enemy and friendly states) to differ in *quality*. That is, we would expect official sources of the United States and its client regimes to be used heavily—and uncritically—in connection with one's own abuses and those of friendly governments, while refugees and other dissident sources will be used in dealing with enemies.[88] We would anticipate the uncritical acceptance of certain premises in dealing with self and friends—such as that one's own state and leaders seek peace and democracy, oppose terrorism, and tell the truth—premises which will not be applied in treating enemy states. We would expect different criteria of evaluation to be employed, so that what is villainy in enemy states will be presented as an incidental background fact in the case of oneself and friends.[89] What is on the agenda in treating one case will be off the agenda in discussing the other.[90] We would also expect great investigatory zeal in the search for enemy villainy and the responsibility of high officials for abuses in enemy states, but diminished enterprise in examining such matters in connection with one's own and friendly states.

The quality of coverage should also be displayed more directly and crudely in placement, headlining, word usage, and other modes of mobilizing interest and outrage. In the opinion columns, we would anticipate sharp restraints on the range of opinion allowed expression. Our hypothesis is that worthy victims will be featured prominently and dramatically, that they will be humanized, and that their victimization will receive the detail and context in story construction that will generate reader interest and sympathetic emotion. In contrast, unworthy victims will merit only slight detail, minimal humanization, and little context that will excite and enrage.

Meanwhile, because of the power of establishment sources, the flak machines, and anti-Communist ideology, we would anticipate outcries that the worthy victims are being sorely neglected, that the unworthy are treated with excessive and uncritical generosity,[91] that the media's liberal, adversarial (if not subversive) hostility to government explains our difficulties in mustering support for the latest national venture in counterrevolutionary intervention.

88 We have noted elsewhere that the *New York Times* regularly relied upon Indonesian officials in "presenting the facts" about East Timor, which was being invaded by Indonesia, and ignored refugees, church sources, etc. In contrast, refugees, not state officials, were the prime source in the *Times*'s reporting on postwar events in Vietnam and Cambodia (*The Washington Connection and Third World Fascism* [Boston: South End Press, 1979], pp. 151–52, 169–76, 184–87). On attempts to evade the obvious implications, see chapter 6 [of *Manufacturing Consent*], under "The Pol Pot Era" (pp. 284–85).

89 Thus when the CIA directs Nicaraguan contras to attack such "soft targets" as farming cooperatives, with explicit State Department approval, the media commentators, including doves, either applaud or offer philosophical disquisitions on whether such targets are legitimate, given that they are defended by lightly armed militia. Terrorist attacks on Israeli kibbutzim, also defended by armed settlers, are regarded somewhat differently. For details, see Noam Chomsky, *The Culture of Terrorism* (Boston: South End Press, 1988).

90 The variable use of agendas and frameworks can be seen with great clarity in the treatment of Third World elections supported and opposed by the United States, as described in Chapter 3 [of *Manufacturing Consent*].

91 Classic in their audacity are Michael Ledeen's assertions that: (1) Qaddafi's word is given more credence in the mass media than that of the U.S. government; and (2) "Relatively minor human rights transgressions in a friendly country (especially if ruled by an authoritarian government of the Right) are given far more attention and more intense criticism than far graver sins of countries hostile to us ..." (*Grave New World* [New York: Oxford University Press, 1985], p. 131; Qaddafi's superior credence is described on pp. 132–33). See chapter 2 [of *Manufacturing Consent*] for documentation on the reality of mass media treatment of abuses by clients and enemy states.

6.9 Gerald Taiaiake Alfred (1964–)

Taiaiake Alfred is an Indigenous scholar and activist from the Bear clan of the Mohawk Nation who grew up in the Kahnawá:ke reserve in Québec, Canada. His work centres around the struggle for Indigenous rights, the preservation and resuscitation of Indigenous cultures, and processes of decolonization. Following colonization by Britain and France beginning in the late sixteenth century, the Indigenous population of what is now Canada fell by 40 to 80 per cent. This, combined with the late-nineteenth-century effort of colonial Canada to forcibly assimilate the remaining Indigenous population into settler culture resulted in the devastation of Indigenous languages and cultures and has led to ongoing social crises in many Indigenous communities. Alfred is a key figure in the current struggle of the Indigenous people of what is now Canada to rebuild their cultures, assert their rights, and fight for fair treatment and independence from Canadian governance.

In *Peace, Power, Righteousness*, Alfred develops a program to encourage and foster the rebuilding of Indigenous traditions in order to push back against the legacy of Canadian colonialism. In particular, Alfred seeks to distill a set of principles that grounded pre-contact Indigenous social and political structures. For Alfred, these principles may be useful tools for challenging some of the injustices inherent in Western colonial societies, and in constructing a new social and political vision, not just for Indigenous peoples, but for the entire world. Interestingly, many of these principles bear a strong resemblance to those developed by Western European thinkers of the Enlightenment tradition, including universal liberty and equality. Alfred's implicit argument is that while European thinkers may have arrived at some of these ideas, European culture has never been very good at putting them into practice, of which colonial oppression stands as a key example. Indigenous societies, argues Alfred, had strong social and political traditions that enacted these principles much more successfully, and it is these traditions that he wishes to bring to light.

One of Alfred's key points in the following excerpt concerns the difference between European and Indigenous conceptions of power. He argues that European thought almost always conceives of power as the domination of one individual or group by another, usually through the threat of violence or the control of vital resources (such as food, water, and land). You will notice that this is precisely the working definition of power proposed in the introduction to this chapter, with a focus on coercive rather than deceptive forms of power. Alfred argues that the traditional Indigenous conception of power is very different. Rather than conceiving of power as a zero-sum game in which one can have power only if another does not, Alfred argues that Indigenous traditions think of power in terms of something we might call reciprocal empowerment: To exercise one's power is to help others to become more powerful. According to Alfred, a successful, powerful traditional leader is one who fosters and nurtures the power of those who are under his or her care, rather than one who suppresses it.

from Peace, Power, Righteousness[1]

Are you a Canadian?

No. Actually, I've tried to search for the moment in time when Canada decided legally—at least legally—that we were considered citizens. Which is kind of a joke, because as I've heard someone say, "Legally, yes, we are regarded as citizens. Yet the same legislation—the Indian Act—is always there to remind us that we're not." To me, you can't look at the Indian Act, and look at the precedents in the courts, and then draw the conclusion that we're citizens.[2]

Well, I think legally they gave Indians the vote in the 1960s. Formal citizenship came before that, but not much before. It wasn't asked for: It was given because they realized that in order to tax and do the things they wanted to do for Indians—or to Indians—they needed them to be citizens. They resisted as long as they could, then they made Indians second-class citizens and imposed the Indian Act on them. I'm not a Canadian. I don't believe in that. I think that if you're strong in your nation, then that's what you are. If you have a good relationship with Canada, fine, so much the better....

Is there a fundamental or inherent difference between indigenous and white society? This is a relevant question, given the tendency of the dominant Western tradition to draw racial distinctions. Indigenous traditions, by contrast, include all human beings as equal members in the regimes of conscience. Yet some Native people have been influenced by the divisive European approach. Representing this perspective in an academic context, Donald Fixico has claimed that white people can never come to terms with indigenous values because they "come from a different place on earth." He writes,

> Anglo-Americans and Natives are fundamentally different. These differences in worldview and in the values that go with them mean that there will always exist an Indian view and a White view of the earth.[3]

I believe, on the contrary, that there is a real danger in believing that views are fixed (and that cultures don't change). Fixico's polarization of Indian and European values suggests he believes that white people are incapable of attaining the level of moral development that indigenous societies promote among their members with respect to, for example, the land. Not only does this dichotomization go against the traditional Native belief in a universal rationality, but it offers a convenient excuse for those who support the state in its colonization of indigenous nations and exploitation of the earth. If Fixico is right, the state can't help it: The establishment's world view is preordained.

Challenging mainstream society to question its own structure, its acquisitive, individualistic values system, and the false premises of colonialism is essential if we are to move beyond the problems plaguing all our societies, Native and white, and rebuild relations between our peoples. A deep reading of tradition points to a moral universe in which all of humanity is accountable to the same standard. Our goal should be

1 The notes to these excerpts have here been converted to footnotes for clarity and consistency.

2 In 1985, Canada amended the Indian Act to restore status to those who had been "enfranchised" (who had given up their status in order to receive the benefits of Canadian society) and to eliminate its discrimination against Indian women who married non-Indians, permitting them to pass on their Indian status to their children. The series of amendments that effected the change also included the partial devolution of control over membership to Indian bands, resulting in what has become known as a two-tiered membership system with a distinction made between Indian status on the federal level and band membership on the local level. The new system created a situation where the federal government defined and imposed membership criteria for those communities that did not design and implement a local code in accordance with the Indian Act. In effect, where the new Indian Act theoretically allowed for band-controlled definitions of membership criteria, only those local membership codes that were acceptable to the minister and that conformed to Canadian laws were ratified and formalized by the Department of Indian Affairs.

3 D.L. Fixico, "The Struggle for Our Homes: Indian and White Values and Tribal Lands," in J. Weaver, ed., *Defending Mother Earth* (Maryknoll, NY: Orbis Books, 1996), 41.

to convince others of the wisdom of the indigenous perspective. Although it may be emotionally satisfying for indigenous people to ascribe a greedy, dominating nature to white people, taking such an approach leaves one in self-defeating intellectual and political positions. It is more hopeful to listen to the way traditional teachings speak of the various human families: They ask that we consider each one to be gifted and powerful in its own way, each with something different to contribute to the achievement of peace and harmony. Far from condemning different cultures, this position challenges each one to discover its gift in itself and realize it fully, to the benefit of humanity as a whole. It is just as important for Europeans as it is for Native people to cultivate the values that promote peace and harmony.

The value of the indigenous critique of the Western world view lies not in the creation of false dichotomies but in the insight that the colonial attitudes and structures imposed on the world by Europeans are not manifestations of an inherent evil: They are merely reflections of white society's understanding of its own power and relationship with nature. The brutal regime of European technological advancement, intent on domination, confronted its opposite in indigenous societies. The resulting near-extinction of indigenous peoples created a vacuum in which the European regime established its political, economic, and philosophical dominance.[4]

The primitive philosophical premises underpinning that regime were not advanced or refined in the deployment of microbes and weapons. At their core, European states and their colonial offspring still embody the same destructive and disrespectful impulses that they did five hundred years ago. For this reason, questions of justice—social, political, and environmental—are best considered outside the framework of classical European thought and legal traditions. The value of breaking away from old patterns of thought and developing innovative responses has been demonstrated with respect to environmental questions. But, in fact, many of these and other pressing questions have been answered before: Indigenous traditions are the repository of vast experience and deep insight on achieving balance and harmony.

At the time of their first contact with Europeans, the vast majority of Native American societies had achieved true civilization: They did not abuse the earth; they promoted communal responsibility; they practised equality in gender relations; and they respected individual freedom. As the Wendat historian Georges Sioui put it in a lucid summary of the basic values of traditional indigenous political and social thought,

> With their awareness of the sacred relations that they, as humans, must help maintain between all beings, New World men and women dictate a philosophy for themselves in which the existence and survival of other beings, especially animals and plants, must not be endangered. They recognize and observe the laws and do not reduce the freedom of other creatures. In this way they ensure the protection of their most precious possession, their own freedom....[5]

In choosing between revitalizing indigenous forms of government and maintaining the European forms imposed on them, Native communities have a choice between two radically different kinds of social organization: One based on conscience and the authority of the good, and the other on coercion and authoritarianism. The Native concept of governance is based on what Russell Barsh, a great student of indigenous societies, has called the "primacy of conscience." There is no central or coercive authority, and decision-making is collective. Leaders rely on their persuasive abilities to achieve a consensus that respects the autonomy of individuals, each of whom is free to dissent from, and remain unaffected by, the collective decision. The clan or family is the basic unit of social organization,

4 On differing perspectives on land and the environment, historically and today: W. Cronan, *Changes in the Land* (New York: Hill and Wang, 1983); and C. Merchant, *Radical Ecology* (New York: Routledge, 1992).

5 G.E. Sioui, *For and American Autohistory* (Montreal: McGill-Queen's University Press, 1992), 9.

and larger forms of organization, from tribe through nation to confederacy, are all predicated on the political autonomy and economic independence of clan units through family-based control of lands and resources.

A crucial feature of the indigenous concept of governance is its respect for individual autonomy. This respect precludes the notion of "sovereignty"—the idea that there can be a permanent transference of power or authority from the individual to an abstraction of the collective called "government." The indigenous tradition sees government as the collective power of the individual members of the nation; there is no separation between society and state. Leadership is exercised by persuading individuals to pool their self-power in the interest of the collective good. By contrast, in the European tradition, power is surrendered to the representatives of the majority, whose decisions on what they think is the collective good are then imposed on all citizens.

In the indigenous tradition, the idea of self-determination truly starts with the self; political identity—with its inherent freedoms, powers, and responsibilities—is not surrendered to any external entity. Individuals alone determine their interests and destinies. There is no coercion, only the compelling force of conscience based on those inherited and collectively refined principles that structure the society. With the collective inheritance of a cohesive spiritual universe and traditional culture, profound dissent is rare and is resolved by exemption of the individual from the implementation and implications of the particular decision. When the difference between individual and collective becomes irreconcilable, the individual leaves the group.

Collective self-determination depends on the conscious coordination of individual powers of self-determination. The governance process consists in the structured interplay of three kinds of power: individual power, persuasive power, and the power of tradition. These power relations are channelled into forms of decision-making and dispute resolution grounded in the recognition that beyond the individual there exists a natural community of interest: the extended family. Thus, in almost all indigenous cultures, the foundational order of government is the clan. And almost all indigenous systems are predicated on a collective decision-making process organized around the clan.

It is erosion of this traditional power relationship and the forced dependence on a central government for provision of sustenance that lie at the root of injustice in the indigenous mind. Barsh recognizes a truth that applies to institutions at both the broad and the local level: "The evil of modern states is their power to decide who eats."[6] Along with armed force, they use dependency—which they have created—to induce people's compliance with the will of an abstract authority structure serving the interests of an economic and political elite. It is an affront to justice that individuals are stripped of their power of self-determination and forced to comply with the decisions of a system based on the consciousness and interests of others.

The principles underlying European-style representative government through coercive force stand in fundamental opposition to the values from which indigenous leadership and power derive. In indigenous cultures, the core values of equality and respect are reflected in the practices of consensus decision-making and dispute resolution through balanced consideration of all interests and views. In indigenous societies, governance results from the interaction of leadership and the autonomous power of the individuals who make up the society. Governance in an indigenist sense can be practised only in a decentralized, small-scale environment among people who share a culture. It centres on the achievement of consensus and the creation of collective power, bounded by six principles:

- Governance depends on the active participation of individuals.
- Governance balances many layers of equal power.
- Governance is dispersed.

6 R.L. Barsh, "The Nature and Spirit of North American Political Systems," *American Indian Quarterly* (Spring 1986), 186.

- Governance is situational.
- Governance is non-coercive.
- Governance respects diversity....

The indigenous tradition is profoundly egalitarian; it does not put any substantial distance between leaders and other people, let alone allow for the exercise of coercive authority. Yet these are fundamental features of the political systems imposed on Native people. The hard truth is that many of those who hold positions of authority in Native communities have come to depend on the colonial framework for their power, employment, and status. How many of them would still hold their positions if the criteria for leadership reflected indigenous values instead of an ability to serve the interests of mainstream society? Very few contemporary Native politicians can honestly claim to possess the qualities and skills needed to lead in a non-coercive, participatory, transparent, consensus-based system. The hunger for power, money, and status prevents many people from seeing what is best for the community in the long run. But even when the people who seek that power do so with the best intentions, for the good of the people, the fact remains that holding non-consensual power over others is contrary to traditional values. Whatever the purpose behind the use of arbitrary authority, the power relationship itself is wrong.

Proponents of an indigenous form of government aim to overturn that unjust power relationship along with the government systems that have been imposed on our communities since colonization. Those systems cannot be defended on grounds of history (they are foreign), morality (they are intended to destabilize), or even practice (they do not work). Yet many people who are entrenched politically or bureaucratically within them resist any attempt to recover the traditional basis for governmental organization. Their defence of the status quo reflects a need to preserve the power relationships of contemporary Native politics. This is both a political and philosophical problem, a corruption that must be addressed if the values embedded in the European/American political system are not to form the general criteria for status, prestige, and leadership in our communities....

In the conventional Western understanding, a leader's power is based on control of certain strategic resources: for example, service provision, connections to the outside, and specific symbols with special meaning within the culture. It is exercised by manipulating various resources to secure changes in a target. Thus, power in the Western sense involves the imposition of an individual's will upon others. Even the most progressive non-indigenous notions of power, such as the one developed by Burns, still involve satisfying the personal motives of the leader.[7] While Burns distinguishes between "naked power," in which there is no engagement of leader to follower, and real leadership, in which the goals of leader and follower are merged, power is still defined in terms of "securing changes in the behaviour of the respondent, human or animal, and in the environment." Especially for indigenous peoples—all too familiar with state power founded on coercion—Burns's naked power seems the norm.[8]

Michel Foucault identified two ways of understanding state power.[9] The first sees state sovereignty as being created through the contractual surrender of individual rights. In this view, it is the abuse of state power—its extension beyond the accepted legal framework—that results in "oppression" of individuals. Most of Western political theory concerns the tensions that arise within a constitutionally regulated matrix of political power.

7 On the traditional notion of power in indigenous societies: R. Barsh, "The Nature and Spirit of North American Political Systems," *American Indian Quarterly* (Spring 1986), 181–98; G.E. Dowd, *A Spirited Resistance* (Baltimore: Johns Hopkins University Press, 1993), 1–22; S. Kan, *Symbolic Immortality* (Seattle: University of Washington Press, 1989); H. Robinson, *Nature/Power* (Toronto: Talon Books, 1992); B. Neidjie et al., *Australia's Kakadu Man* (Cambridge, MA: Terra Nova Press, 1987), 39; and H.K. Trask, *From a Native Daughter* (Honolulu, Latitude 20 Books, 1999).

8 Burns on power: *Leadership* (New York: Harper & Row, 1978), 13–18.

9 Foucault's two approaches to the analysis of power: M. Foucault, *Power/Knowledge* (New York: Vintage Books, 1980), 91–2, and *The Politics of Truth* (Cambridge, MA: MIT Press, 1997), 29–52.

The other, deeper, understanding of power proposed by Foucault sees the overextension of state power within a constitutional framework not as abuse but as the "mere effect and continuation of a relation of domination" that is fundamental—"a perpetual relation of force." Instead of defining oppression as an overextension of state power within a legal framework,

Foucault points to the continual domination by force necessary to maintain that framework itself. This approach is particularly useful for analyzing the relationship between the state and indigenous peoples—an approach in which not only the expression and extension of state power but the entire framework on which the sovereignty of the state depends is in question....

Traditionalists, recognizing the risk of intellectual co-optation, have adopted a traditional solution: focusing not on opposing external power, but on actualizing their own power and preserving their intellectual independence. This is an indigenous approach to empowerment. Unlike the statist version, this conception of power is not predicated on force. It does not involve coercing or inducing other beings to fulfil imperatives external to their own nature; thus, it is not inherently conflictual. Nor does it require a contractual surrender of power, leading to continuous tension between the individual and the state. Furthermore, it is consistent with Foucault's thoughts on the direction away from state sovereignty:

> If one wants to look for a non-disciplinary form of power, or rather, to struggle against disciplines and disciplinary power, it is not toward the ancient right of sovereignty that one should turn, but towards the possibility of a new form of right, one which must indeed be anti-disciplinarian, but at the same time liberated from the principle of sovereignty.[10]

The alternative to state power offered by the indigenous tradition transforms our understanding of power's meaning and use. There are many potential benefits to such a reorientation, not only within Native communities but as the foundation for building a post-colonial relationship with the state....

The Kanien'kehaka Kaswentha (Two-Row Wampum) principle embodies this notion of power in the context of relations between nations. Instead of subjugating one to the other, the Kanien'kehaka who opened their territory to Dutch traders in the early seventeenth century negotiated an original and lasting peace based on coexistence of power in a context of respect for the autonomy and distinctive nature of each partner. The metaphor for this relationship—two vessels, each possessing its own integrity, travelling the river of time together—was conveyed visually on a wampum belt of two parallel purple lines (representing power) on a background of white beads (representing peace). In this respectful (co-equal) friendship and alliance, any interference with the other partner's autonomy, freedom, or powers was expressly forbidden. So long as these principles were respected, the relationship would be peaceful, harmonious, and just.

It is with indigenous notions of power such as these that contemporary Native nationalism seeks to replace the dividing, alienating, and exploitative notions, based on fear, that drive politics inside and outside Native communities today. This goal differs significantly from the revolutionary objectives of earlier phases of the Native movement. Not only is revolution in the classic sense unworkable, given the relatively small numbers of indigenous peoples in North America today, but it is contrary to the basic principles of traditional indigenous philosophies. Indigenous peoples do not seek to destroy the state, but to make it more just and to improve their relations with the mainstream society. The principles embedded in cultural ideals such as the Kaswentha are in fact consistent with some Western principles that have been nearly forgotten in the construction of the modern

10 Foucault, *Power/Knowledge*, 108.

hegemonic state—among them, the original principle of federalism. Indigenous empowerment involves achieving a relationship between peoples founded on the principles of autonomy and interdependence. To accommodate indigenous notions of nationhood and cease its interference in indigenous communities, the state need only refer to the federal principle.

In traditional systems, it was essential for communities to cultivate relationships with their neighbours that would allow for ongoing dialogue and dispute resolution. This principle was embodied in numerous confederal unions that promoted harmony and co-operation. Today, in many cases, such co-operation is hindered by political, racial, and legal differences between neighbouring communities. The time has come to recognize our mutual dependency, to realize that indigenous and non-indigenous communities are permanent features of our political and social landscape, to embrace the notion of respectful co-operation on equal terms, and to apply the peacemaking principles on which were based both the many great precontact North American confederacies and the later alliances that allowed European societies to establish themselves and flourish on this continent.

In addition, we must recognize that we can never achieve the goal of peaceful coexistence as long as we continue to accept the classic notion of sovereignty as the framework for discussions of political relations between indigenous peoples and the state....

Beyond the question of the source of authority and its implications for nationhood, however, there are practical drawbacks to implementing a form of government based on sovereignty in communities with completely different perspectives on the nature and appropriate use of power. According to Deloria, provisions for "self-government" and other state-delegated forms of authority in indigenous communities are not wrong; they are simply inadequate because they do not take into account the spiritual needs of indigenous societies:

> Self-government is not an Indian idea. It originates in the minds of non-Indians who have reduced the traditional ways to dust, or believe they have, and now wish to give, as a gift, a limited measure of local control and responsibility. Self-government is an exceedingly useful concept for Indians to use when dealing with the larger government because it provides a context within which negotiations can take place. Since it will never supplant the intangible, spiritual, and emotional aspirations of American Indians, it cannot be regarded as the final solution to Indian problems.[11]

I would go even further than Deloria on this point. "Sovereignty" as it is currently understood and applied in indigenous–state relations cannot be seen as an appropriate goal or framework, because it has no relevance to indigenous values. The challenge before us is to detach the notion of sovereignty from its current legal meaning and use in the context of the Western understanding of power and relationships. We need to create a meaning for sovereignty that respects the understanding of power in indigenous cultures, one that reflects more of the sense embodied in such Western notions as "personal sovereignty" and "popular sovereignty." Until then, sovereignty can never be part of the language of liberation....

To argue on behalf of indigenous nationhood within the dominant Western paradigm is self-defeating. To frame the struggle to achieve justice in terms of indigenous "claims" against the state is implicitly to accept the fiction of state sovereignty. Indigenous peoples are by definition the original inhabitants of the land. They had complex societies and systems of government. And they never gave consent to European ownership of territory or the establishment of European sovereignty over them (treaties did not do this, according to both historic Native understandings and contemporary legal analysis). These are indisputable realities

11 Vine Deloria, Jr, on nationhood and sovereignty: Deloria and R.M. Lyttle, *The Nations Within* (Austin, TX: University of Texas Press, 1984), 8–15. "Self-government is not an Indian idea," 15.

based on empirically verifiable facts. So why are indigenous efforts to achieve legal recognition of these facts framed as claims? The mythology of the state is hegemonic, and the struggle for justice would be better served by undermining the myth of state sovereignty than by carving out a small and dependent space for indigenous peoples within it.

The need to perpetuate a set of fictive legal premises and fact-denying myths is apparent in every legal act of the state. To justify the establishment of non-indigenous sovereignty, aboriginality in a true sense must necessarily be excluded and denied. Otherwise, it would seem ridiculous that the original inhabitants of a place should be forced to justify their existence to a crude horde of refugees from another continent. As the European scholar Fae Korsmo has pointed out, the loss of collective memory is an essential requirement for creating a colonial reality:

> The people already living in or near the area have no role in the new myths, except perhaps as enemies or a dying race. They represent a noble yet doomed past that must be prevented from becoming a present-day threat. Insofar as the colonial mythology has put the burden on the indigenous societies to justify their claims in terms of their origins and hardy continuity, the doctrine of aboriginal title is part of colonialism and therefore dooms the indigenous claimants to failure.[12]

To summarize the argument thus far, sovereignty is an exclusionary concept rooted in an adversarial and coercive Western notion of power. Indigenous peoples can never match the awesome coercive force of the state; so long as sovereignty remains the goal of indigenous politics. Therefore, Native communities will occupy a dependent and reactionary position relative to the state. Acceptance of Aboriginal rights and title in the context of state sovereignty represents the culmination of white society's efforts to assimilate indigenous peoples....[13]

Native leaders have a responsibility to expose the truth and debunk the imperial pretense that supports the doctrine of state sovereignty and white society's dominion over indigenous nations and their minds. State sovereignty depends on the fabrication of falsehoods that exclude the indigenous voice. Ignorance and racism are the founding principles of the colonial state, and concepts of indigenous sovereignty that don't challenge these principles, in fact, serve to perpetuate them. To claim that the state's legitimacy is based on the rule of law is hypocritical and anti-historic. There is no moral justification for state sovereignty. The truth is that Canada and the United States were established only because indigenous peoples were overwhelmed by imported European diseases and were unable to prevent the massive immigration of European populations. Only recently as indigenous people have learned to manipulate state institutions and gained support from other groups oppressed by the state has the state been forced to change its approach. Recognizing the power of the indigenous challenge and unable to deny it a voice, the state has attempted to pull indigenous people closer to it. It has encouraged them to reframe and moderate their nationhood demands to accept the *fait accompli* of colonization, to collaborate in the development of a "solution" that does not challenge the fundamental imperial lie.

By allowing indigenous peoples a small measure of self-administration, and by forgoing a small portion of the money derived from the exploitation of indigenous nations' lands, the state has created incentives for integration into its own sovereignty framework. Those communities that co-operate are the beneficiaries of a patronizing false altruism that sees indigenous peoples as the anachronistic remnants of nations, the descendants of once independent peoples who by a combination of tenacity and luck have managed to survive and must now be protected as minorities.

12 F. Korsmo, "Claiming Memory in British Columbia: Aboriginal Rights and the State," *American Indian Culture and Research Journal* 20 (4), 72.

13 On sovereignty as a concept and its effect on knowledge and politics: J. Bartelson, *A Genealogy of Sovereignty* (Cambridge, UK: University of Cambridge Press, 1995), 3–7.

By agreeing to live as artifacts, such co-opted communities guarantee themselves a role in the state mythology, through which they hope to secure a limited but perpetual set of rights. In truth, the bargain is a pathetic compromise of principle. The reformulation of nationhood to create historical artifacts that lend legitimacy to the political economy of the modern state is nothing less than a betrayal.

What do traditionalists hope to protect? What have the co-opted ones forsaken? In both cases, the answer is the heart and soul of indigenous nations: a set of values that challenge the destructive and homogenizing force of Western liberalism and free-market capitalism, and that honour the autonomy of individual conscience, non-coercive authority, and the deep interconnection between human beings and the other elements of creation.

Nowhere is the contrast between indigenous and (dominant) Western traditions sharper than in their philosophical approaches to the fundamental issues of power and nature. In indigenous philosophies, power flows from respect for nature and the natural order. In the dominant Western philosophy, power derives from coercion and artifice—in effect, alienation from nature.

A brief detour to consider the relationship of human beings to the earth may serve to illustrate the last point. Indigenous philosophies are premised on the belief that earth was created by a power external to human beings, who have a responsibility to act as stewards; since humans had no hand in making the earth, they have no right to "possess" it or dispose of it as they see fit—possession of land by humankind is unnatural and unjust. The stewardship principle, reflecting a spiritual connection with the land established by the Creator, gives human beings special responsibilities within the areas they occupy as indigenous peoples, linking them in a "natural" way to their territories.

The realities of capitalism make this concept problematic both for the state and for indigenous peoples. But the perceptions of the problem are different. Non-indigenous people may suspect that traditionalist Natives would oppose the types of uses and activities promoted by the state in their nations' territories. In fact, this is not the case. Most Native people do not reject modernization or participation in larger economies. However, traditionalists recognize a responsibility to participate in the economy with the intent of ensuring the long-term health and stability of people and the land; in this context, development for development's sake, consumerism, and unrestrained growth are not justifiable. It is the intense possessive materialism at the heart of Western economies that must be rejected—for the basic reason that it contradicts traditional values aimed at maintaining a respectful balance among people and between human beings and the earth.

The form of distributive or social justice promoted by the state today depends on the development of industry and enterprises to provide jobs for people and revenue for government institutions. Most often—especially on indigenous lands—those industries and enterprises centre on the extraction of natural resources. Trees, rocks, and fish become commodities whose value is calculated solely in monetary terms without reference to the spiritual connections between them and indigenous peoples. From a traditional point of view, this is an extreme devaluation of nature....

The only position on development compatible with a traditional frame of mind is a balanced one, committed at once to using the land in ways that respect the spiritual and cultural connections indigenous peoples have with it and to managing the process so as to ensure a primary benefit for its natural indigenous stewards. The primary goals of an indigenous economy are to sustain the earth and to ensure the health and well-being of the people. Any derogation of that principle—whether in qualitative terms or with reference to the intensity of activity on the land—should be seen as upsetting the balanced ideal that lies at the heart of Native societies....

What is the role of a leader in this? Or, more generally, what are the duties and traits of a real Native leader?

Well, in the old days, a leader made certain that the camp, or longhouse, did not have petty problems that festered. Many a chief called the two parties who were quarrelling together and tried to get them to make up. Sometimes, he had to give them his own horses or some other gift to put everything right.

So I think that the Indian leader, insofar as [it's] possible, should be a figure of reconciliation and futuristic vision. And I think we are getting some people elected now who are acting that way. But a leader also should look at the community, evaluate where the strengths and weaknesses are, and develop a cadre of people who can work together on things—making sure that everyone comes together once in a while to get the general feeling that the community as a whole is moving forward. A leader probably ought also to be someone who enables processes to happen, who realizes that sometimes people are not ready to do things, and [will take the time] to gently educate them, to prepare them. Many of the old tribal chairmen of the 1960s did that, and they were very powerful leaders....

Colonial Mentalities

Despite all the wisdom available within indigenous traditions, most Native lives continue to be lived in a world of ideas imposed on them by others. The same set of factors that creates internalized oppression, blinding people to the true source of their pain and hostility, also allows them to accept, and even to defend, the continuation of an unjust power relationship. The "colonial mentality" is the intellectual dimension in the group of emotional and psychological pathologies associated with internalized oppression. Just as harmful to the society as self-hate and hostility are to individuals, the colonial mentality can be thought of as a mental state that blocks recognition of the existence or viability of traditional perspectives. It prevents people from seeing beyond the conditions created by the white society to serve its own interests.

The colonial mentality is recognizable in the gradual assumption of the values, goals, and perspectives that make up the status quo. The development of such a mentality is almost understandable (if not acceptable), given the structural basis of indigenous–state relations and the necessity for Native people to work through the various institutions of control to achieve their objectives. Native professionals, for example, find it hard to resist the (assimilative) opportunity structure created by the range of state strategies designed to co-opt and weaken challenges to the state's hegemony.

The structural integration and professionalization of Native politics within a bureaucratic framework controlled—financially and politically—by the state is the main reason for the persistence of the colonial mentality. In the Native context, all local governments, regional bodies, and national representative organizations are chartered and funded by the state. In Canada, for example, band councils, tribal councils, and the Assembly of First Nations are all creatures of the federal government. The fact that the very existence of government institutions within Native communities depends on an essentially foreign government goes largely unexamined and unchallenged by Native politicians. This dependence imposes a set of parameters that constrains the actions and even the thoughts of those working within the system.

Attempting to decolonize without addressing the structural imperatives of the colonial system itself is clearly futile. Yet most people accept the idea that we are making steady progress toward the resolution of injustices stemming from colonization. It may take more energy, or more money, than is currently being devoted to the process of decolonization, but the issue is always discussed within existing structural and legal frameworks. Most Native people do not see any need for a massive reorientation of the relationship between themselves and the state. This is symptomatic of the colonial mentality.

6.10 Review Questions

1. How do our three classical authors (Confucius, Plato, and Aristotle) relate discursive thought to collective action and independent judgement?

2. In what ways do our three classical authors set out a framework for Enlightenment-era and contemporary debates about the relationship between power and propaganda?

3. What is Machiavelli's purpose in *The Prince*? And to what extent, if any, does he conceive of that as a moral purpose?

4. According to Machiavelli, how should a Prince relate to moral virtues and vices?

5. How does Mill explain the traditional struggle between individual liberty and political authority? And what special threat to individual liberty is presented by democracy or majority rule?

6. According to Mill, what is the only justification for limiting individual liberty? Why does he restrict it to actions that affect others (and not those which affect only oneself)?

7. What are the three types of traditional power with which Foucault compares and contrasts discipline, and how does each function?

8. What features of discipline are shared with or contrast with traditional forms of power? And what does Foucault argue has happened to disciplinary techniques over time?

9. According to Chomsky and Herman, what are the five filters that operate in privately owned mainstream news media, and what precisely is filtered out by them?

10. What do Chomsky and Herman describe as "dichotomization," and how does it function in their propaganda model?

11. What is Alfred's account of the Native understanding of the difference between Native and European (white) cultures?

12. According to Alfred, how does the Native conception of political power differ from that of the European conception?

6.11 Further Reading

Bernays, Edward. *Propaganda*. Kennikat Press, 1928 [1972].

—. *The Engineering of Consent*. University of Oklahoma Press, 1969.

Drury, Shadia. *Leo Strauss and the American Right*. St. Martin's Press, 1997.

Foucault, Michel. *Security, Territory, Population: Lectures at the Collège de France, 1977–78*. Translated by Graham Burchell, Palgrave Macmillan, 2007.

French, J.R.P., and B. Raven. "The Bases of Social Power." *Studies in Social Power*, edited by D. Cartwright, Institute for Social Research, 1959, pp. 150–67.

McLuhan, Marshall. *Understanding Media*. McGraw-Hill, 1964.

CHAPTER 7

Violence and Civility

Death is nothing to us.

—EPICURUS, MAXIM

The wise man thinks of nothing less than death.

—SPINOZA, *THE ETHICS*

The terrorist hypothesis is that the system itself will commit suicide in response to the multiple challenges posed by deaths and suicides.

—JEAN BAUDRILLARD, *THE SPIRIT OF TERRORISM*, P. 17

Peace is the continuation of war by other means.

—HANNAH ARENDT, *ON VIOLENCE*, P. 9

One's got to get up in the morning thinking of a deviant act, merely to make certain of one's freedom. It needn't be much; kicking the dog will do.

—J.G. BALLARD, INTERVIEW IN *PARIS REVIEW*

There's no such thing as a nonviolent revolution.

—MALCOLM X

7.1 Introduction

This chapter takes up the question of morality in terms of violence, and especially forms of violence that occur between dominant, institutionalized organizations such as nation states, and the subgroups and individuals who are excluded from and dominated by those organizations. When powerful institutions such as nation states deploy violence against threatening or rebellious sub-groups, it is often overlooked, or at best represented as an unfortunate necessity in preventing more and worse forms of violence. For example, the use of force by police in apprehending criminals, the use of military violence to defend the nation state, or military intervention into foreign conflicts in order to secure peace, are all represented by the nation states in question as regrettable but unavoidable uses of violence. Often, the term violence is even avoided in favour of softer language: 'law and order,' 'security,' and 'peace-making.' Meanwhile, when the subgroups in question commit violent acts, it is represented by nation states as a terrible catastrophe that must be avoided. For example, the destruction of the property of wealthy corporations, the throwing of stones at riot police and military personnel, attacks by colonized populations against the colonizers designed to undermine and upset colonial rule, all tend to be labelled as immoral, using terms such as 'anarchist rioting,' 'criminality,' and 'terrorism.'

This double standard is perhaps most visible today in two of the great scandals of the Western European Enlightenment tradition: colonialism and the Holocaust. Somehow, the spirit of modern Enlightenment, based as it is in conceptions of universality, rationality, and critical thinking, went hand in hand with the brutal repression, enslavement, and even extermination of relatively defenceless non-state groups, singled out on the basis of their racial characteristics as convenient targets for state violence. The mass slaughter of indigenous North Americans, the violent enslavement of Africans, and the extermination of Jews, Roma, Poles, and others were all represented by the nation states that participated in them as essentially moral or at worst a regrettable necessity. Meanwhile, any use of violence in the resistance of these populations against their repression is depicted as barbarous, irrational, and even evil. The readings in this chapter have been selected on the basis that they challenge this easy double standard, along with the platitude that "all violence is bad" that usually accompanies it. This chapter raises a series of difficult questions such as: What forms of violence are represented as moral (or even as non-violent) or demonized as evil by the institutions that commit them or are targeted by them? What if one finds oneself part of an institution that is itself violent and evil? Is violence against dominant institutions ever moral?

Saint Thomas Aquinas provides a good starting point for this chapter with his "Whether It Is Always Sinful to Wage War?" which lays out the basic principles according to which modern institutions such as nation states understand their own violence as legitimate and moral while understanding the violence of others as illegitimate and immoral. Aquinas, a pre-Enlightenment theologian, begins from the notion that violence is always sinful and then develops a series of criteria according to which it can be justifiable. These criteria have fundamentally to do with a negative reflexivity. That is to say, Aquinas argues that it is moral to commit violence—to sin—only if its aim is to prevent violence—to prevent sin. This reflexivity is developed into three criteria: to be legitimate, violence must be pursued by a nation state rather than an individual or non-state actor; its target must be someone who deserves punishment, i.e., someone who is guilty of sin; and it must aim at a good, which is to say the war must be waged to establish peace. From the perspective of the majority of the authors in this chapter, these criteria are highly suspect: Aren't nation states just as likely as non-state actors to deploy violence out of self-interest and even cruelty? Isn't sin, like beauty, in the eye of the beholder—something that, even in Christian dogma, only God can judge? And doesn't all war aim at peace in the sense that victory—the decimation and enslavement of the enemy—is the end of war and therefore the beginning of peace?

Thucydides's history of the Peloponnesian War acts as an example here of how precisely the kinds of moral imperatives described by Aquinas can be both put to use and undermined by realpolitik, the rational self-interest of nation states and other institutions which is essentially unconcerned with moral questions. In these excerpts, we have the story of Athens, a military superpower, at war with Sparta, and deciding how to treat two weaker sub-populations: the city of Mitylene and the island of Melos. Mitylene, an ally of Athens, rebelled against the Athenian cause after four years of war and refused to participate in the ongoing struggle. Melos, a putatively neutral island nation, was besieged by Athens and forced to join the war. In the first excerpt we see a debate over what to do with Mitylene between the hawkish Cleon, who advocates a brutal slaughter, and the moderate Diodotus, who argues that only the rebel leaders should be executed.

What is vital here is the fact that Diodotus's argument is not based on moral convictions but on principles of political realism: he argues the moderate approach will be beneficial to Athens's economic interests. In the second excerpt we see a debate between representatives of Melos and Athens, the former of which argues for clemency on moral grounds, the latter of which argues for brutal repression on the basis that might makes right. In both of these historical cases, Athens makes decisions based on its own material interests rather than moral considerations.

Nietzsche, an iconoclastic figure in the context of Western thought, intervenes here with his *On the Genealogy of Morals* precisely in order to challenge the commonsense notion that violence is always immoral. For Nietzsche, this sentiment is characteristic of the weak, decadent society in which he finds himself and that he wishes to critique. This society of 'slave *ressentiment*,' argues Nietzsche, is so fixated on preventing harm that it stifles individual authenticity and self-expression. Nietzsche wishes to celebrate what he calls 'noble morality,' a set of values that he associates with a historically dominant aristocracy that was (in Nietzsche's mind unjustly) overthrown by commoners and slaves. On the one hand, Nietzsche's argument valorizes a terrifying kind of narcissism that legitimizes violence against weak, excluded populations on the basis that strong people are entitled to cruelty as part of their nature. It is on account of this, and Nietzsche's anti-Semitic remarks, that his work has become associated with Nazism. On the other hand, however, Nietzsche's argument provides a cogent critique of supposedly mild-mannered modern liberalism that refuses to acknowledge the violence that it deploys in maintaining control and (supposedly) preventing the violence of others.

Freud disrupts our usual fantasy of a peaceful, non-violent world filled with everyday friendly people by arguing that human beings have a natural drive towards aggression. Rather than a side-effect of self-interested competition, or an aberrant characteristic of sick or deranged individuals, Freud imagines violence as something for which every human being—however 'normal'—has a natural predilection. As such, Freud argues, civilization is constantly threatened with disintegration, and it requires a series of techniques to manage and control aggression. Instead of assuming that violence can be gotten rid of, Freud argues, we should attend to the way that it is redirected and channelled by civilization in its quest for stability. Included among these is the redirection of aggression outside of the social group towards a socially acceptable target—what we might call 'scapegoating'—which is how Freud understood the rise of anti-Semitism in Germany and Austria. He also describes what he calls the 'superego'—our everyday sense of 'conscience'—as another of these techniques, designed to redirect our aggression back at ourselves through guilt as self-punishment. If what we usually take to be our moral compass is actually just a way to get us to take out our aggression on ourselves, this has disturbing implications for our ability to distinguish morality from immorality.

Arendt, Zimbardo, and Himmler together examine the question of how everyday people can be mobilized by their social circumstances to commit acts that they would otherwise understand as deeply immoral. Arendt argues that Nazi official Adolf Eichmann, whose trial she attended and reports upon in *Eichmann in Jerusalem*, was not essentially evil, or crazy, or brainwashed, or even particularly stupid. He, like most Nazis, was an everyday 'normal' person caught up in a situation where the social and cultural coordinates that one would usually use to tell the difference between morality and immorality were deeply corrupted. Zimbardo generalizes from this report and his own infamous Stanford Prison Experiment to describe the social processes that can allow normal people to suspend their ethical judgement and perform immoral acts. These arguments are deeply unsettling for the commonsense notion that 'normal' people are essentially good and would never do anything as evil as participate in the Holocaust. Lastly, Himmler, the top Nazi official in charge of constructing and overseeing the concentration camps in which millions of Jews and others were put to death, provides a fascinating glimpse, in his

"Pozen Speech," into the structure of Nazi ideology: Instead of the duty of compassion being contrasted with the temptation to be cruel, Himmler presents cruelty as the duty of the 'good' Nazi and compassion as the temptation to be resisted. This inversion of standard morality presents unusual challenges for the individual living in such a society.

Lastly, Fanon brings this argument into relation with the example of colonialism, describing the process of decolonization—through which previously colonized populations achieve independence or equal citizenship—as necessarily violent. In contrast to those who argue that decolonization can only be achieved through non-violent protest and reconciliation, Fanon argues that these strategies are ultimately capitulations to colonial rule. Understanding colonialism as driven by precisely the kind of realpolitik described by Thucydides, Fanon argues that colonial powers only deploy moral arguments as a kind of ideological smokescreen, behind which they continue to pursue dominance, usually through economic means. Fanon argues that the only way to achieve true justice for the colonized would be for them to receive back the value that has been extracted from them through colonial genocide, theft, and slavery. However, he argues, this is precisely what colonial powers will never agree to. While they may be willing to recognize the cultural values of previously colonized peoples and allow them to participate in the free market, they will never willingly let go of the wealth and power they generated through colonial exploitation. As such, argues Fanon, the only true decolonization is one achieved through violent struggle and seizure of resources. For Fanon, this is the only violence that is legitimately moral.

7.2 Thucydides (c. 460–c. 400 BCE)

Thucydides was an Athenian historian and general who is most famous for his history of the Peloponnesian War, from which this excerpt is taken. Unlike other historians of the time, Thucydides did not attribute historical events to the Gods. Rather, he claimed to deploy strict standards of objectivity, impartiality, and evidence-gathering in his research. As such, he is sometimes named as the first to use scientific reasoning in the writing of history. Thucydides is also famous for the thesis that international relations are always decided by self-interested calculation. Whether it is called realpolitik or political realism, this argument suggests that references to morality hold at best an ideological function in the realm of international politics and that ultimately the principle that might makes right will always triumph in relations between nation states.

The Mitylenian dialogue (from Book 3) pits the hawkish Cleon against the moderate Diodotus. Mitylene had been a client state under Athenian protection when war between Athens and Sparta erupted four years earlier (it ultimately lasted 29 years). In the fifth year, Mitylene (a city on the island of Lesbos) revolted and abandoned the Athenian cause. The Athenian general, Paches, successfully subdued the Mitylenians, but this put Athens in a dilemma: what to do with former allies who could no longer be trusted? Cleon argues successfully in the Athenian assembly that all of the Mitylenians must be dealt with severely: it is imperative of imperial power that they not exercise leniency. Diodotus argues that Athens must target its response to the crisis by punishing only the leaders of the revolt. The event is quite dramatic, because a contingent had been dispatched by ship to Mitylene the day before with orders to kill all of the males and enslave the female population. When Diodotus manages to convince the assembly to change its mind, a second ship must overtake the first ship in time to prevent the execution of the original punishment. The Melian dialogue (from Book 5) takes place in the sixteenth year of the war. In it Athenian representatives present residents of the island of Melos with an ultimatum: either join the Athenian side or be destroyed. The Melians appeal to justice in an effort to retain some autonomy and negotiate terms that will keep them independent of the hostilities. The Athenian arguments exemplify realpolitik in its essence: we are more powerful, they maintain, and therefore we dictate all the terms.

While the strategies deployed by the Athenians in the course of the Peloponnesian War conform very nicely to the amoral advice on how to gain and retain power offered by Machiavelli in the previous chapter, the notion of suspending one's moral reasoning, especially in matters that concern the interests of one's nation state, are more at home here. In the Athenians' refusal to think of the Mitylenians and Melians in moral terms, facilitating their brutally violent repression, one should read a foreshadowing of Arendt's and Zimbardo's arguments about how ordinary people can be encouraged by social circumstances to suspend their moral reasoning and commit acts they would otherwise experience as evil. Moreover, Diodotus's argument in the first excerpt—the only Athenian who argues in favour of mercy—is based on economic calculation rather than morality, foreshadowing Fanon's argument that oppressive colonial powers will only grant a subject population's political 'independence' if they can guarantee continued dominance in some other fashion.

from The Peloponnesian War *(Melian and Mitylenian Dialogues)*

Book 3—The Mitylenian Dialogue

Arrived at Mitylene, Paches reduced Pyrrha and Eresus; and finding the Lacedaemonian, Salaethus, in hiding in the town, sent him off to Athens, together with the Mitylenians that he had placed in Tenedos, and any other persons that he thought concerned in the revolt. He also sent back the greater part of his forces, remaining with the rest to settle Mitylene and the rest of Lesbos as he thought best.

Upon the arrival of the prisoners with Salaethus, the Athenians at once put the latter to death, although he offered, among other things, to procure the withdrawal of the Peloponnesians from Plataea, which was still under siege; and after deliberating as to what they should do with the former, in the fury of the moment determined to put to death not only the prisoners at Athens, but the whole adult male population of Mitylene, and to make slaves of the women and children. It was remarked that Mitylene had revolted without being, like the rest, subjected to the empire; and what above all swelled the wrath of the Athenians was the fact of the Peloponnesian fleet having ventured over to Ionia to her support, a fact which was held to argue a long-meditated rebellion. They accordingly sent a galley to communicate the decree to Paches, commanding him to lose no time in dispatching the Mitylenians. The morrow brought repentance with it and reflection on the horrid cruelty of a decree, which condemned a whole city to the fate merited only by the guilty. This was no sooner perceived by the Mitylenian ambassadors at Athens and their Athenian supporters, than they moved the authorities to put the question again to the vote; which they the more easily consented to do, as they themselves plainly saw that most of the citizens wished some one to give them an opportunity for reconsidering the matter. An assembly was therefore at once called, and after much expression of opinion upon both sides, Cleon, son of Cleaenetus, the same who had carried the former motion of putting the Mitylenians to death, the most violent man at Athens, and at that time by far the most powerful with the commons, came forward again and spoke as follows:

"I have often before now been convinced that a democracy is incapable of empire, and never more so than by your present change of mind in the matter of Mitylene. Fears or plots being unknown to you in your daily relations with each other, you feel just the same with regard to your allies, and never reflect that the mistakes into which you may be led by listening to their appeals, or by giving way to your own compassion, are full of danger to yourselves, and bring you no thanks for your weakness from your allies; entirely forgetting that your empire is a despotism and your subjects disaffected conspirators, whose obedience is ensured not by your suicidal concessions, but by the superiority given you by your own strength and not their loyalty. The most alarming feature in the case is the constant change of measures with which we appear to be threatened, and our seeming ignorance of the fact that bad laws which are never changed are better for a city than good ones that have no authority; that unlearned loyalty is more serviceable than quick-witted insubordination; and that ordinary men usually manage public affairs better than their more gifted fellows. The latter are always wanting to appear wiser than the laws, and to overrule every proposition brought forward, thinking that they cannot show their wit in more important matters, and by such behaviour too often ruin their country; while those who mistrust their own cleverness are content to be less learned than the laws, and less able to pick holes in the speech of a good speaker; and being fair judges rather than rival athletes, generally conduct affairs successfully. These we ought to imitate, instead of being led on by cleverness and intellectual rivalry to advise your people against our real opinions.

"For myself, I adhere to my former opinion, and wonder at those who have proposed to reopen the case of the Mitylenians, and who are thus causing a delay which is all in favour of the guilty, by making the sufferer proceed against the offender with the edge of his anger blunted; although where vengeance follows most closely upon the wrong, it best equals it and most amply requites it. I wonder also who will be the man who will maintain the contrary, and will pretend to show that the crimes of the Mitylenians are of service to us, and our misfortunes injurious to the allies. Such a man must plainly either have such confidence in his rhetoric as to adventure to prove that what has been once for all decided is still undetermined, or be bribed to try to delude us by elaborate sophisms. In such contests the state gives the rewards to others, and takes the dangers for herself. The persons to blame are you who are so foolish as to institute these contests; who go to see an oration as you would to see a sight, take your facts on hearsay, judge of the practicability of a project by the wit of its advocates, and trust for the truth as to past events not to the fact which you saw more than to the clever strictures which you heard; the easy victims of new-fangled arguments, unwilling to follow received conclusions; slaves to every new paradox, despisers of the commonplace; the first wish of every man being that he could speak himself, the next to rival those who can speak by seeming to be quite up with their ideas by applauding every hit almost before it is made, and by being as quick in catching an argument as you are slow in foreseeing its consequences; asking, if I may so say, for something different from the conditions under which we live, and yet comprehending inadequately those very conditions; very slaves to the pleasure of the ear, and more like the audience of a rhetorician than the council of a city.

"In order to keep you from this, I proceed to show that no one state has ever injured you as much as Mitylene. I can make allowance for those who revolt because they cannot bear our empire, or who have been forced to do so by the enemy. But for those who possessed an island with fortifications; who could fear our enemies only by sea, and there had their own force of galleys to protect them; who were independent and held in the highest honour by you—to act as these have done, this is not revolt—revolt implies oppression; it is deliberate and wanton aggression; an attempt to ruin us by siding with our bitterest enemies; a worse offence than a war undertaken on their own account in the acquisition of power. The fate of those of their neighbours who had already rebelled and had been subdued was no lesson to them; their own prosperity could not dissuade them from affronting danger; but blindly confident in the future, and full of hopes beyond their power though not beyond their ambition, they declared war and made their decision to prefer might to right, their attack being determined not by provocation but by the moment which seemed propitious. The truth is that great good fortune coming suddenly and unexpectedly tends to make a people insolent; in most cases it is safer for mankind to have success in reason than out of reason; and it is easier for them, one may say, to stave off adversity than to preserve prosperity. Our mistake has been to distinguish the Mitylenians as we have done: had they been long ago treated like the rest, they never would have so far forgotten themselves, human nature being as surely made arrogant by consideration as it is awed by firmness. Let them now therefore be punished as their crime requires, and do not, while you condemn the aristocracy, absolve the people. This is certain, that all attacked you without distinction, although they might have come over to us and been now again in possession of their city. But no, they thought it safer to throw in their lot with the aristocracy and so joined their rebellion! Consider therefore: if you subject to the same punishment the ally who is forced to rebel by the enemy, and him who does so by his own free choice, which of them, think you, is there that will not rebel upon the slightest pretext; when the reward of success is freedom, and the penalty of failure nothing so very terrible? We meanwhile shall have to risk our money and our lives against one state after another; and if successful, shall receive a ruined town from which we can no longer draw the revenue upon which our strength depends; while if unsuccessful, we shall have an enemy the more upon our hands, and shall spend the time that might be employed in combating our existing foes in warring with our own allies.

"No hope, therefore, that rhetoric may instil or money purchase, of the mercy due to human infirmity must be held out to the Mitylenians. Their offence was not involuntary, but of malice and deliberate; and mercy is only for unwilling offenders. I therefore, now as before, persist against your reversing your first decision, or giving way to the three failings most fatal to empire—pity, sentiment, and indulgence. Compassion is due to those who can reciprocate the feeling, not to those who will never pity us in return, but are our natural and necessary foes: the orators who charm us with sentiment may find other less important arenas for their talents, in the place of one where the city pays a heavy penalty for a momentary pleasure, themselves receiving fine acknowledgments for their fine phrases; while indulgence should be shown towards those who will be our friends in future, instead of towards men who will remain just what they were, and as much our enemies as before. To sum up shortly, I say that if you follow my advice you will do what is just towards the Mitylenians, and at the same time expedient; while by a different decision you will not oblige them so much as pass sentence upon yourselves. For if they were right in rebelling, you must be wrong in ruling. However, if, right or wrong, you determine to rule, you must carry out your principle and punish the Mitylenians as your interest requires; or else you must give up your empire and cultivate honesty without danger. Make up your minds, therefore, to give them like for like; and do not let the victims who escaped the plot be more insensible than the conspirators who hatched it; but reflect what they would have done if victorious over you, especially as they were the aggressors. It is they who wrong their neighbour without a cause, that pursue their victim to the death, on account of the danger which they foresee in letting their enemy survive; since the object of a wanton wrong is more dangerous, if he escape, than an enemy who has not this to complain of. Do not, therefore, be traitors to yourselves, but recall as nearly as possible the moment of suffering and the supreme importance which you then attached to their reduction; and now pay them back in their turn, without yielding to present weakness or forgetting the peril that once hung over you. Punish them as they deserve, and teach your other allies by a striking example that the penalty of rebellion is death. Let them once understand this and you will not have so often to neglect your enemies while you are fighting with your own confederates."

Such were the words of Cleon. After him Diodotus, son of Eucrates, who had also in the previous assembly spoken most strongly against putting the Mitylenians to death, came forward and spoke as follows:

"I do not blame the persons who have reopened the case of the Mitylenians, nor do I approve the protests which we have heard against important questions being frequently debated. I think the two things most opposed to good counsel are haste and passion; haste usually goes hand in hand with folly, passion with coarseness and narrowness of mind. As for the argument that speech ought not to be the exponent of action, the man who uses it must be either senseless or interested: senseless if he believes it possible to treat of the uncertain future through any other medium; interested if, wishing to carry a disgraceful measure and doubting his ability to speak well in a bad cause, he thinks to frighten opponents and hearers by well-aimed calumny. What is still more intolerable is to accuse a speaker of making a display in order to be paid for it. If ignorance only were imputed, an unsuccessful speaker might retire with a reputation for honesty, if not for wisdom; while the charge of dishonesty makes him suspected, if successful, and thought, if defeated, not only a fool but a rogue. The city is no gainer by such a system, since fear deprives it of its advisers; although in truth, if our speakers are to make such assertions, it would be better for the country if they could not speak at all, as we should then make fewer blunders. The good citizen ought to triumph not by frightening his opponents but by beating them fairly in argument; and a wise city, without over-distinguishing its best advisers, will nevertheless not deprive them of their due, and, far from punishing an unlucky counsellor, will not even regard him as disgraced. In this way successful orators would be least tempted to sacrifice their convictions to popularity, in the hope of still higher honours, and unsuccessful speakers to resort to the same popular arts in order to win over the multitude.

"This is not our way; and, besides, the moment that a man is suspected of giving advice, however good, from corrupt motives, we feel such a grudge against him for the gain which after all we are not certain he will receive, that we deprive the city of its certain benefit. Plain good advice has thus come to be no less suspected than bad; and the advocate of the most monstrous measures is not more obliged to use deceit to gain the people, than the best counsellor is to lie in order to be believed. The city and the city only, owing to these refinements, can never be served openly and without disguise; he who does serve it openly being always suspected of serving himself in some secret way in return. Still, considering the magnitude of the interests involved, and the position of affairs, we orators must make it our business to look a little farther than you who judge offhand; especially as we, your advisers, are responsible, while you, our audience, are not so. For if those who gave the advice, and those who took it, suffered equally, you would judge more calmly; as it is, you visit the disasters into which the whim of the moment may have led you upon the single person of your adviser, not upon yourselves, his numerous companions in error.

"However, I have not come forward either to oppose or to accuse in the matter of Mitylene; indeed, the question before us as sensible men is not their guilt, but our interests. Though I prove them ever so guilty, I shall not, therefore, advise their death, unless it be expedient; nor though they should have claims to indulgence, shall I recommend it, unless it be clearly for the good of the country. I consider that we are deliberating for the future more than for the present; and where Cleon is so positive as to the useful deterrent effects that will follow from making rebellion capital, I, who consider the interests of the future quite as much as he, as positively maintain the contrary. And I require you not to reject my useful considerations for his specious ones: his speech may have the attraction of seeming the more just in your present temper against Mitylene; but we are not in a court of justice, but in a political assembly; and the question is not justice, but how to make the Mitylenians useful to Athens.

"Now of course communities have enacted the penalty of death for many offences far lighter than this: still hope leads men to venture, and no one ever yet put himself in peril without the inward conviction that he would succeed in his design. Again, was there ever city rebelling that did not believe that it possessed either in itself or in its alliances resources adequate to the enterprise? All, states and individuals, are alike prone to err, and there is no law that will prevent them; or why should men have exhausted the list of punishments in search of enactments to protect them from evildoers? It is probable that in early times the penalties for the greatest offences were less severe, and that, as these were disregarded, the penalty of death has been by degrees in most cases arrived at, which is itself disregarded in like manner. Either then some means of terror more terrible than this must be discovered, or it must be owned that this restraint is useless; and that as long as poverty gives men the courage of necessity, or plenty fills them with the ambition which belongs to insolence and pride, and the other conditions of life remain each under the thraldom of some fatal and master passion, so long will the impulse never be wanting to drive men into danger. Hope also and cupidity, the one leading and the other following, the one conceiving the attempt, the other suggesting the facility of succeeding, cause the widest ruin, and, although invisible agents, are far stronger than the dangers that are seen. Fortune, too, powerfully helps the delusion and, by the unexpected aid that she sometimes lends, tempts men to venture with inferior means; and this is especially the case with communities, because the stakes played for are the highest, freedom or empire, and, when all are acting together, each man irrationally magnifies his own capacity. In fine, it is impossible to prevent, and only great simplicity can hope to prevent, human nature doing what it has once set its mind upon, by force of law or by any other deterrent force whatsoever.

"We must not, therefore, commit ourselves to a false policy through a belief in the efficacy of the punishment of death, or exclude rebels from the hope of repentance and an early atonement of their error. Consider a moment. At present, if a city that has already revolted perceive that it cannot succeed, it will come to terms while it is still able to refund expenses, and pay tribute afterwards. In the other case, what city, think you, would not prepare better than is now done, and hold out to the last against its besiegers, if it is all one whether it surrender late or soon? And how can it be otherwise than hurtful to us to be put to the expense of a siege, because surrender is out of the question; and if we take the city, to receive a ruined town from which we can no longer draw the revenue which forms our real strength against the enemy? We must not, therefore, sit as strict judges of the offenders to our own prejudice, but rather see how by moderate chastisements we may be enabled to benefit in future by the revenue-producing powers of our dependencies; and we must make up our minds to look for our protection not to legal terrors but to careful administration. At present we do exactly the opposite. When a free community, held in subjection by force, rises, as is only natural, and asserts its independence, it is no sooner reduced than we fancy ourselves obliged to punish it severely; although the right course with freemen is not to chastise them rigorously when they do rise, but rigorously to watch them before they rise, and to prevent their ever entertaining the idea, and, the insurrection suppressed, to make as few responsible for it as possible.

"Only consider what a blunder you would commit in doing as Cleon recommends. As things are at present, in all the cities the people is your friend, and either does not revolt with the oligarchy, or, if forced to do so, becomes at once the enemy of the insurgents; so that in the war with the hostile city you have the masses on your side. But if you butcher the people of Mitylene, who had nothing to do with the revolt, and who, as soon as they got arms, of their own motion surrendered the town, first you will commit the crime of killing your benefactors; and next you will play directly into the hands of the higher classes, who when they induce their cities to rise, will immediately have the people on their side, through your having announced in advance the same punishment for those who are guilty and for those who are not. On the contrary, even if they were guilty, you ought to seem not to notice it, in order to avoid alienating the only class still friendly to us. In short, I consider it far more useful for the preservation of our empire voluntarily to put up with injustice, than to put to death, however justly, those whom it is our interest to keep alive. As for Cleon's idea that in punishment the claims of justice and expediency can both be satisfied, facts do not confirm the possibility of such a combination.

"Confess, therefore, that this is the wisest course, and without conceding too much either to pity or to indulgence, by neither of which motives do I any more than Cleon wish you to be influenced, upon the plain merits of the case before you, be persuaded by me to try calmly those of the Mitylenians whom Paches sent off as guilty, and to leave the rest undisturbed. This is at once best for the future, and most terrible to your enemies at the present moment; inasmuch as good policy against an adversary is superior to the blind attacks of brute force."

Such were the words of Diodotus. The two opinions thus expressed were the ones that most directly contradicted each other; and the Athenians, notwithstanding their change of feeling, now proceeded to a division, in which the show of hands was almost equal, although the motion of Diodotus carried the day. Another galley was at once sent off in haste, for fear that the first might reach Lesbos in the interval, and the city be found destroyed; the first ship having about a day and a night's start. Wine and barley-cakes were provided for the vessel by the Mitylenian ambassadors, and great promises made if they arrived in time; which caused the men to use such diligence upon the voyage that they took their meals of barley-cakes kneaded with oil and wine as they rowed, and only slept by turns while the others were at the oar. Luckily they met with no contrary wind, and the first ship making no haste upon so horrid an errand, while the second pressed on in the manner described, the first arrived so little before them, that Paches had only just had time to read the decree, and to prepare to execute the sentence, when the second put into port and prevented the massacre. The danger of Mitylene had indeed been great.

The other party whom Paches had sent off as the prime movers in the rebellion, were upon Cleon's motion put to death by the Athenians, the number being rather more than a thousand. The Athenians also demolished the walls of the Mitylenians, and took possession of their ships. Afterwards tribute was not imposed upon the Lesbians; but all their land, except that of the Methymnians, was divided into three thousand allotments, three hundred of which were reserved as sacred for the gods, and the rest assigned by lot to Athenian shareholders, who were sent out to the island. With these the Lesbians agreed to pay a rent of two minae a year for each allotment, and cultivated the land themselves. The Athenians also took possession of the towns on the continent belonging to the Mitylenians, which thus became for the future subject to Athens. Such were the events that took place at Lesbos.

Book 5—The Melian Dialogue

The next summer Alcibiades sailed with twenty ships to Argos and seized the suspected persons still left of the Lacedaemonian faction to the number of three hundred, whom the Athenians forthwith lodged in the neighbouring islands of their empire. The Athenians also made an expedition against the isle of Melos with thirty ships of their own, six Chian, and two Lesbian vessels, sixteen hundred heavy infantry, three hundred archers, and twenty mounted archers from Athens, and about fifteen hundred heavy infantry from the allies and the islanders. The Melians are a colony of Lacedaemon that would not submit to the Athenians like the other islanders, and at first remained neutral and took no part in the struggle, but afterwards upon the Athenians using violence and plundering their territory, assumed an attitude of open hostility. Cleomedes, son of Lycomedes, and Tisias, son of Tisimachus, the generals, encamping in their territory with the above armament, before doing any harm to their land, sent envoys to negotiate. These the Melians did not bring before the people, but bade them state the object of their mission to the magistrates and the few; upon which the Athenian envoys spoke as follows:

Athenians. Since the negotiations are not to go on before the people, in order that we may not be able to speak straight on without interruption, and deceive the ears of the multitude by seductive arguments which would pass without refutation (for we know that this is the meaning of our being brought before the few), what if you who sit there were to pursue a method more cautious still? Make no set speech yourselves, but take us up at whatever you do not like, and settle that before going any farther. And first tell us if this proposition of ours suits you.

The Melian commissioners answered:

Melians. To the fairness of quietly instructing each other as you propose there is nothing to object; but your military preparations are too far advanced to agree with what you say, as we see you are come to be judges in your own cause, and that all we can reasonably expect from this negotiation is war, if we prove to have right on our side and refuse to submit, and in the contrary case, slavery.

Athenians. If you have met to reason about presentiments of the future, or for anything else than to consult for the safety of your state upon the facts that you see before you, we will give over; otherwise we will go on.

Melians. It is natural and excusable for men in our position to turn more ways than one both in thought and utterance. However, the question in this conference is, as you say, the safety of our country; and the discussion, if you please, can proceed in the way which you propose.

Athenians. For ourselves, we shall not trouble you with specious pretences—either of how we have a right to our empire because we overthrew the Mede, or are now attacking you because of wrong that you have done us—and make a long speech which would not be believed; and in return we hope that you, instead of thinking to influence us by saying that you did not join the Lacedaemonians, although their colonists, or that you have done us no wrong, will aim at what is feasible, holding in view the real sentiments of us both; since you know as well as we do that right, as the world goes, is only in question between equals in power, while the strong do what they can and the weak suffer what they must.

Melians. As we think, at any rate, it is expedient—we speak as we are obliged, since you enjoin us to let right alone and talk only of interest—that you should not destroy what is our common protection, the privilege of being allowed in danger to invoke what is fair and right, and even to profit by arguments not strictly valid if they can be got to pass current. And you are as much interested in this as any, as your fall would be a signal for the heaviest vengeance and an example for the world to meditate upon.

Athenians. The end of our empire, if end it should, does not frighten us: a rival empire like Lacedaemon, even if Lacedaemon was our real antagonist, is not so terrible to the vanquished as subjects who by themselves attack and overpower their rulers. This, however, is a risk that we are content to take. We will now proceed to show you that we are come here in the interest of our empire, and that we shall say what we are now going to say, for the preservation of your country; as we would fain exercise that empire over you without trouble, and see you preserved for the good of us both.

Melians. And how, pray, could it turn out as good for us to serve as for you to rule?

Athenians. Because you would have the advantage of submitting before suffering the worst, and we should gain by not destroying you.

Melians. So that you would not consent to our being neutral, friends instead of enemies, but allies of neither side.

Athenians. No; for your hostility cannot so much hurt us as your friendship will be an argument to our subjects of our weakness, and your enmity of our power.

Melians. Is that your subjects' idea of equity, to put those who have nothing to do with you in the same category with peoples that are most of them your own colonists, and some conquered rebels?

Athenians. As far as right goes they think one has as much of it as the other, and that if any maintain their independence it is because they are strong, and that if we do not molest them it is because we are afraid; so that besides extending our empire we should gain in security by your subjection; the fact that you are islanders and weaker than others rendering it all the more important that you should not succeed in baffling the masters of the sea.

Melians. But do you consider that there is no security in the policy which we indicate? For here again if you debar us from talking about justice and invite us to obey your interest, we also must explain ours, and try to persuade you, if the two happen to coincide. How can you avoid making enemies of all existing neutrals who shall look at our case from it that one day or another you will attack them? And what is this but to make greater the enemies that you have already, and to force others to become so who would otherwise have never thought of it?

Athenians. Why, the fact is that continentals generally give us but little alarm; the liberty which they enjoy will long prevent their taking precautions against us; it is rather islanders like yourselves, outside our empire, and subjects smarting under the yoke, who would be the most likely to take a rash step and lead themselves and us into obvious danger.

Melians. Well then, if you risk so much to retain your empire, and your subjects to get rid of it, it were surely great baseness and cowardice in us who are still free not to try everything that can be tried, before submitting to your yoke.

Athenians. Not if you are well advised, the contest not being an equal one, with honour as the prize and shame as the penalty, but a question of self-preservation and of not resisting those who are far stronger than you are.

Melians. But we know that the fortune of war is sometimes more impartial than the disproportion of numbers might lead one to suppose; to submit is to give ourselves over to despair, while action still preserves for us a hope that we may stand erect.

Athenians. Hope, danger's comforter, may be indulged in by those who have abundant resources, if not without loss at all events without ruin; but its nature is to be extravagant, and those who go so far as to put their all upon the venture see it in its true colours only when they are ruined; but so long as the discovery would enable them to guard against it, it is never found wanting. Let not this be the case with you, who are weak and hang on a single turn of the scale; nor be like the vulgar, who, abandoning such security as human means may still afford, when visible hopes fail them in extremity, turn to invisible, to prophecies and oracles, and other such inventions that delude men with hopes to their destruction.

Melians. You may be sure that we are as well aware as you of the difficulty of contending against your power and fortune, unless the terms be equal. But we trust that the gods may grant us fortune as good as yours, since we are just men fighting against unjust, and that what we want in power will be made up by the alliance of the Lacedaemonians, who are bound, if only for very shame, to come to the aid of their kindred. Our confidence, therefore, after all is not so utterly irrational.

Athenians. When you speak of the favour of the gods, we may as fairly hope for that as yourselves; neither our pretensions nor our conduct being in any way contrary to what men believe of the gods, or practise among themselves. Of the gods we believe, and of men we know, that by a necessary law of their nature they rule wherever they can. And it is not as if we were the first to make this law, or to act upon it when made: we found it existing before us, and shall leave it to exist for ever after us; all we do is to make use of it, knowing that you and everybody else, having the same power as we have, would do the same as we do. Thus, as far as the gods are concerned, we have no fear and no reason to fear that we shall be at a disadvantage. But when we come to your notion about the Lacedaemonians, which leads you to believe that shame will make them help you, here we bless your simplicity but do not envy your folly. The Lacedaemonians, when their own interests or their country's laws are in question, are the worthiest men alive; of their conduct towards others much might be said, but no clearer idea of it could be given than by shortly saying that of all the men we know they are most conspicuous in considering what is agreeable honourable, and what is expedient just. Such a way of thinking does not promise much for the safety which you now unreasonably count upon.

Melians. But it is for this very reason that we now trust to their respect for expediency to prevent them from betraying the Melians, their colonists, and thereby losing the confidence of their friends in Hellas and helping their enemies.

Athenians. Then you do not adopt the view that expediency goes with security, while justice and honour cannot be followed without danger; and danger the Lacedaemonians generally court as little as possible.

Melians. But we believe that they would be more likely to face even danger for our sake, and with more confidence than for others, as our nearness to Peloponnese makes it easier for them to act, and our common blood ensures our fidelity.

Athenians. Yes, but what an intending ally trusts to is not the goodwill of those who ask his aid, but a decided superiority of power for action; and the Lacedaemonians look to this even more than others. At least, such is their distrust of their home resources that it is only with numerous allies that they attack a neighbour; now is it likely that while we are masters of the sea they will cross over to an island?

Melians. But they would have others to send. The Cretan Sea is a wide one, and it is more difficult for those who command it to intercept others, than for those who wish to elude them to do so safely. And should the Lacedaemonians miscarry in this, they would fall upon your land, and upon those left of your allies whom Brasidas did not reach; and instead of places which are not yours, you will have to fight for your own country and your own confederacy.

Athenians. Some diversion of the kind you speak of you may one day experience, only to learn, as others have done, that the Athenians never once yet withdrew from a siege for fear of any. But we are struck by the fact that, after saying you would consult for the safety of your country, in all this discussion you have mentioned nothing which men might trust in and think to be saved by. Your strongest arguments depend upon hope and the future, and your actual resources are too scanty, as compared with those arrayed against you, for you to come out victorious. You will therefore show great blindness of judgment, unless, after allowing us to retire, you can find some counsel more prudent than this. You will surely not be caught by that idea of disgrace, which in dangers that are disgraceful, and at the same time too plain to be mistaken, proves so fatal to mankind; since in too many cases the very men that have their eyes perfectly open to what they are rushing into, let the thing called disgrace, by the mere influence of a seductive name, lead them on to a point at which they become so enslaved by the phrase as in fact to fall wilfully into hopeless disaster, and incur disgrace more disgraceful as the companion of error, than when it comes as the result of misfortune. This, if you are well advised, you will guard against; and you will not think it dishonourable to submit to the greatest city in Hellas, when it makes you the moderate offer of becoming its tributary ally, without ceasing to enjoy the country that belongs to you; nor when you have the choice given you between war and security, will you be so blinded as to choose the worse. And it is certain that those who do not yield to their equals, who keep terms with their superiors, and are moderate towards their inferiors, on the whole succeed best. Think over the matter, therefore, after our withdrawal, and reflect once and again that it is for your country that you are consulting, that you have not more than one, and that upon this one deliberation depends its prosperity or ruin.

The Athenians now withdrew from the conference; and the Melians, left to themselves, came to a decision corresponding with what they had maintained in the discussion, and answered: "Our resolution, Athenians, is the same as it was at first. We will not in a moment deprive of freedom a city that has been inhabited these seven hundred years; but we put our trust in the fortune by which the gods have preserved it until now, and in the help of men, that is, of the Lacedaemonians; and so we will try and save ourselves. Meanwhile we invite you to allow us to be friends to you and foes to neither party, and to retire from our country after making such a treaty as shall seem fit to us both."

Such was the answer of the Melians. The Athenians now departing from the conference said: "Well, you alone, as it seems to us, judging from these resolutions, regard what is future as more certain than what is before your eyes, and what is out of sight, in your eagerness, as already coming to pass; and as you have staked most on, and trusted most in, the Lacedaemonians, your fortune, and your hopes, so will you be most completely deceived."

The Athenian envoys now returned to the army; and the Melians showing no signs of yielding, the generals at once betook themselves to hostilities, and drew a line of circumvallation round the Melians, dividing the work among the different states. Subsequently the Athenians returned with most of their army, leaving behind them a certain number of their own citizens and of the allies to keep guard by land and sea. The force thus left stayed on and besieged the place.

About the same time the Argives invaded the territory of Phlius and lost eighty men cut off in an ambush by the Phliasians and Argive exiles. Meanwhile the Athenians at Pylos took so much plunder from the Lacedaemonians that the latter, although they still refrained from breaking off the treaty and going to war with Athens, yet proclaimed that any of their people that chose might plunder the Athenians. The Corinthians also commenced hostilities with the Athenians for private quarrels of their own; but the rest of the Peloponnesians stayed quiet. Meanwhile the Melians attacked by night and took the part of the Athenian lines over against the market, and killed some of the men, and brought in corn and all else that they could find useful to them, and so returned and kept quiet, while the Athenians took measures to keep better guard in future.

Summer was now over. The next winter the Lacedaemonians intended to invade the Argive territory, but arriving at the frontier found the sacrifices for crossing unfavourable, and went back again. This intention of theirs gave the Argives suspicions of certain of their fellow citizens, some of whom they arrested; others, however, escaped them. About the same time the Melians again took another part of the Athenian lines which were but feebly garrisoned. Reinforcements afterwards arriving from Athens in consequence, under the command of Philocrates, son of Demeas, the siege was now pressed vigorously; and some treachery taking place inside, the Melians surrendered at discretion to the Athenians, who put to death all the grown men whom they took, and sold the women and children for slaves, and subsequently sent out five hundred colonists and inhabited the place themselves.

7.3 St. Thomas Aquinas (1225–1274)

St. Thomas Aquinas is an enormously influential philosopher and theologian in the Western tradition. Writing in the Mediaeval era, Aquinas argued that reason was compatible with Christian religion. In this sense, Aquinas laid the groundwork for much of the Western Enlightenment tradition, which insisted on rationality as the basis of right thinking, but usually stopped short of directly challenging Christian dogma. Aquinas drew on the work of Aristotle in developing his philosophy, foreshadowing the links drawn by Renaissance and Enlightenment thought between the emerging modern principles of scientific reason and democratic inclusion, and the Classical European traditions of ancient Greece and Rome. Aquinas's moral philosophy is grounded in first principles drawn from both Christian theology and his notion of natural reason. In this text he famously attempts to deduce from these principles the criteria for a just war.

Interestingly, Aquinas begins his argument for the possibility of just war with the notion that all war is sinful and unlawful. In spite of this, he argues that war can indeed be just if the following three conditions are met: First, that war only be declared by a sovereign rather than private individuals; second, that the enemy against whom the war is waged must in some sense deserve it, i.e., must themselves be guilty of some sin that deserves redemption; and third, that the intent of the aggressor must be good, that war be pursued only in order to produce peace. Many of these reflexive notions of just violence remain with us to this day: the notion that the state should maintain a monopoly on the use of violence, precisely in order to prevent violence among private citizens; the notion of violence committed in self-defence as structurally different from any other form of violence; and the notion of war waged to secure peace, or "peacekeeping" as it has been called in recent decades.

In this chapter, these basic components of the legitimization of state-based violence come under critique from a variety of directions: Arendt and Zimbardo expose the ways in which obedience to the state, the logic of self-defence, and the demonization of the enemy can all serve as ideological screens to allow individuals to commit acts of violence that are categorically evil; Freud will argue that society directs violence towards scapegoats and other socially acceptable targets, not because doing so is morally justified, but simply because this is a way of warding off social collapse; Fanon and will argue that this kind of logic explains how European colonial powers have historically been able to ignore their own violence while accusing resistant native populations of being barbaric and irrationally violent. As such, Aquinas's argument makes an excellent baseline against which to measure the various critiques that make up the bulk of this chapter.

Summa Theologiae, *Question 40. War: Is Some Kind of War Lawful?*

Whether It Is Always Sinful to Wage War?

Objection 1: It would seem that it is always sinful to wage war. Because punishment is not inflicted except for sin. Now those who wage war are threatened by Our Lord with punishment, according to Matt. 26:52: "All that take the sword shall perish with the sword." Therefore all wars are unlawful.

Obj. 2: Further, whatever is contrary to a Divine precept is a sin. But war is contrary to a Divine precept, for it is written (Matt. 5:39): "But I say to you not to resist evil"; and (Rom. 12:19): "Not revenging yourselves, my dearly beloved, but give place unto wrath." Therefore war is always sinful.

Obj. 3: Further, nothing, except sin, is contrary to an act of virtue. But war is contrary to peace. Therefore war is always a sin.

Obj. 4: Further, the exercise of a lawful thing is itself lawful, as is evident in scientific exercises. But warlike exercises which take place in tournaments are forbidden by the Church, since those who are slain in these trials are deprived of ecclesiastical burial. Therefore it seems that war is a sin in itself.

On the contrary, Augustine says in a sermon on the son of the centurion [**Ep. ad Marcel.* cxxxviii]: "If the Christian Religion forbade war altogether, those who sought salutary advice in the Gospel would rather have been counselled to cast aside their arms, and to give up soldiering altogether. *On the contrary*, they were told: 'Do violence to no man ... and be content with your pay' [*Luke 3:14]. If he commanded them to be content with their pay, he did not forbid soldiering."

I answer that, In order for a war to be just, three things are necessary. First, the authority of the sovereign by whose command the war is to be waged. For it is not the business of a private individual to declare war, because he can seek for redress of his rights from the tribunal of his superior. Moreover it is not the business of a private individual to summon together the people, which has to be done in wartime. And as the care of the common weal is committed to those who are in authority, it is their business to watch over the common weal of the city, kingdom or province subject to them. And just as it is lawful for them to have recourse to the sword in defending that common weal against internal disturbances, when they punish evil-doers, according to the words of the Apostle (Rom. 13:4): "He beareth not the sword in vain: for he is God's minister, an avenger to execute wrath upon him that doth evil"; so too, it is their business to have recourse to the sword of war in defending the common weal against external enemies. Hence it is said to those who are in authority (Ps. 81:4): "Rescue the poor: and deliver the needy out of the hand of the sinner"; and for this reason Augustine says (*Contra Faust.* xxii, 75): "The natural order conducive to peace among mortals demands that the power to declare and counsel war should be in the hands of those who hold the supreme authority."

Secondly, a just cause is required, namely that those who are attacked, should be attacked because they deserve it on account of some fault. Wherefore Augustine says (QQ. in *Hept.*, qu. x, super Jos.): "A just war is wont to be described as one that avenges wrongs, when a nation or state has to be punished, for refusing to make amends for the wrongs inflicted by its subjects, or to restore what it has seized unjustly."

Thirdly, it is necessary that the belligerents should have a rightful intention, so that they intend the advancement of good, or the avoidance of evil. Hence Augustine says (*De Verb. Dom.* [*The words quoted are to be found not in St. Augustine's works, but *Can. Apud. Caus.* xxiii, qu. 1]): "True religion looks upon as peaceful those wars that are waged not for motives of aggrandizement, or cruelty, but with the object of securing peace, of punishing evil-doers, and of uplifting the good." For it may happen that the war is declared by the legitimate authority, and for a just cause, and yet be rendered unlawful through a wicked intention. Hence Augustine says (*Contra Faust.* xxii, 74): "The passion for inflicting harm, the cruel thirst for vengeance, an unpacific and relentless spirit, the fever of revolt, the lust of power, and such like things, all these are rightly condemned in war."

Reply Obj. 1: As Augustine says (*Contra Faust.* xxii, 70): "To take the sword is to arm oneself in order to take the life of anyone, without the command or permission of superior or lawful authority." On the other hand, to have recourse to the sword (as a private person) by the authority of the sovereign or judge, or (as a public person) through zeal for justice, and by the authority, so to speak, of God, is not to "take the sword," but to use it as commissioned by another, wherefore it does not deserve punishment. And yet even those who make sinful use of the sword are not always slain with the sword, yet they always perish with their own sword, because, unless they repent, they are punished eternally for their sinful use of the sword.

Reply Obj. 2: Such like precepts, as Augustine observes (*De Serm. Dom. in Monte* i, 19), should always be borne in readiness of mind, so that we be ready to obey them, and, if necessary, to refrain from resistance or self-defense. Nevertheless it is necessary sometimes for a man to act otherwise for the common good, or for the good of those with whom he is fighting. Hence Augustine says (*Ep. Ad Marcellin.* cxxxviii): "Those whom we have to punish with a kindly severity, it is necessary to handle in many ways against their will. For when we are stripping a man of the lawlessness of sin, it is good for him to be vanquished, since nothing is more hopeless than the happiness of sinners, whence arises a guilty impunity, and an evil will, like an internal enemy."

Reply Obj. 3: Those who wage war justly aim at peace, and so they are not opposed to peace, except to the evil peace, which Our Lord "came not to send upon earth" (Matt. 10:34). Hence Augustine says (*Ep. Ad Bonif.* clxxxix): "We do not seek peace in order to be at war, but we go to war that we may have peace. Be peaceful, therefore, in warring, so that you may vanquish those whom you war against, and bring them to the prosperity of peace."

Reply Obj. 4: Manly exercises in warlike feats of arms are not all forbidden, but those which are inordinate and perilous, and end in slaying or plundering. In olden times warlike exercises presented no such danger, and hence they were called "exercises of arms" or "bloodless wars," as Jerome states in an epistle [*Reference incorrect: cf. *Veget., De Re Milit.* i].

7.4 Friedrich Nietzsche (1844–1900)

Nietzsche, a German-born philosopher who began his career in philology, is widely understood to be one of the most important minds in modern Western thought. Nietzsche is famous in part because his ideas explicitly attacked and rejected the prevailing beliefs and sentiments of German society at the time. Among other things, he attacked both Christianity and Judaism, along with the prevailing ethical philosophies of the day: Kantianism and utilitarianism. Nietzsche rejected mainstream moral standards, which valued selflessness and the good of the group in favour of his own, which valued individuality and self-expression. His work celebrates those with the strength to defy social constraints in favour of living according to their own desires and moral standards.

In *On the Genealogy of Morals*, Nietzsche researches the history of the concept of "the good" in order to ground an argument for what he sees as a resuscitation of a pre-modern moral system. He argues that while traditional nobles or Aristocrats used "good" to refer to things that were like themselves or in their own personal interest, the slaves and servile groups over whom they ruled have since taken control of society and redefined the word. Now, argues Nietzsche, "good" refers to anything that is not noble or aristocratic—humility, meekness, obedience, willingness to work for the good of others—while what once was good has been recast as evil—selfishness, narcissism, individuality, aggression. In the first excerpt below, Nietzsche tries to counteract this trend by setting up his own moral opposition between what he calls "noble morality" and "slave *ressentiment*." In the second excerpt he argues that the height of human development and achievement is what he calls "the animal who is allowed to promise," and he associates this ability to promise with the principles of noble morality.

Nietzsche has been a very controversial figure even to this day in part for the reasons mentioned above. But this has been heightened by an association between his thought and the anti-Semitic ideology of Nazism. In part this is because his sister, Elisabeth Förster-Nietzsche, who took control of his work when he suffered a mental collapse at age 44, was a vocal National Socialist and anti-Semite who used her access to her brother's work to spread her own political views. Nietzsche himself explicitly condemns modern anti-Semitism in *On the Genealogy of Morals* and even praises the Jewish people. At the same time, however, Nietzsche is very critical of the moral system he attributes to organized Judaism and, in the excerpt we have chosen, he makes clear that he blames part of what he sees as the corrupted state of modern European society on the influence of historical Judaism.

~

from On the Genealogy of Morals

First Essay
Good and Evil, Good and Bad

...

The judgment "good" does *not* originate from those to whom "goodness" was shown! On the contrary, it was the "good people" themselves, that is, the noble, powerful, higher-ranking, and higher-thinking people who felt and set themselves and their actions up as good, that is to say, of the first rank, in opposition to everything low, low-minded, common, and vulgar. From this *pathos of distance* they first arrogated to themselves the right to create values, to stamp out the names for values. What did they care about usefulness! Particularly in relation to such a hot pouring out of the highest rank-ordering, rank-setting judgments of value, the point of view which considers utility is as foreign and inappropriate as possible. Here the feeling has reached the very opposite of the low level of warmth which is a condition for that calculating shrewdness, that reckoning by utility—and not just for a moment, not for one exceptional hour, but permanently. The pathos of nobility and distance, as I mentioned, the lasting and dominating feeling, something total and fundamental, of a higher ruling nature in relation to a lower type, to a "beneath"—*that* is the origin of the opposition between "good" and "bad." (The right of the master to give names extends so far that we could permit ourselves to grasp the origin of language itself as an expression of the power of the rulers: they say "That *is* such and such"; they seal every object and event with a sound, and in the process, as it were, take possession of it.) Given this origin, the word "good" is from the start *in no way* necessarily tied up with "unegoistic" actions, as it is in the superstition of those genealogists of morality. Instead that occurs for the first time with the *decline* of aristocratic value judgments, when this entire contrast between "egoistic" and "unegoistic" presses itself ever more strongly into the human conscience—it is, to use my own words, the *instinct of the herd* which, through this contrast, finally gets its word (and its *words*)....

I was given a hint of the *right* direction by the following question: What, from an etymological perspective, do the meanings of "good," as manifested in different languages, really signify? There I found that all of them lead back to the *same transformation of ideas*—that everywhere "noble" and "aristocratic" in a social sense is the fundamental idea out of which "good" in the sense of "spiritually noble," "aristocratic," "spiritually high-minded," "spiritually privileged" necessarily develops, a process which always runs in parallel with that other one that finally transforms "common," "vulgar," and "low" into the concept "bad." The most eloquent example of the latter is the German word "*schlect [bad]*" itself, which is identical with the word "*schlicht [plain]*"—compare "*schlectweg [simply]*" and "*schlechterdings [simply]*"—and which originally designated the plain, common man, still without any suspicious side glance, simply in contrast to the noble man. Around the time of the Thirty Years War approximately, hence late enough, this sense changed into the one used now.[1] As far as the genealogy of morals is concerned, this point strikes me as a *fundamental* insight; that it was first discovered so late we can ascribe to the repressive influence which democratic prejudice in the modern world exercises concerning all questions of origin....

With respect to *our* problem—which for good reasons we can call a *quiet* problem and which addresses in a refined manner only a few ears—there is no little interest in establishing the point that often in those words and roots which designate "good" there still shines through the main nuance of what made the nobility feel they were men of higher rank. It's true

1 *Thirty Years War*: a prolonged, devastating, and inconclusive European war over religion (1618–48).

that in most cases they perhaps name themselves simply after their superiority in strength (as "the powerful," "the masters," "those in command") or after the most visible sign of this superiority, for example, as "the rich" or "the owners" (that is the meaning of *arya [noble]*, and the corresponding words in Iranian and Slavic). But they also name themselves after a *typical characteristic*, and this is the case which is our concern here. For instance, they call themselves "the truthful," above all the Greek nobility, whose mouthpiece is the Megarian poet Theogonis.[2] The word developed for this characteristic, ἐσθλος *[esthlos: fine, noble]*, indicates, according to its root meaning, a man who *is*, who possesses reality, who really exists, who is true. Then, with a subjective transformation, it indicates the true man as the truthful man. In this phase of conceptual transformation it becomes the slogan and catch phrase for the nobility, and its sense shifts entirely over to mean "aristocratic," to mark a distinction from the *lying* common man, as Theogonis takes and presents him—until finally, after the decline of the nobility, the word remains as a designation of spiritual *noblesse [nobility]* and becomes, as it were, ripe and sweet. In the word κακός *[kakos: weak, worthless]*, as in the word δειλός *[deilos: cowardly]* (the plebeian in contrast to the αγαθός *[agathos: good man]*), the cowardice is emphasized. This perhaps provides a hint about the direction in which we have to seek the etymological origin for the multiple meanings of αγαθός *[agathos: good]*. In the Latin word *malus [bad]* (which I place alongside μέλας *[melas: black, dark]*) the common man could be designated as the dark-coloured, above all as the dark-haired (*"hic niger est" ["this man is dark"]*), as the pre-Aryan inhabitant of Italian soil, who through this colour stood out most clearly from those who became dominant, the blonds, that is, the conquering races of Aryans. At any rate, Gaelic offers me an exactly corresponding example—the word *fin* (for example, in the name *Fin-Gal*), the term designating nobility and finally the good, noble, and pure, originally referred to the blond-headed man in contrast to the dusky, dark-haired original inhabitants. Incidentally, the Celts were a thoroughly blond race. People are wrong when they link those traces of a basically dark-haired population, which are noticeable on the carefully prepared ethnographic maps of Germany, with any Celtic origin and mixing of blood, as Virchow still does.[3] It is much rather the case that in these places the *pre-Aryan* population of Germany predominates. (The same is true for almost all of Europe: essentially the conquered races have finally attained the upper hand for themselves once again in colour, shortness of skull, perhaps even in the intellectual and social instincts. Who can confirm for us that modern democracy, the even more modern anarchism, and indeed that preference for the "Commune," for the most primitive form of society, which all European socialists now share, does not indicate for the most part a monstrous *throwback [Nachschlag]*—and that the conquering *master race*, the race of Aryans, is not being physiologically defeated, too?) The Latin word *bonus [good]* I believe I can explicate as "the warrior," provided that I am correct in tracing *bonus* back to an older word *duonus* (compare *bellum* [*war*] = duellum [*war*] = *duen-lum*, which seems to me to contain that word *duonus*). Hence, *bonus* as a man of war, of division (*duo [two]*), as a warrior. We see what constituted a man's "goodness" in ancient Rome....

You will have already guessed how easily the priestly way of evaluating can split from the knightly-aristocratic and then continue to develop into its opposite. Such a development receives a special stimulus every time the priestly caste and the warrior caste confront each other jealously and are not willing to agree amongst themselves about the reward. The knightly-aristocratic judgments of value have as their basic assumption a powerful physicality, a blooming, rich, even overflowing health, together with those things required to maintain these qualities—war, adventure, hunting, dancing, war games, and, in general,

2 *Theogonis*: a Greek poet from Megara in the sixth century BCE.
3 *Virchow*: Rudolf Virchow (1821–1902), German doctor and anthropologist.

everything which involves strong, free, and happy action. The priestly-noble method of evaluating has, as we saw, other preconditions: these make it difficult enough for them when it comes to war! As is well known, priests are the *most evil of enemies*—but why? Because they are the most powerless. From their powerlessness, their hate grows among them into something huge and terrifying, to the most spiritual and most poisonous manifestations. The really great haters in world history and also the cleverest haters have always been priests—in comparison with the spirit of priestly revenge all the remaining spirits are hardly worth considering at all. Human history would be a really stupid affair without the spirit that entered it from the powerless. Let us quickly consider the greatest example. Nothing on earth which has been done against "the nobility," "the powerful," "the masters," and "the possessors of power" is worth mentioning in comparison with what *the Jews* have done against them: the Jews, that priestly people, who knew how to get final satisfaction from their enemies and conquerors merely through a radical transformation of their values, that is, through an act of the *most spiritual revenge*. This was appropriate only to a priestly people with the most deeply suppressed priestly desire for revenge. In opposition to the aristocratic value equation (*good = noble = powerful = beautiful = fortunate = loved by god*), the Jews, with a consistency inspiring fear, dared to reverse things and to hang on to that with the teeth of the most profound hatred (the hate of powerlessness), that is, to "only those who suffer are good; the poor, the powerless, the low are the only good people; the suffering, those in need, the sick, the ugly are also the only pious people; only they are blessed by God; for them alone there is salvation.—By contrast, you privileged and powerful people, you are for all eternity the evil, the cruel, the lecherous, the insatiable, the godless; you will also be the unblessed, the cursed, and the damned for all eternity!" ... We know *who* inherited this Judaic transformation of values ... In connection with that huge and immeasurably disastrous initiative which the Jews launched with this most fundamental of all declarations of war, I recall the sentence I wrote at another time (in *Beyond Good and Evil*, page 118 *[Section 195]*)—namely, that with the Jews *the slave rebellion in morality* begins: that rebellion which has a two-thousand-year-old history behind it and which we nowadays no longer even notice because it—has triumphed.[4] ...

Jesus of Nazareth, the personified evangelist of love, this "Saviour" bringing holiness and victory to the poor, to the sick, to the sinners—was he not that very seduction in its most sinister and most irresistible form, the seduction and detour to exactly those *Judaic* values and innovations in ideals? Didn't Israel attain, precisely with the detour of this "Saviour," of this apparent enemy against and dissolver of Israel, the final goal of its sublime thirst for vengeance? Isn't it part of the secret black art of a truly *great* politics of revenge, a farsighted, underground, slowly expropriating, and premeditated revenge, that Israel itself had to disown and nail to the cross, like some mortal enemy, the tool essential to its revenge before all the world, so that "all the world," that is, all Israel's enemies, could then take this particular bait without a second thought? ...

—"But what are you doing still talking about *nobler* ideals! Let's follow the facts: the people have triumphed—or 'the slaves,' or 'the rabble,' or 'the herd,' or whatever you want to call them—if this has taken place because of the Jews, then good for them! No people ever had a more world-historical mission. 'The masters' have been disposed of. The morality of the common man has prevailed. We may also take this victory as a blood poisoning (it did mix the races up together)—I don't deny that. But this intoxication has undoubtedly *been successful*. The 'salvation' of the human race (namely, from 'the masters') is well under way...."

4 *Beyond Good and Evil*: Nietzsche published this work in 1886.

The slave revolt in morality begins when the *ressentiment*[5] itself becomes creative and gives birth to values: the *ressentiment* of those beings who are prevented from a genuine reaction, that is, something active, and who compensate for that with a merely imaginary vengeance. Whereas all noble morality grows out of a triumphant affirmation of one's own self, slave morality from the start says "No" to what is "outside," "other," "not itself." And *this* "No" is its creative act. This transformation of the glance which confers value—this *necessary* projection towards what is outer instead of back onto itself—that is inherent in *ressentiment*. In order to arise, slave morality always requires first an opposing world, a world outside itself. Psychologically speaking, it needs external stimuli in order to act at all—its action is basically reaction. The reverse is the case with the noble method of valuing: it acts and grows spontaneously. It seeks its opposite only to affirm its own self even more thankfully, with even more rejoicing—its negative concept of "low," "common," "bad" is merely a pale contrasting image after the fact in relation to its positive basic concept, thoroughly saturated with life and passion, "We are noble, good, beautiful, and happy!" When the noble way of evaluating makes a mistake and abuses reality, this happens with reference to the sphere which it does *not* know well enough, indeed, the sphere it has strongly resisted learning the truth about: under certain circumstances it misjudges the sphere it despises, the sphere of the common man, of the low people. On the other hand, even if we assume that the feeling of contempt, of looking down, or of looking superior *falsifies* the image of the person despised, we should note that such distortion will fall short by a long way of the distortion with which the suppressed hatred and vengeance of the powerless man assaults his opponent—naturally, in effigy. In fact, contempt contains too much negligence, too much lack of concern, too much looking away and impatience mixed in with it, even too much of a personal feeling of joy, for it to be capable of converting its object into a truly distorted image and monster. We should not fail to hear the almost benevolent nuances which, for example, the Greek nobility places in all the words with which it separates itself from the lower people—how a constant form of pity, consideration, and forbearance is mixed in there, sweetening the words, to the point where almost all words referring to the common man finally remain as expressions for "unhappy" and "worthy of pity" (compare *δειλός [deilos: cowardly]*, *δείλαιος [delaios: mean, low]*, *πονηρός [poneros: oppressed by toil, wretched]*, *μοχθηρός [mochtheros: suffering, wretched]*—the last two basically designating the common man as a slave worker and beast of burden)—and how, on the other hand, for the Greek ear the words "bad," "low," and "unhappy" have never stopped echoing a single note, one tone colour, in which "unhappy" predominates. This is the inheritance of the old, nobler, and aristocratic way of evaluating, which does not betray its principles even in contempt. (—Philologists should recall the sense in which *οϊζυρος [oizuros: miserable]*, *άνολβος [anolbos: unblessed]*, *τλήμων [tlemon: wretched]*, *δυστυχεῖν [dystychein: unfortunate]* and *ξυμφορά [xymfora: misfortune]* were used.) The "well born" simply *felt* they were "the happy ones"; they did not have to construct their happiness artificially first by looking at their enemies, or in some circumstances to talk themselves into it, *to lie to themselves into it* (the way all men of *ressentiment* habitually do). Similarly they knew, as complete men overloaded with power and thus *necessarily* active, that they must not separate action from happiness—they considered being active necessarily associated with happiness (that's where the phrase *εὖ πράττειν [eu prattein: do well, succeed]* derives its origin)—all this is very much the opposite of "happiness" at the level of the powerless and oppressed, those festering with poisonous and hostile feelings, among whom happiness comes out essentially as a narcotic, an anaesthetic, quiet, peace, "Sabbath," relaxing the soul,

5 *ressentiment*: Nietzsche uses this French word, which since his writing, and largely because of it, has entered the English language as an important term in psychology: a short definition is as follows: "deep-seated resentment, frustration, and hostility, accompanied by a sense of being powerless to express these feelings directly" (Merriam-Webster). *Ressentiment* is thus significantly different in meaning from *resentment*.

and stretching one's limbs, in short, as something *passive*. While the noble man lives for himself with trust and candour (*γενναῖος [gennaios]*, meaning "of noble birth," stresses the nuance "upright" and also probably "naive"), the man of *ressentiment* is neither upright nor naive, nor honest and direct with himself. His soul *squints*. His spirit loves hiding places, secret paths, and back doors. Everything furtive attracts him as *his* world, *his* security, *his* refreshment. He understands about remaining silent, not forgetting, waiting, temporarily diminishing himself, humiliating himself. A race of such men of *ressentiment* will inevitably end up *cleverer* than any noble race. It will also value cleverness to a completely different extent, that is, as a condition of existence of the utmost importance; whereas, cleverness among noble men easily acquires a delicate aftertaste of luxury and sophistication about it:—here it is simply far less important than the complete functional certainty of the ruling *unconscious* instincts or even a certain lack of cleverness, something like brave recklessness, whether in the face of danger or of an enemy, or those wildly enthusiastic, sudden fits of anger, love, reverence, thankfulness, and vengeance, by which in all ages noble souls have recognized each other. The *ressentiment* of the noble man himself, if it comes over him, consumes and exhausts itself in an immediate reaction and therefore does not *poison*. On the other hand, in countless cases it just does not appear at all; whereas, in the case of all weak and powerless people it is unavoidable. Being unable to take one's enemies, one's misfortunes, even one's *bad deeds* seriously for any length of time—that is the mark of strong, complete natures, in whom there is a surplus of plastic, creative, healing power, as well as the power to make one forget (a good example for that from the modern world is Mirabeau, who had no memory of the insults and the maliciousness people directed at him and who therefore could not forgive, merely because he—forgot). Such a man with a single shrug simply throws off himself the many worms which eat into other men.[6] Only here is the real "*love* for one's enemy" even possible—provided that it is at all possible on earth.—How much respect a noble man already has for his enemies!—and such a respect is already a bridge to love.... In fact, he demands his enemy for himself, as his mark of honour. Indeed, he has no enemy other than one in whom there is nothing to despise and a *great deal* to respect! By contrast, imagine for yourself "the enemy" as a man of *ressentiment* conceives him—and right here we have his action, his creation: he has conceptualized "the evil enemy," "*the evil one*," as, in fact, a fundamental idea from which he now also thinks his way to a complementary image and counterpart, a "good man"—himself! ...

We see exactly the opposite with the noble man, who conceives the fundamental idea "good" in advance and spontaneously, that is, from himself, and from there he first creates a picture of "bad" for himself! This "bad" originating from the noble man and that "evil" arising out of the stew pot of insatiable hatred—of these the first is a later creation, an afterthought, a complementary colour; by contrast, the second is the original, the beginning, the essential *act* in the conception of a slave morality—although the two words "bad" and "evil" both seem opposite to the same idea of "good," how different they are! But it is *not* the same idea of "good." Instead we should ask *who* the "evil person" really is in the sense of the morality of *ressentiment*. The strict answer to that is as follows: *simply* the "good person" of the other morality, the noble man, the powerful, the ruling man, only coloured over, only re-interpreted, only looked at again through the poisonous eyes of *ressentiment*. Here there is one thing we will be the last to deny: whoever has come to know those "good men" only as enemies, has known them also as nothing but *evil enemies*, and the same people who are kept within such strict limits by custom, honour, habit, gratitude, and even more by mutual surveillance and jealousy *inter pares [among equals]* and who, by contrast, demonstrate in relation to each other such resourceful consideration,

6 *Mirabeau*: Honoré Gabriel Riqueti, comte de Mirabeau (1749–91), French politician and writer at the time of the French Revolution.

self-control, refinement, loyalty, pride, and friendship—to the outside, where the strange world, the world of what is foreign to them, begins, these men are not much better than beasts of prey turned loose. Here they enjoy freedom from all social constraints. In the wilderness they make up for the tension which a long fenced-in confinement within the peace of the community brings about. They go *back* to the innocent conscience of a beast of prey, as joyful monsters, who perhaps walk away from a dreadful sequence of murder, arson, rape, and torture with an exhilaration and spiritual equilibrium, as if they had merely pulled off a student prank, convinced that now the poets once again have something to sing about and praise for a long time to come. At the bottom of all these noble races we cannot fail to recognize the beast of prey, the *blond beast* splendidly roaming around in its lust for loot and victory. This hidden basis from time to time needs to be discharged: the beast must come out again, must go back into the wilderness once more,—Roman, Arab, German, Japanese nobility, Homeric heroes, Scandinavian Vikings—in this need they are all alike. It is the noble races that left behind the concept of the "barbarian" in all their tracks, wherever they went. A consciousness of and even a pride in this fact still reveals itself in their highest culture (for example, when Pericles says to his Athenians, in that famous funeral speech, "our audacity has broken a way through to every land and sea, putting up permanent memorials to itself for good *and ill*"). This "audacity" of the noble races, mad, absurd, and sudden in the way it expresses itself, its unpredictability, even the improbability of its undertakings—Pericles emphatically praises the *ῥαθυμία [rathumia: freedom of anxiety]* of the Athenians—their indifference to and contempt for safety, body, life, comfort, their fearsome cheerfulness and the depth of their joy in all destruction, in all the physical pleasures of victory and cruelty—all this was summed up for those who suffered from such audacity in the image of the "barbarian," of the "evil enemy," of something like the "Goth" or "Vandal."[7] The deep, icy mistrust which the German evokes, as soon as he comes to power, once more again today—is still an after-effect of that unforgettable terror with which for centuries Europe confronted the rage of the blond Germanic beast (although there is hardly any idea linking the old Germanic tribes and we Germans, let alone any blood relationship).... Assuming as true what in any event is taken as "the truth" nowadays, that it is the *point of all culture* simply to breed a tame and civilized animal, a *domestic pet*, out of the beast of prey "man," then we would undoubtedly have to consider all those instincts of reaction and of *ressentiment* with whose help the noble races and all their ideals were finally disgraced and overpowered as the essential *instruments of culture*—though to do that would not yet be to claim that the *bearers* of these instincts also in themselves represented culture. Instead, the opposite would not only be probable—no! nowadays it is *visibly apparent*! These people carrying instincts of oppression and of a lust for revenge, the descendants of all European and non-European slavery, of all pre-Aryan populations in particular—they represent the regression of mankind! These "instruments of culture" are a disgrace to humanity and more a reason to be suspicious of or a counterargument against "culture" in general! We may well be right when we hang onto our fear of the blond beast at the bottom of all noble races and keep up our guard. But who would not find it a hundred times better to fear, if he could at the same time admire, rather than *not* fear but in the process no longer be able to rid himself of the disgusting sight of the failures, the stunted, the emaciated, and the poisoned? And is not that *our* fate? Today what is it that constitutes our aversion to "man"?—For we *suffer* from man. There's no doubt of that. It is *not* a matter of fear. Rather it's the fact that we have nothing more to fear from man, that the maggot "man" is

7 *Pericles* (495–429 BCE), political leader and general in Athens at the outbreak of the Peloponnesian War. He delivered his famous funeral oration at the end of the first year of the war. The *Goths*: tribes from Eastern Germany who attacked the Roman Empire in the third and fourth centuries. Later (as the Visigoths and Ostrogoths) they gained political dominance in parts of Europe, once the Roman Empire collapsed; *Vandals*: Eastern Germanic tribes, allied to the Goths, who invaded the Roman Empire.

in the foreground swarming around, that the "tame man," the hopelessly mediocre and unedifying man, has already learned to feel that he is the goal, the pinnacle, the meaning of history, "the higher man,"—yes indeed, that he has a certain right to feel that about himself, insofar as he feels separate from the excessive number of failed, sick, tired, and spent people, who are nowadays beginning to make Europe stink, so that he senses that he is at least relatively successful, at least still capable of life, of at least saying "Yes" to life....

For matters stand like this: the diminution and levelling of European man conceal *our* greatest danger, since we grow tired at the sight of him.... We see nothing today which wants to be greater. We suspect that things are still going down, down into something thinner, more good-natured, more prudent, more comfortable, more mediocre, more indifferent, more Chinese, more Christian—humanity, there is no doubt, is becoming constantly "better." ... Europe's fate lies right here—with the fear of man we also have lost the love for him, the reverence for him, the hope for him, indeed, our will to him. A glimpse at man nowadays makes us tired—what is contemporary nihilism, if it is not *that*? ... We are weary of *man*....

—But let's come back: the problem with the *other* origin of the "good," of the good man, as the person of *ressentiment* has imagined it for himself, demands its own conclusion.—That the lambs are upset about the great predatory birds is not strange, but the fact that these large birds of prey snatch away small lambs provides no reason for holding anything against them. And if the lambs say among themselves, "These predatory birds are evil, and whoever is least like a predatory bird and instead is like its opposite, a lamb—shouldn't that animal be good?" there is nothing to find fault with in this setting up of an ideal, except for the fact that the birds of prey will look down on them with a little mockery and perhaps say to themselves, "*We* are not at all annoyed with these good lambs. We even love them. Nothing is tastier than a tender lamb." To demand from strength that it does *not* express itself as strength, that it does *not* consist of a will to overpower, a will to throw down, a will to rule, a thirst for enemies and opposition and triumphs, is just as unreasonable as to demand from weakness that it express itself as strength. A quantum of force is simply such a quantum of drive, will, and action—rather, it is nothing but this very driving, willing, and acting itself—and it cannot appear as anything else except through the seduction of language (and the fundamental errors of reason petrified in it), which understands and misunderstands all action as conditioned by something which causes actions, by a "subject." For, in just the same way as people separate lightning from its flash and take the latter as an *action*, as the effect of a subject called lightning, so popular morality separates strength from manifestations of strength, as if behind the strong person there were an indifferent substrate that is *free* to express strength or not. But there is no such substrate; there is no "being" behind the doing, acting, or becoming. "The doer" is merely fabricated and added into the action—the act is everything. People basically duplicate the action: when they see a lightning flash, that is an action-action *[ein Thun-Thun]*: they set up the same event first as the cause and then yet again as its effect. Natural scientists are no better when they say "Force moves, force causes," and so on—our entire scientific knowledge, for all its coolness and freedom from feelings, still remains exposed to the seduction of language and has not gotten rid of the changelings foisted on it, the "subjects" (the atom, for example, is such a changeling, like the Kantian "thing-in-itself"): it's no wonder, then, that the repressed, secretly smouldering feelings of revenge and hate use this belief for their own purposes and even, in fact, maintain a faith in nothing more fervently than in the idea that *the strong person is free* to be weak and that the predatory bird is free to be a lamb:—in so doing, of course, they arrogate to themselves the right to *blame* the bird of prey for being a bird of prey.... When the oppressed, the downtrodden, and the violated say to each other, with the vengeful cunning of the powerless, "Let us be different from evil people, namely, good! And every person is good who does not oppress, who hurts no one, who does not attack, who does not retaliate, who hands revenge over to God, who keeps himself hidden, as we do, the person who avoids all evil and demands little from life in general, like us, the patient, humble, and upright"—what that amounts to, coolly expressed and without bias, is essentially nothing more than "We weak people are merely weak. It's good if we do not do anything *for which we are not strong enough*"—but this bitter state, this shrewdness of the lowest ranks, which even insects possess (when in great danger they act as if they were dead in order not to do "too much"), has, thanks to that counterfeiting and self-deception of powerlessness, dressed itself in the splendour of a self-denying, still, patient virtue, as if the weakness of the weak man himself—that means his *essence*, his actions, his entire single, inevitable, and irredeemable reality—is a voluntary achievement, something willed, chosen, an *action*, *something of merit*....

Let's bring this to a conclusion. The two *opposing* values "good and bad" and "good and evil" have fought a fearful battle on earth for thousands of years. And if it's true that the second value has for a long time had the upper hand, even now there is still no lack of places where the battle goes on without a final decision.... The symbol of this battle, written in a script which has remained legible through all human history up to the present, is called "Rome against Judea, Judea against Rome." To this point there has been no greater event than *this* war, *this* posing of a question, *this* contradiction between deadly enemies. Rome felt that the Jew was like something contrary to nature itself, its monstrous polar opposite, as it were. In Rome the Jew was considered "*convicted* of hatred against the entire human race." And that view was correct, to the extent that we are right to link the health and the future of the human race to the unconditional rule of aristocratic values, to Roman values.... The Romans were indeed strong and noble men, stronger and nobler than any people who had lived on earth up until then or even than any people who had ever been dreamed up. Everything they left as remains, every inscription, is delightful, provided that we can guess *what* is doing the writing there. By contrast, the Jews were *par excellence* that priestly people of *ressentiment*, who possessed an unparalleled genius for popular morality.... This is very remarkable: without doubt Rome has been conquered. It is true that in the Renaissance there was an incredibly brilliant reawakening of the classical ideal, of the noble way of evaluating everything. Rome itself behaved like someone who had woken up from a coma induced by the pressure of the new Jewish Rome built over it, which looked like an ecumenical synagogue and was called "Church." But Judea immediately triumphed again, thanks to that thoroughly vulgar (German and English) movement of *ressentiment* we call the Reformation, together with what had to follow as a result, the re-establishment of the church—as well as the re-establishment of the old grave-like tranquillity of classical Rome. In what is an even more decisive and deeper sense than that, Judea once again was victorious over the classical ideal with the French Revolution. The last political nobility which there was in Europe, in seventeenth and eighteenth century *France*, broke apart under the instincts of popular *ressentiment*—never on earth has there been heard a greater rejoicing, a noisier enthusiasm! It's true that in the midst of all this the most dreadful and most unexpected events took place: the old ideal itself stepped *physically* and with unheard of splendour before the eyes and the conscience of humanity—and once again stronger, simpler, and more urgently than ever rang out, in opposition to the old lying slogan of *ressentiment* about the *privileged rights of the majority*, in opposition to that will for a low condition, for abasement, for equality, for the decline and twilight of mankind—in opposition to all that there rang out the fearsome and delightful counter-slogan about the *privilege of the very few*! As a last signpost to a *different* road, Napoleon appeared, that most singular and late-born man there ever was, and in him the problem of the *noble ideal itself* was made flesh—we should consider well *what* a problem that is: Napoleon, this synthesis of *monster [Unmensch]* and *superman [Übermensch]*....

Second Essay
Guilt, Bad Conscience, and Related Matters

...

Precisely that development is the long history of the origin of *responsibility*. That task of breeding an animal which is permitted to make promises contains within it, as we have already grasped, as a condition and prerequisite, the more precise task of first *making* a human being necessarily uniform to some extent, one among others like him, regular and consequently predictable. The immense task involved in this, what I have called the "morality of custom" (cf. *Daybreak* 9, 14, 16)—the essential work of a man on his own self in the longest-lasting age of the human race, his entire *pre-historical* work, derives its meaning, its grand justification, from the following point, no matter how much hardship, tyranny, monotony, and idiocy it also manifested: with the help of the morality of custom and the social strait jacket, the human being *was made* truly predictable. Let's position ourselves, by contrast, at the end of this immense process, in the place where the tree at last yields its fruit, where society and the morality of custom finally bring to light *the end for which* they were simply the means: then we find, as the ripest fruit on that tree, the *sovereign individual*, something which resembles only itself, which has broken loose again from the morality of custom, the autonomous individual beyond morality (for "autonomous" and "moral" are mutually exclusive terms), in short, the human being who possesses his own independent and enduring will, who is *entitled to make promises*—and in him a consciousness quivering in every muscle, proud of *what* has finally been achieved and has become a living embodiment in him, a real consciousness of power and freedom, a feeling of completion for human beings generally. This man who has become free, who really *is entitled* to make promises, this master of *free* will, this sovereign—how is he not to realize the superiority he enjoys over everything which is not permitted to make a promise and make pledges on its own behalf, knowing how much trust, how much fear, and how much respect he creates—he "*is worthy*" of all three—and how, with this mastery over himself, he has necessarily been given in addition mastery over his circumstances, over nature, and over all less reliable creatures with a shorter will? The "free" man, the owner of an enduring unbreakable will, by possessing this, also acquires his own *standard of value*: he looks out from himself at others and confers respect or contempt. And just as it will be necessary for him to honour those like him, the strong and dependable (who *are entitled* to make promises)—in other words, everyone who makes promises like a sovereign, seriously, rarely, and slowly, who is sparing with his trust, who *honours* another when he does trust, who gives his word as something reliable, because he knows he is strong enough to remain upright even when opposed by misfortune, even when "opposed by fate"—in just the same way it will be necessary for him to keep his foot ready to kick the scrawny unreliable men, who make promises without being entitled to, and to hold his cane ready for the liar, who breaks his word in the very moment it comes out of his mouth. The proud knowledge of the extraordinary privilege of *responsibility*, the consciousness of this rare freedom, of this power over oneself and destiny, has become internalized into the deepest parts of him and grown instinctual, has become an instinct, a dominating instinct:—what will he call it, this dominating instinct, assuming that he finds he needs a word for it? There's no doubt: the sovereign man calls this instinct his *conscience*....

For the most extensive period of human history, punishment was certainly *not* meted out *because* people held the instigator of evil responsible for his actions, and thus it was *not* assumed that only the guilty party should be punished:—it was much more as it still is now when parents punish their children out of anger over some harm they have suffered, anger vented on the perpetrator—but anger restrained and modified through the idea that every injury has some *equivalent* and that compensation for it could, in fact, be paid out, even if that is through the *pain* of the perpetrator.

Where did this primitive, deeply rooted, and perhaps by now ineradicable idea derive its power, the idea of an equivalence between punishment and pain? I have already given away the answer: in the contractual relationship between *creditor* and *debtor*, which is, in general, as ancient as the idea of "legal subject" and which, for its part, refers back to the basic forms of buying, selling, bartering, trading, and exchanging goods....

In order to inspire trust in his promise to pay back, in order to give his promise a guarantee of its seriousness and sanctity, in order to impress on his own conscience the idea of paying back as a duty, an obligation, the debtor, by virtue of a contract, pledges to the creditor, in the event that he does not pay, something else that he still "owns," something else over which he still exercises power, for example, his body or his woman or his freedom or even his life.... Let us clarify for ourselves the logic of this whole method of compensation—it is weird enough. The equivalency is given in this way: instead of an advantage making up directly for the harm (hence, instead of compensation in gold, land, possessions of some sort or another), the creditor is given a kind of *pleasure* as repayment and compensation—the pleasure of being allowed to discharge his power on a powerless person without having to think about it, the delight in "*faire le mal pour le plaisir de le faire*" *[doing wrong for the pleasure of doing it]*, the enjoyment of violation. This enjoyment is more highly prized the lower and baser the creditor stands in the social order, and it can easily seem to him a delicious mouthful, in fact, a foretaste of a higher rank. By means of the "punishment" of the debtor, the creditor participates in a *right belonging to the masters*. Finally he also for once comes to the lofty feeling of despising a being as someone "beneath him," as someone he is entitled to mistreat—or at least, in the event that the real force of punishment, of executing punishment, has already been transferred to the "authorities," the feeling of *seeing* the debtor despised and mistreated. The compensation thus consists of an order for and a right to cruelty....

At this point, I can no longer avoid setting out, in an initial, provisional statement, my own hypothesis about the origin of "bad conscience." It is not easy to get people to attend to it, and it requires them to consider it at length, to guard it, and to sleep on it. I consider bad conscience the profound illness which human beings had to come down with under the pressure of that most fundamental of all the changes which they ever experienced—that change when they finally found themselves locked within the confines of society and peace. Just like the things water animals must have gone though when they were forced either to become land animals or to die off, so events must have played themselves out with this half-beast so happily adapted to the wilderness, war, wandering around, adventure—suddenly all its instincts were devalued and "disengaged." From this point on, these animals were to go on foot and "carry themselves"; whereas previously they had been supported by the water. A terrible heaviness weighed them down. In performing the simplest things they felt ungainly. In dealing with this new unknown world, they no longer had their old leaders, the ruling unconscious drives which guided them safely—these unfortunate creatures were reduced to thinking, inferring, calculating, bringing together cause and effect, reduced to their "consciousness," their most impoverished and error-prone organ! I believe that never on earth has there been such a feeling of misery, such a leaden discomfort—while at the same time those old instincts had not all of a sudden stopped imposing their demands! Only it was difficult and seldom possible to do their bidding. For the most part, they had to find new and, as it were, underground satisfactions for themselves. All instincts which are not discharged to the outside *are turned back inside*—this is what I call the *internalization [Verinnerlichung]* of man. From this first grows in man what people later call his "soul." The entire inner world, originally as thin as if stretched between two layers of skin, expanded and extended itself, acquired depth, width, and height, to the extent that what a person discharged out into the world was *obstructed*. Those frightening fortifications with which the organization of the state protected itself against the old instincts for freedom—punishments belong above all to these fortifications—brought it about that all those instincts of the wild, free, roaming man turned themselves backwards, *against man himself*. Enmity, cruelty, joy in pursuit, in attack, in change, in destruction—all those turned themselves against the possessors of such instincts. *That* is the origin of "bad conscience." The man who, because of a lack of external enemies and opposition, was forced into an oppressive narrowness and regularity of custom impatiently tore himself apart, persecuted himself, gnawed away at himself, grew upset, and did himself damage—this animal which scraped itself raw against the bars of its cage, which people want to "tame," this impoverished creature, consumed with longing for the wild, which had to create out of its own self an adventure, a torture chamber, an uncertain and dangerous wilderness—this fool, this yearning and puzzled prisoner, became the inventor of "bad conscience." But with him was introduced the greatest and weirdest illness, from which humanity up to the present time has not recovered, the suffering of man *from man*, *from himself*, a consequence of the forcible separation from his animal past, a leap and, so to speak, a fall into new situations and living conditions, a declaration of war against the old instincts, on which, up to that point, his power, joy, and ability to inspire fear had been based....

Inherent in this hypothesis about the origin of bad conscience is, firstly, the assumption that the change was not gradual or voluntary and did not manifest itself as an organic growth into new conditions, but as a break, a leap, something forced, an irrefutable disaster, against which there was no struggle, nor even any *ressentiment*. Secondly, however, it assumes that the adaptation of a populace hitherto unchecked and shapeless into a fixed form, just as it was initiated by an act of violence, was carried to its conclusion by nothing but acts of violence—that consequently the oldest "State" emerged as a terrible tyranny, as an oppressive and inconsiderate machinery, and continued working until such raw materials of people and half-animals finally were not only thoroughly kneaded and submissive but also *given a shape*. I used the word "State": it is self-evident who is meant by that term—some pack of blond predatory animals, a race of conquerors and masters, which, organized for war and with the power to organize, without thinking about it, sets its terrifying paws on a subordinate population which may perhaps be vast in numbers but is still without any form, is still wandering about. That is, in fact, the way the "State" begins on earth. I believe that fantasy has been done away with which sees the beginning of the state in a "contract." The man who can command, who is by nature a "master," who comes forward with violence in his actions and gestures—what has he to do with making contracts! We do not negotiate with such beings. They come like fate, without cause, reason, consideration, or pretext. They are present as lightning is present, too fearsome, too sudden, too convincing, too "different" even to become merely hated. Their work is the instinctive creation of forms, the imposition of forms. They are the most involuntary and most unconscious artists in existence:—where they appear something new is soon present, a power structure which *lives*, something in which the parts and functions are demarcated and coordinated, in which there is, in general, no place for anything which does not first derive its "meaning" from its relationship to the totality. These men, these born organizers, have no idea what guilt, responsibility, and consideration are. In them that fearsome egotism of the artist is in charge, which stares out like bronze and knows how to justify itself for all time in the "work," just as a mother does in her child. *They* are not the ones in whom "bad conscience" grew—that point is obvious from the outset. But this hateful plant would not have grown *without them*. It would have failed if an immense amount of freedom had not been driven from the world under the pressure of their hammer blows, their artistic violence, or at least had not been driven from sight and, as it were, made *latent*. This powerful *instinct for freedom*, once made latent—we already understand how—this instinct for freedom driven back, repressed, imprisoned inside, and finally still able to discharge and direct itself only against itself—that and that alone is what *bad conscience* is in its beginning....

You will already have guessed *what* really went on with all this and *under* all this: that will to self-torment, that repressed cruelty of animal man pushed inward and forced back into himself, imprisoned in the "state" to make him tame, who invented bad conscience in order to lacerate himself, after the *more natural* discharge of this will to inflict pain had been blocked—this man of bad conscience seized upon religious assumptions to drive his self-torment to its most horrifying hardship and ferocity. Guilt towards *God*: this idea becomes his instrument of torture. In "God" he seizes on the ultimate contrast he is capable of discovering to his real and indissoluble animal instincts. He interprets these animal instincts themselves as a crime against God (as enmity, rebellion, revolt against the "master," the "father," the original ancestor and beginning of the world).... In this spiritual cruelty there is a kind of insanity of the will which simply has no equal: a man's *will* finding him so guilty and reprehensible that there is no atonement, his *will* to imagine himself punished, but in such a way that the punishment could never be adequate for his crime, his *will* to infect and poison the most fundamental basis of things with the problem of punishment and guilt in order to cut himself off once and for all from any exit out of this labyrinth of "fixed ideas," his *will* to erect an ideal—that of the "holy God"—in order to be tangibly certain of his own absolute worthlessness when confronted with it. O this insane, sad beast man! ...

We modern men, we are the inheritors of thousands of years of vivisection of the conscience and self-inflicted animal torture. That's what we have had the longest practice doing, that is perhaps our artistry; in any case, it's something we have refined, the corruption of our taste. For too long man has looked at his natural inclinations with an "evil eye," so that finally in him they have become twinned with "bad conscience." An attempt to reverse this might, *in itself*, be possible—but who is strong enough for it, that is, to link as siblings bad conscience and the *unnatural* inclinations, all those aspirations for what lies beyond, those things which go against our senses, against our instincts, against nature, against animals—in short, the earlier ideals, all the ideals which are hostile to life, ideals of those who vilify the world? To whom can we turn to today with *such* hopes and demands? ... In this we would have precisely the *good* people against us, as well, of course, as the comfortable, the complacent, the vain, the enthusiastic, the tired.... But what is more deeply offensive, what cuts us off so fundamentally, as letting them take some note of the severity and loftiness with which we deal with ourselves? And, by contrast, how obliging, how friendly all the world is in relation to us, as soon as we act as all the world does and "let ourselves go" just like all the world! To attain the goal I'm talking about requires a *different* sort of spirit from those which are likely to exist at this particular time: spirits empowered by war and victory, for whom conquest, adventure, danger, and even pain have become a need. That would require getting acclimatized to keen, high air, winter wanderings, to ice and mountains in every sense. That would require even a kind of sublime maliciousness, an ultimate self-conscious wilfulness of knowledge, which comes with great health. Simply and seriously put, that would require just this *great health*! ... Is this even possible today? ... But at some time or other, in a more powerful time than this mouldy, self-doubting present, he must nonetheless come to us, the *redeeming* man of great love and contempt, the creative spirit, constantly pushed again and again away from every sideline or from the beyond by his own driving power, whose isolation is misunderstood by people as if it were a flight *from* reality—whereas it is only his immersion, burial, and absorption *in* reality, so that, once he comes out of it into the light again, he brings home the *redemption* of this reality, its redemption from the curse which the previous ideal has laid upon it. This man of the future, who will release us from that earlier ideal just as much as from what *had to grow from it*, from the great loathing, from the will to nothingness, from nihilism—that stroke of noon and of the great decision which makes the will free once again, who gives back to the earth its purpose and to the human being his hope, this anti-Christ and anti-nihilist, this conqueror of God and of nothingness—at some point he must come....

7.5 Sigmund Freud (1856–1939)

Sigmund Freud, an Austrian-born Jew, is the inventor of psychoanalysis, a form of treatment for mental illness that understands psychic disturbances as problems in the patient's universe of meaning rather than his or her biology, and that therefore seeks to treat those disturbances through speech. Arguably Freud's most important and controversial "discovery" is the unconscious: a portion of the individual's thought process that is inaccessible to his or her conscious mind. Pointing to dreams, neurotic symptoms, psychotic hallucinations, and slips of the tongue as evidence, Freud argued that every individual has an entire world of repressed unconscious desires, ideas, and beliefs that he or she is unaware of and likely to reject as part of his or her own identity. Freud argued that by bringing the unconscious to consciousness through a particular kind of conversation (psychoanalysis), various forms of mental illness could be resolved. While many contemporary practitioners in the treatment of mental illness refer to psychoanalysis as a disproven or discredited theory and practice, it continues to be offered as a form of treatment and its theoretical ideas continue to influence several contemporary fields of thought.

In addition to informing the treatment of individuals suffering from mental illness, Freud's psychoanalytic theory had a whole range of implications for understanding human behaviour and social and political organization. Freud did not hesitate to expand on some of these in his voluminous writing, and the current text, *Civilization and Its Discontents*, is an example of this. In this text Freud engages in an argument with the 'discontents,' those who, like Jean-Jacques Rousseau for example, argue that civilization is essentially evil or corrupt and that the pre-civilized state of nature must have been happier and more just. Freud argues that civilization plays a vital role in allowing the social group to restrain and manage the primitive, irrational desires of individuals to use each other as objects of enjoyment. While this argument echoes the ideas of many conservative Enlightenment thinkers such as Hobbes and Burke, Freud adds something new to the equation: the notion of an irrational, instinctual drive to aggression that is natural to human beings. For Freud, every human being has a natural desire to harm others, not as a tool that serves some other purpose, but simply because it feels good.

The flip side of Freud's assertion of a natural aggressive drive is his argument that rational thinking is not strong enough to overcome it. That is to say, unlike Enlightenment thinkers who assume human beings can ultimately be fitted into a perfectly rational social organization, Freud argues that irrational aggression will persist. As such, society needs to find a way to channel or counterbalance aggression in order to remain stable and effective. Much of *Civilization and Its Discontents* is taken up with Freud's enumeration of the various strategies that civilization employs to this end. Not only does this include channelling aggression towards a socially acceptable target, for which Freud blames the horrors of Nazism, it also includes internalizing aggression as superego guilt feeling, which Freud identifies as self-flagellation or a desire for punishment. Freud's theory of the superego is in many ways just as unsettling as his notion of the aggressive drive: it implies that what we usually take to be our moral compass—our conscience—is actually just a tool deployed by civilization to get us to direct our aggressive tendencies against ourselves, a tool that has no necessary relation to morality.

from Civilization and Its Discontents

How have so many people arrived at this strange attitude of hostility to civilization? I believe a deep, long-standing dissatisfaction with the existing state of civilization provided the foundation on which, given certain historical events, this condemnation arose....

It is time for us to consider the nature of this culture, whose value in terms of happiness has been brought into doubt. We will not insist on a formula succinctly expressing that nature until we have learned something from our investigation. It will therefore suffice to reiterate that the word "civilization" designates the whole sum of the achievements and institutions in which our life differs from that of our animal ancestors and which serve two purposes—protecting people from nature and regulating people's relations with one another.[1] ...

It is easy to make a start. We recognize as cultural all activities and items of value that are useful to humans in that they make the earth serviceable to them, protect them from the violence of the forces of nature, etc....

Thus we acknowledge the high cultural level of a country if we find that everything in it that is serviceable in the exploitation of the earth by humanity, and in the protection of humanity from the forces of nature—everything, in short, that is useful to humanity—is cared for and conscientiously nurtured....

Beauty, cleanliness, and order obviously have a special place among the requirements of civilization. No one will assert that they are as important for life as control over the forces of nature or as important as other factors we shall become acquainted with later, but no one would want to demote them to the status of trivialities. That civilization does not concern itself only with usefulness is already shown by the example of beauty, which we consider essential among the interests of civilization....

However, it seems that civilization can be characterized by no trait better than by its appreciation and nurture of the higher mental activities—intellectual, scientific, and artistic achievements—and the leading role assigned to ideas in human life. Among these ideas, religious systems stand in the foreground; I have attempted to cast light on their complex structure elsewhere. Beside them come philosophical speculations; and finally what one might call people's ideals—their conceptions of a possible perfection of the individual person, of a nationality, or of humanity as a whole—and the demands people establish based on these conceptions....

As the last, but certainly not the least important character trait of civilization we must examine how the relations of humans to each other, i.e., social relations, are regulated—relations that affect one as a neighbor, as a provider of help, as the sexual object of another person, and as a member of a family or of a state. Here it is especially hard to disregard certain ideal demands and to grasp what essentially characterizes civilization. Perhaps one should begin by explaining that the element of civilization arises with the first attempt to regulate these social relations. If such an attempt were not made, these relations would be subject to the whim

1 [Freud's note:] See *The Future of an Illusion*, Chapter 1, Paragraph 3.

of the individual, i.e., the physically stronger person would decide them in accordance with his own interests and drive impulses. In this aspect, nothing would be changed if this stronger person, in turn, encountered an even stronger one. Human life in communities is only possible when a majority gathers that is stronger than each individual and holds together against each individual. The power of this community now establishes itself as "law," as opposed to the power of the individual, which is condemned as "brute force." This replacement of the power of the individual by that of a community is the decisive step toward civilization. The essence of this step is that the members of the community restrict themselves in their possibilities of gratification, whereas the individual knew no such limitation. Thus the first demand of civilization is justice, i.e., the assurance that a system of law, once established, will not be broken in favor of an individual. As for the ethical value of such a system, nothing is decided here. The further course of cultural development seems to strive toward a system in which the law is no longer the expression of the will of a small community—a caste, social stratum, or ethnic group—which, in its turn, behaves like a violent individual towards other, perhaps more extensive groups. The final result should be a system of law to which all—at least all who are capable of living in a community—have contributed by sacrificing their drives, and which allows no one (again with the same exception) to become the victim of brute force.

Individual freedom is not a gift of civilization. It was at its greatest before there was any civilization, though then it had essentially no value since the individual was hardly capable of defending it. Through cultural development, individual freedom experiences restrictions, and justice demands that no one be spared these restrictions. What is felt in a human community as a striving for freedom may be opposition to an existing injustice, and thus may prove favorable for the further development of civilization and remain compatible with civilization. But it may also arise from what remains of the original personality, untamed by civilization, and thus may become the basis of hostility to civilization. Thus the striving for freedom is directed against specific forms and demands of civilization, or against civilization in its entirety....

A good part of the struggle of humankind is concentrated on the single task of finding an efficient, i.e., satisfying, reconciliation between the claims of the individual and the cultural claims of the multitude, and one of the problems in the fate of humankind is whether this reconciliation is achievable through a certain form of civilization or whether the conflict is irreconcilable....

Drive sublimation is an especially prominent feature in the development of civilization, and makes it possible for higher mental activities—scientific, artistic, or ideological—to play such a significant role in cultural life. If one yields to the first impression, one will be tempted to say that sublimation is simply a drive outcome imposed by civilization. But it would be better to consider the question a bit more. Thirdly and lastly [after character-development and sublimation]—and this seems the most important—it is impossible to overlook the extent to which civilization is based on the renunciation of drives, that is, the high degree to which it presupposes the non-gratification (suppression, repression, or something else?) of powerful drives. This "cultural frustration" governs the large domain of the social relationships of humans; we know already that it is the cause of the hostility that all civilizations must combat. It will also place difficult demands on our scientific work; we will have much to explain here. It is not easy to understand how it can become possible to deprive a drive of gratification. Doing so is certainly not without risk: if this is not compensated for economically, one can only expect serious disturbances.

But if we want to know what value can be claimed by our view of cultural development as a special process, comparable to the normal maturation of the individual, it is apparent that we must attack another problem and ask ourselves the question: "To what influences does cultural development owe its origin, how did it arise, and by what was its course determined?"

...

V

Psychoanalytic work has taught us that precisely these restrictions on sexual life are not tolerated by so-called neurotics. In their symptoms, they create substitute gratifications for themselves, but these either cause suffering in their own right or become sources of suffering by producing difficulties for them in the environment and in society. The second situation is easy to understand, while the first presents us with a new problem. But civilization demands still other sacrifices beyond giving up sexual gratification.

We have interpreted the difficulty of cultural development as a general developmental difficulty by attributing it to the lethargy of the libido, to its disinclination to relinquish an old position for a new one. We are saying essentially the same thing when we derive the antithesis between civilization and sexuality from the fact that sexual love is a relationship between two persons, in which a third can only be superfluous or disturbing, whereas civilization is based on relationships among a greater number of human beings. At the height of a love-relationship there is no more interest in the environment whatsoever; the two lovers are sufficient unto themselves, and do not even need their shared child in order to be happy. In no other case does Eros reveal so clearly the core of its being—the intention of making one out of many; but when it has achieved this in the proverbial way, in the love of two human beings, it does not want to go beyond this.

Thus far, we can certainly imagine a cultural community consisting of such double individuals, who, libidinally satisfied in themselves, are mutually connected through the bond of common work and common interests. In such a case, civilization would have no need to reduce the energy level of sexuality. But this desirable situation does not exist, and never has. Reality shows us that civilization is not content with the connections it has thus far been allowed to establish, that it also wants to bind together the members of the community in a libidinal way, and that it employs all means to that end, furthers every path toward creating strong identifications among the members of the community, and invokes goal-inhibited libido on a grand scale to strengthen the communal bonds through relations of friendship. For the fulfillment of these aims, the restriction of sexual life is unavoidable. We lack insight into the necessity that forces civilization onto this path and brings about its antagonism to sexuality. It must be due to some disturbing factor we have not yet discovered.

Here, one of the so-called ideal demands of civilized society can show us the way. It proclaims: "Thou shalt love thy neighbor as thyself."[2] It is famous throughout the world—certainly older than Christianity, which presents it as its proudest claim—but is surely not very old; in historical times it was still unknown. Let us consider it in a naïve manner, as if hearing of it for the first time. Then we will be unable to suppress a feeling of surprise and aversion. Why should we obey the precept? How will this help us? But above all, how can we achieve this? How can we manage this? My love is something valuable to me, something I must not throw away without reflection. It imposes duties on me for whose fulfillment I must be prepared to make sacrifices. If I love others, they must deserve it in some way. (I shall disregard their potential usefulness to me, and their possible significance for me as sexual objects; for the precept of love for one's neighbor, these two types of relationships are irrelevant.) Other persons deserve my love if they are so similar to me in important respects that I can love myself in them; they deserve my love if they are so much more

2 The so-called "golden rule" commandment, or the "second great commandment," is derived from Mosaic Law and the Old Testament and, with the first commandment, later forms the basis of Christian ethics. The two commandments appear, for instance, in Mark 12:28–31: "And one of the scribes came, and having heard them reasoning together, and perceiving that he had answered them well, asked him, Which is the first commandment of all? And Jesus answered him, The first of all the commandments *is*, Hear, O Israel; The Lord our God is one Lord: And thou shalt love the Lord thy God with all thy heart, and with all thy soul, and with all thy mind, and with all thy strength: this *is* the first commandment. And the second *is* like, *namely* this, Thou shalt love thy neighbour as thyself. There is none other commandment greater than these."

perfect than I am that I can love my ideal of myself in them; if the other person is my friend's son I must love him, for my friend's pain, should any harm befall his son, would also be mine—a pain I would have to share. But if other persons are strangers to me, and cannot attract me through any worth of their own or any previously gained significance in my emotional life, it will be hard for me to love them. Indeed, it would be wrong for me to do so, for my love is valued by all those in my own group as a preference for them; it is an injustice toward them if I make a stranger their equal. But if I am to love him with this universal love simply because he, too, is an earthly being, like an insect, an earthworm, a grass-snake, then, I fear, only a small measure of love will fall upon him—surely not as much, by the judgment of reason, as I am entitled to retain for myself. Of what use is such a precept, so solemnly proclaimed, if its fulfillment cannot be recommended as reasonable?

If I look more closely, I find still more difficulties. Not only is this stranger generally unworthy of my love: I must honestly confess that he is more deserving of my hostility, even my hatred. He seems not to have the slightest love for me, shows me not the slightest consideration. If he can gain any advantage, he does not hesitate to harm me; he does not consider whether the extent of his advantage is in proportion to the amount of harm he does me. Indeed, he need not even gain any advantage; if he can simply gratify a desire for pleasure, he thinks nothing of mocking me, insulting me, slandering me, and demonstrating his power over me, and the more secure he feels, and the more helpless I am, all the more surely can I expect him to treat me this way. If he behaves otherwise, if he shows me consideration and spares me as a stranger, I am in any case prepared to reciprocate in a similar way toward him—without any precept. Indeed, if this grandiose commandment were "Love thy neighbor as thy neighbor loves thee," then I would have no objection. There is a second commandment, which strikes me as even more incomprehensible and arouses still stronger opposition in me. It is: "Love thine enemies."[3] If I consider this carefully though, it seems that I am wrong to reject it as a greater imposition. It is basically the same thing.[4]

Now I think I hear a dignified voice admonishing me: "*It is precisely because your neighbor is unworthy of love, and should sooner be considered your enemy, that you should love him as yourself.*"[5] Then I understand: this is a case similar to *credo quia absurdum* [I believe because it is absurd]. Now it is very probable that my neighbor, when he is called upon to love me as himself, will answer exactly as I have, and will reject me for the same reasons. I hope he will not have the same objective justification—but that is precisely what he, too, will think....

The bit of truth, so eagerly denied, behind all this is that people are not gentle beings in need of love, who at most can defend themselves if attacked. Rather they must also recognize among their drive impulses a powerful tendency for aggression. Their neighbor, consequently, is not merely a potential helper or sexual object for them. Rather, they are also tempted to gratify their aggression on him, to exploit without compensation his capacity for work, to use him sexually without his consent, to seize his possessions, to humiliate him, to cause him pain, to torture and kill him. *Homo homini lupus* [Man is a wolf to man].[6]

3 Matthew 5:44: "But I say unto you, Love your enemies, bless them that curse you, do good to them that hate you, and do good to them which despitefully use you and persecute you."

4 [Freud's note:] A great poet may permit himself to express heavily criticized psychological truths, at least in jest. Thus Heine confesses: "I have the most peaceable disposition. My wishes are: a humble cottage, a thatched roof, but a good bed, good food, milk and butter, very fresh, flowers before the window, and a few beautiful trees before the door—and if dear God wants to make me completely happy, he will grant me the joy of having six or seven of my enemies hanged from those trees. With emotion in my heart I shall forgive them, before their death, for all the wrong they did me in their lifetime, for indeed, one must forgive one's enemies—but not before they are hanging." (*Gedanken und Einfälle*, 1869) [Thoughts and Ideas (Section 1)] [Christian Johann Heinrich Heine (1797–1856) was a German man of letters, best known for his lyric poetry and for his later works of satire.]

5 Freud adopts the heuristic voice in *The Question of Lay Analysis* (1926) and, similarly, the "imaginary opponent" in *The Future of an Illusion*. For commentary, see the Introduction to the Broadview Edition of *The Future of an Illusion* (2012), especially pp. 26–38 and 49–50.

6 Presumably from the synonymous *lupus est homo homini* (third-/second-century BCE Roman comic poet Plautus, *Asinaria*, 495).

Who, after all the experiences of life and history, will have the courage to dispute this claim? This cruel aggression usually waits for some provocation, or puts itself in the service of some other intention whose goal could also have been attained through milder measures. Given circumstances favorable to this aggression, when the mental counterforces normally inhibiting it have ceased to function, it also expresses itself spontaneously and reveals humankind as a wild beast to whom the sparing of members of the same species is an alien concept. Whoever thinks of the atrocities committed during the migrations of the peoples of Europe, during the invasions of the Huns or of the so-called Mongols under Genghis Khan and Tamerlane, or during the conquest of Jerusalem by the pious Crusaders, or indeed, thinks of the horrors of the last World War, will have to bow humbly before the truth of this view.

The existence of this inclination to aggression, which we can sense in ourselves and correctly assume in others, is the factor that disturbs our relations with our neighbor and forces civilization to exert so much energy. Due to this primary hostility among human beings, civilized society is constantly threatened with disintegration. An interest in communal work would not hold it together; the passions of drives are stronger than reasonable interests. Civilization must do its utmost to hold people's aggressive drives in check and, through mental reaction formations, impede their expression. Hence the use of methods to drive people into identifications and goal-inhibited love-relationships; hence the restriction of sexual life, and hence also the ideal commandment to love one's neighbor as oneself—which is really justified by the fact that nothing else is so contrary to original human nature. Through all of its efforts, this striving of civilization has thus far not achieved very much. It hopes to prevent the crudest excesses of brutal violence by claiming for itself the right to treat criminals with violence, but the law is incapable of grasping the more cautious and finer expressions of human aggression. We each reach the point where we must give up as illusions the expectations which, in our youth, we associated with our fellow humans; then we can learn how much our life is made difficult and painful through their ill will. Yet it would be unfair to accuse civilization of wanting to eliminate strife and competition from human activity. Strife and competition are surely essential, but opposition is not necessarily hostility; it is merely misused as a pretext for hostility.

The communists believe they have found the way to deliverance from evil; human beings are thoroughly good and are well disposed to their neighbor, but the institution of private property has corrupted their nature.[7] The ownership of private property gives power to an individual, and with it the temptation to mistreat his neighbor; those excluded from ownership must oppose the oppressor with hostility. If private property is abolished, if all wealth is made collective, and if everyone is allowed to partake in its enjoyment, ill will and hostility will disappear among humankind. Since all needs will be satisfied, no one will have any reason to see another person as an enemy; everyone will willingly participate in the necessary labor. I shall not undertake any economic criticism of the communist system; I cannot investigate whether the abolition of private property is expedient and advantageous.[8] But I am able to recognize the psychological assumptions of communism as an untenable illusion. In abolishing private property one removes from the human urge to aggression one of its instruments—certainly a strong one, but certainly not the strongest. As for differences in power and influence, which aggression misuses for its own purposes—in these one has changed nothing, not even in their essence. Aggression was not created

7 For more on Freud's discussions of communism, see *The Future of an Illusion* (2012), Chapters 1–2, especially pp. 76–79, and also the Introduction, pp. 17–26.

8 [Freud's note:] Whoever has tasted the misery of poverty in his own youth, and has experienced the indifference and arrogance of the wealthy, should be safe from the suspicion that he has no understanding or good will for efforts to fight against economic inequality among humankind and all its results. If, indeed, in the name of justice, this fight invokes an abstract demand for the equality of all people, there is the obvious objection that nature, in endowing individuals with physical and mental abilities in an extremely unequal way, has established injustices for which there is no remedy.

by property, and reigned nearly unrestricted in primeval times, when property was still very meager....

It is clearly not easy for people to renounce the gratification of their inclination to aggression; they feel uncomfortable in renouncing it. The advantage a relatively small cultural group possesses in allowing this drive the outlet of hostility toward outsiders is not to be underestimated. A larger group of people can always be bound together in love, so long as others remain as targets for the expression of aggression. I have previously examined the phenomenon that precisely those communities that are adjacent and also similar in other ways feud with each other and ridicule each other—such as the Spaniards and the Portuguese, the North Germans and the South Germans, the English and the Scots, etc. I called this phenomenon the "narcissism of minor differences," a name that provides little in terms of explanation. This can now be recognized as a comfortable and relatively harmless gratification of the inclination to aggression, through which cohesion is made easier for the members of the community. In this way the Jewish people, scattered everywhere, have rendered services worthy of recognition to the cultures of the peoples that have hosted them; unfortunately all the massacres of Jews in the Middle Ages were not sufficient to make that period more peaceful and secure for their Christian comrades. After the Apostle Paul had made universal human love the foundation of his Christian community, extreme intolerance by Christendom toward those remaining outside it became an inevitable consequence. To the Romans, who had not founded their collective existence as a state upon love, religious intolerance was foreign, although with them religion was an affair of the state and the state was permeated by religion. Nor was it an incomprehensible coincidence that the dream of Germanic world domination called for anti-Semitism as its complement; and it is comprehensible that the attempt to establish a new, communist civilization in Russia finds its psychological support in the persecution of the bourgeoisie. One can only ask, with concern, what the Soviets will do after they have exterminated their bourgeoisie.

Since civilization imposes such great sacrifices not only on human sexuality but also on the human inclination to aggression, we understand better why it is hard for people to feel happy in it. Indeed, in this sense primal humans had a better situation since they knew no restrictions on drives. On the other hand, they had very little security in which to enjoy such happiness for long. Civilized humans have traded a portion of their possibilities of happiness for a portion of security. But we must not forget that in the primal family only the head of the family enjoyed such freedom of drives; the others lived in slavish oppression. Thus the contrast between a minority enjoying the advantages of culture and a majority robbed of those advantages was, in that primal era of culture, taken to the extreme....

What means does civilization use to hold in check, render harmless, and perhaps eliminate the aggression that opposes it? We have already become acquainted with some of these methods, but not yet with the one that is apparently the most important. We can study it in the history of the development of the individual. What happens in individuals to render harmless their desire for aggression? Something very remarkable, which we would not have guessed and which is nevertheless so obvious. Aggression is introjected, internalized; indeed, it is sent back from where it came—and thus is turned against one's own ego. There it is taken over by a portion of the ego that distinguishes itself from the other portions as superego, and now, as "conscience," treats the ego with the same strict readiness for aggression that the ego would have liked to gratify upon other individuals. The tension between the strict superego and the ego, subject to it, we call the sense of guilt; it expresses itself as a need for punishment. Thus civilization overcomes individuals' dangerous desire for aggression by weakening them, disarming them, and setting up an agency within them to supervise, like an occupying force in a conquered city.

Concerning the origin of the sense of guilt, analysts think differently from other psychologists; but even for analysts, it is not easy to account for it. First of all, if one asks how a person arrives at a sense of guilt, one receives an indisputable answer: people feel guilty (the devout say "sinful") when they have done something they recognize as "bad." But then one notices how little this answer gives us. Perhaps, after some hesitation, one will add that even those who have not done this bad deed, but merely recognize in themselves the intention to do so, may consider themselves guilty; then the question arises as to why the intention is regarded here as equal to the deed. But both cases assume that people have already recognized bad deeds as reprehensible, as something not to be carried out. How do they reach this judgment? We can reject an original—as it were, natural—capacity to distinguish good from bad. Often bad deeds are not at all what is harmful or dangerous to the ego; rather, they are sometimes desirable and pleasurable to the ego. Here, then, an extraneous influence is evident—an influence that determines what is to be called good or bad. Since people's own feelings would not have led them down the same path, they must have a motive for subjecting themselves to this extraneous influence. This motive is easily discovered in people's helplessness and dependence on others, and can best be designated as fear of the loss of love. If one loses the love of another person one depends on, one also loses protection from various dangers and is exposed especially to the danger that this much stronger person will demonstrate his superiority in the form of punishment. Initially, then, what is bad is that for which one is threatened with the loss of love. Due to fear of that loss, one must avoid what is bad. Therefore it makes little difference whether one has already done the bad deed, or merely intends to do so. In both cases, the danger only arises when the authority discovers it, and in both cases the authority would behave in a similar way. This situation is called a "bad conscience," but it actually does not deserve that name, for at this stage the sense of guilt, clearly, is only fear of the loss of love—"social" anxiety. In the small child it can never be anything else, but in many adults as well, the only thing that has changed is that in the place of the father or of both parents the greater human community now stands. Therefore these persons regularly allow themselves to carry out bad deeds that promise them comfort or advantage, provided they are sure that the authority will discover nothing and can hold nothing against them; their fear relates only to being discovered.[9] Present-day society must generally reckon with this situation.

A great change takes place once the authority is internalized by setting up a superego. With this, the phenomena of conscience are raised to a higher level, and it is only at this point that one should actually speak of conscience or a sense of guilt.[10] Here the fear of being discovered disappears, and the distinction between doing something bad and wishing something bad disappears completely, for nothing can hide from the superego—not even thoughts. The real-world seriousness of the situation has faded away, for the new authority, the superego, has no motive we know of for mistreating the ego, with which it is closely bound. But historic influence, which allows what is past and surmounted to live on, expresses itself in that everything remains basically as it was in the beginning. The superego torments the sinful ego with the same feelings of anxiety and lurks, watching for chances to have the ego punished by the external world.

In this second stage of development, the conscience demonstrates a characteristic unknown in the first stage and is no longer easy to explain. Indeed, the more virtuous a person is, the stricter and more suspicious the behavior of the conscience becomes, so that in the end precisely those who have come the furthest in saintliness reproach themselves with the most extreme sinfulness.... Another fact from the field of ethics, so rich in problems, is that misfortune—i.e., external denial of gratification—so greatly promotes

9 [Freud's note:] One is reminded of Rousseau's famous mandarin. [A philosophical-moral conundrum attributed to social philosopher Jean-Jacques Rousseau (1712–78): If, through a simple gesture, and without leaving Paris, one could cause the death of a mandarin in Peking, and if this brought some form of personal advantage, would one do so?]

10 [Freud's note:] Anyone with insight will understand and acknowledge the fact that in this summary things have been sharply separated which in reality occur in fluid stages, and that the issue is not merely the existence of a superego, but its relative strength and sphere of influence. The entire previous discussion of conscience and guilt is, of course, common knowledge and almost undisputed.

the strength of the conscience in the superego. As long as things are going well for people, their conscience is merciful and allows the ego all sorts of things; but when some misfortune has struck them, they examine themselves inwardly, recognize their sinfulness, raise the standards of the conscience, impose abstinences on themselves, and punish themselves with penances.[11] Entire peoples have behaved in this way, and still do. This, however, is easily explained by the original infantile stage of conscience, which, after introjection into the superego, is not abandoned, but persists beside and behind that introjection. Fate is regarded as a substitute for the agency of the parents. If people experience misfortune, this means that they are no longer loved by this highest power; threatened by this potential loss of love, they once again bow before the parental representative in the superego....

Thus we are familiar with two sources of the sense of guilt—that arising in the fear of authority, and the later one arising in the fear of the superego. The first forces people to renounce the gratification of drives, and the second, going beyond that, presses for punishment since the persistence of forbidden wishes cannot be concealed from the superego. We have also heard how one can understand the severity of the superego, i.e., the demands of the conscience. The severity of the superego simply perpetuates the severity of external authority, which has been separated from it and partially replaced by it. We now see in what relation the renunciation of drives stands to the sense of guilt. Originally, of course, the renunciation of drives was the result of the fear of external authority: one renounced gratifications so as not to lose its love. If one has achieved this renunciation, one is paid up with external authority, so to speak; no sense of guilt should remain. But with the fear of the superego things are different. Here, the renunciation of drives is not enough, for the wish persists and cannot be kept secret from the superego. Thus, despite the renunciation that has occurred, a sense of guilt will arise, and this is a great economic disadvantage in the establishment of the superego, or, as one might say, in the formation of the conscience. The renunciation of drives now no longer has a fully liberating effect; virtuous abstinence is no longer rewarded with the assurance of love. A threatening external unhappiness—loss of love and punishment by the external authority—has been traded in for a lasting internal unhappiness, the tension of the sense of guilt.

These interrelations are so complex and at the same time so important that, despite the risk of repetition, I would still like to address them from another side. The chronological sequence would thus be the following: first comes renunciation of drives due to fear of aggression by external authority. (That, of course, is the true nature of the loss of love: love protects one from the aggression of punishment.) Then comes the establishment of an internal authority, and renunciation of drives due to fear of that authority, conscience. In this second case comes the equivalency of bad deeds and bad intent, and hence a sense of guilt and a need for punishment. The aggression of conscience perpetuates the aggression of authority. Thus far, things have presumably become clear, but where does this leave room for the conscience-strengthening influence of misfortune (externally imposed renunciation), and for the extraordinary severity of conscience in the best and most compliant people? We have already explained both of these special characteristics of conscience, but we probably still have the impression that these explanations do not get to the bottom of things, and leave an unexplained remainder. And here, finally, an idea arises which belongs exclusively to psychoanalysis and is foreign to people's usual manner of thinking. This idea is of the type that allows us to understand why the topic necessarily seemed so confused and opaque. Specifically, it tells us the following: initially, conscience (more correctly,

11 [Freud's note:] In one of his delightful little stories, "The first melon I ever stole," Mark Twain illustrates this promotion of morality through misfortune. This first melon happens to be unripe. I heard Mark Twain tell the story himself. After pronouncing the title, he paused and asked himself as if in doubt: "*Was it the first?*" With this, he had said everything. Thus, the first melon was not the only one. [An unpublished anecdote related by Mark Twain during his first public lecture in Vienna, 9 February 1898.]

the anxiety that later becomes conscience) is indeed the cause of drive-renunciation, but later the relationship is reversed. Every renunciation of drives now becomes a dynamic source of conscience, every new renunciation increases the severity and intolerance of the conscience, and if we could only bring it better into harmony with our knowledge of the history of the genesis of conscience, we would be tempted to adopt the paradoxical claim that the conscience is the result of the renunciation of drives, or that the (externally imposed) renunciation of drives creates conscience, which then demands further renunciation of drives.

... [L]et us consider the case of the drive for aggression, and let us assume that in these situations it is always the renunciation of aggression that is involved. This, of course, will only be a temporary assumption. The effect of drive-renunciation on the conscience proceeds in the following manner: every bit of aggression we neglect to gratify is taken over by the superego and increases the aggression of the superego (against the ego). This does not mesh well with the claim that the original aggressiveness of the conscience is the perpetuated severity of external authority and thus has nothing to do with renunciation. But we can make this discrepancy disappear if we assume a different derivation for this first version of the aggression of the superego. Against the authority that blocks the child in the first, but also most important gratifications, a considerable amount of aggressive inclination must have developed in the child, regardless of the nature of the drive deprivations imposed. Of necessity, children must renounce the gratification of this vengeful aggression. They find their way out of this economically difficult situation through well-known mechanisms: they take up this unassailable authority into themselves. It now becomes the superego and comes to possess all the aggression which, as a child, one would have liked to exercise against it. The child's ego must content itself with the sad role of the authority—the father—degraded in this way. This is a reversal of the situation, as so often occurs. "If I were the father and you were the child, I would treat you badly." The relationship between the superego and the ego is the return, distorted by the wish, of real relationships between the still undivided ego and an external object. This is also typical. But the essential difference is that the original severity of the superego is not—or is not so much—the severity one has experienced from the external object or attributes to it, but is rather one's own aggression toward it. If this is correct, one may in fact assert that in the beginning the conscience arose through the suppression of an aggressive impulse, and that it was subsequently strengthened by renewed suppressions of this type.

Which of these two conceptions is correct? The earlier one, which seemed so unassailable historically, or the newer one, which rounds off the theory in such a welcome way?[12] Clearly—as also indicated by the evidence of direct observation—both are justified. They do not contradict one another, and even meet at one point, for children's vengeful aggression will in part be determined by the amount of punishing aggression they expect from their father. Yet experience shows that the severity of the superego—the superego the child develops—in no way reflects the severity of the treatment the child has experienced.[13] The first seems independent of the second; given a very gentle upbringing, a child may acquire a very strict conscience. But it would also be incorrect to exaggerate this independence; it is not difficult to convince oneself that the strictness of the upbringing also exerts a strong influence on the formation of the child's superego. In essence, in the construction of the superego and the genesis of the conscience, innate constitutional factors, and influences from the milieu of the real environment, act together—and this is by

12 Freud is essentially drawing a distinction between the realms of psychoanalysis and metapsychology, respectively.

13 [Freud's note:] As correctly emphasized by Melanie Klein [1882–1960] and other English writers.

no means surprising, but is, rather, the universal etiological condition for all such processes.[14]

...

When one has a sense of guilt after and because one has committed a misdeed, the feeling should sooner be called *remorse*. It relates only to one act, and of course requires that a *conscience*, the readiness to feel guilt, already exist before the act. Such remorse, then, can never help us to find the origin of conscience and of the sense of guilt in general. The course of events in these everyday cases is usually that a drive-need has acquired the strength to achieve gratification despite the conscience, which is also limited in strength, and that with the natural weakening of the need, through gratification, the former relations of strength are restored. Psychoanalysis is thus justified in excluding from this presentation the case of the sense of guilt due to remorse, however often it occurs and however great its practical significance may be.

... The decisive thing is really not whether one has killed one's father or has abstained from the deed. One will feel guilty in both cases, for the sense of guilt is an expression of the conflict of ambivalence, of the eternal struggle between Eros and the drive for destruction or death. This conflict is incited as soon as people are faced with the task of living together. So long as the community knows no other form than the family, the conflict must express itself in the Oedipus complex, give rise to conscience, and create the first sense of guilt. When an expansion of the community is attempted, the same conflict—in forms dependent on the past—is continued and strengthened, leading to a further intensification of the sense of guilt. Since civilization obeys an inner erotic impulse commanding it to unite people in a closely bound mass, it can achieve this goal only through an ever-increasing strengthening of the sense of guilt. What began in relation to the father is completed in relation to the mass. If civilization is the necessary course of development from the family to humanity, then, inextricably bound up with civilization, there is an increase in the sense of guilt, perhaps to heights the individual finds hard to bear—an increase that is due to the inborn conflict of ambivalence and to the eternal struggle between love and strivings toward death....

7.6 Heinrich Himmler (1900–1945)

Heinrich Himmler was the head officer of the Nazi SS paramilitary organization from 1929 to 1945. As one of the highest ranking officials in the Nazi regime, he had a direct role in planning and executing the Holocaust, the Nazi plan to exterminate all the Jews (as well as Roma, Poles, non-heterosexuals, and others) in Germany and eventually all of Europe, which led to the deaths of eleven to fourteen million people. Himmler was directly responsible for setting up the concentration camps in which the victims of the Nazi regime were imprisoned and ultimately put to death. When Himmler realized Germany would lose World War II, he attempted to set up peace talks with the United States without

14 [Freud's note:] In *The Psychoanalysis of the Total Personality* (1927) and in connection with Aichhorn's study of delinquency (1925), Franz Alexander [1881–1964] has accurately addressed the two main types of pathogenic methods of upbringing—over-strictness and spoiling. The "unduly lenient and indulgent father" brings about the development of an over-strict superego in the child because, given the love the child receives, no other outlet remains for the child's aggression but to turn it inward. In delinquent children brought up without love, the tension between ego and superego is absent, and all their aggression can be directed outward. Thus, disregarding a constitutional factor, which may be assumed, one can say that a strict conscience arises from the collaboration of two factors: the frustration of drives, which unleashes aggression, and the experience of love, which turns the aggression inward and transfers it to the superego.

Hitler's approval and was ultimately dismissed by Hitler and targeted for arrest. Himmler was detained by British forces and committed suicide in British custody in May of 1945.

This speech is the first of the two Poznan (Posen) speeches, delivered secretly by Himmler to top Nazi officials in the occupied Polish city of Poznan. This speech is particularly important historically because it is the first recorded document that refers specifically to the Nazi project of genocide without recourse to euphemisms. Rather than the usual "final solution," Himmler refers directly to "the extermination of the Jewish people," proving beyond a shadow of a doubt that the Nazi party knew about, wanted, and planned the Holocaust. The focus of the speech, however, is on providing the listeners with an ideological framework that will allow them to carry out extremely brutal, murderous acts without being obstructed by guilt or moral feeling. Specifically, Himmler repeatedly invokes the notion that resisting sympathy for Nazism's victims is a form of heroic self-sacrifice, and the notion that the listeners' moral duty is only to their own racial-ethnic group, in relation to whom all other racial ethnic-groups constitute a threat.

This speech provides a wonderful illustration, both of Arendt's thesis about the banality of evil and Zimbardo's conclusions about the social contexts that allow ordinary people to suspend their moral judgement. Taking cues from Eichmann's faulty or selective reading of Kant's ethical imperative, Arendt argues that Nazism constitutes a particularly difficult moral challenge: While we are used to the idea that being moral means resisting our own selfish impulses and performing our social duty for others, in the Nazi context it was precisely morality and sympathy that became the temptation (which Himmler here encourages his listeners to resist), while being obedient to one's social duty was immoral. Moreover, Himmler deploys many of the strategies Zimbardo describes that encourage and allow for the suspension of moral judgement: compartmentalization, dehumanization, seemingly moral rhetoric, and more.

from A Speech at Posen, October 1943

In the months which have past since we last met in June of 1942, many comrades have fallen and given their lives for Germany and for the Führer. Before them, in the forefront—I ask you to stand in their honour, and in the honour of all our dead SS men and dead German soldiers, men and women—in the forefront, from our ranks, our old comrade and friend, SS Obergruppenführer Eicke....

For the SS Man, one principle must apply absolutely: we must be honest, decent, loyal, and comradely to members of our own blood, and to no one else. What happens to the Russians, the Czechs, is totally indifferent to me. Whatever is available to us in good blood of our type, we will take for ourselves, that is, we will steal their children and bring them up with us, if necessary. Whether other races live well or die of hunger is only of interest to me insofar as we need them as slaves for our culture; otherwise that doesn't interest me. Whether 10,000 Russian women fall down from exhaustion in building a tank ditch is of interest to me only insofar as the tank ditches are finished for Germany.

We will never be hard and heartless when it is not necessary; that is clear. We Germans, the only ones in the world with a decent attitude towards animals, will also adopt a decent attitude with regards to these human animals; but it is a sin against our own blood to worry about them and give them ideals, so that our sons and grandchildren will have a harder time with them. When somebody comes to me and says, "I can't build tank ditches with children or women. That's inhumane, they'll die doing it." Then I must say: "You are a murderer of your own blood, since, if the tank ditches are not built, then German soldiers will die, and they are the sons of German mothers. That is our blood." That is how I would like to indoctrinate this SS, and, I believe, have indoctrinated, as one of the holiest laws of the future: our concern, our duty, is to our people, and to our blood. That is what we must care for and think about, work for and fight for, and nothing else. Everything else can be indifferent to us. I wish the SS to face the problem of all foreign, non-Germanic peoples, particularly the Russians, with this attitude. Everything else is moonshine, a fraud against our own people, and an obstacle to earlier victory in the war....

When I was appointed Reich's Minister of the Interior, everybody said (since it's so awfully easy to say), "Mister, hit hard, stay tough. The German people expect terrible severity from you." I'm already severe, I don't need any admonitions. It's very easy to say something like that, but: a death sentence means eternal misery for a whole family; it means bringing shame on a name which was once honourable. Imagine for a moment what it will mean to the children and grandchildren of that family, when it is later said (you must always visualize these things as they will look 10 or 15 years after the war): "The father of this family was beheaded for high treason during the Great War, which involved the fate of the Germanic nation." (In the distant future, everything we do today will look heroic. Human weaknesses will then be forgotten. All the cowards will have died off in the meantime, and in the end everybody will be considered a hero.) Such a family will be shamed for all time. I know all that. I know how hard it is; and I therefore try to restrict the necessary educational measures....

I'll never catch every defeatist. I'm perfectly well aware that, in one or two years, when the divisions and regiments withdraw into their garrisons—some of the older veterans having been wounded up to 7 or 8 or 9 or 10 times, while the rest no longer march with us because they lie under the grass; when, I hope, a still decent part of the old SS once again marches back to Germany, I know that many thousands will applaud us then, and perhaps feel themselves to have been much more heroic than we were, or—we don't think of ourselves as heroic—more decent than we were.

It will always be like that. I don't mind. We shouldn't mind either. We should never lose our sense of humour. It is, however, necessary to set an example for the number of cowards who can be found among every people. It is, God knows, unfortunately true that these cowards are always found in the upper, rather than the lower or middle, ranks of a people. Intellect obviously ruins the character in some manner, at least as regards the formation of will and energy. It's enough for me, for such education, if I always grab one out of 100 of the defeatists who later cry "hurrah," and lay his head between his feet. Then the others will shut up for a quarter of a year. Then all the little mommies will say, "For God's sake, don't get yourself killed, don't make us unhappy. Somebody we know was recently beheaded. It's in the newspapers. So just keep quiet, cry 'hurrah' very loud."

Good, let him; we've achieved our objective. We could never storm a fort or a front line position with a person like that anyway. We know that anyway. But the main thing is to keep them from hurting our decent people. Insofar as is necessary, action will be taken brutally and mercilessly. None of us enjoys that. Although we don't like it, you must act mercilessly, gentlemen, without regard to family relationships, or acquaintance, or class, or possible previous earlier service; without regard to whether he is a party comrade or not, when the fate of the nation so requires. Always go after a big fish rather than a little one who's stupid and has been fooled. The domestic front will always be in order if we have the nerve to keep it in order, although it gives us no pleasure to take action personally.

We must be also clear in our minds that we have 6 or 7 million foreigners in Germany. There may even be 8 million. We have prisoners in Germany. They are not all dangerous, as long as we strike hard at the smallest minor problem. It's a small matter to shoot 10 Poles today, instead of maybe having to shoot tens of thousands in their place later, and compared to the fact that shooting those tens of thousands would also cost German blood, too. Every little blaze must be immediately stamped out, smothered, extinguished; otherwise, just as in a real fire, a veritable prairie fire, politically and psychologically, may break out among the people....

... This war will ensure that everything annexed to the German Reich, to Greater Germany, and then to the Germanic Reich in the years since 1938, will remain ours. This war is being carried on to keep the path to the East open; so that Germany may be a world power; to found the Germanic World Empire. That will be the meaning of this war, whether it lasts 5, 6, perhaps even 7 years. We don't know how long it will last. We don't even ask how long. It will be carried on by us for as long as it lasts, and it will be carried on with determination and good humour by us for as long as it lasts. It will be won by the side that stands, that doesn't give up or give in, even in the most difficult situations. To ensure that this never happens, is our principal task....

... As Reichsführer-SS, as Chief of the German Police, and now as Reichsminister of the Interior, I would have no moral right to proceed against any racial comrade, nor could we bring forth the strength to do so, if we did not take care to cleanse our own ranks brutally. You can be sure that I will do this as Reichsminister of the Interior. You can also be sure that I will not go off at a madman's clip, and then maybe pull the bridle so hard that the nag falls down on his hindquarters; rather, the bit will be pulled slowly and gradually, so the horse will be brought to a decent pace again.

... We [the SS] tackle the most ungrateful problems, and I must admit that whether it's in [SS Group Leader Oswald] Pohl's concentration camps or his economic operations, whether outside among the Higher SS and Police Leaders or in the factories of the SS Administrative Main Office, one thing is obvious: we are SS men wherever we are. If something is in a bad way, get right down to it. Educate every subordinate in this direction for me. We want to help without being hindered by jurisdiction, since, after all, we want to win the war. Whatever we do, after all, we're doing for Germany. Whether it involves the building of a street or a tunnel that isn't going ahead somewhere; whether it's an invention which can't come into existence due to sheer bureaucracy, or whether it's something else: wherever we can lend a hand, we're going to do it. Whatever we achieve in our armaments factories will be a considerable accomplishment, one which is worth seeing, even if we can only describe and estimate it at the end of the war.

I want to mention another very difficult matter here before you in all frankness. Among ourselves, it ought to be spoken of quite openly for once; yet we shall never speak of it in public. Just as little as we hesitated to do our duty as ordered on 30 June 1934, and place comrades who had failed against the wall and shoot them, just as little did we ever speak of it, and we shall never speak of it. It was a matter of course, of tact, for us, thank God, never to speak of it, never to talk of it. It made everybody shudder; yet everyone was clear in his mind that he would do it again if ordered to do so, and if it was necessary.

I am thinking now of the evacuation of the Jews, the extirpation of the Jewish people. It is one of those things that's easy to say: "The Jewish people will be extirpated," says every Party comrade, "that's quite clear, it's in our program: elimination of the Jews, extirpation; that's what we're doing." And then they all come along, these 80 million good Germans, and every one of them has his decent Jew. Of course, it's quite clear that the others are pigs, but this one is one first-class Jew. Of all those who speak this way, not one has looked on; not one has lived through it.

Most of you know what it means when 100 bodies lie together, when 500 lie there, or if 1,000 lie there. To have gone through this, and at the same time, apart from exceptions caused by human weaknesses, to have remained decent, that has made us hard. This is a chapter of glory in our history which has never been written, and which never shall be written; since we know how hard it would be for us if we still had the Jews, as secret saboteurs, agitators, and slander-mongers, among us now, in every city—during the bombing raids, with the suffering and deprivations of the war. We would probably already be in the same situation as in 1916/17 if we still had the Jews in the body of the German people.

The riches they had, we've taken away from them. I have given a strict order, which SS Group Leader Pohl has carried out, that these riches shall, of course, be diverted to the Reich without exception. We have taken none of it. Individuals who failed were punished according to an order given by me at the beginning, which threatened: he who takes even one mark of it, that's his death. A number of SS men—not very many—have violated that order, and that will be their death, without mercy. We had the moral right, we had the duty to our own people, to kill this people which wanted to kill us. But we don't have the right to enrich ourselves even with one fur, one watch, one mark, one cigarette, or anything else. Just because we eradicated a bacillus, after all, doesn't mean we want to be infected by the bacillus and die. I will never permit even one little spot of corruption to arise or become established here. Wherever it may form, we shall burn it out together. In general, however, we can say that we have carried out this most difficult task out of love for our own people. And we have suffered no harm to our inner self, our soul, our character in so doing....

We [members of the SS] have arisen through the law of selection. We have selected from the average of our people. Our people arose through the dice game of Fate and history in long primeval times, over generations and centuries. Foreign peoples swept over this people and left their hereditary material in them. Channels of foreign blood flowed into this people; yet this people has nevertheless, through horrifying misery and frightful blows of fate, still had, in their blood vessels, the strength to endure.

Thus, this entire people has been drenched in, and is held together by, Nordic-Faelisch-Germanic blood; so that in the end one could, and still can, continue to speak of a German people. Out of this people, the result of diverse mixtures of hereditary factors, such as was available after the collapse which followed the years of the struggle for freedom, we have now consciously attempted to select the northern Germanic blood, since we could assume that this part of the blood was the bearer of the creative and heroic, of the life-maintaining qualities of our people. We examined the outward appearance on the one hand, and then revised that outward appearance in terms of new requirements on the other hand, through more and more samples, both physical and intellectual, both of character and soul.

We repeatedly sought out and rejected that which was not suitable, that which did not adapt to us. As long as we possess the strength to do so, this Order will remain healthy. The moment we forget the law of the racial foundation of our people, the law of selection and severity with regards to ourselves, then the germ of death will lie within us; in that moment we will perish, just as every human organization, every prime of life in this world, comes to an end at last. To enable this flourishing and bearing of fruit to continue for as long and as blessedly as possible, and—don't be alarmed—for as many thousands of years as possible, must be our aspiration and our inner law. For that reason, it is our duty, whenever we meet and whatever we do, to remember our principle: blood, selection, severity. The law of nature is precisely this: what is hard, is good; what is strong, is good; that which endures out of the struggle for existence, both physically and in terms of will and soul, is good—always viewed from the vantage point of time....

7.7 Hannah Arendt (1906–1975)

Arendt was a German-born Jewish philosopher and academic whose ideas have had a profound impact on Western political thought. She is best remembered for her work on democracy, totalitarianism, and the nature of evil. In the years leading up to Hitler's rise to power, Arendt encountered increasing anti-Semitism in her own country and was briefly imprisoned by the Gestapo—the Nazi secret police—in 1933. On her release, Arendt fled Germany for France, but was detained again when Germany invaded France at the beginning of World War II. In 1941, she escaped and fled to America, and lived in New York for the rest of her life.

Eichmann in Jerusalem began as a journalistic piece in which Arendt reported on the trial of Adolf Eichmann, a Lieutenant Colonel in the Nazi SS, which she had attended. At the end of World War II in 1945, many high-ranking Nazi party members faced prosecution—and many of them were given the death penalty—under international law at the Nuremberg trials. Several of the highest-ranking Nazi leaders, including Hitler, committed suicide in order to escape prosecution, and many escaped into hiding around the world. Eichmann was in this last category. In 1960, members of the Mossad—Israel's secret police—captured Eichmann in Argentina and smuggled him, in contravention of international law, back to Israel to stand trial in Jerusalem. In 1962 Eichmann was found guilty by the Israeli Supreme Court of crimes against Jews, Poles, Slovenes, and Roma, and membership in three different criminal organizations. He was sentenced to execution by hanging.

What Arendt began as a series of magazine articles gradually became a book-length meditation on the nature of evil in which she offered an unsettling answer to the question of what sort of person could participate in a project as horrifying as the Holocaust. In contrast to assumptions common at the time and even to the final ruling of the court, Arendt contended that Eichmann was not an essentially evil person, nor even especially anti-Semitic, but was in fact perfectly normal, hence her book's subtitle "The Banality of Evil." If anything set Eichmann apart it was that he was slightly below average intelligence, had faced a series of humiliating failures in his life, and preferred being told what to do as a member of a large organization to having to make decisions on his own. The unsettling implications of Arendt's argument remain controversial to this day: anyone might become an Eichmann under the right circumstances if they are not vigilant, and precisely those characteristics that our societies tend to hold up as those of a "good citizen" make one more, not less, vulnerable to this possibility.

~

from Eichmann in Jerusalem

II: The Accused

Otto Adolf, son of Karl Adolf Eichmann and Maria, née Schefferling, caught in a suburb of Buenos Aires on the evening of May 11, 1960, flown to Israel nine days later, brought to trial in the District Court in Jerusalem on April 11, 1961, stood accused on fifteen counts: "together with others" he had committed crimes against the Jewish people, crimes against humanity, and war crimes during the whole period of the Nazi regime and especially during the period of the Second World War. The Nazis and Nazi Collaborators (Punishment) Law of 1950, under which he was tried, provides that "a person who has committed one of these ... offenses ... is liable to the death penalty." To each count Eichmann pleaded: "Not guilty in the sense of the indictment."

In what sense then did he think he was guilty? In the long cross-examination of the accused, according to him "the longest ever known," neither the defense nor the prosecution nor, finally, any of the three judges ever bothered to ask him this obvious question. His lawyer, Robert Servatius of Cologne, hired by Eichmann and paid by the Israeli government (following the precedent set at the Nuremberg Trials, where all attorneys for the defense were paid by the Tribunal of the victorious powers), answered the question in a press interview: "Eichmann feels guilty before God, not before the law," but this answer remained without confirmation from the accused himself. The defense would apparently have preferred him to plead not guilty on the grounds that under the then existing Nazi legal system he had not done anything wrong, that what he was accused of were not crimes but "acts of state," over which no other state has jurisdiction (*par in parem imperium non habet*), that it had been his duty to obey and that, in Servatius' words, he had committed acts "for which you are decorated if you win and go to the gallows if you lose." (Thus Goebbels had declared in 1943: "We will go down in history as the greatest statesmen of all times or as their greatest criminals.") Outside Israel (at a meeting of the Catholic Academy in Bavaria, devoted to what the *Rheinischer Merkur* called "the ticklish problem" of the "possibilities and limits in the coping with historical and political guilt through criminal proceedings"), Servatius went a step farther, and declared that "the only legitimate criminal problem of the Eichmann trial lies in pronouncing judgment against his Israeli captors, which so far has not been done"—a statement, incidentally, that is somewhat difficult to reconcile with his repeated and widely publicized utterances in Israel, in which he called the conduct of the trial "a great spiritual achievement," comparing it favorably with the Nuremberg Trials.

Eichmann's own attitude was different. First of all, the indictment for murder was wrong: "With the killing of Jews I had nothing to do. I never killed a Jew, or a non-Jew, for that matter—I never killed any human being. I never gave an order to kill either a Jew or a non-Jew; I just did not do it," or, as he was later to qualify this statement, "It so happened ... that I had not once to do it"—for he left no doubt that he would have killed his own father if he had received an order to that effect. Hence he repeated over and over (what he had already stated in the so-called Sassen documents, the interview that he had given in 1955 in Argentina to the Dutch journalist Sassen, a former S.S. man who was also a fugitive from justice, and that, after Eichmann's capture, had been published in part by *Life* in this country and by *Der Stern* in Germany) that he could be accused only of "aiding and abetting the annihilation of the Jews," which he declared in Jerusalem to have been "one of the greatest crimes in the history of Humanity." The defense paid no attention to Eichmann's own theory, but the prosecution wasted much time in an unsuccessful effort to prove that Eichmann had once, at least, killed with his own hands (a Jewish boy in Hungary), and it spent even more time, and more successfully, on a note that

Franz Rademacher, the Jewish expert in the German Foreign Office, had scribbled on one of the documents dealing with Yugoslavia during a telephone conversation, which read: "Eichmann proposes shooting." This turned out to be the only "order to kill," if that is what it was, for which there existed even a shred of evidence....

Would he then have pleaded guilty if he had been indicted as an accessory to murder? Perhaps, but he would have made important qualifications. What he had done was a crime only in retrospect, and he had always been a law-abiding citizen, because Hitler's orders, which he had certainly executed to the best of his ability, had possessed "the force of law" in the Third Reich. (The defense could have quoted in support of Eichmann's thesis the testimony of one of the best-known experts on constitutional law in the Third Reich, Theodor Maunz, currently Minister of Education and Culture in Bavaria, who stated in 1943 [in *Gestalt und Recht der Polizei*]: "The command of the Führer ... is the absolute center of the present legal order.") Those who today told Eichmann that he could have acted differently simply did not know, or had forgotten, how things had been. He did not want to be one of those who now pretended that "they had always been against it," whereas in fact they had been very eager to do what they were told to do. However, times change, and he, like Professor Maunz, had "arrived at different insights." What he had done he had done, he did not want to deny it; rather, he proposed "to hang myself in public as a warning example for all anti-Semites on this earth." By this he did not mean to say that he regretted anything: "Repentance is for little children. (*Sic!*) ..."

Throughout the trial, Eichmann tried to clarify, mostly without success, this second point in his plea of "not guilty in the sense of the indictment." The indictment implied not only that he had acted on purpose, which he did not deny, but out of base motives and in full knowledge of the criminal nature of his deeds. As for the base motives, he was perfectly sure that he was not what he called an *innerer Schweinehund*, a dirty bastard in the depths of his heart; and as for his conscience, he remembered perfectly well that he would have had a bad conscience only if he had not done what he had been ordered to—to ship millions of men, women, and children to their death with great zeal and the most meticulous care. This, admittedly, was hard to take. Half a dozen psychiatrists had certified him as "normal"—"More normal, at any rate, than I am after having examined him," one of them was said to have exclaimed, while another had found that his whole psychological outlook, his attitude toward his wife and children, mother and father, brothers, sisters, and friends, was "not only normal but most desirable"—and finally the minister who had paid regular visits to him in prison after the Supreme Court had finished hearing his appeal reassured everybody by declaring Eichmann to be "a man with very positive ideas." Behind the comedy of the soul experts lay the hard fact that his was obviously no case of moral let alone legal insanity. (Mr. Hausner's recent revelations in the *Saturday Evening Post* of things he "could not bring out at the trial" have contradicted the information given informally in Jerusalem. Eichmann, we are now told, had been alleged by the psychiatrists to be "a man obsessed with a dangerous and insatiable urge to kill," "a perverted, sadistic personality." In which case he would have belonged in an insane asylum.) Worse, his was obviously also no case of insane hatred of Jews, of fanatical anti-Semitism or indoctrination of any kind. He "personally" never had anything whatever against Jews; on the contrary, he had plenty of "private reasons" for not being a Jew hater. To be sure, there were fanatic anti-Semites among his closest friends, for instance Lászlo Endre, State Secretary in Charge of Political (Jewish) Affairs in Hungary, who was hanged in Budapest in 1946; but this, according to Eichmann, was more or less in the spirit of "some of my best friends are anti-Semites."

Alas, nobody believed him. The prosecutor did not believe him, because that was not his job. Counsel for the defense paid no attention because he, unlike Eichmann, was, to all appearances, not interested in questions of conscience. And the judges did not believe him, because they were too good, and perhaps also too conscious of the very foundations of their profession, to admit that an average, "normal" person, neither feeble-minded nor indoctrinated nor cynical, could be perfectly incapable of telling right from wrong. They preferred to conclude from occasional lies that he was a liar—and missed the greatest moral and even legal challenge of the whole case. Their case rested on the assumption that the defendant, like all "normal persons," must have been aware of the criminal nature of his acts, and Eichmann was indeed normal insofar as he was "no exception within the Nazi regime." However, under the conditions of the Third Reich only "exceptions" could be expected to react "normally." This simple truth of the matter created a dilemma for the judges which they could neither resolve nor escape....

... Eichmann's father, first an accountant for the Tramways and Electricity Company in Solingen and after 1913 an official of the same corporation in Austria, in Linz, had five children, four sons and a daughter, of whom only Adolf, the eldest, it seems, was unable to finish high school, or even to graduate from the vocational school for engineering into which he was then put. Throughout his life, Eichmann deceived people about his early "misfortunes" by hiding behind the more honorable financial misfortunes of his father....

Well, the disasters were ordinary: since he "had not exactly been the most hard-working" pupil—or, one may add, the most gifted—his father had taken him first from high school and then from vocational school, long before graduation. Hence, the profession that appears on all his official documents, construction engineer, had about as much connection with reality as the statement that his birthplace was Palestine and that he was fluent in Hebrew and Yiddish—another outright lie Eichmann had loved to tell both to his S.S. comrades and to his Jewish victims. It was in the same vein that he had always pretended he had been dismissed from his job as salesman for the Vacuum Oil Company in Austria because of membership in the National Socialist Party. The version he confided to Captain Less was less dramatic, though probably not the truth either: he had been fired because it was a time of unemployment, when unmarried employees were the first to lose their jobs. (This explanation, which at first seems plausible, is not very satisfactory, because he lost his job in the spring of 1933, when he had been engaged for two full years to Veronika, or Vera, Liebl, who later became his wife. Why had he not married her before, when he still had a good job? He finally married in March, 1935, probably because bachelors in the S.S., as in the Vacuum Oil Company, were never sure of their jobs and could not be promoted.) Clearly, bragging had always been one of his cardinal vices.

While young Eichmann was doing poorly in school, his father left the Tramway and Electricity Company and went into business for himself. He bought a small mining enterprise and put his unpromising youngster to work in it as an ordinary mining laborer, but only until he found him a job in the sales department of the Oberösterreichischen Elektrobau Company, where Eichmann remained for over two years. He was now about twenty-two years old and without any prospects for a career; the only thing he had learned, perhaps, was how to sell.... A cousin of his stepmother—a man he called "uncle"—who was president of the Austrian Automobile Club and was married to the daughter of a Jewish businessman in Czechoslovakia, had used his connection with the general director of the Austrian Vacuum Oil Company, a Jewish Mr. Weiss, to obtain for his unfortunate relation a job as traveling salesman. Eichmann was properly grateful; the Jews in his family were among his "private reasons" for not hating Jews. Even in 1943 or 1944, when the Final Solution was in full swing, he had not forgotten: "The daughter of this marriage, half-Jewish according to the Nuremberg Laws, ... came to see me in order to obtain my permission for her emigration into Switzerland. Of course, I granted this request, and the same uncle came also to see me to ask me to intervene for some Viennese Jewish couple. I mention this only to show that I myself had no hatred for Jews, for my whole education through my mother and my father had been strictly Christian; my mother, because of her Jewish relatives, held different opinions from those current in S.S. circles." ...

... Had Eichmann been a bit less prim or the police examination (which refrained from cross-examination, presumably to remain assured of his cooperation) less discreet, his "lack of prejudice" might have shown itself in still another aspect. It seems that in Vienna, where he was so extraordinarily successful in arranging the "forced emigration" of Jews, he had a Jewish mistress, an "old flame" from Linz. *Rassenschande*, sexual intercourse with Jews, was probably the greatest crime a member of the S.S. could commit, and though during the war the raping of Jewish girls became a favorite pastime at the front, it was by no means common for a Higher S.S. officer to have an affair with a Jewish woman. Thus, Eichmann's repeated violent denunciations of Julius Streicher, the insane and obscene editor of *Der Stürmer*, and of his pornographic anti-Semitism, were perhaps personally motivated, and the expression of more than the routine contempt an "enlightened" S.S. man was supposed to show toward the vulgar passions of lesser Party luminaries.

... At the end of 1932, he was unexpectedly transferred from Linz to Salzburg, very much against his inclinations: "I lost all joy in my work, I no longer liked to sell, to make calls." From such sudden losses of *Arbeitsfreude* Eichmann was to suffer throughout his life. The worst of them occurred when he was told of the Führer's order for the "physical extermination of the Jews," in which he was to play such an important role. This, too, came unexpectedly; he himself had "never thought of ... such a solution through violence," and he described his reaction in the same words: "I now lost everything, all joy in my work, all initiative, all interest; I was, so to speak, blown out." A similar blowing out must have happened in 1932 in Salzburg, and from his own account it is clear that he cannot have been very surprised when he was fired, though one need not believe his saying that he had been "very happy" about his dismissal....

... Before Eichmann entered the Party and the S.S., he had proved that he was a joiner, and May 8, 1945, the official date of Germany's defeat, was significant for him mainly because it then dawned upon him that thenceforward he would have to live without being a member of something or other. "I sensed I would have to live a leaderless and difficult individual life, I would receive no directives from anybody, no orders and commands would any longer be issued to me, no pertinent ordinances would be there to consult—in brief, a life never known before lay before me." When he was a child, his parents, uninterested in politics, had enrolled him in the Young Men's Christian Association, from which he later went into the German youth movement, the *Wandervogel*. During his four unsuccessful years in high school, he had joined the *Jungfrontkämpfeverband*, the youth section of the German-Austrian organization of war veterans, which, though violently pro-German and anti-republican, was tolerated by the Austrian government. When Kaltenbrunner suggested that he enter the S.S., he was just on the point of becoming a member of an altogether different outfit, the Freemasons' Lodge Schlaraffia, "an association of businessmen, physicians, actors, civil servants, etc., who came together to cultivate merriment and gaiety.... Each member had to give a lecture from time to time whose tenor was to be humor, refined humor." Kaltenbrunner explained to Eichmann that he would have to give up this merry society because as a Nazi he could not be a Freemason—a word that at the time was unknown to him. The choice between the S.S. and Schlaraffia (the name derives from *Schlaraffenland*, the gluttons' Cloud-Cuckoo Land of German fairy tales) might have been hard to make, but he was "kicked out" of Schlaraffia anyhow; he had committed a sin that even now, as he told the story in the Israeli prison, made him blush with shame: "Contrary to my upbringing, I had tried, though I was the youngest, to invite my companions to a glass of wine."

A leaf in the whirlwind of time, he was blown from Schlaraffia, the Never-Never Land of tables set by magic and roast chickens that flew into your mouth—or, more accurately, from the company of respectable philistines with degrees and assured careers and "refined humor," whose worst vice was probably an irrepressible desire for practical jokes—into the marching columns of the Thousand-Year Reich, which lasted exactly twelve years and three months. At any rate, he did not enter the Party out of conviction, nor was he ever convinced by it—whenever he was asked to give his reasons, he repeated the same embarrassed clichés about the Treaty of Versailles and unemployment; rather, as he pointed out in court, "it was like being swallowed up by the Party against all expectations and without previous decision. It happened so quickly and suddenly." He had no time and less desire to be properly informed, he did not even know the Party program, he never read *Mein Kampf*. Kaltenbrunner had said to him: Why not join the S.S.? And he had replied, Why not? That was how it had happened, and that was about all there was to it.

Of course, that was not all there was to it. What Eichmann failed to tell the presiding judge in cross-examination was that he had been an ambitious young man who was fed up with his job as traveling salesman even before the Vacuum Oil Company was fed up with him. From a humdrum life without significance and consequence the wind had blown him into History, as he understood it, namely, into a Movement that always kept moving and in which somebody like him—already a failure in the eyes of his social class, of his family, and hence in his own eyes as well—could start from scratch and still make a career. And if he did not always like what he had to do (for example, dispatching people to their death by the trainload instead of forcing them to emigrate), if he guessed, rather early, that the whole business would come to a bad end, with Germany losing the war, if all his most cherished plans came to nothing (the evacuation of European Jewry to Madagascar, the establishment of a Jewish territory in the Nisko region of Poland, the experiment with carefully built defense installations around his Berlin office to repel Russian tanks), and if, to his greatest "grief and sorrow," he never advanced beyond the grade of S.S. *Obersturmbannführer* (a rank equivalent to lieutenant colonel)—in short, if, with the exception of the year in Vienna, his life was beset with frustrations, he never forgot what the alternative would have been. Not only in Argentina, leading the unhappy existence of a refugee, but also in the courtroom in Jerusalem, with his life as good as forfeited, he might still have preferred—if anybody had asked him—to be hanged as *Obersturmbannführer a.D.* (in retirement) rather than living out his life quietly and normally as a traveling salesman for the Vacuum Oil Company....

VIII: Duties of a Law-Abiding Citizen

So Eichmann's opportunities for feeling like Pontius Pilate were many, and as the months and the years went by, he lost the need to feel anything at all. This was the way things were, this was the new law of the land, based on the Führer's order; whatever he did he did, as far as he could see, as a law-abiding citizen. He did his *duty*, as he told the police and the court over and over again; he not only obeyed *orders*, he also obeyed the *law*. Eichmann had a muddled inkling that this could be an important distinction, but neither the defense nor the judges ever took him up on it. The well-worn coins of "superior orders" versus "acts of state" were handed back and forth; they had governed the whole discussion of these matters during the Nuremberg Trials, for no other reason than that they gave the illusion that the altogether unprecedented could be judged according to precedents and the standards that went with them. Eichmann, with his rather modest mental gifts, was certainly the last man in the courtroom to be expected to challenge these notions and to strike out on his own. Since, in addition to performing what he conceived to be the duties of a law-abiding citizen, he had also acted upon orders—always so careful to be "covered"—he became completely muddled, and ended by stressing alternately the virtues and the vices of blind obedience, or the "obedience of corpses," *Kadavergehorsam*, as he himself called it.

The first indication of Eichmann's vague notion that there was more involved in this whole business than the question of the soldier's carrying out orders that are clearly criminal in nature and intent appeared during the police examination, when he suddenly declared with great emphasis that he had lived his whole life according to Kant's moral precepts, and especially according to a Kantian definition of duty. This was outrageous, on the face of it, and also incomprehensible, since Kant's moral philosophy is so closely bound up with man's faculty of judgment, which rules out blind obedience. The examining officer did not press the point, but Judge Raveh, either out of curiosity or out of indignation at Eichmann's having dared to invoke Kant's name in connection with his crimes, decided to question the accused. And, to the surprise of everybody, Eichmann came up with an approximately correct definition of the categorical imperative: "I meant by my remark about Kant that the principle of my will must always be such that it can become the principle of general laws" (which is not the case with theft or murder, for instance, because the thief or the murderer cannot conceivably wish to live under a legal system that would give others the right to rob or murder him). Upon further questioning, he added that he had read Kant's *Critique of Practical Reason*. He then proceeded to explain that from the moment he was charged with carrying out the Final Solution he had ceased to live according to Kantian principles, that he had known it, and that he had consoled himself with the thought that he no longer "was master of his own deeds," that he was unable "to change anything." What he failed to point out in court was that in this "period of crimes legalized by the state," as he himself now called it, he had not simply dismissed the Kantian formula as no longer applicable, he had distorted it to read: Act as if the principle of your actions were the same as that of the legislator or of the law of the land—or, in Hans Frank's formulation of "the categorical imperative in the Third Reich," which Eichmann might have known: "Act in such a way that the Führer, if he knew your action, would approve it" (*Die Technik des Staates*, 1942, pp. 15–16). Kant, to be sure, had never intended to say anything of the sort; on the contrary, to him every man was a legislator the moment he started to act: by using his "practical reason" man found the principles that could and should be the principles of law. But it is true that Eichmann's unconscious distortion agrees with what he himself called the version of Kant "for the household use of the little man." In this household use, all that is left of Kant's spirit is the demand that a man do more than obey the law, that he go beyond the mere call of obedience and identify his own will with the principle behind the law—the source from which the law sprang. In Kant's philosophy, that source was practical reason; in Eichmann's household use of him, it was the will of the Führer. Much of the horribly painstaking thoroughness in the execution of the Final Solution—a thoroughness that usually strikes the observer as typically German, or else as characteristic of the perfect bureaucrat—can be traced to the odd notion, indeed very common in Germany, that to be law-abiding means not merely to obey the laws but to act as though one were the legislator of the laws that one obeys. Hence the conviction that nothing less than going beyond the call of duty will do.

Whatever Kant's role in the formation of "the little man's" mentality in Germany may have been, there is not the slightest doubt that in one respect Eichmann did indeed follow Kant's precepts: a law was a law, there could be no exceptions. In Jerusalem, he admitted only two such exceptions during the time when "eighty million Germans had each had 'his decent Jew'": he had helped a half-Jewish cousin, and a Jewish couple in Vienna for whom his uncle had intervened. This inconsistency still made him feel somewhat uncomfortable, and when he was questioned about it during cross-examination, he became openly apologetic: he had "confessed his sins" to his superiors. This uncompromising attitude toward the performance of his murderous duties damned him in the eyes of the judges more than anything else, which was comprehensible, but in his own eyes it was precisely what justified him, as it had once silenced whatever conscience he might have had left. No exceptions—this was the proof that he had always acted against his "inclinations," whether they were sentimental or inspired by interest, that he had always done his "duty." ...

That Eichmann had at all times done his best to make the Final Solution final was therefore not in dispute. The question was only whether this was indeed proof of his fanaticism, his boundless hatred of Jews, and whether he had lied to the police and committed perjury in court when he claimed he had always obeyed orders. No other explanation ever occurred to the judges, who tried so hard to understand the accused, and treated him with a consideration and an authentic, shining humanity such as he had probably never encountered before in his whole life.

(Dr. Wechtenbruch told reporters that Eichmann had "great confidence in Judge Landau," as though Landau would be able to sort things out, and ascribed this confidence to Eichmann's need for authority. Whatever its basis, the confidence was apparent throughout the trial, and it may have been the reason the judgment caused Eichmann such great "disappointment"; he had mistaken humanity for softness.) That they never did come to understand him may be proof of the "goodness" of the three men, of their untroubled and slightly old-fashioned faith in the moral foundations of their profession. For the sad and very uncomfortable truth of the matter probably was that it was not his fanaticism but his very conscience that prompted Eichmann to adopt his uncompromising attitude during the last year of the war, as it had prompted him to move in the opposite direction for a short time three years before....

In Jerusalem, confronted with documentary proof of his extraordinary loyalty to Hitler and the Führer's order, Eichmann tried a number of times to explain that during the Third Reich "the Führer's words had the force of law" (*Führerworte haben Gesetzeskraft*), which meant, among other things, that if the order came directly from Hitler it did not have to be in writing. He tried to explain that this was why he had never asked for a written order from Hitler (no such document relating to the Final Solution has ever been found; probably it never existed), but had demanded to see a written order from Himmler. To be sure, this was a fantastic state of affairs, and whole libraries of very "learned" juridical comment have been written, all demonstrating that the Führer's *words*, his oral pronouncements, were the basic law of the land. Within this "legal" framework, every order contrary in letter or spirit to a word spoken by Hitler was, by definition, unlawful. Eichmann's position, therefore, showed a most unpleasant resemblance to that of the often-cited soldier who, acting in a normal legal framework, refuses to carry out orders that run counter to his ordinary experience of lawfulness and hence can be recognized by him as criminal....

... It would be idle to try to figure out which was stronger in him, his admiration for Hitler or his determination to remain a law-abiding citizen of the Third Reich when Germany was already in ruins. Both motives came into play once more during the last days of the war, when he was in Berlin and saw with violent indignation how everybody around him was sensibly enough getting himself fixed up with forged papers before the arrival of the Russians or the Americans. A few weeks later, Eichmann, too, began to travel under an assumed name, but by then Hitler was dead, and the "law of the land" was no longer in existence, and he, as he pointed out, was no longer bound by his oath. For the oath taken by the members of the S.S. differed from the military oath sworn by the soldiers in that it bound them only to Hitler, not to Germany.

The case of the conscience of Adolf Eichmann, which is admittedly complicated but is by no means unique, is scarcely comparable to the case of the German generals, one of whom, when asked at Nuremberg, "How was it possible that all you honorable generals could continue to serve a murderer with such unquestioning loyalty?," replied that it was "not the task of a soldier to act as judge over his supreme commander. Let history do that or God in heaven." (Thus General Alfred Jodl, hanged at Nuremberg.) Eichmann, much less intelligent and without any education to speak of, at least dimly realized that it was not an order but a law which had turned them all into criminals. The distinction between an order and the Führer's word was that the latter's validity was not limited in time and space, which is the outstanding characteristic of the former. This is also the true reason why the Führer's order for the Final Solution was followed by a huge shower of regulations and directives, all drafted by expert lawyers and legal advisers, not by mere administrators; this order, in contrast to ordinary orders, was treated as a law. Needless to add, the resulting legal paraphernalia, far from being a mere symptom of German pedantry or thoroughness, served most effectively to give the whole business its outward appearance of legality.

And just as the law in civilized countries assumes that the voice of conscience tells everybody "Thou shalt not kill," even though man's natural desires and inclinations may at times be murderous, so the law of Hitler's land demanded that the voice of conscience tell everybody: "Thou shalt kill," although the organizers of the massacres knew full well that murder is against the normal desires and inclinations of most people. Evil in the Third Reich had lost the quality by which most people recognize it—the quality of temptation. Many Germans and many Nazis, probably an overwhelming majority of them, must have been tempted *not* to murder, *not* to rob, *not* to let their neighbors go off to their doom (for that the Jews were transported to their doom they knew, of course, even though many of them may not have known the gruesome details), and not to become accomplices in all these crimes by benefiting from them. But, God knows, they had learned how to resist temptation.

7.8 Frantz Fanon (1925–1961)

Frantz Fanon was a philosopher, psychiatrist, and revolutionary whose work is primarily concerned with the project of decolonization. Colonialism, the practice through which European nation-states established colonies throughout Africa, Asia, Australasia, and the Americas, was responsible for the genocide, enslavement, impoverishment, and brutal exploitation of indigenous populations around the world. Decolonization, for Fanon, is the process through which these populations and their descendants are liberated from colonial control and from its deleterious legacy. Fanon was born in Martinique, a French colony in the Caribbean, and in his political life he supported the war for liberation waged by Algeria, a French colony in Africa, against French colonial occupation.

Fanon's most famous and controversial argument, which is well represented in this excerpt from *Wretched of the Earth*, is that true decolonization cannot take place without violent struggle. This places him in contrast with such figures as Martin Luther King, Jr., who argued that non-violent protest was the only moral and effective way to secure freedom and equality for the descendants of Black African slaves in America. Fanon argues that the peaceful, rational negotiation of private interests, usually understood as one of the crowning achievements of Western Enlightenment thought, acts only as a kind of lure or trick in the colonial context. While colonial powers may be willing to recognize the humanity of and grant rights to previously colonized populations, the notion of returning to those populations the wealth and power that was generated by their murder and subjugation is never considered. The moment a decolonizing population makes any claim on the value generated by its colonization, it is accused of being unreasonable, violent, and savage.

In this sense, Fanon follows Marx in shifting the focus of revolutionary (in this case anti-colonial) struggle from the political and cultural spheres to the economic. Educated in the University of Lyon in France, Fanon did not wish to dismiss the premises of Western Enlightenment thought in favour of some "authentic" indigenous culture. But he did insist that both be carefully critiqued and reimagined from the point of view of creating a society that produces actual equality and liberty for all. From this angle, Fanon criticizes colonial powers for usually defining decolonization as the moment in which a previously colonized population is allowed to participate as an "equal" in the international global marketplace. Fanon argues that this equality is illusory: the colonial powers are already masters of the game of global economic competition because they have accumulated an enormous stockpile of wealth precisely through colonialism. The decolonizing population, on the other hand, enters this competition at a ridiculous disadvantage for the same reason. Thus, Fanon concludes that the only way to achieve actual equality is the redistribution of wealth, which must be violently imposed because the colonizers and their descendants will never agree to it.

from Wretched of the Earth, *"Concerning Violence"*

[D]ecolonization is always a violent phenomenon....

... Decolonization is the meeting of two forces, opposed to each other by their very nature, which in fact owe their originality to ... the situation in the colonies. Their first encounter was marked by violence and their existence together—that is to say the exploitation of the native by the settler—was carried on by dint of a great array of bayonets and cannons.

... [I]t is the settler who has brought the native into existence and who perpetuates his existence. The settler owes the fact of his very existence, that is to say, his property, to the colonial system....

In decolonization, there is therefore the need of a complete calling in question of the colonial situation. If we wish to describe it precisely, we might find it in the well-known words: "The last shall be first and the first last." Decolonization is the putting into practice of this sentence.... [I]f the last shall be first, this will only come to pass after a murderous and decisive struggle between the two protagonists. That affirmed intention to place the last at the head of things, and to make them climb at a pace (too quickly, some say) the well-known steps which characterize an organized society, can only triumph if we use all means to turn the scale, including, of course, that of violence....

The colonial world is a world cut in two. The dividing line, the frontiers are shown by barracks and police stations. In the colonies it is the policeman and the soldier who are the official, instituted go-betweens, the spokesmen of the settler and his rule of oppression. In capitalist societies the educational system, whether lay or clerical, the structure of moral reflexes handed down from father to son, the exemplary honesty of workers who are given a medal after fifty years of good and loyal service, and the affection which springs from harmonious relations and good behavior—all these aesthetic expressions of respect for the established order serve to create around the exploited person an atmosphere of submission and of inhibition which lightens the task of policing considerably. In the capitalist countries a multitude of moral teachers, counselors and "bewilderers" separate the exploited from those in power. In the colonial countries, on the contrary, the policeman and the soldier, by their immediate presence and their frequent and direct action maintain contact with the native and advise him by means of rifle butts and napalm not to budge. It is obvious here that the agents of government speak the language of pure force. The intermediary does not lighten the oppression, nor seek to hide the domination; he shows them up and puts them into practice with the clear conscience of an upholder of the peace; yet he is the bringer of violence into the home and into the mind of the native.

The zone where the natives live is not complementary to the zone inhabited by the settlers. The two zones are opposed, but not in the service of a higher unity.

... No conciliation is possible, for of the two terms, one is superfluous. The settlers' town is a strongly built town, all made of stone and steel. It is a brightly lit town; the streets are covered with asphalt, and the garbage cans swallow all the leavings, unseen, unknown and hardly thought about. The settler's feet are never visible, except perhaps in the sea; but there you're never close enough to see them. His feet are protected by strong shoes although the streets of his town are clean and even, with no holes or stones. The settler's town is a well-fed town, an easygoing town; its belly is always full of good things. The settlers' town is a town of white people, of foreigners.

The town belonging to the colonized people, or at least the native town, the Negro village, the medina, the reservation, is a place of ill fame, peopled by men of evil repute. They are born there, it matters little where or how; they die there, it matters not where, nor how. It is a world without spaciousness; men live there on top of each other, and their huts are built one on top of the other. The native town is a hungry town, starved of bread, of meat, of shoes, of coal, of light. The native town is a crouching village, a town on its knees, a town wallowing in the mire. It is a town of niggers and dirty Arabs. The look that the native turns on the settler's town is a look of lust, a look of envy; it expresses his dreams of possession—all manner of possession: to sit at the settler's table, to sleep in the settler's bed, with his wife if possible. The colonized man is an envious man. And this the settler knows very well; when their glances meet he ascertains bitterly, always on the defensive, "They want to take our place." It is true, for there is no native who does not dream at least once a day of setting himself up in the settler's place....

... To break up the colonial world does not mean that after the frontiers have been abolished lines of communication will be set up between the two zones. The destruction of the colonial world is no more and no less that the abolition of one zone, its burial in the depths of the earth or its expulsion from the country.

The natives' challenge to the colonial world is not a rational confrontation of points of view. It is not a treatise on the universal, but the untidy affirmation of an original idea propounded as an absolute....

As soon as the native begins to pull on his moorings, and to cause anxiety to the settler, he is handed over to well-meaning souls who in cultural congresses point out to him the specificity and wealth of Western values.... The violence with which the supremacy of white values is affirmed and the aggressiveness which has permeated the victory of these values over the ways of life and of thought of the native mean that, in revenge, the native laughs in mockery when Western values are mentioned in front of him....

... The colonialist bourgeoisie, when it realizes that it is impossible for it to maintain its domination over the colonial countries, decides to carry out a rearguard action with regard to culture, values, techniques, and so on.... For a colonized people the most essential value, because the most concrete, is first and foremost the land: the land which will bring them bread and, above all, dignity.... As far as the native is concerned, morality is very concrete; it is to silence the settler's defiance, to break his flaunting violence—in a word, to put him out of the picture.

... The intellectual who for his part has followed the colonialist with regard to the universal abstract will fight in order that the settler and the native may live together in peace in a new world. But the thing he does not see, precisely because he is permeated by colonialism and all its ways of thinking, is that the settler, from the moment that the colonial context disappears, has no longer any interest in remaining or in co-existing....

... The colonialist bourgeoisie, in its narcissistic dialogue, expounded by the members of its universities, had in fact deeply implanted in the minds of the colonized intellectual that the essential qualities remain eternal in spite of all the blunders men may make: the essential qualities of the West, of course. The native intellectual accepted the cogency of these ideas, and deep down in his brain you could always find a vigilant sentinel ready to defend the Greco-Latin pedestal. Now it so happens that during the struggle for liberation, at the moment that the native intellectual comes into touch again with his people, this artificial sentinel is turned into dust. All the Mediterranean values—the triumph of the human individual, of clarity and of beauty—become lifeless, colorless knickknacks. All those speeches seem like collections of dead words; those values which seemed to uplift the soul are revealed as worthless, simply because they have nothing to do with the concrete conflict in which the people is engaged.

Individualism is the first to disappear. The native intellectual had learnt from his masters that the individual ought to express himself fully. The colonialist bourgeoisie had hammered into the native's mind the idea of a society of individuals where each person shuts himself up in his own subjectivity, and whose only wealth is individual thought. Now the native who has the opportunity to return to the people during the struggle for freedom will discover the falseness of this theory. The very forms of organization of the struggle will suggest to him a different vocabulary. Brother, sister, friend—these are words outlawed by the colonialist bourgeoisie, because for them my brother is my purse, my friend is part of my scheme for getting on. The native intellectual takes part, in a sort of auto-da-fé, in the destruction of all his idols: egoism, recrimination that springs from pride, and the childish stupidity of those who always want to have the last word. Such a colonized intellectual, dusted over by colonial culture, will in the same way discover the substance of village assemblies, the cohesion of people's committees, and the extraordinary fruitfulness of local meetings and groupments. Henceforward, the interests of one will be the interests of all, for in concrete fact *everyone* will be discovered by the troops, *everyone* will be massacred—or *everyone* will be saved. The motto "look out for yourself," the atheist's method of salvation, is in this context forbidden.

Self-criticism has been much talked about of late, but few people realize that it is an African institution. Whether in the *djemaas*[1] of northern Africa or in the meetings of western Africa, tradition demands that the quarrels which occur in a village should be settled in public. It is communal self-criticism, of course, and with a note of humor, because everybody is relaxed, and because in the last resort we all want the same things. But the more the intellectual imbibes the atmosphere of the people, the more completely he abandons the habits of calculation, of unwonted silence, of mental reservations, and shakes off the spirit of concealment. And it is true that already at that level we can say that the community triumphs, and that it spreads its own light and its own reason....

... The workers, primary schoolteachers, artisans, and small shop-keepers who have begun to profit—at a discount, to be sure—from the colonial setup, have special interests at heart. What this sort of following demands is the betterment of their particular lot: increased salaries, for example. The dialogue between these political parties and colonialism is never broken off. Improvements are discussed, such as full electoral representation, the liberty of the press, and liberty of association. Reforms are debated....

Thus there is very easily brought into being a kind of class of affranchised slaves, or slaves who are individually free. What the intellectual demands is the right to multiply the emancipated, and the opportunity to organize a genuine class of emancipated citizens. On the other hand, the mass of the people have no intention of standing by and watching individuals increase their chances of success. What they demand is not the settler's position of status, but the settler's place. The immense majority of natives want the settler's farm. For them, there is no question of entering into competition with the settler. They want to take his place.

The peasantry is systematically disregarded for the most part by the propaganda put out by the nationalist parties. And it is clear that in the colonial countries the peasants alone are revolutionary, for they have

1 Village assemblies.—*Trans.*

nothing to lose and everything to gain. The starving peasant, outside the class system, is the first among the exploited to discover that only violence pays. For him there is no compromise, no possible coming to terms; colonization and decolonization are simply a question of relative strength....

[G]uerilla warfare would be of no value as opposed to other means of violence if it did not form a new element in the worldwide process of competition between trusts and monopolies.... Capitalism, in its early days, saw in the colonies a source of raw materials which, once turned into manufactured goods, could be distributed on the European market. After a phase of accumulation of capital, capitalism has today come to modify its conception of the profit-earning capacity of a commercial enterprise. The colonies have become a market. The colonial population is a customer who is ready to buy goods; consequently, if the garrison has to be perpetually reinforced, if buying and selling slackens off, that is to say if manufactured and finished goods can no longer be exported, there is clear proof that the solution of military force must be set aside. A blind domination founded on slavery is not economically speaking worthwhile for the bourgeoisie of the mother country. The monopolistic group within this bourgeoisie does not support a government whose policy is solely that of the sword. What the factory-owners and finance magnates of the mother country expect from their government is not that it should decimate the colonial peoples, but that it should safeguard with the help of economic conventions their own "legitimate interests."

... [A]bove all there is competition, that pitiless war which financial groups wage upon each other. A Berlin Conference was able to tear Africa into shreds and divide her up between three or four imperial flags. At the moment, the important thing is not whether such-and-such a region in Africa is under French or Belgian sovereignty, but rather that the economic zones are respected.

7.9 Philip Zimbardo (1933–)

Philip Zimbardo is a psychologist and professor emeritus at Stanford University. He is best known for his infamous "Stanford Prison Experiment," which is often held up as a prime example of unethical social science research and the need for high ethical standards in the use of human subjects for scientific study. The results of the 1971 Stanford Prison Experiment led Zimbardo to several conclusions on the nature of human evil and the role of social structures in permitting and promoting it, which are collected in his 2007 book *The Lucifer Effect*. Zimbardo has also researched and written on the psychology of shyness, psychological relationships to time, and the effects of socialization in military culture. Zimbardo appeared as an expert witness for the defence in trials related to the Abu Ghraib prisoner abuse scandal in 2004.

In the Stanford Prison Experiment, funded by a US Navy grant, 24 male university students, chosen for their psychological normalcy and stability, were recruited to act as guards and inmates in a simulated prison set up in the basement of one of Stanford's university buildings. The experiment was designed to test what effects the prisoner/guard power relationship would have on the behaviour of the volunteers. After only a few days, the volunteers playing the role of guards became increasingly sadistic and inflicted suffering on the prisoners for only the slightest perceived resistance. The students playing prisoners became depressed, tried to stage a prison revolt, and showed signs of extreme psychological stress. Moreover, Zimbardo reported finding his own role as prison superintendent affecting his behaviour in ways that he had difficulty accounting for. The two-week study had to be terminated after only six days.

In *The Lucifer Effect*, Zimbardo offers his conclusions, drawn from the Stanford Prison Experiment and other research. He argues that social context can push even the most normal, stable people into performing acts that they themselves would identify as immoral, even evil, under different circumstances. Phenomena such as compartmentalization, anonymity, the dehumanization of others, and obedience to authority all play a role in allowing normal people to suspend their moral reasoning and participate in evil behaviour. Zimbardo borrows from Arendt's *Eichmann in Jerusalem* and combines her observations with his own theory to explain why everyday Germans were capable of participating in the Nazi project of extermination. He also argues that torture and abuse committed by US military personnel in incidents such as the Abu Ghraib prison scandal should be understood in the same light, suggesting that these situations may even have been fostered intentionally by the US government based on its own research into Zimbardo's theory.

from The Lucifer Effect

Evil: Fixed and Within or Mutable and Without?

The idea that an unbridgeable chasm separates good people from bad people is a source of comfort for at least two reasons. First, it creates a binary logic, in which Evil is *essentialized*. Most of us perceive Evil as an entity, a quality that is inherent in some people and not in others. Bad seeds ultimately produce bad fruits as their destinies unfold....

Upholding a Good–Evil dichotomy also takes "good people" off the responsibility hook. They are freed from even considering their possible role in creating, sustaining, perpetuating, or conceding to the conditions that contribute to delinquency, crime, vandalism, teasing, bullying, rape, torture, terror, and violence. "It's the way of the world, and there's not much that can be done to change it, certainly not by me."

An alternative conception treats evil in *incrementalist* terms, as something of which we are all capable, depending on circumstances.

Alternative Understandings: Dispositional, Situational, and Systemic

Running parallel to this pairing of essentialist and incremental conceptions is the contrast between *dispositional* and *situational* causes of behavior....

The traditional view (among those who come from cultures that emphasize individualism) is to look within for answers—for pathology or heroism. Modern psychiatry is dispositionally oriented. So are clinical psychology and personality and assessment psychology. Most of our institutions are founded on such a perspective, including law, medicine, and religion. Culpability, illness, and sin, they assume, are to be found within the guilty party, the sick person, and the sinner. They begin their quest for understanding with the "Who questions": *Who* is responsible? *Who* caused it? *Who* gets the blame? and *Who* gets the credit?

Social psychologists (such as myself) tend to avoid this rush to dispositional judgment when trying to understand the causes of unusual behaviors. They prefer to begin their search for meaning by asking the "What questions": *What* conditions could be contributing to certain reactions? *What* circumstances might be involved in generating behavior? *What* was the situation like from the perspective of the actors? Social psychologists ask: To what extent can an individual's actions be traced to factors outside the actor, to situational variables and environmental processes unique to a given setting? ... Most of us have a tendency both to overestimate the importance of dispositional qualities and to underestimate the importance of situational qualities when trying to understand the causes of other people's behavior....

Aberrant, illegal, or immoral behavior by individuals in service professions, such as policemen, corrections officers, and soldiers, is typically labeled the misdeeds of "a few bad apples." The implication is that they are a rare exception and must be set on one side of the impermeable line between evil and good, with the majority of good apples set on the other side. But who is making the distinction? Usually it is the guardians of the system, who want to isolate the problem in order to deflect attention and blame away from those at the top who may be responsible for creating untenable working conditions or for a lack of oversight or supervision. Again the bad apple–dispositional view ignores the apple barrel and its potentially corrupting situational impact on those within it. A systems analysis focuses on the barrel makers, on those with the power to design the barrel....

The primary simple lesson the Stanford Prison Experiment teaches is that *situations matter*. Social situations can have more profound effects on the behavior and mental functioning of individuals, groups, and national leaders than we might believe possible. Some situations can exert such powerful influence over us that we can be led to behave in ways we would not, could not, predict was possible in advance.[1] ...

The Power of Rules to Shape Reality

Situational forces in the SPE combined a number of factors, none of which was very dramatic alone but that together were powerful in their aggregation. One of the key features was the power of rules. Rules are formal, simplified ways of controlling informal complex behavior. They work by externalizing regulations, by establishing what is necessary, acceptable, and rewarded and what is unacceptable and therefore punished. Over time, rules come to have an arbitrary life of their own and the force of legal authority even when they are no longer relevant, are vague, or change with the whims of the enforcers.

Some rules are essential for the effective coordination of social behavior, such as audiences listening while performers speak, drivers stopping at red traffic lights, and people not cutting into queues. However, many rules are merely screens for dominance by those who make them or those charged with enforcing them. Naturally, the last rule, as with the SPE rules, always includes punishment for violation of the other rules. Therefore, there must be someone or some agency willing and able to administer such punishment, ideally doing so in a public arena that can serve to deter other potential rule breakers.

When Roles Become Real

> Once you put a uniform on, and are given a role, I mean, a job, saying "your job is to keep these people in line," then you're certainly not the same person if you're in street clothes and in

1 L. Ross and R. Nisbett, *The Person and the Situation* (New York: McGraw-Hill, 1991).

> a different role. You really become that person once you put on the khaki uniform, you put on the glasses, you take the nightstick, and you act the part. That's your costume and you have to act accordingly when you put it on.
> —Guard Hellmann

... Typically, roles are tied to specific situations, jobs, and functions, such as being a professor, doorman, cab driver, minister, social worker, or porn actor. They are enacted when one is in that situation—at home, school, church, or factory, or onstage. Roles can usually be set aside when one returns to his or her "normal" other life. Yet some roles are insidious, are not just scripts that we enact only from time to time: they can become who we are most of the time. They are internalized even as we initially acknowledge them as artificial, temporary, and situationally bound. We become father, mother, son, daughter, neighbor, boss, worker, helper, healer, whore, soldier, beggar man, thief, and many more.... [P]eople can do terrible things when they allow the role they play to have rigid boundaries that circumscribe what is appropriate, expected, and reinforced in a given setting. Such rigidity in the role shuts off the traditional morality and values that govern their lives when they are in "normal mode." The ego-defense mechanism of *compartmentalization* allows us to mentally bind conflicting aspects of our beliefs and experiences into separate chambers that prevent interpretation or cross talk. A good husband can then be a guiltless adulterer; a saintly priest can then be a lifelong pederast; a kindly farmer can then be a heartless slave master. We need to appreciate the power that role-playing can have in shaping our perspectives, for better as well as for worse, as when adopting the teacher or nurse role translates into a life of sacrifice for the good of one's students and patients.

Role Transitions from Healer to Killer

The worst-case scenario was the Nazi SS doctors who were assigned the role of selecting concentration camp inmates for extermination or for "experiments." They were socialized away from their usual healing role into the new role, assisting with killing, by means of a group consensus that their behavior was necessary for the common good....

Framing the genocide of the Jews as the "Final Solution" (*Endlösung*) served a dual psychological purpose: "it stood for mass murder without sounding or feeling like it; and it kept the focus primarily on problem solving." It transformed the whole matter into a difficult problem that had to be solved by whatever means were necessary to achieve a pragmatic goal. The intellectual exercise deleted emotions and compassion from the doctor's daily rounds....

Roles and Responsibility for Transgressions

To the extent that we can both live in the skin of a role and yet be able to separate ourselves from it when necessary, we are in a position to "explain away" our personal responsibility for the damage we cause by our role-based actions. We abdicate responsibility for our actions, blaming them on that role, which we convince ourselves is alien to our usual nature. This is an interesting variant of the Nuremberg Trial defense of the Nazi SS leaders: "I was only following orders." Instead the defense becomes "Don't blame me, I was only playing my role at that time in that place—that isn't the real me...."

Anonymity and Deindividuation

In addition to the power of rules and roles, situational forces mount in power with the introduction of uniforms, costumes, and masks, all disguises of one's usual appearance that promote anonymity and reduce personal accountability. When people feel anonymous in a situation, as if no one is aware of their true identity (and thus that no one probably cares), they can more easily be induced to behave in antisocial ways. This is especially so if the setting grants permission to enact one's impulses or to follow orders or implied guidelines that one would usually disdain....

Cognitive Dissonance That Rationalizes Evil

An interesting consequence of playing a role publicly that is contrary to one's private beliefs is the creation of *cognitive dissonance*. When there is a discrepancy between our behavior and beliefs, and when actions do not follow from relevant attitudes, a condition of cognitive dissonance is created. Dissonance is a state of tension that can powerfully motivate change either in one's public behavior or in one's private views in efforts to reduce the dissonance. People will go to remarkable lengths to bring discrepant beliefs and behavior into some kind of functional coherence. The greater the discrepancy, the stronger the motivation to achieve consonance and the more extreme changes we can expect to see.... When the discrepant action has been public, it cannot be denied or modified. Thus, the pressure to change is exerted on the softer elements of the dissonance equation, the internal, private elements—values, attitudes, beliefs, and even perceptions. An enormous body of research supports such predictions.[2]

How could dissonance motivate the changes we observed in our SPE guards? ... Having made the commitment to some action dissonant with their personal beliefs, guards felt great pressure to make sense of it, to develop reasons why they were doing something contrary to what they really believed and what they stood for morally. Sensible human beings can be deceived into engaging in irrational actions under many disguised dissonance commitment settings. Social psychology offers ample evidence that when that happens, smart people do stupid things, sane people do crazy things, and moral people do immoral things. After they have done them, they offer "good" rationalizations of why they did what they cannot deny having done. People are less rational than they are adept at *rationalizing*—explaining away discrepancies between their private morality and actions contrary to it. Doing so allows them to convince themselves and others that rational considerations guided their decision. They are insensitive to their own strong motivation to maintain consistency in the face of such dissonance.

The Power of Social Approval

Typically, people are also unaware of an even stronger force playing on the strings of their behavioral repertoire: the *need for social approval*. The need to be accepted, liked, and respected—to seem normal and appropriate, to fit in—is so powerful that we are primed to conform to even the most foolish and outlandish behaviors that strangers tell us is the right way to act....

---

2 L. Festinger, *A Theory of Cognitive Dissonance* (Stanford, CA: Stanford University Press, 1957); P.G. Zimbardo and M.R. Leippe, *The Psychology of Attitude Change and Social Influence* (New York: McGraw-Hill, 1991); P.G. Zimbardo, *The Cognitive Control of Motivation* (Glenview, IL: Scott, Foresman, 1969).

Dehumanization: The Other as Nothing Worthwhile

Kill a Gook for God
—Penned on helmet of a U.S. soldier in Vietnam

One of the worst things that we can do to our fellow human beings is deprive them of their humanity, render them worthless by exercising the psychological process of dehumanization. This occurs when the "others" are thought not to possess the same feelings, thoughts, values, and purposes in life that we do. Any human qualities that these "others" share with us are diminished or are erased from our awareness. This is accomplished by the psychological mechanisms of intellectualization, denial, and the isolation of affect. In contrast to human relationships, which are subjective, personal, and emotional, dehumanized relationships are objectifying, analytical, and empty of emotional or empathic content.

To use Martin Buber's terms, humanized relationships are "I–Thou," while dehumanized relationships are "I–It." Over time, the dehumanizing agent is often sucked into the negativity of the experience, and then the "I" itself changes, to produce an "It–It" relationship between objects, or between agency and victim. The misperception of certain others as subhuman, bad humans, inhuman, infrahuman, dispensable, or "animals" is facilitated by means of labels, stereotypes, slogans, and propaganda images.[3]

Sometimes dehumanization serves an adaptive function for an agent who must suspend his or her usual emotional response in an emergency, a crisis, or a work situation that demands invading the privacy of others. Surgeons may have to do so when performing operations that violate another person's body, as may first responders to a disaster. The same is often true when a job requires processing large numbers of people in one's caseload or daily schedule. Within some caring professions, such as clinical psychology, social work, and medicine, this process is called "detached concern." The actor is put into the paradoxical position of having to dehumanize clients in order to better assist or cure them.[4]

Dehumanization typically facilitates abusive and destructive actions toward those so objectified. It is hard to imagine that the following characterizations made by our guards were directed toward their prisoners—other college students who, but for a fateful coin flip, would have been wearing their uniforms: "I made them call each other names and clean toilets out with their bare hands. I practically considered the prisoners *cattle*, and I kept thinking I have to watch out for them in case they try something." ...

Ten Lessons from the Milgram Studies:[5] Creating Evil Traps for Good People

Let's outline some of the procedures in this research paradigm that seduced many ordinary citizens to engage in this apparently harmful behavior. In doing so, I want to draw parallels to compliance strategies used by "influence professionals" in real-world settings, such as salespeople, cult and military recruiters,

---

3 V.W. Bernard, P. Ottenberg, and F. Redl, "Dehumanization: A Composite Psychological Defense in Relation to Modern War," in *The Triple Revolution Emerging: Social Problems in Depth*, ed. R. Perruci and M. Pilisuck (Boston: Little, Brown, 1968), pp. 16–30.

4 H.I. Lief and R.C. Fox, "Training for 'Detached Concern' in Medical Students," in *The Psychological Basis of Practice*, ed. H.I. Lief, V.F. Lief, and N.R. Lief (New York: Harper & Row, 1963); C. Maslach, "'Detached Concern' in Health and Social Service Professions," paper presented at the American Psychological Association annual meeting, Montreal, Canada, August 30, 1973.

5 Stanley Milgram's 1963 experiments in blind obedience were motivated by a desire to understand the complicity of Germans in the Holocaust. Famously, he led volunteers to believe they were being called upon to apply electric shocks of increasing intensity to a scientific test subject in the next room. This test subject was in fact an actor who simulated distress and pain. The experiments sought to see how intense a shock the volunteers would be willing to deliver when encouraged by the researcher. The results suggested that the majority of people are willing to deliver a potentially lethal shock under such circumstances. See S. Milgram, *Obedience to Authority: An Experimental View* (New York: Harper & Row, 1974).

media advertisers, and others.[6] There are ten methods we can extract from Milgram's paradigm for this purpose:

1. Prearranging some form of contractual obligation, verbal or written, to control the individual's behavior in pseudolegal fashion. (In Milgram's experiment, this was done by publicly agreeing to accept the tasks and the procedures.)
2. Giving participants meaningful roles to play ("teacher," "learner") that carry with them previously learned positive values and automatically activate response scripts.
3. Presenting basic rules to be followed that seem to make sense before their actual use but can then be used arbitrarily and impersonally to justify mindless compliance. Also, systems control people by making their rules vague and changing them as necessary but insisting that "rules are rules" and thus must be followed (as the researcher in the lab coat did in Milgram's experiment ...).
4. Altering the semantics of the act, the actor, and the action (from "hurting victims" to "helping the experimenter," punishing the former for the lofty goal of scientific discovery)—replacing unpleasant reality with desirable rhetoric, gilding the frame so that the real picture is disguised. (We can see the same semantic framing at work in advertising, where, for example, bad-tasting mouthwash is framed as good for you because it kills germs and tastes like medicine is expected to taste.)
5. Creating opportunities for the diffusion of responsibility or abdication of responsibility for negative outcomes; others will be responsible, or the actor won't be held liable. (In Milgram's experiment, the authority figure said, when questioned by any "teacher," that he would take responsibility for anything that happened to the "learner.")
6. Starting the path toward the ultimate evil act with a small, seemingly insignificant first step, the easy "foot in the door" that swings open subsequent greater compliance pressures, and leads down a slippery slope.[7] (In the obedience study, the initial shock was only a mild 15 volts.) This is also the operative principle in turning good kids into drug addicts, with that first little hit or sniff.
7. Having successively increasing steps on the pathway that are gradual, so that they are hardly noticeably different from one's most recent prior action. "Just a little bit more." (By increasing each level of aggression in gradual steps of only 15-volt increments, over the thirty switches, no new level of harm seemed like a noticeable difference from the prior level to Milgram's participants.)
8. Gradually changing the nature of the authority figure (the researcher, in Milgram's study) from initially "just" and reasonable to "unjust" and demanding, even irrational. This tactic elicits initial compliance and later confusion, since we expect consistency from authorities and friends. Not acknowledging that this transformation has occurred leads to mindless obedience (and it is part of many "date rape" scenarios and a reason why abused women stay with their abusing spouses).
9. Making the "exit costs" high and making the process of exiting difficult by allowing verbal dissent (which makes people feel better about themselves) while insisting on behavioral compliance.

6 See R. Cialdini, *Influence* (New York: McGraw-Hill, 2001).

7 J.L. Freedman and S.C. Fraser, "Compliance Without Pressure: The Foot-in-the-Door Technique," *Journal of Personality and Social Psychology* 4 (1966): 195–202; see also S.J. Gilbert, "Another Look at the Milgram Obedience Studies: The Role of the Graduated Series of Shocks," *Personality and Social Psychology Bulletin* 4 (1981): 690–95.

10. Offering an ideology, or a big lie, to justify the use of any means to achieve the seemingly desirable, essential goal. (In Milgram's research this came in the form of providing an acceptable justification, or rationale, for engaging in the undesirable action, such as that science wants to help people improve their memory by judicious use of reward and punishment.) In social psychology experiments, this tactic is known as the "cover story" because it is a cover-up for the procedures that follow, which might be challenged because they do not make sense on their own. The real-world equivalent is known as an "ideology." Most nations rely on an ideology, typically, "threats to national security," before going to war or to suppress dissident political opposition....

Obedience to a Powerful Legitimate Authority

In the original obedience studies, the subjects conferred authority status on the person conducting the experiment because he was in an institutional setting and was dressed and acted like a serious scientist, even though he was only a high-school biology teacher paid to play that role. His power came from being perceived as a representative of an authority system. (In Milgram's Bridgeport replication [of the Milgram experiment], the absence of the prestigious institutional setting of Yale reduced the obedience rate to 47.5 percent compared to 65 percent at Yale, although this drop was not a statistically significant one.) Several later studies showed how powerful the obedience effect can be when legitimate authorities exercise their power within their power domains....

Torturers and Executioners: Pathological Types or Situational Imperatives?

There is little doubt that the systematic torture by men of their fellow men and women represents one of the darkest sides of human nature. Surely, my colleagues and I reasoned, here was a place where dispositional evil would be manifest among torturers who did their daily dirty deeds for years in Brazil as policemen sanctioned by the government to get confessions by torturing "subversive" enemies of the state....

What kind of men could do such deeds? Did they need to rely on sadistic impulses and a history of sociopathic life experiences to rip and tear the flesh of fellow beings day in and day out for years on end? ...

The sociologist and Brazil expert Martha Huggins, the Greek psychologist and torture expert Mika Haritos-Fatouros, and I interviewed several dozen of these violence workers in depth at various venues in Brazil. (For a summary of our methods and detailed findings about these violence workers, see Huggins, Haritos-Fatouros, and Zimbardo.[8]) Mika had done a similar, earlier study of torturers trained by the Greek military junta, and our results were largely congruent with hers.[9] We found that sadists are selected out of the training process by trainers because they are not controllable, get off on the pleasure of inflicting pain, and thus do not sustain the focus on the goal of extraction of confessions....

The social philosopher Jean-Jacques Rousseau elaborated this theme of the corrupting influence of social forces by envisioning human beings as "noble, primitive savages" whose virtues were diminished by contact with corrupting society. In stark opposition to this conception of human beings as the innocent victims of an all-powerful, malignant society is the view that people are born evil—genetic bad seeds.

8 M. Huggins, M. Haritos-Fatouros, and P.G. Zimbardo, *Violence Workers: Police Torturers and Murders Reconstruct Brazilian Atrocities* (Berkeley: University of California Press, 2002).

9 M. Haritos-Fatouros, *The Psychological Origins of Institutionalized Torture* (London: Routledge, 2003).

Our species is driven by wanton desires, unlimited appetites, and hostile impulses unless people are transformed into rational, reasonable, compassionate human beings by education, religion, and family, or controlled by the discipline imposed upon them by the authority of the State.

Where do you stand in this ages-old debate? Are we born good and then corrupted by an evil society or born evil and redeemed by a good society? Before casting your ballot, consider an alternative perspective. Maybe each of us has the capacity to be a saint or a sinner, altruistic or selfish, gentle or cruel, dominant or submissive, perpetrator or victim, prisoner or guard. Maybe it is our social circumstances that determine which of our many mental templates, our potentials, we develop. Scientists are discovering that embryonic stem cells are capable of becoming virtually any kind of cell or tissue and ordinary skin cells can be turned into embryonic stem cells. It is tempting to expand these biological concepts and what is now known about the developmental plasticity of the human brain to the "plasticity" of human nature.[10] ...

Deindividuation Transforms Our Apollonian Nature into a Dionysian Nature

Let's assume that the "good" side of people is the rationality, order, coherence, and wisdom of Apollo, while the "bad" side is the chaos, disorganization, irrationality, and libidinous core of Dionysus. The Apollonian central trait is constraint and the inhibition of desire; it is pitted against the Dionysian trait of uninhibited release and lust. People can become evil when they are enmeshed in situations where the cognitive controls that usually guide their behavior in socially desirable and personally acceptable ways are blocked, suspended, or distorted. The suspension of cognitive control has multiple consequences, among them the suspension of: conscience, self-awareness, sense of personal responsibility, obligation, commitment, liability, morality, guilt, shame, fear, and analysis of one's actions in cost-benefit calculations.

The two general strategies for accomplishing this transformation are; (a) reducing the cues of social accountability of the actor (no one knows who I am or cares to) and (b) reducing concern for self-evaluation by the actor. The first cuts out concern for social evaluation, for social approval, doing so by making the actor feel anonymous—the process of deindividuation. It is effective when one is functioning in an environment that conveys anonymity and diffuses personal responsibility. The second strategy stops self-monitoring and consistency monitoring by relying on tactics that alter one's state of consciousness. This is accomplished by means of taking alcohol or drugs, arousing strong emotions, engaging in hyperintense actions, getting into an expanded present-time orientation where there is no concern for past or future, and projecting responsibility outward onto others rather than inward toward oneself.

Deindividuation creates a unique psychological state in which behavior comes under the control of immediate situational demands and biological, hormonal urges. Action replaces thought, seeking immediate pleasure dominates delaying gratification, and mindfully restrained decisions give way to mindless emotional responses. A state of arousal is often both a precursor to and a consequence of deindividuation. Its effects are amplified in novel or unstructured situations where typical response habits and character traits are nullified. One's vulnerability to social models and situational cues is heightened; therefore, it becomes as easy to make love as to make war—it all depends on what the situation demands or elicits. In the extreme,

10 L. Ross, and R. Nisbett, *The Person and the Situation* (New York: McGraw-Hill, 1991).

there is no sense of right and wrong, no thoughts of culpability for illegal acts or Hell for immoral ones.[11] With inner restraints suspended, behavior is totally under external situational control; outer dominates inner. What is possible and available dominates what is right and just. The moral compass of individuals and groups has then lost its polarity....

Mechanisms of Moral Disengagement

This model begins by assuming that most people adopt moral standards because of undergoing normal socialization processes during their upbringing. Those standards act as guides for prosocial behavior and deterrents of antisocial behavior as defined by their family and social community. Over time, these external moral standards imposed by parents, teachers, and other authorities become internalized as codes of personal conduct. People develop personal controls over their thoughts and actions that become satisfying and provide a sense of self-worth. They learn to sanction themselves to prevent acting inhumanely and to foster humane actions. The self-regulatory mechanisms are not fixed and static in their relation to a person's moral standards. Rather, they are governed by a dynamic process in which moral self-censure can be selectively activated to engage in acceptable conduct; or, at other times, moral self-censure can be disengaged from reprehensible conduct. Individuals and groups can maintain their sense of moral standards by simply disengaging their usual moral functioning at certain times, in certain situations, for certain purposes. It is as if they shift their morality into neutral gear and coast along without concern for hitting pedestrians until they later shift back to a higher gear, returning to higher moral ground.

Bandura's model goes further in elucidating the specific psychological mechanisms individuals generate to convert their harmful actions into morally acceptable ones as they selectively disengage the self-sanctions that regulate their behavior. Because this is such a fundamental human process, Bandura argues that it helps to explain not only political, military, and terrorist violence but also "everyday situations in which decent people routinely perform activities that further their interests but have injurious human effects."[12]

It becomes possible for any of us to disengage morally from any sort of destructive or evil conduct when we activate one or more of the following four types of cognitive mechanisms.

First, we can redefine our harmful behavior as honorable. Creating moral justification for the action, by

11 Some relevant references on deindividuation include: E. Diener, "Deindividuation: Causes and Consequences," *Social Behavior and Personality* 5 (1977): 143–56; E. Diener, "Deindividuation: The Absence of Self-Awareness and Self-Regulation in Group Members, in *Psychology of Group Influence*, ed. P.B. Paulus (Hillsdale, NJ: Erlbaum, 1980), pp. 209–42; L. Festinger, A. Pepitone, and T. Newcomb, "Some Consequences of De-individuation in a Group," *Journal of Abnormal and Social Psychology* 47 (1952): 382–89; G. Le Bon, *The Crowd: A Study of the Popular Mind* (London: Transaction, 1995 [1895]); T. Postmes and R. Spears, "Deindividuation and Antinormative Behavior: A Meta-analysis," *Psychological Bulletin* 123 (1998): 238–59; S. Prentice-Dunn and R.W. Rogers, "Deindividuation in Aggression," in *Aggression: Theoretical and Empirical Reviews*, eds. R.G. Geen and E.I. Donnerstein (New York: Academic Press, 1983), pp. 155–72; S. Reicher and M. Levine, "On the Consequences of Deindividuation Manipulations for the Strategic Communication of Self: Identifiability and the Presentation of Social Identity," *European Journal of Social Psychology* 24 (1994): 511–24; J.E. Singer, C.E. Brush and S.C. Lublin, "Some Aspects of Deindividuation: Identification and Conformity," *Journal of Experimental Social Psychology* 1 (1965): 356–78; C.B. Spivey and S. Prentice-Dunn, "Assessing the Directionality of Deindividuated Behavior: Effects of Deindividuation, Modeling, and Private Self-Consciousness on Aggressive and Prosocial Responses," *Basic and Applied Social Psychology* 4 (1990): 387–403.

12 See the extensive writings of Albert Bandura on moral disengagement, among them: A. Bandura, *Social Foundations of Thought and Action: A Social Cognitive Theory* (Englewood Cliffs, NJ: Prentice-Hall, 1986); A. Bandura, "Mechanisms of Moral Disengagement," in *Origins of Terrorism: Psychologies, Ideologies, Theologies, States of Mind*, ed. W. Reich (Cambridge, UK: Cambridge University Press, 1990), pp. 161–91; A. Bandura, "Moral Disengagement in the Perpetration of Inhumanities," *Personality and Social Psychology Review* (Special Issue on Evil and Violence) 3 (1999): 193–209; A. Bandura, "The Role of Selective Moral Disengagement in Terrorism," in *Psychosocial Aspects of Terrorism: Issues, Concepts and Directions*, ed. F.M. Mogahaddam and A.J. Marsella (Washington, DC: American Psychological Association Press, 2004), pp. 121–50; A. Bandura, C. Barbaranelli, G.V. Caprara, and C. Pastorelli, "Mechanisms of Moral Disengagement in the Exercise of Moral Agency," *Journal of Personality and Social Psychology* 71 (1996): 364–74; M. Osofsky, A. Bandura, and P.G. Zimbardo, "The Role of Moral Disengagement in the Execution Process," *Law and Human Behavior* 29 (2005): 371–93.

adopting moral imperatives that sanctify violence, does this. Creating advantageous comparisons that contrast our righteous behavior to the evil behavior of our enemies also does this. (We only torture them; they behead us.) Using euphemistic language that sanitizes the reality of our cruel actions does this as well. ("Collateral damage" means that civilians have been bombed into dust; "friendly fire" means that a soldier has been murdered by the stupidity or intentional efforts of his buddies.)

Second, we can minimize our sense of a direct link between our actions and its harmful outcomes by diffusing or displacing personal responsibility. We spare ourselves self-condemnation if we do not perceive ourselves as the agents of crimes against humanity.

Third, we can change the way we think about the actual harm done by our actions. We can ignore, distort, minimize, or disbelieve any negative consequences of our conduct.

Finally, we can reconstruct our perception of victims as deserving their punishment, by blaming them for the consequences, and of course by dehumanizing them, perceiving them to be beneath the righteous concerns we reserve for fellow human beings....

Here is my ten-step program for resisting the impact of undesirable social influences and at the same time promoting personal resilience and civic virtue. It uses ideas that cut across various influence strategies and provides simple, effective modes of dealing with them. The key to resistance lies in development of the three Ss: self-awareness, situational sensitivity, and street smarts. You will see how they are central to many of these general strategies of resistance....

"*I made a mistake!*" Let's start out by encouraging admission of our mistakes, first to ourselves, then to others.... Doing so openly reduces the need to justify or rationalize our mistakes and thereby to continue to give support to bad or immoral actions. Confession of error undercuts the motivation to reduce cognitive dissonance....

"*I am mindful.*" In many settings smart people do dumb things because they fail to attend to key features in the words or actions of influence agents and fail to notice obvious situational clues. Too often we function on automatic pilot, using outworn scripts that have worked for us in the past, never stopping to evaluate whether they are appropriate in the here and now.[13] Following the advice of the Harvard researcher Ellen Langer, we must transform our usual state of mindless inattention into "mindfulness," especially in new situations.[14] ... For the best results, add "critical thinking" to mindfulness in your resistance.[15] Ask for evidence to support assertions: demand that ideologies be sufficiently elaborated to allow you to separate rhetoric from substance. Try to determine whether the recommended means ever justify potentially harmful ends. Imagine end-game scenarios of the future consequences of any current practice....

"*I am responsible.*" Taking responsibility for one's decisions and actions puts the actor in the driver's seat, for better or for worse. Allowing others to compromise their own responsibility, to diffuse it, makes them powerful backseat drivers and makes the car move recklessly ahead without a responsible driver. We become more resistant to undesirable social influence by always maintaining a sense of personal responsibility and by being willing to be held accountable for our actions. Obedience to authority is less blind to the extent that we are aware that diffusion of responsibility merely disguises our individual complicity in the conduct of questionable actions. Your conformity to antisocial group norms is undercut to the extent that you do not allow displacement of responsibility, when you refuse to spread responsibility around the gang,

13 When a blaze broke out in 1979 in a Woolworth store in the British city of Manchester, most people escaped, but ten died in the fire when they could have readily fled to safety. The fire chief reported that they had died because they were following a "restaurant script" rather than a survival script. They had finished dinner and were waiting to pay their bill; one does not leave a restaurant until one's bill is paid. No one wanted to stand out from the others; no one wanted to be different. So they waited, and they all died. This event is described in one of the vignettes in a British television production in which I was involved, called "The Human Zoo." It is available from Insight Media, New York.

14 E.J. Langer, *Mindfulness* (Reading, MA: Addison-Wesley, 1989).

15 D.F. Halpern, *Thought and Knowledge: An Introduction to Critical Thinking*, 4th ed. (Mahwah, NJ: Erlbaum, 2003).

the frat, the shop, the battalion, or the corporation. Always imagine a future time when today's deed will be on trial and no one will accept your pleas of "only following orders," or "everyone else was doing it."

"*I will assert my unique identity.*" Do not allow others to deindividuate you, to put you into a category, a box, a slot, to turn you into an object.... Make eye contact (remove all eye-concealing sunglasses), and offer information about yourself that reinforces your unique identity. Find common ground with dominant others in influence situations and use it to enhance similarities.

"*I respect just authority but rebel against unjust authority.*" In every situation, work to distinguish between those in authority who, because of their expertise, wisdom, seniority, or special status, deserve respect, and the unjust authority figures who demand our obedience without having any substance. Many who assume the mantel of authority are pseudo-leaders, false prophets, confidence men and women, self-promoters who should not be respected but rather disobeyed and openly exposed to critical evaluation....

"*I want group acceptance, but value my independence.*" ... We are indeed social animals, and usually our social connections benefit us and help us to achieve important goals that we could not achieve alone. However, there are times when conformity to a group norm is counterproductive to the social good. It is imperative to determine when to follow the norm and when to reject it....

"*I will be more frame-vigilant.*" ... The way issues are framed is often more influential than the persuasive arguments within their boundaries. Moreover, effective frames can seem not to be frames at all, just sound bites, visual images, slogans, and logos. They influence us without our being conscious of them, and they shape our orientation toward the ideas or issues they promote.... We desire things that are framed as being "scarce," even when they are plentiful. We are averse to things that are framed as potential losses and prefer what is presented to us as a gain, even when the ratio of positive to negative prognoses is the same.[16] ...

"*I will balance my time perspective.*" We can be led to do things that are not really what we believe in when we allow ourselves to become trapped in an expanded present moment. When we stop relying on our sense of past commitments and our sense of future liabilities, we open ourselves to situational temptations to engage in *Lord of the Flies* excesses. By not "going with the flow" when others around you are being abusive or out of control, you are relying on a temporal perspective that stretches beyond present-oriented hedonism or present-oriented fatalism....

"*I will not sacrifice personal or civic freedoms for the illusion of security.*" The need for security is a powerful determinant of human behavior. We can be manipulated into engaging in actions that are alien to us when faced with alleged threats to our security or the promise of security from danger.... Never sacrifice basic personal freedoms for the promise of security because the sacrifices are real and immediate and the security is a distant illusion....

"*I can oppose unjust systems.*" Individuals falter in the face of the intensity of the systems we have described: the military and prison systems as well as those of gangs, cults, fraternities, corporations, and even dysfunctional families. But individual resistance in concert with that of others of the same mind and resolve can combine to make a difference.... It may involve getting help from other authorities, counselors, investigative reporters, or revolutionary compatriots. Systems have enormous power to resist change and withstand even righteous assault. Here is one place where individual acts of heroism to challenge unjust systems and their bad barrel makers are best performed by soliciting others to join one's cause. The system can redefine individual opposition as delusional, a pair of opponents as sharing a *folie à deux*, but with three on your side, you become a force of ideas to be reckoned with....

16 P.G. Zimbardo and J.N. Boyd, "Putting Time in Perspective: A Valid, Reliable Individual Differences Metric," *Journal of Personality and Social Psychology* 77 (1999): 1271–88.

Heroic Contrasts: The Extraordinary versus the Banal

Fame is no plant that grows on mortal soil.
—John Milton

... [D]oers of heroic deeds typically argue that they were simply taking an action that seemed necessary at the time. They are convinced that anybody would have acted similarly, or else they find it difficult to understand why others did not. Nelson Mandela has said, "I was not a messiah, but an ordinary man who had become a leader because of extraordinary circumstances."[17] Phrases like this are used by people at all levels of society who have acted heroically: "It was nothing special"; "I did what had to be done." These are the refrains of the "ordinary" or everyday warrior, our "banal hero." ...

On the Banality of Heroism[18]

We may now entertain the notion that most people who become perpetrators of evil deeds are directly comparable to those who become perpetrators of heroic deeds, alike in being just ordinary, average people. The banality of evil shares much with the banality of heroism. Neither attribute is the direct consequence of unique dispositional tendencies; there are no special inner attributes of either pathology or goodness residing within the human psyche or the human genome. Both conditions emerge in particular situations at particular times when situational forces play a compelling role in moving particular individuals across a decisional line from inaction to action. There is a decisive decisional moment when a person is caught up in a vector of forces that emanate from a behavioral context. Those forces combine to increase the probability of one's acting to harm others or acting to help others....

This perception implies that any of us could as easily become heroes as perpetrators of evil depending on how we are influenced by situational forces. The imperative becomes discovering how to limit, constrain, and prevent the situational and systemic forces that propel some of us toward social pathology. But equally important is the injunction for every society to foster a "heroic imagination" in its citizenry. It is achieved by conveying the message that every person is a hero in waiting who will be counted upon to do the right thing when the moment of decision comes. The decisive question for each of us is whether to act in help of others, to prevent harm to others, or not to act at all. We should be preparing many laurel wreaths for all those who will discover their reservoir of hidden strengths and virtues enabling them to come forth to act against injustice and cruelty and to stand up for their principled values.

17 Brink, "Leaders and Revolutionaries."

18 This conception of the banality of heroism was first presented in an essay by Zimbardo on *Edge* Annual Question 2006, an annual event sponsored by John Brockman inviting a range of scholars to reply to a provocative question, which that year was "What is your dangerous idea?" See www.edge.org.

7.10 Review Questions

1. How do Cleon, Diodotus, and the Melians each support their arguments for or against violence?
2. Would Aquinas see these arguments as justifying war?
3. Would Nietzsche identify Himmler's speech as practising "noble morality" or "slave *ressentiment*"?
4. What are the similarities and differences between Nietzsche and Freud's account of "bad conscience" or guilt?
5. Which technique for dealing with human aggression would Freud see at work in Himmler's speech?
6. According to Freud's account of the superego, is Adolf Eichmann likely to feel guilty? Why or why not?
7. Arendt argues that Eichmann's "household use of Kant by the little man" was common among Germans under Nazism. Do you see signs of it in Himmler's speech?
8. Why does Fanon believe that the process of decolonization, if it is to be successful, will always have to involve violent struggle?
9. Would Aquinas see Fanon's anti-colonial struggle as a "just war"?
10. How does Fanon understand the "Western Tradition" of enlightened, rational negation of interests in the context of colonialism?
11. Who does Zimbardo argue commits evil acts and why?
12. Which of the techniques that Zimbardo describes for suspending our moral judgement do you see at work in Eichmann's testimony?
13. Would Zimbardo identify Fanon's anti-colonial struggle as evil or heroic?

7.11 Further Reading

Agamben, Giorgio. *Homo Sacer: Sovereign Power and Bare Life*. Stanford University Press, 1998.

Arendt, Hannah. *On Violence*. Harcourt, Brace & World, 1970.

—. *The Origins of Totalitarianism*. New ed., Harcourt Brace Jovanovich, 1966.

Baudrillard, Jean. *The Spirit of Terrorism and Other Essays*. New ed., Verso, 2003.

Benjamin, Walter. "Critique of Violence." *Reflections: Essays, Aphorisms, Autobiographical Writings*. Schocken Books, 1978.

Girard, René. *Violence and the Sacred*. Continuum, 2005.

CHAPTER 8

Political Identity and Human Nature

By nature, men are nearly alike; by practice they get to be wide apart.

—CONFUCIUS

Party is the madness of the many for the gain of a few.

—ALEXANDER POPE

In politics shared hatreds are almost always the basis of friendships.

—ALEXIS DE TOCQUEVILLE

A nation is a society united by a delusion about its ancestry and by a common hatred of its neighbours.

—WILLIAM RALPH INGE

People don't change governments. Governments change. People remain the same.

—WILL ROGERS

Every revolutionary ends up by becoming either an oppressor or a heretic.

—ALBERT CAMUS

The most radical revolutionary will become a conservative the day after the revolution.

—HANNAH ARENDT

A person is a person because he recognizes others as persons.

—DESMOND TUTU

8.1 Introduction

Readings in our final chapter explore the political dynamics of socio-cultural diversity, such diversity being both a fact of global relations and a consequence of international migration. Typically, these dynamics are analyzed in terms of cultural identity and difference. Debates related to diversity arise both internationally, when different countries interact, and domestically, when a diverse array of groups inhabit the same country. The central value at stake in either case is *equality*: (1) Can two separate countries with dissimilar national identities relate to each other as equals? And (2) can a diverse population living within a single state forge a coherent, unifying identity that accommodates all of its constituent groups equally? In one respect, we are here returning to concerns first introduced in Unit II. But whereas the focus in Chapters 4 and 5 falls on legal and economic equality between individuals, readings collected in the present chapter are concerned with inequality due specifically to socio-cultural differences. In such cases, the capacity of states to cooperate with each other or of individuals to live collectively seems to depend on two factors: (i) how the parties involved identify themselves and (ii) how well each party respects others with manifestly different identities. Legal equality and economic equality are still integral elements of the debates in the present chapter, but our primary focus will be socio-cultural identity and difference.

Because international travel, migration, and communication have become commonplace, people with different cultural and national identities interact with one another routinely. What conditions and moral principles govern these interactions? In its elemental form, this problem emerges when two individuals from different backgrounds must find common ground for social intercourse. When meeting, do they shake hands or bow? Is eye contact polite or provocative? When parting, do they wave or kiss? Neither party can depend on their own familiar, parochial conventions to regulate transactions. Considered at the scale of political life, the problem becomes intrinsically more complex, and this political problem is complicated by history. The historical record of international and intercultural relations is marked by deep and abiding animosities, which are often nurtured by glorifying myths of national identity and simplistic stereotypes about other cultures. Western European colonialism, which was first addressed in the previous chapter, reappears here as a glaring example of how one nation can devalue, dehumanize, and even destroy members of other cultures. The brutal legacy of colonialism is something that must be reckoned with in this chapter, both politically and morally.

Complicating the picture further still, socio-cultural identity and difference factor into relations within a single society. No society is homogeneous, and any variegated collection of people requires individuals to occupy different roles. Roles prescribe how we ought to behave with our immediate associates, personally and professionally—as a parent, sibling, civil servant, manager, labourer, customer, shop-keeper, employee, neighbour, and so on. People identify with these socio-functional roles, and each category is potentially laden with codified normative implications (e.g., the obligations of a parent, the decision-making authority of a manager, etc.). In this mix we can observe the operation of such things as gender, race, sexuality, age, religion, ability, and a host of other characteristics. Codified relations between men and women, majority and minority racial groups, conventional and unconventional sexual orientations, etc., are less tangible and often more value-laden than the socio-functional categories specified above. Such valuations pervade social life, often passing without critical scrutiny. Chapter 8 surveys attempts to address these difficult issues.

It is not possible in a single chapter to review the full range of issues related to diversity. For this reason the present chapter concentrates on gender-based and race-based inequality. These two points of focus are sufficiently weighty on their own to merit special consideration, but as it happens these two dimensions of identity have systematic implications for other threats to basic equality. Consider for a moment gender-based inequality.

It is historically accurate to characterize many cultures as traditionally *patriarchal*. What this means, literally, is that a social group is ruled (*archy*) by father-figure men (*patri*). In feudal Europe, for example, women were identified in relation to the dominant male figure in their families rather than as citizens or as persons in their own right. In this context, it seemed natural to value dominant men and submissive women and to denigrate as unnatural submissive men and dominant women. When universality emerged as a normative principle during the Enlightenment, it became possible to challenge and dismantle these traditional gender roles. In the first wave of feminism at the turn of the twentieth century, women in Western European, North American, and other countries fought for equal rights to citizenship, political participation, and personal property. In its second wave (1960s–1980s), feminism challenged unequal gender divisions in the workforce (e.g., unequal pay, limited opportunities for women to advance professionally, stereotyped gender roles, etc.). And lastly in its third wave (1980s–present), feminism has explored complex manifestations of femininity, incorporating into these efforts considerations for race, class, sexual identity, and sexual orientation. Thus, with each successive wave, feminism has expanded its focus to include a wider range of forces that threaten inequality. A similar story can be developed about the career of racism.

Both race-based colonialism and gender-based inequality were in the past thought to be founded on axiomatic natural principles. Recently, these ideas about what's natural have crumbled under critical scrutiny. No respectable biologist today takes seriously ideas that were used in former times to rank intellectual or moral capacities using race or gender. How are we to understand this transformation? Two generic answers to this question present themselves, one Universalist and the other Pluralist. Central to the *Universalist* answer is a narrative in which conventional values of particular societies and groups tend to merge into a single all-encompassing set of moral principles that purport to govern all of humanity. In essence, universalism explains a diminishing prevalence of racism and sexism in terms of a progressive tendency towards identity inclusivity. Central to the *Pluralist* answer is a narrative in which the values of minority groups have been established within a network of independently authoritative principles. In essence, pluralism explains the widespread tendency towards equality as a levelling of formerly disadvantaged groups and formerly privileged groups; in this case, however, different groups remain distinct from each other.

Historical, sociological trends that the Universalist and Pluralist positions attempt to explain are ongoing. For this reason, the debate here is practical as well as theoretical. Besides explaining what has happened, they prescribe what ought to be done. The Universalist approach is informed by an Enlightenment notion that individual human beings are fundamentally the same and therefore entitled to equal status. It makes our shared humanity primary, and consequently both political identities and political differences are secondary: while we may come from different places and endorse different values, we are all essentially the same. In light of this essential similarity, it has become a political priority to bridge differences, effectively making one identity common to all. The Pluralist approach is skeptical about the existence and significance of a purported essential nature. Mutual respect is primary, according to Pluralism, and we are therefore obliged to recognize and tolerate people who are different from us. The Pluralist approach thus accepts differences as an irreducible fact that need not be overcome or transcended. Indeed, Pluralism celebrates this difference as diversity, arguing that people with different cultural backgrounds must find ways to co-exist without minimizing differences or merging their identities. In sum, the Universalist approach corresponds in essential details with the idea that society ought to be a melting pot and the Pluralist approach with the idea that it ought to be a mosaic.

* * *

We commence the present survey with two ancient stoics, Epictetus and Hierocles. Both adopt the Universalist position described above, but they arrive at it from opposite directions. Epictetus begins by articulating the scope of our primary obligations in the widest terms possible: we are all citizens of the world (his term, *kosmo-politos* translates literally as "universe-citizen"; 8.2.1). Local obligations to neighbours, friends, and family follow as a conceptual consequence of our cosmopolitan nature. Hierocles's account, by contrast, begins with the narrowest concerns of all: one's self and one's immediate family relations (8.2.2). Without any natural means to delimit a person's concerns, these concerns ultimately encompass everyone. Even if there are gradational differences between the narrower spheres of concern and the widest, such differences are matters of degree, not kind. Hierocles does not use the term "cosmopolitan," but his account nevertheless ends precisely where Epictetus's began. Thus, Epictetus articulates an abstract and general variant of universalism that yields concrete normative guidance, whereas Hierocles uses familiar normative conventions to elaborate a Universalist position.

Our first Enlightenment-era figures, Mary Wollstonecraft and Toussaint L'Ouverture, invoke Universalist ideals to criticize manifest forms of inequality in the eighteenth century. First, Wollstonecraft complains that women in England were not the legal and political equals of men, despite avowed commitments to Enlightenment principles from British political leaders (8.3; Burke being an exception, 4.9). In essence, she challenges the sincerity of this commitment: if legal and political rights are predicated on the basis of *human* rationality, then political rights must be extended to women. Women deserve the opportunity to participate in the political life of their own country. Despite her own formidable capacities, Wollstonecraft concedes that many of her female contemporaries conform to stereotypes portraying women as irrational, overly emotional, and ill-equipped for this task. This, she insists, is due to inadequate education, not a natural deficiency of her sex. Equal educational opportunities, she is confident, will correct any manifest gender-based differences of ability. Wollstonecraft's pioneering efforts thus prepared ground for suffragette campaigns that later won both educational opportunities and the franchise for women in England and elsewhere.

As leader of a slave rebellion in the French colony that would ultimately become Haiti, Toussaint L'Ouverture was a practical person, not a theorist. Speaking on behalf of black Haitians, his challenge to France was, like Wollstonecraft's challenge to British politicians, fundamentally Universalist: race ought to be no bar to basic political rights. Indeed, liberated Haitian slaves wanted only what the French revolutionaries had claimed as the birthright of all citizens (8.4). Many Haitians (albeit not L'Ouverture himself) were kidnapped Africans. Still, they had no desire to reject European Enlightenment values or to return to their cultural roots. They wanted to be full French citizens with the same rights and protections as white Frenchmen. Failing that, L'Ouverture demanded national independence for Haiti.

In a rhetorical *tour de force*, Sojourner Truth connects gender, race, and class, pointing to the ways in which various forms of exclusion and exploitation reinforce each other (8.5). As a black person, Truth was denied the rights of a white woman. As a woman, she was denied the rights of a black man. And as a former slave, she was often regarded as belonging to an inferior class. The task of rectifying inequalities and redistributing the balance of rights in a society is complicated by the fact that people have complex identities. Many people, like Truth, are engaged simultaneously in several overlapping struggles. Today theorists identify this as the problem of intersectionality. More than a century before the term "intersectionality" took hold in the social sciences, Sojourner Truth introduced the idea: coincidental and interdependent systems of discrimination. This combination of factors constitutes a special kind of political challenge in any society that values equality. At the theoretical level, intersectionality requires examining how any particular form of inequality overlaps with other forms of it, and these intersections must be incorporated in any program to correct historical identity-based forms of inequality. As bell hooks argues later in the chapter, women's equality is inseparable from inequalities based on race and class that intersect with it (8.8). Gains for women, she argues, will not be genuinely beneficial if they come at the expense of other identify factors, such as race or class. Indeed, such modest achievements will not even be gains for women, because racism and classism affect women. Sojourner Truth, addressing a women's conference, for example, still faced disadvantages as a *black* woman in a country dominated by whites and as a *poor* woman in an economy dominated by wealth.

John Stuart Mill is a Pluralist and central figure of modern liberalism. For Mill, modern democracies distribute power to the people in order to avert the formation of an oppressive or negligent elite class (8.6). However, in a modern democracy the majority (who hold power through democratic representation) may yet behave tyrannically towards minorities. Moreover, he worries that this democratic form of tyranny—a tyranny of the majority—will intrude on ever more minute details of day-to-day life. To counteract this possibility, individual liberty must receive the strongest protections. Based in the moral theory of utilitarianism (6.6), he argues that the only justifiable reason for the state (or any individual) to restrict individual freedom is to prevent a person from harming others: as long as you aren't harming another person, you are entitled to live as you please. Taking this a step further, Mill thinks it is vital for a society to accommodate the widest range of voices and personalities possible; social progress depends on the mutual accommodation of different opinions and lifestyles. For this reason, Mill advocates a liberal society in which people can conduct "experiments in lifestyle" without political or conventional fetters. Mill's rationale for individual diversity has been extended in recent year as a rationale for multiculturalism: as long as different cultures can co-exist peacefully within a secure constitutional framework, different sub-communities need not be merged into a unified identity.

Colonial racism and traditional forms of sexism face a different kind of reckoning from our twentieth-century contributors. Edward Said and bell hooks, in particular, advance the case for Pluralism independently of classical liberalism entirely. Working outside the Enlightenment framework, they diagnose problems with universalism as being due not simply to practices that fall short of laudable ideals. This is how Wollstonecraft and L'Ouverture voice their objections to gender-based and race-based inequality. Rather, for both of Said and hooks, Universalism is inherently flawed and thereby cannot serve as an ideal. According to Said, an Oriental/Western distinction within humanity was used to rationalize colonialism: colonial rule was not a well-intentioned effort to expand the fruits of Enlightenment; it was a campaign to impose the Western worldview on purportedly inferior Oriental people (8.7). According to hooks, an exclusive focus on women's issues among second-wave feminists simply elevated *some* women into preeminent positions of power and perpetuated a range of other inequalities (8.8).

For Edward Said, problems with colonialism originate in the Enlightenment assumption that mature human subjects are free rational decision-makers (see 1.3). This assumption is applied to Europeans. Orientals, by contrast, are presumed to be in the grip of irrational cultural traditions and biological drives, incapable of making free and rational decisions. Western European colonial rule was thus based on a false dichotomy: colonial rulers understood themselves as abstract, rational agents, whereas the Oriental "other" was conceived of as embodied, socially embedded, causally-determined, and in need of guidance—the sort of guidance provided by a benevolent imperial power. This reductionist and problematic division is encapsulated by the Rudyard Kipling poem, "The White Man's Burden," which begins:

> Take up the White Man's burden—
> Send forth the best ye breed—
> Go send your sons to exile
> To serve your captives' need

To wait in heavy harness
On fluttered folk and wild—
Your new-caught, sullen peoples,
Half devil and half child....

Colonial rule was profitable for the imperial powers, but as Kipling's poem makes plain, it was defended on paternalist grounds. Accordingly, Said objects in particular to the condescension and paternalism of European colonialism.

For bell hooks, second-wave feminists of the 1960s–1980s concentrated their efforts too narrowly on winning employment opportunities for middle-class women and establishing their own independence from men (8.8). These efforts produced real victories, since they reduced the sorts of economic and social dependence that had hitherto trapped women in abusive relationships and blocked them from employment opportunities that were available to men. However, hooks argues, benefits secured by these campaigns were confined to middle class, white women. Women in impoverished and racialized communities were already on par with the men around them in underpaid, grueling working-class jobs. These women did not experience equality with the men around them as especially liberating. For hooks, the core problem is not simply that men dominate women, but that domination in some form infects a wide range of social relations—sometimes based on gender, sometimes race, sometimes sexual orientation, sometimes class, and usually several of these things simultaneously. This generic underlying tendency toward domination is usually unanalyzed and unquestioned. Effectively, a focus on glass-ceiling issues among second-wave feminists—under-employment and underpay for women in a male-dominated workplace—generated a situation in which one sub-set of women simply rose to dominant roles that were formerly occupied exclusively by men, thereby replicating long-standing forms of dysfunction. Feminism, hooks argues, violates its fundamental commitment to equality when it aims only to give some women an equal opportunity to occupy positions of dominance. In the cause of equality, sexism cannot be isolated from other social issues: anti-sexism thus interrelates with anti-racism, LGBT-rights, anti-capitalism, curbing anthropogenic climate change, and so on.

Glen Coulthard returns to problems identified by Edward Said (8.7), but applied to Canada's relationship with First Nations and analyzed in light of Frantz Fanon's theory of decolonization (see 7.8). In particular, he critically assesses two persistent elements of the Canadian government's position on settler-First Nations relations: (1) that colonial oppression is an unfortunate but nonetheless closed chapter of Canada's history, and (2) that official apologies and limited measures of appeasement have sufficiently prepared the ground for reconciliation (8.9). Coulthard maintains that this position is wrong and skirts the truth of *ongoing* oppression. By his account, Canada continues to violate treaty obligations and fails to respect First Nations communities as independent sovereign nations. Accordingly, while "native resentment" is framed by the Canadian government as a pathological condition to be healed or overcome, it is in his opinion a perfectly reasonable response among First Nations to the historical record of injustice. Not only is resentment morally justified, it is empowering. Moreover, where reconciliation has led to successful decolonization elsewhere (e.g., in South Africa), it has been tied to a proper redistribution of power in favour of an *indigenous majority*. No such redistribution is possible in Canada because European settlers outnumber the First Nations population (as a result of genocidal practices). While the ideal of reconciliation seems reasonable on the surface, the Enlightenment rhetoric of peaceful negotiation invoked by the Canadian government only screens persistent problems.

Murray Bookchin returns to the theme of experimentation that was first developed in the nineteenth century by John Stuart Mill (8.6). In this respect, Bookchin and Mill approach social issues in a way that contrasts discernably from that of seventeenth- and eighteenth-century Enlightenment authors. Thomas Hobbes (4.6), John Locke (5.3) and Immanuel Kant (1.3, 4.8) tended to approach social issues as theoretical problems requiring elegant and systematic solutions. In each case, practical proposals can be traced back to axiomatic first principles: social stability for Hobbes, individual liberty for Locke, and rational duty for Kant. In Bookchin's opinion, these theoretical models for ordering society are mechanical, and the rigid, hierarchical structures they yield are unsuited for *human* communities (8.10). His own political ideas are formulated as ecological principles, according to which social relations are conceived of as lateral networks with multiple overlapping relations and redundancies. Whatever theoretical elegance is lacking in his ecological conception of social life is balanced by its promise of resilience: a hierarchical structure can come to ruin by a fault at a single central point, whereas a complex network—such as a healthy ecosystem—can adjust to changes by virtue of its organic interrelations. If we were to adopt Bookchin's proposals, social relations would be, in effect, too fluid to sustain systematic inequalities. Moreover, the Enlightenment assumption that nature functions primarily as a source of raw materials for narrow human purposes is, for Bookchin, the root cause of pathological relations in both the social and environmental spheres. Accordingly, human life will be more pleasant and healthier if we abandon hierarchical social relations and restore our collective relationship with nature. It might also save the human race from extinction.

Excerpts from Nelson Mandela's 1962 trial in South Africa (8.11) conclude this chapter and unit. Like Socrates, Mandela seems more firmly committed to a moral and political cause than his own personal fate. As a lawyer and life-long activist, Mandela had no reason to believe that he could be acquitted in a South African court, so he used the trial as an opportunity to expose the injustices of colonial rule, racism, legal inequality, and violent oppression. Because of colonial rule, the black majority in South Africa were disenfranchised, deprived of prime land, economically exploited as cheap labour, forbidden from travel abroad without permission, unable to voice discontent in a meaningful way, and deprived of fair legal process. They were not even *second*-class citizens in their own country: "whites" had the most rights, "coloureds" (mostly Indian immigrants) had more rights than black Africans, and "blacks" the fewest rights of all. The system that officially sanctioned this taxonomy was called apartheid (which translates as "apartness"). The racist apartheid system enforced artificial colonial divisions up until Mandela was released from prison in 1990. Its demise came when Mandela was elected president in 1994, in the first national election that extended the right to vote to black South Africans. Mandela's arguments appeal explicitly to a Universalist ideal: as human beings, blacks deserve the opportunity to participate as equals in the political life of their own country. Implicitly, however, the path towards reconciliation that South Africa ultimately pursued was Pluralist, since political reforms in the post-Apartheid era aimed at the mutual accommodation of groups that were formerly stratified hierarchically.

8.2 Stoicism

Ancient stoicism advocates a life guided by divine reason (see 3.6). A virtuous person submits to the dictates of reason, natural law, and duty, and the good life for an individual person is thereby harmoniously integrated with other people. As it happens, stoic voices represent every strata of ancient society: Marcus Aurelius, for example, was Roman emperor (arguably, the most powerful position in the ancient world); Seneca was a renowned playwright, senator, and advisor to the emperor, Nero; and Epictetus was a slave who, after gaining his freedom, taught stoic philosophy. With respect to identity, stoics sought ways to understand one's relations to a distant stranger as being essentially the same as one's relations with a neighbour or family member.

In the first passage included here, Epictetus instructs students to understand their duties first in light of our shared humanity. In this regard, each person is a citizen of the world, a *kosmopolitan* in Greek. Next, they are asked to consider concrete attachments to their intimate relations, in particular, a father and brother. Because the universe and all of its elements are expected to harmonize with each other, Epictetus does not think there is any tension between the first demand upon stoics to identify with a universal community and the second demand to identify with one's family.

The second passage included here, a fragment of Hierocles, portrays different relations in a person's life as a series of concentric circles. Hierocles conceives of human identity as beginning with one's self, expanding outward to one's intimate relations, and extending ultimately to the entire human race. Obligations of benevolence that impel someone to consider kith and kin have no natural limit. Accordingly, ethical agency impels a person outward to the most remote of these circles of concern.

8.2.1 *Epictetus (55–135 CE), from* Discourses 2

Chapter 10: How We May Discover the Duties of Life from Names

Consider who you are. In the first place, you are a man; and this is one who has nothing superior to the faculty of the will, but all other things subjected to it; and the faculty itself he possesses unenslaved and free from subjection. Consider then from what things you have been separated by reason. You have been separated from wild beasts: you have been separated from domestic animals. Further, you are a citizen (*politēs*) of the world (*kosmos*), and a part of it, not one of the subservient, but one of the principal parts, for you are capable of comprehending the divine administration and of considering the connection of things. What then does the character of a citizen promise? To hold nothing as profitable to himself; to deliberate about nothing as if he were detached from the community, but to act as the hand or foot would do, if they had reason and understood the constitution of nature, for they would never put themselves in motion nor desire anything, otherwise than with reference to the whole. Therefore the philosophers say well, that if the good man had foreknowledge of what would happen, he would cooperate toward his own sickness and death and mutilation, since he knows that these things are assigned to him according to the universal arrangement, and that the whole is superior to the part and the state to the citizen. But now, because we do not know the future, it is our duty to stick to the things which are in their nature more suitable for our choice, for we were made among other things for this.

After this, remember that you are a son. What does this character promise? To consider that everything which is the son's belongs to the father, to obey him in all things, never to blame him to another, nor to say or do anything which does him injury, to yield to him in all things and give way, cooperating with him as far as you can. After this know that you are a brother also, and that to this character it is due to make concessions; to be easily persuaded, to speak good of your brother, never to claim in opposition to him any of the things which are independent of the will, but readily to give them up, that you may have the larger share in what is dependent on the will....

Next to this, if you are a senator of any state, remember that you are a senator: if a youth, that you are a youth: if an old man, that you are an old man; for each of such names, if it comes to be examined, marks out the proper duties....

8.2.2 Hierocles (2nd century CE), Fragments Quoted by Stobaeus[1]

How We Ought to Conduct Ourselves towards Our Kindred

The consideration of the duties pertaining to [all] kindred is consequent to the discussion of those that pertain to parents, brothers, wives, and children; for the same things may, in a certain respect, be said of the former as of the latter; and on this account may be concisely explained. For, in short, each of us is, as it were, circumscribed by many circles; some of which are less, but others larger, and some comprehend, but others are comprehended, according to the different and unequal habitudes with respect to each other. For the first, indeed, and most proximate circle is that which every one describes about his own mind as a centre, in which circle the body, and whatever is assumed for the sake of the body, are comprehended. For this is nearly the smallest circle, and almost touches the centre itself. The second from this, and which is at a greater distance from the centre, but comprehends the first circle, is that in which parents, brothers, wife, and children are arranged. The third circle from the centre is that which contains uncles and aunts, grandfathers and grandmothers, and the children of brothers and sisters. After this is the circle which comprehends the remaining relatives. Next to this is that which contains the common people, then that which comprehends those of the same tribe, afterwards that which contains the citizens; and then two other circles follow, one being the circle of those that dwell in the vicinity of the city, and the other, of those of the same province. But the outermost and greatest circle, and which comprehends all the other circles, is that of the whole human race.

These things being thus considered, it is the province of him who strives to conduct himself properly in each of these connections to collect, in a certain respect, the circles, as it were, to one centre, and always to endeavour earnestly to transfer himself from the comprehending circles to the several particulars which they comprehend. It pertains, therefore, to the man who is a lover of kindred [to conduct himself in a becoming manner] towards his parents and brothers; also, according to the same analogy, towards the more elderly of his relatives of both sexes, such as grandfathers, uncles and aunts; towards those of the same age with himself, as his cousins; and towards his juniors, as the children of his cousins. Hence we have summarily shown how we ought to conduct ourselves towards our kindred, having before taught how we should act towards ourselves, our parents, and brothers; and besides these, towards our wife and children. To which it must be added, that those who belong to the third circle must be honoured similarly to these; and again, kindred similarly to those that belong to the third circle. For something of benevolence must be taken away from those who are more distant from us by blood; though at the same time we should endeavour that an assimilation may take place between

1 From *Political Fragments of Archytas and other Ancient Pythagoreans*, by Thomas Taylor, published in 1822. In Taylor's day it was assumed that these works were by the fifth-century Pythagorean author Hierocles of Alexandria. They are now assigned to the second-century Stoic philosopher Hierocles.

us and them. For this distance will become moderate, if, through the diligent attention which we pay to them, we cut off the length of the habitude towards each individual of these. We have unfolded, therefore, that which is most comprehensive and important in the duties pertaining to kindred....

8.3 Mary Wollstonecraft (1759–1797)

Mary Wollstonecraft was an English writer who is best known for the book from which the present selection is drawn, *A Vindication of the Rights of Woman* (1792). Wollstonecraft's family was respectably middle class, but lost its fortune early in her life. She took work as the governess of upper-class children and wrote about her frustration with the limited employment opportunities available to women. Wollstonecraft went to France in 1792 and witnessed the French Revolution. She was sympathetic to Enlightenment ideals of universality and rationality, especially the elimination of class distinctions and the establishment of equal rights in a democratic system.

Wollstonecraft was a proto-feminist, presaging in many ways the ideals and demands of the modern feminist movement. In her time, the right to vote in Britain was restricted to landowners, which effectively excluded women insofar as a woman's property transferred to her husband upon marriage. Moreover, unmarried women were subject to scorn and ostracism, and women were excluded from the majority of wage-earning occupations. As a consequence, women were almost completely subordinated to men. It was presupposed that women were naturally deficient in the capacity to reason. Wollstonecraft challenged conventions, not only in argument, but by demonstrating in her life that women could reason and think critically every bit as well as men.

Some of Wollstonecraft's remarks may surprise a contemporary reader. In particular, she argues that women accepted status as second-class citizens because it made their lives easier and more comfortable to forego politics and paid labour. Because of conventional obstacles to education, she conceded that women at that time were poor at reasoning. Without training and practice at such things, women had to rely on feminine charm. In general, she links gender inequality and class difference. Inequalities of wealth and power, she argues, are harmful to everyone, and so universal equality would improve life across society. Accordingly, women should participate in modern democracy as part of a general commitment to wider egalitarian ideals.

~

from A Vindication of the Rights of Woman, with Strictures on Political and Moral Subjects

Chapter 4: Observations on the State of Degradation to Which Woman Is Reduced by Various Causes

That woman is naturally weak, or degraded by a concurrence of circumstances is, I think, clear. But this position I shall simply contrast with a conclusion, which I have frequently heard fall from sensible men in favour of an aristocracy: that the mass of mankind cannot be any thing, or the obsequious slaves, who patiently allow themselves to be penned up, would feel their own consequence, and spurn their chains. Men, they further observe, submit every where to oppression, when they have only to lift up their heads to throw off the yoke; yet, instead of asserting their birthright, they quietly lick the dust, and say, let us eat and drink, for to-morrow we die. Women, I argue from analogy, are degraded by the same propensity to enjoy the present moment; and, at last, despise the freedom which they have not sufficient virtue to struggle to attain. But I must be more explicit.

... Only "absolute in loveliness," the portion of rationality granted to woman is, indeed, very scanty; for, denying her genius and judgment, it is scarcely possible to divine what remains to characterize intellect.

... Reason is ... the simple power of improvement; or, more properly speaking, of discerning truth. Every individual is in this respect a world in itself. More or less may be conspicuous in one being than other; but the nature of reason must be the same in all, if it be an emanation of divinity, the tie that connects the creature with the Creator; for, can that soul be stamped with the heavenly image, that is not perfected by the exercise of its own reason? Yet outwardly ornamented with elaborate care, and so adorned to delight man ... the soul of woman is not allowed to have this distinction, and man, ever placed between her and reason, she is always represented as only created to ... take things on trust.... The inquiry is, whether she has reason or not. If she has, which, for a moment, I will take for granted, she was not created merely to be the solace of man, and the sexual should not destroy the human character.

Into this error men have, probably, been led by viewing education in a false light; not considering it as the first step to form a being advancing gradually toward perfection ... but only as a preparation for life. On this ... error ... has the false system of female manners been reared, which robs the whole sex of its dignity, and classes the brown and fair with the smiling flowers that only adorn the land. This has ever been the language of men, and the fear of departing from a supposed sexual character, has made even women of superior sense adopt the same sentiments. Thus understanding, strictly speaking, has been denied to woman; and instinct, sublimated into wit and cunning, for the purposes of life, has been substituted in its stead.

The power of generalizing ideas, of drawing comprehensive conclusions from individual observations, is the only acquirement for an immortal being, that really deserves the name of knowledge. Merely to observe, without endeavouring to account for any thing, may, (in a very incomplete manner) serve as the common sense of life....

This power has not only been denied to women; but writers have insisted that it is inconsistent, with a few exceptions, with their sexual character. Let men prove this, and I shall grant that woman only exists for man. I must, however, previously remark, that the power of generalizing ideas, to any great extent, is not very common amongst men or women. But this exercise is the true cultivation of the understanding; and every thing conspires to render the cultivation of the understanding more difficult in the female than the male world.

I am naturally led by this assertion to the main subject of the present chapter, and shall now attempt to point out some of the causes that degrade the sex, and prevent women from generalizing their observations.

I shall not go back to the remote annals of antiquity to trace the history of woman; it is sufficient to allow, that she has always been either a slave or a despot, and to remark, that each of these situations equally retards the progress of reason. The grand source of female folly and vice has ever appeared to me to arise from narrowness of mind; and the very constitution of civil governments has put almost insuperable obstacles in the way to prevent the cultivation of the female understanding: yet virtue can be built on no other foundation! The same obstacles are thrown in the way of the rich, and the same consequences ensue.

Necessity has been proverbially termed the mother of invention; the aphorism may be extended to virtue. It is an acquirement, and an acquirement to which pleasure must be sacrificed, and who sacrifices pleasure when it is within the grasp, whose mind has not been opened and strengthened by adversity, or the pursuit of knowledge goaded on by necessity? Happy is it when people have the cares of life to struggle with; for these struggles prevent their becoming a prey to enervating vices, merely from idleness! ...

Pleasure is the business of a woman's life, according to the present modification of society, and while it continues to be so, little can be expected from such weak beings. Inheriting, in a lineal descent from the first fair defect in nature, the sovereignty of beauty, they have, to maintain their power, resigned their natural rights, which the exercise of reason, might have procured them, and chosen rather to be short-lived queens than labour to attain the sober pleasures that arise from equality. Exalted by their inferiority (this sounds like a contradiction) they constantly demand homage as women, though experience should teach them that the men who pride themselves upon paying this arbitrary insolent respect to the sex, with the most scrupulous exactness, are most inclined to tyrannize over, and despise the very weakness they cherish....

Ah! why do women, I write with affectionate solicitude, condescend to receive a degree of attention and respect from strangers, different from that reciprocation of civility which the dictates of humanity, and the politeness of civilization authorise between man and man? And why do they not discover, when "in the noon of beauty's power," that they are treated like queens only to be deluded by hollow respect, till they are led to resign, or not assume, their natural prerogatives? Confined then in cages, like the feathered race, they have nothing to do but to plume themselves, and stalk with mock-majesty from perch to perch. It is true, they are provided with food and raiment, for which they neither toil nor spin; but health, liberty, and virtue are given in exchange....

The passions of men have thus placed women on thrones; and, till mankind become more reasonable, it is to be feared that women will avail themselves of the power which they attain with the least exertion, and which is the most indisputable....

... With a lover, I grant she should be so, and her sensibility will naturally lead her to endeavour to excite emotion, not to gratify her vanity but her heart. This I do not allow to be coquetry, it is the artless impulse of nature, I only exclaim against the sexual desire of conquest, when the heart is out of the question.

...

I lament that women are systematically degraded by receiving the trivial attentions, which men think it manly to pay to the sex, when, in fact, they are insultingly supporting their own superiority. It is not condescension to bow to an inferior. So ludicrous, in fact, do these ceremonies appear to me, that I scarcely am able to govern my muscles, when I see a man start with eager, and serious solicitude to lift a handkerchief, or shut a door, when the LADY could have done it herself, had she only moved a pace or two.

A wild wish has just flown from my heart to my head, and I will not stifle it though it may excite a horse laugh. I do earnestly wish to see the distinction of sex confounded in society, unless where love animates the behaviour. For this distinction is, I am firmly persuaded, the foundation of the weakness of character ascribed to woman; is the cause why the understanding is neglected, whilst accomplishments are acquired with sedulous care: and the same cause accounts for their preferring the graceful before the heroic virtues.

... Abilities and virtues are absolutely necessary to raise men from the middle rank of life into notice; and the natural consequence is notorious, the middle rank contains most virtue and abilities. Men have thus, in one station, at least, an opportunity of exerting themselves with dignity, and of rising by the exertions which really improve a rational creature; but the whole female sex are, till their character is formed, in the same condition as the rich: for they are born, I now speak of a state of civilization, with certain sexual privileges, and whilst they are gratuitously granted them, few will ever think of works of supererogation, to obtain the esteem of a small number of superior people.

When do we hear of women, who starting out of obscurity, boldly claim respect on account of their great abilities or daring virtues? Where are they to be found? "To be observed, to be attended to, to be taken notice of with sympathy, complacency, and approbation, are all the advantages which they seek." True! my male readers will probably exclaim; but let them, before they draw any conclusion, recollect, that this was not written originally as descriptive of women, but of the rich. In Dr. Smith's Theory of Moral Sentiments, I have found a general character of people of rank and fortune, that in my opinion, might with the greatest propriety be applied to the female sex.... Women, commonly called Ladies, are not to be contradicted in company, are not allowed to exert any manual strength; and from them the negative virtues only are expected, when any virtues are expected, patience, docility, good-humour, and flexibility; virtues incompatible with any vigorous exertion of intellect....

In the middle rank of life, to continue the comparison, men, in their youth, are prepared for professions, and marriage is not considered as the grand feature in their lives; whilst women, on the contrary, have no other scheme to sharpen their faculties. It is not business, extensive plans, or any of the excursive flights of ambition, that engross their attention; no, their thoughts are not employed in rearing such noble structures. To rise in the world, and have the liberty of running from pleasure to pleasure, they must marry advantageously, and to this object their time is sacrificed, and their persons often legally prostituted. A man, when he enters any profession, has his eye steadily fixed on some future advantage (and the mind gains great strength by having all its efforts directed to one point) and, full of his business, pleasure is considered as mere relaxation; whilst women seek for pleasure as the main purpose of existence. In fact, from the education which they receive from society, the love of pleasure may be said to govern them all....

In short, women, in general, as well as the rich of both sexes, have acquired all the follies and vices of civilization, and missed the useful fruit.... Their senses are inflamed, and their understandings neglected; consequently they become the prey of their senses, delicately termed sensibility, and are blown about by every momentary gust of feeling.... Ever restless and anxious, their over exercised sensibility not only renders them uncomfortable themselves, but troublesome, to use a soft phrase, to others. All their thoughts turn on things calculated to excite emotion; and, feeling, when they should reason, their conduct is unstable, and their opinions are wavering, not the wavering produced by deliberation or progressive views, but by contradictory emotions. By fits and starts they are warm in many pursuits; yet this warmth, never concentrated into perseverance, soon exhausts itself; exhaled by its own heat, or meeting with some other fleeting passion, to which reason has never given any specific gravity, neutrality ensues. Miserable, indeed, must be that being whose cultivation of mind has only tended to inflame its passions! A distinction should be made between inflaming and strengthening them. The passions thus pampered, whilst the judgment is left unformed, what can be expected to ensue? Undoubtedly, a mixture of madness and folly!

...

Novels, music, poetry and gallantry, all tend to make women the creatures of sensation, and their character is thus formed during the time they are acquiring accomplishments, the only improvement they are excited, by their station in society, to acquire....

And will moralists pretend to assert, that this is the condition in which one half of the human race should be encouraged to remain with listless inactivity and stupid acquiescence? Kind instructors! what were we created for? To remain, it may be said, innocent; they mean in a state of childhood. We might as well never have been born, unless it were necessary that we should be created to enable man to acquire the noble privilege of reason, the power of discerning good from evil, whilst we lie down in the dust from whence we were taken, never to rise again.

...

I am fully persuaded, that we should hear of none of these infantine airs, if girls were allowed to take sufficient exercise and not confined in close rooms till their muscles are relaxed and their powers of digestion destroyed. To carry the remark still further, if fear in girls, instead of being cherished, perhaps, created, were treated in the same manner as cowardice in boys, we should quickly see women with more dignified aspects. It is true, they could not then with equal propriety be termed the sweet flowers that smile in the walk of man; but they would be more respectable members of society, and discharge the important duties of life by the light of their own reason....

In the same strain have I heard men argue against instructing the poor; for many are the forms that aristocracy assumes. "Teach them to read and write," say they, "and you take them out of the station assigned them by nature...." But they know not, when they make man a brute, that they may expect every instant to see him transformed into a ferocious beast. Without knowledge there can be no morality!

...

To fulfil domestic duties much resolution is necessary, and a serious kind of perseverance that requires a more firm support than emotions, however lively and true to nature. To give an example of order, the soul of virtue, some austerity of behaviour must be adopted, scarcely to be expected from a being who, from its infancy, has been made the weathercock of its own sensations. Whoever rationally means to be useful, must have a plan of conduct; and, in the discharge of the simplest duty, we are often obliged to act contrary to the present impulse of tenderness or compassion. Severity is frequently the most certain, as well as the most sublime proof of affection; and the want of this power over the feelings, and of that lofty, dignified affection, which makes a person prefer the future good of the beloved object to a present gratification, is the reason why so many fond mothers spoil their children....

Mankind seem to agree, that children should be left under the management of women during their childhood. Now, from all the observation that I have been able to make, women of sensibility are the most unfit for this task, because they will infallibly, carried away by their feelings, spoil a child's temper. The management of the temper, the first and most important branch of education, requires the sober steady eye of reason; a plan of conduct equally distant from tyranny and indulgence; yet these are the extremes that people of sensibility alternately fall into; always shooting beyond the mark....

... I shall not lay any great stress upon the example of a few women (Sappho, Eloisa, Mrs. Macaulay, the Empress of Russia, Madame d'Eon, etc. These, and many more, may be reckoned exceptions; and, are not all heroes, as well as heroines, exceptions to general rules? I wish to see women neither heroines nor brutes; but reasonable creatures.) who, from having received a masculine education, have acquired courage and resolution; I only contend that the men who have been placed in similar situations have acquired a similar character, I speak of bodies of men, and that men of genius and talents have started out of a class, in which women have never yet been placed.

Chapter 9: Of the Pernicious Effects Which Arise from the Unnatural Distinctions Established in Society

From the respect paid to property flow, as from a poisoned fountain, most of the evils and vices which render this world such a dreary scene to the contemplative mind. For it is in the most polished society that noisome reptiles and venomous serpents lurk under the rank herbage; and there is voluptuousness pampered by the still sultry air, which relaxes every good disposition before it ripens into virtue.

One class presses on another; for all are aiming to procure respect on account of their property: and property, once gained, will procure the respect due only to talents and virtue. Men neglect the duties incumbent on man, yet are treated like demi-gods; religion is also separated from morality by a ceremonial veil, yet men wonder that the world is almost, literally speaking, a den of sharpers or oppressors.

There is a homely proverb, which speaks a shrewd truth, that whoever the devil finds idle he will employ. And what but habitual idleness can hereditary wealth and titles produce? For man is so constituted that he can only attain a proper use of his faculties by exercising them, and will not exercise them unless necessity, of some kind, first set the wheels in motion. Virtue likewise can only be acquired by the discharge of relative duties; but the importance of these sacred duties will scarcely be felt by the being who is cajoled out of his humanity by the flattery of sycophants. There must be more equality established in society, or morality will never gain ground, and this virtuous equality will not rest firmly even when founded on a rock, if one half of mankind are chained to its bottom by fate, for they will be continually undermining it through ignorance or pride. It is vain to expect virtue from women till they are, in some degree, independent of men; nay, it is vain to expect that strength of natural affection, which would make them good wives and good mothers. Whilst they are absolutely dependent on their husbands, they will be cunning, mean, and selfish, and the men who can be gratified by the fawning fondness, of spaniel-like affection, have not much delicacy, for love is not to be bought, in any sense of the word, its silken wings are instantly shrivelled up when any thing beside a return in kind is sought. Yet whilst wealth enervates men; and women live, as it were, by their personal charms, how, can we expect them to discharge those ennobling duties which equally require exertion and self-denial. Hereditary property sophisticates the mind, and the unfortunate victims to it, if I may so express myself, swathed from their birth, seldom exert the locomotive faculty of body or mind; and, thus viewing every thing through one medium, and that a false one, they are unable to discern in what true merit and happiness consist....

I mean, therefore, to infer, that the society is not properly organized which does not compel men and women to discharge their respective duties, by making it the only way to acquire that countenance from their fellow creatures, which every human being wishes some way to attain. The respect, consequently, which is paid to wealth and mere personal charms, is a true north-east blast, that blights the tender blossoms of affection and virtue. Nature has wisely attached affections to duties, to sweeten toil, and to give that vigour to the exertions of reason which only the heart can give....

Destructive, however, as riches and inherited honours are to the human character, women are more debased and cramped, if possible by them, than men, because men may still, in some degree, unfold their faculties by becoming soldiers and statesmen.

...

The preposterous distinctions of rank, which render civilization a curse, by dividing the world between voluptuous tyrants, and cunning envious dependents, corrupt, almost equally, every class of people, because respectability is not attached to the discharge of the relative duties of life, but to the station, and when the duties are not fulfilled, the affections cannot gain sufficient strength to fortify the virtue of which they are the natural reward. Still there are some loop-holes out of which a man may creep, and dare to think and act for himself; but for a woman it is an herculean task, because she has difficulties peculiar to her sex to overcome, which require almost super-human powers.

A truly benevolent legislator always endeavours to make it the interest of each individual to be virtuous; and thus private virtue becoming the cement of public happiness, an orderly whole is consolidated by the tendency of all the parts towards a common centre.... Is one half of the human species, like the poor African slaves, to be subject to prejudices that brutalize them, when principles would be a surer guard only to sweeten the cup of man? ...

Women are in common with men, rendered weak and luxurious by the relaxing pleasures which wealth procures; but added to this, they are made slaves to their persons, and must render them alluring, that man may lend them his reason to guide their tottering steps aright. Or should they be ambitious, they must govern their tyrants by sinister tricks, for without rights there cannot be any incumbent duties. The laws respecting woman, which I mean to discuss in a future part, make an absurd unit of a man and his wife; and then, by the easy transition of only considering him as responsible, she is reduced to a mere cypher.

...

But, as the whole system of representation is now, in this country, only a convenient handle for despotism, they need not complain, for they are as well represented as a numerous class of hard working mechanics, who pay for the support of royalty when they can scarcely stop their children's mouths with bread.... Taxes on the very necessaries of life, enable an endless tribe of idle princes and princesses to pass with stupid pomp before a gaping crowd, who almost worship the very parade which costs them so dear. This is mere gothic grandeur, something like the barbarous, useless parade of having sentinels on horseback at Whitehall, which I could never view without a mixture of contempt and indignation.

... Women might certainly study the art of healing, and be physicians as well as nurses.... They might, also study politics, and settle their benevolence on the broadest basis....

Business of various kinds, they might likewise pursue, if they were educated in a more orderly manner, which might save many from common and legal prostitution. Women would not then marry for a support, as men accept of places under government, and neglect the implied duties; nor would an attempt to earn their own subsistence, a most laudable one! sink them almost to the level of those poor abandoned creatures who live by prostitution.... The few employments open to women, so far from being liberal, are menial; and when a superior education enables them to take charge of the education of children as governesses, they are not treated like the tutors of sons....

... Is not that government then very defective, and very unmindful of the happiness of one half of its members, that does not provide for honest, independent women, by encouraging them to fill respectable stations? But in order to render their private virtue a public benefit, they must have a civil existence in the state, married or single; else we shall continually see some worthy woman, whose sensibility has been rendered painfully acute by undeserved contempt, droop like "the lily broken down by a plough share."

... How many women thus waste life away, the prey of discontent, who might have practised as physicians, regulated a farm, managed a shop, and stood erect, supported by their own industry, instead of hanging their heads surcharged with the dew of sensibility, that consumes the beauty to which it at first gave luster....

...

Those writers are particularly useful, in my opinion, who make man feel for man, independent of the station he fills, or the drapery of factitious sentiments. I then would fain convince reasonable men of the importance of some of my remarks and prevail on them to weigh dispassionately the whole tenor of my observations. I appeal to their understandings; and, as a fellow-creature claim, in the name of my sex, some interest in their hearts. I entreat them to assist to emancipate their companion to make her a help meet for them!

Would men but generously snap our chains, and be content with rational fellowship, instead of slavish obedience, they would find us more observant daughters, more affectionate sisters, more faithful wives, more reasonable mothers—in a word, better citizens. We should then love them with true affection, because we should learn to respect ourselves; and the peace of mind of a worthy man would not be interrupted by the idle vanity of his wife, nor his babes sent to nestle in a strange bosom, having never found a home in their mother's.

8.4 Toussaint L'Ouverture (1743–1803)

Toussaint L'Ouverture is best known as the leader of the Haitian Revolution. The Caribbean island that is now divided into the nations of Haiti and the Dominican Republic was first colonized by the Spanish in 1492. The western part of the island, which would become Haiti, was ceded to the French and became known as St-Domingue in 1625. The Spanish and the French were brutally repressive to the native population, who died in great numbers from imported diseases. Both colonial powers employed kidnapped Africans as slave labour. The French, in particular, imported thousands of slaves to work the extremely lucrative sugar plantations. At this time, St-Domingue was the wealthiest country, *per capita*, in the world (only the white French colonists owners counted as citizens). In 1791, a slave revolt escalated into a full-scale revolution in which the slave population overthrew their colonial masters and declared national independence, becoming the first nation in history to be born from a successful slave revolution. France tried repeatedly over the next thirteen years to recapture the territory and return the black population to slavery. Toussaint L'Ouverture, a former slave who had been freed fifteen years earlier, became the military and political leader of this revolution. The following selections feature several of L'Ouverture's letters, both to his comrades in arms and to various representatives of the French government.

L'Ouverture's letters are introduced here by Jean-Bertrand Aristide (1953–), a Catholic priest who in 1990 became Haiti's first democratically elected president. Following Haiti's declaration of independence in 1804, France extorted payment of 90 million francs for "lost property," crippling Haiti's economy and reducing it to the poorest country on Earth. Haiti only finished paying this debt in 1947. Following years of political instability, military occupation by the United States, and brutal dictatorial rule by the Duvalier dynasty, Aristide was elected in a landslide victory. Aristide had advocated for the return of the independence debt extorted by France, a demand that was widely dismissed by the international community. In 2004, he was ousted in a coup d'état which, he maintains, was carried out by the American military to protect American economic interests. Aristide continues to argue for economic justice for Haitians and characterizes Haiti's rule by a small, wealthy, mulatto élite as the result of "mental slavery."

L'Ouverture's letters convey first and foremost his identity as a French citizen, drawing on France's traditions of Enlightenment thought and revolutionary democratic politics. In essence, L'Ouverture presents the embattled revolutionaries of St-Domingue as a genuine manifestation of the Enlightenment principles of universality and equality. In this way, L'Ouverture uses France's central place in the Enlightenment and its new commitment to democracy against its own record of legally sanctioning brutal enslavement and exploitation. In this sense, L'Ouverture was simultaneously fighting for black Haitians to participate in the Western Enlightenment and challenging anyone who espoused Enlightenment principles to live by their declared principles.

8.4.1 Jean-Bertrand Aristide, "Introduction," The Haitian Revolution: Toussaint L'Ouverture

In 1804 Haiti emerged as the first black republic from the world's only successful slave revolution. The outstanding leader who charted the course of this historic event was a slave whose name is now a timeless symbol of freedom: Toussaint L'Ouverture. The written works he left, his memoirs and letters, and the constitution he drafted, offer insight into his political, theological and economic legacy. For us, following in Toussaint's footsteps, his written record raises three core questions. To what extent did Toussaint liberate himself not only from physical slavery, but from mental slavery to the colonial system he fought? Second, on the theological plane, does Toussaint's legacy offer a line of liberation that can be implemented today? And lastly, would fulfilling Toussaint's social and economic legacy allow us to eradicate poverty, the modern version of slavery, and move towards real freedom?

From the transatlantic slave trade to today's global system of economic slavery, broad ranges of players have worked to maintain colonialism. Those I would call mental slaves, the colonized who nonetheless defend the interests of white colonizers, have always played a crucial role in upholding slavery, then and now. Perhaps the most powerful criticism that has been levelled at Toussaint was that he was overprotective of the masters and their system. Loved by a majority, feared by a minority, and perceived by some in hindsight as having been too kind, too gentle and too diplomatic towards the colonizers, Toussaint's true personality emerges in his writings and his achievements. Hence our first question: Did this former slave remain a mental slave to the system he sought to overthrow? ...

Toussaint: Former Slave Not Mental Slave

The nervous system of the human body can be disrupted by both intrinsic and extrinsic disorders. The body politic is susceptible to the same disruptions. Since 1492, and continuing to this day, colonialism and neocolonialism have been a permanent source of extrinsic disorder to Haiti. Internally, mental slaves from the Haitian elite have generated intrinsic pathologies throughout the country's social fabric that have blocked sustainable development. For the colonizers, blacks fell into two categories: slave and mental slave. Which of these was Toussaint L'Ouverture?

François Dominique Toussaint L'Ouverture was the son of Gaou-Guinou, an Arada prince born in present-day Benin, Africa, who was shipped to Haiti as a slave.... The uncertainty surrounding Toussaint's date of birth reflects how slaves were reduced to objects in the eyes of the colonizers. At least four different dates have been proposed: 1739, based on a letter Toussaint addressed to the French Directory in 1797;

1746, according to his son Isaac; 1743, based on several sources; and 1745, based on documents from Fort de Joux, the French military installation where he was imprisoned, and ultimately died.

At the time of his birth, whatever the date, few thought that he would survive. His frail physique inspired the nickname *Fatra baton*, meaning a stick so thin that it should be thrown in the garbage. But the child surprised everyone. Toussaint developed exceptional physical and intellectual capacities; very early he distinguished himself from the many others on the Bréda Plantation. 'At first assigned to work with the estate animals, L'Ouverture became coachman to the estate manager and then steward of all the livestock.'[1] In 1799, the plantation owner, Bayon de Libertat, said of Toussaint: 'I entrusted to him the principal branch of my management, and the care of the livestock. Never was my confidence in him disappointed.'

Toussaint had long nurtured good relations with some colonizers, and on the eve of the slave insurrection of 1791 he had even saved some of their lives. His legacy has endured some harsh criticism on this point. But his was essentially a moderate, temperate character, self-controlled and diplomatic in style. Despite the violence of the slave system, Toussaint did not adopt a violent comportment, based in turn on revenge and hatred. How did he manage to cultivate these precious personal qualities while developing skills vital to navigating within the complex political arena in which he found himself?

The watershed moment for Toussaint took shape sometime in 1790 or 1791, perhaps under the glow of the 14 August 1791 ceremony at Bois Caïman. Toussaint himself was already free; nevertheless he opted to stand with the masses, those who had been reduced to the property of their masters. Toussaint could not fully enjoy his own liberty; he shared the suffering of those who were still victims of slavery. For him to be fully free—and to feel fully free—*all* enslaved persons had to be free.

A year earlier, in 1790, Toussaint had chosen not to join the mobilizing efforts of Vincent Ogé, a free coloured man whose vision of freedom was limited only to his own caste of wealthy and free coloureds, and did not extend to the slaves. Colonial France was 'the first empire to have a democratic imperial policy that included slaves and free coloured.... That policy did not last very long.... But it lasted longer in the Caribbean, both before and after it was imperial policy.'[2] Toussaint's vision of liberty was universal at a time when France sought to exploit the divisions (real and created) between the coloured and slave communities....

The slave rebellion that erupted in northern Haiti in the wake of the Bois Caïman ceremony in August 1791 occurred in a region that 'was the earliest densely settled and earliest devoted to sugar, largely because its agricultural plain could support rain-fed sugar cultivation.... The northern region produced roughly two-fifths of the sugar of Haiti by the beginning of the Revolution, a bit less tonnage than, but equal in value to, that of the western region.'[3] This rebellion ignited an insurrection that was a clear and deep expression of a collective call for freedom. Though he was not an instigator of the rebellion, Toussaint followed the will and interests of the slaves, and in late 1791, just one year after refusing to align with Ogé, Toussaint stepped onto the public stage and responded to the historic call of the slaves. The insurrection needed his leadership, and he created an *ouverture* (opening) towards freedom. Indeed, he was 'L'Ouverture' (The Opening). St-Domingue thus became, in the words of Aimé Césaire, 'the first country in modern times to have posed in reality, and to also have posed for human reflection, the great problem that the twentieth century has not yet succeeded in resolving in all

1 Marika Sherwood and Hakim Adi, *Pan-African History: Political Figures from Africa and the Diaspora since 1787* (Routledge, 2003), p. 109.

2 Arthur L. Stinchcombe, *Sugar Island Slavery in the Age of Enlightenment: The Political Economy of the Caribbean World* (Princeton University Press, 1995), p. 201.

3 Stinchcombe, *Sugar Island Slavery*, p. 231.

its social, economic, and racial complexity: the colonial problem'.[4]

At the start of the revolution, with almost half a million enslaved Africans in St-Domingue (100,000 new slaves had arrived in just the three preceding years), the colonizers thought they could resolve the colonial problem by exponentially increasing the number of slaves.

The vision of the rebel slaves, of course, was radically different: to eradicate the colonial problem the slaves began by burning down the plantations—the engine of the slave system—and by courageously fighting the colonial masters. Toussaint's approach was less radical. His first choice included neither fire nor the rejection of all whites. When he realized that his former master's family was in imminent danger, Toussaint took precautions to protect them. This move was characteristic of Toussaint, who, throughout the struggle for freedom, systematically sought alliances that could bring him closer to his goal. For similar strategic reasons, in 1793, during the war between France and Spain, Toussaint joined the Spanish camp, which occupied the eastern two-thirds of the island. Serving as an aide to Georges Biassou, one of the most important insurgent leaders in the northern plains, he quickly rose through the ranks.

Because of his exceptional military talents, his ability to build consensus, train soldiers and find strategic ways to achieve victories, Toussaint was recognized as a great general. His authority in the north was legendary. Meanwhile, the French colonizers were desperate to find a counterweight to his ascension and, at the same time, to repel European forces encroaching on their interests. In addition to the Spanish in the east, a British invasion threatened St-Domingue's coastline. The National Assembly in Paris dispatched Léger-Félicité Sonthonax and Etienne Polverel, two French commissioners, to replace General Etienne Laveaux as governor of the colony. Their mission was to lure rebel slaves from the Spanish with the promise of freedom.

Toussaint saw an opening. However dubious the French offer may have been, he saw the opportunity to strengthen his own strategy by joining the French and abandoning the British and the Spanish, who in any event were stalling on the promise of freedom made to the slaves. On 29 August 1793, the very same day that Sonthonax issued his proclamation abolishing slavery in the north, Toussaint issued his own proclamation: 'I want Liberty and Equality to reign in St-Domingue. I work to bring them into existence. Unite yourselves to us, brothers, and fight with us for the same cause.' With these words, Toussaint 'was positioning himself against Sonthonax as the true defender of liberty in St-Domingue'.[5] He officially aligned himself with the French in 1794, only after the French National Assembly had sanctioned the Sonthonax proclamation against slavery. He then immediately began to pressure the French to put a definitive end to slavery throughout the colony.

Promoted to Général de Brigade by Laveaux, former Governor of St-Domingue, Toussaint led his army of blacks, mulattos and whites and won a number of victories, routing the Spanish from the island.

Meanwhile, in 1794, French forces led by Victor Hugues regained control of the neighbouring island of Guadeloupe from the British, who had briefly occupied it with the support of local plantation owners.[6] This successful restoration of French power in Guadeloupe was a potential threat to Toussaint's plan for the total eradication of slavery in St-Domingue.

> The freedom of planter governments in the colonies means by definition that arbitrary imperial governments do not have the right to interfere with their decisions. The freedom of the planters to do what they want with their

4 Laurent Dubois, *Avengers of the New World* (Belknap Press of Harvard University/Duke University, 2004), p. 3, citing Aimé Césaire, *Toussaint Louverture: La révolution française et le problème colonial* (Le club français du livre, 1960).
5 Dubois, *Avengers of the New World*, p. 176.
6 Chris Bongie, *Islands and Exiles: The Creole Identities of Post/Colonial Literature* (Stanford University Press, 1998, p. 3).

> property means that slaves do not have freedom, the right to do what they want.[7]

Slavery formed the foundation of the colonial economy: the unpaid labour of slaves was the principal source of riches for the colonizers, and St-Domingue stood at the pinnacle of this wealth:

> [In the 1790s, the colony] produced close to one-half of all the sugar and coffee consumed in Europe and the Americas, as well as substantial amounts of cotton, indigo, and ground provisions. Though scarcely larger than Maryland, and little more than twice the size of Jamaica, it had long been the wealthiest colony in the Caribbean and was hailed by publicists as the 'Pearl of the Antilles' or the 'Eden of the Western World.' ... By 1789 Saint Domingue had about 8,000 plantations producing crops for export. They generated some two-fifths of France's foreign trade, a proportion rarely equaled in any colonial empire.[8]

It was clear the colonizers would fight tooth-and-nail to keep this source of wealth.

In 1795, Toussaint found himself in a complex strategic position. As he manoeuvred forward, he had to balance ethics and moral values with strategic planning. He was able to revive the economy of St-Domingue while significantly improving social conditions on the island. He believed that social tensions could be reduced by encouraging unity among blacks, coloureds and whites. Although freed from the whip, the former slaves would have to work hard; Toussaint did not tolerate laziness: 'Work', he said, 'is necessary, it is a virtue.' But now the wealth generated by the former slave would directly benefit them. Unfortunately, this vision did not fit in with colonial plans. Despite economic and social progress made by 1795, the road to freedom was still long. Forever faithful to the masses of slaves, and committed to building alliances to reach his goal, he abandoned whoever thought that he, Toussaint, could be used against his people. In 1797, Toussaint broke ranks with Sonthonax for precisely this reason.

Generally, blacks and mulattos who were of the political, intellectual or economic elite, and who benefited by serving as mental slaves to the colonizers, failed to recognize that the experience of slavery itself 'formed the root of an emergent collective identity through an equally emergent collective memory, one that signified and distinguished a race, a people'.[9] The psychological obsessions and inferiority complexes of internal colonization prevented the colonized from understanding that a transfer of class does not mean a change of self or identity. Such mental slaves, then as now, live in a near permanent state of identity crisis. As feelings of inferiority weaken their sense of identity, they constantly look to the white master with whom they identify—much as Frantz Fanon famously described in his seminal work *Black Skin, White Masks*.[10]

By contrast, hierarchical divisions between enslaved Africans and white colonizers helped raise the slaves' consciousness of their condition. Toussaint knew that the slaves could gain power only through unity, whereas those who remained mentally enslaved were, by definition, powerless. In this respect, Toussaint's perception of power opposed that of Sonthonax. While never forsaking his convictions, Toussaint did have the ability to understand multiple perspectives. He understood that the exercise of power required continuous vigilance and identification of different types of enemies—the immediate enemy and the enemy to come.[11]

At the same time Toussaint showed that he could reach compromises with those who pursued interests broadly compatible with his own. In 1798, Toussaint

7 Stinchcombe, *Sugar Island Slavery*, p. 319.
8 Franklin W. Knight and Colin A. Palmer, eds., *The Modern Caribbean* (University of North Carolina Press, 1989), p. 21.
9 Ron Eyerman, *Cultural Trauma: Slavery and the Formation of African American Identity* (Cambridge University Press, 2001), p. 1.
10 Frantz Fanon, *Black Skin, White Masks*, trans. Charles Lam Markmann (Grove Press, 1967; originally published in 1952).
11 Ben Shalit, *The Psychology of Conflict and Combat* (Praeger, 1988), p. 8.

agreed to negotiate on behalf of France for the withdrawal of British forces from St-Domingue and for greater commercial exchanges with foreign nations. He signed economic agreements with Britain and the United States to sell sugar, coffee and other produce in exchange for needed weapons and foreign manufactured goods. Signed on 22 May 1799, these agreements were a step towards prosperity; they were also a testament to Toussaint's principles and his capacity to think strategically. The two contracting countries offered to recognize Toussaint as king, ruler of an independent nation. Because, as C.L.R. James rightly noted, Toussaint understood that power was a 'means to an end'—in this case, true liberty for all slaves—he refused the offer. He was not obsessed with power for power's sake. Toussaint signed the trade agreements because they could bring something to his people. But he refused to be crowned 'king' by the same white colonizers responsible for the continued enslavement of his people.[12]

In any case, Toussaint did not need to be king. He was loved, even revered, by his people. His view of leadership was expansive; he opened his arms to all—black, mulatto and white—and this empowered him to achieve much during his administration. The increased agricultural production sparked by Toussaint's policies not only brought needed resources to the country, it was a collective expression of the dignity of the former enslaved Africans turned agricultural workers....

For Toussaint, power and leadership operated relationally and reciprocally. In this vision of leadership, to control the balance of power a leader must care about the fundamental needs of his or her followers. Toussaint shaped a strategy that consistently demonstrated that he cared deeply for the dignity and prosperity of his people. Signing trade agreements with the British and the Americans while flatly rejecting the offer to be crowned king was one example. Another was his expulsion of his nominal French superior Gabriel Hédouville and of Hédouville's successor Philippe Roume. When Hédouville first arrived from France with the 'difficult mission to reassert metropolitan control in the colony', Toussaint let Hédouville know exactly what he was thinking: 'There are men who talk as if they support general liberty, but who inside are its sworn enemies.'[13]

Toussaint's commitment to universal liberty was not shared by many of his foreign contemporaries. Two years after signing the trade agreement with Toussaint, Thomas Jefferson would begin to undermine it. Given the social and geopolitical complexity of the context in which Toussaint led the enslaved Africans and their descendants, we are compelled to ask how he managed to become such an outstanding liberator. The political participation of the slaves was certainly an indispensable driving force against the enemies. But so too was Toussaint's character, his personality. I refer here to the essence of his person and his self-consciousness.[14] And in his essence he was a free man. Toussaint consistently demonstrated intellectual independence from the colonizers, even while maintaining the ability to negotiate with them when necessary. Time and again, Toussaint demonstrated his own autonomy, his ability to manoeuvre, to lead, and to *shape* events, rather than merely to respond to them. He set his own course, and this the colonizers ultimately found intolerable.

The fundamental interests of blacks and whites in eighteenth-century St-Domingue were poles apart. To manoeuvre in such complex territory, Toussaint often had to change tactics and modify plans, but he was always consistent in his basic principles. He never took one stand while in the company of the master and the opposite stand when among his own people. Duplicity of this kind is characteristic of mental slaves who define themselves in terms of their dependency on their masters. The social dimensions of their selves betray their distance from their social origins. Within their own societies, mental slaves identify themselves as members of the elite. It is inconceivable to them that

12 C.L.R. James, *The Black Jacobins* (Allison & Busby, 1982), pp. 211–13.
13 Dubois, *Avengers of the New World*, p. 217.
14 Richard Jenkins, *Social Identity* (Routledge, 2004), p. 27.

all people have equal social standing. They internalize and then invert their own psychological subordination.

Anyone who wants to understand the process by which European colonizers succeeded in using the colonized in their indirect rule over the natives they dominated should pay careful attention to the psychological dimensions of colonialism. In this context, the 'self is an object of inquiry—a crucial site of colonial and anti-colonial struggle.'[15] According to William Easterly, in British Nigeria in 1939 there were 1,315 British citizens in charge of 20 million Nigerians, while 2,384 Europeans ruled over 9.4 million Africans in the Belgian Congo and 3,660 Europeans imposed their will on 15 million Africans in French-occupied West Africa.[16] When Toussaint emerged, in 1791, as the great leader of St-Domingue, approximately 40,000 white colonizers there were ruling over 30,000 *machotara*,[17] or coloureds, and 500,000 slaves, two-thirds of whom had been born in Africa. How did the minority manage to control the majority? They certainly could not have succeeded without the help of mental slaves—people who lacked genuine autonomy and a national identity.... Slavery and its attendant economic exploitation were permanent sources of political conflict in the colony. But the issue of identity occupied an important space, because the contours of identity traced by the elite and the mental slave were exclusive: the elites were human, slaves were not. Kenneth Hoover confirms that 'what identity analysis demonstrates is that, independently of economic advantage or disadvantage, considerations of identity have the potential both to tear communities apart and bring them together'.[18]

This legacy is with us still. More than 200 years later, Haitian identity is still split, with the great mass of the Haitian people on one side, and a small elite who remain identified with today's colonizers on the other. In 2004, Toussaint's descendants experienced the destructive powers of this split. White neocolonial forces, allied with today's Haitian mental slaves, vowed to use violence to disrupt and prevent the bicentennial commemoration of the very events around which Haitian mass national identity was formed:

1. Toussaint's constitution proclaiming freedom for all in 1801;
2. Toussaint's assassination in Fort de Joux on 7 April 1803;
3. The birth of Haiti's flag, symbolizing a radical rejection of French colonialism, on 18 May 1803;
4. The last battle of Vertières, marking the historic victory of enslaved Haitians over the then superpower of the world, Napoleon's army, on 18 November 1803;
5. The independence of the world's first black republic, Haiti, on 1 January 1804.

Neocolonizers spent more than US$200 million dollars to ensure that the descendants of Toussaint would not be able to celebrate these historic events. But the masses of the Haitian people, whose identity stems from them, commemorated the Revolution anyway.... Why, then, outside the African diaspora, was the commemoration of the world's only successful slave revolution so little noted? Since the moment the enslaved Africans of Haiti rose up, colonialists and neocolonialists have used every means at their disposal, notably the pens of historians, to keep the world from knowing the truth of the Haitian Revolution, and specifically of how French colonizers kidnapped Toussaint, assassinated his character and then killed him in Fort de Joux.

The mental slaves who continue to serve the colonial order have never had the moral courage to challenge this manipulation. Rather than confront Napoleon's crimes against Toussaint and the Haitian people, they choose actively to promote historical amnesia. Mythomaniacal colonizers and the mental slaves who mimic them share a pathological proclivity towards

15 Karl E. Scheibe, *The Psychology of Self and Identity* (Praeger, 1995), p. 23.
16 William Easterly, *The White Man's Burden* (Penguin, 2006).
17 A Kiswahili word meaning 'coloured people'.
18 Kenneth R. Hoover, James Marcia and Kristen Parris, *The Power of Identity: Politics in a New Key* (Chatham House Publishers, 1997), p. 61.

lying. Together they reinforce the sclerosis of the colonial and neocolonial system. It is not surprising then that neocolonizers recruit mental slaves as they prepare to re-enter the political scene of a former colony.

Both the first coup d'état against Toussaint's successor on 17 October 1806 and the most recent coup in Haiti, on 29 February 2004, illustrate the barbarity that will be used to overthrow any head of state who is neither a mental slave nor a corrupt dictator defending the interests of the wealthy and their foreign masters. In 2004 the neocolonizers demonstrated once again that, for them, a Haitian president must be both a puppet and a mental slave. Unfortunately, they have so far succeeded.

But the Haitian people have achieved a high level of consciousness, and, like Toussaint, they will never give up. To the pertinent question posed by Jean Twenge and Roy Baumeister, 'How do people react to social exclusion and rejection?',[19] The people of Haiti answer simply but profoundly: 'We follow Toussaint L'Ouverture.'

8.4.2 Letters (3, 9, 13, 20)

LETTER 3

This extraordinary document, signed by Toussaint in the name of his fourteen-year-old nephew Belair, was written by the leaders of the slave revolt to the colonial assembly in St-Domingue and the national commissioner Roume. After failed negotiations six months before, the letter testifies to an early and rapid radicalization of the revolution to encompass the call for general liberty based on the logic of indivisible, universal human rights.

~

Letter to the General Assembly from Biassou, Jean-François and Toussaint L'Ouverture

July 1792

Gentlemen,

Those who have the honour to present you with these memoirs are a class of men whom up to the present you have failed to recognize as like yourselves, and whom you have covered in opprobrium by heaping upon them the ignominy attached to their unfortunate lot. These are men who don't know how to choose big words, but who are going to show you and all the world the justice of their cause; finally, they are those whom you call your slaves and who claim the rights to which all men may aspire.

For too long, gentlemen, by way of abuses that one can never too strongly accuse of having taken place because of our lack of understanding and our ignorance—for a very long time, I say—we have been victims of your greed and your avarice. Under the blows of your barbarous whip we have accumulated for you the treasures you enjoy in this colony; the human race has suffered to see with what barbarity you have treated men like yourself—yes, men—over whom you have no other right except that you are stronger and more barbaric than we; you have engaged in [slave] traffic, you have sold men for horses, and even that is the least of your shortcomings in the eyes of humanity; our lives depend on your caprice, and when it's a question of amusing yourselves, the burden falls on men like us,

19 Dominic Abrams, Michael A. Hogg and José M. Marques, eds., *The Social Psychology of Inclusion and Exclusion* (Psychology Press, 2005), p. 27.

who most often are guilty of no other crime than to be under your orders.

We are black, it is true, but tell us, gentlemen, you who are so judicious, what is the law that says that the black man must belong to and be the property of the white man? Certainly you will not be able to make us see where that exists, if it is not in your imaginations—always ready to form new [phantasms] so long as they are to your advantage. Yes, gentlemen, we are free like you, and it is only by your avarice and our ignorance that anyone is still held in slavery up to this day, and we can neither see nor find the right that you pretend to have over us, nor anything that could prove it to us, set down on the earth like you, all being children of the same father created in the same image. We are your equals then, by natural right, and if nature pleases itself to diversify colours within the human race, it is not a crime to be born black nor an advantage to be white. If the abuses in the Colony have gone on for several years, that was before the fortunate revolution that has taken place in the motherland, which has opened for us the road which our courage and labour will enable us to ascend, to arrive at the temple of liberty, like those brave Frenchmen who are our models and whom all the universe is contemplating.

For too long we have borne your chains without thinking of shaking them off, but any authority which is not founded on virtue and humanity, and which only tends to subject one's fellow man to slavery, must come to an end, and that end is yours. You, gentlemen, who pretend to subject us to slavery—have you not sworn to uphold the French Constitution? What does it say, this respectable constitution? What is the fundamental law? Have you forgotten that you have formally vowed the Declaration of the Rights of Man, which says that men are born free, equal in their rights; that their natural rights include liberty, property, security and resistance to oppression? So then, as you cannot deny what you have sworn, we are within our rights, and you ought to recognize yourselves as perjurers; by your decrees you recognize that all men are free, but you want to maintain servitude for 480,000 individuals who allow you to enjoy all that you possess. Through your envoys you offer liberty only to our chiefs; it is still one of your maxims of politics to say that those who have played an equal part in our work should be delivered by us to be your victims. No, we prefer a thousand deaths to acting that way towards our own kind. If you want to accord us the benefits that are due to us, they must also shower onto all of our brothers....

Gentlemen, in very few words you have seen our way of thinking—it is unanimous and it is after consulting everyone to whom we are connected in the same cause that we present to you our demands, as follows.

First: general liberty for all men detained in slavery.

Second: general amnesty for the past.

Third: the guarantee of these articles by the Spanish government.

Fourth: the three articles above are the basis and the sole means to achieve a peace that would be respected by the two parties, and only after they are approved in the name of the Colony and M. the Lieutenant Général, and when the National Civil Commissioners have agreed to present this approval to the king, and to the National Assembly.

If, like us, you desire that the articles above be accepted, we will commit ourselves to the following: first, to lay down our arms; second, that each of us will return to the plantation to which he belongs and resume his work on condition of a wage which will be set by the year for each cultivator who starts work for a fixed term.

Here, gentlemen, is the request of men who are like you, and here is their final resolution: they are resolved to live free or die.

We have the honour to be, gentlemen, your very humble and obedient servants.

Biassou, Jean-François, Belair

LETTER 9: LETTER TO LAVEAUX, 20 FEBRUARY 1796

In February 1796, plantation workers in the northern mountains near Port-de-Paix revolted in response to the dismissal of Etienne Datty, a local black commander. Toussaint, who rode overnight to put down the rebellion, describes in this letter his negotiations with the rebels. The letter is particularly important in its examination of the diverse claims and definitions of freedom being made by the various communities united under the French flag. For Toussaint, freedom is only possible through organized labour under the rule of universal, rights-based law offered by the French Republic (in implicit contrast to the slave-holding Spanish and English states in competition for control of the island). For the rebellious workers, freedom arises instead through a shared communal experience of suffering such as that they have shared with Datty which has no necessary connection, and is even inimical, to large-scale plantation labour.

~

1 Ventôse, An 4

Toussaint L'Ouverture to Etienne Laveaux

[...] As soon as I arrived [in Port-de-Paix], I wrote to Pageot, commander of the Northern Province, to alert him to my arrival, and sent Baptiste Andro with two of my dragoons to deliver the letter. At that moment, a large number of farmers, both men and women, came to me with food, some chickens and eggs. They told me how glad they were to see me and that they hoped I would put an end to all these disorders. I ordered them to get me hay, which they did immediately and seemed to do with pleasure. I took this to be a good sign that it would not be difficult to resolve things.

At seven in the evening, Etienne arrived, in conformity with the order I had sent him, with around five hundred men, many of them armed. I saddled my horse and ordered Etienne to form a circle of all the citizens who had gone with him, as well as those who had just arrived with the hay. I mounted my horse and entered the circle where, after having condemned the murders they had committed, I told them that if they wished to preserve their liberty they would have to submit to the laws of the Republic, and be docile and work, that it was only in this way that they would benefit from their freedom. Furthermore, I said that if they had any claim to make that they would never obtain it in this manner, and that God had said: Ask and ye shall receive, knock and my door will be open to you, but that he has not said to commit crimes to obtain what one needs.

I asked them if they knew me and whether they were glad to see me. They answered yes, that they knew that I was the father of all the blacks, and that they also knew that I had never ceased to work for their happiness and for their liberty, but they begged me to listen to them and that perhaps I would see that they perhaps were not so in the wrong as I believed. I was quiet and listened to them. One of them spoke and said to me: 'General, all of us look upon you as our father, it is you after God who are dearest to us and in whom we have the most confidence.' I told him to be silent and said that if they thought of me in this way they should not have acted as they had, and that if they had feared to address the Governor General [Laveaux] whom we must all regard as our father and the defender of our liberty, they should have come to me. I would then have tried to convince the Governor General to meet their demands if I found them just, and that I would in this way have prevented them from committing such crimes. They answered me that they love the Governor General, but that unfortunately for them, all men are not like him, for then they would surely be happy. They went on to say, 'Since the beginning of the revolution, Etienne has always been our leader, it is he who has always commanded us. He has always shared in our misery in our struggle to win our freedom. Why has his command been taken from him, and why is he seen as so undeserving as to give it to another without our agreement? That is why, general, we took up arms. It is unfortunate for us that there are bad men among us who have committed crimes. But we are by no means accomplices in all that. Alas, general, they wish as well to make us slaves; there is no equality here, as it seems there is with you. Look how the whites and coloured men who are with you are good and are united with the blacks. One would think they were brothers from the same mother. That, general, is what we call equality. Here it is not the same. We are looked down upon, they vex us at every turn. They don't pay us what we are owed for the food we grow. They force us to give away our chickens and pigs for nothing when we go to sell them in the city, and if we complain, they have us arrested by the police, and they throw us in prison without giving us anything to eat, and then make us pay to get out. You see, general, that one is not free if he is treated like this. We are certain from what we observe that all those who are with you are content and love you.'

When he stopped speaking, I asked him if this was all they had to complain about. He answered me: 'Yes.' I asked all the others if what he had said was true. They answered me all together that it was true. I quieted them down and said, 'My friends, I shouldn't treat you in this way, because the shame you bring to me and all the men of our colour makes me see that you are not my friends. All the reasons that you give appear just to me, but if you should give me a house full of them'—I used this expression to make them understand that they could have all the reasons they wished and still they were in the wrong because they had rendered themselves guilty in the eyes of God, of the law, and of men. 'What will I tell the National Convention when it will ask me for an account of what you have just done? How is it possible, when I have just sent deputies to the National Convention to thank them in the name of all the blacks for the magnanimous decree that grants them liberty? How can I assure them, after this, that they will work to deserve this decree and will prove to France and to all nations that they are worthy by their submission to the law, by their work and their docility, that I can answer for them all, and that soon, with the help of France, we shall prove to the entire universe that St-Domingue, worked by free hands, will recover its wealth? Answer me this. My shame will show that I have deceived them; it will prove to them what the enemies of our freedom have tried to make them believe, that blacks are not fit to be free, that if they become free they will no longer work, and that they will steal and kill.'

They answered me that they were wrong and begged me, in all my friendship for them, to repair this mistake, and swore to me never to do wrong again and to be wise and obedient, to do nothing more without consulting me and to stop the first among them who would dare to give bad advice. They said to me as well that it was absolutely essential that I put things back in order before leaving, that I had come too far not to leave them in peace before returning. I promised them that I had come for nothing else, but that it was up to them to prove that they wanted peace and tranquillity by all of them returning immediately to their respective plantations and starting back to work, and that this was entirely up to them. They answered me in a single voice: 'Forgive us, general, we will be so good that you will be forced to forget what we have just done.' So I asked them to go away. To Etienne I said that these were not all the citizens of his parish. He answered me that no, there were still three camps in the mountains. After that, I said to all those I had just sent away to return the next day when those from the mountains had arrived, that I wished to pardon them all together.

It was 9.30 in the evening. I asked Etienne where his secretary was. He said to me that he was also in the mountains. I ordered Etienne to give him the order to return to the plantation with all the citizens who were camped in the mountains to see me.

...

LETTER 13: LETTER TO THE FRENCH DIRECTORY, NOVEMBER 1797

This letter, along with his 1793 proclamation the most famous Toussaint ever wrote, is the culminating document of his republican political philosophy and his steadfast defence of universal human rights. It was written in response to the increasing conservatism of the French Directory, and, in particular, the attacks against Toussaint by the arch-racist, pro-slavery representative Vaublanc.[1]

Toussaint L'Ouverture to the French Directory

When the people of St-Domingue first tasted the fruit of liberty that they hold from the equity of France; when to the violent upheavals of the revolution that announced it succeeded the pleasures of tranquillity; when finally the rule of law took the place of anarchy under which the unfortunate colony had too long suffered, what fatality can have led the greatest enemy of its prosperity and of our happiness still to dare to threaten us with the return of slavery? The impolitic and incendiary speech of Vaublanc has threatened the blacks less than the certainty of the plans meditated upon by the property owners of St-Domingue. Such insidious declamations should have no effect upon the wise legislators who have decreed liberty to humanity. The attacks the colonists propose against this liberty must be feared all the more insofar as they hide their detestable projects under the veil of patriotism. We know that illusory and specious descriptions have been made to you of the renewal of terrible violence. Already, perfidious emissaries have crept among us to foment destruction at the hands of liberticides. They will not succeed, this I swear by all that is most sacred in liberty. My attachment to France, the gratitude that all the blacks conserve for her, make it my duty to hide from you neither the plans being fomented nor the oath that we renew to bury ourselves beneath the ruins of a country revived by liberty rather than suffer the return of slavery.

It is for you, Citizen Directors, to remove from over our heads the storm that the eternal enemies of our liberty are preparing in the shades of silence. It is for you to enlighten the Legislature, it is for you to prevent the enemies of the present system from spreading themselves on our unfortunate shores to sully them with new crimes. Do not allow our brothers, our friends, to be sacrificed to men who wish to reign over the ruins of the human species. But no, your wisdom will enable you to avoid the dangerous snares which our common enemies hold out for you....

I send you with this letter a declaration which will acquaint you with the unity that exists between the proprietors of St-Domingue who are in France, those in the United States, and those who serve under the English banner. You will see there a resolution, unequivocal and carefully constructed, for the restoration of slavery; you will see there that their determination to succeed has led them to envelop themselves in the mantle of liberty in order to strike it more deadly blows. You will see that they are counting heavily on my willingness to espouse perfidious views out of fear for my children. It is not astonishing that these men who sacrifice their country to their interests are unable to conceive how many sacrifices a true love of country can support in a better father than they, since I unhesitatingly base the happiness of my children on that of my country, which they and they alone wish to destroy.

I shall never hesitate in choosing between the safety of St-Domingue and my personal happiness, but I have nothing to fear. It is to the solicitude of the

1 For still-unsurpassed commentary on the world-historical nature of this letter, see C.L.R. James, *The Black Jacobins* (Vintage 1989 [1963]), pp. 194–98.

French government that I have confided my children.... I would tremble with horror if it was into the hands of the colonists that I had sent them as hostages; but even if it were so, let them know that in punishing them for the fidelity of their father, they would only add one degree more to their barbarism, without any hope of making me fail in my duty....

Blind as they are, they cannot see how this odious conduct on their part can become the signal of new disasters and irreparable misfortunes, and that far from it helping them regain what in their eyes liberty for all has made them lose, they expose themselves to total ruin and the colony to its inevitable destruction. Could men who have once enjoyed the benefits of liberty look on calmly while it is taken from them! They bore their chains when they knew no condition of life better than that of slavery. But today when they have left it, if they had a thousand lives, they would sacrifice them all rather than to be subjected again to slavery. But no, the hand that has broken our chains will not subject us to them again. France will not renounce her principles. She shall not permit the perversion of her sublime morality and the destruction of the principles that honour her the most, and the degradation of her most beautiful accomplishment, by rescinding the decree of 16 Pluviôse [4 February 1794, abolishing slavery in the French colonies] that honours so well all of humanity. But if, in order to re-establish servitude in St-Domingue this were to be done, I declare to you that this would be to attempt the impossible. We have known how to confront danger to obtain our liberty, and we will know how to confront death to preserve it. This, Citizens and Directors, is the morality of the people of St-Domingue, these are the principles I transmit to you on their behalf.

Let me renew to you the oath that I have made: to cease to exist before gratitude is stricken from my heart and to remain faithful to France, to my duty, and before the land of liberty be profaned and blackened by the liberticides, before they can wrest from my hands this glaive, these arms that France has confided in me for the defence of her rights, for those of humanity, and for the triumph of liberty and equality.

Greetings and respect

Toussaint L'Ouverture

LETTER 20: LETTER FROM NAPOLEON TO TOUSSAINT, 18 NOVEMBER 1801

This letter was presented to Toussaint at his plantation at Ennery on 8 February 1802, by his two sons, returned from their studies in France, and their tutor Coisnon. The letter had little chance of success, as it named Leclerc as Toussaint's superior officer. In fact, virtually every word of it was either false or highly ambiguous; Leclerc had explicit orders from Napoleon to capture and deport Toussaint and the entire black officer class with him, and to reinstate slavery as soon as possible.

Citizen General

The peace with England and all the European powers, which has established the Republic in the highest degree of power and grandeur, now allows the government to occupy itself with the colony of St-Domingue. We are sending there Citizen Leclerc, our brother-in-law, in his quality as General to serve as first magistrate of the colony. He is accompanied by a considerable force in order to ensure the respect of the sovereignty of the French people.

It is in these circumstances that we hope that you will prove to us, and to all of France, the sincerity of the sentiments that you have regularly expressed in the letters that you wrote to us.

We hold you in esteem, and we are happy to recognize and proclaim the great services that you have rendered the French people. If its banner flies over St-Domingue, it is to you and the brave blacks that this is owed.

Called by your talents and the force of circumstances to the leading position of command, you have done away with civil war, put a brake on persecution by several ferocious men, and returned to its place of honour the cult of God, from which everything emanates.

The constitution you made, while including many good things, contains some that are contrary to the dignity and sovereignty of the French people, of which St-Domingue forms only a portion.

The circumstances in which you found yourself, surrounded on all sides by enemies without the metropole being able to either assist or resupply you, rendered articles of that constitution legitimate that otherwise would not be. But today, when the circumstances have changed for the better, you should be the first to render homage to the sovereignty of the nation that counts you among its most illustrious citizens thanks to the services you have rendered it and by the talents and the force of character with which nature has graced you. A contrary conduct would be irreconcilable with the idea we have conceived of you. It would have you lose the many rights to recognition and the benefits of the republic, and would dig beneath your feet a precipice which, in swallowing you up, could contribute to the misfortune of those brave blacks whose courage we love, and whose rebellion we would, with difficulty, be obliged to be punished.

We have made known to your children and their tutor the sentiments that animate us. We are returning them to you.

Assist the General with your counsels, your influence and your talents. What could you wish for? Freedom for blacks? You know that in all the countries we've been we have given it to people who didn't have it. Consideration, honours, fortune? After the services you have rendered us, that you can yet render us, and the particular sentiments that we have for you, can you possibly be unsure about your fortune and the honours that await you?

And, General, think that if you are the first of your colour to have arrived at such a great power, and to have so distinguished himself for his bravery and military talents, you are also before God and ourselves principally responsible for the conduct of the people of St-Domingue.

If there are evil ones who say to the individuals of St-Domingue that we arrive to investigate what they did during the time of anarchy, assure them that we are informing ourselves only of their conduct in those circumstances, and that we are only investigating the past in order to learn of the traits that distinguished them in the war they carried out against the English and the Spaniards, who were our enemies.

Count without any reservation on our esteem, and conduct yourself as should one of the principal citizens of the greatest nation in the world.
The First Consul, Bonaparte

8.5 Sojourner Truth (1797–1883)

Sojourner Truth was an African American who became an abolitionist and advocate for civil and women's rights after being freed from slavery in 1828. Born Isabella Bomfree, she changed her name to Sojourner Truth in 1843. She was already an influential speaker at religious revivals when in 1851 she began a lecture tour that included the Women's Convention in Akron, Ohio. At that event she gave the speech reported here.

Truth campaigned both for the abolition of slavery and for equal rights for women, and she understood these struggles to be inextricably connected. The Akron speech addresses both causes. It is one of the earliest examples of what we today call "intersectionality," for it addresses how overlapping sociological categories result in special disadvantages to people who face discrimination for more than one reason (see also 8.8). The following speech draws attention to different dimensions of social life that cannot be understood in isolation from each other, in this case, her race and her gender.

In this particular instance, Truth's words are matched by her formidable personality. For this reason, we include not only the speech but a report of the occasion testifying to her oratorical powers.

Speech to the 1851 Women's Convention

One of the most unique and interesting speeches of the Convention was made by Sojourner Truth, an emancipated slave. It is impossible to transfer it to paper, or convey any adequate idea of the effect it produced upon the audience. Those only can appreciate it who saw her powerful form, her whole-souled, earnest gestures, and listened to her strong and truthful tones. She came forward to the platform and addressing the President said with great simplicity: May I say a few words? Receiving an affirmative answer, she proceeded;

I want to say a few words about this matter. I am a woman's rights. I have as much muscle as any man, and can do as much work as any man. I have plowed and reaped and husked and chopped and mowed, and can any man do more than that? I have heard much about the sexes being equal; I can carry as much as any man, and can eat as much too, if I can get it. I am as strong as any man that is now. As for intellect, all I can say is, if woman have a pint and man a quart—why can't she have her little pint full? You need not be afraid to give us our rights for fear we will take too much—for we can't take more than our pint'll hold. The poor men seem to be all in confusion, and don't know what to do. Why children, if you have woman's rights give it to her and you will feel better. You will have your own rights, and they won't be so much trouble. I can't read, but I can hear. I have heard the Bible and have learned that Eve caused man to sin. Well if woman upset the world, do give her a chance to set it right side up again. The Lady has spoken about Jesus, how he never spurned woman from him, and she was right. When Lazarus died, Mary and Martha came to him with faith and love and besought him to raise their brother. And Jesus wept—and Lazarus came forth. And how came Jesus into the world? Through God who created him and woman who bore him. Man, where is your part? But the women are coming up blessed be God and a few of the men are coming up with them. But man is in a tight place, the poor slave is on him, woman is coming on him, and he is surely between a hawk and a buzzard.

8.6 John Stuart Mill (1806–1873)

John Stuart Mill is perhaps the most influential English-speaking philosopher of the nineteenth century. Historically, he fits into the British liberal tradition that includes John Locke (1632–1704; see 5.3) and Adam Smith (1726–1790; see 5.5), especially the utilitarian stream that begins with Jeremy Bentham (1748–1832) and James Mill (1773–1836), John Stuart's father. According to liberalism, individual liberty is the supreme political value. And according to the principle of utility, an action or policy is good if and only if it promotes the greatest happiness for the greatest number of people (i.e., the Greatest Happiness Principle).

J.S. Mill carried on the cause of utilitarianism from Bentham and his own father, but he formulated it to avoid any threat to individuality and individual liberty implicit in the Greatest Happiness Principle. A threat to individual liberty came from the possibility that overall happiness might be achieved by sacrificing the interests of a single person or a minority. This threat is particularly acute in a democracy when a majority has the raw power to disregard the interests of individuals or members of minority groups (see 6.6). This situation was dubbed a tyranny of the majority by Mill's contemporary Alexis de Tocqueville (see 5.6). *On Liberty* begins with the proposal that a society can avoid the tyranny of the majority by respecting the Harm Principle, which asserts that individuals are free to do as they please as long as they do not harm anyone else (which is why it is sometimes called the No-harm principle; 6.6).

In Part III of *On Liberty*, Mill asserts that individuals must determine what the good life is for themselves, and the only limit to the pursuit of this life should be harm to another person. As long as the harm principle is not violated, individual freedom should be fully protected and encouraged. For liberals, freedom consists of the absence of coercion. By starting from the liberty of the individual as opposed to the legitimacy of the majority, Mill refocuses the role of legitimate governance. Ideally, the government will be very small and function within narrowly circumscribed limits: to protect the sovereignty of the individual from others, including both government itself and the coercive and conformist influences of the majority.

According to Mill, there will always be tensions in a democratic society between minorities and majorities. The majority will and should always rule in a representative democracy, but the minority must always be protected both for itself and for the security such protection offers everyone, including members of the majority. For Mill, nonconformists and odd personalities bring new ideas into the world and compel those who subscribe to popular views to reflect. Moreover, majorities have no special access to the truth. There is no reason to suppose that a majority position is true or more credible than a minority one. As with any other action, a person's liberty to speak can only be justifiably limited by the harm principle. In this vein, free speech is good for everyone, since dissent is good for discovery and public debate. According to Mill, a representative government that respects and even encourages freedom of speech thereby advances overall happiness.

~

from On Liberty

Chapter I: Introductory

The subject of this Essay is not the so-called Liberty of the Will, so unfortunately opposed to the misnamed doctrine of Philosophical Necessity; but Civil, or Social Liberty: the nature and limits of the power which can be legitimately exercised by society over the individual. A question seldom stated, and hardly ever discussed, in general terms, but which profoundly influences the practical controversies of the age by its latent presence, and is likely soon to make itself recognised as the vital question of the future. It is so far from being new, that in a certain sense, it has divided mankind, almost from the remotest ages; but in the stage of progress into which the more civilised portions of the species have now entered, it presents itself under new conditions, and requires a different and more fundamental treatment....

The object of this Essay is to assert one very simple principle, as entitled to govern absolutely the dealings of society with the individual in the way of compulsion and control, whether the means used be physical force in the form of legal penalties, or the moral coercion of public opinion. That principle is, that the sole end for which mankind are warranted, individually or collectively, in interfering with the liberty of action of any of their number, is self-protection. That the only purpose for which power can be rightfully exercised over any member of a civilised community, against his will, is to prevent harm to others. His own good, either physical or moral, is not a sufficient warrant. He cannot rightfully be compelled to do or forbear because it will be better for him to do so, because it will make him happier, because, in the opinions of others, to do so would be wise, or even right. These are good reasons for remonstrating with him, or reasoning with him, or persuading him, or entreating him, but not for compelling him, or visiting him with any evil in case he do otherwise. To justify that, the conduct from which it is desired to deter him must be calculated to produce evil to some one else. The only part of the conduct of any one, for which he is amenable to society, is that which concerns others. In the part which merely concerns himself, his independence is, of right, absolute. Over himself, over his own body and mind, the individual is sovereign....

Chapter III: On Individuality, as One of the Elements of Wellbeing

Such being the reasons which make it imperative that human beings should be free to form opinions, and to express their opinions without reserve; and such the baneful consequences to the intellectual, and through that to the moral nature of man, unless this liberty is either conceded, or asserted in spite of prohibition; let us next examine whether the same reasons do not require that men should be free to act upon their opinions—to carry these out in their lives, without hindrance, either physical or moral, from their fellow-men, so long as it is at their own risk and peril. This last proviso is of course indispensable. No one pretends that actions should be as free as opinions. On the contrary, even opinions lose their immunity, when the circumstances in which they are expressed are such as to constitute their expression a positive instigation to some mischievous act. An opinion that corn-dealers are starvers of the poor, or that private property is robbery, ought to be unmolested when simply circulated through the press, but may justly incur punishment when delivered orally to an excited mob assembled before the house of a corn-dealer, or when handed about among the same mob in the form of a placard. Acts, of whatever kind, which, without justifiable cause, do harm to others, may be, and in the more important cases absolutely require to be, controlled by the unfavourable sentiments, and, when needful, by the active interference of mankind. The liberty of the individual must be thus far limited; he must not make himself a nuisance to other people. But if he refrains from molesting others in what concerns them, and merely acts according to his own inclination and judgment in things which concern himself, the same reasons which show that opinion should be free, prove also that he should be allowed, without molestation, to carry his opinions into practice at his own cost. That mankind are not infallible; that their truths, for the most part, are only half-truths; that unity of opinion, unless resulting from the fullest and freest comparison of opposite opinions, is not desirable, and diversity not an evil, but a good, until mankind are much more capable than at present of recognising all sides of the truth, are principles applicable to men's modes of action, not less than to their opinions. As it is useful that while mankind are imperfect there should be different opinions, so is it that there should be different experiments of living; that free scope should be given to varieties of character, short of injury to others; and that the worth of different modes of life should be proved practically, when any one thinks fit to try them. It is desirable, in short, that in things which do not primarily concern others, individuality should assert itself. Where, not the person's own character, but the traditions or customs of other people are the rule of conduct, there is wanting one of the principal ingredients of human happiness, and quite the chief ingredient of individual and social progress.

In maintaining this principle, the greatest difficulty to be encountered does not lie in the appreciation of means towards an acknowledged end, but in the indifference of persons in general to the end itself. If it were felt that the free development of individuality is one of the leading essentials of well-being; that it is not only a co-ordinate element with all that is designated by the terms civilisation, instruction, education, culture, but is itself a necessary part and condition of all those things; there would be no danger that liberty should be under-valued, and the adjustment of the boundaries between it and social control would present no extraordinary difficulty. But the evil is, that individual spontaneity is hardly recognised by the common modes of thinking, as having any intrinsic worth, or deserving any regard on its own account. The majority, being satisfied with the ways of mankind as they now are (for it is they who make them what they are), cannot comprehend why those ways should not be good enough for everybody; and what is more, spontaneity forms no part of the ideal of the majority of moral and social reformers, but is rather looked on with jealousy, as a troublesome and perhaps rebellious obstruction to the general acceptance of what these reformers, in their own judgment, think would be best for mankind....

... The question, one must nevertheless think, can only be one of degree. No one's idea of excellence in conduct is that people should do absolutely nothing but copy one another. No one would assert that people ought not to put into their mode of life, and into the conduct of their concerns, any impress whatever of their own judgment, or of their own individual character. On the other hand, it would be absurd to pretend that people ought to live as if nothing whatever had been known in the world before they came into it; as if experience had as yet done nothing towards showing that one mode of existence, or of conduct, is preferable to another. Nobody denies that people should be so taught and trained in youth, as to know and benefit by the ascertained results of human experience. But it is the privilege and proper condition of a human being, arrived at the maturity of his faculties, to use and interpret experience in his own way. It is for him to find out what part of recorded experience is properly applicable to his own circumstances and character. The traditions and customs of other people are, to a certain extent, evidence of what their experience has taught *them*; presumptive evidence, and as such, have a claim to his deference: but, in the first place, their experience may be too narrow; or they may not have interpreted it rightly. Secondly, their interpretation of experience may be correct, but unsuitable to him. Customs are made for customary circumstances, and customary characters: and his circumstances or his character may be uncustomary.

Thirdly, though the customs be both good as customs, and suitable to him, yet to conform to custom, merely *as* custom, does not educate or develop in him any of the qualities which are the distinctive endowment of a human being. The human faculties of perception, judgment, discriminative feeling, mental activity, and even moral preference, are exercised only in making a choice. He who does anything because it is the custom, makes no choice. He gains no practice either in discerning or in desiring what is best. The mental and moral, like the muscular powers, are improved only by being used. The faculties are called into no exercise by doing a thing merely because others do it, no more than by believing a thing only because others believe it. If the grounds of an opinion are not conclusive to the person's own reason, his reason cannot be strengthened, but is likely to be weakened by his adopting it: and if the inducements to an act are not such as are consentaneous to his own feelings and character (where affection, or the rights of others, are not concerned), it is so much done towards rendering his feelings and character inert and torpid, instead of active and energetic.

It will probably be conceded that it is desirable people should exercise their understandings, and that an intelligent following of custom, or even occasionally an intelligent deviation from custom, is better than a blind and simply mechanical adhesion to it. To a certain extent it is admitted, that our understanding should be our own: but there is not the same willingness to admit that our desires and impulses should be our own likewise; or that to possess impulses of our own, and of any strength, is anything but a peril and a snare. Yet desires and impulses are as much a part of a perfect human being, as beliefs and restraints: and strong impulses are only perilous when not properly balanced; when one set of aims and inclinations is developed into strength, while others, which ought to co-exist with them, remain weak and inactive. It is not because men's desires are strong that they act ill; it is because their consciences are weak. There is no natural connection between strong impulses and a weak conscience....

In some early states of society, these forces might be, and were, too much ahead of the power which society then possessed of disciplining and controlling them. There has been a time when the element of spontaneity and individuality was in excess, and the social principle had a hard struggle with it. The difficulty then was, to induce men of strong bodies or minds to pay obedience to any rules which required them to control their impulses. To overcome this difficulty, law and discipline, like the Popes struggling against the Emperors, asserted a power over the whole man, claiming to control all his life in order to control his character—which society had not found any other sufficient means of binding. But society has now fairly got the better of individuality; and the danger which threatens human nature is not the excess, but the deficiency, of personal impulses and preferences. Things are vastly changed, since the passions of those who were strong by station or by personal endowment were in a state of habitual rebellion against laws and ordinances, and required to be rigorously chained up to enable the persons within their reach to enjoy any particle of security. In our times, from the highest class of society down to the lowest, every one lives as under the eye of a hostile and dreaded censorship. Not only in what concerns others, but in what concerns only themselves, the individual, or the family, do not ask themselves—what do I prefer? or, what would suit my character and disposition? or, what would allow the best and highest in me to have fair-play, and enable it to grow and thrive? They ask themselves, what is suitable to my position? what is usually done by persons of my station and pecuniary circumstances? or (worse still) what is usually done by persons of a station and circumstances superior to mine? I do not mean that they choose what is customary, in preference to what suits their own inclination. It does not occur to them to have any inclination, except for what is customary. Thus the mind itself is bowed to the yoke: even in what people do for pleasure, conformity is the first thing thought of; they like in crowds; they exercise choice only among things commonly done: peculiarity of taste, eccentricity of conduct, are shunned equally with crimes: until by dint of not following their own nature, they have no nature to follow: their human capacities are withered and starved: they become incapable of any strong wishes or native pleasures, and are generally without either opinions or feelings of home growth, or properly their own. Now is this, or is it not, the desirable condition of human nature?

... Doubtless, however, these considerations will not suffice to convince those who most need convincing; and it is necessary further to show, that these developed human beings are of some use to the undeveloped—to point out to those who do not desire liberty, and would not avail themselves of it, that they may be in some intelligible manner rewarded for allowing other people to make use of it without hindrance.

In the first place, then, I would suggest that they might possibly learn something from them. It will not be denied by anybody, that originality is a valuable element in human affairs. There is always need of persons not only to discover new truths, and point out when what were once truths are true no longer, but also to commence new practices, and set the example of more enlightened conduct, and better taste and sense in human life. This cannot well be gainsaid by anybody who does not believe that the world has already attained perfection in all its ways and practices. It is true that this benefit is not capable of being rendered by everybody alike: there are but few persons, in comparison with the whole of mankind, whose experiments, if adopted by others, would be likely to be any improvement on established practice. But these few are the salt of the earth; without them, human life would become a stagnant pool. Not only is it they who introduce good things which did not before exist; it is they who keep the life in those which already existed. If there were nothing new to be done, would human intellect cease to be necessary? Would it be a reason why those who do the old things should forget why they are done, and do them like cattle, not like human beings? There is only too great a tendency in the best beliefs and practices to degenerate into the mechanical; and unless there were a succession of persons whose ever-recurring originality prevents the grounds of those beliefs and practices from becoming merely traditional, such dead matter would not resist the smallest shock from anything really alive, and there would be no reason why civilisation should not die out, as in the Byzantine Empire. Persons of genius, it is true, are, and are always likely to be, a small minority; but in order to have them, it is necessary to preserve the soil in which they grow. Genius can only breathe freely in an *atmosphere* of freedom. Persons of genius are, *ex vi termini*, more individual than any other people—less capable, consequently, of fitting themselves, without hurtful compression, into any of the small number of moulds which society provides in order to save its members the trouble of forming their own character. If from timidity they consent to be forced into one of these moulds, and to let all that part of themselves which cannot expand under the pressure remain unexpanded, society will be little the better for their genius. If they are of a strong character, and break their fetters, they become a mark for the society which has not succeeded in reducing them to commonplace, to point at with solemn warning as "wild," "erratic," and the like; much as if one should complain of the Niagara river for not flowing smoothly between its banks like a Dutch canal.

I insist thus emphatically on the importance of genius, and the necessity of allowing it to unfold itself freely both in thought and in practice, being well aware that no one will deny the position in theory, but knowing also that almost every one, in reality, is totally indifferent to it. People think genius a fine thing if it enables a man to write an exciting poem, or paint a picture. But in its true sense, that of originality in thought and action, though no one says that it is not a thing to be admired, nearly all, at heart, think that they can do very well without it. Unhappily this is too natural to be wondered at. Originality is the one thing which unoriginal minds cannot feel the use of. They cannot see what it is to do for them: how should they? If they could see what it would do for them, it would not be originality. The first service which originality has to render them, is that of opening their eyes:

which being once fully done, they would have a chance of being themselves original. Meanwhile, recollecting that nothing was ever yet done which some one was not the first to do, and that all good things which exist are the fruits of originality, let them be modest enough to believe that there is something still left for it to accomplish, and assure themselves that they are more in need of originality, the less they are conscious of the want.

In sober truth, whatever homage may be professed, or even paid, to real or supposed mental superiority, the general tendency of things throughout the world is to render mediocrity the ascendant power among mankind. In ancient history, in the middle ages, and in a diminishing degree through the long transition from feudality to the present time, the individual was a power in himself; and if he had either great talents or a high social position, he was a considerable power. At present individuals are lost in the crowd. In politics it is almost a triviality to say that public opinion now rules the world. The only power deserving the name is that of masses, and of governments while they make themselves the organ of the tendencies and instincts of masses. This is as true in the moral and social relations of private life as in public transactions. Those whose opinions go by the name of public opinion, are not always the same sort of public: in America they are the whole white population; in England, chiefly the middle class. But they are always a mass, that is to say, collective mediocrity. And what is a still greater novelty, the mass do not now take their opinions from dignitaries in Church or State, from ostensible leaders, or from books. Their thinking is done for them by men much like themselves, addressing them or speaking in their name, on the spur of the moment, through the newspapers. I am not complaining of all this. I do not assert that anything better is compatible, as a general rule, with the present low state of the human mind. But that does not hinder the government of mediocrity from being mediocre government. No government by a democracy or a numerous aristocracy, either in its political acts or in the opinions, qualities, and tone of mind which it fosters, ever did or could rise above mediocrity, except in so far as the sovereign Many have let themselves be guided (which in their best times they always have done) by the counsels and influence of a more highly gifted and instructed One or Few. The initiation of all wise or noble things, comes and must come from individuals; generally at first from some one individual.... It is in these circumstances most especially, that exceptional individuals, instead of being deterred, should be encouraged in acting differently from the mass. In other times there was no advantage in their doing so, unless they acted not only differently, but better. In this age the mere example of nonconformity, the mere refusal to bend the knee to custom, is itself a service. Precisely because the tyranny of opinion is such as to make eccentricity a reproach, it is desirable, in order to break through that tyranny, that people should be eccentric. Eccentricity has always abounded when and where strength of character has abounded; and the amount of eccentricity in a society has generally been proportional to the amount of genius, mental vigour, and moral courage which it contained. That so few now dare to be eccentric, marks the chief danger of the time.

I have said that it is important to give the freest scope possible to uncustomary things, in order that it may in time appear which of these are fit to be converted into customs. But independence of action, and disregard of custom are not solely deserving of encouragement for the chance they afford that better modes of action, and customs more worthy of general adoption, may be struck out; nor is it only persons of decided mental superiority who have a just claim to carry on their lives in their own way. There is no reason that all human existences should be constructed on some one, or some small number of patterns. If a person possesses any tolerable amount of common-sense and experience, his own mode of laying out his existence is the best, not because it is the best in itself, but because it is his own mode. Human beings are not like sheep; and even sheep are not undistinguishably alike. A man cannot get a coat or a pair of boots to fit him, unless they are either made to his measure, or he has a whole warehouseful to choose from: and is it easier to fit him with a life than with a coat, or are human beings more like one another in their whole physical and spiritual conformation than in the shape of their feet? If it were only that people have diversities of taste, that is reason enough for not attempting to shape them all after one model. But different persons also require different conditions for their spiritual development; and can no more exist healthily in the same moral, than all the variety of plants can in the same physical, atmosphere and climate. The same things which are helps to one person towards the cultivation of his higher nature, are hindrances to another. The same mode of life is a healthy excitement to one, keeping all his faculties of action and enjoyment in their best order, while to another it is a distracting burthen, which suspends or crushes all internal life. Such are the differences among human beings in their sources of pleasure, their susceptibilities of pain, and the operation on them of different physical and moral agencies, that unless there is a corresponding diversity in their modes of life, they neither obtain their fair share of happiness, nor grow up to the mental, moral, and aesthetic stature of which their nature is capable. Why then should tolerance, as far as the public sentiment is concerned, extend only to tastes and modes of life which extort acquiescence by the multitude of their adherents? Nowhere (except in some monastic institutions) is diversity of taste entirely unrecognised; a person may, without blame, either like or dislike rowing, or smoking, or music, or athletic exercises, or chess, or cards, or study, because both those who like each of these things, and those who dislike them, are too numerous to be put down. But the man, and still more the woman, who can be accused either of doing "what nobody does," or of not doing "what everybody does," is the subject of as much depreciatory remark as if he or she had committed some grave moral delinquency. Persons require to possess a title, or some other badge of rank, or of the consideration of people of rank, to be able to indulge somewhat in the luxury of doing as they like without detriment to their estimation. To indulge somewhat, I repeat: for whoever allow themselves much of that indulgence, incur the risk of something worse than disparaging speeches—they are in peril of a commission *de lunatico*, and of having their property taken from them and given to their relations.

There is one characteristic of the present direction of public opinion, peculiarly calculated to make it intolerant of any marked demonstration of individuality. The general average of mankind are not only moderate in intellect, but also moderate in inclinations: they have no tastes or wishes strong enough to incline them to do anything unusual, and they consequently do not understand those who have, and class all such with the wild and intemperate whom they are accustomed to look down upon. Now, in addition to this fact which is general, we have only to suppose that a strong movement has set in towards the improvement of morals, and it is evident what we have to expect. In these days such a movement has set in; much has actually been effected in the way of increased regularity of conduct, and discouragement of excesses; and there is a philanthropic spirit abroad, for the exercise of which there is no more inviting field than the moral and prudential improvement of our fellow-creatures. These tendencies of the times cause the public to be more disposed than at most former periods to prescribe general rules of conduct, and endeavour to make every one conform to the approved standard. And that standard, express or tacit, is to desire nothing strongly. Its ideal of character is to be without any marked character....

... There is now scarcely any outlet for energy in this country except business. The energy expended in that may still be regarded as considerable. What little is left from that employment, is expended on some hobby; which may be a useful, even a philanthropic hobby, but is always some one thing, and generally a thing of small dimensions....

The despotism of custom is everywhere the standing hindrance to human advancement, being in unceasing antagonism to that disposition to aim at something better than customary, which is called, according to circumstances, the spirit of liberty, or that of progress or improvement. The spirit of improvement is not always a spirit of liberty, for it may aim at forcing improvements on an unwilling people; and the spirit of liberty, in so far as it resists such attempts, may ally itself locally and temporarily with the opponents of improvement; but the only unfailing and permanent source of improvement is liberty, since by it there are as many possible independent centres of improvement as there are individuals. The progressive principle, however, in either shape, whether as the love of liberty or of improvement, is antagonistic to the sway of Custom, involving at least emancipation from that yoke; and the contest between the two constitutes the chief interest of the history of mankind.... We are eager for improvement in politics, in education, even in morals, though in this last our idea of improvement chiefly consists in persuading or forcing other people to be as good as ourselves. It is not progress that we object to; on the contrary, we flatter ourselves that we are the most progressive people who ever lived. It is individuality that we war against: we should think we had done wonders if we had made ourselves all alike; forgetting that the unlikeness of one person to another is generally the first thing which draws the attention of either to the imperfection of his own type, and the superiority of another, or the possibility, by combining the advantages of both, of producing something better than either....

... M. de Tocqueville, in his last important work, remarks how much more the Frenchmen of the present day resemble one another, than did those even of the last generation. The same remark might be made of Englishmen in a far greater degree.... Formerly, different ranks, different neighbourhoods, different trades and professions, lived in what might be called different worlds; at present, to a great degree in the same. Comparatively speaking, they now read the same things, listen to the same things, see the same things, go to the same places, have their hopes and fears directed to the same objects, have the same rights and liberties, and the same means of asserting them. Great as are the differences of position which remain, they are nothing to those which have ceased. And the assimilation is still proceeding. All the political changes of the age promote it, since they all tend to raise the low and to lower the high. Every extension of education promotes it, because education brings people under common influences, and gives them access to the general stock of facts and sentiments. Improvements in the means of communication promote it, by bringing the inhabitants of distant places into personal contact, and keeping up a rapid flow of changes of residence between one place and another. The increase of commerce and manufactures promotes it, by diffusing more widely the advantages of easy circumstances, and opening all objects of ambition, even the highest, to general competition, whereby the desire of rising becomes no longer the character of a particular class, but of all classes. A more powerful agency than even all these, in bringing about a general similarity among mankind, is the complete establishment, in this and other free countries, of the ascendency of public opinion in the State. As the various social eminences which enabled persons entrenched on them to disregard the opinion of the multitude, gradually become levelled; as the very idea of resisting the will of the public, when it is positively known that they have a will, disappears more and more from the minds of practical politicians; there ceases to be any social support for non-conformity—any substantive power in society, which, itself opposed to the ascendency of numbers, is interested in taking under its protection opinions and tendencies at variance with those of the public.

The combination of all these causes forms so great a mass of influences hostile to Individuality, that it is not easy to see how it can stand its ground. It will do so with increasing difficulty, unless the intelligent part of the public can be made to feel its value—to see that it is good there should be differences, even though not for the better, even though, as it may appear to them, some should be for the worse. If the claims of Individuality are ever to be asserted, the time is now, while much is still wanting to complete the enforced assimilation. It is only in the earlier stages that any stand can be successfully made against the encroachment. The demand that all other people shall resemble ourselves, grows by what it feeds on. If resistance waits till life is reduced *nearly* to one uniform type, all deviations from that type will come to be considered impious, immoral, even monstrous and contrary to nature. Mankind speedily become unable to conceive diversity, when they have been for some time unaccustomed to see it....

8.7 Edward Said (1935–2003)

Professor Edward Said helped to found and made major contributions to the field of postcolonial studies. Between the fifteenth and early twentieth centuries, European nations founded colonies on almost every continent in the world, considerably expanding their own wealth, territory, and influence. Almost invariably, colonization had catastrophic consequences, for the Indigenous peoples in colonized regions were routinely and systematically robbed, enslaved, exploited, oppressed, and subjected to cultural and existential genocide. Postcolonial studies are concerned with understanding both how colonialism happened, and how its ongoing legacy has affected both colonizing and colonized cultures. Said was born in Mandatory Palestine (the temporary political entity set up in what is now Israel and the occupied Palestinian territories by Britain following World War I). There he experienced colonialism first hand. Because Said's father was a veteran of the US army, he was also a citizen of the United States.

Orientalism (1978), which is excerpted here, revolutionized the study of the Middle East by showing how European conceptions of the "Orient" were not neutral and objective. Rather, they were based on a pernicious set of contestable assumptions that simply perpetuated unequal power relationships between the colonizers and the colonized. When Europeans studied the Middle East, they brought with them a series of question-begging assumptions about natural European superiority that entitled them to rule over "Orientals." The first chapter of Orientalism, "Knowing the Oriental," focuses on Britain's colonial occupation of Egypt. The basic, general story is one in which Orientals are largely homogenous, needy, child-like recipients of paternalistic, colonial oversight.

As a consequence of these Orientalist assumptions, the voices of the colonized were silenced and colonial powers are released from the obligation to reflect on their occupation of foreign territory. The Oriental was understood as "almost everywhere nearly the same." Thus, not only could the specific lessons learned in Egypt be taken and used on all colonies in the East, but the powerful stereotypes offered a suitable rationale to dismiss signs of resistance or rebellion. From the Orientalist perspective, "true Egyptians" loved British rule and relied upon Britain for their own good. Any deviation from this standard was deemed unnatural and unrepresentative of genuine Oriental behaviour. In the case of British rule over Egypt, it became easy to dismiss the very reasonable and justified demand for Egyptian national autonomy, along with demands for "free native institutions, the absence of foreign occupation, [and] a self-sustaining national sovereignty." As a result, Egypt did not become independent until 1922.

from Orientalism, *Ch. 1: "Knowing the Oriental"*

On June 13, 1910, Arthur James Balfour lectured the House of Commons on "the problems with which we have to deal in Egypt." These, he said, "belong to a wholly different category" than those "affecting the Isle of Wight or the West Riding of Yorkshire." He spoke with the authority of a long-time member of Parliament, former private secretary to Lord Salisbury, former chief secretary for Ireland, former secretary for Scotland, former prime minister, veteran of numerous overseas crises, achievements, and changes. During his involvement in imperial affairs Balfour served a monarch who in 1877 had been declared Empress of India; he had been especially well placed in positions of uncommon influence to follow the Afghan and Zulu wars, the British occupation of Egypt in 1882, the death of General Gordon in the Sudan, the Fashoda Incident, the battle of Omdurman, the Boer War, the Russo-Japanese War. In addition his remarkable social eminence, the breadth of his learning and wit—he could write on such varied subjects as Bergson, Handel, theism, and golf—his education at Eton and Trinity College, Cambridge, and his apparent command over imperial affairs all gave considerable authority to what he told the Commons in June 1910. But there was still more to Balfour's speech, or at least to his need for giving it so didactically and moralistically. Some members were questioning the necessity for "England in Egypt," the subject of Alfred Milner's enthusiastic book of 1892, but here designating a once-profitable occupation that had become a source of trouble now that Egyptian nationalism was on the rise and the continuing British presence in Egypt no longer so easy to defend. Balfour, then, to inform and explain.

Recalling the challenge of J.M. Robertson, the member of Tyneside, Balfour himself put Robertson's question again: "What right have you to take up these airs of superiority with regard to people whom you choose to call Oriental?" The choice of "Oriental" was canonical; it had been employed by Chaucer and Mandeville, by Shakespeare, Dryden, Pope, and Byron. It designated Asia or the East, geographically, morally, culturally. One could speak in Europe of an Oriental personality, an Oriental atmosphere, an Oriental tale, Oriental despotism, or an Oriental mode of production, and be understood. Marx had used the word, and now Balfour was using it; his choice was understandable and called for no comment whatever.

> I take up no attitude of superiority. But I ask [Robertson and anyone else] ... who has even the most superficial knowledge of history, if they will look in the face the facts with which a British statesman has to deal when he is put in a position of supremacy over great races like the inhabitants of Egypt and countries in the East. We know the civilization of Egypt better than we know the civilization of any other country. We know it further back; we know it more intimately; we know more about it. It goes far beyond the petty span of the history of our race, which is lost in the prehistoric period at a time when the Egyptian civilisation had already passed its prime. Look at all the Oriental countries. Do not talk about superiority or inferiority.

Two great themes dominate his remarks here and in what will follow: knowledge and power, the Baconian themes. As Balfour justifies the necessity for British occupation of Egypt, supremacy in his mind is associated with "our" knowledge of Egypt and not principally with military or economic power. Knowledge to Balfour means surveying a civilization from its origins to its prime to its decline—and of course, it means *being able to do that.* Knowledge means rising above immediacy, beyond self, into the foreign and distant. The object of such knowledge is inherently vulnerable to scrutiny; this object is a "fact" which, if it develops, changes, or otherwise transforms itself in the way that civilizations frequently do, nevertheless is fundamentally, even ontologically stable. To have such knowledge of such a thing is to dominate it, to have authority over it. And authority here means for "us" to deny autonomy to "it"—the Oriental country—since we know it and it exists, in a sense, *as* we know it. British knowledge of Egypt *is* Egypt for Balfour, and the burdens of knowledge make such questions as inferiority and superiority seem petty ones. Balfour nowhere denies British superiority and Egyptian inferiority; he takes them for granted as he describes the consequences of knowledge.

> First of all, look at the facts of the case. Western nations as soon as they emerge into history show the beginnings of those capacities for self-government ... having merits of their own.... You may look through the whole history of the Orientals in what is called, broadly speaking, the East, and you never find traces of self-government. All their great centuries—and they have been very great—have been passed under despotisms, under absolute government. All their great contributions to civilisation—and they have been great—have been made under that form of government. Conqueror has succeeded conqueror; one domination has followed another; but never in all the revolutions of fate and fortune have you seen one of those nations of its own motion establish what we, from a Western point of view, call self-government. That is the fact. It is not a question of superiority and inferiority. I suppose a true Eastern sage would say that the working government which we have taken upon ourselves in Egypt and elsewhere is not a work worthy of a philosopher—that it is the dirty work, the inferior work, of carrying on the necessary labour.

Since these facts are facts, Balfour must then go on to the next part of his argument.

> Is it a good thing for these great nations—I admit their greatness—that this absolute government should be exercised by us? I think it is a good thing. I think that experience shows that they have got under it far better government than in the whole history of the world they ever had before, and which not only is a benefit to them, but is undoubtedly a benefit to the whole of the civilised West.... We are in Egypt not merely for the sake of the Egyptians, though we are there for their sake; we are there also for the sake of Europe at large.

Balfour produces no evidence that Egyptians and "the races with whom we deal" appreciate or even understand the good that is being done them by colonial occupation. It does not occur to Balfour, however, to let the Egyptian speak for himself, since presumably any Egyptian who would speak out is more likely to be "the agitator [who] wishes to raise difficulties" than the good native who overlooks the "difficulties" of foreign domination. And so, having settled the ethical problems, Balfour turns at last to the practical ones. "If it is our business to govern, with or without gratitude, with or without the real and genuine memory of all the loss of which we have relieved the population [Balfour by no means implies, as part of that loss, the loss or at least the indefinite postponement of Egyptian independence] and no vivid imagination of all the benefits which we have given to them; if that is our duty, how is it to be performed?" England exports "our very best to these countries." These selfless administrators do their work "amidst tens of thousands of persons belonging to a different creed, a different race, a different discipline, different conditions of life." What makes their work of governing possible is their sense of being supported at home by a government that endorses what they do. Yet

> directly the native populations have that instinctive feeling that those with whom they have got to deal have not behind them the might, the authority, the sympathy, the full and ungrudging support of the country which sent them there, those populations lose all that sense of order which is the very basis of their civilisation, just as our officers lose all that sense of power and authority, which is the very basis of everything they can do for the benefit of those among whom they have been sent.

Balfour's logic here is interesting, not least for being completely consistent with the premises of his entire speech. England knows Egypt; Egypt is what England knows; England knows that Egypt cannot have self-government; England confirms that by occupying Egypt; for the Egyptians, Egypt is what England has occupied and now governs; foreign occupation therefore becomes "the very basis" of contemporary Egyptian civilization; Egypt requires, indeed insists upon, British occupation. But if the special intimacy between governor and governed in Egypt is disturbed by Parliament's doubts at home, then "the authority of what ... is the dominant race—and as I think ought to remain the dominant race—has been undermined." Not only does English prestige suffer; "it is vain for a handful of British officials—endow them how you like, give them all the qualities of character and genius you can imagine—it is impossible for them to carry out the great task which in Egypt, not we only, but the civilised world have imposed upon them."[1]

As a rhetorical performance Balfour's speech is significant for the way in which he plays the part of, and represents, a variety of characters. There are of course "the English," for whom the pronoun "we" is used with the full weight of a distinguished, powerful man who feels himself to be representative of all that is best in his nation's history. Balfour can also speak for the civilized world, the West, and the relatively small corps of colonial officials in Egypt. If he does not speak directly for the Orientals, it is because they after all speak another language; yet he knows how they feel since he knows their history, their reliance upon such as he, and their expectations. Still, he does speak for them in the sense that what they might have to say, were they to be asked and might they be able to answer, would somewhat uselessly confirm what is already evident: that they are a subject race, dominated by a race that knows them and what is good for them better than they could possibly know themselves. Their great moments were in the past; they are useful in the modern world only because the powerful and up-to-date empires have effectively brought them out of the wretchedness of their decline and turned them into rehabilitated residents of productive colonies.

Egypt in particular was an excellent case in point, and Balfour was perfectly aware of how much right he had to speak as a member of his country's parliament on behalf of England, the West, Western civilization, about modern Egypt. For Egypt was not just another colony: it was the vindication of Western imperialism; it was, until its annexation by England, an almost academic example of Oriental backwardness; it was to become the triumph of English knowledge and power. Between 1882, the year in which England occupied Egypt and put an end to the nationalist rebellion of Colonel Arabi, and 1907, England's representative in Egypt, Egypt's master, was Evelyn Baring (also known as "Over-baring"), Lord Cromer. On July 30, 1907, it was Balfour in the Commons who had supported the project to give Cromer a retirement prize of fifty

1 This and the preceding quotations from Arthur James Balfour's speech to the House of Commons are from Great Britain, *Parliamentary Debates* (Commons), 5th ser., 17 (1910): 1140–46. See also A.P. Thornton, *The Imperial Idea and Its Enemies: A Study in British Power* (London: MacMillan & Co., 1959), pp. 357–60. Balfour's speech was a defense of Eldon Gorst's policy in Egypt; for a discussion of that, see Peter John Dreyfus Mellini, "Sir Eldon Gorst and British Imperial Policy in Egypt," unpublished Ph.D. dissertation, Stanford University, 1971.

thousand pounds as a reward for what he had done in Egypt. Cromer *made* Egypt, said Balfour:

> Everything he has touched he has succeeded in.... Lord Cromer's services during the past quarter of a century have raised Egypt from the lowest pitch of social and economic degradation until it now stands among Oriental nations, I believe, absolutely alone in its prosperity, financial and moral.[2]

How Egypt's moral prosperity was measured, Balfour did not venture to say. British exports to Egypt equaled those to the whole of Africa; that certainly indicated a sort of financial prosperity, for Egypt and England (somewhat unevenly) together. But what really mattered was the unbroken, all-embracing Western tutelage of an Oriental country, from the scholars, missionaries, businessmen, soldiers, and teachers who prepared and then implemented the occupation to the high functionaries like Cromer and Balfour who saw themselves as providing for, directing, and sometimes even forcing Egypt's rise from Oriental neglect to its present lonely eminence.

If British success in Egypt was as exceptional as Balfour said, it was by no means an inexplicable or irrational success. Egyptian affairs had been controlled according to a general theory expressed both by Balfour in his notions about Oriental civilization and by Cromer in his management of everyday business in Egypt. The most important thing about the theory during the first decade of the twentieth century was that it worked, and worked staggeringly well. The argument, when reduced to its simplest form, was clear, it was precise, it was easy to grasp. There are Westerners, and there are Orientals. The former dominate; the latter must be dominated, which usually means having their land occupied, their internal affairs rigidly controlled, their blood and treasure put at the disposal of one or another Western power. That Balfour and Cromer, as we shall soon see, could strip humanity down to such ruthless cultural and racial essences was not at all an indication of their particular viciousness. Rather it was an indication of how streamlined a general doctrine had become by the time they put it to use—how streamlined and effective.

Unlike Balfour, whose theses on Orientals pretended to objective universality, Cromer spoke about Orientals specifically as what he had ruled or had to deal with, first in India, then for the twenty-five years in Egypt during which he emerged as the paramount consulgeneral in England's empire. Balfour's "Orientals" are Cromer's "subject races," which he made the topic of a long essay published in the *Edinburgh Review* in January 1908. Once again, knowledge of subject races or Orientals is what makes their management easy and profitable; knowledge gives power, more power requires more knowledge, and so on in an increasingly profitable dialectic of information and control. Cromer's notion is that England's empire will not dissolve if such things as militarism and commercial egotism at home and "free institutions" in the colony (as opposed to British government "according to the Code of Christian morality") are kept in check. For if, according to Cromer, logic is something "the existence of which the Oriental is disposed altogether to ignore," the proper method of ruling is not to impose ultrascientific measures upon him or to force him bodily to accept logic. It is rather to understand his limitations and "endeavor to find, in the contentment of the subject race, a more worthy and, it may be hoped, a stronger bond of union between the rulers and the ruled." Lurking everywhere behind the pacification of the subject race is imperial might, more effective for its refined understanding and infrequent use than for its soldiers, brutal tax gatherers, and incontinent force. In a word, the Empire must be wise; it must temper its cupidity with selflessness, and its impatience with flexible discipline.

2 Denis Judd, *Balfour and the British Empire: A Study in Imperial Evolution, 1874–1932* (London: MacMillan & Co., 1968), p. 286. See also p. 292: as late as 1926 Balfour spoke—without irony—of Egypt as an "independent nation."

> To be more explicit, what is meant when it is said that the commercial spirit should be under some control is this—that in dealing with Indians or Egyptians, or Shilluks, or Zulus, the first question is to consider what these people, who are all, nationally speaking, more or less *in statu pupillari*, themselves think is best in their own interests, although this is a point which deserves serious consideration. But it is essential that each special issue should be decided mainly with reference to what, by the light of Western knowledge and experience tempered by local considerations, we conscientiously think is best for the subject race, without reference to any real or supposed advantage which may accrue to England as a nation, or—as is more frequently the case—to the special interests represented by some one or more influential classes of Englishmen. If the British nation as a whole persistently bears this principle in mind, and insists sternly on its application, though we can never create a patriotism akin to that based on affinity of race or community of language, we may perhaps foster some sort of cosmopolitan allegiance grounded on the respect always accorded to superior talents and unselfish conduct, and on the gratitude derived both from favours conferred and from those to come. There may then at all events be some hope that the Egyptian will hesitate before he throws in his lot with any future Arabi.... Even the Central African savage may eventually learn to chant a hymn in honour of Astraea Redux, as represented by the British official who denies him gin but gives him justice. More than this, commerce will gain.[3]

How much "serious consideration" the ruler ought to give proposals from the subject race was illustrated in Cromer's total opposition to Egyptian nationalism. Free native institutions, the absence of foreign occupation, a self-sustaining national sovereignty: these unsurprising demands were consistently rejected by Cromer, who asserted unambiguously that "the real future of Egypt ... lies not in the direction of a narrow nationalism, which will only embrace native Egyptians ... but rather in that of an enlarged cosmopolitanism."[4] Subject races did not have it in them to know what was good for them. Most of them were Orientals, of whose characteristics Cromer was very knowledgeable since he had had experience with them both in India and Egypt. One of the convenient things about Orientals for Cromer was that managing them, although circumstances might differ slightly here and there, was almost everywhere nearly the same.[5] This was, of course, because Orientals were almost everywhere nearly the same.

Now at last we approach the long-developing core of essential knowledge, knowledge both academic and practical, which Cromer and Balfour inherited from a century of modern Western Orientalism: knowledge about and knowledge of Orientals, their race, character, culture, history, traditions, society, and possibilities. This knowledge was effective: Cromer believed he had put it to use in governing Egypt. Moreover, it was tested and unchanging knowledge, since "Orientals" for all practical purposes were a Platonic essence, which any Orientalist (or ruler of Orientals) might examine, understand, and expose. Thus in the thirty-fourth chapter of his two-volume work *Modern Egypt*, the magisterial record of his experience and achievement, Cromer puts down a sort of personal canon of Orientalist wisdom:

> Sir Alfred Lyall once said to me: "Accuracy is abhorrent to the Oriental mind. Every Anglo-Indian should always remember that maxim." Want of accuracy, which easily degenerates into

---

3 Evelyn Baring, Lord Cromer, *Political and Literary Essays, 1908–1913* (1913; reprint ed., Freeport, N.Y.: Books for Libraries Press, 1969), pp. 40, 53, 12–14.

4 Ibid, p. 171.

5 Roger Owen, "The Influence of Lord Cromer's Indian Experience on British Policy in Egypt 1883–1907," in *Middle Eastern Affairs, Number Four: St. Antony's Papers Number 17*, ed. Albert Hourani (London: Oxford University Press, 1965), pp. 109–39.

> untruthfulness, is in fact the main characteristic of the Oriental mind.
>
> The European is a close reasoner; his statements of fact are devoid of any ambiguity; he is a natural logician, albeit he may not have studied logic; he is by nature sceptical and requires proof before he can accept the truth of any proposition; his trained intelligence works like a piece of mechanism. The mind of the Oriental, on the other hand, like his picturesque streets, is eminently wanting in symmetry. His reasoning is of the most slipshod description. Although the ancient Arabs acquired in a somewhat higher degree the science of dialectics, their descendants are singularly deficient in the logical faculty. They are often incapable of drawing the most obvious conclusions from any simple premises of which they may admit the truth. Endeavor to elicit a plain statement of facts from any ordinary Egyptian. His explanation will generally be lengthy, and wanting in lucidity. He will probably contradict himself half-a-dozen times before he has finished his story. He will often break down under the mildest process of cross-examination.

Orientals or Arabs are thereafter shown to be gullible, "devoid of energy and initiative," much given to "fulsome flattery," intrigue, cunning, and unkindness to animals; Orientals cannot walk on either a road or a pavement (their disordered minds fail to understand what the clever European grasps immediately, that roads and pavements are made for walking); Orientals are inveterate liars, they are "lethargic and suspicious," and in everything oppose the clarity, directness, and nobility of the Anglo-Saxon race.[6]

Cromer makes no effort to conceal that Orientals for him were always and only the human material he governed in British colonies. "As I am only a diplomatist and an administrator, whose proper study is also man, but from the point of view of governing him," Cromer says, "... I content myself with noting the fact that somehow or other the Oriental generally acts, speaks, and thinks in a manner exactly opposite to the European."[7] Cromer's descriptions are of course based partly on direct observation, yet here and there he refers to orthodox Orientalist authorities (in particular Ernest Renan and Constantin de Volney) to support his views. To these authorities he also defers when it comes to explaining why Orientals are the way they are. He has no doubt that *any* knowledge of the Oriental will confirm his views, which, to judge from his description of the Egyptian breaking under cross-examination, find the Oriental to be guilty. The crime was that the Oriental was an Oriental, and it is an accurate sign of how commonly acceptable such a tautology was that it could be written without even an appeal to European logic or symmetry of mind. Thus any deviation from what were considered the norms of Oriental behavior was believed to be unnatural; Cromer's last annual report from Egypt consequently proclaimed Egyptian nationalism to be an "entirely novel idea" and "a plant of exotic rather than of indigenous growth."[8]

We would be wrong, I think, to underestimate the reservoir of accredited knowledge, the codes of Orientalist orthodoxy, to which Cromer and Balfour refer everywhere in their writing and in their public policy. To say simply that Orientalism was a rationalization of colonial rule is to ignore the extent to which colonial rule was justified in advance by Orientalism, rather than after the fact. Men have always divided the world up into regions having either real or imagined distinction from each other. The absolute demarcation between East and West, which Balfour and Cromer accept with such complacency, had been years, even centuries, in the making. There were of course

6 Evelyn Baring, Lord Cromer, *Modern Egypt* (New York: Macmillan Co., 1908), 2: 146–67. For a British view of British policy in Egypt that runs totally counter to Cromer's, see Wilfrid Scawen Blunt, *Secret History of the English Occupation of Egypt: Being a Personal Narrative of Events* (New York: Alfred A. Knopf, 1922). There is a valuable discussion of Egyptian opposition to British rule in Mounah A. Khouri, *Poetry and the Making of Modern Egypt, 1882–1922* (Leiden: E.J. Brill, 1971).

7 Cromer, *Modern Egypt*, 2: 164.

8 Cited in John Marlowe, *Cromer in Egypt* (London: Elek Books, 1970), p. 271.

innumerable voyages of discovery; there were contacts through trade and war. But more than this, since the middle of the eighteenth century there had been two principal elements in the relation between East and West. One was a growing systematic knowledge in Europe about the Orient, knowledge reinforced by the colonial encounter as well as by the widespread interest in the alien and unusual, exploited by the developing sciences of ethnology, comparative anatomy, philology, and history; furthermore, to this systematic knowledge was added a sizable body of literature produced by novelists, poets, translators, and gifted travelers. The other feature of Oriental-European relations was that Europe was always in a position of strength, not to say domination. There is no way of putting this euphemistically. True, the relationship of strong to weak could be disguised or mitigated, as when Balfour acknowledged the "greatness" of Oriental civilizations. But the essential relationship, on political, cultural, and even religious grounds, was seen—in the West, which is what concerns us here—to be one between a strong and a weak partner.

Many terms were used to express the relation: Balfour and Cromer, typically, used several. The Oriental is irrational, depraved (fallen), childlike, "different"; thus the European is rational, virtuous, mature, "normal." But the way of enlivening the relationship was everywhere to stress the fact that the Oriental lived in a different but thoroughly organized world of his own, a world with its own national, cultural, and epistemological boundaries and principles of internal coherence. Yet what gave the Oriental's world its intelligibility and identity was not the result of his own efforts but rather the whole complex series of knowledgeable manipulations by which the Orient was identified by the West. Thus the two features of cultural relationship I have been discussing come together. Knowledge of the Orient, because generated out of strength, in a sense *creates* the Orient, the Oriental, and his world. In Cromer's and Balfour's language the Oriental is depicted as something one judges (as in a court of law), something one studies and depicts (as in a curriculum), something one disciplines (as in a school or prison), something one illustrates (as in a zoological manual). The point is that in each of these cases the Oriental is *contained* and *represented* by dominating frameworks. Where do these come from?

Cultural strength is not something we can discuss very easily—and one of the purposes of the present work is to illustrate, analyze, and reflect upon Orientalism as an exercise of cultural strength. In other words, it is better not to risk generalizations about so vague and yet so important a notion as cultural strength until a good deal of material has been analyzed first. But at the outset one can say that so far as the West was concerned during the nineteenth and twentieth centuries, an assumption had been made that the Orient and everything in it was, if not patently inferior to, then in need of corrective study by the West. The Orient was viewed as if framed by the classroom, the criminal court, the prison, the illustrated manual. Orientalism, then, is knowledge of the Orient that places things Oriental in class, court, prison, or manual for scrutiny, study, judgment, discipline, or governing.

During the early years of the twentieth century, men like Balfour and Cromer could say what they said, in the way they did, because a still earlier tradition of Orientalism than the nineteenth-century one provided them with a vocabulary, imagery, rhetoric, and figures with which to say it. Yet Orientalism reinforced, and was reinforced by, the certain knowledge that Europe or the West literally commanded the vastly greater part of the earth's surface. The period of immense advance in the institutions and content of Orientalism coincides exactly with the period of unparalleled European expansion; from 1815 to 1914 European direct colonial dominion expanded from about 35 percent of the earth's surface to about 85 percent of it.[9] Every continent was affected, none

9 Harry Magdoff, "Colonialism (1763–c. 1970)," *Encyclopaedia Britannica*, 15th ed. (1974), pp. 893–4. See also D.K. Fieldhouse, *The Colonial Empires: A Comparative Survey from the Eighteenth Century* (New York: Delacorte Press, 1967), p. 178.

more so than Africa and Asia. The two greatest empires were the British and the French; allies and partners in some things, in others they were hostile rivals. In the Orient, from the eastern shores of Mediterranean to Indochina and Malaya, their colonial possessions and imperial spheres of influence were adjacent, frequently overlapped, often were fought over. But it was in the Near Orient, the lands of the Arab Near East, where Islam was supposed to define cultural and racial characteristics, that the British and the French encountered each other and "the Orient" with the greatest intensity, familiarity, and complexity. For much of the nineteenth century, as Lord Salisbury put it in 1881, their common view of the Orient was intricately problematic: "When you have got a … faithful ally who is bent on meddling in a country in which you are deeply interested—you have three courses open to you. You may renounce—or monopolize—or share. Renouncing would have been to place the French across our road to India. Monopolizing would have been very near the risk of war. So we resolved to share."[10]

And share they did, in ways that we shall investigate presently. What they shared, however, was not only land or profit or rule; it was the kind of intellectual power I have been calling Orientalism. In a sense Orientalism was a library or archive of information commonly and, in some of its aspects, unanimously held. What bound the archive together was a family of ideas.[11] …

8.8 bell hooks (1952–)

Gloria Jean Watkins, better known by her pen name, bell hooks, is an author, activist, and feminist scholar. The pseudonym bell hooks is a tribute to her great-grandmother, and it is purposely never capitalized in order for her work and ideas to be the focus of attention rather than her name or personality.

In the following excerpt, hooks contends that early feminist theory and practice failed to realize the potential of feminism. Because it never developed a universally acceptable definition of what feminism means, the movement was taken over by middle class white activists. The demands of these activists were overly narrow and class-specific, focusing on greater inclusivity for their own class and right-to-work privileges. The movement thus excluded non-middle-class and non-white perspectives, and by limiting the scope of feminism obscured its radical and politically revolutionary prospects.

hooks argues that feminism can benefit both men and women if it accepts a radical agenda and sets itself against cultural, political, economic repression as such. Only radical feminism can accomplish this, and to do so it must draw connections between myriad forms of domination and oppression that affect women, including capitalist exploitation, imperialist oppression, and sexist prejudice. For hooks, to be a feminist one must also be an anti-racist, a peace activist, an environmentalist, and so forth. In time, these numerous

10 Quoted in Afaf Lutfi al-Sayyid, *Egypt and Cromer: A Study in AngloEgyptian Relations* (New York: Frederick A. Praeger, 1969), p. 3.

11 The phrase is to be found in Ian Hacking, *The Emergence of Probability: A Philosophical Study of Early Ideas About Probability, Induction and Statistical Inference* (London: Cambridge University Press, 1975), p. 17.

movements may be expected to coalesce into a genuine pluralist force working against all the forms of domination that structure contemporary society.

from Feminist Theory: From Margin to Center

Feminism: A Movement to End Sexist Oppression

A central problem within feminist discourse has been our inability to either arrive at a consensus of opinion about what feminism is or accept definition(s) that could serve as points of unification. Without agreed-upon definition(s), we lack a sound foundation on which to construct theory or engage in overall meaningful praxis. Expressing her frustrations with the absence of clear definitions in a recent essay, "Towards a Revolutionary Ethics," Carmen Vazquez comments:

> We can't even agree on what a "Feminist" is, never mind what she would believe in and how she defines the principles that constitute honor among us. In key with the American capitalist obsession for individualism and anything goes so long as it gets you what you want, feminism in America has come to mean anything you like, honey. There are as many definitions of Feminism as there are feminists, some of my sisters say, with a chuckle. I don't think it's funny.

It is not funny. It indicates a growing lack of interest in feminism as a radical political movement. It is a despairing gesture expressive of the belief that solidarity among women is not possible. It is a sign that the political naïveté which has traditionally characterized woman's lot in male-dominated culture abounds.

Most people in the United States think of feminism, or the more commonly used term "women's lib," as a movement that aims to make women the social equals of men. This broad definition, popularized by the media and mainstream segments of the movement, raises problematic questions. Since men are not equals in white supremacist, capitalist, patriarchal class structure, which men do women want to be equal to? Do women share a common vision of what equality means? Implicit in this simplistic definition of women's liberation is a dismissal of race and class as factors that, in conjunction with sexism, determine the extent to which an individual will be discriminated against, exploited, or oppressed. Bourgeois white women interested in women's rights issues have been satisfied with simple definitions for obvious reasons. Rhetorically placing themselves in the same social category as oppressed women, they are not anxious to call attention to race and class privilege.

Women in lower-class and poor groups, particularly those who are non-white, would not have defined women's liberation as women gaining social equality with men, since they are continually reminded in their everyday lives that all women do not share a common social status. Concurrently, they know that many males in their social groups are exploited and oppressed. Knowing that men in their groups do not have social, political, and economic power, they would not deem it liberatory to share their social status. While they are aware that sexism enables men in their respective groups to have privileges that are denied them, they are more likely to see exaggerated expressions of male chauvinism among their peers as stemming from the male's sense of himself as powerless and ineffectual in relation to ruling male groups, rather than an expression of an overall privileged social status. From the very onset of the women's liberation movement, these women were suspicious of feminism precisely because they recognized the limitations inherent in its definition. They recognized the possibility that feminism defined as social equality with men might easily become a movement that would primarily affect the social standing of white women in middle- and upper-class groups while affecting only in a very marginal way the social status of working-class and poor women.

Not all the women who were at the forefront of organized women's movement, shaping definitions, were content with making women's liberation synonymous with women gaining social equality with men. On the opening pages of *Woman Power: The Movement for Women's Liberation*, Cellestine Ware, a black woman active in the movement, wrote under the heading "Goals":

> Radical feminism is working for the eradication of domination and elitism in all human relationships. This would make self-determination the ultimate good and require the downfall of society as we know it today.

Individual radical feminists like Charlotte Bunch based their analyses on an informed understanding of the politics of domination and a recognition of the interconnections among various systems of domination even as they focused primarily on sexism. Their perspectives were not valued by those organizers and participants in women's movement who were more interested in social reforms....

... Even though Zillah Eisenstein can optimistically point to the potential radicalism of liberal women who work for social reform in *The Radical Future of Liberal Feminism*, the process by which radicalism will surface is unclear. Eisenstein offers as an example of the radical implications of liberal feminist programs the demands made at the government-sponsored Houston conference on women's rights issues which took place in 1978:

> The Houston report demands as a human right a full voice and role for women in determining the destiny of our world, our nation; our families, and our individual lives. It specifically calls for (1) the elimination of violence in the home and the development of shelters for battered women, (2) support for women's business, (3) a solution to child abuse, (4) federally funded nonsexist child care, (5) a policy of full employment so that all women who wish and are able to work may do so, (6) the protection of homemakers so that marriage is a partnership, (7) an end to the sexist portrayal of women in the media, (8) establishment of reproductive freedom and the end to involuntary sterilization, (9) a remedy to the double discrimination against minority women, (10) a revision of criminal codes dealing with rape, (11) elimination of discrimination on the basis of sexual preference, (12) the establishment of nonsexist education, and (13) an examination of all welfare reform proposals for their specific impact on women.

The positive impact of liberal reforms on women's lives should not lead to the assumption that they eradicate systems of domination. Nowhere in these demands is there an emphasis on eradicating the politic of domination, yet it would need to be abolished if any of these demands were to be met. The lack of any emphasis on domination is consistent with the liberal feminist belief that women can achieve equality with men of their class without challenging and changing the cultural basis of group oppression. It is this belief that negates the likelihood that the potential radicalism of liberal feminism will ever be realized. Writing as early as 1967, Brazilian scholar Heleieth Saffioti emphasized that bourgeois feminism has always been "fundamentally and unconsciously a feminism of the ruling class," that:

> Whatever revolutionary content there is in petty-bourgeois feminist praxis, it has been put there by the efforts of the middle strata, especially the less well-off, to move up socially. To do this, however, they sought merely to expand the existing social structures, and

> never went so far as to challenge the status quo. Thus, while petty-bourgeois feminism may always have aimed at establishing social equality between the sexes, the consciousness it represented has remained utopian in its desire for and struggle to bring about a partial transformation of society; this, it believed, could be done without disturbing the foundations on which it rested.... In this sense, petty-bourgeois feminism is not feminism at all; indeed it has helped to consolidate class society by giving camouflage to its internal contradictions.

... Philosopher Mihailo Markovic discusses the limitations of liberalism in his essay "Women's Liberation and Human Emancipation":

> Another basic characteristic of liberalism which constitutes a formidable obstacle to an oppressed social group's emancipation is its conception of human nature. If selfishness, aggressiveness, the drive to conquer and dominate, really are among defining human traits, as every liberal philosopher since Locke tries to convince us, the oppression in civil society—i.e. in the social sphere not regulated by the state—is a fact of life, and the basic civil relationship between a man and a woman will always remain a battlefield. Woman, being less aggressive, is then either the less human of the two and doomed to subjugation, or else she must get more power-hungry herself and try to dominate man. Liberation for both is not feasible.

Although liberal perspectives on feminism include reforms that would have radical implications for society, these are the reforms that will be resisted precisely because they would set the stage for revolutionary transformation were they implemented. It is evident that society is more responsive to those "feminist" demands that are not threatening, that may even help maintain the status quo. Jeanne Gross gives an example of this co-optation of feminist strategy in her essay "Feminist Ethics from a Marxist Perspective," published in 1977:

> If we as women want change in all aspects of our lives, we must recognize that capitalism is uniquely capable of co-opting piecemeal change.... Capitalism is capable of taking our visionary changes and using them against us. For example, many married women, recognizing their oppression in the family, have divorced. They are thrown, with no preparation or protection, into the labor market. For many women this has meant taking their places at the row of typewriters. Corporations are now recognizing the capacity for exploitation in divorced women. The turnover in such jobs is incredibly high. "If she complains, she can be replaced."

Particularly as regards work, many liberal feminist reforms simply reinforced capitalist, materialist values (illustrating the flexibility of capitalism) without truly liberating women economically....

In an article, "Sisters—Under the Skin," in a San Francisco newspaper, columnist Bob Greene commented on the aversion many women apparently have to the term "feminism." Greene finds it curious that many women "who obviously believe in everything that proud feminists believe in dismiss the term 'feminist' as something unpleasant; something with which they do not wish to be associated." Even though such women often acknowledge that they have benefited from feminist-generated reform measures that have improved the social status of specific groups of women, they do not wish to be seen as participants in feminist movements:

> There is no getting around it. After all this time, the term "feminist" makes many bright, ambitious, intelligent women embarrassed and uncomfortable. They simply don't want to be associated with it.
>
> It's as if it has an unpleasant connotation that they want no connection with. Chances

> are if you were to present them with every mainstream feminist belief, they would go along with the beliefs to the letter—and even if they consider themselves feminists, they hasten to say no.

Many women are reluctant to advocate feminism because they are uncertain about the meaning of the term. Other women from exploited and oppressed ethnic groups dismiss the term because they do not wish to be perceived as supporting a racist movement; feminism is often equated with white women's rights efforts. Large numbers of women see feminism as synonymous with lesbianism; their homophobia leads them to reject association with any group identified as pro-lesbian. Some women fear the word "feminism" because they shun identification with any political movement, especially one perceived as radical. Of course there are women who do not wish to be associated with women's rights movement in any form, so they reject and oppose feminist movement. Most women are more familiar with negative perspectives on "women's lib" than with the positive significations of feminism. It is this term's positive political significance and power that we must now struggle to recover and maintain.

Currently feminism seems to be a term without any clear significance. The "anything goes" approach to the definition of the word has rendered it practically meaningless. What is meant by "anything goes" is usually that any woman who wants social equality with men regardless of her political perspective (she can be a conservative right-winger or a nationalist communist) can label herself feminist. Most attempts at defining feminism reflect the class nature of the movement. Definitions are usually liberal in origin and focus on the individual woman's right to freedom and self-determination....

Many feminist radicals now know that neither a feminism that focuses on woman as an autonomous human being worthy of personal freedom nor one that focuses on the attainment of equality of opportunity with men can rid society of sexism and male domination. Feminism is a struggle to end sexist oppression. Therefore, it is necessarily a struggle to eradicate the ideology of domination that permeates Western culture on various levels, as well as a commitment to reorganizing society so that the self-development of people can take precedence over imperialism, economic expansion, and material desires. Defined in this way, it is unlikely that women would join feminist movement simply because we are biologically the same. A commitment to feminism so defined would demand that each individual participant acquire a critical political consciousness based on ideas and beliefs....

... By repudiating the popular notion that the focus of feminist movement should be social equality of the sexes and by emphasizing eradication of the cultural basis of group oppression, our own analysis would require an exploration of all aspects of women's political reality. This would mean that race and class oppression would be recognized as feminist issues with as much relevance as sexism.

... Lack of adequate definition made it easy for bourgeois women, whether liberal or radical in perspective, to maintain their dominance over the leadership of the movement and its direction. This hegemony continues to exist in most feminist organizations. Exploited and oppressed groups of women are usually encouraged by those in power to feel that their situation is hopeless, that they can do nothing to break the pattern of domination. Given such socialization, these women have often felt that our only response to white, bourgeois, hegemonic dominance of feminist movement is to trash, reject, or dismiss feminism. This reaction is in no way threatening to the women who wish to maintain control over the direction of feminist theory and praxis. They prefer us to be silent, passively accepting their ideas. They prefer us speaking against "them" rather than developing our own ideas about feminist movement.

Feminism is the struggle to end sexist oppression. Its aim is not to benefit solely any specific group of women, any particular race or class of women. It does not privilege women over men. It has the power to transform in a meaningful way all our lives. Most importantly, feminism is neither a lifestyle nor a ready-made identity or role one can step into....

To emphasize that engagement with feminist struggle as political commitment, we could avoid using the phrase "I am a feminist" (a linguistic structure designed to refer to some personal aspect of identity and self-definition) and could state, "I advocate feminism." Because there has been undue emphasis placed on feminism as an identity or lifestyle, people usually resort to stereotyped perspectives on feminism. Deflecting attention away from stereotypes is necessary if we are to revise our strategy and direction. I have found that saying "I am a feminist" usually means I am plugged into preconceived notions of identity, role, or behavior. When I say, "I advocate feminism," the response is usually, "What is feminism?" A phrase like "I advocate" does not imply the kind of absolutism that is suggested by "I am." It does not engage us in the either/or dualistic thinking that is the central ideological component of all systems of domination in Western society. It implies that a choice has been made, that commitment to feminism is an act of will. It does not suggest that by committing oneself to feminism, the possibility of supporting other political movements is negated....

7
Rethinking the Nature of Work

Attitudes towards work in much feminist writing reflect bourgeois class biases. Middle-class women shaping feminist thought assumed that the most pressing problem for women was the need to get outside the home and work—to cease being "just" housewives. This was a central tenet of Betty Friedan's groundbreaking book, *The Feminine Mystique*. Work outside the home, feminist activists declared, was the key to liberation. Work, they argued, would allow women to break the bonds of economic dependency on men, which would in turn enable them to resist sexist domination. When these women talked about work they were equating it with high-paying careers; they were not referring to low-paying jobs or so-called "menial" labor. They were so blinded by their own experiences that they ignored the fact that a vast majority of women were (even at the time *The Feminine Mystique* was published [in 1963]) already working outside the home, working in jobs that neither liberated them from dependence on men nor made them economically self-sufficient. Benjamin Barber makes this point in his critique of the women's movement, *Liberating Feminism*:

> Work clearly means something very different to women in search of an escape from leisure than it has to most of the human race for most of history. For a few lucky men, for far fewer women, work has occasionally been a source of meaning and creativity. But for most of the race it remains even now forced drudgery in front of ploughs, machines, words, or numbers—pushing products, pushing switches, pushing papers to eke out the wherewithal of material existence.

Critiques like Barber's did not lead feminist thinkers at that time to re-examine their perspectives on women and work. Even though the notion of work as liberation had little significance for exploited, underpaid, working women, it provided ideological motivation for college-educated white women to enter, or re-enter, the work force. It gave many non-college-educated white women who had been taught that a woman's place is in the home the support to tolerate low-paying jobs, primarily to boost household incomes and break into personal isolation. They could see themselves as exercising new freedom. In many cases, they were struggling to maintain middle-class lifestyles that could no longer be supported solely by the income of husbands. Caroline Bird explains the motivating forces behind their entry into the work force in *The Two-Paycheck Marriage*:

> Whether professional or "pink collar" work, wives didn't think of themselves in the context of economic history. They had no idea they were creating a revolution and had no intention of doing so. Most of them drifted into jobs "to help out" at home, to save for the down payment on a house, buy clothes for the children, or to meet the rising expenses of college. They eagerly sought part-time jobs, work that wouldn't "interfere" with their families. Instead of keeping women at home, children of the 1970s were the expense that drove women to earn, for wives with children at home were more apt to be earning than women in general.

Although many of these women never participated in feminist movement, they did think of themselves as challenging the old-fashioned ideas about women's place.

Early feminist perpetuation of the notion "work liberates women" alienated many poor and working-class women, especially non-white women, from feminist movement for a number of reasons....

Black women and men were among the first groups to express fears that the influx of married, white women into the job market would mean fewer hirings of qualified black people, given the extent to which white supremacy has worked to prevent and exclude non-white people from certain jobs. By grouping white women of all classes with non-white people in affirmative-action programs, a system was effectively institutionalized that allowed employers to continue discriminating against non-white peoples and maintain white supremacy by hiring white women. Employers could satisfy affirmative-action guidelines without hiring any non-white people....

Approached in the right way, attacking poverty could become one of the issues that could unite women from various ethnic groups and cultural backgrounds. Ehrenreich and Stallard assert:

> The feminization of poverty—or, to put it the other way, the impoverishment of women—may be the most crucial challenge facing feminism today....

Ehrenreich and Stallard suggest that women should work to envision new economic programs, but they avoid explicitly criticizing capitalism in this essay. We must accept that it is a system that depends on the exploitation of underclass groups for its survival. We must accept that within that system, masses of women are and will be victims of class oppression.

Most women active in feminist movement do not have radical political perspectives and are unwilling to face these realities, especially when they, as individuals, gain economic self-sufficiency within the existing structure. They are reluctant, even unwilling, to acknowledge that supporting capitalist patriarchy or even a non-sexist capitalist system would not end the economic exploitation of underclass groups. These women fear the loss of their material privilege. As more middle-class white women lose status and enter the ranks of the poor, they may find it necessary to criticize capitalism. One of the women described by Ehrenreich and Stallard acknowledges that "hard times have a remarkable way of opening your eyes." ...

Feminist consciousness-raising has not significantly pushed women in the direction of revolutionary politics. For the most part, it has not helped women understand capitalism—how it works as a system that exploits female labor and its interconnections with sexist oppression. It has not urged women to learn about different political systems like socialism or encouraged women to invent and envision new political systems. It has not attacked materialism and our society's addiction to overconsumption. It has not shown women how we benefit from the exploitation and oppression of women and men globally or shown us ways to oppose imperialism. Most importantly, is has not continually confronted women with the understanding that feminist movement to end sexist oppression can be successful only if we are committed to revolution, to the establishment of a new social order.

New social orders are established gradually. This is hard for individuals in the United States to accept.

We have either been socialized to believe that revolutions are always characterized by extreme violence between the oppressed and their oppressors or that revolutions happen quickly. We have also been taught to crave immediate gratification of our desires and swift responses to our demands. Like every other liberation movement in this society, feminism has suffered because these attitudes keep participants from forming the kind of commitment to protracted struggle that makes revolution possible. As a consequence, feminist movement has not sustained its revolutionary momentum. It has been a successful rebellion. Differentiating between rebellion and revolution, Grace Lee Boggs and James Boggs emphasize:

> Rebellion is a stage in the development of revolution, but it is not revolution. It is an important stage because it represents the "standing up," the assertion of their humanity on the part of the oppressed. Rebellion informs both the oppressed and everybody else that a situation has become intolerable. They establish a form of communication among the oppressed themselves and at the same time open the eyes and ears of people who have been blind and deaf to the fate of their fellow citizens. Rebellions break the threads that have been holding the system together and throw into question the legitimacy and the supposed permanence of existing institutions. They shake up old values so that relations between individuals and between groups within the society are unlikely ever to be the same again. The inertia of the society has been interrupted. Only by understanding what a rebellion accomplishes can we see its limitations. A rebellion disrupts the society, but it does not provide what is necessary to establish a new social order....

To build a mass-based feminist movement, we need to have a liberatory ideology that can be shared with everyone. That revolutionary ideology can be created only if the experiences of people on the margin who suffer sexist oppression and other forms of group oppression are understood, addressed, and incorporated. They must participate in feminist movement as makers of theory and as leaders of action. In past feminist practice, we have been satisfied with relying on self-appointed individuals, some of whom are more concerned about exercising authority and power than with communicating with people from various backgrounds and political perspectives. Such individuals do not choose to learn about collective female experience, but impose their own ideas and values. Leaders are needed, and should be individuals who acknowledge their relationship to the group and who are accountable to it. They should have the ability to show love and compassion, show this love through their actions, and be able to engage in successful dialogue....

... Feminist activists would do well to heed the words of Susan Griffin when she reminds us in her essay "The Way of All Ideology":

> A deeply political knowledge of the world does not lead to a creation of an enemy. Indeed, to create monsters unexplained by circumstance is to forget the political vision which above all explains behavior as emanating from circumstance, a vision which believes in a capacity born to all human beings for creation, joys, and kindness, in a human nature which, under the right circumstances, can bloom. When a movement for liberation inspires itself chiefly by a hatred for an enemy rather than from this vision of possibility, it begins to defeat itself. Its very notions cease to be healing. Despite the fact that it declares itself in favor of liberation, its language is no longer liberatory. It begins to require a censorship within itself. Its ideas of truth become more and more narrow. And the movement that began with a moving evocation of truth begins to appear fraudulent from the outside, begins to mirror all that it says it opposes, for now it, too, is an oppressor of certain truths, and speakers, and begins, like the old oppressors, to hide from itself....

8.9 Glen Coulthard (1974–)

Glen Coulthard is a member of the Yellowknives Dene First Nation as well as an associate professor of political science and Indigenous Studies at the University of British Columbia in Vancouver. "Seeing Red" is the fourth chapter in Coulthard's *Red Skin, White Masks: Rejecting the Colonial Politics of Recognition* (2014). Both its title and focus pay homage to Frantz Fanon's *Black Skin, White Masks*, which examines the experience of black men and women living in white-controlled societies (see 7.8).

Coulthard focuses on settler-colonialism in the Canadian context, in particular following the *Indian Act* (1951), the *Statement of the Government of Canada on Indian Policy* (the White Paper of 1969), and the *Royal Commission on Aboriginal Peoples* (1996). He argues that this series of commissions and inquiries has failed to diagnose or undo the damage caused to First Nations peoples by European colonialism. Rather, these efforts have legitimized and obfuscated ongoing colonial rule. Their unwarrented focus on reconciliation and forgiveness obscures ongoing practices of colonial oppression. In this context, First Nations resentment and opposition accurately reflect the non-reconciled relationship they find themselves in. Eliminating resentment and opposition may be desirable for the Canadian government, but it is not for Indigenous people.

Essentially, reconciliation means different things to First Nations people and to the Canadian government. Coulthard argues that for Indigenous people, reconciliation requires a sort of self-healing to overcome the violent nation-to-nation relationship built into the settler state. This necessarily means challenging the legitimacy of colonial rule. For the Canadian government, on the other hand, reconciliation means apologizing for the past and moving on to make the country more inclusive and just along conventional lines. Decolonization is oppositional at its core because it requires a restoration of Indigenous cultural practices in a way that departs from conventional conceptions of inclusivity and justice. This, Coulthard argues, can never occur within the restricted confines imposed by the Canadian government.

~

from Red Skin, White Masks

Seeing Red: Reconciliation and Resentment

On June 11, 2008, the Conservative prime minister of Canada, Stephen J. Harper, issued an official apology on behalf of the Canadian state to Indigenous survivors of the Indian residential school system.[1] ...

The benefit of the doubt that was originally afforded the authenticity of the prime minister's apology has since dissipated. Public distrust began to escalate following a well-scrutinized address by Harper at a gathering of the G20 in Pittsburgh, Pennsylvania, on September 25, 2009. It was there that Harper made the somewhat astonishing (but typically arrogant and self-congratulatory) claim that Canadians had "no history of colonialism." ...

Over the last three decades, a global industry has emerged promoting the issuing of official apologies advocating "forgiveness" and "reconciliation" as an important precondition for resolving the deleterious social impacts of intra-state violence, mass atrocity, and historical injustice.[2] Originally, this industry was developed in state contexts that sought to undergo a formal "transition" from the violent history of openly authoritarian regimes to more democratic forms of rule—known in the literature as "transitional justice"—but more recently has been imported by somewhat stable, liberal-democratic settler polities like Canada and Australia.[3] In Canada, we have witnessed this relatively recent "reconciliation politics" converge with a slightly older "politics of recognition," advocating the institutional recognition and accommodation of Indigenous cultural difference as an important means of reconciling the colonial relationship between Indigenous peoples and the state. Political theorist Andrew Schaap explains the convergence of these two discourses well: "In societies divided by a history of political violence, political reconciliation depends on transforming a relation of enmity into one of civic friendship. In such contexts the discourse of *recognition* provides a ready frame in terms of which reconciliation might be conceived."[4]

In Canada "reconciliation" tends to be invoked in three distinct yet interrelated ways when deployed in the context of Indigenous peoples' struggles for self-determination. First, "reconciliation" is frequently used to refer to the diversity of individual or collective practices that Indigenous people undertake to reestablish a positive "relation-to-self" in situations where this relation has been damaged or distorted by some form of symbolic or structural violence. Acquiring or being afforded due "recognition" by another subject (or subjects) is often said to play a fundamental role in facilitating reconciliation in this first sense.[5] Second, "reconciliation" is also commonly referred to as the act of restoring estranged or damaged social and political relationships. It is frequently inferred by proponents of political reconciliation that restoring these relationships requires that individuals and

---

1 Prime Minister of Canada, "Statement and Apology" (Ottawa: Indian Affairs and Northern Development, 2008). Online as "Prime Minister Harper Offers Full Apology on Behalf of Canadians for the Indian Residential Schools System," Prime Minister of Canada website, June 11, 2008, http://www.pm.gc.ca/eng/news/2008/06/11/pm-offers-full-apology-behalf-canadians-indian-residential-schools-system.

2 Jeff Corntassel and Cindy Holder, "Who's Sorry Now? Government Apologies, Truth Commissions and Indigenous Self-Determination in Australia, Canada, Guatemala, and Peru," *Human Rights Review* 9, no. 4 (2008): 465–89.

3 For a genealogy of the emergence of "the field of transitional justice," see Paige Arthur, "How 'Transitions' Reshaped Human Rights: A Conceptual History of Transitional Justice," *Human Rights Quarterly* 31 (2009): 321–67. For a discussion of the application of transitional justice concepts and mechanisms to the context of Indigenous–state relations, see C. Young, "Canada and the Legacy of Indian Residential Schools"; Will Kymlicka and Bashir Bashir, eds., *The Politics of Reconciliation in Multicultural Societies* (Oxford: Oxford University Press, 2008); Damian Short, *Reconciliation and Colonial Power: Indigenous Rights in Australia* (Burlington, Vt.: Ashgate Publishers, 2008).

4 Andrew Schaap, "Political Reconciliation through a Struggle for Recognition?," *Social and Legal Studies* 13, no. 4 (2004): 523 (emphasis added).

5 For example, see Axel Honneth, "Integrity and Disrespect: Principles of the Concept of Morality Based on the Theory of Recognition," *Political Theory* 20, no. 2 (1992): 187–201. For a discussion of Honneth's approach, see Fraser and Honneth, *Redistribution or Recognition?* Indigenous people often equate this form of reconciliation with individual and collective "healing."

groups work to overcome the debilitating pain, anger, and resentment that frequently persist in the wake of being injured or harmed by a perceived or real injustice.[6] In settler-state contexts, "truth and reconciliation" commissions, coupled with state arrangements that claim to recognize and accommodate Indigenous identity-related differences, are viewed as important institutional means to facilitate reconciliation in these first two senses.[7] These institutional mechanisms are also seen as a crucial way to help evade the cycles of violence that can occur when societal cultural differences are suppressed and when so-called "negative" emotions such as anger and resentment are left to fester within and between disparate social groups.[8] The third notion of "reconciliation" commonly invoked in the Canadian context refers to the process by which things are brought "to agreement, concord, or harmony; the fact of being made consistent or compatible."[9] As Anishinaabe political philosopher Dale Turner's recent work reminds us, this third form of reconciliation—the act of rendering things *consistent*—is the one that lies at the core of Canada's legal and political understanding of the term: namely, rendering consistent Indigenous assertions of nationhood with the state's unilateral assertion of sovereignty over Native peoples' lands and populations. It is the state's attempt to impose this third understanding of reconciliation on the institutional and discursive field of Indigenous–non-Indigenous relations that is effectively undermining the realization of the previous two forms of reconciliation.

Thomas Brudholm's recent [2008] book, *Resentment's Virtue: Jean Améry and the Refusal to Forgive*, offers an important critique of the global turn to reconciliation politics that has emerged in the last thirty years. Specifically, Brudholm's study provides a much-needed "counterpoint" to the "near-hegemonic status" afforded "the logic of forgiveness in the literatures on transitional justice and reconciliation."[10] Focusing on the Truth and Reconciliation Commission of South Africa, Brudholm shows how advocates of transitional justice often base their normative assumptions about the presumed "good" of forgiveness and reconciliation on a number of uncritical assumptions about the supposed "bad" of harboring reactive emotions like anger and resentment: that these feelings are physically and mentally unhealthy, irrational, retrograde, and, when collectively expressed, prone to producing increased social instability and political violence. Brudholm challenges these assumptions through a fascinating engagement with the writings of essayist and holocaust survivor Jean Améry, whose own work challenges the scathing and very influential portrayal of *ressentiment* as an irredeemably vengeful, reactionary, and backward-looking force by Friedrich Nietzsche in *On the Genealogy of Morals* (1887).[11] According to Brudholm, Améry's work forces us to consider that under certain conditions a disciplined maintenance of resentment in the wake of historical injustice can signify "the reflex expression of a moral protest" that is as "permissible and admirable as the posture of forgiveness."[12]

---

6 Trudy Govier, *Forgiveness and Revenge* (New York: Routledge, 2002), viii.

7 Will Kymlicka and Bashir Bashir, "Introduction: Struggles for Inclusion and Reconciliation in Modern Democracies," in Kymlicka and Bashir, *The Politics of Reconciliation in Multicultural Societies*, 1–24.

8 Trudy Govier, *Forgiveness and Revenge*; Govier, "Acknowledgement and Truth Commissions: The Case of Canada," in *Philosophy and Aboriginal Rights: Critical Dialogues*, ed. Sandra Tomsons and Lorraine Mayer (Don Mills, Ont.: Oxford University Press, 2013). Also see Thomas Brudholm, *Resentment's Virtue: Jean Améry and the Refusal to Forgive* (Philadelphia: Temple University Press, 2008).

9 Oxford English Dictionary quoted in Dale Turner, "Aboriginal Relations in Canada: The Importance of Political Reconciliation," Federation for the Humanities and Social Sciences Blog, *Equity Matters*, May 3, 2011, http://www.idees-ideas.ca/ blog/ aboriginal-relations-canada-importance-political-reconciliationx.

10 Brudholm, *Resentment's Virtue*, 3.

11 Jean Améry, *At the Mind's Limit: Contemplations by a Survivor on Auschwitz and Its Realities*, trans. Sidney and Stella Rosenfeld (Bloomington: Indiana University Press, 1980). Also see Friedrich Nietzsche, *On the Genealogy of Morals and Ecce Homo*, ed. Walter Kaufmann (New York: Vintage, 1989).

12 Brudholm, *Resentment's Virtue*, 4.

In this chapter, I undertake a similar line of argumentation, although with two significant differences. First, as a critique of the field and practice of *transitional justice*, Brudholm's study is "limited to the *aftermath* of mass atrocities" and to the "*time after* the violence has been brought to an end."[13] In the following pages, the political import of Indigenous peoples' emotional responses to settler colonization is instead explored against the "nontransitional" backdrop of the state's approach to reconciliation that began to explicitly inform government policy following the release of the *Report of the Royal Commission on Aboriginal Peoples* (RCAP) in 1996.[14] I show that in settler-colonial contexts—where there is no period marking a clear or formal transition from an authoritarian past to a democratic present—state-sanctioned approaches to reconciliation must ideologically manufacture such a transition by allocating the abuses of settler colonization to the dustbins of history, and/or purposely disentangle processes of reconciliation from questions of settler-coloniality as such. Once either or both of these conceptual obfuscations have been accomplished, holding the contradictory position that Canada has "no history of colonialism" following an official government apology to Indigenous survivors of one of the state's most notoriously brutal colonial institutions begins to make sense; indeed, one could argue that this form of conceptual revisionism is *required* of an approach that attempts to apply transitional justice mechanisms to nontransitional circumstances. In such conditions, reconciliation takes on a temporal character as the individual and collective process of overcoming the subsequent *legacy* of past abuse, not the abusive colonial structure itself. And what are we to make of those who refuse to forgive and/or reconcile in these situations? They are typically cast as being saddled by the damaging psychological residue of this legacy, of which anger and resentment are frequently highlighted.

The second difference is that I use the work of Frantz Fanon as my central theoretical referent instead of that of Jean Améry. As Améry himself perceptively noted in an important 1969 essay, Fanon held a very nuanced perspective on both the potentially transformative and retrograde aspects of colonized peoples' "hatred, contempt and resentment" when expressed within and against the subjective and structural features of colonial power.[15] This chapter builds on Fanon's insights to demonstrate two things. First, far from being a largely disempowering and unhealthy affliction, I show that under certain conditions Indigenous peoples' individual and collective expressions of anger and resentment can help prompt the very forms of self-affirmative praxis that generate rehabilitated Indigenous subjectivities and decolonized forms of life in ways that the combined politics of recognition and reconciliation has so far proven itself incapable of doing. And second, in light of Canada's failure to deliver on its emancipatory promise of postcolonial reconciliation, I suggest that what implicitly gets interpreted by the state as Indigenous peoples' *ressentiment*—understood as an incapacitating inability or unwillingness to get over the past—is actually an entirely appropriate manifestation of our *resentment*: a politicized expression of Indigenous anger and outrage directed at a structural and symbolic violence that still structures our lives, our relations with others, and our relationships with land....

DWELLING ON THE NEGATIVE: RESENTMENT AND RECONCILIATION

In common usage, "resentment" is usually referenced negatively to indicate a feeling closely associated with

---

13 Ibid., 4–5.

14 I say "explicitly" here because achieving reconciliation in the three senses noted above always implicitly informed the turn to recognition politics that began in the early 1970s. Also, I borrow the term "nontransitional" from Courtney Young, "Transitional Justice for Indigenous People in a Non-Transitional Society," Research Brief for Identities in Transition, *International Center for Transitional Justice*, October 2009.

15 Jean Améry, "The Birth of Man from the Spirit of Violence: Frantz Fanon the Revolutionary," *Wasafiri* 44 (2005): 14.

anger.[16] However, where one can be *angry* with any number of things, resentment is typically reserved for and directed against instances of perceived wrongdoing. The *Oxford English Dictionary*, for example, defines resentment as a feeling of "bitter indignation at having been treated *unfairly*."[17] One could argue, then, that resentment, unlike anger, has an in-built *political* component to it, given that it is often expressed in response to an alleged slight, instance of maltreatment, or injustice. Seen from this angle, resentment can be understood as a particularly virulent expression of *politicized anger*.[18]

The political dimension of resentment has not gone unnoticed within the Western philosophical tradition; philosophers such as Adam Smith, John Rawls, Robert Solomon, Jeffrie Murphy, Alice MacLachlan, and Thomas Brudholm (to name only a few) have all written extensively on the "moral" significance of emotions like resentment.[19] In *A Theory of Justice*, for example, Rawls writes that "resentment is a moral feeling. If we resent our having less than others, it must be because we think that their being better off is the result of unjust institutions, or wrongful conduct on their part."[20] In a similar vein, Jeffrie Murphy argues that resentment can be both a legitimate and valuable expression of anger in response to the unjust abrogation of one's rights; it is an affective indicator of our sense of self-worth or self-respect.[21] And Alice MacLachlan writes: "In emphasizing the moral function of resentment as one kind of anger ... philosophers have offered an important service to angry victims of political violence, who are often voiceless except in their ability to articulate and express resentment."[22] Thomas Brudholm notes that, although these theorists vary regarding "the conditions and circumstances under which anger or resentment is appropriate," they nonetheless all draw an important "distinction between excessive and pathological forms of anger and resentment, on the one hand, and appropriate and valuable forms, on the other hand."[23]

Discussions within the field of recognition and reconciliation politics, however, rarely treat reactive emotions like anger and resentment even-handedly. Indeed, in such contexts, anger and resentment are more likely to be seen as pathologies that need to be overcome. However, given the genealogical association of feelings like resentment with political and moral protest, why have they received such bad press in the literature on reconciliation? I think there are at least two reasons to consider here. First, as several scholars have noted, in the transitional justice and reconciliation literature our understanding of resentment has been deeply shaded by Nietzsche's profoundly influential characterization of *ressentiment* in *On the Genealogy of Morals*.[24] There, *ressentiment* is portrayed as a reactive, backward, and passive orientation to the world, which, for Nietzsche, signifies the abnegation of freedom as self-valorizing, life-affirming action. To be saddled with *ressentiment* is to be irrationally preoccupied with and incapacitated by offences suffered in the past. "*Ressentiment*," writes Jean Améry, "nails" its victims to "the past," it "blocks the exit

16 Thomas Brudholm, "Revisiting Resentments: Jean Améry and the Dark Side of Forgiveness," *Journal of Human Rights* 5, no. 1 (2006): 7–26; Robert Solomon, *Living with Nietzsche: What the Great "Immoralist" Has to Teach Us* (Oxford: Oxford University Press, 2003); Alice MacLachlan, "Unreasonable Resentments," *Journal of Social Philosophy* 41, no. 4 (2010): 422–41.

17 See under "resentment," http://oxforddictionaries.com (emphasis added).

18 On the political significance of anger in the face of gendered and racial oppression, I have learned much from the foundational analysis in Audre Lorde, "The Uses of Anger," *Women Studies Quarterly* 25, nos. 1/2 (1997): 278–85. Also see the fierce poem by queer Menominee poet Chrystos, "They're Always Telling Me I'm Too Angry," *Fugitive Colors* (Cleveland: Cleveland State University Poetry Center, 1995), 44.

19 Adam Smith, *The Theory of Moral Sentiments* (New York: Penguin Modern Classics, 2010); John Rawls, *A Theory of Justice* (Cambridge, Mass.: Harvard University Press, 2005); Solomon, *Living with Nietzsche*; Jeffrie Murphy, *Getting Even: Forgiveness and Its Limits* (New York: Oxford University Press, 2003); MacLachlan, "Unreasonable Resentments"; Brudholm, *Resentment's Virtue*.

20 John Rawls, *A Theory of Justice* (Cambridge, Mass.: Harvard University Press, 1971), 533.

21 Murphy, *Getting Even*.

22 MacLachlan, "Unreasonable Resentments," 422–23.

23 Brudholm, *Resentment's Virtue*, 9–10.

24 For example, in the context of post-Holocaust demands for reconciliation, Jean Améry wrote: there "seems to be general agreement that the final say on resentment is that of Friedrich Nietzsche" (Améry, *At the Mind's Limit*, 67).

... to the future" and "twists" the "time-sense" of those trapped in it.[25] This theme is taken up again in *Thus Spoke Zarathustra*, where Nietzsche describes the so-called "man of *ressentiment*" as an "angry *spectator* of everything past."[26] For Nietzsche, *ressentiment* is an expression of one's "impotence" against "that which *has been*."[27] For the resenting subject, "memory" is a "festering wound."[28] In Nietzsche's view, to wallow in resentment is to deny one's capacity to actively "forget," to "let go," to *get on with life*.[29] In the third section below I show how state reconciliation policy in Canada is deeply invested in the view that Indigenous peoples suffer from *ressentiment* in a way not entirely unlike Nietzsche describes.

The second reason why negative emotions like anger and resentment find few defenders in the field of reconciliation politics is because they sometimes *can* manifest themselves in unhealthy and disempowering ways. My argument here does not deny this. Individual narratives highlighting the perils associated with clinging to one's anger and resentment appear too frequently in the Canadian reconciliation literature to do so. Consider, for example, the following account by Ojibwe author Richard Wagamese, which speaks to the personal necessity of overcoming anger and resentment as a precondition in his own healing journey:

> For years I carried simmering anger and resentment. The more I learned about the implementation of [Indian residential school] policy and how it affected Aboriginal people across the country, the more anger I felt. I ascribed all my pain to residential schools and those responsible.... But when I was in my late forties, I had enough of the anger. I was tired of being drunk and blaming the residential schools and those responsible.... My life was slipping away on me and I did not want to become an older person still clinging to [such] disempowering emotion[s].[30]

Taken together, these are all very serious concerns. It makes no sense at all to affirm the worth of resentment over a politics of recognition and reconciliation if doing so increases the likelihood of reproducing internalized forms of violence. Nor could one possibly affirm the political significance of Nietzschean *ressentiment* if doing so means irrationally chaining ourselves "to the past." While I recognize that Indigenous peoples' negative emotional responses to settler colonization can play out in some of these problematic ways, it is important to recognize that they do not always do so. As we shall see in the next section, these affective reactions can also lead to forms of anticolonial resistance grounded on transformed Indigenous political subjectivities. I suggest that the transformative potential of these emotions is also why Frantz Fanon refused to dismiss or condemn them; instead he demanded that they be *understood*, that their transformative potential be *harnessed*, and that their structural referent be *identified* and *uprooted*.

THE RESENTMENT OF THE COLONIZED AND THE RISE OF RECONCILIATION POLITICS IN CANADA

Understanding Fanon's views regarding the political significance of what he calls "emotional factors" in the formation of anticolonial subjectivities and decolonizing practices requires that we briefly revisit his theory of internalized colonialism.[31] Recall from chapter 1 [of *Red Skin, White Masks*] that, for Fanon, in contexts where the reproduction of colonial rule does not rely

25 Ibid., 68.
26 Friedrich Nietzsche, *Thus Spoke Zarathustra*, ed. Adrian Del Caro and Robert Pipin (Cambridge: Cambridge University Press, 2006), 111.
27 Ibid. (emphasis added).
28 Nietzsche, *On the Genealogy of Morals and Ecce Homo*, 230.
29 Ibid, 38–39, 57–58.
30 Richard Wagamese, "Returning to Harmony," in *Response, Responsibility and Renewal*, ed. Aboriginal Healing Foundation (Ottawa: Aboriginal Healing Foundation Research Series, 2009), 144.
31 Fanon, *The Wretched of the Earth*, 89.

solely on force, it requires the production of "colonial subjects" that acquiesce to the forms of power that have been imposed on them. "Internalization" thus occurs when the social relations of colonialism, along with the forms of recognition and representation that serve to legitimate them, come to be seen as "true" or "natural" to the colonized themselves. "The status of 'native' is a neurosis," explains Sartre in his preface to *The Wretched of the Earth*, "introduced and maintained by the colonist in the colonized *with their consent*."[32] Similar to how the Italian Marxist theorist Antonio Gramsci viewed the reproduction of class dominance in situations absent ongoing state violence, colonial hegemony is maintained through a combination of coercion and consent.[33] Under such conditions, colonial domination appears "more subtle, less bloody," to use Fanon's words.[34]

For Fanon, this "psychological-economic structure" is what produces the condition of stagnancy and inertia that characterizes the colonial world.[35] *The Wretched of the Earth*, for example, is littered with passages that highlight the fundamentally passive and lethargic condition that the colonial situation produces. The "colonial world," writes Fanon, is "compartmentalized, Manichaean and *petrified*"; it is a world in which the "colonial subject" is "penned in," lies "coiled and robbed," taught "to remain in his place and not overstep his limits."[36] In *Black Skin, White Masks*, Fanon describes this Manichaean relation as "locked" or "fixed" by the assumptions of racial and cultural inferiority and superiority held by the colonized and colonizer, respectively.[37] Unlike racist arguments that attribute the supposed inertia of colonized societies to the cultural and technological underdevelopment of the colonized themselves, Fanon identifies the colonial social structure as the source of this immobility.[38]

Although the internalized negative energy produced by this "hostile" situation will first express itself against the colonized's "own people"—"This is the period when black turns on black," writes Fanon, when colonial violence "assumes a black or Arab face"—over time, it begins to incite a negative *reaction* in the colonial subject.[39] It is my claim that this reaction indicates a breakdown of the psychological structure of internalized colonialism. The colonized subject, degraded, impoverished, and abused, begins to look at the colonist's world of "lights and paved roads" with envy, contempt, and resentment.[40] The colonized begin to *desire* what has been denied them: land, freedom, and dignity. They begin dreaming of revenge, of taking their oppressor's place:

> The gaze that the colonized subject casts at the colonist's sector is a look of lust, a look of envy. Dreams of possession. Every type of possession: at sitting at the colonist's table and sleeping in his bed, preferably with his wife. The colonized man is an envious man. The colonist is aware of this as he catches the furtive glance, and constantly on his guard, realizes bitterly that: "They want to take our place." And it is true that there is not one colonized subject who at least once a day does not dream of taking the place of the colonist.[41]

Although Fanon is quick to insist that the "legitimate desire for revenge" borne of the colonized subject's nascent "hatred" and "resentment" toward the colonist cannot alone "nurture a war of liberation," I

32 Jean-Paul Sartre, preface to Fanon, *The Wretched of the Earth*, liv.
33 See Antonio Gramsci, *Selections from the Prison Notebooks* (New York: International Publishers, 1999).
34 Fanon, *The Wretched of the Earth*, 27.
35 Frantz Fanon, *Black Skin, White Masks*, trans. Richard Philcox (Boston: Grove Press, 2008), 18.
36 Fanon, *The Wretched of the Earth*, 15 (emphasis added).
37 Fanon, *Black Skin, White Masks* (2008), xiii–xiv.
38 The arguments of both Hegel and early Marx are paradigmatic of the former view.
39 Fanon, *The Wretched of the Earth*, 15–16, 94.
40 Ibid., 4, 5, 16, 89.
41 Ibid., 5. On "envy" and its close relationship to "resentment," see Marguerite La Caze, "Envy and Resentment," *Philosophical Explorations: An International Journal for the Philosophy of Mind and Action* 4, no. 1 (2007): 141–47.

suggest that these negative emotions nonetheless mark an important turning point in the individual and collective coming-to-consciousness of the colonized.[42] More specifically, I think that they represent the *externalization* of that which was previously *internalized*: a purging, if you will, of the so-called "inferiority complex" of the colonized subject. In the context of internalized colonialism, the material conditions of poverty and violence that condition the colonial situation appear muted to the colonized because they are understood to be the product of one's own cultural deficiencies. In such a context, the formation of a colonial "enemy"—that is, a source external to ourselves that we come to associate with "our misfortunes"—signifies a collapse of this internalized colonial psychic structure.[43] For Fanon, only once this rupture has occurred—or, to use Jean Améry's phrase, once these "sterile" emotions "come to recognize themselves" for "what they really are ... consequences of social repression"[44]—can the colonized then cast their "exasperated hatred and rage in this new direction."[45]

Importantly, Fanon insists that these reactive emotions can also prompt the colonized to revalue and affirm Indigenous cultural traditions and social practices that are systematically denigrated yet never fully destroyed in situations of colonial rule. After years of dehumanization the colonized begin to resent the assumed "supremacy of white values" that has served to ideologically justify their continued exploitation and domination. "In the period of decolonization," writes Fanon, "the colonized masses thumb their noses at these very values, shower them with insults and vomit them up."[46] Eventually, this newfound resentment of colonial values prompts the colonized to affirm the worth of their own traditions, of their own civilizations, which in turn generates feelings of pride and self-certainty unknown in the colonial period. For Fanon, this "anti-racist racism" or "the determination to defends one's skin" is "characteristic of the colonized's response to colonial oppression" and provides them with the motivating "reason the join the struggle."[47] Although Fanon ultimately saw this example of Indigenous cultural self-recognition as an expression akin to Nietzschean *ressentiment*—that is, as a limited and retrograde "reaction" to colonial power—he nonetheless claimed it as necessary for the same reason he affirmed the transformative potential of emotional factors like anger and resentment: they signify an important "break" in the forms of colonial subjection that have hitherto kept the colonized "in their place."[48] In the following chapters [not included here], I delve further into what I claim to be Fanon's overly "instrumental" view of culture's value vis-à-vis decolonization in light of the more substantive position held by contemporary theorists and activists of Indigenous resurgence....

MANAGING THE CRISIS: RECONCILIATION AND *THE ROYAL COMMISSION ON ABORIGINAL PEOPLES*

The federal government was forced to establish [the] RCAP in the wake of two national crises that erupted in the tumultuous "Indian summer" of 1990. The first involved the legislative stonewalling of the Meech Lake Accord by Cree Manitoba Member of the Legislative Assembly (MLA) Elijah Harper....

The second crisis involved a seventy-eight-day armed "standoff" beginning on July 11, 1990, between the Mohawk nation of Kanesatake, the Quebec provincial police (Sûreté du Québec, or SQ), and the Canadian armed forces near the town of Oka, Quebec. On June 30, 1990, the municipality of Oka was granted a court injunction to dismantle a peaceful barricade erected by

42 Fanon, *Wretched of the Earth*, 89.
43 Ibid., 31.
44 Améry, "The Birth of Man from the Spirit of Violence," 15.
45 Fanon, *Wretched of the Earth*, 31.
46 Ibid., 8.
47 Ibid., 89.
48 In the following chapter [not included here] I explore the limitations of Fanon's views on the instrumentality of Indigenous cultural politics in more detail.

the people of Kanesatake in an effort to defend their sacred lands from further encroachment by non-Native developers. The territory in question was slotted for development by a local golf course, which planned on extending nine holes onto land the Mohawks had been fighting to have recognized as their own for almost three hundred years.[49] Eleven days later, on July 11, one hundred heavily armed members of the SQ stormed the community. The police invasion culminated in a twenty-four-second exchange of gunfire that killed SQ Corporal Marcel Lemay.[50] In a display of solidarity, the neighboring Mohawk nation of Kahnawake set up their own barricades, including one that blocked the Mercier Bridge leading into the greater Montreal area. Galvanized by the Mohawk resistance, Indigenous peoples from across the continent followed suit, engaging in a diverse array of solidarity actions that ranged from information leafleting to the establishment of peace encampments to the erection of blockades on several major Canadian transport corridors, both road and rail. Although polls conducted during the standoff showed some support by non-Native Canadians outside of Quebec for the Mohawk cause,[51] most received their information about the so-called "Oka Crisis" through the corporate media, which overwhelmingly represented the event as a "law and order" issue fundamentally undermined by Indigenous peoples' uncontrollable anger and resentment.[52]

For many Indigenous people and their supporters, however, these two national crises were seen as the inevitable culmination of a near decade-long escalation of Native frustration with a colonial state that steadfastly refused to uphold the rights that had been recently "recognized and affirmed" in section 35 (1) of the Constitution Act, 1982. By the late 1980s this frustration was clearly boiling over, resulting in a marked rise in First Nations' militancy and land-based direct action.[53] ...

From the vantage point of the colonial state, by the time the seventy-eight-day standoff at Kanesatake started, things were already out of control in Indian Country. If settler-state stability and authority is required to ensure "certainty" over Indigenous lands and resources to create an investment climate friendly for expanded capitalist accumulation, then the barrage of Indigenous practices of disruptive countersovereignty that emerged with increased frequency in the 1980s was an embarrassing demonstration that Canada no longer had its shit together with respect to managing the so-called "Indian Problem." On top of this, the material form that these expressions of Indigenous sovereignty took on the ground—*the blockade*, explicitly erected to impede the power of state and capital from entering and leaving Indigenous territories respectively—must have been particularly troubling to the settler-colonial establishment. All of this activity was an indication that Indigenous people and communities were no longer willing to wait for Canada (or even their own leaders) to negotiate a just relationship with them in good faith. In Fanon's terms, Indigenous peoples were no longer willing to "remain in their place."[54] There was also growing concern that Indigenous youth in particular were no longer willing to play by Canada's rules—especially regarding the potential use of violence—when it came to advancing their communities' rights and interests. As Georges Erasmus, then national chief of the Assembly of First Nations, warned in 1988: "Canada,

49 Kiera Ladner and Leanne Simpson, eds., *This Is an Honour Song: Twenty Years since the Barricades* (Winnipeg: Arbeiter Ring Press, 2010), 1–2.

50 Linda Pertusati, *In Defence of Mohawk Land: Ethnopolitical Conflict in Native North America* (New York: State University of New York Press, 1997), 101–2.

51 "Oka Costs Natives Canada's Sympathy," *Toronto Star*, November 27, 1990, A9.

52 For examples of such representations, see Mark Kennedy, "PM Brands Warriors 'Terrorists,' Calls for Surrender," *Ottawa Citizen*, August 29, 1990, A2; "Army Moving In on Mohawks; 'No One above the Law' PM Says of Warriors," *Edmonton Journal*, August 29, 1990, A1; William Johnson, "Oka Symbolizes Meech Aftermath," *Edmonton Journal*, July 24, 1990, A7; "Judge Recognizes Native 'Rage' as Oka Standoff Leaders Jailed," *Toronto Star*, February 20, 1992, A13; "Thousands of Okas Loom," *The Gazette*, September 28, 1990, A4. For critical analyses of such representations, see James Winter, *Common Cents: The Media's Portrayal of the Gulf War and Other Issues* (Montreal: Black Rose Press, 1992); Gail Valaskakis, "Rights and Warriors," *Ariel: A Review of International English Literature* 25, no. 1 (1994): 60–72.

53 Boyce Richardson, ed., *Drumbeat: Anger and Renewal in Indian Country* (Ottawa: Summerhill Press and the Assembly of First Nations, 1989).

54 Fanon, *The Wretched of the Earth*, 15.

if you do not deal with this generation of leaders, then we cannot promise that you are going to like the kind of violent political action that we can just about guarantee the next generation is going to bring to you." Consider this "a warning," Erasmus continued: "We want to let you know that you're playing with fire. We may be the last generation of leaders that are prepared to sit down and peacefully negotiate our concerns with you."[55] Erasmus's warning was ignored, and the siege at Kanasatake occurred two years later.

In the wake of having to engage in one of the largest and costliest military operations since the Korean War, the federal government announced on August 23, 1991, that a royal commission would be established with a sprawling sixteen-point mandate to investigate the abusive relationship that had clearly developed between Indigenous peoples and the state.[56] Published two years behind schedule in November 1996, the $58-million, five-volume, approximately four-thousand-page *Report of the Royal Commission on Aboriginal Peoples* offers a vision of reconciliation between Aboriginal peoples and Canada based on the core principles of "mutual recognition, mutual respect, sharing and mutual responsibility."[57] Of the 440 recommendations made by RCAP, the following are some of the more noteworthy:

> Legislation, including issuing a new Royal Proclamation, stating Canada's commitment to a new relationship with companion legislation establishing a new treaty process and recognition of Aboriginal Nations' governments;
>
> Recognition of an Aboriginal order of government, subject to the Charter of Rights and Freedoms, with authority over matters relating to the good government and welfare of Aboriginal peoples and their territories;
>
> Replacement of the federal Department of Indian Affairs with two departments, one to implement the new relationship with Aboriginal nations and one to provide services to non-self-governing communities;
>
> Creation of an Aboriginal parliament;
>
> Expansion of the Aboriginal land and resource base;
>
> Recognition of Metis self-government, provision of a land base, and recognition of Metis rights to hunt and fish on Crown land;
>
> Initiatives to address social, education, health, and housing needs, including the training of ten thousand health professionals over a ten-year period, the establishment of an Aboriginal peoples' university, and recognition of Aboriginal peoples' authority over child welfare.[58] ...

The decade of heightened First Nations militancy that culminated in the resistance at Kanesatake created the political and cultural context that RCAP's call for recognition and reconciliation sought to mitigate—namely, the simmering anger and resentment of the colonized transformed into a resurgent affirmation of Indigenous difference that threatened to disrupt settler-colonialism's sovereign claim over Indigenous peoples and our lands. In light of this, to suggest that we replace these emotions by a more conciliatory and constructive attitude like "forgiveness" seems misplaced to me.[59] Of course, individual and collective expressions of anticolonial anger and resentment can be destructive and harmful to relationships; but these emotional forces are rarely, if ever, as destructive and violent as the colonial relationship they critically call into question. "The responsibility for violence," argues Taiaiake Alfred, "begins and ends with the state, not with the people who are challenging the

---

55 "Act or Face Threat of Violence, Native Leader Warns Ottawa," *Toronto Star*, June 1, 1988, A1.

56 In Commonwealth countries a "royal commission" is a major commission of inquiry into an issue of perceived national public importance.

57 Royal Commission on Aboriginal Peoples, *Report of the Royal Commission on Aboriginal Peoples*, 5 vols. (Ottawa: Minister of Supply and Services, 1996); available online at http://www.collectionscanada.gc.ca and http://www.aadnc-aandc.gc.ca.

58 Mary Hurley and Jill Wherrett, *The Report of the Royal Commission on Aboriginal Peoples* (Ottawa: Parliamentary Information and Research Service, 2000), 2.

59 Trudy Govier, "Acknowledgement and Truth Commissions: The Case of Canada," in Tomsons and Mayer, *Philosophy and Aboriginal Rights*, 44.

inherent injustices perpetrated by the state."[60] Yet, as the history of First Nations' struggle that led to RCAP demonstrates, these emotions can also play an important role in generating practices of resistance and cultural resurgence, both of which are required to build a more just relationship with non-Indigenous peoples on and in relation to the lands that we now share....

RIGHTEOUS RESENTMENT? THE FAILURE OF RECONCILIATION FROM GATHERING STRENGTH TO CANADA'S RESIDENTIAL SCHOOL APOLOGY

The critical importance of Indigenous peoples' emotional reactions to settler colonization appears even more pronounced in light of Canada's problematic approach to conceptualizing and implementing reconciliation in the wake of the RCAP report. There have been two broad criticisms of the federal government's approach to reconciling its relationship with Indigenous peoples: the first involves the state's rigid historical temporalization of the problem in need of reconciling (colonial injustice), which in turn leads to, second, the current politics of reconciliation's inability to adequately transform the structure of dispossession that continues to frame Indigenous peoples' relationship with the state.[61] Stephanie Irlbacher-Fox captures these concerns well when she writes that "by conflating specific unjust events, policies, and laws with 'history,' what is unjust becomes temporally separate from the present, unchangeable. This narrows options for restitution: we cannot change the past."[62] In such a context, I argue that Indigenous peoples' anger and resentment represents an entirely understandable—and, in Fanon's words, "legitimate"—response to our settler-colonial present.[63]

The federal government officially responded to the recommendations of RCAP in January of 1998 with *Gathering Strength: Canada's Aboriginal Action Plan*.[64] Claiming to "build on" RCAP's core principles of "mutual respect, mutual recognition, mutual responsibility, and sharing," *Gathering Strength* begins with a "Statement of Reconciliation" in which the Government of Canada recognizes "the mistakes and injustices of the past" in order "to set a new course in its policies for Aboriginal peoples."[65] This is the first policy statement by the federal government that explicitly applies the conceptual language typically associated with "transitional justice" to the non-transitional context of a formally liberal democratic settler state. The result, I suggest, is an approach to reconciliation that goes out of its way to fabricate a sharp divide between Canada's unscrupulous "past" and the unfortunate "legacy" this past has produced for Indigenous people and communities in the present.

The policy implications of the state's historical framing of colonialism are troubling. If there is no colonial present, as *Gathering Strength* insists, but only a colonial past that continues to have adverse effects on Indigenous people and communities, then the federal government need not undertake the actions required to transform the current institutional and social relationships that have been shown to produce the suffering we currently see reverberating at pandemic levels within and across Indigenous communities today.[66] Rather than addressing these structural issues, state policy has instead focused its reconciliation efforts on repairing the psychologically injured or damaged status of Indigenous people themselves.

60 Taiaiake Alfred, Wasáse: *Indigenous Path - ways of Actions and Freedom* (Peterborough, ON: Broadview Press, 2005), 53.

61 Taiaiake Alfred, "Restitution is the Real Pathway for Justice of Indigenous Peoples," in Aboriginal Healing Foundation, *Response, Responsibility, and Renewal*, 179–87; Stephanie Irlbacher-Fox, *Finding Dahshaa: Self-Government, Social Suffering, and Aboriginal Policy in Canada* (Vancouver: University of British Columbia Press, 2009). These two texts embody both of these criticisms.

62 Irlbacher-Fox, *Finding Dahshaa*, 33.

63 Fanon, *The Wretched of the Earth*, 89.

64 Department of Indian Affairs and Northern Development, *Gathering Strength: Canada's Aboriginal Action Plan* (Ottawa: Minister of Public Works and Government Services Canada, 1998).

65 Ibid., 1.

66 Irlbacher-Fox, *Finding Dahshaa*, 106–8.

Sam McKegney links this policy orientation to the increased public interest placed on the "discourse of healing" in the 1990s, which positioned Aboriginal *people* as the "primary objects of study rather than the system of acculturative violence."[67] Hence, the only concrete monetary commitment made in *Gathering Strength* includes a one-time grant payment of $350 million allocated "for community-based healing as a first step to deal with the legacy of physical and sexual abuse at residential schools."[68] The grant was used to establish the Aboriginal Healing Foundation in March of 1998.[69] The Conservative government of Canada announced in 2010 that additional funding for the Aboriginal Healing Foundation would not be provided.

According to Taiaiake Alfred, Canada's approach to reconciliation has clearly failed to implement the "massive restitution, including land, financial transfers, and other forms of assistance to compensate for past and continuing injustices against our peoples."[70] The state's lack of commitment in this regard is particularly evident in *Gathering Strength*'s stated position on Canada's land claims and self-government policies. Rather than affirm Aboriginal title and substantially redistribute lands and resources to Indigenous communities through a renewed treaty process, or recognize Indigenous autonomy and redistribute political authority from the state to Indigenous nations based on the principle of Indigenous self-determination, *Gathering Strength* essentially reiterates, more or less unmodified, its present policy position as evidence of the essentially just nature of the current relationship between Indigenous peoples and the state.

For example, regarding the comprehensive claims process, although *Gathering Strength* states Canada's "willingness to discuss its current approach with Aboriginal, provincial, and territorial partners in order to respond to concerns about the existing policy," the "alternatives" that have since been pursued are even more restrictive than was the original policy.[71] At the time of *Gathering Strength*'s publication in 1998, the "concerns" alluded to by the federal government involved more than two decades' worth of First Nations' criticisms regarding the comprehensive claims policy's "extinguishment" provisions, which at the time explicitly required Aboriginal peoples to "cede, release and surrender" all undefined Aboriginal rights and title in exchange for the benefits clearly delineated in the text of the settlement itself. The state has pursued two alternatives to formal extinguishment: the so-called "modified" rights approach developed during negotiations over the Nisga'a Final Agreement (2000), and the "nonassertion" approach developed during negotiations over the Tlicho Agreement (2003).

With respect to the former, Aboriginal rights and title are no longer formally "extinguished" in the settlement but rather "modified" to include *only* those rights and benefits outlined in the claim package. The provisions detailed in the settlement are the only legally binding rights that the signatory First Nation can claim after the agreement has been ratified. Regarding the latter, in order to reach a settlement a First Nation must legally agree to not "assert" or "claim" any Aboriginal rights that are not already detailed in the text of the agreement. Again, the provisions specified in the settlement exhaust all claimable Aboriginal rights. Although the semantics of the comprehensive claims policy have changed, the legal and political outcomes remain the same.[72] Peter Kulchyski suggests that these alternative

67 Sam McKegney, "From Trickster Poetics to Transgressive Politics: Substantiating Survivance in Tomson Highway's *Kiss of the Fur Queen*," *Studies in American Indian Literatures* 17, no. 4 (2005): 85.

68 Department of Indian Affairs and Northern Development website, "Notes for an Address by the Honourable Jane Stewart, Minister of Indian Affairs and Northern Development, on the Occasion of the Unveiling of *Gathering Strength—Canada's Aboriginal Action Plan*," Ottawa, January 7, 1998, http://www.aadnc-aandc.gc.ca/eng/1100100015725/1100100015726.

69 Aboriginal Healing Foundation, *FAQs*, http://www.ahf.ca/faqs.

70 Alfred, *Wasáse*, 152.

71 Department of Indian Affairs and Northern Development, *Gathering Strength*, 11.

72 Bonita Lawrence, *Fractured Homeland: Federal Recognition and Algonquin Identity in Ontario* (Vancouver: University of British Columbia Press, 2012), 71. Lawrence offers a discussion of "alternative" comprehensive claim options.

approaches to formal extinguishment may be even worse than the original policy, given that the latter at least left open the possibility of making a claim for an Aboriginal right that was originally unforeseen at the time of signing an extinguishment agreement. "Leave it to the state," Kulchyski concludes, "to find a way to replace one of its oldest, most outdated, ineffective and unjust policies—the extinguishment clause—with something worse."[73]

A similar colonial trend can be seen in *Gathering Strength*'s stated commitment to implementing an Aboriginal right to self-government. Here the federal government simply reaffirms its previous 1995 policy position on the matter, which claims to "recognize" the "inherent right of self-government for Aboriginal people as an existing Aboriginal right within section 35 of the *Constitution Act, 1982*." The use of the term "inherent" here is nonsense when considered in light of the scope of the policy, as there is really nothing "inherent" about the limited range of rights that Canada claims to recognize. The stated purpose of the federal government's position is to clearly establish the terms under which Aboriginal governments might negotiate "practical" governing arrangements in relation to their own communities and with other governments and jurisdictions. In setting out these terms, however, the state unilaterally curtails the jurisdictional authority made available to Aboriginal nations through the so-called "negotiation" process. As a result, Indigenous sovereignty and the right of self-determination based on the principle of equality between peoples is explicitly rejected as a foundation for negotiations: "The inherent right of self-government *does not* include a right of sovereignty in the international law sense." Instead, what the state grants is recognition of an Aboriginal right "to govern themselves in relation to matters that are *internal to their communities, integral to their unique cultures, identities, traditions, languages and institutions*."[74]

One should recognize a familiar pattern here. Instead of proceeding with negotiations based on the principle of Indigenous self-determination, Canada's policy framework is grounded in the assumption that Aboriginal rights are subordinately positioned within the ultimate sovereign authority of the Crown. On this point, Michael Asch has suggested that the policy clearly takes its cues from recent Aboriginal rights jurisprudence: "All court decisions rest on the presumption that, while it must be quite careful to protect Aboriginal rights, Parliament has the ultimate legislative authority to act with respect to any of them."[75] This restrictive premise coincides with the Supreme Court of Canada's own articulation of the meaning and purpose of "reconciliation" outlined in *R. v. Van der Peet* in 1996. As the court states, "what s. 35(1) does is provide the constitutional framework through which the fact that aboriginals lived on the land in distinctive societies, with their own practices, traditions and cultures, is acknowledged and reconciled with the Crown. The substantive rights that fall within the provision must be defined in light of this purpose; the aboriginal rights recognized and affirmed by s. 35(1) must be directed towards reconciliation of the pre-existence of Aboriginal societies with the sovereignty of the Crown."[76] And how, might we ask, does the court propose to "reconcile" the "pre-existence of Aboriginal societies with the sovereignty of the Crown"? Or, stated slightly differently, how does the court propose to *render consistent* Indigenous nationhood with state sovereignty? By refusing that the "aboriginal

---

73 Peter Kulchyski, *Like the Sound of a Drum: Aboriginal Cultural Politics in Denendeh and Nunavut* (Winnipeg: University of Manitoba Press, 2005), 100.

74 Department of Indian Affairs and Northern Development website, *The Government of Canada's Approach to Implementation of the Inherent Right and Negotiation of Self-Government* (Ottawa: Department of Indian Affairs and Northern Development, 1995), http://www.aadnc-aandc.gc.ca/eng/1100100031843/1100100031844 (emphasis added).

75 Michael Asch, "Self-Government in the New Millennium," in *Nation to Nation: Aboriginal Sovereignty and the Future of Canada*, ed. John Bird, Lorraine Land, and Murray MacAdam (Toronto: Irwin Publishing, 2002), 70.

76 *R. v. Van der Peet* (1996), Supreme Court Ruling, 507, 539.

societies" in question had anything akin to sovereignty worth recognizing to begin with. Instead, what the court offers up is an interpretation of Aboriginal rights as narrowly construed "cultural" rights that can be "infringed" on by the state for any number of legislative reasons—ranging from conservation to settlement, to capitalist nonrenewable resource development, and even to protect white interests from the potential economic fallout of recognizing Aboriginal rights to land and water-based economic pursuits. Like all Aboriginal rights in Canada, then, the right of self-government is not absolute; even if such a right is found to be constitutionally protected, it can be transgressed in accordance with the justifiable infringement test laid out in *R. v. Sparrow* in 1990 and later expanded on in decisions like *R. v. Gladstone* in 1996, *Delgamuukw v. British Columbia* in 1997 and *R. v. Marshall (No. 2)* in 1999.[77] When all of these considerations are taken into account it becomes clear that there is nothing "inherent" about the right to self-government recognized in Canada's "Inherent Right" policy.

At least in *Gathering Strength* the federal government acknowledges that Canada has a colonial past. The same cannot be said about the state's next major gesture of reconciliation: the federal government's official 2008 "apology" to Indigenous survivors of the Indian residential school system. Informed by a similarly restrictive temporal frame, the 2008 "apology" focuses exclusively on the tragedy of residential schools, the last of which officially closed its doors in 1996. There is no recognition of a colonial past or present, nor is there any mention of the much broader system of land dispossession, political domination, and cultural genocide of which the residential school system formed only a part. Harper's apology is thus able, like *Gathering Strength* before it, to comfortably frame reconciliation in terms of overcoming a "sad chapter" in our shared history. "Forgiveness" and "reconciliation" are posited as a fundamental step in transcending the painful "legacy" that has hampered our collective efforts to "move on"; they are necessary to "begin anew" so that Indigenous peoples can start to build "new partnerships" together with non-Indigenous peoples on what is now unapologetically declared to be "our land."[78]

Thus, insofar as the above two examples even implicitly address the problem of settler-colonialism, they do so, to borrow Patrick Wolfe's useful formulation, as an "event" and not "a structure": that is, as a temporally situated experience which occurred at some relatively fixed period in history but which unfortunately continues to have negative consequences for our communities in the present.[79] By Wolfe's definition, however, there is nothing "historical" about the character of settler colonization in the sense just described. Settler-colonial formations are *territorially acquisitive in perpetuity*. As Wolfe explains, "settler colonialism has both negative and positive dimensions. Negatively, it strives for the dissolution of native societies. Positively, it erects a new colonial society on the expropriated land base—as I put it, settler colonizers come to stay: invasion is a structure not an event. In its positive aspect, elimination is an organizing principle of settler-colonial society rather than a one-off (and superseded) occurrence."[80] In the specific context of Canadian settler-colonialism, although the *means* by which the colonial state has sought to eliminate Indigenous peoples in order to gain access to our lands and resources have modified over the last two centuries—ranging from violent dispossession to the legislative elimination of First Nations legal status under sexist and racist provisions of the Indian Act to the "negotiation" of what are still essentially land surrenders under the present comprehensive land claims policy—the *ends*

77 Lisa Dufraimont, "From Regulation to Recolonization: Justifiable Infringement of Aboriginal Rights at the Supreme Court of Canada," *University of Toronto Faculty of Law Review*, 58, no. 1 (2000): 1–30.

78 Prime Minister of Canada, "Statement and Apology."

79 Wolfe, "Settler Colonialism and the Elimination of the Native," 388.

80 Ibid.

have always remained the same: to shore up continued access to Indigenous peoples' territories for the purposes of state formation, settlement, and capitalist development....

... In the context of Canadian settler-colonialism, I contend that what gets implicitly represented by the state as a form of Indigenous *ressentiment*—namely, Indigenous peoples' seemingly pathological inability to get over harms inflicted in the past—is actually a manifestation of our *righteous resentment*: that is, our bitter indignation and persistent anger at being treated unjustly by a colonial state both historically and in the present. In other words, what is treated in the Canadian discourse of reconciliation as an unhealthy and debilitating incapacity to forgive and move on is actually a sign of our *critical consciousness*, of our sense of justice and injustice, and of our awareness of and unwillingness to *reconcile* ourselves with a structural and symbolic violence that is still very much present in our lives. Viewed in this light, I suggest that Indigenous peoples' individual and collective resentment—expressed as an angry and vigilant *unwillingness to forgive*—ought to be seen as an affective indication that we care deeply about ourselves, about our land and cultural communities, and about the rights and obligations we hold as First Peoples.

CONCLUSION

... The specific commemorative and educational goals outlined in the Truth and Reconciliation Commission of Canada's (TRC) mandate are important and admirable. However, many of the shortcomings that plagued both *Gathering Strength* and the 2008 apology also plague the mandate's terms of reference. In particular, the TRC temporally situates the harms of settler-colonialism in the past and focuses the bulk of its reconciliatory efforts on repairing the injurious legacy left in the wake of this history. Indigenous subjects are the primary object of repair, not the colonial relationship. These shortcomings have produced many critics of the TRC. Taiaiake Alfred, for example, warns that genuine reconciliation is impossible without recognizing Indigenous peoples' right to freedom and self-determination, instituting restitution by returning enough of our lands so that we can regain economic self-sufficiency, and honoring our treaty relationships. Without these commitments reconciliation will remain a "pacifying discourse" that functions to assuage settler guilt, on the one hand, and absolve the federal government's responsibility to transform the colonial relationship between Canada and Indigenous nations, on the other.[81] ...

8.10 Murray Bookchin (1921–2006)

Murray Bookchin was born in New York City to Russian Jewish immigrant parents. He considered himself an anarchist, and he participated in eco-anarchist and anti-capitalist movements as both an activist and author.

In the excerpt included here, "Ecology and Revolutionary Thought," Bookchin argues that we cannot deal with the domination of the natural world by humans without simultaneously dealing with the domination of humans by humans. According to Bookchin, the idea that human beings can dominate nature comes from the idea of domination in a hierarchical society. As a result, we find ourselves in potentially fatal political and environmental crises. The best hope out of the ecological crisis is to create decentralized,

81 Alfred, "Restitution Is the Real Pathway to Justice for Indigenous Peoples," 182–84.

democratic, and communal societies based on mutual aid and care. While this cannot guarantee an ecologically harmonious relationship between humans and the natural environment, it is proposed as offering more hope than any of those based on capitalist principles.

Bookchin was critical of the current state of human progress (particularly under capitalism), but his efforts to reconcile the relationship between human and non-human nature were premised on the promise of human rationality. In this respect, his arguments retain the spirit of the Enlightenment. For Bookchin, human nature is not the problem, but the systems of hierarchy, domination, and capitalism that structure current social relationships and our thinking. In this respect, his anarchism is an idealistic, utopian project to re-enchant humanity and realize its potential.

from Post-Scarcity Anarchism

What we are seeing today is a crisis in social ecology. Modern society, especially as we know it in the United States and Europe, is being organized around immense urban belts, a highly industrialized agriculture and, capping both, a swollen, bureaucratized, anonymous state apparatus. If we put all moral considerations aside for the moment and examine the physical structure of this society, what must necessarily impress us is the incredible logistical problems it is obliged to solve—problems of transportation, of density, of supply (of raw materials, manufactured commodities and foodstuffs), of economic and political organization, of industrial location, and so forth. The burden this type of urbanized and centralized society places on any continental area is enormous....

From the standpoint of ecology, man is dangerously over-simplifying his environment. The modern city represents a regressive encroachment of the synthetic on the natural, of the inorganic (concrete, metals, and glass) on the organic, of crude, elemental stimuli on variegated, wide-ranging ones. The vast urban belts now developing in industrialized areas of the world are not only grossly offensive to the eye and the ear, they are chronically smog-ridden, noisy, and virtually immobilized by congestion.

The process of simplifying man's environment and rendering it increasingly elemental and crude has a cultural as well as a physical dimension. The need to manipulate immense urban populations—to transport, feed, employ, educate and somehow entertain millions of densely concentrated people—leads to a crucial decline in civic and social standards. A mass concept of human relations—totalitarian, centralistic and regimented in orientation—tends to dominate the more individuated concepts of the past. Bureaucratic techniques of social management tend to replace humanistic approaches. All that is spontaneous, creative and individuated is circumscribed by the standardized, the regulated and the massified. The space of the individual is steadily narrowed by restrictions imposed upon him by a faceless, impersonal social apparatus. Any recognition of unique personal qualities is increasingly surrendered to the manipulation of the lowest common denominator of the mass. A quantitative, statistical approach, a beehive manner of dealing with man, tends to triumph over the precious individualized and qualitative approach which places the strongest emphasis on personal uniqueness, free expression and cultural complexity.

The same regressive simplification of the environment occurs in modern agriculture.[1] The manipulated people in modern cities must be fed, and to feed them involves an extension of industrial farming. Food plants must be cultivated in a manner that allows for a high degree of mechanization—not to reduce human toil but to increase productivity and efficiency, to maximize investments, and to exploit the biosphere. Accordingly, the terrain must be reduced to a flat plain—to a factory floor, if you will—and natural variations in topography must be diminished as much as possible. Plant growth must be closely regulated to meet the tight schedules of food-processing factories. Plowing, soil fertilization, sowing and harvesting must be handled on a mass scale, often in total disregard of the natural ecology of an area. Large areas of the land must be used to cultivate a single crop—a form of plantation agriculture that not only lends itself to mechanization but also to pest infestation. A single crop is the ideal environment for the proliferation of pest species. Finally, chemical agents must be used lavishly to deal with the problems created by insects, weeds, and plant diseases, to regulate crop production, and to maximize soil exploitation....

The simplification process is carried still further by an exaggerated regional (indeed, national) division of labor. Immense areas of the planet are increasingly reserved for specific industrial tasks or reduced to depots for raw materials. Others are turned into centers of urban population, largely occupied with commerce and trade. Cities and regions (in fact, countries and continents) are specifically identified with special products—Pittsburgh, Cleveland and Youngstown with steel, New York with finance, Bolivia with tin, Arabia with oil, Europe and the U.S. with industrial goods, and the rest of the world with raw materials of one kind or another. The complex ecosystems which make up the regions of a continent are submerged by an organization of entire nations into economically rationalized entities, each a way station in a vast industrial belt-system, global in its dimensions....

The point is that man is undoing the work of organic evolution. By creating vast urban agglomerations of concrete, metal and glass, by overriding and undermining the complex, subtly organized ecosystems that constitute local differences in the natural world—in short, by replacing a highly complex, organic environment with a simplified, inorganic one—man is disassembling the biotic pyramid that supported humanity for countless millennia. In the course of replacing the complex ecological relationships, on which all advanced living things depend, for more elementary relationships, man is steadily restoring the biosphere to a stage which will be able to support only simpler forms of life. If this great reversal of the evolutionary process continues, it is by no means fanciful to suppose that the preconditions for higher forms of life will be irreparably destroyed and the earth will become incapable of supporting man himself.

Ecology derives its critical edge not only from the fact that it alone, among all the sciences, presents this awesome message to humanity, but also because it presents this message in a new social dimension. From an ecological viewpoint, the reversal of organic evolution is the result of appalling contradictions between town and country, state and community, industry and husbandry, mass manufacture and craftsmanship, centralism and regionalism, the bureaucratic scale and the human scale....

... Wherever feasible, industrial agriculture must give way to soil and agricultural husbandry; the factory floor must yield to gardening and horticulture. I do not wish to imply that we must surrender the gains acquired by large-scale agriculture and mechanization. What I do contend, however, is that the land must be cultivated as though it were a garden; its flora must be diversified and carefully tended, balanced by fauna and tree shelter appropriate to the region. Decentralization

1 For insight into this problem the reader may consult *The Ecology of Invasions* by Charles S. Elton (Wiley; New York, 1958), *Soil and Civilisation* by Edward Hyams (Thames and Hudson; London, 1952), *Our Synthetic Environment* by Murray Bookchin [pseud. Lewis Herber] (Knopf; New York, 1962), and *Silent Spring* by Rachel Carson (Houghton Mifflin; Boston, 1962). The last should be read not as a diatribe against pesticides but as a plea for ecological diversification.

is important, moreover, for the development of the agriculturist as well as for the development of agriculture. Food cultivation, practiced in a truly ecological sense, presupposes that the agriculturist is familiar with all the features and subtleties of the terrain on which the crops are grown. He must have a thorough knowledge of the physiography of the land, its variegated soils—crop land, forest land, pasture land—its mineral and organic content and its micro-climate, and he must be engaged in a continuing study of the effects produced by new flora and fauna. He must develop his sensitivity to the land's possibilities and needs while he becomes an organic part of the agricultural situation. We can hardly hope to achieve this high degree of sensitivity and integration in the food cultivator without reducing agriculture to a human scale, without bringing agriculture within the scope of the individual. To meet the demands of an ecological approach to food cultivation, agriculture must be re-scaled from huge industrial farms to moderate-sized units....

As in the case of agriculture, however, the application of ecological principles to energy resources presupposes a far-reaching decentralization of society and a truly regional concept of social organization. To maintain a large city requires immense quantities of coal and petroleum. By contrast, solar, wind and tidal energy reach us mainly in small packets.... If homes and factories are heavily concentrated, devices for using clean sources of energy will probably remain mere playthings; but if urban communities are reduced in size and widely dispersed over the land, there is no reason why these devices cannot be combined to provide us with all the amenities of an industrialized civilization. To use solar, wind and tidal power effectively, the megalopolis must be decentralized. A new type of community, carefully tailored to the characteristics and resources of a region, must replace the sprawling urban belts that are emerging today....

There is more to anarchism than decentralized communities. If I have examined this possibility in some detail, it has been to demonstrate that an anarchist society, far from being a remote ideal, has become a precondition for the practice of ecological principles. To sum up the critical message of ecology: if we diminish variety in the natural world, we debase its unity and wholeness; we destroy the forces making for natural harmony and for a lasting equilibrium; and, what is even more significant, we introduce an absolute retrogression in the development of the natural world which may eventually render the environment unfit for advanced forms of life. To sum up the reconstructive message of ecology: if we wish to advance the unity and stability of the natural world, if we wish to harmonize it, we must conserve and promote variety. To be sure, mere variety for its own sake is a vacuous goal. In nature, variety emerges spontaneously. The capacities of a new species are tested by the rigors of climate, by its ability to deal with predators and by its capacity to establish and enlarge its niche. *Yet the species that succeeds in enlarging its niche in the environment also enlarges the ecological situation as a whole.* To borrow E.A. Gutkind's phrase, it "expands the environment," both for itself and for the species with which it enters into a balanced relationship.

How do these concepts apply to social theory? ... In presenting his "measure of progress," Read observes: "Progress is measured by the degree of differentiation within a society. If the individual is a unit in a corporate mass, his life will be limited, dull, and mechanical. If the individual is a unit on his own, with space and potentiality for separate action, then he may be more subject to accident or chance, but at least he can expand and express himself. He can develop—develop in the only real meaning of the word—develop in consciousness of strength, vitality, and joy." ...

Just as the ecologist seeks to expand the range of an ecosystem and promote a free interplay between species, so the anarchist seeks to expand the range of social experience and remove all fetters to its development. Anarchism is not only a stateless society but also a harmonized society which exposes man to the stimuli provided by both agrarian and urban life, to physical activity and mental activity, to unrepressed sensuality and self-directed spirituality, to communal solidarity and individual development, to regional uniqueness and worldwide brotherhood, to spontaneity and self-discipline, to the elimination of toil and the promotion of craftsmanship. In our schizoid society, these goals are regarded as mutually exclusive, indeed as sharply opposed. They appear as dualities because of the very logistics of present-day society—the separation of town and country, the specialization of labor, the atomization of man—and it would be preposterous to believe that these dualities could be resolved without a general idea of the *physical* structure of an anarchist society....

An anarchist society should be a decentralized society, not only to establish a lasting basis for the harmonization of man and nature, *but also to add new dimensions to the harmonization of man and man*. The Greeks, we are often reminded, would have been horrified by a city whose size and population precluded a face-to-face, often familiar, relationship between citizens. There is plainly a need to reduce the dimensions of the human community—partly to solve our pollution and transportation problems, partly also to create *real* communities. In a sense, we must *humanize* humanity. Electronic devices such as telephones, telegraphs, radios and television receivers should be used as little as possible to mediate the relations between people. In making collective decisions—the ancient Athenian ecclesia was, in some ways, a model for making social decisions—all members of the community should have an opportunity to acquire in full the measure of anyone who addresses the assembly. They should be in a position to absorb his attitudes, study his expressions, and weigh his motives as well as his ideas in a direct personal encounter and through face-to-face discussion.

Our small communities should be economically balanced and well rounded, partly so that they can make full use of local raw materials and energy resources, partly also to enlarge the agricultural and industrial stimuli to which individuals are exposed. The member of a community who has a predilection for engineering, for instance, should be encouraged to steep his hands in humus; the man of ideas should be encouraged to employ his musculature; the "inborn" farmer should gain a familiarity with the workings of a rolling mill. To separate the engineer from the soil, the thinker from the spade, and the farmer from the industrial plant promotes a degree of vocational overspecialization that leads to a dangerous measure of social control by specialists. What is equally important, professional and vocational specialization prevents society from achieving a vital goal: the humanization of nature by the technician and the naturalization of society by the biologist.

I submit that an anarchist community would approximate a clearly definable ecosystem; it would be diversified, balanced and harmonious. It is arguable whether such an ecosystem would acquire the configuration of an urban entity with a distinct center, such as we find in the Greek *polis* or the medieval commune, or whether, as Gurkind proposes, society would consist of widely dispersed communities without a distinct center. In any case, the ecological scale for any of these communities would be determined by the smallest ecosystem capable of supporting a population of moderate size.

A relatively self-sufficient community, visibly dependent on its environment for the means of life, would gain a new respect for the organic interrelationships that sustain it. In the long run, the attempt to approximate self-sufficiency would, I think, prove more efficient than the exaggerated national division of labor that prevails today. Although there would doubtless be many duplications of small industrial facilities from community to community, the familiarity of each group with its local environment and its ecological roots would make for a more intelligent and more loving use of its environment. I submit that, far from producing provincialism, relative self-sufficiency would create a new matrix for individual and communal development—a oneness with the surroundings that would vitalize the community.

The rotation of civic, vocational and professional responsibilities would stimulate the senses in the being of the individual, creating and rounding out new dimensions in self-development. In a complete society we could hope to create complete men;

in a rounded society, rounded men. In the Western world, the Athenians, for all their shortcomings and limitations, were the first to give us a notion of this completeness. "The *polis* was made for the amateur," H.D.F. Kitto tells us. "Its ideal was that every citizen (more or less, according as the *polis* was democratic or oligarchic) should play his part in all of its many activities—an ideal that is recognizably descended from the generous Homeric conception of *arete* as an all-round excellence and an all-round activity. It implies a respect for the wholeness or the oneness of life, and a consequent dislike of specialization. It implies a contempt for efficiency—or rather a much higher ideal of efficiency; and efficiency which exists not in one department of life, but in life itself." An anarchist society, although it would surely aspire to more, could hardly hope to achieve less than this state of mind.

If the ecological community is ever achieved in practice, social life will yield a sensitive development of human and natural diversity, falling together into a well balanced, harmonious whole. Ranging from community through region to entire continents, we will see a colorful differentiation of human groups and ecosystems, each developing its unique potentialities and exposing members of the community to a wide spectrum of economic, cultural and behavioral stimuli. Falling within our purview will be an exciting, often dramatic, variety of communal forms—here marked by architectural and industrial adaptations to semi-arid ecosystems, there to grasslands, elsewhere by adaptation to forested areas. We will witness a creative interplay between individual and group, community and environment, humanity and nature. The cast of mind that today organizes differences among humans and other life forms along hierarchical lines, defining the external in terms of its "superiority" or "inferiority," will give way to an outlook that deals with diversity in an ecological manner. Differences among people will be respected, indeed fostered, as elements that enrich the unity of experience and phenomena. The traditional relationship which pits subject against object will be altered qualitatively; the "external," the "different," the "other" will be conceived of as individual parts of a whole all the richer because of its complexity. This sense of unity will reflect the harmonization of interests between individuals and between society and nature. Freed from an oppressive routine, from paralyzing repressions and insecurities, from the burdens of toil and false needs, from the trammels of authority and irrational compulsion, individuals will finally, for the first time in history; be in a position to realize their potentialities as members of the human community and the natural world.

New York
February 1965

8.11 Nelson Mandela (1918–2013)

Nelson Mandela was a trained lawyer and leader in the anti-apartheid revolutionary movement in South Africa all of his adult life. He was repeatedly arrested and jailed for his political activism, and in 1964 he was sentenced to life in prison for sabotage (having been convicted on other charges earlier). After 27 years in prison, Mandela was released and went on to become the first black South African head of state, serving as president from 1994 to 1999. The system Mandela opposed was called apartheid (Afrikaans for "separateness") because it enshrined in law racial differences between whites (descendants of European colonials), blacks (native Africans), and coloureds (people of mixed descent, and Asians). The system was dismantled after his release from prison.

Included here are excerpts from Mandela's 1962 trial for inciting an illegal protest (i.e., not having a license to stage a national strike) and leaving the country without permission (when he left to get international support for the anti-apartheid cause). He begins by trying to establish that the trial against him violates fundamental principles of law: as a disenfranchised black in South Africa he has not consented to the laws he is accused of violating, and because whites control the legal system the court cannot satisfy a standard of impartiality in his case. Every citizen is entitled to be tried by a jury of peers, but the court before which Mandela stands accused is composed entirely of white South Africans. As such, he argues, the court has not the legitimate authority to try his case. In particular, the judge ought to recuse himself, because a white judge cannot preside impartially over the trial of a black defendant in a racist system. However, because black lawyers were barred from rising to a magistrate's position in South Africa, grounds for recusal in this instance would apply to any other judge in the legal system at the time. In effect, Mandela's objections to this particular magistrate constitute objections to the entire apartheid system.

The authority of a legal system is premised, Mandela insists, on the democratic participation of the people subject to it laws. So because black South Africans have been denied representation in government, its legislation does not legitimately apply to him. This point is emphasized in the autobiographical details of Mandela's penalty speech, in which he contrasts the uncivilized treatment of black Africans in their own land with the treatment he personally received in other countries and in the traditional African modes of governance prior to colonial rule.

~

from South African Trial Transcripts (1962), "Black Man in a White Man's Court"[1]

MANDELA: Your Worship, before I plead to the charge, there are one or two points I would like to raise.

Firstly, Your Worship will recall that this matter was postponed last Monday at my request until today, to enable Counsel to make the arrangements to be available here today. Although Counsel is now available, after consultation with him and my attorneys, I have elected to conduct my own defence. Some time during the progress of these proceedings, I hope to be able to indicate that this case is a trial of the aspirations of the African people, and because of that I thought it proper to conduct my own defence. Nevertheless, I have decided to retain the services of Counsel, who will be here throughout these proceedings, and I also would like my attorney to be available in the course of these proceedings as well, but subject to that I will conduct my own defence.

The second point I would like to raise is an application which is addressed to Your Worship. Now at the outset, I want to make it perfectly clear that the remarks I am going to make are not addressed to Your Worship in his personal capacity, nor are they

1 Extracts from the court record of the trial of Mandela held in the Old Synagogue court, Pretoria, from 15 October to 7 November 1962. Mandela was accused on two counts, that of inciting persons to strike illegally (during the 1961 stay at home) and that of leaving the country without a valid passport. He conducted his own defence.

intended to reflect upon the integrity of the court. I hold Your Worship in high esteem and I do not for one single moment doubt your sense of fairness and justice. I must also mention that nothing I am going to raise in this application is intended to reflect against the Prosecutor in his personal capacity.

The point I wish to raise in my argument is based not on personal considerations, but on important questions that go beyond the scope of this present trial. I might also mention that in the course of this application I am frequently going to refer to the white man and the white people. I want at once to make it clear that I am no racialist, and I detest racialism, because I regard it as a barbaric thing, whether it comes from a black man or from a white man. The terminology that I am going to employ will be compelled on me by the nature of the application I am making.

I want to apply for Your Worship's recusal from this case. I challenge the right of this court to hear my case on two grounds.

Firstly, I challenge it because I fear that I will not be given a fair and proper trial. Secondly, I consider myself neither legally nor morally bound to obey laws made by a parliament in which I have no representation.

In a political trial such as this one, which involves a clash of the aspirations of the African people and those of whites, the country's courts, as presently constituted, cannot be impartial and fair.

In such cases, whites are interested parties. To have a white judicial officer presiding, however high his esteem, and however strong his sense of fairness and justice, is to make whites judges in their own case.

It is improper and against the elementary principles of justice to entrust whites with cases involving the denial by them of basic human rights to the African people.

What sort of justice is this that enables the aggrieved to sit in judgement over those against whom they have laid a charge?

A judiciary controlled entirely by whites and enforcing laws enacted by a white parliament in which Africans have no representation—laws which in most cases are passed in the face of unanimous opposition from Africans—

MAGISTRATE: I am wondering whether I shouldn't interfere with you at this stage, Mr Mandela. Aren't we going beyond the scope of the proceedings? After all is said and done, there is only one court today and that is the White Man's court. There is no other court. What purpose does it serve you to make an application when there is only one court, as you know yourself. What court do you wish to be tried by?

MANDELA: Well, Your Worship, firstly I would like Your Worship to bear in mind that in a series of cases our courts have laid it down that the right of a litigant to ask for a recusal of a judicial officer is an extremely important right, which must be given full protection by the court, as long as that right is exercised honestly. Now I honestly have apprehensions, as I am going to demonstrate just now, that this unfair discrimination throughout my life has been responsible for very grave injustices, and I am going to contend that that race discrimination which outside this court has been responsible for all my troubles, I fear in this court is going to do me the same injustice. Now Your Worship may disagree with that, but Your Worship is perfectly entitled, in fact, obliged to listen to me and because of that I feel that Your Worship—

MAGISTRATE: I would like to listen, but I would like you to give me the grounds for your application for me to recuse myself.

MANDELA: Well, these are the grounds, I am developing them, sir. If Your Worship will give me time—

MAGISTRATE: I don't wish to go out of the scope of the proceedings.

MANDELA: Of the scope of the application. I am within the scope of the application, because I am putting forward grounds which in my opinion are likely not to give me a fair and proper trial.

MAGISTRATE: Anyway proceed.

MANDELA: As your Worship pleases. I was developing the point that a judiciary controlled entirely by whites and enforcing laws enacted by a white parliament in which we have no representation, laws which in most cases are passed in the face of unanimous opposition from Africans, cannot be regarded as an impartial tribunal in a political trial where an African stands as an accused.

The Universal Declaration of Human Rights provides that all men are equal before the law, and are entitled without any discrimination to equal protection of the law. In May 1951, Dr D F Malan, then Prime Minister, told the Union parliament that this provision of the Declaration applies in this country. Similar statements have been made on numerous occasions in the past by prominent whites in this country, including judges and magistrates. But the real truth is that there is in fact no equality before the law whatsoever as far as our people are concerned, and statements to the contrary are definitely incorrect and misleading.

It is true that an African who is charged in a court of law enjoys, on the surface, the same rights and privileges as an accused who is white in so far as the conduct of this trial is concerned. He is governed by the same rules of procedure and evidence as apply to a white accused. But it would be grossly inaccurate to conclude from this fact that an African consequently enjoys equality before the law.

In its proper meaning equality before the law means the right to participate in the making of the laws by which one is governed, a constitution which guarantees democratic rights to all sections of the population, the right to approach the court for protection or relief in the case of the violation of rights guaranteed in the constitution, and the right to take part in the administration of justice as judges, magistrates, attorneys-general, law advisers and similar positions.

In the absence of these safeguards the phrase 'equality before the law', in so far as it is intended to apply to us, is meaningless and misleading. All the rights and privileges to which I have referred are monopolised by whites, and we enjoy none of them.

The white man makes all the laws, he drags us before his courts and accuses us, and he sits in judgement over us.

It is fit and proper to raise the question sharply, what is this rigid colour-bar in the administration of justice? Why is it that in this courtroom I face a white magistrate, am confronted by a white prosecutor, and escorted into the dock by a white orderly? Can anyone honestly and seriously suggest that in this type of atmosphere the scales of justice are evenly balanced?

Why is it that no African in the history of this country has ever had the honour of being tried by his own kith and kin, by his own flesh and blood?

I will tell Your Worship why: the real purpose of this rigid colour-bar is to ensure that the justice dispensed by the courts should conform to the policy of the country, however much that policy might be in conflict with the norms of justice accepted in judiciaries throughout the civilised world.

I feel oppressed by the atmosphere of white domination that lurks all around in this courtroom. Somehow this atmosphere calls to mind the inhuman injustices caused to my people outside this courtroom by this same white domination.

It reminds me that I am voteless because there is a parliament in this country that is white-controlled. I am without land because the white minority has taken a lion's share of my country and forced me to occupy poverty-stricken Reserves, over-populated and over-stocked. We are ravaged by starvation and disease....

MAGISTRATE: What has that got to do with the case, Mr Mandela?

MANDELA: With the last point, Sir, it hangs together, if Your Worship will give me the chance to develop it.

MAGISTRATE: You have been developing it for quite a while now, and I feel you are going beyond the scope of your application.

MANDELA: Your Worship, this to me is an extremely important ground which the court must consider.

MAGISTRATE: I fully realise your position, Mr Mandela, but you must confine yourself to the application and not go beyond it. I don't want to know about starvation. That in my view has got nothing to do with the case at the present moment.

MANDELA: Well, Your Worship has already raised the point that here in this country there is only a white court. What is the point of all this? Now if I can demonstrate to Your Worship that outside this courtroom race discrimination has been used in such a way as to deprive me of my rights, not to treat me fairly, certainly this is a relevant fact from which to infer that wherever race discrimination is practised, this will be the same result, and this is the only reason why I am using this point.

MAGISTRATE: I am afraid that I will have to interrupt you, and you will have to confine yourself to the reasons, the real reasons for asking me to recuse myself.

MANDELA: Your Worship, the next point which I want to make is this: I raise the question, how can I be expected to believe that this same racial discrimination which has been the cause of so much injustice and suffering right through the years should now operate here to give me a fair and open trial? Is there no danger that an African accused may regard the courts not as impartial tribunals, dispensing justice without fear or favour, but as instruments used by the white man to punish those amongst us who clamour for deliverance from the fiery furnace of white rule. I have grave fears that this system of justice may enable the guilty to drag the innocent before the courts. It enables the unjust to prosecute and demand vengeance against the just. It may tend to lower the standards of fairness and justice applied in the country's courts by white judicial officers to black litigants. This is the first ground for this application: that I will not receive a fair and proper trial.

The second ground of my objection is that I consider myself neither morally nor legally obliged to obey laws made by a parliament in which I am not represented.

That the will of the people is the basis of the authority of government is a principle universally acknowledged as sacred throughout the civilised world, and constitutes the basic foundations of freedom and justice. It is understandable why citizens, who have the vote as well as the right to direct representation in the country's governing bodies, should be morally and legally bound by the laws governing the country.

It should be equally understandable why we, as Africans, should adopt the attitude that we are neither morally nor legally bound to obey laws which we have not made, nor can we be expected to have confidence in courts which enforce such laws.

I am aware that in many cases of this nature in the past, South African courts have upheld the right of the African people to work for democratic changes. Some of our judicial officers have even openly criticised the policy which refuses to acknowledge that all men are born free and equal, and fearlessly condemned the denial of opportunities to our people.

But such exceptions exist in spite of, not because of, the grotesque system of justice that has been built up in this country. These exceptions furnish yet another proof that even among the country's whites there are honest men whose sense of fairness and justice revolts against the cruelty perpetrated by their own white brothers to our people.

The existence of genuine democratic values among some of the country's whites in the judiciary, however slender they may be, is welcomed by me. But I have no illusions about the significance of this fact, healthy a sign as it might be. Such honest and upright whites are few and they have certainly not succeeded in convincing the vast majority of the rest of the white population that white supremacy leads to dangers and disaster.

However, it would be a hopeless commandant who relied for his victories on the few soldiers in the enemy camp who sympathise with his cause. A competent general pins his faith on the superior striking power he commands and on the justness of his cause which he must pursue uncompromisingly to the bitter end.

I hate race discrimination most intensely and in all its manifestations. I have fought it all during my life; I fight it now, and will do so until the end of my days. Even although I now happen to be tried by one whose opinion I hold in high esteem, I detest most violently the set up that surrounds me here. It makes me feel that I am a black man in a white man's court. This should not be. I should feel perfectly at ease and at home with the assurance that I am being tried by a fellow South African who does not regard me as an inferior, entitled to a special type of justice.

This is not the type of atmosphere most conducive to feelings of security and confidence in the impartiality of a court.

The court might reply to this part of my argument by assuring me that it will try my case fairly and without fear or favour, that in deciding whether or not I am guilty of the offence charged by the State, the court will not be influenced by the colour of my skin or by any other improper motive.

That might well be so. But such a reply would completely miss the point of my argument.

As already indicated, my objection is not directed to Your Worship in his personal capacity, nor is it intended to reflect upon the integrity of the court. My objection is based upon the fact that our courts, as presently constituted, create grave doubts in the minds of an African accused, whether he will receive a fair and proper trial.

This doubt springs from objective facts relating to the practice of unfair discrimination against the black man in the constitution of the country's courts. Such doubts cannot be allayed by mere verbal assurances from a presiding officer, however sincere such assurances might be. There is only one way, and one way only, of allaying such doubts, namely, by removing unfair discrimination in judicial appointments. This is my first difficulty.

I have yet another difficulty about similar assurances Your Worship might give. Broadly speaking, Africans and whites in this country have no common standard of fairness, morality, and ethics, and it would be very difficult to determine on my part what standard of fairness and justice Your Worship has in mind.

In their relationship with us, South African whites regard it as fair and just to pursue policies which have outraged the conscience of mankind and of honest and upright men throughout the civilised world. They suppress our aspirations, bar our way to freedom, and deny us opportunities to promote our moral and material progress, to secure ourselves from fear and want. All the good things of life are reserved for the white folk and we blacks are expected to be content to nourish our bodies with such pieces of food as drop from the tables of men with white skins. This is the white man's standard of justice and fairness. Herein lies his conceptions of ethics. Whatever he himself may say in his defence, the white man's moral standards in this country must be judged by the extent to which he has condemned the vast majority of its inhabitants to serfdom and inferiority.

We, on the other hand, regard the struggle against colour discrimination and for the pursuit of freedom and happiness as the highest aspiration of all men. Through bitter experience, we have learnt to regard the white man as a harsh and merciless type of human being whose contempt for our rights, and whose utter indifference to the promotion of our welfare, makes his assurances to us absolutely meaningless and hypocritical.

I have the hope and confidence that Your Worship will not hear this objection lightly nor regard it as frivolous. I have decided to speak frankly and honestly because the injustice I have referred to contains the seeds of an extremely dangerous situation for our country and people. I make no threat when I say that unless these wrongs are remedied without delay, we might well find that even plain talk before the country's courts is too timid a method to draw the attention of the country to our political demands.

Finally, I need only to say that the courts have said that the possibility of bias and not actual bias is all that needs be proved to ground an application of this nature. In this application I have merely referred to certain objective facts, from which I submit that the possibility be inferred that I will not receive a fair and proper trial.

MAGISTRATE: Mr Prosecutor, have you anything to say?

PROSECUTOR: Very briefly, Your Worship, I just wish to point out that there are certain legal grounds upon which an accused person is entitled to apply for the recusal of a judicial officer from the case in which he is to be tried. I submit that the Accused's application is not based on one of those principles, and I ask the Court to reject it.

MAGISTRATE: [to Mandela] Your application is dismissed. Will you now plead to your case.

MANDELA: I plead NOT GUILTY to both charges, to all the charges.

[Mandela was convicted of both charges against him. The following excerpt comes from his address to the court in the penalty phase of the trial. It concerns the charge that he incited people to commit illegal acts in staging a national strike.]

MANDELA: I am charged with inciting people to commit an offense by way of protest against the law, a law which neither I nor any of my people had any say in preparing. The law against which the protest was directed is the law which established a republic in the Union of South Africa. I am also charged with leaving the country without a passport. This court has found that I am guilty of incitement to commit an offense in opposition to this law as well as of leaving the country. But in weighing up the decision as to the sentence which is to be imposed for such an offense, the court must take into account the question of responsibility, whether it is I who is responsible or whether, in fact, a large measure of the responsibility does not lie on the shoulders of the government which promulgated that law, knowing that my people, who constitute the majority of the population of this country, were opposed to that law, and knowing further that every legal means of demonstrating that opposition had been closed to them by prior legislation, and by government administrative action.

The starting point in the case against me is the holding of the conference in Pietermaritzburg on 25 and 26 March last year [1961], known as the All-in African Conference, which was called by a committee which had been established by leading people and spokesmen of the whole African population, to consider the situation which was being created by the promulgation of the republic in the country, without consultation with us, and without our consent. That conference unanimously rejected the decision of the government, acting only in the name of and with the agreement of the white minority of this country, to establish a republic.

It is common knowledge that the conference decided that, in place of the unilateral proclamation of a republic by the white minority of South Africans only, it would demand in the name of the African people the calling of a truly national convention representative of all South Africans, irrespective of their colour, black and white, to sit amicably round a table, to debate a new constitution for South Africa, which was in essence what the government was doing by the proclamation of a republic, and furthermore, to press on behalf of the African people, that such new constitution should differ from the constitution of the proposed South African Republic by guaranteeing democratic rights on a basis of full equality to all South Africans of adult age. The conference had assembled, knowing full well that for a long period the present National Party Government of the Union of South Africa had refused to deal with, to discuss with, or to take into consideration the views of, the overwhelming majority of the South African population on this question. And, therefore, it was not enough for this conference just to proclaim its aim, but it was also necessary for the conference to find a means of stating that aim strongly and powerfully, despite the government's unwillingness to listen.

Accordingly, it was decided that should the government fail to summon such a National Convention before 31 May 1961, all sections of the population would be called on to stage a general strike for a period of three days, both to mark our protest against the establishment of a republic, based completely on white domination over a non-white majority, and also, in a last attempt to persuade the government to heed our legitimate claims, and thus to avoid a period of increasing bitterness and hostility and discord in South Africa.

At that conference, an Action Council was elected, and I became its secretary. It was my duty, as secretary of the committee, to establish the machinery necessary for publicizing the decision of this conference and for directing the campaign of propaganda, publicity, and organization which would flow from it.

The court is aware of the fact that I am an attorney by profession and no doubt the question will be asked why I, as an attorney who is bound, as part of my code of behaviour, to observe the laws of the country and to respect its customs and traditions, should willingly lend myself to a campaign whose ultimate aim was to bring about a strike against the proclaimed policy of the government of this country.

In order that the court shall understand the frame of mind which leads me to action such as this, it is necessary for me to explain the background to my own political development and to try to make this court aware of the factors which influenced me in deciding to act as I did.

Many years ago, when I was a boy brought up in my village in the Transkei, I listened to the elders of the tribe telling stories about the good old days, before the arrival of the white man. Then our people lived peacefully, under the democratic rule of their kings and their amapakati, and moved freely and confidently up and down the country without let or hindrance. Then the country was ours, in our own name and right. We occupied the land, the forests, the rivers; we extracted the mineral wealth beneath the soil and all the riches of this beautiful country. We set up and operated our own government, we controlled our own armies and we organized our own trade and commerce. The elders would tell tales of the wars fought by our ancestors in defence of the fatherland, as well as the acts of valor performed by generals and soldiers during those epic days. The names of Dingane and Bambata, among the Zulus, of Hintsa, Makana, Ndlambe of the AmaXhosa, of Sekhukhuni and others in the north, were mentioned as the pride and glory of the entire African nation.

I hoped and vowed then that, among the treasures that life might offer me, would be the opportunity to serve my people and make my own humble contribution to their freedom struggles.

The structure and organization of early African societies in this country fascinated me very much and greatly influenced the evolution of my political outlook. The land, then the main means of production, belonged to the whole tribe, and there was no individual ownership whatsoever. There were no classes, no rich or poor and no exploitation of man by man. All men were free and equal and this was the foundation of government. Recognition of this general principle found expression in the constitution of the council, variously called Imbizo, or Pitso, or Kgotla, which governs the affairs of the tribe. The council was so completely democratic that all members of the tribe could participate in its deliberations. Chief and subject, warrior and medicine man, all took part and endeavoured to influence its decisions. It was so weighty and influential a body that no step of any importance could ever be taken by the tribe without reference to It.

There was much in such a society that was primitive and insecure and it certainly could never measure up to the demands of the present epoch. But in such a society are contained the seeds of revolutionary democracy in which none will be held in slavery or servitude, and in which poverty, want, and insecurity shall be no more. This is the inspiration which, even today, inspires me and my colleagues in our political struggle.

When I reached adult stature, I became a member of the African National Congress. That was in 1944 and I have followed its policy, supported it, and believed in its aims and outlook for eighteen years. Its policy was one which appealed to my deepest inner convictions. It sought for the unity of all Africans, overriding tribal differences among them. It sought the acquisition of political power for Africans in the land of their birth. The African National Congress further believed that all people, irrespective of the national groups to which they may belong, and irrespective of the colour of their skins, all people whose home is South Africa and who believe in the principles of democracy and of equality of men, should be treated as Africans; that all South Africans are entitled to live a free life on the basis of fullest equality of the rights and opportunities in every field, of full democratic rights, with a direct say in the affairs of the government.

These principles have been embodied in the Freedom Charter, which none in this country will dare challenge for its place as the most democratic program of political principles ever enunciated by any political party or organization in this country. It was for me a matter of joy and pride to be a member of an organization which has proclaimed so democratic a policy and which campaigned for it militantly and fearlessly. The principles enumerated in the Charter have not been those of African people alone, for whom the African National Congress has always been the spokesman. Those principles have been adopted as well by the Indian people and the South African Indian Congress; by a section of the Coloured people, through the South African Coloured People's Congress, and also by a farsighted, forward-looking section of the European population, whose organization in days gone by was the South African Congress of Democrats. All these organizations, like the African National Congress, supported completely the demand for one man, one vote.

Right at the beginning of my career as an attorney I encountered difficulties imposed on me because of the colour of my skin, and further difficulty surrounding me because of my membership and support of the African National Congress. I discovered, for example, that, unlike a white attorney, I could not occupy business premises in the city unless I first obtained ministerial consent in terms of the Urban Areas Act. I applied for that consent, but it was never granted. Although I subsequently obtained a permit, for a limited period, in terms of the Group Areas Act, that soon expired, and the authorities refused to renew it. They insisted that my partner, Oliver Tambo, and I should leave the city and practise in an African location at the back of beyond, miles away from where clients could reach us during working hours. This was tantamount to asking us to abandon our legal practice, to give up the legal service of our people, for which we had spent many years training. No attorney worth his salt will agree easily to do so. For some years, therefore, we continued to occupy premises in the city, illegally. The threat of prosecution and ejection hung menacingly over us throughout that period. It was an act of defiance of the law. We were aware that it was, but, nevertheless, that act had been forced on us against our wishes, and we could do no other than to choose between compliance with the law and compliance with our consciences.

In the courts where we practised we were treated courteously by many officials but we were very often discriminated against by some and treated with resentment and hostility by others. We were constantly aware that no matter how well, how correctly, how adequately we pursued our career of law, we could not become a prosecutor, or a magistrate, or a judge. We became aware of the fact that as attorneys we often dealt with officials whose competence and attainments were no higher than ours, but whose superior position was maintained and protected by a white skin.

I regarded it as a duty which I owed, not just to my people, but also to my profession, to the practice of law, and to justice for all mankind, to cry out against this discrimination, which is essentially unjust and opposed to the whole basis of the attitude towards justice which is part of the tradition of legal training in this country. I believed that in taking up a stand against this injustice I was upholding the dignity of what should be an honorable profession.

Nine years ago the Transvaal Law Society applied to the Supreme Court to have my name struck off the roll because of the part I had played in a campaign initiated by the African National Congress, a campaign for the Defiance of Unjust Laws. During the campaign more than eight thousand of the most advanced and farseeing of my people deliberately courted arrest and imprisonment by breaking specified laws, which we regarded then, as we still do now, as unjust and repressive. In the opinion of the Law Society, my activity in connection with that campaign did not conform to the standards of conduct expected from members of our honourable profession, but on this occasion the Supreme Court held that I had been within my rights as an attorney, that there was nothing dishonourable in an attorney identifying himself with his people in their struggle for political rights, even if his activities should infringe upon the laws of the country; the Supreme Court rejected the application of the Law Society.

It would not be expected that with such a verdict in my favour I should discontinue my political activities. But Your Worship may well wonder why it is that I should find it necessary to persist with such conduct, which has not only brought me the difficulties I have referred to, but which has resulted in my spending some four years on a charge before the courts of high treason, of which I was subsequently acquitted, and of many months in jail on no charge at all, merely on the basis of the government's dislike of my views and of my activities during the whole period of the Emergency of 1960.

Your Worship, I would say that the whole life of any thinking African in this country drives him continuously to a conflict between his conscience on the one hand and the law on the other. This is not a conflict peculiar to this country. The conflict arises for men of conscience, for men who think and who feel deeply in every country. Recently in Britain, a peer of the realm, Earl Russell, probably the most respected philosopher of the Western world, was sentenced, convicted for precisely the type of activities for which I stand before you today, for following his conscience in defiance of the law, as a protest against a nuclear weapons policy being followed by his own government. For him, his duty to the public, his belief in the morality of the essential rightness of the cause for which he stood, rose superior to this high respect for the law. He could not do other than to oppose the law and to suffer the consequences for it. Nor can I. Nor can many Africans in this country. The law as it is applied, the law as it has been developed over a long period of history, and especially the law as it is written and designed by the Nationalist government, is a law which, in our view, is immoral, unjust, and intolerable. Our consciences dictate that we must protest against it, that we must oppose it, and that we must attempt to alter it.

Always we have been conscious of our obligations as citizens to avoid breaches of the law, where such breaches can be avoided, to prevent a clash between the authorities and our people, where such clash can be prevented, but nevertheless, we have been driven to speak up for what we believe is right, and to work for it and to try and bring about changes which will satisfy our human conscience.

Throughout its fifty years of existence the African National Congress, for instance, has done everything possible to bring its demands to the attention of successive South African governments. It has sought at all times peaceful solutions for all the country's ills and problems. The history of the ANC is filled with instances where deputations were sent to South African governments either on specific issues or on the general political demands of our people. I do not wish to burden Your Worship by enunciating the occasions when such deputations were sent; all that I wish to indicate at this stage is that, in addition to the efforts made by former presidents of the ANC, when Mr. Strijdom became Prime Minister of this country, my leader, Chief A J Lutuli, then President of our organization, made yet another effort to persuade this government to consider and to heed our point of view. In his letter to the Prime Minister at the time, Chief Lutuli exhaustively reviewed the country's relations and its dangers, and expressed the view that a meeting between the government and African leaders had become necessary and urgent.

This statesmanlike and correct behaviour on the part of the leader of the majority of the South African population did not find an appropriate answer from the leader of the South African government. The standard of behaviour of the South African government towards my people and its aspirations has not always been what it should have been, and is not always the standard which is to be expected in serious high-level dealings between civilized peoples. Chief Lutuli's letter was not even favoured with the courtesy of an acknowledgement from the Prime Minister's office.

This experience was repeated after the Pietermaritzburg conference, when I, as Secretary of the Action Council, elected at that conference, addressed a letter to the Prime Minister, Dr Verwoerd, informing him of the resolution which had been taken, and calling on him to initiate steps for the convening of such a national convention as we suggested, before the date specified in the resolution. In a civilized country one would be outraged by the failure of the head of government even to acknowledge receipt of a letter, or to consider such a reasonable request put to him by a broadly representative collection of important personalities and leaders of the most important community of the country. Once again, government standards in dealing with my people fell below what the civilized world would expect. No reply, no response whatsoever, was received to our letter, no indication was even given that it had received any consideration whatsoever. Here we, the African people, and especially we of the National Action Council, who had been entrusted with the tremendous responsibility of safeguarding the interests of the African people, were faced with this conflict between the law and our conscience. In the face of the complete failure of the government to heed, to consider, or even to respond to our seriously proposed objections and our solutions to the forthcoming republic, what were we to do? Were we to allow the law which states that you shall not commit an offence by way of protest, to take its course and thus betray our conscience and our belief? Were we to uphold our conscience and our beliefs to strive for what we believe is right, not just for us, but for all the people who live in this country, both the present generation and for generations to come, and thus transgress against the law? This is the dilemma which faced us, and in such a dilemma, men of honesty, men of purpose, and men of public morality and of conscience can only have one answer. They must follow the dictates of their conscience irrespective of the consequences which might overtake them for it. We of the Action Council, and I particularly as Secretary, followed my conscience.

If I had my time over I would do the same again, so would any man who dares call himself a man. We went ahead with our campaign as instructed by the conference and in accordance with its decisions....

I do not believe, Your Worship, that this court, in inflicting penalties on me for the crimes for which I am convicted, should be moved by the belief that penalties deter men from the course that they believe is right. History shows that penalties do not deter men when their conscience is aroused, nor will they deter my people or the colleagues with whom I have worked before.

I am prepared to pay the penalty even though I know how bitter and desperate is the situation of an African in the prisons of this country. I have been in these prisons and I know how gross is the discrimination, even behind the prison walls, against Africans, how much worse is the treatment meted out to African prisoners than that accorded to whites. Nevertheless, these considerations do not sway me from the path that I have taken, nor will they sway others like me. For to men, freedom in their own land is the pinnacle of their ambitions, from which nothing can turn men of conviction aside. More powerful than my fear of the dreadful conditions to which I might be subjected is my hatred for the dreadful conditions to which my people are subjected outside prison throughout this country.

I hate the practice of race discrimination, and in my hatred I am sustained by the fact that the overwhelming majority of mankind hate it equally. I hate the systematic inculcation of children with colour prejudice and I am sustained in that hatred by the fact that the overwhelming majority of mankind, here and abroad, are with me in that. I hate the racial arrogance which decrees that the good things of life shall be retained as the exclusive right of a minority of the population, and which reduces the majority of the population to a position of subservience and inferiority, and maintains them as voteless chattels to work where they are told and behave as they are told by the ruling minority. I am sustained in that hatred by the fact that the overwhelming majority of mankind both in this country and abroad are with me.

Nothing that this court can do to me will change in any way that hatred in me, which can only be removed by the removal of the injustice and the inhumanity which I have sought to remove from the political and social life of this country.

Whatever sentence Your Worship sees fit to impose upon me for the crime for which I have been convicted before this court, may it rest assured that when my sentence has been completed I will still be moved, as men are always moved, by their consciences; I will still be moved by my dislike of the race discrimination against my people when I come out from serving my sentence, to take up again, as best I can, the struggle for the removal of those injustices until they are finally abolished once and for all.

8.12 Review Questions

1. How does Mill relate freedom of action, freedom of opinion, and custom in his account of happiness?
2. Why does Mill believe that society should permit "different experiments of living"? What good will this accomplish and how?
3. Why does Wollstonecraft argue women in her society have not demanded equality with men?
4. How does Wollstonecraft compare unequal gender relations to unequal class relations, and what does she suggest are the effects of unequal class relations?
5. Whose interests does hooks argue mainstream feminism has served and whose interests has it ignored and why?
6. Why does hooks argue that feminism must link up with other struggles and what should it fight for if not the right of women to participate in society equally with men?
7. What does L'Ouverture argue is the relationship between the rebellious black slaves of Haiti and the French Revolution that led to the declaration of the rights of man?
8. How does Aristide define "mental slavery" and how does he see it playing out in Haiti's more recent history?
9. How does Coulthard argue "native resentment" is usually understood in Canada and how does he argue it should be understood?

10. How does Coulthard understand the process of reconciliation that has happened in former colonies like South Africa and why does he argue that such a reconciliation is impossible in the current Canadian context?

11. According to Bookchin, what advantages do complex redundant networks have over simple hierarchies?

12. What is Bookchin's vision for a sustainable human society, and why is it superior to alternatives?

13. How does Nelson Mandela's request that his trial judge recuse himself echo themes from Socrates's speech on behalf of the laws in Plato's *Crito*? In what respects does Mandela's situation differ from Socrates's situation?

14. How do Mandela's arguments pick up themes and principles articulated by L'Ouverture?

8.13 Further Reading

Beck, Ulrich. "World Citizens of All Countries, Unite!" *The Time*, no. 30, 1998.

Butler, Judith. *The Psychic Life of Power*. Stanford University Press, 1997.

Davis, Angela. *Women, Race & Class*. Vintage Books, 1981.

de Beauvoir, Simone. *The Second Sex*. Vintage Books, 1952.

Edelman, Less. *Homographesis: Essays in Gay Literary and Cultural Theory*. Routledge, 1994.

Government of Canada. *Royal Commission on Aboriginal Peoples 1991*.

Kymlicka, William. *Politics in the Vernacular*. Oxford University Press, 2001.

Schmitt, Carl. *The Concept of the Political*. Translated by George Schwab, University of Chicago Press, 1996.

Stanley, Jason. *How Fascism Works*. Random House, 2018.

Taylor, Charles. *Multiculturalism and the Politics of Recognition*. Princeton University Press, 1992.

APPENDIX

Timeline of Authors and Figures

Ancient and Medieval Figures

Solomon	(tenth century BCE)
Siddhartha Gautama	(563/480?–483/400? BCE)
Confucius	(551–479 BCE)
Herodotus	(490?–425? BCE)
Socrates	(470–399 BCE)
Thucydides	(460?–400? BCE)
Plato	(427?–347? BCE)
Aristotle	(384?–322? BCE)
Epicurus	(341?–271/270? BCE)
Cleanthes	(331?–232? BCE)
Philo Judaeus	(20? BCE–40? CE)
Epictetus	(55–135 CE)
Hierocles	(2nd century CE)
Sextus Empiricus	(160?–210? CE)
Diogenes Laertius	(300? CE)
Thomas Aquinas	(1225?–1274)

Modern Figures (Renaissance-Enlightenment)

Niccolò Machiavelli	(1469–1527)
Francis Bacon	(1561–1626)
Galileo Galilei	(1564–1642)
Thomas Hobbes	(1588–1679)
Zar'a Yaqob	(1599–1692)
John Locke	(1632–1704)
Isaac Newton	(1643–1727)
Baron de La Brède et de Montesquieu	(1689–1755)
David Hume	(1711–1776)
Jean-Jacques Rousseau	(1712–1778)

Adam Smith	(1723–1790)
Immanuel Kant	(1724–1804)
Edmund Burke	(1730–1797)
Toussaint L'Ouverture	(1743–1803)
Mary Wollstonecraft	(1759–1797)
Sojourner Truth	(1797–1883)
Alexis de Tocqueville	(1805–1859)
John Stuart Mill	(1806–1873)
Charles Darwin	(1809–1882)
Karl Marx	(1818–1883)
Friedrich Engels	(1820–1893)

Post-Enlightenment Figures

Friedrich Nietzsche	(1844–1900)
Sigmund Freud	(1854–1939)
Svante Arrhenius	(1859–1927)
Albert Einstein	(1879–1955)
Heinrich Himmler	(1900–1945)
Karl Popper	(1902–1994)
Hannah Arendt	(1906–1975)
Albert Camus	(1913–1960)
Nelson Mandela	(1918–2013)
Murray Bookchin	(1921–2006)
Thomas Kuhn	(1922–1996)
Edward S. Herman	(1925–2017)
Frantz Fanon	(1925–1961)
Michel Foucault	(1926–1984)
Noam Chomsky	(1928–)
Martin Luther King, Jr.	(1929–1968)
Philip Zimbardo	(1933–)
David Harvey	(1935–)
Edward Said	(1935–2003)
bell hooks	(1952–)
Jean Bertrand Aristide	(1953–)
Gerard Taiaiake Alfred	(1964–)
Naomi Klein	(1970–)
Glen Coulthard	(1974–)

Permissions Acknowledgements

Alfred, Gerald Taiaiake. From *Peace, Power, Righteousness*, 2nd ed. Copyright © Oxford University Press Canada, 2008. Reprinted by permission of the publisher.

Arendt, Hannah. From *Eichmann in Jerusalem*. Copyright © 1963, 1964 by Hannah Arendt; copyright renewed © 1991, 1992 by Lotte Kohler. Used by permission of Viking Books, an imprint of Penguin Publishing Group, a division of Penguin Random House LLC. All rights reserved.

Aristide, Jean-Bertrand. From "Introduction," in *Toussaint L'Ouverture: The Haitian Revolution*, edited by Nick Nesbit. New York: Verso, 2008. Reprinted with the permission of Verso Books UK.

Aristotle. From "Metaphysics," in *The Oxford Translation of Aristotle*, translated by W.D. Ross (Volume 8, 1928). Reprinted with the permission of Oxford University Press. From "Analytica Posteriora," in *The Oxford Translation of Aristotle*, translated by G.R.G. Mure, edited by W.D. Ross (Volume 1). Reprinted with the permission of Oxford University Press. From *Nicomachean Ethics*, Book VI, translated by D.P. Chase, http://www.gutenberg.org/cache/epub/8438/pg8438.txt). From "Politics," translated by Benjamin Jowett, http://classics.mit.edu/Aristotle/politics.1.one.html. From "Rhetoric," in *The Works of Aristotle: Volume XI*, translated by Rhys Roberts. Oxford: The Clarendon Press, 1924. From "Physics," translated by R.P. Hardie and R.K. Gaye, http://classics.mit.edu/Aristotle/physics.2.ii.html.

Arrhenius, Svante. From "On the Influence of Carbonic Acid in the Air upon the Temperature of the Ground," in *The London, Edinburgh, and Dublin Philosophical Magazine and Journal of Science*, Fifth Series, April 1896, https://www.rsc.org/images/Arrhenius1896_tcm18-173546.pdf.

Bacon, Francis. From *Novum Organum*, http://www.gutenberg.org/files/45988/45988-h/45988-h.htm.

Bookchin, Murray. From *Ecology and Revolutionary Thought in Post-Scarcity Anarchism*. Ramparts Press, 1971. Copyright © 2019 The Bookchin Trust. Used with permission.

Burke, Edmund. From "The Reflections on the Revolution in France," 1790.

Camus, Albert. From "The Myth of Sisyphus," from *The Myth of Sisyphus and Other Essays*, translated by Justin O'Brien. Translation copyright © 1955, renewed 1983 by Penguin Random House LLC. Used by permission of Alfred A. Knopf, an imprint of the Knopf Doubleday Publishing Group, a division of Penguin Random House LLC. All rights reserved.

Cleanthes. "Hymn to Zeus," translated by E.H. Blakeney, 1921, https://en.wikisource.org/wiki/Hymn_to_Zeus.

Confucius. From *The Analects*, translated by James Legge, 1861, 1893, https://en.wikisource.org/wiki/Confucian_Analects.

Coulthard, Glen Sean. From *Red Skin, White Masks: Rejecting the Colonial Politics of Recognition*. University of Minnesota Press, 2014. Copyright © 2014 by the Regents of the University of Minnesota. Reprinted with permission.

Darwin, Charles. From *The Origin of Species*, https://en.wikisource.org/wiki/The_Origin_of_Species_(1872).

de Tocqueville, Alexis. From *Democracy in America*, translated by Henry Reeve, 1838.

Diogenes Laertius. From *Lives of the Eminent Philosophers*, translated by C.D. Yonge, M.A. London: G. Bell and Sons, 1915, http://www.gutenberg.org/files/57342/57342-0.txt.

Einstein, Albert. From "The Meaning of Relativity," in *Relativity: The Special and General Theory*, translated by Robert William Lawson. London: Methuen & Co., 1916, https://en.wikisource.org/wiki/Relativity:_The_Special_and_General_Theory/Part_II.

Epictetus. From "Discourses 2," http://classics.mit.edu/Epictetus/discourses.2.two.html.

Epicurus. "Letter to Menoeceus," translated by Robert Drew Hicks.

Fanon, Frantz. From *The Wretched of the Earth*, translated by Constance Farrington. Penguin Classics, 1967, 2001. *Les damnés de la terre* first published in France by François Maspéro éditeur 1961. Copyright © *Présence Africaine*, 1963.

Foucault, Michel. From *Discipline and Punish: The Birth of the Prison*, translated by Alan Sheridan. Translation copyright © 1977 by Alan Sheridan. Used by permission of Pantheon Books, an imprint of the Knopf Doubleday Publishing Group, a division of Penguin Random House LLC. All rights reserved.

Freud, Sigmund. From *Civilization and Its Discontents*, translated by Gregory C. Richter and edited by Todd Dufresne. Broadview Press, 2015.

Galileo Galilei. From "The Assayer," and "Letter to the Grand Duchess Christina," in *Discoveries and Opinions of Galileo*, translated by Stillman Drake. Translation copyright © 1957 by Stillman Drake. Used by permission of Doubleday, an imprint of the Knopf Doubleday Publishing Group, a division of Penguin Random House LLC. All rights reserved.

Harvey, David. From *A Brief History of Neoliberalism*. Copyright © David Harvey 2005. Oxford University Press, 2007. Reproduced with permission of Oxford University Press through PLSclear.

Herman, Edward S., and Noam Chomsky. From *Manufacturing Consent*. Copyright © 1988 by Edward S. Herman and Noam Chomsky. Used by permission of Pantheon Books, an imprint of the Knopf Doubleday Publishing Group, a division of Penguin Random House LLC. All rights reserved.

Herodotus. From "Histories 3.38," in *The History of Herodotus*, translated by George Rawlinson. London: J.M. Dent, 1910, https://en.wikisource.org/wiki/The_History_of_Herodotus_(Rawlinson)/Book_3.

Hierocles. From *Political Fragments of Archytas and Other Ancient Pythagoreans*, translated by Thomas Taylor, 1822, https://en.wikisource.org/wiki/

Political_fragments_of_Archytas_and_other_ancient_Pythagoreans/How_we_ought_to_conduct_ourselves_towards_our_kindred.

Himmler, Heinrich. From the speech to SS-Gruppenführer at Posen, Poland, October 4th, 1943, translated by Stephane Bruchfeld, Gordon McFee, and Dr. Ulrich Rössler. US National Archives document 242.256, reel 2 of 3, https://www.jewishvirtuallibrary.org/himmler-s-posen-speech-quot-extermination-quot.

Hobbes, Thomas. From *Leviathan*, 1651.

hooks, bell. From *Feminist Theory: From Margin to Center*. Routledge, 2015. Copyright © 1984, 2000, 2015, Gloria Watkins. Reproduced by permission of Taylor and Francis Group, LLC, a division of Informa PLC, via Copyright Clearance Center, Inc.

Hume, David. From *A Treatise of Human Nature*, http://www.gutenberg.org/cache/epub/4705/pg4705.txt.

Kant, Immanuel. "What Is Enlightenment?," translated by Mary Campbell Smith. Allen and Unwin, 1903. From *The Foundation of the Metaphysics of Morals*, translated by T.K. Abbott.

King, Martin Luther Jr. "Letter from Birmingham Jail," in *Why We Can't Wait*. HarperCollins, 1963. Copyright © 1963 by Dr. Martin Luther King, Jr. Copyright © 1991 Coretta Scott King. Reprinted by arrangement with The Heirs to the Estate of Martin Luther King Jr., c/o Writers House as agent for the proprietor, New York, NY.

Klein, Naomi. From *This Changes Everything: Capitalism vs. the Climate*. Copyright © 2014 by Naomi Klein. Reprinted in Canada by permission of Vintage Canada/Alfred A. Knopf Canada, a division of Penguin Random House Canada Limited. All rights reserved. Any third party use of this material, outside of this publication, is prohibited. Interested parties must apply directly to Penguin Random House Canada Limited for permission. Reprinted in the United States with the permission of the author via ICM Partners, New York.

Kuhn, Thomas S. From *The Structure of Scientific Revolutions*, 2nd ed. Chicago: University of Chicago Press, 1962. Copyright © 1962, 1970, 1996, 2012 by The University of Chicago. Reprinted with permission.

Locke, John. From *Second Treatise on Government*, 1689.

L'Ouverture, Toussaint. From *Toussaint L'Ouverture: The Haitian Revolution*, introduced by Jean-Bertrand Aristide, edited by Nick Nesbit. New York: Verso, 2008. Reprinted with the permission of Verso Books UK.

Machiavelli, Niccolò. From *The Prince*, translated by W.K. Marriott, 1908.

Mandela, Nelson. "Black Man in a White Man's Court," extracts from the court record of the trial of Mandela held in the Old Synagogue court, Pretoria, from October 15 to November 7, 1962.

Marx, Karl. *The Communist Manifesto*, translated by Samuel Moore with Frederich Engels, 1888, https://www.marxists.org/archive/marx/works/1848/communist-manifesto/index.htm. From *Kapital*, translated by Samuel Moore and Edward Aveling, edited by Frederich Engels, 1887, https://www.marxists.org/archive/marx/works/1867-c1/index.htm.

Mill, John Stuart. From *On Liberty*, 1859.

Montesquieu. From *The Spirit of Laws* (1748), translated by Thomas Nugent (1758).

Newton, Isaac. From *The Mathematical Principles of Natural Philosophy*, translated by Andrew Motte, carefully revised and corrected, with a life of the author, by N.W. Chittenden. New York: Daniel Adee, 1846. (1st American ed.), https://en.wikisource.org/wiki/The_Mathematical_Principles_of_Natural_Philosophy_(1846).

Nietzsche, Friedrich. From *The Antichrist*, translated by Anthony M. Ludovici. Amherst, NY: Prometheus Books, 2000. From *On the Genealogy of Morals* and *Beyond Good and Evil*, in *The Broadview Anthology of Social and Political Thought*, Volume 1, translated by Ian Johnston. Broadview Press, 2008. From *The Joyful Wisdom*, translated by Thomas Common, 1910. From *Human, All Too Human*, translated by Zimmern & Cohn, 1915.

Nuremberg Laws. From "Reich Citizenship Law of September 15, 1935" and "Law for the Protection of German Blood and German Honor of September 15, 1935," https://encyclopedia.ushmm.org/content/en/article/nuremberg-laws, United States Holocaust Memorial Museum website. Reprinted with permission.

Philo. From *The Works of Philo Judaeus*, Volume I, translated by C.D. Yonge. London: George Bell & Sons, 1890.

Plato. From *The Apology* and *Crito*, in *The Apology and Related Dialogues*, translated by Cathal Woods and Ryan Pack. Copyright © 2016, Andrew Bailey, Cathal Woods, and Ryan Pack. Broadview Press, 2016. From *Meno*, http://classics.mit.edu/Plato/meno.html. From *Gorgias*, http://classics.mit.edu/Plato/gorgias.html, and *Phaedrus* http://classics.mit.edu/Plato/phaedrus.html, translated by Benjamin Jowett.

Popper, Karl. From "The Logic and Evolution of Scientific Theory," in *All Life Is Problem Solving*. New York: Routledge, 1999. Reprinted with the permission of the University of Klagenfurt/Karl Popper Library.

Rousseau, Jean-Jacques. From *Discourse on the Origin and Basis of Inequality among Men*, in *Jean-Jacques Rousseau: Fundamental Political Writings*, translated by Ian Johnston and edited by Matthew Maguire and David Williams. Broadview Press, 2018.

Said, Edward W. From *Orientalism*, copyright © 1978 by Edward W. Said. Used by permission of Pantheon Books, an imprint of the Knopf Doubleday Publishing Group, a division of Penguin Random House LLC. All rights reserved.

Sextus Empiricus. From "Outline of Pyrrhonism," in *Sextus Empiricus: Selections from the Major Writings on Scepticism, Man, & God*, translated by Sanford G. Etheridge. Copyright © 1985 by Avatar Books of Cambridge. Reprinted by permission of Hackett Publishing Company, Inc. All rights reserved. From "Against the Ethicists," in *Sextus Empiricus III*, translated by R.G. Bury. Loeb Classical Library 273. Cambridge, MA: Harvard University Press, 1933, 1960.

Siddhartha Gautama. From *A Source Book in Indian Philosophy*, edited by Sarvepalli Radhakrishnan and Charles A. Moore. Princeton University Press, 1957; 6th printing 1967. Republished with the permission of Princeton University Press via Copyright Clearance Center, Inc.

Smith, Adam. From *The Wealth of Nations*, 1776.

Sojourner Truth. "Ain't I a Woman?," from "On Women's Rights" by Marius Robinson in *The Anti-Slavery Bugle*, June 21, 1851.

Solomon. From *Proverbs*, from The Holy Bible, Douay-Rheims Version, 1609–10.

Thomas Aquinas. From *The Summary against the Gentiles*, translated by Anthony C. Pegis and Vernon J. Bourke. Copyright © 1955 by Doubleday and Company, Inc. From *Summary of Theology*, translated anonymously by Fathers of the English Dominican Province.

Thucydides. From *The Peloponnesian War*, translated by Richard Crawley, 1866.

United Nations. Universal Declaration of Human Rights, https://www.un.org/en/universal-declaration-human-rights/.

Wollstonecraft, Mary. From *A Vindication of the Rights of Woman*, 1792.

Zar'a Yaqob. Excerpt from "Treatise of Zar'a Yaquob," in *Classical Ethiopian Philosophy* by Claude Sumner. Copyright © 1985 Fr. Claude Sumner. Reprinted with the permission of Jésuites du Canada–Jesuits of Canada.

Zimbardo, Philip. From *The Lucifer Effect: Understanding How Good People Turn Evil.* Copyright © 2007 by Philip G. Zimbardo, Inc. Used by permission of Random House, an imprint and division of Penguin Random House LLC. All rights reserved.

The publisher has made every attempt to locate all copyright holders of the material published in this book, and would be grateful for information that would allow correction of any errors or omissions in subsequent editions of the work.

From the Publisher

A name never says it all, but the word "Broadview" expresses a good deal of the philosophy behind our company. We are open to a broad range of academic approaches and political viewpoints. We pay attention to the broad impact book publishing and book printing has in the wider world; for some years now we have used 100% recycled paper for most titles. Our publishing program is internationally oriented and broad-ranging. Our individual titles often appeal to a broad readership too; many are of interest as much to general readers as to academics and students.

Founded in 1985, Broadview remains a fully independent company owned by its shareholders—not an imprint or subsidiary of a larger multinational.

For the most accurate information on our books (including information on pricing, editions, and formats) please visit our website at www.broadviewpress.com. Our print books and ebooks are available for sale on our site.

broadview press

www.broadviewpress.com

This book is made of paper from well-managed FSC® - certified forests, recycled materials, and other controlled sources.